To Kaye

With sincere

compliments

RCHweedie

London

22/11/91

MAKERS OF MODERN AFRICA
Profiles in History

MAKERS OF MODERN AFRICA

Profiles in History

Produced by Africa Books Ltd.

Publisher & Editor-in-Chief: Raph Uwechue

Senior Editors:

Adotey Bing
Jonathan Derrick
Godwin Matatu

Consulting Editors:

Pramila Bennett
Ikhenemho Okomilo
Appiah Sackey

Contributing Editors:

Ad'Obe Obe
Lionel Ngakane

Second Edition 1991

Published by
Africa Books Ltd
3 Galena Road
Hammersmith
London W6 0LT
United Kingdom

ISBN 0 903274 18 3
ISBN 0 903274 19 1 Know Africa Books (Set)

Photoset in England by S.B. Datagraphics, Colchester
Printed and bound in Italy by Poligrafici Calderara, Bologna

MAKERS OF MODERN AFRICA
Profiles in History

Published by Africa Books Limited

PUBLISHER'S PREFACE

The KNOW AFRICA books are the result of two decades of research and extensive travels throughout Africa by teams of African scholars, writers and journalists who, under the auspices of AFRICA JOURNAL and AFRICA BOOKS, have accomplished one of the most important tasks in the field of general information and education in Africa. KNOW AFRICA aims at terminating the era of publications on Africa which reflect the colonial perception of the continent. Our hope is that it will become the cutting edge of a new approach towards the understanding of Africa, its history, its people and its vast potential. Ours is a time of change. Yet, until now very little has changed in the way that Africa has been portrayed in numerous books, press, radio and TV reports both inside and outside the continent.

Hence, to most Africans as well as outsiders, Africa still remains, as it did in colonial times, a hotch-potch of countries which differ in culture, religion, language and politics, each too weak to be truly independent. While most African countries are weak and therefore ineffective on their own, united they constitute a formidable force which has both the political and economic potential for improving the quality of life of Africans at home and at the same time assuring their security and dignity on the international plane. But unity will not come until we break the barriers of ignorance which still divide us.

Comprising three volumes, the books provide well-researched information about the people and the present conditions in one of the fastest developing but least documented continents. Taken together, the three volumes in the series are the only works of their class that treat the continent as a whole and look at Africa as one geo-political unit.

Africa Today, the first volume in the series, is a comprehensive reference book on all the 54 countries that comprise the continent of Africa. It begins with an overview of Africa as a unit, reporting on its regional and continental organisations. Then it proceeds to present a detailed record of modern African history, and the political, economic and social development of each African country examined from an African viewpoint. At the same time, it provides basic information on the activities of each country as an integral part of the continent as well as the role of Africa itself as part of the international community.

Africa Who's Who, the second volume, provides extensive and up-to-date biographical data on some 12,000 Africans from all walks of life. The first and only publication of its kind, it is an invaluable reference book on almost everybody who is somebody in Africa.

Makers of Modern Africa, the third volume, has been written by African historians. It consists of some 680 life histories of eminent Africans, now dead, who in their various ways occupy a special place in modern history. For the first time, it provides access, on a pan-African scale, to the social, cultural and political history of Africa as humanly reflected in the lives of those Africans who shaped the destiny of modern Africa.

Inevitably, in the course of production some errors could easily have occurred. Any mis-representation due to such errors is entirely unintentional. It is a work that is intended to be regularly revised and updated.

Raph Uwechue
Publisher and Editor-in-chief

FOREWORD
by
General Ibrahim Badamasi Babangida
President of the Federal Republic of Nigeria

Today, a whole quarter-century beyond the independence of most of the African nations from European overlordship and the founding of the OAU, our fundamental struggle for the total liberation of the continent can be said to have passed into a second stage. The Lagos Plan of Action established a decade ago signified that critical shift. Africa's leadership has since moved on from concentrating on the earlier and essential political primacy of the expulsion of imperial armies and administrators from our soil and the dismantling of the inappropriate colonial structures they left behind, to focus instead on the no less urgent economic and social needs of Africa's second generation: famine and agriculture, health and AIDS, drought and deforestation, and the piteous plight of the millions of refugees driven to mass migration by both natural and man-made disasters.

Yet for all the intense activity by African states to purge the past out of our soul and to purify the present, one relic of the colonial presence remains to be liquidated. Persistent and pernicious, it may be the hardest legacy of all to eradicate. The ultimate and permanent liberation of Africa can come only with the liberation of the African mind from the baneful psychological aftermath of imperial subjugation and racial oppression.

Viewed from this angle, the KNOW AFRICA books comprising AFRICA TODAY, AFRICA WHO's WHO and MAKERS OF MODERN AFRICA are a timely and impressive intellectual contribution by dedicated African scholars to the continuing struggle for the liberation of our continent and its peoples. Furthermore, as an exercise in African self-discovery, they represent an expression of faith in our common heritage and common destiny as Africans. Indeed, the unique attribute of KNOW AFRICA lies in its pan-African concept and continental perspective. It provides an overview of Africa in its totality and inter-connectedness, something usually absent in the general portrayal of the continent.

Even as these books go to press, the world scenario, which for the lifetime of most of us has been that against which Africa's quest for recognition and unity has been played out, has itself changed with the suddeness of a tropical thunderstorm. Most immediately, there is the crisis in the Gulf. As I said at the time, the Gulf War must serve as an object lesson for Africa. If our common task is to restore dignity to the African and to make Africa proud of her role in history, we must accept that the challenge of self-reliance which we all speak about is now here for the Third World. The moment of decision to take our own destiny into our own hands can no longer be postponed.

Nearer home, the independence of the so-called 'last colony' of Namibia, the rapturous release of Nelson Mandela and the shaft of light at last visible at the end of the long and dark tunnel that has been South Africa must give us not only hope but also renewed determination.

Again, the demolition of the Berlin Wall at the end of 1989 shattered the context of international politics as we have known it for almost half a century. Africa, no more than partitioned Europe, was not immune to the sinister consequences of ideological divide and the struggle for hegemony. Today Africa, too, is exercised by a re-examination of the claims of Communism and a reconsideration of the merits of multi-partyism. In Nigeria, as in many other countries, the restoration of democracy constitutes a priority programme.

Overall and everywhere, the state of the international system makes it imperative for us quickly to translate our dreams of dynamic cooperation among African and South-South countries into reality if we are to remain relevant actors in international relations. Africa has no time for the "Afro-Pessimism" that is sometimes discernible in our community. Talk of the continent's "marginalisation" could lead to defeatism. The continent's decolonisation cannot be considered complete until we have achieved what can be called the decolonisation of the mind. Only then can an independent Africa be called a free Africa.

This is where the KNOW AFRICA books come in. It is in their dual role of projecting an objective African image on the international scene, thereby increasing understanding within the world community, and promoting African unity at home through greater pan-African awareness, that I commend KNOW AFRICA books to fellow Africans, peoples of African descent everywhere and the international community at large.

Ibrahim Badamasi Babangida

State House
Dodan Barracks
Lagos

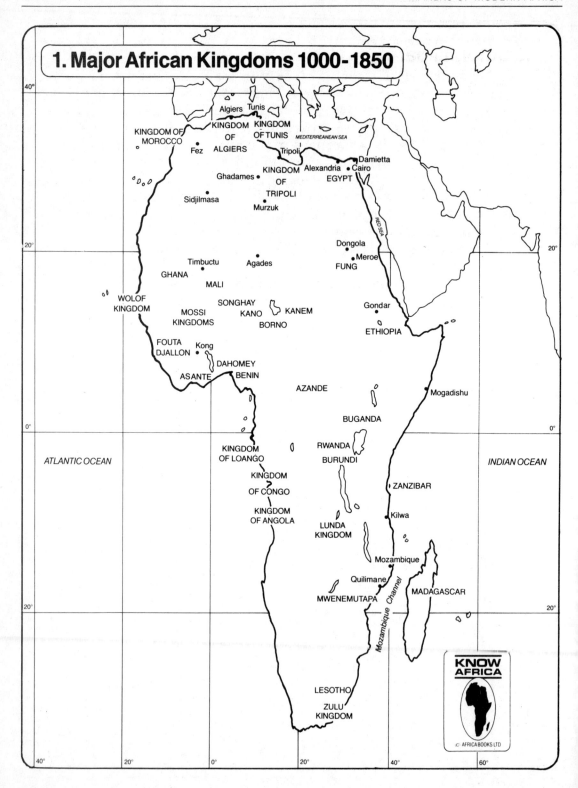

1. Major African Kingdoms 1000-1850

Algiers Tunis

KINGDOM OF MOROCCO

KINGDOM OF ALGIERS

KINGDOM OF TUNIS

MEDITERREANEAN SEA

Fez

Tripoli

Ghadames

KINGDOM OF TRIPOLI

Alexandria • Cairo

• Damietta

EGYPT

Sidjilmasa

Murzuk

RED SEA

Dongola

• Meroe

Timbuctu

Agades

FUNG

GHANA

MALI

WOLOF KINGDOM

SONGHAY

KANO

KANEM

Gondar

MOSSI KINGDOMS

BORNO

ETHIOPIA

FOUTA DJALLON

Kong •

DAHOMEY

ASANTE

BENIN

AZANDE

Mogadishu

BUGANDA

ATLANTIC OCEAN

KINGDOM OF LOANGO

RWANDA

BURUNDI

INDIAN OCEAN

KINGDOM OF CONGO

ZANZIBAR

KINGDOM OF ANGOLA

Kilwa

LUNDA KINGDOM

Mozambique

Quilimane

MWENEMUTAPA

MADAGASCAR

Mozambique Channel

LESOTHO

ZULU KINGDOM

KNOW AFRICA

(C) AFRICA BOOKS LTD

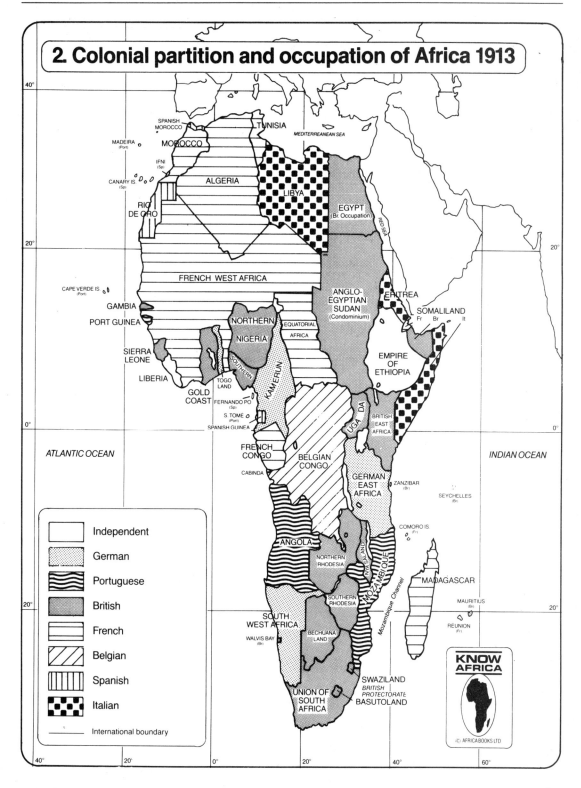

2. Colonial partition and occupation of Africa 1913

Legend:
- Independent
- German
- Portuguese
- British
- French
- Belgian
- Spanish
- Italian
- International boundary

KNOW AFRICA

© AFRICA BOOKS LTD

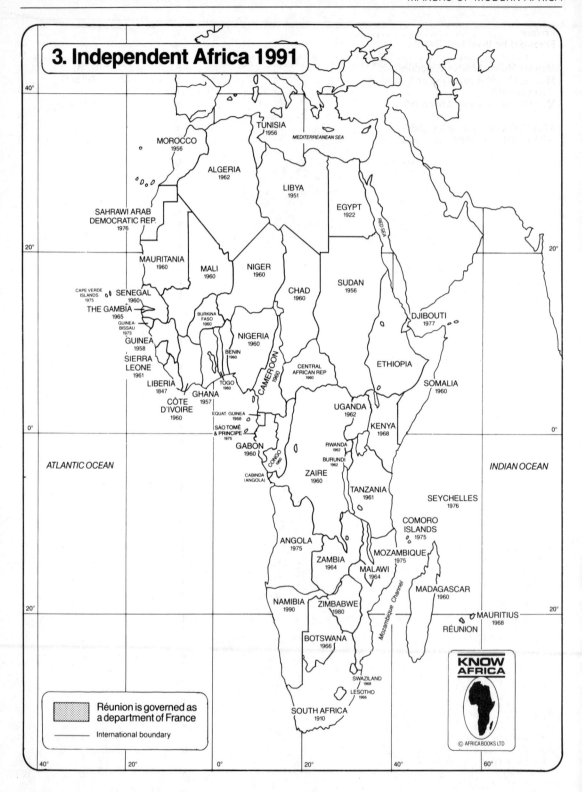

3. Independent Africa 1991

40°

TUNISIA
1956

MEDITERRANEAN SEA

MOROCCO
1956

ALGERIA
1962

LIBYA
1951

EGYPT
1922

SAHRAWI ARAB
DEMOCRATIC REP.
1976

RED SEA

20°   20°

MAURITANIA
1960

MALI
1960

NIGER
1960

CHAD
1960

SUDAN
1956

DJIBOUTI
1977

CAPE VERDE
ISLANDS
1975

SENEGAL
1960

THE GAMBIA
1965

GUINEA-
BISSAU
1973

BURKINA
FASO
1960

NIGERIA
1960

CENTRAL
AFRICAN REP
1960

ETHIOPIA

GUINEA
1958

BENIN
1960

CAMEROON
1960

SIERRA
LEONE
1961

LIBERIA
1847

TOGO
1960

GHANA
1957

SOMALIA
1960

CÔTE
D'IVOIRE
1960

EQUAT. GUINEA
1968

UGANDA
1962

SÃO TOMÉ
& PRINCIPE
1975

KENYA
1968

0°   0°

GABON
1960

CONGO
1960

RWANDA
1962

BURUNDI
1962

ATLANTIC OCEAN

CABINDA
(ANGOLA)

ZAIRE
1960

TANZANIA
1961

INDIAN OCEAN

SEYCHELLES
1976

COMORO
ISLANDS
1975

ANGOLA
1975

ZAMBIA
1964

MOZAMBIQUE
1975

MALAWI
1964

MADAGASCAR
1960

NAMIBIA
1990

ZIMBABWE
1980

Mozambique Channel

MAURITIUS
1968

20°   20°

RÉUNION

BOTSWANA
1966

KNOW
AFRICA

SWAZILAND
1968

LESOTHO
1966

Réunion is governed as
a department of France

International boundary

SOUTH AFRICA
1910

© AFRICA BOOKS LTD

40°   20°   0°   20°   40°   60°

CONTENTS

xvi

MAKERS OF MODERN AFRICA

Profiles in History

Abatcha, I. (died 1968)

ABATCHA, Ibrahim (died 1968).

CHADIAN politician who co-founded the *Front de Libération Nationale du Tchad* (FROLINAT), the main opposition movement in armed struggle against the Chadian government. The movement was formed in 1966 as an alliance between the radical *Union Nationale Tchadienne* (UNT) of Ibrahim Abatcha and the *Mouvement National de Libération du Tchad*, a Moslem-dominated group, to co-ordinate opposition to the single party constitution introduced in 1963 by President Ngartha Tombalbaye (q.v.). The establishment of the *Parti Progressiste Tchadien* (PPT) as the sole political organ in the country was generally supported in the south but opposed in the north by influential Moslem politicians who had been prominent in Chad's pre-independence politics. In 1966 Abatcha emerged as the first national leader of these opposition politicians who had regrouped under FROLINAT.

Little is known about his early life but he was a Moslem, from Bornu, Nigeria. He worked in various positions, achieving prominence as a radical trade unionist. His radicalism led to an early association with the militant UNT whose leadership fell upon him in 1962 when the movement, along with all Chadian parties, was dissolved at the commencement of the one-party system. He led the remnants of UNT into exile in Khartoum, Sudan, where he himself had fled in 1962 after a short period of detention in Fort Lamy (now Ndjamena) for militant activities.

Abatcha spent the next two years in Sudan and Nasser's Egypt and during that period his political ideals were greatly strengthened as was his opposition to the Tombalbaye government. In 1965 he went to Ghana, then under President Nkrumah, and received military training, in preparation for the armed struggle against the Chadian government; he stayed there until 1966. Returning to his exile base in Sudan, in June 1966 he merged UNT with the *Mouvement National de Libération du Tchad* of Ahmed Moussa and other Chadian opposition groups, to form FROLINAT. He became head of the joint movement, and also its first field commander. However within a short period, disagreements broke out among the various groups and the movement was split into two, with Abatcha continuing to head the FROLINAT section.

For the next two years he organised and fought in several guerrilla attacks against government forces in eastern Chad. He was killed during one of these operations in Abéché in March 1968. Abatcha's death was followed by a major power struggle in the hierarchy of FROLINAT, resulting in the joint leadership between Alhaji Abdel Issaka, who became its military commander, and Dr. Abba Siddick who became political head. ■

Abayomi, K.A. (1896-1979)

ABAYOMI, Sir Kofoworola Adekunle (1896-1979).

NIGERIAN doctor and politician. Born on 10 July 1896 in Lagos, son of J. N. John, he attended the UNA School and then, from 1909, the Wesleyan College (now Methodist Boys' High School) in Lagos, where he became a pupil teacher, on completion in 1912. He later transferred to a similar job at the Eko Boy's School.

He joined the civil service as a government dispenser in 1914, working first at the African Hospital in Lagos. A few months later, when the First World War broke out, he worked as a dispenser with the Nigerian forces which fought for the British in the Cameroons Campaign. He was decorated for this service.

Sir Kofo Abayomi

In 1922 he went to Edinburgh University, where several other West African doctors had already qualified, to study medicine. He completed those studies at Moorfields Eye Hospital in London, and specialised as an ophthalmologist. He won the M.B. and Ch.B. of Edinburgh in 1928, and the M.D. in 1936. From 1928 to 1930 he was demonstrator in Physiological Methods at Edinburgh.

Returning to Nigeria in 1930, he combined private medical practice with politics. In 1938 he took over from the deceased Dr. J. C. Vaughn the presidency of the Nigeria Youth Movement (NYM) which he had joined on its foundation as the Lagos Youth Movement in 1933. Also in 1938 he was elected to the Legislative Council as an NYM member for Lagos. He served for two years but resigned in 1940 to go to Britain for further studies.

He served on the Yaba Higher College Advisory Board, the Liquor Licence Board,

the Board of Medical Examiners and the Film Censorship Committee, and was a member of the University College of Ibadan Council from 1947 to 1961; for a time he was chairman of the Lagos Executive Development Board. From 1948 he was president of Nigeria's Society for the Blind. He was awarded the chieftancy title of Onashoku of Oyo. His wife Oyinkan, daughter of Sir Kitoyi Ajasa, was prominent in the Nigerian Girl Guides' Movement. Sir Kofo Abayomi died on 1 January 1979.■

Abayomi, O. (1897-1990)

ABAYOMI, Lady Oyinkan (1897-1990).

NIGERIAN educationist, social worker, philanthropist and politician. She was born on 6 March 1897, the only child of Sir Kitoyi Ajasa (q.v.; a pioneer of the legal and journalistic professions in Nigeria) and Olayinka Ajasa (née Moore) of the Egba royal family of Abeokuta. She began her education at the CMS Girls' Seminary in Lagos and later went to England to study at the Young Ladies Academy at Ryford Hall, Stonehouse, Gloucestershire. In 1917-19 she went for professional training in music and was awarded the Academic Diploma of the Associated London College of Music. It was while she was in London that she developed interest in youth work and social services. Consequently when she returned to Nigeria in 1920, she spent time between teaching music at school and engaging in social services in Lagos.

Her first marriage to the lawyer Moronfolu Abayomi in 1923 ended abruptly with the tragic death of her husband within the first year of their married life. She married, seven years later, a medical doctor who had the same surname as her first husband. Her marriage to Dr. Kofoworola Abayomi (q.v.) was a very happy one, and with his support, she became involved in the struggle for better education for women. She was also preoccupied with the development of the Girl Guides movement and the organisation of Unions of Market Women, the Young Women's Christian Association

Lady Abayomi

(YWCA), and the Nigerian Council of Women's Societies.

Lady Abayomi (her husband was knighted by the Queen of England in 1954) lived a full life of activity in her community and her career was a distinguished one. As an educationist, she taught at New Era Girls' School and Queen's College, Lagos. She was a member of the Lagos Women's Organisation which was in the forefront of the demand for better education for girls that resulted in the founding of Queen's College. She ran a boarding house at home for boys and girls; many people who later became prominent citizens in Nigeria lived in her boarding house where they were brought up with discipline mingled with affection.

She became the protem President of the National Council of Women's Societies when it was founded in 1959; later she became the head of the Lagos branch of this association. She helped to nurture the Nigerian Girl Guides' Association from which she retired in 1982. Although from that year she relinquished her office as the Chief

Commissioner for the Girl Guides' Association, she was elected the life President of the organisation.

In politics she was the founder of the Nigerian Women's Party, an all-female party. She served for seven years as a councillor representing women's interests in the Lagos City Council. In 1954 she was appointed a special member to represent women's interests in the regional legislature of the then Western Region. She was the founder of the British West African Educated Girls' Club which later became known as the Ladies Progressive Club.

Her life of dedicated service to her community and country was recognised by Britain as well as by her country. She was made Member of the Order of the British Empire by the Queen of England. In Nigeria she became one of the few women honoured with Officer of the Federal Republic of Nigeria (OFR). She was showered with distinguished chieftaincy titles in various parts of Yorubaland: Uya Eko (Mother of Lagos) of Lagos, Iya Abiye (the mother of us all) of Egbaland, etc. The prestigious Queens's Drive on Ikoyi waterfront was renamed Oyinkan Abayomi Drive in a further mark of recognition by the Lagos State Government.

Lady Abayomi was a dynamic personality who in spite of her wealthy background was able to mingle with people from different backgrounds with remarkable humility and humanity, dedicating her life to the service of her community. By the time she died on 19 March 1990, at the ripe age of 93, she had immortalised her name in the nation through her life of dedicated service.■

Abbas II (1874-1944)

ABBAS II (1874-1944).

EGYPTIAN monarch, often called Abbas Hilmi. He was born in Cairo on 14 July 1874, son of Tewfik, who became Khedive of Egypt five years later, and his wife Emine. He went to Europe for schooling, spending some time at the Theresianum College in Vienna. During that time the British occupied Egypt and in 1882 established complete control there, while nominally respecting the sovereignty of the Sultan of Turkey, whose representative the Khedive or Viceroy still was in theory. Tewfik, appointed by the Sultan, Britain and France in 1879, submitted to the later imposition of virtual colonial rule by Britain alone. But he died in January 1892, and his son and successor, Abbas Hilmi, showed early on that he resented British domination.

Abbas II

Increasing bad relations between him and Sir Evelyn Baring (later Lord Cromer), who ruled Egypt as Britain's Consul-General and Agent, culminated in a dispute over the appointments of ministers early in 1893. While the Khedive secured the sacking of Prime Minister Fahmi which he desired, he had to accept British control over appointments from then on. The British also placed advisers in key ministries, virtually running them. Abbas unwillingly accepted all this.

In 1894, when inspecting the army, under the overall command of the British General Kitchener, he deliberately criticised its officers, as a criticism of Britain. Kitchener offered to resign but this was refused and Cromer forced Abbas to sack his Under-Secretary for War. Abbas continued to make secret contacts with Turkey, where British control of a country still nominally under Ottoman rule was resented, and with "Pan-Islamic" circles who opposed Britain's rule in Egypt; also with France, resentful of British control of Egypt.

Between 1896 and 1898 the reconquest of the Sudan pleased Egyptians, but the virtually complete British occupation under the "Condominium" was a further grievance to nationalists, who also attacked Britain for denying sufficient Western education to Egyptians, for alleged hostility to Islam, and other acts. Nationalism grew in strength in the following few years, led particularly by Mustafa Kamil (q.v.), his newspaper *al-Liwa'*, and other newspapers. Abbas gave encouragement and help to him and another nationalist editor, Sheikh Ali Yusuf of *al-Mu'ayyad*.

France ended its support of Egyptian nationalism in 1904, but Turkish and German support followed, and indigenous support was massive by 1906, when the Turco-Egyptian frontier incident and the Dinshawai case raised anti-British feeling to a peak. In October 1906 Abbas, whose attitude to the nationalists had been cautious and ambiguous, made a pact with Kamil, providing money for *al-Liwa'*.

Abbas's life style was exploited by the British, who instigated press attacks on business dealings involving the Khedivial palace. This vulnerability isolated him from the more radical nationalists. In 1907 he switched support from Kamil's Nationalists, the most anti-British, to Ali Yusuf's new Constitutional Reform Party, which called for eventual self-rule under the Khedive.

In mid-1914, when he was visiting Constantinople, an attempt was made on Abbas's life. He was in the Turkish capital when Turkey joined Germany in war against Britain. Following this the British declared Ottoman rule in Egypt formally ended, installed a "Protectorate", and on 18 December 1914 deposed Abbas II. Refusing to accept the loss of his throne, Abbas called on Egyptians and Sudanese to rise against Britain. In Egypt, where this did not happen, his uncle Hussain became ruler with the title "Sultan". Abbas remained in exile during the First World War and afterwards.

There were some pro-Abbas elements in the nationalist upsurge of the early 1920's that led to legal independence of Egypt, but not enough to restore him to his throne which he eventually renounced in 1931. He died at Geneva on 21 December 1944.∎

Abbas, F. (1899-1985)

ABBAS, Ferhat (1899-1985).

A LGERIAN nationalist, pharmacist and writer; historic leader (one of the nine) of the Algerian War of Independence in the middle 50's who became the first President of the Provisional Government of the Republic of Algeria, established in Cairo on 19 September, 1958. An intelligent leader, conscious of his responsibilities, he was a passionate campaigner of human rights.

Ferhat Abbas was born on 24 October 1899 in Taher, Sétif, and his father was a Caid. He was first educated in Djidjelli and then went to the Lycée in Philippeville (now Skikda) on the eastern coast in 1909. After three years in the French Army Medical Service he studied pharmacy at the University of Algiers. His political career began in 1937.

A municipal councillor for Sétif, Abbas formed in 1938, the *Union Populaire Algérienne*, which was for a French-Algerian Union. He served as a volunteer in World War II (1939–45) but took a more militant stand when his beliefs in assimilation were shattered with the French refusal to enlist Muslims on an equal basis. He was imprisoned for publishing the Algerian People's Union Manifesto in 1943. He founded the *Amis du Manifeste et de la Liberté* (AML) in March 1944 which protested that de Gaulle's wartime reforms did not provide Algerians with enough freedom. The AML enjoyed wide support during its brief existence; it was dissolved in 1945 following the 8 May 1945 uprising in Sétif and the neighbouring region against the French. The party was blamed for the disturbances and Abbas was arrested, but later released on bail.

Abbas, however, still sought Algerian autonomy within the French system, an independent Algeria federated to France and in 1946 was a founder member of the *Union Democratique du Manifeste Algé*rien (UDMA), an integrationist party. In 1946 he was elected to the French Constituent Assembly. But by 1954 Abbas, completely disillusioned, realised the French were not prepared to give way to appeals for reform and when the Algerian war broke out,

F. Abbas

though opposed to violence, he joined the *Front de Libération Nationale* (FNL) in April 1956 having disbanded the UDMA. He was convinced that the FLN was the only force capable of liberating Algeria, and because 'insurrection had become the most sacred of man's duties'.

Abbas left Algeria in April 1956, travelling to Cairo. He became a member of the *Comité National de la Révolution Algérienne* (CNRA) in August that same year, and of the *Comité de Coordination et d'Exécution* (CCE) in August 1957. From Cairo, Abbas went to Switzerland via Rabat and then Tunis where he remained for some time. He was in charge of FLN publicity in those years, 1956 to 1958.

When the FLN formed a Provisional Government of the Republic of Algeria (GPRA) in 1958, Ferhat Abbas was elected its president, a post which he occupied till 1961, the year in which negotiations with France started.

Abbas's brilliant diplomacy in those intervening years helped to kindle international interest and bring recognition to the Algerian cause, and esteem for him increased both nationally and internationally.

In January 1961, Abbas attended an African Conference in Casablanca of seven African states – Ghana, Libya, Mali, Guinea, Morocco, the GPRA, and the United Arab Republic and Ceylon (Sri Lanka) to establish a programme of cooperation, and formulate an African Charter. Shortly thereafter he was dropped from the GPRA leadership. The FLN achieved power in Algeria itself just over a year later. In a referendum on 1 July 1962, 91 per cent of the electorate voted for Independence which was proclaimed on 3 July 1962. Abbas was elected president of the first Algerian National Assembly with Ben Bella as first Prime Minister. Abbas clashed with Ben Bella over the establishment of a one-party system of government which he rejected, and resigned shortly after the Algerian constitution was adopted and approved by referendum and Ben Bella was elected President of the Republic.

Abbas was detained from 1964 to 1965, following an alleged attempt to undermine Ben Bella in July 1964. Abbas could probably have rejoined the government when a military coup in June 1965 brought Houari Boumedienne (q.v.) as head of the Algerian State. He did not completely disappear from the political scene, and later, in 1976, he was placed under house arrest for having been involved in the publication of manifestos asking for what he called more democratic institutions in Algeria, a stop to inter-Maghreb conflicts; he wished to see a unified Maghreb. The ban was lifted in 1979.

For the next few years Abbas led a quiet life in Kouba on the hills around Algiers, writing and publishing his last work *L'Indépendance confisquée* in 1984, on the 30th anniversary of the outbreak of the National Liberation War in November 1954. That same year he was awarded the *Médaille de Résistance* by President Chadli.

Abbas was a known writer, the author of several books among which were *Le Jeune Algérien* (1931), *La Nuit Coloniale* (1962). He was the editor of *L'Entente* in 1939 and became editor of the newspaper *Egalité* in 1946; *Egalité* changed its name to *La République Algérienne* in 1948. Abbas was eloquent in speech as in his writing; he did not like making light-hearted promises and was scrupulous.

Abbas's was a very full life. His constant struggle for social and economic freedom and agricultural reforms and fight for land redistribution were not altogether in vain. He lived to see a lot of it happen. A generous, open-hearted man who had a passion for truth and was devoted to his work, he was held in high esteem. Abbas died in December 1985 and was buried in the presence of an official delegation of the FLN in the Martyrs Area in El Alia Cemetery, next to Colonel H. Boumedienne, Abd el Kader (q.v.) and other prominent national figures.■

Abbega, F.F.B. (c1836-1916)

ABBEGA, Frederick Fowell Buxton (c1836-1916).

NIGERIAN traveller, interpreter and chief, whose unusual career took him from the hill country now on the Nigeria-Cameroon border in the north to Europe, and to Lokoja, where he ended up as chief. He was of the Margi people, who now live mainly in Borno and Gongola states, and began life as a slave. He and a younger boy from Damagoram (a Hausa province now in the Niger Republic), named Dorugu, were redeemed from slavery by the German traveller Adolf Overweg, who arrived in Borno in 1851 with his more famous colleague Dr Heirrich Barth. They served Overweg and, when he died in 1852, worked for Barth, who continued for a further three years his remarkable travels as a representative of the British government.

After those extensive travels between Borno and Timbuctu, recorded in a voluminous book, Barth returned to Europe in 1855, taking Abbega and Dorugu with him. Both spent some time in England in the household of the Rev. J. F. Schön, a German missionary of the Church Missionary Society (CMS), who was a leading scholar of Hausa and had been on the 1841 expedition which attempted to found a British colony and base at the Niger-Benue confluence. Dorugu helped Schön in his Hausa studies, while Abbega, whose mother tongue was not Hausa, gave the churchman some Margi vocabulary and stories. It was hoped that the two would be pioneers for Christianity in Hausaland and neighbouring countries where it had not yet penetrated. In 1857 both were baptised, being named James Henry Dorugu and Frederick Fowell Buxton Abbega. The latter's names came from those of Frederick Schön and of Thomas Fowell Buxton, the great anti-slave-trade campaigner and main advocate of the 1841 Niger expedition.

Later that same year Abbega returned to what is now Nigeria, by sea from England, but did not try to return to the Margi homeland. He settled at Lokoja, the settlement founded in 1859-60 on the site of the 1841 venture. Lokoja expanded in the 1860s as a commercial centre, visited by African and European merchants, and was peopled by Sierra Leoneans and others redeemed from slavery locally. It was also a centre for missionary work, especially, for some time, that of the CMS under Bishop Crowther (q.v.), and of British and Christian influence, though Islam and the Hausa language were already dominant in the interior of Nigeria by that time. Abbega seems to have married soon after returning from Britain, and had several children. He fitted well into the community there. An interpreter at first, he worked for some time for the CMS, reading the New Testament to people from the Hausa version, at Rabbu, then capital of the Etsu Nupe who was overlord of Lokoja. He was said to have known five languages.

In the 1860s he was a personal messenger for the British Consul (the Lokoja consulate was ended in 1869); in the 1880s, he was a courier for the French Consul in the Delta area, who was also agent-general for the *Campagnie Française de l'Afrique Equatoriale*. He seems to have been an unofficial go-between with the Etsu Nupe, and conducted negotiations with him, including one for permission for a Catholic Mission to be installed at Lokoja in 1884, though he himself gave up Christianity and adopted Islam.

Unlike Dorugu, who remet Abbega at Lokoja in 1864 after returning from Britain and later went to Kano (where he died in 1912), Abbega seems not to have thought of revisiting his homeland. Instead, he remained at Lokoja and became prominent there. In 1896 The Royal Niger Company, then ruling at Lokoja, appointed him Chief of the town, to succeed David Mieux, a Sierra Leone-born interpreter who had held the post from 1870 to his death in 1896.

The following year Abbega was dismissed for alleged malpractice, but in 1898 he was restored again. Thus he was a chief when, on 1 January 1900, British rule over the Northern Nigerian "Protectorate" was proclaimed in a ceremony at Lokoja. The town was then more important than ever because of the extensive Niger river traffic. In 1904 Abbega was deposed again, this time by Lugard's Northern Nigeria Government, and banished to Asaba; he was replaced by Hansa Mieux, son of the previous chief.

In 1905, Abbega was recalled and turbanned as Chief once more. Lokoja had grown by then, with many British officials and a battalion of troops based there, and commercial firms multiplying in the town. Faded old-colonial buildings still abound in Lokoja and are reminiscent of that important bygone era. Abbega presided over it as chief until his death in 1916. He was, however, too old for work in his last years and Momadu Maikarifi took over real power and eventually succeeded Abbega.

A son of Abbega's daughter, Muhammadu Maimaina (1864-1964), worked as an interpreter and political agent for the British in Borno, and then became Chief of the Margi District, ruling over his maternal grandfather's people. ■

Abd al-Quddus, I. (1919-90)

ABD AL-QUDDUS, Ihsan (1919-90).

EGYPTIAN writer and journalist. He was born on 1 January 1919, son of Muhammad Abd al-Quddus, a civil engineer who became an actor and a writer for the stage and screen, and his wife Rose al-Youssuf, a famous woman in her own right—Egypt's leading lady of the theatre and also editor of an influential weekly called after her, *Rose al-Youssuf*. She and her husband were divorced soon after Ihsan's birth, and so he was brought up by his paternal grandfather, a traditional-minded graduate of Al Azhar University.

He studied Law at Cairo University, but practised Law only for a short time after qualifying in 1942; then he wrote for newspapers and magazines, and joined his mother's magazine. In 1945 he was imprisoned for attacks on the government and its allies or masters, the British. After his release his mother appointed him editor-in-chief of *Rose al-Youssuf* and he continued his radical nationalist attacks on the government and the British. He attacked King Farouk (q.v.) and his entourage, criticised the Arab states' conduct of the unsuccessful war against Israel in 1948-9, and also campaigned against Israel. In 1950-51 he was imprisoned again.

Abd al-Quddus' writings voiced the Egyptian nationalist feelings that led to the revolution of 1952 under the leadership of Colonel Nasser (q.v.). However, the new regime was also unwilling to tolerate his criticism, and before long it too had put Abd al-Quddus in gaol. He was badly treated in prison, but he remained dedicated to freedom of speech and thought. His first novel, published in 1954, was entitled *Ana Hurrah* ("I am free"). He had written short stories before, but now he concentrated on novels, of which he eventually published twenty.

In his novels he attacked political corruption and also social prejudices. In attacking those prejudices he produced what some Egyptians considered too erotic writings, and there were calls for banning one of the novels, *Anf wa-Thalath Uyun* ("A nose and three eyes", 1966). But he spoke before the National Assembly and argued successfully against a ban, with the support of President Nasser. Later Islamic fundamentalism, which Abd al-Quddus' own son adopted with many other Egyptians, gathered strength in stark opposition to the writer's ideas. But Egypt remained a relatively tolerant country and his writings were always popular.

He wrote a weekly column in Egypt's leading daily newspaper, *Al-Ahram,* in the 1970s, and in 1974 became Editor-in-Chief of *Akhbar al-Yom,* another prominent newspaper. In 1975 he was made chairman of *al-Ahram.* But while he held this high position for a time, he was best known for his novels and short stories and the ideas he put forward in them. He died in Cairo on 11 January 1990. ■

Abdallah, A. (1919-89)

ABDALLAH, Ahmed (1919-89).

COMOROS statesman, President of the island state of the Comoros for 12 years. He was born in Anjouan, the second island of the four Comoro islands, on 12 June 1919 (by official reckoning), but had some education in Madagascar, the great island nearby. Many Comorians went to Madagascar during French colonial rule over both territories, and it was at Majunga in Madagascar that Abdallah began work as a trader.

Later he developed an import and export business in the Comoros, trading in vanilla, copra and other goods. He became rich, but he took up the land reform movement in Anjouan, supporting the *wamatsaha* (dispossessed) of whom he was one by birth; he was never accepted by the traditional Comorian upper class. Abdallah, who married his wife Ghamyat in 1944 (they had nine children), always remained a businessman

A. Abdullah

during his political career, which began when he served on the *Conseil Général*, the local government council for the Comoros, from 1947 to 1949. The Comoros obtained representation in the French parliament like other colonies, and in 1959 Ahmed Abdallah was elected to the French Senate, where he served until 1972.

After self-government was conceded in 1961 Abdallah became leader of the *Union Démocratique des Comores* (UDC), which for long favoured continued ties with France but in 1972 joined with two other parties to form a "Union" calling for independence from France. In elections at the end of 1972 the Union won on all the four islands except Mayotte, which from then on supported the French connection against the wishes of the majority of Comorians.

Abdallah then became Prime Minister on 26 December 1972. Talks were held with the French government which led to an agreement on 15 June 1973 on independence in five years if approved by a referendum.

When the referendum was held in December 1974 voters on Mayotte voted against independence, while those on the other islands agreed to it. Discussions were held to solve the problem, but while the French called for decentralised government which Mayotte might accept, Abdallah opposed this. Relations between his government and France worsened, and on 6 July 1975 the Comoros parliament declared independence. The next day Ahmad Abdallah was chosen as President.

A month later, on 3 August 1975, a coup d'état carried out by mercenaries led by the Belgian Bob Denard deposed Abdallah and installed Ali Soilih (q.v.) in power. While the coup was believed to have French backing, France retained control of Mayotte, despite continued OAU and other protests; and Soilih's regime broke most ties with France and attempted to establish a self-sufficient, socialist system. Abdallah was arrested by Soilih's regime but then allowed to leave for France in 1976.

On 13 May 1978 a force of mercenaries, headed by the same Denard who had helped overthrow Abdallah (and, it was reported, wanted to kill him) in 1975, overthrew Soilih's regime, Soilih being mysteriously killed a little later. Ahmed Abdallah returned and became co-president with Mohammed Ahmed. The coup was probably aided by the French secret service, and

Abdallah established relations with France which sent plenty of aid (but did not consider restoring Mayotte). However, African states were shocked at the mercenaries' role, the Comoros delegation was at first refused admission to the OAU Council of Ministers in 1978, and Abdallah had to proclaim that he was ordering Denard's hired gunmen to leave. In October 1978 a new constitution for a Federal Islamic Republic was approved by referendum, and Ahmed Abdallah was elected president for a six-year term.

Other African states accepted the legitimacy of Abdallah's regime, but governments of radical ideas which had been friendly to Soilih—those of Tanzania and Seychelles—did not reconcile themselves to it for many years. It became clear later that Denard had returned, if he had ever left, and with other mercenaries had trained and officered a special presidential guard for Abdallah. The President apparently trusted those people to deal with internal opposition. This continued for years, with a plot involving other mercenaries in 1983, a coup attempt in 1985, and another coup attempt in November 1987. Abdallah was believed to have covert help from South Africa in suppressing such challenges.

Besides the opposition Abdallah, who was re-elected unopposed in 1984, had to deal with the country's chronic and serious economic problems. While these were due to factors beyond his control, they did not stop him from continuing in business profitably; on returning to power he reacquired a monopoly of rice imports. Yet despite his self-enrichment, he had qualities which appealed to Comorians, such as his colourful style of dress and direct manner of speech.

In November 1989 a referendum approved a constitutional amendment to allow the President to serve more than two six-year terms. But on the night of 26-7 November 1989 President Abdallah was killed in an attack on his palace in Moroni. Very soon afterwards Col. Denard and his mercenaries seized control, and it was believed, though he denied it, that Denard had killed the President. France and South Africa, now embarrassed by mercenaries who had served them in the past, forced Denard and his men to leave the Comoros. To some Africans their activities tarnished the memory of Ahmed Abdallah who had employed them. But he had support in his own country and was in a way its founding father. ∎

Abd el-Kader (1808-83)

ABD EL-KADER (1808-83).

ALGERIAN resistance leader who led several battles against the French colonial forces. He was the son of Muhyi el-Din of the Hashim ethnic group in western Algeria, a sheikh of the major Sufi Islamic order in Algeria then, the Qadiriyya. He and his father made the pilgrimage to Mecca before both became involved in resistance to the French who landed at Algiers in 1830. In 1831 his father was recognised as leader of a *Jihad* against the French in the Oran area, but he himself led the attacks, and in view of his father's age and failing health he was recognised as Sultan by a number of ethnic groups. He rapidly extended his following. In the next few years he alternately fought the French and made agreements with them, being well informed about them. In France, on the other hand, many saw him as a hero for his resistance to their own country's aggression.

Abd el-Kader

An agreement in 1834 recognised him as ruler of a large western area, where he ruled as Amir. But in 1835-6 the French attacked Mascara and Tlemcen, in that area. In 1837 another agreement, the Treaty of Tafna, was signed. Amir Abd el-Kader extended his authority eastwards in the next few years. He ruled a considerable part of Algeria for a time, ruling through Khalifas (deputies) and traditional chiefs (agha). He had a standing army of a few thousand, reinforced by traditional levies for campaigns.

In late 1839 war resumed and Abd el-Kader's forces advanced on Algiers, killing many French settlers. In late 1840 France sent General Bugeaud to carry out a policy of full occupation of Algeria. This involved a long campaign (February 1841 to June 1847) against Abd el-Kader. The French used brutal methods which eventually succeeded in wearing down the strong resistance. Abd el-Kader fled to Morocco in 1843; Moroccan forces were sent to support the resistance but were defeated in 1844. In 1846 Abd el-Kader led a new rising, but in 1847 he was finally defeated. He surrendered on 23 December 1847 and, in spite of a promise of safe conduct, he was detained in France until 1852 when he was allowed to leave for Damascus in Turkish Syria.

He used his influence to prevent a massacre of Christians in 1860. French admiration for this led to French proposals for an Arab state carved out of the Ottoman empire, under his rule, but he refused. He also refused to support the 1871 rising in Algeria, repudiating one of his sons' action in joining the rising. He died in Damascus on 26 May 1883. ■

Abd el-Krim (1882-1963)

ABD EL-KRIM (1882-1963).

MOROCCAN resistance leader in the struggle against Spanish occupation. His full name was Sidi Mohammed ben Abdel Krim el-Khettabi. His father was a Moslem judge (*qadi*) in Ajdir in northern Morocco, which was occupied by Spain in 1909, just after the young Sidi Mohammed had com-

For five years thereafter Abd el-Krim fought one of the fiercest wars of resistance in colonised Africa, arousing admiration in the Arab world and outside. He ruled with the title of Amin over a large part of the Rif, heading a government termed "Republic State of the Rif."

He abolished slavery and created a constitutional government. The area under him had universal military service, and there was a standing army of some thousands, armed with modern weapons.

In 1924 Abd el-Krim won more victories over the Spanish forces. He refrained for long from attacking the more powerful French. But when talks with Spain broke down because Abd el-Krim insisted on full independence, he attacked French Morocco. In 1925 France and Spain combined to defeat his guerrillas, and he surrendered to the French in May 1926. He, his brother, some of the ministers of his free Rifi government, and their families, were deported to Réunion.

In 1947 the French agreed to allow him back to Morocco, but when his ship stopped in Egypt, he and his party, who were only lightly guarded, went ashore and stayed, urged on by the many exiled nationalists from French North Africa then in Egypt.

After independence the Rifis, dissatisfied with King Mohammed V's government, called for Abd el-Krim's return. The government also wanted this, but he refused to while any foreign troops were on Moroccan soil. King Mohammed V (q.v.) visited him in Egypt in 1960, but he still would not return to Morocco. He died in Cairo on 5/6 February 1963. ■

Abd el-Krim

pleted his studies (1905-09) at the ancient Karaouine University of Fez. He worked for the Spanish authorities as a teacher, as an official of the 'bureau of native affairs", and in 1915 as judge of the court for "native" cases at Melilla. But he turned against Spanish rule, contacting the Germans who in the 1914-18 war encouraged Moroccan resistance, particularly against the French who had occupied most of Morocco. When the authorities found out, Abd el-Krim was arrested in 1916. Freed the same year, he worked in Melilla again and later returned to Ajdir, where he succeeded his father as *qadi* in 1920.

In 1920-21 he personally toured the various section of the Rifis, his Berber countrymen, who fiercely cherished their independence in the high Rif mountains and had not yet been defeated by Spain. The Berbers united under Abd el-Krim to fight against a large Spanish army sent to establish full control over Spanish Morocco. In July 1921 his forces won a tremendous victory over the Spanish army at the Battle of Anual.

Abduh, M. (1849-1905)

ABDUH, Muhammed (1849-1905).

EGYPTIAN religious leader. Born in a village near Tanta in the Nile Delta, of Turkish origin on his father's side, he went at the age of 13 to study at the Sayed Ahmed al-Badami Mosque at Tanta. He also received training and inspiration from a great-uncle who followed Sufism, the pursuit of holiness through personal communion with God. In 1866 he went to al-Azhar, one of the leading centres of Islamic learning, in Cairo. The al-Azhar mosque and University were by then being influenced by the modernisation which was transforming Egypt generally. It started the teaching of modern subjects in 1872, and about then the question of Islam's place in the modern world was the subject of active interest at the University.

From 1871 to 1879 Jamal al-Din al-Afghani, a distinguished scholar, taught at al-Azhar, preaching a way in which Moslems could adopt some European knowledge. Abduh followed his teaching, whose main element was a stress on the use of reason for the correct understanding of Islam; Abduh rejected the customary teaching of the Koran by rote, and passive and uncomprehending acceptance of Islam. He taught that a Moslem must use his reason and comprehend his religion properly and in doing so a Moslem could adopt harmless ideas from the non-Moslem world.

Abduh passed his final examination and a diploma qualifying him as an *alim* (teacher) at al-Azhar in 1877. He then taught at the University. Before then he had begun his numerous writings. He published two works on religion, one on Sufism, and a series of articles in 1876, stressing the need for modern knowledge. He was noted for his views, which challenged the established habits of many Moslems (contrary to true Islam in his view) and governments. On account of his views he was briefly confined to his village by order of Khedive Tewfik in 1879.

Back in Cairo soon afterwards, he became editor of the official gazette. He was active in the events of 1879-82, when a nationalist movement arose in reaction to the Anglo-French "Dual Control." While not closely involved with the military nationalist leader Urabi Pasha (q.v.), he was sentenced to three years' exile after the intervention of British forces and the defeat of the nationalists in 1882. He went to Beirut and then to Paris where he and al-Afghani worked together on a magazine called *al-'Urwa al-wuthqa*, which closed down in 1884 after publishing 18 issues. The magazine was influential in calling on all Moslems to unite against danger which, it said, came especially from British imperialism, and to overcome their own weakness; this, the two scholars said, was due to corruption and self-seeking among Moslem leaders, and unthinking obedience to the teachings of Islam instead of reasoned efforts to understand them.

Later Abduh separated from al-Afghani and gave up active politics, concentrating on the preaching of religious reform (which, of course, had political implications for Moslems). He travelled via Tunis to Beirut, where he stayed for three years, publicizing ideas for reform of religious education, did some teaching, and published works on Arabic literature. In 1888 he returned to Egypt.

He was appointed a judge of the "Native Courts" set up under the British occupation. Later he was a judge of the Court of Appeal. In 1899 he was given the important post of Mufti of Egypt, the country's main official adviser on points of Moslem law. He had good working relations with the British Consul-General, Cromer, seeing British domination as a necessary evil from which some good could come. He was for some years on the administrative council of al-Azhar and helped carry out further reforms there.

Reform of Islam was his main message, from which other ideas, political ones included, were derived. He died in 1905. His influence was profound in Egypt, where Zaghlul Pasha (q.v.) was a noted disciple who became a political leader, and also in Algeria, especially through Ben Badis (q.v.), and other Moslem countries.■

Abdullahi, al-Khalifa (c. 1846-99)

ABDULLAHI,   al-Ta'ish   al-Khalifa (c. 1846-99).

SUDANESE nationalist and religious leader, successor as Khalifa to Muhammed Ahmad al-Mahdi (q.v.). He hailed from a family of religious notables among the Ta'isha, a Baggara ethnic group in Darfur. He was born around 1846 and his belief that the coming of the Mahdi, foretold by Islamic theology, was imminent drove him to search for this figure. He met, and became the disciple of, Muhammed Ahmad, and was an early enthusiast in the Mahdist revolution which started in 1880-81.

Al-Khalifa Abdullahi

After further victories over the Egyptians, the Khalifa suppressed internal resistance, the strongest being in Darfur, and in 1889 his forces defeated the Ethiopians when these withdrew after the death in battle of Emperor John IV. The Khalifa was then at the height of his power. But a major famine hit the Sudan in 1889. Later the Khalifa ordered concentrated efforts on agriculture and there was enough grain. The British in Egypt, anxiously watching the Khalifa's state and thinking of reconquering the Sudan one day, defeated the Mahdists in the Suakin area in 1891. In that year a plot against the Khalifa was foiled.

The contemporary European view of him as a mere tyrant has been modified, and A.B. Theobald in his book, *The Mahdiya*, says, "He created a system of government out of chaos, and with whatever creakings, the system worked for thirteen years, through war, revolution, famine and pestilence." He considers that "the Khalifa 'Abd Abdullahi was not a lovable man; but he was certainly a formidable one."

In 1896 an Anglo-Egyptian force began a slow advance into the Sudan, building a railway as it went. After several battles in which the Mahdists fought well but lost, the Khalifa sent an army of 52,000 to face Kitchener's forces on 2 September 1898. Half the Sudanese army was killed or wounded in an overwhelming defeat at Omdurman. The Khalifa escaped the carnage and eluded the occupying forces for over a year with a few followers. But on 24 November 1899 he was killed by British forces under Col. Sir Reginald Wingate at Umm Diwaikarat, 40 miles from Aba Island. ■

As a competent organiser and commander he became the most important assistant to the Mahdi. The Mahdist revolt originally started from Aba Island in the Nile and was partly a protest against alien rule; the senior posts in the Egyptian administration, though Ottoman in character, were staffed by members of the Europeanised, Turkish-speaking Egyptian ruling class whose way of life was opposed by the Sudanese religious leaders. From 1881 the Mahdist revolution, nationalist and religious, drove back the Egyptians and their European officials and advisers. Britain's occupation of Egypt in 1882 did not stem the Mahdist advance to the south. Britain ordered an evacuation and sent General Charles Gordon to organise it; but Gordon was killed when the Mahdists took Khartoum early in 1885.

On 20 June 1885 the Mahdi died. By his wish Abdullahi became his successor, at the head of the victorious revolution. For thirteen years the Khalifa ruled one of the largest states in Africa. His foreign relations were determined by the belief that such a religious state should not have dealings with bad Moslems or unbelievers. Internally he improved the judicial system, which like taxation and most other aspects of the state was based on Islam.

Abdurahman, A. (1872-1940)

ABDURAHMAN, Dr. Abdulla (1872-1940).

SOUTH AFRICAN political leader; President of the African People's Organisation and the first elected Coloured representative in the Cape Town City Council. The son of a teacher, Abdurahman was born in 1872 of Malay parentage in District Six in Cape Town. After elementary school, he attended the Marist Brothers College, Cape Town, and later the South African College, founded in 1829 as the first secondary school in the country that later developed to become the University of Cape Town. No sooner had Abdurahman graduated from the secondary school than the government introduced measures which barred non-whites from the institution. His family soon migrated to Britain where Abdurahman studied for a medical degree, graduating as a doctor from the University of Glasgow in Scotland in 1893.

It was during that period that he married his Scottish wife, with whom he returned to South Africa in 1895. That same year Dr. Abdurahman set up in private practice in Cape Town and soon earned an outstanding reputation because of the success of his surgery. With this came the inclination to join the growing combined African and Coloured opposition to the discriminatory measures of the government. He entered politics in 1902 as a founding member of the African People's Organisation (APO), formed in Cape Town. A politician of sharp perception and organisational ability, he was elected its President in 1905. The previous year Abdurahman had been elected to the Cape Town City Council, becoming the first Coloured representative in the Council. This was followed in 1914 with his election to the Cape Provincial Council; Abdurahman served on both councils until his death.

Abdurahman commanded the respect of his constituents, cutting across the volatile racial divide emanating from the discriminatory measures of the settler administration. As such he was able to argue for a unitary constitution to safeguard the Cape's non-racial policy while advocating political unity between the Indian, the Coloured and the African communities. He began efforts aimed at achieving the latter through a series of conferences, convened by him and Davidson Don Tengo Jabavu (q.v.) and other African leaders, that met between 1927 and 1934. The outcome of these early efforts was the formation of the non-European Unity Movement which became affiliated with the African National Congress (ANC) in 1943. Earlier in 1906 and 1909 Abdurahman had joined the African leaders in the non-European delegations to London to protest against the creation of the Union of South African and the subsequent introduction of the colour bar.

Throughout his political career he remained committed to the unity of all South African non-white races, believing it was the most effective way of fighting the repressive measures of the white-minority regime. Abdurahman was an admirer of General Jan Christian Smuts (q.v.) and his United Party that later became the Unionist Party, and this may have influenced his opposition to the apartheid policy of the settler admin-

Dr. A. Abdurahman

istration. Nevertheless he used his political influence to oppose many of its measures, like in 1918 when he came out strongly against South Africa's claim to govern Namibia (South West Africa).

In his later years, however, his leadership of the APO came under serious challenge from its younger and more radical elements, which included his daughter Zainunnissa "Cissie" Gool. Gool, in association with James La Guma and John Gomas, later founded the National Liberation League following the unsuccessful bid to unseat Abdurahman. The daughter became the president of a rival movement, the Non-European United Front, but Abdurahman remained at the presidency of the APO until his death in 1940.■

Abebe, A. (1918-74)

ABEBE, Lieutenant-General Abiye (1918-74).

ETHIOPIAN military officer, diplomat and President of the Senate. Of distinguished background, he was the son of Abebe Atnaf Sagad who was also an officer in the Imperial Army; he fought alongside Emperor Haile Selassie (q.v.) in the 1916 Battle of Sagalle. Abiye's nephew, Dejazmatch Wube Atnaf Sagad (died 1913), married Zawditu, daughter of Emperor Menelik II (q.v.) who was proclaimed Empress of Ethiopia in 1916 with Ras Tafari Makonnen (later Emperor Haile Selassie) as Crown Prince and Regent Plenipotentiary.

Abiye Abebe was born in 1918 in Addis Ababa where he was educated; the Emperor took special care of him and supervised his education through the Officer's Training School in Holetta, following which he fought in 1941 in the Ethiopian army during the Italian occupation of the country. After 1942 when the Emperor regained his throne, Abebe was very close to Haile Selassie. After the war of liberation he was appointed governor of Wollega Province and served there between 1942 and 1943. On the eve of his posting to Wollega he married the Emperor's second daughter Princess Tsahal in the Ethiopian capital on 26 April 1942, but the Princess died in childbirth later that same year. Between 1943 and 1947 Abebe became acting Minister of War, becoming a substantive holder of the portfolio in 1949. Three years before he had reverted to military duties as a divisional commander, in addition to his function as acting War Minister.

In 1955 he was appointed Ethiopian Ambassador to France. He remained in Paris until 1958 when the Emperor recalled him to become Minister of Justice. That same year he was made Lieutenant-General in the Imperial Army.

In 1959 Abebe was appointed Minister of the Interior and also Viceroy of Eritrea, the troubled former Italian colony that was annexed by a 1952 United Nations resolution; Eritrea was formally made a province of Ethiopia on 14 November 1962 while Abebe was serving there. It was a measure of

General Abebe's shrewdness that the Eritrean struggle for secession did not develop to open rebellion before 1970 when the Ethiopian government subsequently placed Eritrea under martial law. He was recalled from Asmara in 1964 and made President of the Senate in Addis Ababa.

This new posting, too, did not prove less difficult for Abebe. For the culminative effect of the war in Eritrea and, in particular, of the general dissatisfaction generated by the severe drought and famine of 1973 in which an estimated 100,000 people died resulted in widespread rebellion against the Emperor and his government.

In the subsequent efforts to contain the uprising General Abebe was co-opted in February 1974 by the Emperor into the Council of Ministers which had Aklilu Habte-Wolde (q.v.) as its head; Abebe was appointed Minister of Defence and given the additional post of Chief-of-Staff of the Armed Forces. On 31 March 1974 he announced over Ethiopia radio and television that a plot "by criminal and irresponsible elements, aimed at plunging the country into war" had been foiled the previous week.

When some members of the Armed Forces eventually took a more active role in the running of the government in April 1974 and formed the Military Co-ordinating Committee (MCC), later named the Dergue, General Abebe was among those members of the Emperor's regime who were arrested. Radio Ethiopia announced on 16 July 1974 that the Army had arrested the Defence Minister after being accused by a young officer of being at home and refusing to go to his office at the ministry. He was subsequently executed, together with several senior military officers and ministers in the Emperor's administration, in Addis Ababa on 23 November 1974. The new military authorities charged him with "abuse of authority". ■

Abid, S. (1933-67)

ABID, Said (1933-67).

ALGERIAN army officer who played a prominent role in the armed struggle for independence; he was Commander of the first military region. Said Abid was born in 1933 of peasant parents in Khenchela, south-east of Constantine. At the age of 21 he abandoned his studies in favour of the nationalist struggle that was being launched by the *Front de Libération Nationale* (FLN).

He joined FLN's military wing, the *Armée de Libération Nationale* (ALN) and was posted to the Aurès military region, *Wilaya I*, along the Algerian-Tunisian bor-der. The military regions, six in all, which were established to facilitate war efforts and systemise military organisation, were placed under the militant vanguard of the ALN. After independence was achieved in 1962, Abid was made First Commander of the Aurès military district. He was in this post when the Ben Bella regime was overthrown in a bloodless coup d'état in 1965, and after that his military duties included the guard-ing of the deposed President. Following the coup Abid became a close associate of the new Head of State, Colonel Houari Boumedienne (q.v.), who regarded Abid as the model for the new Algerian military officer.

Abid's own devotion to the new mili-tary leadership was demonstrated during the abortive coup of December 1967 in which he died while attempting to prevent the rebel-lious troops from marching on Algiers. According to an official post-coup report, the coup-makers, headed by Colonel Tahir Zbiri, a former army Chief-of-Staff, had planned to seize power with the aid of the troops in the first military region under Abid's command.

On 14 November 1967 Abid was said to have reported to President Boumedienne that an armoured battalion from El-Asnam was moving towards the Algerian capital, led by Zbiri's brother-in-law, Layachi Haouss-nia. After conferring with the President, Abid returned to his Blida military base to ensure the loyalty of troops under his command but learned that units from Mi-liana and Medea had defied his authority and were heading towards Algiers. He again contacted Boumedienne on the telephone to request permission to attempt peaceful nego-tiations with the rebels.

In an inteview with *Al-Ahram*, Bou-medienne said he granted Abid's request to negotiate with the rebels, provided that they did not continue their march to Algiers. Efforts at negotiation failed on 15 December and the mutineers began their advance, firing at loyalist forces. At this time, Abid was reported by the *Algérie Presse* Service to

be "in constant contact with the Minister of National Defence to inform him of events and how orders were being carried out". A communiqué concerning his death said that Abid committed suicide at his post in Blida, leaving a note in which he said he "could not bear the rebellion of his own commanders". The communiqué added that "Commander Said Abid gave precise orders to his staff to put themselves at the service of the state and nation and to refuse to obey any order which did not come from the government".

Abid was buried with full military honours in his Constantine home region and the funeral was attended by President Bou-medienne and a host of senior ministers. ■

Abubakar III (1903-88)

ABUBAKAR III, Sir Siddiq (1903-88).

NIGERIAN Muslim leader, traditional ruler (Sultan) of Sokoto. Siddiq Abuba-kar was born at Dange, some 60 km from Sokoto, on 15 March 1903, the same day on which the British finally subdued the Sokoto Caliphate.

Siddiq Abubakar III was the son of Usman Shehu, an eminent personality whose father, Mu'azu, was the Sultan of Sokoto (1877-81) and a direct descendant of Usman Dan Fodio (q.v.) who founded the caliphate in 1809.

Siddiq Abubakar had an Islamic edu-cation; he attended the local Koranic schools and held several administrative posts before succeeding his uncle, Hassan Ibn Muazu, as the Sultan of Sokoto at the early age of 35. He first came to Sultan Hassan's attention when he was district scribe, and in 1931 he was appointed a local authority councillor of the Sokoto Native Administration. Later, as head of Talata Mafara, a most important district which included the commercial town of Gusau, he distinguished himself by his administrative competence and the able way he dealt with appeals from traditional courts and supervised district and village heads.

In recognition of his ability and usefulness to the emirate, Siddiq Abubakar was appointed Sardauna of Sokoto, a posi-tion he held until 17 June 1938 when he became the Sultan of Sokoto, Abubakar III.

As the 17th Sultan of Sokoto and *Sarkin Musulmi* (Commander of the Faithful) he became the most important Islamic personality south of the Sahara and was highly respected. Not only was he the descendant and successor of Usman Dan Fodio, whose grave still attracts pilgrims from all over the world, but he was also the leader of 50 million adherents of the Islamic faith who live in West Africa, and who

Abubakar III

looked to him for the definitive dates on which Islamic observances, rituals and ceremonies had to be held.

Although he did not occupy a visible political position in Nigeria, his de facto political influence was considerable and throughout his life he worked towards the promotion of Nigeria's unity and territorial integrity. Moreover, a nationalist and firm believer in Nigerian unity, he used his decisive influence over public affairs for the political and social advancement of Nigeria as one nation. In this regard he contributed a great deal to the maintenance of order and calm among the population of the then Northern Region after the 1966 coup in which Sir Ahmadu Bello (q.v.) was killed.

Later during the civil war he helped to mobilise men for the Federal Forces.

Abubakar saw the development of his country in a different light from many of his more conservative co-religionists. He encouraged further education for females and voting for women in purdah, and urged the liberation of women in these respects. As a result the Women Teachers' Training College in Sokoto was founded. His faith in and identification with the quest for knowledge led to his appointment as Chancellor of the University of Nigeria, Nsukka, which awarded him an honorary LlD degree.

During his life, however, Abubakar, in common with other traditional rulers, witnessed several inroads into his power-base, such as loss of control over local courts, prisons and police. But because of his mature outlook he did not allow these developments to affect his concern for the welfare of his people. He saw these changes as inevitable in the wider context of the country's politics and in the overall interest of Nigeria's development. So when the Northern People's Congress was formed in 1951 and his support was needed to launch the new party and mobilise the Northern people for the independence movement, he readily gave it. Similarly, Abubakar took the post of Minister without Portfolio in the Northern Regional Government in order to give the new administration headed by Sir Ahmadu Bello, whom he had earlier appointed the Sardauna of Sokoto, the stamp of religious acceptability. And yet his involvement was never such as to identify him with the partisan politics of his time. He stood head and shoulders above the politicians of all hues, in a way that allowed him to be accessible to all. When party politics became really divisive he stepped out of it to safeguard his role as the spiritual leader, but continued to be looked up to by other leaders on certain governmental issues.

Abubakar III was a much honoured and respected man. He was knighted by the British in 1944 and after Nigeria attained independence was made Grand Commander of the Order of Niger by the Federal Government. He had a great love of poetry and, as a traditionalist, kept the culture of his people alive while recognising the need to develop their potential and achieve progress in the modern world.

He ruled the emirate for one of the longest reigns in its history, from 17 June

1938 to 1 November 1988 when he died, having celebrated only four months earlier his fiftieth year on the throne. He left behind 52 children and 320 direct grandchildren.

Sultan Abubakar III is best remembered by his compatriots as a religious leader who rose above the religious dissensions of his day and throughout his life played the role of peace-maker and father of all.■

Abushiri (c.1845-89)

ABUSHIRI (c.1845-89).

TANZANIAN resistance leader. His full name was Abushiri ben Salim al-Harthi. Born in about 1845, he was a son of the important clan of the Harthi, of Omani Arab descent; his mother was African. He was one of the Swahili coastal community, of mixed origin and Islamic religion, which in the 19th century was subject to the Sultan of Zanzibar and traded on his behalf extensively between the coast, opposite Zanzibar, and the interior of Tanzania.

His early life is obscure but he is said to have lived at Tabora and Ujiji (on the shore of Lake Tanganyika), two important centres of the ivory and slave trade. Later he moved to Pangani (an ancient town thought to have been the first to be referred to in the writings of the early Portuguese explorers, on the coast of Tanzania, south of the town of Tanga, and became prominent in its local affairs. He claimed to have taken part in an expedition sent by the Sultan in the 1870s against Mirambo (q.v.)) of the Nyamwezi in what is now the Tabora region.

In 1888 the German East Africa Company (a chartered company like others which started colonial occupation) signed an agreement with the Sultan, under which it was given some rights on the mainland coast. This was a move to establish German claims in the area, which Karl Peters had begun to stake in 1885. Ignoring the letter of the agreement, the East Africa Company acted as if it ruled the Swahili coast. Its harsh and domineering acts quickly led to a rising in which the Company's agents were driven from all the seven points where they were stationed, except for Dar-es-Salaam and Bagamoyo.

Abushiri

Abushiri, then apparently in his early forties, emerged as a leader of the insurgents. With an army of 6-8,000 men, he sought to complete the success of the rebellion by marching to the south, attacking the Germans at Bagamoyo and Dar-es-Salaam. These attacks failed and the interior rulers whom Abushiri contacted did not join him, though they sent some help. In 1889 there was a truce between him and the Germans but in talks which followed the Germans rejected Abushiri's peace proposals. In May 1889 the Germans counter-attacked.

Aided by reinforcements from Germany, the invaders drove back the Africans. Abushiri recruited Mbunga warriors (an offshoot of the Ngoni warriors) from the interior but these did more harm to the local population than to the Germans. He contacted another chief fighting the Germans, Bwana Heri, but could not join him in guerilla resistance because of serious elephantiasis. Hindered by this, Abushiri moved north and, with the rebel forces scattered by late 1889, decided to flee to the then British East Africa (Kenya). By then the Africans had turned against him and the Germans had offered a big reward for his arrest. So he was handed over to the Germans, who hanged him on 15 December 1889 at Pangani. The suppression of his rising was followed by full German government control over Tanganyika.■

Acheampong, I.K. (1931-79)

ACHEAMPONG, General Ignatius Kutu
(1931-79).

Gen. I.K. Acheampong

GHANAIAN military ruler who led the country's second coup. General Acheampong was born on 23 September 1931 at Mwamase, Kumasi in the Ashanti Region of Ghana. His father, a cocoa broker, was a devout Roman Catholic and Ignatius Acheampong grew up a firm believer. He received his early education in the Ashanti Region where he studied initially at the elementary school at Trabuom, and later at St. Peter's Catholic School at Kumasi and the Roman Catholic School at Ejisu. He completed his education at the Central College of Commerce, Agona Swedru, in Ghana's Central Region.

He began his career as a tutor at Kumasi Commercial College in 1949. The following year he was appointed Vice-Principal of the Central College of Commerce where he was previously a pupil, and he became Principal of the Western Commercial Institute at Achiose in 1951-52. In 1953 he left the field of education and joined the Ghana Army.

After five years in the Army, he was selected to attend Mons Officer Cadet Training School at Aldershot in England in 1958-59. He then went on a period of attachment with a British battalion before attending the General Staff College at Fort Leavenworth in Kansas, USA. He returned to Ghana and joined the 2nd Battalion in 1961. Between 1962-63 he was a member of the Ghanaian Contingent of the United Nations Peace Keeping Force in the Congo (now Zaire), and by 1966 he had been promoted to Commanding Officer of the 6th Battalion.

By this time Acheampong's interest in politics had deepened and although he played no major role in the 1966 coup, he supported its objectives and was appointed chairman of the administration in the Western Region by the new regime. He became Commanding Officer of the 5th Battalion in 1969, and in November 1971 he was promoted to Brigade Commander of the strategic 1st Infantry Brigade in Accra from which position he engineered a coup against the then Prime Minister Kofi Busia becoming Head of State and Government on 13 January 1972.

After the coup his initial priority was agricultural development to achieve self-sufficiency in food, while attempting to establish an effective agro-industrial sector. With this in mind he initiated the Self-Reliance Programme and Operation Feed the Nation, and in January 1973, he formulated a Charter of Redemption comprising seven courses of action to achieve economic stability. Meanwhile he took responsibility for the portfolios of Finance, Economic Affairs, Defence and Public Relations.

In 1975 Acheampong became Chairman of the Supreme Military Council and in 1976 he was promoted to the rank of General. In October 1976 he put forward proposals for a Union Government which many saw as a ruse to perpetuate military rule, since it advocated a governing union between the military and the civilian sections of society and by the time a referendum was held on this issue in April 1978, it had become very controversial. In the referendum, 1,103,423 people were reported having voted for the concept of Union Government, with 880,255 against. As 57 per cent of the electorate did not vote and doubts were expressed by many people on the conduct of the referendum, workers, students, professionals and the outlawed political parties continued to campaign against Union Government, a campaign which the military Government met with increasing force.

This split in opinion over the political future of Ghana, combined with the now serious economic situation in the country evidenced by a high rate of inflation and a serious shortage of essential commodities on the one hand, together with an increase in smuggling and hoarding and a thriving blackmarket on the other, as well as Acheampong's growing reputation for corruption, caused a group of officers of Ghana's Supreme Military Council to force General Acheampong to resign as Chairman of the Supreme Military Council and retire from the Army on 5 July 1978. He was then sent to the Presidential retreat overlooking the Volta River at Akosombo. Almost one year later, following the coup of 4 June 1979, Ignatius Acheampong was brought out of retirement and executed by a firing squad on 16 June 1979 for alleged economic crimes against his country. ■

Acyl, A. (1944-82)

ACYL, Ahmat (1944-82).

CHADIAN politician, one of the most prominent in the country at the time of his death. He served as Deputy in the National Assembly before being appointed Foreign Minister in the *Gouvernement d'Unité Nationale de Transition* (GUNT) under Goukhouni Oueddei; that government was formed in 1979 and lasted until 1982 when it was overrun by Hissène Habré's *Forces Armées du Nord* (FAN), the other major force in Chad's running civil war at that time.

Ahmat Acyl was a protagonist in that war. Originating from the Salamat zone of south-eastern Chad where he was born in 1944, he was one of the principal Arab ethnic leaders of that area which has always been a main element of the Chad equation. Ahmed Koulamallah, one of the fathers of Chadian independence, was from Acyl's area, and his

fall from power and detention in 1963 by the regime of Ngartha Tombalbaye (q.v.) is one of the reasons behind Chad's civil war. Acyl himself was a co-founder of the *Front de Libération Nationale du Tchad* (FROLINAT), one of the main organisations in the struggle for political power.

A. Acyl

In 1976 he joined the guerillas in the war that had been going on since 1965. Just over a year later during the fiercest fighting, Acyl led the January 1978 major guerilla offensive in the Borkou-Ennedi-Tibesti region, which resulted in the capture of its headquarters, Faya-Largeau. Two months later, this successful operation was followed by the opening of talks which led to the agreements signed on 27 March 1978 in Libya between FROLINAT and the Supreme Military Council under General Félix Malloum.

These agreements were the first stage in the drawing up of a National Charter promulgated at Ndjamena on 29 August 1978, confirming General Malloum as Head of State while Hissène Habré became Prime Minister.

From then on, Ahmat Acyl was constantly in the news concerning developments in Chad, right up to his death. Notably, he was with the *Forces Armeés Populaires* (FAP) under Goukhouni Oueddei in the battle of Ndjamena following the split between Malloum and Habré on 19 February 1979. Soon after the cease-fire of 5 March 1979, the first national reconciliation conference was held at Kano in Nigeria. Acyl was absent at that conference but was a prominent figure at the following Lagos conference that convened under the auspices of Nigeria, Cameroon, Libya, Niger and Sudan.

On 29 April 1979, Goukhouni Oueddei and Hissène Habré formed a Government of National Union whose presidency was conferred on Lal Mahamat Shawa. Acyl joined that government, but it was boycotted by neighbouring states and by the OAU which preferred broader negotiations for peace in Chad. When these negotiations opened in Lagos on 13 August 1979, eleven "tendencies" were represented, among them Ahmat Acyl's *Conseil Démocratique Révolutionnaire* (CDR) which emerged from the so-called Vulcan army in the former FRO-LINAT coalition. The GUNT arose from the Lagos conference. It was entrusted with creating, over the 18 months assigned to it, conditions suitable for the organisation of democratic elections. Constituted on 11 November 1979, it was presided over by Goukhouni Oueddei while Colonel Wadal Kamougue was Vice-President, Hissène Habré Minister of Defence and Ahmat Acyl Minister of Foreign Affairs.

The CDR leader, often presented as the representative of the Arab ethnic elements in Chad, held that post until the fall of the GUNT on 7 June 1982, when Habré's forces (in opposition to the government since March 1980) marched on Ndjamena, before the helpless gaze of a peace-keeping force sent to Chad by the OAU.

Ahmat Acyl was not in Ndjamena when the FAN arrived, but his statements afterwards indicated a willingness to make efforts for reconciliation with Habré, although his own CDR's bases at Guelandeng were being attacked by FAN at the time. He was going to Lai for talks with Colonel Kamougue to seek a possible common approach to the complex politico-military situation in Chad when he died on 19 July 1982 in a plane accident. He was reported to have been killed when struck by a propeller as he was getting out of the plane at Lai, but some press reports said that the former ebullient Foreign Minister was shot down by machine gun fire when he opened the doors of the aircraft. ■

Adegbenro, D.S. (1909-75)

ADEGBENRO, Alhaji Chief Dauda Soroye (1909-75).

NIGERIAN politician, a leading figure in the former Western Nigeria, he emerged as national leader of the now defunct Action Group (AG) party in the 1960s. His rise in the party hierarchy was precipitated by the leadership crisis between him and Chief Samuel Ladoke Akintola (q.v.), following the imprisonment of its leader Chief Obafemi Awolowo for treason in 1963.

Dauda Soroye Adegbenro was born in 1909 in the famous Egba town, in the former Western Region, now capital of Ogun State. He was educated at the local Baptist Boys' High School and Grammar School. His first job was with the Nigerian Railway Corporation as a clerk. He later worked as a storekeeper for the United African Company, the British multi-national with widespread interests in Africa.

Adegbenro took an early interest in the nationalist campaign to win indepen-

Alhaji D.S. Adegbenro

dence from Britain, but he did not commit himself to active politics until the 1940s. It was then that he joined the rank of Awolowo, Akintola and others whose pioneering Nigerian Youth Movement (formed in the 1930s) became the nucleus of the Action Group. The new party was launched as a national movement in April 1951 with a programme of "Freedom for all, life more abundant." The AG demanded, in addition to the end of British rule, freedom from ignorance, hunger and disease. It was with this laudable programme that the party contested the 1951 elections to the Western Region House of Assembly. Though the results of those elections favoured the National Council of Nigeria and the Cameroons (NCNC), led in the Region by Adegoke Adelabu (q.v.), post-election defections gave the AG the majority.

Adegbenro, however, was easily elected, having been prominent in local Egba politics. He was soon selected by the Regional Assembly as one of its representatives in the Federal House of Representatives in Lagos. In 1954 he returned to the Western legislature to serve as Parliamentary Secretary to the Minister of Justice and later as Minister of Land and Labour and then Minister of Local Government. An able administrator, trusted and articulate, he built up an intimate partnership with his party and government leaders, particularly Chief Awolowo who was then Premier of the Region. He was to remain a devoted collaborator of the Chief even when the latter moved unto the national plane as Opposition Leader in the Federal House of Representatives.

Following Awolowo's move to Lagos in 1959, Akintola, his deputy, became Premier at Ibadan. But soon the government was threatened by internal crisis, resulting from the new Premier's resentment of alleged interference by his predecessor in the affairs of the Ibadan government. There followed an open clash in the Western parliament between the supporters of Awolowo and Akintola who soon formed a new party, the Nigerian National Democratic Party, in alliance with the Northern People's Congress of Sir Ahmadu Bello (q.v.). Adegbenro then became leader of the AG and Premier of the Western Region, elected by pro-Awolowo parliamentarians. This was strongly contested by Akintola and the ensuing crisis developed rapidly to widespread violence and breakdown of law and order. Thus was Western Nigeria plunged into deep political crisis which subsequently engulfed the whole country. Akintola was assassinated in the ensuing military coup of 1966 while Adegbenro, like all other Nigerian politicians of that time, was suspended from office. He died in 1975.

He was greatly respected in his Egba community who conferred on him the traditional titles of Balogun of Owu and Ekerin of Egbaland. ■

Adelabu, A.O.A. (1915-58)

ADELABU, Alhaji Adegoke Oduola Akande (1915-58).

NIGERIAN politician, known for his dynamism as the "Lion of the West". He was born on or about 3 September 1915, the only son of a trading family in Ibadan, Oyo State. Adelabu was converted to Christianity at an early age and baptised and christened Joseph, a name which he renounced later when he became a Moslem; he performed his pilgrimage to Mecca in 1957.

After his elementary education at Mapo Central School in Ibadan, he entered Ibadan Government College in 1931 on a government scholarship. His record there showed that Adelabu "possessed a fine critical ability and preferred to draw his own conclusions from fundamentals. He could have passed through the college in less than five years had he been allowed to". The brilliant student left the college with distinction in 1935 and proceeded to the Yaba Higher College in Lagos, then the highest educational institution in the country. And, this time, Adelabu won the United Africa Company (UAC) scholarship of which he was the first Nigerian recipient.

In June 1935, however, he gave up his studies and returned to Ibadan to be appointed secretary to the regional manager of UAC. By October of the following year, Adelabu became an assistant produce manager, but he resigned from UAC in 1939 to join the Union of Co-operative Societies as produce inspector. He rejoined UAC in 1945, this time posted to Lagos as production assistant manager. Always very fond of Ibadan, where

Alhaji A.O.A. Adelabu

he developed an interest in the local politics, Adelabu left UAC again in 1946 to return to his home to further his political ambition.

In 1949 he co-founded the Egbe Omo Ibile, a movement of about 150 organisations with interest in the affairs of Ibadan. Two years later, Adelabu moved into national politics when he enlisted in the National Council of Nigerian Citizens (NCNC) under the leadership of Nnamdi Azikiwe. Adelabu was elected the party's assistant secretary for Western Nigeria and later rose to its national executive committee when he became the First National Vice-President.

In the 1951 elections to the regional House of Assembly in Ibadan, Adelabu led his party to victory, but a series of post-election defections by his colleagues to the Action Group (AG) of Chief Obafemi Awolowo forced the NCNC into opposition; Adelabu became the leader of the NCNC opposition. He was elected in 1954 to the Federal House of Representatives in Lagos where he was appointed Minister of Natural Resources and Social Services in the national government of Alhaji Abubakar Tafawa Balewa

(q.v.). In the same year 1954, Adelabu was elected to the Ibadan District Council (IDC) whose chairman he also became, thus combining the role of federal minister with that of head of the IDC.

Adelabu resigned from both offices in early 1956 following allegation of administrative irregularities in the IDC. Later he was re-elected to the Western House of Assembly where he resumed his earlier role of opposition leader.

An able and hard-working politician, Adelabu's capabilities endeared him in the dual role of federal minister and chairman of the IDC. These qualities, and his characteristic oratory, gave him great importance for some time in the nationalist movement. His strong personality was felt all over the country and he had his own followers as well as enemies.

In 1957 he led the Western Nigeria NCNC delegation to the Constitutional Conference in London. But on 23 March 1958, the "Lion of the West" died in a car accident.∎

Adele II (1893-1964)

ADELE II, Adeniji, Oba of Lagos (1893-1964).

NIGERIAN traditional ruler. Adeniji Adele was a grandson of Adele I, who reigned briefly as Oba of Lagos (or Eleko) in the 19th century, before the British occupation, but whose direct family did not occupy the throne for some time afterwards. He went to the Church Missionary Society (CMS) Grammar School in Lagos and later worked as a surveyor for the British colonial government. As a surveyor and draughtsman he travelled to the northern and eastern Provinces of Nigeria. He won a prize for a novel at an exhibition in Calabar in 1914.

He volunteered for military service in the First World War and served as a sapper with the Royal Engineers in the Cameroons Campaign (1914-15), being decorated three times. Later he worked again at the Survey Department, before joining the Treasury staff as one of the then subordinate Nigerian civil servants. He was transferred to the

Oba Adele II

Ademola II (1872-1962)

ADEMOLA II, Oba Sir Oladipo Samuel, Alake of Abeokuta (1872-1962).

NIGERIAN traditional ruler. He was born on 20 September 1872 to Alake Ademola I and his wife Hannah Adeyombo Ademola, in Afin Ake in Abeokuta. After education at Igbore and Ikerelun Schools, and later at St. Paul's, Breadfruit Street, Lagos, he took to business. He traded for some time, returning to trading after learning printing as an apprentice to R. B. Blaize (q.v.). While living in Lagos he became well known among the Egbas. At the age of 21 he started taking part in the politics of Abeokuta, which at that time (1893) had its

secretariat in 1937, working as chief clerk and later as acting assistant secretary.

Later Prince Adeniji Adele worked for the Inland Revenue Department and then once again for the Treasury, where he was an accountant. He was working as Provincial Treasurer in Kano in September 1949 when he learnt that he had been chosen as Oba of Lagos to succeed Oba Falolu. His succession was contested and he was not crowned until three years later.

He then became a much respected traditional ruler in Nigeria's federal capital, where the indigenes whose traditional government the Oba heads are now a small minority because of the city's expansion, but still very influential. In 1952 he became a member of the Western Region House of Chiefs (Lagos being separated from that Region in 1954). Under the Lagos Local Government Law of 1953 the Oba became President of the Town Council.

Oba Adeniji Adele died in September 1964 and was succeeded by Oba Oyekan. ■

Oba Ademola II

independence guaranteed for a while by Britain in a treaty, and was governed by an "Egba United Government."

A crisis over the succession to the position of Basorun in 1897 was resolved with the help of the young Prince Ademola and the Lagos government representative, Mr. W. Allen. A few years later the Prince helped secure the traditional authorities' permission for the new railway from Lagos to pass through Abeokuta. In 1904 Prince Ademola was one of the party that accompanied the reigning Alake, Gbadebo, on his visit to Britain at the invitation of the Colonial Secretary. The Prince's stay in Britain had a great impact on his government when he became Oba. Before then he had considerable local opposition and for some time he stayed in his village, where he became a successful farmer.

Following the death of Oba Gbadebo on 28 May 1920, Prince Samuel Ademola was chosen as the new Alake by the Egba Council, and he was crowned on 27 September 1920 at a spectacular ceremony attended by the British governor and a crowd of 10,000. Although annexed to Nigeria in 1914, Abeokuta retained much of its earlier traditional system, which nevertheless was altered by the early impact of Christianity and Western education. Oba Ademola is recalled as having fitted well the somewhat unusual requirements of the natural ruler of the Egbas, who in 1930 celebrated under him the centenary of Abeokuta. Educated men were appointed to traditional positions by the Oba. And he favoured Western education, allowing his own son Adetokunboh (born in 1906) to go to England to complete his education, and providing help for others' schooling. In 1935 he was awarded the CBE.

In 1948 a protest against him by market women led by Mrs. Funmilayo Ransome-Kuti (q.v.), daughter-in-law of the Reverend Josiah Ransome-Kuti (q.v.) who had been a friend of the Alake, forced him to retire from Abeokuta for two years. But the Alake re-gained control and later became a senior member of the Western Region House of Chiefs.

He died towards the end of 1961. His children by his marriage in 1904 to Tejumade Assumpçao (Alakija), a sister of the famous Adeyemo and Olayinka Alakija, include Sir Adetukunboh Ademola, a former Chief Justice of Nigeria. ∎

Adeniyi-Jones, C.C. (1876-1957)

ADENIYI-JONES, Dr Curtis Crispin (1876-1957).

NIGERIAN doctor and politician. He was born at Waterloo in Freetown, Sierra Leone, of Yoruba ("Aku") parents of the Creole community. He was educated first in Freetown, where he went to the CMS Grammar School. Then he went to Britain, where he qualified as a doctor at Durham University. He studied further at the Rotunda Hospital, Dublin, and the newly founded Liverpool School of Tropical Medicine. After being awarded the M.B. and B.Surg. qualifications, he returned to West Africa and, like many Sierra Leone Creoles, went to work in Nigeria (at a time when many people belonged equally to either country). He entered Government Medical Service at Lagos in 1904. There were already many African doctors in Nigeria then, but a new British policy adopted about that time relegated them to junior ranks in the colonial medical service, and subordinate to

Dr. C.C. Adeniyi-Jones

European doctors regardless of relative ability and qualifications.

After working for the government for several years he resigned to set up in private practice. In 1914 he added hospital wards, for male and female patients, to his house, Priscilla Hall, and later an operating theatre, to what became one of the leading private clinics in Lagos. After starting it Dr Adeniyi-Jones decided, a few years later, to go into politics. In Lagos the lively politics of the 1920s centred on the traditional throne of the Oba or Eleko and on representation, newly agreed by the British, for Africans on the Town Council and in the Nigerian Legislative Council (Legco). The acceptance by the colonial rulers of popular election of four Africans to Legco, three from Lagos and one from Calabar, gave Adeniyi-Jones, his opportunity to enter politics.

In the first elections of 1923 he was elected to Legco in Lagos, as a prominent member of the Nigerian National Democratic Paty (NNDP) led by Herbert Macaulay (q.v.). The other members elected for Lagos, the lawyers J. Egerton Shyngle and Eric Moore, were also of the NNDP. Adeniyi-Jones polled 1,281 votes, Egerton Shyngle 1,301 and Moore 1,298. Macaulay could not stand for election because of a criminal conviction a few years earlier, and although he was the outstanding leader, the post of President of the NNDP was held by Egerton Shyngle. On the latter's death in 1926 Dr Adeniyi-Jones succeeded him as President.

He was on Legco for 15 years in all, and was one of the most prominent citizens of Lagos. He spoke on many public occasions and sometimes acted as a spokesman for Nigerian or at least Lagosian interests, as in 1934 when he proposed more African representation on the Lagos Town Council, which the colonial government accepted. In the 1928 elections he became the "First Lagos Member" after polling more votes than the other two Lagos members, T. A. Doherty (another lawyer) and Moore. In 1933 Moore polled more votes and became the First Lagos Member, Adeniyi-Jones being the second member and Doherty the third.

Dr Adeniyi-Jones did not limit his interests to politics; for some time in the 1930s he engaged in commercial ventures aimed at giving African farmers and exporters a bigger role and a better deal in the overseas trade dominated by expatriate firms. He was a director of West African Co-operative Producers Ltd. and chairman of the Nigerian Mercantile Bank.

In the 1938 Legco elections the domination of Nigeria's limited elective politics by the NNDP was challenged and ended by the Nigerian Youth Movement (NYM). In the election campaign the NYM said that Adeniyi-Jones, who was seeking re-election, was not a Nigerian. This propaganda charge overlooked the fact that very many prominent Nigerians of the early Lagos and Abeokuta élites, while born in Sierra Leone, were of Yoruba descent and had never forgotten their ancestral origins. But in the 1938 elections Adeniyi-Jones and the other two NNDP candidates were defeated. The NYM won all the Lagos seats.

In 1940, on the death of Olayinka Alakija, a NYM member, Adeniyi-Jones contested the by-election. When it was again said that he was not a Nigerian, he said, "Of course I was born in the Sierra Leone, in the village of Waterloo, and I am proud of it. And prouder still that I was born there of pure Yoruba parents". He was defeated by the NYM candidate, Jibril Martin (1888-1959).

Adeniyi-Jones did not contest any election after that. He died in March 1957 in Lagos, where the Adeniyi-Jones family is still prominent.■

Aderemi II (1889-1980)

ADEREMI II, Sir Adesoji, Oni of Ife (1889-1980).

NIGERIAN traditional ruler, the longest-reigning major Oba (king) in Yorubaland in recent times. He was born to a Christian family on 15 November 1889 in Iremo Ward, Ile-Ife; his father was Prince Osundeyi Gbadebo. He completed primary education at the CMS School and in 1909 joined the Nigerian Railway, rising to become a stationmaster, a solid achievement in those days. In 1921 he retired to establish a produce-buying and transport business, soon becoming one of the wealthiest men in his community and a very prominent leader of enlightened opinion there.

He came to the throne of Oni of Ife (spiritually the most important Oba, ruling at the legendary first home of the Yoruba people) in 1930, and was crowned on 25 September 1930. On his accession to the throne, he took immediate steps to modernise

Sir Adesoji Aderemi II

many Ife customs and tradition and was physically and financially involved in bringing educational opportunities to the ancient-town of Ile-Ife. Oduduwa College, Ife's premier secondary school, was achieved through his effort in 1932 and he was a main force behind the founding of many others. He is credited with the introduction of public amenities, such as telephones (1930), pipe borne water (1946) and electricity in 1955.

His intelligence, energy and geniality made him the indispensable man on various consultative bodies of the colonial government in the 1940s. Awarded the King's Medal for African Chiefs in 1936 and made CMG in 1943, he soon advanced from the smaller stage of Oyo Province to the old Western House of Assembly in 1946 and the Legislative Council of Nigeria in 1947. He was a delegate to the African Conference in London in 1948, led Nigeria's delegation to Queen Elizabeth II's coronation in 1953, and was a delegate to the various Nigerian constitutional conferences from 1953 to 1958.

He became an active and leading member of Egbe Omo Oduduwa, the Yoruba cultural organisation founded in 1948, and in the Action Group, which grew from it to become, in 1951, the dominant political party in the Western Region. In 1951 he was invited to become a central government Minister without portfolio irrespective of his position as an Oba, and he held this post until 1955. In 1954 he was appointed president of the Western House of Chiefs, a position he held until 1960.

Oba Aderemi was the first Nigerian to be appointed Governor of Western Nigeria; he was also knighted as KCMG. Through his influence, Ife was marked out as the site for the Western Region's own university.

A "good mixer", he had visited the Moor Plantation agricultural station at Ibadan, with the Emir of Ilorin, at an early date, and also met Obas from Ekiti Division, thereby breaking the tradition of the secluded lives of Yoruba traditional rulers. He attended the first conference of the Obas held at Oyo in 1937 and was an ideal and hospitable host at Ile-Ife when the second conference was held there in 1938.

In the report of the Southern Province of Nigeria for 1936, the section on Oyo Province by G. H. Findlay, Senior Resident in charge of the province, described Oba Aderemi and his administration like this: "Ile-Ife with a population of 48,000 is administered by the Oni, assisted by a council of chiefs. The Oni's crown is the oldest among the Yoruba-speaking people. He is an educated and sensible man with progressive and sound ideas and a keen sense of humour. The Oni's administration is sound. His personal supervision over the Treasury and the department of Native Administration and his control of the expenditure of his native treasury is less restricted than the other native authorities."

Many decades later he was still a respected and revered figure in the former Western State. In June 1980 big celebrations on the 50th anniversary of his accession showed this. But soon after those celebrations he died on 7 July 1980; a few days later a formal announcement was made as a signal for widespread mourning at Ile-ife and elsewhere. ■

Adesuyi, S.L. (1923-76)

ADESUYI, Dr. Samuel Lawrence (1923-76).

Dr. S.L. Adesuyi

NIGERIAN medical practitioner who became the Chief Medical Officer of the Federation. He was born on 30 November 1923 in Ile-Oluji in what is now Ondo State. After primary education at the Ile-Oluji St. Peter's School, he attended Ibadan Government College from 1937 until 1942 and proceeded to Yaba Higher College and later to Achimota College in Accra, Ghana. He commenced medical studies in 1945 at the Yaba School of Medicine in Lagos where he received the Sir Walter Johnson's Prize in Anatomy and Physiology in 1946.

In 1949 he entered the University College of Ibadan Medical School, becoming a Licentiate in Medicine and Surgery in 1950. There, he received the Sir Walter Johnson's Prize in Public Health and Forensic Medicine, the Blair Aitkens Memorial Prize in Medicine, and the May and Baker prize in Surgery.

His first appointment in 1950 was as House Physician and Surgeon at Adeoyo Hospital in Ibadan, he left in 1951 to become Medical Officer at the Federal Ministry of Health in Lagos. Dr. Adesuyi went to Britain in 1953 for a year's attachment with the West London Hospital Medical School. He became a Member of the Royal College of Surgeons and Licentiate of the Royal College of Physicians in 1954, and returned to Nigeria to the post of Medical Officer, which he held until 1956 when he joined the Lagos General Hospital as Medical Superintendent. From 1957 to 1958 he worked at the Yaba Mental Hospital, returning to Britain at the end of 1958 for postgraduate studies at the London School of Hygiene and Tropical Medicine and at the Royal Institute of Public Health and Hygiene, where, again, he won the Tanner Memorial Prize for Public Health, in addition to the Diploma in Public Health, which was followed in 1959 with the Certificate in Medical Statistics and Epidemiology.

Dr. Adesuyi was appointed Federal Government Medical Statistician in 1959 and, from 1962 to 1965, became Consultant Medical Statistician to the Federal Ministry of Health. In 1965 he became Deputy Chief Medical officer to the Federal Government and was elevated the following year to the post of Chief Medical Officer and Director of Health Services and Training. He held the two offices until his death in 1976.

Between 1963 and 1975, Dr. Adesuyi was an associate lecturer in Biostatistics at the College of Medicine of the University of Lagos while, at the same time, serving on the Advisory Panel on Health Statistics of the WHO. In 1973 WHO awarded him the World Physicians' Day Gold Medal for Public Health. He held other public appointments also: he was secretary of the Nigerian National Council on Health; president of the Institute of Medical Laboratory Technology of Nigeria; chairman of the Midwives Board; and chairman of the Medical Research Council of Nigeria. He was also a member of the Board of Governors of the College of Medicine of Lagos University, of the Board of Management of the Lagos University Teaching Hospital, and of the National Advisory Committee on the Prerogative of Mercy. A man of varied interests, he was a former chairman of the International Committee of the National Sports Council of Nigeria as well as past vice-president of the Nigeria Olympic Association.

Dr. Adesuyi died on 17 July 1976, in Lagos. ■

Adjetey, C.F. (1893-1948)

ADJETEY, Sergeant Cornelius Frederick (1893-1948).

G HANAIAN soldier, a symbolic figure in the nationalist struggle for independence. He was born in 1893 in Labadi, east of Accra, and was educated at the Osu Presbyterian School in the Ghanaian capital.

After his elementary education, Adjetey joined the Royal West African Frontier Force, the British colonial force on the West

C.F. Adjetey

Coast. He served in East Africa in the 1915 campaign against the Germans during the First World War, returning to the battlefield in Burma against the Axis forces between 1942 and 1945. Before his demobilisation at the end of the Second World War he had been decorated by the British for his service and promoted sergeant in 1944.

The immediate post-war years saw the rise of nationalist reaction against European colonialism in Africa. In the Gold Coast (now Ghana) this opposition to British rule manifested itself in political mobilisation, which included joint action of the workers and the United Gold Coast Convention (UGCC) that had just appointed Kwame Nkrumah (q.v.) as its general secretary. This political mobilisation culminated in a workers' strike and mass demonstrations in 1947 and 1948.

During one of these demonstrations on 28 February 1948, organised by workers and former servicemen against high prices and post-war conditions in the Gold Coast, the colonial police opened fire, killing 29 demonstrators and wounding 237. Sergeant Adjetey, who was at the head of a column of ex-soldiers marching towards Christianborg Castle where they intended to present a petition to the British Governor, Sir Gerald Creasy, was among those shot dead at the crossroads at Osu. Two other former soldiers, Corporal Attipoe and Private Odartey Lamptey, later died from the injuries sustained during the shooting.

The incident caused widespread protest and condemnation in the Gold Coast, forcing the establishment of the Watson Commission to inquire into the causes of the disturbances. Following the demonstration, Nkrumah and other members of UGCC were arrested and detained at Lawra on 1 March 1948 after allegations that the party was responsible for the agitations and riots. This, however, could not reverse the trend of events that subsequently led to political freedom for the Gold Coast.

Even before 1957 when the country became independent Ghana, Sergeant Adjetey had become a symbol of the resistance to colonial rule. On 12 June 1949, before about six thousand people, Kwame Nkrumah launched the Convention People's Party (CPP) ". . . in the name of the chiefs and the people, the rank and file of the Convention, the Labour Movement, our valiant ex-servicemen, the youth movement throughout the country, the man in the street, our children and those yet unborn, the new Ghana that is to be, Sergeant Adjetey and his comrades who died at the crossroads of Christianborg during the riots of 1948 . . ."

At independence Adjetey was honoured as a martyr, with a monument erected in his memory at the Osu crossroads in Accra. The street where the demonstrators marched on that fateful day has also been renamed the "28th February Road". ■

Adoula, C. (1921-78)

ADOULA, Cyrille (1921-78).

C. Adoula

ZAIREAN trade unionist and politician who played a crucial role during the 1960s crisis when he served as Prime Minister. Cyrille Adoula was born on 13 September 1921 at Leopoldville (Kinshasa) in the Congo (now Zaire). His father was a dockworker from Equateur Province while his mother came from the Kasai region. He attended a Catholic Mission Primary School in Leopoldville and the St. Joseph Institute until 1941. He worked in various companies in Leopoldville before joining the Congolese Central Bank as a clerk.

He then became a member of the Congolese Division of the *Fédération Générale des Travailleurs Belges*, the only trade union movement operating in the country at that time. His active participation led to his election as secretary-general of the organisation.

When the *Mouvement National Congolais* (MNC), one of the first political groupings in the Congo, was formed in 1958, Adoula was one of its founding members. In July 1959 internal tensions caused a small group of moderates, including Adoula, to break away and form the MNC-Kalonji (so named after its leader) in Elisabethville (now Lubumbashi). Because of his interest in reforms he became a member of the new party's economic and social commission.

In December 1959 he was elected vice-president of the newly-formed Abako Cartel, an alliance of various political and cultural groupings including the MNC-Kalonji. Lat-

er in the month he travelled to Brussels as a member of the Cartel delegation and remained there till January 1960, to attend a conference of the International Confederation of Free Trade Unions (ICFTU).

Shortly afterwards he left the MNC-Kalonji on the grounds that it was moving away from its original objectives and was developing an ethnic bias. He continued his work in the trade union movement, helping to establish the *Fédération Générale des Travailleurs du Kongo* (FGTK) out of the *Fédération Générale des Travailleurs Belges*, in preparation for independence. He was again appointed Secretary-General of the new organisation, and was a member of the Executive Committee of the ICFTU, with which the FGTK was associated.

He also joined the *Parti de l'Unité Nationale* and was elected Senator for Equateur Province in May 1960. After a change of government on 5 September 1960 Adoula was appointed minister of the Interior. However, the new government was dismissed a week later following the seizure of power by Sergeant Mobutu of the Congolese Armed Forces. Adoula was appointed one of the delegates to work in close co-operation with the United Nations, becoming leader of the delegation to the United Nations General Assembly in March 1961.

In the same month he went to a conference of Congolese politicians held in Madagascar, and was afterwards one of the negotiators for the reconvening of the Congolese central parliament at Leopoldville. Meanwhile Kasavubu had resumed his position as Head of State in February 1961, and the following August he appointed Adoula Prime Minister.

Adoula, a determined and dedicated supporter of national unity, gained general support at a time when the country was in deep crisis. All the opposing factions were represented in his government apart from the ethnic groups allied in Tshombe's Conakat in the Katanga, the mineral-rich region of the country that had seceded from the Congo and refused to participate in a central government. Adoula was opposed to the break up of the country and by June 1963, when the Katanga secession attempt had been crushed with the help of UN troops, two other regions' attempts to gain independence had also been overcome and a semblance of national unity was beginning to emerge.

In June 1964 he left the office of Prime Minister and spent some time abroad pursuing a career as a diplomat and serving as ambassador to Belgium, Luxembourg, the European Economic Community and the USA. He returned to Zaire in August 1969 and was appointed Foreign Minister with responsibility for External Trade. The following year he was taken ill. He went for medical treatment to Lausanne, Switzerland. He died eight years later on 24 May 1978, at the age of 56.■

Adu, A.L. (1914-77)

ADU, Amishadai Larson (1914-77).

GHANAIAN administrator, one of Africa's top international civil servants. He was born on 22 October 1914 at Anum, Ghana. After his elementary education in various public schools in Ghana, he attended Achimota College from 1931 to 1936. From Achimota a scholarship took him to Queen's College, Cambridge University, England, where he achieved a brilliant academic record and graduated with Honours in the Natural Sciences in 1939.

He returned to Ghana in 1939, taught science at Achimota College for three years, and then joined the colonial administrative service in 1942. He was one of the first

A.L. Adu

Africans to be appointed to the senior rank of District Commissioner, and served in that capacity in various places until 1949, when he was appointed joint secretary to the Coussey Constitutional Committee, which laid the constitutional foundation for independent Ghana. He became Commissioner for Africanisation in 1950, Director of Recruitment and Training in 1952, and Secretary for External Affairs in 1955.

When Ghana became independent in 1957, he was the first Permanent Secretary in the Ministry of Foreign Affairs and served there until 1959, when he was appointed Secretary to the Cabinet and Head of the Ghana Civil Service. He was Secretary to the National Council for Higher Education and Research from 1961 to 1962.

He headed the Tanganyika Salary Commission in 1961, and was Secretary-General of the East African Common Services Organisation (a forerunner of the East African Community) in 1962-1963; Regional Representative of the UN Technical Assistance Board and Director, Special Fund Programmes in East Africa, in 1964-65; and Deputy Secretary-General of the Commonwealth Secretariat in London from 1966 to 1970. He returned to Ghana in 1970 to become Managing Director of the Ghana Consolidated Diamonds Limited. In July 1975 he returned to the UN as Deputy Chairman of the International Civil Service Commission, a post he held until his death on 2 September 1977 in New York.

He wrote *The Civil Service in New African States* (1969) and *The Public Service and the Administration of Public Affairs in Ghana* (1973).

Adu was a lifelong and devout member of the Presbyterian Church and took the teachings of Christ to be a guide for his life. He served with distinction through the colonial period and through the difficult days of early independence in both East and West Africa, then as a regional civil servant and finally in the international civil service.

His integrity was tested over and over again especially when he served as Resident Director of the Consolidated African Selection Trust Limited in Ghana, a major subsidiary of one of the great transnational corporations, Selection Trust Limited. To him administration was not a matter of textbooks, codes or regulations, procedures or priorities; administration was a matter of arranging both simple and difficult situations towards a successful outcome with neatness, thoroughness, humanity and justice. ∎

Afrifa, O.A.A. (1936-79)

AFRIFA, General Okatakyie Akwasi Amankwa (1936-79).

GHANAIAN soldier and politician; he and Colonel Kotoka plotted the coup that ended Ghana's first civilian administration. He was born on 24 April 1936 at Mampong in Ashanti, and educated at the Presbyterian Primary School, Mampong, from 1948 to 1951. He gained a scholarship to Adisadel College in Cape Coast where he studied between 1952 and 1956.

In 1957 Afrifa enlisted in the Ghanaian army, starting his military training at the Regular Officers Special Training School at Teshie in Ghana before going to the Royal Military Academy, Sandhurst, England, a country he would later praise highly in his book, *The Ghana Coup*, published in 1966. He came out from Sandhurst in 1960 as the third best Commonwealth cadet. His military training continued at the School of Infantry in England and later at the Ghana Defence College in Accra in 1964.

On his return from military training abroad in 1961, Afrifa served in the Ghana contingent of the United Nations Peace Keeping Force in the Congo, now Zaire. In 1962 he was commanding officer of the 2nd Battalion of Infantry before being posted to the 2nd Brigade Headquarters at Kumasi where he met Colonel Kotoka (q.v.) with whom he later plotted the overthrow of President Nkrumah (q.v.) in February 1966. Afrifa's role was regarded as crucial to the success of the coup; he personally took control of the radio station in Accra and told listeners to "Stand by for Colonel Kotoka".

Gen. O.A.A. Afrifa

Subsequent reports had it that Afrifa had long nourished the idea of overthrowing the Government of Nkrumah because he had felt, on his return from active service in the Congo, that the Congo affair was none of Ghana's business.

In *The Ghana Coup*, General Afrifa did not conceal his admiration for Britain, institutions such as Sandhurst Military Academy, and the Commonwealth, which President Nkrumah had invariably classed as instruments of neo-colonialism. Relating his experiences at Sandhurst and how he became a loyal supporter of the British tradition, he said, Sandhurst was "a wonderful and mysterious institution with traditions going back to 1802. One cannot appreciate its mystery unless one experiences Sandhurst . . . . No one cared whether one was a prince, lord, commoner, foreigner, Muslim or black man. There were quite a number of lords and princes at Sandhurst. Everyone was treated according to his own merits . . . . The food at Sandhurst was good; I loved the companionship of the people of identical calling, and the English breakfast . . . . Now I look back on Sandhurst with nostalgia. It is one of the greatest institutions in the world. Through its doors have passed famous generals, kings and rulers".

On Britain and the Commonwealth, General Afrifa said, "I have been trained in the United Kingdom as a soldier, and I am ever prepared to fight alongside my friends in the United Kingdom in the same way as Canadians and Australians will do. How would we be friends belonging to the Commonwealth and stay out in time of Commonwealth adversity, and when this great Union is in danger?"

In the wake of the coup, Afrifa, the youngest member of the National Liberation Council (NCL) under the chairmanship of General Ankrah, was given the portfolio of Finance, Economic Affairs and Trade. A year later he was made Commandant of the Military Academy and other military training establishments in Ghana. When General Ankrah resigned on 2 April 1969, following the finding of a commission which enquired into alleged "slush funds" from politicians, Afrifa took over as Chairman of the NCL; by May he had lifted the ban on political parties and set 29 August 1969 as the date for the elections of the Second Republic which brought Dr. Busia's Progress Party to power. General Afrifa became the chairman

of the three-man Presidential Commission which maintained a supervisory role over the newly elected civilian Government. In 1970, when the Commission was dissolved, Afrifa said it is a "lesson for those in power not to perpetuate their positions. Now our rifles are down and we believe they are down for ever", and retired from the army.

In December of the same year, he joined the Council of State, the advisory body to President Akufo-Addo (q.v.) and remained in office till Dr. Busia's Government was ousted by General Acheampong (q.v.) in a coup on 13 January 1972. Afrifa attempted to launch an attack on Accra in a bid to restore Dr. Busia (q.v.) but was arrested and detained in the James Fort prison where he remained till 3 July 1973.

Following his release, General Afrifa played a leading part in the People's Movement for Freedom and Justice which was instrumental in undermining General Acheampong's position by its determined opposition to Union Government. But he lost because the referendum on "Unigov" of 1978 favoured Acheampong. However, in the elections of 18 June 1979, held under Acheampong's successor, General Akuffo, he won a seat in Parliament on the ticket of Victor Owusu's Popular Front Party. The newly-elected civilian Government was not convened before General Afrifa and eight others including General Acheampong, General Akuffo and Colonel Felli were executed on 16 June 1979 after being found guilty of corruption by the Armed Forces Revolutionary Council, chaired by Flight-Lieutenant Jerry John Rawlings. No details of any trial were published, though Jerry Rawlings said charges in the case of General Afrifa, which caused much disquiet, would be published. His widow Christina called for him to be vindicated. ∎

Agbaje, S. (1880-1953)

AGBAJE, Salami (1880-1953).

NIGERIAN businessman, he was for many years the wealthiest man in Ibadan, then Nigeria's largest city and a leading commercial centre. He was born in 1880 in

Lagos, his father being from Iseyin and his mother probably from Ibadan. Without actually attending school he learned to read, write and speak English. In 1904 he went to Ibadan,. where he first worked for a European sawmill operation and then took over the sawmill. He later became prominent as a middleman for the buying of produce, especially cocoa, whose cultivation was being fast expanded by the Yorubas.

For several decades Agbaje had continued business success and wealth, above all as a produce trader. In those days European companies bought a good deal of Nigeria's exportable agricultural produce, but Agbaje, aided by his literacy and his use of modern business organisation in which he had a number of employees, was able to hold his own against the expatriate firms. As his wealth grew he loaned money to many Ibadan traders and chiefs, thus expanding a network of dependents.

In the 1920s Agbaje, himself a Moslem, had close contacts with some educated people, mainly Christians, of Ibadan who formed a group interested in modernisation and political advance. Some of them, notably Isaac Akinyele (q.v.) and Akinpelu Obisesan, formed in 1914 a group called the Egba Agba O'Tan. This group planned an enterprise for the manufacture of roof tiles, and Agbaje promised to put up capital for it, but they feared he would then control the enterprise and rejected the offer. He had by then already acquired a reputation as a shrewd business operator. This reputation grew. He bought a press for a planned newspaper to be launched by members of the Egba, and handed it to them, but the project soon collapsed. Later, he earned a reputation for ruthless business methods.

After the separation of Ibadan from Oyo, the British allowed the election of an Oba (King) for Ibadan, which had previously only had a lower-ranking Bale. The first Oba or Olubadan was enthroned in 1936. Salami Agbaje was from then on prominent in traditional politics. He became President of a Native Court in 1936 and began to climb up the hierarchy of traditional titles in the kingdom. In Ibadan there is usually automatic promotion from one title to the next, ending with the Obaship itself. Thus, when Agbaje acquired the title of Otua Balogun, he was well on the way to becoming Olubadan, a possibility which aroused negative reaction from his many enemies.

A petition, organised by Adegoke Adelabu (q.v.), Obisesan and others, against Agbaje was presented to the Oba and the Ibadan Council in 1949. At first Agbaje was suspended from membership of the Council. But in 1951 a British official, H. L. M. Butcher, investigated the complaints against Agbaje and dismissed them. They were largely complaints for sharp business practice and other behaviour resented by other Ibadan citizens, and did not amount to any serious charge. But while it lasted the "Agbaje Agitation" had dominated Ibadan politics from 1949 to 1951.

Having successfully defied his enemies, who had been concerned with the possibility of his becoming Oba, Salami Agbaje proceeded to the title of Balogun. But in late 1953 he died. Of his several sons, Dr S. A. Agbaje was the first Ibadan man to become a doctor, and Chief Mojeed Agbaje was a lawyer and a prominent politician in the National Council of Nigerian Citizens (NCNC) and eventually a Minister in the Western Region Government; he was just re-entering politics at the end of military rule when he died in a road accident in late 1978. ■

Agbebi, M. (1860-1917)

AGBEBI, Dr Mojola (1860-1917).

NIGERIAN activist in the Pan-African Movement at the turn of the century. Agbebi, one of the children of Sierra Leone Creoles, Yoruba "Recaptives" who went back to their native Nigeria, is regarded today in nationalist circles as a pioneer of African nationalism, the anticipator of later cultural nationalism which he showed in his personal life by changing his original Creole names, David Brown Vincent and persistently wore African clothes. He is also renowned as a newspaperman, who edited several publications in Lagos.

Mojola Agbebi was born at Ilesha, a famous Yoruba town in what is now Oyo State in Nigeria, on 10 April 1860. His father was an emigrant from Sierra Leone, but he originally came from Oye in Ekiti Division. Eight years after Mojola's birth, he was sent to Lagos to be educated at the CMS Faji Day School which he attended until 1874. He then entered the CMS Training School where he studied for three years. In 1877, at 17, he became a CMS school master at the Faji Day School. Between 1880 and 1883 he worked

Dr. M. Agbebi

with various Church missions in Porto Novo, after being dismissed from his teaching post at Faji by the CMS authorities in 1880 over matters of routine.

His disagreement with the CMS led to his association with not only the Catholic, Methodist and American Baptist missions, all of whom he worked for at Porto Novo but also with the First Independent Native Baptist Church, a progressive African movement, becoming its leader in 1888, though he later left it in 1903 to start his own Araromi Church. He rejoined the American Baptists to which he belonged for the rest of his life.

In 1908 he married Adeotan Sikuade, and had several children by her. Four of these died in 1916, a year before his own death in 1917. This tragic loss, coupled with declining interest in church activities at the time, had a profound effect on his overburdened life. He was a man of varied interests, participating in a number of local and international events and organisations

working for the emancipation of the African race. He visited Liberia in the 1890s, at the invitation of E. W. Blyden (q.v.), and was honoured with honorary degrees of MA and PhD for his "racial fidelity" and literary ability. His literary activities included poems which won commendations from the British authorities in Lagos.

Following his experiences in Liberia and in New York where he also receivd an honorary DD degree from the University of New York in 1903, Agbebi dropped his European names for Yoruba ones. From that period also he abandoned European clothes in favour of his native ones, thus anticipating the cultural nationalism which later nationalists like Ojike (q.v.), the "Boycott King", consolidated.

Agbebi presented a paper, *The West African Problem*, at the Universal Races Congress held in London in 1911. A year before he had co-founded the Lagos Auxiliary of the Anti-Slavery and Aborigines Protection Society, a quasi-political organisation whose other leading members included Herbert Macaulay and Sapara-Williams (qq.v.).

His activities in Lagos included the editing of several (more than one source had it that he edited all) newspapers published in Lagos between 1880 and 1914. From 1880 to 1883 he worked with R. B. Blaize (q.v.), on *The Lagos Times*, and during that period until the 1890s worked on the most successful Lagos newspaper, *The Lagos Observer*. Agbebi was associated with J. P. Jackson on *The Lagos Weekly Times*, then *The Lagos Weekly Record* from 1891 onwards. He edited, for one year from 1889, the *Iwe Irohin Eko*, a newspaper published in English and Yoruba at the time which, in later years, was published only in Yoruba.

Mojola Agbebi died in Lagos on Thursday 17 May 1917.■

Aggrey, J.E.K. (1875-1927)

AGGREY, Dr. James Emman Kwegyir (1875-1927).

G HANAIAN educationist and celebrated exponent of inter-racial unity, J.E.K. Aggrey was born on 18 October 1875 at

Anomabu in the south of the Gold Coast (now Ghana). His father worked as an agent to various merchants and was also one of the spokesmen of the Chief of Anomabu. In 1884 the family was converted to Christianity, soon after which Aggrey began his education at the Cape Coast Methodist School, during the five years he spent at the school he showed an aptitude for his studies. He was sent to live with the missionary family at the Cape Coast Mission House when he was 13 years old, he left two years later to become a teacher at Abura Dunkwa.

In 1892 he returned to the Cape Coast Methodist School as an assistant teacher and continued his own education in his spare time, passing the Teacher's Certificate with distinction three years later and also receiving the Gold Coast Legislative Council Prize for his studies at the same time. He then joined the Telegraph Corps of a British expeditionary force to Kumasi as an interpreter, remaining in this post until 1896 when he was appointed headmaster of his old school.

While he held this position he was also involved in the translation of the Bible into

Dr. J.E.K. Aggrey

the Fante language, as well as working as the sub-editor of the *Gold Coast Methodist Times*. He became one of the secretaries of the Aborigines' Rights Protection Society (ARPS) after its establishment in 1897, and helped that organisation's eventual success in their campaign against the proposed 1897 Lands Bill by publicising their case in the *Gold Coast Methodist Times*.

In 1898 he was awarded a scholarship by the African Methodist Episcopal Zion (AMEZ) Church to study religion at the Livingstone College in Salisbury, North Carolina, USA, so that he would be able to continue his missionary and educational activities in the Gold Coast more effectively. He was an excellent scholar and graduated from his college with distinction in 1902, gaining a BA degree and a gold medal for his academic achievements.

He did not immediately return to the Gold Coast to continue his previous activities as expected, but stayed in North Carolina working at the Livingstone College as a registrar and later a financial secretary and lecturer. During his holidays he continued his own studies at the prestigious Columbia University at Morningside Heights, New York. He was enrolled at the Hood Theological Seminary at Charlotte, North Carolina from where he graduated in 1912 with a DD degree. While studying for his doctorate he also worked on a part-time basis for the AMEZ Publishing House in Charlotte.

During the next few years he continued to teach at the Livingstone College and his reputation and prestige grew to the extent that he was considered for the position of President of the College in 1917, although it was later decided that he was not eligible because of his nationality.

In 1920 he became the only African member of a Commission of Inquiry into Education in Africa under the auspices of the Phelps-Stokes Fund. While serving on this Commission he travelled first to Britain and thence to Sierra Leone, Liberia, the Gold Coast, Nigeria, the Congo, Angola and South Africa, gaining an insight into the educational needs of these countries. He was very well received in these countries and was offered the position of Professor of Sociology at the College of Fort Hare in Cape Province, South Africa, a position which he refused as he wanted to be able to continue his own studies and participate in the development of new educational facilities on the continent.

The findings of the Commission were published in 1922 and, as a result, an Advisory Committee on Education was established by the British government, along with educational programmes for British colonies in Africa. Aggrey meanwhile returned to America to carry on with his studies, and gained an MA degree and a Diploma in Education from Columbia University later in the year.

Another Phelps-Stokes Commission was established to investigate education in East Africa and Aggrey was once again selected to be one of its members. His work on this Commission took him to Ethiopia, Kenya, Tanganyika, Uganda, Northern and Southern Rhodesia, Nyasaland and again to South Africa. As with his first trip, he received a very favourable reception in these countries and his international prestige was greatly enhanced by the favourable response to his public speeches.

In 1924 he was offered the position of President of the Livingstone College for which he had been ineligible seven years earlier, but declined as he had decided to return to the Gold Coast. In October 1924 he arrived in Accra to help establish a college of higher education near Accra, after which he would take the appointment of assistant vice-principal in this institution.

From this time until 18 January 1927 when the Achimota College was opened, Aggrey worked very hard in assisting with the organisation of the establishment of the college, and in overcoming suspicions among African nationalists as to the British government's motives in setting up such an institution. He was very successful in this, being able to articulate effectively his strong belief that the establishment of higher education institutions for Africans in Africa was vitally important to the development of the country.

The emblem of the college became a symbol of black and white piano keys, a reference to his much-quoted saying that although the different coloured keys could be played on their own, they had to be played together to achieve perfect harmony.

Shortly after the opening of the college, Aggrey went on a brief visit to England, after which he travelled to the USA to visit his wife and four children, and to complete his thesis entitled "British Relations with Africa" for presentation to the Columbia University for a PhD. After a very brief period he fell ill and he died on 30 July 1927, at Harlem Hospital in New York, of pneumococcous meningitis.

He was an amiable personality who had achieved great prestige as a brilliant scholar and was fluent in many languages. During his life he adhered to his religious beliefs which included the conviction that the different races could live in harmony through Christian doctrine. He worked very hard to bring about understanding between black and white people and as his reputation grew he became known as the "Interpreter of Races", promoting mutual respect between white and black societies through increasing their knowledge of each other.

To Aggrey the role of education was of crucial importance and even up to his death he was still continuing his own studies. Although he published no books, many books have been written about him and his wise sayings are still known and often repeated. He gained great respect for his views on racial understanding and his promotion of higher education in Africa, and his influence and inspiration to others have stretched far beyond his national boundaries. ∎

Ahidjo, A. (1924-89)

AHIDJO, El Hadj Ahmadou (1924-89).

CAMEROONIAN statesman and first President of the independent Republic. He was born in August 1924 at Garoua in northern Cameroon, son of a Fulani chief. After completing the Yaounde Higher Primary School in 1941, he started work as a radio operator at the post office. He got involved in the youth activism of the time and soon became the leader of the *Jeunes Musulmans* movement.

Ahidjo's long political career took off in January 1947 when he was elected to the French Cameroon Territorial Assembly, then only a consultative body with no real power. He became leader of the *Union Camerounaise* (UC), at that time the party of his fellow northerners. Ahidjo was re-elected in March 1952, when the assembly became the Representative Assembly with legislative powers. In October 1953 he was also elected to represent the territory in the Assembly of the French Union in Paris. At home, Ahidjo became the president of the Assembly by a unanimous vote among its members in December 1956. By then he had become one of the most prominent members of the *Bloc Démocratique Camerounais* (BDC) led by André-Marie Mbida (q.v.).

A. Ahidjo

Mbida became Prime Minister in the first African government in May 1957 when Cameroon attained internal self-rule. Ahidjo's next step up the political ladder came in February 1958 when he took office as Prime Minister following the dismissal of Mbida. The latter had been accused of using excessive force to repress the rival nationalist movement, the *Union des Populations du Cameroun* (UPC) led by Reuben Um Nyobe (q.v.), which had unleashed a campaign of armed resistance in the rural areas, especially in the Sanaga-Maritime and Bamileke

areas; but Ahidjo, then vice-premier and Minister of the Interior, was responsible for the security forces which crushed the UPC, and when in power was to continue the harsh repression. He was 33 years old when he became Prime Minister.

On becoming premier, Ahidjo proposed a political solution and programme for the attainment of independence. He initiated negotiations with France and the United Nations, and in May 1958 proposed that Cameroon should be given full independence from the colonial power. He also adopted the slogan of "reunification" with British Cameroons which the UPC had first popularised. Despite opposition demands for new elections prior to self-rule, Cameroon became an independent republic on 1 January 1960, and Ahidjo became its first President. The southern section of British Cameroons later became part (the Western region) of the Federal Republic after a plebiscite in 1961, in which the northern half of the territory opted to join Nigeria.

Under President Ahidjo, Cameroon pursued broadly liberal economic policies and achieved modest social progress on many fronts. Ahidjo maintained good relations with France, the main former colonial power, and established new ties with a broad range of other countries. A one-party system was established over the whole country in 1966 when the *Union Nationale Camerounaise* (UNC) was formed, by the absorption of all other parties into the UC. In May 1972 Ahidjo announced a proposal for a unitary state to replace the federal system; this was approved by the population in a referendum and the United Republic of Cameroon came into being on 2 June 1972, with both French and English as its official languages. A unitary Constitution ended the West and East state governments at Buea and Yaounde, centralising more power in the President's hands. Although the 1972 Constitution did not create a one-party state by law, the UNC remained the sole party and only UNC candidates stood in the May 1973 elections, for example.

Even though he was elected for a further five-year term in 1980, President Ahidjo unexpectedly resigned on grounds of ill-health on 6 November 1982 and handed over the presidency to his Prime Minister, Paul Biya. He however retained his position as chairman of the UNC. Ahidjo's resignation surprised Cameroonians, but the changeover was smoothly effected. Paul Biya soon began to be his own man in his elevated position, rather than a front man for the retired president; and rumours began to spread of tensions between the new President and his predecessor.

In 1983 President Biya announced that he had foiled a plot to overthrow him, involving close associates of Ahidjo. In a power struggle Ahidjo lost out and Paul Biya was elected as chairman of the UNC at an extraordinary party congress in September 1983. In February 1984 Ahidjo was tried *in absentia* alongside two others for the alleged coup plot and sentenced to death. Biya was able to establish his supremacy by quelling a rebellion in early April 1984, in which Ahidjo's involvement was suspected but not proved.

Ahidjo spent the rest of his last years in exile, mainly in France and Senegal. He died in Dakar, Senegal, on 30 November 1989. For about three decades the leading political figure in his country, Ahidjo will be remembered as the "founding father" of a unified country. ∎

appointed Vice-President of this Council in 1967 and became Minister of the Interior in 1968.

On the return of civilian rule in July 1968, Aikpe returned to his army duties where he remained until 1972 when another military coup toppled the government. Major Mathieu Kerekou became Head of State, and Aikpe was once again appointed Minister of the Interior with the additional portfolio of Security as well as serving as Commander of the Ouidah Parachute Commandos. He was a member of the Marxist group in the Army and in 1975 he was promoted to the rank of Major. By this time his popularity and influence in the political field had grown considerably but on 20 June 1975, he was shot dead in Porto Novo by the Presidential Guards, for allegedly committing adultery with President Kerekou's wife. However some of his supporters are sceptical as to whether this was the real reason for his killing or just a cover for the elimination of a political rival. ∎

Aikpe, M. (1942-75)

AIKPE, Major Michel (1942-75).

BENINESE soldier who, following a coup d'état in 1967, became Vice-President of the Revolutionary Military Council and Minister of the Interior. He was born in 1942 in Bohicon, Benin (then Dahomey). He received his primary education in Bohicon and then trained at the technical military school in Bingerville, Côte d'Ivoire, before proceeding for further military training in Strasbourg in France. He gained a diploma in experimental science from St. Cyr Military Academy, and later received training as instructor at the military training centre in Mont Louis in France.

Returning to Dahomey he was made Commander of the First Company of Parachute Commandos based in Ouidah. In 1966 Aikpe became a member of the Revolutionary Military Council which had the previous year taken power in a coup d'état. He was

---

el-Aïnin, Ma' (c. 1838-1910)

EL-AININ, Sheikh Ma' (c. 1838-1910).

SAHRAWI resistance leader who played a distinguished part in the movement against Spanish and French colonisation of the region of modern Mauritania, Morocco and the Sahrawi Republic (formerly Western Sahara). His influence in these countries was enormous and remained so for several years between 1884 and the time of his death in 1910. He was a marabout (Moslem scholar and teacher) with a considerable reputation for piety and Islamic learning; he preached the need to purify Islam and to unify the brotherhoods. For this and the exploits of his army in the anti-colonial struggle, he is remembered as the warrior-saint.

He was born around 1838 at Oualata, the twelfth son of Sheikh Mohammed Fadel, and named Mohammed Mustafa. He was given an early religious education at Fez in

Morocco and Chinguetti in Mauritania, the famous old centre of Islamic learning and intellectual centre of the Maghreb, where he was taught by sages who preached the return to the pure sources of Islam. Shortly before entering the University of Tindouf, Algeria, he made the pilgrimage to Mecca in 1857, when he was just nineteen years old.

After going to Tindouf he established close ties with Saguiet el-Hamra, west of Tindouf and south of Morocco, and the Reguibat nomads who live in that area and neighbouring areas (now partly included in the Sahrawi Republic). This became the centre of his support, his birthplace being far to the south, in what is now south-east Mauritania.

Mohammed Mustafa, who was called Ma' el-Aïnin ("dew of the eyes") and is remembered by that name, helped organise resistance to Spanish occupation in Saguiet el-Hamra after 1884. This was the beginning of his career as a champion of Islam and independence against European penetration. He was based for some time at Smara, a centre of trade which Ma' el-Aïnin developed with Moroccan help in the still independent Saguiet el-Hamra. By the 1890s he had established close links with Morocco.

In earlier centuries, the Sultans of Morocco had had some spiritual influence over the desert territories between the Senegal valley and the Moroccan Atlas mountains. In some areas they were respected as religious leaders, but they seldom, if ever, had effective rule in that large region, and even acknowledgement of their spiritual supremacy had ended long before the lifetime of Ma' el-Aïnin, in much of Trab-le-Bidan, the area which later became Mauritania.

Further north, however, there was possibly a stronger traditional attachment to Morocco. All the people of this desert area were nomads, the Hassaruija Arabs being the most numerous. Fiercely independent, the various warrior and nomadic peoples were loosely ruled by emirs; they did not come under French rule during the three centuries of close commercial contact with the French in Senegal, until the beginning of the 20th century. The Saguiet el-Hamra and Rio de Oro areas nominally claimed by Spain from 1884 were not occupied till long afterwards.

Thus it was a large region still free from colonial rule that the religious leader Ma' el-Aïnin became a resistance leader of after 1900, in collaboration with Morocco which was also then still independent. His influence was strong in Adrar (in central Mauritania) when the French coloniser Coppolari advanced French power northwards from Senegal after 1900. Two other renowned Islamic leaders were influential in Trab-le-Bidan then, Sheikh Sidiya Baba and Sheikh Sa'd Bou, but they accepted a French 'protectorate' at Coppolari's persuasion at an early date. In 1902-3, the French gradually occupied Trarza and other areas in southern Mauritania, defeating many efforts at resistance.

After the defeat in 1904 of a coalition of Moorish leaders including Emir Bakar of the Idaw 'Aych people, that people sent an appeal for help to Ma' el-Aïnin. Later Ma' told Bakar that Moroccan arms were on the way. But the French attacked Tagart, defeated the Idaw 'Aych and killed Bakar. After that Coppolari was ready to move north into Adrar, where Ma' el-Aïnin was determined to resist them. On May 1905 Coppolari was murdered, apparently by a member of a Moslem sect founded by Ma' el-Aïnin's father; Ma' had possibly instigated the act. He now rallied the Moors to resist French occupation and told them Morocco had offered help.

Ma' el-Aïnin recognised Moroccan sovereignty over the area now covered by Mauritania, and other areas; this fact was to be used by later rulers of Morocco to justify a claim that that region (part of Mauritania and Western Sahara) belonged to Morocco, though Ma's action can also be seen as a tactical move against French occupation, rather than an expression of a desire for Moroccan rule for its own sake. Morocco did send him arms and in 1905, sent Moulay Idris, a relative of Sultan Moulay Abdel Aziz of Morocco, to proceed south bearing 14 decrees appointing emirs and kaids (local governors). In 1906 he visited Atar, the "holy" city of Chinguetti and other areas of Mauritania.

Ma' also obtained arms from Germany and Spain, which were jealous of France's effort to secure domination of Morocco. Spain obtained the "right" to occupy a northern strip of Morocco from other Europeans, but the greater part was recognised by the 1906 Algeciras Conference as a sphere of French influence. Germany, whose opposition to French protection had led to that conference, continued with Spain to allow and even encourage arms shipments to forces resisting French occupation. Sultan Abdel Aziz, unable to fight the French himself because of their domination over his weak central administration, encouraged Ma' el-Aïnin. In 1906-7 Ma' visited Morocco, and anti-French feelings aroused during his visit to Casablanca in January 1907 led to killings of Frenchmen there.

Later in 1907 France landed forces at Casablanca and forced the Sultan at Fez to recall Idris. Soon afterwards Sultan Abdel Aziz was replaced by his brother Abdel Hafid. Ma' el-Aïnin, who had gone at the time (September 1907) to Mogador and Safi, approved the change or, according to one account, even helped bring it about. He organised effective resistance to the French.

From 1906 to 1909 the French made only limited progress in Mauritania. With arms continuing to come by sea to the Saguiet el-Hamra coast in 1908, Ma' el-Aïnin's Moorish warriors were able to harass the French, launch raids and kill and mob Moors who submitted to French rule. Despite French pressure on the new Sultan, Morocco's aid to Ma' was reported still continuing into 1909.

On 9 January 1909 the French occupied Atar, west of Chinguetti with their 'Adrar column'. Ma' defeated a French force under Captain Bablon at Rars-Remt. But then the French took Chinguetti and occupied the Adrar palm groves. This forced the nomadic warriors, unable to live without access to the oasis, to fight. They did so and lost on 28 July 1909.

Later that year Ma' left Smara, his base in those years, for Tiznit, a Moroccan town 80 kilometres south of Agadir, with 700 men. In the Sous valley around Tiznit he organized meetings and aroused support. He then advanced on Marrakesh and aimed to reach Fez; it was reported that he seemed to be aiming to become Sultan. But the French forces already in Morocco under General Moinier halted Ma's advance on 23 June 1910. As Ma' el-Aïnin retreated many supporters left him. He died, old, beaten and ill at Tiznit on 28 October 1910.

Ma' el-Aïnin was responsible for the development of Smara in the Saguiet el Hamra region as a great commercial city – on the trans-Saharan caravan route – making it the central market place for transactions between Morocco, Senegal and the Soudan regions.■

Ajasa, K. (1866-1937)

AJASA, Sir Kitoyi (1866-1937).

NIGERIAN journalist and lawyer. He was originally named Edmund Macaulay, and was the son of Thomas Benjamin Macaulay, a Sierra Leone "Recaptive" (slave freed from a slave ship) of Dahomean birth who died at Lagos in 1899. He went to Dulwich College in London and then to the Inner Temple (London), where he was called to the Bar in 1893. He won a case in a British court before returning to Lagos and setting up in legal practice there.

At some date he changed his name, presumably following a trend towards reversion to Yoruba names that were quite widespread among Sierra Leone and Lagosian Creoles at the end of the 19th century. He took a major part in the launching in 1894 of the newspaper *The Lagos Standard*, an important addition to the already lively Lagos press scene, but soon broke with its owner, George Alfred Williams, apparently because of disagreement over how much the British administration should be criticised. During the next twenty years Ajasa made his attitude to the British administration clear: he wanted it to make concessions to the Africans, and was not uncritical, but did not agree with vocal criticism and sharp press attacks such as were favoured by many of the Lagos elite. The British in apparent appreciation of his support, appointed him to the Board of Health in 1902 and secretary of the Lagos Institute set up with official encouragement for discussion of public issues. In 1906 he was appointed to the Legislative Council, to which he was frequently reappointed thereafter.

In 1914, on the amalgamation of Northern and Southern Nigeria, Governor-General Lugard created an advisory "Nigerian Council" which, as it turned out, was an ineffective body. Ajasa was appointed to it, and was for years a friend as well as a political ally of Sir Frederick Lugard, whom the Lathe Lagos elite generally loathed. Later in 1914 Ajasa started a new newspaper, the *Nigerian Pioneer* which operated in partnership with European business firms and was edited by him.

Sir Kitoyi Ajasa

For years, the *Pioneer* was a leading Lagos weekly, noted for its moderate and cautious approach to the government, very different from the vigorous and often abusive criticism which Ajasa and Lugard deplored in other newspapers. Its attitude was strongly criticised by those other newspapers. Their allegations of a subsidy from Lugard were unproven, but Ajasa and his newspaper were certainly close to the Governor-General. In the Legislative Council Ajasa did not oppose a measure providing for press censorship in 1917 (not passed into law then), though he had opposed a Seditious Offences Ordinance in 1909. Ajasa intervened to have the critical editor Bright Davies (q.v.) released from prison during the First World War, but remained Bright Davies' political enemy.

He had other political enemies also, especially during the feverish political activity after 1918. Then his Reform Club grouped together persons who, like himself believed more in co-operation than in the confrontational style of politicians like Herbert Macaulay (q.v.). In 1923, when the first elected Lagos representatives entered the Legislative Council, Ajasa was renominated to sit with the elected nationalists there. In the

same year the British government awarded him the OBE.

He was knighted in 1929. His newspaper continued to do well for over 20 years and played a major role in the Eleko Controversy (in which Ajasa backed the suspension of the Oba of Lagos, the Eleko) and other Lagos political developments in the 1920s. In the 1930s it acquired its own printing press. In 1936 Sir Kitoyi was charged with contempt of court, but when he apologised the charge was withdrawn.

Sir Kitoyi Ajasa married Lucretia Cornelia Layinka Moore in 1896. He died on 31 August 1937, and has since come to be respected, more than in his controversial lifetime, as a distinguished Nigerian who genuinely sought the interests of his people. ■

Akenzua II (1899-1978)

AKENZUA II, Oba Uku Akpolokpolo, Omo n'Oba n'Edo (1899-1978).

NIGERIAN traditional ruler of the Edo people. He was born as Edokparhogbuyunmun at Benin in 1899; his father was Oba Eweka II who ruled Benin from 1914 until 1933, and his grandfather the great Oba Ovonramwen (q.v.) who was the last independent king of Benin. He studied at Benin Government School between 1907 and 1915 and later at King's College, Lagos, from 1918 to 1921. On leaving school, he became employed as a transport clerk in the Benin Native Authority on a wage of ₦6 per month.

His training for the future office of Oba began when he became confidential secretary to his father, Eweka II, whose death in 1933 introduced Akenzua II to the rigour of office. Before then, in 1925, he worked under the supervision of the late Alake of Abeokuta, Oba Ademola II (q.v.). Following this, he was appointed to head the Ekiadolor District, the present Iyekuselu; he was in this office when his father died. In the same year Prince Okoro was installed Oba of Benin with the title of Akenzua II.

Between 1946 and 1966, the formative years of the new political system in the country, the Oba was a member of the Legislative Council of Nigeria, member of the Western House of Assembly, a member of the Western House of Chiefs and a cabinet minister.

Oba Akenzua was instrumental in the creation of the Midwest Region; it was his view that the two provinces of Benin and Delta in the Western Region could constitute the Bendel State by which the Midwest later became known. In October 1953 he formed the Benin-Delta People's Party to campaign for the unification of the two provinces. With the creation of the region he became the first President of the Midwest House of Chiefs in 1964.

His contributions to the politics and policies that shaped the content of Nigerian formative politics were rewarded by awards and honours bestowed on him: he was decorated with the insignia of Commander of the Republic of Nigeria and was made a Justice of Peace. From 1966 to 1972 he served as Chancellor of Ahmadu Bello University.

As the Oba of Benin, Akenzua II was the custodian of the rich Bini tradition and

Oba Akenzua II

culture whose study and promotion he personally encouraged; it was to this end he volunteered whatever bronze or ivory carvings under his jurisdiction for the success of the Black Arts and Culture Festival, FESTAC, that was held in the Nigerian capital in 1977. He died in late 1978 and was succeeded by Solomon Igbinoghodua Aisiokuoba who became Oba Erediauwa I of Benin in 1979. ■

Akintola, S.L. (1910-66)

AKINTOLA, Chief Samuel Ladoke (1910-66).

NIGERIAN politician; he was the second Premier of Western Nigeria, succeeding Chief Obafemi Awolowo in 1959. He was born on 6 July 1910 at Ogbomosho in Western Nigeria. After primary and secondary education at Ogbomosho, he worked for some time as editor of the *Nigerian Baptist*, a magazine published by the Baptist mission in Lagos. Working as a clerk in the Nigerian Railway and then as an editor of the *Daily Service*, of Lagos, the newspaper of the Nigerian Youth Movement, he left in 1946 for England where he studied public administration at Oxford and later qualified as a lawyer. He returned to Nigeria in 1949. Like most of his contemporaries with a good education, he was quickly drawn into politics and was a founding member of the Action Group (AG) under the leadership of Chief Obafemi Awolowo. As deputy leader of that party, he was for several years leader of the Action Group parliamentary group in the Federal House of Representatives, where he served as Minister of Health and Minister of Communications and Aviation.

In preparation for independence, scheduled for 1960, the Action Group took a decision that was to change the career of Akintola and the history of that party. Following the 1959 eve-of-independence elections and in order to project the party's image at the national level, Chief Awolowo, the party leader, was elected to the Federal House of Representatives where he became

Chief S.L. Akintola

regime. Three months of bloody rioting followed the announcement that his government had won the elections. The chaos was put to an abrupt end by his assassination in Ibadan on 15 January 1966 by the military coup makers.

A Yoruba like Chief Awolowo, brilliant and diplomatic, Chief Akintola was widely acknowledged as the most astute Nigerian politician of his day.■

Akinyele I. (1880-1965)

AKINYELE, Oba Isaac, Olubadan of Ibadan (1880-1965).

NIGERIAN traditional ruler of Ibadan, one of the largest cities in West Africa. He was the son of Josiah Akinyele, an Ibadan convert to Christianity; his brother Alexander became a clergyman, founder of Ibadan Grammar School, and later Bishop. Isaac entered government service, in the junior ranks to which Nigerians were confined in those days, becoming a Customs inspector for the Ibadan District Council in 1903. Later he worked as a farmer for a time. He and his brother formed the *Egba Agba O'Tan*, a small association, in 1914.

Isaac Akinyele became an active member of the Christ Apostolic Church and was, for long, its head in Ibadan. He also became a chief and thus rose steadily in the traditional hierarchy headed from 1936 by an Oba, the Olubadan. He became Otun Balogun and then, in late 1953, Balogun. Problems were expected because the title had close associations with the traditional Yoruba religion, which might make it difficult for a devout Christian to hold it. But the problems were overcome and Akinyele rose steadily towards the Oba's throne.

He was involved in politics, as a party supporter of the Action Group (AG). His political interests conflicted with those of the National Council of Nigeria and the Cameroons (NCNC) which controlled the Ibadan District Council, and its local boss, Adegoke Adelabu (q.v.). In February 1955, he was elected Olubadan of Ibadan having previously served as chief judge.

Leader of Opposition. Chief Akintola took Awolowo's place as the Premier of the Western Region. This division of roles later led to a conflict over the implementation of AG's policies in the West Regional Government. In 1962, things came to a head when there was an open clash in the Western parliament between the supporters of the two leaders. Chief Akintola, supported by the NPC-controlled federal government, won the day. He later formed a new party consisting of his followers in the AG and the former Western Regional branch of the National Council of Nigerian Citizens (NCNC), and called it the Nigerian National Democratic Party (NNDP); it entered into alliance with the Northern People's Congress (NPC).

Chief Akintola's alliance with the conservative NPC was unpopular among the progressives in the country and particularly in his own Western Region, where Chief Awolowo's Action Group was still very popular. The regional elections held in October 1965 brought to a fatal climax popular discontent against Chief Akintola's

Oba Akinyele's rule was soon engulfed in the turbulent political developments in Western Nigeria, the result of the growing rift in the Action Group between its leader, Chief Obafemi Awolowo (q.v.), and his deputy and Premier of the Western Region, Chief Samuel Ladoke Akintola (q.v.) in 1962. This came to a head when Alhaji Adegbenro (q.v.),

Oba I. Akinyele

Awolowo's supporter, was appointed premier by Governor Sir Adesoji Aderemi, the Oni of Ife (q.v.). Disorder broke out in the House of Assembly as the new premier was presenting his government for vote of confidence, and following the subsequent outbreak of violence both among the parliamentarians in the Assembly and among their supporters outside, the Region was placed under a state of emergency. The government was suspended and a sole Administrator of the West was appointed in the person of Dr. Moses A. Majekodunmi.

Throughout the entire political crisis Oba Akinyele remained aloof, placing himself at the disposal of any peace initiative for which Ibadan was a venue on several occasions. He ruled for only ten years but left a big reputation behind when he died in May 1965. ■

Akou, M. (1913-70)

AKOU, Dr Martin (1913-70).

TOGOLESE doctor and politician. He was Togo's first deputy in the French National Assembly. Born in 1913, he was a son of the famous Pastor Akou of the Evangelical Church, who started working in Lomé for the Bremen Mission in 1895 and continued the work it had started in both French and British Togoland later, becoming head of the Ho Seminary of the Ewe Presbyterian Church (in British Togoland) in 1944.

Martin Akou, after primary school, was taken by a missionary to Germany and went to schol at Westheim. He continued studies at Basle in Switzerland, and after the end of the Second World War completed medical studies in France.

In 1946 Dr. Akou became Togo's first deputy in the French National Assembly. As the candidate of the *Comité de l'Unité Togolaise* (CUT) of Sylvanus Olympio (q.v.), he defeated his rival Nicolas Grunitzky (q.v.). In the 1951 elections, however, the tables were turned and Grunitzky was elected. He originally had French government backing, but when the French turned against the CUT Akou joined the *Indépendants d'Outre-Mer*, a group including other African deputies, notably Senghor of Senegal and Apithy of Dahomey, during his five years in the French parliament.

After losing the 1951 election he retired from politics and re-established a medical practice in Gold Coast (Ghana), being one of the many Togolese who belonged on both sides of the border (a border finally fixed in 1956, but still challenged by some). He died in 1970. ■

Akuffo, F.W.K. (1937-79)

AKUFFO, General Frederick William Kwasi (1937-79).

GHANAIAN military ruler. He was born on 21 March 1937 at Akropong near

Gen. F.W.K. Akuffo

Accra. After completing his primary and secondary education in the Presbyterian Secondary School at Odumase Krobo, Akuffo enlisted in the Ghana army as an officer cadet in 1957.

His military training began with a two-year engagement from 1958 to 1960, at the Royal Military Academy, Sandhurst, England. He remained in Britain for another year for training in parachuting, followed in 1967 by another course at Britain's Staff College and at the National Defence College in India in 1973.

Returning to Ghana, Akuffo served in various capacities in the army, culminating in his appointment in 1974 as army commander. He succeeded Lieutenant-General Lawrence Okai in November 1976 as Chief of Defence Staff. Following the 1972 coup in which the Busia (q.v.) administration was overthrown, General Akuffo became the second in the six-man Supreme Military Council (SMC) headed by General Acheampong (q.v.). He won national attention in Ghana in 1974 when he was placed in charge of the change-over in the country's traffic laws, from driving on the left side to driving

on the right. Abroad, too, General Akuffo was becoming a familiar figure at international conferences like the June 1977 Commonwealth Heads of Government in London where he headed the Ghana delegation.

On 5 July 1978 the General ousted his superior, Acheampong, as Head of State in a bloodless coup. Statement issued by the new Government said that Acheampong had resigned and retired with immediate effect from the army. General Akuffo justified forcing Acheampong out of office in a broadcast to the nation by saying that "the channel of communication between him and the rest of his colleagues had virtually broken down and the whole of governmental activity had become a one-man show". The former Head of State, General Akuffo added, had also "unilaterally varied decisions that had been taken collectively at SMC meetings" as well as taking several important decisions "without consulting or even informing his colleagues. . . . We, his colleagues on the SMC, therefore, had no alternative, in this context, but to demand his exit from the scene".

General Akuffo, who emphasised the necessity of national unity and stability, declared that "Our primary task now as a government is to heal the wounds of our country". He ordered a general amnesty for all exiled Ghanaians not wanted for criminal offences and released some 40 Ghanaians who had been incarcerated for actively campaigning for a rejection of the non-party "Union Government" in the run up to the referendum in March 1978. Among those freed were Komla Gbedemah, a former Finance Minister in President Nkrumah's Government, and William Ofori-Atta and Victor Owusu, who both served in Dr. Kofi Busia's administration, and several professionals and academics.

The new Head of State added that his administration would return the country to civilian rule by July 1979. Accordingly, Akuffo accepted the report of the Constitutional Commission set up by his predecessor in early July, and lifted the ban on political parties that had been in effect since 1972. Earlier, on 15 December 1978, Akuffo had inaugurated the Constituent Assembly to set the final stage for the new constitution.

The Akuffo administration was only a few weeks away from the elections of 18 June 1979 to produce a civilian successor when it was overthrown by a group of young officers led by Flight-Lieutenant Jerry Rawlings on 4 June after an earlier futile attempt on 15 May. A few days later, on 26 June 1979, General Akuffo, along with his predecessors, General Afrifa, General Acheampong and five other senior military officers, Major-General Utuka, Rear Admiral Amedume, Air Vice-Marshal Boakye, Major-General Kotei and Colonel Felli were executed for alleged corruption by the new government. ■

Akufo-Addo, E. (1906-79)

AKUFO-ADDO, Edward (1906-79).

G HANAIAN statesman, President of Ghana from August 1970 to January 1972. Born on 26 June 1906 at Akwapim, a centre of early education in Ghana, he was educated at the Presbyterian Middle School, the Presbyterian Training College and the Theological Seminary, all at Akropong, and was then trained as a catechist before going to Achimota College. From there he went to St. Peter's Hall (as it then was), Oxford, to read mathematics. He studied at the Middle Temple, London, and was called to the Bar in 1940, returning then to set up a private practice in the Gold Coast (now Ghana).

His political career began with the formation of the United Gold Coast Convention (UGCC) of which he was a founder member in 1947. He was one of six UGCC leaders detained in 1948. He was a member of the Legislative Council of Gold Coast in 1949-1950 and member of the Coussey Constitutional Commission for Gold Coast in 1949.

After 21 years of legal practice he became a Judge of the Ghana Supreme Court in 1962 and held the post until 1964. Then he was sacked with other judges by the Nkrumah (q.v.) regime, after their acquittal of some politicians on trial. Akufo-Addo was appointed in September 1966 to be the Chief Justice of Ghana on the dismissal of his predecessor by the National Liberation Council (NLC), and served in that post and as well as chairman of the General Legal Council of Ghana, from 1966 to 1970. He was also appointed chairman of the Council of the University of Ghana in 1966. He headed the Political Committee of the NLC, and the

E. Akufo-Addo

Constitutional Commission which drafted a constitution for discussion by the Constituent Assembly. The agreed new Constitution came into force in 1969.

He became the President of the Republic of Ghana in August 1970, retiring in 1972 when the government of Dr. Kofi Busia (q.v.), was overthrown in a military coup. He was conferred with a national honour, Member of the Order of the Volta, and was an honorary fellow of St. Peter's College, Oxford.

He died in July 1979. ■

Alakija, A. (1884-1952)

ALAKIJA, Sir Adeyemo (1884-1952).

N IGERIAN lawyer and newspaper entrepreneur, a founding member of the Nigerian *Daily Times*, now one of Africa's leading daily newspapers. He was a son of one of the "Brazilian" families of Lagos: black repatriates from Brazil, using Brazilian

(Portuguese) names but usually remembering their African ancestry, which was often Yoruba. His family was of Egba origin and named Assumpçao. He was born on 25 May 1884 to Ribeiro and Maximiliana Assumpçao and named Placido Adeyemo. He had a famous brother Olayinka, and his sister Tejumade married Alake Ademola II (q.v.) of Abeokuta.

Placido Assumpçao's family were Catholics like other "Brazilians", but after going to the famous Catholic school in Lagos, St. Gregory's, he went on to the CMS Grammar School (Anglican). On leaving school he entered the government service as a clerical worker in 1900; he spent ten years in that service, mainly with the Posts. He married Christina Ayodele George in 1907.

In 1910 he began legal studies at the Middle Temple in London, where he was called to the Bar in 1913. In that year he and his brother, Olayinka, abandoned their Portuguese name for a Yoruba one, Alakija.

Adeyemo Alakija practised successfully as a lawyer. He went into politics, first a close colleague of Herbert Macaulay (q.v.), with whom he later broke over the issue of the British government's action against the Oba of Lagos (Eleko), a major issue in Lagos

Sir Adeyemo Alakija

politics in the 1920s. In 1923 and in 1926 he unsuccessfully stood for election to the Legislative Council (Legco), as an independent. His brother was a prominent elected member of Legco later. Adeyemo also joined it but only as an appointed member, representing Egba Division from 1933 to 1941.

In 1926 he made his most famous contribution to history by playing an active part in the foundation of the *Daily Times*, now Nigeria's leading daily newspaper. He planned it with Ernest Ikoli (q.v.), an already successful young editor, and Richard Barrow, agent of Jurgen's Colonial Products Limited and chairman of the Lagos Chamber of Commerce. A new daily newspaper was planned, to take Reuters and radio reports among other news coverage. The idea was supported by Barrow's expatriate business colleagues and approved by the government. Thus the Nigerian Printing and Publishing Company (NPPC) was formed, with a nominal share capital of £3,000, to start the *Daily Times* and take over Ikoli's *African Messenger*. The new newspaper started on 1 June 1926 with Ikoli as editor.

Alakija was chairman of the Board of the NPPC. It succeeded in bringing out a popular newspaper using modern techniques, with the help of advertising by the European firms. Its success was in spite of a pro-government attitude that was not usual among Nigerian editors at that time apart from Alakija's friend Sir Kitoyi Ajasa (q.v.). In 1936 the NPPC was merged with West African Newspapers Limited of London and Liverpool, publishers of *West Africa* and the *West African Review*. Later, in 1948, the International Publishing Corporation of London took over the *Daily Times* enterprise.

Alakija won the traditional titles of Bariyun of Ake (Abeokuta) in 1932, and Woje Ileri of Ife in 1935. The British government also honoured him with the Jubilee Medal, the Coronation Medal, and in 1939 the CBE. He attended King George VI's coronation in 1937. In 1942, having ceased the previous year to be an appointed Legco member, he was appointed to the Executive Council. In 1945 he was knighted, with the KBE. He went to Britain in 1949 to receive the knighthood from George VI.

Sir Adeyemo's contribution to Nigerian politics included the formation, in 1945, of the Egbe Omo Oduduwa, of which he became the first President. This Yoruba organisation ("League of the Sons of Oduduwa") became the nucleus of the Action Group.

But Sir Adeyemo was most famous as head of the leading newspaper, and as a major figure in Lagos society. He was a prominent Freemason, the first Nigerian to become Grand Master of the Nigerian Freemasons, who were influential among the Lagos elite.

Sir Adeyemo Alakija died on 10 May 1952. His widow, Lady Alakija, was for years afterwards an active Director of the Daily Times of Nigeria Limited and a living link with its early days under her husband.■

Alegre, C.C. (1864-90)

ALEGRE, Caetano da Costa (1864-90).

C.C. Alegre

SÃO TOMÉ poet. He was born in 1864 in São Tomé. He came from a background of wealthy landowners of mixed African and European stock, his father being a Portuguese settler who married an indigene of the colony. The Berlin Conference of 1884-5 formally affirmed Portugal's colonial "rights" over these islands, where her occupation lasted for 400 years. These events, coupled with the Portuguese "assimilation" policy and its attendant racist overtones, were to have a profound influence on Alegre's life.

After formal elementary and secondary schooling in São Tomé he was sent to Lisbon in 1882, enrolling there as a medical student. But the young student soon became despondent with Portugal because of the prevalent racism. This disappointment led to a feeling of alienation which infuenced the theme of his poetry, written between 1882 and 1889 in Lisbon. He died there a year later in 1890, at the early age of 26.

Alegre was the first writer in Portuguese to highlight the cruel subjugation and feeling of alienation of the African in the Portuguese colonies. With his own unhappy experiences both in São Tomé and Portugal, he dwelt at length on the feeling of hopelessness and isolation in a European culture that was reluctant to recognise the African

whose heritage received remarkable exaltation in Alegre's poetry. Some of the poems were published posthumously in 1916 in Lisbon as a collected work under the title *Versos*. The book was reprinted in 1950, followed by a second edition in 1951, while the poet and his works have become the subject of increasing critical literary evaluation. In 1963 a criticism of his poems appeared in *Poetas e Contistas de expressão portuguesa*, while 1967 saw another evaluation in *Literatura africana de expressão portuguesa*.■

Ali, A.I. (1917-74)

ALI, Field-Marshal Ahmed Ismail (1917-74).

EGYPTIAN soldier who served as War Minister from 1972 until his death. Field-Marshal Ali was also Commander-in-Chief of the Egyptian Armed Forces.

Field-Marshal A.I. Ali

He was born on 14 October 1917 in Cairo, and had his education in the Egyptian capital. He then enlisted in the army and trained at the Cairo Military Academy where he graduated in 1938. He returned to the Staff College for further training and earned the MA degree in military science in 1950; he later taught at the premier Egyptian military institution from 1950 until 1953. He was to undertake further courses in Britain and at the Frunze Military Academy in Moscow.

During the Second World War, Ali served as Intelligence officer with the British forces in north Africa. He played active roles in the subsequent four wars between his country and Israel – 1948, 1956, 1967 and 1973. In the Palestine War of 1948 he was at the head of an Egyptian command in Gaza, after which he was appointed a brigade commander. Returning from further military training abroad in 1957, he was made commander of the Port Said Forces. Four years later he was seconded by President Nasser (q.v.) as military adviser to the then Congo government of Prime Minister Patrice Lumumba (q.v.).

In the 1967 Six-Day War, Ali was Chief of Staff on the Jordanian front where he commanded Egyptian forces against Isra-el. An expert on battle tactics, he was made Chief of Military Operations in 1968; the following year he succeeded Abdel Moneim Riad as Chief of Staff of the Egyptian Armed Forces. He was replaced in 1969 by President Nasser after a serious military setback in the 1967 war with Israel. During the hostilities the Israelis landed on the Shadwan island, at the mouth of the Gulf of Suez, and seized an Egyptian radar installation, for which he was reprimanded for not having taken necessary preventive measures; he was removed from office but was allowed to remain in the army.

Following Nasser's death, President Sadat (q.v.) appointed Ali, who was then a Major-General, as head of the Intelligence. He was appointed Commander-in-Chief of the Egyptian Armed Forces in 1972 when he was also returned to the cabinet as War Minister. As head of the army, he organised the impressive crossing of the Suez Canal by the Egyptian Third Army during the 1973 war with Israel. Prior to the October offensive, on 21 January 1973, Ali had been made Commander-in-Chief of the combined Armed Forces of Egypt, Libya and Syria; this was followed on 28 January 1973 with the appointment as Commander-in-Chief of the entire Arab Fronts.

Field-Marshal Ali died on 26 December 1974 in a London clinic where he was receiving treatment for cancer. Announcing his death to Egyptians, President Sadat said that Field-Marshal Ali was a "hero whose name will forever be linked with the stories of the Egyptian military and the heroic feats of the great crossing to victory." The Field-Marshal was given a state funeral in Cairo on 27 December 1974. ■

Alli, A. F. (1929-89)

ALLI, Professor Ambrose Folorunsho (1929-89).

NIGERIAN doctor and politician who became well known nationally during the Second Republic in the years 1979 to 1983. Born on 22 September 1929 at Ekpoma in Bendel State, Ambrose Alli was educated at the Immaculate Conception College in

Benin City before going to St. Patrick's College at Asaba, and to the School of Agriculture in Ibadan. He trained as a medical laboratory technologist at the University College Medical Laboratory, Ibadan, from 1950 to 1953, and studied medicine at the University College of Ibadan from 1953 to 1960. Alli did further medical studies in Britain after that and worked in hospitals there and in Zimbabwe (1960-62).

Alli returned to Nigeria in 1966 to begin a distinguished academic career. He was professor of Morbid Anatomy at Ahmadu Bello University, Zaria from 1969 to 1971, and at the University of Ibadan from 1971 to 1974. From 1974 to 1979 he was head of the Department of Pathology at the University of Benin.

But it was through his career in politics that Ambrose Alli rose to prominence. With the lifting of the ban on formal activity by political parties in 1978 he became more involved in politics, in preparation for the return to civilian rule in 1979. He was a member of the 1977-78 Constituent Assembly which deliberated the 1979 Constitution leading to the Second Republic. He was a foundation member of the Unity Party of Nigeria led by Obafemi Awolowo (q.v.) on whose platform he was elected as Governor of Bendel State in July 1979. He served in that office until September 1983 when he lost the gubernatorial elections to another candidate.

During his term as Governor Ambrose Alli vigorously implemented his party's programme of free education for all in his state. The Bendel State University, situated in Ekpoma, was founded during this period. Alli's practical and personal involvement is said to have literally made the founding of this university possible, and it is perhaps the most remarkable achievement for which he will be remembered.

When the civilian regime of President Shehu Shagari was overthrown on 31 December 1983, Professor Alli was detained alongside many other civilian politicians. He was tried on corruption charges and sentenced to a total of 66 years' imprisonment. The sentence was later reviewed and reduced to seven years. His health deteriorated while in gaol. Alli was released on 13 February 1988 only after the payment of 983,000 naira raised by his friends into the government chest. Alli died on 22 September 1989 (his 60th birthday) at the Lagos Univer-

A.F. Alli

sity Teaching Hospital. Calls have been made for the Bendel State University to be renamed after Alli as a tribute to him.■

Alves, N.B. (1945-77)

ALVES, Nito Baptista (1945-77).

ANGOLAN politician, the Commander of MPLA's 1st Military Region who at independence became a member of the Central Committee and Minister of the Interior. He was born in 1945 in Piri, northern Angola. After primary education at the Evangelical Mission near Piri, he went to Luanda in 1960 for further studies, completing his secondary education in 1965. It was in the middle of the 1960s that Alves commenced his political activities, centred on the nationalist underground campaign to dislodge Portuguese colonialism.

In 1966 he escaped arrest by the colonial police, PIDE, and fled north to join MPLA guerrillas in Dembos where the movement had established its first military command. His star quickly rose as the anti-colonial war gathered momentum. In 1967 he was appointed a co-commander of the Centre for Revolutionary Instruction (CIR) and in 1971 became commander of the 1st Military Region. As such he was able to establish a strong following among the members of the FAPLA, the military organ of the MPLA.

After the 1974 coup in Lisbon and the installation of Angola's shortlived transitional government in 1975, Alves was a key figure in forming the *poder popular* (people's power) groups, which played a crucial role in the re-establishment of the MPLA in government. Shortly after he returned from his postings in the north to Luanda he participated in the MPLA Congress held in Lusaka, Zambia, which proved an unsuccessful attempt to reconcile the internal rifts within the movement on the eve of its ascension to power. Here, as at successive MPLA congresses, Alves expounded ideological directives which President Neto (q.v.) later described as "ultra revolutionary".

Following the establishment of the MPLA government in November 1975, Alves was brought into the Central Committee and appointed Minister of Interior Administration, a position which placed him in contact with the mass organs of the MPLA. His task was to disband the far-left unofficial groups such as the Angolan Communist Organisation (OCA), the Henda Committees, named after an MPLA combatant who was killed in 1968, and the Amilcar Cabral Committees, all of which did not share a common ideological thread with the MPLA. Alves was accused of using his office to set up a personal power base among the youth, trade union and women's organisations of the movement. MPLA sources complained that this was often accompanied by attacks on the leadership. The rift with his colleagues in the Central Committee came to a head during the urban elections of 1976 when he was charged with attempting to organise a base among Luanda's *muceques*, the shanties, and suburbs. He was subsequently dismissed from office in October 1976, and though retaining his membership fo the Central Committee, was removed from the Political Bureau of the MPLA. Nevertheless, he continued to exercise some political influence through his position in the Central Committee and retained support within the FAPLA and the *muceques*, his traditional stronghold.

According to MPLA leadership, the "Nitistas", as Alves's followers were known, began to plan to overthrow President Neto; the "Nitistas" clandestine meetings had been going on for some time in Luanda and FAPLA before Alves was formally ostracised from the MPLA leadership on 21 May 1977. At that meeting where Alves and one of his colleagues, José Van Dunem (q.v.), were ousted from the Central Committee, the "Nitistas" leaders attacked what was commonly referred to in the *muceques* as the "petty bourgeoisie". This attack had racial undertones against the Whites and Mulattoes in the Neto administration – Alves openly advocated an all-Black administration, a view which the MPLA leadership had consistently rejected.

Following his expulsion from the MPLA, Alves was placed under arrest, with José Van Dunem. This precipitated the abortive coup of 27 May 1977, which was aimed, according to MPLA sources, at "installing Nito Alves as President and Van Dunen as Prime Minister". The two men were released from São Paulo prison in Luanda where they were detained by a group which identified itself as the "MPLA Action Committee". Several MPLA leaders, including Siady Mingas (q.v.), Minister of Finance, were killed by the plotters. Following the unsuccessful bid for power, Alves went into hiding, but was apprehended, tried by military tribunal and executed. ∎

Amer, M.A. (1919-67)

AMER, Field-Marshal Mohammed Abdel-Hakim (1919-67).

EGYPTIAN soldier, who became Vice-President under Abdul Nasser (q.v.). Amer was born on 11 December 1919 in Istal in the Minya province of Egypt. He, like Nasser whom he was to serve for 15 years, trained at the Cairo Military Academy and was commissioned as a second lieutenant in 1939. In 1948 he graduated from the Staff Officers' College and took part in the Palestine War of that year.

In the following years both Amer and Nasser became important members in the Free Officers' Movement whose objectives included the elimination of British imperialism, the abolition of feudalism and capitalism and the establishment of a democratic state

Field-Marshal M.A. Amer

apparatus. Following the coup d'état of 23 July 1952 which replaced King Farouk with General Neguib, Amer was appointed director of the new Head of State's office. He became a major-general the following year, and from then on until 1958 was Commander-in-Chief of Egypt's armed forces. Promoted Field-Marshal in 1957, he served from 1958 to 1962 as Commander-in-Chief of the United Arab Republic Forces, during the political union of Syria and Egypt. Amer also served as governor of Syria until the union with Egypt was dissolved in 1961.

After 1961 he became Second Vice-President to Nasser, also taking charge of the ministry of War. In 1964 he was appointed to the new post of First Vice-President, which he held along with that of Deputy

Supreme Commander of the Armed Forces. In these capacities Amer took charge of the military operations during the Six Day War of June 1967, in which Egypt lost the Sinai Peninsula and part of the Gaza Strip to Israel. The defeat caused considerable crisis of confidence within the Egyptian government, with President Nasser offering to step down (but popular demonstration persuaded him to remain in office). Amer and other senior military officers also tendered their resignations which were accepted.

On 14 September 1967, Amer was reported to have committed suicide. It was officially announced next day that he had poisoned himself. He had been placed under house arrest in early September on suspicion of plotting to overthrow the government. A statement from the ministry of National Guidance said that the Field-Marshal had taken large quantities of poison on 13 September as he was about to testify before a military tribunal investigating the alleged plot.

Until his resignation in June 1967 Amer was a close friend and confidant of President Nasser. The two army colleagues organised the 1952 coup and governed Egypt together. Amer's daughter married one of Nasser's brothers, while the President named one of his sons after Field-Marshal Amer. After his death Nasser told his cabinet that Amer was "closer than a brother" to him. It was later reported by *Al-Ahram*, the authoritative Egyptian daily, that when President Nasser decided to re-organise the armed forces after the June 1967 setback he invited Amer to stay on as Vice-President, but Amer refused, insisting on retaining his military post. ■

Anchouey, L. (1896/97-1929)

ANCHOUEY, Laurent (1896/97-1929).

GABONESE politician. He was of the Omyeme people who were the first to seek Western education in large numbers after the establishment of the first French settlement in Gabon in 1843. Although few, these early French-educated Gabonese were an older elite than those of any other French colony except Senegal, Dahomey (Benin) and Madagascar. Thus nationalist protests started earlier there and in the other three territories mentioned (see, e.g., Diouf; Hunkanrin; Ravoahangy).

In 1919 Anchouey founded a branch of the *Ligue des Droits de l'Homme*, a very influential organisation in France, in Libreville, French colonial headquarters in Gabon. This helped to get the Ligue interested in French colonial repression, which was very severe in the interior of Gabon in the 1920s.

In the early 1920s Anchouey spent some time in France, where he founded and edited *L'Echo Gabonais*, a newspaper critical of French colonial methods. It is said to have been started either in Dakar (where one source says some West Indians helped start it in 1922) or in France itself. Anchouey's activity is said to have included also the editing of another newspaper, called the *Voix Coloniale* or the *Voix Africaine*, in France. He was also associated with *Jeune Gabon*, an organisation in the colony in the 1920s.

The establishment of "Committees for *L'Echo Gabonais*", which were similar to the sections of the *Ligue des Droits de l'Homme*, Gabon branch, was practical expression of Anchouey's political ideas. While keeping a watch on him the French authorities apparently had to tolerate some of his activity as the Ligue was powerful in France.

Generally Anchouey had a co-operative attitude towards the French administration. He opposed French colonial oppression but blamed the administrators on the spot, calling for Africans to be freed from these by closer integration with France. He called for more education and more spread of French "civilisation". He believed that sympathisers within the colonial ruling country represented better ideals to which they could appeal against ill-treatment by colonial officials in Africa: "Frenchmen of France, we appeal to you", he wrote in *L'Echo Gabonais*.

By 1925 Anchouey was back in Gabon, where he tried to revive political activity centred around the branch of the Ligue. This activity and that of the Jeune Gabon movement did not last long, and Anchouey himself died an early death in 1929. ∎

Andom, A.M. (1924-74)

ANDOM, Lieutenant-General Aman Michael (1924-74).

ETHIOPIAN soldier and statesman. Aman Michael Andom was born in 1924 in Eritrea, now a province of Ethiopia, to a family of Lutherans. He was educated at an American school in Khartoum, Sudan. On completing his studies he joined the resistance movement against the Italian occupation of Ethiopia, remaining on as a regular soldier in the Ethiopian Armed Forces after liberation was achieved in 1941.

He rapidly gained a reputation as an able soldier and was sent to the Cadet Training School in Khartoum. He later travelled to England for officer training at the military academies in Camberley and Sandhurst, and by 1962 was promoted to Major-General.

By this time he had become critical of some aspects of Emperor Haile Selassie's reign, and although he was uninvolved in the revolt of the Imperial Guards in 1960, serving at the time on the Ethiopian-Somali border, his unorthodox views began to be known. As a result he was appointed military attaché in the Ethiopian Embassy in the USA in 1964, and the following year he was "retired" from the army and made a member of the Senate.

While he was in the Senate he continued his outspoken criticism of the autocratic regime of the Emperor and its attendant bureaucratic inefficiency and corruption. He had also retained his popularity with the armed forces during this period, and following the popular uprising, he was promoted to the rank of Lieutenant-General in July 1974. At the same time he was appointed Chief-of-Staff and Minister of Defence and became a member of the Armed Forces Co-ordinating Committee.

Being an Eritrean, he was particularly concerned with the long-standing strife in that region. In August 1974, 23 deputies from the provinces resigned from the Ethiopian Parliament in protest against what they saw as a lack of government interest in the Eritrean problem. Andom decided to visit the province to study the situation there.

Meanwhile, the Emperor's powers were becoming more and more restricted as the Armed Forces Co-ordinating Committee gradually gained more power. After the Emperor was deposed on 12 September, a Provisional Military Administrative Council (PMAC) was set up to rule the country. Andom was made Chairman of the PMAC, thus becoming the first military Head of State in Ethiopia, while also retaining his positions of Chief of Staff of the Armed Forces and Minister of Defence.

Gen. A.M. Andom

On gaining power, the PMAC issued a declaration of the aims of the revolution, some of which were to remove injustices and inequalities existing in the country, especially those related to land ownership, income distribution, educational opportunity and membership of ethnic or religious groups, so as to build a nation united on the basis of co-operation and equality. Andom was in complete support of these aims, although he was the figurehead rather than the dominating force of the revolution. Part of his duties was to receive accredited ambassadors and other international dignatories, but he did so on behalf of the whole PMAC.

However, by November disagreements had begun to emerge between Andom and the PMAC. After his visit to Eritrea he believed that a peacefully negotiated solution to the problem was possible and he refused to sign an order to send 5,000 extra troops to the area. He also refused to sanction the execution without trial of those under arrest for opposition to the revolution, and he resigned from the Government as well as from his position as army Chief-of-Staff.

He was placed under house arrest a week later on 22 November 1974 and the following day he was shot dead after his house was attacked by machine gun, tank and mortar fire.■

Andrade, M. de (1928-90)

ANDRADE, Mário de (1928-90).

ANGOLAN nationalist leader. Born on 21 August 1928 at Golungo Alto (North Kwanza region), he was of Angolan and Portuguese parentage, *mestiço*; in Angola, unlike Africa generally, this fact automatically conferred certain favours and privileges under highly repressive Portuguese rule.

Mário Coelho Pinto de Andrade, as he was named in full, went to Lisbon in 1948 to study Philology. He was linked with the group of young literary people in Luanda who in 1952 published a journal, *Mensagem,* until it was banned. In Portugal he was in contact with other Africans who, having obtained higher education which almost all Africans were denied under Portuguese rule, were conscious of their people's subjugation and began protest activity.

In 1954 Mário de Andrade went to France, where he studied sociology at the Sorbonne in Paris and wrote under the name "Buanga Fele" for the famous journal *Présence Africaine* edited by Alioune Diop (q.v.). A poet himself, he also edited an anthology of African poetry in Portuguese. In Paris he developed his nationalist activity against Portuguese misrule in Angola and other colonies. He organised a *Movimento Anti-Colonialista* (MAC) grouping nationalists from several Portuguese territories. He was also involved in early moves to organise

African protests in Angola; there were two short-lived early organisations, the *Partido Comunista Angolano* and the *Partido da Luta Unida dos Africanos de Angola* (PLUA), but these were not very effective, and in December 1956 the *Movimento Popular de Libertação de Angola* (MPLA) was founded, destined to last until it became the ruling party of independent Angola.

Mário de Andrade was a founder member of the MPLA and one of its main leaders in exile; he was joined in France in 1957 by Viriato da Cruz. He made many contacts, for example with Portuguese opponents of the Salazar dictatorship, to spread the MPLA message. From 1960 to 1962 he was president of the MPLA. During that time the armed struggle was launched in Angola in February 1961. de Andrade continued to travel to seek support for the struggle. At a meeting in Morocco in April 1961 a Conference of Nationalist Organisations of the Portuguese Colonies (Portuguese initials CONCP), a development from the MAC, was set up, and de Andrade became its President.

In December 1962, at the first national conference of the MPLA in Léopoldville (now Kinshasa), de Andrade was replaced as President by Agostinho Neto (q.v.), who was to become President of Angola at independence. In the early 1960s victory seemed far off and the MPLA, besides being in conflict with the rival UPA which became the GRAE under Holden Roberto, was also internally divided. Mário de Andrade parted company with Neto's leadership in 1963. He rejoined the party in Brazzaville the following year, but this time as a rank and file member.

During the struggle of the next ten years de Andrade co-authored a book, published in Paris in 1971: *La guerre en Angola: Etude socio-économique.* He participated in a brief guerrilla operation in Angola, operating from Zambia, but otherwise his contribution to the military aspect of the resistance was small. In 1974 Mário de Andrade's elder brother Father Joaquim Pinto de Andrade, a priest gaoled for years for nationalist activity and chosen as honorary President by the MPLA, was able to join the MPLA exiles based in Brazzaville. Then, however, the two brothers joined with others to form an opposition group within the MPLA, *Revolta Activa,* against Neto's leadership, which they said was too authoritarian. This organisation rejoined the body of the MPLA a few months later, during the momentous developments following the Portuguese revolution of April 1974.

Mário de Andrade played no further significant role in those developments, which led to Portugal's withdrawal from Angola in 1975 amid civil war among the liberation movements: MPLA, FLNA (i.e. GRAE) and UNITA. The MPLA defeated the FNLA quickly but UNITA survived with South African aid to fight against Dr. Neto's MPLA government, bringing years of war and ruin to Angola. Throughout all this de Andrade was in exile, estranged from the MPLA government but never supporting UNITA. He spent some time in Guinea-Bissau and Cape Verde, occupying guest ministerial positions, and writing a biography of Amilcar Cabral (q.v.). He also spent some time in Mozambique, researching into the history of the nationalist movement.

He died after a long illness in London, on 26 August 1990. His body was taken home for a hero's funeral in Luanda, in recognition of his role as a pioneer nationalist and the MPLA's first President. ∎

Anionwu, L.O.V. (1921-80)

ANIONWU, Lawrence Odiatu Victor (1921-80).

NIGERIAN administrator and diplomat, he was the first Nigerian Permanent Secretary of the Ministry of External Affairs, and his country's first Ambassador to Rome. These achievements made Anionwu outstanding in the history of administration in modern Nigeria, for he not only oversaw the work of an important government department during the formative years of Nigeria's independent foreign policy, but also rose to become one of the leading envoys of Nigeria.

Lawrence Anionwu was born on 5 May 1921 in Onitsha, the famous market town now in Anambra State. After his primary education he attended Nigeria's premier secondary school of the time, King's College, Lagos. He later studied at Trinity

Hall, Cambridge, England, where he graduated with the M.A. degree in 1946,and an LLB in 1948, and was called to the Bar at Lincoln's Inn in London in the same year.

He returned to Nigeria in 1949 and set himself up in private legal practice at Jos, now the capital of Plateau State but at that time a divisional headquarters in the former Northern Nigeria. From then until the late 1950s, when he returned to Onitsha, Anionwu practised there while also being a coroner for the Jos Division. At the same time, he served on the Jos Township Advisory Board, the Plateau Provincial Liquor Board, the Provincial Education Committee and the Jos Local Education Committee. During that period Anionwu was also manager of the Jos Township School and president of the Jos African Club which, after independence, became known as the Jos Club.

On his return to Onitsha in the late 1950s, he was appointed a Senior Crown Counsel by the former Eastern Region Government, an appointment which was a major achievement for Anionwu in particular and for Nigerian lawyers in general, for although they had had remarkable success in private practice very few had been encouraged by the British administration to join the public service. Anionwu was among the few appointed by that administration and given prominent positions. He was serving as Crown Counsel at Enugu when, on the eve of independence in 1960, he was appointed into the Federal Public Service signalling the commencement of its Nigerianisation. He had the distinction of being the first Nigerian administrator to be appointed with the specific purpose of redirecting the work of a government department to meet the requirements of a newly independent country.

He was sent for further training to the Imperial Defence College in London, and on his return to Lagos, was posted to the Ministry of External Affairs where he served as the first Nigerian Permanent Secretary from 1960 until 1963. An able officer, he soon displayed the exemplary qualities that won the admiration and respect of his colleagues. Three years later he was given the task of opening the Nigerian Embassy in Rome where he was the country's first representative. He was to go to London as High Commissioner in 1967 when civil war broke out in Nigeria, thus interrupting his diplomatic career.

Anionwu retired from the public service when the civil war ended in 1970, but continued to make generous contributions towards community development in his home town, Onitsha. Among the projects he was involved in was the reconstruction of the Emmanuel Church. He also served on the Board of the Central Water Transportation Service based there. He died from a stroke in London, where he was visiting, in 1980 and his body was flown to Onitsha for burial.■

Anyogu, J.C. (1898-1967)

ANYOGU, Right Reverend John Cross (1898-1967).

NIGERIAN clergyman who, on being consecrated Bishop on 9 June 1957, became the first member of his Igbo community to attain the rank. He also had the distinction of being the first Igbo to be ordained a priest, in 1930, and the first Bishop of the Catholic diocese of Enugu which had been created in 1963, the year of his installation. Through his efforts Enugu became a very important mission centre administering to several thousand Christians in and around the town – the parish had the second largest concentration of Catholics, coming only after Owerri in Nigeria.

He was born on 11 March 1898 in Onitsha, another early mission settlement on the bank of the River Niger, some 96 kilometres from Enugu. His parents, Jacob and Ama Fatima Anyogu, were prominent worshippers at the Onitsha mission where their contribution to its growth, both as a base for European missionaries arriving in Nigeria as well as a training ground for prospective priests, was well known. Their offspring John was not slow in noticing this dedication for by 1912, when he was only 14, he too had resolved to serve God. "As my New Year resolution", he wrote to his father on 1 January 1912, "I want to serve God all my life. I want to be a priest". His father took the matter up with the European priests at the mission, asking whether an African could be a priest. The positive response led to

Rev. J.C. Anyogu

Nigeria, from where he was posted to Oguta in 1948. The following year Anyogu was transferred to Nteje where, in addition to other mission duties, he taught the Igbo language to Irish priests.

In 1956 he was honoured by the British Queen, Elizabeth II, with the Order of the British Empire (OBE). A year later, on 9 June 1957, Father Anyogu was consecrated Bishop, becoming the first member of his community to attain the rank. Subsequently when he was installed Bishop of Enugu on 15 January 1963, he became the first Bishop of the new diocese which, before his death on 5 July 1967, had become an important Catholic centre not only for the eastern region which Enugu served as the administrative headquarters but also for Nigeria as a whole. ■

John and his brother Luke being sent to England in March 1913 for training.

John had attended the Holy Trinity School at Onitsha for his elementary education. In 1912 he passed the then Standard VI as well as the Junior Civil Entrance Examinations which showed his exemplary brilliance.

In Britain he studied at the Junior Seminary of St. Mary's, in Grange-over-Sands, in the industrial Lancashire belt. Five years later, he went to Ireland to read philosophy in Dublin and matriculated with distinction.

He returned to Nigeria in 1919 to continue his studies for the priesthood at Onitsha; he was one of the first crop of priests to graduate from the Igbariam Seminary there. Alongside his studies there John Anyogu taught Latin to junior seminarians, using his own quarters as a make-shift classroom. Also during this period, in 1922, he was sent to Ogoja, some 320 kilometres from Onitsha – a distance he did on foot – to spread the gospel. Then on 8 December 1930 he was ordained at Onitsha by Bishop Shanahan, at the age of 32, becoming the first priest from Eastern Nigeria.

Father Anyogu was first located to the Adazi parish as a curate. He served there for five years before being relocated to take charge of the Nnewi parish. In 1940 he went to Idah, a southerly town of then Northern

Apithy, S. M. (1913-89)

APITHY, Sourou Migan (1913-89).

BENINESE statesman who was for a time President of his country, formerly called Dahomey. Born on 8 April 1913 in Porto Novo, he was of the Goun people, who with the neighbouring Nagos (Yorubas) formed his power base in his political activity. That began after he spent twelve years, 1933 to 1945, in France for studies, at a time when only a few Africans from the French territories were able to study in Europe. He studied at Bordeaux and Paris, and obtained a diploma in accountancy.

He was elected in 1945 to the French Constituent Assembly as one of Dahomey's two representatives, the other being a French missionary who took up African interests, Father Aupiais. For many years following, Apithy was one of the Africans from the colonies who sat in two French Constituent Assemblies and then in the National Assembly of the Fourth Republic. He served there until 1958. At the same time he sat in the Dahomey assembly, called the *Conseil Général* and then the *Assemblée Territoriale*, from 1946 to 1960, and in the *Grand Conseil* for French West Africa from 1947 to 1957.

Apithy joined the *Rassemblement Démocratique Africain* (RDA) at first, but in 1948 left to join the *Indépendants d'Outre-Mer* (IOM), a group of African deputies in Paris without a party organisation. Later he left this group and remained unattached to the inter-territorial African parties. In Dahomey he was a founder of the *Union Progressiste Dahoméenne* (UPD), but in 1951 established his own new party, the *Parti Républicain Dahoméen* (PRD). He was Mayor of Porto Novo in 1956 and President of Dahomey's Territorial Assembly in 1956-7. Thus he was one of Dahomey's leading politicians, but by 1957, when elections prior to internal self-government were held in French Africa, he was seriously challenged by Justin Ahomadegbe and his *Union Démocratique Dahoméenne* (UDD).

In the 1957 elections the PRD won a small majority in Dahomey's Assembly, 35 seats out of 60, but Apithy formed a coalition with the northern-based party led by Hubert Maga, the *Mouvement Démocratique Dahoméen* (MDD). Apithy became vice-chairman of the Executive Council, then chairman in July 1958. In that year his party and the MDD were joined to form the *Parti Progressiste Dahoméen* (PPD), but they split soon afterwards, partly because of disagreement over the proposed Mali Federation; after discussions, Apithy decided Dahomey should not join the proposed federal union.

Elections were held in April 1959 with Apithy leading his own separate PRD again. The UDD protested at early results which gave the PRD 37 seats, and the results were changed; it also refused to agree to Apithy becoming Prime Minister, and so Hubert Maga took the post and led the country into independence in 1960, at the head of a coalition. Apithy served briefly as Foreign Minister, then went briefly into opposition, and in late 1960 became Finance Minister. His party and Maga's then merged into the *Parti Dahoméen de l'Unité* (PDU), which won elections in December 1960 held on the "list" system, which meant that the losers, the UDD, were eliminated from the Assembly. Maga then became President and Apithy Vice-President.

Later Apithy became ambassador to France, while still being Vice-President. But in October 1963 Maga was overthrown. In January 1964 Sourou Migan Apithy became President. But he ruled in uneasy alliance with his opponent for many years, Ahoma-

S.M. Apithy

degbe, and when they fell out in 1965 over the appointment of a head of the Supreme Court, a crisis followed which led to an army takeover. Apithy then went into exile.

In 1970, to resolve a crisis following new elections, the three veteran political leaders Apithy, Maga and Ahomadegbe formed a three-man joint presidency to be headed by each in turn for two years. Maga served his two-year term first, but Ahomadegbe had only just begun his when the army took power again in October 1972 under Col. Matthieu Kérékou. Apithy thus never got his chance to be head of state again, and he did not return to politics, but lived mainly in Paris until he died there on 3 December 1989. ■

Appiah, J. E.(1918-90)

APPIAH, Joseph Emmanuel (1918-90).

GHANAIAN politician. He was born on 16 November 1918 in Kumasi, capital of Ashanti, his father J.W.K. Appiah being a leading figure in the court of the Asantehene (King of Asante, or Ashanti) when he was restored to his throne in 1935, and chief secretary of the Asanteman Council of the

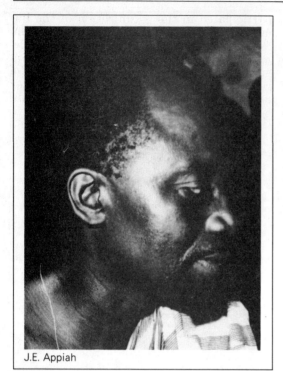

J.E. Appiah

The following year Joe Appiah, as he was usually called, was called to the Bar. Still working with the CPP, he returned to Gold Coast with his wife, but about then a National Liberation Movement arose in the Ashanti Region to oppose the CPP, and in February 1955 Appiah joined it. Other CPP leaders from Ashanti did the same, but Appiah's move (possibly influenced by his father) was a special boost to the NLM and blow to Nkrumah. Despite extreme organised violence by its supporters, the NLM failed in its campaign against the CPP. But Appiah, a member of the NLM's Inner Council, was elected to parliament in 1956 as an NLM member to represent Atwima Amansie.

Gold Coast became independent as Ghana, under the rule of Nkrumah and the CPP, on 6 March 1957. On 3 November of that year a new opposition party under Dr K.A. Busia (q.v.) was created, the United Party, and Appiah joined its executive. He strongly opposed the Preventive Detention Act in 1958, having declared that he had left the CPP because of its dictatorial tendencies. In 1961-2 he was himself detained without trial under the Act. When Ghana was made a one-party state in 1964 Appiah returned to Kumasi to practise law.

After the overthrow of President Nkrumah in 1966 Appiah worked with the National Liberation Council (NLC) as roving ambassador and then as a member of the committee preparing for a return to civilian rule. Before elections were held in 1969 he broke with Busia and formed the United National Party, which had no success at the polls; later in 1969 he became the leader outside parliament of the Justice Party opposing Busia's ruling Progress Party (PP).

Appiah became a roving ambassador again after the army overthrew Busia and formed the National Redemption Council (NRC) under General Acheampong (q.v.). He also joined a committee formed by the NRC to gather ideas on its proposal for non-party Union Government ("Unigov"), eventually dropped. In these ways Appiah came to be associated with an unpopular regime that eventually fell in 1979 to popular acclaim. Appiah, no longer working with the regime by then, took no further part in politics afterwards. As a lawyer he served for years as President of the Ghana Bar Association, and as an active churchman he became a member of the synod of the Methodist

historic kingdom. The young Joseph Appiah attended Mfantsipim Secondary School in Cape Coast and then worked as a trainee manager for the United Africa Co. at Takoradi and Freetown.

In 1943 he went to London to study Law. While a student he became President of the West African Students' Union (WASU). He attended the Manchester Pan-African Conference of 1945 with Kwame Nkrumah (q.v.) among others, and was a close ally of Nkrumah for many years. When Nkrumah returned to Gold Coast (as it was then) in 1947 to form the Convention Peoples Party (CPP), Appiah remained in London as his personal representative. By 1953 he was thus representing the Prime Minister of Gold Coast, and making important political contacts.

In 1953 he married Peggy Cripps, daughter of the British Labour politician Sir Stafford Cripps. The wedding aroused much attention in Britain at the time, and was a big Labour Party social occasion, attended by leading members of the party as well as by K.A. Gbedemah, a CPP leader, and George Padmore, the Trinidadian activist who was Kwame Nkrumah's political adviser for many years.

Church in Ghana. He died on 8 July 1990, survived by his wife, a son and three daughters. When he died his completed *Autobiography of an African Patriot* was in the process of publication. ■

d'Arboussier, G. (1908-76)

d'ARBOUSSIER, Gabriel (1908-76).

SENEGALESE politician who became his country's first Minister of Justice. Born in January 1908 in Djenne in what was then French Soudan (now Mali), d'Arboussier was educated in France, qualifying as a lawyer and later as an administrator from the Ecole Nationale de la France d'Outre-Mer.

He joined the colonial administration in French West Africa, where his father, Henri d'Arboussier, was a distinguished administrator, and in 1945 was elected to the French Constituent Assembly as a representative from French Equatorial Africa. Once in the Assembly, d'Arboussier became involved in the nationalist politics that had begun to emerge in the French colonies. He

G. d'Arboussier

participated in the organisation of the Bamako Conference of 1946 which led to the formation of the inter-territorial *Rassemblement Démocratique Africain* (RDA). The aim of the RDA was to "free Africa from the colonial yoke by the affirmation of her personality and by the association – freely agreed to – of a union of nations".

Gabriel d'Arboussier was elected one of the Vice-Presidents of RDA by the Bamako Conference which also elected Félix Houphouet-Boigny, who later became first President of Côte d'Ivoire, President of RDA. In 1948, d'Arboussier told his party colleagues that the "RDA should be the unflagging instrument in organising the African masses in their struggle against colonialism and imperialism". He became General Secretary of the RDA in 1949 and at the same time was appointed editor of *Réveil*, the party's journal.

He was re-elected to the French National Assembly in 1947 and from that time also represented Côte d'Ivoire in the Grand Council of the French Union, where he served as Vice-President from 1947 to 1950, when he began a campaign against the colonial authorities in Côte d'Ivoire.. This campaign was ruthlessly repressed by French forces. The cumulative consequence of the agitation was a split in the RDA, with Houphouet-Boigny choosing to co-operate with the French and allowing the radical elements to be purged. d'Arboussier was dismissed as General Secretary, and in 1952 was expelled from the party after challenging the decision to dismiss him.

He set up in private practice in Senegal where he worked for several years. In 1957 he was elected a representative for Niger in the Grand Council of French West Africa and became Vice-President and later President of the Council. With the disintegration of the federation of Mali (Senegal and Soudan) in August 1960 and subsequent national independence from France, d'Arboussier chose to remain in Senegal, where he became the first Minister of Justice. He held this post until 1963/4, when he was made Ambassador to France.

In 1965 he became a top international diplomat, as Director of the United Nations Institute for Training and Research. In 1968 he was again made an Ambassador of Senegal, now to West Germany, Austria and Switzerland. He held this post until 1972. He died in December 1976. ■

Armattoe, R.E.G. (1913-53)

ARMATTOE, Dr. Raphael Ernest Grail (1913-53).

GHANAIAN scientist who was runner-up for the Nobel Prize in Physiology in 1948. He was also a prolific author of more than seventeen books which include professional publications and a novel.

He was born on 20 August 1913 at Keta on the south-east border with Togoland, of a Palime trading family. He had his elementary education in schools at Lomé, capital of Togo, and at Denu in the then Gold Coast. In 1925 he obtained his Cambridge School Certificate with distinction, a year ahead before the time he was expected to enter for the examination at the Mfantsipim School in Cape Coast which he attended for three years from 1925. He then studied at various universities in Europe: medicine at Berlin University in Germany, French literature at Lille University in France, anthropology at the Sorbonne, also in France, and science and medicine at the universities of Lausanne in Switzerland and Edinburgh in Scotland respectively. He did his post-graduate studies in, among other places, Londonderry in Northern Ireland, and he held doctorate degrees in philosophy, medicine and anthropology.

In 1941 Armattoe was admitted to the fellowship of the Royal Society of Edinburgh and seven years later became a Senior Travelling Research Fellow for the Warner Bond Foundation of Anthropology and Race Biology. In 1948 he was a candidate for the Nobel Prize in Physiology for whch he was subsequently a runner-up. Armattoe spent his working life in Europe, based at the Lomoshie Research Centre in Londonderry where as Director, he was head of a team of European scientists who carried out research for various governments and institutions.

He is reputed for having found a cure for guinea-worm, a water-borne disease that was rampant in his native West Africa, in the *Abochi* drug whose formula he discovered. Armattoe also carried out extensive research into the possible application of different species of African herbs and roots for medicinal use. In the late 1940s he was

Dr. R.E.G. Armattoe

commissioned by the home-rule government of the Gold Coast to look into ways of eradicating the swollen shoot disease that was affecting the country's main economic crop, cocoa. Though he was reported to have found a remedy, the project was not implemented before his death.

Armattoe was a man of many talents and untiring energy, belonging to many professional organisations in which he played an active role. But he also found time to become involved in the Pan-Africanist movement in the 1940s, a movement that culminated in the Fifth Pan-African Conference that was held in Manchester, England, in 1945 and attended by Kwame Nkrumah (q.v.) and other future African leaders. It was here that plans were made to achieve independence for Africa through mass political organisation, and Armattoe participated in these deliberations.

Though he remained to continue his work in Europe during the subsequent anti-colonial struggle in the continent he never ceased to voice these aspirations through his work and several books on Africa. Among these are *The Golden Age of West African Civilisation* which was published in 1946, *Deep Down the Black Man's Mind* published posthumously in 1954, *The Ewes In Eweland,* an anthropological study of the Ewe peoples in Ghana and Togo, and *Dawn Over Africa*, his only novel, which was also published after his death. These publications reflect the African's view of the continent in relation to the incursion of the colonial powers. Armattoe's own view on the subjugation of the African was demonstrated in his reaction to the racist measures that were being implemented by the white supremacist regime in South Africa in the 1940s: "Let honest men say openly that they are in power not because of any inherent aptitude but because they happen to be born among the privileged and they do not intend to share power with other races. To pretend that non-Europeans have no capacity for civilisation and that it would not be in their own interest to be educated is a mere balderdash. Happily for the world there are a few rational elements in every country who see that this world is one and that it cannot remain half free and half slave."

Armattoe died in December 1953 in Germany and was buried in Hamburg, leaving his Swiss wife Leony and their two daughters.■

Arrisol, J. (1888-1953)

ARRISOL, Joachim (1888-1953).

S EYCHELLOIS politician. He was born on 18 August 1888 at Anse Boileau, Seychelles. His parents were of African descent. He was employed by the Union Lighterage Company in Victoria for 43 years and on 28 November 1940 was appointed unofficial member of the Legislative Council. He was reappointed to this position on 7 December 1943 and again on 7 July 1944 and 1 May 1947.

While he was unofficial member of the Legislative Council he received the authority to sign passport applications, a privilege which was enjoyed by members of the Executive Council and Justices of the Peace. On 11 March 1948 he was appointed to that Council for one year. He was nominated as a temporary member of the Legislative Council on 28 February 1949, to take the place of C.E. Collet who was on leave of absence. Later on in the year on 5 November he was

nominated a full member of the Legislative Council in place of Collet who had resigned. He died on 11 July 1953, at the age of 64.■

Asafu-Adjaye, E.O. (1903-76)

ASAFU-ADJAYE, Sir Edward Okyere (1903-76).

G HANAIAN lawyer, the first Ghana High Commissioner to Britain. Born at Calabar, Nigeria, where his father was working, he was of a royal family of Ashanti, and went to school in Gold Coast (Ghana), first at Kumasi Government Boys' School and then at the SPG Grammar School (now Adisadel College) at Cape Coast. He and his elder brother Isaac became the first sons of Ashanti to go overseas for education after the British occupation and introduction of Western schooling in 1896. Edward went to University College, London, and in 1927 was called to the Bar at Lincoln's Inn.

He first practised law in the Accra chambers of the late Sir Henley Coussey. Until 1935 he had to practise in Gold Coast Colony because trained lawyers were excluded by the British from the "Native Courts" of Ashanti and the Northern Territories. In 1935 a change in the law allowed him to set up his Odarten Chambers in the Ashanti capital, Kumasi. Earlier he had joined a protest delegation against the Sedition and Waterworks Bills (1934).

There were other important events in Ashanti in 1935. The traditional throne of the Asantehene was restored by the British government and Prempeh II (q.v.) was enthroned. A Confederacy Council to assist in the traditional government was created, and Mr. Asafu-Adjaye was a member of it for over 15 years. He was also a member of the Kumasi Town Council established in 1943. He attended the coronation of George VI in 1937 and that of Elizabeth II in 1953.

In 1946 he was nominated by the Confederacy Council as an Ashanti representative on the Gold Coast Legislative Council. Nominated again in 1951, he then became Minister of Local Government in the first predominantly African government in the Gold Coast, headed by Kwame Nkrumah

Sir Edward O. Asafu-Adjaye

(q.v.). In that position, which he held until 1955 after reappointment in 1954, he sponsored an important Local Government Ordinance altering the role of traditional rulers (with which he had been so closely associated). In 1954 he was elected to parliament. He became Minister of Trade and Labour in 1955. He did not seek re-election to parliament in 1956.

In 1957 he went to London as the first High Commissioner of the first newly independent Black African State. Knighted by the Queen in 1960, he retired in 1961. Returning to legal practice he later headed the inquiry ordered by the National Liberation Council into prison conditions under President Nkrumah; its report was published in 1967. Sir Edward was a member of the Council of the University of Ghana.

He died on 27 February 1976. ■

Atangana, C. (died 1943)

ATANGANA, Charles (died 1943).

CAMEROONIAN traditional ruler. Born probably in the early 1880s at Mvolye, he came from the Ewondo, the main section of the Beti ethnic group which is called "Yaounde" in common Cameroon usage and lives around the city of Yaounde. Atangana Ntsona, as he was called, grew up at the time when the Germans founded the modern Yaounde town (1889) and gradually imposed their rule on the Betis. An orphan, he travelled to the coast once before being presented by a chief, claiming to be his father, to the German colonist, Major Hans Dominik. A rising in 1895 was put down by Dominik with the ferocity for which he is still remembered today. He decided to train Atangana as one of the first collaborators of the Germans among the Beti people, to ensure their permanent submission and achieve some sort of progress. Thus he sent him to the Kribi area for Catholic missionary schooling.

Atangana had to flee from his school because of a Bulu uprising, and worked for a time as male nurse at Douala, where he made an un-customary marriage with Maria Biloa, a Beti girl, having by now been baptised as Karl Friedrich Otto. Later he worked as a clerk at the German capital of Buea. Returning to Yaounde, he advanced rapidly in the Germans' service there. He became an interpreter, helping to reorganise local government among his people. When Major Dominik returned in 1904 Karl Atangana helped him govern the Betis. He was the main spokesman and representative of the colonial regime in the area. He was appointed a judge in 1911 and then given the task of appointing chiefs. In 1912-13 he went on a long tour of Germany.

On 25 March 1914 the Germans regularised his effective position by making him paramount chief of the Ewondos. This title was quite untraditional, the Ewondos and other Betis having only had many small independent chieftaincies before colonial rule. While he had considerable local support, Atangana then and later derived his power from the colonial rulers and his own intelligent and modern outlook. This led him to start modern plantations before 1914 and to build a new house at Mvolye near Yaounde, and to use the first private telephone in the town.

But Atangana's efforts at modernising the amenities within the community were interrupted in 1915-16 when he and many Betis followed the retreating Germans into Spanish Guinea. For the rest of the First World War he was in charge of most of the

Cameroonian soldiers and civilians interned on Fernando Po.

Later he spent some time in Spain. The French who now ruled most of former German Kamerun, and moved their capital to Yaounde in 1921, at first refused to allow Atangana to return. They relented in 1921, on condition that he should first help organise a road-building project between Nkongsamba and Dschang. After passing this test – a clear sign of what was expected of a chief under French colonial rule – he was allowed to return to Yaounde, where he had a triumphal reception on 26 November 1921, and resumed his paramount chieftaincy. He was for twenty years the most powerful chief in French Cameroon. In 1925 he was placed over seven *chefs de groupement* and 80 other chiefs.

Atangana was a firm ruler who believed in co-operation with the French. He had his own strongarm men and recruited workers for French forced labour projects which included the construction of the Douala-Yaounde railway. He also employed many people to work on his own farms. He was certainly a major agent of colonial repression. He and lesser chiefs helped organise large levies of food for forced labourers and the Yaounde urban population.

Chiefs were allowed to collect money from their subjects to buy cars in 1925, and by 1926 Charles (as he now was) Atangana had a car and three lorries. He continued to enrich himself as before. In 1924 he had personally 500 hectares of food crops, 110 of palm trees, and 100 of cocoa, and also 500 head of livestock.

Atangana was a moderniser, encouraging cocoa growing by the Betis and aiding the massive anti-sleeping-sickness campaign conducted among them by Dr. Eugène Jamot (a campaign, however, that had very dubious aspects). He was a follower of the Catholic mission and helped it secure, during his reign, the mass conversion of almost all the Ewondos.

The French paid him 24,000 francs per year in 1938 and awarded him the *Légion d'Honneur* decoration in 1939. He died on 1 September 1943. His paramount chieftaincy never had the same power later as in his day. He is commemorated with a statue in Yaounde. One of his children, Catherine, (educated by nuns in Germany), lived to be a much respected elder citizen of the Cameroonian capital. ■

Atta, A.A. (1920-72)

ATTA, Abdul Aziz (1920-72).

NIGERIAN administrator. Born on 1 April 1920 at Lokoja, he was the son of the late Alhaji Ibrahim, Attah of Igbirra, a traditional ruler in what is now Kwara State. He was educated at Okene Elementary and Middle Schools between 1926 and 1935. In 1936 he entered Achimota College, Ghana, and studied there until 1944 when he went to Balliol College, Oxford, England, graduating in 1947 in Politics, Philosophy and Economics.

Returning to Nigeria the following year, he entered the government service as Cadet Administrative Officer in the then unified Nigeria Public Service. He served in Calabar, Opobo, Ikot-Ekpene and former Southern Cameroons, all then under the Eastern Region, and after the division of the Public Service continued to serve in that Region; he was District Officer in Umuahia before obtaining the important post of Pri-

A.A. Atta

vate Secretary to Dr. Nnamdi Azikiwe, Premier of the Eastern Region. Then he was Secretary to the Agent-General for the Region in Britain; Training Officer in the Regional Ministry of Finance, Enugu; and Secretary for Annang Province.

He moved to the Federal Public Service as Administrative Officer, Class III, in 1958 and was promoted Permanent Secretary in 1960, and headed in turn the ministries of Defence, Communications, Industries and Finance. He occupied the vital post of Permanent Secretary, Finance, from 1966 through the years of civil war with all its effects on the country's finances. In December 1970 he was appointed Administrative Officer (Principal Grade), and became Secretary to the Federal Military Government and Head of the Federal Civil Service.

Atta died on 12 June 1972 at the Royal Free Hospital, London, after two years in the highest administrative post in Nigeria, and was buried in his home country. He had four daughters and a son by his wife Iyabo. One of his brothers Alhaji Abdul Maliki (q.v.) was another famous public servant. ■

Attahiru I, Sultan of Sokoto

Attahiru I (died 1903)

ATTAHIRU I, Muhammadu, Sultan of Sokoto (died 1903).

NIGERIAN traditional ruler of Sokoto, which ranks first among the emirates of northern Nigeria. Son of Sarkin Musulmi (Commander of the Faithful) Ahmadu Atiku who reigned from 1859 to 1866, Attahiru was elected the 11th Sultan in 1902 to succeed Sarkin Musulmi Abdurahman. His father Atiku was the 4th Sultan of Sokoto and the 5th Sarkin Musulmi, both offices to which he himself later succeeded. But unlike Atiku who achieved fame as founder of new towns, namely Acida, Sabo Birni and Cimola, Attahiru's short reign of less than twelve months was devoted to resisting British colonialism. Thus, like his grandfather Sultan Abubakar Atiku (reigned 1837-42) who defended the Sultanate against the Habes' intermittent attacks, he is fondly remembered as a great resistance leader.

There is not much documentation relating to Attahiru's early life, though he is recorded as one of several children. His accession in November 1902 when he became the 11th Sultan of Sokoto and the 12th Sarkin Musulmi was overshadowed by a major political development in the history of Nigeria – British military penetration of the hinterland in the north.

When his predecessor died in October 1902 there was a dispute over succession in which, by the sheer force of his personality, Attahiru emerged victorious. Around that time British forces, under Frederick Lugard, were advancing on Sokoto, having subdued Kano. Against this background of uncertainty Sultan Attahiru prepared his people, still disunited following the succession dispute, for battle. On 15 March 1903 he personally led his army into the famous Battle of Sokoto in which the Fulani cavalry engaged the British in an heroic encounter just outside Sokoto town. According to some sources the battle lasted only 90 minutes; largely because of the British superior military power (they used Maxim guns) and partly because of internal disunity, the Sokoto resistance soon collapsed.

But the opposition to the British presence produced its heroism. According to the Nigerian historian Obaro Ikime, in his book, *The Fall of Nigeria*, the resistance, and the courage and devotion of the Fulani soldiers who led it, surprised the British. "When the Sokoto army marched out of the city walls to await the British they took with them the flag of the Caliph. The main body of the army was already in flight within half an hour of the beginning of the battle. However, a small group stood its ground to defend the flag, the symbol of the Caliphate. The British themselves praised the courage and devotion of this small group. One British source describes how, as the British opened fire on the group, one soldier after another took over the flag and held on to it till he in turn was shot down. And so it continued until the last of the group, the fiftieth, so goes a British account, fell dead and the flag fell on him. The British thereupon captured the flag. But such was the importance of the flag to the people, that someone managed to seize it back and take it to the Caliph in flight".

The Caliph commenced his flight as the British entered Sokoto city; he left, marching his forces eastwards and reminding his citizens that the founder of the Caliphate, Usman dan Fodio (q.v.), had prophesied that the faithful would one day have to take the *hijra* (flight) to the east. Thousands, including the Alkali and other officials of his government and also some Emirs deposed by the British, joined him in a remarkable mass show of opposition to the British occupation. He and his followers stopped at Gusau and then moved on, with a British force in pursuit. The latter were beaten off several times, with several casualties.

As the exodus progressed through Zaira, Katagum and other emirates, several others joined the fleeing Caliph. At Burmi Attahiru I and his party made a last stand. A first British attack, on 13 May 1903, was successfully repelled. But in the second Battle of Burmi on 27 July 1903 Burmi fell to the Europeans after fierce resistance in which over 600 were thought to have died, Caliph Attahiru was among those who fell. The diverse character of his supporters, who had come from Sokoto, Kano, Gombe, Kontagora, Nupe, Katagum, Misau, Bauchi and other parts of the Caliphate – testified to the unequivocal opposition to the British presence.

Attahiru's son, Mai Wurno, was among the many survivors who refused to submit to British rule. They continued their flight till they reached the Blue Nile in modern Sudan where they settled. ■

Attoh Ahuma, S.R.B. (1863-1921)

ATTOH AHUMA Rev. Samuel Richard Brew (1863-1921).

GHANAIAN churchman, journalist and celebrated nationalist campaigner. He was originally Samuel R.B. Solomon, born on 22 December 1863, son of the Reverend James Solomon of the Wesleyan Methodist Church. After education at the Wesleyan elementary school and high school in Cape Coast, and then (1886-8) at Richmond College in the same town, he was ordained a minister in 1888.

In the 1890s he became celebrated as a journalist and a nationalist campaigner. He edited the *Gold Coast Methodist Times* and used it as an organ of protest against British rule. In 1897 the newspaper headed the campaign against the Lands Bill, and the Reverend Solomon helped found the Aborigines Rights Protection Society (ARPS) to protest against the bill. After an article entitled "Colony or Protectorate, which?"

Rev. S.R.B. Attoh Ahuma

in that year the Wesleyan Mission authorities, upset at the Reverend Solomon's political activism, removed him from the ministry. The *Methodist Times* collapsed when he ceased to be editor.

About then he visited England, though early in 1898 he joined the staff of *The Gold Coast Aborigines* when it was started as the ARPS' organ. He joined the African Methodist Episcopal Zion (AMEZ) mission, an Afro-American one, and in 1898 he and James E.K. Aggrey (q.v.) were chosen by that mission to go to the USA for studies. In that same year he changed his name to Attoh Ahuma. He spent four years at Livingstone College, Salisbury, North Carolina, where he graduated BA in 1902; he later completed an MA thesis for the same college.

Returning to Gold Coast, he became Principal of Accra Grammar School, but this closed down soon afterwards. Then he became Principal of the AMEZ Secondary School, at Cape Coast. In these and the succeeding years he published a number of books: *Memoirs of West African Celebrities* (1903), *Cruel as the Grave* (1913), *His Quest and Conquest* (1917), and, most famous, *The Gold Coast Nation and National Consciousness* (1911). The latter, especially, marked him out as a leading pioneer nationalist like his contemporary J. Casely-Hayford (q.v.).

In 1912 he founded a new nationalist newspaper, *The Gold Coast Nation*. He continued to be active in the ARPS and became its Secretary in 1913, and its dominant member from then until his death. But despite his political activity he wished to return to the work of a minister of the Methodist Church. He was allowed to do this in 1914 and worked for the missionary church at Axim, Elmina and other places in south-western Gold Coast.

He died at Elmina on 15 December 1921. ∎

Dr. E.A. Awoliyi

Awoliyi, E.A. (1910-71)

AWOLIYI, Dr. Elizabeth Abimbola (1910-71).

NIGERIAN doctor, the first West African woman to qualify in modern medical science. She was born on 4 November 1910 in Lagos, daughter of David Evaristo Akerele. She began her education at St. Mary's Catholic Convent School in Lagos. Then she went to Queen's College, Lagos, before going overseas for further studies which, unusually for a Nigerian in those days, were in Ireland. She first went to St. Joseph's Convent School, then to the University of Dublin (Cafrey's College, then the College of Surgeons) where she graduated with First Class Honours and a Medal in Medicine. She obtained the Licentiate of the Royal College of Surgeons, Dublin; Diploma in Gynaecology and Obstetrics, Dublin; Diploma in Child Health; and membership of the Royal College of Physicians, UK. She did a course in Child Welfare at Birmingham in England.

Early in 1938 she returned to Nigeria and was appointed Junior Medical Officer at Massey Street Dispensary. She was steadily promoted from then on. She married Dr. S.O. Awoliyi, another doctor, who became Chief Medical Adviser to the Federal Government and died in 1965. They had two children, a son and a daughter.

She was prominent in Catholic lay organisations in Lagos and became president of the Lagos branch of the National Council of Women, president of the Business and Professional Women's Association, and president of the Child Care Voluntary Association. She was a director of the Commercial Medicine Store in Lagos and was awarded the traditional titles of Iya Ibiye of Lagos and Iyalaje of Oyo.

In 1962 Dr. (Mrs.) Awoliyi was appointed Senior Specialist Gynaecologist and Obstetrician in the Federal Ministry of Health. In the same year she won a scholarship for study at the Mayo Clinic, Rochester, Minn., USA.

Dr. (Mrs.) Awoliyi died on 14 September 1971.■

Awolowo, O. (1909-87)

AWOLOWO, Chief Obafemi (1909-87).

NIGERIAN political leader first of the Action Group then of the Unity Party of Nigeria, Chief Obafemi Awolowo was born at Ikenne, Ogun State, on 6 March 1909. The son of a Yoruba farmer, he was one of the truly self-made men among his contemporaries in Nigeria.

Chief O. Awolowo

A popular, if controversial figure in Nigerian politics, Awolowo earned himself a coveted place in his country's history as one of the founding fathers of the nation. The conferment on him, in 1980, of Nigeria's highest honour, Grand Commander of the Federal Republic (GCFR), was in clear recognition of his contribution to his country.

During a checkered career as a teacher, short-hand typist, newspaper reporter, businessman, and then trade unionist, he studied in his spare time, gaining a bachelor's degree in commerce in 1944. Even as a young man, Awolowo showed an inclination to politics. In June 1940 he became Secretary of the Ibadan branch of the Nigeria Youth Movement, and three years later he was one of the founders of the Trade Union Congress of Nigeria. In 1944 he left the country to study law in England.

On his return, he plunged into politics and in 1951 founded the Action Group. In the 1951 Western Regional elections, Awolowo was elected to represent the Ijebu Remo division and, as the head of his party, became Leader of Government Business and Minister for Local Government in the region. Making use of his organizational ability, he carried out a complete reform of local government. He established a modern system of elective councils, with seats reserved for traditional chiefs.

It is his reforms in education that have, perhaps, left a more lasting mark in Nigeria. As Premier of the Western Region, he passed a comprehensive education law in 1954 which introduced, in 1955, free primary education. His government shortened the primary school course from eight to six years and made promotions from one class to the next automatic. Awolowo who, himself, had acquired education the hard way, believed that "every Nigerian citizen must be educated at public expense to the limits of his natural ability to enable him to be in the finest possible state to produce the utmost he is capable of".

Awolowo seized the chance of his Premiership of the Western Region to build the Action Group into a strong national political force. He forged alliances with the minorities in the other regions in the hope of achieving federal power. In the pre-independence elections of 1959 the party failed, however, to make the necessary impact outside the Western Region, and Awolowo became Leader of the Opposition in the

Federal House of Representatives. A tussle for power between him and his deputy, Chief S. L. Akintola, who replaced him as Premier of the Western Region, coupled with his firm opposition to the NPC (Northern People's Congress)-controlled Federal Government, brought an alliance of his opponents which led to his trial and a ten-year prison sentence on charges of treason in 1963.

He served three years of his sentence, spending most of the time writing his book *Thoughts on the Nigerian Constitution* (Oxford University Press, 1968). This was a follow-up to two earlier books he wrote: *Path to Nigerian Freedom* (1947) and *Awo: The Autobiography of Chief Obafemi Awolowo* (1960). Awolowo wrote several other books later, among them: *My Early Life* (1968), *The People's Republic* (1968), *The Strategy and Tactics of the People's Republic* (1970), *Awo on the Civil War* (1981), *Path to Nigerian Greatness* (1981), *Voice of Reason: Selected Speeches of Chief Obafemi Awolowo* (1981), *Voice of Courage: Selected Speeches of Chief Obafemi Awolowo* (1981), *My March Through Prison* (1985) and *For the Good of the People*.

Awolowo was pardoned and released by General Yakubu Gowon soon after the military coup of July 1966. Gowon told him: "We need you for the wealth of your experience". Not long after, he was appointed Federal Commissioner for Finance and Vice-Chairman of the Federal Executive Council. He held both posts throughout the duration of the Civil War. As commissioner for Finance, he was a great exponent of the fiscalist approach to the management of the economy. Disappointed in his hopes for an early return to civilian rule after the war, Awolowo quit Gowon's government in 1971 to resume his law practice.

When the ban on political activities was lifted in 1978, Awo, as he was popularly known, founded the Unity Party of Nigeria (UPN) and was chosen as the party's presidential candidate for the 1979 general election. He lost, but the failure did not dampen the fervour of his quest for Nigeria's presidency. He ran again unsuccessfully in the 1983 general election. Both times he maintained that the elections were rigged and that he had been cheated out of victory.

Whether in government or out of it, Awolowo continued to campaign for free education. In January 1974, Gowon's government announced the Universal Primary Education Programme (UPE), and in the 1979 election Awolowo's party, the UPN, made free education at all levels throughout the country a campaign issue. Although Awolowo failed to become President, the UPN, under his unflagging inspiration, introduced free education in the five states it controlled.

Awolowo the astute politician was also a successful businessman. His business empire centred mainly on investment, and revolved around four principal companies: Dideolu Estates Limited, Industrial Promotions and Consultancy Limited, Sopolu Investment and Services Limited, and Liberty Press, with a combined turnover running into several millions of naira at the time of his death. As in politics, Awolowo ran his business with the thoroughness and zeal that were the hallmarks of the man himself.

Indeed, Awolowo's vast business interests often obscured the fact that he was a lawyer with an equally vast practice. As a lawyer he earned the reputation of seldom rejecting a case from a client because of his belief that anybody able to afford the legal fees should have his or her case handled by a lawyer. However, that did not prevent him from advising in favour of an out of court settlement when he saw that pursuing a case was fruitless.

For nearly all of his political career, Awolowo believed that it was the destiny of the intelligentsia of each of Nigeria's ethnic groups to organize the groups and come into some federal arrangement for governing the nation. He was convinced that "If a country is bilingual or multilingual, the Constitution must be federal and the constituent states must be organized on a linguistic basis". In pursuance of this philosophy, he was co-founder and first General Secretary of *Egbe Omo Oduduwa*, the Yoruba cultural organization which laid the foundation of his political party, the Action Group. His abiding attachment to linguistic groupings secured for Chief Awolowo the acknowledged leadership of the Yorubas of Nigeria, as well as the opposition of some of his non-Yoruba compatriots.

Politics and business were the two best known sides of Awolowo. But he was also a devout Christian. Religion and metaphysics formed the single most vital thread that connected the remarkable events of his career. These religious and metaphysical influences deeply affected the kind of personality Awolowo had. A man of towering principles, he combined a steely interior with a brutal frankness which at times worked to his political disadvantage.

His personal philosophy rested on doggedness and resilience. He once wrote: "The great glory is not in never falling, but in rising each time you fall. In this connection, I am profusely thankful to God for giving me the strength and the grace each time I had fallen and lifting me after each fall, that I am now what I am". Chief Awolowo died suddenly but peacefully on 9 May 1987.

His life-long promotion of education at all levels in Nigeria was immortalized soon after when the Federal Government renamed the prestigious University of Ife, Ile-Ife, as Obafemi Awolowo University.■

Ayachi, H. (1873-1958)

AYACHI, Hassouna (1873-1958).

TUNISIAN politician and pioneer leader of the anti-colonial movement. A native of Sousse, he was educated there and at the famous Sadiqiyya College, founded by Khair el-Din (q.v.) in 1875 for combined Islamic and modern education, and attended by generations of Tunisians including, later, Habib Bourguiba. Then he went to the *Ecole Normale Supérieure*, a teacher training college, and in 1893 began working as a teacher at Monastir. In 1894 he became a teacher of Arabic at the Lycée Carnot.

He then went into government service as an interpreter for the French colonial ("Protectorate") regime, but only for a short time, as he went in 1896 for higher studies in France. In 1898 he qualified as a lawyer in Paris. He set up a flourishing practice in Sousse and took part in other activities in the area of that city. With others he encouraged agricultural and other activities by the Arabs.

He contributed to *El-Hadira*, an important Arabic-language newspaper founded in 1888, and to *Ez-Zohra*; also to the French-language newspaper founded in 1907, *Le Tunisien*. He thus supported the early nationalists, organised for a time in the

"Young Tunisian" party, who called for reforms while declaring loyalty to France until repression following a strike in Tunis in 1912. When nationalism revived after the First World War, he was once more prominent in it.

H. Ayachi

In 1919-20 nationalists led by Sheikh Abdul-Aziz el-Tha'alibi (q.v.) founded the Destour Party, which called for a constitution (*destour* in Arabic) to be granted by France conferring more rights on the Tunisians. Two delegations were sent to France, one under el-Tha'alibi and then another under Ayachi. Both failed to change French policies, which were aimed at total domination of the interests of the European settlers.

The Destour Party, strictly confining itself to constitutional protests and not appealing for mass support, made no headway against the colonial regime. But in 1934 a breakaway movement committed to mass organisation and radical protest was formed, named Neo-Destour. From the start its leader was Habib Bourguiba, but Ayachi chaired some of its early meetings. In 1938, when the French clamped down on the new nationalist movement, Ayachi was among those arrested. He was detained at Sousse and then at Tunis, but was freed in 1939. Thereafter, being ill and ageing, he withdrew from active politics. He lived to see the Neo-Destour win independence in 1956, dying two years later. ▨

Al-Azhari, I. (1902-69)

AL-AZHARI, Ismail (1902-69).

SUDANESE nationalist and politician who was Prime Minister from 1953 until 1956. He was born at Omdurman in the Sudan in 1902, into a fairly wealthy family. On completing his primary and secondary education he studied at the Gordon Memorial College in Khartoum until 1921, when he joined the Department of Education as a mathematics teacher. The department later sponsored his studies at the American University at Beirut, and on graduating he returned to Sudan to continue his work in the Department of Education until 1946.

His interest in nationalist politics led him to join the Graduates Congress, an association formed in 1938 by educated Sudanese nationalists campaigning for independence. In 1939 he served as Secretary of this organisation; he became its President in the following year. He remained in this position until 1942 when he and other more militant members of the organisation broke away to set up the Ashigga Party, with el-Azhari as its President. At that time he supported Nile Valley unity with Egypt as a means of ending British administration in the Sudan. A militant nationalist, he served a prison sentence during this period for his role in political activities and demonstrations.

In 1952 the Ashigga Party joined forces with other pro-Union with Egypt groups and founded the National Unionist Party (NUP) with al-Azhari as President. The NUP received much financial assistance from Egypt as well as support from the powerful Khatmiya Moslem sect, and in the ensuing elections held in 1953, the party was victorious. Al-Azhari became Prime Minister and Minister of the Interior and began preparations for Sudanese self-determina-

I. Al-Azhari

tion. On the opening of Parliament in 1954 a violent demonstration was held by the influential Mahdists, calling for complete independence in the country. The measure of support for this, combined with the feeling that a great many people who supported solidarity with the Egyptians did so as a means of gaining independence from Britain, caused al-Azhari to decide against union with Egypt, and on 1 January 1956 Sudan became independent.

Al-Azhari continued as Prime Minister but he faced immediate problems, not only from his strong political opponents but also from a number of his own political allies who were angered by the change of policy towards Egypt, combined with hostility from the Egyptian government. As a result, in February 1956 he was compelled to form a coalition government. However, the political tensions did not diminish and in July 1956, following a split in the NUP, he was forced to resign.

He continued to be active in the country's politics and became leader of the parliamentary Opposition after his party's defeat in the 1958 elections. Meanwhile, political disagreements and strains were increasing between all the parties and in November 1958 the Armed Forces took over the government and banned all political organisations. Al-Azhari received a pension from the new government and went into private business.

Two years later he joined other former leading political figures in calling on the government to hold national elections to return the country to civilian rule. This caused the military government to stop his pension and on 11 July 1961 he was arrested and detained along with other former politicians.

The ban on political parties was lifted in 1964 following the return to civilian rule and once again al-Azhari, having retained his strong following in the towns, led the NUP to political prominence. He was elected President of the Supreme Council, a five-man committee which collectively acted as head of state, and remained in this position until the revolution of May 1969 when he was again arrested and detained. He died shortly afterwards on 26 August 1969, following a heart attack.■

B

Bâ, Ma (died 1867)

BA, Ma (died 1867).

GAMBIAN religious leader of the nineteenth century. He was of a religious family; his father was a Moslem teacher in Baddibu, one of the most important Gambian kingdoms in the nineteenth century situated on the north bank of the Gambia River. He was educated in the coastal state of Cayor and then became a religious teacher in the Wolof region where he married the niece of the Bourba Jolof (paramount ruler of the Wolofs or Jolofs).

He returned to Baddibu on the death of his father and continued his religious teachings, building up a large following and later becoming the representative of the great Tijaniyya Islamic sect in the kingdom.

By 1861 tensions were building up between the King of Baddibu and the British, due to the King's opposition to the latter's trade at Bathurst (now Banjul). Bâ participated in the peace negotiations and the King, fearing that he was becoming too powerful, ordered his death. Bâ and his followers rose against the monarchy, killed the King and his son, scattered their followers and took over the government of the kingdom.

The following year he provided military help to Moslems in the strategic Niumi state. This help was withdrawn shortly afterwards following the attack on his territory by the King of Saloum. He was able to successfully repel this invasion and counterattacked, with the help of Moslem supporters living in Saloum. By 1864 the area under his authority had extended northwards to the Saloum River (in present day Senegal) with the exception of Niumi territory. Later, he began to work for the establishment of a united Islamic state while continuing to expand northwards.

Meanwhile French interests in Saloum had become perturbed at Bâ's growing power. An agreement was worked out whereby Bâ's authority was recognised in October 1865 in return for his concession to French interests and trading rights in the area. However, the following month the French organised a revolt in Saloum and gathered a large force to attack Bâ's army. Bâ was able to crush this rebellion and continued with his plans for the expansion of his state. In 1866 a section of his army took Niumi and offered support to other Moslem leaders' attempts to gain control of Cayor. In 1867 he decided to attack the kingdom of Sine. His troops were defeated in the invasion during which Bâ died. ■

Babalola, J.A. (1904-60)

BABALOLA, Joseph Ayo (1904-60).

NIGERIAN churchman; he was a prime mover in the indigenous religious movement which resulted in the Aladura Church. He later founded the Christ Apostolic Church where as a leading evangelist he displayed both spiritual and organisational leadership. His movement swept through his Yorubaland home region in the 1930s and, by 1958, rose to become the third largest religious movement in Western Nigeria, with some 83,000 followers. By 1963, three years after Babalola's death, the Christ Apostolic Church had established numerous church schools: 110 primary schools, 22 secondary modern schools, four grammar schools and a teacher training college in Western Nigeria, while the movement had continued to grow and to attract big followings all along the West African coast.

Joseph Ayo Babalola, a native of Ilofa in Ilorin Province in modern Kwara State, was born in 1904. His father was a local

J.A. Babalola

Church Missionary Society (CMS) official, known to his Yoruba compatriots as Baba Egbe. Joseph Babalola thus had a Christian background, attending various church schools in Lagos and elsewhere. In 1928 he stopped schooling, at Standard IV, and gained employment with the Public Works Department (PWD), as a steam-roller driver based in the Ekiti area of Western Nigeria.

It was while on location work along the Ilesha-Akure road in October 1929 that he had a prophetic vision. It is said that on that day Babalola's steam-roller stopped working and he heard a voice calling out his name and telling him to preach the Gospel. Leaving his job, naked and covered with ashes, he returned to his Ilofa home where he was thought to be insane and was imprisoned

for two weeks. He emerged from there and left for Ibadan to be received by notable church leaders like Isaac B. Akinyele (q.v.), of the Faith Tabernacle, an independent Yoruba church that had seceded from the Anglican Church and contacted the Faith Tabernacle Church of the USA.

Babalola became active in this church in Lagos and on 9 December 1929, he was baptised by Pastor Odunjo at Ebute-Metta, a Lagos base of the Tabernacle church.

In the 1930s, Babalola led a revival which came to be known as the Aladura movement. The name, Aladura (one who prays), emphasises the concept of prayer which is foremost in the movement's teachings. His disagreement with the Faith Tabernacle was over the doctrine of divine healing, Babalola objected to the use of all medicine. His movement quickly gained a large following among the Yorubas and on 13 July 1941 he and his followers named their church the Christ Apostolic Church. Its phenomenal growth soon alarmed both the established churches and the colonial authorities, though the latter had no cause for anxiety since the Aladura movement posed no immediate political threat. Yet fear of its potential led to the arrest and imprisonment of Babalola in 1942; he was charged with taking part in a "witch-testing" exercise and imprisoned for six months.

But unlike Simon Kimbangu (q.v.) in the Congo, Babalola returned to active evangelism after a short prison sentence. He baptised more followers (by August 1941 he had already baptised as many as 1,596 men and 6,000 women) and converted many more. The prophet died in 1960 when his church was at its peak, with followers in many parts of Nigeria as well as along the West African coast such as Sierra Leone. ■

Babana, H.O. (died 1979)

BABANA, Horma Ould (died 1979).

MAURITANIAN politician, who was prominent in the early days of his country's opposition to French rule. He was the first Mauritanian to be elected to the French National Assembly. He worked as an interpreter in the French colonial service in his country before embarking on a political career which quickly earned him recognition as a critic of French policies, especially the absorption of the traditional chiefs into the colonial administrative structure as a means of consolidating French rule over the territory. He was also an active supporter of Morocco's claim to Mauritania, as a part of "Greater Morocco", which was opposed by both the French authorities and many of Babana's compatriots.

It was not until 1946 however that Babana's serious political involvement began with the development of organised nationalism in French West Africa. In November of that year he contested the elections to the French constituent assemblies on the platform of the French Socialists (SFIO) and won, thus becoming the first Mauritanian to be elected deputy to the French National Assembly. Babana first formed part of the parliamentary group of the SFIO but in 1948, when the party withheld its support for the Palestinian cause, he left and joined the *Union Démocratique et Sociale de la Résistance* (UDSR) led by François Mitterand.

He also formed a political party in Mauritania, the *Entente Mauritanienne*, essentially to serve as a forum of expression for his nationalist policies. The party soon became the focal point of nationalist reaction against French rule, gaining popular support among the workers and intellectuals. The *Entente Mauritanienne*, however, failed to win the 1951 elections in which Babana also lost his deputyship. It again lost the elections of 1956, to the *Union Progressiste Mauritanienne* (UPM) of Mokhtar Ould Daddah, and after unsuccessfully trying to have the elections annulled, on the grounds that they were manipulated by the French authorities, Babana went into exile in Morocco, where he made repeated calls for the revision of the boundary with Mauritania. His party was merged in June 1958 with the UPM to become the *Parti du Regroupement Mauritanien* (PRM). He remained in exile, largely in Morocco and partly in France where he spent sometime receiving treatment, having been taken ill.

Horma Ould Babana's support for Morocco's expansionism, especially at a time when that policy was being revived by Moroccan nationalists, made him a welcome guest in that country. The concept of "Greater Morocco" emanates from the country's imperial past that at one stage of its history saw its empire stretched eastwards across Algeria to Egypt and southwards across the Sahara. Today the policy involves periodic claims to be rightful ruler of the territories of the immediate neighbours, Mauritania and the Sahrawi Republic.

Aged, ill and weak, Babana returned to his country which became independent of France in November 1960, with Ould Daddah as leader. Babana died in 1979.■

Babiiha, J.K. (1913-82)

BABIIHA, John Kabwimukya (1913-82).

UGANDAN politician who served as first Vice-President of the Republic from 1966 until 1971. Before then he led a political party, the Uganda People's Union Party, which merged with Milton Obote's Uganda People's Congress (UPC) in 1960. Babiiha combined a crowded political career with a keen scientific interest in veterinary affairs. He was trained in veterinary science at Makerere University and served as Chairman of the East African Council of Veterinary Education.

He was born in Toro, Western Uganda, on 17 April 1913 and attended St. Leo's High School in Virika before entering St. Joseph's College at Mbarara and later St. Mary's College, Kisubi. From 1934 he studied veterinary science at Makerere University, gaining a diploma in 1938. For seven years he worked as assistant veterinary officer in the British colonial administration and in 1946 joined the Toro kingdom government as its secretary and later as assistant treasurer to the Rukurato, the Toro local parliament. He studied for a BA degree at the University of South Africa between 1950 and 1953 when he returned to his political career.

Babiiha was nominated in 1954 to represent Toro in the Uganda Legislative Council. Four years later he led his party in the first parliamentary elections to the Uganda Parliament; he won a seat and was re-elected as member for Toro in the general elections of March 1961. During that time, with Uganda moving closer to independence, he also took an active part in the constitutional arrangements towards independence for his country, and presented in 1950 a manifesto to the British government.

J.K. Babiiha

Babiiha urged the colonial authorities to effect a constitution which would give Uganda a Central Parliament and autonomous regional assemblies and allow for a Council of State to be made up of traditional rulers who would be chosen in rotation to serve as Head of State for a specified period. The 1962 independence constitution did in fact include Babiiha's proposal for a ceremonial Head of State. But that constitution was replaced in 1966 with one which abolished traditional kingdoms, thus ending the presidency of King Edward Mutesa II (q.v.), and Obote became the executive Head of State.

Earlier in 1960 Babiiha had been instrumental in the formation of Obote's

UPC and became its first national Chairman. After independence in 1962, he was a member of the country's first Cabinet as minister of Animal Husbandry, Game and Fisheries. A man who had already shown a deep interest in veterinary affairs and farming (he kept a successful ranch in his Toro home) he built up his department, with remarkable enthusiasm and skill, into a very successful Ministry.

He also had the distinction of being the oldest member of Obote's government. His ability, and loyalty to Obote during the constitutional crisis which resulted in the 1966 constitution, brought him respect and admiration as well as reward. He was made Vice-President of Uganda when Mutesa II fell from power following the 1966 constitution, and held that post until January 1971 when Obote's administration was overthrown in the military coup led by Idi Amin.

Before then there had been other attempts to topple the government, with assassination attempts on the lives of both President Obote and Vice-President Babiiha. Obote was shot on the cheek in December 1969 and Babiiha, his deputy, assumed control of government during his absence. He himself had earlier narrowly escaped an attempt on his life. Following the 1971 coup he retired to his farm in western Uganda but reappeared briefly on the public scene in 1973 when he served on Amin's international public relations delegation to Europe and the Americas.

Babiiha had a tremendous capacity for both political and academic pursuits. Between the late 1940s and mid-1950s he did various short-time courses at several universities in Europe and the USA. In 1958 he published a historical book, *Abayaga Clan in Western Uganda*, which was revised in 1975. For this, and for his contribution to the evolvement of a united, independent Uganda, he was rewarded with national and foreign honours including the Uganda Independence Commemoration Medal as well as the Uganda Republic Medal of Distinguished Service.

Babiiha's death in February 1982 was widely mourned in Kampala where President Obote, who was once again President, led the long procession of dignitaries and public mourners who paid their last respect to the former Vice-President as his body lay in state at Parliament Buildings.∎

Bakin Zuwo, S. (1934-89)

BAKIN ZUWO, Alhaji Sabo (1934-89).

NIGERIAN politician who was well known in northern Nigerian politics since pre-independence days and who rose to national prominence in the Second Republic. Born on 31 December 1934 in the Bakin Zuwo quarter of Kano, Bakin Zuwo began his education at a Koranic school. He subsequently attended evening classes at the Shauchi Primary School and then the Holy Trinity School in Sabon Gari in Kano. In 1952 he undertook a course in local government administration at the Institute of Administration in Zaria. However, the political tutelage that proved more directly crucial to his later political career began when Bakin Zuwo enrolled at the Mallam Aminu School of Political Thought at Sudawa in Kano at the age of 16. Young though he was, he became the political secretary of Alhaji Aminu Kano (q.v.), the progressive leader in Northern Nigerian politics, in the same year, 1950. This association prepared him for an active role in the Northern Elements Progressive Union (NEPU), founded and led by Aminu Kano.

S. Bakin Zuwo

The nationalist politics of the day, as advocated by Aminu Kano and espoused by his followers like Bakin Zuwo, combined demands for freedom from colonial rule with agitation for what was perceived as the legitimate interests of Northerners within the Federation of Nigeria. In 1953 Bakin Zuwo fell foul of the laws of the British colonialists and was sentenced to six months' imprisonment for alleged sedition. He was again arrested in Kano, Kaduna, Sokoto, Gashua, Burina, Hadejia and Ngwu for political activities.

Like many African nationalists of the time, Bakin Zuwo became involved in active trade unionism and served as president of the local branch of the then United Labour Congress. In 1960, the year of Nigeria's independence, he became the secretary-general of NEPU in Kano Province, and then from 1960 to 1963 president of NEPU's Positive Action Wing.

When the military took over the administration of Nigeria in 1966, Bakin Zuwo first turned to journalism and then to running his own business. He remained, however, active in the trade union movement and became national vice-chairman of the Nigerian Labour Congress in 1974. He also participated in the leadership of various social and cultural bodies.

With the lifting of the ban on political parties in 1978, Bakin Zuwo once again became the political secretary of Alhaji Aminu Kano and was one of the leading figures in the People's Redemption Party (PRP). In 1979 Bakin Zuwo was elected Senator for Kano Central under the Second Republic Constitution and later chosen to be the PRP leader in the Senate. In October 1983 he was elected Governor of Kano State, the peak of his political career. But he did not last long in that position as the army coup of December 1983, led by General Buhari, swept out the civilian regime from office.

Bakin Zuwo was one of those caught in the net of the new military regime in their early bid to rid the country of corruption. He was tried and sentenced to 23 years in prison on charges of corruption by the Kaduna Zone of the Special Military Tribunal on the Recovery of Public Property, set up after the coup. The concurrent sentences, totalling over 60 years, were reduced to five years by the military government in October 1984.

Bakin Zuwo was released from gaol in January 1988. He died on 16 February 1989 in a West German hospital, where he had been taken after being injured in a fall. He was buried in Kano, his beloved city, in whose politics he had featured prominently for several decades. Alhaji Bakin Zuwo was survived by three wives and 26 children.

The significance of Bakin Zuwo in modern Africa is that he was able with little formal education to rise to the top of the political ladder, in a nation which boasted a large number of articulate graduates and professionals in all fields.■

Bako, A. (1924-80)

BAKO, Alhaji Audu (1924-80).

NIGERIAN police officer and Military Governor of Kano State (one of the most populous of Nigeria's 19 states) for eight years. Born at Kaduna on 24 November 1924, son of a policeman, he was educated at Kaduna Government School and Zaria Mid-

dle School. He enlisted in the Nigeria Police Force (NPF) on 24 June 1942. He became instructor in police law at Kaduna Police College (1946-49), prosecuting officer (1949-54) and later deputy police commissioner in charge of Native Authority (NA) Police (the traditional Emirate *dogarai*, placed under NPF control) in the Northern Region. He received training at the Metropolitan Police School and the Senior Police Officers Training Course at Rython-on-Dunesmore, both in Britain, and attended a Forensic Science Course for police in 1955, among other training. In 1963 he was Assistant Commissioner in charge of Kano and Katsina provinces. He rose to become deputy Commissioner of Police for the former Northern Region.

In May 1967 he was appointed Military Governor of Kano State following the creation of new states. His administration, despite controversial aspects, included many positive achievements well remembered in the state. He was retired in the July 1975 coup, dismissed in February 1976, and criticised in an inquiry report. But after his death early in 1980 the Tiga irrigation dam, built during his governorship, was renamed the Audu Bako Dam.

Following his retirement in 1975 he began farming and died at a farm he had in Sokoto State, leaving a widow and eleven children including Dr. Lawal Bako, a doctor, and Hajiya Fatima Yusuf Imam Wara, acting deputy solicitor-general of Sokoto State. Alhaji Audu Bako published a *History of the NativeNative Authority Police and Guide to Native Authority Police Duties.*■

Alhaji A. Bako

Balewa, A.T. (1912-66)

BALEWA, Alhaji Sir Abubakar Tafawa (1912-66).

NIGERIAN politician, the first Prime Minister of the Federal Republic of Nigeria. He was born in 1912 in the small town of Tafawa Balewa in what is now Bauchi State in the north-east of Nigeria. After receiving his elementary education at Bauchi Provincial School, he went to Katsina Higher College in 1928. He qualified as a teacher in 1933 and went to teach at Bauchi Middle School. In 1945 he won a scholarship to Britain where he spent a year at the Institute of Education of the University of London, and on his return was appointed education officer for Bauchi Province.

He quickly became involved in the politics of Nigeria's Northern Region. In Bauchi he joined the Bauchi Discussion Circle, which soon became a forum for voicing African aspirations. Constitutional development in Nigeria brought the need for indigenous legislators and he soon became a member of the first Northern House of Assembly, from which he was elected to the Nigerian Legislative Council in Lagos in 1946. Further constitutional changes made him in 1952, as Minister of Works, one of the first group of central government ministers. In 1954 he was appointed Minister of Transport, in this capacity he was responsible for the building of the new Government Coastal Agency, and for creating the Inland Waterways Department.

As a parliamentary leader of the Northern Peoples' Congress (NPC), the biggest party in the Federal Parliament, he was appointed on 2 September 1957 the first Prime Minister of Nigeria. He formed a national government, consisting of six ministers from the National Council of Nigeria and the Cameroons (NCNC), four from the NPC, two from the Action Group (AG), and one from the Kamerun National Congress (KNC). He strongly believed that it was most essential that the three major political parties should work together in close co-operation on all matters of policy and planning if Nigeria were to achieve independence. After the 1959 independence elections Abubakar became, on 1 October 1960, the first Prime Minister of independent Nigeria and was knighted by the British queen.

After a stormy Federal election in 1964, he was re-appointed Prime Minister, a post which he retained until his assassination on 15 January 1966.

In Nigeria's turbulent and complex politics, Sir Abubakar remained a cool figure preoccupied with the problem of holding together the country's 250 ethnic groups. In September 1957, in his first parliamentary speech as Prime Minister, he characteristically declared: "Today unity is our greatest concern and it is the duty of every one of us to work to strengthen it. Bitterness due to political differences will carry Nigeria no-

where and I appeal to all political leaders throughout the country to try to control their extremists. Nigeria is large enough to accommodate us all in spite of our political differences."

Yet unity and stability eluded Sir Abubakar during his tenure of office. Shortly after independence, on 25 May 1962, a split in the AG government in the Western Region led to fighting on the floor of the regional House of Assembly and subsequent-

Sir Abubakar Tafawa Balewa

ly to disorder in the region. Sir Abubakar declared a State of Emergency, suspended the government and appointed an administrator to run the region's affairs for six months. But the crisis did not subside; it was followed by a major political upheaval involving the leader of the AG opposition in the Federal House of Representatives, Chief Obafemi Awolowo, and his supporters who, it was alleged, planned to overthrow the government of Sir Abubakar. On 2 November 1962 Chief Awolowo and 27 others were arrested and charged with treason, tried and sentenced on 11 September 1963 to terms of imprisonment.

Although he was Nigeria's federal Prime Minister, on the purely party political plane he was always number two in his own party, the NPC, under the shadow of Sir Ahmadu Bello (q.v.), that party's powerful and aristocratic chief. Critics of his government blamed its weakness on the excessive influence of Sir Ahmadu Bello.

But outside the country, as within it, many saw Sir Abubakar's government as guided by a sense of moderation. Opposed to what he considered extreme and hasty Pan-Africanism, he is remembered as stating at the inaugural meeting of the Organisation of African Unity (OAU) in Addis Ababa in 1963 that he did not believe in the African Personality or the African nationalism as defined by Kwame Nkrumah (q.v.) of Ghana. Earlier, on independence day, 1 October 1960, Sir Abubakar had struck a similar if divergent note, contrary to the elated and victorious mood of celebration of Independence when he said that Nigeria's pride in its achievement was "tempered by feelings of sincere gratitude to all who have shared in the task of developing Nigeria politically, socially and economically."

If Balewa was ready to praise the British for granting independence, he was also prepared to defend Nigerian and African interests when challenged by foreign countries. It is in this regard that he convened and chaired the extraordinary session of the Commonwealth Heads of Government in Lagos in January 1966 to discuss the crisis brought about by Rhodesia's Unilateral Declaration of Independence (UDI). He was the first African to preside over such a gathering.

While he was chairing that conference that was torn between African demands for an immediate end to Rhodesia's three-month-old UDI and lethargic British opinion, his country's political stability was on the verge of collapse following disorder arising from the disputed October 1965 elections in the Western Region. What had been assumed to be an isolated problem of law and order had escalated into chaos, posing perhaps the greatest challenge to Balewa's government. He sent the Army to restore law and order in the Region, but the task was never accomplished, for a section of the Army mutinied on 15 January 1966, killing Balewa in an attempt to overthrow his government. His body was discovered on 21 January. The rebellious troops who had kidnapped him on 15 January later surrendered to the authoritiy of Major-General Aguiyi-Ironsi (q.v.)

A devout Moslem, popularly known as "Balewa the good," Sir Abubakar was a simple man. In 1952 he was made Officer of the Order of the British Empire (OBE) and in 1955 Commander of the Order of the British Empire (CBE). In 1960, the year of Nigeria's independence, he was made Knight Commander of the Order of the British Empire (KBE) and appointed Privy Councillor in 1961. In a North of feudal Fulani aristocracy, he was born a commoner, belonging to the small Jere ethnic group (a branch of the Hausa), and throughout his life reflected the humility and native shrewdness that this background gave him. His assassination was perhaps the most regretted in Nigeria, where few people had anything against him as a person. ■

Bamba, A. (c. 1850-1927)

BAMBA, Ahmadou (c.1850-1927).

SENEGALESE religious leader. He came from a family of Wolof marabouts or preachers, and his father, Mamor Anta Selly, was a leading Moslem teacher linked to the courts of Ma Bâ and Lat Dior (qq.v.); he was close to Lat Dior, marrying his niece, and stayed with him until his own death about 1880. After that his son, Bamba, became well known as a preacher and until 1886, a religious confidant of Lat Dior who was killed in that year.

Ahmadou Bamba then returned to his family's village of Mbacke-Baol, where disciples began to gather to hear his preaching. Conflicts forced him to leave and he founded a village nearby, calling it Darou Salam. It was about 1889 when he was initiated into the Qadiriyya Moslem religious order by Sheikh Sidiya Baba of Mauritania. Soon afterwards, about 1890, he claimed to have had a revelation.

Although Bamba never preached opposition to French rule, the size of his following worried the French authorities, who broke it up in 1891. But the followers reassembled; they included ex-soldiers of the Bourba Jolof (paramount ruler of the Wolofs) and others whose lives had been disrupted or disturbed by colonial conquest; these seem to have been attracted to the marabout Bamba, and the French accordingly re-

A. Bamba

groundnut growing and to a great extent organised its expansion into the interior. This brought in money for the order.

While always suspicious of a spontaneous African movement, the French were very pleased at the Mourides' groundnut farming, and also at Ahmadou Bamba's help in recruiting soldiers in the First World War; for this he was decorated (*Croix de la Légion d'Honneur*) in 1918. In that year 20,000 pilgrims visited him on the Prophet's Birthday. In 1924 he began work on a grand new mosque at Touba, authorised by the government in 1926, with donations from the faithful. By 1927 the movement was estimated to have about 100,000 members.

On 19 July 1927 Ahmadou Bamba died at Diourbel. His sons Mamadou Mustafa (1927-45) and Falilou (1945-68) in turn succeeded him as Khalifa General, leader of the Mourides. Their brother Abdoul Ahad Mbacke (q.v.) succeeded Falilou in 1968. Under these sons of the founder the Mourides expanded, growing more and more groundnuts, and numbered over 450,000 thirty years after the founder's death.■

mained suspicious. From early on his followers worked for him as well as bringing gifts which he distributed.

When France established direct rule in Baol in 1895 Ahmadou Bamba moved on to Jolof, which still retained some autonomy. But the French arrested him there, and after a trial on vague charges he was deported to Gabon where he spent seven years. His return was greeted by his followers as a miracle, and he was quickly deported again by a government very nervous of someone with such influence among Senegal's recently conquered Moslems. He was sent to Mauritania, where he stayed at the camp of Sheikh Sidiya.

He was allowed to return in 1907, and went to Cheyen village in Jolof where he was kept under surveillance. His following became greater than ever. While he never broke with the Qadiriyya he virtually founded a new order, the Muridiyya (Mourides). Its preaching stressed above all hard work for the common good in the service of God. Thus attention was concentrated above all on growing of groundnuts, already Senegal's leading cash crop. The Mourides expanded

Bamina, J. (c.1925-65)

BAMINA, Joseph (c.1925-65).

BURUNDIAN politician, President of the Senate and Prime Minister. Born in about 1925 into an eminent Hutu family, he was educated at the Burasira Seminary before attending the Lovanium University in the Congo (now Zaire). Bamina belonged to the *Parti de l'Unité et du Progrès National* (UPRONA) at its inception and played an important role in the formation of its policies which, to an extent, were aimed at safeguarding the interests of the noble class to which he belonged. He was a member of the younger privileged activists who formed the personal entourage of Prince Louis Rwagasore (q.v.) whose premiership of Burundi came to an abrupt end in 1961 when he was assassinated. Bamina was one of the Prime Minister's advisers.

In 1961 Bamina was elected to the National Assembly as an UPRONA deputy; he was elected again in 1965, this time to the

Senate whose President he became. He was elected president of the UPRONA party in September 1962, but this was followed by a split within the party when the defeated contender for the presidency, Paul Mirere-kano (q.v.), organised a rival wing of UPRONA. Reconciliation was not achieved until the Kitega Conference of September 1964 where an agreement on a new executive committee was reached, with Bamina retaining the presidency of the party.

But the intra-party feud continued and the party suffered another blow in 1965 with the assassination of another of its Prime Ministers, Pierre Ngendandumwe (q.v.).

Following the assassination of Ngendandumwe, Joseph Bamina was appointed by Mwami Mwambutsa to head a new administration in late January 1965. Ngendandumwe's death highlighted the involvement of external powers in the domestic politics of Burundi. The Chinese were alleged to have been involved in the assassination, because Ngendandumwe had temporarily halted the relations between the Chinese and his government. The succeeding administration of Bamina served notice to the Chinese Ambassador and his staff to leave Burundi within two days.

Bamina's government was dissolved in March of the same year to allow for a general election. In October 1965 he was arrested, following an abortive coup d'état and revolt in which the Hutu community wanted to put an end to Tutsi's extended control over government. Joseph Bamina was executed in December 1965 for complicity in the coup attempt. ■

Brig. J.A. Bangura

Bangura, J.A. (1930-71)

BANGURA, Brigadier John Ahmadu (1930-71).

SIERRA LEONEAN soldier, Chairman of the National Interim Council in April 1968. Born on 8 March 1930 at Kalangba in the Northern Province of Sierra Leone, he was educated at the American Wesleyan Methodist School, after which he went to the Central School at Koyeima and the Bo Government School. On completing his secondary education in 1950 he enlisted as a private in the Army. He was sent on various military courses in West Africa, and after excelling at his studies he travelled to England for officer cadet training at the Sandhurst Military Academy. He was the first Sierra Leonean to graduate from this Academy, and remained in England to attend the Mons Officer Cadet School until 1954, when he reached the rank of second-lieutenant.

In 1955 he returned to Sierra Leone where he joined the Royal Sierra Leone Regiment, commanding a platoon of the First Battalion Rifle Company. He was promoted to captain three years later and in 1963 he served with the United Nations Emergency Force in the Congo (now Zaire), after which he was promoted to major. He was appointed commander of the First Battalion with the rank of lieutenant-colonel in 1964 and two years later he was made a full colonel.

By 1967 the political tensions in the country were rising, and just before the elections held in that year took place, he was detained and charged with mutiny. He was released shortly afterwards and assigned to the Sierra Leone Embassy in the USA as a counsellor. Meanwhile, the newly elected government had been overthrown by the military and Bangura went to Guinea where he organised opposition to the new military administration of the National Reformation Council (NRC). The following year a group of junior officers seized power in Sierra Leone and Bangura was recalled to Freetown to head the new government as Chairman of the National Interim Council. He immediately reassured the nation that civilian rule would be restored as soon as possible, and a week later he handed over the government to Siaka Stevens, who had been prevented from assuming the premiership the previous year.

Bangura then returned to his previous position with the First Battalion and was also appointed commander of the Military Forces. Shortly afterwards he became a brigadier and in 1970 he was awarded the CBE. In March 1971 there was a coup attempt against the government and a number of high-ranking officers, including Bangura, were arrested and charged with treason. He was found guilty and was executed on 29 June 1971 at Pademba Road Prison. ■

Bangura, S.L. (1930-79)

BANGURA, Samuel Lansana (1930-79).

SIERRA LEONEAN banker who became Governor of the Bank of Sierra Leone. Born on 7 June 1930 at Yele, Sierra Leone, he had his early education at the SDA Mission School, Yele, and Bo Government School. He went to Hull University, England where he read economics, graduating in 1957. The following year Sam Bangura proceeded to Queen's College, Oxford, for post-graduate studies, finishing in 1959.

That same year he returned to Sierra Leone and joined the government service, first as Assistant District Commissioner and later as District Commissioner of Bonthe. In 1962 he was attached to the Ministry of Finance, where he rose to the rank of Deputy Financial Secretary. In 1964 he was appointed Permanent Secretary, Development Office.

Bangura was transferred to the Bank of Sierra Leone on 1 June 1966 as Deputy Governor. He was appointed Governor in November 1970, a post he held until his death. Sam Bangura worked hard for his country, representing it most effectively in international financial circles, he believed that the necessities of domestic policies

S.L. Bangura

should not obscure the genuine need for international assistance to Sierra Leone. He had a notable political sense and did his best to assuage creditors while maintaining progress for the country. Bangura's efforts were aided by the West African Clearing House, established in Freetown, and the African Association of Central Bankers.

Sam Bangura was found dead at his home in Freetown early on the morning of Saturday, 22 December 1979. He was buried on 30 December, and was widely mourned in Freetown. Great unease about the circumstances of his death led to an inquest which concluded that he had been murdered. Four people, including his niece, were charged with the deed and later convicted. ■

Bankole-Bright, H.C. (1883-1958)

BANKOLE-BRIGHT, Dr. Herbert Christian (1883-1958).

SIERRA LEONEAN physician and politician. He co-founded the National Congress of British West Africa (NCBWA). Born on 23 August 1883 at Okrika, Nigeria, his parents were wealthy Creoles from Sierra Leone. At the time of his birth, his father was working in Nigeria for a Sierra Leonean company. While he was still young, the family returned to Freetown and established a prosperous business. Bankole-Bright was educated at the Wesleyan Boys' School in Freetown, after which he travelled to Scotland to study medicine at the University of Edinburgh. He passed his final examinations

Dr. H.C. Bankole-Bright

in 1910 and established a private medical practice in Freetown.

In 1918 he became the proprietor and editor of *The Aurora*, a newspaper which reflected his moderate anti-colonialism. Two years later he was one of the founding members of the National Congress of British West Africa (NCBWA), and following its inaugural conference in Accra in 1920 he went to London as secretary of the NCBWA delegation that unsuccessfully placed various demands before the British Secretary of State for the Colonies. He remained very active in the NCBWA, becoming Secretary-General of its Sierra Leone branch, while continuing his medical practice and running a nursing home.

An able public speaker, he was elected to the Legislative Council in 1924, remaining a member of this body until 1939. During this period he called for constitutional changes that would eventually lead to self-determination. He also campaigned for better pay and conditions for African workers and the establishment of a Court of Appeal in West Africa.

The influence which he had built up in 1920s and early 1930s began to diminish as his attitude began to change. He did not support Wallace-Johnson's (q.v.) Youth League, opposing, among other things, an organisation that appealed to mass support, thus threatening the political framework in which he operated. During the Freetown City Council elections in 1938 open conflict flared up between the two men. The following year Bankole-Bright supported three bills concerned with sedition, subversive literature and expulsion that were proposed by the British administration in an attempt to combat the effectiveness of Wallace-Johnson's activities. As a result of his support for these unpopular measures, he was forced by his constituency to resign from the Legislative Council.

He then devoted his time to his medical practice until the late 1940s when he once again became active in politics. He was one of the co-founders of the National Council of Sierra Leone (NCSL) in 1950 and the following year he was re-elected member of the Legislative Council, representing Freetown Central. He established the *Evening Despatch* and remained on the Legislative Council until the 1957 elections, when the NCSL lost all its seats. He died shortly afterwards on 12 December 1958, aged 75. ■

Bante, T. (1921-77)

BANTE, Brigadier-General Teferi (1921-77).

ETHIOPIAN soldier and statesman. Teferi Bante was born in the Legedadi suburb of Addis Ababa in 1921. His parents were members of the Galla ethnic group. With the liberation of Ethiopia from Italian occupation and the return of Emperor Haile Selassie I (q.v.) in 1941, Bante enlisted as a private in the Ethiopian Armed Forces. He was sent to study at the Guenet Military School from where he graduated as a second-lieutenant in 1943.

He then joined the ground forces, serving in various units based in the Hararghe Administrative Region. He later became a training officer in the 4th Army Brigade, after which he joined the 12th Battalion for a period until joining the 3rd Army Division, again as a training officer.

Brig-Gen. T. Bante

Later he transferred to the Headquarters of the 4th Army in Addis Ababa and was appointed director of Training at the Guenet Military School. During this period his unorthodox views of the government came to the attention of the authorities, and he was sent to Washington as a military attaché at the Ethiopia Embassy there. He remained in the USA in this position for five years and on his return was appointed second-in-command of the 4th Army Division. He also became a commanding officer at the Harar Military Academy.

In September 1974, after the deposition of Emperor Haile Selassie I, he was made commander of the 2nd Army Division based in Asmara, Eritrea. During his long army career he had risen through the ranks to the position of Brigadier-General and had gained a reputation for good conduct and leadership as well as for patriotism. As a result he was called from Eritrea to become Chairman of the Provisional Military Administrative Council (PMAC) on 28 November 1974. On the same day, 5,000 extra troops were sent to reinforce the existing military contingent in Eritrea, where there had been strife for many years. This was one of the main issues that led to the resignation, arrest and subsequent death of the previous Head of State, Lieutenant-General Andom (q.v.), who disagreed with the PMAC on the need for extra troops being sent to that region.

One of Bante's early commitments as Head of State was to overcome and eradicate the maladministration and corruption that were features of the previous governments. To help solve this problem 207 new administrators were sworn in on 3 December 1974. Two days later a Civilian Council consisting of 50 men was established to begin work on a new constitution and to draw up plans for the eventual establishment of a representative government and the introduction of land reforms.

In December the Government's policy for the reconstruction of Ethiopia along socialist lines was announced, whereby the administration of the country would be based on the participation of the workers, national unity, equality and co-operation. The progress of the country would be in line with the watchword of the revolution, *Ethiopia Tikdem* (Ethiopia First).

In order to begin this national reconstruction, Bante launched a National Work

Campaign on 21 December 1974. Under it an initial 25,000 (the target being 60,000) teachers, university students and senior school pupils would go to rural areas to try to remedy the lack of education there as well as to explain the aims of the revolution, to encourage self-reliance through co-operation, and to help carry out famine relief programmes. This effort helped to enforce the land reform measure of March 1975.

Meanwhile, there was still the problem of Eritrea. In January 1975 the situation became more serious when two of Eritrea's separatist movements combined in a common front, to intensify their offensive. The Government tried unsucccessfully to resolve the problem while appealing to certain Arab states not to continue giving support to the Eritreans.

As the conflict continued, tying down half the Ethiopian army in the region, opposition to the military Government grew inside the country. In April 1976 a detailed political programme was published, stating the aims of the revolution which would eventually lead to a people's democratic republic along socialist lines. The Government warned that progress of the programme would be slow because of the problems facing the country, the need to re-educate the masses and the need to counter the subversive work of enemies of the revolution.

The following month Bante once again attempted to find a peaceful solution to the problem of Eritrea, issuing an eight point plan which offered regional autonomy, the release of political prisoners, the lifting of the State of Emergency once peace was guaranteed, and government help in the rehabilitation of exiled Eritreans and for those who had lost property or other means of livelihood during the struggle. These proposals received support within Ethiopia, but the Eritreans rejected them, arguing that they were intended to influence world opinion while an offensive was being planned.

Despite the refusal of the Eritreans to accept the proposals, Bante continued to search for a solution to the strife in that region. He was also concerned over the growing dispute with Somalia over Ethiopia's Ogaden region to which Somalia laid claim. In September 1976 dialogue began between the two countries with a view to settling the dispute peacefully.

In December 1976 the PMAC was re-organised so as to be more effective in carrying out the Government's revolutionary programme, and to restore collective responsibility. This reorganisation reassigned power in the top leadership of the PMAC to the benefit of Bante, who, apart from being Head of State, was also head of the three newly established bodies of the PMAC. He was also Commander-in-Chief of the Armed Forces, and was in charge of the appointment and promotion of senior personnel. This shift in the power structure undermined the authority of leading figures in the PMAC and intensified the power struggle within the leadership.

During this period Bante also began to show a softening of his attitude towards the Ethiopian People's Revolutionary Party, a clandestine organisation operating within the country for a return to civilian rule, a move that the PMAC did not feel could benefit the revolution until the masses were ready for it. On 3 February 1977 Bante was shot dead at his official headquarters after being accused of working against the revolution. ■

Banza, A. (1932-69)

BANZA, Lieutenant-Colonel Alexandre (1932-69).

CENTRAL AFRICAN REPUBLIC soldier and politician. He was born at Carnot in the west of the country in October 1932, the oldest of nine children. Educated in French Cameroon and Congo Brazzaville (now the People's Republic of Congo), he entered the army when he was 18, joining the First Battalion of the Congo-Gabon Rifles. After gaining a commission, he was tranferred in 1962 to the Central African Republic Army. He was promoted lieutenant in 1963 and captain in 1964.

At the time of the military coup d'état in which Jean-Bedel Bokassa took power on 1 January 1966, he was commander of an Infantry battalion and was one of the masterminds of the coup. Bokassa formed a new government in early January 1966, known as the Revolutionary Council. Banza was first named Minister of State in charge of Finance and ex-Servicemen, and later, in a reshuffle, was named Minister of State for Finance and National Economy. He brought considerable authority to the task, and for the first six months of 1966, Bokassa allowed him, like other ministers, to assume full responsibility for his department.

Lt-Col. A. Banza

Lieutenant-Colonel Banza, as he now was, was a close friend of President Bokassa, being the latter's second in command. As such, it was he who, on a journey to Paris in May 1966, explained the reasons for the coup d'état and succeeded in giving some reassurance to French political and economic circles. The way was then open for President Bokassa to make a private visit to Paris in July 1966, in a further effort to obtain recognition for his regime.

It was not only France which had been slow to recognise the new military regime; Colonel Bokassa felt that the country was being left in isolation and during the latter half of 1966 left the country in the care of Colonel Banza in order to make a series of visits in Africa and Europe.

During the course of 1967 and 1968, Bokassa began to feel that French aid was inadequate and the conditions placed on it too restrictive. He wished to move out of the franc zone and create a Central African currency linked to the Congo and Zaire. In mid-1966 Bokassa and Banza opened negotiations with a number of international bankers in order to raise additional finance, and agreements were reached in October for a loan of US $50,000,000 for the financing of various projects. Pressure from France caused Bokassa to drop the arrangements. At the beginning of 1967, Banza was given the additional portfolio of Economic Affairs.

In April 1968 President Bokassa reshuffled his government; Banza vacated the Ministries of Finance and Economic Affairs and was given the Ministry of Health.

The year 1968 was marked by a series of quarrels and reconciliations with neighbouring states; relations with the Congolese Republic and with Chad were particularly strained. In October, with fresh rumours of plots, Bokassa sent for a contingent, the second since he came to power, of French troops.

The invitation to pay an official visit to France in February 1969 gave Bokassa the boost that he had been awaiting for three years. In April he decided to consolidate his position still further and Lieutenant-Colonel Banza was arrested on the night of 10 April at Bangui and tried, on charges of planning to murder the Head of State and seize power for himself. He was sentenced to death on the 11th and was officially said to have been executed at dawn on 12 April 1969. ■

Baptiste, J. (died c. 1970)

BAPTISTE, Jean (died c. 1970).

CHADIAN politician, co-founder of the *Union Démocratique Indépendante du Tchad* in 1954. He was born in the Ouaddai region of eastern Chad. After working in a transporting business he joined the *Union Démocratique du Tchad* (UDT). He was elected to represent part of the Borkou-Ennedi-Tibesti region in the Territorial Assembly in 1952 and at the same time was chosen as a delegate to the Grand Council of the *Afrique Equatoriale Française* (AEF). He later broke away from the UDT and helped to found the *Union Démocratique Indépendante du Tchad* (UDIT). He was re-elected to the Territorial Assembly and also became deputy mayor, and later mayor, of Fort Lamy, now Ndjamena.

Meanwhile the UDIT had allied with other political parties in the country and, following the March 1957 elections, Baptiste was appointed Minister of Planning in the coalition government. He remained in this position until early 1958 when he resigned after disagreeing with the Government. However he continued to be active in the Territorial Assembly and when the Provisional Government was formed in December 1958 he became Minister of the Economy.

At that time the political situation in the country was very unsettled. In February 1959 another Provisional Government was formed with Baptiste heading the Ministry of Public Works. This new government lasted one month, after which a third Provisional Government was formed, headed by one of Baptiste's long-standing political rivals. Baptiste was not given a ministerial position in this administration. On 24 March, twelve days after its formation, the government was dissolved and in the fourth Provisional Government Baptiste was once again appointed Minister of Economics with the additional portfolios of Tourism and Health. By June 1959 the situation had stabilised enough for a more secure government to be formed and Baptiste was transferred to the position of Minister of Social Affairs, Health and Labour.

In the following months he helped form the *Parti National Africain* (PNA), consisting of Moslem opposition groups including factions of his own party, the UDIT. The PNA finally came into being at the end of January 1961 with Baptiste as its executive President. He had hoped that there would be mutual co-operation between the PNA and other political parties, particularly the now dominant *Parti Progressiste Tchadien* (PPT), but as a result of his involvement in the PNA he was sacked from government and shortly afterwards was also expelled from the PNA for his "treasonable" sympathies. He remained a deputy in the Territorial Assembly but these events caused his political influence to decline sharply.

Later on in the year he was arrested and briefly detained. After his release his movements and activites were closely watched and his citizenship was withdrawn. He was re-arrested in September 1963, following a series of violent anti-government demonstrations and riots, and was imprisoned in the Borkou-Ennedi-Tibesti region. His death was announced in 1970, although it is believed that he was killed soon after his arrest. ■

Barclay, A. (1856-1938)

BARCLAY, Arthur (1856-1938).

LIBERIAN statesman, lawyer and journalist. He was born on the island of Barbados in the Caribbean in 1856. When he

A. Barclay

was nine years old his family decided to return to Africa. They landed in Monrovia on 10 May 1865 and were among the founders of the Crozierville settlement. After attending secondary school, Barclay went to the Liberia College to study law, receiving a Bachelor of Arts degree on 9 December 1873. While he was still studying he began to teach, and on graduating he remained at the College, becoming principal of the Preparatory Department, and later professor of Mathematics and Languages. Shortly after graduating he was also appointed private secretary to Joseph Jenkins Roberts (q.v.) a position he held until he became the Chief Clerk of the House of Representatives.

In 1878 Barclay, now a practising attorney-at-law, entered into partnership with Henry W. Grimes, and their law firm became one of the most reputable in Monrovia. In this period he was also an editor of *The Observer*, a popular Liberian newspaper.

He left the House of Representatives in 1883 and was appointed judge of the Montserrado County Court of Quarter Sessions and Common Pleas by the President of the Republic. Two years later he became sub-treasurer of Montserrado County, and in 1892 he was appointed Postmaster-General. Later he was made Secretary of State.

In the 1904 elections he was elected President of the Republic. He was re-elected in 1906 and 1908, by which time the Constitution had been amended to extend the presidential term from two to four years.

He pursued policies which were aimed at improving relations between the indigenous ethnic groups and the Liberian settlers. Early in his administration he called the first conference of ethnic leaders and Government officials. He evolved a system whereby the people in the interior continued to be governed according to customary law, while the Government appointed paramount chiefs, helped by district commissioners who would liaise between them and the central government. The conference also helped to establish better trading relations with the indigenous people.

However, these efforts did not quite satisfy the indigenous population of the interior and they continued to resist the Monrovia government. The government, realising that its voluntary militia was inadequate for its security needs, established a more effective defence force to deal with both interior fighting and encroachments on

Liberian territory from outside. In 1908 the Liberian Frontier Force was formed, initially with British and later American assistance. In addition to social unrest, the country faced economic difficulties. Customs revenues were dwindling and the debt repayments that the administration had inherited were becoming increasingly difficult to meet.

In order to stimulate the economy, Barclay established a Bureau of Agriculture to encourage the production of various crops. A rubber growing concession was granted to a British-controlled firm in 1904; it began planting in 1910.

In 1906 a private British loan was negotiated for £100,000, with Liberian customs revenues pledged as security. The money received under the loan was partly intended for arrears repayments and partly for economic development with 40 per cent of the loan allocated to a British concession company operating in Liberia.

Barclay appealed to the USA for further assistance and in 1909 an American fact finding Commission was sent to Liberia. On receiving the Commission's report, the USA agreed to help Liberia overcome its immediate financial problems. In 1912 an international loan of $1,700,000 was negotiated to pay Liberia's outstanding debts, with the country's customs revenue put under international (American, British, French and German) receivership until the loan was repaid.

When Barclay left office at the end of his eight-year term of office in 1912, the situation in Liberia had markedly improved. For many years afterwards his advice and opinion on public affairs were sought by those who succeeded him. He was a very energetic person, commanding the respect of many.

He served briefly as president of the Liberia College and remained an active member of the College's Board of Trustees until his death. A deeply religious man, he was a member of the Episcopal Church, in which he rose from vestryman to junior warden and later senior warden. A man of immense integrity, he was selected to represent Liberia on the League of Nations Commission established to investigate allegations of a slave trade scandal in Liberia in 1930. In his later years he was fondly referred to as "Liberia's Great Old Man!" He died in July 1938 at the age of 81.■

Barclay, E.J. (1882-1955)

BARCLAY, Edwin J. (1882-1955).

LIBERIAN lawyer and statesman. He was born on 5 January 1882 at Brewerville in Montserrado County, Liberia. On completing his secondary education, he studied law at the Liberia College, graduating with honours.

He joined the government service and was soon promoted Secretary of State. On 3 December 1930 he was sworn in as President of the Republic of Liberia following the resignation of President King.

At that time Liberia was facing serious economic difficulties which were exacerbated by the general world depression. His position was made more difficult as Britain and the USA would not recognise his presidential authority because they asserted he had not been elected. They suggested that

E.J. Barclay

Liberia should be governed by a commission appointed by the League of Nations. Barclay was fundamentally opposed to this proposal and was determined to remain in office and defend his country's sovereignty. However, he did agree to the League of Nations sending three experts to Liberia to make a six months' study of its administration, economy and public health problems.

On completing their investigation, the three experts proposed a series of internal reforms, some of which were later carried out. A plan to deal with Liberia's financial difficulties was formulated under which it was proposed that Liberian debts would be refinanced by Firestone, and a group of foreign advisers would be selected by the League to supervise the country's internal administration.

Barclay was not in favour of these proposals, fearing that they could lead to the end of Liberian independence, and expressed grave reservations in this matter. Taking this as a rejection of their recommendations, the Council of the League of Nations withdrew their offers of assistance, and the USA broke off diplomatic relations. Meanwhile the country's economic situation further deteriorated, giving rise to social unrest.

By 1934 strong measures were clearly imperative. The Government passed a Moratorium Act, suspending the repayments of a 1926 loan. As a result, negotiations were begun between the Government, Firestone and the Finance Company of America, resulting in the revision of the terms of the 1926 loan. By 1935 Barclay had successfully fought his way out of the crisis without seriously jeopardising Liberian autonomy. He restored domestic order and gained recognition of his presidency by the USA.

In 1935 the Constitution was amended, extending the life of a presidential administration from four to eight years, but providing that a president could not serve two consecutive terms. In the same year Barclay, having finished President King's term, was elected President. By this time the economic effects of the world depression on the Liberian economy were diminishing and the Government began to receive revenues from Firestone rubber production, enabling the country to achieve and maintain a balanced budget.

During his presidency, Barclay also turned his attention to relations with the indigenous peoples, and established interior councils as well as improved educational and health facilities in the rural areas.

On the outbreak of the Second World War, Barclay decided that Liberia should remain neutral as her size and resources made her totally unprepared for such a conflict. However, following the sinking of ships in Liberian coastal waters by German U-boats, Barclay granted the USA and Britain permission to build and operate an air-field in Liberia. In 1943 President Roosevelt visited Barclay on his return journey from the Casablanca Conference. During this meeting, Barclay was assured of American assistance in the construction of a deep water port and in exploring the possibilities of exploiting the country's rich iron ore deposits.

In May 1943 presidential elections were held with Barclay, unable constitutionally to stand for re-election, supporting the successful True Whig Party candidate, W.V.S. Tubman (q.v.). Barclay then left public service, but in 1954 when the Independent True Whig Party was formed to contest the 1955 elections he agreed to stand as its presidential candidate. He campaigned against the Government's intention to increase foreign participation in the economy, and what he considered to be extravagant government expenditure. He polled few votes and his party faced total eclipse, especially following the implication of some of the leaders of the Independent True Whig Party in an attempted assassination plot against the President. Shortly afterwards he fell ill and died on 6 November 1955. ■

Al-Baruni, S. (1870-1940)

AL-BARUNI, Sulayman (1870-1940).

LIBYAN leader who fought against the Italian occupation of his country. Al-Baruni was particularly active in his efforts to liberate Libya, especially Tripolitania from which region he came, during the Turco-Italian war. When the news of peace between Italy and the Ottoman Porte reached Libya, Tripolitanian leaders were divided from the onset on whether to contin-

ue the war effort or whether to enter into negotiations with Italy on the basis of the independence granted by the Turkish Sultan. Sulayman al-Baruni, heading the war supporters, prevailed, on the assumption that Italy was not going to recognise Tripolitanian independence without war. He believed that Italy would only become "reason-

S. Al-Baruni

able" once Libyan nationalists were in a position to negotiate with Italy from a position of strength.

Baruni was a daring leader, yet he was unable to unite the people behind him and when the Italians overran the country, Baruni was forced to leave for Istanbul, Turkey, in March of 1913. But Italy's control of Tripolitania during World War I (1914-1918) hardly extended beyond the city of Tripoli, and al-Baruni returned in 1915 as Turkey's new Governor of Libya, and continued the struggle against Italy to the end of the war. He refused further compromises with Italy.

When the war came to an end, Baruni and Ramadan al-Suwayhili (q.v.), another Libyan leader, proclaimed their country a republic and threatened to continue the war if Italy refused to recognise their independence. A national convention was held in November 1918 when it was decided, owing to rivalry among the leaders, to appoint a Council of Four composed of Baruni, Suwayhili, Murayyid and Bilkayr, assisted by Abd al-Rahman Azzam, rather than one head of State.

Italy was formally notified of the establishment of the republic and she agreed to recognise this régime, and a statute to that effect was issued on 1 June 1919. The Italians actually aimed at controlling the country through the local leaders, and dissension among the Four soon prevailed and the attempt to establish a republic was abortive. Together with the Ottoman representatives Nuri Bey and Ja'afir Bey al-Askari, Baruni played a critical role in influencing the Sanusi leader, Sayyid Ahmad al-Sharif (q.v.), to wage a guerilla campaign against the Italians.

He even gained Turkish support for Libya's liberation. He was adept at manoeuvering between powers though his position was an uncompromising one. He was determined to see the end of the Italian occupation of Libya, and thus eliminate the dependencies that were being created in the country. He refused to shave his beard until his country was rid of the colonial invaders.

When the Libyan resistance to Italy collapsed in the early thirties, Baruni went into exile first to Turkey, Iraq and later to Bombay, India, where he died in 1940, without having seen his country liberated from Italy.■

Emir A. Bayero

Bayero, A. (1881-1953)

BAYERO, Alhaji Abdullahi, Emir of Kano (1881-1953).

NIGERIAN traditional ruler. Son of Emir Muhammadu Abbas (who ruled from 1903-1919), he was district head of Bichi before he was appointed the tenth Fulani Emir of Kano in 1926. He was officially installed in February 1927.

Under British supervision, he carried out some reforms of the Emirate government. The economic prosperity continued in his reign despite the slump going on in the post-Second World War years and considerable development was financed from Native Authority funds; by the early 1950s the Kano NA was spending over £1 million annually for its programmes. Under the Emir, whose good relations with the British were shown by a procession in which he and the governor took part in 1936, Kano became important to the British as a civil air route terminal (1936), an air base in the Second World War, and a major groundnut centre as it had been since 1912. Near the end of his reign politics developed rapidly in this largely commercial city.

In 1934 he visited Britain and was received by King George V. He went to Mecca twice; the first time, in 1937, he travelled by car and became the first ever Emir of Kano to perform the Hajj; he performed it again in 1951, that time by air, and on his return opened a new mosque. He followed the Reformed Tijaniyya Moslem confraternity, and was much influenced by Sheikh Ibrahim Niass of Kaolack (Senegal), who preached it in Kano.

This well remembered Emir died on 25 December 1953. Bayero University, Kano, is named after him. He was succeeded by his son Muhammad Sanusi (born 1900).■

Beavogui, L.L. (1923-84)

BEAVOGUI, Louis Lansana (1923-84).

GUINEAN politician, ex-Prime Minister and Minister of Planning and Statistics. Beavogui was one of the closest associates of the late President Sekou Touré (q.v.) serving in the most important ministerial portfolios, until the latter's death. He was dedicated and hardworking, and an articulate and serious-minded administrator.

Born in Macenta in the south near the Liberian border in 1923, Louis Lansana Beavogui went to the School of Medicine and Pharmacy in Dakar where he trained as a doctor. He worked first as Assistant Medical Officer in Guékedou, southern Guinea and then as medical officer in Kissidougou, north of Guékedou. It was there that Beavogui's political career began in 1953 as a town councillor and a year later as Mayor of Kissidougou. In 1956 he was elected to one of the three Guinean seats to the French National Assembly, Sekou Touré and Saifoulaye Diallo being the other two. The following year he was appointed Minister of Trade, Industry and Mining.

In 1958 Guinea became an independent republic with Sekou Touré as Head of State and Bevavogui was appointed Minister for Economic Affairs and Planning. In 1961 he became Minister of Foreign Affairs which catapulted him into the international arena for eight years, during which he helped to shape the deeply nationalist foreign policy of Guinea at the time. A man of strong convictions at the Conference of Non-Aligned Nations in Belgrade in 1961, he proposed the admission of China to the United Nations. He was involved in the UN debate on the Congo in 1965 where his contribution was highly appreciated.

Beavogui reflected the nationalism of his President and his vision of the continent, and while Sekou Touré was alive was widely regarded as his natural political successor.

In a government reshuffle in 1969 he was appointed Minister of Economic Affairs, a vital ministry considering the pallid state of the Guinean economy. At the ninth Congress of the *Parti Démocratique de Guinée* (PDG) in 1972, the post of Prime Minister was created and Beavogui was appointed to it, as well as being in charge of the Army, Foreign Affairs, Financial Control and Information. Two months later the Ministry of Foreign Affairs was given to Fily Cissoko. Beavogui was still Prime Minister when Sekou Touré died in 1984, and it fell to Beavogui to head the government as

L. Beavogui

interim Head of State. Within a week, however, on 3 April 1984, the military took over and Beavogui and other members of the government were placed under arrest. He died that same year at the age of 62 in hospital in Conakry, having been transferred, because of ill-health, from prison in Kindia where he had been detained since the coup.■

Behanzin (1845-1906)

BEHANZIN, King (1845-1906).

BENINI monarch. He was the last independent King of Dahomey (now in modern Benin), heir to the powerful kingdom centred at Abomey since the early 18th century. He adopted the name Behanzin (Gbehanzin) on his accession, being previously called Ahokponu and Kondo. He was the son of King Glele who reigned from 1858 to 1889.

Glele, resolved to maintain Dahomey's independence as well as control the trade with Europeans, came into increasing conflict with the French from 1878, when they began asserting control over Porto-Novo and Cotonou. France occupied Porto-Novo in alliance with its King Toffa, in 1883, but Glele refused to recognise any French sovereignty in the area. In 1889 talks began on the dispute and others arising from it. Towards the end of 1889, Glele died (it was rumoured he had committed suicide) and was succeeded immediately by Behanzin.

The crisis with the French continued, resulting in a battle with Cotonou in 1890. Then there was a truce. But Behanzin approved continued sales of prisoners to the Germans, who sent them to work in other parts of Africa without offically calling them slaves, and this was added to other French complaints. In March 1892 a boat carrying France's Lt.-Governor on the Dahomey coast was attacked, and this was a pretext for a major French expedition approved by France's parliament in April 1892.

French forces commanded by Gen. Dodds fought their way slowly inland towards Abomey. The Dahomey forces, including the women warriors ("Amazons"), fought back well, delaying the French advance and winning some local victories. But the French captured Abomey. For some time then they negotiated with Behanzin on surrender on terms which would include a continued role for the King. These negotiations failed and the French attacked the remnants of Behanzin's forces. On 26 January 1894 he surrendered.

Shortly before then his brother Agoli-Agbo had been proclaimed King under

French sovereignty. The old kingdom was steadily reduced in area and weakened, and in 1900 Agoli-Agbo was deposed and the kingdom abolished permanently. Behanzin was then in exile in Martinique with several of his family. After several years there they

King Behanzin

were moved to Algeria, where Behanzin died in Algiers on 10 December 1906.

In 1928 his son Wanilo, who had accompanied him and been for long forbidden to return, was allowed finally to go back and take Behanzin's ashes to Abomey for reburial. Wanilo had qualified as a lawyer in France and begun to practise there. He successfully had his father's ashes reburied near the burial place of earlier kings of Dahomey.■

Bekkai, M. (1907-61)

BEKKAI, M'barek (1907-61).

MOROCCAN politician. The first Prime Minister of independent Morocco, he was born in Morocco in 1907, into a family of the nomadic Beni Snassen ethnic group which had, in the last generation, settled and grown rich. After completing his education he decided on a military career and joined the French Army. He rose through the ranks, serving with distinction in the Second World War, and he attained the rank of lieutenant-colonel before leaving the service, after being badly wounded and losing a leg.

M. Bekkai

On leaving the French Army he became the Pasha of Sefrou, a position he held until 1953, when he resigned in protest against the deposition and exile of Sultan Mohammed V (q.v.) by the French Government. At this time Bekkai, an independent nationalist, became increasingly involved in his country's politics. His unswerving loyalty to the Sultan caused him to play a leading role as the Sultan's representative in the subsequent negotiations with the French.

A temporary Council of the Throne was established on 15 October 1955 with Bekkai as one of its members, and although this was dissolved on 2 November 1955 in preparation for Mohammed V's triumphant return to Morocco, it indicated the growing trend that the legitimist and moderate policies put forward by Bekkai were coming to the fore in the country.

On 7 December 1955, three weeks after the Sultan's return, a government of national unity was formed, with Bekkai as Prime Minister and the twenty ministerial posts being shared between the various Moroccan political parties. The political parties had their differences over many issues, but open disagreements were kept to a minimum while the independence negotiations were in progress.

The independence talks began early in 1956, and on 2 March 1956 Bekkai and the French Foreign Minister, M. Pineau, signed an agreement under which the French Government recognised the independence and territorial integrity of Morocco. Bekkai, who believed in co-operation with the French, signed protocols for co-operation in economic, technical and defence matters.

One of the early problems of independent Morocco was the establishment of an effective army and, shortly after independence, Bekkai established a commission for military discussions. After a long working session, a Ministry of National Defence was formed and the commission was adjourned, although Bekkai, along with the Ministers of Defence and the Interior, was among the members of the newly established High Committee of National Defence.

By the summer of 1956 however, the differences between members of the Cabinet were beginning to emerge, and a bitter political antagonism arose between ministers of the Istiqlal Party and the Democratic Istiqlal Party, with Bekkai, an independent,

caught in the middle. The situation deteriorated and on 10 August Bekkai talked openly
of resigning. The Sultan intervened and
insisted that he should remain in the government until the preparations for electing a
National Assembly were complete. In October 1956 a new government was formed
without representatives from the Democratic Istiqlal Party and Bekkai remained Prime
Minister.

The following eighteen months were
difficult for Bekkai as no satisfactory working relationship developed between the Istiqlal Party and Mohammed V and he often had
to act as a buffer between these two sides.
Political rivalry grew and on 16 April 1958
Bekkai resigned as Prime Minister after
supporting a declaration which was both in
favour of free political association and
against his government's ban on the Popular
Movement, an action which caused all ministers belonging to the Istiqlal Party to resign.

On 26 May 1960 a new government
was sworn in and Bekkai became Minister of
the Interior, a position he held until his
death on 12 April 1961 following a heart
attack.■

H. Belkhodja

Belkhodja, H. (1916-81)

BELKHODJA, Hassan (1916-81).

TUNISIAN diplomat and banker, who
held numerous political posts and wielded considerable behind-the-scenes influence
over President Habib Bourguiba. In his
youth he joined Bourguiba's Neo-Destour
Party, which was to lead the country to
independence. He was the Neo-Destour representative in Paris for some time, with
Mohamed Masmoudi, and was involved in
the independence talks with the French
government.

Born at Ras Jebel in the Bizerta
region on 10 March 1916, he attended the
Lycée Carnot in Tunis and then went to
Paris for university studies, obtaining a
Doctorate in Law in 1950. He was president
of the North African Moslem Students'
Association in France (AEMNA).

On his return to Tunisia, Hassan
Belkhodja was for a long time close to Salah

Ben Youssef (q.v.), then Bourguiba's com-
rade but later his rival. When Ben Youssef
was dismissed with other members of the
Chenik government by the French in 1952,
he escaped from France to Belgium in
Belkhodja's car. Later when Bourguiba and
Ben Youssef clashed over progress towards
self-government and then independence,
Belhodja backed Bourguiba. After independence in 1956 he was Tunisia's ambassador to
France. When in 1958, relations between
France and Tunisia were severed because of
the French air raid on Sakhiet (a response to
Tunisia's aid to the Algerian *Front de
Libération Nationale* (FLN) fighting against
French rule), Belkhodja returned to Tunisia.
He was accused of conspiracy, but an inquiry
cleared him. For a time he served as ambassador to Spain. Then, returning to Tunisia,
from 1959 he concentrated his efforts on the
economy of the country, in a number of ways.
Having always been interested in agriculture, he developed the idea of a National
Agricultural Bank, and proceeded to found
it in 1959 and served as its Director for

several years. He also founded the *Société Tunisienne de l'Industrie Laitière* for the dairy industry.

Hassan Belhodja was always on close terms with Bourguiba, and thus had important political influence. Having first collaborated with the Minister of Economic Affairs, Ahmed Ben Salah in the 1960s, he came to disagree with Ben Salah's economic policies, centred on compulsory cooperatives for agriculture (i.e. collectivisation). When World Bank representatives criticised the way in which the development of cooperatives, for which the Bank had provided aid, had proceeded, Belkhodja and others saw that the President knew of their report. In 1969 the powerful Ben Salah fell. In November of that year Hassan Belkhodja became Minister of Economic Affairs, but he was soon removed from that post in 1970 by the new Prime Minister, Hedi Nouira.

Soon afterwards, however, he became Chairman and Director-General of Tunisia's major bank, the *Société Tunisienne de Banques* (STB). He remained an important behind-the-scenes figure in politics, and in 1974 returned to ministerial office, first as Minister of Agriculture. Later he was Minister of Transport and then, from April 1980 to April 1981, Foreign Minister. After that short spell he left the government but was re-elected in April 1981 to the *Parti Socialiste Destourien* (PSD, former Neo-Destour) political bureau. He returned to the directorship of the STB, but only for a short time for on 29 November 1981 he died of a heart attack. ■

beginning of the nineteenth century. After primary education in Sokoto, he attended Katsina Higher College where he was a contemporary of Sir Abubakar Tafawa Balewa (q.v.), Nigeria's first Prime Minister. For three years he taught at Sokoto Middle

Sir Ahmadu Bello

Bello, A. (1909-66)

BELLO, Alhaji Sir Ahmadu (1909-66).

NIGERIAN statesman, the Sardauna of Sokoto, and the first Premier of Northern Nigeria. As leader of the Northern People's Congress (NPC) he wielded enormous influence on national politics in the fifties and early sixties.

He was born on 12 June 1909 in Rabbah, near Sokoto. His father Ibrahim, the chief of Rabbah, was a grandson of Usman dan Fodio (q.v.), the Fulani religious leader who founded the Sokoto Empire at the

School. Later, he became the district head of Rabbah. After a course in Local Government in England, he was appointed secretary to the Sokoto Native Authority.

Like many of his contemporaries among the small élite in Northern Nigeria, he quickly became involved with politics, participating actively in the rapid political changes that preceded Nigeria's independence. He was one of the founders of the Northern People's Congress (NPC) in 1949. His aristocratic background (the Sardauna is a traditional title which means war leader) combined with his powerful personalilty made him an easy choice for the leadership of the party. He was successively regional Minister of Works, of Local Government and

Community Development. In 1954 he was appointed the first Premier of Northern Nigeria. By that time, the fact that his party controlled the vast and dominant Northern Region had made him the most powerful political figure in Nigeria. Imperious in manner and gifted with a keen political sense, Sir Ahmadu was to dominate Nigeria's political life until his death on 15 January 1966.

Although his predominant image is one of a feudal Moslem religious leader, he was really first and foremost a politician. His conservatism and near-ostentatious attention to religion were carefully cultivated attitudes calculated to appeal to the realities of the Northern Nigeria of his time. His personal private life and the basic enlightenment of his policies on education and industrialisation in the North did not reveal a man opposed to change. By temperament a natural leader, born into a ruling family, he was ambitious for power. The dominance of the North in the old federation left the seat of power in Nigeria in Kaduna, the North's capital. The Sardauna knew this and preferred to keep direct personal control of the North. "I would rather be called the Sultan of Sokoto than the president of Nigeria," he was quoted as saying as late as 1965. He was said to hope to succeed his relative, Sultan Abubakar.

As the leader of the NPC, which controlled the federal government from independence in 1960 until the military coup in 1966, it was normally his place to assume the post of federal Prime Minister. This he left to his deputy, Sir Abubakar Tafawa Balewa, over whose activities in Lagos he exercised considerable influence. Personally charming, Sir Ahmadu was admired by many, feared by many more and respected by all. His attachment to the old North, however, and his undisguised attempt to use that Region as a base for controlling the whole of Nigeria made him unpopular in the rest of the country. He had many opponents in the North also – in Kano province, among the Tivs, etc. – although these were repressed harshly.

The assassination of this gifted and certainly most forceful Nigerian politician of his time was a direct attempt to dislodge a man whose grip on the lever of power appeared so strong that it led many idealistic progressives to think that it would be permanent as long as he lived. By killing him on 15 January 1966, the coup leader Major Nzeogwu (q.v.) ended Nigeria's First Republic.■

Bello, Sultan (1781-1837)

BELLO, Muhammadu, Sultan of Sokoto (1781-1837).

NIGERIAN traditional ruler, son and successor of Usman dan Fodio (q.v.) and the first holder of the title of Sultan of Sokoto, denoting sovereignty over all the area conquered by dan Fodio's Islamic *Jihad*. Bello was a leading colleague of his father in the *Jihad*. He fought in many of its major campaigns, including the one which defeated Gobir in 1808.

In 1809 Shehu Usman dan Fodio made a division of the territory conquered by the *Jihad*, with the western part assigned to his brother Abdullahi and the eastern part to Bello. Bello established his headquarters at Sokoto and dan Fodio moved there about 1814.

Sultan M. Bello

In April 1817, on his death, Usman dan Fodio left the supremacy over the empire, and the title *Sarkin Musulmi*, Commander of the Faithful, to Bello. This angered Abdullahi who considered that by Fulani tradition he should have succeeded his brother. But Bello was able to assert his authority, he adopted the title of Sultan. In 1822, Sultan Bello built an alternative capital, Wurno, also erected as a bastion against the formidable Tuareg to the north, his fondness for Wurno earned him the name of Mai Wurno.

Revolts against Sultan Bello's rule began very early and continued for much of his reign. He organised eleven expeditions against Kebbi, whose king was eventually killed in 1831. A major expedition led to the defeat and death of the claimants to the thrones of Gobir and Katsina (the latter being based at Maradi) at the battle of Gawakuke near Rabbah, possibly in 1835.

While Sultan Bello also made his mark as a scholar, theologian and writer, he continued his father's drive to reform government, law and society on Islamic lines and destroy remnants of paganism. He took a particular interest in the Sharia, Islamic law, and the Sharia courts and the enforcement of justice. His reputation as a scholar matched that of his father as was noted by the visiting British traveller Clapperton in the 1820s. He wrote over eighty known publications and also poems in praise of the Prophet Mohammed and the *Jihad*. His most famous work is the *Infaq el-maisuri*, a historical work on the area eventually ruled by him, dealing especially with the *Jihad*.

Sultan Bello died in 1837 and was buried at Wurno. He was succeeded by his brother Abubakar Atiku and then his (Bello's) son, Aliyu Baba, who reigned from 1842 until 1859. ■

Ben Ammar, T. (1885-1985)

BEN AMMAR, Tahar (1885-1985).

TUNISIAN nationalist and agricultural reformer, Tahar Ben Ammar held office as premier in the period prior to Tunisia's independence from France. He was the one who signed the agreement protocol on 20 March 1956 for Tunisia's accession to independence. Well before becoming Prime Minister, he was known as a champion of the Tunisian peasant whose life he did a lot to improve. He rescued him from the claws of usurers, being the force behind the creation of credit agencies, especially the *"Caisse foncière"* (Land Bank) which at the time enabled 30,000 Tunisians to stay as owners of their lands. Again later, on his initiative, the *Office national des Céréales* was created. And it was thanks to him that Tunisians began to be admitted to the *Ecole coloniale d'Agriculture*, and that land which had been given to French settlers were in part restituted to them.

Ben Ammar was born in Tunis on 25 November 1885, the son of a middle-class family with landed property. After studying at the Carnot School, he turned to agriculture and was among the first to use modern equipment in that area. He became himself one of the country's biggest landowners and was president of the Tunisian Chamber of Agriculture from 1928 for several years.

Ben Ammar entered politics just before World War I (1914-1919). He joined the Destour Nationalist Party in 1920, but left it in 1924 due to internal quarrels. He became a member of the Consultative Conference which, in 1922, became the Grand Council of Tunis. He was elected President of the Tunisian section of that Council a number of times, the last time being in December 1951.

Though a known friend of France, Ben Ammar was an outspoken advocate of internal self-government for Tunisia. In 1945 in Algiers he put forward to General de Gaulle of France a formula for self-government in Tunisia, which he had already defended with the French Resident General. That same year when Bourguiba and other leaders of the Neo-Destour were arrested, the whole country flared up and Ben Ammar succeeded in getting a commission of inquiry established. Edgar Faure entrusted this to his then Minister of State, François Mitterand, who was in charge of the Tunisian question, and the report advised on the granting of internal autonomy. Negotiations followed and an agreement was reached which was signed by T. Ben Ammar. But this did not go through when E. Faure's government fell from power. Ben Ammar did not give up; in May 1952, he renewed the demand for autonomy to E. Faure's successor, Pinay.

In the summer of 1952, in Ben Ammar's home outside Tunis, the leaders of the Neo and old Destour parties gathered to discuss the reforms proposed by France and decided to reject the "packet", and because of this Ben Ammar's life was in danger for some time from those in favour of it. Then de Gaulle met Ben Ammar and there followed a new

T. Ben Ammar

series of proposals by the French Government. And so, not surprisingly, he was one of the first men requested by the Bey to become a member of the Commission of Forty.

On 2 August 1952, the Bey of Tunis, Sidi Mohammed el Amin, charged Tahar Ben Ammar with the task of forming a new Tunisian Government. He was then nearly 70 and until this appointment as Premier, had held no public position for some time though he had acted as a representative of the Neo-Destour party in the absence of its arrested and exiled leaders. He had, moreover, often been useful behind the scenes and was one of those who helped most to solve the

deadlock with France, taking a prominent position in favour of the nationalists.

As Premier of the first Tunisian regime he was empowered to negotiate with France for self-government and had consultations with the Minister for Tunisian and Moroccan Affairs, which led to Tunisia being granted home rule. But it was nearly two years later in July 1954 that the newly formed French government led by Pierre Mendes France offered internal autonomy for Tunisia, with France retaining responsibility for defence and foreign affairs. The French proposals were accepted and in August 1954 a new Tunisian Government headed by Ben Ammar was formed. He held office until March 1956 when he signed the independence agreement with France.

Ben Ammar, no longer young, led a quiet life after that, until his death on 10 May 1985 at his home in Tunis.■

Ben Badis, A. (1889-1940)

BEN BADIS, Abd-el-Hamid (1889-1940).

ALGERIAN religious leader and reformer. He came from a prominent Moslem family in Constantine. He studied at the famous Islamic university in Tunis, Zaitouna, and later went on the pilgrimage to Mecca and spent some months in Egypt. He was influenced by the Egyptian preacher of Islamic reform, Mohammed Abduh (q.v.), and others with similar ideas.

Back in Algeria he began teaching at Constantine in 1914. Besides being a popular preacher, he was a poet and hymn writer. His concern for the reform of Islam and the betterment of the Moslems' position led him to start on 2 July 1925 the newspaper *el-Mountaqid*. This expressed his ideas, which were widely supported and which inevitably involved protest against the French settlers who had oppressed the Moslem Algerians for a century. Ben Badis also attacked the *Marabouts*, religious leaders who claimed special holiness and even occult and magical powers, and who, so the reformers said, led Moslems into superstition contrary to true Islam. The French who approved the *Marabouts*, saw the Islamic conflict as threatening France's hold over the Moslem Algerians.

Thus Ben Badis was a nationalist, and was seen as such by the French, who banned *el-Mountaqid* after its 18th issue. A new journal, almost identical, was immediately started, *El-Chihab*, and this continued until 1939 to give expression to the ideas of the

Ben Badis

growing movement for reform headed by Ben Badis.

On 5 May 1931 Ben Badis formed the *Association des Oulemas Musulmans Algériens*. This organisation of *oulemas* (teachers) was committed to reform and became an influential representative body for Moslem Algerians. It was the force behind the popular unrest in 1934/5, but despite severe harassment it was able to hold a congress at Algiers in September 1935. Then, with more freedom accorded by the 1936 Popular Front government in France, the first Algerian Moslem Congress was held in Algiers on 7 June 1936, organised principally by the *oulemas*.

Ben Badis's association was by now a leading nationalist organisation. Its followers' slogan was "Algeria is my country, Arabic is my language, Islam is my religion". In mosques and Moslem schools its influence spread far. Ben Badis was disappointed that his collaboration in late 1930s with other nationalist leaders did not materialise in reforms by the Popular Front government of France.

Ben Badis died on 16 April 1940. His successor, Sheikh Bachir Ibrahimi (1889-1965), led the *oulemas'* association into the era of the war for independence. ∎

Ben Barka, M. (1920-65)

BEN BARKA, el-Mehdi (1920-65).

MOROCCAN politician. Born in Rabat in 1920, he was active in the 1930s nationalist reaction against French colonialism while he was still at school. He was first a member of Morocco's first political movement, the *Comité d'Action Marocaine*, and later joined the newly formed Istiqlal (Independence) Party in 1944. The Istiqlal Party, under the leadership of Allal el-Fassi (q.v.), brought together intellectuals, trade unionists and religious leaders who signed the Istiqlal Manifesto that demanded an end to the Protectorate Agreement. Ben Barka was among the signatories, an action for which he was imprisoned.

Following his release he was made secretary of the Rabat branch of the Istiqlal and was able to build the organisation into a mass movement. When the party's activities were suspended by the French authorities, and King Mohammed V (q.v.) exiled to Madagascar, Ben Barka was banished to southern Morocco, but he was allowed to participate in the negotiations that led to the Sultan's return in 1955. He became President of independent Morocco's Consultative Assembly in 1956 and held the office, in addition to the post of political director of the party's weekly newspaper *El-Istiqlal*, until 1959, when he resigned from the Istiqlal Party Directorate over major ideological differences with the relatively more conservative elements in the party. He headed a rival faction, which in September 1959 became a new party, the *Union Nationale des Forces Populaires* (UNFP), that grouped all dissident movements in parliament into an opposition of strength. As leader of the UNFP he continued his criticism of the policies of Abdallah Ibrahim's government, which received the support of King Mohammed V, calling for constitutional reforms.

Ben Barka

Outside Morocco, Ben Barka's reputation had grown considerably, especially among the progressive Arab states and the nationalist African countries. In January 1960 he led the UNFP delegation to the Second All African Peoples' Conference held in Tunis, and the following April he attended the Afro-Asian Solidarity Conference that took place in Conakry. He fled to Paris in January 1961, following disagreements with King Hassan. He returned home a year later and successfully contested elections to the National Assembly. But soon Ben Barka fled Morocco again, following announcement of a plot against the King. Back in Paris, he remained external leader of the UNFP. In October 1965 he was kidnapped and presumably murdered in the French capital. A French court charged General Mohammed Oufkir (q.v.), who was then Morocco's Minister of the Interior, and a former head of

security, with complicity in Ben Barka's disappearance, and sentenced him *in absentia.* ■

Ben El-Mehdi, M.H. (1911-84)

BEN EL-MEHDI, Prince Moulay Hassan (1911-84).

Moroccan nationalist, firm supporter of the monarchy who was instrumental in the return of Mohammed V (q.v.) to the Moroccan throne and Morocco's independence in 1956. A cousin of King Hassan II and a career diplomat, he was governor of the Bank of Morocco when he died in November 1984.

Born in Fez in the Zerbtana district in 1911, Prince Moulay Hassan Ben El-Mehdi was educated in Arabic as well as in Spanish and his teacher was the famous Aleme Mohamed Daoud. His father Moulay El-Mehdi was appointed Khalifa at Tetouan in the "Spanish zone" of influence in Morocco following the Franco-Spanish accord of 1904 on the division of Morocco, and the application of the 27 November 1912 convention when Morocco became a Protectorate of France; Prince Moulay Hassan accompanied him there. After his father's death in 1923, the post remained vacant till 1926 when Ben El-Mehdi was appointed Khalifa at the age of 15, not only of the northern zone but of all the regions which fell under the Spanish administration, Ifni, Ait Baamrane, Tarfaya and the Saharan provinces. The 1912 convention meant that Spain now received her zones of influence in Morocco from France as the 'protecting power' and not from the Sultan.

Ben El-Mehdi lent his support to the nationalist movement that began to be felt in the Spanish occupied territory in the 1930s, at first as a supporter of the *Comité d'Action Marocaine* (until 1934), then of the *Hizb Al-Islah* (The Reformist Party) led by Abdelkhalek Torres, which later demanded an end to the Protectorate.

Ben El-Mehdi remained loyal to His Majesty Mohammed V (q.v.), Sultan of Morocco from 1927 to 1953 and again in 1956, who in fact supported the nationalist movement.

So when the latter was forced into exile to Europe in 1953, he corresponded secretly with him and was after that in permanent contact, resisting all pressures by the authorities to join a meeting of all the Caids in 1954 because he saw it as a means of perpetuating Morocco's division. Thus Tetouan under his leadership became the headquarters of political and military resistance and the refuge of nationalists. Nationalist fervour ran high with the exile of Mohammed Ibn Yusuf (Mohammed V), and there were outbreaks of violence throughout Morocco in 1954-55.

In 1955 Sultan Mohammed Ibn Arafa renounced the throne and withdrew to Tangiers, and Mohammed V returned as the legitimate Sultan and Morocco became independent in 1956. Tetouan reverted to provincial capital status under a royal governor, and Ben El-Mehdi was appointed his country's ambassador to Great Britain in 1957. He held this post until 1965 when he was accredited to Rome. In 1967 he became director-general of the *Banque Nationale pour le Développement Economique*. Later, in 1969, King Hassan II appointed him Governor of the Bank of Morocco, which position he occupied until his death in November 1984. ■

Benjamin, S. (1945-67)

BENJAMIN, Seti (1945-67).

TANZANIAN political activist in the TANU Youth League (TYL), who died during the 1967 campaign in support of the newly announced Arusha Declaration.

Benjamin was born in July 1945 in the Singida region in central Tanzania where he had part of his elementary education, his family having moved north to settle at Usa River in Arusha when he was only ten years old. There he continued his education, becoming a head prefect at his school, but his ambitions for education were frustrated when he was not selected to proceed to Standard V. He developed early interest in the politics of TANU which centred on gaining independence for Tanganyika. The party had just been reconstructed, in 1954, from the Tanganyika African Association

(TAA) by Julius Nyerere, as an effective political organisation whose aims were to demand independence from Britain. Having defined its goals the party sought to facilitate the demands through mass political mobilisation of the people. To that effect the

S. Benjamin

TYL was created, and Benjamin, like most of the Tanzanian youth then, became a member of the new youth wing. He joined the Usa River branch and soon rose to become its leader.

The TYL's purpose was to strengthen the activities of the parent organisation through political rallies, marches, lectures and other general duties that would promote TANU's objectives. In independent Tanzania the TYL developed into a mass movement playing effective role in various institutions like the army and schools where, for an example, TYL cells carry out political education while serving as a link between the institutions and the public on the one hand

and between the bodies and the Party on the other. Its members, who constitute a great part of the Tanzanian People's Defence Force (TPDF), were seen as reservists for the armed forces during emergencies.

Benjamin was leader of the TYL branch in Arusha, where he also worked as a messenger in the regional office of Tanzania's ruling party, the Tanganyika (later Tanzania) African National Union (TANU), which became the Chama Cha Mapinduzi (CCM, Party of the Revolution) in February 1977 following a merger with Zanzibar's Afro-Shirazi Party.

Following the Arusha Declaration in February 1967, the TYL embarked on developing a spirit of support for the newly proclaimed socialist ideology and organised several marches from various parts of Tanzania to express their solidarity with the Party. It was in the process of one of these marches that Benjamin, who was leading the Arusha team of TYL marchers from Arusha to Dar-es-Salaam, fell ill. He was taken to the Mawenzi Hospital in Moshi where he died in mid-February 1967. ■

Ben M'hidi, M.L. (c.1922-57)

BEN M'HIDI, Mohammed Larbi (c.1922-57).

ALGERIAN politician whose ideas shaped the theoretical framework for the Revolution against the French. A Berber by origin, he was an actor for some time, playing minor roles in Algiers radio plays, before joining the opposition to French rule. He joined the *Organisation Spéciale* started by members of the *Mouvement pour le Triomphe des Libertés Démocratiques* (MTLD) and operating as a small underground movement against French rule in the early 1950s.

Ben M'hidi was one of the nine members of the *Comité Révolutionnaire pour l'Unité et l'Action* (CRUA) which launched the guerrilla war against French rule on 1 November 1954. The *Front de Libération Nationale* (FLN) which emerged from the CRUA made him commander of *Wilaya* 5 (guerrilla military district), in the Oran area. His position as a leader of the FLN was

confirmed by his election to its executive committee after the Soumman Congress of 1956. He was the main theorist of the Algerian revolution and an ardent idealistic believer in it.

In 1956 he and FLN colleagues launched an urban guerrilla campaign in Algiers using indiscriminate tactics which Ben M'hidi considered regrettable but justified. The French forces counter-attacked in the famous "Battle of Algiers". Repression was entrusted mainly to paratroopers who used torture on a massive scale. In February 1957 Ben M'hidi, political leader of the campaign, was arrested. In March 1957 the authorities alleged that he had committed suicide. In fact he was killed by the French – shot, according to one account, by an unknown authority's order. After Algeria became independent in 1962 the rue d'Isly, one of the smartest streets in Algiers, was renamed after Ben M'hidi. ■

Benson, S.A. (1816-65)

BENSON, Stephen Allen (1816-65).

LIBERIAN statesman. He was born at Cambridge, Dorchester County, Maryland, USA, in March 1816. His family decided to return to Africa to start a new life when he was six years old. They were among the early settlers in Liberia, arriving at Monrovia in August 1822. On 11 November 1822, about three months after their arrival, the Monrovia settlement was attacked by indigenous chiefs hostile to the settlers. His eldest brother was killed along with one of his sisters, and his father was injured in the arm. Benson was one of seven children captured during the attack, and was taken off to King Bromley's Town, one of the indigenous settlements.

He remained a prisoner of war in this village (later to become the Virginia settlement) for four months, during which time he was treated very well and cured of fever from which he had been suffering at the time of his captivity. After negotiations between the chiefs and the settlers, he was returned safely to the Monrovia settlement with the other children.

Up to 1830 he was educated at schools operated by the American Colonisation Society, while also helping his mother nurse his father back to health, and, after her death in 1825, assisting with the responsibilities of caring for his younger brothers and sisters.

S.A. Benson

When he left school he worked for a period with his father who was responsible for purchasing cattle, palm oil and rice in Grand Bassa for the settlers in Monrovia.

In 1832 Benson joined the Liberian Militia in its military campaign against King Willey and his men who had repeatedly recaptured and sold into slavery people who had previously been freed. During the campaign Benson was placed at the head of a company.

He then moved to Monrovia, working in the mercantile business, and through business connections with Joseph Jenkins Roberts' (q.v.) trading company, a close friendship began between these two men. In 1835, following the Bassa Grove killings when his father narrowly escaped death, Benson joined the volunteers who went to help the Grand Bassa settlers. When the trouble was over Benson remained in Grand Bassa working with his father. They built up an extensive farm and a flourishing business,

particularly in coffee and palm oil which they exported in their own ships.

In 1838 trouble once again flared up in Grand Bassa and Benson served as a first-lieutenant in the militia. In May 1839 Benson was chosen to convey the offer of peace negotiations which were shortly followed by a peace treaty.

Benson became a member of the Colonial Council in 1842 and while he served on this body he worked closely with Joseph Jenkins Roberts, then governor, on preparations for the formal removal of the American Colonisation Society's control over Liberia to clear the way for independence. He was appointed judge of the Court of Quarter Sessions and Admiralty in Grand Bassa County in 1848, and also became general superintendent of the county for a while.

In the May 1853 elections he was elected Vice-President of Liberia and his popularity with the people enabled him to be elected President of the Republic in May 1855. By the time of his inauguration in January 1856, war had broken out in Sinoe. He immediately organised and led a group of soldiers to the area. However, pressing duties soon forced him to relinquish command of the soldiers and return to Monrovia. Trouble also broke out in Cape Mount, and on 4 May 1856 he travelled to the area, successfully resolving the problem in two weeks.

He then returned to Sinoe where on 23 June 1856 he signed a peace treaty with the indigenous chiefs at Greenville. The successful conclusion of the Sinoe and the Cape Mount problems increased the area of the Republic by several hundred square miles. Later in the year, war broke out in Maryland, and the Government sent troops there. In 1857 Maryland decided to join the Republic, almost doubling the size of Liberia.

Once the internal problems were resolved, he was able to attend to other matters. During his administration he sponsored the exploration and settlement of the interior of the country, the expansion of education, agricultural development and improved internal and external relations. Under his encouragement many schools were established, particularly by the missions.

He also greatly encouraged the development of agriculture and agricultural processing industries, realising as a farmer himself that this sector would largely provide the wealth for the country. On 14 December 1857 he opened the first National Fair, later to become an annual event, designed to stimulate agricultural activities. Each successive National Fair showed a growth in farms and their productivity, with agricultural exports to the USA and Europe during 1859 being greater than the total exported since the settlement of Liberia.

Despite the increase in the prosperity of the country, Benson's presidency was beset by difficulties caused by encroachment on Liberian territory. A British trader established a trading station east of the Sewa River in 1860 and refused to pay customs duties on the trade. In retaliation the Liberian Government seized two of his schooners, but had to give them up when the British governor in neighbouring Sierra Leone sent gunboats to retrieve them.

Benson then travelled to London to try and resolve the problem, but only received vague commitments from the British government. The trader's bad treatment of the local Vai people caused them to rise up against him, and the Sierra Leonean governor claimed a protectorate of the area, stretching between the Mano and Sewa Rivers, stating that Liberia could not maintain order there.

After serving three two-year terms as President, Benson returned to his farm and business in Grand Bassa where he died on 24 January 1865.■

M.S. Ben Yahia

Ben Yahia, M.S. (1934-82)

BEN YAHIA, Mohammed Seddick (1934-82).

ALGERIAN politician and diplomat; he was appointed his country's first Ambassador to Moscow in 1963. One of the most skilful and respected politicians in Algeria, he became Foreign Minister in 1979. Ben Yahia conducted Algeria's foreign policy skilfully, maintaining cordial relations with Morocco, Tunisia, and Libya.

He was born at Djidjelli in lower Kabylia on the Mediterranean coast in 1934, twenty years before the *Front de Libération Nationale* (FLN) emerged as the central force behind Algerian nationalism to lead the war

against French colonialism. After studying law at the University of Algiers, he joined the FLN. It was while at university that Ben Yahia became involved in nationalist politics, becoming secretary-general of the General Union of Algerian Moslem Students that had been created by the FLN to support its struggle through diplomatic and non-military means. In 1956, he joined the parent organisation and was posted at the age of 22 to the Far East as its diplomatic representative based in Djakarta, Indonesia.

Three years later Ben Yahia became a member of the *Conseil National de la Révolution Algérienne* (CNRA), the wartime parliamentary body which the FLN created at its Soummam Valley Congress. He was given the influential post of Secretary-General in the provisional government based at Cairo. He was thus an important factor in both the Tripoli Charter, which he helped to draft, and the Evian accord with the French, that led to Algeria's independence on 3 July 1962.

He was close to both Ben Bella and Houari Boumedienne (q.v.), the political and military leaders of the FLN respectively. Under the former's administration, he was posted to Moscow as Algeria's first Ambassador in 1963, but two years later he supported Boumedienne's coup d'état, and was posted to London but never took up the post owing to a diplomatic break between his country and Britain. He was named Minister of Information in 1966, then successively Minister of Higher Education and Minister of Finance.

A leading intellectual, noted for his great sense of good political judgement, Ben Yahia was a committed socialist and was one of the architects of the Algerian National Charter which appeared in 1977. In 1979 he was made Minister of Foreign Affairs, taking control of the Foreign Ministry after its 16 years under Abdelaziz Bouteflika, with remarkable skill.

He was held in high esteem in the Arab World in general, for helping to shape an Arab strategy in response to the existence and policies of Israel and, in 1981, he won international acclaim for the role he played in securing the release of the American hostages taken by Iran after the seizure of the US Embassy in Teheran 1980.

Ben Yahia died on 3 May 1982, in a mysterious plane crash during a visit to Iran where he was mediating in the war between that country and Iraq.■

Ben Youssef, S. (1908-61)

BEN YOUSSEF, Salah (1908-61).

TUNISIAN politician, the first Minister of Justice in Muhammad Chenik's 1950 government. Born on the island of Djerba in 1908, in his youth he joined the Neo-Destour founded, as a breakaway from the Destour nationalist party, by Habib Bourguiba and others in 1934.

He rose to prominence as secretary-general of the Neo-Destour, and its real leader in the absence of Bourguiba, in the late 1940s. A militant nationalist and popular orator, he aroused mass support for the campaign to end French rule. The Neo-Destour under his effective leadership (1945-9), and the *Union Générale des Travailleurs*

Tunisiens (UGTT) whose leaders (including Farhat Hached, q.v.) were closely allied with him, were committed to an early end of the French "Protectorate." The dynamic Ben Youssef was thought to be a possible rival to Bourguiba, but he visited the party's leader in Egypt, and later submitted to his leader-

S. Ben Youssef

ship on his return to Tunisia in 1949. Ben Youssef virtually created the *Union Tunisienne de l'Artisanat et du Commerce* (UTAC) and the *Union Générale des Agriculteurs Tunisiens* (UGAT), traders' and farmers' organisations linked to the Neo-Destour.

In 1950 the French authorities conceded some self-government and a government was formed under Muhammad Chenik; Ben Youssef was Minister of Justice. Talks between the government and the French on more concessions broke down, and early in 1952 the French began a policy of repression directed at the Neo-Destour. Before long they arrested many members of the Tunisian government. Ben Youssef, in Paris at the time after presenting a protest to the United Nations, escaped to avoid arrest, and went to

Egypt. He stayed there, working with other exiled nationalists from French North Africa, while the Neo-Destour opposition to France led to limited guerrilla war.

In 1954 France agreed to more autonomy. Ben Youssef returned in 1955, but immediately clashed with his colleageus in the Neo-Destour Party. Most of these, led by Bourguiba, favoured co-operation with France to progress eventually from self-government to independence. Ben Youssef, more pan-Arabist and less pro-French in sympathy, favoured calling for immediate independence. A serious split in the nationalist party followed, with the leadership following Bourguiba while Ben Youssef was followed by the Djerba people (prominent in commerce), the urban youth in Tunis, and some Tunisian landowners and Moslem traditionalists.

Bourguiba organised concerted efforts to win over Ben Youssef's supporters, and with the help of the well-developed party machinery he succeeded. A congress of the party at Sfax in November 1955 led to a triumph for Bourguiba. Ben Youssef then tried to establish rival branches of the Neo-Destour. His supporters and Bourguiba's resorted to terrorism in late 1955, and from January 1956 some "Youssefists"were in the hills as guerrillas. He had many supporters still, but after the arrest of 120 prominent ones in late January Ben Youssef fled to Libya.

In March 1956 Tunisia became independent, but some guerrillas fought on. French troops which remained in the country launched an operation in the Matmata area before the last Youssefists surrendered in June 1956. Their leader went to Egypt, where for long President Nasser (q.v.) sympathised more with him than with Bourguiba. The Tunisian government feared for years that the Algerian FLN, which had large forces in Tunisia during its war with the French and had disagreements with Bourguiba might help Ben Youssef try to return. On 16 January 1957 he was sentenced to death. In 1958 Tunisia left the Arab League because he was allowed to stay in Egypt.

There was a meeting between Ben Youssef and Bourguiba in Switzerland in March 1961. On 12 August 1961, Salah Ben Youssef was murdered in a hotel in Frankfurt. He was said to have been enticed there by a telephone call; three suspects with Tunisian passports were mentioned. It was widely believed that the Bourguiba government had ordered the death of its main opponent. ∎

Biayenda, E. (1927-77)

BIAYENDA, Cardinal Emile (1927-77).

CONGOLESE clergyman, created cardinal by Pope Paul VI on 5 March 1973. He was ordained priest on 26 October 1958 and consecrated titular Archbishop of Garba on 17 May 1970. Biayenda became the Archbishop of Brazzaville on 14 July 1971, a post he held until his death. He was famous for his radical social views which he often expressed publicly.

Cardinal Emile Biayenda was a native of Mpangala, Vinza, in the north of the Congo where he was born in 1927. He attended the Catholic Mission School at Kindamba from 1937 to 1942 and between then and 1944 studied at the Mission of Boundji. In late 1944 he entered the minor

Cardinal E. Biayenda

seminary of St. Paul in Mbamou, proceeding in 1950 to the major seminary of Brazzaville where he completed his studies in 1959. Six years later he was sent to Europe for further studies at the University of Lyons in France where he read and obtained the Licentiate in Theology and Sociology in 1969.

After his ordination in October 1958, he served as vicar of the Parish of Santa Maria in Wenge from 1959 until March 1962, and then as parish priest of St. John Mary Vianney parish in Muleke between 1962 and July 1965. In May 1969, he was made parish priest of the Parish of the Holy Spirit in Mongali. On 18 February 1970 Biayenda was chosen by his confreres Vicar with the rank of bishop and responsibility for co-ordinating the works of the apostolate and the various diocesan commissions. In March 1970 he was nominated titular Archbishop of Garba and Coadjutor with the right of succession to Brazzaville. Just over a year later, after the death of Archbishop Théophile Mbemba, he became Archbishop of Brazzaville. Biayenda participated in the 1971 Synod of the Episcopal Conference and, in 1972, together with all other bishops of the Congo, sent a Pastoral Letter on the theme of development and the role of a Christian in the nation.

His views on various ecclesiastical and humanitarian issues were critical of the government of his country. In the 1960s such opposition from clergymen led to tension in the relations between the Church and the State. Consequently, Catholic-backed organisations were dissolved on government orders while mission schools were taken over and some church leaders were jailed, exiled or forced to operate clandestinely. During this period and the period after the subsequent change of government, Biayenda continued to speak critically against state injustices and persecution.

He was abducted and killed on the night of 22/23 March 1977. The following day Pope Paul VI announced the Cardinal's death at the Vatican, saying, "In making this most painful announcement to you, we ask you to join us to share all the sorrow resulting therefrom, and to pray God for the eternal repose of that elect soul of father and pastor, as well as the constructive pacification and concord of hearts and deeds in that nation so dear to us, and at present so much tormented".

The Pope sent a telegram to the Bishop of Fort Rousset and the dean of the Bishops of the Congo, Most Reverend Georges Singha, in which he expressed shock. "In this so grievous hour, ardently wishing that calm may return to your country, we ask God to welcome into his peace this zealous servant of the Gospel, to comfort his family, the members of the diocese of Brazzaville and the Church of the Congo, and we impart to you, in witness of our closeness in prayer and in trial, a special Apostolic Blessing," the Pope said. ■

Bikila, A. (1932-73)

BIKILA, Abebe (1932-73).

ETHIOPIAN athlete, his country's first Olympic champion and world record holder. Abebe Bikila was born in the Mout province in Ethiopia in 1932. Unknown outside his own country until the Rome Olympics in 1960, Abebe surmounted the lack of adequate training facilities with a strong will and determination to win. Abebe was a member of Emperor Haile Selassie's (q.v.) household guard, whose only sport then was football. The absence of track or field sports

A. Bikila

made his victory in the 1960 marathon in Rome a complete surprise as no one expected a serious challenger to come from Ethiopia.

In 1960 Abebe ran the gruelling marathon event in the record winning time of 2 hours, 15 minutes, 15.2 seconds. He gained his victory by pulling away barefoot in the last 1,000 metres in accordance with the advice of his coach to make his sprint effort late. He returned to Ethiopia to be honoured as his country's first Olympic champion and was promoted to the rank of corporal of the Imperial Guards.

On 21 October 1964, at the Tokyo Olympics, he broke his own record when he ran 2 hours, 12 minutes, 11.2 seconds. This time he was wearing warm-up shoes. On his victory salute lap at the end of the 26 miles and 385 yard race, he went through a series of acrobatics to the delight of the crowd. Bikila had won his second gold medal less than a month after he had had his appendix removed.

Bikila went to Mexico for the Games of 1968 but an ankle injury from which he had been suffering for much of the year forced him to drop out of the race after a few kilometres.

In 1969 Abebe was involved in a car accident which left him virtually paralysed. He also suffered multiple injuries including a broken neck and had to be flown to Stoke Mandeville Hospital in Britain for treatment. Later he founded the Ethiopian Paraplegic Sports Association and continued to participate in international paraplegic games such as archery and javelin throwing.

In 1972, the German Olympic Association specially invited Captain Abebe and made arrangements for him to be at the Munich Olympic Games.

On 25 October 1973 Bikila died of a brain haemorrhage. He was given a state funeral. He was survived by a wife and four children. ■

Biko, S. (1946-77)

BIKO, Stephen (1946-77).

SOUTH AFRICAN politician and founder/leader of the Black Consciousness movement. Stephen Biko was born on 18

S. Biko

December 1946 in King William's Town, Eastern Cape, South Africa. He attended the Brownlee Primary School for two years, followed by four years at the Charles Morgan Higher Primary School. He began his matriculation studies at the Lovedale Institute, but three months later it was closed down because of senior pupils' strikes and Biko went to the Marianhill Catholic Institute in Natal, where he matriculated in 1965.

Between 1966 and 1972 Biko studied medicine at the University of Natal. As his interest and involvement in politics grew he spent less and less time on his studies. He was one of the principal proponents of the Black Consciousness movement which emerged in South Africa in the later 1960s. Black Consciousness arose as an assertion of black identity in a society that denied it, and its leaders strove to harness the latent political power they had to effect change in the political system of South Africa.

Biko firmly believed that "black liberation" had to start with "black psychological self-reliance" and that as the consciousness of Africans increased, white liberals could not continue to act as spokesmen for the black population. He also believed that in South Africa it is impossible for a white person to put himself or herself into a black person's situation in the same way as it was impossible to have a true black spokesman in a white context. He did not reject white liberals as such, but considered that anyone opposing the system of apartheid was not automatically an ally. Biko did not believe that real black liberation could be won under a white liberal leadership who would inhibit the struggle with too gentle and inadequate solutions. The ideology of Black Consciousness was not racist but an attempt to adjust to the conditions of the society in which it operated. The myth that white is superior and black inferior in South Africa convinced Biko that the black population needed their own organisations to develop a group pride and feelings of humanity from which the psychological and physical oppression of the system could begin to be overcome. These views were bound to bring supporters and leaders of the movement into direct conflict with Nationalist Party policies.

As the Black Consciousness movement developed, Biko became one of the founders of the all-black South African Students' Organisation (SASO), the constitution of which was formally adopted at a conference at the University of the North in July 1969, with Biko as its first president. SASO aimed to develop the political self-reliance and solidarity of black students in the universities. A year later SASO broke its affiliations with the National Union of South African Students (NUSAS) while still technically recognising it as the national student organisation.

After the formation of SASO the Black Consciousness movement gained momentum, not only among students but also among other black people. Biko helped to found other Black Consciousness organisations, such as the Black Community Programmes, all-black sports bodies, and trust funds to provide assistance to families of political prisoners. In 1972 the Black People's Convention was established, a coalition of over 70 black organisations, with Steve Biko as its honorary president.

In the same year, Biko contributed to a volume entitled *Student Perspectives in South Africa*. This book was published in association with the Bailey Institute of Inter-racial Studies, but was later banned in South Africa. He had also written an essay, *Black Theology: The South African Voice*, published in London by C. Hurst and edited by Basil Moore.

Before his medical studies were completed, Biko was expelled from the University of Natal in August 1972. He then became a full-time organiser of the Black Community Programmes in Durban until a banning order was served on him in March 1973. Under this order his movements were restricted to King William's Town magisterial district; he was not allowed to speak to more than one person at a time, could not write publicly or be quoted, and was carefully watched by the Security Police.

While in King William's Town he registered for a correspondence course with the University of South Africa to study law, and during the next few years he passed a number of examinations. He also established Black Community Programmes in his restricted area and worked there as the executive director for the Eastern Cape until December 1975, when his banning restrictions were increased to prohibit him from doing this work.

Between 1974 and 1977, as well as being banned, Biko was detained four times, twice briefly, once for 101 days, and finally when he met his death. He was prosecuted five times in this period, with the charges ranging from traffic offences to breaking his banning restrictions and allegedly convincing witnesses to alter their sworn statements. He won all these cases, although he often found it difficult to raise the money to pay court costs and sometimes had to depend on the finances of the Black People's Convention.

On 19 August 1977, Biko was stopped at a Security Police roadblock near Grahamstown, outside his restricted area, and was arrested. He was taken to Port Elizabeth where he was detained without trial for questioning concerning his alleged involvement in the riots in Port Elizabeth, and drafting and distributing pamphlets inciting disorder and violence. It was alleged that during his detention, Biko was kept in chains so that he would not injure himself, and was not allowed exercise in the fresh air. On 7 September, he went into a coma following 22 hours of intensive interrogation, torture and beatings. In the following days he was examined by doctors who stated that, notwithstanding his case history, they found nothing seriously wrong with him. On 11 September, having noticed that Biko had been unable to eat or drink properly for five days, the Security Police decided to take him for treatment to Pretoria, 600 miles away. It was alleged that no ambulances were available. He was transported, still manacled and naked, in the back of a Land Rover on a pile of mats. He died on 12 September 1977 of a brain haemorrhage caused by head injuries sustained during his detention in police custody. A post-mortem report signed by four pathologists, one of whom was acting on behalf of the Biko family, also found that Biko had suffered injuries to his left ribs and had more than a dozen abrasions and bruises.

Although 30 years old when he died, Steve Biko was an undisputed leader of the Black Consciouness movement, and made a great impact, both in South Africa and abroad. He was quick thinking, articulate and intelligent and had great charisma. In spite of this he kept in the background, not wanting a leadership cult to grow up around him and detract from the struggle. He had an uncompromising contempt for the Nationalist Party policies but wanted to avoid violence if possible, fearing that this could engender bitterness that could affect the transition to a new system in South Africa. However, he was also realistic, accepting that violence could not be ruled out in future, as situations and circumstances changed. People and their welfare were important to him and this was reflected in his work for the Black Community Programmes and in his commitment to the Black Consciousness movement. ∎

Blaize, R.B.O. (1845-1904)

BLAIZE, Richard Beale Olamilege (1845-1904).

NIGERIAN businessman, one of the richest Africans in Lagos in the early 20th century. Born in Freetown, son of the merchant John Blaize (an important Creole

"recaptive"), he went to Lagos in 1862 and worked first as a printer for Robert Campbell, editor of the *Anglo-African*. In 1863 he started work for the government press of Lagos Colony, where he was head printer for twelve years. In 1875 he resigned from the government service to set up in private business.

He had a well-known store in Breadfruit Street in Lagos island, where he sold cloths with designs that had African motifs specially ordered by him and manufactured in Manchester, Britain. Soon his store was one of the biggest in the Colony. In 1886 it was moved, with his adjoining house, to the Marina. He joined the Lagos Chamber of Commerce in 1888 and was described by Governor Carter in 1896 as "undoubtedly the wealthiest native merchant in Lagos," worth about £150,000.

He bought a commercial press and from 1880 to 1883 ran the *Lagos Times and Gold Coast Colony Advertiser*. From 1883 to 1890 he owned the *Lagos Weekly Record*, edited by J.P. Jackson (q.v.), a Liberian, one of the early non-Nigerian nationalists who promoted Pan-Africanism from Lagos. The *Record* was constantly attacking the British authorities. Blaize himself had an independent mind and criticised the colonial government, and defended the interests of the Egbas in particular and Nigerians in general. Shortly before his death he visited Britain with the Alake of Abeokuta in 1904.

He married Emily Cole (died 1895). Their daughter Charlotte Olajumoke Blaize (1872-1952) married Dr. C. Obasa and was a businesswoman in Lagos. ∎

Blyden, E.W. (1832-1912)

BLYDEN, Edward Wilmot (1832-1912).

LIBERIAN educationist, politician, journalist and a very prolific Pan-Africanist writer noted for his beliefs and strong ideas about the "African Personality". He was born in Charlotte-Amalie, the capital of St. Thomas, one of the Virgin Islands in the West Indies, on 3 August 1832. Although his parents were born in the West Indies, the family originally descended from Eastern

Nigeria. His father was a tailor and his mother a school teacher who supplemented Blyden's primary school education with private studies at home. When he was ten years old the family moved to Venezuela where they lived for two years, returning to

E.W. Blyden

St. Thomas in 1844. During this period Blyden showed an early aptitude for languages, learning to speak fluent Spanish. On his return he continued his schooling while being apprenticed to a tailor.

His parents were deeply religious and all the family were members of the Dutch Reformed Church. In 1849 Blyden decided to join the ministry. The following year he went to the USA and applied for entrance to Rutgers' Theological College. He was refused admission because he was black, and following rejections on similar grounds from two other theological colleges he gave up. He was forced to leave the USA because of racial discrimination and the Fugitive Slave Law under which free men were sometimes captured as runaway slaves. As opportunities were very limited on St. Thomas, Blyden, who already had developed great pride in the

black race and its culture, decided to emigrate to Liberia. He sailed from Baltimore in December 1850, arriving in Monrovia on 26 January 1851.

After recovering from a bout of fever, he began working as a part-time clerk to a merchant, while continuing his education at the Presbyterian Alexander High School. He soon won a scholarship and was able to study full time.

At the same time he also became a correspondent for the only newspaper in the country at that time, the *Liberia Herald*, and his articles reflected his determination that the Republic should succeed. He also became a lay preacher in 1853, and in the same year, joined the Liberian Militia for an expedition to resolve problems with the indigenous Vai people. This was his first contact with the people of the interior and he came back impressed and eager to work towards the greater integration of the Republic.

In 1854 he became a teacher at the Alexander High School, where he was also principal on occasion. He was also active in public life, gaining the admiration and respect of leading Liberians. In 1855 he was appointed editor of the *Liberia Herald* by President Roberts (q.v.), a position he held for one year.

His belief in the potential of Liberia becoming the first great black republic gathered momentum and in 1856 he published a 33-page pamphlet entitled *A Voice from Bleeding Africa on Behalf of Her Exiled Children*. This was the first of many pamphlets that he published during his lifetime covering a variety of themes all of which reflected his deep commitments: to restore confidence, pride and self-respect to his race, and to overcome the low morale caused by years of slavery and humiliation; to disprove the myth of black inferiority that was propounded by whites to justify their oppression; to develop the "African Personality"; to rediscover black history and to correct misrepresentations in books on this subject; to preserve African customs, culture and institutions.

In later works he expanded on the theme that Christianity, because of its lack of regard for the values he extolled, had retarded the emergence of the "African Personality", while Islam, contrary to the views of the missionaries, had had the opposite effect. As well as pamphlets, he published articles expressing these ideas and appealing for an increase in emigration to Liberia. He did not believe that opportunities existed for different races to live together in harmony, and felt that it was preferable to emigrate and help build a black republic than to live in a society where one's existence was merely tolerated. He believed that the establishment of the Republic was the first pre-requisite for ensuring that the derogatory arguments against his race would be finally overcome.

Apart from being a prolific writer, he was also involved in many other activities. He was principal of the Alexander High School and a minister in the Presbyterian Church in 1858. His belief in the importance of education led him in March 1861 to be appointed educational commissioner to Britain and the USA. He visited both countries during 1861 and succeeded in raising funds for the establishment of a girls' school, as well as scholarships at Edinburgh University, Scotland, for two of his students. He himself was offered a scholarship for full time studies in England, but turned it down to return to Liberia.

However, he did not neglect his own studies whenever he found the time. In 1861 he was appointed professor of Greek and Latin at the newly-established Liberia College. He did not take up this position until the following year as his simultaneous appointment as commissioner to encourage emigration from the USA to Liberia caused him to travel again to America. However, his efforts were impeded by the outbreak of the American Civil War.

In 1863 he returned to Liberia and took up his position as professor of Classics at the Liberia College, a position he held until 1871. During this period he became involved in the growing conflict between blacks and people of mixed descent in Liberia. It was felt that the latter considered themselves to be superior to the former and had formed a ruling elite in the country which few blacks were allowed to penetrate.

After he became Secretary of State in 1864, he promoted the emigration of skilled blacks from Barbados, each new family being promised 25 acres. One boat arrived under his scheme (one of the passengers being Arthur Barclay (q.v.), a future President of Liberia), but opposition, especially from people of mixed descent, led to the scheme being finally dropped.

As Secretary of State he was also involved in the dispute with Britain over Liberia's boundaries with Sierra Leone. In 1866 he was forced to relinquish his post on the grounds that it was incompatible with his professorship at the Liberia College.

In May 1866 he bagan a tour of Lebanon, England, Gibraltar, Malta and Syria, where he remained for three months studying at the Syrian Protestant College to improve his knowledge of Arabic. On his return to Liberia he extended his course to include the study of Arabic so that the Republic would be better equipped to establish relations with the Moslem community of the country's interior.

By 1870, when his close friend Roye (q.v.) became President of the Republic, Blyden's unpopularity with the people of mixed descent had increased, particularly following an article that he wrote for the Smithsonian Institute Annual Report, entitled *Mixed Races of Liberia*. In May 1871 his opponents accused him of committing adultery with President Roye's wife. Public feeling was stirred up against him, forcing him to flee to Sierra Leone where he remained until 1873 when he was cleared of this charge. By this time his views on race had further developed, to the point where he believed that "miscegenation" was not only contrary to nature, but also led to the creation of a weak and immoral race. Blyden had himself married a wife of mixed-descent family in 1856, but over the years their relationship had deteriorated.

During his stay in Freetown he was appointed editor of the *Negro*, a new paper aimed at fostering racial awareness and solidarity. Between January and October 1873 he was also appointed government agent to the interior to help establish good relations with the indigenous people of Sierra Leone.

He returned to Liberia in 1873 and after turning down an offer of appointment as Secretary of State under President Roberts, he revisited the USA where he was awarded an honorary LLD degree by Lincoln University in Pennsylvania. He also tried to persuade the American Colonisation Society to only settle "pure" blacks in Liberia, and although he received a sympathetic response they did not want this view expressed publicly for political reasons.

In 1875 he once again became principal of the Alexander High School, holding this post until his appointment as Ambassador to

Britain in 1877. The Legislature was opposed to this appointment and would not grant a salary for it. Undeterred, he accepted the position. While in London he gained recognition for his literary works and became an honorary member of the Athenaeum, one of London's most exclusive clubs.

He was recalled in 1878 and was appointed president of Liberia College in 1880. This was a position he had long wanted because he hoped to widen the scope of the College and transform it into a school of learning which would attract blacks from all over the world. However, although he managed to stimulate new life and interest in the College, his efforts were impeded by lack of funds and interrupted by his appointment as Minister of the Interior in 1880.

As Minister of the Interior he was once again involved in the boundary dispute between Liberia and Sierra Leone, and the treaty he negotiated ceding part of the North West Liberia to Sierra Leone was not ratified by the Senate. He did not attach much importance to the loss of this territory because he believed that the British protectorate over Sierra Leone would eventually lapse when the two countries merged into one large black republic.

However, there was fierce opposition to his handling of this matter and in 1882 Blyden was forced to resign. Between 1880 and 1882 he received three more honours in recognition of his work: in 1880 he was made a fellow of the American Philological Association, received an honorary DD degree from Lincoln University, and in 1882 became an honorary member of the Society of Science and Letters in Bengal, India.

On leaving the Ministry of the Interior he resumed his duties at the Liberia College and visited the USA for nine months to raise money for his educational projects. He returned to Liberia in June 1883 and came into conflict with two new professors who had joined the College in his absence. The President of the Republic supported the two professors, forcing Blyden to leave his post for six months and resign as president of the College.

He became vice-president of the American Colonisation Society in 1884, and the following year he decided to stand in the presidential elections, being the nominated candidate of the Republic Party. This party, ironically, was dominated by politicians of mixed blood, but Blyden felt that party politics were less important than the platform of the candidate. It was a hard-fought campaign in which Blyden lost.

Shortly afterwards he returned to Sierra Leone, and as his conviction grew that Christianity had retarded African development, he resigned as minister of the Presbyterian Church. In 1887 a collection of his articles were published in book form in London, entitled *Christianity, Islam and the Negro Race*. This book was acclaimed as being of great scholastic merit, and the first edition sold 500 copies. In recognition of his writings on religion he was made honorary member of the American Society of Comparative Religion in 1889.

He was re-appointed Ambassador to Britain in 1892. During his stay in London he tried to encourage British interest in Liberia to safeguard the possible break up of the Republic by European imperialism.

In 1896-97 he was Agent of Local Affairs in Lagos. He had travelled to that country twice before and his writings had been well received there. While in this post he established a school for Moslem children that taught a secular English education, thus helping to overcome the traditional Moslem distrust of Western education. From Lagos he went to Sierra Leone to continue teaching and writing, and returned to Liberia in 1889 to help re-organise Liberia College for its re-opening in 1900, when he was appointed professor of Classics. The following year he returned to Sierra Leone to become director of Mohammedan Education.

In July 1905, President Barclay appointed him Minister Plenipotentiary and Ambassador Extraordinary in London and Paris, to help negotiate a settlement for the boundary dispute between Liberia and French West Africa. Blyden once again felt that Liberia was in danger of disintegration at the hands of the imperialist powers and suggested that Britain and France should maintain an economic and administrative presence in Liberia while retaining her independence and boundaries. This proposal was rejected by the Liberian Government and shortly afterwards, in September 1905, he was recalled.

For the remainder of his life he lived in Sierra Leone, where he died on 7 February 1912. For his life's work he had gained international respect and esteem and had been awarded Knight Commander of the

Humane Order of African Redemption by the Liberian Government, Grand Band of the Order of the Green Dragon of Annam by the French Government, the Order of the Medijidieh by Turkey, the National Order of Tunisia, and the Coronation Medal from Edward VII of Britain.

Although Blyden's writings and ideas were aimed at blacks everywhere, his attention was focussed to the English-speaking areas of Africa. Apart from his belief that Sierra Leone and Liberia would eventually become one, he also foresaw a future where all the Africans in West Africa would belong to one community. He believed that as the African personality developed through educational and cultural independence, so their racial solidarity would grow, enhancing the conditions for political independence and the emergence of a larger West African state.

He was a controversial figure who spent his life attempting to disprove myths of racial superiority and advancing interest in an understanding of African customs and institutions, while trying to instill a sense of pride and dignity in his fellows. He was a highly intelligent man who became learned despite his lack of advanced formal education. His lifetime of perseverance for the advancement of his race, his efforts to bring about unity and solidarity and his outstanding literary and academic achievements earned him great respect, even from those who did not always agree with his views.■

Boavida, A. (1923-68)

BOAVIDA, Dr. Americo (1923-68).

ANGOLAN gynaecologist and politician, renowned theorist of his country's struggle for independence from Portugal.

Americo Boavida was born in Luanda on 20 November 1923. He completed primary and secondary schooling and was one of the first Angolan graduates of the *Liceau de Luanda*. Boavida represented the local athletics club and led his group to sporting successes. In 1952 he obtained a degree in medicine from the University of Lisbon, followed by a diploma in tropical medicine and hygiene. Between 1954 and 1958, he worked in the clinical hospital of the medical faculty of the University of Barcelona, Spain, and in 1965, he specialised in gynaecology and obstetrics at the Institute for Postgraduate Medical Studies in Prague.

From 1955 to 1960, Boavida practised in Luanda, where he became known for his professional ability and commitment as a nationalist. His involvement in politics led him to abandon his medical profession in order to devote his attention to the struggle for national independence. In August 1960 he joined the *Movimento Popular de Libertação de Angola* (MPLA), and was assigned to the Department of Foreign Relations, as president of the Angolan Volunteer Corps for Assistance of Refugees (CVAAR) in Kinshasa. He was also a member of the National Committee. He was one of the first doctors to respond to the nationalist cause which his wife, a Portuguese national, supported; she accompanied him in all his activities.

Boavida's services to the MPLA's Eastern Front included setting up a number of dispensaries and making scientific analyses of health problems in Angola. Dr. Boavida also made profound contributions to the analysis of Portuguese colonialism in many articles and in his book *Angola: Cinco Sécolos de Exploração Portuguesa*, published in Brazil by Editora Civilização Brasiliera. He analysed Portugal's own backwardness and economic dependence on her overseas provinces. Boavida saw Portugal's relationship to her colonies as one of "collective colonialism" through which Portugal, especially since 1961 and since the inception of armed struggle in Angola, mortgaged the natural wealth of Angola and Mozambique in exchange for military, financial and political support from NATO. Lacking capital of her own to sustain a viable colonial empire, Boavida saw Portugal in the role of a visible but increasingly junior partner in a multinational effort to defeat the liberation movements and maintain economic exploitation of Angola, Mozambique and Guinea. He saw support from Portugal's "partners" as clearly the factor which enabled Portugal to hang on to her African colonies. However an accelerated exodus of young people (which Dr. Boavida documented) and the emergence of Armed Revolutionary Action (ARA) in Portugal, among other things, convinced him that it would be difficult for the Lisbon regime to play adequately its role as an occupying power. This led Boavida to offer the prediction that Portuguese colonialism was entering its final days.

Boavida argued that the historical meaning of the war in Angola, where the Angolan people opposed colonialism, lay in the class struggle. It was a war of an oppressed community against an oppressing minority with contradictory and irreconcilable economic interests. This point and others are explored in a detailed socio-economic analysis of the relationship between Portugal and Angola in his book *Angola: Five Centuries of Portuguese Exploitation.*

At 8.00 in the morning of 25 September 1968, during an attempt to escape the Portuguese air and ground attack on the "Hanoi 2" MPLA base (which marked the start of the Portuguese regime's late dry-season offensive against the MPLA's liberated zones in eastern Angola), a piece of shrapnel from a Portuguese fragmentation bomb pierced Boavida's brain and killed him.■

Boganda, B. (1910-59)

BOGANDA, Barthélemy (1910-59).

CENTRAL AFRICAN REPUBLIC statesman who is honoured as the founder of the Republic. He was born in Boubangui in Lobaye, Ubangi-Shari (now Central African Republic), on 4 April 1910. After the murder of his mother by guards in charge of rubber gathering for the *Compagnie Forestière Sangha-Oubangui*, he was adopted by Catholic missionaries and baptised on 24 December 1922. He studied first at *St. Paul des Rapides* at Bangui, and later at the seminaries of Kisantu in the Belgian Congo (now Zaire), Brazzaville, and Yaounde. After being ordained priest on 17 March 1938, he worked in various missions, including Grimari and Bakala. With the encouragement of his bishop, he decided to enter politics to fight for equal rights for Africans, and was elected first African member for Ubangi-Shari on 10 November 1946.

At the time of his election, Ubangi-Shari was one of the four territories comprising French Equatorial Africa (AEF), the other three being Chad, Gabon and Middle Congo. At the end of the Second World War

the French Constituent Assembly passed laws which improved African conditions in their colonies, such as the abolition of forced labour. The French settlers of Ubangi-Shari fought a fierce rear-guard action against these liberalising moves. Boganda, on his

B. Boganda

first visit to France in 1947, discovered a different mentality from that of the colonialists in Ubangi-Shari.

His first speech to the Assembly, on 4 August 1947, was unambiguous about the course he intended to pursue. "The Africans must certainly seem very strange, because they will not be satisfied with speeches alone. They judge only the facts. . . . We are the citizens of one nation and we all share equal duties. We must also share equal rights."

At the end of 1947 he wrote a letter to the Minister for French Overseas Territories, denouncing the various abuses to be found in Ubangi, including conscription of labour, arbitrary arrest and violence, low salaries, segregation in public places, compulsory cultivation of cotton, and unfair distribution of the capitation tax. Although Boganda was a member of the French Mouvement Républicain Populaire (MRP), such speeches were sufficient for the colonialists to brand him a Communist and an agitator.

Boganda wished to create a political party that would not depend on external subsidy or on contributions from his poverty-stricken supporters. He therefore sought to encourage the setting up of a system of consumer-producer co-operative societies, which he saw as a means of increasing the income of the rural masses. Thus the Socoulole (*Société Co-opérative de l'Oubangui-Lobaye-Lesse*) was founded along with a cotton co-operative and a transport co-operative, to try and break the monopoly of the expatriate-controlled export-import, cotton and transport companies. However, these ventures proved unsuccessful.

Realising that the goal of political autonomy was a long way off, because of the lack of trained and educated people, Boganda and Antoine Darlan, the vice-president of the Grand Council of AEF, also an Ubangian and a trade unionist, decided to press for the accession of all Ubangi-Shari Africans to French citizenship. To this end a Union Oubanguienne was formed. On 28 September 1949, Boganda and a few educated compatriots formed the *Mouvement d'Evolution Sociale de l'Afrique Noire* (MESAN), which in Boganda's perception was to be a popular mass movement.

In the French Assembly he continued to advocate measures that would remove the coercive labour practices of the colony. But Boganda soon realised that he was making little headway in getting the territory's Europeans to do anything about improving conditions for the people. The cotton companies remained powerful enough to obtain the removal of administrators who refused to send armed guards to the cotton fields. Many of the settlers believed the granting of political liberties to be incompatible with economic development. In 1950 and 1951, therefore, Boganda decided a change of strategy was needed, and began a territory-wide campaign fomenting unrest.

This campaign and the creation of MESAN provoked hostile reactions from the colonial authorities and any official suspected of being in contact with Boganda was immediately dismissed, while he himself was subjected to surveillance to see whether any legal action could be taken against him. A trumped-up charge of disturbing the public order was brought against him in January 1951, and in March he was condemned to two months in prison and his French wife, whom he had married in 1949, to two weeks for complicity. But in the elections to the French Assembly held on 17 June 1951, Boganda won by a large majority. From then on, he sought to make MESAN a mass movement.

When, in March 1952, MESAN secured control of the Territorial Assembly, there was little the colonial administration could do, although they found themselves under attack from the settlers and traders. The French administration tried to improve the Africans' position. But it was still almost obligatory to grow cotton, which most people resented bitterly. Anger over this and other oppression caused tension in 1952-54. In May 1954, serious racial disturbances broke out at Berberati in the south-west. Boganda, who had not been popular there, was called on by the governor to calm the situation, and did so; although he was disappointed when the African leaders of the disturbances were jailed.

However, Boganda continued to enjoy the confidence of a majority of Ubangians and had become a charismatic figure. The elections to the French Assembly on 2 January 1956 saw him win again, with a convincing 84.7 per cent of the votes. The *loi-cadre*, the enabling law which established the institutional framework for autonomy in France's colonies, was voted by the French Assembly on 23 June 1956. On 18 November 1956, the first single electoral college municipal elections were held in Bangui; Boganda, running in a mainly white constituency, against well-known white candidates, was elected deputy mayor of Bangui.

In the elections to the Territorial Assembly of 31 March 1957, Boganda's MESAN party won all the seats. The next stage, under the provision of the *loi-cadre*, was the setting up of a Council of Government; Boganda was determined that autonomy, now to be fairly complete, should not involve the breaking up of French Equatorial Africa, and chose to devote himself to the Grand Council of the AEF to which he had just been elected president, assigning the post of vice-president of the Ubangi-Shari Council of Government to Abel Goumba.

The six ministers chosen by Boganda for Ubangi-Shari and designated by the Assembly took up their posts on 17 May 1957 and were in charge of "local" services, while state services were still under the governor's control. This system led to considerable number of problems, mainly because of the lack of trained personnel. (Of the 5,000 indigenous administrators in 1957, very few held the certificate of primary education).

On French rule, Boganda said in 1957, "For the last six years in this Assembly, I have heard a great deal about wood and manganese, about everything which man can produce or exploit by his work. But about him for whom everything on earth was created, about he who suffers and sweats, who exploits and produces, about man himself, not a word". But he did not want to see the AEF cut off from France. A programme of economic recovery, based on coffee, was put forward by M. Guérillot, the French administrator in charge of economic and administrative affairs.

Boganda's rather hasty endorsement of the plan dented his reputation and that of the Council of Government. Indeed, demonstrations broke out when details of the plans became known and Boganda travelled to the cotton zones to explain the meaning of the "work crusade". He virtually left political life for a time to travel all over the country, explaining to the people that they could no longer count on French assistance and that the country's only hope lay in increasing its agricultural production.

In a speech to the Territorial Assembly on 8 July 1958, he declared that Ubangi-Shari, and indeed the whole of French Black Africa, considered the *loi-cadre* as outdated and irrelevant, and in the name of MESAN, demanded total independence. In August 1958, in order to avoid the risk of political isolation, he put MESAN under the umbrella of Senghor's *Parti du Regroupement Africain* (PRA) and sent a delegation to the PRA's Congress in Cotonou.

In the referendum of September 1958, Boganda secured a vote against immediate independence. His idea of unity of the AEF countries in the French Community collapsed when the Assemblies of Congo, Gabon and Chad voted to become individual member states of the Community. On 1 December 1958, therefore, Boganda was obliged to proclaim the Central African Republic (consisting only of Ubangi-Shari) as a member state of the French Community and he became the Head of the new Government. Final attempts at unity in the following months failed.

Legislative elections in the CAR were fixed for 5 April 1959. It was during the campaign for these elections that Barthélemy Boganda was killed. On Easter Day, 29 March 1959, he died in an air crash, the circumstances of which remain mysterious to this day. It was a death that was deeply mourned by the entire country.■

Boka, E. (1928-64)

BOKA, Ernest (1928-64).

IVORIAN lawyer and politician. He was born in Azaguie, near Abidjan, on 7 December 1928. After elementary education in Bingerville, the former capital of Côte d'Ivoire, he was sent to France, where he went first to the Lycée at Avignon, then to another Lycée at Briançon.

He later studied law and political science at Grenoble, and obtained a law degree in 1954. The following year he obtained two doctorate diplomas in the same Faculty of Law and Political Science at the University of Grenbole, one in Roman Law and History of Law, the other in Private Law. These two doctorates allowed Ernest Boka, who thus completed his studies at the age of 27, to choose between a private legal career and an administrative one. At first he considered the opportunities for private practice, and in 1955 he became a trainee lawyer at the Bar of Grenoble.

He returned to Côte d'Ivoire in 1956 and entered government service. In November of that year he was appointed *Chef de Cabinet* to the governor of Côte d'Ivoire, and from then on was an important figure in the French Overseas Territories.

Amid the rapid changes which occurred over the next few years in Côte d'Ivoire Boka was directly involved in politics and followed the country's development with lively interest. In 1957, at the age of 29, he was appointed Minister of Public Instruction (equivalent to Minister of National Education) of Côte d'Ivoire.

He made clear his views on education when giving prizes at the Cocody Lycée in Abidjan in July 1957; in a speech entitled "The importance of education for the new institutions in French Africa", he said: "An education policy must be started on the basis of the country's social structures and rate of development, its resources and its needs. The plan laid down for Côte d'Ivoire should

E. Boka

permit a rise in the school attendance rate for children of primary school age from 20 to 50 per cent by 1962 . . . The difficulty lies in the lack of teachers and buildings. The answer lies in the expansion of teacher training colleges and ten-year bonds for their graduates; also in the starting of new primary and technical classes." Boka, as Minister of Education, planned to make education universal by introducing compulsory schooling. In the two years he served in office he worked on this objective to develop and raise the level of education.

In 1959 he became Minister Delegate (special assistant) in the Prime Minister's Office, in charge of the Civil Service. In the same year he was appointed a member of Côte d'Ivoire's delegation to the UN. With the efficiency he had already shown Boka carried out, for two years, the tasks of both

offices. On 3 January 1961, at the age of just over 30, he became President of the Supreme Court of his country. His legal studies and brilliant mind might be said to have marked him out for this high office.

In his speech at his swearing-in, Boka spoke of the Supreme Court's role and his own: "In reality, it will not be by claiming to take over the functions of political institutions, still less by opposing necessary changes, that the Supreme Court keeps its moral authority. It will be by remaining true to its own function, that of a regulator, a qualified adviser and an independent judge, that it proves its true vitality and its permanent adaptation to the needs of the State, and merits the indispensable confidence of the citizens in the law and justice. That is a difficult task, but also a great honour, and we shall try to remain worthy of it."

He was implicated in the plot against the Government which was uncovered in January 1963, and was removed from office. He was arrested and detained in prison in Yamoussokro, where the Government said that he committed suicide on 6 April 1964. Announcing Boka's death in the National Assembly, President Houphouet-Boigny told members that the former Supreme Court chief left a suicide note in which he admitted having been corrupt and ambitious to become Head of State. ■

Bokwe, J.K. (1855-1922)

BOKWE, John Knox (1855-1922).

SOUTH AFRICAN clergyman, writer and pioneer music composer. He was born on 18 March 1855 in Ntshelamanzi, near Lovedale, Cape Province, South Africa. The third son and youngest child of Colwepi Joseph Bokwe who was a councillor for Ngqika, he studied at the Lovedale College between 1869 and 1872. In 1870 he joined the *Isigidimi* magazine and later became the official interpreter to the Commissioner of Ngqika, after which he was appointed controller of the Lovedale telegraph office in 1873.

In 1875 he began to compose music, and in 1885 published a collection of hymns and songs, *Amaculo ase Lovedale* (Lovedale Music). He later composed the masterpieces "Vuka Deborah" and "Plea for Africa". He visited Scotland in 1892. In 1897 he resigned his post at the Lovedale telegraph office. He joined Tengo Jabavu (q.v.) in the *Imvo Zabatsundu*, a weekly newspaper but soon

J.K. Bokwe

turned to the ministry where he served as an evangelical pastor, having been ordained earlier in the Presbyterian church. He was in charge of the Presbyterian mission at Ugie, where he won the confidence of the European and African population. During his period of service there he directed a programme establishing new mission stations in Ugie, Macleans and Tsolo districts.

He continued to compose music as well as write. Among his publications were *Ntsikana: The story of an African Convert* and *Ntsikanu: The story of an African hymn* (Lovedale 1904). He retired in 1920 to Lovedale, where he died in 1922. ■

Boni, N. (1912-69)

BONI, Nazi (1912-69).

BURKINABE writer and politician who was a prominent activist in pre-independence politics and became in 1957 President of the Territorial Assembly. A Bwa, born in 1912 near Dedougou in the Bobo-Dioulasso region of Upper Volta (now Burkina Faso), Nazi Boni had his primary education at Ouagadougou, and then proceeded to Dakar to study at the William Ponty Teachers Training College. On completion of his studies, he returned to Ouagadougou where he was a teacher from 1931 to 1941. His teaching career was interrupted by the Second World War, when he was at Abidjan, capital of Côte d'Ivoire which then included much of Upper Volta's territory.

Boni returned to Ouagadougou after the war and took to politics, joining at first the *Union Voltaique* party and later becoming a member of *Mouvement Populaire de l'Evolution Africaine* (MPEA) which he was to lead for several years. He was elected deputy for the Bobo-Dioulasso region in the French National Assembly in 1946, and re-elected in 1951 and again in 1956. During most of the same period Boni was also serving in the Territorial Assembly of Upper Volta, which was reconstituted as a separate colony in 1947. He was President of the Territorial Assembly from 1957 to 1958.

Most of his political career was spent campaigning for a division of Upper Volta into two autonomous territories, Mossi and non-Mossi, which would be integrated in a proposed Federation of Mali, Senegal, Dahomey and Soudan. His policy was thus at variance with that of the ruling governing party, the local section of Félix Houphouet-Boigny's inter-territorial *Rassemblement Démocratique Africain* (RDA), which was led in Upper Volta by Maurice Yameogo. His attempt to strengthen his opposition against the RDA was foiled in 1960 when his new *Parti Républicain de la Liberté*, affiliated to the governing party in Mali, was banned by Yameogo.

In July 1960 Boni went into exile in Mali and later Senegal, where he wrote a historical novel, *Crépuscule des temps anciens* (The Twilight of Former Times), about

N. Boni

cine graduating in 1962. He then returned home and established a medical practice in Fort Lamy (now Ndjamena), at the same time becoming a member of the political bureau of the *Parti Progressiste Tchadien* (PPT). He was openly critical of some of the government's policies and in March 1963 he was arrested and charged with treason. A special criminal court found him guilty and sentenced him to death, although this was later commuted to life imprisonment. In August 1965 he was released.

Dr. O. Bono

his people. He returned to Upper Volta in 1966 after the deposition of Yameogo in a military coup, but lived in relative political obscurity until he was killed in a car accident in May 1969. ■

Bono, O. (1934-73)

BONO, Dr. Outel (1934-73).

CHADIAN physician who in 1962 became the second Chadian to qualify as a doctor (the first being Dr. Bojoglo Baroum who was also his country's Foreign Minister). Dr. Bono achieved prominence in political life as a leading member of the political bureau of the government party, the *Parti Progressiste Tchadien* (PPT), which he represented in the National Assembly.

Of Sara origins, he was born in 1934 at Fort Archambault (now Sarh) in southern Chad. After receiving his early education in Chad he travelled to France to study medi-

For the next four years Dr. Bono held the position of Director of Public Health, while also working as a doctor at Fort Lamy Hospital. He continued to oppose various aspects of the government policies, especially the cotton policy which he saw as benefiting chiefs and officials but not the farmers, and the continued presence of French troops in Chad. He was once again arrested in May 1969, and this time received a five-year prison sentence. He was released after a short period, although the police thereafter kept a close watch on his activities.

He resumed his previous medical appointments until mid-1972 when he once again travelled to France to study at a Paris hospital. While in France he developed relations with the *Front de Libération Nationale du Tchad* (FROLINAT), the major opposition movement in armed struggle against the Chadian government. But as he did not agree with all their aims he began to make preparations to establish his own political party, the *Mouvement Démocrtique de la Rénovation Tchadienne* (MDRT). This organisation aimed to achieve administrative and social reforms, freedom of speech and a change in the relationship between France and Chad, which Dr. Bono considered to be neo-colonialist. However, just before the new movement was inaugurated Bono was murdered in Paris on 26 August 1973. ∎

Bouceif, A. (1934-79)

BOUCEIF, Lieutenant-Colonel Ahmed Ould (1934-79).

MAURITANIAN military ruler. He was born in 1934 at Kiffa in central Mauritania, and came from the Moorish ethnic group. He joined the army in 1962 and underwent special training courses in France, including one at the *Ecole d'Armes Blindées et de Cavalerie* at Saumur and the *Ecole d'Application d'Infanterie* at Saint-Maixent.

After returning to Mauritania, he became a prefect at Bir-Moghrein, in the north of the country and assistant governor of Nouadhibou. He was later appointed governor at F'Derik, near Zouerate.

On 24 June 1976, President Moktar Ould Daddah appointed him army Chief of Staff and in October of the same year promoted him lieutenant-colonel. He was put in charge of the second Military Region of Zouerate, near the border with Western Sahara, where POLISARIO had been fighting for independence since Spain ceded the region to Mauritania and Morocco in 1976. A few months before President Ould Daddah was overthrown on 10 July 1978, lieutenant-colonel Bouceif was appointed commander of

Nema, the fifth Military Region, in the south-east of the country.

After the military coup of July 1978, he was appointed Minister of Fisheries and Marine Economy. Serious differences within the government over the Western Sahara

Lt-Col. A. Bouceif

and over Mauritania's ethnic problems brought about a major government reshuffle in April 1979, in which leading civilian ministers were ousted and a Military Committee for National Salvation was established. On 6 April 1979, Ould Bouceif was named Prime Minister and became Vice-President of the ruling military committee. At the time of his appointment he said that "Military orthodoxy is re-established. Before, there was fiction and reality: on one side a Military Committee, on the other movements other than military which exercised the real power. The association with civilians had developed a system of government unsuited to face up to present difficulties".

Though the new rulers' main worry was safeguarding the territorial integrity of their country, the Government of Ould Bouceif made immediate determined efforts to seek a peaceful solution to the problem of Western Sahara. And while declaring Mauritania's intention of maintaining its alliance with Morocco and its willingness to call on French military assistance in the war against POLISARIO in the neighbouring country, Bouceif sent envoys to Tripoli for talks with POLISARIO representatives. On 23 April 1979, Mauritania reached agreement with the POLISARIO in which it renounced its claim to any part of Western Sahara. A government statement issued from Nouakchott said that Mauritania "recognised the right to self-determination of the Saharan people and favoured the dialogue with the POLISARIO Front and all parties interested in the Western Saharan conflict". According to Bouceif however, "All other understanding or interpretation is null and void and does not express therefore the official position of Mauritania." The Prime Minister later flew to Rabat for talks with King Hassan of Morocco and to Paris for talks with the President of France.

Bouceif met his untimely death on his way to attend a meeting of the Heads of State of the Economic Community of West African States (ECOWAS) at Dakar on 27 May 1979. His plane crashed into the sea in a violent sand-storm, after overshooting the runway at Dakar airport. ■

Col. H. Boumedienne

Boumedienne, H. (1927-78)

BOUMEDIENNE, Colonel Houari (1927-78).

ALGERIAN freedom fighter and statesman, who, during his 14 years as president of his country, became one of the leading African statesmen of recent times. He was born Mohamed Brahim Boukharrouba on 23 August 1927, in the small village of Heliopolis in the Constantinois. His father was a poor peasant and he had six brothers and sisters. He was 18 when the French colonial authorities perpetrated massacres in the aftermath of the popular rioting of May 1945. He underwent an Islamic secondary education and in 1951 left the country to study in Tunis and Cairo. He joined Messali Hadj's nationalist *Parti Populaire Algérien* (PPA) at an early age, and in Cairo associated with other Maghreb nationalists.

Following the outbreak of the armed struggle in Algeria in 1954, he undertook military training offered by President Nasser's army. He returned via Morocco in 1958 and worked for the *Front de Libération Nationale* (FLN) as an arms supplier and guerrilla organiser, later becoming commander of the *Wilaya* (guerrilla military district) that was stationed at Oran. In 1960 he was appointed Chief of Staff of the *Armée de Libération Nationale* (ALN).

In this post his socialist beliefs led him to criticise the FLN political leadership, which led to his dismissal from the ALN, by President Ben Khedda, on the eve of independence. During the period of conflict between the political and military elements of the FLN at the declaration of independence, Boumedienne threw his weight behind Ben Bella against other members of the Provisional Revolutionary Government (GPRA) led by Ben Khedda. There followed a *coup de force* which placed Ben Bella in power.

Boumedienne was at first a shy and hesitant public speaker. He always spoke in Arabic and used earthy images to clarify complex issues. Intelligence, background knowledge and great force, characterised his speeches. His popularity among ordinary people grew in direct proportion to his image as someone who could produce results. On 19 June 1965, Boumedienne overthrew Ahmed Ben Bella in a coup d'état which he called the "Revolutionary Resurgence".

President Boumedienne became the moving spirit behind a regime of officers and technocrats who radically changed Algeria's economy, transforming it from a war-ruined, export-oriented agricultural country into one that began to enjoy one of the most sound industrial bases in the Third World.

Efforts at transforming its agrarian system included sweeping land reforms as well as plans to halt and eventually reverse the northward encroachment of the Sahara Desert. The government's radical development programmes in the social and cultural areas, took roads, schools, housing and electricity to a population which at the country's independence from France in July 1962 was to a large extent starving, brutalised and illiterate.

These revolutionary strides were taken in the aftermath of a seven year war of independence in which a million Algerians and 40,000 French troops and colonists lost their lives, a terrible struggle whose memory is still vivid on both sides.

Under Boumedienne, Algerian foreign policy was a dynamic one, with a militant anti-imperialist stand, supporting liberation struggles in the developing countries, and a belief in setting an example of practical and principled conduct for anyone willing to follow it. It nevertheless remained genuinely non-aligned, pursuing technical, cultural, trade and military relations with capitalist as well as communist states. It maintained simultaneous dialogues with Europe, the Maghreb, the Arab world and Africa, showing both pragmatism and determination.

The problems and disruption attending all this change, stemming from external factors and from the changes themselves, were not denied by the regime. On the contrary, Boumedienne tried to encourage criticism and to carry on a dialogue with the population without losing his grip on events or giving ammunition to some Algerians who felt that the "socialist options" had gone too far. This produced the interesting spectacle of a military-based regime trying to create a non-military vanguard political party with a view to a gradual transfer of power to democratically elected representatives. The task was difficult, and was not made any easier, in the immediate short term, by the untimely death of Houari Boumedienne on 27 December 1978, after a short illness.■

Braide, G.S.M. (died 1918)

BRAIDE, Garrick Sokari Marian (died 1918).

NIGERIAN churchman, leader of a remarkable indigenous Christian movement in the area of modern Rivers State in 1915-16. He was a canoe seller of Bakana, an Ijaw town near the heads of the New Calabar and Bonny Rivers. He followed the Anglican Christian Mission of the Niger Delta Pastorate. This was a Nigerian-run Anglican body headed from 1900 to 1917 by Bishop James Johnson (q.v.), not a secession from the Church Missionary Society (CMS), but with some autonomy granted as a concession to nationalist feelings among West African Anglicans, after the conversion of many Ijaws, from the 1860s by African preachers under Bishop Samuel Ajayi Crowther (q.v.) and his mission. They were partially satisfied by the creation of the Delta Pastorate to continue the evangelisation of the Ijaws.

Garrick Braide, son of pagans, was a catechist for the Pastorate and a zealous and devout Christian. He worked under Bishop Johnson from 1908 and enjoyed fame for prayers for the sick; these, apparently, often cured people, and Braide did not accept any payment from them. By 1915 people were coming to him from far and wide, and a touch of his hand was said to achieve cures. In 1908 he was already said to have predicted calamities which would fall on people who did not heed his preaching. Later besides being an active worker for the Delta Pastorate, he was a member of a District Council and Board of the Pastorate. He won many converts. He persuaded the Ijaws to throw away their traditional objects of worship ("idols") and successfully preached rejection of strong liquor, which had been popular in the area.

In late 1915 Braide, and the very numerous other Rivers people who already venerated him, parted company with the Niger Delta Pastorate. He claimed that he was the second Elijah referred to in Malachi 4, 5: "Behold, I will send you Elijah the prophet before the coming of the great and dreadful day of the Lord." The Bishop rejected this claim and criticised many other aspects of the cult of which Braide was the leader. But the cult became a mass movement which spread over the Rivers area in a few months.

Braide was believed to be a prophet with supernatural powers. Many people in Abonema, Bakana, Bonny and other Ijaw towns and villages followed him, deserting the Delta Pastorate. According to Johnson's biographer E. A. Ayandele, Ijaws had come to resent the control of their local Anglican church by "outsiders" even though those were fellow Nigerians, as they were not Ijaws and had, despite Johnson's own determination, failed to train Ijaw church leaders. But there was much more than that to the Ijaws' veneration of Garrick Braide.

Braide had two lieutenants, a former clerk and schoolmaster of Bakana named Ngangia, and Moses Hart of Bonny. One called himself a "son of the prophet" and the other a "servant of the prophet". Belief in them and their leader Braide spread both among Ijaws of the Delta Pastorate and among hitherto unconverted pagans. Between November 1915 and February 1916 Braide succeeded far more than the Anglican mission had done in fifty years in making people abandon the traditional religion. "Idols" and charms were destroyed in vast quantities. Wherever he went Braide successfully preached proper Sunday observance, regular prayers, peace and harmony through an end to litigation, and abandonment of drinking and selling of spirits. Even chiefs renounced strong liquor and the sale

of gin by European traders whom Braide denounced fell dramatically. As did the British government's revenues, derived from import duties on alcoholic drinks.

Veneration of Braide was so great that his bath water was thought to have healing and other virtues, and was used for washing, or rubbing mixed with earth on the skin, and even drinking. Chiefs and everyone else honoured the "prophet" wherever he passed. Bishop Johnson, who had lost two-thirds of his Delta Pastorate congregation, turned strongly against the Braide movement.

The government considered it to be anti-white. Braide was alleged to have said he could stop the First World War, which was then raging, and added, "power is now passing from the whites to the blacks." His followers seemed to the British to be expressing frustration at British rule. The British, with the Chilembwe (q.v.) nationalist church movement in Nyasaland (Malawi) in mind, feared an African movement like Braide's at a time when they were doing badly in the War (as Braide's followers and other Nigerians certainly knew).

Thus Garrick Braide was imprisoned in 1916 for sedition and extortion. He was given several six-month prison sentences, later halved by the Lieutenant-Governor. Many of his followers were also arrested. But his following continued to spread and in 1916 became an organised new church, the Christ Army Church. Josephus D. Manuel, a former government clerk, was ordained a minister.

In November 1918 Garrick Braide was killed by a stroke of lightning. His followers were in later years divided, some forming a Garrick Braide Church while others continued with the Christ Army Church. Later the Christ Army Church split. Some branches mixed pre-Christian with Christian beliefs but others followed Braide's own teaching, which was strongly Christian. The phenomenal success of his teaching which was sternly moralistic, calling for abandonment of engrained beliefs and habits, showed that Braide met a religious need the missionaries had not met. It disproved the theory that African indigenous church movements are inevitably rebellions against the severity of Christian teachings. Although he left no united new church in the long term, Braide's Christian influence was very profound. ■

Brewah, L.A.M. (1924-78)

BREWAH, Luseni Alfred Morlu (1924-78).

SIERRA LEONEAN politician and lawyer, who became his country's first Attorney-General under the 1971 Republican Constitution. Born on 21 April 1924 in Taima Kori in the district of Moyamba, he was the son of the paramount chief Morlu Brewah of Kori. After primary schooling at the Bo Government School, he attended the Prince of Wales School in Freetown before proceeding to the USA where he studied at Northwestern University and then the University of Chicago. He later came to Britain to read Law at King's College (University of London) and was called to the Bar at Lincoln's Inn in 1959.

Returning to Freetown in 1960, Brewah set up in private legal practice. Two years later he entered politics when he stood for Parliament as an independent candidate in the 1962 elections: he was elected unopposed in the Moyamba North constituency. He retained his parliamentary seat, again unopposed, in subsequent general elections in March 1967 and 1973. His political career was interrupted in 1967 and 1968, during military rule, but he returned to Parliament in 1968 on the re-establishment of parliamentary democracy. In April of that year, Brewah was given a ministerial post in the Government of President Siaka Stevens as Minister of External Affairs. In the immediate aftermath of the military interregnum he was, as the holder of the External Affairs portfolio, responsible for rebuilding his country's image among the international community.

Following his appointment to the Cabinet he joined the ruling party, the All People's Congress (APC). In the Cabinet reshuffle in April 1969 he was named Minister of Health, a portfolio he retained until April 1971 when the country adopted a Republican status. Following this Brewah was appointed Attorney-General with Cabinet rank, the first Sierra Leonean to so serve under the Republican Constitution. It was during his tenure that some military officers who opposed the Republican Constitution and tried to topple the government were tried for treason, found guilty and executed. Among those executed in June 1971 was Brigadier John Ahmadu Bangura (q.v.), the former commander of the Sierra Leonean army. Brewah retained the Ministry after the 1973 general elections in which he was re-elected to Parliament.

Brewah was made Minister of Works following major changes in the Government in 1974 and in 1976 he was relieved of his ministerial duties. He however remained in the legislative assembly as a minor member on the Government bench. He did not seek re-election in the May 1977 general elections but instead retired to private legal practice. He died in 1978 at the Serabu Hospital in Freetown after a short illness.■

L.A.M. Brewah

Briggs, W.O. (1918-87)

BRIGGS, Wenike Opurum (1918-87).

NIGERIAN lawyer, journalist and politician who championed minority rights and campaigned for the creation of more states in the Federation. He served as a federal commissioner in General Gowon's administration.

Wenike Opurum Briggs was born on 10 March 1918, at Abbonnema the son of Abel Opurum Briggs who was a trader and

Dr. W. Briggs

Madam Obuta Dafinasi Oruwari. His wife was Agnes Alaerebola.

Having successfully completed his early education at Nyemoni primary school and at King's College, Lagos, he began earning a living as a postal clerk with the Posts and Telegraphs department. Between 1942 and 1945 he worked as a customs officer in the department of Customs and Excise, joining the politically active Nigerian Youth Movement in 1944. By this time he had developed an interest in politics and his resignation from his promising job with Customs and Excise in 1945 to become a sub-editor of the *Daily Service* was not unconnected with it. During the years 1945 to 1947 which he spent with the *Daily Service* he underwent his political as well as his journalistic apprenticeship serving under Chief

S. L. Akintola (q.v.), a brilliant and articulate politician who was for a long time deputy leader of the Action Group and later founder of the Nigerian National Democratic Party (NNDP).

Before the end of 1947 Wenike Briggs had started his own weekly, *The Nigerian Statesman*, and it was as its editor and the secretary general of the Lagos branch of the Nigerian Youth Movement that he joined a team of journalists who represented the West African press, on the invitation of the Colonial Office, in a tour of Britain. It was during this visit that he made up his mind to equip himself better for politics and journalism. He went on to study journalism in 1951 at the Regent Street Polytechnic, London, where he obtained a Diploma. He then took up legal studies, and after obtaining the LLB from the University of Sheffield and having been called to the Bar at Gray's Inn, London, in 1958, he returned home.

While Briggs was in Britain he joined the United Nigeria Committee whose members advocated the creation of more states, and became its secretary general.

In Nigeria he established his legal practice in Port Harcourt and also found time to work for COR (Calabar, Ogoja, Rivers) State Movement whose secretary general he became. He was elected parliamentary member for Degema division in 1959, standing for a party in alliance with the Action Group (AG) of Chief Obafemi Awolowo (q.v.). He was re-elected in 1964 as a candidate for the United Progressive Grand Alliance (UPGA) which was an alliance of the NCNC (National Council of Nigerian Citizens) and the AG. He retained his parliamentary seat until the military intervention of 1966, when, undaunted by the civil strife, including a short arrest in Biafra, he was soon back in Lagos campaigning for more states. He shot into limelight with his appointment by General Gowon, first as federal commissioner for Education in October 1967, and then as federal commissioner for Trade, a post he held from October 1971 to 1974.

Wenike Briggs took no active part in his country's politics after 1974, though he did live to see the creation of more states. He died on 21 April 1987. He is remembered by many of his compatriots for the great impact he made in his zealous and consistent advocacy of the rights of Nigeria's ethnic minorities. ◾

Bright, C. (1929-80)

BRIGHT, Dr. Cyril (1929-80).

LIBERIAN economist. He was born on 25 April 1929 in Freetown, Sierra Leone, but had his early education at the College of West Africa, Monrovia, from 1945 to 1947, and on completion worked in the American health mission in Liberia. In 1951 he went to the University of Nebraska, USA, to study for a BSc degree awarded in 1953. He returned to Liberia in 1956 and was appointed chairman of the Exploration Team for the Agricultural Development National Production Council.

In 1962 he became economic affairs officer with the United Nations' Economic Commission for Africa and in 1966 an Under-Secretary in Liberia's Ministry of Planning and Economic Affairs. In February of the following year Bright was made head of the department. In the same year, he was appointed Secretary-General of the Mano River Union, which embraces Liberia, Sierra Leone and Guinea. When William Tolbert (q.v.) succeeded as President of Liberia in 1971 he remained at his old Ministry where he implemented Liberia's first comprehensive development plan.

In November 1972 he resigned from the Tolbert administration after the President had expressed a loss of confidence in him. He was executed on 22 April 1980 following the military overthrow of President Tolbert's government. ■

Dr. C. Bright

Bright Davies, J. (1848-1920)

BRIGHT DAVIES, James (1848-1920).

SIERRA LEONEAN administrator and a prominent journalist in the early development of journalism in Sierra Leone, Ghana and Nigeria. Born at Freetown on 20 June 1848, of Ibo origin like Africanus Horton (q.v.), he was a foundation student at the CMS Grammar School from 1864; after completing education he worked as a clerk in the government service in British West Africa where he rose rapidly to be Financial Secretary to the governor of Sierra Leone. But he found Governor Rowe incompatible as an employer and resigned. Having already contributed in 1873-5 to the *Independent*, he now went in for full-time journalism. He edited the *West African Reporter*, one of Sierra Leone's most important early newspaper, published from 1876 to 1886.

He later moved to Gold Coast and worked as chief clerk in the Secretariat. He was at one time acting Colonial Secretary but he was conscious of the growing preference for Europeans in the civil service, which hit him personally when he was placed on a lower salary than a European in a comparable post. This intensified his anti-colonial feelings. The British government, which had suspected him of contributing anonymously to the *Western Echo*, took action against him in 1886 for signing a farewell address for a police inspector that was alleged to contain damaging innuendos; when he refused to answer a query he was suspended.

He helped to found the Gold Coast Printing and Publishing Co., which in 1895 brought out a new newspaper, the *Gold Coast Independent*, with him as manager and editor. Three years later, however, he resigned after a disagreement with a Liverpool firm for which he was agent. In 1899 he left Gold Coast and went to Northern Nigeria. He was a transport clerk during Lugard's occupation, becoming Chief Transport Clerk at Jebba (Lugard's first base); later he worked in Southern Nigeria as senior Marine Clerk at Burutu. In 1906 he left government service and settled at Lagos.

He inspired the formation in 1909 of the Nigerian Shipping Corporation, to run steamers between Lagos and Forcados and Lokoja and break into the European monopoly of African shipping. He became a Corresponding Secretary of the Lagos Anti-Slavery and Aborigines Protection Society, founded in 1910.

Bright Davies was most remembered in Lagos for returning to journalism and founding the *Nigerian Times* in 1910. During the First World War the newspaper ran into difficulties again, and eventually its proprietor had to sell it in 1917 to Adamu Idrisu Animashaun. But this was not before his writings in the newspaper had brought down the wrath of the British government, then headed by Governor-General Lugard who was particularly upset at criticism during wartime. After an article criticising British rule in Nigeria, Bright Davies was charged with attempting to bring the government into hatred and contempt and inciting disaffection, disloyalty and feelings of enmity towards it. He was fined £100 and bound over on 9 February 1916. In August 1916 he wrote an article criticising British trading firms. A court found that he had again incited to disaffection in breach of the binding-over order of the earlier judgement, and he was sentenced to six months' imprisonment. According to Prof. F. Omu in his *The Press and Politics in Nigeria, 1880-1937*, he was the first Nigerian journalist to go to prison.

He was freed before his sentence expired, after many pleas on his behalf. He was not able to revive his newspaper before he died on 17 January 1920. ■

Bubiriza, P. (1932-72)

BUBIRIZA, Pascal (1932-72).

BURUNDIAN administrator who in 1962 became his country's first Ambassador to the United Nations, immediately prior to which he was *chef de Cabinet* in the government of Premier André Muhirwa who succeeded the assassinated Prince Louis Rwagasore (q.v.) in October 1961.

Pascal Bubiriza was born in November 1932 at Rugazi to a Hutu family. After early education he went to the Groupe Scolaire d'Astrida created in 1929 at Butare in Rwanda to serve the Belgian twin-territories of Rwanda-Urundi; the League of Nations had mandated the countries to Belgium in 1924. The Groupe Scolaire d'Astrida was established primarily to train administrators for the two countries. Thus, like Bubiriza, most of the early educated élites of Burundi were products of that institution and, like him, most were absorbed into the colonial administration.

Between 1954 and 1956 he served at Bujumbura and Muyinga before being promoted assistant administrator of the Bubanza district in late 1956. Four years later he was appointed assistant provincial administrator of the area and held that post until a few months before independence in 1962. Rwanda-Urundi had been split in 1959 into the separate states of Rwanda and Burundi and each was granted internal self-government that year. Then on 1 July 1962 Burundi became an independent state, ending 42 years of Belgian trusteeship.

A very capable administrator, respected by his colleagues for his diligence, Bubiriza was appointed his country's first Ambassador to the UN in August of that same year. The next year, however, following the appointment of Pierre Ngendandumwe (q.v.) as successor to Premier Muhirwa, Bubiriza was recalled and made Minister of the Interior. He held that important Ministry until April 1964, when he was again reassigned diplomatic duties. He was scheduled to be posted to Zaire but his implication in an alleged plot to oust the government delayed his posting until 1965. He was eventually posted to Ethiopia where he represented his country until 1967.

Bubiriza returned to Bujumbura to be appointed Minister of Communications in the new government of Captain Michel Micombero (q.v.) who had come to power in November 1966. Soon he was implicated in a Hutu plot against that administration, for which he was executed in 1972.■

Bureh (c. 1840-c. 1908)

BUREH, Bai (c.1840-c.1908).

SIERRA LEONEAN resistance leader. Originally named Kebalai, he was of the Loko people to the north of Freetown, who retained independence until the 1890s but long before then had contact with the British, and from the 1860s with the French further north also. Kebalai commanded the forces of Bokari, ruler at Forekaria, before becoming chief of Kasse and taking the title Bai Bureh. His chieftancy was not large but his influence had spread widely even before he became a leader of resistance to British penetration.

For some decades the British in Freetown made treaties with interior rulers, without claiming overall sovereignty. Bai Bureh respected his own agreements with the British. However, during a war, started in 1889, against Karimu and his "Mureteis", Bai Bureh was nearly arrested by the British, though he had thought he was fighting on their side; he escaped. In 1890 the British began enforcing their informal control of a part of the hinterland (that part reserved to Britain under an 1889 agreement with France) with a new force of Sierra Leone Frontier Police. Bai Bureh's troops joined this force in a campaign against Tambi in 1892.

As a result of such campaigns the British declared Sierra Leone a Protectorate in 1896, a declaration which Bai Bureh accepted minimally and reluctantly. In 1894, after soldiers supplied by him had raided French Guinea territory, he escaped arrest

by the British a second time, but then met Governor Cardew at Port Loko and submitted to an order to hand over 50 guns.

Then the British imposed a Hut Tax on the Protectorate. Early in 1898 an order to Bai Bureh to collect the tax from his

Bai Bureh

subjects met a hostile reaction; Bai Bureh's soldiers turned back the messenger with the order and the British then sent forces to arrest him.

Bai Bureh, who later said he had never received an order to levy the tax and had fought only when attacked, escaped capture and became the resistance leader among the northern Temnes and Lokos in the rising called ever since "the Hut Tax War". Regular forces were sent to join the "Frontiers" in Bai Bureh's country around Karene. Fighting was on a considerable scale from February 1898. The resistance forces set up good defensive positions with palm logs and trenches, and fired trade guns from cover with good effect. They evaded capture and repeatedly fought back from the bush in true guerrilla style. Bai Bureh maintained discipline, and although his forces killed a missionary it was not on his orders. He is reported to have responded to an offer of £100 reward for his arrest with a counter offer of £500 for the governor's arrest.

In late April 1898 Mende, Sherbro, Gallinas, Vai and other peoples in the south joined the uprising. They had no leader and committed widespread undisciplined murders of Europeans and Creoles. Despite the killing of Creoles, the governor accused the Creoles of inciting the rising. There was in fact some admiration for Bai Bureh, whose forces committed very few murders, in Freetown. There opinion blamed Cardew and the tax for the war, and this was a widely held view in Britain also. In renewed operations in the Karene areas in October 1898 the West Africa Regiment pursued Bai Bureh until he was captured on 16 November. A few months later the rising ended. While the bloodstained Mende rising was punished by 96 hangings, Bai Bureh could not be charged with murder, the idea of charging him with treason was dropped because the Protectorate was not legally a part of the Queen's Dominions and he had no duty of allegiance to her. He was detained in Freetown and then, with a wife and a few other deportees, was sent to Gold Coast, on 30 July 1899. Remaining in exile for six years he died shortly after his return.∎

Dr. K.A. Busia

Busia, K.A. (1913-78)

BUSIA, Dr. Kofi Abrefa (1913-78).

GHANAIAN scholar and politician. Born on 11 July 1913, at Wenchi in the Brong Ahafo region north west of Ashanti, Busia attended the Presbyterian and Methodist primary schools at Kumasi before winning a scholarship to Mfantsipim Secondary School in Cape Coast where he gained his Junior and Senior School certificates with honours. He trained as a teacher at Wesley College, Kumasi, and joined the staff of the Prince of Wales College in Achimota in 1936. In 1939 he obtained, through a correspondence course, his first degree with honours in medieval and modern history and won a scholarship to Oxford where he obtained a BA in Politics, Philosophy and Economics, and subsequently became a Carnegie Research Fellow in 1941.

Busia returned to Ghana in 1942 as Assistant District Commissioner, but soon fell out with the colonial administration. He returned to Oxford as a Nuffield Research Fellow and obtained a doctorate in Philosophy. His thesis, "The Position of the Chief in the Modern Political System of the Ashanti", was later published as a standard text in 1951.

On his return to Ghana in 1947, he was for two years officer-in-charge of social survey for the colonial government – it was during this time he produced his book the *Social Survey of Sekondi-Takoradi*. In 1949 Dr. Busia was appointed the first lecturer in African Studies at the Ghana University College. In 1954 he became the first African to hold a chair in Ghana when he was appointed professor and head of the sociology department.

In 1951, he was indirectly elected by the Ashanti Confederacy Council to the Legislative Council. In 1952 he assumed leadership of the Ghana Congress Party (GCP). In 1956, Dr. Busia gave up his professorship for full-time politics. In the same year the GCP merged with the National Liberation Movement, fusing again at independence in 1957 with other opposition groups to form the United Party (UP). Dr. Busia established himself as the main opposition leader against the Convention People's Party (CPP) of Dr. Kwame Nkrumah (q.v.), but his position was severely weakened by massive defections to the ruling CPP. In 1959 Busia left Ghana for the Hague in Holland to become Professor of Sociology and Culture of Africa at the University of Leiden.

In 1961 he returned to Oxford as a senior member of St. Anthony's College, and remained there until 1966, setting out his political philosophy in his book, *Africa in Search of Democracy*, published in 1967. Apart from Oxford, Dr. Busia had other leading academic appointments, including that of Director of Studies for the World Council of Churches where he surveyed the churches' role in Birmingham, England, and wrote *Urban Churches in Britain* in 1966. Dr. Busia's rich and rewarding academic career gives him a place of prominence in the growing world of African scholars and men of letters. A prolific writer, his publications include *Self-Government, Education for Citizenship, Industrialisation in West Africa* (1955); *Challenge of Africa* (1962); and *Purposeful Education for Africa* (1964).

Following the overthrow of President Nkrumah in February 1966, Busia returned to Ghana in March to serve in the National Liberation Council (NLC) of General Ankrah. He was appointed chairman of the Political Advisory Committee of the NLC, becoming in July 1967 chairman of the National Advisory Committee after the inclusion of 14 civilian members in the Executive Council. Between 1967 and 1968 he served as chairman of the Centre for Civic Education and became a member of the Constituent Assembly appointed to draw up a new constitution in preparation for a return to civilian rule.

In the elections of August 1969, Busia was elected member of Parliament for Wenchi East constituency while his new party, the Progress Party, won 105 seats against 35 of its rival, the National Alliance of Liberals led by Komla Gbedemah. Busia became Prime Minister. But soon afterwards his efforts to handle the country's rough and turbulent politics came under severe criticism. In 1969 he expelled African "aliens" from Ghana in an unprecedented move; in 1970 he dismissed 568 Ghanaians from the civil service for having served under the Government of the First Republic, he dismembered the Trade Union Congress whom he clashed with, and he also dismissed several senior military officers.

At the same time a large section of the population were disappointed by the Prime Minister's inability to make much headway with the country's economy which was taking a turn for the worse. To deal with rapid inflation, a deteriorating balance of payments deficit, coupled with growing pressure of the external debt, Busia devalued the currency by 44 per cent, only to be confronted with resentment arising from high prices of basic commodities. While he was on a visit to Britain on 13 January 1972 the army, led by General Acheampong (q.v.), ousted him in a bloodless coup. Dr. Busia remained in Britain, eventually retiring to his Standlake home in Oxfordshire. He died in Oxford on 28 August 1978. ■

Buta, A. (died 1915)

BUTA, Alvaro (died 1915).

ANGOLAN chief and leader of the resistance to colonialism. He was of the Baxikongo section of the great Kongo (Bakongo) people living on both sides of the lowest part of the Congo (Zaire) river. The kingdom of Kongo, in which a king entitled Manikongo ruled over this numerous people, was powerful in the 16th century, when it was closely allied with Portugal and its kings were for some time Catholics. Later the kingdom declined but a remnant of it survived with the capital at São Salvador. Some of the nobility bore the title *Tulante*, derived from the Portuguese military rank *Tenente* (lieutenant). Alvaro Buta bore this title and is remembered as "Tulante Buta".

He was a chief of the Madimba region in 1911, when the Portuguese had nominal control of the Bakongo, although they were able to intervene in the choice of a successor to the King at São Salvador, which was on the Portuguese side of the border designed by the colonial partition. When King Pedro VI died in 1910 the Portuguese did not allow choice of a new king because Portugal had become a republic. On 1 July 1911, the choice of the kingmakers, Manuel Martins Kiditu, was installed, but not as a king, only as a judge. In that same year Portuguese rule was further enforced on the peoples of northern Angola, and protests gathered strength. In 1912 many areas refused to pay the colonial tax. Some people fled into the Belgian Congo (now Zaire) from increasing oppression. Then, in 1913, there was a major uprising among the Bakongo in Angola, and very soon Alvaro Buta emerged as the main leader.

The final provocation to the rising was a demand by the Portuguese for labourers for São Tomé, where cocoa was grown by imported Angolan workers who were virtually slaves. Manuel Kiditu provided some and was paid. The revolt which followed spread from the Bassorongo, another Kongo section, to the Baxikongo and then others further east. Most of the 250,000 Bakongo in Angola slipped from precarious Portuguese rule. From December 1913 Buta's insurgents fought the Portuguese as well as the judge/king Manuel Kiditu, whom Buta accused of "selling the country" and told him to pay back the money paid for the labourers sent to São Tomé.

The British Baptist missionaries, working at São Salvador since 1878 and a powerful force by 1913, were suspected by the Portuguese of encouraging the revolt. One of them, Reverend Bowskill, mediated with the insurgents. As a result Buta entered São Salvador in December 1913 with a force which rose to 2,000 men, and engaged in talks with the Portuguese representative, Moreira. He demanded the dethronement of Manuel Kiditu and his advisers, the end of the recruitment of "contract labourers", and a reduction in taxation. Manuel immediately fled. The Portuguese replaced Moreira, but although they suspended recruitment for São Tomé they also abolished the ancient monarchy and detained some African leaders of the Baptist Mission congregation.

Buta then attacked São Salvador continually in early 1914, but failed to take it. The uprising spread and won the sympathy of the Bakongo across the border in the Belgian Congo and French Equatorial Africa. A Portuguese offensive in mid-1914 had some success and Buta had to withdraw

to his home area, but he remained at large with many followers. Later events have not been fully recorded in history (the best accounts are in R. Pélissier, *les Guerres Grises*, and J. Marcum, *The Angolan Revolution vol. I*). But it is clear that Baptist Mission mediation led to surrender by some leading colleagues of Buta early in 1915, after which, however, they were arrested with another colleague, Simon Seke, who had stayed in São Salvador. He and another Baptist, Miguel Nekaka, who had been arrested earlier were suspected of being instigators by the government, whose relations with that Mission had usually been bad.

Some time about mid-1915 Buta was invited to a meeting with some Portuguese, who arrested him. He was taken to Cabinda and then to Luanda, where he died of influenza later in 1915. He and Mandume (q.v.), who was also defeated in 1915, were the last and among the greatest of the major resistance leaders in the region. Although it had been defeated by 1916, the Kongo rising in Angola was among the biggest uprisings in Africa in the war against colonialism.∎

Bwanausi, A.W. (1930-68)

BWANAUSI, Augustine Willard (1930-68).

MALAWIAN politician. He was born in 1930 in Blantyre into a Yao family with a long association with the struggle for the independence of Malawi; his grandfather had been involved in the Reverend John Chilembwe's (q.v.) armed rebellion of 1915 against colonial domination and his uncle, Chief Lundu, was one of the chiefs who opposed the Federation of Rhodesia and Nyasaland that was imposed in August 1953 by the British government.

After successfully finishing his primary education at the famous Henry Henderson Institute, Bwanausi entered the equally famous Blantyre Secondary School and came out as the leading student of his final year. In 1951 he won a government scholarship to Makerere University College in Uganda, majoring in Physics, Mathematics and Chemistry. Declared the best student of the year after his second year examinations at Makerere, he graduated with a BSc degree in 1954. He later did a post-graduate course in education at Bristol University, England.

Bwanausi took an active part in

A.W. Bwanausi

Makerere students' politics and other activities. He was a leading member of the Makerere College Political Society which, in 1952, organised the first demonstration held in solidarity with the people of South Africa on the occasion of the third centenary of the arrival of the first European settlers in that country.

The Makerere protest was bitterly criticised by the then European-dominated administration of the College and the Kenya settlers who formed the backbone of settler obduracy in the East Africa region. For his role in the demonstration and later for what was called the "Mammoth Petition" and the subsequent hunger strike in protest against

bad food at the College, Bwanausi was expelled, together with other student leaders. He was however reinstated later in the year.

But it was in the organisation of the Makerere College branch of NYASA, the Nyasaland African Students Association (whose headquarters was at Fort Hare College in South Africa) that Bwanausi's leadership ability excelled. With his colleagues in the branch, he spent tireless nights to produce the organisation's magazine, also called NYASA, which in the absence of an African paper back home in Nyasaland (now Malawi) played a significant role in mobilising public opinion against the Central African Federation and for the independence of Nyasaland. As a member of NYASA he toured many parts of East Africa to address Malawi groups. They also did a lot of research on the question of the Federation of Rhodesia and Nyasaland and helped the Nyasaland African Congress, the parent body of NYASA, in preparing memoranda against the scheme.

He returned to Nyasaland after qualifying at Makerere and worked as a teacher at his old secondary school in Blantyre. He also took an increasing part in political activities and was soon elected to the Central Committee of the Nyasaland African Congress under the leadership of J.F. Sangala. He was also a member of the Nyasa College Association which launched a fund to start a college for poor Malawi students – the funds were later handed over to the Malawi University Fund, launched after self-government.

Still actively promoting the Nyasaland African Congress' twin objectives of secession from the Federation and independence for Nyasaland, Bwanausi contested the elections to the self-government parliament and won the Blantyre Urban seat for the party. He was appointed Minister of Social Development in the Government headed by Dr. Hastings K. Banda. He later held the portfolio of Development, Housing and Works and was thus responsible for implementing Malawi's first three year development plan.

He later however fell out with Prime Minister Banda over the government's fraternisation with South Africa and on 7 September 1964 he and two other ministers were dismissed for "instigating a split in the Cabinet". Bwanausi went into exile in Tanzania where he became a teacher at Pugu

Secondary School near Dar-es-Salaam. He later moved to Zambia to teach and was preparing a book on Mathematics for Zambia's Ministry of Education when he died in a motor accident in the Copperbelt in 1968.

Bwanausi was active in his exile days in the Pan-African Democratic Party led by another Malawian exile, Henry Masauko Chipembere (q.v.), who had resigned in protest at the dismissals of 1964.■

Cabral, A. (1924-73)

CABRAL, Amilcar (1924-73).

G UINEA-BISSAU politician and leading ideologist of the liberation struggle; he founded the Partido Africano da Independencia da Guiné e Cabo Verde (PAIGC), the political movement that led the country to independence. He was born in the Cape Verde Islands, which were then attached for administrative purposes to Portuguese Guinea. After attending the local school, he became one of the few who succeeded in going for higher education in Lisbon where he first trained as an agronomist and later as a hydraulics engineer. In 1952, Cabral went to Portuguese Guinea, where he was one of that colony's few educated Africans, and worked as an agricultural engineer. Between 1952 and 1954, he was director of a team which carried out the first agricultural census in Portuguese Africa, the results of which were published in the *Boletim Cultural da Guiné* Volume XI, Number 43.

As director of the census, Cabral gained first hand knowledge of the land and people of Guinea, it was an experience he would later draw upon when he became secretary-general of the PAIGC. While still a civil servant, Cabral wrote articles in which he identified problems, located blame and recommended solutions. Two of his articles were published in *Boletim Cultural da Guiné Portuguesa* Volume IX, Numbers 34 and 36, under the titles of "On the Utilisation of Land in Africa" and "The Contribution of the Guinean Peoples to the Agricultural Production of Guinea."

Cabral's active contribution to the liberation struggle began in 1953 when he tried, under the guise of a legal sporting organisation, to initiate clandestine ac-

tivity. He differed from some of his contemporaries by advocating a long programme of preparing the peasants for revolution before – rather than after – launching the struggle. During 1956-1959 he was involved in the organisation of cells in the main urban areas of Bafata, Bolama and Bissau. In 1959, after the failure of the dock strike of Pidjiguiti where Portuguese troops killed 50 workers and injured hundreds of others, Cabral was convinced that a strategy which focused on the building of an urban party was bound to fail.

PAIGC cells were heavily infiltrated and repressed by PIDE, the Portuguese secret police. The President of the party at

A. Cabral

that time, Rafael Barbosa, was under arrest as were many other members of the party. Cabral then left for Conakry following ex-French Guinea's independence in 1958. He decided to introduce the strategy of guerrilla warfare within rural areas inside Portuguese Guinea. Cabral realised that nationalism based on limited economic demands would fail and needed to be replaced by a revolutionary nationalism aspiring to the assumption of power. This made imperative a search for a suitable strategy for mobilising the peasants.

In 1959, in a special school, 1,000 cadres drawn from wage-earners, members of the petty bourgeoisie, merchants and peasants were trained, active recruitment of young men was started, especially the unemployed and migrant workers who had a rural background. These changes made the PAIGC a strong force in Guinea, and after three years of fighting that started in 1963 more than two thirds of the country was under PAIGC control.

Cabral examined the internal structure of the different socio-economic zones in order to determine the role which each social group could play in the revolution. From this analysis Cabral concluded that no class was strong enough to accomplish the revolution on its own. The diverse material interests and aspirations of the different groups had to be united against Portuguese colonialism. This necessitated the building of a strong party which Cabral and six others, including his brother Luis Cabral, formed in 1956.

Cabral also had to deal with the question of which social stratum his party could rely on in order to fight. Most peasants in Guinea-Bissau could not read or write and they had almost no direct contact with the colonial power apart from paying taxes. Furthermore, the country was a trading colony and had no settler group which might have deprived peasants of their land. These conditions increased the magnitude of the work involved in convincing the peasants to fight, and so Cabral concluded that in the specific context of Guinea-Bissau, the peasants did not represent a revolutionary force.

Cabral also recognised that the colonial situation did not conduce to the formation of a vanguard party, consisting of a class of conscious workers, which was aware of its role and the real aims of the liberation struggle. As regards the bourgeoisie, he noted that there was no economically viable bourgeoisie because imperialism had prevented its proper formation, that those in existence owed their status to involvement in the colonial state apparatus: the African petty bourgeoisie. This was the only stratum which had access to the instruments which the colonial authority used to oppress the people. While the petty bourgeoisie enjoyed privileges which placed them above the masses, in their day-to-day lives they were confronted by colonialism's humiliation and discrimination.

Cabral saw the petty bourgeoisie as having two possibilities – either allying themselves with imperialism in order to preserve their group, or joining the workers and peasants.

In a speech delivered at the Frantz Fanon Centre in Freviglio, Milan, Italy, in May 1964, Cabral argued that his analysis was closely connected with actual struggle. The central aspects of his analytical method were:

  i) defining the position of each group in relation to their dependence upon the Portuguese colonialists;
  ii) determining the basis of the position each group adopts;
  iii) understanding each group's nationalist capacity, and
  iv) assessing their revolutionary capacity in the post-independence period.

Using this analysis, Cabral noted that in the specific situation of Guinea-Bissau, the proletariat was not well-formed. He categorised urban Africans into higher officials, middle officials, and professionals. Next came minor officials, clerks with contracts and small farm owners. Lastly, there were the wage earners employed in commerce without a contract such as dock workers, boat porters, domestic servants, and so on. Cabral called the last group *déclassés* and divided them into two categories. The *déclassés* proper included beggars and prostitutes who would normally be the "lumpen-proletariat" if there were a developed proletariat. Then there were the nominal *déclassés* consisting of the urban, uprooted recent arrivals, mostly young people connected to the petty bourgeoisie or workers' families but who were themselves unemployed and retained closer ties with rural areas. Cabral saw this latter group as vital to the liberation movement because of its link with the peasants.

Cabral's theoretical analysis represented an important contribution to liberation literature. Differing somewhat with Marxism-Leninism's insistence on the dictatorship of the proletariat, Cabral argued that a decisive role can be played by the petty bourgeoisie, the revolutionary or semi-revolutionary intellectuals forming the vanguard of the revolution.

In a speech delivered in Havana in January 1966, "The Weapon of Theory" (an address to the first Tricontinental Conference of the Peoples of Asia, Africa and Latin America) Cabral emphasised that the most difficult task was "the struggle against our weaknesses," the result of internal contradictions in the economic, social, cultural/historical reality of a people. However great the similarities between various situations, however identical each people's enemies, national liberation and social revolution were not exportable. They differed according to local and national circumstances, and were influenced by the historical reality of each people.

Cabral's major concern was that the people of Guinea-Bissau might regain their own history, i.e. the right to control the national productive forces. This was the only guarantee for genuine liberation as it enabled productive forces to evolve within a people's historical process.

Cabral saw culture as a product as well as a determinant of a people's history. He saw foreign domination's success as dependent upon an organised repression of a people's culture. This in turn made culture the vital factor in national liberation. Since imperialist domination must oppress indigenous culture, national liberation became an act of culture, the organised political expression of the culture of the people undertaking the struggle. To Cabral, the cultural characteristics of each group are important in that each group's attitudes towards the liberation movement are not dictated by its economic interests only, but also but its culture.

Moreover, Cabral pointed out that some of the peoples of Guinea-Bissau were not differentiated in terms of classes. According to Marx, the motor of history is the class struggle. Some societal groups, though having no class (e.g. the Balante), are a part of history nonetheless but in a different framework, following their own dialectic. In his speech of 1970 at Syracuse, USA, on "National Culture and Liberation", Cabral set forth some original ideas on the impact of colonialism. He further elaborated in October 1972 at Lincoln University, Pennsylvania, on the question of class and culture.

Under Cabral the PAIGC did not start armed struggle in one particular place. There was a wide zone of guerrilla activity from the very beginning of 1963, from both the Senegal and Guinea frontiers. Cabral did not consider the liberated zones as only militarily liberated, but as areas with modified administrative and political structures. At the village level, a new administration and legitimacy were set up. Two women and three men were elected to head village committees, local militias were placed in charge of local production, communications, logistics, etc. A health officer, often a woman, was sent for every half dozen villages. Cabral also set up people's stores where peasants could barter rice for clothes. This was the administrative structure that continued to be developed with more complexity and sophistication until the 1972 elections in the liberated areas.

Cabral strove to improve the status of women. He forbade such practices as forced marriages and succeeded in encouraging many women to join the party.

Cabral was also a diplomat. He reached agreements on many issues with neighbouring countries. He was able to explain to other African countries that they too were fighting against Portuguese colonialism. On the international level he was careful to avoid being involved in schisms such as the Sino-Soviet dispute. The movement drew support from both socialist and capitalist countries.

Cabral never stopped emphasising that his people were not fighting against the Whites or the Portuguese people as such. They were fighting against a system and the domination of Portuguese colonialism and all those who supported it. He worked closely with Portuguese leftist groups and accepted that not everything Portuguese was necessarily bad.

From 1963 the PAIGC's main rear base was in Guinea (Conakry), though Senegal later provided another. Cabral was in Conakry when not in the zone of combat or on tour elsewhere. In November 1970 the anti-government Guinean exiles and Portuguese forces who attacked Conakry assaulted the PAIGC office there, but Cabral was not present. However, early in 1973 he was murdered in Conakry. It is believed that the Portuguese colonial authorities persuaded a member of the PAIGC, Innocente Camil, to assassinate Cabral by falsely promising that upon the liquidation of the PAIGC, they would grant independence to Guinea-Bissau. Despite Portugal's denial, it was widely believed that the assassination of Cabral on 20 January 1973 was master-minded by the Portuguese secret police.■

Carr, H.R. (1863-1945)

CARR, Henry Rawlingson (1863-1945).

NIGERIAN educationist who made major contributions to the development of education in the country. He was the first student of Fourah Bay College to gain an honours degree, and the first African Resident (Commissioner) of the Colony of Lagos.

H.R. Carr

Born on 15 August 1863, in Lagos, he was the son of a Sierra Leonean emigrant of Egba origins, Amuwo Carr, and Rebecca Carr. He had his elementary education at the St. Paul's (Breadfruit) School betwen 1869 and 1870, but finished schooling at the Olowogbowo Wesleyan Elementary School, also in Lagos, where he attended from 1871 until 1873. In 1874, he enrolled at the newly-opened Wesleyan Boys' High School in Freetown, Sierra Leone. He entered Fourah Bay College in 1877 and obtained with honours the Bachelor of Arts degree in mathematics and physics in 1882, at the age of 19. He was the first student of the College to gain an honours degree. He left for Britain and enrolled at Lincoln's Inn, St. Mark's College in Chelsea and the Royal College of Science in South Kensington, also in London.

On his return to Nigeria in June 1885, after an absence of 12 years, Carr was appointed senior assistant master at the Church Missionary Society (CMS) Grammar School in Lagos. In 1889, he was invited by the colonial governor to join the civil service as Chief Clerk and Sub-Inspector of Schools for Lagos, in the following year he became the Assistant Colonial Secretary for Native Affairs. He later returned to the department of Education as Provincial Inspector, then Chief Inspector of Schools in Southern Nigeria and Commissioner (Resident) of the Colony of Lagos, from which post he retired on 1 August 1924, at the age of 61.

In 1898 he married Sarah Henrietta Robbin, daughter of Henry Robbin who was a Justice of the Peace of Abeokuta and Freetown. He had written his first book, *Key to Lock's Trigonometry* (published by Macmillan), in 1889, followed by the *General Reports of Education in Lagos* which he compiled and published between 1891 and 1903.

Carr's main interest was education and this was obvious in his reluctance to accept other assignments in the public service. He advocated that education should feature prominently in government programmes because he believed it was necessary for the development of the individual and the nation. This devotion led to his appointment to the Legislative Council in 1928 where, with his wide knowledge of the subject, he became adviser until 1941. He also served in many other capacities in the church, including the Chancellorship of the Diocese of Lagos of the Anglican Church from 1906 until his death in 1945. He held many memberships of the board of governors or advisers of several educational institutions in Nigeria. In 1906, he received the Master of Arts and Bachelor of Civil Law degrees from Durham University. In the King's Birthday Honours of 1920 he was made a Companion of the Imperial Service Order. Later he received the Commander of the Order of the British Empire and also the honorary degrees of Master of Science and Doctor of Civil Law.

Henry Carr died on 6 March 1945. ■

Casely-Hayford, A. (1898-1977)

CASELY-HAYFORD, Archie (1898-1977).

A. Casely-Hayford

GHANAIAN politician. He was a son of the veteran nationalist Joseph Ephraim Casely-Hayford (q.v.) by his first wife, Beatrice Madeline, who died in 1902. Born at Axim, he was educated at Mfantsipim College, Cape Coast, and later in Britain, at Dulwich College in London and then at the University of Cambridge, where he was at Clare College and received the MA degree in law and economics. Returning home, he practised at the Bar in Gold Coast from 1921 to 1936.

He became a member of Sekondi Town Council in 1926. In 1936 he was appointed a district magistrate; he had risen to be senior district magistrate by 1948, when he returned to private legal practice. Then he entered nationalist politics, joining the Convention People's Party (CPP) of Kwame Nkrumah (q.v.), a choice that was in apparent contradiction to Casely-Hayford's upper class background.

Before the 1951 elections he acted as defence counsel for Nkrumah and some other CPP leaders; the party gave him the title D.V.B. (Defender of the Verandah Boys). In 1951 he was elected a CPP member of the Legislative Council for Kumasi, a sign of the CPP's anti-tribalism as he was a Fanti, not an Ashanti. He was re-elected there in 1954, but in 1956, when the Ashantis had largely turned against the CPP, a "safe" seat was found for him.

When Nkrumah formed his first government in 1951 Casely-Hayford was appointed Minister of Agriculture. In that position he was responsible for CPP efforts to persuade cocoa farmers to agree to the destruction of trees to halt the spread of "swollen shoot"; this had some immediate success, though many cocoa farmers later turned against the CPP. He was moved to the ministry of communications. In 1954, as minister of the interior, he had some responsibility (divided, however, with the colonial government still in power) in dealing with the virtual insurrection in Ashanti.

After independence he did not play any important role in politics. But much later, under the rule of the National Reformation Council (NRC) which took over in 1972, he was chairman of the Committee which recommended ways to honour the memory of Kwame Nkrumah. He also became Chancellor of the University of Cape Coast, a post he held at the time of his death in August 1977.

He was involved in many voluntary activities, being chairman of the Ghana Legion of Ex-Servicemen, chairman of the

National Awards and Honours Committee, and a keen rugby player and supporter. He was awarded the Grand Medal in his own country and the Queen's Coronation Medal from Britain. His wife was Thyra Jones-Quartey, sister of the late Prof. K. Jones-Quartey.■

Casely-Hayford, J.E. (1866-1930)

CASELY-HAYFORD, Joseph Ephraim (1866-1930).

GHANAIAN writer, lawyer, politician and founder of the National Congress of British West Africa, J.E. Casely-Hayford was born on 28 September 1866 at Cape Coast in the then Gold Coast, the son of a minister in the Methodist Church. The family's original name of Kwamina Afua had been anglicised through the influence of Christian missionaries.

After attending the local Wesleyan Boys' High School, he travelled to Sierra Leone to study at Fourah Bay College in Freetown. On completing his studies he was appointed headmaster of the Wesleyan Boys'

J.E. Casely-Hayford

High School in Accra, after which he returned to Cape Coast to become headmaster of his old school there.

In 1885 Casely-Hayford left the teaching profession and became a journalist for the *Western Echo* which was owned by his uncle. He remained in this position until 1887 when he left to establish his own newspaper, the *Gold Coast Echo* which began publishing in 1888. Just over a year later he stopped producing the *Gold Coast Echo* and in 1890 became co-proprietor of the *Gold Coast Chronicle*, until 1896. During this time he also contributed articles to the *Wesleyan Methodist Times*.

Desiring to join the legal profession, he had studied law while at the *Gold Coast Chronicle* and became an articled clerk to a Cape Coast lawyer. Later he travelled to England to complete his law studies in London and was called to the Bar at the Inner Temple Inn of Court in 1896. During his stay in England he also studied economics as an external student at Cambridge University. On completing his studies he returned home and set up in legal practice.

In 1897 he joined the newly-established Aborigines' Rights Protection Society (ARPS) and he acted as its legal adviser in its successful campaign against the proposed Lands Bill during the same year. He gradually built up a busy legal practice, and continued writing in his spare time. In 1903 he published his first book, *Gold Coast Native Institutions*, which he dedicated to his first wife, Beatrice Madeline, who had died the previous year.

He published *Ethiopia Unbound* in 1911 and in the same year was one of an ARPS delegation whose opposition to the Forest Lands Bill in the Legislative Council prevented the British Governor from passing that Bill into law.

As his interest and involvement in politics grew, he began to see the need for the Africanisation of education and institutions so as to promote African culture and to restore African self-confidence and self-respect and overcome the cultural oppression of colonialism. To this end he established the Gold Coast National Research Association in 1915.

Between 1916 and 1925 he was a nominated member of the Gold Coast Legislative Council. He was inspired by Mahatma Gandhi and his advocacy for nationalism through non-violence, and Edward Wilmot

Blyden (q.v.), who worked to dispel the myth of negro inferiority and to develop the African personality, as well as by Marcus Garvey.

He felt that an organisation should be established to constitutionally promote the political, social and economic aims of Africans, both in his own country and in the other British West African colonies of Gambia, Nigeria and Sierra Leone. Along with a few others he began preparations for a West African Conference which later became the National Congress of British West Africa (NCBWA), holding its first meeting in March 1920. Casely-Hayford became vice-president of this organisation, and later in 1920 he travelled to London as part of a delegation from the NCBWA to request constitutional and policy changes leading to self-government from the British colonial authorities. The Secretary of State for the Colonies refused to meet the delegation, but they were able to publicise their objectives through the League of Nations' Union.

From 1927 he represented Sekondi Takoradi on the Legislative Council until 1930, the year of his death. During this time he was also a member of the Takoradi Harbour Committee of the Council which was involved in the creation of a deep water harbour as part of a development plan. Throughout the 1920s there had been opposition between the intelligentsia such as Casely-Hayford and the traditional chiefs. The former strongly opposed the 1925 Constitution and the 1927 Native Administration Ordinance as these pieces of colonial legislation strengthened the traditional authority of the chiefs. However, some of these difficulties were overcome, partly through the appointment of educated chiefs.

During the later years of his life he became involved in the production of the *Gold Coast Leader*, a fortnightly journal which supported the political advancement of Africans. He also helped found the Gold Coast Youth Conference, the precursor to political parties in Ghana. He died the following year on 11 August 1930 at the age of 63. He had made a major contribution to the development of nationalist politics in his country and was also in the unique position of being supported by politicians in all four British West African colonies.

He was survived by his second wife Adelaide and their daughter Gladys and son Victor and by another son by his first marriage, the late Archie Casely-Hayford (q.v.), who served in a number of ministerial positions under Kwame Nkrumah. ∎

Cetshwayo (1832-84)

CETSHWAYO (1832-84).

ZULU King whose reign coincided with the economic revolution that transformed South Africa politically as well. The British, anxious to control the sub-continent through a federation with the Boers, sought to subjugate the remaining still independent African nations. Cetshwayo, an obstruction to this plan, was invaded and when defeated exiled to Cape Town. Though he later returned to head the Zulu nation, he did so under British tutelage, and died leaving behind him a broken kingdom.

Born in 1832, Cetshwayo was the eldest son of Mpande (q.v.). When he was about eight years old his father was installed King of the Zulus. In his youth he served his father in the élite Thulwana regiment and by the time he reached manhood, had his own Zulu followers known as Usuthu. As he

Cetshwayo

became increasingly influential in Zulu affairs, there developed during the 1850s rivalry between Cetshwayo and his brother Mbuyazi as to who would succeed as King. This culminated in the battle of Ndondaku-suka where many thousands, including Mbuyazi, died, and Cetshwayo became the acknowledged successor of his father.

By the early 1860s increasing border disputes with the Boers in Transvaal led Mpande and Cetshwayo to seek the support of the British in Natal, which they obtained for some years. When Cetshwayo succeeded to the throne in 1872 on the death of his father, he wanted his position to be recognized by the British so as to substantiate their promises of support against Boer incursions into Zululand and the following August this was achieved during a visit to his country by Natal's Secretary for Native Affairs, Theophilus Shepstone. The Zulu state at that time was economically independent, as well as having a strong political and military infrastructure.

In 1877, as part of the British confederation policy for southern Africa, Transvaal was annexed with Shepstone becoming its administrator. As a result, his policy of friendship towards Cetshwayo changed.

Shepstone's position was buttressed when he was joined by Sir Bartle Frere, the newly appointed British High Commissioner in southern Africa, whose brief was to help form the confederation. Frere regarded Cetshwayo as another Chaka (q.v.), a threat to the British plans for the region, and sent a damning report to London to this effect. In an attempt to weaken the Zulu state, Frere and Shepstone accepted the validity of the Boers' claims to land in Zululand. A boundary commission was appointed by the British Government to investigate the dispute. This was welcomed by Cetshwayo, and in June 1878 it reported that the Boers had no legal claim to the disputed land. Frere suppressed this report for some time, instead exaggerating minor border incidents to prove the aggression of the Zulus and the consequent threat to the stability of the region as a white-dominated confederation.

Acting on his own initiative, Frere contacted Cetshwayo in 1878 and demanded that the Zulu military system be dismantled. Cetshwayo refused and began to amass his forces in his capital Ulundi. The following January, miscalculating the military strength of the Zulus, Frere sent in troops to try to enforce his demands. The battle of Isandlwana followed during which the British suffered a crushing defeat. Cetshwayo tried to no avail to reach a settlement with the British forces as he realised the economic strains of keeping his large army permanently mobilised. His orders not to attack the invaders were disobeyed and subsequent battles proved disastrous.

Meanwhile public opinion in Britain was going against this conflict and the plan for confederation was abandoned. Frere was replaced by Sir Garnet Wolseley who was charged with bringing about peace. He did this by claiming that the war was against Cetshwayo and not the Zulu people. The presence of British troops in Zululand and the need for the resumption of food production to ward off starvation caused most of the Zulu soldiers to return to their farms, and two months later, in August 1879, Cetshwayo was captured and taken to Cape Town where he was imprisoned. Wolseley thus ended the rule of the Zulu royal house. He set about breaking up the political and military infrastructure that had been the source of the Zulus' strength, by replacing it with 13 separate and weaker individual territories. While in Cape Town, Cetshwayo resumed contact with the Bishop of Natal, Bishop Colenso, who was really angered by the way Shepstone and Frere had manoeuvred the invasion of Zululand. He began to campaign vigorously for Cetshwayo's release and return to his rightful position. Cetshwayo also sent several letters to the British Government asking to return home.

By the end of 1881 it became apparent that Wolseley's new order in Zululand was not working. Internal rivalries were bringing about increasing violence and bloodshed and the British began to consider the possibility of Cetshwayo's return. In the summer of 1882 he was invited to London for talks. Arriving there in July, he impressed everyone with his dignity and behaviour. A report from the Special Commissioner for Zululand arrived during the talks. This recommended Cetshwayo's return to his home, provided the country was partitioned to avoid confrontation with those groups that had risen to power through Cetshwayo's exile and were thus opposed to his return. The exact areas of partition were not finalised. Cetshwayo protested vigorously against this proposal but was unable to stop its implementation.

On his return to Cape Town in September 1882 the details of the partition of Zululand were revealed. Cetshwayo finally and reluctantly agreed to the plan and he arrived in Zululand in January 1883. He remained in contact with the British Government, though he continued to strongly object to his loss of land. Moreover, the partitioning did not resolve the internal rivalry problem; soon increased violence broke out, followed by civil war. In July his house at Ulundi was attacked and many of the leading men of the Zulu people were killed. Cetshwayo escaped to Nkandla with a few followers. He moved to Eshowe in October 1883 under the protection of Osborn, the British Resident Commissioner. The following February he died, officially of a heart attack although there were rumours that he had been poisoned. The Zulus' great nation and independence died with him.■

King Chaka

Chaka (c.1788-1828)

CHAKA, King (c.1788-1828).

FOUNDER of the Zulu Empire, the son of Senzangakhona, a Zulu prince, and Nandi, a princess of the Langeni clan. Chaka grew up among his mother's people because his parents, who belonged to the same Langeni clan, had separated when he was six owing to the fact that their marriage had violated Zulu law and custom. Most of his boyhood was characterised by incessant humiliations based on the circumstances of his birth. In 1802 Chaka and his mother left the Langenis and found refuge among the Mtetwa.

At the age of 23, Chaka entered military training under Dingiswayo, paramount chief of the Mtetwa, who was soon immensely impressed by Chaka's military genius and skill. In 1816, Chaka's father Senzangakhona died, leaving a vacant throne for which Dingiswayo encouraged Chaka to make a bid. Chaka ascended to the throne and immediately set about introducing stern discipline into a disorganised army. He forbade his soldiers to marry in order that family commitment may not interfere with military duty. He was opposed to the wearing

of sandals as he saw them as an impediment to fast movement. His motto was "Either return from battle with your weapons or not return at all". With these and other measures of stern discipline, Chaka commanded an army of over 60,000 men and 10,000 women.

He equipped his soldiers each with a shield and *assegai*, a long-bladed short-handled dagger that enabled Chaka's army to engage the enemy at close quarters with devastating effect. He organised the army into *impi* (regiments) based on age groups and billeted in separate kraals. In one swift campaign after another, Chaka's army brought many groups under the rule of the Zulu political empire, which emanated from present-day Natal. Chaka's army inspired such great fear among other clans that many of them fled and set in motion their own destruction which came to be known as *Mfecane*, the Crushing.

In 1827 Chaka's mother, Nandi, died and it is said that the King ordered the death of many people to mourn and mark the occasion. On 24 September 1828, two of Chaka's half brothers, Dingane and Mhlangana, and an *induna* or army commander, Mbopa, assassinated the King, allegedly in order to put a stop to Chaka's incessant calls for army operations. Chaka left an empire so strong that it lasted for 50 years after the death of its founder. A memorial has been erected in Couper Street, Stanger, a town that was built after Chaka's death, in the approximate position of his assassination. The Chaka memorial was built in 1932 by public subscription and declared a historical monument by the South African government in 1938, and it is inscribed: "In memory of Tshaka ka Senzangakona, the founder, king, and ruler of the Zulu nation. Born about 1788. Died on 24 September, 1828. Erected by his descendant and heir Solomon ka Dinuzulu and the Zulu Nation. A.D. 1932."■

Champion, A.W.G. (1893-1975)

CHAMPION, Allison Wessells George (1893-1975).

SOUTH AFRICAN pioneering trade unionist. Born on 4 December 1893 in Lower Tugela in the Natal Province, he was named after an American missionary for whom his father worked as an interpreter. Champion was educated at mission schools before entering Adams College where he was expelled in 1913 for rebellious activity. He gained employment as a police constable in Johannesburg but soon moved to Dundee in his birth province, as a Special Branch investigator.

After that he returned to Johannesburg in 1916 to work in the gold mines as a clerk. Here he participated in the formation of the Native Mine Clerks' Association in 1920 and was elected its first president. He soon gained recognition for his exceptional leadership and organisational abilities which in 1925 brought him into Clements Kadalie's (q.v.) Industrial and Commercial Workers Union of Africa (ICU) as its Transvaal branch secretary. Second in command to Kadalie, Champion acted as national secretary of the ICU during the former's trip to Europe in 1927. During this period Champion succeeded in forcing through many changes on behalf of his members in the ICU. In Natal and Transvaal he challenged many laws and government orders which impinged on the rights of workers. For example, he

successfully fought for the revocation of the law which prevented African drivers from driving European passengers. His activities also compelled many employers to improve the working conditions of their African employees.

A.W.G. Champion

The ICU grew into a powerful organisation, alarming the white minority regime. Its activities led in 1929, to riots in Durban when many African workers and two Europeans were killed during a labour unrest. After these riots the government set up the de Waal Commission whose report described Champion as a man of great influence who could do both much good and harm. The report recommended that immediate measures be taken to improve the conditions of the African workers.

In 1928 at the height of its power the ICU split because of internal disputes that included allegations of financial irregularities. Champion led the Natal branch which formed the core of an "independent" ICU and for which he became secretary. This however declined, when he was banned from Natal in 1930 as a result of the 1929 riots. He stayed in Johannesburg until 1933 when the banning order expired, returning to Durban for active involvement in the African National Congress (ANC). During the 1920s he was elected into the executive committee of the movement, then being led by Josiah T. Gumede (q.v.). In 1937 he was voted back into the executive where he served for the next 14 years, becoming president of its Natal branch in 1945. Between 1940 and 1947 he acted as president-general of the movement.

In 1942 Champion was elected to the Natives' Representative Council. He also served on the Durban combined Location Advisory Board and the Urban Bantu Councils whose chairman he was for ten years. He deliberated in many succession disputes between ruling houses in Natal and Zululand and, for this, was highly respected by many chiefs in South Africa. He was an adviser to Chief Gatsha Buthelezi of KwaZulu. Champion died in 1975. ■

Chilembwe, J. (1870-1915)

CHILEMBWE, Reverend John (1870-1915).

Rev. J. Chilembwe

MALAWIAN clergyman, politician and anti-colonialist hero whose life was a source of inspiration for many of his compatriots. A Yao, he was born at Sangano in 1870. Largely a self-taught man, he embraced a philosophy which called for "Africa for the Africans".

He was a student at the Church of Scotland mission at Blantyre. In 1892 he came into contact with Joseph Booth's Baptist mission and acted as Booth's assistant, interpreter and pupil. In 1897 Chilembwe accompanied Booth to Britain and the USA. Under the auspices of the Black Baptist Church, Chilembwe enrolled at a seminary in Virginia. While in America he came into contact with contemporary Afro-American ideas.

He returned to Chiradzulu in Nyasaland (now Malawi) as an ordained minister in 1900 and founded the Ajana Providence Industrial Mission at Mbombwe, near Blantyre, with Afro-American Baptists' help. His following grew. One school enrolled 1,000 pupils and the adult education section had 800 people by 1912.

Chilembwe's aims were to improve the standard of living and quality of life of his people. He also attempted to modernise the social and economic institutions in rural Malawi. His teachings concentrated on improved methods of growing crops and personal and environmental health while at the same time he encouraged people to work hard and discouraged the drinking of alcoholic beverages.

Chilembwe's idea of operating within the framework of the colonial system had been shattered by 1914. The situation was aggravated by the famine of 1913 and the outbreak of the First World War. Chilembwe vociferously protested, both on public platforms and in the local press, against the forced participation of Africans in the war.

White plantation farmers accused Chilembwe of fomenting nationalism among the people. Some farmers went to the extent of burning down the buildings and schools that Chilembwe had erected for the education of the people. Such was the ill-treatment of Africans by the European settlers in the neighbourhood that Chilembwe decided to mobilise armed opposition to the planters and also against conscription into the British colonial army. In doing so, Chilembwe became one of the first Western-educated Africans to attempt a mass-based resistance movement against colonial domination. It was said that Chilembwe's objective was not to overthrow the government but only to highlight the grievances of his people in the most dramatic fashion.

In the uprisings which followed in January 1915, with limited attacks in a few places, three Europeans died. But the response of the colonial administration was swift and savage, many people were killed by the troops which were deployed to contain the uprising. On 3 February 1915, Chilembwe was found, with his nephew Morris Chilembwe, by the police, and both were shot dead while allegedly resisting arrest. Chilembwe's name is a legend in independent Malawi where he is regarded as a hero of anti-colonialism. ■

Chinamano, J.M. (1922-84)

CHINAMANO, Josiah Mushore (1922-84).

ZIMBABWEAN politician, educationist and nationalist leader who was Joshua Nkomo's colleague and right-hand man in the Zimbabwe liberation struggle. Subjected to long periods of detention together with his wife Ruth, he survived the many years of political struggle to become Minister of Transport for a period in the Zimbabwean government as one of the four members of Zimbabwe African People's Union (ZAPU) in Prime Minister Robert Mugabe's cabinet.

Born on 29 October 1922 near Salisbury (now Harare), he was a diligent student at the missionary schools he attended, being usually top of the class. This diligence was to characterise him throughout his life. He taught at Waddilove Institute where he studied for the Bachelor of Arts degree through correspondence courses of the University of South Africa. Later, in detention, he studied for another degree in Economics. In 1953 he spent a year in London teaching missionary teachers who were preparing to teach in African missionary schools. Thereafter, he became headmaster of a Methodist

school. But dissatisfied with the educational policies of the government, which not only provided inferior education for Blacks but also did not provide sufficient schools, he went on to found a non-governmental school in Highfields which became the largest of its

J. Chinamano

kind with over 1400 pupils. Alongside it he established a co-operative and shopping centre. The school attracted teachers from Scotland and assistants from the white liberal Rhodesians.

Chinamano and his wife were active members of ZAPU and as such were exposed to frequent harassment by the Rhodesian security police. They were arrested and detained in April 1964 with other leaders of ZAPU, on the instructions of Ian Smith who had become Prime Minister three days before. The Chinamanos, Joshua Nkomo, and Joseph Msika were flown out to a wild life reserve where they were joined by other political detainees. They were released a year later but their freedom was to be short-lived. They were detained under "preventive detention" orders two months later and became separated from their children for five years, whose education and upkeep were taken care of by International Defence and Aid. Meanwhile, Highfields school had been closed for alleged political indoctrination of the pupils.

When they were released in 1970 they were restricted to a four-mile radius of their house in Highlands. Chinamano was also banned from teaching; he opened a small store.

After Ian Smith declared unilateral independence on 11 November 1965, the Conservative government of Britain hoped that they could persuade the Rhodesian Africans to accept a new constitution (drawn up without their participation). A commission of inquiry was set up under the British judge, Lord Pearce in 1972, to test African opinion on the proposed constitutional changes. If the Africans accepted the changes the illegal regime would then have been legalized. Joshua Nkomo and the vast majority of ZAPU executives were in detention, so Chinamano was ordered by Nkomo to set up a front organisation to co-ordinate opposition to the proposed constitutional changes, ZAPU having been proscribed. Chinamano became treasurer of the organisation, African National Council (ANC), and Bishop Muzorewa its chairman. The Africans rejected the proposed settlement and Pearce had to report that the Africans opposed the handing of power to a White minority.

In 1972 Chinamano and his wife were again detained following disturbances during the Pearce Commission enquiry. They were confined to a detention centre and later transferred to Marandellas prison reserve. The Pearce Report said: "The Chinamanos were of importance to the African National Council. We have no evidence that they were planning disorders".

In September 1975 the leaders of the ANC as well as the ZAPU leaders, among them Nkomo, met in Lusaka to hold elections for the leadership that would create a unified African National Council. Bishop Muzorewa returned to Salisbury before the Congress. The ZAPU element of the Council then decided to hold its own Congress. Joshua Nkomo was elected President and Chinamano Vice-President. In December that year Chinamano was part of a delegation that had an abortive meeting with Ian Smith to persuade him to hand over power to the nationalist organisations.

When the Zimbabwe liberation war was ended by the Lancaster House Conference in London on 21 December 1979, Chinamano was dispatched by ZAPU to Maputo to discuss unity with Robert Mugabe's Zimbabwe African National Union (ZANU), but this was not to be. ZANU won the elections by a wide margin. The Prime Minister elect Robert Mugabe appointed two White members of Ian Smith's party and four members of ZAPU into his twenty-two member cabinet with Josiah Chinamano becoming Minister of Transport.

In February 1982 large dumps of arms were found and the government accused ZAPU of plotting to overthrow it. Eleven days after the find, Joshua Nkomo, Josiah Chinamano, Joseph Msika and Jini Ntuta were dismissed from their cabinet posts.

He died in 1984 while he was still politically active within ZAPU.■

Chinsinga (died 1902)

CHINSINGA, King (died 1902).

MOZAMBICAN ruler of Makanga, a nineteenth century state north of the Zambezi River. The area is now a province in the Republic of Mozambique. Chinsinga was a contemporary of Gungunyane and Makombe Hanga (qq.v.), the legendary politicians and celebrated soldiers of freedom who resisted Portuguese colonialism. Like these great men, King Chinsinga led his people into battle to defend the sovereignty of Makanga against European colonialist incursions.

As a young man Chinsinga was sent by his father, King Saka-Saka, to train at Quelimane, now a major port on the Indian Ocean coast, and later at Tete on the Zambezi. The Portuguese were very active in these regions at that time and, apart from being exposed to their influence, the young prince was able to witness at close quarter the harsh, oppressive measures of the Europeans. This experience influenced his policies when he became king.

He did not immediately ascend the throne upon his father's assassination in 1885 by a European. The royal council of Makanga elected his cousin, Chicucuru II, as successor but the new king was killed by a Portuguese invading army four years later. Chicucuru's death led to submission to Portugal and to the commercial activities of the Companhia da Zambézia, one of the powerful companies which helped enforce colonial occupation.

Chinsinga, who had been exiled by his cousin to Tete, returned in 1892 and fought the new ruler Chigaga. He overthrew him and ascended the throne. Shrewd in diplomacy and an able organiser, he was cautious not to provoke the wrath of the Companhia da Zambézia. He indeed encouraged their involvement in Makanga's affairs through the company's local representative, Joao Martins. Trade flourished as Europeans flooded Makanga for ivory, wax, rubber and slaves.

In return for Chinsinga's loyalty to the Companhia, Portugal granted funds for the development of the region. But his subjects were then beginning to oppose the subjugation of Makanga to the colonial authorities; the King was criticised for having betrayed his ancestors. In 1897 he acknowledged the criticism and reassured his citizens that future policies would be motivated by Makanga's interests. Thus began his anti-colonial policy which culminated in the Makanga rising of 1901.

Early in 1897 he repudiated the 1893 treaty nominally accepting Portuguese rule. He said then "Since Makanga does not belong to the Companhia da Zambézia no one can order anything to be done without my approval". The Europeans responded by invading Makanga in December 1901 and for the following five months engaged King Chinsinga's army in battle. The resistance was fierce but, outpowered by the European arsenal, Makanga was subdued. King Chinsinga attempted to flee to Blantyre in Malawi but committed suicide midway by the Revube River in 1902. ■

Chipembere, H.M. (1900-76)

CHIPEMBERE, Reverend Habil Matthew (1900-76).

MALAWIAN clergyman and educationist. He was born in Masiye Village, Chiwanga Niassa Province, Mozambique, on the eastern shore of Lake Malawi directly opposite Nkota Kota on the other side. His parents, who belonged to the same people as the famous Undi Chief whose land was later parcelled between Nyasaland (now Malawi)

and Northern Rhodesia (now Zambia), fled from the Ngoni invasion of Malawi. These people, the original Nyanja (so called because of their association with the lake, *nyanja* in the local language, and great fishermen) arrived on the Mozambique side of Lake

Rev. H.M. Chipembere

Malawi just after the partition of Africa. They were the bearers of the original name of Malawi. They were strong followers of the Anglican Church, the first African translation of the Bible was into their language, and the population had a very high number of Anglican priests.

Habil was enrolled at the Chiwanga (Msumba) lakeshore mission school and attended Sunday school as well, in preparation for admission into the Christian faith, before he was baptised (dropping his traditional names) Habil Matthew Chipembere. While he had given his children religious freedom, their father remained a polygamist and a famous trader (known as Faida) in the area and the coast of Tanzania, trading in elephant tusks, handicrafts and possibly slaves in exchange for cloth, beads and other commodities; he was not baptised until later in life and even then insisted on being called Yusuf, the Moslem or Swahili version of his baptismal name Joseph. Habil made rapid progress at school and easily passed the Saint Michael Teachers' Training College Entrance Examination; the school had been transferred from Kango, on the Mozambican side of Lake Nyasa, to Likoma Island in what was then Nyasaland, after the murder of its principal, the Reverend Arthur (after whom he named his first son), by Portuguese authorities for refusing to allow the local officers free access to the girl students. Habil was admitted into St. Michael's College, Makulawe, in 1915, being one of the two youngest students of the year. The College, however, was closed during part of the First World War period; he thus did not finish his studies until 1919 (the year he married Drusilla Salim) instead of 1917.

Since missionaries were transferred freely then between Tanganyika, Mozambique and Nyasaland, teachers and other members of staff could also be freely transferred from one territory to another. Thus after working for one year or so at his old school in Msumba (in Mozambique) Habil was transferred to various mission stations in Nyasaland and at one time in Tanganyika before he was eventually transferred to Fort Johnston (now Mangochi), where he and his family finally settled among his people, who had also emigrated back to Nyasaland. Habil also had a spell as tutor at his former Teachers' Training College in Likoma before he enrolled as a deacon in 1933; qualifying in 1935, he was ordained on 25 January 1938. His first station was in Liuli in Tanganyika, then within the Diocese of South-West Tanganyika which also included Mozambique, Malawi and Northern Rhodesia. During World War II, he was chaplain to soldiers in Kenya and in that capacity he travelled widely, as far as India. In 1960 he was installed Canon by Bishop Frank Thorne.

Such was the impact of his work as a priest that Habil was promoted in 1963 the first Anglican Archdeacon of the South-West Nyasa province of the Anglican church. At this time, however, his family was already heavily engulfed in the politics of Nyasaland with his son Henry Masauko Blasius Chipembere (q.v.) already in the forefront of the struggle for the liberation and a Member of the Legislative Council as well as Treasurer-General of the Nyasaland African Congress. When Masauko was jailed for three years, the Malawi Congress Party formed after the then banned Nyasaland African Congress, unanimously nominated

Habil for the Fort Johnston constituency (the stronghold of Masauko), and he was elected unopposed. He served as one of the respected old members of parliament in a self-governing Malawi, until Masauko was released to take up the seat himself in 1963.

Habil, however, went on to serve as a father figure in Malawi politics, particularly in the Mangochi (Fort Johnston) District. And thus, after the Malawi 1964 Cabinet crisis in which three senior members of Government were sacked and three others, including Masauko, resigned in sympathy, Habil fell out of favour with the Banda regime after several attempts by Banda to woo him and even intimidate him to his favour. When finally Masauko, Silombela and others took up armed resistance against Banda, Habil (already under various threats) felt that he and his family were in danger. He was eventually banished from Likoma Island and chose to live in exile in Tanzania where he served as a priest at his old station Mbamba Bay from 1966 to 1969, when he retired. He joined his son Masauko (also in exile) in Dar-es-Salaam. Habil died in exile there in 1976; at his funeral ceremony at St. Alban's Church eight fellow Anglican priests officiated, including Archbishop John Sepeku of the Anglican Church.∎

Chipembere, H.M.B. (1930-75)

CHIPEMBERE, Henry Masauko Blasius (1930-75).

MALAWIAN politician. He was born on 5 August 1930 at Kayoyo, Malawi, the fourth son of the Rev. H.M. Chipembere (q.v.). He received his education at Blantyre Secondary School and Goromonzi Secondary School in Zimbabwe (Southern Rhodesia). He then went to the University of Fort Hare in South Africa where he obtained a BA degree.

On his return to the then Nyasaland in 1954, Chipembere became an assistant district commissioner at Domasi, near Zomba. He however became very active in the Nyasaland African Congress at a time when the issue of the Federation of Rhodesia and Nyasaland was dominant. The Federation had been created in 1953 and many African politicians were convinced that it reinforced white settler control based in the then Southern Rhodesia. He was among the five people (all on the Congress ticket) who were elected to the Legislative Council through the indirect vote of the African Provincial Councils in March 1956. In 1957,

H.M.B. Chipembere

Chipembere married Catherine Ambali from Likoma Island, and they had seven children.

Chipembere argued that members of the Nyasaland African Congress should not sit in the Assembly of the Federation of Rhodesia and Nyasaland. The two Congress members who refused to resign their seats in the Assembly were expelled later from the party.

Chipembere was impressed by Dr. Hasting K. Banda's campaigns against the Federation in London. He started correspondence with him and spearheaded the drive to get Banda to return to Nyasaland. For his part, Banda insisted that he would return only if he were guaranteed the leadership of Congress. Chipembere was instrumental in enabling Congress to meet this demand and in 1958 Banda returned to Malawi and duly assumed the presidency of Congress.

A powerful orator and able organiser, Chipembere was the elected treasurer-general of the Malawi Congress Party (MCP), and was among those who organised the Emergency Conference of 24 and 25 January 1959 which was followed by a series of disturbances throughout Malawi. On 3 March 1959, Chipembere was arrested along with others and detained in Gwelo in Southern Rhodesia (Zimbabwe) together with Dr. Banda and the two Chisiza brothers (qq.v.) under the State of Emergency Act.

On his release in September 1960, still general treasurer of the MCP, he continued to advocate militant action against the colonial government. In February 1961 he was sentenced to three years' imprisonment in Zomba after being convicted of sedition and inciting violence.

In February 1963, a new constitution brought internal self-government, and when Chipembere was released in 1963 Banda appointed him Minister of Local Government. He was later transferred to head the Ministry of Education. In an ensuing Cabinet crisis in 1964, Chipembere appealed to Prime Minister Banda to become less autocratic, to encourage corporate leadership and to democratise the decision-making process.

The issues facing the government were the question of recognising Communist China and Malawi's relationship with South Africa. China had proposed to give Malawi an £18m loan which most of the Cabinet members were ready to accept, but which Dr. Banda was reluctant to receive. Banda said that China was attempting to bribe his government into recognition but that he did not understand the language of bribery. Ministers present at the Cabinet meetings at the time however later claimed that the Prime Minister was using the issue of China as an excuse, a diversion from the unanimous cabinet opposition to his policy of appeasing South Africa.

At the time of the Cabinet revolt, Chipembere was in Canada attending an education conference. On his return he adopted a conciliatory stance. In a speech later in Parliament, Chipembere made an appeal for a rational approach to the crisis. This was a debate which preceded a vote of confidence in Dr. Banda.

In September 1964 three ministers were dismissed. Chipembere and two others resigned in protest against the dismissals.

Chipembere was later put under house arrest at his home in Malindi, Fort Johnston, but escaped into Mozambique where he organised a resistance movement. In Malawi, Chipembere became a wanted man, and a reward of £500 was put on his head, dead or alive. In February 1965 Chipembere led an armed attack on Fort Johnston. He managed to capture a police station, some arms and ammunition, and vehicles. His army destroyed the telecommuncations system, but the rebels' march on Zomba, the capital of the province, which was some 150 miles to the south, was forestalled by security forces at Liwonde, 30 miles from Zomba. Chipembere's men later adopted guerrilla tactics, but they were eventually defeated when Chipembere's lieutenant and chief of operations Medson Evans Silombela was captured. Silombela was sentenced to death and his execution was witnessed by the public, including relatives of the people who died during the brief period of the resistance.

Following the abortive advance on Zomba, Chipembere fled the country to the United States. He later joined other Malawian exiles in Tanzania where he taught at TANU's ideological colleges at Kirukoni and founded the Pan-African Democratic Party of Malawi. In 1969 he went back to America to research for a PhD degree in History at the University of California, Los Angeles. He was later offered the position of assistant professor in History at the California State University, Los Angeles. He died in Los Angeles, due to a worsening of his diabetic condition, on 24 September 1975. ■

he toured the then Belgian Congo (now Zaire) as part of a United States study team. He then moved to Salisbury where he worked in the Indian High Commission as an information officer. For a time he was a member of the Baha'i sect but left it because of its opposition to political involvement.

D.K. Chisiza

Chisiza, D.K. (1930-62)

CHISIZA, Dunduza Kaluli (1930-62).

MALAWIAN politician, Dunduza Chisiza was born on 8 August 1930 at Karonga, Malawi (then called Nyasaland). He was educated at the Livingstonia Mission and Aggrey Memorial College, Uganda. In 1949 he worked as a clerk in the Dar-es-Salaam police records office. Between 1952 and 1953

After helping to found the Southern Rhodesia African National Youth League in 1955, which was a precursor to the African National Congress two years later, he was deported to Nyasaland in 1956. There he joined the Nyasaland African Congress. Between 1957 and 1958 he studied Third World economies at Fircroft College, Birmingham, England.

On his return, he became the secretary-general of the Nyasaland African National Congress, and organised an emergency conference of Congress in January 1959. This led to political unrest during which Chisiza, together with over 1,500 other

Congress leaders, were arrested on 3 March 1959. He was detained in Gwelo in Southern Rhodesia (Zimbabwe) with Dr. Banda, his brother Yatuta Chisiza (q.v.) and Henry Chipembere (q.v.).

While in prison he busied himself with writing. In a pamphlet entitled *Africa: What lies ahead*, he wrote that in its drive towards independence a nationalist movement needed to elevate the leader above all others, that colleagues needed to assume a subordinate role and pledge their loyalty to his leadership. Arguing that leadership involved following as well as leading, Chisiza stated that once the goal of independence was achieved the problem would arise of reconciling subordination with individual initiative on the part of second level leaders. Such an exercise of initiative could be mistakenly construed as a sign of rivalry and disloyalty by the leader. These fears were proven right by the Cabinet crisis which engulfed the government in 1964.

On his release in September 1960 he was appointed secretary-general of the Malawi Congress Party. He attended the Federal Review Conference of December 1960 as part of the Nyasaland delegation. Elected member of Parliament for Karonga district in the first Nyasaland general elections, he served as parliamentary secretary in the Ministry of Finance between 1961 and 1962. A voracious reader, Chisiza believed that Nyasaland's economy required a strong agricultural base, in a mixed economy in which cooperatives would be dominant. He organised an international economic symposium in 1962. On 2 September 1962 Chisiza was killed in a car crash near Zomba, less than two years before the independence of Malawi.■

Malawi's independence and later held the post of Minister of Home Affairs.

He was born in 1926 in Karonga District in the then Nyasaland (renamed Malawi at independence on 6 July, 1964). He and his younger brother Dunduza had their early education locally before attending the Livingstonia Institution, a Scottish mission institute in Nyasaland, and both later

Y.K. Chisiza

Chisiza,Y.K. (1926-67)

CHISIZA, Yatuta Kaluli (1926-67).

MALAWIAN politician who, like his brother Dunduza Kaluli Chisiza (q.v.), was prominent in the nationalist struggle for

left their country for the then Tanganyika, now mainland Tanzania, where in 1948 Chisiza joined the British colonial police force.

Yatuta Kaluli Chisiza rose to the rank of Inspector of Police, which was very rare for an African in those colonial days when Europeans had a monopoly of senior positions. He however turned down a request by the Tanganyika African National Union

(TANU) to stay as head of a future independent Tanzania's police force, in favour of joining the independence struggle of his country.

He returned to Nyasaland in 1957 to join forces with his brother and other nationalists in the campaign against British rule there. He was a full-time member of the Nyasaland African Congress (NAC) which at the time had a programme centred on a policy of non-co-operation with the colonial authorities; nationalist feelings had been rising against British plans to create the Federation of Rhodesia and Nyasaland, and its imposition in August 1953 brought African opposition to the verge of new militancy. On 24 and 25 January 1959 NAC held an emergency Action Conference at Soche, to deliberate on its strategy. This meeting was followed by a series of anti-British demonstrations in several parts of the protectorate.

The following month the British authorities declared a state of emergency and banned the NAC, alleging that the movement had at the Soche meeting plotted the massacre of the British governor and top British administrators in Nyasaland. Some 1,500 leaders and prominent members of the NAC were subsequently arrested in a dawn swoop on 3 March 1959. Among these were Yatuta Chisiza, who was serving as chief of security and private secretary to Dr Hastings Banda. Others detained included Banda himself, Dunduza Chisiza and Henry Chipembere (q.v.). They were all detained in Gwelo prison in Southern Rhodesia (now Zimbabwe).

While in detention Chisiza was reported to have been angered by his exclusion from the independence "Gwelo Cabinet" which nationalist inmates were plotting. Meanwhile the Malawi Congress Party (MCP) had been formed to succeed the banned NAC, with the aim of continuing the campaign for independence as well as for the release of the detained NAC leaders. Dr Banda was released in April 1960; this was followed by the ending of the state of emergency in June, but it was not until September of that same year that Chisiza and the last seven other detainees were freed.

He was re-elected administrative secretary of the MCP which had begun negotiations on Nyasaland's independence with the British. In the general elections on the eve of independence, Chisiza was elected a member for the Karonga constituency, becoming Minister of Home Affairs, with responsibility for Local Government, the Police and Prison Services, in the first administration of independent Malawi. He retained the post until 1964, also serving on various party and government delegations which represented Malawi abroad.

With Augustine Bwanausi (q.v.), Minister of Development and Housing, and Kanyama Chiume who was Minister of External Affairs, Chisiza was one of the prime movers of the anti-Banda parliamentary debate which precipitated a Cabinet crisis in 1964. Some senior Cabinet ministers disagreed with Dr Banda on various policy issues, including the Prime Minister's alleged refusal to accept aid from China while pursuing a policy of extreme fraternisation with Portugal which was then at war with the nationalists to keep its hold over Mozambique, Angola and Guinea-Bissau. They also accused Banda of treating the Malawian government as his personal estate and refusing to permit adequate consultation within the Cabinet.

On 7 September 1964, Dr Banda sacked Bwanausi, Chiume and the Minister of Justice and Attorney-General, Mr Chirwa, after accusing them of instigating a split in his government. The same day, Chisiza resigned from the government out of sympathy with his dismissed colleagues. He stated then that the MCP of which Banda was life-president had strayed from its programme as a nationalist party. He accused Dr Banda of going too far in his dealings with Portugal and South Africa at a time when independent African opinion was unanimous in its condemnation of the former's continued colonial rule in Africa and of the latter's racist policies.

After a brief period in Malawi, Chisiza and his dismissed colleagues went into exile in Tanzania. He left there for a six-month stay in China and returned to Dar-es-Salaam to organise opposition to President Banda. During that same period Chipembere, the other Minister who had resigned from the government, led an armed revolt against President Banda, which was defeated. In October 1967 Chisiza led a small group of armed supporters in a rebellion in southwest Malawi. This, too, was quickly put down by government forces, who killed Chisiza and his followers near Blantyre. ∎

Chitepo, H.T. (1923-75)

CHITEPO, Herbert Tapfumanei (1923-75).

ZIMBABWEAN lawyer and nationalist politician. A leading political activist and organiser of the Zimbabwe African National Union, the nationalist movement that came to power on the attainment of Zimbabwe's independence. He was born at Inyanga on 5 June 1923, and educated at the St. David's Mission, Bonda and St. Augustine's Secondary School, Penhalonga, before he moved to Adams College, Natal,

H.T. Chitepo

South Africa where he matriculated. Chitepo obtained a BA degree in English and History at the University of Fort Hare, South Africa in 1949. Later he was appointed research assistant in Shona at the Universty of London's School of Oriental and African Studies. He also attended King's College, London, and read Law at the Inns of Court

during 1952 and 1953. He became Southern Rhodesia's first African barrister in 1954.

The Land Apportionment Act which restricted Africans from operating businesses in urban areas had to be amended to allow Chitepo to occupy his law chambers in the centre of Salisbury (now Harare). Later in 1954 Chitepo was admitted as an advocate of the Southern Rhodesia High Court. Practising law in a country where there was an unequal dispensation of political and economic powers and privilege was a daunting task for Chitepo.

Initially Chitepo's clients were mainly Africans on criminal charges. The government clampdown on nationalist activities saw Chitepo handling more political cases of African nationalists accused of violating restriction orders or the Land Husbandry Act. Chitepo was affected by the double standards that were prevalent in Rhodesian courts. Once after defending a white client in a divorce case, Chitepo was shocked at the uproar in the local press which commented, "Let Africans practise but don't let them into the sanctity of our marriages." Chitepo resolved never to accept a case from another European client.

In 1959 he travelled to New Delhi, India, to attend the conference of the International Commission of Jurists. In the same year he appeared before the Beadle Tribunal to defend nationalists who had been arrested under the Emergency Powers Act.

He joined the National Democratic Party (NDP) formed on 1 January 1960 to replace the African National Congress which had been banned. He was co-opted to the NDP's National Council as an adviser, in which capacity he presented a paper to the National Convention on "The impact of legislation on the community". Whitehead (q.v.), the Southern Rhodesian premier at the time, wished to include Chitepo on his delegation to the Federal Review Conference, but Chitepo insisted that he could only go as part of an NDP delegation, which he did. Chitepo acted as adviser to Rev. Ndabaningi Sithole and Joshua Nkomo during the 1961 constitutional talks.

When the NDP was banned in December 1961 Chitepo helped to form the Zimbabwe African People's Union (ZAPU). Chitepo then moved to Tanzania in 1962 where he became the Director of Public Prosecutions. In 1963 the ZAPU president, Joshua

Nkomo, suspended Chitepo from ZAPU for the latter's criticisms of party policy and management. Chitepo was elected national Chairman of the Zimbabwe African National Union (ZANU) when it was formed on 8 August 1963, following the split within ZAPU.

Chitepo was authorised by ZANU's Sikombela Forest Central Committee Decree of 1964 to organise and lead the liberation of Zimbabwe through armed struggle while most of the ZANU leaders were detained at Sikombela. In 1965 Chitepo established a base in Lusaka, Zambia, from where the liberation struggle was launched.

Under Chitepo's leadership the team embarked on a massive recruitment campaign and training programmes. Guerrilla incursions into Rhodesia were heralded by the battle of Sinoia on 28-29 April 1966. This took Smith's forces by surprise. Chitepo had launched a new era in the battle for freedom in Zimbabwe. However, Chitepo still believed that the war for the liberation of Zimbabwe could be fought on many fronts and urged at the Commonwealth Conference of 1966 that economic sanctions against Rhodesia should be intensified.

The period between 1966 and 1970 saw the inception of *Chimurenga*, the war of liberation. Between 1970 and 1972, the Zimbabwe Revolutionary Council, *Dare re Chimurenga*, of ZANU reappraised the situaton. Chitepo called these years "the period of the Great Debate". The *Dare* under Chitepo realised that the party, ZANU, was not doing enough politisation among the peasants, that the training programmes for the guerrillas needed improvement, and that the inadequate deployment of the guerrilla forces and arms was a contributory factor to the relatively limited impact of the operations. Chitepo recognised the necessity for consolidating the party's ideology through greater emphasis on study.

The vitality with which the Zimbabwe African National Liberation Army (ZANLA) waged the war from 1972 bore testimony to Chitepo's efforts. While in Zambia he had made strenuous efforts to unify the progressive Zimbabwean liberation movements and rejected dealings with James Chikerema's Front for the Liberation of Zimbabwe (FROLIZI) because of its parochialism and divisive orientation. Chitepo succeeded in establishing a Joint Military Command with ZAPU. ZANLA's pressure on the regime of Ian Smith forced it to appeal to South Africa for military help. Faced with continued guerrilla pressure Rhodesia and South Africa decided to turn to diplomacy, leading to the emergence of so-called "détente".

International pressure saw the uniting of ZANU, ZAPU and FROLIZI under Bishop Muzorewa. Herbert Chitepo had vigorously objected to this shotgun marriage of parties. The Lusaka Unity Declaration of December 1974 led to the formation of the African National Council (ANC). The ANC represented the Zimbabweans at the abortive Victoria Falls Conference of 1975, leading to the failure of detente at that stage.

Chitepo was assassinated on 18 March 1975, when a bomb exploded in his car outside his house in Lusaka. He was survived by his wife and six children. Controversy surrounded the circumstances of his death. An international commission set up by the Zambian government declared that Chitepo's death was the result of a power struggle within ZANU. Subsequent evidence however suggests that his assassination was the work of agents of the former white minority government of Rhodesia.∎

Cissoko, S. (1929-86)

CISSOKO, Seydou (1929-86).

SENEGALESE political activist and anti-colonialist who was president of the *Parti de l'Indépendance et du Travail* (PIT) and a leading political figure in opposition to the Senegalese government for over three decades.

Cissoko was born on 6 September 1929 in Bakel in a working class family. After attending the primary schools in Bakel and Matam, he went to the Lycée Blanchot and then to William Ponty Teachers' Training College from where he qualified as a teacher, and where also began his political education and career.

In the 50s Cissoko militated actively within the *Union Démocratique Sénégalaise*, affiliated to the *Rassemblement Démocratique Africain* (RDA). He was also engaged in trade union activities as a member of the *Syndicat Unic de l'Enseignement Laïc*.

In 1957 Cissoko was one of the signatories to the founding manifesto of the *Parti Africain de l'Indépendance* (PAI) of Mahjemout Diop, a young pharmacist and author, which was a small, intellectual political party, allied to the French Communist Party.

S. Cissoko

nist Party. A member of the central executive committee, he was chief editor and managing director of the party's two papers *La Lutte* and *Monsarev* (Wolof for Independence, literally "own your country"). Cissoko fought within the PAI for independence and was opposed to the de Gaulle form of union with France which the governing *Union Progressiste Sénégalaise* (UPS) decided to advocate acceptance of.

In 1960, after independence, the PAI was banned, but it continued to operate clandestinely until 1976 when with the constitutional revision to reinstate freedom of the parties, it was one of the four legally recognized parties including the government's *Parti Socialiste* (formerly UPS). Cissoko was known as a political analyst and a journalist and during those years he conti-

nued to devote his time to achieving the aims of the party, constantly opposing the government through his writings. In 1972 at the PAI's second congress he was elected its secretary-general, but soon thereafter he became ill and went to the Soviet Union for medical treatment.

Cissoko returned to Senegal six years later, in 1981, in time to be elected secretary-general at the constitutional congress of PIT, which was formed when internal disagreement brought a split in the PAI leadership. He continued his political activities as an overt revolutionary because by then multi-partyism was not restricted to a few or those with specified political leanings.

However, Cissoko's health deteriorated again, and taking into account his abilities and loyalties, PIT at its 1984 congress created the post of president of the party and elected him to it. He had to go again to Moscow for medical treatment soon after that, however, and he remained there until his death on 9 March 1986.

A leading figure in the International Communist Movement, Cissoko was much loved by his colleagues, and on his death the Central Committee of the Soviet Communist Party issued a communique describing him as "an eminent figure in the international and African communist, working class movement for their liberation". ■

Clinton, J.V. (1902-73)

CLINTON, James Vivian (1902-73).

NIGERIAN journalist who came from a family typical of the old "coastal" elite, being of varied origins and moving freely between many parts of West Africa. He came to belong to Nigeria and more especially to Calabar. "All Calabar people know me and regard me as one of them", he said.

His grandfather, James Clerk Clinton, was a West Indian from St. Vincent, who was a pioneer of the mahogany trade in the Gold Coast (now Ghana), Liberia and Côte d'Ivoire, and his father C. W. Clinton, who was born in Liberia, and received his early education in Sierra Leone, practised law in

Calabar, where he was also a member of the Legislative Council from 1928 to 1938.

Born on 6 February 1902 at Axim, James Vivian Clinton went to school at Calabar from the age of eight to 11, when he went to England for schooling, at Bexhill in

J.V. Clinton

Sussex and then at Taunton in Somerset. He went on to Cambridge University where he obtained the B.A. in History and Law. In 1924 he was, like his father, called to the Bar.

On his return to Calabar, he joined his father as a partner in legal business, and then, in late 1926, moved to Port Harcourt, already an expanding seaport town though it had only been founded in 1913, to set up his own practice. But only a few months later, misfortune struck him. He became deaf after a protracted malaria attack and had to give up the law practice. His mother took him to Britain and Austria for treatment, and in Vienna the leading ear specialist at the time said he could not be cured, though his hearing might come back suddenly, which however it never did.

He first joined the London Institute of Estate Management to train as a surveyor, but failed the examinations and after dabbling in accountancy, decided to take up journalism. After five years in England working in Fleet Street, he returned to West Africa and joined the staff of the *Daily Mail* of Sierra Leone, then owned by the father-in-law of one of his uncles. He worked there for three years and then returned to Calabar where he had persuaded his father to help him start his own newspaper. So, in 1935, he started the *Nigerian Eastern Mail* in Enugu. For years he was one of the leading editors in the Eastern Provinces, though the *Eastern Mail* was soon challenged by Nnamdi Azikiwe's new newspapers and, in comparison with them, was seen as conservative.

In 1951 Clinton sold the *Eastern Mail*, by then losing money, to the Eastern Press Syndicate, and agreed to edit a daily newspaper for the same Syndicate from Enugu. Before starting on that job he built up a fishing business based at Ibeno; this took him to nearby British Southern Cameroons in 1952-53. When he eventually took up his post as editor of the new daily in Enugu, lack of capital and trouble with machinery bedevilled the *Nigerian Daily Record*, as it was called, and after six months it collapsed. Then J. V. Clinton concentrated on his fishing venture, which nevertheless was financially precarious.

In 1954 Clinton became Senior Publicity Officer in the Federal Ministry of Information in Lagos, serving in that post until June 1962, when he retired. He briefly came out of retirement during the "Emergency" of 1962 in the Western Region, following the Action Group split, when he served as Chairman of the Western Nigeria Housing Corporation, an appointment he held until 1965. This last post, held at a time of crisis by a deaf and now ageing man, was typical of the versatile talents of one whose career spanned many walks of life and many different places also.

In 1965 the family moved back to Lagos where Clinton settled to life as a freelance journalist. He turned out a weekly editorial with the *Sunday Times* writing about his experiences and on varied subjects. He also wrote a novel published by Heinemann Publishers – *The Rescue of Charlie Kalu*, and had started a draft on his autobiography, *The Fisherman's Story*, before his death. He was an atheist, but believed in the principles of buddhism, and was a practising yogi. His interests were diverse but related to philosophy and the betterment of man.

He died in Lagos on 18 May 1973 and was survived by one son. ■

Coleman, W.D. (1842-1908)

COLEMAN, William David (1842-1908).

LIBERIAN statesman. Worked, during his term as President of Liberia, to improve educational facilities and the circumstances of the indigenous peoples. Born on 18 July 1842 in Kentucky, USA, Coleman was the son of poor working class and religious parents. His father died while he was still a boy and his mother decided to emigrate to Africa with her children. They arrived in Liberia in 1853 and settled in Clay-Ashland.

Coleman was sent to the local Presbyterian Mission School, but had to leave a year later because of lack of money. He got a job as a manual worker to help his mother support the family and continued his studies in the evenings, gradually gaining a good education. Four years later, at the age of 16, he decided to become a skilled worker and became apprenticed to a carpenter, eventually working his way up to becoming a master craftsman.

After a while he bought some land for cultivation, while continuing to work as a carpenter, and the success of his agricultural activities enabled him to branch out into commerce. He built up his enterprise and by the time he was 44 he was a wealthy farmer and businessman. He was involved in many civic activities and his interest in politics led him to join the True Whig Party, of whose Clay-Ashland branch he was to become leader.

He was elected a member of the House of Representatives three consecutive times, serving for six years before being elected to the Senate for two four-year terms. In the May 1891 elections he was elected Vice-President of the Republic, having the support of both the True Whig and the Republi-

can Parties. He remained in this position until 12 November 1896 when he became President following the death of the former incumbent. He gained much popularity while serving the remainder of this term before beginning his own as duly elected President in May 1897.

He believed in the importance of education for the development of the

W.D. Coleman

country and was determined to re-open Liberia College which had been closed during the previous administration because of unfavourable reports sent to the Board of Trustees. He also wanted the College to have financial security, and when it was finally re-opened in 1900 he allocated funds to it to enable it to continue on a more viable basis. He was the first Liberian President to come from the rural interior and he was deeply concerned for its development as well as for the advancement of the indigenous peoples of the country. He tried to gain effective administrative control in order to facilitate the integration and unity of the Liberian nation. However, his endeavours encountered much opposition, both from the Americo-Liberian section of the population who feared that by sheer numbers the indigenous peoples would become dominant, and from the ethnic groups themselves who were fearful of the effects which change might have on their traditions.

As a result ethnic conflicts broke out, and Coleman's inability to quell the disturbances infuriated his Cabinet and other politicians. On 5 December 1900, a meeting was held by leading citizens and politicians during which Coleman was confronted with bitter criticism of his interior policy.

Shortly afterwards he resigned from the presidency and returned to his business activities in Clay-Ashland where he died in July 1908. He retained deep religious beliefs throughout his life, and paid for the construction of an Episcopal church in his home town. He was deeply concerned with the development and welfare of his country and gained a reputation for being very generous and understanding.∎

Combes, C.A. (1891-1968)

COMBES, Charles Alphonse (1891-1968).

IVORIAN sculptor and influential artistic figure of his day. He was born on 30 September 1891, in Paris. He completed his early education at the Ecole Alsacienne after which he enrolled at the University of Paris where he obtained an arts degree. He studied medicine at the University and at the same time exhibited various works of art and sculptures in Paris, particularly at the Salon des Indépendants. During this period he also learned to fly and obtained a pilot's licence just before the outbreak of the First World War.

In 1914 he joined the Medical Corps of the French Air Force and was later seriously wounded in action. He then began to manufacture spare parts for aircraft. In the meantime he became involved in local community work and gave much of his money to those he saw as less fortunate than himself.

He arrived in Bingerville, then the capital of the French colony of Côte d'Ivoire, in 1925. In 1928 he moved into the hinterland and for the next four years lived at Toumodi and Danané, studying the customs and rituals of the Yacoba people.

In 1932 he taught at M'batto and later moved back to Bingerville where he opened a painting and sculpting workshop and also taught art at the *Ecole Primaire Supérieure*. Throughout this period he continued to be creative artistically and a number of his works of art were exhibited at both the 1934 and 1935 Exhibitions held in Abidjan.

Following the achievement of independence by Côte d'Ivoire in August 1960, Combes took up Ivorian nationality thus relinquishing his French citizenship. Shortly afterwards he was appointed director of the National School of Art at Bingerville. In 1962 he was made Commander of the National Order of Côte d'Ivoire and three years later Commander of the Order of Merit for National Education. He died on 6 October 1968, aged 77.∎

Couchoro, F.K.D. (1900-68)

COUCHORO, Félix Komla Dossa (1900-68).

TOGOLESE writer and activist in the independence movement. Born at Ouidah in Dahomey (Benin) on 30 January 1900, he spent most of his life in neighbouring Togo where he went to the Catholic primary school at Grand Popo. He returned to Dahomey to attend the Catholic seminary of Ste. Jeanne d'Arc at Ouidah. Later he worked as a school teacher at Grand Popo from 1917 to 1939.

In 1939 he set up business at Anecho and began his literary career. He was also a public letter writer and an early activist with Olympio's (q.v.) *Comité de l'Unité Togolaise* (CUT). When the French government turned against the CUT, Couchoro fled to Aflao in Gold Coast (Ghana) in 1951. He returned after M. Olympio became Prime Minister in 1958.

Félix Couchoro published his first novel, *L'Esclave*, in 1930. His other famous novels were *L'Amour de Féticheuse* and *L'Héritage, cette Peste*. When Togo progressed to self-government and then independence in 1960, Couchoro became assistant editor in the Information Service and then director of information, it was in this role that he campaigned vigorously for African unity. He published many novelettes in *Togo-Presse*, and the chapters later gathered to form the novel *L'Héritage, cette Peste*. He retired in 1965, and on 5 April 1968 died at home. Some of his works continued to be published in the newspaper *Togo-Presse* after his death, until 1970. He is regarded by many as Togo's most famous literary figure. ■

Coulibaly, D.O. (1909-58)

COULIBALY, Daniel Ouezzin (1909-58).

BURKINABE politician and Pan-Africanist, a founder of the first trade union in French-speaking West Africa. He was born in 1909 at Nouna, in north-west Burkina Faso (formerly Upper Volta). He did his secondary and higher studies at the Ecole William Ponty in Dakar, graduating first in his class and served the school from 1935 to 1942 as director of studies. In 1937, with Mamadou Konate (q.v.) of French Soudan (Mali), he formed the first French-speaking West African trade union to protect the collective interests of teachers.

On leaving Ponty, he went to Côte d'Ivoire, where a chance meeting with Félix Houphouet-Boigny on a train led to what was to be a lifelong friendship. Houphouet-Boigny became President in 1944 of the *Syndicat Agricole Africain* (SAA), established to represent the interests of the African planters of Côte d'Ivoire. When political reforms made it legal for Africans to form parties, the SAA and various radical town groups organised the campaign of Houphouet-Boigny as candidate for the deputyship to the French National Assembly in the 1945 elections. Houphouet would probably not have won the election without the support of the voters in the Bobo-Dioulasso area, and here the campaign for his election was organised by Ouezzin Coulibaly against considerable French official oppositon. Coulibaly was even subjected to personal harassment and humiliation.

In August 1945, prior to the municipal council elections, educated Africans in Abidjan united in a *Bloc Africain* of which the

Groupe d'Etudes Communistes (GEC) gained control and which became, in 1946, a formal party, the *Parti Démocratique de la Côte d'Ivoire* (PDCI). October 1946 saw the founding in Bamako of the inter-territorial *Rassemblement démocratique Africain* (RDA),

D.O. Coulibaly

for which Houphouet-Boigny became president by acclamation, and Coulibaly its political secretary. The RDA embodied the recognition that the struggle for independence could be more effectively fought on a common front, and aimed to ensure that the proposals for constitutional reform of 1946 were actually carried out.

Coulibaly stood as a candidate in the 1946 elections to the French Assembly and was elected deputy from the Bobo region. It was in 1947, after fifteen years of having its territory divided between Côte d'Ivoire, Niger and Soudan, that Upper Volta again became a separate territorial entity. Coulibaly was one of those whose efforts helped to create new branch sections of the RDA. His major commitment, however, was to the inter-territorial ideal embodied in the RDA, which explains why he remained so long absent from Upper Volta.

From 1947 onwards, there was an official campaign on the part of the French administration to defeat the RDA and thwart its progress. This took a particularly unpleasant form in Côte d'Ivoire and included assisting the formation of opposition parties; in early 1950 there were serious incidents during political meetings convened by the anti-RDA parties. Charges of slander were brought against Coulibaly as director of the RDA newspaper, *Le Démocrate*, by Governor Péchoux. Coulibaly was protected by his immunity as a deputy. In 1949 and 1950 he also escaped attempts on his life, attempts made because of his prominent position as RDA political secretary. Other members or sympathizers of the RDA were not so fortunate. The methods of harassment and obstruction were legion and by May 1950 many Africans had been killed, hundreds wounded and thousands of RDA members and supporters imprisoned.

The RDA experienced a crisis in the months following September 1950 when it disaffiliated from the French Communist Party. This meant, on the one hand, that greater cooperation was now possible between the administration and the RDA. On the other hand, this cooperation was bitterly resented both by the Communists and the settlers. Gabriel d'Arboussier (q.v.), the movement's secretary-general, broke with it. This opposition was given vivid illustration in February 1951, with the opening of the newly completed port of Abidjan. The communist lawyers acting on behalf of RDA political prisoners urged them to dissuade the RDA deputies from attending the official ceremonies on the same platform as the French governor. Ouezzin Coulibaly's defence of their presence at the ceremonies was, "the port stays when the French go"; the lawyers were subsequently dismissed.

In the elections to the French Parliament held in June 1951, Houphouet-Boigny was again returned; Ouezzin Coulibaly lost his seat to a chief who had the backing of the administration. This was attributable, in large degree, to widespread and well-documented electoral falsification on the part of the authorities. The election of Coulibaly's opponent was challenged, unsuccessfully, in the French Parliament.

These elections, however, marked the end of official repression of the PDCI and the RDA. The PDCI leadership, however, had been seriously weakened by the years of repression, not only in its upper ranks, but down to village level and Ouezzin Coulibaly was asked, at the end of the PDCI conference in 1952, to undertake its reorganisation. In 1953 Ouezzin Coulibaly was elected a Senator to the French Parliament by the territorial assembly of Côte d'Ivoire.

His role as political director of the RDA took him, for most of 1954, to Guinea, where the RDA sought to demonstrate its solidarity with the *Parti Démocratique de Guinée* (PDG), which had been the victim of electoral rigging by the authorities in the 1954 parliamentary elections. He toured with Sekou Touré (q.v.) and helped organise the PDG; he was also partially instrumental in moving the PDG towards dialogue with the administration and away from total opposition, urging it, like the PDCI, towards greater flexibility.

It was in June 1956 that the *loi-cadre* or enabling law which proposed important constitutional changes in the territories of French West Africa, including Executive Councils with African vice-presidents, was voted in the French Parliament. After the adoption of the *loi-cadre* provisions, Ouezzin Coulibaly turned his attention to the policies of his native Upper Volta. He negotiated an alliance between the RDA, whose support in Upper Volta had hitherto come principally from the Bobo-Dioulasso area in the west, and the *Parti Social d'Education des Masses Africaines* (PSEMA), supported in the east and backed by the Mogho Naba, traditional ruler of the Mossi. These two groups formed the *Parti Démocratque Unifié* (PDU-RDA) and won the March territorial elections by a narrow majority. Ouezzin Coulibaly, elected member for Banfora in south-west Upper Volta, became the head of Upper Volta's first African government.

In 1958, General de Gaulle proposed a referendum, under which each territory was offered complete independence or autonomy within the French Community. Côte d'Ivoire insisted that each territory should have direct, separate links with France, while the other members of the RDA were in favour of autonomy within a federal framework. Coulibaly's position on this remained unclear. However, having devoted much of his life to the inter-territorial ideal of the RDA as a force for change, he was rather unwilling to see it split over the issue of federalism versus separatism. It was while planning a meeting of the RDA's Co-ordinating Committee to work out a common policy on the referendum, a meeting that might conceivably have avoided the subsequent break-up of the RDA, that Ouezzin Coulibably died unexpectedly on 7 September 1958, in Paris, just three weeks before the referendum. ∎

Coulibaly, G. (c.1860-1962)

COULIBALY, Gbon (Peleforo Soro) (c.1860-1962).

IVORIAN traditional ruler and an important figure in the French system of colonial administration in West Africa. Son of Zouacognon Soro, chief of the Tiembara state of Korhogo, he was born as Peleforo Soro in about 1860 but acquired the nickname Gbon ("chimpanzee" in the Senufo language), by which he became known. He succeeded his father as a result of Korhogo's involvement in the 1870s wars in the Western Soudan where he led his father's army that was helping Sikasso, under its ruler, Tieba, to resist Samory Toure (q.v.). In 1894 Zouacognon died in a smallpox epidemic and

G. Coulibaly

Babemba, successor to Tieba, had Coulibaly installed as ruler of Korhogo. He later broke with his Sikasso sponsor and went over to Samory, who was then resisting French occupation. Soon, however, he ended co-operation with Samory and switched over to the French.

The French colony of Côte d'Ivoire was then extended northwards, to include Korhogo, which in 1900 became capital of an administrative *cercle*. At first Coulibaly was effective ruler over many of his subjects, under French control. The French administration, in its early military phase, found it easy to rule through this state on the "indirect rule" principle. In 1905 civilian administration was introduced, with units of government called regions, *cercles*, and districts, *circonscriptions*; chiefs ruled over *cantons*, their rule depending strictly on French satisfaction with their loyalty. Coulibaly enjoyed a special relation with the colonialists who saw him as a powerful chief with extensive authority. He later became a Moslem, employed Islamic scholars as advisers and adopted the Islamic name Coulibaly. This change worried the French as many of his people followed his example and became Moslems.

Coulibaly established assemblies of village representatives as part of his government system, a move that was supported by the French government. He set an example to his subjects by popularising cash crop production on a farm manned by trained personnel. In the judicial field Coulibaly's powers were reduced by the appointment of elders after the reorganisation of the courts, which were now at the village, *canton* and *cercle* level, and were supposed to be outside his traditional power.

For many years during his reign he had power and honour heaped on him by the French rulers. He was made *Chevalier de la Légion d'Honneur*, and was taken on country-wide tours of Côte d'Ivoire and to France. After 1930, however, the French changed their policy towards the chief of Korhogo, which affected their relations. Coulibaly did not want to share power in the manner demanded by the colonial government's reforms of chieftancy all over French West Africa in 1932. He was, however, awarded the *Etoile Noire du Bénin* decoration in 1938, and in 1942 was appointed provincial chief of all the 13 cantons of Korhogo.

From 1942, he turned to the Côte d'Ivoire section of the *Rassemblement Démocratique Africain* (RDA) which was being led by Félix Houphouet-Boigny, whom he supported until he was forced by the colonial authorities to renounce party politics. By 1960, when the country became independent, Coulibaly was a hundred years old, and very weak. He died on 19 September 1962 after a reign of 68 years over the Tiembaras of Korhogo. The next day President Houphouet-Boigny honoured him posthumously with the decoraton of Grand Officer of the National Order. He is buried at the Korhogo mosque. ∎

Crowther, S.A. (c. 1806-91)

CROWTHER, Bishop Samuel Ajayi (c.1806-91).

Bishop S.A. Crowther

NIGERIAN clergyman, the celebrated first African Anglican bishop of West Africa. He was born in or around 1806 in Oshogun village in Abeokuta, now in Ogun State of Nigeria, in the heyday of the transatlantic slave trade. His family were sold into slavery in 1821 but were intercepted on the journey to the Americas by a British anti-slavery patrol force and resettled in Freetown, capital of Sierra Leone. Ajayi was placed under the care of a Christian Missionary Society (CMS) schoolmaster of the Freetown region in Sierra Leone. He was converted to Christianity, learnt to read the bible and was baptised on 11 December 1825 with the adopted name of Samuel Crowther.

In 1826 he went to England to study at a school in Liverpool Street, Islington, London, where he was the first Nigerian to be schooled together with English children. He returned to Freetown and was appointed schoolmaster by the government. In 1827, he entered the newly founded Fourah Bay Institution of the CMS, where his brilliance and hard work prompted his principal to comment that Ajayi "is a lad of uncommon ability and steady conduct and has a thirst for knowledge and indefatigable industry". He later became a tutor in the college and was soon made the first African evangelist. He joined an ill-fated missionary expedition

to Lokoja in 1841. In 1843, Ajayi revisited England where he was received into deacon's orders and was ordained a priest the following year.

In 1845, 25 years after he had been taken away, Ayaji re-joined his mother in his hometown of Abeokuta. He could still remember his Yoruba language into which he translated the New Testament while serving in the parish of the newly formed Christian Mission.

On 29 June 1864 he was consecrated the Bishop of Western Equatorial Africa by the Archbishop of Canterbury in Canterbury Cathedral, becoming the first African Anglican bishop. In appreciation for his translation of the Bible into Yoruba, the University of Oxford awarded him the honorary degree of Doctor of Divinity. During subsequent visits to Britain he was honoured by Queen Victoria who received him at Windsor Castle, and also by British government ministers.

As Bishop he devoted his efforts to establishing a Christian community and spent the rest of his life looking after his diocese, which covered especially the lower Niger area. The Anglican mission spread in that area, where he and others had established the CMS at Onitsha in 1857, and in many other places. Crowther was a tireless preacher who was said to be truly saintly in character. In the late 1880s an inquiry into allegations against the clergy and other staff of his diocese turned into a hostile inquisition by white missionaries, which greatly grieved the Bishop. He died in the middle of this unhappy episode on 31 December 1891.

His son, Archdeacon Dandeson Crowther, was also a prominent CMS churchman in the lower Niger area. A daughter became the mother of Herbert Macaulay (q.v.).■

Curé, M. (1886-1978)

CURE, Dr. Maurice (1886-1978).

MAURITIAN medical doctor who is remembered as the founder of the Mauritius Labour Party (MLP), and as a politician who, though unsuccessful in achieving practical results, awakened the consciousness of the Mauritian people to British colonial rule. From the moment he started can be traced the development of the path to independence and the subsequent pattern of politics in the island today.

Born on 3 September 1886, Curé was first educated at the Royal College of Curepipe. He won a scholarship in 1907 and went to Britain where he studied medicine at St. Bartholomew's Hospital, London. When the First World War of 1914-1918 broke out, he offered to serve in the British Army but he was turned down, and that influenced his political ideas and affiliations. He returned to Mauritius in 1919. His first contact with politics was through the Mauritius Retrocession Movement organised by the Mauritian professionals of mixed origins (Creoles) who believed that Mauritius had been ignored by the British during the war and assumed that the French would have treated them differently and aimed at a return of Mauritius to France.

However the idea of "retrocession" did not gain much ground and its candidates were heavily defeated in the 1921 elections. But Curé, well known by then, concentrated his political energies and effort in other directions. While he practised medicine in Mauritius, Curé became increasingly shocked by the conditions of the works,

especially the Hindu sugar cane labourers (mainly of Indian origin). He organized marches to Government House and presented petitions to the Governor for the introduction of measures to improve the labourers' working conditions. He demanded

Dr. M. Curé

an extension of the franchise to include the working classes, modifications in labour legislation to conform with International Labour Organization conventions and the establishment of an agricultural bank to make loans to small planters.

Curé ran in the municipal elections in 1924 and Council of Government elections of 1926 and 1931 but was defeated. He won a by-election to the Council of Government in 1934 but lost his seat two years later. Freed from the obligations of an elected deputy he concentrated his efforts on expanding the activities of the Mauritius Labour Party which he had founded in 1936, and of which he was the President. The main objective of the party was to ensure "the representation of the workers in Mauritius" whose political consciousness he aroused by telling them that they were entitled to higher wages, better housing, improved hospital care and the right to form trade unions.

Even then the colonial Government did not take him seriously. His indictment of the management of the sugar industry, however, antagonised both Franco-Mauritians (White Mauritians who were of French origin) and the Creole bourgeoisie who labelled him a Soviet agent. The total lack of interest and indifference of the colonial administration contributed to the outbreak of the serious labour riots of 1937 which involved not only labourers but also small cane planters.

Curé was then accused of having created an atmosphere of unrest through systematic subversive agitation. However, a commission which was set up to look into the problem, among the workers, found most of the workers' and planters' complaints justified. Recommendations were made and important measures were taken to improve the conditions of both planters and labourers.

Dr Curé was again accused in September 1938 of having provoked a dock strike. The British Governor determined to prevent him from causing any further trouble, and placed him under house arrest for a month. His friend, Anquetil, another very active trade unionist was deported to the island of Rodrigues for three months. He did not remain long on the political scene after that,

and in the last few years of his political career Curé found himself without any money and without any legal support to fight several court cases brought against him. What was to be his last effort to revive interest in the Party was the publication of a newspaper called *Le Peuple Mauricien*. But very soon, an accumulation of debts forced him to sell his press. He resigned as leader of the Party in May 1941.

Apart from improving the economic conditions of the workers, the Labour Party later managed to obtain major constitutional reforms which brought a realignment in Mauritian politics. The constitution of 1947 provided for a Legislative Council of 34, of which 19 were to be elected members; 12 nominated and 3 would be appointed officially. Political representation ceased to be the preserve of the economically powerful and the formally educated.

Curé was cut off from the Labour Party from the 1950s, and when he stood as a candidate, in the crucial general elections of 1967 which decided on the country's independence it was not on the MLP platform. Despite his previous record of political involvement, he polled less than one per cent of the votes. He never rejoined the MLP, and died in 1978, at the age of 92.■

D

Dadié, G. (1891-1953)

DADIE, Gabriel (1891-1953).

IVORIAN politician, a leading figure in the political development that brought his country to independence. He was born on 14 May 1891 at Assinie, on the south coast not far from the border of the then Gold Coast (Ghana). He attended the Assinie Catholic School for his primary school education, he then went on to the Grand Bassam government school where he was noted for his intelligence and alertness, a record which helped him into an appointment in the French colonial government.

Under the direction of Captain Chiffer he helped install the first telephones

G. Dadié

in the Baoule *cercle* (the French colonial administrative unit). He soon rose to the position of instructor at the training centre for postal and telecommunications officials at Bingerville, simultaneously occupying the position of postmaster.

Later he was posted to his home village of Assinie to take the jobs of postmaster and officer in charge of an administrative *subdivision*. For this he had the distinction in 1916 of being the first Ivorian to occupy such a high post in the hierachy of the colonial administration, such high office being normally reserved for the Europeans.

Dadié fought for France in the First World War, serving with the Tours engineers' regiment. He returned to Côte d' Ivoire in 1922 as a non-commissioned officer. During his stay in Paris, he became interested in anti-colonial politics and established links with the Black Diaspora in France. Among these was Satineau, a politician from the French West Indies, whom he succeeded in persuading to stand as a candidate for the *Conseil Supérieur des Colonies* as a representative of Côte d'Ivoire. But Satineau was defeated by the white settlers, who formed most of the electorate for the Council.

Dadié himself returned to the postal department, still as postmaster. He was posted in 1923 to Dimbokro where he formed part of an educated elite who sought to modify colonial policies in force in the colony. Disenchanted with these policies he resigned from government service in 1924 and set up as a planter at Agboville. The example of Dadié was followed by other Africans and even some Europeans, who resigned from the government to become planters or traders. From 1930 he worked as a planter and timber concessionaire, and became successful and respected by Europeans and Africans alike.

As a member of the Chamber of Agriculture he took the opportunity offered by the crisis of 1942, over the sale, at a loss, of coffee and cocoa, to join with some other leading African planters to reassert their objection to colonial measures. He co-founded the *Syndicat Agricole Africain* (African Farmers' Union). With other founder members of the organisation, he was entrusted with the important mission of asking the young medical officer Félix Houphouet-Boigny to become chairman of the union. Houphouet-Boigny refused the offer at first but later agreed. Dadié himself became the union's adviser and propaganda secretary.

When Boa Kouassi, the paramount of chief of Indenie, was appointed a member of the General Executive Council of French West Africa, he took Dadié with him on his journeys. They travelled together first to Dakar, then to Paris to visit the International Colonial Exhibition at Vincennes. Having already been in Paris, Dadié lost no time in introducing Chief Boa Kouassi to West Indian politicians whom he considered natural allies in the anti-colonial struggle.

When the African Farmers' Union grew into a major voice in the opposition to French rule, Dadié's leadership saw it through the government's repressive measures of 1949. The respect which he enjoyed among the people was enormous and he became popularly known as "Father Dadié". He was in fact rightly seen as the first "active militant" of the nationalist movement.

Dadié became a central personality in the formation of the *Rassemblement Démocratique Africain* (RDA), under Houphouet-Boigny whom he accompanied on his election campaign all over Côte d'Ivoire territory. Between 1945 and 1946 he travelled widely throughout the country, winning supporters to the cause of independence. Philippe Yace, who later became chairman of the National Assembly of Côte d'Ivoire, says "Dadié was an extraordinary man who foresaw events and therefore prepared to face them. So generous as to be able to sacrifice all his belongings for others, he did not attach much importance to material wealth." Another contemporary, Mamadou Coulibaly, recalled that "he will be remembered prominently in the history of the decolonisation of Africa as one of the greatest torch-bearers of our continent."

The Senegalese doctor Doudou Gueye, who knew him in 1944 at Agboville, recalls that he joined that year in the creation of the *Comité d'Etudes Franco-Africaines* (CEFA)

and adds that "if he never agreed to be enslaved, so also he never wanted to enslave another either, or to enslave himself." His son Bernard Dadié, who became Minister of Cultural Affairs of independent Côte d'Ivoire, said his father "spent his life breaking down barriers, lifting restrictions which made Africans untouchables in their own country".

Gabriel Dadié devoted all his life to farming and politics; in moments of leisure he played the accordion, with which he livened up the Bingerville students' evenings. Weakened by illness in 1950, he continued to lead young Ivorians, as in the past, giving them the benefit of his political experience. He was taken to hospital at Treichville in Abidjan in 1952, at the same time as his son Bernard was imprisoned by the French at Grand Bassam for the second time. On 16 May 1953, at the age of 62, "Father Gabriel Dadié" died.∎

Dadoo, Y.M. (1909-83)

DADOO, Dr Yusuf Mohamed (1909-83).

SOUTH AFRICAN national political leader who for almost 50 years was in the forefront of the struggle against racism and oppression in South Africa. He played a pivotal role in influencing the South Africans of Indian origin, to which community he himself belonged, towards co-operation with the Black South Africans in a united front of action and resistance to apartheid rule. A patriot as well as a dynamic leader, Dr Yusuf Dadoo led by example; he was very popular and able to guide and inspire others to commit themselves fully to the struggle for freedom and justice. Elected in 1969, he was vice-chairman of the Revolutionary Council of the African National Congress (ANC) for 14 years, and until his death vice-chairman of the Politico-Military Council as well as chairman of the South African Communist Party (SACP), and President of the South African Indian Congress (SAIC) from 1948 to 1952, when he was banned by the Government under the Suppression of Communism Act from all gatherings and forbidden to hold office in the SAIC.

Born in Krugersdorp, Transvaal, on 5 September 1909, he attended schools locally and in Johannesburg and India before going to the UK to study medicine. After being arrested for demonstrating against imperialism in 1929 in London, he went to Edin-

Dr. Y.M. Dadoo

burgh, Scotland, where he qualified in 1936. Returning to South Africa as a doctor that same year, Dadoo soon became involved in radical politics, working as he did among the poverty-stricken and victims of the apartheid régime, first as a leader of the Transvaal Indian Congress, but soon as a national leader. He saw the need for a united front of all fighters against the régime, and advocated strongly closer co-operation between Indians, Africans and Coloureds, pointing out the fact that the solution to their own community's problems lay within the context of a broader national struggle which should comprise all sections of oppressed South Africans.

To this effect, he took the initiative and formed the Non-European United Front

in Johannesburg in 1938; though this was short-lived, it paved the way for the subsequent full support pact in 1947 betweeen the ANC, Dadoo's Transvaal Indian Congress and Naicker's (q.v.) Natal Indian Congress, leading to the joint planning Council for the Defiance Campaign of 1952 and the Congress Alliance, the Congress of the People and the adoption of the Freedom Charter in 1955.

Dadoo was a socialist; he joined the Communist Party in 1939 and became a member of the Central Committee of the Communist Party of South Africa in the 1940s. His total commitment and eloquence soon established him as a leader; he spoke at meetings and was convicted many times for political offences, undergoing several terms of imprisonment. In 1940 he was jailed for four months with hard labour for leading protests against the recruitment of non-white soldiers for the Second World War on different pay scales and conditions of service. He served three separate terms of imprisonment of three to six months as a result of his participation in the 1946 Passive Resistance Campaign by the South African Indians, and was arrested and imprisoned and banned again several times between 1952 and 1960, amongst others on a charge of sedition for organising a strike of African mineworkers.

In 1945 Dadoo was elected vice-chairman of the National Anti-Pass Council formed to protest against the pass laws. He became president of the SAIC in 1950 and in 1952 was one of the five members of the Joint Planning Committee of the ANC and the SAIC for the Campaign of Defiance against the apartheid laws. The Communist Party of South Africa was banned in 1950, but it reappeared as the SACP in 1960, when it became an active underground organization. Dadoo in the meantime continued to be active and exercised considerable influence behind the scenes, and was elected SACP's chairman in 1972.

After the Sharpeville massacre of 1960, Dadoo left South Africa for Britain to organize international solidarity and co-operation and alert world opinion. During the rest of his life, he worked tirelessly, leading SACP delegations all over the world, attending meetings and was an active member of the ANC. A planner as well as an organiser, he was well-known for his dedication to the South African cause and struggle. His last message to the SACP's Central

Committee, the first since 1953 that he could not attend, was a few days before his death on 19 September 1983 in London. In it he told them they must never give up, but must fight to the end.

Dadoo received many honours in his lifetime. At the Congress of the People at Kliptown in the Transvaal in 1955 when the Freedom Charter was adopted, as a token of the appreciation for his work, he was awarded the traditional African title of *Isitwalandwe Seaparankoe* which means 'the one who wears the plumes of the rare bird', an honour awarded only to the bravest of warriors and leaders. Amongst others were the Order of Dimitrov by Bulgaria, the Order of Karl Marx by the German Democratic Republic, the Order of Friendship of the People by the USSR, the Gold Medal of the Afro-Asian People's Solidarity Organisation, the Scroll of Honour of the World Peace Council, the Decoration of the Hungarian Peace Movement and the Wielki Proletariat from Poland.■

Danquah, J.K.K.B. (1895-1965)

DANQUAH, Dr. Joseph Kwame Kyeretwi Boakye (1895-1965).

GHANAIAN lawyer and politician, one of the most important early nationalist politicians instrumental in the constitutional development of the Gold Coast and later Ghana. He was born on 21 December 1895 at Bepong, Kwahu, in Ghana. His family, who belonged to the Presbyterian Church, sent him to the Basel Mission schools at Kyebi and Begoro. He left school at the age of 17 and became a law clerk to a barrister in Accra, leaving this position in 1914 to become a clerk in the Supreme Court.

The following year he was appointed secretary to his older brother, Nana Sir Ofori Atta I, the Paramount Chief of Akyem Abuakwa, serving in this post until 1921.

In 1921 he travelled to England to study law and philosophy at the University of London, where he graduated with a BA degree and was awarded the John Stuart Mill Scholarship in the Philosophy of Mind and Logic. He continued his studies at the University and received an LLB degree as

well as being called to the Bar at the Inner Temple Inn of Court in 1926. The following year he gained a PhD for his thesis entitled "The Moral End as Moral Excellence".

He left England in 1927 and travelled to Finland, Germany, Holland, France and

Dr. J.K.K.B. Danquah

Switzerland. On his return to the Gold Coast, as Ghana was then called, he established a private legal practice after turning down a teaching position at Achimota College. He soon built up a solid reputation as an able lawyer of customary and constitutional law. A year later, in 1928, he published two books, *Akan Laws and Customs* and *Cases in Akan Law*. In 1944 he published his third book, *Akan Doctrine of God*. In 1929 he became a founding member of the Gold Coast Youth Conference and two years later he established the *Times of West Africa*, a daily newspaper which gained popularity and influence during the 1930s.

He became active in the campaign against two proposed bills, one widening the definition of "sedition" and the other shifting costs of supplying water in the coastal districts from the colonial government to the people, and went to London in 1934 as part of a delegation to protest against these. He remained in London until 1936, carrying out further research on his people's origins. This research was partly the basis for the change of name from Gold Coast to Ghana at the time of independence.

In 1937 he resumed his activities with the Gold Coast Youth Conference, becoming its secretary and gaining a wide measure of popularity with the country's younger generation. Through his work with the Youth Conference he was linked with the Joint Provincial council of Paramount Chiefs, which appointed him in 1942 to a three-man committee to work out a draft constitution for the Gold Coast. The proposals made by this committee were rejected by the British colonialists.

Danquah was elected to the Legislative Council in 1946 and during the next four years was active in campaigning for rural development schemes and improved marketing and distribution of agricultural produce for farmers. Although his efforts were partly responsible for the establishment of a Cocoa Marketing Board in 1947, he realised that there was a need for self-government before any real changes could be brought about.

Apart from his position on the Legislative Council, he was also involved in other associations, being the representative of the Farmers' Union on the Cocoa Marketing Board and legal advisor of the Ex-Servicemen's Union. Seeing the need for the establishment of a political organisation to unite these interests, he became one of the founders of the United Gold Coast Convention (UGCC), a nationalist movement that was established on 4 August 1947. A weekly newspaper originally called the *Star* but later renamed the *Statesman* was also set up to put the views of the organisation across to the people. Danquah became Vice-President of the UGCC and Dr. Kwame Nkrumah (q.v.), more radical than the other leaders of the organisation, returned from abroad to become its General Secretary.

Meanwhile tension was growing in the country against the British administration and in February 1948 riots broke out. The leaders of the UGCC seized the opportunity to campaign for self-government and other political demands. A state of emergency was declared and Danquah was arrested with five other leading members of the

organisaton. After the riots Danquah was a member of the Coussey Committee established to make constitutional proposals. The recommendations of this Committee formed the basis of the 1951 Constitution and were also an important preparatory move towards eventual self-government.

However, during this period disagreements among leading members of the UGCC led to a split, with Kwame Nkrumah leaving the UGCC to form the Convention People's Party (CPP) in June 1949. This new party gained a broader base of support than the UGCC which confined its appeal to lawyers, merchants, academics and other members of the professional classes.

Under the new constitution, parliamentary elections were held in February 1951. Danquah was elected member for Akyem Abuakwa, but the majority of seats went to Nkrumah's Convention People's Party. In 1952 the UGCC formed a parliamentary opposition by combining with the Ghana Congress Party and the Northern People's Party. Until 1954, when he lost his seat in the election, Danquah was an active member of this opposition.

In November 1954 he travelled to New York under a United Nations Fellowship, remaining there until February 1955. Returning to the Gold Coast, he became a member of the National Liberation Movement, an organisation that opposed the Convention People's Party, and which stood for the establishment of a federal constitution.

Elections were once again held in 1956 but Danquah failed to regain his seat. The following year, in March 1957, Ghana gained independence under Nkrumah. Danquah continued to be opposed to the CPP's policies, arguing that they were eroding democracy, the principles of the rule of law and individual freedom. In the same year the opposition parties merged into the Unity Party, and Danquah was selected as candidate for this party in the 1960 presidential elections but lost to Nkrumah who won with an overwhelming majority.

Danquah continued to be opposed to the CPP government. His open criticisms of it, along with his efforts to bring about a change of government, caused him to be detained under the Preventive Detention Act on 3 October 1961. On his release on 22 June 1962 he resumed his criticism of the increasing powers of President Nkrumah. He became president of the Ghana Bar Association but in January 1964 was re-arrested in a wave of detentions after an assassination attempt on the President.

He was detained in Nwasam Prison near Accra, where he died after a heart attack on 4 February 1965. ■

Dantata, A. (c.1880-1955)

DANTATA, Alhassan (c.1880-1955).

NIGERIAN entrepreneur and pioneer in Northern Nigeria's business community. Born at Bebedji, son of a woman trader, he became a kola trader and by 1912 had developed an important business in Kumasi, terminus of the old Hausa kola trade route, from where he shipped kola to Nigeria by sea. He returned to Kano in time for the great groundnut boom of 1912. He was one of the most prominent Hausa traders to benefit by that boom, and by 1917-18 he was the main supplier of groundnuts to the Royal Niger Company.

Soon after the end of the First World War he went on the pilgrimage to Mecca, via Britain where he was presented to King George V. Back in Kano, he steadily built up his commercial empire based on groundnut and kola trading. He bought groundnuts through many agents for sale to the purchasers for export: first the commercial firms, then, from 1947, the marketing boards. In his last years he was the second in importance among the Licensed Buying Agents of the marketing board for groundnuts.

His role in the purchase of kola nuts from forest areas of Nigeria for sale in the North was so great that eventually whole "kola trains" from the Western Region were filled with his nuts alone.

He founded, with other merchants (*attajirai*), the Kano Citizens' Trading Company, for industrial undertakings; it started Nigeria's first-ever textile mill, in Kano in 1950. For years he advanced money to young businessmen who re-paid him from their profits. As a devout Moslem however, he was against interest as contrary to Islamic moral teaching, and his bank account bore no interest, at his instructions.

Near the end of his life he was appointed a director of the Railway Corporation. He was for some time a member of the Emir of Kano's Council. At the time of his death in October 1955, he had the reputation of being Nigeria's wealthiest citizen.

His many sons shared out his business empire. ■

A. Dantata

Davies, H. O. (1905-89)

DAVIES, Hezekiah Oladapo (1905-89).

NIGERIAN lawyer and politician. H.O. Davies, or H.O.D., as he was called, was born in Lagos on 5 April 1905, descended partly from the Ogunmade ruling house of Lagos and from other Yoruba ruling families, those of Ilesha and Efon-Alaaye. His father worked for the Elder Dempster shipping line. He went to the Elementary Wesleyan School, the Baptist School in Broad Street, and Wesleyan Boys' School; he was an active member of the Wesleyan (Methodist) Church all his life. He also attended King's College, Lagos, and taught there for a time (1924).

H.O. Davies

He worked as a civil servant, in the Kaduna Secretariat and later in the Survey Department in Kaduna and Lagos, before going to Britain for further studies in 1934. He studied at the London School of Economics and obtained the Bachelor of Commerce degree in 1937, after an active student life in which he took part in many organisations; he was President of the West African Students' Union (WASU) in 1935-6. Already married by then, he rejoined his wife and children on his return to Nigeria in 1937. He worked as Assistant Manager at the CMS Bookshop in Lagos, but also corresponded for British papers and began political activity with the Nigerian Youth Movement (NYM) founded in 1933.

He helped found the NYM's newspaper, the *Daily Service*. and before the Second World War he also helped organise trade unions, such as the Railway Workers' Union under Michael Imoudu. During the war he was involved in organising the workers' agitation over the COLA (Cost of Living Allowance), but also worked for a time for the government as a marketing officer under the Department of Agriculture.

In 1944 he returned to London to read for the Bar. Among his other activities were efforts to raise funds for strikers during Nigeria's general strike of 1945, and attendance with Obafemi Awolowo (q.v.) at the Manchester Pan-African Conference, also in 1945. He was called to the Bar in 1946 at the same time as Awolowo and T.O. Elias, later Chief Justice of Nigeria. Back in Nigeria from 1947, he worked as a solicitor and advocate. He prosecuted in several important cases, and was one of the defence counsel for Oba Adele II (q.v.) of Lagos in his case (which he won) for possession of the traditional royal palace in 1949. In 1953 he went to Kenya to join the defence team for Jomo Kenyatta (q.v.) who, however, was gaoled by the colonial government.

In the rapidly developing nationalist politics of Nigeria, Davies was chairman of the NYM from 1946 to 1948, but later left the Movement. In 1953-6 he was a leader of the movement to stop inclusion of Lagos in the Western Region; he headed a delegation to Britain for that purpose, which was achieved. Although he was not among the frontline political leaders as Nigeria attained independence, he was eminent throughout as a lawyer, and was made a QC in 1959. About the time of independence in 1960 he wrote *Nigeria: The Prospects for Democracy.*

In 1961 he became chairman of the Nigerian National Press, government-owned publishers of the *Morning Post* and *Sunday Post.* He entered the Federal House of Representatives in 1964 as Nigerian National Alliance (NNA) member for Ekiti West. The NNA government of the Federation, under Sir Abubakar Tafawa Balewa (q.v.), then sent him to New York to head Nigeria's delegation to the UN Economic and Social Council. Among his other work in these years was heading a committee for the review of company law in Nigeria.

During the Nigerian Civil War Davies was sent to East Africa as a Federal Government representative in 1968. He carried out the same assignment in France, using contacts he had made through work with the French oil company CFP. He sought to persuade the French government, which showed support for the Biafrans, to refrain from actual recognition of their secession. He continued to work for companies for years, but did not return to active politics. However, as an elder statesman he gave advice on politics and matters of national interest in his last years. He died on 22 November 1989. ■

Davies, J.P.L. (c.1828-1906)

DAVIES, James Pinson Labulo
(c.1828-1906).

NIGERIAN businessman, an example of successful entrepreneurship in Lagos' emergent business circles. He was one of the community of people taken off slave ships and resettled at Freetown, where he may have been born to Yoruba parents on an unknown date. His decision to eventually settle in Lagos was typical of the desire to reverse the damaging effects of slave trade by those lucky enough to escape it en route.

He went to the Church Missionary Society (CMS) Grammar School in Freetown. From 1849 to 1852 he served in Royal Navy vessels along the African coasts, learn-

J.P.L. Davies

ing navigation and seamanship and rising to the rank of lieutenant. He left the Navy in 1852, apparently because he was unhappy with taking part in the bombardment of Lagos by H.M.S. *Bloodhound* at the end of 1851. Then he worked as captain or master for several merchant ships owned by African traders for traffic along the West African coast. After losing a ship in 1855 he decided to settle down in Lagos to a successful business career.

He traded at first in partnership with a West Indian firm, then on his own from 1857. By the time formal British rule was imposed in Lagos in 1861 he was already a successful import-export businessman, exporting palm oil and cotton. He traded along the lower Niger from an early date. In 1863 he was Treasurer of the African Commercial Association, founded to encourage the interior peoples to end fighting in the interests of "Peace, Commerce and Civilisation."

Davies was one of the most successful African businessmen in Lagos in the latter part of the 19th century. There were others too, notably R.B. Blaize (q.v.), at that time when European firms had not yet established their later dominance. Like their brothers the Creoles of Sierra Leone, the elite of Lagos – merchants, professional men, clergy – tended to see British rule as beneficial, since they, at the time, fared better under it than many other Africans. There were, however, disagreements; in 1865 Governor Glover considered Davies to be among the leaders of *Saro* – a term used to refer to re-emigrants from Sierra Leone – Lagosians whom he saw as trouble-makers, though Davies did sign an oath of loyalty demanded by the governor. In 1872 Davies was appointed to the Lagos Colony Legislative Council; but that Council was abolished, temporarily, in 1874. In the 1870s he was a Justice of the Peace and an Assessor of the Court of Requests.

His firm, called at various times Davies Bros. and W.G. Christie & Co., was said to be – under the latter name – one of the "principal commercial houses" in Lagos in 1894. He started a cocoa and coffee farm in 1892 but concentrated mainly on trade, and did well despite the exclusion of African businessmen from the Niger by the Royal Niger Company in the 1880s and 90s.

He was a pillar of the CMS and contributed £100 to the foundation of the CMS Grammar School at Lagos. He supported the Rev. James Johnson (q.v.) in his efforts to defend and expand African initiative in the Anglican church in West Africa, and protested at the hostile attitude of white missionaries to Johnson. He was one of that churchman's main lay allies in Lagos.

After a first marriage to a wife who died an early death in 1860, he married at Brighton in England, in 1862, Miss Ina Sarah Forbes Bonetta, who was a "Recaptive" of an unusual sort: a captive Yoruba girl, she had been prepared at the age of nine for human sacrifice in Dahomey, but then King Gezo (q.v.) gave her to Captain Forbes of H.M.S. *Bonetta*, a British government representative who protested at the human sacrifices in Dahomey, and he sent her to Britain and Sierra Leone for education. Queen Victoria had taken an interest in her and acted as godmother to her daughter by Captain Davies, christened Victoria. Sarah Davies died in 1880. After that Captain Davies married Catherine Kofoworola Raffle.

Captain J.P.L. Davies, a leading figure in Lagos, died on 30 April 1906. ■

I.O. Delano

Delano, I.O. (1904-79)

DELANO, Isaac Oluwole (1904-79).

NIGERIAN writer and educationist and moving spirit in the development of African studies scholarship. Born on 4 November 1904 in Igbore, Abeokuta (now in Ogun State), he attended the Lagos Grammar School in 1919, and later went to King's College, Lagos. From 1952-54 he studied at the School of Oriental and African Studies, University of London, England.

He was a school teacher and also full-time Administrative Secretary of the Egbe Omo Oduduwa, the former Yoruba cultural society, from 1948 to 1951. Delano served on various government committees; he was the first Chairman of the Egba-Ifo District Council. While in London he was an Assistant Research Officer in Yoruba. Later he was appointed lecturer at the University of Ife, and he was an Examiner in Yoruba language for both the University of London (1953-78) and the West African Examinations Council. He was a Research Fellow in Yoruba and Associate of the Hansberry College of African Studies, University of

Nigeria, Nsukka (1962-66), and Research Fellow in Yoruba Studies, University of Ife.

Later he was Honorary Research Associate and part time Yoruba Specialist, Institute of African Studies, Universty of Ife, receiving an honorary degree of the University of Ife in 1974. A statue of him was erected in his honour by the Institute of African Studies, University of Ife, in gratitude for Delano's contributions to the cause of African Studies.

He was a popular broadcaster and published several articles in newspapers and magazines. He also worked on various historical research projects with Professor Saburi O. Biobaku and was the author of several publications, which include *The Soul of Nigeria* (London 1937), *Aiye D'aiye Oyinbo, L'ojo ojo Un, The Singing Minister of Nigeria* (London 1942), *Notes and Comments from Nigeria* (London 1944), *An African* (London 1945), *One Church for Nigeria* (London 1945), *Atumo Ede-Yoruba* (London 1958), *Agbeka oro Yoruba* (London 1960), *Iranti anfani, Itan Egba* (London 1963), *Itan Oyo* (London 1964), *Owe L'esin Oro* (Ibadan 1966), *Conversation in Yoruba and in English* (New York 1963), *A modern Yoruba grammar* (London 1965).

Isaac Oluwole Delano died on 15 December 1979. He is survived by several eminent children including Honourable Justice I.B. Delano of Ilaro High Court, Ogun State of Nigeria.■

Deng, W. (died 1968)

DENG, William (died 1968).

SUDANESE politician and influential exponent of national unity. Born in southern Sudan, he became interested in politics from an early age. He was convinced that a federal system in the country would solve the problem of southern Sudan which originated from geographical and social differences between the North and South of the country, and which were exacerbated by the British administration's Southern Policy. This policy attempted to separate the South from the Arabic and Moslem influences in the North, partly to prevent the spread of nationalism but also so that the region could eventually be assimilated into other British territories to the south of the country.

He became a District Commissioner in the Upper Nile Province and remained in this position until 1961 when he went into voluntary exile following disagreements with the military regime of General Abboud. The following year he founded the Sudan African National Union (SANU), becoming its president. This party reflected Deng's federalist beliefs. He remained in exile until 1964 and during this period he co-authored a book entitled *The Problem of Southern Sudan* in which he expressed his views on the political and racial differences between northern and southern Sudan.

In 1964 the military regime was overthrown and Deng returned to Sudan under a general amnesty granted by the new government. He continued to be active in southern politics and in 1967 he was one of the 36 southern Sudanese who were elected members of the Constituent Assembly in a supplementary election. Along with Siddick el-Mahdi he became one of the leaders of the powerful opposition in parliament.

He was re-elected member of the Assembly for Rumbeck in Bahr el Ghazal Province in April 1968. Meanwhile conflict continued in the South and shortly afterwards, on 5 May 1968, he was shot dead in an ambush outside Rumbeck.■

W. Deng

Dennis, C.C. (1931-80)

DENNIS, Charles Cecil Jr (1931-80).

LIBERIAN lawyer and politician who, from 1973 until his death, served as Minister of Foreign Affairs and was active in the formulation of OAU policy on South Africa and the liberation movements. This was a period of intensive political activities for Liberia, particularly in its regional and international relations.

Dennis was born on 21 February 1931 and attended the College of West Africa, Liberia, from where he entered Lincoln University, Pennsylvania, USA. He completed his education at George Washington University in Washington. On completion, he was called to the Bar of the Supreme Court of Liberia.

In 1960 he was appointed director of the Legislative Drafting Service of the Liberian Senate. Five years later he established himself in private legal business as C. Cecil Dennis Jr. Law firm in Monrovia. Also in 1965 Dennis was made professor at the Louis Arthur Grimes School of Law, Universty of Liberia. Between that time and the period he was appointed Foreign Minister, he served on several boards and organisations; he was chairman of the Board of Directors of the Bank of Liberia, and vice-president of the Liberian-American-Swedish Minerals Company (LAMCO), which was the largest of the five mining companies that operated in the country at the time.

He was appointed in 1973 Minister of Foreign Affairs by President Tolbert (q.v.), and this post he held until 1980. One of the young new breed of ministers in the Tolbert's new-wave government, Dennis played a major part in strengthening his country's relations with its neighbours. He formulated the policy of regional cooperation between Liberia and its two immediate neighbours – Sierra Leone and Guinea. This led to the establishment in October 1973 of the Mano River Union (MRU), a sub-regional economic grouping of, initially, Liberia and Sierra Leone, and later Guinea who joined it in November 1980. The MRU's aim, as reiterated by Sierra Leone's President Siaka Stevens on the occasion of Guinea's entry, is to create "a positive and constructive move towards economic self-reliance, and social and cultural integration at a sub-regional level."

The same principle led to intensification of ties between Liberia and other countries in West Africa and the continent in general. As Foreign Minister, Dennis was responsible for Liberia's role in the formation in 1975 of the Economic Community of West African States (ECOWAS), of which Liberia is one of the sixteen member countries. On the continental plane, Dennis was equally active in the Pan-African politics of the Organisation of African Unity (OAU). After Liberia's earlier attempt to establish a form of dialogue with South Africa, which the Liberian authorities then believed could pave the way for that country's change of its apartheid policy, Liberia soon re-identified with the majority African opinion of no dealings with Pretoria.

Dennis was instrumental in re-establishing his country's image in Africa and also played a significant part in the subsequent OAU policies on South Africa and the liberation movements. It was he who pre-

C.C. Dennis

pared the groundwork for the OAU 16th Summit Conference which took place in Monrovia in 1979.

Dennis was a member of the Liberian Codification Commission. He was accorded national honours – Commander, Order of the Star of African Redemption; Knight Grand Commander, Most Venerable Order of Pioneers; and foreign honours – Grand Gross Commander of the Order of Orange-Nassau, Netherlands, and Honorary Consul-General of the Republic of South Korea.

He was executed on 22 April 1980 following the overthrow of President William Tolbert and a trial of leading members of the fallen regime. He is survived by a widow and three children.■

Diagne, B. (1872-1934)

DIAGNE, Blaise (1872-1934).

SENEGALESE politician and leading African administrator in French colonial West Africa, the first to be elected deputy to the French Assembly in Paris. Blaise Diagne was born in 1872 on the island of Gorée, off the coast of Senegal, near Dakar. His father was a cook and his mother a housemaid. While still very young he was adopted by a wealthy Catholic Creole family who sent him to the local Catholic school and later to Aix-en-Provence in France to finish his secondary studies. He later returned to Senegal, where he graduated first in his class at Saint-Louis in 1890.

B. Diagne

Encouraged by his academic success, he decided to compete for a post in France's colonial Customs service. He passed the examination and in 1892 was sent as a second-class clerk to the then Dahomey (now Benin). His career in the Customs took him to Gabon, Congo, Réunion, Madagascar, and, finally, to French Guiana in South America. In each country, the colonial authorities regarded him as a trouble-maker. He did not hesitate to speak out against oppression and racial discrimination, but this behaviour earned him suspension or blocked his promotion on several occasions.

In 1908 he fell ill and underwent an operation in France. His fifteen months' sick leave gave him the opportunity to see French politics and colonial lobbies in action. In 1908 he married a French girl, Odette Villian, and in 1910 he was assigned to French Guiana.

There again, although his superiors were at first more than satisfied with his work, Diagne's crusade on behalf of the oppressed led to bitter confrontation with his superiors. Moreover, local merchants were unused to agents they could not bribe. On leave in France, in 1912, he lectured on France's colonial problems and engaged in public debate with some influential figures in colonial life and thinking. It was also during this leave that he first put forward the idea that he might run for political office in Senegal. Later that year he returned to French Guiana to take the examination for the rank of Inspector of Customs. On a six months' leave in France, Diagne, although his chances looked slim, decided to seek election as deputy for Senegal in the French Parliament.

His most immediate problem was how to build strong bases of support in Dakar and Saint-Louis. He had to win the support of the Young Senegalese, Senegal's first political party, founded in Saint-Louis in 1912.

Diagne had achieved equality and success within the "assimilationist" system applied in the historic "four communes" of Senegal. His compelling oratory and promises to work for the abolition of all oppressive laws and taxes against the African soon won him the support of the Young Senegalese. Although a native of Senegal, Diagne's long absence from his birthplace meant that he was unknown to most people to whom his name had to be brought. He toured the country, appealing to all ethnic groups and projecting himself as the first African candidate who could best represent the people of Senegal as a whole.

Until 1912, all Africans born in the four communes (Saint-Louis, Goree, Dakar and Rufisque), or of parents born there, were French citizens (known as "*originaires*"), whereas those born in the protectorate were French subjects, with minimal rights. A controversial decree of 1912 had placed the status of the *originaires* in some doubt. In the 1914 elections Diagne campaigned on the basis of seeking clarification of his constituents' political rights. His other demands were the abolition of the head tax, pensions for older workers, recognition of the Africans' right to organise trade unions, and the alteration of the customs rates to encourage small businessmen.

The first vote produced a convincing victory for Diagne over the French incumbent. However, as he was not supported by a majority of registered voters, a runoff was set for 10 May. Diagne won the second ballot with a narrower margin but became the first African deputy to the French Assembly. His election gave birth to new African aspirations, in a country whose political life had hitherto been dominated by the French and the Creole community, but colonialists saw it as a dangerous precedent for their other colonies.

Diagne took up his seat with the Socialists in the French Parliament. He had served for only six weeks when France entered the First World War. He proposed that the Senegalese should be enlisted into the French corps stationed in Senegal for the duration of the war. Diagne urged acceptance of the idea that the *originaires* should not be asked to fight unless given full rights and privileges including citizenship, and urged them not to join up until their status had been clarified. He finally won largely due to his persistence, oratory and skill, but also because of the enormous manpower demands of the war. The Law of 19 October 1915 came to be known as the first of the "Blaise Diagne laws".

In September 1916, Diagne introduced a resolution in Parliament: "The natives of the four communes of Senegal, and their descendants, are and remain French citizens subject to the military obligations imposed by the Law of 19 October 1915". It was passed, virtually without debate, thus resolving the citizenship question which had been around since 1848.

At the end of 1917, when Clemenceau became Minister of War as well as Prime Minister, Diagne was asked to join the Cabinet in a junior capacity and to lead a recruitment mission in West Africa. He accepted the post, but did not leave until a certain number of concessions had been made over the treatment of Africans serving in France, such as exemption from taxation, and the setting up in Senegal of veterans' hospitals, agricultural schools and a medical school. He returned to Paris in August 1918, having enlisted 60,000 men compared with the 40,000 he had been sent to recruit.

Although this was a triumph, and his name became familiar throughout West Africa, some saw him as a collaborator with the colonialists. The concessions he had won were seen as not worth the thousands of African lives lost in the war.

The 1919 elections to the French Assembly after the war were again bitterly contested, with the French and Creole community seeking to restore their respective influences. Diagne's platform included the demand for the abolition of the distinction between Senegalese civil servants and those workers on the basis of merit, not race.

The vote on 30 November resulted in an overwhelming victory for Diagne. In the municipal elections the following month, Diagne's newly-found Republican-Socialist party won complete control of local government in the four communes. The French press soon began to use the word "Diagnism" as a synonym for Africanisation and nationalism.

Diagne consistently advocated constitutional reforms as well as the setting up of mixed communes endowed with municipal councils and a single electoral college of all citizen voters. He also proposed the election of a deputy for each of the French West African colonies, one for French Equatorial Africa and one for Madagascar; both proposals were regarded with alarm by the French colonialists.

Although he could not obtain enough support for further reforms outside Senegal, however, he supported the setting up of an enlarged Council in Senegal composed of elected *originaires* and appointed members from the Protectorate. It came into being by the decree of 4 December 1920, enabling the non-citizen Senegalese of the Protectorate to be directly involved in politics for the first time. In the Council elections of June 1921, Diagne's Republican-Socialist party won a majority of seats. The result of these victories was increased antagonism on the part of the French administration and officials in France as well as the Bordeaux merchants who traded in Senegal. Diagne made a much-criticised pact with the latter in 1923 under which they agreed to support him in return for representation on his councils and party. Galandou Diouf (q.v.), the first African elected to the General Council of the four communes in 1909, and until the early 1920s Diagne's loyal lieutenant, stood against Diagne in the elections for the French Parliament. He failed in the 1928 and 1932 elections and was not elected until after Diagne's death.

Diagne came closer than ever to the French government in later years, until in the early 1930s he served as Under Secretary of State for the Colonies in that government. Earlier he had defended French forced labour in Africa before the International Labour Organisation (ILO) in Geneva. He had many African critics and Diouf seriously challenged him for the Senegalese voters' support. But although Diagne adopted a somewhat more conservative stance in his later years, this did not greatly detract from the immense contribution of this capable and committed leader to the evolution of political life in Senegal. He died in 1934. ■

Diakite, Y. (1932-73)

DIAKITE, Captain Yoro (1932-73).

MALIAN soldier and politician, born in 1932 in Bangassi, a small village in the Kita *Cercle*. He had his education at the Ecole Rurale in Kassaro and the Ecole des Enfants de Troupe in Kati. He joined the army in 1951 and served in Senegal and Indo-China. Diakite went to the Ecole de Fréjus as an officer cadet in 1956. On his return from France, he was stationed at Thiès in Senegal, and in 1960 he served in Congo with the United Nations peace-keeping mission.

When he returned to Mali, Diakite was promoted lieutenant and posted to Timbuctu and later to Bamako at the Etat Major (General Staff). Appointed director of the Ecole Militaire Interarmes at Kati, he played a key role in planning the 1966 coup d'état, having earlier on several occasions attempted to organise a coup against Modibo Keita (q.v.). He was made Vice-President of the Military Committee of National Liberation (CMLN) after the coup. Later, he was made Minister of Transport, Telecommunications and Tourism, until September 1970 when he became Minister of the Interior, Security and Defence. Diakite held this portfolio until April 1971.

He was later expelled from the government, the army and the committee after he was accused by the CMLN, along wth Malik

Diallo, of plotting against the "security of the state". He was then sentenced to life imprisonment with hard labour on 31 July 1972. Diakite had on many occasions come into conflict with those members of the Military Committee who supported maintaining Mali's long-standing special relationships with the Communist bloc, while he favoured closer ties wth France and the West. He was the author of a novel, *Une Main Amie* (1969), whose preface was written by former President Modibo Keita. He died in prison in 1973 of undisclosed causes. ■

Diallo, S. (1923-81)

DIALLO, El-Hadj Saifoulaye (1923-81)

GUINEAN politician, a founder member of the inter-territorial *Rassemblement Démocratique Africain* (RDA) and its Guinean section the *Parti Démocratique de Guinée* (PDG). When he was elected to the Guinean National Assembly in 1957 he became its first President. Since then he remained prominent, and powerful in Guinean politics, always close to the first President of the Republic, Sékou Touré (q.v.).

Saifoulaye Daillo was born in 1923 in Diari near Labe, into a noble Fulani family in the Foutah Djallon, mouth of the River Niger. His father was a local chief, and Diallo was educated at Timbo and Labe. He had his post-primary education at the Camille Guy School in the Guinean capital, Conakry. Following in the footsteps of his contemporaries in French-speaking West and Central African regions, he completed his education at the prestigious Ecole William Ponty in Dakar, and like many of them joined the French colonial administration. He served as a clerk first at Niamey in Niger from 1947 to 1949, then at Bobo-Dioulasso in Burkina Faso (formerly Upper Volta) between 1949 and 1955, and lastly at Mamou in his native Guinea in 1955 for one year. Never promoted to a responsible position in those years, he was frequently transferred from one station to another because of his militant activities in the RDA. He gave up his job in the colonial service in 1956 to devote himself to full-time politics.

El-Hadj S. Diallo

Guinea was voting in General de Gaulle's referendum (1958) on whether Guineans preferred complete independence to limited autonomy, Diallo threw his influence behind Sékou Touré's campaign for independence. And the result was the massive vote which led to French withdrawal from Guinea in 1958. Following that he played a prominent role as political power broker, rallying Guinea's various ethnic groups and their leaders behind the Government of President Touré.

At independence in 1958 he was re-appointed President of the National Assembly, in addition to holding the post of Political Secretary of the PDG which at the time was the policy-making body of the country. He was appointed to the Cabinet in 1963 as Minister of State for Finance and Planning. This was a difficult posting at a time when Guinea's choice for total independence led to France's hasty and punitive retreat which left the new Republic without funds and economic foundation. But Diallo directed the economy to offset the large credit repayments which had accumulated after five years of extensive foreign borrowing. Three years later he was moved to the ministry of Foreign Affairs where he replaced Louis Lansana Beavogui (q.v.) as Minister of State.

Ill health caused him in later years to be less active. But in 1972 President Touré made him Minister at the Presidency, and from then until his death on 25 September 1981 he held other ministerial ranks in the administration.■

His political activities were, of course, important to the RDA which he had helped to found in October 1946. At the inaugural congress in Bamako that year, when he was only 23, Diallo was elected secretary-general of the Niamey branch. He then became the political secretary of the Conakry branch and joint secretary-general of the Bobo-Dioulasso branch, and finally the administrative secretary of the Mamou branch. In January 1956 he was elected with Sékou Touré as Deputy for his country to the French National Assembly, coming closely behind the latter on the electoral list. In November of the same year he was elected Mayor of Mamou.

In March 1957 he was voted into the Guinean Territorial Assembly of which he became the first President. This was followed three months later with his election to the Grand Council of French West Africa. When

Dibongue, R.G.K. (1896-1974)

DIBONGUE, Robert Gabea Kum (1896-1974).

CAMEROONIAN administrator and politician, a leading figure in the debate about the fate of British ruled Southern Cameroons. Born in Douala under German rule, he went to a German school there and in 1912 was appointed a First Class Clerk, working at Buea, the German government headquarters. He was at Douala when Anglo-French forces landed there in September

1914 in the campaign against the Germans in their colony of "Kamerun", in the First World War. The French kept Douala, as part of French Cameroon, but Dibongue, who had learned English with the help of a Nigerian friend, went to British Southern Cameroons. In that territory, ruled by Britain for 40 years as a Mandated Territory and then as a Trust Territory, Dibongue had a distinguished administrative career within the limits laid down for Africans in the colonial period.

He worked at the Buea headquarters of the British mandate administration and Cameroons Province. He rose from being a probationary clerk in the Provincial Office to reach the post of Assistant Chief Clerk. In 1944 he was transferred to Enugu, capital of the Eastern provinces of Nigeria, to which Southern Cameroons was attached for many purposes. He became Chief Clerk there but, seeing no prospect of further promotion, retired in 1947 and returned to Douala.

Two years later he was back in British Cameroons, active in the emerging political life there. The people there, with close ties linking them to Nigeria and particularly the Eastern Region, joined in Nigerian demands for self-government. But the question arose among them of whether their long-term future lay with Nigeria, or in independence on their own or union with French Cameroon. Dibongue was one of the early supporters of the last idea.

A French Cameroons Welfare Union (FCWU) was co-founded by Dibongue, and in 1949 sent a petition to a visiting mission of the United Nations, which supervised the British and French administrations of Cameroon. It was a group formed by some of the very many emigrants from French Cameroon who had gone for decades to British Southern Cameroons. Besides seeking to advance these people's position in Southern Cameroons, the FCWU also supported unification between the British and French Trust Territories. This was also a major demand of the *Union des Populations du Cameroun* (UPC), the main nationalist party in French Cameroun, led by Reuben Um Nyobe (q.v.). It was called "Re-unification" because it sought to restore the unity of the former German colony, and, to stress its point, it favoured use of the German spelling "Kamerun." The FCWU supported the demand, and in the 1949 petition attacked French misrule in particular.

In 1950/51 Dibongue became Honorary General President of the FCWU. He strongly supported the cause of "Re-unification", and was himself a symbol of the ties between the British and French territories; besides migrants like him there were indigenous ethnic groups related to each other on either side of the border. In 1951 he and N.N. Mbile organised a conference at Kumba with representatives (Abel Kingue and Ernest Ouandié) of the UPC. The conference agreed on the aim of "Re-unification" but not on a specific programme for achieving it. Dibongue and Mbile, who had supported Dr Emmanuel Endeley's Cameroons National Federation, now left it to form the Kamerun United National Congress.

Later in 1951, at another meeting at Kumba, Um Nyobe called for unity among nationalists in both British and French zones, and for a "national committee" as an initial step, but no action was taken in this direction. Nor did any such action follow a meeting of Dibongue and other FCWU leaders with Um Nyobe and Kingue at Tiko in 1952. And from then on Dibongue's support for "Re-unification" faded away. Mbile, who was less keen on the idea, later abandoned it, and his Kamerun People's Party (KPP) supported union with Nigeria, to which British Southern Cameroons was still closely linked although it was a separate Region after 1954. Its ally the Kamerun National Congress of Endeley (even though it, too, used the German spelling) also came to favour union with Nigeria. And so did their supporter Dibongue, who came to argue that the advantages for British Southern Cameroons now lay in permanent union with Nigeria.

When the 1959 elections brought to power the Kamerun National Democratic Party (KNDP) of J.N. Foncha, which favoured union with French Cameroun, Dibongue was removed from the post of Chairman of the Southern Cameroons Development Agency, to which he had been appointed earlier. He and Dr Endeley were on the losing side, as in February 1961 a referundum produced a clear majority in British Southern Cameroons in favour of union with ex-French Cameroun (independent since 1 January 1960) rather than with Nigeria. Re-unification, which he had advocated earlier, came about on 1 October 1961. Dibongue died in 1974 and is buried in Douala. ■

Dike, K.O. (1917-83)

DIKE, Professor Kenneth Onwuka (1917-83).

NIGERIAN educationist, a renowned historian and distinguished university administrator who was the first Vice-Chancellor of his country's premier institution of higher learning, the University of Ibadan. Dike's death in 1983 brought to a close an important chapter in the history of scholarship in not only Nigeria but also Africa; he was the prime mover in the promotion of African history as an essential ingredient of African education.

He was born on 17 December 1917, in Awka in Anambra State. After early schooling and secondary education at the Dennis Memorial Grammar School, Onitsha, he went to Achimota College in Ghana. From there he attended Fourah Bay College, Freetown, in Sierra Leone, and successively the University of Durham, the University of Aberdeen and the University of London, all in Britain.

While in London Dike chose a theme focusing on the activities of Africans which required the study of Oral Traditions as the subject for his Ph.D thesis, at a time when it was not yet academically acceptable to use oral material for historical study. But Dike, "with a background in folklore, especially traditions of famous itinerant Awka blacksmiths, could not accept that Africans had no history beyond the activities of Europeans". Thus he pressed ahead with his research, drawing from oral material which he was the first to get accepted as a valid part of scholarly work. The resultant study, *Trade and Politics in the Niger Delta 1830-1890*, accordingly assumes a unique significance in the evolution of historiography not only in Africa but also worldwide. The work which was subsequently published in 1956, marks an important milestone in the appreciation of African history as seen through an African eye.

Dike's other pioneering works include *Reports on the Preservation and Administration of Historical Records in Nigeria*, published earlier in 1953, *A Hundred Years of British Rule in Nigeria* which came out in 1957 and *The Origins of the Niger Mission*, in 1958. These works became the blueprint for historical studies and set a tradition of sustained scholarship which came to be known as the 'Ibadan School' of History Studies.

Prof. K.O. Dike

It was also at Ibadan that Dike left his most lasting tradition as an Africanist, educationist and administrator. He joined the University's Department of History as a lecturer in 1950, when it was an affiliate of the University of London and called University College, Ibadan. At the time the only courses available there were British History, European History and the history of European colonization of Africa. And Dike's immediate aim was to correct the anomaly by introducing courses in African History but the absence of relevant textbooks frustrated his efforts. Two years later he left the University for a senior research fellow post with the West African (now Nigerian) Institute of Social and Economic Research where, in addition to his duties, he did the preliminary work for the establishment of the National Archives of which he became the first Director in 1952.

In 1954 he returned to the University and became, two years later, its first Nigerian Head and Professor of History. From then on he began to Africanise the department by recruiting staff who under his administrative leadership and intellectual guidance reformed the curriculum to create a truly African approach to the teaching of African History. He also initiated several scholarly research projects which included the Benin Research Scheme and pursued publications, all which combined to make Ibadan's History Department renowned for pioneering the new historiography in Africa. According to J. F. Ade Ajayi, "the series of monographs in the Ibadan History Series of which Dike was the first General-Editor, remains a monument to this achievement."

In 1955 Dike founded the Historical Society of Nigeria, of which he was the first President. The Society's aim was to encourage interaction among scholars and to promote the proper study of history at all levels in the country. Indeed the first issue of the Society's *Journal* in 1956 was devoted to the question of what history to teach in Nigerian schools. This subsequently led to a joint effort by Dike's Department of History, the West African Examination Council and the Society to prepare new syllabuses in African History for secondary schools in West Africa. The three bodies also convened a Workshop for teachers from all over English-speaking West Africa and the resultant papers were published as *A Thousand Years of West African History*, and *Africa in the 19th and 20th Centuries* which quickly became essential reference materials. Professor Dike remained the President of the Historical Society until 1966 when he was forced to leave Ibadan as a result of the national crisis which found him on the side of breakaway Biafra.

Before then however Dike had made his mark as a successful administrator. In 1958 he was appointed the first African Principal of University College which he steered through a most difficult time when the institution was becoming autonomous of the University of London. When in 1962 it became the University of Ibadan, Professor Dike became its first Vice-Chancellor.

Dike was a man of outstanding qualities; a distinguished scholar who pioneered African historiography, an eminent educationist who established the blueprint for the study of truly African history and a success-

ful administrator who presided over the transition from a colonial University College to the University of Ibadan and made it an influential seat of learning through sustained scholarship. His foresight led to the creation of national as well as international institutions. He created the Department of Antiquities which became the National Museum, the National Archives, the Institute of African Studies and the International School – the last two being attached to the University of Ibadan. He was a prime mover in the establishment of the Nigerian Institute of International Affairs and the International Congress of African Historical Society.

He reappeared on the international scene in 1970 when, after the collapse of Biafra, he took up a post as Professor of History at Harvard University, Cambridge, in the United States. In 1980 he returned to Nigeria to be appointed the first President of the new University of Technology in Enugu, Anambra State. He was laying the foundation for that young institution when he died on 26 October 1983. ∎

Dikko, M. (1865-1944)

DIKKO, Muhammadu, Emir of Katsina (1865-1944).

NIGERIAN traditional ruler. He was appointed by the British in 1906, though his family, the Sulibawa, had not been the ruling family hitherto. His father Gidado, a noted soldier, had held the office of Durbi, and Muhammadu was later appointed to the same title by Emir Abubakar (deposed 1904). He is said to have helped the British build a fort in 1906, while he was a District Head, and thus to have favourably impressed the newly installed colonial authorities, who in the same year made him the ninth Fulani Emir of Katsina.

In 1934 Katsina became a separate province in British Northern Nigeria. The Katsina Emirate under Muhammadu Dikko was noted for a progressive attitude towards education. Unlike most Emirs, Dikko allowed the spread of Western education. It was in Katsina in 1921 that the new secon-

M. Dikko, Emir of Katsina

dary school for Northern Nigeria was opened, Katsina Training College (transferred later to Kaduna and, as Barewa College, to Zaria). The first elementary teacher training college for the Moslem North was opened at Katsina in 1930. There was a girls' school which was housed for a time in the Emir's compound in Muhammadu Dikko's reign.

In 1921 and again in 1933 Muhammadu Dikko went to Mecca and Europe. He died on 29 January 1944, and was succeeded by his son Usman Nagogo (q.v.).■

Dikko, R.A.B. (1912-77)

DIKKO, Dr. Russell Aliyu Barau (1912-77).

NIGERIAN politician and medical doctor. Born at Zaria on 15 June 1912, he adhered to the small CMS (Anglican) mission following at Wusasa outside Zaria, and was educated at its school from 1922 to 1929. He went to King's College, Lagos, from 1929 to 1931, and then to the University of Birmingham, England, where he became the first person from Northern Nigeria to qua-

lify in European medicine, after passing the examinations of the London Joint Medical Board in 1934. He obtained the MRCS and LCRP.

He joined the government medical service, as a Junior Medical Officer (1940), later becoming Medical Officer (1941), and Senior Medical Officer (1953); he was then made Principal Medical Officer in the Endemic Diseases Division in the Northern Region. He had before then played a major role in the rise of party politics in the North. In 1948-9 he organised meetings leading to the creation in 1949 of the Jamiyar Mutanen Arewa, the body which became the Northern People's Congress (NPC). He headed it for over two years, but when the NPC became a political party in 1951 he had to resign because he was a civil servant.

In 1960 he was posted to the Curative Service Division, and in 1962 he was appointed Permanent Secretary to the Northern Region Ministry of Health. In June 1967 he joined the Federal Executive Council as Commissioner for Mines and Power. In 1971 he became Commissioner for Transport. He left the Federal Government in January 1975 and died two years later.■

Dr. R.A.B. Dikko

Dinar, A. (c.1865-1916)

DINAR, Sultan Ali (c.1865-1916).

SUDANESE traditional ruler, Sultan of Darfur which, under him, was one of the last parts of Africa to submit to effective European occupation. He was born at Shuwaiya near the Mellum into the family of the Sultans who had ruled Darfur as an independent state and which, at the time of his birth, had not yet been annexed to the Egyptian Sudan. He was named Ali Dinar Zakariya Muhammad el-Fadi.

In 1874 Darfur, a large savanna region between Kordofan and Wadai, was annexed to the Egyptian Sudan through the efforts of Zubair, who defeated and killed Sultan Ibrahim. In 1881 Rudolf Slatin, one of many Europeans who worked for Egypt in the government of the Sudan, was appointed governor of Darfur. But in 1883 he surrendered to the forces of the Mahdi (q.v.). A

Sultan A. Dinar

cousin of Ali Dinar, Abu Khairat, challenged that rule in 1889, at first with Ali's help; but then they quarrelled and Abu Khairat was killed, possibly by Ali Dinar, who then became titular Sultan (1890) although he submitted to the Khalifa a year later.

His opportunity came with the Anglo-Egyptian victory over the Khalifa in 1898. He went to El Fasher, capital of Darfur, and took power as Sultan. He recognised the authority of the Governor-General in Khartoum, who ruled over the Anglo-Egyptian Condominium – in reality a British colony – of the Sudan. This Governor-General, Sir Reginald Wingate, and his Inspector-General, Slatin Pasha, decided to leave Ali Dinar in power as a virtually independent ruler, in return for formal submission and regular tribute, which Ali Dinar paid (fixed at £500 per annum in 1901).

Accepting this situation as enough, the British left Darfur without any colonial administration whatever, recognising the Sultan who ruled in the traditional way unhindered and was even helped by the British against his local enemies. He ruled with the aid of a Wazir (who commanded his army), a Qadi (chief judge) and other officials, and an advisory Council; and of personal representatives – manadib, provincial military commanders – who collected taxes for him and otherwise enforced his rule.

Ali Dinar launched many military expeditions against sedentary and nomadic Arab ethnic groups. The government in Khartoum approved, or at any rate acquiesced in, these expeditions, and in 1913 helped him enforce his rule over the Rizaiqat nomads even when he failed to defeat them militarily.

Ali Dinar failed to defeat Dar Marsalit to the west in 1905-7. Later the French, after occupying Wadai (added to Chad Territory) between 1902 and 1909, claimed territory in some areas west of Darfur, including Dar Marsalit. The dispute, which led to discussions between Britain and France, was complicated by the lack of real British rule in Darfur, and was not solved by 1914.

When the First World War broke out, the informal relationship between Ali and the British rapidly broke down. Ali Dinar decided to support the call by Turkey on all Moslems to rise against British rule. He was contacted by the Turks and by the Sanusiya of Libya, but only very little help reached him from them before he clashed finally with the British. In April 1915 the Sultan refused allegiance or tribute to Britain. In March 1916, the British invaded Darfur with a force of about 2,000 men, supported by aircraft which dropped proclamations calling on Ali Dinar's men to surrender. Ali Dinar's forces, about 3,000 infantry and 800 cavalry with irregulars added, were driven back in several engagements. In May 1916 El Fasher was occupied. Ali Dinar escaped, but was later pursued by the British, and on 6 November 1916 he was killed in a last stand.

To the British this was a small episode in the 1914-18 war, but from another viewpoint the occupation of Darfur, which on 1 January 1917 was formally annexed to the Anglo-Egyptian Sudan for the first time, was one of the last acts in the occupation of Africa. Dinar can be seen as one of the last leaders of "primary resistance" to colonial rule, except for Abdullah Hassan (q.v.) of Somalia. ■

King Dinuzulu

Dinuzulu (1869-1913)

DINUZULU ka Cetshwayo (1869-1913).

KING of the Zulus who is remembered for his political activities against white occupation of South Africa.

He was born in 1869, the eldest son of Cetshwayo (q.v.) who ruled Zululand as an entity until 1879 when the kingdom was occupied by the British and partitioned into 13 territories, each placed under a chief who was responsible to the British government. The Zulu King Cetshwayo was banished to Cape Town and allowed to return home in 1883, a year before he died. Following Cetshwayo's death Dinuzulu, now fifteen years old, contested the throne against his father's arch-rival, his half-cousin Zibhebhu of the Manedlakazi people, who was leader of the other Zulu royal house. Supported by the royal councillors who had proclaimed him king of the Zulus, Dinuzulu sought, and got, the help of some Transvaal Boers, in exchange for large territorial concessions to the Afrikaner farmers who had infiltrated Zululand, and succeeded in becoming king on 21 May 1884.

He succeeded to the kingship at a time of intense rivalry between the Boers and the British who were competing for influence in the area, and while the former had recognised Dinuzulu as paramount chief of the Zulus, the latter extended their authority over the part of Zululand that was incorporated into the Transvaal, on 19 May 1887. By 1888, Zululand was wholly annexed and partitioned into districts which were headed by British magistrates. Dinuzulu resisted the annexation into the British Protectorate but his efforts were defeated. On 15 November 1888 he surrendered at Pietermaritzburg and in 1889 he was tried and found guilty of treason and deported to the island of St. Helena for ten years.

In 1898 Dinuzulu was permitted to return to Zululand, but only as a minor chief with a government salary. During his absence Zululand had been incorporated into Natal, under a British colonial government. In 1906 Chief Bambata of the Zondi in the province led an armed revolt against the imposition of a poll tax. The "Bambata Rebellion", often regarded as the last attempt by the Zulus to mount military resistance to European invasion, was ruthlessly suppressed by the British. Though Bambata himself was killed in the uprising, the revolt continued throughout Zululand for several years, culminating in the arrest and trial of Dinuzulu who had played no role in the spontaneous revolt. He was nevertheless found guilty of high treason, and in March 1909 was deposed again and sentenced to four years imprisonment.

Dinuzulu was given a free pardon after the Union of 1910 and released to settle on the Uitkyk in the Transvaal where he died on 18 October 1913. A year before his death, he was made one of the seven honorary presidents of the ANC at its founding. His daughter's son, Chief Gatsha Buthelezi, became prime minister of the KwaZulu "Homeland" in 1972. ■

Diop, A. (1910-80)

DIOP, Alioune (1910-80).

A. Diop

SENEGALESE publisher, famous as founder and head of the *Présence Africaine* publishing company in Paris. A man of great conviction and obstinate dedication, Alioune Diop spent almost forty years of his life towards the rehabilitation of Black people and their culture in the world.

Born on 10 January 1910 at Saint-Louis in Senegal, he went to school locally, and, at the age of twenty-one, left Senegal to go and study classical literature at the Universities of Algiers and Paris. After obtaining his Licence ès lettres, he worked as a teacher in France before returning home and joining the civil service of French West Africa.

In 1946 he was elected to the Council of the Republic (Senate) in Paris as a Socialist representative of Senegal. In Paris he started the journal *Présence Africaine* in 1947, and, the following year, left active politics to devote all his energies to the journal and the publishing company that built up around it. He ran these for the rest of his life.

The journal *Présence Africaine* was intended as a mouthpiece for Black people in the world to voice their opinions and ideas, and as a forum for discussion on the future of Black civilization in the face of the encroachment by Western culture and values. It was also to help the Black personality and culture to blossom with the emergence of a "new humanism" through the opportunities for expression it afforded it. Launched under the patronage of eminent Black as well as White intellectuals, such as L. S. Senghor, R. Wright, P. Hazoumé (q.v.), Albert Camus, André Gide and Jean-Paul Sartre, it made a mark from the beginning and has published hundreds of articles on all sorts of subjects relating to Africa. It has particularly helped to publish literary efforts by Africans and West Indians in French, but this is not its exclusive aim, and it is not all in French, having an English edition also. Among the famous writers who have written for *Présence Africaine*, and been published by the publishing company attached to it, are L. S. Senghor, Jacques Rabemanjara, Dadié, Aimé Césaire, and there have also been publications in English.

Alioune Diop was a key figure in French African circles. He had his own ideas about African culture, about what Senghor termed *"négritude"* and Black people's contribution to the world. He gave some expression to his concern for the latter in his introduction to the first issue of the journal: "The Black man shines by his absence in the making of modern life, he can now gradually affirm his presence by contributing to its humanism. There can be no genuine universalism if it is to consist solely of European subjectivism. Tomorrow's world must be built by *all* men."

Présence Africaine became a literary institution and Diop as its director was a key figure in organising cultural congresses of Africans, Afro-Americans and West Indians. First there was the Congress of Negro Writers and Artists in 1956 in Paris where in the opening speech Diop made a moving appeal to the unity and solidarity of Black peoples as the basis for not only their political but, just as importantly, also for their cultural freedom and liberation. The aim was to call upon all Black intellectuals to put their heads together and think about the conditions and future of Black peoples. The *Société Africaine de Culture* was founded after the Paris Congress with Diop as secretary-general. Its concern was to encourage Black nations to defend and enrich their natural cultures by affirming the values that affect the daily life of their people.

A second Congress of Negro Writers and Artists took place in Rome in 1959 and in 1966, Diop was chairman of the Negro Arts Festival in Dakar, and was active in helping to organise its successor, the 1977 Festival of Black and African Arts and Culture (FESTAC) in Lagos. He was for a time secretary-general of FESTAC, but in 1976 he was replaced by the Nigerian President of the Festival, after disagreements between Senegal and Nigeria about its organisation.

Though Alioune Diop himself wrote no books, the forewords to the journal and books he published reflect his philosophy. All his energies were concentrated on "creating" an exclusively Negro-African community of which everybody would be proud and which would bring its own contribution to

the world. His efforts took several directions and though they took concrete form mainly in the journal *Présence Africaine* and the company's publications, other avenues were through the many cultural gatherings he sponsored in Africa.

Diop's influence over a whole generation of prominent Africans, mainly but not wholly in French-speaking Africa, was very great. There were many African tributes when he died in Paris on 2 May 1980. He left behind a wife and children.■

Diop, C.A. (1923-86)

DIOP, Professor Cheikh Anta (1923-86).

SENEGALESE celebrated historian and politician; his monumental work on African cultural unity and his exposition of ancient Egyptian civilization as purely African has earned him a place of pride among the greats of this world. He was the first one to point out that ancient Egypt was not "a foreign implant on African soil", but rather the blossoming of a genuinely African civilization.

C.A. Diop

Born in Diourbel, west-central Senegal, in December 1923, Cheikh Anta Diop was educated first in his country and later at the citadel of French radical intellectualism, the Sorbonne University in Paris. There is little doubt that his sojourn at the Sorbonne of the time with the prevalent radical political fervour which encouraged mass African nationalist movements for independence, left an impact on the young student. From 1946 to 1960, he was active in the growing anti-colonial and pan-African movements of African students in the French capital. He was a founding member of the student branch of the *Rassemblement Démocratique Africain* (RDA), the first French-speaking pan-African political movement founded in 1946 at the Bamako Congress to agitate for independence from France. Diop served as its Secretary-General from 1950 for three years. In 1951 he co-organized the first pan-African students' political congress in Paris. Meanwhile Diop had completed his studies, culminating in a doctoral dissertation on the Egyptian origin of African civilization. The thesis was rejected by the French academic authorities, but after publication in 1955 in *Présence Africaine* under the title *Negro Nations and Culture*, it drew world-wide acclaim for its exposition and established Diop as a most distinctive historian, and since, he has been identified with the reconstruction of Africa's place in history; he was awarded the doctorate degree by the Sorbonne in 1960 for his theses, *L'Afrique noire précoloniale* and *L'Unité culturelle de l'Afrique noire*, two other works of research.

The dissertation expounded the theory that contemporary European civilization drew heavily from Pharaonic Egypt through the latter's contact with ancient Greece and Rome. Black Africa, Diop reasoned, is therefore the intellectual and scientific granary from which Europe learnt mathematics, laws of astronomy and chemistry, and developed the studies of human physiology; early European scholars were informed by the Greeks and Romans who had borrowed from Pharaonic Egypt. Diop argued that the Egyptians, whom he stated were Black Africans, were the forerunners in the fields of science, arts, thought and religion of which Ancient Egypt had advanced knowledge.

Diop's findings were considered revolutionary at the time, and they infuriated the French establishment riding on the wave of a prevailing assumption of European cultural superiority over the African. The rejection of the thesis and the subsequent prolonged prohibition of Diop from working at the University of Dakar, for a long time the only university in French-speaking Africa, were part of the reactions.

But, significantly, the appearance of *Negro Nations and Culture* in the 1950s constituted a new area of research into a subject that received scholarship had considered settled. More importantly Diop's theory helped to galvanize the struggle for independence at a time when anti-colonial feelings needed a solid cultural basis. Thus its political and intellectual implications combined to become a unifying force for the African, and Black peoples in other parts of the world while, at the same time, giving Diop a place as a leading articulator of the Black cause. This strong desire to locate Africa in its rightful place in history remained the major influence in Diop's future career in research and politics. Having produced his second major work, *L'unité culturelle de l'Afrique noire; domaines du patriarcat et du matriarcat dans l'antiquité classique*, in 1959, he returned to Senegal in 1960, when the country became independent. Later that same year he published another important work, *L'Afrique noire précoloniale*.

In 1961 he was appointed researcher at the *Institut Fondamental d'Afrique Noire* (IFAN) where, with the assistance of the Egyptian authorities and generous contributions from scientific organizations in Europe, particularly Scandinavia, he founded a radio-carbon laboratory. He worked progressively to establish his theory that ancient Egypt was the forerunner of modern civilization, and his research culminated in the publication in 1974 of *The African Origin of Civilization: Myth or Reality*.

By the early 1980s, Diop had become renowned for his free carbon-dating work for scholars from all over Africa who sent him archaeological specimens for analysis.

For his achievements he was honoured at the 1966 First World Festival of Black Arts held in Dakar, being the African author who had the most profound influence in modern African and international history. He was subsequently involved in the organization of the 1977 Second Festival of Black and African Arts and Culture (FESTAC) in Lagos of which his collaborator and publisher, *Présence Africaine*'s Alioune Diop (q.v.), was for a while Secretary-General.

Politically Cheikh Diop maintained his opposition to the pro-French policies of the government of President Léopold Senghor, and this took shape in 1961 in the foundation of the *Bloc des Masses Sénégalaises* of which he was the first Secretary-General. The party was made up of intellectual and socialist colleagues of Diop who, following its dissolution in 1963, regrouped in 1976 as the *Rassemblement National Démocratique* (RND). He had earlier founded the *Front National du Sénégal* which continued to oppose President Senghor; the *Front*, along with other opposition parties in the country, was banned in 1965.

During this period Diop established a Wolof language journal, *Taxaw,* to articulate his criticism of government policies, but it did not however succeed in changing the pro-French leaning of the country. Outside the political mainstream however, *Taxaw*, which in Wolof means Stand Up!, became the platform for intellectuals and academics who like Diop disagreed with the policy of retaining French as the medium of education in Senegalese schools and colleges. By the early 1970s the demands of the Wolof language movement had become loud and urgent enough to result in a nation-wide strike by school teachers which severely shook the Senghor's government. The compelling urge of nationalism led Diop to translate Albert Einstein's theory of relativity as well as several other foreign works into Wolof.

The vigorous cultural agitation notwithstanding, Diop and his RND Party were for a long time suppressed. In 1979 Diop was charged for breaches of a law which prohibited the formation of political organizations outside the permitted four-party framework. The RND had been denied official recognition, three other opposition parties having been granted it; the government described the RND as a "personality cult". In October 1977 Diop made a public denunciation of the prohibition law in a petition signed by Senegalese intellectuals and politicians and published in the Paris-based *Le Monde* newspaper; it demanded immediate legalization of all parties in the country. This was denied the RND until 1981 when after the retirement of President Senghor in 1980 his successor, Abdou Diouf, revoked the banning order. The following year the RND won

a parliamentary seat in the elections to the National Assembly, but Diop refused to take the seat, leaving it to his deputy who then broke away and formed his own party.

He remained outside the political mainstream until his death, even though the Diouf presidency permitted relative freedom. On 7 February 1986, Diop died of a heart attack in Dakar and was widely mourned in Africa as well as outside the Continent. One eloquent tribute in the United States held him to be "the very pinnacle of great African figures of the era of African rebirth." His own country paid public homage at the historian's home where a large governmental delegation, trade unionists, university teachers and students, members of parliament as well as members of the diplomatic corps heard a Presidential address describe Diop as "Senegal's most fertile and brilliant son, one of the fiercest fighters for Black culture, one of the most persuasive exponents of Black cultural identity, one of the most prestigious and respected heralds of refound Black dignity." IFAN, where he had spent his working life, has been renamed after him. There is also a Cheikh Anta Diop Foundation in Yaoundé, Cameroon, founded in his honour. ■

Diop, D.M. (1927-60)

DIOP, David Mandessi (1927-60).

SENEGALESE writer. He was born on 9 July 1927 at Bordeaux, France, son of a Senegalese technician at Douala harbour in Cameroon, Mamadou Diop, and Maria née Mandessi Bell, daughter of a Cameroonian businessman.

He received his education in France where he spent a considerable part of his youth, the rest being spent in West Africa. He studied medicine, but later taught the History of Literature at secondary schools.

Diop's experience in Europe and in French West Africa formed the basis of his literary work. His book *Coups de Pilon*, containing his seventeen poems, is his only legacy and consists only a small part of what he wrote. The appearance of *Coups de Pilon* in 1956 aroused hopes of a career that was tragically cut short, but the unifying passion and the fire of these few poems earned Diop a place as the spokesman of a new age, the age of the Guinean Revolution in particular and the era of African rejection of colonialism and many of its facets of assimilation and subjugation in general. When Guinea obtained independence outside the French commonwealth in 1958, Diop went to the new Republic as a teacher at the Ecole Normale of Kindia, Guinea.

His poems project a rejection of his assimilationist background and show the new spirit of Africans towards a fresh beginning at the demise of colonial rule. President Léopold Senghor talked of Diop's poems as "the simple force of his verse and a humour which scourges, quickly like the lash of a whip". According to Gerald Moore "He is the Mayakovsky of the African Revolution" in *Modern Poetry from Africa* edited by Moore and Ulli Beier adds that Diop's poetry has "no room for gentle nostalgia or forgiveness. His poems move inexorably towards a triumphant affirmation. He does not hope for better things, he commands them by the power of the word, just as Agostinho Neto [q.v.] does from the coffee-fields of Angola".

Diop died in a plane crash in Dakar, on 25 August 1960, his family and manuscripts perishing with him. ∎

H. Diori

young Diori's formal education started in the Niamey Regional School under Boubou Hama (q.v.), later to become one of the leading nationalist figures of Niger, and continued at the Victor Ballot School in Porto Novo in modern Benin and then at the William Ponty Teachers' Training College in Dakar, Senegal.

On returning to Niger in 1936, Diori began work as a teacher in Niamey and Maradi until 1938. Then he went to Paris to teach Djerma and Hausa at the French Institute of Overseas Studies between 1938 and 1946. He became the headmaster of a school in Niamey after his stint in Paris. Diori's participation in nationalist politics began around that time. He joined with his former teacher Boubou Hama to found the *Parti Progressiste Nigérien* (PPN) as the Niger section of Houphouët-Boigny's *Rassemblement Démocratique Africain* (RDA) in 1946. Within the RDA, Diori became one of the closest allies of F. Houphouët-Boigny, later to be the first President of the Republic of Côte d'Ivoire, and their friendship continued well into the independence era.

In 1946 Diori was elected deputy to the French National Assembly in Paris under the very limited franchise given to the French colonies. But his former colleague,

Diori, H. (1916-89)

DIORI, El-Hadj Hamani (1916-89)

NIGER statesman and nationalist who led his country to independence and became its first President. He remained in office until a military coup toppled his regime in 1974.

Hamani Diori was born on 6 June 1916 at Soudoure, near Niamey, to a Djerma family. His father, Sidibe Diori, had joined the French colonial service as a public health official and so his family was well placed to take advantage of the changing political order in that West African region. The

Djibo Bakary, split from Diori and the PPN and went on to form the rival and more radical *Union Démocratique Nigérienne* (UDN), and Diori's political fortunes wavered. He failed to be re-elected to the French National Assembly in 1951; moreover, the French administration supported Bakary, who happened to be a cousin of Diori.

Diori went back to teaching as director of the Hamani Diori School in Niamey from 1951 to 1958, during which period he also devoted much attention to the reorganisation of the PPN into a more effective force. He was eventually re-elected to the French National Assembly in January 1956 when he narrowly defeated Bakary, and became a Deputy President of the Assembly. In the following year, he joined the Niger Territorial Assembly as deputy for Zinder although Bakary's UDN won 41 seats in that assembly compared to the PPN's 19 seats. Diori also became a municipal councillor in Niamey in 1956.

But Djibo Bakary, despite his position at the time as head of government, was defeated in de Gaulle's 1958 referendum on the future of the French colonial empire, concerning independence within the French Community. Diori's PPN successfully campaigned for a "yes" vote, rallying together a coalition of chiefs and traditional elements among the Hausas, Djermas and Fulanis. This time the PPN had the backing of the French administration, and Hamani Diori swept back to power. On 18 December 1958 Niger became an "autonomous republic" with Hamani Diori as Prime Minister. Two years later, on 3 August 1960, the independent Republic of Niger was proclaimed and Diori became Head of State.

In the first three years of independence, Diori held the ministerial portfolios of Foreign Affairs and Defence, and acquired a reputation as mediator in inter-African problems. He also served in the leadership of various Francophone groupings in Africa; he was chairman of OCAM (*Organisation Commune Africaine et Malgache*) in 1966-67 and president of the Entente Council from 1966 to 1974. However, the French began to lose confidence in him, for despite the pressure put on him, Diori gave his support to the Federal Government in Nigeria's civil war of 1967-70 as he did not want to alienate the Hausa population on both sides of Niger's border with its southern neighbour.

However, Diori's position at home became increasingly precarious in contrast with his high international reputation. His regime began to develop agriculture and, after many years of tolerating French paternalism, began to assert its independence. But these efforts seemed to have come too late. The Diori regime was accused of mismanaging drought aid to the country, tolerating corruption in high places and becoming politically repressive. The *Sawaba* (Freedom) Party, formed out of the *Mouvement Socialiste Africain* (MSA) as the UDN had become, had been banned as early as October 1959 and its leader Bakary driven into exile. Attempts by some *Sawaba* elements to overthrow the government through force in 1963-65 did not succeed.

Over the years, although his original political rivals had long since left the scene, local sympathy had become scant for Diori who appeared to have lost touch with the ordinary people of Niger. Eventually toppled on 15 April 1974 in an army coup led by Lt.-Col. Seyni Kountché (q.v.), in which Diori's wife Aissa was killed, Diori himself was put under house arrest together with several of his cabinet ministers. He was not finally released until after Kountché's death and chose to live mainly in Morocco thereafter.

Hamani Diori died in a Rabat hospital on 23 April 1989 after many years of failing health. He will be remembered for the many diplomatic successes Niger scored during his presidency.■

Diouf, G. (1874-1941)

DIOUF, Galandou (1874-1941).

SENEGALESE politician and anti-colonial activist. Born in Saint-Louis, he held many jobs at first, eventually working as an accountant for Abdou Salam Boughreb, the main Moroccan merchant in Dakar, and then as chief accountant with the French firm of Buhan and Teisseire at Rufisque. Dakar and Rufisque, with Saint-Louis and Gorée, were the "four communes" where a few thousand Africans had the vote for a General Council (for local government) and for the French Parliament.

G. Diouf

in 1920, crystallising around himself all opposition to colonial rule and Diagne. He had been radical (by the standards of that time) since joining the General Council.

In 1928 he stood against Diagne in the elections for deputyship, for which the latter was re-elected amidst allegations of electoral fraud. Diouf's campaign was aided by two weekly newspapers, *L'Afrique Occidentale Française* and the strongly anti-colonialist *Périscope Africain*, which was published in Dakar. They rallied round him again in the 1932 elections which saw Diagne returned to the Chamber of Deputies, but in 1934 Diouf was elected after Diagne's death.

Like his predecessor, Diouf was soon to change sides, for no sooner was he elected deputy than he declared support for French policies. And, like Diagne, he too was ostracised by his supporters in Senegal who in 1936 campaigned for the election of Lamine Gueye (q.v.), a former ally in the movement, as their deputy. But, again like Diagne, Diouf defeated his opponent with the help of French administrators who were said to have rigged the elections in his favour.

Galandou Diouf served as deputy until the suspension of representative politics in 1940, following the defeat of France by the Germans and the creation of the Vichy regime which then ruled French West Africa. He died in 1941.■

In 1909 Diouf was elected to the General Council. To halt the threatened disfranchisement by the French of the African voters of the four communes, and redress the inherent anomalies in the colonial system, Diouf allied with a group of radical African civil servants to form the Young Senegalese, a pressure group which advocated equal pay for equal work, more political participation, and more African access to education.

Diouf's first major political impact came in 1914 when he enlisted the Young Senegalese's support for the election of Blaise Diagne (q.v.) as the first African deputy to be sent to the French parliament by the four communes of Senegal. He himself was later elected mayor of Rufisque. But it did not take long before the colonial authority fomented discord in the new movement.

The French successfully won Diagne over to their side. Diouf broke with Diagne

Dipcharima, Z.B.S. (1917-69)

DIPCHARIMA, Zanna Bukar Suloma (1917-69).

NIGERIAN politician. He was born in 1917 in Dipcharima village in the Bornu Province of northern Nigeria (now in Borno State, the official spelling "Borno" being used today). Dipcharima attended the Maiduguri Middle School and later trained as a teacher at the Katsina Higher Training College, the former Northern Nigeria's highest institution of learning at the time.

He began teaching in 1938, working at various schools until 1946 when he embarked on a political career. He first joined the National Council of Nigeria and the Came-

roon (NCNC) being led by Dr Nnamdi Azikiwe, and was in the party's delegation to
Britain in 1947. He left the NCNC to become
a manager for John Holt. Dipcharima re-
entered politics in 1954, this time as a
member of the Northern People's Congress

Z.B.S. Dipcharima

(NPC) on whose platform he was elected to
the Bornu Native Authority. An extremely
popular politician, Dipcharima soon rose to
become president of Bornu Province branch
of the NPC and head of the Yerwa District in
1956, taking the traditional title of Zana.

He won a seat in the Federal House of
Representatives in Lagos in 1954 and was
made Parliamentary Secretary in the Ministry of Transport. In 1957, he became Minister
of State without Portfolio and later Minister
of Commerce and Industry, before taking the
portfolio of Transport in 1964. Dipcharima
was holding this office when the federal
civilian government was overthrown in the
military coup of 5 January 1966; he made the
headlines when, in the absence of the

abducted Prime Minister Tafawa Balewa
(q.v.), he presided over the Cabinet that
handed over power to the armed forces.
Dipcharima died in an air accident in 1969. ■

Disengomoka, E.A. (1915-65)

DISENGOMOKA, Emile Adolphe
(1915-65).

ZAIREAN educationist and author of an
important sociological work on the family in his country. One of his other books won
the coveted Margaret Wrong literary prize
in 1948. Disengomoka also had the distinction of being the first Zairean to receive the
Régent Littéraire which is equivalent to an
MA degree.

His father was a Protestant pastor at
Ngombe Lutete, who had trained at the
Evangelical Training Institute at Kimpese
where he qualified with a diploma in 1922.
Disengomoka had been born seven years
before, on 31 March 1915, at Kingemba. He
first went to school in his father's Ngombe
Lutete Parish and then left in 1928 to study
French at the Ecole des Moniteurs in Madzia
in neighbouring Congo, then a French
colony. From 1931 to 1934 he worked as
regional administrator of the Protestant
elementary schools in Ngombe Lutete, but
returned to college for further training at
the Kimpese Evangelical Pedagogical Institute where he remained until 1942. He
continued his studies at the Pastor's School,
also at Kimpese, until 1944 before becoming
headmaster of Thysville (now Mbanza-
Ngungu) Primary School for five years.

His brilliance and insatiable quest for
education spurred him on to seek admission
to higher institutions which at that time
were not available in the Belgian Congo. He
was admitted to the Ecole Normale
Moyenne, a teachers' training college at
Nivelles in Belgium, in 1949. From there he
proceeded to the Ecole de Régence de Nivelles in 1951 and read for his Régent
Littéraire diploma. In July 1954 he was
awarded that degree, an achievement which
none of his country people had attained
before then. It was, for Disengomoka, the

crowning glory of the long and difficult efforts that began at Ngombe Lutete in the mid-1920s and, for his country, the first positive step towards breaking down the colonial barriers imposed by the Belgians.

Before then Africans were denied education beyond the middle level, except for the clergy (there were 366 Congolese Catholic priests in 1958), and were kept in the lower ranks in the civil service and the army, and excluded from most commercial activity by the Belgian firms and settlers who came in large numbers in the 1940s and 50s. African political development, severely restricted by the Belgians, found expression through cultural organizations. With time, however, and with more Africans following in the footsteps of Disengomoka, open political activity followed, giving rise to articulated demands for political rights and later independence (see Patrice Lumumba).

Politics in the Congo then developed among Africans, as the coercive and regimenting power of the Belgians was relaxed. The heavy restrictions on higher education were gradually ended; the Lovanium University centre at Kisantu started giving more advanced courses. A state university was created at Elisabethville (now Lubumbashi) in 1956, but the number of Congolese graduates was still trivial by 1960 when Congo became independent.

Disengomoka returned to his country in 1955 with his degree to become headteacher of the Central School at Ngombe Lutete. Three years later he went to teach French at the Athénée de Nqiri Nqiri (secondary school) in Kinshasa and then became, in 1965, Principal of the Institut Polytechnique Congolais in the capital.

Though not overtly involved in the politics of the time, he took an active part in civic duties as member of the Council of Léopoldville (now Kinshasa) and of the Council of the Central Government. He was a member of the Board of Governors at the Free University of the Congo, from 1963 to 1964.

He wrote his first novel *Ku nlwulu* (The Future) in 1942, one of the first Zairean novels. In 1943 his award winning novel, *Kwenkwenda (Where shall I go?)*, was published, followed in 1948 with his sociological work on the family, *Luvuvamu mu rizo* (Peace in the House). All these books reflect his interest in the socio-politico development of his country, which he so greatly inspired

by his own educational achievement. He died on 15 March 1965, five years after Zaire achieved independence from Belgium. ∎

Diwani, R. (1910-78)

DIWANI, Rajabu (1910-78).

TANZANIAN political leader in the anticolonial movement, being an early member of the Tanganyika African National Union (TANU), the forerunner of the Chama Cha Mapinduzi (CCM). He served on the National Executive and Central Committees of both organs, and was a founder member of the TANU Youth League.

Diwani was born in 1910, a member of the Zaramo ethnic group, in the Kisarawe district near Dar-es-Salaam. After formal education he set himself up in private business but he was soon attracted to the growing African nationalism that was reacting against British colonial domination of Tanganyika (now incorporating Zanzibar in the United Republic of Tanzania). Diwani joined TANU, founded in 1954 by President Julius Nyerere as a successor to the Tanganyika African Association (TAA). While the earlier association was formed in 1929 by the African elite in the colonial civil service as a discussion forum for indigenous opinion, TANU was conceived as a political party that overtly sought independence for Tanganyika. It adopted the slogan "Uhuru" (Freedom), later "Uhuru na Kazi" (Freedom and Work), with which it agitated for African advancement, an end to colonial rule and the creation of a united non-racial society. With these objectives the TANU leadership successfully built the party into a mass movement which drew large support from the European and Asian communities.

Diwani, a leading activist in the new party, was elected to both its National Executive and Central Committees under the leadership of Nyerere, and there began a working relationship between the two leaders which survived all political vicissitudes. Diwani set out to organise the youth into the Bantu Youth that later developed into the TANU Youth League (TYL). Like

R. Diwani

its parent movement, the TYL was effective and energetic, and its activities had repercussions on the results of the 1958 Legislative Council elections in which TANU emerged victorious. Its activities in post-colonial Tanzania include developing a spirit of support for and a commitment to the socialist policies of TANU, through its many local branches in the form of lectures, rallies, marches and other general duties like maintaining law and order at public meetings.

These activities have caught the imagination of other nationalist movements in Africa, notably those in Angola, Mozambique, Namibia and South Africa who have used, and still use, Tanzania as rear base in the anti-colonial struggle. Some of these have tacitly applied to the Tanzanian experience in the formation of their youth movements. Thus Diwani, the founder and leader of the TYL, is generally regarded as a folk hero of the African youth movement. Among his compatriots he has been variously de-

scribed as "commander", "grand patron" and "grandfather" of the Tanzanian youth.

Diwani remained a central figure in the TANU leadership throughout his political career, where he was a close confidant of President Nyerere. He played an important role in the development of TANU's policies that resulted in the political merger of Tanganyika and Zanzibar in 1964, the 1967 Arusha Declaration which proclaimed the policy of "Socialism and Self-Reliance", and the *Mwongozo* (Party Guidelines) of 1967. A year later, when the TANU merged with the Afro-Shirazi Party of Zanzibar to become the Chama Cha Mapinduzi (CCM – Party of the Revolution), Diwani was again elected to both its National Executive and Central Committees; he served in these roles until his death on 6 August 1978, following a car accident. ■

Dlamini, M. (1914-78)

DLAMINI, Prince Makhosini (1914-78).

SWAZI politician and first Prime Minister in the first self government cabinet. He was born in 1914 at Enhletsheni, Swaziland, the son of Prince Majosi, a relative of the King. He studied at the Franson Christian Memorial School and the National School at Matsafa. Between 1938 and 1940 Prince Makhosini trained as a teacher at the Umphumulo Teacher Training Institute in Natal, South Africa. He taught in Swaziland for several years and became headmaster of Bethel Mission School and principal of the Swazi National School at Lobamba.

In 1947 he resigned from teaching to devote more time to farming and politics. When his father died in 1950 Prince Makhosini was appointed chief. He also served as a rural development officer for the colonial administration.

Makhosini was a member of the Constitutional Committee which produced the "50-50 Constitution" proposals for the British Protectorate. The proposals provided for the establishment of a Legislative Council consisting of 24 members: 12 Europeans and 12 Swazi. Eight of the Swazi seats were to be filled by the King's nominees, according to Swazi custom. Eight European seats were to be elected by voters on the European roll. The remaining 4 Swazi and 4 European seats were to be elected on a common roll of 4 double member constituencies. These proposals were presented at the constitutional talks of November 1961, but the colonial administration rejected them.

Prince M. Dlamini

King Sobhuza II appointed Prince Makhosini Prime Minister in the first self-government Parliament, *imbokodvo*, in 1964. He retained this position in the fully autonomous government of April 1967 and after independence in September 1968. The Makhosini administration did not replace the traditional system of local government. They complemented each other. The *imbokodvo* manifesto which was produced by Prince Makhosini's government demonstrated the non-subservient position of the Swazi National Council to white opinion.

Prince Makhosini represented Swaziland at the OAU meeting in October 1965 in Accra. His government's close ties with South Africa has been understood by the OAU to be unavoidable because of the country's geographical location.

Makhosini was a popular leader who gained the respect of most politicians in Swaziland. A prominent opposition member Sishaya Nxanala, crossed the floor in a gesture of support for him. However, the opposition under Dr Ambrose Zwane had gained strength by the time the King, in April 1973, abrogated the Constitution, dissolved Parliament, and assumed full power himself. When that happened Prince Makhosini remained Prime Minister. In March 1976 he was replaced by Maphevu Dlamini (q.v.), a relative. He died in Mbabane on 28 April 1978, following a heart attack.■

Dlamini, M. (1922-79)

DLAMINI, Major-General Maphevu (1922-79).

S WAZI soldier and politician who in 1967 became the first Commander of the Umbutfo Defence Force. He became the second Swazi to hold the office of Prime Minister in 1976.

He was born on 31 March 1922 at Egocweni near Zombodze, Swaziland, the son of the late Prince Phenduka, a descendant of Ndwandwa, King Mswati's brother. He received his education at Zombodze National School, St. Joseph's School, Mzimpofu, and the Swazi National High School, Matsafa. After graduating from high school, he was

Maj-Gen. M. Dlamini

invited to teach school age children the "three Rs" at King Sobhuza II's Lozitha Royal Residence. He left teaching to go to South Africa where he was first employed as a salesman and later by the American War Information Office. When the office closed at the end of the Second World War, Dlamini found a job in the dispensary department of the Johannesburg General Hospital.

His experience in medical surroundings spurred his interest in veterinary medicine. On returning to Swaziland in 1951 he began to train as a veterinary assistant, his effort bearing fruit in 1962 when he was appointed Stock Inspector. Following Swaziland's independence in September 1968, Dlamini was made Chief Stock Inspector. His role in the country's public life also increased with his appointment to membership and later chairmanship of the Land Speculation Control Board and the Tibiyo Taka Ngwane Fund.

In 1973, Swaziland's Constitution was abrogated and political parties banned. The same year also saw the formation of a Swazi army, the Umbutfo Defence Force, consisting of 650 men trained, supplied and equipped with South African assistance. Dlamini joined this army and rose to become colonel in November 1975. In January 1976, King Sobhuza II appointed Colonel Dlamini the first Commander of the Umbutfo Defence Force. In March of the same year he was appointed Prime Minister, the second man to hold this portfolio since the country's independence in 1968. In June 1976 he undertook his first official trip outside Swaziland and toured Mozambique, Botswana, Tanzania, Zambia, Kenya and Mauritius. In February 1979 he was reappointed Prime Minister following the general elections. He died on 24 October 1979.■

Dodo, J. (1918-86)

DODO, Jean (1918-86).

IVORIAN author and journalist, who, in the years leading to his country's independence, was also active in politics. Educated at the Bingerville Junior Seminary, Dodo was a militant as a young man. He accompanied the future President Houphouet-Boigny to Bamako for the founding congress of the *Rassemblement Démocratique Africain* (RDA) in 1946, and later headed the Daloa departmental committee of the ruling party in Côte d'Ivoire, the *Parti Démocratique de la Côte d'Ivoire* (PDCI).

J. Dodo

Though a political career was opened to him, Dodo chose rather to devote his life to journalism and literature, and he became known for his writings where the recurring theme was the universality of man. He disliked polemics, and hoped for African unity, world unity, a harmonious world where peace and love would reign.

Dodo, who became known as the "dean of the press" in Côte d'Ivoire, was for five years President of the country's *Association Nationale des Journalistes*. He was literary director of the publishing company NEA, *Nouvelles Editions Africaines*, and secretary-general of the Côte d'Ivoire section of the International Pen Club.

Jean Dodo wrote three novels, *Wazzi*, *Sacrés Dieux d'Afrique* and *Le Médiateur*. He also wrote poems, published in a collection entitled *Symphonie en Noir et Blanc*, which was awarded the Broquette-Gonin Prize. He was an officer of the *Palmes Académiques Françaises*, and *Chevalier du Mérite Français*. Dodo believed strongly that African writers in French should use the purest correct

French, without altering it as some did; but he favoured writing in African languages, though admitting he could not do it himself.

Jean Dodo died on 5 May 1986 in Abidjan, aged 67, and was buried at Williamsville. ■

Doe, S. K. (1952-90)

DOE, Samuel Kanyon (1952-90).

LIBERIAN soldier and President, leader of the coup which ended the long rule of

S.K. Doe

the Americo-Liberians and the True Whig Party in 1980, then head of a new regime which ruled with violence and after ten years fell by violence.

Born on 6 May 1952 at Topleu, he was of the Krahn ethnic group, one of several groups of indigenous Liberians. He described himself as a "poor up-country boy". Like many other "Tribesmen" (as the rulers of Liberia called the indigenous people) he joined the army, in 1969; NCOs and privates of the army were generally "Tribesmen". In the later 1970s opposition mounted to the TWP regime under President William Tolbert (q.v.), whose reforms of the situation still left Americo-Liberian supremacy largely intact. On 12 April 1980 troops led by Doe, then a Master-Sergeant, overthrew the regime. Tolbert was killed, and soon afterwards 13 of his leading colleagues were executed by firing squad.

Doe, then only 27, formed a People's Redemption Council with other NCOs of the army, who were promoted to senior officer rank as Doe himself was (to General and Commander-in-Chief) later on. The PRC had some popularity in proclaiming an end to the previous situation of the indigenous majority, and at first radical civilian opponents of TWP rule joined Doe's government.

Several African rulers, upset by the murder of Tolbert who was incumbent OAU chairman, showed hostility to Doe for some time; but this had abated by 1981, when he attended the OAU summit. The USA, despite its intimate links with the former regime, quickly resumed and indeed greatly increased aid to Liberia.

From the start Doe's rule was marked by violence, caprice and uncertainty. The crude violence of the early executions was to be followed by other such acts. In-fighting among the new rulers led to killings from 1981, when Doe's vice-chairman, Thomas Weh Syen, and four others were executed. At the same time Doe and his comrades adopted some of the traits and luxurious life style of the former rulers. In 1981 the radical civilians parted company with Doe, and leading figures of the old regime began to return to official favour.

In foreign relations he followed a consistent policy of close relations with the USA; restoration of relations with Israel fitted in with this. US aid of all sorts flowed in, despite his oppressive acts, during Reagan's presidency. In 1987 American experts were appointed to some key posts to draft Liberia's budget, in response to a worsening economic crisis which added to Liberians' problems under Doe's rule.

Thomas Quiwonkpa (q.v.), Army Commander, was sacked in 1983 after being accused of a plot. He attempted a coup d'état in 1985, after which he was brutally killed. Another leader of the 1980 coup, Nicholas Podier, was killed in 1988, allegedly while attempting a new coup though it may in fact have been a summary execution. On one count there were nine plots against Doe's ten-year rule.

The PRC was dissolved in 1984, when a new Constitution was approved by referendum; political parties were then legalised, and elections were held on 15 October 1985, Doe being elected President with 50.9 per cent of the votes. He was inaugurated on 6 January 1986. The outward installation of democratic and civilian rule did not alter the character of Doe's rule. His rule was not only violent but also crude and capricious.

In December 1989 insurgents led by Charles Taylor and the National Patriotic Front of Liberia began a rising in Nimba County. The rebels were mainly from the Gio and Mano peoples, and opposed the domination of Doe's Krahn ethnic group, whom Doe had recruited into the army in large numbers to back his rule. The rebels killed Krahns and the Liberian army killed many civilians in Nimba County. As the rebels advanced the army, undisciplined and skilled mainly in indiscriminate killing, retreated to Monrovia. By July 1990 Taylor and his insurgent forces were in the capital, but a split among the rebels, with Prince Johnson leading a new faction, helped delay final victory over President Doe, who held out in his Executive Mansion with his Krahn guard. Anarchy and mindless murder descended on Monrovia. Doe agreed to talks but these were inconclusive, and in August a peace-keeping force from five African states was sent to Monrovia in the hope of restoring order.

Samuel Doe himself was invited to meet Prince Johnson at the headquarters of the West African intervention force as part of the peace process. But when he arrived there he was kidnapped by Johnson's men without the intervention force being able to save him. Then, on 10 September, he was put to death in a hideous sadistic manner. He left a widow, Nancy, and five children. ■

Douala Manga Bell, A.N. (1897-1966)

DOUALA MANGA BELL, Prince Alexandre N'doumb'a (1897-1966).

CAMEROONIAN traditional ruler. Of the Duala ethnic group, he was born on 3 December 1897, son of Rudolf Douala Manga Bell (q.v.) and Emma Engome.

He went to Germany for education in 1902, eventually attending a Prussian military academy. In Douala's absence his father became Paramount Chief of the Bonadoo or "Bell" section of the Dualas in 1908 and was later hanged in 1914 by the Germans for an alleged plot, after opposing expropriation of his people's land. N'doumb'a Douala also attended a German medical school. He married a Cuban wife, Andrea; the marriage did not last long but produced two children.

In 1919 the French, now rulers at Douala after the partition of former German Cameroon, allowed him to return to a hero's welcome. But they refused to let him succeed to his martyred father's paramount chieftaincy. In the 1930s he was unofficially acknowledged as being the ruler of the Bonadoo, and was appointed to the Administrative Council of French Cameroon. He was widely respected because of his personal accomplishments. He was said to know a dozen languages and to be an accomplished musician.

In 1939 he became a French citizen, and joined the French forces on the outbreak of the Second World War. He was cut off from Cameroon by the events of 1940 and stayed in Senegal until 1943. In 1945 Prince Alexandre entered politics and became at first highly popular among the Cameroonian ethnic groups. He was elected to the French National Assembly. However, he was not a nationalist leader and never used his great personal following to form a political party. In fact he defended French rule before the United Nations, in reply to the revolutionary *Union des Populations du Cameroun* (UPC). But even the UPC had to reckon with his personal standing.

In 1952 he finally became Paramount Chief of the Bonadoo in Douala. His popularity in his home city continued during the troubled years leading to independence and after. He was as politically docile under President Ahidjo as under the French, but had real power as an individual "character". He was elected to the Cameroon National Assembly in 1960. He died on 20 September 1966 and was buried before a crowd of 100,000 people. ■

Douala Manga Bell, R. (1873-1914)

DOUALA MANGA BELL, Paramount Chief Rudolf (1873-1914).

CAMEROONIAN traditional ruler, recalled today as a hero of resistance to colonial rule. He was a Paramount Chief of the Duala people, indigenous inhabitants of the major seaport of (in the French spelling) Douala. The senior of the four major segments of the Dualas, the Bonadoo, was called "Bell" by Europeans. Their ruler Ndumb'a Lobe Bele, "King Bell" to Europeans, signed with other Duala rulers a treaty with

R. Douala Manga Bell

Germany in 1884, surrendering sovereignty on certain conditions. He died in 1897 and was succeeded by his son Manga Ndumbe or Manga Bell, who had been educated in England.

Manga Bell had about fifty children by various wives. One, brought up by the Protestant missionaires who converted most of the Dualas in the German colonial period, was named Rudolf Douala Manga Bell, but is remembered among the Dualas simply as Douala Manga. Born in 1873, he was considered by his people and the Germans to be next but one in line for the leading chiefly title among the Dualas. The Germans decided to send him for higher education before he eventually acceded to the title. So he went to Germany for studies, ending at a university according to one account.

On returning to Douala he married in 1896 Emma Engome, daughter of a British sea captain, Thomas Dayas, and his Duala wife. Their first son was to become as famous as his father, under the name of Prince Alexandre Douala Manga Bell (q.v.).

While his father Manga Bell ruled over the Bonadoo, Douala Manga won the good opinion of the Germans, who gladly approved his succession on his father's death in 1908. They had been hoping for close collaboration between their representative, the Bezirksamtmann (District Officer) for Douala, and a ruler with a thorough German education. They did not know that a ruler of the Dualas could not fail to voice the increasing dissatisfaction of his people with colonial rule. Probably Douala Manga always shared these feelings. The Dualas had adopted Christianity and Western education on a large scale, and had done well with trade, cash crop plantations, and building and property renting in a leading commercial centre, as well as clerical employment. But they were highly critical of German rule, which they said had broken many of the agreements made in 1884. In 1902 a delegation of three of the four Duala paramount chiefs went to Germany to protest at these breaches; Douala Manga accompanied them.

Rudolf Bell owned many properties and had solid houses, one let to a European to use as a hotel. He had every prospect of a very comfortable existence if he collaborated with the Germans, whom he respected so far as to send his eldest son to Germany for his entire education. However, he led the protests at German actions when, in 1910, the government decided to make a "European zone" along the left bank of the Wouri in Douala, in the area where the Dualas lived. The plan involved wholesale removal of the Africans to new settlements further inland.

For three years after 1911 the Dualas held meetings and organised protests at this eviction and expropriation plan, saying it was contrary to the 1884 Treaty and to their interests. Rudolf Manga Bell led the protests of all the people likely to be affected. Clan loyalties were set aside, and when African owners of modern-style houses like Rudolf Bell were exempted personally this did not weaken his stand on behalf of the others. Eventually he and his fellow leaders of the protest contacted lawyers in Germany and had their views brought before the German parliament. But the protests only delayed the government actions which began on March 1914 with the removal of the Africans from much of the Bonadoo (Bell) area to a new town called "New Bell".

By then Rudolf Douala Manga had been suspended from his chiefly functions, in mid-1913. He remained the real leader of the Dualas, and as protests continued after the first stage of the expropriation, the Germans arrested him and others. He and his secretary, Ngosso Din, were charged with a plot for a rising against German rule. Rudolf Bell and Ngosso Din were tried hastily and secretly, convicted and sentenced to death. The German governor, Ebermaier, confirmed the sentences. Rudolf Douala Manga Bell was hanged on 8 August 1914. Later, under French rule, the hero and martyr of the Dualas was reburied in a new tomb on 8 March 1935. On 8 August 1936 an obelisk, still standing by the main square at Bonanjo in Douala, was inaugurated. ■

Duarte, F.C. (1903-53)

DUARTE, Fausto Castilho (1903-53).

CAPE VERDEAN writer whose poetry embodies the cultural heritage of his people. He was born at Santiago in the Cape Verde Islands in 1903. After spending his early years on the islands he moved to Guinea-Bissau where he became an adminis-

trative officer in the Portuguese colonial government. He was very interested in Cape Verdean literature and during this period he began writing stories based on the lives of African peoples. He gave a lecture entitled *Da Literatura colonial e da 'Morna' de Capo Verde* at a conference on literature in the Portuguese colonies in 1934, and in the same year his first book, *Auá (novela negra)* was published by Livraria Clássica in Lisbon. The third edition of this work came out in 1945, published by *Editôria Marítimo-Colonial* in Lisbon, and it was awarded a prize in a Portuguese competition for colonial literature.

In 1935 Livraria Clássica published his second novel, *O negro sem alma* and four years later *Rumo au degrêdo* was published by the Portuguese company Guimar. His last novel *A revolt* was published by Livraria Latina in 1945 and in the same year a collection of his stories entitled *Foram estes os vencidos* was accepted for publication. He went to Portugal where he died in 1953. ■

Dube, J.L. (1871-1946)

DUBE, Reverend John Langalibalele (1871-1946).

SOUTH AFRICAN writer, clergyman and first President of the African National Congress. Born on 12 February 1871 to Reverend James and Elizabeth Dube, in Inanda in the Natal province, he had his elementary education at local missions before going to the Amanzimtoti (now Adams) College. He entered Oberlin College, Ohio, USA in 1889, and published his first book, *A Talk Upon My Native Land*, in 1892. He obtained a Bachelor of Arts degree in 1893, and was ordained in 1897.

It was during his stay in America that he met contemporary Black intellectuals, Booker T. Washington, W.E.B. du Bois and John Hope, who were to influence him in his later life. He returned to South Africa to found the Zulu Christian Industrial School (renamed the Ohlange Institute) in Natal in 1901. This institution, organised in emula-

Rev. J.L. Dube

Right and England's Duty, which called on the British government to face up to its legal responsibility in South Africa and to halt repression in the colony.

At its inaugural meeting on 8 January 1912, in Bloemfontein, Dube was elected the first President-General of the South African Native National Congress which later became the African National Congress (ANC). The following year saw the most important and fundamental policy of the government come into force, the Lands Act of 1913 which gave legal sanction to white possession of land and denied the African the right to either own or purchase land in white areas. Under Dube's leadership the ANC launched vigorous protests which culminated with a visit to London in 1914. But Dube and members of his delegation were not favourably received at the Colonial Office. Returning to South Africa in disgust, their immediate efforts in the campaign were to be interrupted by the outbreak of the First World War.

Dube was elected in 1942 to the Native Representation Council as a member for Natal. In the Council he was a senior spokesman, and was succeeded in that capacity in 1946 by Chief Albert Luthuli (q.v.).

In literature and scholarship, as in politics, Dube showed immense quality and energy. He wrote Zulu folk and dance songs and published *Isita esikhulu somuntu omnyama nguye ugobo lwake (The Greatest Enemy of the Black is Himself)* in 1922, which is generally regarded as the first Zulu work in grammatical form. He wrote a novel in English, *Clash of colour* in 1926, followed in 1933 by his classical historical novel, *Uieque isila ka Tshaka,* depicting the working of Chaka's court and the life of the great Zulu King himself. It was translated into English in 1951 as *Jeqe, the Body-servant of King Tshaka.* His last works, *U-Shembe,* a biography of the famous Zulu prophet Isaiah Sembe, and *Ukuziphatha Kahle* (Good Manners) were published in 1935.

Dube was highly regarded for his scholarship and political exploits; in 1926, he was a guest participant at the International Conference of Christian Missions held in Belgium which dealt with religion and race relations. In 1936 he became the first African to be awarded an honorary PhD degree by the University of South Africa. He died in Umhlanga, Natal, on 11 February 1946, at the age of 75. ■

tion of Washington's famous Tuskeegee Institute with a strong bias for industrial arts, grew to become the focal point of education for young African males and females in the country.

In 1903, with the eminent African journalist, Nganzana Luthuli, Dube cofounded the *Ilanga lase Natal* (The Natal Sun), the first Zulu language newspaper, of which he became editor. Dube used the columns of the journal, which also carried articles in English, to voice the aspirations of the Zulu whose rights were being usurped by the white settlers. This won him wide support among Africans but great disfavour from the white supremacist government. The paper was closed down for a while after Dube had vigorously supported Chief Bambata's campaign against the erosion of African rights. In 1909 he published his most important political treatise, *Zulu's Appeal for*

Dundulu, M. (c. 1865-1938)

DUNDULU, Mantantu (c. 1865-1938).

ZAIREAN literary figure who collaborated with the Baptist Missionary Society (BMS) in the translation of the Bible from English to Kikongo. With the BMS representative in the Belgian Congo (now Zaire), William H. Bentley, he also compiled the first *Dictionary and Grammar of the Kongo Language* in English. Though Dundulu was converted to Christianity as an adult, he was the first Protestant Christian in Zaire; he was baptised in 1888 at the Ngombe-Lutete BMS Mission.

Dundulu was born about 1865 at Padwa, a border locality now in modern Angola. His family was a distinguished one, his uncle Tulante Mbidi was chief of the Lemvo community. Mantantu Dundulu was brought up by Mbidi, his father having died when he was still very young. In 1879 he met up with Bentley, an English missionary who was accompanying King Don Pedro V (ruler of the historic Kingdom of Kongo, the state of the Bakongo people) on his visit to the Congo, when the latter travelled to Lemvo. From then on he worked with Bentley as an interpreter and later as a collaborator in major literary works.

The two men established the first English mission school at Mbanza Kongo (Sao Salvador), the traditional capital of the Kongo Kingdom and, in 1883, built a BMS base at Malebo. Yet Dundulu did not become a convert until the previous year, 1882. And even then he did not receive his baptism until six years later when on 19 February 1888 he became the first person to be baptised at the newly established BMS mission at Ngombe-Lutete. The late arrival of Protestant missionaries in this part of modern Zaire, due to the hesitation of King Pedro to open up the Kingdom of Bakongo (covering areas within Angola and modern Zaire) to them, prevented early mission activities in the area and, consequently, resulted in few African converts by the late nineteenth century. Thus when Dundulu was converted to the protestant faith in April 1882, becoming one of the first African converts in his country, he was following a pattern that had already been established in the Congo Kingdom and other parts of the neighbouring Portuguese state of Angola where Catholic missionaries had long been active.

Soon after his conversion, Dundulu, and Bentley, set to work on the compilation of a dictionary of the Kongo language. They both travelled to England in 1884, and in the course of this, visited Belgium as well, where Dundulu was received by King Leopold II. He was to revisit England in 1892, and spent a year working with Bentley on the translation of the New Testament into Kikongo. That achieved, they began work on the translation of the entire bible, which necessitated Dundulu's third trip to Britain in the early 1900s. Though suffering from bad eyesight by that time, he actively participated in the revision of the Kikongo Bible that was published in 1926. He also assisted Mrs Bentley on other translations which included the Proverbs and Psalms, while collaborating with other missionaries to translate the Acts of the Apostles into Kikongo. His last major literary effort was his autobiography, *Mpungwilu*.

Dundulu died in February 1938 and was honoured posthumously by the Belgian colonial administration with the medal of the Royal Order of the Lion in appreciation of his achievements.∎

Duse, M.A. (1866-1945)

DUSE, Mohammed Ali (1866-1945).

EGYPTIAN journalist and ardent believer in Pan-Africanism. Born in November 1866 in Alexandria, of Sudanese descent, he was given the name of a French captain named Duse (his full name was variously arranged). At the age of nine he was sent to Britain for education. His father was killed in the British operations in Egypt in 1882. He stayed in Britain and lived as an actor, playwright and journalist.

In 1911 he published a book critical of Britain's occupation of Egypt, *In the Land of the Pharaohs*. From 1912 to 1914 he was editor of the *African Times and Orient Review*, giving critical coverage of events in the colonies; based in London, he was financially backed by J. Eldred Taylor of Sierra Leone and then by other West Africans. The *Review* was revived briefly between 1917 and 1919. He was a major figure in the then small African community in Britain.

In 1920 Duse Mohammed went to the USA. He collaborated with Marcus Garvey, the Afro-American leader then at the height of his influence, on the journal *The Negro World*. He attempted various business schemes to try to organise African export trade independently of the expatriate firms, but without success. He formed various associations in the USA as he had done in Britain, e.g. the Universal Islamic Society in Detroit in 1926.

In 1931 he went to West Africa, where, on being refused entry into Gold Coast (Ghana), he settled in Lagos with his wife. In Lagos, which he had visited before, he became prominent among the Western-educated elite, who had had their newspapers for fifty years, and in partnership with Nigerian colleagues started a new newspaper, *The Comet*, in 1933, after editing the *Nigerian Daily Telegraph* in 1932. For a time *The Comet* was an organ of the Nigeria Youth Movement. It played a role in early nationalism; in 1945 it was bought by Nnamdi Azikiwe (for a time it was edited from Kano by Anthony Enahoro).

On 26 August 1944 Duse Mohammed presided over the founding meeting, in Lagos, of the National Council of Nigeria and the Cameroons (NCNC). Thus he was closely involved with the Nigerian nationalist movement when he died on 25 June 1945, and a huge crowd attended his funeral in Lagos. ■

Easmon, J.F. (1856-1900)

EASMON, Dr John Farrell (1856-1900).

SIERRA LEONEAN doctor, a strong opponent of racialism in colonial medical service. Born on 30 June 1856, he was the son of Walter Richard Easmon, a Freetown Creole trader possibly descended from one of the early Nova Scotian immigrants, and his wife Mary Ann, daughter of a distinguished Irish resident in Sierra Leone, John McCormack. He went to the Catholic primary school in Freetown and then to the CMS Grammar School. After working at the Colonial Hospital in Freetown as a learner dispenser and nurse, he went to Europe for medical studies, paid for from money left by his maternal grandfather.

He studied at University College, London, and was awarded the MD in 1879. He returned to Sierra Leone in 1880 but soon afterwards moved to Gold Coast (Ghana), where in 1881 he was appointed Assistant Colonial Surgeon; in the following years he acted as Chief Medical Officer of Gold Coast Colony eight times. He published in 1886 the results of his research into Blackwater Fever.

He applied for the post of Chief Medical Officer in Sierra Leone, but was rejected on the grounds that an African was not suitable for the post. This was the beginning of a change in British Colonial policy that was to result during the 1890's, in the replacement of Africans who had previously been allowed to rise to the highest civil service posts. In the Gold Coast the same happened, but the controversy around Dr Easmon was more complicated there when, in 1892, he applied for the position of that colony's Chief Medical Officer. The Governor strongly supported his candidacy and he was appointed in 1893. But the Ga people of Accra opposed the appointment of a Sierra Leonean, arguing that if an African was to hold the post it should be their own son, Dr B.W. Quartey Papafio.

The disagreement between Gold Coasters and Sierra Leoneans continued for years over this issue, with a local newspaper, the *Gold Coast Chronicle*, attacking Dr Easmon in 1894. A group of Sierra Leoneans including James Bright Davies (q.v.) formed the new *Gold Coast Independent* partly to counter the *Chronicle*. In 1897 Dr Easmon was suspended by the government for being too closely linked with the management of the *Independent*, and for conducting a private medical practice contrary to regulations.

He travelled to Britain and saw the Colonial Secretary, Mr J. Chamberlain, who told him to return to his post. But a European – not Dr Quartey Papafio as the Ghanaians had wanted – had already been appointed to replace him. Dr Easmon was offered a government job in newly occupied Kumasi but refused. He decided to open a private practice and started one at Cape Coast, with a retainer fee of £1,000 p.a., paid by a local African businessman. He died at Cape Coast on 9 June 1900. By his wife Annette he had a son, Dr McCormack Charles Farrell Easmon (1890-1973), who followed him both as a doctor and as an opponent of British racialism in the government medical service, mainly in Sierra Leone.

John F. Easmon led an eventful life in his 44 years: he was not only a member of the early generation of doctors in West Africa, he was also among the first of the educated elite in the region who used their influence to oppose the discriminatory practices of the colonial authorities. True that these racist measures prevailed until national independence, many years after his death, but Easmon evidently inspired future nationalism in the region.■

Ebeya, E. (1919-64)

EBEYA, Eugène (1919-64).

ZAIREAN gallant soldier and patriot; he led his country's army against the secessionist forces of Christophe Gbenye and Pierre Mulele (q.v.) in the war to keep Zaire a united country. He was killed in that war in the 1960s. Before then Eugène Ebeya had distinguished himself as an exemplary officer who despite the repressive and discriminatory measures of the Belgian colonial rulers attained the highest rank an African could achieve in the *Force Publique* (the colonial army) for which he earned the *First Sergeant's Star*. He subsequently rose to become Chief of Staff of the *Armée Nationale Congolaise* (ANC) after independence in 1960.

Eugène Ebeya was honoured posthumously by the Zairean government when it renamed the important military Camp Hardy at Mbanza Ngungu Camp Lieutenant-Colonel Ebeya. Also, the M.S. *Baron Liebrechts* ship was rechristened M.S. *Ebeya* in memory of the officer whom General Mobutu Sese Seko, Zaire's Head of State and Commander-in-Chief, said will continue to serve as a model. "He died so that the Congo could live. Let us not forget this. Very soon, I will recommend Colonel Ebeya for our country's highest honours. But for now, the best homage we can pay is to show ourselves worthy of him", Mobutu said at Ebeya's death on 5 February 1964.

Eugène Ebeya was born in 1919 in the Equateur province, in the Bangala ethnic group. At the age of 20 he enlisted in the *Force Publique* which took him to battle in World War II. After the war, in the 1950s, Ebeya was made Chief Superintendent at the Ecole des Cadets at Katanga where his qualities prompted the Belgian commander to recommend him for the *First Sergeant's Star* in 1954. The recommendation read, in part, that "his moral values will always be an example to our future officers".

Following the demise of Belgian rule on 30 June 1960, Ebeya was made Commander of the 13th Infantry Battalion. In 1961, he was promoted to Major and placed in charge of the Second Division based at Kinshasa. Then the following year, after being appointed Chief of Staff, he led his army on Katanga (now renamed Shaba) to consolidate government control over the province that Moise Tshombe (q.v.) had declared independent of the Congo. Ebeya had been active in that campaign against the seccessionist forces in Katanga, who were finally defeated, with UN assistance, in June 1963. His exploits there enhanced his reputation as a valiant and patriotic soldier dedicated to the survival of a united, viable Zaire. Shortly after that he acted as Commander-in-Chief for Mobutu, on the latter's absence from the country.

Meanwhile the Gbenye-Mulele rebellion in the Kwilu area was growing, eventually breaking out in December 1963. Government forces marched on Stanleyville (now Kisangani) where the Gbenye-Mulele's "People's Republic of the Congo" was based, reinforcing Ebeya's Third Division that was stationed there. Ebeya had been acting for Colonel Malumba as Commander of that Division and so played a very crucial part in suppressing the uprising. Colonel Eugène Ebeya was killed in action there on 5 February 1964. His body was brought to Kinshasa and buried with full military honours at Gombe cemetery. ■

Edet, L.O. (1913-79)

EDET, Louis Orok (1913-79).

NIGERIAN police officer who after Nigeria's independence in 1960 became head of Africa's largest police force, the Nigerian Police Force (NPF). Louis Orok Edet was born on 29 August 1913 at Duke Town in Calabar, now in Cross River State in Nigeria. His father was Chief William Edet Duke while his mother was Madam Geraldine Affiong Orok. He received his primary education at the Sacred Heart School, Calabar, and went on to attend Bonny Grammar School.

He joined the NPF as a clerk in 1931 and was transferred to general dutes as a Sub-Inspector in August 1945. During the Second World War he worked in the Immigration Department. His service took him to Enugu, Ibadan, Akure, Ilesha and other towns, as well as Lagos. He worked on the suppression of the "leopard-men" murder gang in the lower Cross River area.

In 1948 he moved to the Western provinces; he was promoted Assistant Superintendent of Police in 1949. He attended training courses at Rython-on-Dunesmore

Louis O. Edet

in Britain in 1953 and 1957, and again in 1960. He commanded at various times the Railway Police and the Port Authority Police, among other commands, and rose to the ranks of Assistant Commissioner and Deputy Commissioner in 1960.

In December 1960 Edet commanded the first contingent of the NPF to serve under the UN in the Congo. The Nigerian police won an excellent reputation during the Congo crisis and stayed after withdrawal of UN military contingents, leaving only in early January 1966. Edet himself returned to Nigeria in 1961 and became Commissioner in charge of the police in the Federal capital.

Promoted Deputy Inspector-General in 1962, he was appointed in March 1964 Inspector-General of Police, the first Nigerian to hold that post. He commanded the NPF during the period of civil strife in the Western Region in 1965. After the coup d'état of January 1966 Edet served as a member of the Federal Executive and Supreme Military Council until he retired in July 1966.

He was appointed recruitment attaché in the Nigeria High Commission in

London, a post he held until 1968. In the same year, Edet was appointed Commissioner for Home Affairs and Information in the then South-Eastern state of Nigeria. He relinquished this post in 1972 after playing a significant role in the reconstuction and rehabilitation of the civil-war-torn State.

In appreciation of Edet's service to the nation as well as to his own community he was made Chief by the Duke House in 1970, and later rose to become president of the Executive Council of the House as well as deputy Etubom. The distinguished public career of Louis Edet also earned him several national and international honours, including the Order of the Federal Republic (OFR), the Queen's Police Medal (QPM), and Commander of the British Empire (CBE). Louis Edet was also awarded a medal by the late Pope Paul VI. He was an executive committee member of the International Police Organisation, life patron and former chairman of the Caretaker Committee of the Nigerian Football Association, member of the National Council for Arts and Culture, director of the United Africa Company and chairman of the National Oil Producers Association.

Louis Edet died on 17 January 1979, and was survived by five children and eleven grandchildren. ■

Edusei, K. (1915-84)

EDUSEI, Krobo (1915-84).

GHANAIAN politician known as "Moke" who was a forceful and outspoken nationalist very much one of the "old guard" nationalist politicians with their strengths and weaknesses. He was decisive and articulate, and attracted a personal following whose loyalty he retained through a career often highly controversial.

Krobo Edusei was born in December 1915 in Ashanti, and was brought up in the house of a Kumasi Chief, the Bantamahene. He attended the Kumasi Government Boys' school and on leaving worked briefly as a debt collector. His first important employment was as a reporter on the Ashanti Pioneer, a local newspaper, an experience useful in both political and stylistic terms.

This too, however, did not last very long, for he decided to set up business as a small-scale druggist.

The late 'forties in what was then the Gold Coast were a time of increasing political ferment, as elsewhere in Africa; expecta-

K. Edusei

tions were aroused, and increased political consciousness led to demands for a greater share in the power still exclusively in the hands of the British administration. In 1947 Krobo Edusei was one of the founders of the Ashanti Youth Organisation – a radical organisation set up to fight for the rights of the Ashantis. Vigorous and eloquent, with a popular style, Krobo Edusei soon attracted the notice of other politicians and nationalists, among them Kwame Nkrumah (q.v.).

In the following year Edusei joined Nii Kwabena Bonne's campaign for a national boycott of European and Syrian traders in an effort to force down high prices originally justified by the austerities of the Second World War. Edusei became Chairman of the Kumasi committee of the Anti-inflation campaign and Bonne's chief assistant. He even established his own 'Courts' which

imposed fines on people who did not cooperate. With considerable support from many local administrations, the campaign was a success, and was perhaps the first flexing of political muscle within the African Colonial political context, with consequences more far-reaching than most people realised at the time. Government-supervised negotiations between the Chamber of Commerce and the Nii Bonne Committee eventually led to an announcement that prices would be reduced and the boycott ended. But the movement had by that time acquired political overtones and when expectations of the scale of the reductions were not met, a demonstration rapidly escalated into violence in Accra and other towns. The Government announced a State of Emergency and arrested the six main leaders of the United Gold Coast Convention, a party which had very little to do with the Anti-Inflation campaign. Among these was Kwame Nkrumah, who was arrested in Kumasi, but had to be removed thence when Edusei threatened to come and release him.

In 1949 Kwame Nkrumah founded the Convention People's Party which Edusei joined, becoming a member of the Central Committee. The following year, as a result of their Positive Action Campaign in favour of immediate self-government Nkrumah and Edusei, and others, were imprisoned. In the elections of 1951 Edusei won the Kumasi North-West seat and became Chief Whip of the CPP and Ministerial Secretary at the Ministry of Justice. He was re-elected in 1954. The nationalist parties were still at that time deeply divided, however, and Ashanti as a whole was by no means solidly in favour of the CPP. As National Propaganda Secretary, Edusei did a great deal to contain opposition to the CPP in Ashanti and he managed to keep Kumasi loyal to the CPP. In 1956 he was again re-elected and became Minister Without Portfolio.

From September 1957 to November 1958 as Minister of the Interior, he introduced a number of what was regarded as highly contentious and repressive legislation in Parliament, which he nevertheless implemented, to considerable opposition at home and criticism abroad. He eventually went so far as to personally threaten individual opponents, and had to be removed to another less prominent ministry. He retained his value, however, to the CPP because of his great influence in Ashanti. He was later Minister of Communications. Unfortunately, his earlier actions came to be overshadowed by a most controversial happening during Nkrumah's government, known as the 'Golden Bed' affair. His wife had ordered a solid gold bed in London for delivery to Ghana. The news caused a major furore and the bed had to be returned.

With the military coup of 1966 which brought down Nkrumah's government, Krobo Edusei's fortunes also underwent a considerable change. He was arrested and imprisoned, and only released on agreeing to restore to the nation some £2 million of local and overseas assets. He was generally held to have accepted bribes as a 'normal' part of political life. He was, however, generous in turn and is said often to have given large sums to those who asked him for help: he was seen thus as endearing rather than criminal in his behaviour. He was banned from politics by the military régime of General Ankrah and lived subsequently as a private citizen.

In 1978 he re-emerged from his private life to become a founding member of the People's National Party (PNP). He was influential in getting Limann selected as leader. But under subsequent military administrations he again experienced difficulties, and in 1982 he was one of three PNP officials convicted of illegally negotiating and accepting a $1 million loan from Dr Mario Chiavelli, an Italian businessman on behalf of the PNP. For this he was sentenced to 11 years' imprisonment. But in August 1983 he was released on the grounds of ill-health, from which he died six months later. ■

Emokpae, E.O. (1934-84)

EMOKPAE, Erhabor Ogieva (1934-84).

NIGERIAN celebrated sculptor and artist whose important works include the copper murals at the headquarters of the United Nations Economic Commission for Africa (ECA) in Addis Ababa, Ethiopia, and the replica of the 16th century Benin Ivory Mask which was used as the emblem for the 1977 Second World Black and African Festival of Arts and Culture (FESTAC). His murals and mosaics are also prominent features of the Nigerian National Theatre and the Murtala Muhammed International Airport in Lagos. Emokpae was a leading exponent of the school of artistic expression which deliberately sought to give a positive direction to art in post-colonial Africa.

He was born on 9 May 1934 in Benin city, seat of the ancient Benin Kingdom and capital of modern Bendel State. Benin's own prominence in Africa's cultural almanac go back to the early centuries' ivory and brass and bronze-casting craftsmen whose influence can be seen in Emokpae's works. After eight years of elementary education at the local Government School which he left in 1949, he entered the Western Boys High School, also in Benin, the same year and passed out in 1951. He then studied art at the Government Trade Centre (now Yaba College of Technology) in Lagos from 1951 to 1953.

That same year he commenced his career as a graphic artist in the Government service, attached to the Ministry of Information. Five years later he joined the Lagos office of the West African Publicity Company; in later years this Lagos agency, as Lintas Advertising Agency, grew to become the largest of its kind in Africa, with Emokpae directing its creative output as the Artistic Director. He retired from Lintas in 1976.

Emokpae was a leading member in the vanguard of African artists who consciously sought to give hope to their people. To him the artist should inspire hope and confidence among those around him. In his prescient words, his work is "a gold tooth in a mouth full of decay".

His works revolved round the abstract areas of human experiences which he expressed through a form he called 'dualism'. He defined dualism as "an attempt to explain fact by reference to two co-existing principles; we have positive and negative, and we find that throughout the system of creation the two opposites permeate the entire spectrum. In metaphysics it is mind and matter. In ethics it is right and wrong. For every action there is a reaction; you laugh, you cry, you succeed and you fail. So you have a situation where the dynamics of your action and your thoughts are determined by the dualistic nature of life". In other words, where there is confusion there also exists

E.O. Emokpae

hope for orderly, viable options.

This philosophy permeates Emokpae's works which can be seen today in various important centres of Africa, Europe, and America. His first major commission was by the Nigerian Institute of International Affairs where his giant mural now stands imposingly outside its Lagos premises. This was followed with the interior decoration of two major banks in the Nigerian capital. Later he was commissioned to do a replica of the 16th century Ivory Mask from Benin as the emblem for FESTAC. The Mask has emerged through the years as one of the finest examples of known African and Black art – it was worn as a pectoral by Benin Kings in royal ancestral ceremonies and was last worn by King Ovonramwen (q.v.) who was dethroned by the British. The Mask now rests in the British Museum, while Emokpae's replica is on display at the National Museum in Lagos.

Subsequently, between 1974 and 1975, Emokpae did the bronze friezes at the National Theatre of Nigeria. The following year came his first major international commission; he was asked to do the copper murals for the United Nations building, which houses the ECA, in Addis Ababa. Among his other remarkable works are the murals and friezes at the Murtala Muhammed International Airport in Lagos and at the Unilever House in Blackfriars, London. Emokpae also designed the maces of the universities of Lagos and Benin.

In between these engagements Emokpae held several one-man and joint exhibitions in many cities of Nigeria, Britain, Brazil, Germany and Canada where his works drew wide critical acclaim.

A man of untiring activity, he was also the Secretary of the Nigerian Arts Council between 1967 and 1975; he had earlier held the same position in the Lagos Arts Council. For his artistic achievements and contribution to the development of art in general, he was conferred with the national honour of Officer of the Order of the Niger in 1980. Four years later, at the height of his fame, Emokpae died in Lagos in February 1984. He was buried in his hometown, Benin, amid national mourning. One of the eulogists at the burial credited him as a modern master of the chisel and brush: "Emokpae represented a level of African civilization. The passage of time will place him on the same pedestal as past masters like Michelangelo and the rest". ■

Endeley, E. L. M. (1916-88)

ENDELEY, Dr Emmanuel Lifafe Mbele (1916-88).

CAMEROONIAN politician, an outstanding political leader in the 1950s and 1960s who became the first prime minister of Southern Cameroons under British Trusteeship. Born at Buea on 10 April 1916, son of a chief of the Bakweri people, he was educated at Buea government school and then the Bojongo Catholic mission school. At that time and until 1961 the British-ruled portion of the former German territory of Kamerun was a Mandated Territory and then a Trust Territory, but was for practical purposes linked closely with British-administered Nigeria. Many people from British Cameroons went to school in Nigeria, including Emmanuel Endeley, who went to Government College, Umuahia, then on to the new Yaba Higher College in Lagos in 1934. This college trained Nigerians and other West Africans for post-secondary qualifications.

Emmanuel Endeley completed his education at the Yaba Higher College, qualifying in surgery and medicine in 1943. While he was a student he and about 20 other Cameroonians, mostly students at Yaba, formed the Cameroons Youth League (CYL)

Dr. E.L.M. Endeley

in 1939, to defend the interests of British Cameroons. He was appointed assistant medical officer in Lagos in 1943 and then in Buea soon afterwards. In 1944, Dr Endeley and others from the CYL became founding members of the National Council of Nigeria and the Cameroons (NCNC), for a time Nigeria's leading nationalist party. Later renamed the National Council of Nigerian Citizens, it included the name of Cameroons for years, to show that British Cameroons' future was seen as linked with Nigeria's. That was Endeley's own view in the succeeding years. He wanted British Cameroons to be an autonomous administrative region within Nigeria.

Dr Endeley's next posting was to Port Harcourt, but in 1946 he was removed from the Nigerian medical register, allegedly for professional misconduct. He was, however, later reinstated. He returned to British Southern Cameroons and became active in

politics, first of all in the trade union movement. In 1948 he became general secretary of the Cameroons Development Corporation Workers' Union representing employees on the plantations around Mount Cameroon which were started by the Germans. He also worked with the Bakweri Land Claim Committee and the Bakweri Improvement Union, and was the Bakweri people's spokesman in their long-standing claim for the return of land expropriated by the Germans in the 1890s for these plantations.

In 1947 Endeley founded the Cameroons Federation Union, which advocated "reunification" of the two British Cameroonian trust territories, though his main concern was for separate regional status for British Southern Cameroons within Nigeria. When the Cameroons National Federation (CNF) was formed in 1949, grouping several existing organisations and including representatives from French Cameroun, Endeley became one of the leaders with N. N. Mbile, S. T. Muna and S. A. George. The idea of "reunification" of the two parts of the British territory (British Northern and Southern Cameroons under United Nations Trusteeship) was by then supported in British Cameroons by some sections of the CNF, but for some years its political development was within the context of changes in Nigeria.

Endeley was elected to the House of Assembly of the Eastern Region of Nigeria in 1951, as one of Southern Cameroons' representatives. Later from there with N. N. Mbile and S. T. Muna he was also elected to the House of Representatives in Lagos, serving as minister without Portfolio, and then as minister of Labour, in the Federal Council of Ministers of Nigeria. In 1952, the CNF merged with the Kamerun United National Congress (KUNC), founded by Mbile and R. G. K. Dibongue (q.v.), to form the Kamerun National Congress (KNC); this used the German spelling, as other parties did, to express the idea of unity of the whole of the former German territory. Endeley, however, favoured continued links with Nigeria, with the region retaining its own distinctive Cameroonian identity, rather than with French Cameroun. By supporting this line, the KNC won all 13 seats in the 1953 elections and in the following year British Southern Cameroons obtained a separate regional status inside Nigeria. Endeley was appointed leader of Government business in the new Southern Cameroons House of Assembly. During the Nigerian Eastern Region crisis of 1953, Endeley supported Dr Azikiwe's opponents and eventually left the NCNC and allied with the Action Group under Obafemi Awolowo (q.v.).

In 1955 in British Southern Cameroons, J. N. Foncha parted company with Endeley over the question of secession from Nigeria and federation with French Cameroun, and formed the Kamerun National Democratic Party (KNDP). The KNC, in alliance with a smaller party (the KPP, Kamerun People's Party), narrowly won the elections to Southern Cameroons' Assembly in 1957, and Dr Endeley became Premier of British Southern Cameroons. The KNC backed continued association with Nigeria as a separate region, while the KNDP called for separation of both British Northern and Southern Cameroons from Nigeria, and their union, as a prelude to ultimate "reunification" with French Cameroun. In the January 1959 elections Foncha and the KNDP won a narrow majority in the enlarged (26 seats) Assembly of Southern Cameroons, and Foncha became head of government in Buea.

After both Nigeria and French Cameroun became independent in 1960, British Cameroons was offered the choice of union with one or other of those countries, separate independence being ruled out by most parties. Endeley joined his KNC to the KPP to form the Cameroon People's National Congress (CPNC), which campaigned for union with Nigeria. In a plebiscite under the auspices of the United Nations, on 11 February 1961, British Northern Cameroons for long linked for practical purposes with Northern Nigeria, voted for union with Nigeria. But Southern Cameroons voted by a considerable majority for union with the Cameroun Republic. This took effect on 1 October 1961 with the creation of the Federal Republic of Cameroon.

After the "reunification", which he had opposed, Endeley continued to be active in politics. The KNPC continued until 1966 in West Cameroon (i.e. former British Southern Cameroons); in that year with other West Cameroon parties, it merged with the Union Camerounaise of President Ahmadou Ahidjo, effectively the sole party in East (ex-French) Cameroun, to form the *Union Nationale Camerounaise* (UNC) – a move which

Dr Endeley, adapting himself to the realities of the new political situation, openly endorsed.

Endeley was the UNC president for his native Fako division and served for a time as assistant national treasurer of the new party, as well as a national vice-chairman for many years. In 1972 Cameroon became a unitary state and West Camerooon lost its separate parliament, of which Endeley had been a member since "reunification". In the following year he was elected a deputy in the new National Assembly for the United Republic of Cameroon, and he was re-elected in 1978. He finally retired from politics in the early 1980s. He died on 30 June 1988.

Ensala (died 1926)

ENSALA, Chief (died 1926).

ZAIREAN traditional ruler of the Bobangi chiefdom, who in the manner of Nigeria's King Jaja (q.v.) of Opobo and Sierra Leone's John Ezzidio (q.v.) rose from slavery to prominence in public service. Like these two great West Africans, Ensala gained the reward for resourcefulness and diligence which so distinguished their lives, during servitude and after.

Not much is known of Ensala's early life, except that he came from the area around Mbandaka, a north-western confluence locality where the River Busira empties into the River Zaire. He was sold as a slave into the Dangi household in the Bobangi territory on the north-west shore of the River Zaire; that territory, now demarcated by the Zaire-Congo border, extended from the mouth of the Ubangui River in the south to beyond the confluence of the Rivers Ubangui and Giri. It was customary in Bobangi society, as it was in Jaja's Bonny, for able slaves to work up their way to position of responsibility in their household, particularly in the fields of commerce and politics, and then to position of wealth and influence and subsequently freedom. Hence during his years of servitude Jaja's leadership and organisational qualities became the asset that aided his phenomenal rise in the late 1880s to the headship of the Anna Pepple house in Bonny. Ensala, like Jaja before him, was to show similar qualities that in 1910 led to his succession to the chieftancy of Bobangi, following the death of Chief Bolangwa that year.

The Bobangi chiefdom was important to the Belgian colonial authorities, who sanctioned Ensala's accession, because of its enormous size in relation to neighbouring polities but primarily for its strategic location on the River Zaire that provided the trade route to the entire Congo's commercial products. Bobangi itself was then famous for its large quantity of copal, which many from nearby and far away states came to exploit. Trade was thus important to the territory, and Chief Ensala was, through shrewd management, able to develop this even further as well as consolidate his reign amidst colonial encroachment. Even in 1918 when his territory was demarcated and a large portion in the north was made autonomous of Bobangi, Chief Ensala's authority was unchallenged.

Indeed, his leadership was so admired that the colonial authorities in 1926 planned to re-enlarge his domain by annexing a neighbouring southern territory to Bobangi. The report recommending that annexation said that Ensala enjoyed "great influence among his tribe as well as beyond. Furthermore, he had incontestable chiefly qualities; calmness, a certain uprightness of spirit in relation to his subjects, and a great deal of common sense".

Chief Ensala did not, however, live to see the enlargement of his chiefdom, for he died that same year, 1926. ∎

Eseko (died 1901)

ESEKO, Chief (died 1901).

ZAIREAN traditional ruler of the Budja polity in the Mongala and Lulonga river basins north of the Zaire River. He distinguished himself in the war of resistance to Belgian colonialism; his exploits particularly in the climatic Budja rising at the beginning of this century qualified him as one of the most celebrated soldiers for freedom in the central African region. Indeed Chief Eseko could easily be grouped in the category of Africa's distinguished freedom fighters, like Paitando Mapondera (q.v.) of Zimbabwe; Makombe Hanga (q.v.) of Mozambique; Bai Bureh (q.v.) of Sierra Leone; Lat Dior (q.v.) of Senegal; and Abd el-Kader (q.v.) of Algeria, whose multi-faceted campaigns against colonialist encroachment paved way for the second wave of African nationalists who after the second world war successfully combated colonializations.

The Belgians' misrule of the Congo Free State was characterised by oppression and exploitation. An 1891 decree by King Leopold II of Belgium assigned large areas of the Congo to Concessionary Companies, each of which was given a full monopoly of forest produce and allowed to collect it in the way it liked; the other areas were exploited directly by the State. One of these companies was the *Société Anversoise de Commerce au Congo*, an Antwerp trading firm which obtained the contract to monopolize the rubber of Budja.

Like the other concessionary companies operating in the country, the Anversoise was in practice a state within the state, with boundless powers to police and extort taxes which were collected in the form of wild rubber that Eseko's subjects were forced to harvest in the forest. Huge amounts of this produce were demanded from the villagers; they had to go all over the forest to find often impossible quantities. It was reported that sometimes the women and children were held as hostages while the men looked for rubber. Those failing to find rubber as ordered were often killed by the *Force Publique* (the Colonial Army), irregular forces often including criminal elements, and company police. These militia were believed to have used unlimited brutality.

Under the pressure of increasingly heavy rubber demands the Congolese began to revolt against the Belgian tyranny. There were sporadic mutinies by the Africans from the late 1890s; the Batetela soldiers of the *Force Publique* in 1895-96 and a bigger mutiny occurred in 1897, lasting for several years. The Luba and Azande polities also began resisting the exploitation while from 1898 Chief Eseko and other Budja rulers led the celebrated Budja rising against the Anversoise's rubber tyranny. All this however did not curb the colonial excesses and Belgian rule continued to be extremely repressive, and unpopular with the Congolese, long after.

Chief Eseko's rebellion began in 1898 when the principal Budja chiefs organised an armed resistance that was to last for seven years. They attacked and killed the European agents of the Anversoise company and also captured its Dundusana, Mankika, and Yakombo trading posts. The company's armed units, supported by the *Force Publique*, retaliated with punitive expeditions in which several Budja chiefs were killed. Eseko and some others at first escaped to continue the resistance.

In January 1901 the troops of the Congo Free State launched a major offensive in the Budja district which, after five months of fierce fighting, fell to the superior militamilitary power of the Europeans. Eseko and his two other principal collaborators, Chiefs Zengo and Ekwalanga, were executed soon after, but their people fought on until 1905, three years before King Leopold II formally handed the Congo Free State to Belgium; henceforth it was known as the "Belgian Congo", and is now Zaire. ∎

Esua, E.E. (1901-73)

ESUA, Eyo Eyo (1901-73).

NIGERIAN leading educationist and founder member of the Nigerian Union of Teachers (NUT) which, with over 300,000 subscribers, is the largest professional organisation in Africa. Esua was its first full-time general secretary, from 1942 until his retirement in 1964. He was the first African to hold such a position in Black Africa. Thus, along with the NUT founder president Reverend Israel O. Ransome-Kuti and Alvan Ikoku (qq.v.), Esua helped to shape the Union having a profound effect on its activities.

Eyo Eyo Esua was born on 14 January 1901 in Calabar, of Efik parents. After attending local primary and secondary schools, he entered the Hope-Waddell Training Institute also in Calabar to train as a teacher, receiving the Institute's certificate in 1920. For the following two years he taught at Ikpe, then at his former Institute which was the leading educational establishment in the region then. From 1925 until 1942 Esua was a teacher, headmaster and

acting principal of the Baptist Boys' Academy in Lagos, where he had moved .

Concurrently from 1934 until 1942 he served as honorary secretary of the NUT which he had helped to create in 1931. During the next two decades, he served as

E.E. Esua

the Union's first full-time General Secretary, becoming the first holder of that office. He was returned to the post at subsequent elections of officers; he remained there until he retired on 31 December 1964, shortly before the NUT's 34th Annual Conference in February 1965.

From the time he joined the NUT he expended so much effort in its cause that he was very much associated with the organisation. Articulate, an able administrator and organiser with boundless energy, he worked tirelessly in building its fortunes. His grasp of all pertinent legislation, coupled with the above qualities, made him a formidable negotiator with the various government officials he dealt with.

No sooner had he taken office than he began to solicit unaffiliated local teachers' organisations to join the NUT which in the early 1940s had about 20,000 members. In addition to this membership drive, he sought support among international organisations for the NUT cause. This resulted in several tours of Britain and America where he built up a large following of supporters. During one of these overseas visits, he participated in the first Oxford Commonwealth Educational Conference and was Chairman of the Conference's Teacher Training Group. From there he went on to attend another conference in Washington, where he again chaired the African group.

Esua's capacity for leadership was soon recognised outside the ranks of his Union and as a consequence he was invited to sit on a number of official educational boards and commissions both in Nigeria and abroad. In 1960 he served on the British-appointed Philips Commission which reviewed primary education for Nyasaland (now Malawi).

On 1 May 1965, Esua was recalled from retirement by the Federal Government to head the Electoral Commission. Three years later he was made Commissioner of Federal Pensions. He served there and later in other honorary positions until his death in December 1973.

Esua was widely honoured; he gained the British CBE and in 1972 received the William Russel Distinguished Service Medal from the World Conference of Organisations of the Teaching Profession (WCOTP).

Glowing tributes were paid to him on his retirement in 1964. One, by the then President of the NUT, Ikoku, read: "As true assessment of the work of Mr. Esua for the Nigerian teacher in particular and Nigerian education in general will be an intriguing exercise for historians of the immediate future, suffice it to say that we his contemporaries have never had his better. I hereby place on record the unbounded appreciation of this Union for his unique services and indebtedness to his sterling qualities". ■

Eyegue Ntutumu,M. (1933-79)

EYEGUE NTUTUMU, Miguel (1933-79).

EQUATORIAL GUINEAN politician. Born in May 1933 in Chaman (Mikomeseng), he was a cousin to Macias Nguema (q.v.) and of the former Interior Minister, Masie Ntutumu. He was godson to a national hero of the struggle for independence, Enrique Nvo Okenve, co-founder of the *Cruzada Nacional de Liberación*. Eyegue Ntutumu went to Higher Provincial College in 1947 but a year later interrupted his studies to join the territorial guard of the Spanish colonial army. He left the army in 1950 and worked in several commercial companies. He later joined the government service, becoming an administrator in 1959.

In 1968 he was elected deputy, then president of the Provincial Council of Rio Muni. But in the purge that followed Anatasio Ndongo Miyone's (q.v.) alleged coup d'état on 5 March 1969, Eyegue Ntutumu was arrested and detained. Following his release he assisted in the establishment of the people's militia, a paramilitary unit of the *Partido Unico Nacional de Trabajadores* (PUNT).

The PUNT, of which he was an active member, replaced all existing parties in the country in 1970 when President Macias Nguema introduced a one-party system. Eyegue Ntutumu was appointed governor of Rio Muni in 1970 but ill-health forced him out of office in 1972 when he was replaced by Nsue Micha. He returned to active politics in 1973 and in the following year, after the assassination of Bosio Dioco, was made Vice-President of the Republic under Macias Nguema.

By 1975, however, the President fell out with his cousin after accusing Ntutuma's wife, Margarita Nanzu, of plotting to poison him, Nguema, and replace him with her husband. Eyegue Ntutumu was dismissed in September 1975. He was arrested in December 1976, following a senior civil servants' petition to President Nguema which warned about the disastrous consequences of the government's economic policies, and placed in the Bata prison. But he was released as a result of intervention by the Sociedad Forestal del Rio Muni, a French company with operations in the forest reserves in Equatorial Guinea and through which France had offered considerable loans to the government of President Nguema.

Eyegue Ntutumu was brought before a military tribunal in September 1979 after President Macias Nguema had been overthrown in a military coup. He was executed on 29 September 1979. ■

Ezzidio, J. (died 1872)

EZZIDIO, John (died 1872).

SIERRA LEONEAN businessman and the first African to participate in representative government in that country. Originally from what is now Nigeria, he was freed from a Brazilian slave ship by the British Navy in 1827, when he was about 15. Like other slaves taken off slave ships by the navy's "Preventive Squadron", he was settled free in Freetown where he was then apprenticed to a French trader, Jean Billaud, who renamed him John Isadore, following the normal custom of conferring new European names; Isadore was later changed to Ezzidio. After the death of Billaud the young Ezzidio worked for two other Europeans as shopboy and then as agent. Then he set up as a trader on his own.

He was one of many "Recaptives" in Freetown who found conditions favourable for Africans in mercantile business in West Africa for much of the 19th century. By 1841 he had saved enough to buy a house where he met businessmen and established links which led to regular direct orders from London or Manchester. By 1850 he was importing goods worth £3-4,000 per year. In 1859, when about to visit Britain again, Ezzidio was said to have taken space in the *New Era* to advertise the sale of a large stock to be sold at reduced prices – the traditional cottons for up country trade, ladies' shawls and silk bonnets, gentlemen's suiting, patent leather boots, hams, tea, mixed biscuits, patent medicines, sherry, port, and stout.

Ezzidio was converted to Methodist Christianity and became a pillar of the Wesleyan Mission. He was a preacher, and in 1856 he helped acquire land for a new Methodist Church whose foundation stone was laid in the same year. He also took an active part in the politics of Freetown. He was mayor of the town in 1845. He organised and signed petitions from leading Creoles and others on several occasions as in the criticism of Governor Macdonald in 1847. In 1853, they criticised proposals to abolish grand juries and impose a property qualification for petty jurors, and opposed the compulsory registration of alien children in Freetown ordered by the British government which alleged that such children, working as "servants" or "apprentices," were sometimes slaves. In each case Ezzidio defended the legal rights of the inhabitants of Sierra Leone Colony, while sharing their general loyalty to Britain.

In 1863, when a Legislative Council (Legco) was created, John Ezzidio was elected to it by the Freetown business community. He was an active and respected member. He was an effectve preacher of unity among the Creoles. He tried to act as a representative of the business community, but this was not the British view of his role in Legco; and so his idea that annual estimates should be submitted first to the Chamber of Commerce was rejected.

In 1864 Ezzidio succeeded in having a European superintendent appointed for the Wesleyan Mission. But this superintendent, the Rev. B. Trevaskis, wished to dominate the mission and saw Ezzidio as a rival. He was against the government grant for the Anglican CMS Native Pastorate, which Ezzidio, though not an Anglican, voted for in Legco. Trevaskis even stopped work on the Wesley Church started through Ezzidio's efforts.

Suffering from the rivalry of the domineering churchman he had invited, Ezzidio began in the 1860s to suffer a decline in health also. Then, too his business began to run into difficulties, and in a few years he lost £3,000. In 1870 he went to Britain for a rest. He returned very ill, and in October 1872 died in Freetown.■

F

Fadahunsi, J.O. (1901-86)

FADAHUNSI, Sir Joseph Odeleye
(1901-86).

NIGERIAN politician and businessman, the first national vice-president of the National Council of Nigerian Citizens (NCNC) and later the second indigenous governor of the defunct Western Region of Nigeria. He held the office of governor until 1966 when the army took control of the government. For a while Fadahunsi remained as adviser to the new military governor of the Region.

Fadahunsi was born in Ilesha, Oyo State, Nigeria, in 1901. He was educated at Oshun Methodist School before going to the

J.O. Fadahunsi

Wesley Teacher Training College in Ibadan. From 1925 to 1926 he taught at Methodist schools in Ikorodu and Lagos. He soon gave up teaching altogether and became a produce buyer, later a storekeeper and a salesman. In 1948, by then a successful businessman, he was appointed managing director of Ijesha United Trading and Transport Company. He was director of the Nigerian Produce Marketing Board in 1952-53, and chairman of Nigeria Airways Corporation in 1962-63.

Earlier, Fadahunsi had become involved in nationalist politics as a member of the NCNC (formerly National Council for Nigeria and the Cameroons). He was elected to the Western House of Assembly in Nigeria's first general elections in 1951, and remained a member of Parliament for the next ten years. A staunch supporter of the NCNC whose dominant policy was the achievement of independence for a unitary Nigeria, and opposed to excessive regionalism, he was deputy leader of the Opposition in the regional House of Assembly for some time as well as the party's national vice-president, to which office he was also elected in 1951.

In 1962 a rift in the ruling party of the region, the Action Group (AG), between its national leader, Obafemi Awolowo (q.v.), and its deputy leader and Premier of the Western Region, Samuel Akintola (q.v.), came to a head. The Oni of Ife, Oba Adesoji Aderemi (q.v.), who was then governor of the region, was removed from office in the wake of this political crisis which prompted the Federal Government of Abubakar Tafawa Balewa (q.v.) to declare a state of emergency throughout the region. Fadahunsi was appointed governor in 1963, and held the post for three years.

Fadahunsi believed in development through education, and during his governorship and life in general he paid particular attention to the provision of education for a larger majority. He himself founded and was the proprietor of two schools; the Ilesha Grammar School and Obokun High School. His work in the field of education was widely recognised and he was appointed president of the Ilesha Higher Education Committee. He was also a member of the Methodist Synod. Nationally honoured as Grand Commander of the Order of the Niger, he was knighted in 1963.

Fadahunsi devoted the rest of his life to his business affairs and education development after the 1966 military coup, and died at the age of 85 on 12 May 1986, at his Ilesha home. He was mourned by thousands.■

Faduma, O. (1860-1946)

FADUMA, Rev. Orishatukeh (1860-1946).

SIERRA LEONEAN teacher, clergyman and leading nationalist. He was born in British Guiana (now Guyana), son of freed Yoruba slaves from what is now Nigeria, named John and Omolofi Faduma. At a young age he was resettled in Freetown, Sierra Leone. There, like others of the Creole community, he was given a British name, William James Davies. He attended the Methodist Boys' High School in Sierra Leone and then Wesley College, Taunton, England, from there he went on to acquire the BA of London University.

On returning to Sierra Leone he became Senior Master at the Wesleyan Boys' High School. While there he changed his name, adopting his father's surname and a traditional Yoruba forename. He also helped found the Dress Reform Society in 1887. These were both acts in support of a movement to rehabilitate African customs after decades of adopting British customs.

In 1891 Faduma went to the USA, where he spent much of the rest of his life. He went to Yale University Divinity School, where in 1895 he was awarded a degree, followed by postgraduate studies in religion. He may have joined the African Methodist Episcopal (AME) Church about this time, and become a pastor of it. In 1895 he married an Afro-American, Henrietta Adams, and until 1914 he was Principal of the Peabody

Academy, Troy, North Carolina, besides working as a pastor.

He retained his earlier belief in "cultural nationalism" as preached by Dr. E.W. Blyden (q.v.) in particular. At a Missionary conference on Africa in Atlanta, Georgia, in 1895 he deplored the abandonment of African names, dress and food by African converts and evangelists. In 1914 he said Christianity had been too closely linked to imperialism and Europe; missionaries had travelled in the ships carrying rum and whisky.

He returned to Sierra Leone in 1915 and became Principal of the Collegiate School of the United Methodist Church. From 1918 to 1923 he was Inspector of Schools in Sierra Leone Colony; he was also in charge of the Model School. In 1923 he attended the second conference of the National Congress of British West Africa organised in Freetown by Dr. H.C. Bankole-Bright. In 1924 he returned to the USA, where he taught Latin, French, African history and other subjects at a number of institutions. He stayed in the USA until his death in January 1946.■

Fajemirokun, H.O. (1926-78)

FAJEMIROKUN, Henry Oloyede (1926-78).

NIGERIAN businessman. He was born in Ile-Oluji in Ondo State, Nigeria, on 14 July 1926. Between 1932 and 1936, he obtained primary education in his home town and went on to CMS Grammar School, Lagos, and Ondo Boys' High School.

In April 1944, Fajemirokun enlisted in the old Royal West African Frontier Force and in 1945 served with the 2nd Echelon at Jhansi GHQ in India. After army service in 1946, he pursued an accountancy career, joining the post and telecommunications division of the colonial civil service. He was elected president of the Post and Telecommunications Ex-servicemen's Union in 1948, and later became president-general of the Nigerian Civil Service Union until 1956, when he left to start a business career, which at the time of his death in March 1978 spanned a whole spectrum of ventures from insurance and engineering to shipping, centred around Henry Stephens and Sons.

In 1970, he was appointed president of the Lagos Chamber of Commerce and Industry; in 1972 he became president of the

H.O. Fajemirokun

Nigerian Associaton of Chambers of Commerce, Industry and Mines; the same year he was elected the first president of the Federation of West African Chambers of Commerce, followed in 1974 with the vice-presidency of the Federation of Commonwealth Chambers of Commerce. Henry Fajemirokun was one of the two co-presidents of the Nigerian-British Chamber of Commerce and also a member of the Board of Governors of the Nigerian-American Chamber of Commerce.

In 1968, in appreciation of his contributions to the development of his province, the Jegun of Ile-Oluji conferred the chieftaincy title of Yegbato of Ile-Oluji on him. In 1971 he was given the title of Asiwaju of

Okeigbo and the University of Ife conferred on him the honorary degree of Doctor of Science. ■

Fajuyi, A. (1926-66)

FAJUYI, Lt.-Col. Adekunle (1926-66).

NIGERIAN army officer and military ruler. Born in Ado-Ekiti (now in Ondo State) on 26 June 1926, he was the son of a farmer and carpenter, Isaiah Fajuyi, and his wife Felicia, a trader. He enlisted in the army in 1943 after working as a clerk. He received training at the command Training School at Teshie, Ghana. Before rising to officer rank he won the British Empire Medal for dealing with an incident of unrest among troops in 1951. He was commissioned in 1954 and, after completing a course at the Officer Cadets' School, Chester, England where he was the first African to be made an under officer, became a Lieutenant. He was attached to the British Army of the Rhine in 1955 and then returned to Nigeria and joined the 3rd Battalion of what was then the Queen's Own Nigerian Regiment. Fajuyi was also awarded the Second World War Medal, the Nigerian Independence Medal, the Congo Service Medal and the Nigerian Forces Star.

He was Regimental Signal Officer for about two and a half years. Later he was Weapon Training Officer with the same 3rd Battalion, then based at Enugu. He then became Company Commander and returned to Britain for training in Platoon Tactics at Warminster and a course with the Regular Officers' Commission Board. Back in Nigeria he served at various times as Signal Officer, Company Commander, and Chief Instructor in the Infantry Wing of Military Training College, Kaduna.

As a Major with the Nigerian contingent, Fajuyî played a distinguished role in the UN Operations in the Congo from 1960 to 1964. He won the Military Cross for personal courage and gallantry in two actions at the head of a company in North Katanga, the first Nigerian army officer to win it, and became Military Assistant to the Supreme commander of the UN forces.

In 1964 he was made Commander of the 1st Battalion, 2 Brigade of the Nigerian

Army, based at Enugu. Shortly before the January 1966 coup, Fajuyi now a Lieutenant-Colonel, was transferred to command the Abeokuta Garrison. Following Gen. Aguiyi-Ironsi's (q.v.) takeover, he was appointed Military Governor of the Western

Lt.-Col. A. Fajuyi

Region. He presided over the restoration of peace following the region's civil strife in mid-1966, and the rigorous implementation there of the military regime's policies of attacking corruption and other evils of the old regime, many of whose leaders in the West were detained. Fajuyi also attempted to tackle the problems that at the time beset the University of Ife (now Obafemi Awolowo University). Freedom was curtailed and serious academic work and pursuits had been almost impossible in 1965. He restored its autonomy and allocated it the necessary funds for its academic programmes.

On 29 July 1966, he was arrested with the Head of State, Gen. Ironsi, who was his guest at Government House, Ibadan, by mutineers supporting Nigeria's second coup d'état. Fajuyi was said to have told them they must take him too if they arrested Gen. Ironsi. Both were assassinated.

In January 1967 his body, like Gen. Ironsi's, was disinterred from a temporary grave for an official burial. Lt.-Col. Fajuyi became a hero in the former Western State, with a popular song in his honour composed by the musician I.K. Dairo. ∎

Farouk (1920-65)

FAROUK, King (1920-65).

EGYPTIAN monarch, the last king of the Mohammed Ali dynasty. He was born on 11 February 1920 to Fuad I, then reigning as Sultan, and his wife Nazli. He was almost immediately declared heir apparent by the British, then ruling Egypt. In 1922 Egypt became independent and Fuad was restyled King. On his death he was succeeded by Farouk, who became King on 6 May 1936.

Later that year an Anglo-Egyptian Treaty reduced Britain's *de facto* control over nominally independent Egypt, but this was still considerable. As he grew up Farouk tried to assert his own power, clashing with the main political party, the Wafd. He dismissed the Wafd Prime Minister, Nahas Pasha (q.v.), in 1937. But during the Second World War, when the British presence was reinforced, the British ambassador, on 4 February 1942, forced the King to recall Nahas, even sending troops to surround the palace. However, the King and his entou-

King Farouk

rage, headed by his tutor, aide-de-camp and adviser Ahmad Hasanayn, retained some power in their own right in the early 1940s and Nahas was sacked again in 1944.

In the succeeding years the political situation was confused, with many other political parties and groups challenging the Wafd, while unrest mounted because of the continued British presence and other grievances. Farouk was for a time a rallying point for nationalists opposing Britain's military installations (much reduced in 1947) and demanding the return to Egypt of the Sudan. Successive governments made some concessions to Egyptian sentiment and also joined the Arab attack on Israel (1948-49). But corruption on a vast scale, revealed conspicuously in the conduct of the war, discredited the politicians. The king came to arouse contempt for his devious and underhand methods, the self-enrichment of all his entourage, and his "playboy" life style.

In 1950-1 a new Wafd government started overdue social and economic reforms and adopted a popular hostile attitude to Britain. Farouk joined in the new policy by declaring himself ruler of the Sudan. Guerrilla attacks on British forces in the Suez Canal zone led to a crisis in which a part of Cairo was burned down in January 1952. But the popular feelings thus revealed were turning against the monarchy too, and the "Free Officers" movement decided to carry out its plans for a coup d'état. On 23 July 1952 they took over power. On 26 July Farouk abdicated in favour of his infant son Fuad, himself deposed a year later on the declaration of a Republic, and left the country. He died in Rome on 18 March 1965. ■

M.A. El-Fassi

El-Fassi, M.A. (1906-74)

EL-FASSI, Mohammed Allal (1906-74).

MOROCCAN politician, founder of the Istiqlal (Independence) Party. He was born in 1906, the son of a former professor at the University of Karaouine in Fez who later became a judge. He received an early Islamic education at the university before reading law. He took to politics in 1930 while still a student; and was twice imprisoned for taking part in anti-colonial demonstrations. He later became a teacher of theology at the university, until 1933 when he was exiled to Paris by the French colonial authorities.

El-Fassi returned to Morocco in 1934 to join the nationalist struggle, first joining the *Comité d'Action Marocain* (CAM) and later founding the Istiqlal Party. He was again arrested during a demonstration in Casablanca in November 1936 and banished to Gabon for nine years. During this period he wrote many nationalist poems and songs that became very popular in the Arab world. Returning to Morocco in 1946, he continued as leader of the Istiqlal Party and visited Egypt, Europe and America to mobilise support for the Party's cause. He returned to Egypt in 1947 after the Istiqlal was banned, and from there appealed to Moroccans through broadcasts from Cairo to take up arms against the colonial administration.

He did not participate in the subsequent 1955 independence negotiations with France because of his objection to French proposals to leave part of what he called Moroccan territory to Mauritania and Algeria. By independence, in March 1956, his reputation earned him an appointment as adviser to the Sultan (King) Mohammed V.

In 1960 he was elected president of the Istiqlal, and on the accession of King Hassan II in 1961 he was appointed Minister of State. In later years he remained critical of the presence of French executives in the administration of independent Morocco and continued to advocate the annexation of the Spanish territories in the Sahara.

El-Fassi resigned from the government in 1963 and took the Istiqlal into opposition. He also returned to teaching Islamic law at Rabat University. He died of a heart attack on 13 May 1974. ■

H. Fathy

Fathy, H. (1900-89)

FATHY, Hassan (1900-89).

EGYPTIAN architect. He became well known for his efforts to apply Egypt's traditional mud brick building to modern use, and was a leading lecturer and writer on architectural affairs. Born at Alexandria on 23 March 1900, he obtained a Diploma from the Architectural Section of the High School of Engineering at Cairo in 1926, and then worked as an architect with the Cairo Department of Municipal Affairs from 1926 to 1930.

From 1930 to 1946, while lecturing at the Cairo Faculty of Fine Arts, he also carried out research and practised privately as an architect. He had noted that traditional village building in mud brick had great virtues. While working on the design of an experimental farm at Bahtim he studied use of old Nubian techniques of building arches and domes in mud brick. He consistently advocated that style of building as being better suited, on economic and environmental grounds, to Third World and tropical countries. There was some interest outside Egypt in his ideas, but his main success was in applying them in his country.

His greatest achievement was the building of a new settlement at Gourna, opposite the ancient Egyptian monuments of Luxor on the Nile. The Department of Antiquities commissioned this work in 1945, to rehouse people who were finding robbery of antiquities more profitable than farming. The project used traditional building methods, but it was left incomplete, partly because of withdrawal of government funding. Fathy described it in his book *Gourna, A Tale of Two Villages* (Cairo, 1969).

Fathy was Director of School Buildings at the Ministry of Education from 1949 to 1952, and was on the staff of Cairo University Faculty of Fine Arts from 1949, becoming Dean of the Faculty's Architectural Section (1953-57). From 1957 to 1962 he was a member of a research project on "The City of the Future", and then (1963-65) he was Director of Housing Pilot Projects in Egypt's Ministry of Scientific Research. He did work for the United Nations as a Consultant to the Relief and Works Agency (UNRWA) and later as Director of the UN Committee for Housing in South Arabia (1965-66), working in what later became South Yemen (now part of united Yemen), a country with an old tradition of mud brick building.

In 1966 he was appointed Lecturer in the Philosophy of Town Planning at the 1,000-year-old Al Azhar University in Cairo. For many years he attracted young architects from several countries to study under him at his house in Cairo. He published more books including *The Arab House in the Urban Setting* and *Constancy, Transposition and Change in the Arab City*. He died in Cairo on 30 November 1989. ■

Fawzi, M. (1900-81)

FAWZI, Mahmoud (1900-81).

EGYPTIAN diplomat, fondly remembered as "the Dean of Diplomacy". He was the epitome of international diplomacy, having rendered distinguished service to successive Egyptian regimes, first under Kings Fuad

M. Fawzi

and Farouk (q.v.) and later under Presidents Nasser and Sadat (qq.v.). He was Prime Minister under Sadat from 1970 for two years before becoming Vice-President.

Mahmoud Fawzi's diplomatic career began in the 1920s and took him to various postings abroad as a representative of Egypt. When the monarchy fell in the 1952 Revolution his diplomatic experience became an asset to the new Free Officers' regime which he served with equal distinction. Under Nasser he displayed exemplary qualities during the protracted negotiations with the British vis-à-vis the Condominium with Sudan and the withdrawal of British troops from the Suez Canal. The result was the Anglo-Egyptian agreement of 1953 which ended the Condominium and that of 1954 which resulted in British withdrawal from Egypt. Fawzi then began to formulate an independent foreign policy, in line with the objectives of the new regime. This soon gave Egypt an influential voice in world affairs; her non-aligned policy enabled her to deal with both the Western and Eastern blocs. Soon, too, Egypt gained influence in the Arab world, the African and Third World circles. For all these activities and his role in subsequent developments leading to the emergence of Pan-Arabism, the Non-Aligned Movement and the Organisation of African Unity, Fawzi gained credit and became known as the "diplomat of the century".

He was born on 19 September 1900 and educated at the universities of Cairo, Rome and Liverpool as well as at Columbia University in the United States. He graduated in Law in 1923 and studied for a Doctorate in Criminal Law. He entered the Egyptian foreign service in 1924, his first posting being New York and New Orleans as Vice-Consul. He subsequently served as consul at Kobe in Japan between 1929 and 1936; as second secretary at the Egyptian Embassy in Athens; and then as consul, later consul-general, at Liverpool, UK, from 1937 until 1940. He returned to Cairo in 1940 to become Director of the Department of Nationalities in the Ministry of Foreign Affairs.

Fawzi had a flair for languages and made the most of his wide range of postings to become fluent in English, French, Italian, Greek, Spanish and Japanese. Thus equipped he was soon re-posted abroad, becoming in 1941 consul-general in Jerusalem. In 1944 he became the Egyptian representative to the United Nations Security Council, and later his country's Permanent Representative to the UN. He was serving as ambassador to Britain when the 1952 Revolution ended the Egyptian monarchy. Later that year he was made Minister of Foreign Affairs by the new regime and from that time until his retirement from public service in 1974 was almost constantly in charge of Egypt's foreign affairs, either as Minister or Vice-President.

From 1954 to 1958 he headed the Ministry of Foreign Affairs and later, from 1958 until 1964, was Minister of Foreign Affairs of the United Arab Republic proclaimed in February 1958 and consisting of Egypt and Syria.

He held that post, becoming as well Deputy Prime Minister and Vice-President, throughout Nasser's (q.v.) rule. When Sadat succeeded the first President in 1970 Fawzi became his Prime Minister during the difficult period of his succession. His appointment was seen then as a sign that President Sadat was going to accord greater importance to diplomacy as a means of solving the Arab-Israeli crisis. Fawzi, however, soon found his position too political for his apolitical diplomatic taste and was switched to the vice-presidency in 1972. Two years later he retired from public life and died on 12 June 1981, at the age of 81.■

Col. R.J.A. Felli

Felli, R.J.A. (1938-79)

FELLI, Colonel Roger Joseph Atogetipoli (1938-79).

GHANAIAN soldier, one of the youngest and longest serving officers in the successive military administrations that followed the overthrow of President Kwame Nkrumah in 1966. He was born on 2 May 1938 in Navrongo in the Upper Region of Ghana, and educated at the Tamale Government Secondary School where he gained his West African School Certificate.

Felli enlisted in the Ghana army as officer cadet in 1960. After a brief training in the country he went to the Royal Military Academy, Sandhurst in Britain from 1961 to 1963. He was commissioned regular officer in 1963 and did a number of further training courses in Ghana and abroad, specialising in signals. In 1964, he returned to Britain for the Signals qualifying course, followed by the No 1 Overseas' Officers' Communications course at the School of Signals, Blandford, from 1968 to 1969. A year before, Felli had attended the Company Commanders' course at the Military Academy Training School at Teshie, near Accra.

With these technical qualifications Felli was well equipped for his future appointments as adjutant of the No 1 Signals Regiment, General Staff officer (operations and training), and later director of Communications in the army. Following the 1966 coup he was given the first of a series of civilian appointments when he became the Commissioner for Works and Housing and member of the National Liberation Council headed by General Ankrah. In May 1972 the second military regime appointed him to the Ministry of Trade and Tourism where he was placed in charge of Ghana's trade and economic problems and developing an almost entirely new department of tourism. He was later moved to the Ministry of Economic Planning, and in 1975 was made Commissioner for Foreign Affairs. He held this portfolio till he retired from the armed forces in March 1979. His retirement in March was only three months from the elections of 18 June when a civilian administration was chosen to succeed the regime of General Akuffo (q.v.) who had been ousted on 4 June 1979, in a coup led by Flight-Lieutenant Jerry John Rawlings.

Colonel Felli was among the six senior officers tried by the new regime for alleged corruption under the Armed Forces Revolutionary Council Special Courts Decree. They were found guilty of acquiring and obtaining loans, properties, material goods, favours and advantages, and committing abuses by virtue of their official positions in the public service. They were also found guilty of gross negligence and intentional or reckless dissipation of public property. On 26 June 1979 Colonel Felli and the others were executed.■

First, R. (1925-82)

FIRST, Ruth (1925-82).

SOUTH AFRICAN politician, a leading activist in the struggle for political and social change in her country. Her involvement with the African National Congress (ANC) spanned decades and, like most members of that organisation, Ruth First was arrested, detained and tortured under South African draconian measures aimed at suppressing Black political activity. She was also a prolific journalist and author of several books in which she articulated African grievances.

Ruth First was born in 1925 in Johannesburg, the daughter of Jewish immigrants whose radical opposition to racial discrimination was strong. She was educated at the Jeppe High School for Girls and later read Sociology at the University of Witwatersrand. At university she was active in student politics, and through her contact

with Black students became aware of the appalling conditions of Africans. She became a co-founder of the Federation of Progressive Students and subsequently joined the Young Communist League (YCL). As a very leading member of these organisations Ruth addressed political rallies and immersed herself even more vigorously in the problems of the African workers.

For a short period after leaving university she worked as research officer in Johannesburg while also teaching politics in the evening at African night schools. She

R. First

soon also started to work for the Communist Party, and to write for the liberal *Advance*, *New Age*, *Spark*, and *Guardian* newspapers. All these papers were in turn banned by the regime and had finally to be abandoned because the staff were harrassed by the authorities. Throughout her period with these publications Ruth First was a tireless, tenacious, investigative journalist whose reports became renowned for exposing discrimination and judicial malpractices against Africans, and the appalling labour conditions of Black farm workers, and the harrowing consequences of the myriad of laws that govern the lives of urban Africans.

The most celebrated investigation by Ruth First was the report on the hiring out of short-term offenders, convicted under the Tax and Pass Laws, to White-owned farms where they worked as slave labourers, stripped of clothes, flogged and often killed, and accommodated in cowsheds. Her article on the Bethal potato farms led to a month long national boycott of potatoes by Africans at the instigation of the African National Congress.

In 1950 the Communist Party was banned, but Ms First and her husband, Joe Slovo, whom she married in 1949 and with whom she had three daughters, continued their political activities, this time under the Congress Alliance headed by the ANC. She was among the one hundred and fifty ANC leaders arrested and charged in 1956 with high treason. The ensuing famous treason trial lasted four years and, at the end, all defendants were acquitted. The trial was a reaction to the adoption of the Freedom Charter by the ANC at Kliptown on 25 June 1955.

On 31 March 1960 the ANC launched an anti-pass campaign. Ten days earlier the Pan-Africanist Congress (PAC) had launched a similar campaign with a massive demonstration at Sharpeville, to which the police responded with unprecedented violence, killing sixty-nine demonstrators.

The massacre sparked off several demonstrations and riots, and on 30 March 1960 the government declared a State of Emergency and detained several ANC and PAC leaders. Ruth First escaped to Swaziland, but returned home shortly before the end of the emergency to continue political activity underground.

In 1963 she was again arrested, this time for allegedly recruiting people for training in guerrilla warfare and sabotage with the aims of furthering the aims of communism in South Africa. She was kept in solitary confinement for 117 days, and brutally tortured. On her release she was banned and restricted geographically, socially and professionally.

She then left South Africa for Britain where she involved herself with the external activities of the ANC. She represented the organisation at the UN and at several other international conferences. In 1973 she joined the Department of Sociology of Durham University, England, where she taught Development Theory and the Sociology of Under-Developed Societies.

Following the independence of Mozambique in 1975 she went to Maputo as senior lecturer at the Centre for African Studies at the Eduardo Mondlane University. Her work there entailed studies on projects for the political, economic and social development of Mozambique in particular and Africa in general.

Her books on the same subject include *The Barrel of a Gun: 117 Days*; *South-West Africa*; and *Libya, the Elusive Revolution*. She also edited the autobiographies of Gevan Mbeki and Oginga Odinga, the veteran Kenyan politician.

Ruth First was killed by a parcel bomb in her Maputo office on 18 August 1982. Her assassination, widely attributed to the South African authorities, is a tragic testimony of her dedication to the struggle for political justice in her country.∎

Fischer, B. (1908-75)

FISCHER, Bram (1908-75).

SOUTH AFRICAN lawyer, politician and anti-apartheid campaigner, Bram Fischer was born in 1908 in the Orange Free State, South Africa. He came from an establishment family. He was the son of a judge and the grandson of a prime minister. After his education at Grey College and Grey University in the Orange Free State where he obtained a law degree, he worked for two years as a registrar. Between 1931 and 1934 he read jurisprudence and economics at New College, Oxford under a Rhodes Scholarship. After his studies at Oxford, he became a member of the Johannesburg Bar where he soon acquired the reputation of an able barrister and an unyielding fighter against apartheid.

Throughout his law career he readily accepted cases of non-whites who were arrested for violating pass laws and other enactments of the South African regime. A former chairman and longest serving member of the Johannesburg Bar Council, he also joined the South African Communist Party in the 1930s. In 1946 Fischer along with other members of the Central Committee of the Communist Party were charged with having incited mine workers to strike and were fined £50 each. Under the 1950 Suppression of Communism Act, Fischer and his wife were forbidden to attend any political meet-

B. Fischer

ing or activity. He and his wife struggled for racial equality in both word and deed. They adopted an African child and Fischer's wife taught for years at the Indian High School in Johannesburg without pay. In 1960, when she was jailed with other whites and non-whites without charge for months, Fischer visited them and arranged to care for their families and children.

He was one of the defence counsel in the 1956-61 "treason trial" and it was at this time that his political genius became known beyond the confines of South Africa. His success in the treason case of 156 anti-apartheid leaders became an impetus for the liberation movement. Unfortunately, after the discharge of the accused in that case, Mrs Molly Fischer died in a motor accident. Two weeks later Mr. Bram Fischer was arrested. He was released after three days.

His second arrest came on 23 September 1964 when he was charged along with twelve whites with being members of the illegal Communist Party of South Africa. He applied for bail which was granted at £5,000. At the court he prudently and courageously stated that he was an African and hailed from South Africa. He went further to say that he would not leave his country because his political beliefs were opposed to his government. On 25 January 1965 he left his home and drafted a note to his counsel that he had gone underground to continue his struggle against apartheid, though he repaid the bail to avoid causing his guarantor trouble. In his letter to the court he stated that if he could convince a few people to deviate from apartheid policies, he would not regret any punishment incurred by him. He predicted disaster, terrific bloodshed and civil war if the persecution of the blacks did not stop. His resolution to leave was a result of the introduction of the 90-day no-trial clause in the 1963 General Law Amendment Act; this clause he defined as "legalised torture".

His disappearance from his home in 1965 was officially regarded as an act of "sabotage" and he was declared a wanted man. He was captured the same year and brought to trial under the 1963 Act and the Suppression of Communism Act. His statement from the dock on 28 March 1966 was an irritation to the authors of apartheid. He was sentenced to life imprisonment. Whilst in prison with other political prisoners in Pretoria he was assigned to cleaning of the prison lavatories and when his only son died he was not allowed to attend his funeral. In 1974 it was discovered that he was suffering from acute cancer but the unforgiving apartheid government would not immediately release him. When he was eventually released, as it turned out, just six weeks before he died, it was on condition that while he lived the officials of the prisons department were free to visit him, and that after his death, his ashes should be at the disposal of the Prisons Department. Mr. Kruger, the Minister of Justice, was forced to reverse his decision by national and international protest. Bram Fischer died in May 1975. ■

Fitzjohn, W. H. (1915-90)

FITZJOHN, Rev. William Henry (1915-90).

SIERRA LEONEAN churchman, educator and diplomat. He was born on 5 November 1915 to an aristocratic Creole family of Freetown. He was educated at Albert Academy, Freetown and later graduated from Lincoln University, Pennsylvania, USA in 1943. He later studied at Columbia University (New York), securing the MA and PhD.

He was ordained minister of the Evangelical United Brethren in Christ Church in 1946. His teaching career took him to the Albert Academy where he was acting Principal from 1946 to 1949. He lectured at the famous Fourah Bay College (now part of the University of Sierra Leone) from 1950 to 1959. His political career involved membership of the Legislative Council to represent Moyamba, 1965-8.

He became the first Sierra Leonean diplomatic representative in the USA from 1959 to 1961. In 1961, the year of independence, he was appointed High Commissioner to the United Kingdom, serving until 1964; and later he was High Commissioner to Nigeria for many years from 1972.

His competence as an accomplished diplomat was clearly illustrated by his activities in Britain and Nigeria. He assisted many penniless Sierra Leonean students in Britain to continue and complete their education. He helped many Sierra Leonean residents in Britain and established a Consular office in Liverpool. He was a vice-president of the Anglo-Sierra Leonean Society in the UK until his death. In Nigeria, his posting came when the relationship between Sierra Leone and Nigeria was at a low ebb (after Sierra Leone's policy in the civil war) and he helped to effect rapid reconciliation.

He lived a life of industry and excelled in politics and pastoral duties. He was a very active churchman and preached extensively in various churches, especially when he was in Lagos. He was a kind and thoughtful man whose life was an inspiration to many. His wife Alice was also ordained to the church ministry. He wrote two autobiographical books, *Chief Gbondo* and *Ambassador of Christ and Caesar*. He died in Freetown early in 1990. ■

Fonlon, B. N. (1924-86)

FONLON, Dr Bernard Nsokika (1924-86).

CAMEROONIAN politician who is also remembered as an educationist for his keen interest in and work on the development of bilingualism in his country, as shown in his writings and academic career.

Bernard Fonlon was born on 19 November 1924, at Kumbo Nso in what is now the North-Western Province of Cameroon, and went to Catholic schools in the then British Southern Cameroons. After working as an assistant teacher at a Catholic school in 1940-41 he had his secondary schooling at Christ the King College, Onitsha (now in Anambra state) in Eastern Nigeria as many people from British Southern Cameroons did in those days when the territory was administratively linked to Eastern Nigeria.

In 1946-47 Fonlon taught at the leading Catholic school for boys in former British Cameroons, St. Joseph's College, Sasse (Buea). Then he decided to study for the priesthood and went to Bigard Memorial Seminary at Enugu in Anambra State, Nigeria, to study philosophy and theology. But after five years there, when he was already a deacon and was about to be ordained priest, he was dismissed for having written a book "unworthy of his priestly status". He reverted to lay life, but he kept the vow of celibacy that he had taken, and never married. In 1954, the year after leaving the seminary, he went to Ireland to study literature at the National University of Ireland, Dublin, where he received a Master of Arts degree, then he did further studies at the Sorbonne University, Paris, and at Oxford, England. He obtained his PhD in literature at Dublin in 1961.

In that year, 1961, in a referendum British Southern Cameroons voters chose union with former French Cameroon, now independent, while Northern Cameroons chose to integrate with Nigeria. This was in accordance with the policy of the Prime Minister of Southern Cameroons, John Ngu Foncha, who became Vice-President of the Federal Republic of Cameroon which came into being when the merger took effect on 1 October 1961.

During that important year Dr Fonlon, who had returned to the Cameroons, was

Dr. B.N. Fonlon

Will We make or Mar? (1964), *To Every Son of Nso* (1965), *Under the Sign of the Rising Sun* (1965), *The Tasks of Today* (1966), *The Nature, End and Purpose of University Studies* (1969).

Dr Fonlon died on 27 August 1986 in Ottawa, Canada, where he had gone as a visiting professor. He was buried at Kumbo Nso amid widespread mourning. ∎

Franco (1939-89)

FRANCO (Luambo Makiadi) (1939-89).

ZAIREAN musician. He and Tabu Ley Rochereau were the most outstanding of the musicians who made Zairean music popular all over Africa and beyond. Born on 6 June 1939 at Sona Bata in the Bas-Zaïre region, son of a railwayman who later moved to the capital Léopoldville (now Kinshasa), he began playing music very early, playing a home-made guitar to attract customers to his mother's market stall. He joined a group called Bikunda or later Watam, which brought out its first record in 1953.

In 1956 Luambo Makiadi and seven others joined to found OK Jazz, which was to be his famous band, among the most famous in Zaire and in all Africa. Luambo Makiadi took the stage name Franco. The music he popularised was strongly influenced, like other Zairean music, by Latin American rhythms and especially the rumba; it was also influenced from the 1960s by Zairean traditional music. He was both solo singer and guitarist, with a special individual guitar style. He sang in Lingala, the language which has come to be widespread all over Zaire, partly because of its use in popular music.

OK Jazz is also called TPOK Jazz (TP = *tout puissant*, "all-mighty"); "OK" means *Orchestre Kinois,* i.e. "Kinshasa band", and was also the initials of an early sponsor, a bar keeper named Omar Kashana. The bars of Kinshasa were the first home of Zairean music, which as "Congo music" spread over much of Africa from the 1960s. In early days OK Jazz was supreme, Tabu Ley Rochereau being the only rival, though there were other popular artists like "Dr" Nico (q.v.). Franco and Tabu Ley had some rivalry for years, each attacking the other in songs.

Foncha's private secretary; he was later appointed *chargé de mission* under President Ahidjo. Fonlon, who himself spoke both English and French well, held several posts in the government of the first of Africa's states officially bilingual in English and French. He was appointed deputy minister of Foreign Affairs in 1964, minister of Transport, Posts and Telecommunications in 1968, and minister of Health and Social Welfare in 1970. In 1972, however, he left the government following the formation of the unitary state after a national referendum which formally constituted the United Republic of Cameroon. Fonlon did not go back into politics after this. He became professor of Literature and head of the Department of Negro-African Literature at the University of Yaoundé.

Well before this Dr Fonlon had begun to be noted as a writer. He helped to found *Abbia*, a cultural periodical published in Yaoundé. He took particular interest in the implications of Cameroon's "bilingualism" — which was really, he wrote at one time, "trilingualism", as a Cameroonian who spoke English and French also spoke his or her African language. He published many books: *A Case of Early Bilingualism* (1963),

Many other Zairean musicians began their careers in OK Jazz, while from outside Zaire the trumpeter Hugh Masekela played with them for a time. Sam Mangwana, later

Franco

famous in his own right, was with TPOK Jazz in the 1970s, when it became a 30-piece band. Franco's former saxophonist, Kiamuangana Verckys, left to become the leader of the music business in Zaire, sponsoring other bands.

Franco's fame spread outside Africa, especially in the 1980s. He performed with OK Jazz in Belgium, Britain and other countries. In 1983 he marked reconciliation with his former rival Tabu Ley with an album *Incroyable! mais Vrai! Rochereau et Franco à Paris*. In all he recorded over 100 albums, possibly as many as 150.

Franco supported President Mobutu with his art. For example, he supported the "Authenticity" campaign to revive African tradition in 1972, when he changed his own name to L'Okanga La Nju Pene Luambo Makiadi (but keeping his stage name). In 1984 he sang *Candidat na Biso Mobutu* for elections in which Mobutu was the sole presidential candidate. However, it was said that he was not merely a praise-singer, but hinted at criticisms of the powerful in his songs. One song was said, for example, to criticise Zaire's prime minister. He may have been arrested more often than the two well known occasions (once for a driving offence, once, with all the band, for a song considered indecent). But he remained on good terms with Mobutu's regime, while most of his songs were non-political, about love and marriage for example, as in his hit song *12,000 Lettres*; he was said to blame women too much.

Franco lived in style in Kinshasa. A very wealthy man and literally a very big one (weighing 22 stone at one point), he had a luxurious two-storey house and owned a club called Un Deux Trois. He had 18 children. By 1989 TPOK Jazz had become three bands, two in Zaire and one in Belgium. In that year he went on a European tour but fell seriously ill with kidney failure and diabetes. He died at Namur in Belgium on 12 October 1989; the President of Zaire ordered four days of national mourning in recognition of his contribution to the world of music in general and his nation in particular. ■

Gadama, A.E. (1934-83)

GADAMA, Aaron Elliot (1934-83).

MALAWIAN politician who enjoyed vast personal support from the Chewas in the Central Region, and, who, though believed to have been a cousin of President Banda, opposed him later in his career.

Born on 6 August 1934 in the village of Kawinga, Kasungu district in the Central Region of Malawi, Gadama was educated at Mdabwi, Chipaso and Pherere primary schools before he went to Zomba Catholic Secondary School. In 1959, he qualified as a teacher, after two years' training at Bosco Teachers' Training College and then for five years taught in primary schools in the Central Region. In 1964 he went to Moray House College of Education, Edinburgh, Scotland, where he obtained a Diploma in Education, and after also obtaining a Certificate in Modern Mathematics at a college in Nairobi, he returned to Malawi as headmaster of a primary school in Kasungu district.

Gadama's political career began when he joined the Malawi Congress Party, soon becoming its chairman for Kasungu District, later regional secretary for the Central Province and eventually appointed a member of the Party's 10-man National Executive Committee. He entered the Malawi National Assembly as the deputy for Kasungu in 1971 and in 1972 was promoted to the Cabinet as Minister for Community Development and Social Welfare. Six months later he became Minister without portfolio so that he could be available for special assignments and thus take some burden off the President when he travelled at home and abroad.

In his ministerial role Gadama was anxious to avoid mistakes made by other ministers "who had talents but not tact" in handling problems for President Banda; and was a strongly conservative minister. In February 1983, at a meeting of the Zambia-Malawi Joint Permanent Commission in Lusaka, he said a lot to cement good relationships between the two countries. He also led a three-man Malawi Congress Party delegation, invited for the first time since Malawi independence, to attend the Chama Cha Mapinduzi Annual Conference in Dar es Salaam in October 1982. Before then he had acted as Minister for Natural Resources, a portfolio almost always held by Banda himself, and once as Minister for Transport. He

A.E. Gadama

was also deputy chairman of the Board of Governors of the Kamuzu Academy, deputy Government Chief Whip in the Malawi National Assembly and Chairman of the Board of Directors of the Agricultural Development and Marketing Board.

In 1983, like Matenje (q.v.), Gadama was vehemently opposed to Banda's choice of John Tembo to succeed him ad interim during his then proposed sabbatical of a year in the United Kingdom. Matenje was at the time Secretary-General of the Malawi Congress Party. He was not long in opposition, however, for a few weeks later, in May 1983, he was killed in an accident along with Matenje and John Chiwanga and John Sangala, other ministers who had protested against the choice. Many believed that their death was no accident nor a coincidence but a direct "result" of their stand. ■

Galega II, V.S. (1903-85)

GALEGA II, Vincent Samdala (1903-85).

CAMEROONIAN traditional ruler and political figure. Born Vincent Samdala, he attended public school in Bali and worked as a dispenser in Batibo before succeeding his father, Fonyanga II, on 3 September 1940 as Gagela II, fifth Fon of Bali Nyonga, a well-known kingdom in the Bamenda Grassfields of what was then the British Cameroons. He was the first literate occupant of the office, a keen reformer who brought many changes to the kingdom.

Abroad, he sought to improve the rather notorious reputation of his people as ruthless warriors: he launched a sustained peace drive that won him friendship and respect among his peers. And at home, he worked hard to modernize the kingdom. A new maternity hospital and dispensary, built at his instigation, improved health facilities. So did a new drinking water supply system. Transport was also improved with the opening of an airport. But it was education that remained his first priority. His attention to it was duly rewarded with the very first college in the entire Cameroon Grassfields – the Cameroon Protestant College, Bali, opened in 1949 – and several primary schools.

Galega II

Galega II also had a keen sense of history. In 1960 he established a History Committee to reconstruct, harmonize and preserve the history of Bali-Nyonga.

That was just as well because one of the chronic problems of his entire reign was basically a historical problem. Bali Nyonga had never been on the best of terms with some of its neighbours of the Widikum ethnic group who found themselves at the rough end of a long nineteenth century migration that had brought columns of Bali raiders from the upper middle Benue into the Bamenda grassfields. Widikum memories of these raids were immortalised when the Bali chose to settle in their midst, on some of the land they had won from them by conquest.

There was no love lost between the two communities as one Widikum village after another laid claim to portions of Bali conquered land. But when successive British administrators and eventually the Supreme Court upheld Bali ownership of the land in dispute, Widikum frustrations boiled over. In March 1952 they attacked Bali in a concerted effort to seize the land themselves.

In the week-long civil war that followed, Galega personally organized and directed Bali resistance. The war claimed fifteen lives and widespread damage to property. Galega emerged from it with his integrity unimpaired, even enhanced by the fact that Bali alone had resisted the determined onslaught of a dozen Widikum villages all round it. It was awarded £9000 in damages, collected from the defeated villages.

The 1950s also witnessed the beginning of the nationalist movement in the British Cameroons, as the political fate of the trust territory became a matter of common concern and public discussion. Galega II found himself at the forefront of that debate, as one of the first traditional rulers to board the train of national politics. He took a very active part in all the conferences that were held at different venues to determine the future of the territory, acting as a calming influence in often very agitated debates.

This political involvement led Galega to work closely with the then Premier of the Southern Cameroons, Dr E. M. L. Endeley (q.v.). But the latter's attitude towards traditional authority caused undue tension between them, until finally one act of discourtesy during a visit to London led to a celebrated break with Galega that has been widely regarded as the watershed of Southern Cameroons politics. For just then, the fate of the territory had narrowed down to a straight choice between union with Nigeria, supported by Endeley's Kamerun National Convention (KNC) government, and union with Cameroon under French administration supported by J. N. Foncha's Kamerun National Democratic Party (KNDP). The balance seemed poised between the two, with Endeley having a slight lead, narrowly winning the 1957 general elections. Then Galega joined Foncha, taking the vast majority of grassfields chiefs with him. When the questions were finally put to the people of the Southern Cameroons in a plebicite in 1961, Foncha won by a landslide. The Southern Cameroons then joined the Republic of Cameroun to form the Federal Republic of Cameroon, the only country in Africa to unite territories formerly administered by France and Britain.

Galega II continued to play an active role in the Federated State of West Cameroon (formerly Southern Cameroons), as well as in the Federal Republic. In the former, he served as Vice-President of the venerable House of Chiefs. And when the one-party system was created in the federation with the formation of the Cameroon National Party, Galega was elected President of the section for Bamenda Division.

With time, however, his political influence waned as the emphasis shifted from traditional to administrative authority, a shift epitomised by the closure of the House of Chiefs in 1972. Galega's health also began to fail as old age set in. He died in September 1985 after nearly half a century on one of the most important thrones in Cameroon. ∎

Gebre-Egzy, T. (1924-74)

GEBRE-EGZY, Dr. Tesfaye (1924-74).

ETHIOPIAN diplomat, who served as provisional Secretary-General of the Organisation of African Unity (OAU) at the organisation's inception. He was born in July 1924 in Arada in the Ethiopian capital where he had his primary and secondary education. He later entered the American University in Beirut, Lebanon, and proceeded to America to study at Stanford University, California, and at the Fletcher School of International Law and Diplomacy where he obtained a doctorate in public and international law.

He entered the Ethiopian government service in 1955 as a deputy in the Ministry of Foreign Affairs, from where he later played a major part in shaping his country's foreign policies, especially in the areas of Pan-African unity. In 1958 Gebre-Egzy was co-secretary-general of the first conference of independent African states consisting of Ethiopia, Ghana, Egypt, Liberia, Morocco, Libya, Sudan and Tunisia, convened by Kwame Nkrumah in Accra.

This conference laid the ground for the subsequent ones hosted by Ethiopia in 1960 and 1963, the latter being the first summit of African Heads of State where the Charter of the OAU was ratified. The following year Addis Ababa was formally adopted as the OAU headquarters and, as chief host of the conference Gebre-Egzy was retained as the Organisation's interim Secretary-General, serving until the appointment in August 1964 of Diallo Telli (q.v.) of Guinea.

Gebre-Egzy was appointed Ethiopia's Ambassador and Permanent Representative to the United Nations in New York in 1960. This was the year Ethiopia, together with Liberia, took South Africa before the International Court of Justice to try to obtain a ruling on the legality of South Africa's continued occupation of Namibia and on apartheid. The Court's decision in 1966 did not rule on these issues but only asserted that the two countries had no legal interest in the matter.

He was executed on 23 November 1974 in Addis Ababa, along with 28 other senior civilian officials of the Imperial government deposed by the military. The new Provisional Military Administrative Council said the executed officials were guilty of "gross abuse of authority". ■

Gezo (1797-1858)

GEZO, King (1797-1858).

BENINESE monarch. Born in 1797, Gezo immediately took on the task of freeing his kingdom when he took the throne in 1818. For many years Dahomey (now in

King Gezo

independent Benin) had been under the economic domination of the Yoruba kingdom of Oyo in south-western Nigeria, to whom the Dahomeans had to pay annual tribute. A successful re-assertion of independence vis-à-vis Oyo depended on a reformed army which Gezo undertook to create. He organised the "Amazons", female warriors, many of whom were the King's wives, into a powerful, well-trained fighting corps. With their male counterparts they won a series of battles. The battle of Paonignan, near Canna, in 1827, marked a decisive victory for Gezo over the Oyo forces, breaking Oyo domination which had existed since 1748. To mark this victory he built a palace at Canna to be used for annual ceremonies of remembrance and thanksgiving.

This victory over the Oyo encouraged Gezo to extend his kingdom in other directions. He brought the Mahees in the north under Dahomean domination, to the west he defeated the Ashanti, while to the south and east he sought to bring the Popo, Awori and Egbado under his control. In 1840 he conquered Atakpame, a strategic territory in the south of present-day Togo, and took its king, Komlau, prisoner.

In 1848, he captured Oke Odan and in 1851 launched the Dahomey-Abeokuta war because he perceived the presence of the British in Abeokuta as an economic threat to Dahomey. He formed an alliance with King Kosoko (q.v.) of Lagos whereby the latter would attack Badagry, while Gezo would attack Abeokuta should the Britsh fail to abandon Abeokuta in compliance with Gezo's demand. Gezo suffered a defeat at Abeokuta on 3 March 1851.

The second sphere in which Gezo proved his ability as a ruler was that of economics. At his succession the country's economic position was depressed. His strategy for restoring prosperity was two-fold: on the one hand a vigorous prosecution of the slave trade, and on the other boosting the production of and trade in palm-oil. Recognising that an immediate cessation of the slave trade, as the Europeans were urging, would have a disastrous effect on his kingdom, including probably the loss of his throne, Gezo nevertheless agreed to phase out this activity gradually, at the same time introducing the cash crops, especially cotton, in which the Europeans wished to trade. He encouraged agriculture and other economic activities, such as weaving, with the hope that these would eventually lead to a more stable society. He was not pleased when the British refused money in compensation for loss of the slave trade.

After a long reign, which saw the economic and political bases of the kingdom strengthened at a period when other kingdoms were beginning to yield to European penetration, King Gezo died in 1858, shortly after the war against the Po, to the north of the kingdom. ■

Ghali Pasha (1846-1910)

GHALI PASHA, Boutros (1846-1910).

EGYPTIAN politician, instrumental in the British administration of Egypt. He was one of the Coptic Christian minority in Egypt. He went to an American mission school at Asyut, and was also educated in Switzerland, before entering government service, in which the Copts had a very prominent position by the late 19th century. He worked as a clerk in Cairo and rose rapidly to become Under-Minister of Justice in 1886. He later became Minister of Justice.

British control was established over Egypt under the reign of Khedive Tewfik from 1879 to 1892 and Boutros Ghali was one of many Egyptians who collaborated with the British. From 1893 he served Khedive Abbas II (q.v.) and his British overlords as a minister in the Khedivial government, starting as minister of Finance. The British virtually controlled the Ministries and denied Khedive Abbas, who was hostile to Britain, any control over them. They found Ghali a reliable and willing collaborator in this system. He served as Foreign Minister and Minister of Justice. He was a talented minister, "tenacious and slippery" according to one historian, and impressed Consul-General Cromer favourably.

Egyptian views of him were affected by the nationalist movement protesting against the regime in which Cromer really ruled as a colonial governor, and also by the position of the Copts. Despite Kamil's (q.v.) hope of uniting Moslems and Copts, the Islamic character of much of the nationalist feeling and the role of the Copts in the administration caused a gradually increas-

ing communal rift. In 1906, there came the "Dinshawai Incident" in which some villagers attacked British soldiers who had injured a woman while shooting pigeons, one officer being killed. As Minister of Justice, Boutros Ghali Pasha presided over a special court at Shibin el-Kom, convened under a special regulation of 1895 dealing with offences against British servicemen in Egypt. The trial of 52 villagers ended in very heavy sentences including four death sentences carried out on 28 June 1906. The outcry against this action in Egypt was directed against Boutros Ghali as well as the British.

The nationalist movement, however, was declining by the time that Boutros Ghali was appointed Prime Minister in 1909, succeeding Mustafa Fahmi who had held the post for 14 years. Ghali was said to be the first Prime Minister of wholly indigenous descent in Khedivial Egypt.

Boutros Ghali revived the press law of 1881 to deal with the very outspoken anti-government press, and in June 1909 had Shaykh Abdul Aziz El-Shawish, editor of al-Liwa', sent into "administrative exile" under that law. In 1909 he further angered the Nationalist Party by starting negotiations with the Suez Canal Company on the extension of its Concession, already granted until 1968, to last until 2008.

Boutros Ghali Pasha was assassinated by a Nationalist activist, Ibrahim Wardani, dying of bullet wounds on 21 February 1910. ■

Gibanda, G. (c.1865-1931)

GIBANDA, Chief Gabanda (c.1865-1931).

ZAIREAN traditional ruler who was chief of the Bapende people at the time of the Belgian occupation; and remembered for leading a revolt against the colonial authorities following the imposition of punitive taxation in 1931.

Born in about 1865, Gibanda belonged to the Kimbai ethnic group and rose to be head of the Musanga chiefdom, an important Lunda centre on the Kwilu River. He came to the throne in the early part of the 20th century, at a time of intensive activities by the colonial powers who sought to estabish their control. He soon established contact with the Belgians whose commercial activities and forced labour along the Congo (Zaire) River and the Kasai tributary were forcing the local people to migrate southwards to Musanga country. The worst instances of this oppression were in King Leopold's Congo Free State until 1908, but some of it was continued under the Belgian colonial administration which followed.

The Belgian authorities accorded Gibanda official recognition in December 1920, in return he granted certain concessions to the Europeans to develop Musanga's palm kernels and oil industry. But by the late 1920s relations with the colonial authorities became strained as the Bapende people were being moved from their homes and relocated in infertile areas to make room for the development of roads and industries. The resulting dislocation of community life, and the exploitative conditions under which the members of the community were made to work in the government plantations, provoked resentment. The situation was escalated by punitive taxation, imposed by the colonial government on the plantation workers who were already hard hit by low wages.

The resentment against these measures culminated in an open revolt against the government in 1931. The so-called Bapende Revolt began on 8 June 1931 with a peaceful demonstration against the taxes being levied by the colonial authorities. As tempers rose, however, the tax collection post in Kilimba was attacked and the tax agent, Maximilien Ballot, a Belgian, was killed. Government troops were quickly despatched to suppress the rebellion and to recover Ballot's body from the demonstrators. Chief Gibanda and several of his sub-chiefs and headmen were later arrested and charged for complicity in the death of Ballot. Together with the leaders of the revolt, they were tortured in prison while awaiting trial; some of the accused died in custody from ill-treatment.

In October 1931, the chief was brought to trial for allegedly hiding one of the leaders of the revolt, which he denied. He also pleaded that he had no prior knowledge of the revolt. But he was found guilty and condemned to death, his execution being carried out by the Force Publique (the colonial army) who tortured him, severed his

genitals and weighted him down naked in the sun. He subsequently died a slow, agonising death. A year after his death, in November 1932, the Belgian authorities admitted that Chief Gibanda was in fact in the neighbouring Chokwe country during the uprising and that he was unjustly tortured and executed.

The execution of Gibanda is but one of the indiscriminate atrocities of colonialism in Africa. In Belgian Congo, as in the countries ruled by other European states, resistance, or even mild criticism by erstwhile collaborators like the Bapende chief, was brutally crushed. But this did not curb the tide of nationalism.■

Gichuru, J.S. (1914-82)

GICHURU, James Samuel (1914-82).

KENYAN leading politician, one of the founding fathers of modern Kenya.

James Samuel Gichuru was born of Kikuyu parents in 1914 at Thogoto in the Kiambu area. After primary schooling at the Church of Scotland Mission in Kikuyu, where his father was teaching, he attended

J.S. Gichuru

the Alliance High School and later Makerere College in Uganda, where he gained a teacher's diploma. He returned to teach at the Alliance High School in 1935, for five years, and among his pupils were Oginga Odinga and Ronald Ngala (q.v.) who later distinguished themselves in Kenyan politics. Gichuru remained in the teaching profession until he joined full-time active politics, but not before becoming principal of the Church of Scotland Mission in 1951. Before then he had been involved in the nationalist movement that was reacting against continuing British colonial rule.

He was a founding member of the Kenya African Union (KAU), formed in 1944 under the leadership of Harry Thuku (q.v.) who resigned three months later and paved the way for Gichuru's rise to the presidency. He thus became the first President of KAU and held the post until 1947 when Kenyatta was able to assume it. Gichuru was elected to the first Kenyan self-government legislature and was a member of the delegation to the Lancaster House constitutional conference for Kenya's independence. In 1950 he was appointed Chief of Dagoretti, a central Kiambu locality, where he had his own father serving under him as a headman. He was dismissed from that post in 1952 by the colonial authorities for nationalist activities, but unlike Kenyatta and others he was not detained then; he returned to teaching. In 1955, however, Gichuru was placed in detention until January 1960. When KAU became the Kenya African National Union (KANU) on the eve of independence Gichuru had the distinction of being its first President on March 1960, but again relinquished the office in favour of veteran Kenyatta. From that time on Gichuru remained a regular feature in his country's political scene, emerging as a pivotal figure in the independent government which he served as its first Minister of Finance.

Later, in December 1969, he became Minister of Defence and he oversaw the expansion and modernisation of Kenya's armed forces. He attended to defence matters even after the Ministry was scrapped and turned into a department in the Office of the President.

Keeping his place in the hierarchy of Kenyan politics was not easy for Gichuru, especially in the closing years of his life. He was in poor health and his advanced age made life more difficult. But it is a tribute to his astuteness as a politician that he was always able to manage to ward off vigorous challenges to his leadership from younger and more dynamic rivals. He was able to retain both his Central Kimbu Limum constituency seat and KANU branch chairmanship since he first took both offices. In heated and sometimes aggressive election campaigns, his younger opponents took time off to tell the electorate that a diabetic like Gichuru was an unfit representative for them in Parliament. Gichuru's retort, which always saw him carry the day, was: "Nobody goes to Parliament to play football". Until his death in August 1982 in a Nairobi hospital after a long illness, he was a Minister of State under President Daniel arap Moi.

A wily politician, his combined toughness and compromise always put him one step ahead of his rivals. Determined to carry out his duties to the very last in spite of his poor health, he bore out the old Kikuyu saying that "A stream does not pass over an old stone". ■

Giwa, O. (1947-86)

GIWA, Oladele (1947-86).

NIGERIAN journalist and founder of *Newswatch* magazine. He was born in Ife, Oyo State, on 16 March 1947. Giwa's life is a tale of the transition from obscurity to celebrity, of the rewards of perserverance, the hazards of courage and the vicissitudes of the investigative journalism that he practised. He will be remembered especially for sensitizing national consciousness to the responsibilities of public office.

The son of an Afenmai washerman from the Bendel State of Nigeria, Giwa's childhood was one of penury and deprivation. The father provided the barest necessities of life for the family from his earnings as a washerman in the palace of the Ooni of Ife, Oba Adesoji Aderemi. Dele, as the eldest child, shared his time between his studies and helping with clothes washing by the Esinmirin riverside near Ife. The early acquaintance with hardship fortified his resilience and instilled in him the resolve to succeed and to rise above the humble circumstances of his birth. His ambition was aided by his brilliance and sociability.

From 1955 to 1960 he attended Ansar-Udeen Primary School. Then at great financial cost to the family, but in acknowledgement of Dele's thirst for knowledge, he was

D. Giwa

enrolled at the Local Authority Secondary Modern School in Lagere, Ile-Ife. In 1964 he was admitted into Oduduwa College, Ife. It was in this college that Giwa acquired his zeal for and initiation into journalism. He became one of the editors of the school magazine, *The Torch*, founded by a West Indian teacher, Hartley Sutton. He passed the West African School Certificate examination in 1967.

He worked for a year as a clerk at the Barclays Bank (now Union Bank) in Lagos and for five months at the Nigerian Tobacco Company, Ibadan. From there, he secured employment with the Nigerian Broadcasting Corporation, Ibadan, as a news assistant, a job in harmony with his journalistic leaning. His duties at NBC included taking phoned-in reports from correspondents in Abeokuta, Oyo, Ikeja, Warri and other major towns that fell under the jurisdiction of NBC Ibadan. He was also in charge of recasting wire service reports and monitoring such foreign stations as the British Broadcasting Corporation, the Voice of America and the Ghana Broadcasting Corporation.

He proceeded to the United States in

1971, where he read for a Bachelor of Arts degree in English at Brooklyn College, New York. In 1974 he secured employment with the *New York Times*. From the *New York Times* he moved to the *Daily Times* of Nigeria through the instrumentality of Patrick Dele Cole and Stanley Macebuh, then managing director and editor-in-chief respectively of the *Daily Times* of Nigeria, who impressed on him the patriotic need to come home and contribute in his professional capacity to his country's upliftment.

Giwa joined the *Daily Times* in 1979 and discharged his duties as features editor with a vigour and an enthusiasm that readily infected all who worked with him. He was part of a team of talented and exciting writers like Stanley Macebuh and Olatunji Dare under the inspiring leadership of Dele Cole. This "competitiveness" brought out the best in him. His two columns, *Parallax View* and *Press Snaps*, were very popular.

Apprehensive that the country's return to civilian rule in 1979 might endanger press freedom and frustrate initiative at the *Daily Times*, Giwa accepted the offer of Chief M. K. O. Abiola to work for him as the founding editor of the *Sunday Concord* on the condition that the management would not interfere with the editorial policy. He, along with the nucleus of the staff he attracted, nurtured the *Sunday Concord* to fame. After some time Giwa began to feel that there were limitations to the assurances of immunity from interference and the primacy of journalistic considerations over other interests, and he decided to leave the *Concord* newspapers. His friends, Ray Ekpu and Yakubu Mohammed, joined him in a new venture.

Giwa had worked for the *Concord* newspapers for four and a half years, 1980 to 1984, and resolved this time to be his own master. Together with Ray Ekpu, Yakubu Mohammed and Dan Agbese, former editor of the *New Nigerian*, he established *Newswatch* magazine, whose maiden issue, dated 4 February 1985, appeared on the stands on 28 January 1985. *Newswatch* was an instant success.

Unfettered by any government or other proprietary interests or control, *Newswatch* magazine pursued its policy of "first with the news" with a singularity of purpose, forthrightness and a crusading zeal that kept it very much in the public's eye. With *Newswatch*, investigative journalism attained new dimensions. It did not shy away from sensitive or controversial issues, nor did it prevaricate on issues of major national import.

One of the magazine's first entanglements with the authorities arose over the comment that Justice Uwaifo's Judicial Panel, which exonerated the former President Shehu Shagari, was a "Kangaroo Court" indulging in "a hollow ritual". The author, Ray Ekpu, was convicted for contempt of the tribunal and fined ₦20.

Giwa himself was not given to equivocation. His unwavering commitment to whatever cause he believed in, his abundant, some would say reckless, courage, his forthright, if sometimes strident, expression of his ideas, was to bring him into confrontation with the police and security agencies. One of his first contacts with them ended in his detention on 29 October 1982. It was for his publication in the *Sunday Concord* of 24 October 1982, before the government had officially released it to the public, of the Government White Paper on the report of a commission of enquiry that investigated the destruction by fire of the Republic Building in Lagos. The Lagos High Court later ruled on 20 July 1984, that the detention was illegal. Giwa was awarded ₦10,000 damages and the Inspector General of Police was asked to tender a public apology to him.

Conflict with the security authorities attained a new height when on 17 October 1986, he was invited to the headquarters of the security organisation (SSS) where he was reportedly confronted with four allegations, namely, that he was publishing a follow-up story on the removal of Commodore Ebite Ukiwe; espousing the cause of CSP Alozie Ogugbuaja, the Lagos State police public relations officer, who was having trouble with the police command; holding talks with labour unions, students groups and other leftist groups to destabilize the country; and finally that he was holding talks with some people with the possible intention of importing arms into the country.

Giwa denied all four allegations and complained to the minister of Information, Tony Momoh, and the new chief of General Staff, Rear-Admiral Aikhomu, about this harassment. Notwithstanding reassurances from the minister, Giwa promptly wrote to his lawyer, Gani Fawehinmi, to take necessary action "to clear my good name and disabuse the mind of the government".

It was at this point in his relations with the security authorities that Giwa was killed in his residence in Lagos by a letter bomb on 19 October 1986. He left five children and a widow, Funmi, whom he had married in 1984.

Giwa's death provoked nationwide consternation, as well as indignation and condemnation. The security authorities quickly and stoutly denied any involvement. The Federal Government promised to carry out a thorough investigation.

Giwa's lawyer, Gani Fawehinmi, gave concrete expression to his suspicion of the involvement of the security organisation by initiating proceedings to compel the prosecution of two of their officers for the murder of his client.

Some people may have disagreed with Giwa's abrasive style, a few may have criticised his method, but none doubted his patriotic motivation in his search for the truth and in the articulation of his perception of objectives in the national cause. But it was the tragic circumstances of his violent death in the prime of his life and career that turned Giwa in the eyes of many of his compatriots into a symbol of courage in the minefield of investigative journalism in Africa.■

El-Glaoui, S.T.B.M. (1879-1956)

EL-GLAOUI, Siddi Hadji Thami Ben Mohammed (1879-1956).

MOROCCAN politician. He was born at Telouet in the Great Atlas, where his father had been a Berber chief. He was the adversary of Sidi Mohammed V, Sultan of Morocco (q.v.). He instigated the 1953 revolt against the Sultan, the hereditary enemy of his family. He was appointed Pasha of Marrakesh and the neighbouring areas in 1908 by the French colonial authorities. These areas had been brought under Berber suzerainty following battles in which it is said that el-Glaoui participated as a young boy. When the French declared a protectorate over part of Morocco, el-Glaoui supported them in their efforts to contain Berber resistance. During World War I, when French troops were needed elsewhere, el-

Glaoui undertook to maintain law and order in the French protectorate.

He had vast interests in agricultural and mining concerns and led what came to be known as the traditionalists against Moroccan nationalists demanding independence

S.T.B.M. El-Glaoui

from France. In 1951, he deployed a contingent of ethnic forces against nationalist positions in Fez and Rabat and succeeded in forcing the Sultan to dismiss his militant advisers. In 1953 he spearheaded the deposition of the Sultan who was subsequently exiled to Corsica and later Madagascar. In his absence, the tide of nationalism grew and violence broke out in Marrakesh and other urban centres in 1955. An attempt was made on the life of el-Glaoui, who then supported the return of the Sultan. Later he underwent a serious operation and died on 23 January 1956, just after the Sultan was restored to the throne in November 1955.■

Gobir, Y.A. (1934-75)

GOBIR, Alhaji Yusuf Amuda (1934-75).

NIGERIAN administrator, generally regarded as one of the ablest public officers in the Nigerian federal structure. He worked his way up from state service to become a federal Permanent Secretary, first in the Ministry of Defence and then Establishments. Yusuf Gobir was born on 2 October 1934 at Ilorin, now capital of Kwara State. He had his education at the Ilorin Provincial (later Government) Secondary School, and the Institute of Administration in Zaria in 1951-2. Shortly after he did an administrative service course at Oxford University, England.

Like most educated Nigerians of the time Gobir was attracted to the civil service which he joined in 1950. He was at first in the federal Nigerian Public Service but when the Northern Region Public Service was created in 1954 he went to the North. After several years in the service there he read law and was called to the Bar at Inner Temple, London, in 1964.

On the creation of new states in 1967-8 Gobir served in his home state, Kwara. Already well-known for his industry and efficiency, he was one of the senior administrators who established a structure for the

Y.A. Gobir

new state's civil service, and was the Permanent Secretary in the Governor's Office. In April 1969 he was transferred to the Federal Service and was appointed Permanent Secretary to the Ministry of Defence, a vital post during the Civil War. In 1971 he was posted to the Federal Ministry of Establishments and later to the Federal Ministry of Transport. He served there until his death on 28 December 1975, in a road accident while on holiday in Spain. His body was flown to Nigeria, amid widespread mourning, for burial at Ilorin. ■

Gomwalk, J.D. (1935-76)

GOMWALK, Joseph Deshi (1935-76).

NIGERIAN police officer and Military Governor. He was born on 13 April 1935 at Amper, Pankshin Division, now in Plateau State of Nigeria, son of a Native Authority scribe, and was educated at the Sudan United Mission (SUM) school in Amper from 1943 for three years. Then he went to the SUM's schools at Gindiri, finishing at the secondary school there (1950-55). He went on to the Nigerian College of Arts, Science and technology, Zaria (1956-58), and then to University College, Ibadan, where he matriculated in 1958 and in 1961 was awarded a BSc in Zoology (with specialisation in Parasitology).

He worked as research officer at the Kaduna Veterinary School, but three months later transferred to the Northern Nigerian Administrative Service, for which he worked in Mambilla in what is now Gongola State (he pioneered construction of the escarpment road to Mambilla Plateau), from 1961 to 1965. In February 1966 he joined the Nigeria Police Force (NPF). He rose to the rank of Chief Superintendent.

On the creation of new states in May 1967 he was appointed Military Governor of Benue-Plateau State. He was compulsorily retired, as were the other state military governors who had held office for eight years, in July 1975, on the fall of the regime of Gen. Gowon whose home area was very close to Mr. Gomwalk's (they were said to be related). Shortly afterwards he and his family were denounced in an inquiry report

J.D. Gomwalk

for malpractices. He was dismissed from the NPF on 3 February 1976.

After General Murtala Muhammed (q.v.) was killed on 13 February 1976 in a coup attempt, Mr. Gomwalk was arrested and tried for being involved in the plot. He was executed on 14 May 1976. ■

Gore-Browne, S. (1883-1967)

GORE-BROWNE, Sir Stewart (1883-1967).

ZAMBIAN settler politician, famous as a white farmer who took the side of Africans, and particularly of Kenneth Kaunda's United National Independence Party (UNIP) in the struggle for independence and the end of colonial rule. For this he was greatly honoured when he died in independent Zambia, and President Kaunda wrote later, "Gore-Browne is a legend in Zambia – a country which he helped to construct, a country he loved, a country in which his spirit will long live".

Born in England in 1883, the son of a lawyer and grandson of a governor of New

Zealand, he went to the famous Public School at Harrow and then joined the army. He served with the army in South Africa from 1902 to 1904. Back in Britain, for a few years he was responsible, as a motoring enthusiast, for the building of the Brooklands car racing circuit. In 1911 he joined a commission to survey one of the new artificial borders between recently occupied European colonies in Africa: that between the Belgian Congo (now Zaire) and Northern Rhodesia (now Zambia). This was to prove a turning point in his life.

While in Northern Rhodesia, then ruled by the British South Africa Company (BSAC), he decided to acquire land and settle, and he picked on a site at Shiwa Ngandu in the Bemba people's country in the north-east. His plans to settle were interrupted by the First World War, which began when he was in Britain. He fought on the Western Front, held training and staff posts, was decorated, and rose to the rank of Lieutenant-Colonel.

In 1920 he returned to Northern Rhodesia, where the BSAC allotted him 10,000 acres at Shiwa Ngandu. He struggled for years to make his farm there a success, trying to grow among other crops roses for "attar" perfume. But little success came his way until the 1930s, when his lime crops did well. By then he was a well known figure among the White settlers. But from the beginning he sought to establish, by his own example, a different treatment of Africans. He had been appalled by the racism and brutality of the Whites who had gone to the area, and believed in benevolent paternalism. He learned Cibemba and acquired a good reputation among his Bemba neighbours. However, he shared many of the prejudices of his time, and his attitude was respected by Africans because the average settler attitude was much worse. In his early days in Northern Rhodesia he rejected any idea of African self-government but thought "partnership" between them and the settlers possible.

Lt-Colonel Gore-Browne, who married Lorna Goldman in England in 1927 (they had two daughters), was also respected by the other White settlers and in 1935 he became one of their representatives on the Legislative Council (Legco) of Northern Rhodesia, which had become an ordinary colony after the end of BSAC rule in 1924. In 1933 he had completed a magnificent "manor

house" at Shiwa Ngandu, built in British style and well known all over Northern Rhodesia during the decades when its owner was involved in politics. In Legco he was a self-appointed champion of Africans, while for years also satisfying his settler constituents who relied on him to defend some of

Sir S. Gore-Browne

their selfish interests before the government. For long Gore-Browne thought settlers could cater for African interests and the two could work together instead of clashing, although he persistently denounced injustice favouring Whites at Africans' expense. He said, "A prosperous blackman means a prosperous whiteman and *vice versa*".

He criticised the impact of taxation on Africans – which took no account of the inability of many to pay – and called for better health services and more aid to African farmers. He listened to Africans and agreed with them in opposing plans for a merger of the Rhodesias which would involve domination by the Southern Rhodesia (now Zimbabwe) settler parliament. But he retained enough respect among settlers to become leader of the *unofficial* members (then all whites) of Legco, from 1939 to 1946.

During the Second World War years he was very close to the colonial administration. He did much to defuse the 1940 crisis on the Copperbelt, when African mineworkers went on strike, the "colour bar" being their major grievance. Gore-Browne was against that too, but it was to last for a long time, especially in the mining industry, in which the top jobs were reserved for whites. He worked to reduce discrimination against strong White obstruction. He advocated permission for Africans to join trade unions before this was granted in 1948. He advocated increased representation of Africans, and at his suggestion the African Representative Council came into being in 1946. In that year he told Legco of the Africans' grievances, including loss of the best land to Whites and the colour bar. In that year, too, Sir Stewart Gore-Browne, having recently been knighted, resigned as leader of the *unofficials* because he could not agree to the call for "amalgamation" with Southern Rhodesia; his successor, Roy Welensky, had been Gore-Browne's friend and political ally, but now parted company with him politically over the "amalgamation" issue. Gore-Browne at first favoured a Rhodesian "federation" and, when he proposed an alternative new constitition to that decreed by Britain for Northern Rhodesia in 1948, found that African leaders opposed it as they feared it would lead to "amalgamation". But the African Representative Council voted in 1948 to retain Gore-Browne as their representative, and in the next few years he came to oppose strongly the Federation as it was finally established in 1953.

Until then Gore-Browne, whose advocacy of African interests had been appreciated by many, had retained his paternalist approach. But, with his eyes open to a changing situation, he noted the rising "political consciousness" of Africans. In 1951 he decided not to seek re-election to Legco, seeing that he was now out of touch with "African opinion as well as white", since the Africans called for majority rule. He did not fully retire, and was much visited in Shiwa Ngandu.

He took long to accept the idea of African self-rule but eventually he rejected plans for White "liberals" to head a pro-African political organisation, and came to see that the Africans were organising themselves and Whites should seek to help, not direct them. He met Kenneth Kaunda in Britain in 1957, and in 1958 invited him to dinner in Lusaka, which was a significant gesture at that time.

After that Kaunda, as well as Hastings Banda of Nyasaland (Malawi), was in regular contact with him, while struggling to separate their countries from the White-ruled Central African Federation. In March 1960 Sir Stewart said, "African opposition to Federation is now so strong that it could be disastrous to force it on them any longer". He urged this point on the then British Colonial Secretatry, Macleod.

In March 1961, Sir Stewart Gore-Browne became a member of Kaunda's United National Independence Party (UNIP). Thus the former settler representative identified himself with the African struggle against Federation and for independence. Later in 1961 he attended a UNIP meeting at Mulungushi, but he did not know of the decision taken there to organise sabotage, arson and destruction of property to back up the party's campaign. Shaken by that violence, the British government made concessions which led to African self-government and independence and the end of Federation.

Elections were held in 1962 under complex procedures aimed at ensuring representation of Whites out of proportion to their numbers. Sir Stewart was a UNIP candidate; he won the African vote massively but under the regulations he had to win the Whites' votes too, and as they were generally against him he did not win a seat. Gore-Browne, who had accompanied Kaunda to New York earlier in 1962, played no active role in politics after failing to enter parliament. However, when he died on 4 August 1967, at the age of 84, he received a state funeral, and President Kaunda attended and delivered an oration, saying, "Born an Englishman, he died a Zambian". ▪

Gouveia (died 1899)

GOUVEIA, King (died 1899).

MOZAMBICAN King of the Gorongosa who united several kingdoms in Mozambique against Portuguese and British imperialism. Gouveia, who was born in Goa, started his climb to power with a well-armed private army which he used to harass the

Portuguese and protect vulnerable chieftains. His first significant conquest was the protection of the Sena who were invaded by the Ngoni. Not only did he protect but he also subjugated minor chieftains thus becoming a territorial overlord.

Within a short period he ruled over the Sena and Tonga people and even maintained the symbols of Kingship such as the royal drum and stool. He married the daughter of the Sena chief thus providing himself with prestigious kin. He controlled a secondary state that encompassed most of the Zambezi valley.

Some of the Tonga chiefs under Gouveia had been subjects of King Makombe Chipapata of the Barue nation. To thwart Gouveia's imperial ambitions, Chipapata formed an alliance with Gouveia's archenemy Bonga of the Massangano. Their attack on Gouveia failed and Chipapata in his defeat offered to aid Gouveia in his invasion of the Ngoni. Having eliminated the Ngoni thirty-five year threat, Chipapata gave his daughter Adriana in marriage to Gouveia. Some of the Barue disapproved of Chipapata's appeasement and rebelled, gathering around his son Hanga (q.v.). They organised a coup against Gouveia, which failed. Despite Hanga's treachery Gouveia named him his successor as ruler in preference to his eldest son.

During that entire period Lisbon was offering Gouveia a number of gratuities in exchange for nominal loyalty and collaboration. These included legal titles to land he had conquered, exemption from taxes and cash payments. He was also given a prestigious title, Capitão-Môr, and was allowed to carry out clandestine slave trade if he so wished. In 1877 he went to Lisbon where he was received as a hero and made an official of the Companhia da Zambesia. On his return he refused to surrender his independence to the Portuguese. It was at that point that Lisbon abandoned its policy of imposing its authority by agreement. It embarked on a strategy of divide and conquer. This also proved a failure. It then started a campaign of conquests. With the help of Gouveia the Portuguese attacked the Massangano, but poor leadership and malaria debilitated the European soldiers. This coupled with the tenacity of the Massangano caused the defeat of the Portuguese. However Gouveia still clung to his independence.

In 1890 he was arrested by the British South African police. Hanga used this period to mobilise the disaffected Barue in a rebellion against Gouveia. When Gouveia was released, a year later, he led a force of 4,000 against Hanga. In the ensuing battle his forces were routed and he was killed. His death ushered in a new period of anticolonial strife led by Hanga.■

Graham-Douglas, N.B. (1926-83)

GRAHAM-DOUGLAS, Dr. Nabo Bekinbo (1926-83).

NIGERIAN lawyer; in 1966 he became the Attorney-General of the then Eastern Nigeria. He later held a similar post in the Rivers State and subsequently became Federal Attorney-General and Commissioner for Justice in 1972.

He was born on 15 July 1926, in Abonnema, near Port Harcourt in Rivers State. After elementary schooling at the Nyemoni School in his birthplace, he went to the Kalabari National College in Buguma from where he proceeded to Exeter University in England for legal studies. He then entered King's College, University of Lon-

Dr. N.B. Graham-Douglas

don, and later the Institute of Advanced Studies, also in London. He was called to the Bar there at the Inner Temple.

Returning to Nigeria soon after, Graham-Douglas set up in private practice and soon won recognition for numerous successful cases he defended. In March 1966, in the wake of the first military coup which overthrew the Government of Alhaji Abubakar Tafawa Balewa (q.v.) in January of the same year, he was appointed by the succeeding Military Government to serve as Attorney-General for Eastern Nigeria, succeeding another eminent jurist, Dr. Christopher Chukwuemeka Mojekwu (q.v.). But the hostilities between the Federal authorities and the break-away Biafra meant that he could not retain his office. He was unequivocally opposed to the secession of the region and subsequently resigned his post. For this he was detained briefly by the secessionists, thus ending his tenure as Attorney-General of the region in September 1967. He was later to publish an account of his involvement in the crisis, entitled *Triumph or Turpitude?* A man of immense talent and with an imposing personality, he also later wrote a specialised book, *Forensic Aspects of Nigerian Land Law*, published in 1972.

Following constitutional re-arrangements which allowed for the break-up of Nigeria's four regions into 12 units, the Eastern Region was split into East-Central, Cross Rivers, and Rivers State. Graham-Douglas was appointed the Attorney-General and Commissioner for Justice of his home state Rivers, in 1969. There he employed his now widely recognised experience and ability in creating a legal structure for the new state. He remained in that post for three years, then in 1972 was appointed Attorney-General for the Federation in the regime of General Yakubu Gowon. He was concurrently Commissioner for Justice in the same government.

Graham-Douglas fell with that regime in the coup of July 1975, following which he went once more into private practice until his death on 18 December 1983. His last major national assignment was with the Committee of Friends of Gowon which was charged with the responsibility of making arrangements for the deposed leader's return to Nigeria after several years in exile. Graham-Douglas died before Gowon's arrival in Nigeria in late December, but the former Head of State said that he "cannot pay him

any greater tribute than to say that he was as great as his stature. Let's rejoice that he has played his part well". ■

Grant, G.A. (1878-1956)

GRANT, George Alfred (1878-1956).

GHANAIAN businessman and nationalist leader; founding member of the United Gold Coast Convention, Ghana's first nationalist movement. He was born at Beyin, son of William Minneaux Grant and grandson of the merchant Francis Chapman Grant, famous as proprietor of the *Gold Coast Times*, a member of the Legislative Council, and Treasurer of the Fanti Confederation of 1871. His schooling at the Cape Coast Wesleyan School was followed by private tuition by an African businessman so that the young Grant could follow in the footsteps of his father. He went to study the timber trade first at Axim, then, for five years, with a British firm in Côte d'Ivoire.

Armed with knowledge of the important trade in tropical timber, Grant entered

G.A. Grant

253

the business on his own from a young age. He became one of the most remarkable West African businessmen of the first half of the 20th century, maintaining a flourishing timber export business throughout the period when European firms were dominating African trade almost entirely and handling much of the Gold Coast timber trade. In 1903 Grant began exporting mahogany to Britain. He visited Britain in 1905 and expanded his business contacts. By 1909 his business was well established at Axim.

Between 1914 and 1919 he chartered ships for transport of timber to Britain and the USA. Between 1920 and 1922 he opened his own offices at London, Liverpool and Hamburg. He used a former German navy minesweeper for oceanic trade, and motor launches for local coastal trade. In Gold Coast he expanded operations to Dunkwa, Sekondi and later Akim Abuakwa.

He was appointed to the Legislative Council in 1926, to represent Sekondi. He retained his seat until the following year, deciding then to concentrate on his business, and became known everywhere as "Pa Grant."

In the Second World War he was a member of the committee to control timber exports. But he resented the general discrimination against African businessmen during the War years and after. He was also concerned about the inadequacy of representation of African interests. In 1947 he took his own steps to deal with that situation. He invited J.B. Danquah (q.v.) and others to a meeting to launch a nationalist party. As a result, at a meeting of 40 people at Canaan Lodge at Saltpond, the United Gold Coast Convention (UGCC) was formed on 4 August 1947.

Grant was among the UGCC leaders who invited Kwame Nkrumah (q.v.) to return to be the party's secretary-general. In 1948 Nkrumah, Danquah and four other UGCC leaders, not including Grant, were detained after the riots in Accra which led to the Watson Commisson before which Grant gave evidence, concentrating among other things on the general discrimination against African businessmen. Following this an all-African Committee, the Coussey Committee on Constitutional Reform, was formed, with Grant and 5 other UGCC leaders among the 40 members. With progress towards self-government under changes recommended by the Coussey Committee, Nkrumah and other

radicals in the UGCC parted company with the main leaders of the Convention, including Grant. Pa Grant died on 30 October 1956. ■

Greene, J.E. (1915-77)

GREENE, James Edward (1915-77).

LIBERIAN politician, who abandoned a teaching career in 1952 for politics and rose to become his country's Vice-President in 1972. He was born in Greenville in Sinoe County in eastern Liberia on 6 July 1915.

He was educated locally at St. Paul's High School before going to the University of Liberia where he graduated with a Bachelor of Arts in 1940. He later pursued a course in legal studies and was admitted to the Bar as an attorney in the Third Judicial Circuit in Sinoe County in 1946. In 1961, he became counsellor in the Supreme Court.

Son of a former Commissioner for

J.E. Greene

Sinoe County, Greene made his debut in politics in 1961 when he became member for Sinoe County in the House of Senate, having started his working life as a teacher in 1941 in Sinoe High School and becoming its principal from 1949 to 1952. Greene's ability and drive were quickly recognised in the True Whig Party where he was very popular with his colleagues. In 1963, he was elected national vice-chairman of the Party. Four years later he became its chairman.

He was a member of many fraternities and lodges and served on various boards, including the Board of Trustees of the University of Liberia who awarded him an honorary LLB.

In the Senate he was chairman of the Armed Forces Committee and Enrolled Bills Committee. A quiet, unassuming but able politician with exacting qualities, he represented his constituency in the Senate till 4 April 1972, when he was appointed Vice-President of the Republic of Liberia. He held that office till his death in July 1977. ■

N. Grunitzky

Grunitzky, N. (1913-69)

GRUNITZKY, Nicolas (1913-69).

TOGOLESE politician who served as Prime Minister of autonomous Togo within the French Union and later as President after independence. He was born to a Polish officer in the German army and a Togolese mother in Akatpame on 5 April 1913, the eve of the co-ordinated attack by British and French forces on Germany that had ruled Togo since 1884. In 1914 the territory was surrendered to Britain and France who divided it up between themselves.

Grunitzky had his elementary education in Togo and became one of the first Togolese to win a scholarship to study in France, where he gained his *baccalauréat* and later obtained an engineering degree in 1937.

On returning to Togo, he worked in the civil service as a Public Works engineer with the Togo railways, but he resigned to take up a successful business career in transport and construction. When Togo

came under the control of the Vichy French government during the Second World War, Grunitzky became an active Gaullist, a role which earned him French support in his later political career. However, in spite of the French backing, Grunitzky failed to get elected as Togo's deputy in the French National Assembly in 1946, being defeated by Martin Akou (q.v.) who ran under the auspices of Olympio's (q.v.) nationalist movement, the *Comité de l'Unité Togolaise* (CUT). But between 1951 and 1958, Grunitzky, a founding member and leader of the conservative *Parti Togolais du Progrès* (PTP), represented Togo in the French Chamber.

In 1952 he suffered several political setbacks when his candidacy for Togo's territorial assembly was rejected by his constituents in the Ewe, Kpessi and Kabre districts. Following this he was expelled by the PTP, but re-emerged in 1955 with the assistance of the colonial administration, who opposed the CUT's agitation for independence. In the elections to the Togo Assembly in 1955 Grunitzky benefited from the French administration's apprehension of CUT and was elected to become the first Prime Minister of autonomous Togo within the French Union. However, the United Nations-supervised elections of April 1958 proved a decisive defeat for the Grunitzky Government; the PTP won only three seats to CUT's 33. Olympio dislodged Grunitzky as Prime Minister, leading Togo to independence in 1960.

In the wake of the 1958 defeat, Grunitzky merged the PTP with the *Union des Chefs et des Populations du Nord* (UCPN) to form a new party named the *Union Démocratique des Populations Togolaises* (UDPT). But in the 1961 elections the new party was unable to win a seat in the National Assembly. Grunitzky left Togo for Côte d'Ivoire in 1962 to carry on his business. He returned to the country in 1963 and became president following the otherthrow and assassination of Olympio.

Opposition to Grunitzky's administration however continued. The next four years saw demonstrations against it by Olympio's supporters who would not accept the presence of Olympio's alleged assassins in the hierarchy of the armed forces, or cooperate with the new Government. The regime was also unpopular because the economy was suffering as a result of the closure of Togo's border with Ghana. Meanwhile, the rift between Grunitzky and Vice-President Meatchi (q.v.), who enjoyed the support of CUT elements in the Government, was developing into open conflict and culminated in the resignation from the Cabinet of all CUT ministers. Faced with these crises, President Grunitzky dismissed the Government on 1 November 1966 and formed a new administration with himself as Minister of Defence, Mines, Public Works, Transport and Telecommunication in addition to being the President. But the new Government survived for only two months before it was overthrown by the army on 13 January 1967, the fourth anniversary of his predecessor's assassination.

Following the coup, Grunitzky again went into self-exile in Côte d'Ivoire, where he had established a flourishing transport and construction business. He died on 27 September 1969 in a Paris hospital, where he was being treated for injuries sustained in a car accident in Côte d'Ivoire.∎

Gueye, A.L. (1891-1968)

GUEYE, Amadou Lamine (1891-1968).

SENEGALESE politician, active in early anti-colonial politics. He was born on 20 September 1891 at Médine, in the then French Soudan, although his family came from Saint-Louis, Senegal. He developed an interest in politics at an early age and was one of the founding members, in 1912, of the Young Senegalese (*Jeunes Sénégalais*). This group met regularly at first to discuss ideas and engage in cultural activities and soon formed a political section. In 1914 they endorsed the candidacy of Blaise Diagne (q.v.), the first African to be elected deputy to the French Assembly, and put their weight behind his election campaign. During the First World War he served in the French

A.L. Gueye

army and fought in France. He qualified as a lawyer in Paris in 1921 and gained a doctorate in juridical, political and economic science. On returning to Senegal, he became an advocate at the Court of Appeal in Dakar and later served as a magistrate in Réunion and Martinique. In the early 1920s, dissatisfied with what they considered to be collaboration with the colonial authorities on the part of Blaise Diagne, a number of dissidents from the 1921 General Council elections joined forces with Gueye to oppose Diagne. Maitre Gueye was elected mayor of Saint-Louis in 1924.

It was during the 1930's that Gueye entered mainstream politics, twice contesting the Senegal seat in the French Parliament, in 1934 and 1936, though not elected. In 1937 he became the political director of the Senegalese Federation of the *Section Française de l'Internationale Ouvrière* (SFIO, French Socialist Party). In 1945, with the resumption of political activity, virtually at a standstill during the war years, Gueye was elected secretary-general of the SFIO federation of Senegal-Mauritania, and also as deputy for Senegal to the French Constituent Asssembly. This election precipitated the formation of a loosely structured coalition of urban associations, called the *Bloc Africain.*

One of the features of Senegalese life which exercised a determining influence on the course of the country's political life during the pre-war period was that of a two-tier status for Africans. Senegalese in the coastal communities of Saint-Louis, Goree, Dakar and Rufisque, were regarded by France as "Citizens" and had the same political rights as citizens of metropolitan France. They had a General Council and elected a deputy to the French National Assembly. With the exception of these four communes, all other Africans throughout the countries which made up the *Afrique Occidentale Française* (AOF, French West Africa) had the status of "subjects"; they had few of the rights enjoyed by "citizens" and were liable to forced labour and conscription

In the Constituent Assembly Lamine Gueye introduced a resolution which became known as the Lamine Gueye Law, on 7 May 1946. It declared all inhabitants of the colonies, including Algeria, to be French citizens "in the same category as the French nations of the metropole or of the overseas territories." Thus the old status of *sujet* was

ended and all Africans under French rule were French citizens.

This law stood even though the Constitution drawn up by the first Constituent Assembly was rejected by French voters and a new Constituent Assembly had to be elected. Gueye was a member of this also, and in 1946 he became Mayor of Dakar, a post he was to hold until 1961.

October 1946 saw the birth of a political movement which was to be of major importance in the coming struggle for independence. This was the *Rassemblement Démocratique Africain* (RDA), formed under the leadership of Félix Houphouet-Boigny of Côte d'Ivoire; as its name suggested, it was intended to be an inter-territorial union of all progressive African forces. However, the SFIO, fearing that the RDA would come under Communist control, persuaded their African deputies, and in particular Gueye and Léopold Senghor, to stay away from the founding meeting held in Bamako. This decision was crucial to the subsequent political evolution of Senegal, since for the next 12 years it divided those leaders with mass support in Senegal from their counterparts in other countries of French West Africa who adhered to the RDA.

Although elections for the Senegalese General Council in 1946 were held on a territory-wide basis, at least 35 of the 50 SFIO candidates elected were former "citizens" from the historic Four Communes. Further, all the representatives to the Assembly of the French Union and the French Senate designated by the Senegalese General Council in 1947 were pre-1946 "citizens", leaving Senghor and a small group of SFIO members in the General Council as the only elected representatives for rural "subject" voters. This continued cleavage between "citizens" of the old communes and the peasant masses, despite the Lamine Gueye Law, became more pronounced after the SFIO party congress held in September 1947, when Senghor called for a greater decentralisation in order to ensure a more equitable participation by all regional, ethnic and economic interests. He denounced what he termed Gueye's "dictatorial" leadership, alleging nepotism and the practice of clan politics in the running of the SFIO's affairs.

In 1948 Senghor led his dissident faction out of the SFIO to form the *Bloc Démocratique Sénégalais* (BDS). With its explicit objective of mass membership and multi-ethnic support, the BDS grew in popularity at the expense of the SFIO with its more elitist character. Such was the decline of the SFIO that in the 1951 elections Gueye lost his seat in the French National Assembly, while in 1952 the SFIO suffered heavy losses in the elections to the Senegalese Territorial Assembly. But while in the French Parliament Gueye had put forward a second law whch bore his name, passed in 1950, ending discrimination between Europeans and Africans in the civil service in the "Overseas territories".

Meanwhile the RDA had been carefully building up its organisation and influence at grass roots level, so that in the 1956 elections to the French Assembly, RDA candidates won 9 seats. As a result, Houphouet-Boigny was given a full cabinet post and was directly involved in drafting the colonial *loi-cadre* (enabling law) of 23 June 1956. This was the law which established the institutional framework for autonomy in France's associated territories. It proved to be a turning point in the political evolution of West Africa, bringing to a head the issues of federation and independence, over which opinion in West Africa was deeply divided. The law's introduction of universal suffrage and the conferment of much extended powers to local assemblies constituted a definite step forward, but it was criticised as granting inadequate autonomy and likely to lead to the balkanisation of West Africa. The reaction of the Socialists to the proposals of the *loi-cadre* differed sharply from those of the RDA and of Senghor. At a meeting in Conakry in January 1957, Gueye founded a new party, the *Mouvement Socialiste Africain* (MSA) together with Djibo Bakary of Niger and Fily Dabo Sissoko (q.v.) of the Soudan. The MSA declared itself satisfied with the proposals of the *loi-cadre*, which involved the break-up of the former territorial entities, and willing to suspend any decision on federation. In the March 1957 elections to implement the terms of the *loi-cadre*, the RDA, with its firm anti-federalist stance, won the majority of seats in French West Africa as a whole, although Senghor's inter-territorial *Convention Africaine* party, in favour of a federal solution, made the best showing in Senegal.

In early 1958 the MSA joined with the *Convention Africaine* on the inter-territorial plane to create the *Parti du Regroupement Africain* (PRA). In the same year also, faced

with the strength of the RDA, Gueye decided to merge his party with Senghor's *Bloc Populaire Sénégalais* (formerly the *Bloc Démocratique Sénégalais*) to form a new party, the *Union Progressiste Sénégalaise* (UPS).

At the PRA's congress held in Cotonou, in July 1958, Gueye declared himself in favour of unconditional independence and the congress adopted a resolution in favour of immediate independence. However, a later PRA meeting in Niamey decided to allow each territorial section in Africa a free vote in de Gaulle's September 1958 referendum: this poll resulted in a vote against immediate independence, except in French Guinea.

In January 1959 Senegal joined with the Soudan to form the Mali Federation. In March of the same year the UPS won all the seats in the Senegal elections and Lamine Gueye was elected President of the Senegal National Asssembly, a position which he held until his death. The Mali Federation became independent on 20 June 1960 only to break up two months later in August. One reported reason for the break-up was that Modibo Keita (q.v.), President of Mali and Prime Minister of the Soudan, had decided to back Lamine Gueye for President of the Federation in place of Senghor, as had formerly been agreed.

Gueye died on 10 June 1968 and was buried in a great official funeral. He had earlier published his life story as *Itinéraire Africain*.■

Gumede, J.T. (1870-1947)

GUMEDE, Josiah Tshangana (c.1870-1947).

SOUTH AFRICAN journalist and nationalist politician. He was editor of the first Zulu newspaper *Ilanga Lase Natal* (The Natal Sun). Born in about 1870, he had his early education at the Natal College in Grahamstown in the Cape Province, and on completion went into teaching in Somerset East and then Natal. He left the profession and took on various jobs, first as a land agent for a white-owned company in Pietermaritzburg and later as a storekeeper. He subsequently took to singing, and toured Europe in 1892 on singing engagements with a Zulu choir. During this period Gumede developed interest in the nationalist politics of his country, and took the first steps towards a political career when he became an adviser to various chiefs in Natal and the Orange

J.T. Gumede

Free State. In this capacity he joined the African delegation which visited London in 1906 to petition the British government about the acquisition of Sotho land in the Orange Free State.

Gumede co-founded the Natal Native Congress (NNC) in 1901, serving at various times as its secretary and vice-president under Reverend John Lengalibalele Dube (q.v.). Between 1914 and 1918 Gumede worked as editor of the *Ilanga Lase Natal*, the first African newspaper to be published in South Africa, founded in 1903 by Dube to support the campaign of the Natal Native Congress. The newspaper was printed in Ohlanga and issued in both Zulu and English. The two leaders parted company in the early 1920s when they had a policy disagree-

ment over what direction the NNC should follow. Gumede then formed the Natal branch of the ANC in 1926, having been a co-founder of the South African Native National Congress that became the ANC in 1912. Gumede was an important organiser in the 1920 African mine workers' strike in the Rand.

He was elected president of the ANC between 1927 and 1930 and during this period encouraged grass-roots participation in the activities of the movement. In 1927 he led the ANC delegation to the first international conference of the League Against Imperialism that was held in Brussels, Belgium, and visited Moscow later that same year as guest of the Soviet government. Gumede developed closer links with the South African Communist Party and openly supported some of its positions. He joined the party's League of African Rights in 1929 and became president of the association.

This overt fraternisation with the Communist Party and Gumede's radical propositions which included the demand for a "Native Republic" caused a backlash among the ranks of the ANC who wanted to maintain its independent status. He was subsequently voted out of the presidency of the movement at its 1930 annual conference where his re-election was contested by Pixley ka Isaka Seme (q.v.) who was supported by Dube. Gumede lost to Seme by a vote of 39 to 14, but he remained loyal to the movement. He retained his position as proprietor of its organ, the *Abantu-Batho* and continued to make regular contributions to it until his death in 1947. ■

Gungunyane (c. 1850-1906)

GUNGUNYANE, King (c.1850-1906).

MOZAMBICAN resistance leader, last independent ruler of the Gaza kingdom before its integration into modern Mozambique. His father, Umzila, ruled the empire until 1884 and it was during his reign that Gungunyane was born, in about 1850. When Umzila died in 1884 the heir to the kingship was 35 years old. He assumed power after a bitter battle for succession. The defeated candidates took refuge in neighbouring hostile countries where their presence and the incursions of the European colonial powers posed a two-pronged challenge to the new king.

Gungunyane succeeded to a large extent in preserving the unity of his empire

King Gungunyane

by suppressing rebellions, notably among the Chope in the south. But maintaining the independence of the Gaza Empire, in the face of the intensive activities of the Portuguese

and the British on its borders, proved less successful. In 1889 he relocated the seat of his government at the mouth of the River Limpopo in the south. The move from the Manica highlands, involving Gungunyane's household and some sixty thousand people, had a tremendous effect on the empire's troubled state; its social life was destabilised while the economy, already strained by war, was dislocated. The ensuing vulnerability was exploited by the Portuguese the following years in the war to establish their rule; and the decline of the Gaza kingdom was rapid.

Still hoping to maintain links with the British, Gungunyane in 1890 welcomed an agent of Cecil Rhodes's British South Africa Company, thinking he was a representative of the British government. The agent was seeking mining concessions in the country, like the one the company had obtained from Lobengula (q.v.), King of the Ndebele, in 1888, which facilitated the creation of Rhodesia (now Zimbabwe), under British rule. Some records have indicated that Gungunyane was willing to enter into a treaty with the British South Africa Company, but an agreement between Britain and Portugal in 1891 placed Mozambique under the influence of the Portuguese, thus ending the rivalry between the two colonial powers and the commencement of the military campaign against Gungunyane.

After a protracted battle lasting four years, Gungunyane's army succumbed to the superior fire-power of the Portuguese in 1895. The king was captured, dethroned and deported that year. During his exile in the Azores, a Portuguese possession in the north Atlantic, his troops, commanded by Maguiguana, revolted against the Portuguese in 1898 but were ruthlessly suppressed. Gungunyane died in captivity in 1906.■

H

Habte-Wolde, A. (1912-74)

HABTE-WOLDE, Aklilu (1912-74).

ETHIOPIAN politician. He was born on 12 March 1912, in Addis Ababa, where he attended the Menelik School before reading law at the Sorbonne in Paris. He joined government service in 1936 and, following the Italian occupation of Ethiopia the same year, became head of the Ethiopian Legation in Paris, but in 1940, when the Germans occupied the French capital, Habte-Wolde joined Emperor Haile Selassie (q.v.) in exile.

After the liberation of Ethiopia from the Italians, he returned to the country in 1941 and was appointed to the government as Vice-Minister for Foreign Affairs. For

A. Habte-Wolde

the next 30 years Habte-Wolde played an important role in formulating and executing Ethiopia's foreign policy, a role that aided his election as the first African Vice-Chairman of the United Nations General Assembly.

Habte-Wolde's ability and influence were of significance in 1950 when he successfully argued for the UN adoption of his government's proposal for the reunification of the former Italian colony of Eritrea with Ethiopia. In later years he played an equally prominent role in the realisation of the desire of the newly independent African countries to form a Pan-African forum, officially constituted as the Organisation of African Unity (OAU) in Addis Ababa in 1963.

Habte-Wolde was appointed Deputy Prime Minister in 1957, in addition to the portfolio of Foreign Affairs. Following the mutiny by the Imperial Guards in 1960, he was appointed Prime Minister and the Emperor's spokesman in 1961.

As head of government he had to deal with Ethiopia's immediate problems of widespread clamour for reforms and the growing accusations of corruption in the administration. Added to this was the tension on the border with Somalia, incited and supported by the Eritreans who opposed their annexation with Ethiopia, which was at its worst in 1963. But after the 1969 military coup in Somalia, Habte-Wolde worked hard to improve relations with the country and even visited it. In 1972 his peace efforts with the Sudan were more successful.

In the late sixties, Habte-Wolde had made himself rather unpopular when he had supported the Land tax, and the Ministry of Planning and Development was merged with his own office. The problems were made worse by the disastrous famine of 1973, and the government's handling of the relief operation brought further discontent and unrest. Habte-Wolde was forced to resign as

Prime Minister in February 1974, paving way for the gradual accession of the military. He was later arrested and executed on 23 November 1974, in the purge that followed the overthrow of Emperor Haile Selassie. ■

Hached, F. (1914-52)

HACHED, Farhat (1914-52).

TUNISIAN trade unionist, who founded his country's first independent trade union body. He was born on 2 February 1914 in Abasssa, a village in the Kerkennah Islands off Sfax.

After completing primary education in 1929 Farhat Hached went to Sousse where he joined the Tunisian Automobile Transport Company of the Sahel (STTAS) as a

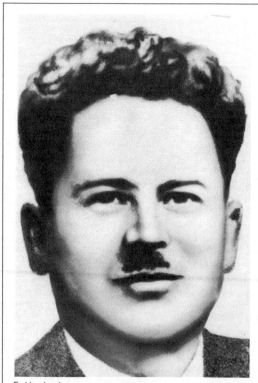

F. Hached

clerk and later as inspector of roads until 1939. It was during this period that he began his trade union activities, facilitated by a 1932 law which allowed the formation of unions in Tunisia and Algeria.

In 1939 Hached began efforts to organise a new trade union organisation to be independent of the French *Confédération Générale du Travail* (CGT), which started a branch in Tunisia in 1938. After the Second World War his efforts succeeded in the formation of the *Union Générale des Travailleurs Tunisiens* (UGTT). The UGTT, constituted in January 1946, was and still is the umbrella organisation for the various independent unions in the country; its activities in the late 1940s and early 1950s were directed essentially against French colonialism. As leader of the UGTT, Hached worked closely with the leaders of Tunisia's nationalist movements, the Destour Party and the Neo-Destour Party, especially the latter, as in 1951 when the three-day nation-wide strike he organised to support the demand for independence was backed by the parties. In fact the UGTT was by then a firm ally of the Neo-Destour.

Hached is best remembered for having established his country's first national union that had no ties with the unions of the metropolis. The CGT had for years a Tunisian branch, rival of the UGTT. Against strong opposition from the French CGT, he succeeded in bringing the UGTT into the World Federation of Trade Unions (WFTU) where he was to seek international support for the Tunisian cause; and in 1950 the UGTT moved into the rival International Confederation of Free Trade Unions (ICFTU). Such was Hached's influence that the French feared that he could pressurize the United Nations into accepting a Tunisian complaint lodged against France at the General Assembly. The backing of the ICFTU, which was in turn backed by the USA, inhibited French action against the UGTT. But he was assassinated in Tunisia on 5 December 1952, on the eve of the UN debate.

This was during unrest that was directed against French rule, in which the Neo-Destour and its close ally the UGTT led the opposition. A French settlers' terrorist organisation, determined to oppose Tunisian self-government through violent means, was found to have been responsible for the trade union leader's death. ■

Haile Selassie I (1892-1975)

HAILE SELASSIE I, Emperor (1892-1975).

ETHIOPIAN monarch. He was born in Ejersa Goro, Harar Province, on 23 July 1892, the son of Ras (Prince) Makonnen, cousin of Emperor Menelik II (q.v.). His name at birth was Lij Tafari Makonnen but he chose his name of Haile Selassie I, "Power of the Trinity", on ascending the throne in 1930. He became the 225th ruler of Ethiopia, in direct descent from King Solomon and the Queen of Sheba.

Ras Tafari's early education consisted of private lessons in Amharic and Geez and later in French, arithmetic, geography and history, taught by a priest from the French Mission in Harar, followed by formal schooling at Menelik School in Addis Ababa. In 1906, at the age of 13, Tafari's father named him his heir and appointed him governor of Gara Muleta. At 14, he became governor of

Emperor Haile Selassie

Selalie, at 16 governor of Sidamo, and later governor of Harar in 1910, succeeding his father who had died in 1906.

As governor of Harar and Sidamo, then Ethiopia's richest province, he tried to introduce a programme of social and economic reform. His ideas were not welcomed by the powerful conservative forces of oligarchy, but against stiff opposition Tafari instituted reforms to reduce feudal influence.

In 1916 Tafari was proclaimed regent and heir to the throne on the deposition of Menelik's grandson Lij Yasu. On 2 November 1930 the 38-year-old Tafari succeeded Empress Zawditu to the Imperial Throne and was crowned Haile Selassie I, Emperor of Ethiopia, Elect of God, King of Kings (*Negusa Nagast*), and Conquering Lion of the Tribe of Judah. The new Emperor set out to introduce a centralised system of government. In the first year of his reign he introduced proposals for a written constitution, a parliament and an independent judicial system. He outlawed slave trading and encouraged parents to send their sons to school. He paid particular attention to the development of health services and broadening of the educational system. Unfortunately, he could not do much before Italy, in violation of international law, invaded Ethiopia in October 1935.

The Emperor went into exile, but not without first resisting the occupation of his country. However, the arms embargo imposed by the European powers and the Emperor's unsuccessful appeals to the League of Nations to intervene made the country virtually helpless. In May 1936 he left Addis Ababa for Britain, from where he would return in 1940 to lead the war of liberation. He re-entered Ethiopia from the Sudan at the head of the resistance. Three months later, the Ethiopians defeated the Italians and on 5 May 1941, five years after the invasion, the Emperor returned in triumph to Addis Ababa.

A deeply religious man, the Emperor proclaimed that his people must follow Christian principles and forego acts of revenge against the captured Italian soldiers, about sixty thousand of them, despite the atrocities this army is said to have committed during the occupation. He immediately embarked on strengthening Ethiopia's independence and by 1945 he had firmly established the supremacy of the central government.

In 1950, Haile Selassie introduced a three-point programme for the expansion of education, improvement of communications and development of more opportunities for employment. In 1930, when he became Emperor, Ethiopia had less than ten schools. By 1954, there were ten thousand elementary church schools, 416 state schools, 24 secondary schools and ten schools of higher educaton.

Once stability had been restored (apart from occasional regional uprisings) the conditions for reform improved. In 1955, he promulgated a new constitution which brought Ethiopia its first parliament, elected in 1957. Yet the Emperor was fearful of the consequences of too sweeping reform, and he relinquished very little of his absolute power to the directly elected Assembly of Deputies. As it turned out, this policy worked to his detriment, for in 1960 while he was on a state visit to Brazil, there was a revolt by a section of the Imperial Guards who attempted to dethrone him. The army and the air force remained loyal to the Emperor, who returned to Addis Ababa and crushed the attempted coup. This was the first major challenge to his authority. The widespread sympathy expresssed for the rebels, especially by the young educated Ethiopians, was not only an indication of serious political opposition to his authority, but also an expression of resentment at his lack of realistic comprehension of the ills afflicting Ethiopian society.

As the years went by the ageing Emperor became disengaged from the affairs of the state. This disengagement continued with the relinquishment in 1966 of the Ministry of Foreign Affairs which he had held since becoming Emperor. His foreign policy was aimed at securing not only peace and independence for his country but also international respect for Ethiopia which was admitted into the League of Nations in 1923, and later into its successor the United Nations Organisation (UN). In 1950 Ethiopian troops were part of the UN contingent in Korea; there was a similar contribution later in the Congo.

In the Africa of the early 1960s Selassie's influence could be seen on emerging states. The Emperor modified his foreign policy partly, from pro-West to pan-African and non-aligned, in tune with the growing African opinion.

He visited many African capitals, participating in successful mediation in interstate disputes, and helped pave the way for the evolution of continental unity. In 1963, he played a leading role in convening the first conference of African Heads of State, which led to the formation of the OAU. Earlier, in 1962, he had led the Ethiopian delegation to a similar conference of African states in Lagos. In later years the Emperor turned increasingly to the role of mediator in African disputes, as in the 1967-70 Nigerian civil war, when he helped organise peace talks in Addis Ababa in 1968. In 1972, he played a major part in ending Sudan's internal war between the Khartoum government and the Anya Nya guerrillas. Ethiopia's own dispute with Somalia had died down by 1970.

At home success was more remote, as the challenge to his authority increased. In 1962 Eritreans, opposed to the 1952 union of the province with Ethiopia, formed the Eritrean Liberation Front (ELF) to fight against what they regarded as "Ethiopia's annexation". They intensified their campaign in early 1970 and by November the Emperor declared a state of emergency in the province, deploying half of the Ethiopian Army and Air Force against the guerrillas.

Matters came to a head in 1973 when the country was hit by severe drought and famine, killing, according to some estimates, about 100,000 people. There was general discontent at the government's apparent failure to recognise the severity of the crisis, and there followed a wave of strikes in the towns, students' demonstrations and a mutiny of the armed forces.

In April 1974, members of the armed forces formed the Military Co-ordinating Committee (MCC), later named the Dergue. The MCC succeeded in making itself a permanent body working with the Cabinet on 3 July 1974. It then called for a new constitution stripping the Emperor of many of his traditional powers. A series of arrests were later announced which affected government ministers and other civil servants. The MCC explained that the aim of the arrests was to pave the way for reforms and legal action against suspected wrongdoers in government, without touching the Crown to which they said they remained loyal. Proposals for a new constitution were announced on 7 August 1974 and the MCC later moved to further reduce the power of the Emperor. On 17 August the commander of the Emperor's Imperial Guards was arrested, the Emperor's governing body, the Crown Council, was dissolved on 18 August and his residence, the Jubilee Palace, was nationalised on 25 August. On 12 September 1974 the Dergue announced the deposition of the Emperor and the formation of a provisional military government headed by Lieutenant-General Aman Michael Andom (q.v.).

Throughout 1974 Emperor Haile Selassie went through the final stages of his eclipse as all his officials and associates were dismissed or abandoned him. Even the church leaders with whom he had worked closely, dissociated themselves from him, and the process of his isolation received acceleration from the popular indignation caused by reports that he and his family had enriched themselves at the expense of the Ethiopian people. He was later accused by the Dergue of having used public funds for his personal benefit and of having amassed several hundred million pounds in Swiss bank accounts. He signed approval for transfer of his money to the country as a whole after he was deposed. He was then kept in the military barracks in Addis Ababa. Later he was returned to the former Palace, where he died on 27 August 1975.

His wife Menen predeceased him in 1962. His son Asfa Wossen nominally succeeded him as King in 1974, before the declaration of a Republic in early 1975. Haile Selassie left other children, and grandchildren. Asfa Wossen and many of the family went into exile.■

Hainyeko, T. (1932-67)

HAINYEKO, Tobias (1932-67).

NAMIBIAN political and military leader. He was the first commander of the People's Liberation Army of Namibia (PLAN), the military wing of the South West Africa People's Organisation (SWAPO), the nationalist movement dedicated to achieving independence for Namibia and putting an end to South African colonial rule. PLAN was founded in the mid-1960s.

Hainyeko was born in 1932 in northern

T. Hainyeko

Namibia, where he grew up. In the early 1950s he moved to Cape Town in South Africa. He worked there for some time, and met other Namibians working or studying in the Cape Town area. Cape Town was then an important centre for Namibians who had left their country to escape the brutal contract labour system imposed by South Africa. It was also a centre of political and cultural activities in which the Namibians became involved. Later Namibian leaders such as Herman ya Toivo, Jariretunda Kozonguizi, Jacob Kuhangua, and many others, as well as Hainyeko, spent valuable years in Cape Town, sharing political experience and work. Most of them were either members or sympathisers of the forerunner of SWAPO, the Ovambo People's Congress (OPC).

He returned to Namibia but left the country in the early 1960s to promote the cause of Namibian independence in international circles. In December 1959 the South African occupation force shot at a peaceful demonstration of Namibians in Windhoek, killing eleven people and wounding many more. The demonstrations were against the forced removal of Namibians from the Old Location to the new apartheid-built township of Katutura. The brutality of the South African response to the demonstration itself, and to the political activities which followed it, forced many Namibians to leave the country to work politically from abroad.

In April 1960 SWAPO was formed as an expression of the will of the Namibian people to act in unity to end South African rule. From its inception SWAPO foresaw the need to train Namibians for both military and logistic operations to achieve its aims. The end result of this was the formation of PLAN in which Hainyeko played a key part.

When Hainyeko left Namibia he went to Dar-es-Salaam together with others, and was one of the first SWAPO cadres to volunteer for military training. He proved himself, during training in the Soviet Union, to be not only a skilful and courageous fighter, but also a man of tremendous leadership quality. He returned to East Africa to help set up a military training centre for PLAN. It was from here that Hainyeko brought all the trained cadres together and moved to establish the first guerrilla force for the liberation of Namibia. Shortly thereafter, in 1965, through careful planning under Hainyeko, SWAPO established a key base at Omgulumbashe in northern Namibia, as well as training centres within the country. It was from the Omgulumbashe base that SWAPO launched its armed struggle against the South African occupation regime on 26 August 1966.

SWAPO's early military attacks on South African occupation troops in Namibia were occasional incidents carried out by small groups of cadres. PLAN grew into an army many thousands strong, equipped with sophisticated artillery, enabling SWAPO to establish bases within Namibia and control large areas, especially in the north, where South African troops only operated with massive air cover.

Hainyeko was killed in action on the Zambezi River on 27 May 1967, while on a routine mission to the eastern region (Caprivi strip). He is remembered and honoured by the Namibian people as a brave fighter and a hero of the liberation struggle, who gave his life for his country.∎

Hama, B. (1906-82)

HAMA, Boubou (1906-82).

NIGER politician and historian, the right-hand man of Hamani Diori who ruled the country for 15 years. Boubou Hama

was equally famous as a scholar who worked for years on recording Niger's history from oral and written sources.

He was born in 1906 at Foneko in the Tera area, son of the village head, about the time of the French occupation. Boubou

B. Hama

Hama went to French schools first at Tera, then at Dori and Ouagadougou in Burkina Faso (formerly Upper Volta). Then, from 1926 to 1929, he studied at the William Ponty teachers' training college in Dakar, where he qualified as a government school teacher. He taught for nearly twenty years at Niamey and Tillabery in Niger, and in Burkina Faso, among other places. His pupils included Hamani Diori (q.v.), ten years his junior, who later also became a teacher.

In 1946, when political activity was allowed for Africans in the French territories, Hama took part in the foundation of the *Rassemblement Démocratique Africain* (RDA). He and Hamani Diori worked closely together in the *Parti Progressiste Nigérien* (PPN), founded in 1946 as the Niger branch of the RDA. At first the PPN and other branches of the RDA were strongly opposed to the French colonial regime, and Hama, still working as a teacher, clashed frequently with the government and was threatened with sacking. He never gave in to pressure; later he said, "the RDA was not only a political movement for me, it was my country, even my family".

However, the PPN followed most of the RDA policies in establishing good relations with the colonial government in 1951. In Niger one faction, headed by Djibo Bakary, broke away in protest at this and formed another party, the *Mouvement Socialiste Africain* (MSA), later called Sawaba. Diori and Hama remained leaders of the PPN; with Diamballa Maiga, they were at its head for about 20 years. Hama became a member of the Niger Territorial Council in 1947 and then a member of the Grand Council of French West Africa (*Afrique Occidentale Française* – AOF); he served there until 1958. He was also a member until 1952 of the Council of the French Union, a consultative body representing the French empire (then called the French Union) in Paris.

The PPN lost the elections to the French National Assembly in Niger in 1956; following the grant of internal self-government under the 1956 *Loi-Cadre* (Enabling Law) for French colonies, the elections to Niger's new Assembly in 1957 led to another PPN defeat and Bakary, leader of the victorious MSA, became vice-president of the Executive Council, with a Frenchman at its head. In 1956, however, Hama was elected to the Niamey town council; he served as deputy mayor of the capital until 1959.

In 1959, Boubou Hama was appointed director of the Niger section of the *Institut Français de l'Afrique Noire* (IFAN). IFAN was later renamed *Institut Fondamental d'Afrique Noire*), a Dakar-based research institute dealing with scientific research and also historical studies for which Hama was to become famous. He held that post until 1957.

In 1958, after the return of de Gaulle to power in France, a referendum was held in the colonies asking them to decide for or against de Gaulle's planned French Community, in which each colony would have full internal self-government but not complete independence. In Niger, the Sawaba party which was then in power, campaigned for rejection, but the PPN succeeded in securing a majority vote in favour. Three months later in December 1958, elections in Niger led to a heavy defeat for Sawaba. The PPN came to power, with 49 out of the 60 Assembly seats. Niger thus obtained full self-government within the French Community under a PPN government, headed by Diori. Boubou Hama became president of the National Assembly of Niger and also a member of the Senate of the French Community.

The French Community and its Senate soon disappeared and Niger, with other French African territories, became independent in 1960. Hama retained his presidency of the Assembly continuously until 1974. He was President Diori's closest colleague and, it was said, a power behind the throne. The Assembly over which he presided soon became a one-party parliament; Sawaba was banned in October 1959 and after years of resistance, which was at its strongest in 1963-64, was effectively suppressed. The one-party regime of the PPN came to be resented for what its critics termed dictatorship and corruption, and Boubou Hama was said to have become an unpopular character in Niamey.

However, he also became well known in his country and elsewhere as a scholar. He took particular interest in the oral traditions of the peoples of Niger. He built up a collection of manuscripts and published books and articles of traditional accounts of history. His book *Kotia Nima*, a semi-biographical novel published by *Présence Africaine* of Paris, won the *Grand Prix Littéraire de l'Afrique Noire* in 1970. He helped in the selection of an editorial board for the *Histoire Générale de l'Afrique Noire*, a multi-volume work under the auspices of UNESCO, whose first volumes have now appeared.

Besides writing historical and ethnographic works, he also wrote a number of fictitious stories, some being traditional legends. These stories include *l'Aventure extraordinaire de Bi Kado, fils de noirs* (1971) and, most important, the six-volume *Contes et légendes du Niger*, (1972-76) by *Présence Africaine*. His other writings include *Histoire du Gobir et de Sokoto* (1967); *Recherche sur l'histoire des Touareg sahariens et soudanais* (1967); *l'Exode rural un problème de fond* about the "drift to the towns" (1968); *Contribution à la connaissance de l'Histoire des Peuls*, on the Fulanis' history (1968); *Histoire des Songhay*, recalling his people's past (1968); *Essai d'Analyse de l'éducation africaine* (1968); *Histoire Traditionnelle d'un village Songhay: Fonéko* (1970); *le Retard de l'Afrique* (1972); *L'Empire Songhay: ses ethnies, ses légendes et ses personnages historiques* (1974); *les Grands Problèmes de l'Afrique des Indépendances* (1974). In all he published about fifty titles, very many of them when he was an active politician.

On 15 April 1974, in the midst of serious famine caused by the great Sahara drought, the Diori regime was overthrown, accused of adding to the people's sufferings through corruption, hoarding of food, and inefficiency. The new military regime under Colonel Seyni Kountche arrested Boubou Hama among other leaders of the fallen regime. Later he was convicted of embezzlement of 26 million CFA francs and tax evasion amounting to 12 million. He was detained first at Agadez in the far north, then at the Bagadji Iya camp in Niamey. When interviewed there he said, "One cannot regret having handed over power to one's children. These officers were all our pupils and are our children. We can only wish them every success". While in detention he asked only for paper; this was to continue his scholarly writing, and he recalled, "I never worked so well".

In July 1977 he was released, partly because of his age and partly in response to quiet pleading on his behalf. He lived in Niamey for a few years where he died on 29 January 1982. President Kountche paid his respects to "the old Boubou", who had been a well-known figure in Niamey. By the time of his death, having paid the penalty for involvement in a discredited government through imprisonment, he was generally respected as a scholar and a patriarchal character. ■

Hamallah, A. (c.1883-1943)

HAMALLAH (HAMAHOULLAH), Sheikh Ahmedou (c.1883-1943).

MAURITANIAN religious leader. He was of the Ahel Moh'ammed Mohammed Sidi Cherif clan of Tichitt, Mauritania, but his grandfather moved to a place about 40 miles north of Nora, in territory which became part of French Soudan after the conquest which began at the time of Ahmedou Hamahoullah's birth. Later he followed his father to Nioro, an important town in French Soudan, near the border with Mauritania. Ahmedou Hamahoullah and his brother went back to what later became

Mauritania (then not yet colonised) in 1895 for Islamic schooling. He did very well and became noted for precocious understanding of his religion. On returning to Nioro Hamahoullah who came to be known as Hamallah, maintained this reputation. He joined the Tijaniyya order,which like other Islamic orders or brotherhoods (*turuq*) preached a special way of contact with God. It was founded by an Algerian, at-Tijani, and later spread in the upper Niger-Senegal area by the conquering scholar and preacher al-Hajj 'Umar (q.v.) who died in 1864. It continued to spread in 'Umar's former domains, and other areas nearby, before and after the French occupation.

In 1900 an Algerian sent from the home country of the Tijaniyya to help the "Western Soudan" disciples, Sheikh Sidi Mohammed Lakhdar, arrived in Nioro. He had been told to find the man already destined to lead the local Tijaniyya as Khalifa. According to his followers' account, Ahmedou Hamallah was the man selected, after a test which apparently related to particular beliefs of the Tijaniyya. The Algerian chose him as successor and, on his death in 1909, Hamallah became Khalifa of a number of Tijaniyya Moslems around Nioro.

In the next few years he was renowned as a devout, pious and simple *marabout*(Moslem teacher and spiritual leader), who received many gifts but also gave out many. His followers were soon found over a wide area, including his country of origin, Mauritania. This popularity worried the French, and Hamallah also showed an attitude of reserve to the colonial authorities. He did not oppose them as rival leaders alleged, but he did keep cooperation with them to the minimum and encourage his followers to do the same. His followers, however, frequently fought with other Moslems, and this was used by the French as a pretext for action against a *marabout* whom they had been watching suspiciously from an early date.

After several clashes between 1917 and 1923, a major one occurred in Nioro in 1924, and in the following year Hamallah was arrested. He was deported from French Soudan for ten years' internment in Mauritania. He was well treated there, at Mederda, but after a clash between his supporters and other Moslems in another part of Mauritania, at Kaedi, in 1930, he was accused of fomenting them. He was then deported to

Côte d'Ivoire, where he remained until 1936. Then – like another *marabout*, Ahmadou Bamba (q.v.) of Senegal, before him – he returned from deportation to a hero's welcome. He returned to Nioro, whence he still commanded a large following.

Once again, however, a clash involving "Hamallists" was used by the French as a pretext for action against their leader. This time it was on the border of French Soudan and Mauritania. The Vichy French government, in control of French West Africa after the events of mid-1940, decided that Hamallah should be deported for ten years. He was arrested in June 1941, with most leading "Hamallists" at Nioro. Hamallah was deported to Algeria and then, in 1942, to France.

He was detained with French politicians held by the Vichy regime, at Evaux-les-Bains, where he fell ill and died on 16 January 1943, although Africans of French West Africa were not officially told of his death until 1945. An Ivorian later located Hamallah's grave in France and had his remains reinterred in a new one, still in France. Hamallah's followers remained active after 1943, and were said to have formed the core of the *Rassemblement Démocratique Africain* (RDA), the main political party which coordinated the campaign for independence in French West Africa.■

Hanga, M. (died 1910)

HANGA, Makombe (died 1910).

MOZAMBICAN resistance leader who for twenty three years, from 1887 till his death, led a number of anti-colonial campaigns. King of the Barue country, a Shona-related polity south of the Zambezi River, now in modern Mozambique, he was the last independent ruler of Barue before it fell to the Portuguese. His father Makombe Chipapata ruled Barue from about 1845 until he was killed in battle in 1887 against Portuguese agents.

No sooner had Hanga commenced his reign in 1887 than there emerged a prolonged succession crisis, in which the new King had battles with European-backed contenders for the throne such as Samancande, Chipituta, Cassiche, and Cavunda. In the decisive 1901 battle, Hanga succeeded in ending the challenge to his authority by forcing Cavunda into exile. This achieved, he turned his attention to establishing relations with German and British agents in the region. Hanga was particularly interested in establishing diplomatic relations with the British as a safeguard against possible Portuguese invasion. In 1898 he sought British assurances of military assistance in the event of war but his request was rejected. The British officials instead assured him safety in British-controlled Rhodesia (Zimbabwe) if he should seek refuge there.

Hanga's preoccupation with Barue's independence led to further diplomatic contacts, this time with his neighbours. He was aware that the survival of Barue was inextricably linked to that of the neighbours and, accordingly, entered into marriage and political alliances with them. Among these polities was the Mazoe, under Paitando Mapondera (q.v.), across the Zambezi River in Rhodesia. The alliance with Mapondera proved a decisive force in the subsequent 1902 war against the Portuguese. Prior to the battle Hanga had built a fort of about 10,000 soldiers armed with more than seven thousand guns which he acquired from European dealers who bought Barue's ivory and gold. Prior to the war also he encouraged the development of small ammunition factories at Mungari and Missongue, two important Barue centres.

During the Portuguese military incursion which began on 30 July 1902, Hanga's son Cantete was killed. By the end of that year Barue's army had surrendered to the superior power of the colonial forces. Hanga led his followers into exile in Southern Rhodesia where they were later to mastermind the 1904 Shona rebellion against the British. His lieutenants that were captured in the 1902 Barue war were deported to Portuguese territories in West Africa.

The 1902 defeat and Hanga's exile marked the end of Barue's independence and autonomy. With little or no resistance the polity was brought under Portuguese rule. But before he died in 1910 Hanga named his oldest son Chikuwore as successor and gave him the praise name *Nongwe-Nongwe*, which means "you shall have to". In 1917 *Nongwe-Nongwe* led his people against the Portuguese, in what became known as the Barue Insurrection.

Hanga's gallant resistance evidently

inspired later generations of Mozambican politicians who resisted Portuguese rule continuously until 1975 when the *Frente de Libertaçao de Mocambique* (FRELIMO) brought the country to independence.

At independence, President Samora Machel acknowledged this when he said, "From the resistance of the Muenemutapa to the insurrecton of Barue, Mozambican history prides itself on the glorious deeds of the masses in the struggle for the defence of freedom and independence. The defeat of the historic resistance of the People is due exclusively to the treason of the feudal ruling classes, to their greed and ambition, which allowed the enemy to divide the People and so conquer it". ■

Harbi, M. (1921-60)

HARBI, Mahmoud (1921-60).

DJIBOUTI politician. He was born at Ali-Sabieh in southern French Somaliland (later renamed Djibouti) in 1921. His parents were Somali Issa. He became a shopkeeper in his birthplace and his early interest in nationalist politics led him to become a leading member of the Somali and Dankali Youth Organisaton. He rapidly became a radical nationalist leader and his great oratorical skills, combined with his anti-colonial sentiments, gained him great popularity.

In 1951 he was nominated by the Dalols to become a Somaliland representative in the Senate of the French Republic. However, the Abgal nominated Hassan Gouled, later the territory's first President, for this position and although Harbi tried to challenge this decision, he was unsuccessful. Harbi then became involved in the Somali labour movement and under his leadership a strike was held in the Port of Djibouti, stopping the movement of goods for four days. The government agreed to all the demands of the strikers and this greatly increased Harbi's popularity. He also received a great deal of support from the many non-European foreign communities living in Djibouti. In 1956 he was elected member of the French National Assembly.

The following year elections were held for a new territorial Assembly. Harbi founded the *Union Républicaine* to contest these elections on a platform of independence for French Somaliland and the eventual unification of Somali territories. His party won all 30 seats in the Assembly and Harbi became Vice-President of the newly established Council of Ministers under the presidency of the French governor, as well as Prime Minister and Minister of the Port and Public Works.

In September 1958 a referendum was held regarding the future status of the colony: whether it should become completely independent from France or have limited autonomy within the French Community. Harbi campaigned vigorously for independence so as to pave the way for a union with Somalia, but the majority of the people voted to stay as part of the French Community. Harbi's stand for independence and his defeat in the referendum led the French authorities to consider that his government was unrepresentative and the territorial Assembly was dissolved and new elections were held in November 1958. There was much tension in Djibouti at this time and after violent demonstrations the *Union Républicaine* was banned. Harbi formed a new party, the *Union Démocratique Somalienne*, but gained only seven seats in the new Assembly.

Shortly afterwards he went to Paris and while he was there many of his supporters in French Somaliland were imprisoned. He himself was sentenced *in absentia* to ten years' imprisonment and rather than return home, he went into voluntary exile in Cairo. While there he continued to work for a union of Somali territories and in 1959 moved to Mogadishu, becoming a founding member of the National Pan-Somali Movement. He later visited the People's Republic of China and Eastern Europe, and was killed on his way back to Mogadishu in a plane crash on 29 September 1960. ■

Harris, W.W. (c.1865-1929)

HARRIS, William Wade (c.1865-1929).

LIBERIAN clergyman. Born about 1865 at Half-Graway, he received part of his education from the Reverend Jesse Lowris of the Methodist Episcopal Mission. He first worked for a time on ships, before becoming a Methodist Episcopal lay preacher at Cape Palmas.

He worked his way from being an assistant teacher and catechist to becoming in charge of the Mission's boarding school at Half-Graway. In 1907 he was appointed a government interpreter. But he was dismissed from that post in 1908, in the following year he was suspected by the Liberian government of complicity in an alleged plot by the British Consul and the British commander of the Frontier Force. Despite lack of evidence he spent some time in prison where he later claimed to have had a vision in which the Archangel Gabriel said he would be a prophet.

On his release in 1912 Harris put on a white robe and began to preach on his own. In the south-east part of French Côte d'Ivoire, at Grand Lahou, Dabou, the Gold Coast (Ghana) and other places, he won many adherents by preaching a Christian doctrine that stressed the abandonment of witchcraft beliefs and related practices.

In the latter part of 1914 he returned to Côte d'Ivoire and conducted his most spectacular conversion effort. In a few months thousands of people followed his form of Christianity and were baptised by him and his disciples. He was believed to have power of exorcism. He told people to obey the French government, which at first approved his teaching, especially for his advocacy of hard work and temperance. But the French became worried about the possible results of the mass religious movement, and at the end of 1914 he was arrested and apparently ill-treated, and then deported back to Liberia.

The mass conversion in Côte d'Ivoire had lasting effects despite French persecution, including burning of churches in 1915. Catholic and Methodist missions preached to people already baptised by Harris and converted many. In 1926, back in Liberia (where he had stayed except for a journey to Sierra Leone in 1917), Harris told his followers to become Methodists rather than Catholics. But John Ahui later claimed that on 23 March 1929 he was ordained by Harris in Liberia, to succeed him as head of an independent church in Côte d'Ivoire. Later in 1929 "The Prophet Harris" died in Liberia.

Many Ivorians converted by Harris in 1914 remained Christians independent of the missions, they are now called "Eglise Harriste", an important church in modern Côte d'Ivoire. The Golden Jubilee of the conversions was widely celebrated in 1964.■

W.W. Harris

Hashoongo, H.P. (1952-77)

HASHOONGO, Hilite Penny (1952-77).

NAMIBIAN activist in the national liberation struggle led by the South West Africa People's Organisation (SWAPO) for an end to South Africa's illegal occupation of the country. Hashoongo's special contribution was in the youth and women's sections of SWAPO. She exemplified the spirit of the Namibian people, their commitment to the building of a new society through the process of the liberation struggles, and the changing role of Namibian women through their participation in that process. Her sudden death through illness, at the age of 25, places her among her fellow countrymen and women who gave their lives to the cause for freedom.

Born at Onamunama village in the north of Namibia, Hashoongo was the daughter of Moses Hashoongo, a miner at the American-owned Tsumeb mine, where he died underground when a rock fell on him from the roof, two days before Hilite was born. Her widowed mother, Lucia Ndalyatapeni Nanghama, worked as a shop-clerk, and within her limited means made efforts for her daughter to be educated. This was only possible, however, within the Bantu education system designed and imposed by South Africa to make Africans fit only for manual labour.

H.P. Hashoongo

Hashoongo attended elementary school at Onamunama from 1957 to 1960, and then went to stay with her uncle in Tsumeb where she completed her primary school education. In 1964 she went to the Anglican St. Mary's Secondary School at Odibo in northern Namibia, one of the country's few independent and English-language, as opposed to Afrikaans, schools.

The early 1970s saw a great upsurge in nationalist activity in Namibia. SWAPO had grown in strength within the country as it waged the armed struggle against the South African regime. The general stike of 1971-72 mobilised workers throughout the country and brought the economy to a standstill and the plight of the Namibian people to international attention. Demonstrations and protests continued within the country, in which

Namibian youth and students played a leading role.

Hashoongo immersed herself in these anti-colonial activities, working with the SWAPO Youth League (SYL) in particular. Because of her political activities she was not allowed to continue her studies in any Government schools, so she decided to do nursing, and in 1973 attended the Nursing School at Onandjokwe Missionary Hospital. Her identification with the oppressed Namibian people became much stronger in the course of her training, as she had to attend to so many victims of the South African police repression. In the same year, 1973, she was also elected a member of the local co-ordinating committee of the SYL at Onandjokwe, attending many meetings and demonstrations, some of which she addressed. In August that year she was arrested and detained for two months, and later was handed over to the South African-appointed tribal chiefs in Ovamboland, at whose hands she suffered public flogging.

Following the independence of Angola, thousands of Namibians left their country to join SWAPO's campaign and armed struggle from abroad. Hashoongo was amongst them. At SWAPO's Provisional Headquarters, then in Zambia, she became active in the programmes of both the SYL and the SWAPO's Women's Council. She attended many conferences on behalf of SWAPO, and headed the SWAPO delegation to the international conference to mark International Women's Year, held in Mexico City in 1975.

In September 1975 Hashoongo was recommended by SWAPO for a scholarship to study at the High Komsomol School in Moscow, where she studied politics, economics, Russian, typing and photography.

In early 1977 Hashoongo was appointed co-ordinating Secretary of SWAPO's Women's Council. Her tasks included organising women in SWAPO's Health and Education Centres in Zambia and Angola. She also made trips to Europe and to many African countries, campaigning for material assistance for Namibian women, and helped to draft the constitution of the Women's Council which was later adopted by the SWAPO Central Committee.

In September 1977, at its meeting at Lubango, Angola, the Central Committee of SWAPO elected Hashoongo as Secretary of the Women's Council. Before she could really embark on her duties, however, she became ill, and in November 1977 was admitted to Lusaka University Teaching Hospital where she died shortly afterwards.■

Hassan I (1836-94)

HASSAN I, King Abu (1836-94).

KING of Morocco. Moulay Hassan was born in 1836 and was the favourite son of his father, Sultan Sidi Mohammed ben Abderrahman. He and his six brothers received a strict education at the University of Fez. His father designated him heir to the throne as soon as Hassan attained the age of majority and, from an early age, involved him in the affairs of the kingdom.

During the 18th and the first half of the 19th century, Morocco remained in self-imposed isolation. During the 1860s, however, it was forced to come to terms with the fact that its territory was the object of European imperialist ambitions. Britain saw Morocco as an outlet for her manufactured goods and sought control over the Mediterranean sea route; France wished to consolidate its control of the Maghreb and form a link with its West African possessions. Morocco was thus obliged to clarify its relations with the principal European colonial powers. A trade treaty was signed with Britain in 1856, a peace treaty with Spain in 1860 and a convention with France in 1863.

Moulay Hassan's father, Sultan Sidi Mohammed ben Abderrahman (1859-1873), aware of the implications of these dealings with Europe, initiated a programme of modernisation, calling on European technical assistance and giving impetus to a modest industrial development. The years 1867-1869 were economically difficult and the programme suffered a considerable setback as a result.

Hassan's training for his future role as King included involvement with the attempts at creating industrial enterprise and frequent contact with European diplomats and traders, and also had a military component, for he led several military expeditions in the south of the country.

His accession to the throne on 12 September 1873 aroused some opposition which he had to suppress by force of arms.

According to contemporary accounts, it was not simply his father's nomination, nor his knowledge of the kingdom's affairs which fitted Hassan for this role, but also his character, intelligence and impressive bearing. He was known for his generosity, simplicity, sense of humour and religious piety. Although he had a deep knowledge of Islamic culture, he never learned a European language and his knowledge of European affairs came from a few European counsellors and from his reading of newspapers.

Hassan was determined to preserve the territorial integrity of his empire. He decided early, therefore, that a policy of limited co-operation with the European powers was the best means of ensuring this and he continued the innovatory programmes of his father, in terms of the country's economy and administrative structures. The political situation in the Mediterranean was more favourable to such a policy than a few years previously: the defeat of France by the Germans in 1870 had removed the French threat from Morocco's eastern border; Spain's political and financial crisis meant that Morocco was safe from the north, while Britain was merely concerned to maintain the status quo. The task facing Hassan, therefore, was that of helping Morocco adapt to a technically advanced world so that she would be able to withstand the ambitions of the imperialist European powers.

Ensuring the kingdom's territorial integrity depended to a large extent on obtaining and maintaining the loyalty to the crown of the various rival and warring ethnic groups. Hassan achieved this by employing a mixture of threats, force and truly skilful diplomacy. His prestige in the south was so great that there was no major revolt there during his entire reign. He introduced greater administrative flexibility and control in the plains by splitting up large provinces into a series of small administrative units. Stability also depended on a careful control of the power wielded by the various religious leaders and sects; here again, Hassan demonstrated considerable skill in reassuring some groups while restricting the activity of others. Towards the end of his reign he made several visits to border areas of the country, conscious that this reaffirmation of his concern for all parts of the empire would strengthen resistance to any European attempt at incursion.

Hassan's financial policies were just as successful. He ensured the regular collection of taxes, and despite the payment of war reparations to Spain until 1886, the payment of indemnities to European powers and a severe economic crisis between 1878 and 1882, the Treasury was richer than ever before. With such financial reserves at his disposal, Hassan was able to strengthen and reorganise the army, a reform which is regarded as the most important achievement of his reign. He altered traditional recruitment procedures, created a standing army on the European model, called in European instructors, sent the officer corps to Europe for training and purchased modern arms and equipment. He also laid the foundations of an armaments industry and navy.

Hassan took vigorous measures towards improving Morocco's economy. Trade was given a boost by the authorisation of grain exports, by improvements to the ports and by altering customs duties in Morocco's favour. Despite falling prices, external trade increased by 40 per cent overall during Hassan's reign. Incentives were given to the production of cash crops, as also to private industrial enterprise, and a postal service was organised.

If Hassan was not able to extend his reforms as far or as fast as he himself would have wished, this was due in part to the traditionalism of his people and of those who were the intermediaries of change, but it can also be ascribed to pressures exerted by the European colonial powers. Hassan's dilemma was that he could only hope to resist these pressures by modernising his country, but that modernisation made inevitable European assistance in achieving this goal and thus unleashed diplomatic and economic rivalry. Moulay Hassan had established his own sovereignty in the traditional manner by obtaining the sworn allegiance of the country's tribes and minor sultanates, to whom in return he pledged his protection. This right to protection in return for a pledge of allegiance came to be manipulated by the European powers for their own ends and although Hassan sought, both at the Tangiers Conference (1877) and at the International Conference of Madrid (19 May-3 July 1880) to obtain the suppression of this "right to protection", he failed. Thousands of Moroccans subsequently came under French "protection", including several important personalities and the Sherif of Ouez-

zane, a strategicaly important area on the border between Algeria (already a French possession) and Morocco. Thus was Moroccan sovereignty subtly undermined by the use of those same traditional structures that Hassan would have wished to eliminate.

Acceding to Spanish and French demands for financial reparation simply removed one pretext these owners might have had for annexation or conquest. However, it had the negative effect of putting a brake on economic growth and the effort towards modernisation. Yet another means used by Hassan was to play the rival powers off against each other by seeking an alliance with whichever power seemed the least dangerous. He turned first to Britain, then to Germany and later to France. The necessity of defending and strengthening Morocco's borders was yet another brake on modernisation because of a drain on resources.

Moulay Hassan died on 6 June 1894, after returning from an expedition to Tafilalet. In his twenty years' reign he had not only ensured his country's continued independence, but had initiated a programme of important reforms and modernisation. But he himself admitted that, although he had succeeded in holding the European powers at bay, he had not been able to build up the modern state which would be the only guarantee of future independence. It was eighteen years after his death, in 1912, that Morocco became a French Protectorate; "pacification" was not achieved until 1934. But opposition to the colonialists continued, centred around Allal el-Fassi (q.v.) and his nationalist followers. These were instrumental in regaining Morocco's independence in 1956. ■

Hassan, Abdullah (1864-1920)

HASSAN, Sayyid Mohammed Abdullah (1864-1920).

SOMALI nationalist and religious leader. He was born in 1864 in the Nogal valley area, into the Darod section of the nomadic Somali people of the "Horn of Africa". He went to Aden for Islamic studies and travelled to other places also, making the Mecca pilgrimage several times. He was influenced by reports of the Mahdist movement in the Sudan and other Islamic revival and reform movements. In Aden he was particularly influenced by the puritan Ahmadiyya sect (not to be confused with the missionary "Ahmadiyya movement in Islam", founded in India and established now in Nigeria and Ghana). He followed its teacher Muhammed Salih, who broke with the sect and founded his own, the Salihiya, whose doctrine Abdullah Hassan would later preach.

In 1884, Britain occupied a part of Somalia, on the coast east of the new French territory around Djibouti. Further inland Ethiopia began expanding soon after then in the Ogaden, peopled by Somalis. East of there, on the coast stretching southwards from Cape Guardafui, Italy started establishing its rule in 1889, with treaties with two important rival Sultans, those of the Mijertein Somalis and of Obbia.

By the time he returned from Aden to Somali territory in 1895, Abdullah Hassan found it increasingly threatened by Christian powers' occupation. His preaching led to heightened Islamic resistance to this occupation. His reform doctrines, being strict, were not popular at Berbera where he started a school on his return, but later he lived among the Dolbahanta and his influence spread among the Darod. He became a Mullah, a Moslem judge and theologian, and by 1899 he had about 3,000 followers, with whom he occupied important watering holes at Burao and declared a *Jihad*. The "holy war" was apparently at first against the Somalis (the majority) who followed the Qadiriyya school of Islam, which he considered lax, but soon it was directed against the British and Ethiopians.

He dominated the Ogaden and obtained arms from the Sultan of the Mijerteins and from raids. In 1901 a joint Anglo-Ethiopian expedition of about 17,000 troops drove him into the Mijertein area. The Italians, nominal rulers of that area, allowed the British to land forces at Obbia to attack the Mullah. But they were defeated and withdrew in mid-1903. The Mullah, whom the British contemptuously called the "Mad Mullah", then occupied all the Nogal valley from Halin to Ilig.

A fourth British expedition, in 1904, drove Abdullah Hassan into the Mijertein country again. 500 British troops were then landed at Ilig. Thinking the Mullah was nearly finished, the British offered him a safe conduct into exile at Mecca, but he ignored the offer. Instead he sought to divide his enemies by making an agreement with the Italians. The latter, anxious to maintain "indirect rule" and not be obliged to commit large forces to Somalia, responded to an offer of talks. Under an agreement signed on 3 March 1905, the Mullah occupied territory in the Nogal valley, between Mijertein and the Obbia Sultanate territory. The British agreed to this and allowed Hassan's followers to enter British Somaliland in dry-season migrations. For three years there was relative peace, though the Italians, like the British, feared Abdullah Hassan's religious and political power.

In 1908 the Mullah's followers, who like those of the Sudanese Mahdi were called "Dervishes", attacked the Mudugh area to establlsh contact with the Bah Ceri in the Ogaden further inland. This was the time Abdullah Shahari, a leading colleague of the Mullah, left him to visit Muhammed Salih at Mecca and brought back a letter, purportedly from Salih, accusing the Mullah of various misdeeds and telling him to repent or be expelled from the Salihiyya. Some Dervishes said the letter was a forgery, but others who believed it left the Mullah's following.

In British Somaliland, most of the Mullah's followers stayed with him. Efforts to persuade him to surrender failed in 1909, and at the end of that year the British evacuated their forces from the interior of the colony. The Mullah, with 6,000 rifles, was thus still very powerful. But in 1910 the Sultan of the Mijerteins, Yusuf Ali, turned against him; the Mullah, in one of his acts of personal cruelty, killed a daughter of Yusuf Ali whom he had taken as a wife earlier. The British and Italians now coordinated action, the Italians established formal rule over the Mijertein Somalis, and the latter agreed with the Warsangeli to cooperate against the Mullah. Seaborne arms shipments to him were stopped, and after 1911 the Ethiopians at Harar became a greater threat to him under Tafari (Haile Selassie (q.v.)). In 1911 Abdullah was driven out of Italian Somalia altogether.

However, he was still a formidable effective ruler over part of British Somaliland and almost all the Ogaden claimed by Ethiopia. Dervishes raided as far as Berbera once. In January 1913 he moved to Taleh, where Yemeni stone masons had helped to build a massive fortress that would be his base for the next seven years. Early in 1920, the British attacked, using aircraft which were unfamiliar to the Dervishes. After the bombing of Taleh the Mullah evacuated it and the British occupied the fortress on 12 February 1920.

Abdulla Hassan retreated into the Ogaden, where about 3,000 Somalis of the British forces pursued him with Ethiopia's permission. Defeated in a battle with those forces, Abdullah Hassan and his now small band, hit by disease and starvation, retreated to the banks of the Shebelli, where he died. News reached Mogadishu on 10 February 1921 that he had died on 21 December 1920.

Today Abdullah Hassan is remembered as a hero who led a united force against three occupiers of Somali territory. He is also remembered as a poet as well as a reformer and resistance leader whose activities dominated most of the British and Italians' attention for a considerable period. ■

Hazoumé, P. (1890-1980)

HAZOUME, Paul (1890-1980).

BENINESE teacher, anthropologist, author and politician. Born in Porto Novo on 16 April 1890, descended from the nobility of the old kingdom of Porto Novo, he was educated at the St. Joseph's Elementary School in his birthplace before attending the Ecole William Ponty in Dakar, Senegal, from 1907 to 1910. He became a primary school teacher in Ouidah and later in Cotonou. During World War I Hazoumé worked for some time in the African department of the Musée de l'Homme in Paris.

In 1915 he started an underground anti-government newspaper, *Le Récadaire de Béhanzin*, with Emile Zinsou Bode. In the 1930s, while in Paris, he combined journalism with work on a famous anthropological study of Dahomey (Benin) people, *Le Pacte du Sang au Dahomey* (1937). His other work, *Doguicimi*, a novel, was published in 1938 and tells a story of King Gezo's court in Abomey. In 1931, he represented Dahomey at a Congress on "native societies" organised in Paris in connection with the Colonial Exhibition.

After the Second World War, he was active in nationalist politics. He was secretary of the *Comité Central d'Organisation Electorale de Cotonou*, which arose like other such organisations in 1945 to nominate and support candidates for elections now allowed for Africans. He became a leader of the *Union Démocratique Dahoméenne*, (UDD), a major nationalist party. In 1947 he became a member of the Dahomey Territorial Assembly and of the consultative body in France

P. Hazoumé

representing the colonies, the Council of the French Union. He remained a councillor until 1958 when he retired to Cotonou. His literary efforts included a history of the Catholic mission in Dahomey, *Cinquante Ans d'Apostolat au Dahomey*. He also helped in launching the famous journal, *Présence Africaine* in 1947.

He was a candidate for the presidency in the elections in 1968, but after failing to be elected, retired and concentrated on his memoirs until his death in April 1980. ■

Head, B. (1938-86)

HEAD, Bessie (1938-86).

SOUTH AFRICAN novelist whose books reflect the traumas and social problems caused by the inhuman apartheid régime of South Africa. Her writing was deeply in-fluenced by her own experiences, and she saw her own life as a microcosm of the lives of many Black South Africans.

Bessie Head was born in Pietermaritz-burg, South Africa, in 1938. Her maiden name was Emery, and she was of mixed parentage, her mother the daughter of a wealthy, white Natal raceowner and her father a Zulu stablehand. She was born in a mental asylum where her mother was com-mitted and where, rejected by her family, she died in 1943. She was fostered until she was thirteen and then grew up, lonely and bookish, in a Mission orphanage until she was eighteen. After a teacher training course, she taught for four years and then worked as a journalist for two years on Drum magazine.

She married Harold Head, a journa-list, and was for a time active in African nationalist circles. Her marriage broke up and in 1964 she went with her son to Botswana to start anew. There with her refugee status which lasted fifteen years (she was granted Botswanan citizenship in 1979), she taught and wrote her first novel When Rainclouds Gather, which was published in 1969. That novel grew out of her experience in a refugee community and narrates the story of a Black South African refugee having to adjust himself to life in the village with people able to make demands and have a certain control over their actions, he who was denied all human rights in his own country. The theme of "outcast" recurs later.

When Rainclouds Gather, which was published simultaneously in London and New York, was widely acclaimed and gave her the break she needed. Maru, her second novel, was published in 1971 and deals with the question of racialism, not between White and Black, but as seen in the prejudice against a people, the Bushmen or Masarwas, who were believed to be isolated in Botswana.

By that time Bessie had got involved in community development in Botswana, especially in Patrick van Rensburg's now famous Swaneng Hill project in community farming and education at Serowe which was being set up in the sixties. From this was to come "peace of mind" and a growing interest and involvement in rural life particularly in the lives and position of women, rural women in particular, which found expres-sion in the short story collection, The Collector of Treasures in 1977, and Serowe: The Village of the Rainwind in 1981.

B. Head

But it is her third novel A Question of Power, published in 1974, which is the best known and most powerful. It is a disturbing account of mental breakdown and suffering and personality disintegration through evil. Bessie Head herself had suffered tremendous mental agony, and Elizabeth, the central character, echoes the author's experiences.

Concerned with the broad sweep of migrations in Southern Africa, her latest work is a historical chronicle; *A Bewitched Crossroad: an African Saga*, was published in 1984.

Bessie Head's writing was influenced by Russian and Indian novelists and Britain's D. H. Lawrence. Her style is deceptively simple; anger and sadness are often not far from the surface. She has an uncanny grasp of the complexity of character and spins great webs of imagery and symbol around the painful conflicts between men and women, ancient custom and modernity which she describes in her books. This is what makes her novels so gripping and touching, though not without hope; she longed for social reform, for a humane solution to the divisive policies of this world.

Bessie Head died in Serowe, Botswana, her adopted country on 17 April 1986. She was 48 and had been suffering from hepatitis. She was at the time researching in the Bama Ngwato archives in Gaborone while working on her autobiography.■

Henries, R.A. (1908-80)

HENRIES, Richard Abrom (1908-80).

L IBERIAN politician. He was born on 16 September 1908 in Monrovia, and was educated at Liberia College (now University of Liberia). Henries was professor of Mathematics, Liberia College, in 1932 and chief clerk, Commonwealth District of Monrovia till 1934 when he was appointed supervisor of schools for Sinoe and Maryland counties.

In 1943 Henries was elected to the House of Representatives of the Liberian Legislature, and was made chairman of the Committee on Foreign Affairs and on Education. He was president of the Board of Trustees of the University of Liberia in 1952 and a president of the Liberian National Bar Association in 1958. He established the Henries Law firm in 1943.

Henries, as a member of Liberia's Congress, was elected president of the Interparliamentary Union (Liberian group) in 1959. He attended the organisational conference of the United Nations at San Francisco,

USA, in 1945 and was a signatory to the Charter. He became the Speaker of the House of Representatives of the Republic of Liberia in 1951 and this post he held until his death. He was former Grand Master, Ancient Free and Accepted Masons of Liberia (33 degree). He was also a member of the Liberian Scholastic Honours Society and the American Society of International Law. He was True Whig Party leader for Montserrado county, and legal adviser of the party.

He was awarded the honorary degrees of Doctor of Law, Doctor of Civil Laws and

R.A. Henries

Doctor of Education by the University of Liberia. Apart from honorary degrees, he was also accorded all the Liberian national honours, including that of Grand Cordon of the Most Venerable Order of the Knighthood of the Pioneers.

Henries was executed on 22 April 1980, in the purge that followed the overthrow of the administration of President William Tolbert (q.v.).■

Hertzog, J.B.M. (1866-1942)

HERTZOG, General James Barry Munnik (1866-1942).

SOUTH AFRICAN soldier and politician who was Prime Minister from 1924 until 1939. Hertzog wanted an independent South Africa outside the British Empire whose interests, he claimed, should not be placed above those of South Africa.

Born on 3 April 1866 in Soetendal, near Groenberg in Wellington in the Cape Province, he was the son of a German immigrant from Brunswick. Hertzog was educated in Kimberley and Stellenbosch before reading for a BA degree which he obtained in 1889. He later trained as a lawyer in Amsterdam in Holland where he gained the degree of Doctor Juris in 1892.

Returning to South Africa that same year, he settled in private practice in Pretoria and in 1895 he was made a judge in the Orange Free State. When war broke out in 1899 between Britain and the Boers he joined the forces of the latter as legal adviser to the military commander, but a year later he was appointed a general following the implementation of the disciplinary measures which he had introduced into the army while serving in his legal capacity. He took part in the subsequent peace talks with the British at Vereeniging in 1902 where his insistence led to the acceptance of the Dutch language as an official language to be used in South African public schools and courts of law. He signed the Treaty of Vereeniging of 1902 on behalf of the Orange Free State.

After the war Hertzog went into politics, emphasising the issues of recognition for the Dutch language and granting of self-government to the Afrikaners by Britain. When self-government was granted in 1907, he was appointed Attorney-General and Minister of Education, after having been elected to Parliament. As Minister of Education he enforced his controversial language policy while, at the same time, maintaining his opposition to any conciliatory move towards Britain, which was at variance with the policy of the government headed by Louis Botha.

Despite the differences between him and the governing South African Party, he was given an additional responsibility in the government in 1912 when he was made Minister of Native Affairs which he held in conjunction with the portfolio of Justice. The full effect of Hertzog's commitment to Afrikaners' ambitions was felt the following year when he introduced the country's first

Gen. J.B.M. Hertzog

racially discriminatory legislation that culminated in the Natives Land Act of 1913. The Act, regarded by Africans as the "Act of Dispossession", effectively reduced African land possession to a mere 7.9 per cent of the total surface area of South Africa while consolidating the economic and political power of the Afrikaners.

Hertzog broke from the South African Party in 1914 and founded the National Party which became the major party in the coalition government with the Labour Party in 1924. He became Prime Minster that year, leading the National/Labour coalition until 1939. During this period Afrikaans was declared an official language and South Africa was given a national flag, while racial measures that further segregated the Africans from the political and economic life of the country were implemented. His tacit support for Nazi Germany during the Second World War, though winning considerable approval from his fellow Afrikaners, further alienated him from Africans and the British. He fell from power in 1939 and died in 1942 in Pretoria. ■

Honesty II, E. (died 1858)

HONESTY II, King Eyo (died 1858).

NIGERIAN ruler, he was a prominent king of Creek Town which for centuries before the nineteenth was an important Efik trading community in pre-colonial Calabar. King Honesty built his reputation and that of his society on trade, in which, through industry and shrewd diplomacy, he out-manoeuvered his neighbours in Duke Town and Europeans alike to accumulate wealth and influence.

Eyo Honesty was an Efik, born between the late eighteenth and early nineteenth centuries. The mode of life of his people had been determined by their location on the Atlantic coastline, the swampy land and numerous rivers which traverse the hinterland and provide water transport to the port of Calabar. This environment encouraged the early development of trade and agriculture which the Efiks have practised, and still do, with outstanding success. Their geographical location made them middlemen in the trade between the hinterland and European traders who visited Calabar markets as early as the fifteenth century. At that time these Europeans traded mainly in slaves, but the abolition of the slave trade in the nineteenth century gave rise to trade in oil palm commodities, for which Creek Town still remained prosperous.

However, as the palm oil trade developed, so did the rivalry between Creek

Town and Duke Town, the two Efik trading communities in Calabar at the time. This rivalry intensified with the pressure of European officials, traders and missionaries who were anxious to gain influence in the area. King Honesty was eager to welcome the Europeans in the hope that their presence would attract more trade and make his state the centre of activities. He thus welcomed

King E. Honesty II

the Church of Scotland mission on its arrival in 1846, and encouraged the missionaries to build schools and churches; he even personally interpreted the Gospel at church services.

He also invited the British, in preference to the French, to establish a consulate in Creek Town. To this request, but largely for reasons of self-interest the British responded partially in 1849 with the appointment of John Beecroft as Consul, resident in nearby Fernando Po; he and subsequent Consuls often intervened in Calabar affairs. In 1850 King Honesty put an end to the offering of human sacrifice at state ceremonies and also to the killing of twins, both of which were the practice in the Calabar of the time. The king hoped that these actions would impress the British officials and missionaries and encourage them to develop modern industries in Creek Town. He even sought their aid to build a sugar refinery plan to process the sugar cane that was grown extensively in the area. However, very few of these hopes were realised but Creek Town nevertheless grew rich on the new palm oil trade.

In spite of his willingness to allow the Europeans into his domain, King Honesty remained firmly committed to the independence and traditions of his people. He never allowed the missionaries and officials to interfere with his faith and with the smooth running of his state. For one he refused to be converted to Christianity, maintaining his belief in Efik traditions. Secondly, and perhaps more important for him, he made sure his people's middleman position in the trade between the Europeans and the hinterland was not disturbed. He forbade all Europeans operating in his country to deal directly with the traders inland. To do this effectively he restricted the movement of every foreigner, including the Consul, to a certain limit within his centre.

King Honesty succeeded to a large extent in ruling his society independently until his death. He did this largely by appeasing the British when it suited him and defending Creek Town's interests when challenged by the new arrangements. The welfare of his people was his primary interest and he spent his reign developing ways in which they would prosper through modern education and commerce.

The independence of Creek Town, however, did not continue for long after Honesty's death. The determined thrust of the British from the late nineteenth century to establish effective control over the Niger area did not spare Calabar. Even in the 1850s colonial pressure was such in the area that King Honesty's authority was increasingly being undermined under the new arrangements. His trading system was gradually being reorganised, and was finally replaced, after his death, with the direct approach and domination of British firms. It was not only the Efiks, but all the trading communities in the Niger Delta, who consequently lost their prominence as traders and middlemen and were finally ousted in the 1880s because of the British occupation. ■

Horton, J.A.B. (1835-83)

HORTON, Dr. James Africanus Beale (1835-83).

SIERRA LEONEAN medical practitioner, author and pioneer of nationalism in West Africa. Born in 1835 in Freetown to a family of "Recaptives" (people freed from slave ships), originally from what is now Nigeria, he attended the Freetown CMS Grammar School and then the Fourah Bay Institution. He studied medicine in London and Edinburgh – and graduated in 1859. He had adopted the name "Africanus" as a student.

Dr. J.A.B. Horton

In 1859 he joined the British army's medical service. For several years he served in the Gold Coast (now Ghana) where he combined private practice with writing. In 1859 he published *The Medical Topography of the West Coast of Africa, with sketches of its Botany*. He later published *The Physical and Medical Climatology and Meteorology of the*

West Coast of Africa (1866) and *Guinea Worm, or Dracunculus* (1868). He spent some time in Gambia but returned to Gold Coast in 1868.

In 1865 he published *The Political Economy of British West Africa*, the first expression of his political views in which he saw British rule and Christian missions as beneficial for Africa, while insisting on the Africans' capacity for self-government. This first political work was the basis of a more famous one in 1868, *West African Countries and Peoples*.

Between 1868 and 1871 Dr. Horton advised and encouraged the leaders of the Fanti Confederation, an organisation of traditional Fanti states in Gold Coast, led by Chiefs and educated leaders. His letters to British officials urging their support of the confederation were published as *Letters on the Political Condition of the Gold Coast*. But by 1872 the British authorities turned against this movement and there developed official suspicion of Dr. Horton. But he served as Civil Commmandant at Sekondi in 1872-3. Then he accompanied the Ashanti expedition of 1873-74. In 1875, while at Cape Coast, he was promoted Surgeon-Major. In 1874 he published *The Diseases of Tropical Climates and their Treatment*.

Always interested in geology, he explored for minerals in Gold Coast in 1878 and took out mining concessions, one of which was sold to a company in 1880. Business activity was his main interest after he retired from the army in 1879. He settled in Freetown but spent some time in Britain. He helped start a new Commercial Bank of West Africa, which was opened on 15 January 1883 in Freetown. On 15 October 1883 he died in Freetown. ■

Howells, A.W. (1866-1938)

HOWELLS, Bishop Adolphus Williamson (1866-1938).

NIGERIAN clergyman who in 1919 became the first African vicar of the Pro-Cathedral Christ Church in Lagos. He was born in Abeokuta on 9 August 1866 and attended the Ake School there before entering the CMS Training Institute in Lagos in

1882. He then became a teacher at a mission school in Badagry where he worked for one year from 1886.

In 1887 he was posted to St. Paul's School (Breadfruit Street), Lagos, leaving in 1891 to study at Fourah Bay College, Freetown, and later at Durham University in

Bishop A.W. Howells

England. Returning to Lagos in 1894 he was appointed tutor at the CMS Grammar School and was later given responsibility of supervising the mission's training institutions in Lagos.

Howells was made deacon in 1897 and ordained priest two years later. In 1900 he became curate of Christ Church Pro-Cathedral in Lagos and later pastor of St. John's Parish, Aroloya, where he served for several years before his posting in 1919 as the first African vicar of the Pro-Cathedral Church of Christ. His work there was highly regarded in the Church, and on 24 June 1920 the Archbishop of Canterbury consecrated him Bishop at St. Paul's Cathedral in London. Bishop Howells was posted to the Niger Diocese and served there until 1933. He returned to the Lagos Diocese to become assistant to Bishop Melville Jones who was the Bishop of Lagos. On 10 March 1933 he was made the first resident Bishop of Abeokuta. He served there till his retirement on 10 August 1936. Bishop Howells died on 3 December 1938. ■

administration for two articles considered to be seditious which were published in *La Voix du Dahomey*.

During World War II he was an active supporter of the Free French Movement and in 1941 was sentenced to death on charges of spying. He was reprieved and sent into exile in French Soudan (Mali) until 1947 when he returned to Dahomey. He became chairman of the influential *Union des Anciens du Dahomey* in 1950 as well as editor of *L'Eveil* newspaper.

When Dahomey became independent in 1960, despite his advancing years (74), he became Presidential and Vice-Presidential Special Consultant, remaining in this position until his death on 28 May 1964 in Porto Novo. ■

Hunkanrin, L. (1886-1964)

HUNKANRIN, Louis (1886-1964).

BENINESE nationalist and journalist. He was born in Porto Novo in 1886. His family was fairly wealthy and after completing his primary and secondary education in local schools, he went to Senegal to study at the Dakar Teachers' Training College until 1906. He then went back to Dahomey, as Benin was then called, and took up a teaching appointment in Ouidah, near Cotonou. He remained in this position until 1910 when, following a dispute with the school's principal, he returned to Dakar and went into private business.

By this time he was very active in anti-colonial activities and expressed his views in various newspaper articles. Between 1914 and 1918 he became one of the editors of the *Messager du Dahomey* newspaper and continued his criticisms of French rule, while becoming involved in the establishment of an organisaton in Dahomey affiliated to the League of Human Rights.

As a result of his anti-French activities he was detained for a while in France. After his realease he returned to Dahomey in 1923 where he was once again arrested, after riots provoked by taxation, and sent into exile in Mauritania for ten years. He returned to Dahomey in 1933 but the following year he was sued and fined by the French

Hussein, T. (1889-1972)

HUSSEIN, Dr. Taha (1889-1972).

EGYPTIAN educationist. Although blind since the age of three, Taha Hussein became an outstanding Islamic scholar. He devoted his life to achieving academic freedom and the introduction of modern education in his country.

Taha Hussein was born on 14 November 1889 at Maghagha, a mill town in the province of Minya, Upper Egypt. He was the fifth of the eleven children of Aly Hussein, an employee in a sugar factory. Hussein became blind after an illness. In his autobiographical work, *An Egyptian Childhood*, he recalls his sadness over the fact that his brothers and sisters were able to do things which he found impossible. He nevertheless refused to be defeated by his handicap and one of his first accomplishments was to memorise the Koran.

In choosing his life work, Hussein relates that for a blind man like himself there were only two courses open. He could either study at the theological university, al-Azhar, in Cairo, until he earned a degree which would assure him of a livelihood from the daily allowance of loaves and the monthly pension, or he could make a trade of reading the Koran at funerals and in private houses. Hussein enrolled at al-Azhar at the age of 13 and soon became interested in the controversy between the followers of the Moslem tradition and the disciples of Muhammed 'Abduh (q.v.), who was advocating the introduction of modern subjects.

In 1908 a university in the modern sense, the Egyptian University (nationalised in 1925, renamed Fuad I University in 1928, renamed again Cairo University following the 23 July 1952 Revolution) was founded in Cairo. Hussein became a student of the new university and was the first to graduate with a doctor's degree in 1914. The university awarded him a scholarship to study at the University of Paris (Sorbonne), from where he received a post-graduate degree in 1919.

With the aid of his wife, Suzanne Bressau, a fellow student whom he married in Paris in 1917, he began to write. *The Leaders of Knowledge* was published in 1925, followed by *Pre-Islamic Literature*. In 1930 he became dean of the Faculty of Arts. On being appointed minister of Education in 1942, he immediately set about translating his ideas into political practice. In 1943 he abolished fees in primary schools as part of a programme to open schools to all Egyptian children. Free schooling was extended to secondary schools in 1950, bringing the appropriation for education in the Egyptian budget to a level equal to that of the entire national budget less than 20 years earlier.

Hussein opened private schools to the public with the support of the national treasury. These reforms met with some opposition, not only in Egypt but in the Arab world. However, the Arab Cultural Conference at Alexandria in August 1950 approved Hussein's programme in principle. In Egypt, primary school enrolments increased tenfold and projects were initiated to translate the history and culture of Europe into Arabic, and to allow Egyptians to study in Europe. He established an Egyptian Institute in Madrid, Spain, a department of Arabic literature at Athens University, and another on Mediterranean problems at the Centre Universitaire Méditerranéen at Nice, France. He also established an Institute for Desert Questions and the Ibrahim University.

Taha Hussein has the reputation of having done more for the education of Islamic people than any other individual. He wrote over forty books including novels, literary and social studies. His biography *Stream of Days* has been translated into fifteen languages.

He was vice-president of the Academy of Arabic Language, president of the *Institut d'Egypte* (founded by Napoleon Bonaparte), corresponding member of the *Académie des Inscriptions et Belles Lettres*, Paris, member of the *Academia dei Lincei*, Rome and

Dr. T. Hussein

member of the Academies of Mainz, Teheran, Damascus and Baghdad, and the Royal Academy of History. He was honoured by the governments of France, Belgium, Lebanon, Greece, Spain and Iran, and held honorary degees from the universities of Oxford, Athens, Madrid, Rome, Montpellier and Lyons. He died in 1972. ∎

Hutchinson, A. (1924-72)

HUTCHINSON, Alfred (1924-72).

SOUTH AFRICAN writer and activist in the African National Congress (ANC). He was known to many of his colleagues simply as "Hutch". Hutchinson was born in 1924 in the Hectorspruit district in the Transvaal, South Africa, of mixed Swazi and Coloured parentage. He attended a local primary school and later St. Peter's Secondary School in Johannesburg. In 1948 he obtained a BA degree from the University of Fort Hare and worked as a teacher at Pimville High School from where he was dismissed in 1952 for his involvement in political activities.

Hutchinson had been active in the 1950s Campaign for the Defiance of Unjust Laws and was imprisoned for his role, followed by his dismissal from teaching by the Transvaal education authorities. He later joined the staff of the Johannesburg Indian School, as a protest against the Group Areas Act. During this period he had been elected Transvaal branch secretary of the ANC and became a member of the National Executive Committee of the movement. In 1956 he was one of the accused in the celebrated Treason Trial in which 156 African, Indian and Coloured leaders were charged with subversion. Hutchinson was acquitted in 1958.

During the trial he wrote *It Could Never Be In Vain*, a short story published in the *Fighting Talk* magazine in 1957. In it he wrote: "I am waiting in a cell at the Magistrate's Court. I used to think that pacing cells was theatrical stuff. Now I am doing the same. Will the waiting ever come to an end? It ends and I am among friends again. Is this another Congress of the People – drawing all South Africans together? Now we are swinging in the huge singing and I am singing too Izokunyathela: Afrika... Afrika will trample you underfoot. Unrepentant. People seen through the mesh: Surprise and dawning understanding. The thumb raised in reply. Mayibuye i Afrika!

"The Minister of Justice has placed the figure at two hundred. The Fort has room for many more. Who will be next? More come, singing and in groups. Walter, Moses, Ruth, Duma, Rusty, Jack, Ismail Meer... Children suddenly orphaned. The morning and evening papers bring drifts of the outside world. There is widespread agitation, a ferment...

"Tomorrow, December 19th, is 'Treason Day'. The days of waiting are drawing to

A. Hutchinson

an end. A tide of excitement is rising. Bail or no bail we will leave the Fort for a while... There are crowds, huge crowds, outside the Drill Hall and their warmth beats on you like strong sunlight after rain-planting life. And you know, as you never knew before, that you could never be lost: that if you fell another would take your place: that the struggle could never be lost. It could never have been in vain."

Hutchinson was a prolific writer, best known for his short stories which depict the African life in his country, portrayed with great compassion and vivid imagery. His major work, *Road to Ghana*, published in 1960, dealt with, apart from being an account of his escape from South Africa, the measures that precipitated his departure.

Hutchinson escaped from South Africa, without a passport, after the declaration of the State of Emergency following the Sharpeville Massacre of 1960. He made his way to Nkrumah's Ghana where he taught at the University of Ghana, Accra. He later went to Britain to teach in Brighton and London, returning to West Africa in 1971, this time to Nigeria as a lecturer. He died there in October 1972.■

I

Ibekwe, D.O. (1919-78)

IBEKWE, Dan Onuora (1919-78).

NIGERIAN lawyer. Born on 23 June 1919 in Onitsha, in what is now Anambra State of Nigeria, he had his early education at St. Mary's School, Onitsha and then at Christ the King College, Onitsha. After his secondary education, Ibekwe proceeded to the Council of Legal Education Law School, London. He was called to the Bar in 1951.

From 1951 to 1954 Ibekwe and the late J.I.C. Taylor were partners in private legal practice; in 1954 he moved to Aba, where he set up a successful practice of his own. In 1956 he became the legal adviser to the Premier of the Eastern Region, and in 1958 was promoted Solicitor-General of the Eastern Region. He held this portfolio until 1964, when he resigned after the constitutional crisis following controversial Federal elections; he gave advice, for which he was famous afterwards, on the limits to the constitutional powers of President Azikiwe in dealing with the crisis. In 1965, when a Federal Senator, he was appointed Federal Minister in charge of Commonwealth Relations, a role in which he organised the Commonwealth Prime Ministers' Conference in Lagos in January 1966. After Nigeria's first coup which came soon after, he was a solicitor with the firm of Messrs. Irving and Bonnar in 1966, but later in the same year he was detained by the rebel government of Eastern Nigeria (Biafra). He was released in 1970, and appointed Commissioner for Works, Housing and Transport in the East Central State.

In 1972 he was made a Justice of the Supreme Court of Nigeria. Later, in 1975, Ibekwe was appointed the Federal Attorney-

D.O. Ibekwe

General and Commissioner for Justice. He was appointed President of the Federal Court of Appeal in 1976 when he also became Chairman of the Nigerian Institute of International Affairs, posts he held until his death. Apart from his national assignments, Ibekwe published a book, *Justice in Blunderland*. He died on 23 March 1978. He is survived by his wife, Cecilia Nkemdilim, two sons, and six daughters. ■

287

Ibrahim, B. (1940-79)

IBRAHIM, Ba (1940-79).

MAURITANIAN politician in the years following the country's independence in 1960. Born in 1940 in Maghana, southern Mauritania, Ibrahim went to school in the regional capital, Kaedi. In 1961 he went to France to continue his studies and obtained a degree in petrochemical engineering before returning to Mauritania in 1966.

Ba Ibrahim joined the government service as director of the Fisheries Office based in Nouadhibou, an important post considering the importance of the fishing industry in the country's economy. During his period in office a modern infrastructure for the industry began to be developed. In addition to the directorship of the Fisheries Office, Ibrahim was also director of the Planning Office. By 1976 he was economic and financial adviser to the government of President Mokhtar Ould Daddah.

He later entered the cabinet as Minister of Planning, Handicrafts and Tourism, and following a cabinet reshuffle in May 1977, Ibrahim was made Minister of Finance. In January 1978 his portfolio was extended to include Trade as well. He remained Minister of Finance and Trade until May 1978 when he was replaced by President Ould Daddah's brother, Ahmed Ould Daddah.

Following the military coup in July that year, when the Ould Daddah administration was overthrown, Ibrahim was appointed adviser to the new government headed by Lt.-Col. Mustapha Ould Mohamed Salek. In 1979, he was appointed ambassador to France and Britain (with residence in Paris), but he did not take up this post before his tragic death. Ibrahim was one of 13 people in the entourage of Prime Minister Ould Bouceif (q.v.) for the summit meeting of the Economic Community of West African States (ECOWAS) in May 1979, who were killed when their Buffalo military aircraft plunged into the sea off Dakar airport, Senegal.

Ba Ibrahim was one of a generation of Mauritanian politicians who sought to reactivate their country's role in the international community, and his death was widely mourned in Nouakchott. ∎

Ibrahim, K. (1910-90)

IBRAHIM, Sir Kashim (1910-90).

NIGERIAN statesman and educationist, also a prominent traditional office holder in one of the oldest kingdoms in Africa, Borno. He was born at Yerwa, the old quarter of Maiduguri, which became capital of Borno State; Yerwa was and remains the seat of the King or Shehu of Borno. Born into the aristocracy of that famous kingdom, Kashim Ibrahim attended Koranic school, necessary for the traditional office of Shettima for which he was groomed by his father. He was to take this office (overseer of traditional judicial officers) in 1935.

At an early age, however, he embarked on Western education to fit him for the new order installed by the British. By deliberate British policy few Muslim northerners were allowed to receive Western education in his time, although some young

Sir K. Ibrahim

Hausa-Fulani or (in Borno) Kanuri aristocrats were trained in British government schools. Kashim Ibrahim went first to Borno Provincial School and then, from 1925 to 1929, to the famous Katsina Teacher Training College, where almost all the prominent Western-educated men of the first generation in northern Nigeria went. He qualified as a teacher there and then taught at Borno Provincial School. He became a Visiting Teacher in 1933, Senior Visiting Teacher from 1938 to 1947, and Education Officer from 1947 to 1949. During this teaching career he married his first and second wives, Halina and Khadina; by them and a third wife, Zainaba, he had seven daughters and seven sons.

His educational work included considerable expansion of schools in Borno, the creation of the Maiduguri Teachers College in 1952, and the writing of primary school textbooks in Kanuri and English. He was a great believer in Western education, which all his children received.

Shettima Kashim, as he was always known then, naturally became one of the more prominent Northern Region politicians. Among the founders of the Northern Peoples Congress (NPC), he was elected to the Northern Region House of Assembly in 1951 and from there to the Federal House of Representatives, where he served from 1952 to 1955; later he was in the Federal Senate. He was Federal Minister of Social Services in 1952-3, and Federal Minister of Education from 1953 to 1955. In 1955 he joined Sir Ahmadu Bello's (q.v.) Northern Region Government in Kaduna as Minister of Social Welfare, Cooperatives, and Surveys.

In 1956, however, he returned to Maiduguri to assume the traditional office of Waziri (prime minister) under the Shehu. He carried out very necessary reforms in the traditional local government. He was chairman of the Provisional Council of Ahmadu Bello University, Zaria, for the two years before the new university opened in 1962.

In 1962 he was appointed the first Nigerian Governor of the Northern Region. He was knighted by the Queen of England in the same year. Though greatly respected, he had no real power in that post in the last years of Sir Ahmadu Bello's rule over the Northern Region. When that rule was ended with the killing of the Premier in the first coup of 1966, Sir Kashim was briefly arrested. On his release he was appointed Adviser to the Military Governor of the Region, which however was soon afterwards abolished with the creation of states in 1967-8.

Sir Kashim Ibrahim served as Chancellor of the University of Ibadan from 1966 to 1977, and then as Chancellor of the University of Lagos from 1977 to 1984. He did not return to politics. He acquired little material wealth and had to sue for his pension as former Governor of the Northern Region. When he died on 25 July 1990 his reputation was shown by the great gathering at his funeral in Maiduguri, and by the appointment of his son, an architect, as Shettima of Borno soon afterwards. He is remembered as an ardent educationist who in spite of his strong traditional upbringing clearly perceived and promoted the values and virtues of modern education. ∎

Idris I, King (1890-1983)

IDRIS I, Mohammed el-Sanusi (1890-1983).

LIBYAN monarch from independence in 1951 until his overthrow in 1969. He was the first and only King of Libya; the country came into existence formally only in 1951, and became a centralised State under him. It was also under him that, with its vast oil reserves, Libya assumed more strategic importance to the West. Idris was a pious and an intelligent man but suspicious, and in his 18 year reign there were 11 governments.

He was born in March 1890 at Jaghbub, a desert oasis in the south of Cyrenaica into a family which claimed descent from the prophet Mohammed. His grandfather was Muhammad bin Ali al-Sanusi (q.v.) who founded the Sanusiyya or Senoussi, a highly orthodox Islamic brotherhood which preached Islamic unity and a purified practice of the faith. Son of al-Mahdi al-Sanusi (q.v.), Idris received a Koranic education.

At the time when Idris was born, Libya was under Turkish domination. In 1911 when he was just 21, the Italians attacked and conquered Cyrenaica and Tripolitania, the western coastal province. The Italian occupation met with a divided response – the coastal towns assuming a defeatist stance while there was strong

King Idris I

assistance, offering Idris recognition as Emir of all Libya in April 1922. This placed Idris in a dilemma, should he accept and worsen his already strained relations with Italy, or offend Tripolitania by refusing? He played for time before accepting the offer in November 1922, by which time it was too late as the Italians had re-established military control over the area and were threatening Cyrenaica and Fezzan. With the accession to power of Mussolini in 1925, Idris left Cyrenaica for exile in Egypt, not returning until 1943. The Sanusiyya continued a prolonged and bloody military style campaign against Italian rule.

During the Second World War, Idris assisted the Allies by recruiting scouts and guerrilla fighters to guide the troops in the desert campaigns, and returned to Libya in 1943 when the Italian army was routed in Cyrenaica. Cyrenaica and Tripolitania were then occupied by the British, and Fezzan, the southern province, by the French.

There was much discussion on the future of the territories at the end of the War. The UN finally adopted a resolution in November 1949 under which all three territories (Tripolitania, Cyrenaica and Fezzan) were to become independent, with a UN Commission to frame a constitution. Ten weeks before the UN resolution on Libyan independence was passed, Britain granted internal autonomy to Cyrenaica, recognising Idris as Emir of Cyrenaica. Cultivating the Sanusi monarchy in the person of Idris seemed the ideal way of ensuring the future Libya's reliance on the Western powers. Even before the drafting of the constitution, Britain was engaged in long-term negotiations with Idris which would allow British forces to remain on Cyrenaican soil in return for much-needed financial aid.

It was decided that the only means of creating a unified state was the recognition of Idris as monarch: Tripolitania was forced to recognise that if she did not accept the Sanusi crown, Cyrenaica would go her own way and it would not be possible to achieve a unified state. Federation was the only form of state Idris would accept, hence, despite widespread opposition from nationalist groupings, the Constitution provided for a federal form of government. It also provided for an elected House of Representatives and nominated Senate, with the King as Head of State. As well as being empowered to name the Prime Minister, and on his advice nominate other Ministers, the King could

opposition from the interior of the country led by the Sanusiyya in alliance with the Turks. In 1912, Italy and Turkey negotiated a peace which ostensibly granted self-government to Tripolitania and Cyrenaica while still placing them under Italian sovereignty. The Sanusiyya continued to fight the Italians with aid from Turkey and Germany, and in 1916, Idris succeeded his cousin as the spiritual leader of the brotherhood. The following year a truce was negotiated with the help and mediation of the British, and in November 1920, Idris was recognized by the Italians as Emir of Cyrenaica. In return the people were to disarm and disband. Meanwhile, following the First World War (1914-18), Tripolitania had declared itself an Arab Republic.

In the early twenties, however, Tripolitania was once again threatened by the Italians and turned to the Sanusiyya for

appoint provincial governors who were answerable neither to an executive nor to a
legislative body. Laws could be initiated by
the elected House of Representatives, by the
nominated Senate or by the King himself
who had the power to veto legislation and
dissolve the elected Parliament at his sole
discretion.

It was under this Constitution, with
King Idris as Head of State, that the United
Kingdom of Libya came into existence on 24
December 1951. Elections were held, though
not on political lines except in Tripolitania.
Riots followed the allegation by the National
Congress Party that the election results had
been rigged, and the Party's leader was
deported. The King was not prepared to
tolerate political parties; political gatherings were banned by law, meetings were
forbidden, trade union activity restricted
and the press brought under government
control. By the end of its first year of
independence, Libya had become a non-party
state. The second elections, held in January
1956, were conducted not on political lines,
but rather on personality, family influence
and factional interests.

The Constitution and the powers
vested in the King ensured that in practice a
"palace system" of power would operate.
However, since political parties and programmes were suppressed, and the government was immune from public pressure,
governments fell one after another in rapid
succession through conflict with this "palace system".

The problems facing Libya at independence were formidable. Economically it was
possibly the poorest country in the world.
Apart from having no apparent natural
resources, the battles of the Second World
War had left its infrastructure in ruins.
King Idris also faced the political problem of
unifying three entirely different provinces,
with the old traditional rivalry between
Tripolitania and Cyrenaica. In addition,
there was an acute deficiency of trained
administrators, for Italian colonialism had,
as a matter of policy, made no effort to form
an elite.

Another potentially destabilising factor, which led to endless palace intrigues was
the lack of an heir apparent. King Idris had
married his cousin Emira Fatima in 1933, but
was to remain without a son.

It was the discovery of oil (the first
strike was made in 1955) that brought the

federal system to an end. It proved impossible
to manage oil exploitation and the funds that
derived from it without a centralised state.
Thus, in 1963, by royal decree, the Kingdom
of Libya was made a unified and centralised
state under a new Constitution.

Economically, oil proved of little benefit to the mass of the people. It promoted,
rather, the emergence of a new rich class
who benefitted from oil alongside the traditional oligarchy. The new found wealth
tended to be diverted into commercial and
speculative economic activity, while graft
and corruption flourished. Idris's response
to student criticism of government oil policy
and demands for the withdrawal of British
and American bases, which boiled over in
1964 and 1966 into violent demonstrations,
was to ignore it rather than seek confrontation. It was not until the Six-Day War, in
1967, that Arab nationalism really gripped
Libya, and demands for the removal of
foreign military bases were renewed. The
Libyan government threatened to expel the
Americans from Wheelus (an American air
base outside Tripoli) and temporarily shut
off oil production. Despite the voicing of
these anti-western sentiments however, the
bases remained, negotiations for withdrawal
only lasting as long as opposition to the bases
remained vocal.

Libya continued to be strategically
important to the West. Further, by 1968 she
was Britain's and Italy's biggest oil supplier
and France's third biggest. In May 1968 it
was announced that Britain had won an
order to supply a complete missile air defence
system to Libya. For King Idris, this was an
ideal solution to his defence problems, since a
sophisticated missile system could not be
turned into a coup-making instrument. Idris
distrusted the notion of a regular army. In
1956 the army was only 6,500 men strong and
by 1969 still no more than 10,000 in strength,
although it was top-heavy with 'officers.
However, many of the officers had received
their military training in Egypt or from
Egyptian instructors and had therefore been
exposed to the socialist ideas of Nasser's
Egypt and the ideals of Arab nationalism.
Apart from this, there were members of the
officer corps who objected to the re-training
element that went with the defence package
and saw themselves being relegated, and also
young technocrats in positions of influence
who were urging numerical expansion of the
army.

The King was by now an old man and was felt to be losing his judgement, while still more power was amassed by the already powerful Shalhi family. Omar Shalhi was the King's special adviser, while his brother, Colonel Abdul Aziz Shalhi, was in control of the army. The widespread corruption and nepotism, the inequitable distribution of the oil wealth, the continued presence of foreign military bases and the general subservience to foreign interests, all served to increase the growing unpopularity of the monarchy.

On 1 September 1969, King Idris was overthrown by a military coup d'état, led by Colonel Muammar Gaddafi. The King was out of the country at the time, resting at a Turkish spa. He moved to Greece and later to exile in Cairo. He was still there in October 1971 when a Libyan People's Court trying cases of corruption sentenced him to death *in absentia*. He died at the age of 93 in a Cairo hospital on 26 May 1983. ■

Ikoku, A.A. (1900-71)

IKOKU, Alvan Azimwa (1900-71).

NIGERIAN educationist. Born in the small town of Amanagwu in Arochukwu on 1 August 1900, to a wealthy merchant family, he was educated at Government School, Calabar, and later proceeded to a teacher training course at the Hope Waddell College in Calabar. His first appointment was in 1920 with the Presbyterian Church of Scotland in Itigidi, from where he joined the staff of St. Paul's Teacher Training College in Awka in 1924 as senior tutor. While teaching at Awka Ikoku also took private lessons with the Wolsey Hall Correspondence Course and earned the University of London degree in Philosophy in 1928.

In 1931, Ikoku resigned from the mission to establish his own college in Arochukwu, the Aggrey Memorial College, in order to facilitate the secondary education of young Nigerians. An admirer of the eminent Ghanaian educationist, Dr. Aggrey (q.v.), after whom he named his institution, Ikoku believed that education was essential to the development of the country.

Meanwhile the growth of educational institutions in the country had brought about the need to expand the activities of the Lagos-based Nigerian Union of Teachers (NUT) to the regions. Ikoku was a founder member of the newly opened branch in Calabar. His capacity for work, organisation and leadership was quickly recognised in Lagos and in November 1940 he was elected national Second Vice-President of the NUT.

A.A. Ikoku

By 1944, following government recognition of the union, he was one of the three officials appointed onto the Board of Education for the Southern Provinces.

When constitutional changes in 1946 allowed for the election of more Nigerians to the legislative chambers Ikoku was nominated to the Eastern Nigeria House of Assembly and given the Ministry of Education. Further constitutional developments in 1947 brought him to the Legislative Council in Lagos, where he was one of the three representatives of the Eastern Region. Once in government he applied his influence to foster the interests of the NUT in particular and education in general – he is remembered for being instrumental in the Legislative Council's acceptance of 44 of the Union's 45 proposals for amendments to various educational ordinances during a debate in the Lagos chamber.

In 1955, Alvan Ikoku became President of the NUT. It was during this time that the union made recommendations for a uniform system of education in Nigeria, which though rejected by the colonial government later became the basis of the official policy of independent Nigeria. In March 1966, the new military government that had seized power from the civilian administration in January set up a Study Group to look into the feasibility of evolving a unified education policy. Ikoku was appointed a member of the group whose work was interrupted by the Civil War. The advent of hostilities in 1967 saw the door closed between Nigeria and her illustrious son Ikoku, who retired home to Arochukwu in the breakaway region. He was however not to conceal his commitment to the progress of the NUT whose President he remained; from Arochukwu he kept close contact by correspondence with the Lagos Headquarters until his death on 18 November 1971.

Ikoku served on various bodies in the country. He was a member of the West African Examinations Council and the Council of the University of Ibadan, and chairman of the Board of Governors of the Aviation Training Centre. In 1965, he was awarded an honorary degree of Doctor of Laws at a special convocation of the University of Ibadan to whose fortunes he had made enormous contribution.■

E.S. Ikoli

Ikoli, E.S. (1893-1960)

IKOLI, Ernest Sesei (1893-1960).

NIGERIAN journalist; he was the first editor of the *Daily Times*, Nigeria's leading national daily newspaper. Born on 25 March 1893 at Brass (now in Rivers State), he was the son of an illustrious merchant who traded on the coast of south-east Nigeria. His mother was among the first women from the Niger Delta to receive Western education. The young Ikoli went to Bonny Primary School and then to King's

College in Lagos, where he was one of the foundation students on its opening in 1909; later he taught there, becoming assistant Mathematics master in 1913. But in 1919 he resigned over an incident involving European racial arrogance at the college; a European master had spoken rather harshly to Ikoli, which he considered an insult to himself and his race.

He then went into journalism as editorial assistant at the *Lagos Weekly Record* under the editorship of Thomas Horatio Jackson, who had taken over from his father John Payne Jackson (q.v.) who founded the paper in 1889. After two years with the *Record* Ikoli founded his own newspaper, the *African Messenger*, in 1921. He remained its editor and proprietor until 1926 when he was appointed the first editor of the newly founded *Daily Times*, whose first editorial he wrote on 1 June 1926. The previous year the *Daily Times* had taken over Ikoli's *African Messenger*. In 1928 he left the *Daily Times* to found the Nigerian *Daily Mail* until 1931 when it ceased publication.

Ikoli also took part in politics in Lagos, starting as secretary of the local branch of the Universal Negro Improvement Association (UNIA) of Marcus Garvey. In

1934 he, Vaughn, H.O. Davies and others became the leaders of the new Lagos Youth Movement (NYM), which in 1938 was renamed the Nigerian Youth Movement and came under the leadership of Dr. K. Abayomi (q.v.). Three years later he was elected to the Legislative Council in Lagos, in a bitterly contested election in which he was opposed by Samuel Akinsanya (who later became Odemo of Ishara). He was elected president of the NYM in 1943. Meanwhile from 1938 to 1944 he edited another newspaper, the *Daily Service*, the NYM organ, with Samuel Ladoke Akintola (q.v.). Ikoli was re-elected to the Legislative Council as an Independent in 1946, because of the disqualification of his opponent; in 1947 he decided not to seek re-election again.

While Ikoli's active political life was short-lived, he is remembered by his former political colleagues as a foremost politician with a determined mind. One of these, a former political opponent who became a prominent traditional ruler, Oba Samuel Akinsanya, Odemo of Ishara, said of him in the first yearly Ernest Ikoli Memorial Lecture inaugurated by the *Sunday Times* of Nigeria in 1979: "I worked together with Ernest Ikoli for many years. We did many things together. We fought many a fight together. And I cannot remember any political agitation or representation to the colonial government in those days with which Ikoli was not associated. In fact he would be one of the foremost leaders."

After leaving politics Ikoli became chairman of the Rediffusion Service and Public Relations Adviser to the Nigeria Railway Corporation. He was awarded the MBE by the British crown. On 21 October 1960, three weeks after Nigeria became independent Ernest Ikoli died and was widely mourned.■

Ironsi, J.T.U. (1924-66)

IRONSI, General Johnson Thomas Umanakwe Aguiyi (1924-66).

NIGERIAN soldier and statesman. General Aguiyi-Ironsi was born in March 1924, at Umuahia in Eastern Nigeria (now in Imo State). After primary education

he joined the Nigerian army as a private in 1942. By 1946, he had risen to the rank of company sergeant-major. In 1948, he went to Camberley Staff College in England; he returned a year later a 2nd Lieutenant of the Royal West African Frontier Force.

Gen. J.T.U. Aguiyi Ironsi

Aguiyi Ironsi served first at Accra (Ghana) before being posted to Lagos. He was promoted captain in 1953, major in 1955 and lieutenant-colonel in 1960. He was appointed commander of the 5th battalion of the army, stationed in Kano, and later in the year was placed at the head of the Nigerian contingent of the United Nations' force in the Congo (now Zaire).

From 1961 to 1962, he was the military attaché to the Nigeria High Commission, London; during this period he was promoted Brigadier. After a course at the Imperial Defence College, UK, he returned to the Congo in 1964 as commander of the United Nations peace-keeping force. He returned to Nigeria in 1965, and with the complete Nigerianisation of the army he was promoted Major-General and, as the most senior indigenous officer, became head of the Nigerian army in February 1965.

The coup of January 1966 brought the army to power and as its head, Ironsi became the head of the Nigerian government. Although power was handed to him as the leader of the forces loyal to the Balewa administration, the government he inherited was a poisoned gift. Acute political differences and tribal distrust made his position untenable. He failed to satisfy the supporters of Major Nzeogwu (q.v.) and the other coup-makers, who had almost certainly intended to kill him, and whom he detained; while as he was an Ibo, governing in the charged atmosphere that followed the "Ibo coup", the Hausa-Fulani North distrusted him. His attempts at conciliation only made his overthrow easy for his opponents, the officers and other soldiers who carried out the "second coup" barely seven months after he had come to power. He was kidnapped and assassinated in Ibadan on 29 July 1966.

In January 1967, following the Aburi meeting of the military governors, Gen. Ironsi's body was disinterred and reburied in the Eastern Region. ∎

Ismail Pasha (1830-95)

ISMAIL PASHA (1830-95).

KHEDIVE of Egypt under Turkish suzerainty. Born in Cairo on 31 December 1830, the second son of the viceroy Ibrahim Pasha, he was educated in Paris, after which he undertook various diplomatic missions in Europe for the viceroy Mohamed Said Pasha whom he succeeded in 1863. Anxious to increase his prestige he obtained from the Ottoman Sultan in 1867 the hereditary title of Khedive, an honorific title adopted by his successors until 1914.

During his reign the Suez Canal was completed (1869) and he inaugurated it with lavish ceremonies to which all the crowned heads of Europe were invited. The cultivation of cotton was developed under the stimulus of the rising prices during the American Civil War. These two developments were of far-reaching importance for the future economic development of Egypt.

Under his modernising domestic policy, irrigation canals were built, sugar factories, docks, ports and water and gas works were built in Cairo, Suez and Alexandria. An astute landowner of vast estates and an enthusiastic town-planner, he laid the foundations of modern Cairo and in 1869 granted Alexandria its municipal charter. His greatest contribution lay in the development of communications; he extended the railways and nationalised the postal services in 1865.

Progress was also made in the field of education during Ismail's reign; the first girls' school was founded, a school of medicine was opened, a military academy established and schools were increased from 185 to 4,187.

Between 1870 and 1875 Ismail extended Egyptian authority down the Red Sea coast, establishing garrisons at Harar and Berbera, but his attempt to occupy Kismayu was prevented by Britain. In 1869 he commissioned Sir Samuel Baker to annex part of Uganda; in 1874 Darfur was added to the Egyptian dominions. But his forward march was thwarted in Equatoria and in Ethiopia where two Egyptian armies were defeated.

In 1875 he sold his Suez Canal shares to Great Britain for £4,000,000 which Disraeli, Britain's Prime Minister at the time, had obtained from the Rothschilds, a family of international bankers. Yet by 1876 the

Ismail Pasha

foreign debt, which was £3,000,000 in 1863, had soared to £100,000,000. Accordingly, in April 1876 Ismail stopped paying interest on his debts, paid no salaries to his officials and doubled the tax on the people.

The European Court in Alexandria, which had succeeded the consular court by the judicial organisation approved by the Sultan, now ordered Ismail to pay his debt and attached his palace at Ramleh, Alexandria. Britain and France appointed a commission to investigate his finances, as a result of which the "Caisse de la Dette" was established as a supervisory machinery to control Ismail's spending. In October 1876 formal Anglo-French dual control was put into effect. In 1878 Ismail and his relatives were forced to surrender most of their estates and to exact no further taxes unless approved by a committee of Egyptians and foreigners. A new government was formed under the Armenian-born Nubar Pasha, an Englishman was put in charge of finance, and a Frenchman in charge of public works. Ismail's resistance to the resulting encroachments upon his power and independence, culminating in his dismissal of his European commissioners, led to his deposition by the Sultan at the insistence of the powers on 26 June 1879. He died in exile in Istanbul on 21 March 1895. ■

tence at first. After spending some time at Ogbomosho, where he taught but also wrote pamphlets and press articles, he returned in 1938 to Calabar, where a National Institute had been founded by local educated people, and he became its head. Then he started his own West African People's Institute, an educational institution for which he became famous. It had a press which published his works: *The Assurance of Freedom* (1949), *Crusade for Freedom* (1949), *The Revolt of the Liberal Spirit in Nigeria* (1949), *Sterile Truths and Fertile Lies* (1949), *Two Vital Fronts in Nigeria's Advancement* (1949), *National Youth Renaissance* (undated), *Theory of Social Symbiosis* (1951), etc.

He was a leading member of the National Council for Nigeria and the Cameroons (NCNC) after its foundation in 1944, and was elected to the Eastern Nigeria House of Assembly in 1951 on the party's ticket. In 1948 he became First National Vice-President of the NCNC. After elections in 1951, which the NCNC won in the Eastern Region, he became Minister for Natural Resources and Leader of Government Business for that Region. A year later there was a crisis within the NCNC, in January 1953, the nine NCNC ministers in the East resigned, but Ita and five others withdrew their resignations, and stayed as ministers despite

Ita, E. (1902-72)

ITA, Eyo (1902-72).

NIGERIAN educationist, the founder of the Nigeria Youth League Movement. Born in Calabar, he went to Duke Town School in that town and then to Calabar's famous Hope Waddell Training Institute. After teaching at the Baptist Academy at Lagos, 1926 to 1928, he went to the USA where he studied at the Teacher's College of Columbia University, majoring in religion and education. He later read for a BA in Canada. On his return in 1933 he became active as an educationist, a pamphleteer, and a nationalist who believed strongly in a role for Nigeria's youth.

He formed the Nigeria Youth League Movement, which had little effective exis-

E. Ita

a hostile House of Assembly, until new elections in the same year installed a government under the NCNC leader, Nnamdi Azikiwe.

Before that, Ita had formed a National Independence Party (NIP) with Dr. E.U. Udoma and Jaja Wachukwu. Later in 1953 the Calabar-Ogoja-Rivers (COR) movement was founded to call for separation of the non-Ibo minorities from the Eastern Region, and Ita was one of its leading figures for some years. Later his NIP joined the United National Party (UNP) of Alvan Ikoku (q.v.) to form the United National Independence Party.

In 1959 he announced he was leaving the COR movement, and returned to the NCNC. The "professor", as he was called, was not prominent in politics thereafter. After independence he devoted his time to developing and improving his school. During the Civil War he was on the side of the Biafran secessionists and acted as one of their travelling representatives. He died after the return of peace, towards the end of 1972. ■

J

Jabavu, D.D.T. (1885-1959)

JABAVU, Davidson Don Tengo (1885-1959).

SOUTH AFRICAN educationist and politician who was a founder of the All African Convention which sought to unite all non-European opposition to the segregationist measures of the South African government. The eldest son of one of the leading Africans for many years, John Tengo Jabavu (q.v.), he was born in 1885 in King Williams Town. After failing in 1901 to gain admission for his son in an all-white school in King Williams Town, Jabavu senior sent the young Jabavu to be educated at Morija

D.D.T. Jabavu

Institution, a mission centre in Basutoland (now Lesotho). He later studied at Lovedale in the Cape Province before proceeding to the United Kingdom to complete his matriculation at Colwyn Bay in Wales. He entered the University of London in 1906, obtained a degree in English, followed by a diploma in Education from the University of Birmingham.

While studying in London Jabavu attended the 1911 meeting of the Universal Races Congress where he met leading Afro-Americans and Africans, including his father who was on the South African delegation. Before returning home in 1915 he visited America on a tour of Booker T. Washington's renowned Tuskegee Institute and other black centres of learning to acquaint himself with their services to the Afro-American community.

In South Africa, the University of Fort Hare was formally opened in 1916, Jabavu was a founding member of staff, and the only African academic in the institution; he remained there as professor of African languages until 1944. During this period he combined his teaching with extra-curricular activities like promoting student organisations and generally participating actively in African politics. He took part in various projects aimed at furthering the advancement and cause of the Africans: he founded the South African Native Farmers' Association to encourage the development of farming standards; he founded the Cape African Teachers' Association and the South African Teachers' Association and the South African Native Teachers' Federation which he led for a considerable number of years. He was also president of the Cape Native Voters' Convention, which campaigned vigorously in the 1920s and 1930s for the retention of Africans' voting rights.

Although Jabavu was not a regular member of the African National Congress (ANC), he participated in many meetings of the Congress, like the one in December 1935 where the objectives of the All African Convention (AAC) were discussed. The following year, when these were formally endorsed, he was elected first president of the AAC which sought to consolidate all non-European opposition to the proposed abolition of African vote. He led several AAC delegations to Parliament in Cape Town to argue its case for the common voters' roll, but the Convention's subsequent acceptance of a separate roll for Africans was construed by the ANC as damaging to African interests. The ANC parted company with the AAC. In 1948, the year Jabavu retired from public life, attempts were made to reconcile the differences under a joint ANC-AAC "Call for Unity". Jabavu was signatory to the "Call for Unity", on behalf of the AAC, but the move failed and he retired from its presidency.

He devoted his later years to running a private insurance business. A man of untiring energy, he wrote several books and articles on the African struggle. In 1953, in recognition of his contribution towards the creation of a just society in South Africa, Rhodes University awarded him an honorary doctorate. He died in 1959, at the age of 74. ■

J.T. Jabavu

Jabavu, J.T. (1839-1921)

JABAVU, John Tengo (1839-1921).

SOUTH AFRICAN politician and newspaper proprietor and journalist, who edited the first Xhosa newspaper in South Africa. Born of Methodist parents in Fort Beaufort in 1839, Jabavu was educated at the Healdtown Missionary Institution.

In 1875 he qualified as a teacher and from 1876 to 1881 he taught at the Mission Primary School in Somerset East. He took up a part-time job at the printing department of a local newspaper, and in this way he not only augmented the meagre renumeration paid to African teachers but also began a journalistic career with occasional contribution to the prestigious *Cape Argus* newspaper. His writing flair was soon recognised and in 1881 he was offered the position of

editor of *Isigidimi Sama Xhosa*, the Xhosa edition of the *Christian Express* which was being published by Lovedale Mission authorities. He relinquished the office, three years later, because the Lovedale Mission discouraged political commentary.

He then started another African paper, *Imvo Zabantsundu*, which was published weekly in King Williams with the financial assistance of some white liberal politicians who relied on African votes in the Cape Colony. Also in 1884 Jabavu had formed the Native Electoral Association with which he sought to mobilise the minority African vote behind his financiers. He was severely criticised for refusing to stand as a candidate in the 1884 elections even though popular opinion had urged him to do so. The criticism which said he was parochially concerned with Cape Colony politics was compounded by his absence at the launching of the African National Congress (ANC) in 1912; he however participated in its subsequent campaign against the discriminatory measures of the government.

In 1909 he accompanied the ANC leaders to London to protest against the proposed colour bar measures of the newly instituted Union government. He was to return to the British capital two years later as a delegate to the Universal Races Congress which was attended by prominent black leaders from Africa and the United States. In 1912 he founded the South African Races Congress, but his political standing began to wane the following year when he used his newspaper to support the Native Land Act which was widely condemned by African opinion. The popularity of *Imvo Zabantsundu* as the organ of the Africans declined and it was soon taken over by another paper, *Izwe Labantu*, founded by Walter Benson Rubusana (q.v.) and other ANC leaders. Jabavu suffered a further political setback in 1914 when he fought the election of that year to the Cape Provincial Council against Rubusana, the only African member of the Council. Though he did not succeed in getting elected, he succeeded in preventing the re-election of Rubusana by splitting the African vote in the Tembuland constituency in favour of a European candidate, who won the seat.

Jabavu then left politics to concentrate on the task of establishing a university for Africans, which had been his other preoccupation in the past. He was later appointed to the governing council of the University College of Fort Hare which was opened in 1916 and served there until his death in 1921. His eldest son, Davidson Don Tengo Jabavu (q.v.), later worked at the University where he became the first African professor in South Africa. ■

and take a job with the *Lagos Times* owned by R.B. Blaize (q.v.) in 1882. He was later dismissed, but the two men reached an agreement in 1890 to revive the *Times* after it had collapsed. The agreement failed and Jackson and Blaize broke up in recrimination. Then in 1891 Jackson founded the *Lagos Weekly Record*.

For 24 years he edited this paper, making it the most influential newspaper of its time in West Africa with Jackson's unrivalled influence over the coastal elites of British West Africa. He was recalled later with admiration, as a person with a thorough grasp of fact. For nearly ten years his newspaper received a subsidy in the form of regular government advertisements from the British authorities. This did not clash with the general Lagos elite view, expressed by the *Record*, which was in favour of British expansion; or with the views of Dr. E.W. Blyden (q.v.), Jackson's fellow countryman and hero, who combined admiration for African tradition with support for colonialism.

After 1900, when the subsidy ended, Jackson was more critical of the British. He was closely involved in petitions and other protest activities in Lagos, his newspaper being their main means of expression. In 1915 at the height of the *Lagos Weekly Record's* influence he died, leaving it to his son Thomas Horatio Jackson (1879-1936) who developed it even further. ■

Jackson, J.P. (died 1915)

JACKSON, John Payne (died 1915).

LIBERIAN journalist, celebrated editor of anti-colonial newspapers in Lagos. Born at Cape Palmas, he was the son of an Afro-American settler in Liberia, Thomas John Jackson, who became well known as a judge and preacher and who died when John was four years old. John Jackson was able to attend the Training Institute on the Cavalla river. Then he went into business, travelling to the Gold Coast (Ghana) and Lagos in the 1880s. His attempt to become an independent palm produce trader was defeated by European competition. This led him to go to Lagos

---

Jaja (c.1821-91)

JAJA, King of Opobo (c.1821-91).

NIGERIAN traditional ruler, famous for his resistance to the imposition of colonial domination. He was a slave sold into the house of Anna Pepple of Bonny and rose to the headship of his master's "house". He later established himself as the most dominant figure in the politics of the Delta states when he became King of the newly founded kingdom of Opobo. Succession to the headship of an Ijaw trading "house" was not based on heredity but on one's ability to provide for the welfare of the members of the house. Jaja's accession to the headship around 1869 caused resentment in other members of the Anna Pepple house. This culminated in a civil war from which Jaja emerged the victor.

After the civil war in Bonny Jaja led his house to the Opobo river where he founded the Kingdom of Opobo. Here his business acumen and capacity found full

King Jaja

scope; he soon established plantations and built a port and strategically placed trading settlements on the creeks which not only enabled him to control the supply of palm oil to the European merchants along the coast but also made Opobo one of the richest Delta states. With the wealth came political influence and military power. Such was the strength of Jaja's army that during the Ashanti War he committed a contingent of his soldiers to the British effort, for which he was awarded a sword of honour by Queen Victoria in 1875.

In 1870, having consolidated his new settlement, he proclaimed Opobo an independent state consisting of 14 of the 18 houses of Bonny. Three years later the new state was recognised by Britain which in 1884 entered into a "treaty" with Opobo, placing the latter under the protection of the British Crown. However the proclamation of a British Protectorate over the Oil Rivers in 1885 not only heralded the demise of the independence of the coast city-states but also precipitated a quarrel between Jaja and the British.

Jaja was the only ruler in the Delta area who questioned the new political order by seeking a definition of the word "protectorate" from the British, who replied vaguely that Her Majesty's Government would only extend to his kingdom her "gracious favour and protection". He accepted the explanation, believing that Opobo's new relationship with Britain would not affect its independence. Accordingly, he continued to monopolise the oil trade, forbidding anyone to deal directly with the European merchants on the coast while continuing his direct exports to Britain. As a result Jaja saw the British insistence on "free" trade as interference and a violation of the 1884 treaty.

The British Consul in the Oil Rivers, Harry Johnston, was opposed to Jaja's continued independence. In 1887, Johnston abrogated his power to impose customs duties on oil exports from the state. Jaja sent a delegation to London to protest to the Secretary of State for the Colonies. Meanwhile Consul Johnston had written to the British Government requesting permission to expel Jaja who had resisted successive threats to compel him to meet British demands. The King was "invited" on board a British gunboat, HMS *Goshawk*, to meet Consul Johnston. Jaja was reassured by Johnston on the eve of their meeting that "I hereby assure you that whether you accept or reject my proposals tomorrow no restraint whatever will be put on you – you will be free to go as soon as you have heard the message of the Government". But once on board, Jaja was asked to choose between being tried for violating the treaty and seeing Opobo bombed by the British Navy. The King opted for trial, which was then held in Accra. He was found guilty and banished in 1887 to the West Indies on a pension of £800 per annum. This paved the way for the establishment of an effective colonial authority over the region which in the first year provided nearly £90,000 from import duties alone.

Jaja's deportation caused much discontent in the Oil Rivers states. After repeated appeals to the British Government, the Colonial Secretary set up a commission to investigate and make recommendations for the administration of the new colony. In 1891, the commission, headed by Major Claude MacDonald, recommended that, in response to popular demand in Opobo, Jaja should be returned and reinstated. In the same year, Jaja was allowed to return, but died on the way back on 7 July 1891. His body was subsequently transported to Opobo where it was buried. ■

Jaja, Amanyanabo of Opobo (1915-80)

JAJA, Chief Douglas, Amanyanabo of Opobo (1915-80).

Chief D.A. Jaja

NIGERIAN traditional ruler. A descendant of the great King Jaja (q.v.), he ruled Opobo, having succeeded his father as the Amanyanabo, from 1936 until his death in 1980. He is regarded as one of the leading traditional rulers in modern Nigeria.

Douglas Jaja was born on 29 April 1915 in Opobo Town, the son of Chief Arthur Macpepple Jaja (1872-1936) of the Jaja Royal House made famous by its founder and first king of the Opobo kingdom, King Jaja. Douglas Jaja was educated at the Government School, Opobo Town, and then at the Aggrey Memorial College in Arochukwu. He left that College at Class III in 1936 to succeed his father, becoming at the age of 21 the fourth ruler of Opobo after King Jaja. Like his father the new Amanyanabo soon became involved in national affairs. Undaunted by the might of the colonial authorities he gave his support to the nationalist movement of Dr Nnamdi Azikiwe, the National Council of Nigeria and the Cameroons (NCNC) that was campaigning against British rule. It was perhaps because of this involvement in politics that he renounced his chieftancy temporarily between 1943 and 1951. He reassumed his throne in 1952.

Chief Douglas Jaja was appointed to the administration of the defunct Eastern Region, where, as minister of State in the premier's office, he displayed immense industry and influence. He represented that region at the 1957 London Constitutional Conference on Nigeria's independence whose attainment in 1960 brought the Amanyanabo more state functions, and also rewards. He was made a foundation member of the Eastern Region House of Chiefs when that chamber was created shortly after independence. Chief Jaja was a member of the two-chamber legislature of Eastern Nigeria. From there, and as Minister of State he made valuable contributions to the development of the region's political and economic institutions. He performed these functions until the suspension of parliamentary activities by the army in January 1966.

The Amanyanabo, however, remained prominent in national affairs. He was one of the leading traditional rulers who attended the meeting with the new military rulers on 29 July 1966 at Ibadan. It was during that meeting that the first change of leadership within the military regime occurred with the assassinations of General Aguiyi-Ironsi and Colonel Adekunle Fajuyi (qq.v.) Thereafter Chief Jaja's role, like that of all other traditional rulers in the country, was largely dictated by subsequent rearrangements under the new order. Generally this meant less effective voice in state matters, but the chiefs retained influence in local affairs and as such their support was sought throughout Nigeria by the new military authorities. Some, like the Amanyanabo, were even called upon to perform state duties. Chief Jaja was made director of the Opobo Boatyard as well as being appointed a member of the Rivers State Traditional Chiefs Council. Some years before his death on 31 July 1980 he was made Chancellor of the University of Jos in Plateau State.

Chief Douglas Jaja was extremely popular among his subjects and colleagues alike; he was respected for his talent, experience and fairmindedness. The Amanyanabo was as charismatic as he was humble. This humility, coupled with a penchant for simple life-style, had sometimes given a contradictory impression about the Chief's noble background. Chief Jaja was loved the more for that by the people of Opobo who gave him a royal burial in December 1980. ■

Johnson, H.R.W. (1837-98)

JOHNSON, Hilary Richard Wright (1837-98).

LIBERIAN statesman. He was born in Liberia in 1837, his parents being among the early settlers from America who had come to Liberia with the American Colonisation Society. They were devout Methodists and he grew up in a deeply religious environment.

He was educated in Liberia at the Alexander High School, after which he joined the government service, holding a variety of positions until 1858 when he became private secretary to President Benson. He worked very closely with the President, gaining a reputation for efficiency. In 1863 he was appointed Secretary of State.

Four months later he resigned and went to Liberia College to continue his education, receiving a Master of Arts degree. After graduating he remained at the College on teaching commitments.

In 1870 he became Secretary of the Interior, a new Cabinet position which had been created by President Roye. While in this post he was selected as one of the negotiators for the country's first foreign loan between a private group of London bankers and the Liberian Government. These negotiations were completed in 1871 and despite the unpopularity of the loan among leading Liberians, he was appointed Secretary of State under President Roberts (q.v.)in 1872. He remained in this position for one year, and then resigned following his

opposition to the appointment of an ambassador to the Court of St James.

He was selected as president of Liberia College by the Boston Board of Trustees in 1877, but within one year he resigned after disagreements with the Board. He returned to the College in 1880 and was awarded an honorary Doctorate of Laws in 1882.

In the 1883 elections Johnson was the successful presidential candidate and he was inaugurated on 7 January 1884, being the first President of the Republic to be born in Africa. His immediate concern was to resolve the long-standing dispute between his country and Britain over the boundary between Liberia and Sierra Leone. In the previous year, Britain had seized a portion of territory claimed to be in North West Liberia, and international protests by the Liberian Government against this action had been of no avail. Johnson asked the USA for advice, and was told that it would be best to accept the new boundaries. The President did so after receiving authorisation for this move from the Liberian Senate and in November 1885 the Havelock Draft Conven-

H.R.W. Johnson

tion was eventually signed, under which the Mano River became the border between Liberia and Sierra Leone.

This was not the end of his administration's territorial problems. On 26 October 1891 France claimed possession of the Liberian territory between the San Pedro and Cavalla Rivers in the South East of the country. Once again the Government protested in vain and had to accept the situation as it lacked the means to oppose this action with force.

Altogether Johnson served four terms as President between 1884 and 1892, he retired from office after failing to gain re-election. He died in 1898 with the reputation of an astute and able politician and a man of oratorical skills. ■

Johnson, J. (c.1838-1917)

JOHNSON, Bishop James (c.1838-1917).

NIGERIAN churchman, a celebrated Anglican bishop. Born in Freetown to "Recaptive" parents, after completing studies at the Fourah Bay Institution (1857) he became a clergyman under the Anglican Church Missionary Society (CMS). He worked with the CMS "Native pastorate", started in 1861, and believed strongly in it as a means for African advancement, for he was a lifelong defender of African interests in church and state. Although he was often in conflict with the missionaries, they saw him as being basically loyal to them and believed he could channel the nationalist feelings of Christians in Lagos and avert a secession from the Mission. So he was transferred in 1874 to Lagos.

In Lagos he expanded the local Native Pastorate, including several Anglican parishes in it, such as that of St. Paul's in Breadfruit Street. As parson there he was for years a leader of the Lagos elite. His strong opposition to imperialism and advocacy of African initiative and autonomy in church matters aroused a wide following. He joined the Lagos Colony Legislative Council in 1886 and constantly criticised the British government. He believed Africa must be converted by Africans without European conquest. A

fervent and rigorous Christian, he feared no man and the West Coast elite had their disagreements with him, as the missionaries did.

When in 1891 some Anglicans formed the independent United Native African (UNA) Church, Johnson refused to join them. He opposed the CMS' action against the Niger mission of Bishop Crowther (q.v.), but stayed with the CMS and worked with its Delta Pastorate in a part of Bishop Crowther's former diocese. In 1900 he was consecrated Assistant Bishop of the Niger Delta. He was very popular in Nigeria then and there was at first strong support for his scheme to raise money for Africans to finance their own church organisation under the CMS, but missionaries did not agree with Johnson's nationalist view of the scheme. Bishop Johnson, who wrote a book *Yoruba Heathendom* in 1899, advocated greater recognition by the Church of a good deal of African tradition; for example, he would baptise children with Yoruba names.

Johnson was always a strong opponent of imperialism. He left the Legislative Council in 1894 after attacking the 1892 Ijebu expedition. He also denounced the Aro expedition of 1901-2. He criticised the oppression in South Africa and the Congo Free State. He and the dissident Baptist church-

Bishop J. Johnson

man Mojola Agbebi (q.v.) were prominent in the Lagos Branch of the London Aborigines Rights Protection Society (ARPS).

"Holy Johnson" died, after years of active evangelisation in the Niger Delta, in May 1917. ■

Johnson, O. (1849-1920)

JOHNSON, Dr. Obadiah (1849-1920).

NIGERIAN doctor, the second Nigerian to qualify as a doctor (the first one being Dr. Nathaniel King), and the first African to be appointed Assistant Surgeon in colonial Lagos in 1889.

The son of a Nigerian freed slave Erugun (later christened Henry Johnson) who laid claim to descent from the Oyo royal

Dr. O. Johnson

family, Obadiah was the fourth of six children, all born in Sierra Leone where their father was resettled. The other two children of Henry Johnson who distinguished themselves in scholarship were the Venerable Archdeacon Henry Johnson (1840-1901) of the Upper Niger, and Reverend Samuel Johnson (q.v.) who was pastor of Oyo and wrote the classical *History of the Yorubas*. Archdeacon Henry Johnson translated the *Book of Common Prayer* into the Mende language and the Psalms and Catechism into Nupe and Igbirra.

Obadiah Johnson had part of his primary education at Hastings (the village in Sierra Leone where he was born) Village School from 1855 to 1857. He later attended the Kudeti School, Ibadan, in Nigeria where his father died in 1865, and proceeded to Faji Day School in Lagos, and then the Church Missionary Society (CMS) Grammar School there. In 1876 he enrolled at the Fourah Bay College, Freetown, and went later to study at King's College in London and the University of Edinburgh. He excelled at these two British institutions, gaining all the major prizes in science and surgery.

He returned to Nigeria in 1886 and established a private medical practice in Lagos. For one year, from 1887 to 1888, he worked in Sierra Leone as Assistant Colonial Surgeon. During this period he was assistant medical officer at Sherbro, and also served as Justice of the Peace, registrar of Births and Deaths and commissioner of the Court of Requests.

Returning to his private practice in Lagos in 1888, Johnson was appointed in June of that year to the Colonial Medical Service, thus becoming the first African to be so appointed (before that time African doctors were, as a matter of colonial policy, excluded from public employment in Lagos). He was made the first Assistant Colonial Surgeon; later appointees included Dr. Oguntola Odunbaku Sapara (q.v.), Dr. John Randle and Dr. C.J. Lumpkin. Johnson left the public service in 1897, against a background of colonial discriminatory policy, to return to private practice. In 1901 he, with others including Sapara-Williams (q.v.), was nominated to the Lagos Legislative Council where he served until 1913, when he again disagreed with colonial policies.

A devout member of the Church of England, Dr. Johnson was an influential figure in the Christian community in Lagos.

He died in September 1920 in London, and in a tribute the following year Bishop Isaac Oluwole said in Lagos that "The Church in this diocese has suffered a great loss by the death of Dr. Obadiah Johnson. He was a member of the old church committee of Lagos before the constitution of the synod. He was on the committee which drafted the constitution by which our church is now governed, and played an active part in its work ... He has made a bequest of £5,000 to Fourah Bay which will, in due course, be available for the endowment of a chair of science in that college. He loved the Yoruba language and was most jealous for its purity. His professional responsibilities debarred him from serving on our translation committee, but whenever he had the opportunity, he made valuable suggestions".

Dr. Obadiah Johnson was responsible for the publication of *The History of the Yorubas*, in 1921, when he rewrote his brother's manuscripts from notes prepared by him (Samuel Johnson) in 1897.∎

Johnson, S. (1846-1901)

JOHNSON, Reverend Samuel (1846-1901).

NIGERIAN churchman and historian, famous for his *History of the Yorubas*. He was one of the *Saros*, the people who went to Nigeria in the 1840s from Sierra Leone having lived there as "Recaptives" taken off slave ships by the British Navy or as children born to such people in Freetown. They usually originated from areas within modern Nigeria, many of them being Yorubas. One such was from the Oyo area and claimed descent from the Alafin Abiodun of Oyo. He was enslaved, freed at sea and resettled in Freetown, and like other Recaptives was given the European names Henry Johnson when baptised.

Henry Johnson and his wife Sarah had several sons who became famous in Nigeria, where they moved in 1857 to join the Church Missionary Society (CMS) mission under Rev. David Hinderer at Ibadan. The first, Henry, became a famous Archdeacon with the CMS. The second, Nathaniel, worked for the CMS as a teacher and catechist. The third, Samuel, was a clergyman and historian, and the fourth, Obadiah (q.v.), was the second Nigerian in the country's history to qualify as a medical doctor.

Samuel was born at Hastings, Freetown, on 24 June 1846. Moving to Yorubaland with his family, he spent some time with them at Ibadan, longer than planned because of the Ibadan-Ijaiye war of 1860-62: one of many wars among Yoruba kingdoms after the 1820s. From 1863 to 1865 he completed his education at the CMS's Training Institution in Abeokuta.

From 1866 he worked as a schoolmaster under the CMS at Ibadan becoming in 1867, assistant to the Yoruba CMS deacon, Daniel Olubi. He became superintendent of the Anglican Mission's schools at the Kudeti and Aremo stations in Ibadan, and in 1873 he visited Oyo, his ancestral homeland. In 1875 Samuel Johnson became a catechist, and came to be involved in the Yoruba conflicts. The greatest of all the wars among Yoruba states, the Ekiti Parapo War, broke out in 1877. Johnson was to call it the "Sixteen Years' War," and it involved Ibadan, the dominant military power, and Egbaland as well as the Ekiti states which joined to form the Ekiti Parapo. Educated Yorubas, including *Saros* in particular, were involved. Johnson played the role of a peace-maker. In 1881 he carried letters to Lagos from the Alafin of Oyo suggesting British intervention to restore peace. This effort failed but Johnson and others continued their peace efforts. In 1885 he was a British government representative for mediation between Ibadan and the Ijesha and Ekiti states. In 1886 the war ended in some parts, though it was to continue in others until 1893. British interventions to restore peace were to pave the way for British annexation.

In 1880 Johnson became a deacon. The following year he was sent to Oyo as pastor, and in 1888 was ordained a minister. He helped to spread the CMS and Christianity in Oyo, where the Training Institution formerly at Abeokuta was eventually moved in 1896 as St. Andrew's College. That followed the British occupation of Yorubaland, at first by Treaties signed by Obas in 1893, later, in Oyo, by military action in 1895 to ensure full submission. Thus the Alafin of Oyo, who had been a nominal ruler of the Yorubas from his capital at New Oyo from the 1840s, was subordinated to British rule. By then Samuel Johnson, studying carefully the traditions of his countrymen while at Oyo had gone far towards completion of a major general history of the Yorubas. Completed in 1897 the manuscript was sent in 1899 to the CMS headquarters in London, where it got lost without trace. The Rev. Samuel Johnson himself died on 29 April 1901. He had been married twice, the second marriage with Martha Garba was celebrated at Lagos in 1895.

His brother Dr Obadiah Johnson ensured that his work on the Yorubas' history was not wasted after the mysterious loss of the manuscript. Over the years he recompiled the book again from Samuel Johnson's notes. Obadiah Johnson died in London in 1920, and the book was published in London in 1921 by George Routledge & Sons, as a *History of the Yorubas, from the Earliest Times to the Beginning of the British Protectorate*, written by Samuel Johnson and edited by his brother. It is recognised as a pioneering historical study of high quality, and has ensured Samuel Johnson's fame. ■

Jonathan, J.L. (1914-87)

JONATHAN, Chief Joseph Leabua (1914-87).

LESOTHO traditional Chief and first Prime Minister, Leabua Jonathan dominated his country's politics throughout the 21 years he was in power, combining both orthodox and unorthodox methods to neutralise opposition to his regime until a military take-over deposed him on 20 January 1986.

He was born in September 1914, at Leribe, 50 miles north east of Maseru, the capital, the son of Chief Jonathan Molapo and great grandson of Moshoeshoe I (q.v.), founder of the Basotho nation. He left school at the age of 19 and, like most young Basotho men of his age, went to work in the mines in South Africa, as a clerk. He did not remain there for long. In 1937 he was called back to Lesotho to help with local administration. Then came the big break and turning point in his career when, in 1951, he was appointed assessor to the Judicial Commissioner of

Lesotho, Patrick Duncan, who persuaded him to join politics. In 1956 he was elected to the district council at Leribe, and through it to the National Council.

It was about this time that the wind of change began blowing across Africa, bringing with it the rise of African nationalism. The need for getting together and channelling the people's nationalist aspirations led Jonathan to form in 1959, the Basutoland National Party (BNP). In 1964 he led a delegation to London to demand responsible government which was granted in 1965 following general elections in which the Basutoland Congress Party (BCP) of Ntsu Mokhehle also took part. The BNP won overwhelmingly, though Chief Leabua was himself defeated in his constituency. A bye-election at Mphanane however, gave him his seat and on 5 July, 1965 Jonathan became Prime Minister. A year later, on 4 October 1966, Lesotho became independent.

Post-independence politics showed Jonathan to be a shrewd and able operator, and he continued to have an absolute majority until the general elections of 1970 when it was clear, as the votes were being counted, that the BNP would lose power to the BCP. Rather than accept the people's verdict, Jonathan decided to continue as Prime Minister by force. He suspended the independence constitution, declared a state of emergency, and put Lesotho's King, Moshoeshoe II, under house arrest before driving him into eight months of exile in Holland. The BCP went underground, and Mokhehle into exile in South Africa from where he was later to mount an unsuccessful guerrilla campaign against the regime of Chief Leabua Jonathan.

The 1970 constitutional crisis marked a watershed in the political fortunes of Lesotho and of Jonathan. Rule by decree and in the face of mounting opposition forced Jonathan down the road of repression, and the presence of Basotho rebels in South Africa strained relations with the Pretoria regime whose financial and organizational assistance was believed to have helped the BNP win the 1965 elections.

Caught between the geopolitical reality of Lesotho, which is totally surrounded by and economically dependent on South Africa, and the Organization of African Unity's championship of the struggle for decolonization and against apartheid, Jonathan trod so cautious a path in the early years of his career that he was sometimes accused of being Pretoria's stooge.

For most of the first decade in power, Jonathan argued strongly that his country's geographical position dictated a policy of peaceful co-existence with Pretoria. But when he realized Pretoria's intentions were to deal with Lesotho just as one of South Africa's bantustans, and when it became clear that Pretoria's apartheid policies in themselves represented seeds of unavoidable political confrontation in southern Africa, Jonathan became more assertive in defence of the greater political and economic objectives of Lesotho.

One of these was to take as great a part as possible in the struggle by the majority against apartheid in South Africa. By providing refuge for South Africans fleeing repression by the white minority regime, Jonathan ignored the demand by Pretoria that he should expel such people because they were, in the South African regime's eyes, members of the outlawed African National Congress (ANC) organizing terrorism against Pretoria. Jonathan's refusal to comply, for which he won great admiration within the OAU and from many other people abroad, led to frequent raids by South African commandos on suspected ANC houses in Maseru.

Jonathan also succeeded in raising Pretoria's temper by his deliberate move to establish diplomatic relations between his country and the Soviet Union, North Korea and other communist block countries in the face of the white minority regime's supposed crusade against the spread of communism in southern Africa.

By adopting such a position, Jonathan exposed himself as a target for Pretoria's guns. Economic sanctions, which had been used on and off against Lesotho as 'punishment' for its 'misdemeanours' were tightened even more towards the last months of Jonathan's power. Matters came to a head in December 1985 when Pretoria, claiming that ANC guerrillas were being allowed to use Lesotho as a staging post for attacks against South Africa, imposed a blockade. After three weeks almost all economic activity in the mountain Kingdom came to a halt. The army intervened and deposed Jonathan. After his overthrow the controversial Prime Minister retired to his home village where for some time his movements were under close observations by the authorities. He

Chief J. L. Jonathan

died of ill health on 5 April 1987, aged 73, leaving a widow and four daughters. ■

Jua, A.N. (1924-78)

JUA, Augustine Ngom (1924-78).

CAMEROONIAN politician who served as Prime Minister of West Cameroon from 1965 until 1967. Born at Wum in former British Southern Cameroons, which became West Cameroon in 1961, he went to local schools and worked as a teacher in the Bamenda area. In 1952 he became a member of the Wum Native Authority Council under the British Trusteeship administration.

In 1954 British Southern Cameroons was separated from Eastern Nigeria for administrative and political purposes, and given its own House of Assembly for which Jua became an elected member. In 1955 he helped Mr. J.N. Foncha found the Kamerun National Democratic Party (KNDP), which came to favour "reunification" with former French Cameroon. The referendum of 1961 led to that "reunification" under a Federal system in which West Cameroon retained some autonomy with its own government and parliament.

The KNDP suffered from internal conflicts from 1963 when Jua was elected vice-president of the party in a contest with

A. Ngom Jua

Mr. S.T. Muna. In the disagreements Jua was believed to favour more continued autonomy and less centralisation in Yaounde, in contrast to Muna.

In 1965, after a constitutional amendment, President Ahmadu Ahidjo appointed Mr. Jua, who had recently become Secretary of State for Finance in the Buea regional government, Prime Minister.

He headed that government for less than three years. During that time the rivalry among parties in the free party politics of the West at first increased; there was already the opposition Cameroon People's National Congress (CPNC), and now in 1965 Muna and Emmanuel Tabi Egbe formed a Cameroon United Congress (CUC). Jua's government was a coalition in which the CPNC leader Emmanuel Endeley was Leader of Government Business. In 1966, however, all the three Western parties peacefully agreed to join the dominant East Cameroon party, the *Union Camerounaise* (UC), to form the *Union Nationale Camerounaise* (Cameroon National Union, CNU) on 1 September 1966.

The creation of the Federal single party did not immediately affect the autonomy of the West. Jua, however, was now only one of many Western collaborators of the overwhelmingly dominant central government. Others of these, including Muna, joined the CNU provisional steering committee with him in 1967. In December 1967 West Cameroon had elections, the first to be held with one CNU candidate for each constituency. After the elections Jua was replaced as Prime Minister by Mr. S.T. Muna.

Jua then retired, and lived to see a unitary state created. He died at the end of 1978. ■

K

Kabarega (c.1850-1923)

KABAREGA, Mukama (c.1850-1923).

UGANDAN monarch, the 23rd Mukama and last ruler of independent Bunyoro-Kitara, who vigorously resisted the British conquest that led to the colonisation of Uganda. Born in or about 1850, he succeeded his father Mukama Kamurasi after a strenuous war of succession in which he sought the aid of Khartoum slavers to defeat his brother Kabugumiye in 1869.

A ruler of tremendous energy and ambition, he was determined from 1869 to stamp out internal rivalries which had weakened the kingdom and, above all, to recoup the territories of Bunyoro which were lost during the reigns of his weaker predecessors. To accomplish this the Mukama built up a standing army, the first in Bunyoro's history, of about ten regiments with each consisting of between 1,000 and 2,000 men. The Barasura, as the army was called, was largely made up of Banyoro, and Kabarega employed some Khartoum visitors to train the force in the use of modern weapons.

His dependence on the Khartoumers notwithstanding, the Mukama was very conscious of the inherent dangers of dealing with foreigners in general and the Europeans in particular. His apprehensions were realised in 1872 when Sir Samuel Baker, a British representative of the Khedive of Egypt, proclaimed Bunyoro an Egyptian protectorate. The Mukama resisted the Egyptian expeditionary force, whereupon Egypt withdrew recognition of Kabarega in favour of a rebel chief, Ruyonga, as ruler of Bunyoro. Kabarega succeeded in repelling the intruders. At the same time his army was suppressing rebellious elements in the pro-vinces where the apprehended chiefs were replaced with commoners, thus consolidating his reign through the loyalty of well trusted subjects.

By 1880, with internal revolts subdued and threats of Egyptian invasion receding with Egypt's withdrawal from northern Uganda, Mukama Kabarega's army took on Buganda, defeating in 1886 Mwanga's desperate attack on Bunyoro. Next came the British whom the Mukama fought between 1891 and 1898. British occupation of neighbouring kingdoms had proved partially successful, including Toro which Kabarega claimed as a subordinate state. In 1893, when the British moved their military post from the territory, it was quickly overrun by

Mukama Kabarega

Kabarega's army. British troops, reinforced by Buganda, then attacked and defeated Bunyoro after a protracted guerrilla war. The Mukama was arrested in 1899, dethroned, and banished to the Seychelles until 1923. He was permitted to return to his homeland in February 1923 as a private citizen, but died on 7 April 1923 in Jinja, on the journey home from exile. ■

Kabobi, M. (1940-72)

KABOBI, Makanda (1940-72).

ZAIREAN educationist and leading member of the *Mouvement Populaire de la Révolution* (MPR). The son of an interpreter for the Belgian colonial authorities for whom he had earlier served as a soldier during the First World War, Kabobi was

M. Kabobi

born on 16 March 1940 in Kayaya, south of Ilebo, in the Kasai province. He was educated at the Oblate Fathers of Mary Immaculate Mission School in Mwembe before entering the minor seminary in Laba where he matriculated in 1953. He then studied philosophy between 1954 and 1959 at the Oblates' major seminary in Mayidi and proceeded to do economics at the Lovanium University in Leopoldville (later renamed Kinshasa).

He took an active part in student politics at the university, becoming, between 1953 and 1965, the president of the *Association Générale des Etudiants de Lovanium* (AGEL). As such he was at the centre of the 1964 students' demonstration which won considerable concessionary measures from the government, one of these being student participation in the university administration.

Following his graduation with a diploma in 1965, Kabobi went to the USA for further studies in economics at the University of Pittsburgh, Pennsylvania. He later attended Columbia University in New York before returning home in 1968 as research officer in the National Office of Research and Development. In 1970, he became economic adviser to the MPR, a party formed by President Joseph Mobutu and recognised in the Zairean constitution as the sole political party. An articulate theoretician and able organiser, he soon made impression on the leadership of the MPR. He was made chief adviser to the party and in December 1970 he became national secretary of its youth wing. Two years later he was appointed a Political Commissioner, which brought him into the Executive Council of the MPR.

He played an important role in the organisation of the first extraordinary congress of the MPR in May 1972. At this congress, held in Nsele, Kabobi presented the party with new ideas designed to raise political consciousness in the establishment. Among these measures was the establishment of an ideological institute for the MPR. This was accepted by congress and implemented after his death and the institute was named after him. The other measures adopted at the congress under the direction of the MPR's political bureau included the reorganisation of the former provinces into regions and strengthening of the national organs so as to allow for effective control from the centre. Kabobi died on 25 September 1972. ■

Kadalie, C. (c.1896-1951)

KADALIE, Clements (c.1896-1951).

MALAWIAN trade unionist, famous for his trade union activities in South Africa in the 1920s. Born near the Blantyre mission in what was then Nyasaland, he was the son of Chiweyu, paramount chief of the Atonga people of Nkota Bay district in northern Malawi. He completed schooling at Livingstonia Missionary Institute in 1912, qualifying as a teacher. After a year as a teacher he left to travel southwards like many other Nyasas, to Mozambique, Southern Rhodesia, and in 1918 South Africa, where he went to Cape Town.

In 1918-19 he launched the Industrial and Commercial Workers' Union of Africa, normally called the Industrial and Commercial Union (ICU). It rapidly became the biggest trade union for non-whites, especially Africans, that South Africa had ever seen. It launched its first industrial action in December 1919. Strikes and other industrial actions followed in the Rand in 1919-20. In 1921 he succeeded in becoming the national secretary, and the young but very dynamic leader, a powerful orator, built up the ICU into a formidable organisation.

As a powerful African organisation in the political as well as the industrial field, the ICU alarmed the white supremacist regime. An attempt to deport Kadalie in 1920 however, failed. South Africa's repressive laws were unable to stop the rapid expansion of the ICU and it had 17 regional branches by the time of its Cape Town Conference in 1923. In the following year Kadalie sought to profit by the divisions among the whites, and gave what backing an African organisation could give to the Afrikaner nationalists in an election won by them. This move may have ensured a few more years' freedom to organise the ICU, but did not alter the fundamental determination of white South Africans to remain dominant, backed by the white trade unions whose defence of "job reservation" made them enemies of the ICU.

Kadalie toured South Africa in 1924 and then set up his base in the Rand in 1925. Membership of the ICU swelled to reach a peak of 100,000 in 1927, and alarmed whites, who began propaganda over its Communist

C. Kadalie

Party links although these links had been cut in 1926. In 1927 Kadalie was barred from entering Natal, but he openly defied the ban and won a court case. From 1923 Kadalie edited a popular newspaper, *The Workers' Herald*.

In 1927, after the ICU had been forbidden to send a recognised delegation to the International Labour Organisation meeting, Kadalie travelled alone to Geneva, and also to Britain, where he was well received by anti-colonial circles. A British adviser, William Ballinger, was sent for the ICU. But his relations with Kadalie quickly soured. The ICU also had to face persecution of its agricultural members, and a new Native Administration Act (1927) was introduced with the sole aim of punishing militant speeches like Kadalie's. He was charged under the Act in 1928, after a speech about a possible protest against the Pass Laws, but was acquitted.

In 1928, at the height of its power, the ICU was split when the Natal branch under A.W.G. Champion (q.v.) broke off. Ballinger backed the critics and opponents of Kadalie. Early in 1929 Kadalie resigned as secretary. He tried to make a come-back but failed, and in March 1929 formed his own "Independent

ICU", which operated effectively only in East London where it organised a major general strike in 1930. At a subsequent trial at Grahamstown he was acquitted on all counts except one, for which he was sentenced to three months' hard labour or a £25 fine. He served two months' imprisonment.

Later in 1930, barred from attending or addressing meetings on the Rand, he moved to East London. He remained active in politics as a member of the African National Congress, with which he had cooperated when leader of the united ICU. He opposed the new measures against Africans' rights in 1935-36 (the "Hertzog Bills"), but was unable to seek election to the Native Representative Council created then, being debarred because of his non-South African birth; however, an effort to deny him the right to stay in East London failed. After writing his autobiography, published in London in 1970 as *My Life and the ICU*, he died in East London in 1951.■

Kagame, A. (1912-81)

KAGAME, Reverend Professor Alexis (1912-81).

RWANDAN clergyman and philosopher. He was the intellectual leader of the Rwanda Tutsis, defending their traditions and position, from the 1940s, against colonial and missionary control.

Kagame was born on 15 May 1912 at Kiyanza, of a family of Abirus, traditional historians of the court of the Mwami (King) of Rwanda. His family, like that of the Mwami, were not only of the Tutsi people, the minority people who ruled in the Kingdoms of Rwanda and Burundi with the Hutu majority kept in subjection, but also of the highest aristocracy of the Kingdom. The Mwami and his aristocracy in Rwanda, as in Burundi, were maintained in power by the German colonial rulers who were in control when Kagame was born.

When German rule gave way to the Belgians, under a Mandate and later a Trusteeship, in the first World War, the Catholic missionary effort which had begun under the Germans continued with great success. Thousands of people became Catholics and the White Fathers mission became a power in the land. The young Alexis Kagame, after attending the Nganzo Nygrutoru Catholic Primary School in Ruhengeri district and then from 1923 to 1928 the government school established for chiefs' sons also in Ruhengeri, decided to study for the Catholic priesthood.

In 1929 he went to the Junior Seminary at Kabgayi and on to the Major Seminary in 1933. His studies at Kabgayi and later at Nyakibanda, where the seminary was moved in 1936, lasted for many years, before he was ordained in 1941 as a priest, one of the first in Rwanda. In 1938 he became editor of *Kinyamateka*, a Catholic newspaper started in 1933. Also, in 1938-39, he taught French at the Noviciate of the St. Joseph's Brothers, a religious order which many Africans joined after the mass conversion to Catholicism.

He taught at the same Noviciate after ordination in July 1941, for five years. At that time he became one of the most prominent Catholic Rwandans, partly because of his friendship with Mwami Mutara III. With the conversion of the Tutsis as well as the Hutus, leading to the baptism of Mutara in 1943, the Catholic church was predominant in Rwandan society by the 1940s. In 1948 there were 81 Rwandan diocesan clergy, 58 Rwandan religious brothers (of St. Joseph) and 155 Rwandan nuns.

Kagame became prominent among the African churchmen through his writings, in which he recorded, interpreted and, to some extent, defended the Tutsi traditions. One of his books, *Le Code des Institutions Politiques au Rwanda*, was a defence of the old social order as reformed along Christian lines.

In 1950-52 he was director of the *Kinyamateka* newspaper and for a time personal secretary to the Vicar Apostolic, Mgr. Deprimoc. Then he began to acquire widespread fame for his writings. In 1951 his *La Poésie Dynastique au Rwanda* was published in Brussels by the *Académie Royale des Sciences d'Outre-Mer* (ARSOM) of which he became a member. In the succeeding years, while doing higher studies in Rome at the Pontifical Gregorian University (1952-55), he began publication of a massive multi-volume work, *La Divine Pastorale*. This was a long epic on the creation and history of the world from Rwandan tradition. In writing this Kagame revealed how much traditional thought had in common with Christian teaching. He became noted for his recording of traditional African beliefs and for high-lighting their common ground with Christianity, following years in which missionaries had rather tended to stress the differences. In Rome he wrote his doctorate thesis on the *Rwanda Bantu Philosphy of Being.*

Back in Rwanda, he lectured in Rwandan Literature at the Kaasi Junior Seminary (1955-57) and became a lecturer in philosophy and general history at the *Astrida groupe scolaire.* He went on writing and, besides publishing *Histoire du Rwanda* in 1958, became a noted expert in his Kinyarwanda language. In 1960 his book *La Langue du Rwanda et du Burundi expliquée aux autochtones* appeared. By then Rwanda was going through serious internal turmoil. The Hutu majority, encouraged by the spread of Christianity and education, began to resent their subordinate status and followed the Parmehutu party dedicated to their advancement. It was led by Grégoire Kayibanda (q.v.), who had succeeded Kagame a few years before as editor of a Catholic newspaper, *L'Ami.*

A few months after the death of Mwami Mutara III (q.v.) in July 1959, a great uprising of Hutus occurred in November 1959; many Tutsis were killed. The 1960 elections were won by Parmehutu. The Hutus' overthrow of the feudal order was completed in 1961, when a Republic was proclaimed on 28 January and, on 25 September a referendum under UN auspices led to a massive vote to end the Tutsi monarchy. On 1 July 1962 the UN Trust Territories of Rwanda and Burundi became independent, with Kayibanda as President of Rwanda.

Although Alexis Kagame was not only a Tutsi but a champion of the old Tutsi ruling class, closely linked with the fallen monarchy, and although many more Tutsis were murdered in 1961, he not only survived but retained his eminent role in independent Rwanda. When the National University of Rwanda was founded at Butare (formerly Astrida) in 1963, he became its Professor of Rwandan Literature and History, and Professor of Rwandan Language at the attached teacher training college (National Institute of Pedagogy). The murder or flight of many more Tutsis in 1963-64 did not affect his position. This was presumably because of his intellectual eminence. He was in fact well known in many countries by then. In 1964 he published *Le Colonialisme face à la doctrine missionaire à l'heure de Vatican II*, at Butare. He published *Introduction aux grands genres lyriques de l'ancien Rwanda* at Butare in 1969, and *Un Abrégé de l'Ethno-Histoire du Rwanda (Vol. 1)*, in 1972, also at Butare.

Besides retaining his University of Rwanda chair, he also became Professor of African Cultures at the Inter-diocesan Major Seminary at Nyakibanda in 1971, and he was Visiting Professor of the History of East Africa at the University of Zaire (Lubumbashi Campus) in December 1972. He was a member of ARSOM in Brussels as well as a member of the *Académie des Sciences d'Outre-Mer* in Paris, the International African Institute in London, and other learned bodies. At Butare he was an Associate Researcher at the Institute for Scientific Research. A member of UNESCO's International Scientific Committee for the writing of a General History of Africa he had his writings published under UNESCO auspices; a contribution to *Les Cultures et Temps* (1975), and his own *La Philosophie Bantu Comparée* (1976). This was a crowning contribution to scholarship in a field in which he had become an expert. He also produced Catholic church missals in Kinyarwanda in 1975 and 1976.

Professor Alexis Kagame died on 2 December 1981.∎

Kagwa, A. (1865-1927)

KAGWA, Sir Apolo (1865-1927).

UGANDAN politician who was for long traditional Prime Minister, Katikiro, of the kingdom of Buganda, serving various Kings (Kabaka) at the critical time of European occupation. He was converted to Protestant Christianity by the Church Missionary Society. He suffered a mere thrashing during Mwanga's persecution of Christians, and lived to be the outstanding Baganda Protestant leader. He wrote valuable chronicles on the subsequent events.

In the confused civil strife of 1888/9 he played an important role, commanding the

Kisigula regiment of troops. In October 1889 Christian Baganda leaders took over, restoring their former persecutor Mwanga, and then Kagwa became Katikiro, a post he was to hold for 37 years. In the 1890s the Protestant leaders came to dominate the country in alliance with the British, and

Sir Apolo Kagwa

Kagwa was the kingdom's leading figure after the fall of Mwanga.

In 1900 Buganda signed a treaty with Great Britain under which it retained much of its traditional government. As Kabaka Daudi Chwa was an infant Kagwa was for long the most powerful man in a kingdom whose allegiance was crucial to the British; he was one of three regents until the Kabaka's installation in 1914. He tried to assert that the treaty was a genuine treaty between equals, and his resentment at the subordination of Baganda in practice led to tension in 1911. Despite the disagreements he was highly regarded by the CMS and the British. He attended the coronation of King Edward VII in 1902 and was knighted on 5 June 1905. Within Buganda his position became more and more contested in the 1920s; there was opposition by the Bataka

chiefs, and Kabaka Daudi Chwa began to part company with the Prime Minister, though they agreed to some extent on Buganda's privileges.

In 1926 Kagwa resigned over a disagreement over beer permits which raised the whole question of whether Buganda was an ally of Britain, as Kagwa continued persistently to maintain until the last, or a vassal as Britain thought. He died a few months later, in 1927.

Kagwa was a notable example of the marriage of Christianity, development on Western lines, and tradition which was the common aim of the Baganda under his leadership. John Roscoe wrote of him in his book *Twenty-five Years in East Africa* that he "stands out as a leader, not only in religious matters, but also in civil and political life; he has been a wise guide and faithful leader in everything that would lead to progressive development."

To a later generation, Kagwa seemed an outright "collaborator" with the colonial rulers.

Kagwa was survived by thirty children, one of whom later became Katikiro of Buganda.■

Kaid, A. (1924-78)

KAID, Ahmed (1924-78).

ALGERIAN politician; a leader of the resistance against French rule who became Minister of Tourism in the second (1963) administration of Ben Bella and later Minister of Finance and Planning in the government of Colonel Houari Boumedienne (q.v.). Also known as Slimane Dhiles, which he used as a *nom de guerre* during the struggle for Algeria's independence, he was born in Tiaret, northern Algeria, on 17 March 1924.

He entered nationalist politics at an early stage, becoming a member of the *Union Démocratique du Manifeste Algérien* (UDMA) which sought an autonomous independent Algeria within the French system. Formed in 1946 by Ferhat Abbas (q.v.), the UDMA succeeded the *Amis du Manifeste et de la Liberté* (AML) which he created in 1944 to agitate for political reform. By 1945 the AML had over one million members and it continued to grow until its proscription after the May 1945 Sétif riots in which 88 Frenchmen and 1,500 Algerians were officially reported killed in the combined police and military operations to halt anti-French demonstrations.

In March of that year Abbas formed the UDMA; the party polled 71 per cent of the votes and captured eleven of the eighteen seats in the June 1946 elections to the French Constituent Assembly. Further development in nationalist politics brought a fusion of the UDMA with some of its rivals and subsequently its decline and absorption into the *Front de Libération Nationale* (FLN) which appeared in 1954.

In 1956, two years after the FLN launched the armed struggle, Kaid was among the several UDMA partisans who joined the new insurgent force. He was active in its military wing, the *Armée de Libération Nationale* (ALN), which at its inception had only 2,500 poorly trained and inadequately armed guerrillas. After a few years of guerrilla warfare, the ALN developed into a highly organised military force which fought more than 500,000 French troops to a negotiated truce in 1962.

In the ALN, Kaid, now operating as Slimane Dhiles, rose rapidly through the ranks; between 1958 and 1960 he was commander of the 4th Military Region (*wilaya IV*) in south Oran and then the Western General Staff. He was made major, later colonel, and in 1960 served as adjutant to Boumedienne at the ALN Ghardimaou base in Tunisia.

Before then Kaid was a member of the *Conseil National de la Révolution Algérienne* (CNRA), the wartime legislative body of the FLN that was created by the Soummam Valley Congress of 1956. The CNRA, which had authority to consider and approve general decisions, had seventeen regular members consisting of the original members of the FLN who are assisted by seventeen deputies, and Kaid was one of the military commanders who served as the substitute members. The CNRA sanctioned the 1962 peace/independence negotiations between the Algerian Provisional Government (GPRA) created in exile in September 1958 and the French government. Kaid took part in the negotiations that were conducted in Evian, Switzerland, where agreements on

A. Kaid

cease-fire and independence were reached and signed.

After independence was proclaimed in July 1962, Kaid sought and won election as parliamentary deputy for his Tiaret constituency. A month earlier, however, he had been removed, with Boumedienne and another senior army officer, from the ALN General Staff by Ben Bella following the crisis in FLN authority that pitted the GPRA against the Political Bureau. Kaid was arrested and detained briefly. In 1963 he was appointed Minister of Tourism in the Ben Bella government. He held the office until December 1964 when continuing policy differences forced him to resign.

In June 1965 Kaid announced the overthrow of the Ben Bella administration on Algerian radio. Ben Bella was arrested, Boumedienne became head of state and leader of the new Revolutionary Command Council (RCC) of which Kaid became a member. In July 1965 he was appointed Minister of Finance and Planning, and in late 1967 a government communiqué announced that Kaid would supervise the reorganisation of the FLN. By the 1970s however he had become restless about the FLN which he said had become the "bureaucratic appendage of the state". The government announced on 20 December 1972 that

Kaid had resigned from government "for compelling reasons of health".

He went into exile in Paris where he tried to organise opposition to President Boumedienne, but was expelled by French authorities on 25 March 1976 for anti-Algeria activities. He went to Switzerland and later to Morocco where he continued his opposition activities. He died in Rabat on 5 March 1978 and was buried in his Tiaret home where some 10,000 people reportedly attended his funeral.■

Kakonge, J.B.T. (1934-72)

KAKONGE, John Byabazaire Tinkasimire (1934-72).

UGANDAN politician and one of that country's youngest ever cabinet ministers. He was born in Hoima, Bunyoro Kingdom, Uganda. After his primary education John was educated at the famous King's College, Budo, before going to the University of Delhi in India where he obtained an MA in economics.

While at the University of Delhi, John took active part in East African students' politics and was one of their leaders. His political activities there came to the notice of political leaders of Uganda at that time and when he came back, he went straight into politics, sidestepping the tradition of passing through the colonial civil service. He joined the Uganda National Congress (UNC), then the only mass political movement in Uganda under the veteran politician Ignitius Musazi. When the movement split in 1959, Kakonge joined the radical wing led by Dr. Milton Obote, later first Prime Minister of independent Uganda, and in 1960 he was a founder member of the Uganda People's Congress (UPC) with Obote as President-General and he himself its Assistant Secretary-General, a post he held till 1964.

In the first pre-independence general elections in Uganda, Kakonge was elected to the National Assembly as UPC candidate for South Mengo, Buganda, and after independence he became the second most powerful man in the party. He was elected to Parliament in subsequent elections, becoming Mi-

nister for Economic Development and Planning and later Minister for Agriculture, Forestry and Cooperatives.

Though he played a leading role in his party's victory in the general elections prior to independence in 1962, he did not contest for a seat in that election because, as he claimed later, he had been wrongly excluded from the party's list for specially selected members. Following a minor controversy that ensued, he resigned from the UPC and visited Tanganyika from where he returned, twelve days later, after discussions and advice from friends. Following this he rejoined the party and was returned unopposed as its Secretary-General. In 1963 he was also appointed Director of Planning in the Prime Minister's Office – a post specially created for him.

Kakonge continued as Director of Planning until May 1965 when he was given a specially created seat in Parliament. He did not, however, become a Cabinet member till May 1966, on the introduction of a new constitution which made Dr. Obote executive President. When he became the Minister of Planning and Economic Development, at the age of 32, he was Uganda's youngest

J.B.T. Kakonge

Cabinet minister. At the UPC's election in 1965, he lost the secretaryship of the party and was later one of the five Cabinet ministers arrested in February 1966 for allegedly trying to overthrow the Government. He was accused of leading a group in the UPC which was imbibing communism.

He always looked at Uganda as part of the East African complex and actively worked for that ideal not only with colleagues in his movement but also with those in Kenya and in Tanzania. He was thus the leader of the working party for the formation of an East African Federation and made tremendous contributions in such forums as the Pan-African Freedom Movement of East and Central Africa (PAFMECA).

Kakonge was released from detention by Idi Amin who had overthrown the Obote administration, but no sooner had this occurred than he was brutally murdered by the new military regime. A very likeable character in the East Africa region, his death in 1972, together with several other prominent Ugandans, was greatly mourned in neighbouring countries. Such was the esteem in which he was held by his colleagues that when the UPC was returned to power in 1980, after the fall of Amin, the re-elected President Obote and the party leadership paid tribute, with full party honours, to Kakonge. ■

Kamara-Taylor, C.A. (1917-85)

KAMARA-TAYLOR, Christian Alusine (1917-85).

SIERRA LEONEAN politician who was one of the central figures in the political development of the All People's Congress (APC) and in post-independence Sierra Leone. He was very much a man of the people, politically dedicated, determined, with many of the values of the old soldier who fought for democracy in the Second World War.

Kamara-Taylor was born in 1917 at Kathana, Kambia district in the north of the country where his father was a farmer. He had his schooling at the Methodist Boys' High School in Freetown and later obtained

a Diploma in Business Studies from the London School of Accountancy.

On 14 April 1937, he joined the Sierra Leone Development Company digging iron ore at Marampa. There, he rose from messenger in the Telephone Exchange to clerk. That same year, he met his life-long friend and later political colleague, Sierra Leone's former President, Siaka Stevens (q.v.), from whom he took over as station master at the Company Railway.

In 1940, at the outbreak of the Second World War, he joined the first battalion of the Royal Sierra Leone Regiment and served in Nigeria, Ghana, India, and finally, in the Burma Campaign, ending with the rank of Sergeant.

After a brief spell in the Labour Department of the Civil Service, in 1945, he joined the United Africa Company as secretary to the general manager, working his way up to become its first African Public Relations officer in 1958. By then, however, interested in the political developments of

C.A. Kamara-Taylor

the time, he had begun to be involved in nationalist activities.

Kamara-Taylor entered full-time politics in 1960 and was with Siaka Stevens at the constitutional conference of that year. They both insisted that fresh elections be held before independence, refused to sign the conference report, and formed the "Elections before independence movement" which later became the APC. Later Kamara-Taylor became its Secretary-General, a post he held until he was replaced by ET Kamara.

In the 1962 elections, following the country's independence in 1961, he won the seat for Kambia district East, but as the APC did not get a majority, he became an opposition MP. He was re-elected in the 1967 elections, but was prevented from taking his seat by a coup organised in favour of Sir Albert Margai's (q.v.) defeated Sierra Leone People's Party (SLPP), by Brigadier David Lansana. Kamara-Taylor followed Siaka Stevens in exile to London and Guinea. The National Reformation Council which was then formed did not last long; Warrant Officer Patrick Conteh's coup d'état of April 1968 restored civilian rule. The APC came back to power, having won the 1967 elections, with Siaka Stevens as Prime Minister, while Kamara-Taylor was appointed Minister of Lands, Mines and Labour. He succeeded the Finance Minister, Sembu Forna, in May 1971, holding this office until 1978 when he was officially appointed Second Vice-President.

Kamara-Taylor remained in this post until 1984 when he retired due to ill-health. He, however, stayed on as vice-chairman of the party and member of the central committee and governing council until his death on 27 March 1985. ■

Kamil, M. (1874-1908)

KAMIL, Mustafa (1874-1908).

EGYPTIAN journalist and politician. He went to the Khedivial School of Law, and while a student met literary and political figures opposed to British domination. He was influenced by the writer Abd Allah Nadim, a former colleague of Urabi Pasha

(q.v.). Kamil studied in France and was awarded a law degree at Toulouse in 1894. After briefly returning home he went to France again in 1895 to seek support for the Egyptian movement against British rule. Selected speeches by the young nationalist were later published in Paris under the title *Egyptiens et Anglais* (1906). Back in Egypt from 1896, he was soon deeply involved in nationalist activity closely connected, at that time, with Khedive Abbas II. He visited Turkey frequently and, like other Egyptians, respected the Turkish Sultan, still nominal overlord of Egypt despite the British occupation, as a part of his anti-British standpoint with which the Sultan sympathised.

From 1900 to 1907, he was publisher and editor of *al-Liwa'*, a strongly nationalistic newspaper. He was then the leading figure in the Nationalist Party, *al-Hizb al-Watani*, founded in 1892. He remained sympathetic to Turkey and, with many other Egyptians, showed this sympathy during the frontier incident between Turkey and the British authorities in Egypt in 1906. His ideas were to some extent Pan-Islamic, seeking to arouse Islamic sentiments against European imperialism and in support of the Sultan-Caliph of Turkey. The Sultan made him Pasha in 1904.

Kamil and his newspaper aroused strong feelings against the British over the Dinshawai "incident" of 1906, when some Egyptian farmers were hanged for the killing of a British soldier, against strong protests. Nationalist feelings were high, but about then two rivals – Sheikh Ali Yusuf (1863-1913), with his newspaper *al-Mu'ayyad*, and Kamil – competed for leadership. By 1907 Kamil was clearly on the side of immediate British evacuation, while Ali Yusuf was more cautious on that subject. In that year Lord Cromer, virtual governor of Egypt for 24 years, left to an angry send-off by *al-Liwa'*. A new Umma Party, more moderate than the Nationalists in its attitude to British rule, was founded then, as was a Reform Party under Ali Yusuf. Neither had any following comparable to that of the Nationalist Party, which held its first general assembly in December 1907.

As France was no longer supporting the Egyptian nationalists as it had before 1904, now Turkey and Germany were said to be behind Kamil. But his movement was a genuine indigenous national one, and in 1906/7 Khedive Abbas, whose attitude to the nationalists had varied, agreed to pay for French and English versions of *al-Liwa'*: *L'Etendard Egyptien* and *The Egyptian Standard*.

Kamil started a "Nationalist School" which, with aid from voluntary subscriptions, taught 300 pupils in its first years. In January 1905 he put forward a plan for a National University; later the government took over the plan and started a university different from what Kamil had planned. In the last part of his life Kamil and his colleagues operated their own agricultural credit scheme for small farmers.

At the height of his popularity, Mustafa Kamil died on 10 February 1908, after an illness of several months. Half a million people attended his funeral. ■

El-Kanemi (c. 1779-1835)

EL-KANEMI, Sheikh Muhammed el-Amin (c.1779-1835).

RELIGIOUS and political leader in Borno, now in a state of that name in Nigeria. A son of Sheikh Ninga from Fezzan (of Kanembu origin), he became a Moslem scholar and returned from the pilgrimage about the time that the Fulani *Jihad* forces (*see* dan Fodio) attacked and occupied the Borno capital, Birni Ngazargamu (1808). He organised forces to help the defeated Mai (king) of Borno, Dunama, fight back against the invaders. In 1809 Birni Ngazargamu was recaptured.

El-Kanemi, as he was now called, is said to have asked for no reward except the control of four major ethnic groups, the Kanembu, Sugurti, Zedbo and Tubu, and to have been granted it. Although he became the most important personality in the old Borno kingdom, he never became the Mai. As *de facto* ruler he continued wars with the new Hausa-Fulani empire and also engaged in a famous correspondence with dan Fodio, arguing that no war for religious reform was needed in Borno. The correspondence was recorded in the contemporary *Infaq el-Maisuri*.

After Birni Ngazargamu had been again occupied and retaken, el-Kanemi for-

Sheikh El-Kanemi

bade the return of the Mai there, and from 1814 the capital was at Kukawa. From there el-Kanemi, ruling through a puppet Mai, organised military expeditions, including one against Baghirmi and then a major one against the Sokoto Caliphate, defeated in 1826 by Emir Yakubu of Bauchi. He also organised a formidable centralised administration with stricter adherence to Islam. He was renowned for his religious piety, and the British traveller Denham said that he was "greatly loved and respected on account of the extreme correctness of his life and the benevolence of his disposition . . . . compared to all around him, he is an angel, and subdued more by his generosity, mildness and benevolent disposition than by force of arms."

He died around 1835 (a date disputed, but considered certain in Borno tradition). His son Sheikh (Shehu) Umar deposed the last Mai of the Maghumi dynasty in 1846 and established the el-Kanemi dynasty of Shehus of Borno, still ruling today. ■

Kangiwa, S.M. (1939-81)

KANGIWA, Alhaji Shehu Mohammed (1939-81).

NIGERIAN politician, the first executive head of Sokoto State, being elected its Governor in July 1979 in Nigeria's first parliamentary elections since the army overthrew the Federal Government and suspended political activities in 1966. In the intervening years of military rule the Federal structure was re-organised, in two phases, from four to 19 units. Sokoto State was created during the second of these re-organisations in 1976 when the twelve states established in 1967 were further increased.

Shehu Kangiwa was born in that state on 13 November 1939, in Kangiwa village in the Argungu Emirate, famous throughout West Africa for its annual fishing and cultural festival. He had his Islamic and formal education in Sokoto and Zaria. He later trained at the Gombe Teachers' Training College in Bauchi State and then worked

Alhaji S.M. Kangiwa

for two years at the Farfaru and Kotorkoshi Senior Primary Schools. In 1961 he left teaching and joined the civil service, becoming private secretary to Nigeria's first Prime Minister, Sir Alhaji Abubakar Tafawa Balewa (q.v.). In 1963 he left the service to read Law at Ahmadu Bello University, Zaria, and was called to the Bar at Lincoln's Inn, London, in 1966.

From 1966 to 1969, he worked with the Nigerian Railway Corporation as its assistant secretary and later as its representative in London until 1977. He returned to Nigeria that year and became secretary to the newly established Kaduna Polytechnic. He held that post until 1976 when he was appointed permanent secretary in the Sokoto State military government. In August 1978, Shehu Kangiwa was appointed Federal Commissioner for Mines and Power by the military government of General Olusegun Obasanjo. He resigned this appointment five months later to become a founding member of the National Party of Nigeria (NPN), on whose platform he won a landslide victory for the governorship of Sokoto State in July 1979.

As a civil servant and politician, Shehu Kangiwa was very much at home with government business. His several years in the public service had enabled him to build up an intimate knowledge of the levers of power and this, coupled with the over-riding desire to serve, was to serve him in good stead when he became Governor. For nearly two years he displayed a deep understanding of his citizens' aspirations; his governorship was directed essentially to providing for the villagers of Sokoto State under a massive rural development programme which he saw as a beneficial substitute for the over-concentration of projects in the urban areas. He expanded the State's health, agriculture and education sectors, without losing sight of the primary objective to develop the necessary skill to run the machinery. He believed, as he once said, that Africans can best develop their continent if they do it themselves, referring to the recruitment of teachers from abroad whom he said "como with the main aim of earning a living and lack proper orientation".

Shehu Kangiwa was a keen sportsman, known for his love of polo. He fell off his horse while playing a game in November 1981 and died from the injuries he sustained. President Shagari led the funeral of the Governor amid popular mourning.■

Kano, M.A. (1920-83)

KANO, Alhaji Muhammadu Aminu (1920-83).

NIGERIAN politician noted as the champion of radical political changes in the former Northern Region and leader of the Northern Elements Progressive Union (NEPU) from 1950 to 1966, and of the People's Redemption Party (PRP) from 1978 until his death.

He was born on 9 August 1920 of a distinguished Fulani family in Kano city; his father, Malam Yusufu, was at one time Acting Chief Alkali (Islamic judge) of Kano. He went to Kaduna College, originally at Katsina and now (under the name Barewa College) at Zaria, which trained most of the early Moslem Northern Nigerian elite.

Aminu Kano became a teacher, after obtaining a diploma in 1942, at Bauchi Middle School. Another teacher there was Abubakar Tafawa Balewa (q.v.) and the two went in 1946-47 for a course at the University of London Institute of Education. Back in Bauchi they founded the Bauchi General Improvement Union, the start of a long political career.

In Bauchi Aminu Kano became Secretary of another small élite association, the Bauchi Discussion Circle, which soon began to express overt criticisms of the Native Authority (NA) system, i.e. the traditional Hausa-Fulani system as preserved, developed and enforced by the colonial rulers in the Northern Region. The flat-rate taxation from which the *talakawa* (Commoners) suffered caused much discontent and Aminu Kano came to voice it. Around that time, Aminu wrote a pamphlet, *Kano under the Hammer of Native Administration*. This and the Bauchi Discussion Circle annoyed the British authorities. By then political parties were rapidly expanding in Nigeria, with the National Council of Nigeria and the Cameroons (later National Council of Nigerian Citizens, NCNC) gaining much popular support.

In the Northern Region there emerged a new association, the *Jami'iyyar Mutanen Arewa* (JMA, Hausa for the Northern People's Congress (NPC), which it became in 1951) formed in 1948 with Aminu

Alhaji M.A. Kano

Kano as one of its office holders and head of its Maru branch. Overtly non-political and "purely cultural" this body was dedicated to opposing "ignorance, idleness and oppression" in the north. But its support by the traditional rulers and their growing influence did not allow it to become a platform for political reform. And on 8 August 1950 Aminu Kano and others formed the NEPU at a meeting in Kano, dedicated to radical change, which proclaimed a "class struggle", aimed at "the emancipation of the *talakawa* through "reform of the present autocratic political institutions". Later in 1950 Aminu resigned as a teacher to work full-time for NEPU.

Aminu Kano became vice-president of NEPU in 1951 and its president-general in 1953, and as such was the outstanding leader of radical Hausa-Fulani politics whose main area of strength was his home region, Kano Province (now Kano State). Small traders and semi-employed urban youths were among its supporters. Aminu who was the voice of the opposition, led a delegation to protest at market fee increases in Bauchi in 1954. In rural areas NEPU campaigned against the misuse of compulsory communal labour for the authorities.

The reformed Tijaniyya "school" of Islam was to some extent on the side of NEPU, and from an early date its followers were persecuted and harassed by the traditional rulers and the NPC, which had won the 1951 elections. Their tactics ensured that NEPU had only limited success in elections, even in Kano. Though popular support for Aminu was widespread in that city, it failed to secure his election either to the Federal House of Representatives in 1954, or to the Northern Region Assembly in 1956.

However, NEPU remained a formidable champion of the oppressed, and a notable force in Northern Nigerian politics. Aminu Kano led NEPU delegations to constitutional conferences, leading eventually to independence. From 1954 NEPU was allied to the National Council of Nigerian Citizens (NCNC). In 1959, when Aminu became life-president of the party, the NEPU-NCNC alliance won eight seats in the North in the federal elections, and he was elected for Kano East. When the NCNC and NPC joined to form the federal coalition, headed by Aminu's former colleague Tafawa Balewa, NEPU was involved in an alliance, at the federal level, with the Sardauna's NPC. Independence, 1960 found Aminu Kano in the anomalous situation of holding the position of Government Chief Whip in the Federal House.

However, in the Northern Region, NEPU was still the dedicated opponent of NPC rule, though they failed to win any seats there in 1961 and 1964. But Kano's constant opposition to most Northern Region government policies culminated in that government's deposition of Emir Muhammadu Sanusi of Kano in 1963.

Aminu Kano became first vice-president of the NCNC in 1963, but he failed to secure re-election to the Federal parliament in December 1964. He nevertheless remained an influential extra-parliamentary opposition leader, known for his egalitarian ideas. Under him in foreign policy NEPU was pan-Africanist and favoured Non-Alignment. It also favoured increased central government powers in the Federation, in contrast to the NPC.

In the aftermath of the 15 January 1966 coup led by Major Nzeogwu (q.v.) and civil war Aminu Kano was appointed Federal Commissioner for Communications by General Gowon in June 1967. Gowon's government instituted changes which in the North responded in part to Aminu Kano's policies; for example the creation of six states (later increased to ten) out of the Northern Region, and the ending of the separate NA Police. In 1971 he became Federal Commissioner for Health. He left the government a few months before it fell in the 1975 coup. In the following year the military regime's local government reform ended the previous role of the traditional rulers in local government in the north.

In 1978, when the ban on political parties was lifted, the People's Redemption Party (PRP), led by Alhaji Aminu Kano as National President, was recognized as one of the five legal political parties to contest the 1979 elections, in which it was successful mainly in the north and most of all in Kano State. The PRP won all the five elections in Kano State – the State Assembly and Governorship, the Federal Senate and House of Representatives, and the Presidency. Alhaji Aminu was one of the five presidential candidates; for a time disqualified because of the alleged tax arrears, he was later allowed to stand, and polled 1,732,113 votes (10.3 per cent of the total votes cast), including 932,803 (76.41 per cent of the state's votes) in Kano State.

The sweeping PRP victory in Kano State was a peaceful revolution which to some extent fulfilled Alhaji Aminu Kano's dreams. The new PRP state government under Governor Abubakar Rimi abolished flat-rate tax, and while the Emirs remained, the old order was ended.

In 1980, however, a major split occurred in the PRP, under Aminu's leadership; he expelled Kano's and Kaduna's state governors, and PRP legislators at the federal and state level were sharply divided. The split arose from the participation by Abubakar Rimi and Balarabe Musa in meetings with the other "progressive" UPN (Unity Party of Nigeria), and GNPP (Great Nigerian People's Party) governors. By opposing the two PRP governors on that issue, Aminu Kano incurred the charge of betraying his own principles, but the PRP split did great harm to Nigeria's main left-wing party and was doubtless a major blow to Aminu himself. He, however, remained a popular figure in Kano city. People constantly called at his well-known Mambaya house in the city, and found the "Mallam", as always, a simple and accessible person. While the PRP-dominated

State Assembly was for long loyal to Governor Rimi, many other Kano people were loyal to Aminu.

In early 1982, Aminu Kano attended two important conferences of party leaders, called by President Shagari, to discuss the creation of new states. In May 1982 the PRP was registered as a legal party again under his leadership, to contest the 1983 elections. After this many people were reported to have transferred their allegiance to Aminu Kano. Early in 1983 Michael Imoudu – the veteran trade union leader who had headed the faction including Governor Musa, his successor Abba Rimi, and Kano's Governor Abubakar Rimi – submitted to Aminu's leadership and he again became a presidential candidate for the PRP. He chose as his "running mate" a woman who was already deputy national president of the PRP, Mrs Bola Ogunboh. But a few months before the elections, on 17 April 1983, Alhaji Aminu Kano died.■

Kaocen

Kaocen (c.1880-1919)

KAOCEN, Ag Mohammed Wau Teguida (c.1880-1919).

NIGER resistance leader, who led the Tuareg in resistance against colonial domination. He was born around 1880 in Damergou. The insatiable quest of the French for natural wealth and the zeal for conquest in Africa were not liked by the Tuareg, who at that time had gained supremacy over much of the Sahara and Sahel of West Africa. Kaocen was Amenokal (paramount chief) of the Ikazkazan branch of the Kel Owey confederation of the Tuareg. He was converted in 1909 to the militant Sanusiyya order of Islam (based in Libya), and became one of the order's most ardent supporters in the Niger region. He helped in several anti-French assaults in Borkou-Ennedi-Tibesti (Chad) the same year, taking part in the bitter fighting. In 1910, he was given command of the defence of Ennedi by the Grand Sanusi, head of the order. Though defeated there, and chased by French troops into Darfur in Sudan, from there he returned first to Ounianga Kabir in Chad and then to the interior of the Libyan Fezzan in 1913, where he made his plan for the attack against the French in Niger. These operations were a part of the Sanusiyya's war against both the Italians, who invaded Libya in 1911, and the French.

The declaration of the Holy War in October 1914 by the Grand Sanusi in support of the Sultan of Turkey, then at war with Britain and France, was ardently picked up by many including Kaocen Ag Mohammed, whose idea was to free Air from "infidel" rule. In collaboration with the Sultan of Agadez, a mountainous desert area of Niger, Tagama, who had completely convinced the Agadez French commander of the loyalty of the Tuareg, Kaocen on 17 December 1916 surprised the French garrison at Agadez, placing the town under perpetual siege until 3 March 1917, when the French brought up reinforcements from Zinder. During this period of siege Kaocen's troops of 1,000 had defeated several intermittent attacks launched to break the siege.

The hardships inflicted on the French troops by Kaocen and his men brought retaliation when the French finally re-entered Agadez; and later Gall, where they instituted several highly arbitrary and savage reprisals. The *marabouts* who in many instances had actually argued against the upheaval, were rounded up and most were massacred.

Kaocen escaped and with his followers beat a fighting retreat, clashing with French forces. His uprising was accompanied by several others in the Sahara, while the Sanusiyya fought the Italians until 1917; some of this activity was helped and encouraged by the Turks and Germans, anxious to tie down French and Italian forces in Africa, but direct Turco-German involvement in Kaocen's own operations was apparently negligible. However, the British and French, as wartime allies, collaborated to destroy him as a common threat.

While the French reinforced their troops in the Niger territory, the British reinforced theirs across the border in Nigeria, anxious that his Islamic war effort should not influence the Hausa-Fulani population. The British forces (in fact West African in the "other ranks") were sent into French territory early in 1917 while the French fought Kaocen. However, Kaocen escaped to the Tibesti Mountains in Northern Chad. In 1918 he was in Fezzan, then nominally part of Italian Libya where he was eventually captured in local fighting, and on 5 January 1919 he was hanged at Murzuq in Libya. Tuareg resistance to French rule in the Sahara and Sahel did not end then but its most active phase was over after 1917-19. ∎

Kapuuo, C.M. (1923-78)

KAPUUO, Chief Clemens Mutuurunge (1923-78).

NAMIBIAN politician, leader of the National Unity Democratic Organisation. He was born on 16 March 1923, at Ozondjona in the district of Okahandja. Kapuuo was educated at the St. Barnabas (Anglican) Mission School for Africans at Windhoek and later went to Stofberg near Johannesburg, where he attended a teachers' training course. He returned to Namibia and taught English at Waterberg and Katibib primary schools before setting up business as a general dealer in Windhoek. He played an active role in the Teachers' Association which campaigned for a non-discriminatory form of education as opposed to the Bantu system of education, and better treatment for African teachers.

Kapuuo became an activist in politics in the early 1950s, initially as a member and translator to the Herero Chief Council. By 1960 he was already regarded as the likely successor to Chief Kutako (q.v.) and, when the latter died on 20 July 1970, Kapuuo succeeded him.

In his early years as chief, he mobilised opposition to South Africa's plan to consign the Herero people to a barren "homeland" on the edge of the Omakeke Desert in eastern Namibia. He emerged as a national leader during the nationwide strike of December 1971, against the South African government's imposition of the "Contract Labour" system in Namibia.

As leader of the National Unity Democratic Organisation (NUDO), the Herero political organ, Kapuuo played an important role in the setting up in 1971 of the National Convention which sought to bring all the nationalist groups, including the South West Africa People's Organisation (SWAPO), under one umbrella. The Convention's primary aim was to strengthen Africa's opposition to South Africa's continued presence in Namibia. Thus Kapuuo started

Chief C.M. Kapuuo

his political career as a strong anti-colonialist and opponent of South African domination.

But in later years, he became more and more associated with the South African regime's plan for an internal settlement, as opposed to the efforts of SWAPO, the mainstream of the Namibian liberation struggle, and the United Nations. In September 1973, Chief Kapuuo had talks with Mr. Dirk Mudge, leader of the all-white South West African Legislative Assembly (SWALA). The two leaders later issued a joint statement which rejected violence in favour of contact and dialogue at a reasonable level. SWAPO rejected Chief Kapuuo's initiatives and withdrew from the National Convention in December 1974.

Kapuuo attended the South African-sponsored Turnhalle conference in Windhoek in 1975 where the Democratic Turnhalle Alliance (DTA) was formed with him as President and Mudge as Chairman. Kapuuo's participation in the conference was highly valued by South Africa, and seen by many as a means by which the status quo could be legitimised under a new guise.

Chief Kapuuo was a frequent visitor to Europe and USA, mainly calling at the UN; the visits were sponsored by either the South African government or multinational companies with interests in Namibia. He addressed the UN Committee dealing with the question of Namibia, and was received on several occasions by UN Officials.

Kapuuo was assassinated in Windhoek on 27 March 1978, at a time when he seemed to agree with African opinion that he would be better situated if he distanced himself from the DTA.■

Kapwepwe, S.M. (1922-80)

KAPWEPWE, Simon Mwansa (1922-80).

ZAMBIAN politician who at independence became his country's first Minister of Foreign Affairs. The son of a police officer, Kapwepwe was born on 12 April 1922 in Chinsali. He had his early education at Luwa Mission School, where he was a contemporary of Kenneth Kaunda, and later, from 1951 to 1955, studied at the University of Bombay in India on an African National Congress (ANC) bursary. He taught briefly at a mission school in Kitwe on the Copperbelt, where he entered politics as a member of the ANC which he co-founded in 1946 with Kenneth Kaunda, who became first President of Zambia.

A childhood friend of the Zambian leader, Kapwepwe was perhaps President Kaunda's closest colleague in the nationalist struggle for independence. From Chinsali, their common home, the two politicians travelled the length and breadth of the then British colony, sometimes on bicycle, mobilising Zambians to the cause of majority rule. Together, they formed Zambia's most articulate opposition against the then extant Federation between Southern Rhodesia (Zimbabwe), Nyasaland (Malawi) and Northern Rhodesia (Zambia), that was imposed by Britain on the countries in a manner that many Africans regarded as a ruse to consolidate and maintain White domination in the region.

Together, they shared the wrath of the colonial administration, often ending up being cell-mates. Together, they also won independence for Zambia in 1964, after which Kapwepwe became the second most influen-

S.M. Kapwepwe

tial politician, next to President Kaunda, in the political hierarchy of post-colonial Zambia.

The organisational and leadership qualities of the man who became Vice-President of Zambia from 1967 until 1970 was demonstrated during the nationalist struggle. In 1956, he was made treasurer of the ANC and in 1958, disagreeing with Harry Nkumbula's (q.v.) leadership over a lack of radicalism in the party programme, resigned, and together with Kaunda formed the Zambia African National Congress (ZANC). Kapwepwe became treasurer of the new party. He was arrested in March 1959 for political activities and was banished to Mongu until December 1959, when he was released to become the treasurer of the United National Independence Party (UNIP), the successor to ZANC.

Kapwepwe was on the UNIP delegation to the 1960 London Conference where he played an important role with Kaunda in the deliberations that led to the dissolution of the Federation of Rhodesia and Nyasaland. In 1960, he was elected to Parliament, and with the advent of self-government he became Minister of Agriculture and later Minister of Home Affairs before taking the portfolio of Foreign Affairs at independence in 1964.

As Foreign Minister of one of the African front-line states bordering the white minority regimes in southern Africa, Kapwepwe was very critical of British policy towards Rhodesia and the Unilateral Declaration of Independence (UDI) by Ian Smith.

In line with consensus African opinion, which he voiced at Commonwealth conferences and at the United Nations, he urged Britain not to grant independence to Rhodesia before majority rule. The dynamic eloquence with which he argued the African cause was sustained by the Zambian government long after his departure from the Cabinet on 21 August 1970.

From 1970 onwards he became the pivot of opposition to President Kaunda's government, challenging the President for the leadership twice. First he formed the United Progressive Party (UPP) in 1971, which was banned after a period of political unrest in the country in 1972.

Kapwepwe was detained in February 1972 for eleven months and released in January 1973. When a one-party system was adopted the same year he re-joined the ruling

UNIP, but in 1978 once again challenged President Kaunda for the presidency. This however was prevented by the party's constitution, and Kapwepwe spent his last years outside the mainstream of Zambia's politics. He died of a stroke on 26 January 1980.∎

Kariuki, J.M. (1929-75)

KARIUKI, Josiah Mwangi (1929-75).

KENYAN politician. He was born on 3 March 1929 in the Rift Valley province. He had his early education at Kariwa and at Kerogoya Secondary School before attending King's College, Budo, Uganda. He was active in the Mau Mau movement at an early age and between 1952 and 1960 was detained in the emergency imposed by the British colonial authorities. On his release he started a private secretarial business firm in Nairobi and later served as President Jomo Kenyatta's (q.v.) private secretary from 1961 to 1963.

In the May 1963 elections Kariuki was elected to the House of Representatives, to which he was re-elected in 1966, 1969 and 1974. Following his re-election in 1966 he was appointed Assistant Minister in the Ministry of Agriculture and Animal Husbandry, and from 1969 to 1974 served as Assistant Minister for Wildlife and Tourism. His consistency as member of the government notwithstanding, Kariuki became one of the most outspoken critics of the administration.

No sooner had he entered Parliament than he became noted for his criticism of corruption and the widening gap between rich and poor Kenyans. He once said that "A small but powerful group, a greedy self-seeking elite in the form of politicians, civil servants and businessmen, has steadily but very surely monopolised the fruits of independence to the exclusion of the majority of the people. We do not want a Kenya of ten millionaires and ten million beggars".

Following the election of a new Parliament in 1974 he was dropped from the government and he took a back-bench seat in the Assembly where, because of his continued criticism of the system and style of government, he was known as leader of the unofficial opposition. But in spite of all this he remained a loyal member of the ruling party, Kenya African National Union (KANU) which he had joined in the 1960s.

J.M. Kariuki

On 11 March 1975 he was reported dead after he had been missing for ten days. His bullet-riddled and mutilated body was found by the police in Ngong Hills, not far from Nairobi, and he was buried on 16 March at an emotional funeral in Gilgil attended by thousands of Kenyans. The mysterious circumstances in which he died prompted controversies in both government and private circles.

Kariuki wrote an autobiographical book *Mau Mau Detainee*, which was published in 1963 by Oxford University Press, England, and for which he was awarded a Medal of Honour by the Soviet Writers' Union in 1970. ■

Karnou (c.1890-1928)

KARNOU (c.1890-1928).

CENTRAL AFRICAN resistance leader. More of a spiritual leader, he said he had been given a special mission to oppose White rule by a revelation – a star falling, he said, into the Lobaye River. Karnou refused to use anything coming from Europe, even money, and called on the people to do likewise. However, he opposed violence. He said, "If the commandant comes, I shall await him unarmed and I shall say to him: Kill me if you wish, I shall not defend myself. Blood must not be shed." But the people, driven beyond endurance by oppression, did not long pay heed and rebelled violently.

Little is known about Karnou's early life except that he was a "native doctor" born at Nahing, near Bouar, at the start of the French colonial occupation of Ubangi-Shari (now the Central African Republic), and was named Ngaikoumsey Barka. In 1926 he took the name Karnou, meaning "he who can change the world" and became a leader of a great uprising of Africans against French misrule.

The uprising was particularly strong among the Baya people, a large ethnic group occupying the western part of the country, west of Bangui, and also found across the border in Cameroon. They and others had suffered a lot from colonial rule. In Ubangi-Shari, as in the Middle Congo (now the Congo Republic), much of the area was for long controlled by Concessionary Companies which had unlimited powers over the Africans whom they forced by violent means to bring goods for export, usually wild rubber. The French administration added to the oppression through heavy taxes, conscription of porters, forcible cotton growing, military conscription and other forced labour. These impositions were very serious in Ubangi-Shari which in fact had one of the worst colonial regimes Africa ever knew. There were many other revolts before the Baya rising of 1928.

In the few years before 1928 conditions grew worse with the conscription of labourers to build the railway from Brazzaville to Pointe Noire. Thousands of the labourers brought by force from Ubangi-

Shari died, and continued efforts by the French to find more produced desperation. In the Ubangi-Shari subdivisions of Baikokoum, Bouar and Baboua, the French had withdrawn their local administrative staff between 1924 and 1927; an agricultural officer was put in charge of Bouar and Baboua in 1928. There was hardly any French presence in the area to oppose the rising when it started in June 1928. A fight in the Bouar area between Bayas and Fulanis (whom the French were accused by the Bayas of favouring) led to more incidents, and eventually to attacks on French traders and the chiefs and soldiers employed by the French. From then on the rising spread rapidly. It spread to neighbouring areas of Ubangi-Shari, and into the Middle Congo. Bouar was evacuated by the French and burned by Karnou's men. The French administrator of Berberati was wounded and had to flee. French forces started to counter-attack in late 1928 but the insurgents fought on.

On 11 November 1928 Karnou was killed in action. But the rising spread fast in 1929, to cover the whole region between Bangui and Camot. The Africans fought well under several leaders such as André Zaouele and Berondjoko. The insurrection spread to areas of Cameroon and Chad. Only slowly did the French suppress it with reinforcements from other colonies. The French troops used the most atrocious methods to re-establish French rule. By 1931 one of the biggest ever risings against colonial rule in Africa was over. But two of Karnou's lieutenants, Bissi and Yandjere, were not caught until 1935. ∎

Karume, A.A. (1905-72)

KARUME, Sheikh Abeid Amani (1905-72).

TANZANIAN politician, who became the first President of Zanzibar in 1964. A powerfully built former merchant seaman, he was born on 4 August 1905, about seven miles from Zanzibar town. Karume's father died when he was only eight years old, a fact which decidedly affected his economic ability to pursue his education. After completing only a year of secondary schooling, Karume took to sailing.

Seventeen years as a sailor sent him to many parts of the world, mostly in Europe and Asia, and it was during this time in his career that Karume, an ardent footballer and boxer, developed his ability for organisation. In 1938 he led a small but militant labour movement for dock workers and sailors known as the Syndicate.

In 1954 he entered politics, soon after becoming president of Zanzibar's African Association, one of a small number of nationalist movements which had sprung up to demand independence of the islands from the British colonialists. In 1957 the African Association united with the Shirazi (indigenous African) Association to form the Afro-Shirazi Party (ASP). Karume became the leader of the new party.

In an all-party caretaker government following elections in 1961, Karume was appointed Minister of Health and Administration. He assumed two years later leadership of the Oppositon in the National Assembly, following the ASP's defeat in the July 1963 elections despite its having won a majority of votes. Karume considered the results unfair, but the ASP was outvoted in parliament by a coalition of the Zanzibar Nationalist Party and the Zanzibar and Pemba People's Party. Under that govern-

Sheikh A.A. Karume

ment Zanzibar regained independence on 10 December 1963 under its newly acceded Sultan, Sir Jamshid bin Abdullah.

The new government, largely Arab-based, seemed set to perpetuate Arab political and economic supremacy in Zanzibar, a situation which the African leadership, headed by Karume, deeply resented. On 12 January 1964, ASP militants overthrew the government of Sir Jamshid, formed a Revolutionary Council, appointed Karume its Chairman, and declared Zanzibar a People's Republic.

With the proclamation of the Republic, Karume became Zanzibar's first President. Three months later he led his country into a union with Tanganyika to form the United Republic of Tanzania under the leadership of President Julius Kambarage Nyerere on 26 April 1964. In this union, which undoubtedly remains one distinguished example of practical political African unity of the continent, and to whose spirit Karume held very fast, he was the First Vice-President. His government of Zanzibar was considered authoritarian by some. He held this position until his assassination by gunmen on 7 April 1972. But his death did not remove the revolutionary regime whose new leader, Aboud Jumbe, carried on where Karume had left.■

He served as General Secretary of the *Association des Anciens Elèves des Pères de Scheut*, while becoming a key member of the *Union des Intérêts Sociaux Congolais* (UN-ISCO). His early political ambition was the reunification of the Bakongo people who inhabited the French Congo (now the People's Republic of the Congo), the Belgian Congo (now Zaire) and Portuguese Angola. In 1946 he delivered a paper to UNISCO entitled "The Right of the First Inhabitant", in which he claimed that the Bakongo should own and control the Congo by right of first possession.

In 1950, Edmond Nzeza-Landu founded the *Association des Bakongo pour l'Unification, l'Expansion et la Défense de la Langue Kikongo*, soon called ABAKO, as a purely cultural society. Kasavubu took an active part in the activities of the movement and became its president in 1955. In August 1956, Kasavubu, on behalf of ABAKO, demanded independence of the Congolese and their freedom to form political parties.

In December 1957 the Belgians introduced democratic elections. Kasavubu became Mayor of Dendale, one of the communes, and in April 1958 after his installation began to campaign for the freedom of press, national democratic elections and self-government. In August 1958, General de Gaulle paid a visit to Brazzaville just across the river from Leopoldville (now Kinshasa), and offered the French Congo the

Kasavubu, J. (1913-69)

KASAVUBU, Joseph (1913-69).

ZAIREAN statesman. He was a leading protagonist in the "Congo crisis" of the early sixties which received much international attention. He was born in 1913 at Tshela in Leopoldville Province and educated to primary level at Kizu by the Roman Catholic Pères de Scheut. From 1928 to 1936 he studied at a seminary in Mbata Keila and then went to Kabwe Seminary in Kasai, to study philosophy and theology. He spent a year at school in Kangu where he qualified as a teacher in 1940. He taught for two years and in 1942 entered the Belgian administration in the Congo in the treasury department.

J. Kasavubu

choice between membership of the French community as an autonomous republic and complete independence. This had an immediate impact on Congolese opinion.

Patrice Lumumba (q.v.), who had been President of the African Staff Association in Stanleyville (now Kisangani), addressed a firm memorandum to the governor-general of the Belgian Congo. This demanded eventual independence and representative African leaders to formulate a new policy for the Congo. In October 1958 he founded the *Mouvement National Congolais* (MNC) to prepare the national takeover of public affairs. This policy directly contradicted that of the ABAKO party which was based on ethnicity.

In December Kasavubu made plans to attend the first All-African Peoples Conference in Accra, but was unable to go because his papers were not in order. Lumumba went instead and, returning to Leopoldville, addressed a mass meeting on 3 January 1959 where he demanded immediate independence. On 4 January, after an ABAKO meeting was cancelled by the authorities, violent rioting broke out in Leopoldville (Kinshasa), following a march of 30,000 unemployed workers through the city. Kasavubu was arrested along with most of the other leaders of ABAKO on 8 January. On 12 January the association was disbanded.

Imprisoned without trial, Kasavubu was later released at the personal intervention of the Minister for the Congo, Van Hemelrijk, and taken to Belgium along with Daniel Kanza, the vice-president of ABAKO, and Simon Nzeza, the treasurer. In May charges against him were dropped and he returned to the Congo to take up his duties as Mayor of Dendale and to rebuild ABAKO under the new name of the *Alliance des Bakongo*. By the end of 1959 the two main forces in Congolese politics were Lumumba's MNC, which advocated a unitary state, and the separatist ABAKO.

In December, Kasavubu formed the ABAKO Cartel comprising ABAKO, the *Parti de la Solidarité Africaine* (PSA) of Antoine Gizenga, the MNC-Kalonji, a breakaway movement from the MNC under Albert Kalonji of Kasai, and other groups calling for a federal form of government. Kasavubu was elected its President by forty-two votes out of sixty, and on 20 January he led the delegation of the ABAKO Cartel to the Round Table Conference in Brussels. He pressed strongly for a federal constitution, but withdrew from the talks altogether when he failed to persuade the Belgian government to set up a provisional constituent assembly.

Lumumba emerged as the dominant figure at the Conference. Kasavubu returned to Leopoldville and became Finance Minister in the Executive College attached to the governor-general. In the national elections of May 1960, Lumumba's MNC won with 33 seats compared to ABAKO's 12 in the National Assembly. The first National Government was formed on 24 June 1960 with Kasavubu as Head of State and Lumumba as Prime Minister. Mr Kasavubu was elected as Head of State on a joint vote of the two Houses by 159 votes to 43.

On 29 June 1960, the day before independence, a Belgian-Congolese treaty of friendship was signed which stated, inter alia, that Belgian troops stationed on bases in the Congo could only be used in the Congo at the request of the Congolese Minister of Defence.

Within two weeks of independence, mutinies and riots had broken out in various parts of the Congo, largely due to the refusal of the Belgian commander of the Congolese Army to consider improvements in the pay and living conditions of the troops. Panic-stricken Europeans began to leave the country as Belgian troops intervened, seizing Matadi and Leopoldville airport.

On 11 July the provincial leader of Katanga (now Shaba), Moise Tshombe (q.v.), declared the province independent. He was supported in his secessionist stand by the Belgians in Elisabethville (Lubumbashi), thus further deepening the crisis throughout the country. On 12 July Kasavubu and Lumumba sent a cable to the UN, requesting military aid to repel what they regarded as Belgian aggression. "We accuse the Belgian government of carefully preparing the Katanga secession to retain control over our country", the cable said.

There was growing tension between Lumumba and the UN Secretary-General on the one hand and Lumumba and Kasavubu on the other. On 5 September 1960, Kasavubu broadcast an announcement dismissing the appointment of Lumumba as Prime Minister, alleging that the latter had betrayed his office and was the cause of civil war in the country. Kasavubu then appointed Joseph Ileo, a key member of the MNC-Kalonji, as

Prime Minister. Later that evening Lumumba made a counter-broadcast saying that Kasavubu had no constitutional power to revoke his appointment and that Kasavubu's appointment as Head of State was in turn revoked. He called on the people, workers and the Army to rise.

During the night of 5 September, the Council of Ministers issued a communiqué depriving Kasavubu of his functions and accusing him of high treason. At 1.30 p.m. on 6 September, the UN forces temporarily closed Leopoldville radio station. This deprived Lumumba of the means to address the people while Kasavubu broadcast freely on Brazzaville radio.

On 6 September the Chamber of Representatives met and revoked both dismissals. On 8 September the Senate gave Lumumba a vote of confidence. The same day Kasavubu issued a declaration rejecting the votes of the Senate and the Chamber of Representatives on the ground that the decisions of the Head of State were not subject to the approval of either House. On 11 September, the President of the Chamber of Representatives and the Acting President of the Senate informed the UN that the votes of their separate bodies constituted a sovereign determination of renewal of confidence in the Government of Lumumba and an annulment of Kasavubu's ordinance.

On 14 September, Joseph Mobutu of the *Force Publique* – now known as the *Armée Nationale Congolaise* (ANC) – announced that the army was "neutralising all politicians". Later he ordered the occupants of the Communist states' embassies to leave the country, and set up a "*collège des universitaires*" (College of University Men) to run the country.

On 16 September, Kasavubu sent a telegram to the UN Security Council in which he complained of UN interference in the domestic affairs of the Congo and the protection given to Lumumba by Ghanaian troops. Kasavubu was desperately trying to consolidate his own position and sent another telegram to President Kwame Nkrumah of Ghana (q.v.) appealing to him and other African countries to recognise the government of Prime Minister Joseph Ileo.

Kasavubu and Ileo began to associate themselves more closely with Mobutu and in November the United Nations General Assembly agreed to seat the delegation of Kasavubu rather than that of Lumumba.

Belgium, France, South Africa, the United Kingdom and the USA were among those states who voted in favour of Kasavubu's delegation. This recognition by the UN of the Kasavubu/Mobutu régime encouraged the Lumumbists to abandon Leopoldville and try to set up their own government in Stanleyville where their support was strong. While trying to escape to Stanleyville Lumumba was captured by Mobutu's troops and imprisoned in Thysville. Later he was sent to Katanga and held there.

On 13 February 1961 he was reported killed "while trying to escape", and Kasavubu came in for much of the bitter condemnation that swept the world at the news of Lumumba's death.

On 21 February 1961, the United Nations Security Council adopted a resolution which authorised the use of force by the UN to prevent civil war and urged measures to remove all foreign military and political advisers not under UN command from the Congo. On 8 March a Round Table Conference was held in Tananarive (Antananarivo) in Madagascar to consider a new constitution for the Congo. A few days later agreement was reached on a constitution, embodying a confederation of sovereign states under the presidency of Joseph Kasavubu.

On 17 April Kasavubu announced that the Congolese Central Government would accept the resolution and was willing to co-operate with the United Nations. When, at the second Round Table Conference opened in Coquilhatville on 24 April, Tshombe demanded a repudiation of the agreement with the United Nations, Kasavubu and his associates refused. Tshombe walked out of the Conference and was arrested at the airport on 26 April but was later released on 22 June.

The Kasavubu regime negotiated with Gizenga, Lumumba's successor, and the Lumumbists, and as a result parliament was reassembled under United Nations protection in July 1961. On 2 August Kasavubu announced that a new national Government had been formed with Cyrille Adoula (q.v.) as Prime Minister and Antoine Gizenga as his deputy.

On 20 October 1963, after three years of much discontent and unrest in the country, Kasavubu declared a State of Emergency. In July 1964 Kasavubu appointed Tshombe as Prime Minister for a transitional period until elections could be held.

On 13 October 1965 Kasavubu sacked Tshombe, on the ground that it was necessary to have a new national government. The dismissal came just in time to allow Kasavubu to go to Accra for the OAU Summit.

On 25 November 1965 Kasavubu was dismissed, following General Mobutu's second coup. By announcing that his regime would head the administration for the next five years Mobutu had in fact seen to it that Tshombe would not be active for that time. This partly accounted for Kasavubu's willingness to serve the nation and support the new regime by assuming his new role as Senator. He died in Boma on 24 March 1969, of a brain haemorrhage. ■

Kassa, Ras (1922-74)

KASSA, Ras Asserate-Medhin (1922-74).

ETHIOPIAN politician and President of the Imperial Crown Council. Born on 1 May 1922 in Fiché, Selalie, he was of the royal house of Shoa, being the youngest son of Prince Kassa Hailu, himself a past President of the Crown Council and a former governor-general of the Selalie province who was given the coveted royal title of Ras in 1916, and Princess Tsige Mariam Beshah of the Marabetie house. His father voluntarily surrendered his rights to the throne in 1916 to his cousin Lij Tafari Makonnen, later Emperor Haile Selassie I (q.v.). Asserate-Medhin Kassa was educated at Monkton Combe College in Bath, England, before entering the Ethiopian Military Academy in Soba.

He enlisted in the Ethiopian army that was resisting Italian occupation, but following the death of his three brothers at the hands of the Italians Kassa joined Haile Selassie (q.v.) in exile in Britain. In 1941 he returned with the Emperor at the head of the liberation army and a year later he was promoted colonel in the Imperial Ethiopian Army.

After the liberation he was appointed in 1942 into the first post-war administration, serving as governor of Selalie, his home province. Gifted as a linguist, he was fluent in English, French and Italian, in addition to Amharic and other Ethiopian languages like Tigrinya which is spoken in Eritrea. This became an asset in his later political engagements which in late 1942 saw his posting from Selalie to Begemder where he became deputy governor until 1944.

After several political assignments he was made a prince and later given the title Ras in 1966, which was preceded by his promotion to the highest rank of Leul Ras; this title is next only to that of Emperor. He was made Vice-President of the Ethiopian Senate in 1957.

During the attempted coup d'état of 13 December 1960 Kassa, generally considered as one of the most ardent defenders of Ethiopian feudal aristocracy, played an important part in crushing the rebellion of the Imperial Guards. He took the lead in mobilising the loyalist forces behind Emperor Haile Selassie who was on a visit to Brazil. In the subsequent 1961 cabinet reshuffle aimed at strengthening the position of the government, Kassa was named President of the Senate.

Ras Kassa

In 1964 he was appointed governor-general of Eritrea, a sensitive posting in the tense climate of the war between the Eritrean secessionist movements and the Imperial government. The early part of his governorship was a period of relative calm, fostered by his rejection of the official policy of military solution to Eritrean secessionism; he favoured a civic approach as he regarded the problem as a socio-economic one.

He was dismissed from the governorship in May 1970 for opposing the declaration of a state of emergency in the northern province but in August of the same year, he was appointed President of the Crown Council, the body that advised the Emperor on constitutional and political matters. He was at this post when he was arrested on 29 June 1974 by the Provisional Military Government that deposed the Emperor.

Kassa was executed on 23 November 1974 with 29 other civilian officials of the Imperial government for what the new administration described as "gross abuse of authority". ■

to a union. In 1940 he led strikes to press for union rights generally whilst also demanding a minimum wage of five shillings per day, better working conditions and the discontinuation of compulsory food rations for which the European mine owners charged exorbitant prices. During one of these strikes, the police were called in and 80 miners were killed.

Katilungu left the country shortly after for the then Belgian Congo, now Zaire, to work as paymaster in a fish transport company. He returned in 1947 to his old employer at Nkhana, as a clerk and later as senior interpreter, and in the same year, was elected chairman of the newly formed African Mineworkers Trade Union.

These were the formative years of nationalism in Zambia. Trade unions formed the nucleus of the movement which attracted radical Africans from other professions and culminated in 1948 in the creation of the first political party, the Northern Rhodesia African Congress (later renamed African National Congress, ANC). Katilungu became chairman of the Kitwe branch of the ANC in

---

Katilungu, L. (1914-61)

KATILUNGU, Lawrence (1914-61).

ZAMBIAN politician who in 1950 became the first President of the Northern Rhodesia (now Zambia) Trade Union Congress. He was born in 1914 in Chipalo, of a Bemba royal house in Zambia. After primary schooling he trained as a teacher at Roman Catholic missions where he later taught. He became a headmaster at the age of 20, earning 25 shillings a month.

He left teaching in 1936 for a less prestigious engagement at the Nkhana copper mines as a "spanner boy" for 9d a day, inclusive of bonus. It was here, however, that his organisational and leadership qualities came to be recognised. For no sooner had he joined the mines than his influence began to be felt in the organisation of the workers who had been fighting for the right to belong

L. Katilungu

1948, but was sacked from the mines the following year on the grounds of involvement in politics.

He was then appointed assistant Township Manager, a position which he used to advance the interests of trade unionism. When the all-embracing Northern Rhodesia Trade Union Congress was established, he was elected its first President in 1950, while also serving as chairman of Kitwe ANC branch, member of the Urban Advisory Council, and member of the African Representative Council. His rating in the political stakes led to his selection as a member of the ANC Supreme Action Council. He campaigned vehemently against the proposed Federation of Rhodesia and Nyasaland in 1952. The following year he opted for full-time trade unionism, thrusting himself into the forefront of a successful campaign to abolish the Tribal Representative Organisation which the employers preferred to a union.

By the middle of 1952 he had built up a membership of 50,000, a phenomenal boost which brought him criticism from the ANC for luring away its members. When the party itself split, Katilungu stayed with Harry Nkumbula (q.v.), the president of the ANC, whilst attacking the break-away radical elements who regrouped under Kenneth Kaunda in the Zambia African National Congress that was succeeded by the United National Independence Party.

In 1959, he stood for the African Reserved Seat of Kitwe, but he was defeated. In what proved a major dent in his political career in the same year, the TUC split in opposition to his moderate leadership and his opposition to participation in direct political action. Katilungu's political influence suffered a further setback when he agreed to serve on the Monckton Commission which was set up by the British to monitor African opinion on independence. He did so against a background of massive African opposition that led to a boycott of the commission's proceedings.

In December 1960, Katilungu attended Northern Rhodesia's Constitutional Conference in London as an ANC delegate. The same month he lost the presidency of the TUC, having been resoundingly rejected by a members' vote. His loyalty to the ANC however continued, and led to his election in early 1961. He died in November of the same year. ■

Kayamba, M. (1891-1939)

KAYAMBA, Martin (1891-1939).

TANZANIAN teacher, administrator and founder of the first African trade union and welfare organisation in Tanganyika, then under British rule. Called in full Hugh Martin Thackeray Kayamba Mduni, he was born on 2 February 1891 at Mbweni in Zanzibar.

He followed the Anglican Universities Mission to Central Africa (UMCA) and worked as a teacher for that Mission and later as a clerk for the British government in Uganda and Tanganyika.

After the outbreak of the First World War he was interned by the Germans. He was freed when Belgian forces occupied Tabora in 1916 and then went to work for the British at Tanga, becoming an interpreter in 1917. In that year he married his second wife, Dorothy Mary Mnubi; the first one, Mary Syble, died in 1911. He rose steadily in the clerical service, becoming a correspondence clerk in 1919 and, in 1923, head clerk at Tanga, where the British then gave clerical jobs to Africans instead of Asians.

M. Kayamba

Kayamba formed the first African trade union and welfare organisation in Tanganyika Territory under British rule. He became a member of the Provisional Committee on African education in 1928, and in 1929 a member of the Advisory Committee on African education for the whole of Tanganyika. He persistently called for more provision of education for Africans, including more schooling for girls. In 1931 he was chosen as an African witness from Tanganyika before the Joint Parliamentary Committee on East Africa in London.

His journey to Britain for the Committee's hearings was described in detail by him in *Ten Africans*, edited by Margery Perham (1936). He travelled with two other Tanganyika witnesses, Chief Makwaya of Shinyanga and Mwami Lwangisa of Bukaba. He argued strongly against the planned union of Tanganyika with Kenya and Uganda. Eventually the plans for this, despite strong advocacy in some colonial circles, were dropped.

On his return he was made an assistant secretary to the Secretariat of Tanganyika; he was the senior African in the civil service there. He was usually pro-British, but became less so later on. In 1938 he retired to a farm near Tanga. He wrote, in retirement, a short book, *African Problems*. He was prominent in the early African elite which in his day was still small and new in East Africa, after a much later start than in West Africa. ■

Kayibanda, G. (1924-76)

KAYIBANDA, Grégoire (1924-76).

R WANDAN politician, the first President of the country. He was born on 1 May 1924, in Tare in the Gritarana region, and was educated at the Kabgayi Catholic Mission school which he left in 1943 for the Grand Seminary in Nyakibanda. He chose the teaching profession, commencing work in 1949 at Leon Chase Institute in Kigali and rose to the rank of inspector of schools in 1953. He later became a government information officer and in 1955 assumed the editorship of two diocesan newspapers, *L'Ami* and *Kinyamateka*. During this period, he founded the Rwanda Co-operative Movement, the predecessor of his political party, the Muhutu Social Movement (MSM), formed in 1957 to campaign for better conditions for his fellow Hutus.

Kayibanda left Rwanda in 1958 to do a course in journalism at Brussels, returning the following year to devote his time to full-time politics. On 9 October 1959 he re-named his MSM the *Parti du Mouvement de l'Emancipation Hutu* (PARMEHUTU), and extended its activities nationwide. The party won a majority of seats in the Belgian supervised elections in June 1960, and in October 1960 Kayibanda was appointed Prime Minister of a provisional government. On 28 January 1961, when Rwanda was proclaimed a Republic on the abolition of the monarchy, he became the first President. He organised a referendum in September 1961, which overwhelmingly confirmed the Republic and his

G. Kayibanda

presidency. Following a formal declaration of independence on 1 July 1962, he was re-elected President in October 1965 and re-confirmed yet again in October 1969. On both occasions the PARMEHUTU won all 47 seats in the National Assembly.

But his efforts to build national unity and consolidate peace between the Hutu majority and the Tutsi minority suffered a setback in February 1973 when an estimated 300 people were killed during clashes between the two communities. The army intervened and President Kayibanda's government was deposed in a bloodless coup on 5 July 1973. The new Head of State, General Juvenal Habyarimana, a former Defence Minister, dissolved all political organisations and placed Kayibanda and his ministers under house arrest. He was later accused of being responsible for the clashes and sentenced to death, but his sentence was commuted in 1974. He died of a heart condition on 22 December 1976.■

Keita, F. (1921-69)

KEITA, Fodeba (1921-69).

GUINEAN politician and poet. He was born at Siguiri, Guinea, in February 1921. His parents belonged to the Malinke ethnic group. After being educated in local mission schools he went to Senegal to attend the Ecole William Ponty in Dakar. On completing his studies there he became a teacher until 1948, when he travelled to France and enrolled at the Sorbonne in Paris to study law. As he did not receive a grant he worked in his spare time, publishing short stories and poems, as well as performing African dance and music in several Paris nightclubs.

In 1950, Seghers in Paris published a collection of his works entitled *Poèmes Africains*. These poems reflected his militant nationalism which led in the following year to his works being banned throughout French Africa. *Le Maître d'Ecole* and *Minuit* were both published by Seghers in 1953 and he wrote the introduction to *Les Hommes de la Danse* by Michel Huet in 1954.

Later he decided to leave his legal studies at the Sorbonne and founded the *Ballets Africains*, a world-renowned group of West African dancers and singers. He wrote many songs for this group and arranged its choreography and music.

He returned to Guinea in 1957 to take up the appointment of Minister of the Interior, and after independence in 1958 the *Ballets Africains* became the country's national dance company. In 1960 his portfolio was extended to cover National Defence and Security and he held these responsibilities until 1965 when he was appointed Minister of Development, Rural Economy and Labour.

Throughout this period he continued to write music, poetry and prose, celebrating his country's independence and outlining its recent history as well as its culture. In 1965 Seghers published his *Le Théâtre Africain*. He also wrote an unpublished play entitled *Grain de Soel*.

He remained Minister of Development, Rural Economy and Labour until March 1969 when he was arrested and charged with plotting to overthrow the government. He was sentenced to death and

F. Keita

imprisoned in Camayenne Prison where he died, according to one report on 27 May 1969, aged 48. It was later reported that he had been left to starve to death in his cell, but no announcement of this, or his alleged execution was made at the time. ▪

Keita, Modibo (1915-77)

KEITA, Modibo (1915-77).

MALIAN statesman and first President of his country. He was born on 4 June 1915 at Bamako, the descendant of the rulers of the 13th century Mali Empire. He attended local Koranic and primary schools and later studied at the William Ponty School in Dakar, which moulded many of the future leaders of the independence movements in French-ruled West Africa. He graduated with honours from William Ponty in 1930 and worked as a teacher. He was later appointed school inspector.

In 1937, he played an important part in organising the *Arts et Travail*, a militant cultural youth society in Bamako. He was transferred to Sikasso by the authorities who already considered him to be subversive.

After a lull in political activity during World War II Keita stood as a candidate for the Soudan-Niger deputyship to the French Constituent Assembly in October 1945 but was not successful. After the elections, he helped to found the *Bloc Soudanais* party in 1946. The elected deputies to the French constituent Assembly called for a rassemblement, or grouping together, of progressive forces throughout French West Africa and in October 1946, the founding congress of the interterritorial *Rassemblement Démocratique Africain* (RDA) was held in Bamako. During this congress, the delegates of the Mali parties – the *Parti Progressiste Soudanais* (PSP), the *Parti Démocratique Soudanais* (PDS) and the *Bloc Soudanais* – decided to unite under the *Union Soudanaise* (*US*), the Soudan section of the RDA.

However, it soon split over the question of selecting candidates for the November 1946 French National Assembly elections and the territorial *Conseil Général* elections. One seat in the French Assembly was won for the US by Mamadou Konate (q.v.), the two others being won by Fily Dabo Sissoko (q.v.) and Jean Silvandre of the PSP. In the elections to the territorial *Conseil Général*, however, the US won only two seats. After the elections, the PSP and the *Union Soudanaise* continued to be rivals for the next ten years, with the US gradually gaining in popular support.

In 1947, the French indicted Keita on a charge of contempt. In an effort to have the indictment dropped, Konate took Keita with him to Paris, but Keita was arrested and imprisoned for 20 days. He returned to Mali and became Secretary-General of the US in 1948 and a member of the Territorial Assembly.

Under Keita's leadership, the US began to extend its influence and ideas. Its rival party, the PSP, led by Sissoko, was generally less concerned with ideas and issues than with personalities. During 1948 and 1949 the RDA, which was closely linked to the French Communist Party, clashed violently with the French administration in all the AOF (*Afrique Occidentale Française* – French West Africa) territories. Keita was accused of being a Communist and transferred by the colonial government from Sikasso to organise nomadic schools in a remote region near Timbuctu.

Modibo Keita

In 1952 he was able to return to Bamako because the RDA had broken its links with the French Communist Party, and he was elected to the Territorial Assembly in 1956. Although he himself was not altogether in agreement with the disaffiliation from the Communist Party, he bowed to the wish of the majority. Keita urged *Union Soudanaise* members to take pride in their dedication to the party. He gave lucid expression to this sentiment at the Congress of 1952: "Comrades, when you find yourselves ready to weaken, tell yourselves the eyes of the world are fixed upon you, a world which judges you, a world which depending upon your action will laugh at Africa or respect her; think of our hundreds of martyrs, whom we remember, those who have known prison and those who died, whose sacrifice shall not have been in vain and should urge us on; think of the hundreds of thousands of Africans whom we projected into the political arena in 1946 who count on us to tear them from the grasp of the colonialists and to guide them to a better future, who have confidence in us, for the construction of an Africa where words express real things and acts, an Africa drawing strength from the immense resources she hugs jealously to her breast, that will dazzle the world. 'We shall no longer be of this world,' some will say. But we shall have marked the road to be followed, we shall have known the first pricks of the thorns, for we shall have been the first to break the path."

The leaders were also determined not to remain a party of intellectuals and theories. In his political report of 1955, Keita said: "We speak always of the masses. But have we penetrated the masses so as to know their way of life, so as to have wiped away the hostility with which they look at those who went to the schools of the French, and finally so as to have sensed their vital needs and measured the extent of their ability to resist oppression? How many comrades agree to enter a dark and smoky hut, to sit on a mat which in colour and crust resemble the earth, to dip by hand, without the slightest repugnance, into the doubtful platter of rice, to carry to lip and drink without fear the milk on which swims a thin layer of dust?"

Another feature of the party was its adherence to the principles of accountability and collective leadership. As Secretary-General of the US, Modibo Keita rarely spent a week in Bamako; most of the time he was on tour in the interior, keeping in close touch with grass-roots support.

The success of the US can be attributed largely to its responsiveness to the grassroots. This in turn was made possible by a tight organisation, a system of collective discussion and decision-making and an effective communications network that included a newspaper, *L'Essor*, which came out daily from 1949 onwards.

The steady gain in popularlity by the *Union Soudanaise* was reflected in the results of the elections for deputies to the French Assembly, held in January 1956. The US won 49.5 per cent of the votes and Modibo Keita was elected as deputy in place of Jean Silvandre of the PSP. Keita became the first African Vice-President of the French Assembly, resigning after one year to become Secretary of State for Overseas France in the Cabinet of Bourgès-Maunoury and later Secretary of State at the Prime Minister's office in the Gaillard government until May 1958. In 1956 Keita also took over the leadership of the *Union Soudanaise* after the death of Mamadou Konate and in the municipal elections of November 1956 became mayor of Bamako.

In June 1956 the famous *loi-cadre* or enabling law was passed in France. Under its provisions Executive Councils with African vice-presidents were to be established in each French territory. In the territorial elections held in March 1957 to implement these provisions, the *Union Soudanaise* won 64 out of 70 seats. At the RDA Congress held later that year, serious differences emerged between countries in favour of separate ties with France (led by Houphouet-Boigny of Côte d'Ivoire) and those who wanted a Federation and joint links with France (led by Sekou Toure (q.v.) of Guinea). Keita tried to mediate between the two groups.

The next major advance towards self-government came in June 1958, shortly after General de Gaulle came to power in France. He proposed the formation of a French Community, to be composed of autonomous states which would share with each other and France a common foreign policy, through the instrumentality of a joint executive of heads of the associated states. The acceptability of these proposals was to be tested by referendum. Keita, fearing the break-up of the association of French West Africa, encouraged *Union Soudanaise* members to vote in favour of the proposals, resulting in a massive 97% vote in favour. This led to a split with Guinea which voted overwhelmingly for complete independence.

In conformity with the timetable for the implementation of the proposals, Mali became a self-governing Republic in November 1958, with Jean-Marie Koné as President, while Modibo Keita remained in the French government. The concept of a West African Federation was still very much in his mind. Accordingly, he called a conference in Bamako in December 1958 of the RDA parties in Soudan and Upper Volta (now Burkina Faso) and the *Parti du Regroupement Africain* parties in the then Dahomey (now Benin) and Senegal, in order to discuss the establishment of a Federation which would take the name of Mali.

Meanwhile, following Houphouet-Boigny's pressure on Dahomey and Upper Volta to vote against Keita's proposals for a Mali Federation, the two countries withdrew, leaving only Soudan and Senegal. The *Union Soudanaise* and *Union Progressiste Sénégalaise* parties accordingly joined together to form the *Parti de la Fédération Africaine*, of which Keita became Secretary-General. The Federation came into existence in January 1959 and Keita was elected its President. This Federation became independent on 20 June 1960.

In the Soudan territorial elections of March 1959 US candidates won all the seats. In April 1959, Keita proposed a unitary government for the Mali Federation but Senegal was not well disposed to the idea, favouring a loose federation. The two began to drift apart. The final split occurred in August 1960 when Senegal seceded on the occasion of its independence. It came partly as a result of differences over executive appointments. There were other differences, however, going beyond mere personality clashes.

The US leaders regarded the Senegalese leadership as reluctant to pursue social reforms and attacked Senegal's unequal distribution of wealth. Nor did they like Senegal's support of French foreign policy, including the war in Algeria. Mali went on to become an independent Republic on 27 September 1960, with Keita as its first President. In his speech to the first session of the National Assembly of Mali, he said: "In giving the name of Mali to our young Republic we have sworn before history to rehabilitate the moral values which formerly made the grandeur of Africa. This oath my government will keep and that is why we refuse to be passive spectators before the great problems of the world or simple pawns on the international chess-board."

The break with Senegal foreshadowed a rapprochement with the two radical states of West Africa: Ghana and Guinea. In November 1960, Keita held discussions with President Nkrumah (q.v.) in Bamako, where it was agreed that Ghana and Mali would consider long-term union and, further, that Ghana would make available to Mali a long term loan to meet her most urgent needs. A month later, Keita met Presidents Sekou Toure and Nkrumah in Conakry, and agreed to form the Ghana-Guinea-Mali Union.

In January 1961 President Keita attended the Casablanca Conference which brought together the Heads of State of Ghana, Guinea, Mali, Morocco and the United Arab Republic, as well as the Foreign Minister of Libya. The Conference declared its determination to fight neo-colonialism, and, amongst other things, established a Joint African High Command as well as committees for economic, political and cultural co-operation. A charter was drawn up, linking Arab states of North Africa and the socialist states of Black Africa. This was dissolved when the OAU was founded in 1963, as was the Ghana-Guinea-Mali Union. In 1963 Keita successfully mediated in the border war between Algeria and Morocco. In the same year, he was awarded the Lenin Peace Prize.

On the economic front Keita's government introduced austerity measures. The break with Senegal and the resulting need to transport by road raised export costs and the price of imported goods. In 1962 Keita withdrew Mali from the West Africa Monetary Union (UMOA) and the franc zone and established an independent currency. He initiated a system of State socialism, establishing a series of State corporations to run the economy's most important activities.

He was re-elected President in 1964, although there was mounting criticism of his socialist policies. Economic difficulties obliged Mali to look to France for financial aid. In 1967 the currency was devalued by 50 per cent and an austerity budget adopted. It was agreed with France that after one year of transition, Mali would re-enter the franc zone.

Many people viewed these measures as compromising the party's basic principles. But Keita launched a Cultural Revolution on 22 August 1967. The National Political Bureau was dissolved and the *Comité National de Défense de la Révolution* (CNDR) created. These *comités* were established at regional and local level and the People's Militia, the armed section of the party, revitalised. A series of purges was initiated against high officials accused of corruption. On 16 January 1968, the National Assembly dissolved itself and authorised Keita to appoint a legislative delegation. The People's Militia were given greatly increased powers, on the pattern of China's "Cultural Revolution"; this, regrettably, led to certain abuses of power.

Keita's socialist stance, in foreign affairs as well as internally, was not to France's liking. By 1968 the group which felt most alienated was the military. The officers were not in favour of Keita's socialist policies or the government's proposed cuts in the defence budget. On 19 November 1968, the army, led by Colonel Moussa Traore, acted to remove Keita from power; he was arrested after returning by river from Mopti. From then until near the time of his death he was held in detention. He was released in February 1977, during the state visit of President Giscard d'Estaing of France and died in a Bamako hospital on 16 May 1977. ∎

Kenyatta, Jomo (c.1891-1978)

KENYATTA, Jomo (c.1891-1978).

KENYAN statesman, father of the independence struggle in Kenya. He was born Kamau wa Muigai, at Ngenda village near Nairobi in Kiambu District. After education at Dagoretti Scottish Mission School, he became a Christian and was baptised Johnstone Kamau. He was a clerk and meter-reader for Nairobi Municipality from 1921 to 1926.

He entered politics in 1924 as a member of the Kikuyu Central Association (KCA), an organisation formed to press for changes in the British colonial land policies. He served in the KCA as a translator, drafter

of memoranda and later editor of *Mwigwith-ania*, a Kikuyu political journal, 1924-29. In February 1929 he visited England to urge the British Government to recognise African rights in Kenya, and allow Africans to establish their own schools. While in Britain Kenyatta was connected with the League Against Imperialism and was regarded as a trouble-maker by the British authorities. He returned to Kenya in September 1930, and established the first of many African independent schools, a move which brought him into conflict with the colonial administration which opposed African schools.

Kenyatta (who adopted that new name in the 1920s) made a second visit to Britain in April 1931, sent by the KCA to petition the British for more land and political rights. He remained in Britain for the next 15 years, during which time he continued his political campaigns against British colonialism. In 1932-33 he travelled to the Soviet Union and studied at a Communist International (Comintern) Institute. On his return to Britain, Kenyatta studied at the London School of Economics and Political Science, his interest in anthropology culminating in the publication of his book *Facing Mount Kenya; An Anthropological Study of the Kikuyu*. At this time Kenyatta rejected his name Johnstone and called himself Jomo Kenyatta.

In May 1942 Kenyatta married Edna Clarke at Storrington, West Sussex, where he had moved from London after the outbreak of World War II. In the meanwhile he had written another book, *My People of Kikuyu and the Life of Chief Wangombe*, an analytical history of the Kikuyu. He was one of the organisers of the Fifth Pan-African Congress held in Manchester, England, in October 1945. Kenyatta then left for Kenya in September 1946. For the next six years he worked variously as a teacher and a political activist among the Kikuyu, becoming vice-principal of the Independent Teachers College, Githunguri, in 1946, and principal in 1947. In the same year he became president of the Kenya African Union, the forerunner of the Kenya African National Union (KANU).

Alarmed at increased African political activity, centred especially on the fast-expanding KANU, and the tension between the European settlers and Africans, the colonial government took military action in 1952, when violence broke out in the Kikuyu areas. A state of emergency was declared on

20 October 1952. Kenyatta was arrested on charges of managing an illegal organisation, the Mau Mau, a secret association which had been formed to oppose colonial policies. Tried on the basis of what later turned out to be perjured evidence, and in circumstances which did not allow a proper defence, he was convicted and jailed for 10 years; he served seven years, mostly in Lodwar, a remote and arid colonial outpost in northern Kenya. Meanwhile, the Mau Mau guerrillas were largely defeated by 1957, after a campaign of great brutality by the British forces, but the "Emergency" forced the British to make concessions to the Africans.

Kenyatta was finally released in 1961 and appointed Minister of State for Constitutional Affairs and Economic Planning in the part-African colonial government. During this time he actively participated in the Lancaster House constitutional conferences leading to Kenya's independence in 1963. Kenyatta became Prime Minister from 1963 to 1964 and President of Kenya on 12 December 1964. Although constitutionally a multi-party state, at the time of his death Kenya had only one political party, the ruling KANU. All forms of political opposition were discouraged under much of his presidency and recalcitrant opponents were liable to be gaoled under the country's Preventive Detention Act. Kenyatta later became Life President of KANU. He was awarded the British honour of Knight of Grace, Order of St. John of Jerusalem. In 1968, he wrote *Suffering Without Bitterness: the Founding of the Kenya Nation* (Nairobi, East Africa Publishing House). He was awarded a doctorate degree by the university of Manchester.

Under Kenyatta's rule Kenya was very friendly to Britain and committed to capitalist development, in a way surprising to those who had passed superficial judgements on Kenyatta earlier. Expansion brought economic and social problems which led to criticisms by Oginga Odinga and, within KANU, J.M. Kariuki (q.v.), among others. President Kenyatta was reputed to be very wealthy and there was certainly corruption and self-enrichment among the leaders of his regime. But despite murky incidents such as the murders of Tom Mboya (q.v.) and Kariuki, Kenya under Kenyatta was not a strongly repressive state; and criticisms of the regime did not reduce the veneration of the *Mzee*, as he was called.

Jomo Kenyatta

He died on 22 August 1978 at Mombasa on the Kenyan coast, from a heart attack. His children included one son, Peter (died 1979), by his first (Kenyan) wife; another son, also called Peter, by his British wife Edna; and a daughter, Margaret, who was for a time mayor of Nairobi.∎

Khairallah, C. (1898-1972)

KHAIRALLAH, Chedly (1898-1972).

TUNISIAN politician; a leading anti-colonial campaigner and founder of the prominent nationalist newspaper, *L'Etendard Tunisien*. He was born in Tunis on 10 March 1898, son of Khairallah Ben Mustapha, who was active in politics like his father, Hassouna Ben Mustapha, before him. He studied at Sadiqiyya College, the famous secondary school founded in 1875, and then at the Lycée Carnot.

He entered government service in 1924 but also started on a distinguished literary career. He gave lectures to the Sadiqiyya Old Boys' Association, an important group of educated Tunisians. He wrote for *Le Libéral*, newspaper of the Destour Party founded in 1920 by Tha'alibi (q.v.) and others. In 1926, at the height of tension between the Destour and the French resident-general, Khairallah wrote articles which attracted wide attention: an "Open letter to the Resident-General", full of strong criticism, and an article entitled "Damascus, the Martyred City" about French repression of nationalists in another Arab country, Syria. This earned him his share of the punishments imposed on the nationalist leaders. After a trial and conviction he left government service and went to France.

In France, as in Britain, people from the colonies had more freedom than in the colonies themselves, and people from French North Africa were able to form, in Paris, the nationalist organisation *Etoile Nord-Africaine* (ENA), whose outstanding leader was Messali (q.v.) of Algeria. Khairallah, however, was the first chairman of the ENA, and editor of its newspaper, *al-Ikdam*. He also became the representative of the Destour in France, and as such attended the founding Congress, in Brussels in February 1927, of the League Against Imperialism, which was attended by many anti-colonial activists of that period.

On 27 December 1927 he was deported from France after being accused of fomenting incidents at the Paris mosque in June of that year. Back in Tunisia, he resumed nationalist activity. The laws applied against nationalists, though severe, did not prevent him from starting in 1929 a weekly newspaper, *L'Etendard Tunisien*, which criticised French rule persistently, with the collaboration of young nationalists including Habib Bourguiba. In 1930 this newspaper was replaced by *La Voix du Tunisien*, which in 1932 became a daily. This was a considerable journalistic achievement and an important contribution by Khairallah to the nationalist movement. His father was on the editorial committee which started *La Voix*.

Although critical of the French, Khairallah's newspaper did not openly challenge French rule. In 1932 he and Bourguiba began to disagree strongly over this point. After government action against the nationalist newspapers, including summoning of the *La Voix* editorial Board before the resident-general, increased this disagreement, Bourguiba and others parted company with Khairallah's newspaper to form their own, *L'Action Tunisienne*, on 1 November 1932. This separation was due very much to

Khairallah's independent views, which made him unable to agree fully with either of two main factions of the nationalists which emerged openly with the Ksar-Hellal Congress of March 1934 and the formation of the Neo-Destour under Bourguiba.

However, as the more radical Neo-Destour group aroused massive support, as evidenced by the big demonstrations, it was hit by French repressive measures, and two of its Political Bureaux were arrested and deported to the south of the Protectorate *en masse*; Chedly Khairallah was then invited to fill the gap by heading a third Political Bureau, early in 1935. As chairman he met the French Resident-General Peyrouton, with his colleagues, and obtained some compromises. He was suspected by the detained leaders but was allowed to visit them and secured their agreement to his policy for the party. He then told Tunisians to remain calm and avoid demonstrations for the time being. M. Peyrouton had promised the release of the detainees in return for this, but when he failed to free them despite a massive demonstration on 28 March 1935, dissensions among the Neo-Destour revived.

Soon afterwards Khairallah, after three months as leader of the nationalists, was forced by the French to leave for Italy. This was effectively the end of his political career, for he had little part in the events following the legal revival of the Neo-Destour in 1936. But he lived until 1972 and is remembered for literary works, including a philosophical essay, *La Clef des Mirages*, and a two-volume, historical work: *Le Mouvement Jeune-Tunisien* and *Le Mouvement Evolutionniste Tunisien*. ∎

Khair el-Din, A.M. (c.1822-90)

KHAIR EL-DIN, Abu Muhammad (c.1822-90).

TUNISIAN politician. He was most famous as a leader of the 19th century reform movement which sought to bring some necessary modernisation and preserve independence. He was originally a slave, taken from the Caucasus area (now in Russia) to

Turkey. Thence he was taken around 1839 to Tunisia, which was nominally Turkish. He joined the army and rose rapidly as a cavalry officer, becoming colonel in 1846 and general in 1853.

In the 1850s Khair el-Din spent over two years in France. He learned French and became the leader of those Tunisians who wanted to borrow modern developments, from France particularly, while remaining loyal to Islam.

He was a leading reformer when Minister of Marine under Muhammed el-Sadiq Bey in 1862. As a member of the Supreme Council in the early 1860s he opposed the policies of the powerful Vizir Khaznadar, which were leading to increasing foreign debts among other problems. But in 1869 the debts led to an International Financial Commission under which Tunisia's finances came under foreign supervision. The Commission's executive committee was headed by Khair el-Din, who worked with his French colleague effectively and secured improvements in the financial situation.

In 1871 Khair el-Din went to Turkey (as he had done in 1859 and 1864, without success then) to seek regularisation of Tunisia's status as self-governing but subject to the Porte; this was successfully obtained.

In 1873 Khaznadar was removed from office after 36 years, and Khair el-Din became Prime Minister. He sought to assert government authority, curb corruption and other abuses which were rampant under his predecessor, and encourage agriculture. In 1875 he founded Sadiqiyya College, for combined Islamic and Western education. After some years of economic revival and other favourable developments, difficulties increased and Europeans' encroachments, with their quarrels over "concessions", worsened. Combined hostile forces, local and foreign, forced the Bey to remove him in July 1877. Later there was a quarrel over land sold by him to a French company, and this was one factor leading to the French occupation in 1881.

In 1878 he was summoned to Turkey by the Ottoman Sultan, whose subject he had remained while in Tunisia, and in December 1878 he was appointed Grand Vizir of the Ottoman Empire. A few months later he resigned. He died in Constantinople on 30 January 1890. He married four times and left several children.

In Tunisia Khair el-Din's most famous monument was Sadiqiyya College, whose pupils included Habib Bourguiba and others, on whom the influence of the late 19th century movement to combine Islam with modern development seems to have been profound. With the Egyptian theologian Muhammad Abduh (q.v.), and others, Khair el-Din was a leader of that movement.■

Khaled (1875-1936)

KHALED, Emir (1875-1936).

ALGERIAN soldier and politician. Named in full Khaled ibn el-Hachemi ibn al Hadj Abd el-Kader, he was the grandson of Abd el-Kader (q.v.) who led resistance to French rule in the 1840s and later lived in Damascus.

Khaled was born in Damascus on 20 February 1875. His grandfather said he should be trained for a military career. In 1892 the young Khaled returned with his father, el-Hachemi, to Algeria. He soon reacted against the French colonial regime which was by then fully established, with settlers holding the best land and totally dominating the country, depriving the Moslem Algerians of basic rights.

The French kept a close eye on Khaled and his father, who enjoyed wide popularity because of the memories of Abd el-Kader. In view of the situation in his country, Khaled at first did not want to have a French officer's training as his father wished, but later he agreed to go to the famous French military academy, St. Cyr. However, he left it in 1895 and became known as "Emir". He protested at French harassment of his father, but it persisted and all the family moved to Bou Saada at one point; a plan to escape to Egypt with his father failed.

Later Khaled returned to St. Cyr and was allowed to continue his military training, although by now he was noted as a bitter critic of French colonialism. He graduated and was promoted sub-lieutenant. But he was an officer in the separate "native" category, because he refused to apply for French citizenship which would have entitled him to full equality with French officers.

Although he served well in the French army he was still suspect to the authorities; they accused him of sympathising with Sultan Abdul Aziz when French forces, including him, began intervention in Morocco in 1907. He was promoted Captain in 1908. Later he was refused permission to travel to Syria; Algerian Moslems were for long obliged to seek permission to leave their country whenever they travelled to Syria, where Arab nationalism was developing and where hundreds of Algerians did go in 1911 as a protest at French misrule.

In the 1914-18 war Khaled served on the Western Front and won the *Croix de Guerre*. While his uncles were among the Algerians who tried to take advantage of the war to call for revolt against French rule, he himself fought for France. But he and others who, like the Jeunes Algériens group formed before 1914, were loyal to France but called for reforms to benefit the Moslems, were to be greatly disappointed when their hopes for reforms after the end of the war were dashed. The French government in 1919 granted a small increase in the number of Moslems entitled to vote in elections, but they were still very few compared with the settlers, who all had the vote like Frenchmen in France, Algeria being legally considered (apart from the Sahara) as three French departments.

Emir Khaled left the army in 1919 and went into the limited political activity allowed at that time for Moslem Algerians. He was elected by Moslem voters to the Algiers City Council, the Algiers department *Conseil Général*, and the Financial Delegations, all of which had limited Moslem representation. Politics surrounding this representation was in 1919-22 dominated by the question of French citizenship. Some Algerians believed their people should seek French citizenship and the full rights it entailed, but others, led by Khaled, strongly opposed the idea as Moslem North Africans under French rule had usually done, arguing that no practising Moslem could become a French citizen without renouncing his faith and France should accord them rights without requiring such a step.

Khaled and other Moslems adopting this view won the Algiers City Council

elections but were declared ineligible by the authorities. In January 1921 they were elected again. Their supporters won other elections, and this strengthened the calls for reforms. The demands included the extension of the franchise, the end to the separate system of justice for Moslems, and equal duties and rights in military service. They failed to secure even the smallest consideration of such demands. They repeated the demands in the newspaper *al-Ikdam*, with which Khaled worked from 1920 to 1923; it attacked the regular election rigging by French officials, the subservient Arab chiefs, and much else.

Khaled briefly came into the limelight, as an Algerian spokesman, when in 1922 he gave an official speech of welcome to the visiting French president, on behalf of members of the Algiers City Council. In the speech he openly mentioned the demand for Moslem representation in the French parliament. There was an angry French reaction and Khaled resigned, together with his supporters who had elected posts. He continued to call for reforms of a sort which, however limited they may seem in retrospect, in fact could threaten the whole regime of settler domination and were therefore refused firmly. He started a new newspaper, *Fraternité Algérienne*, to continue to press the demands for such reforms, which included compulsory education and application of French social and labour laws to Algeria. While not calling for open resistance, he warned that eventually Moslem Algerians would rise up if oppression went on, citing the contemporary example of Ireland.

Eventually he was deported to Egypt where he was given a big welcome. But the French consular court, which like other such courts still had jurisdiction in Egypt, tried him at Alexandria; a conviction and sentence were, however, quashed on an appeal heard in France. Khaled was allowed to go to France, where he met other North Africans. He denounced colonialism at a mass meeting, and helped found the *Etoile Nord Africaine*, a movement among North Africans in France, in 1924 (*see* Messali). After that, in 1924-25, he left for Syria, where his relatives lived. He stayed there until his death in 1936 plunged Moslem Algerians into mourning for one who had, even if unsuccessfully, stood up for his people's interests at a time of advancing colonial rule. ∎

Khalifa II (1879-1960)

KHALIFA II, Sultan (1879-1960).

SULTAN of Zanzibar. He was born Seyyid Khalifa bin-Harub-bin-Thuwaini-bin-Said in 1879 in Oman in Arabia, which was ruled together with Muscat by a dynasty which from 1693 ruled Zanzibar also, with a different branch ruling independently in Zanzibar from 1856. He came to Zanzibar in 1893, and was proclaimed Sultan on 9 December 1911 and installed on 16 December, after the abdication of his cousin, Sultan Ali. His reign, under British "Protectorate", was characterised by a gradual process of modernisation which saw the creation in 1923 of the Legislative Council, and the building of schools, roads and harbour works. By 1926 the Sultan was president of the Protectorate Council, sitting with principal British officials and three non-official members. He thus wielded great influence which he used to the advantage of his island.

He expanded the clove industry, Zanzibar's main crop and revenue earner. During the two World Wars, the Sultan supported the Allies; he incurred the anger of the Germans then ruling Tanganyika by his call to all Moslems to support the Allies in the First World War. For support to the Allies in general and Britain in particular, the Sultan received honours and respect from the British. He was honoured with invitations to the coronation ceremonies of three British monarchs, King George V in 1911, King George VI in 1937, and Queen Elizabeth II in 1953. He was also bestowed with the honours of GCB, GCMG and GBE.

On 9 October 1960, the Sultan died after reigning for 49 years. His son Abdullah succeeded him but died only three years later, and was in turn succeeded by Khalifa's grandson Jamshid, who ruled briefly for some months before the Revolution supervened on 12 January 1964. This Revolution ended centuries of Arab rule under the dynasty to which Sultan Khalifa II had belonged. ■

Sultan Khalifa II

Khama, Sir Seretse (1921-80)

KHAMA, Sir Seretse (1921-80).

BOTSWANA statesman, first President of independent Botswana. He was born on 1 July 1921 in Serowe, the grandson of Khama the Great who ruled the Bamangwato people for 50 years and repelled the invasions of the Boers. Seretse's father, Sekgoma II, died in 1925, after ruling for only two years and as Seretse was a minor, his uncle, Tshekedi Khama (q.v.), became Regent. Seretse was educated at local schools and later at Tiger Kloof and Lovedale College in South Africa. He entered Fort Hare University in 1941 and graduated with a degree in history in 1944. He proceeded to Britain to continue his studies which in 1945 took him to Balliol College, Oxford, where he read law. He was called to the Bar at the Middle Temple Inn in 1948.

During the later years he met and became engaged to Ruth Williams, an English girl, and in spite of the bitter political controversy which the relationship provoked, married her in London on 28 September 1948. The marriage was opposed by some Bamangwato traditional leaders who believed that the action would lead Seretse to abandon the customs of his people. The opposition was led by Regent Tshekedi who had expressed claim to the Ngwato chieftaincy and was strongly supported by the British colonial administration in Bechuanaland (as Botswana was then called).

Seretse returned home in a bid to persuade his people to accept his marriage, and succeeded, first by gaining the approval of the elders who agreed that they would accept his wife as the Queen rather than lose their rightful ruler and, secondly, in winning the overwhelming support of the Bamangwato at a public rally in Serowe on 13 July 1949.

The verdict was not however accepted by the British government who, under strong pressure from the South African government not to allow the rule of an African chief married to a White woman in a neighbouring country, demanded his abdication. He was offered a pension of £1,100 a year tax-free if he would renounce the chieftancy, but again, Seretse refused. On 5 February 1950 Seretse and his uncle Tshekedi were deprived of their hereditary rights and banished into exile. Seretse, with his wife and their newly born first child, arrived in Britain in August 1950; he was to remain in exile until 1956.

Seretse's deposition led to popular agitation in Bechuanaland, with the Bamangwato resisting pressure from the British government to elect a successor. Nevertheless, the colonial authorities appointed Rasebolai Kgamane, who was third in line of succession, as chief of Native Administration. Then in September 1956 Seretse renounced all claim to the chieftancy for himself and his family, following which he was allowed to return home as a private citizen on 10 October 1956.

During that exile African nationalism was developing and reacting against British rule, the nationalists, both in London and in Africa, had developed a common front in their struggle. Seretse played a leading role in these developments in London and his experiences there formed the background against which he entered politics on his return to Bechuanaland. He took the first cautious steps as a politician in 1957 when he became a member of the Tribal Council.

Constitutional re-arrangements in 1960 paved the way for his election to Bechuanaland's new Legislative Assembly, where he served as one of the five African members. In June 1962 he founded the Bechuanaland Democratic Party (BDP) which swept the board in the country's first popular elections in 1965 by gaining 28 of the 31 seats in the Assembly. In March of that year he was appointed Prime Minister, regaining a leadership role of which he was deprived as a traditional chief. He soon negotiated the terms of independence, which was achieved on 30 September 1966, and he became the first President of the Republic of Botswana, a post he held until his death in 1980. At his country's independence in 1966 he received a British knighthood. Throughout his rule he allowed free elections at intervals and at his death left an official opposition in parliament.

Sir Seretse Khama

President Sir Seretse pursued remarkably bold policies in the face of his country's underdeveloped economy and its virtual dependence on the hostile minority regimes in South Africa and Rhodesia (now independent Zimbabwe). For though he recognised the geographical compulsion of economic links with its white-ruled neighbours, President Khama maintained that Botswana should not sacrifice its national interests and obligations to independent Africa's resolve to eliminate apartheid and to work towards majority rule.

The early years of Seretse's presidency were spent on developing the economy that had largely been dependent on cattle for its income. He encouraged the prospecting for diamonds, nickel and copper, whose discovery brought the country to a new level of prosperity. In the bid to weaken economic ties with South Africa, he took Botswana out of South Africa's monetary union by introducing a national currency, *pula*, and intensified its links with Zambia and the independent countries to the north.

He kept Botswana's doors open to political refugees from South Africa, Namibia and Rhodesia, and while not openly allowing these countries' guerrillas to operate from Botswana he nevertheless granted them transit facilities to and from training camps in Zambia. For this Botswana took its share of the cross-border raids by both the Rhodesian and South African forces, but Sir Seretse continued his role as leader of one of the five countries comprising the African Frontline States. He participated in the tedious and protracted negotiations that subsequently led to majority rule in Zimbabwe in early 1980.

During all this time there was concern about his health. In 1965, he suffered a serious attack of pneumonia and again in 1968 was treated for liver trouble in a Johannesburg hospital. In late June 1980 he entered a London hospital where it was revealed that he was suffering from incurable cancer of the stomach. He returned to Gaborone where he died on 13 July 1980, leaving a widow, three daughters and three sons, including Ian Khama who served as a brigadier in the Botswana army.

President Khama was chancellor of the jointly owned University of Botswana and Swaziland and was given honorary fellowship of Balliol College in 1959. ∎

Khama III (1838-1923)

KHAMA III (1838-1923).

BOTSWANA traditional ruler. He was born in 1838, the son of Sekgoma Khama. In May 1862, he married Elisabeta, the daughter of Tshukuru, a Bamangwato headman. After Elisabeta's death in 1889, Khama married Gasekete, in 1892, the sister of Chief Bathoen and widow of Chief Sebele's son, Semane. She too died two years later.

On 6 May 1862, at the age of twenty-four, Khama, the heir to the Ngwato chieftaincy, accepted the Christian faith. By this action many believed that Khama had abandoned the customs of his people and contradicted the wishes of the ancestors. In April 1865, Sekgoma summoned all the young men of the Ngwato to the traditional ceremony of *boquera* which Khama and his brother as Christians refused to attend, whereupon they were disqualified from the chieftancy. In order to prevent Khama from growing

Khama III

into a challenge against him, Sekgoma enlisted the help of a former chief, Macheng. The latter then made a bid for power and succeeded in displacing Sekgoma in 1867.

In 1872 Khama succeeded in ascending to the Ngwato chieftaincy after he had outmanoeuvred Macheng. A year later Sekgoma and Khamane, Khama's father and brother respectively, mobilised opposition against Khama on the grounds of his acceptance of Christianity and exiled him to Serowe. In January 1875 Khama returned at the head of an army. After defeating the armies of his father and brother, Khama restored himself to the Ngwato chieftaincy and immediately set out to bring Ngwato customs in line with Christian ideas and ways of life. Khama refused to perform some traditional activities, with the result that those that needed to be performed by the chief, e.g. *boquera* and *boyale*, eventually died out after 1876. He established Christianity as the official religion of the Ngwato, and commanded his people to observe the Sabbath. In February 1885 Britain declared a protectorate over Ngwato territory in order to forestall possible German annexation of the area. Khama accepted the declaration.

In 1889 the British South Africa Company (BSAC) of Cecil Rhodes obtained permission to prospect for minerals in areas which formed Britain's sphere of influence. The Ngwato territory which had been designated as such in 1888 formed part of this area. In 1890 Khama cooperated with the company by supplying a regiment of Ngwato troops to guide the company's forces into Mashonaland. During the Matabele war of 1893, Khama sent a force of warriors to help the BSAC crush the resistance of Lobengula (q.v.). But Khama discovered soon after the defeat of the Matabele that the BSAC had designs on his territory. In an effort to stop the BSAC, Khama, accompanied by chiefs Bathoen and Sebele, decided to travel to England to appeal personally to Queen Victoria. In England, Khama and his delegation were first advised by the British colonial government to agree to the territorial aims of the BSAC. They rejected the plan, whereupon Ngwato territory was partitioned into two regions, one for the BSAC and one for Khama, both being under British protectorateship.

In 1902 Khama moved his headquarters from Palapye to Serowe. On 21 February 1923 Khama died of pneumonia. ∎

Khama, T. (1906-59)

KHAMA, Tshekedi (1906-59).

BOTSWANA politician; he acted as Regent for Seretse Khama (q.v.) from 1926 to 1950. He was born in 1906 at Serowe to Khama III (q.v.), a chief of the Bamangwato people. He attended the Church of Scotland College in Lovedale, South Africa, and then enrolled at Fort Hare College in Cape Province, but, in 1926, before he had finished his studies, he was asked to return home to act as Regent for Seretse Khama, the four-

T. Khama

year old son of his elder brother Chief Sekgoma II, who had died.

While he was Regent, educational and transport facilities were improved, communal granaries were set up and a large livestock centre was established. He was also concerned with mineral concessions granted to the British South African Company (BSAC) in 1893, and in 1930 he visited London to discuss the matter with the British Secretary of State for the Colonies. He stressed his people's opposition to mining activities on their territory and after negotiations the BSAC finally abandoned the Bamangwato concessions in 1934.

In 1933 he was suspended from his duties as Regent by the British Commissioner after a white boy, having been found guilty of assaulting an indigenous boy and consorting with a girl from the Bamangwato people, was sentenced to be whipped. By this time he was held in great esteem by his people and the public outcry at his deposition caused the British Commissioner to reinstate Khama shortly afterwards.

As well as watching over the interests of his people he was also concerned with the future of his nephew, Seretse, for whom he was acting as Regent. He was bitterly opposed to Seretse's marriage to an English woman in 1948, believing that not only would it be unacceptable to the Bamangwato people, but would also in fact be detrimental to them in the light of opposition to the match in both London and Pretoria. However, by 1949 the Bamangwato people had indicated their willingness to accept the marriage and Tshekedi's continued opposition lost him popular support.

The following year Tshekedi was sent into exile where, with the support of his nephew, he continued to press for ethnic councils in Bechuanaland to facilitate communication and understanding between the people and the government. He was allowed to return to the Protectorate in 1952 provided he did not resume his involvement in politics there. Despite this he remained active on the African Advisory Council and continued to campaign for the establishment of a legislative council in his country.

He died on 10 June 1959 at the age of 53 while undergoing treatment in a London hospital. During his life he gained great respect among both his people and the British authorities as a man of intelligence and integrity. ■

Khefacha, M.H. (1916-76)

KHEFACHA, Mohammed el-Hedi (1916-76).

TUNISIAN politician and lawyer. He was famous for his defence of Tunisian nationalists fighting for independence from France. He was born on 11 October 1916 in Monastir in northern Tunisia. He attended the Lycée Carnot in Tunis and studied law at the University of Algiers. He was called to the Bar in 1942 and started private legal practice, and soon became noted for his defence of nationalists.

In 1950, Khefacha was elected President of the Union of Young Lawyers of Tunisia. He had also joined the Neo-Destour Party being led by Habid Bourguiba, who later became first President of independent Tunisia. With the attainment of independence in 1956, Khefacha was appointed General Inspector of Customs. He was elect-

M.H. Khefacha

ed to the National Assembly and, in 1958, was appointed Secretary of State in the Ministry of Justice. It was during his term of office that the government abolished the multiple jurisdictions of religious tribunals which were integrated into a single jurisdiction of civil courts. The other important innovation of Khefacha's Ministry was the Personal Status Code that both abolished polygamy and made divorce subject to court decision.

He was re-assigned to the Ministry of Public Health in 1966 where he introduced a family planning programme. In 1969, he was made Minister of the Interior, a post which he occupied until 1973 when he became Minister of Works and Housing. He later took the portfolio of Defence in January 1974 and was still holding this office when he died on 25 May 1976 in a Paris hospital. ■

Khemisti, M. (1930-63)

KHEMISTI, Mohammed (1930-63).

ALGERIAN politician who became Foreign Minister at independence. Though a member of a relatively younger generation of Algerian nationalist leaders, Khemisti was active in the struggle for his country's independence as a student leader. He was born in 1930 in Marnia (the birthplace of the Algerian resistance leader Ben Bella), near Oran. After early education in Algeria he went to France to study medicine at the University of Montpellier; while he was there the armed struggle for independence broke out in the mid-1950s.

Responding to the call of the *Front de Libération Nationale* (FLN) he joined nationalist politics as member of the *Union Générale des Etudiants Musulmans Algériens* (UGEMA), the Moslem student movement created in 1955 by the FLN to support the internal struggle through diplomatic and non-military means. The UGEMA was made an integral part of the FLN by the Soummam Valley Congress of August 1956, and from then on ended its associations with the liberal metropolitan *Union Nationale des Etudiants Français* (UNEF).

UGEMA's role during the war involved pleading the Algerian cause to inter-

national student bodies. At the Sixth International Student Conference which met in Ceylon (now Sri Lanka) in September 1956 it gained both official recognition and support for its objectives. Following this the UGEMA won numerous international scholarships for its members to study abroad. After the anti-colonial struggle the organisation changed its name to the *Union Nationale des Etudiants Algériens* (UNEA) at its fifth congress in Algiers in April 1963 and then decided to unite with other youth organisations in the National Youth Committee under the guidance of the FLN's Political Bureau.

Khemisti was UGEMA's secretary when he was arrested while studying in France. Following his release in 1962 he joined the FLN, aligning himself with Ben Bella in the leadership dispute. He became Algeria's first Minister of Foreign Affairs at independence in 1962. In this capacity he was very much involved in shaping the ideological contours of the newly independent state's foreign policy which was declared as total commitment to non-alignment and the liberation of Africa. Indeed, the years following the defeat of the French in Africa's most

M. Khemisti

violent war of national liberation saw Algeria a leading advocate of the cause of liberation in remaining colonies on the continent. Matching its words with deeds, it offered both material support and office facilities for the liberation movements of southern Africa and the Portuguese colonies of Angola, Mozambique and Guinea-Bissau. At the founding summit conference of the OAU, Algeria appealed to Africa: "Let us all agree to die a little so that the peoples still under colonial domination may be free and African Unity may not be a vain word." Khemisti, as Foreign Minister, was an architect of this policy, though he himself died a month before his country signed the Charter establishing the Organisation of African Unity (OAU) in Addis Ababa on 26 May 1963.

Khemisti was shot by an assassin on 11 April 1963 outside the National Assembly in Algiers. He died in hospital on 5 May 1963. President Gamal Abdul Nasser (q.v.) of Egypt, who was on a state visit to Algeria at the time, accompanied Ben Bella in the mile-long funeral procession through Algiers' Belcourt district to the Sidi Mohammed Cemetery where Khemisti's body was buried. ∎

Khider, M. (1914-67)

KHIDER, Mohammed (1914-67).

ALGERIAN resistance leader in the war against France. He became head of the Political Bureau of the *Front de Libération Nationale* (FLN) at independence. A former factory labourer he was, at thirty-four, the oldest founding member of the clandestine paramilitary force, the *Organisation Spéciale* (OS), organised by Algerian militant nationalists in May 1948.

His prominent associates in the OS, which was inaugurated to advance the nationalist cause through armed struggle, included Belkacem Krim (q.v.), Ahmed Ben Bella, Rabah Bitat, Mohammmed Boudiaf, and Khider's relative, Hocine Ait Ahmed, who was then only twenty-two years old. An intellectual, Ait Ahmed was the driving force behind the creation of the OS and he rose to become its early commander. All these men belonged to the *Mouvement pour le Triomphe des Libertés Démocratiques* (MTLD) of Hadj Ben Ahmed Messali (q.v.), but they rejected the party's moderate posture in favour of militant nationalism.

Khider was also the most politically experienced of the team, having been a past representative for an Algiers' district in the French Chamber of Deputies. He applied this experience in the development of the OS which soon, though still operating underground, attracted a large following. By 1950 when the French discovered its existence, it had an estimated 1,800 members and several cells in central and northern Algeria. It was proscribed and many of its leaders arrested.

Its surviving leaders, Khider, Ben Bella, Ait Ahmed, Boudiaf, Krim, and Bitat (later known popularly in liberation circles as the "historic chiefs"), regrouped in the *Comité Révolutionnaire d'Unité et d'Action* (CRUA) that was renamed the FLN in 1954 and Khider became one of the external leaders who campaigned for international support. In October 1956 the French forced down the aeroplane in which Khider, Ben Bella and three other external leaders were flying across Algerian air-space from Morocco to Tunisia for a meeting with King Hassan and the Tunisian government. The FLN leaders were arrested and imprisoned in France where they stayed for the duration of the war of independence. In 1958, while

M. Khider

still serving his prison term, he was appointed honorary Minister of State in the FLN Provisional Government (GPRA) formed in Tunis in September 1958.

Khider was released from prison by the French in March 1962, at the time of the signing of the Accords d'Evian which provided for independence. Back in independent Algeria he aligned with Ben Bella in the leadership tussle in the FLN. He took part in the historic May 1962 Tripoli Conference which constituted the Tripoli Programme that set out Algeria's socialist option and articulated the supreme role of the Political Bureau in independent Algeria.

When the Political Bureau was created in July 1962 Khider, in addition to the responsibility of re-organising the FLN, was placed at its head. He worked hard at transforming the FLN's wartime machinery into a governing organ, building its basis among the peasants in the cantons. During this period he regularly toured rural Algeria, establishing cells and exhorting guerrillas to choose between a military career and party membership.

He succeeded in building FLN into a mass movement with between 200,000 and 300,000 paid members. He also consolidated its preponderence over all other state institutions. By April 1963 the Political Bureau had become the supreme decision-making body and head of the new party machinery. Thus, in the immediate post-independence era, Khider's success brought him into a powerful position in the hierarchy of government.

He however soon fell out with President Ben Bella over the relationship between the party and government. He resigned his post as Secretary-General of the FLN on 17 April 1963, attributing his resignation to "fundamental divergences in viewpoints." He left Algeria for Switzerland in 1964, where the FLN's funds, estimated at about $12 million, were kept, and Khider was also the party's treasurer. He withdrew the money to support opposition to Ben Bella, even though the Ben Bella government had unsuccessfully sued for possession of the money in April 1966. The immediate repercussion of the litigation was that Khider's residence permit was suspended by the Swiss government. He went to France and later Spain, where he continued to finance external opposition groups who operated from France.

In July 1964 he was formally removed from the FLN for alleged misuse of party funds and in April 1965 he was sentenced in his absence to death for his role in an abortive coup against the Algerian government. Khider was shot dead in Spain on 3 January 1967 as he was leaving his Madrid home. Spanish police later said that the exiled leader's killer was a 40 year-old Algerian, Youcef Darkmouche. Khider's body was buried in Casablanca, Morocco, on 6 January. ■

Kigeri IV (1860-95)

KIGERI IV, Rwabugiri (1860-95).

KING of Rwanda. The history of Rwanda's monarchs dates back to the fourteenth century, although it was not until later that the country's peoples, the Bahutu, Batutsi and Batwa, were all brought under a single Kingdom under one Mwami (King). The principal architect of the centralised Kingdom was King Rwabugiri Kigeri IV whose military prowess brought Rwanda's Tutsi kingship to the peak of its power in the second half of the 19th century. He was born in 1860, of the powerful dynasty which had provided successive Rwandan monarchs.

He ascended the throne after the death of Rwogera Mutara II. Kigeri's reign was characterised by continuous warfare which he waged in order to consolidate the Batutsi oligarchy over the expanded kingdom. For this purpose he rebuilt the army and acquired large quantities of firearms with which he made repeated incursions into the neighbouring states of what are now Uganda and Tanzania to the north and Burundi to the south. Contrary to the practice of his predecessors, King Kigeri initiated a policy designed to facilitate effective administration of the new, centralised kingdom by non-hereditary officials, while maintaining supreme authority over the state. By the 1880s he had established a well developed administrative machinery in Rwanda which was not only conducive to smooth government but was also useful in checking the encroachment of European imperialism. He successfully kept out the European traders and explorers until 1894, when he received the first visitor to Rwanda. Afterwards King Kigeri ensured that successive European visitors did not unduly interfere in the affairs of his Kingdom.

Kigeri died in 1895 by which time he had established himself as the most powerful ruler in the region. ■

Kimalando, J. (c.1900-1980)

KIMALANDO, Joseph (c.1900-1980).

J. Kimalando

TANZANIAN political leader in the struggle for independence. A founder member of the Tanganyika African Association (TAA) that became the Tanganyika African National Union (TANU) in 1954, he was born to a Kibosho family in the Kilimanjaro area. He went to a local Roman Catholic Mission school where he was taught to write Swahili and German, Tanganyika being under the Germans then; he became a convert to Christianity during his attendance there. About 1920 Kimalando went to Nairobi, Kenya, and continued his education there at night school while working as a clerk in a government department. It was during this sojourn that he met the Kenyan political leader, Harry Thuku (q.v.). Kimalando returned to Tanganyika in 1922 to undertake various jobs as time-keeper (1922-23), store-keeper (1923), probationary sub-inspector in the police in Dar-es-Salaam, and later as clerk in the railways where he was to serve for the next fifteen years.

By 1925 Kimalando, like his other compatriots in the government sevice, began to take interest in the activities of the British and started reacting to colonial measures that tended to consolidate European supremacy over Tanganyika. As Kimalando was to recall later in an interview, there were a number of incidents of racial discrimination, maltreatment and downright contempt of Africans by the British administrators and the Europeans in general. The African civil servants in Dar-es-Salaam then, according to Kimalando's interview published in *Tanzania Notes and Records* (no. 70) of 1969, realising the African predica-

ment, formed the African Association (AA) in 1929 as a vehicle for expressing disapproval to colonial abuses. The AA, the first African political organisation in the country, later became known as the Tanganyika African Association (TAA), and among its early demands were compulsory education for Africans, recruitment of black teachers from America and South Africa, establishment and recognition of African trade unions, Africans' participation in government and an end to European settler domination of political and economic life of Tanganyika. In later years it became opposed to the planned union of the three East African territories, namely Kenya, Tanganyika and Uganda, for which it sent a delegation to London to put forward its case.

A founder and leading member of the TAA, Kimalando was elected its vice-president in 1936, and between 1937 and 1938 succeeded to its presidency. He got married (1931) and left the railways in 1938 to set himself up in private business in Moshi where he later supervised the opening of a TAA branch and several sub-branches at Machame, Kibosho, Mbokomu and Sanya Chini. He then worked as a clerk in an Indian advocate's office while devoting more time to the activities of the Moshi TAA branch whose secretary he had become. At the same time he was elected vice-president of the Chagga Cultural Association, another quasi-political organisation, in 1949. In 1953 Kimalando was in the TAA delegation led by its newly elected president, Julius Nyerere, that met in Dar-es-Salaam the British Royal Commission which had been appointed to investigate the causes of Mau Mau activities in neighbouring Kenya.

On 7 July of the following year he was among the seventeen delegates that attended the annual meeting, held in Dar-es-Salaam, of the TAA; it was at this four-day conference that the association became the Tanganyika African National Union (TANU), thus transforming itself from a social union to a political movement. It was from there also that Nyerere, elected first president of TANU, rose to political prominence with a maiden speech which demanded self-government and independence from Britain. Kimalando was to reiterate this call for African rule in late 1954 when as a leader of the Northern Province branch of TANU he presented his party's demands to a visiting United Nations Mission; it was he and Kirilo Japhet who handed the TANU written memorandum to the UN team in Arusha.

As the momentum grew, however, Kimalando, now a member of the older generation of politicians whose moderate and cautious approach conflicted with the more aggressive nationalism of the new leadership, was edged out of position of prominence. He retired from active politics to work as a clerk in Majengo near Moshi where he died on 25 May 1980. ■

Kimathi, D. (1920-57)

KIMATHI, Dedan (1920-57).

KENYAN legendary freedom fighter and politician. He was born on 31 October 1920 at North Tetu in Nyeri district, Kenya. He left school at eighteen and held several jobs including manual labour on various European estates in the so-called "White Highlands". In 1941 he joined the colonial army for a short time.

He later became a member of Kenya's two principal post-war political movements;

on 2 June 1952 he became secretary of the Thompson's Falls branch of the Kenya African Union (KAU). He had already sworn the Mau Mau oath twice prior to this and had himself become an administrator of the oath. At that time the Kenya African Union was a firmly established multi-ethnic mass movement with at least 100,000 members, whose goals were explicitly political as well as economic. From 1946-52, the movement used "legitimate" means, such as petitions and the few institutions to which Africans had access to further their demands, but to no avail.

It was the disillusionment of KAU's more aware members that gave birth to the secret, and almost exclusively Kikuyu, Mau Mau movement. The term "Mau Mau" was used for the first time in 1948 in an official report of the Kenyan secret service and referred to an organisation which was then only loosely structured and without any publicly declared central authority.

Members were recruited among the "squatters" on the European farms of the "White Highlands", their principal grievance was the temporary nature of the contracts they signed with the European farmers allowing them access to the land on which they and their fathers had been born. Oath-swearing bound those who took the oath to keep the movement's secrets and to promote Kikuyu unity.

Towards 1950, some KAU leaders, impressed by the unity forged by the oath, decided to use this oath-swearing campaign for political mobilisation, although at this stage the "Kiambu Parliament", as it was known, was still relatively moderate and its actions conceived of in non-violent terms.

Events took a somewhat more violent turn in 1951 and 1952 when a group of militant youthful trade unionists tried to seize control of the party; they partially succeeded in this aim in the latter half of 1951 by placing some of their members in KAU's central committee, and they gained complete control over the Nairobi branch. They extended the oath-taking campaign from Nairobi to the northern Kikuyu districts of Fort Hall and Nyeri, and started preparations for a campaign of violence to be conducted from the forest areas, by building up stocks of arms.

A few isolated incidents had led the colonial authorities to suspect that a general insurrection was imminent. Thus the pace of events was hastened with the declaration of a state of emergency on 20 October 1952. The colonial authorities called on Britain for assistance and military reinforcements were sent to Nairobi; on the night of 19 October, about 100 African political leaders were arrested, including Jomo Kenyatta (q.v.) and most of the "Kiambu Parliament".

The forest-based resistance was, at this point, still unorganised, but the harsh, repressive measures taken against Kikuyu peasants in the so-called Kikuyu Land Unit caused hundreds of young men to flee to the forest.

It was at this point that Kimathi emerged from relative obscurity within the movement to become a nationally-known figure. Until October 1952 he was a local commander, unknown in Nairobi, although occupying a sufficiently important position to have been included on an expedition to the Aberdare mountains for the purpose of assessing the area's potential as a guerrilla base.

When the state of emergency was declared, Kimathi was returning to Nyeri after this expedition; he lost no time, and on 22 October organised an oath-taking ceremony on the banks of the River Guara at which several hundred Kikuyus were initiated.

Pro-government chiefs and guards who visited this ceremony with the intention of putting a stop to it were murdered; the next day Kimathi's description was issued by the authorities and a reward of £500 was offered for information leading to his arrest. This had the effect of increasing Kimathi's prestige among those who had fled to the forest and helped him establish his leadership.

His rival for the leadership of the roughly 15,000 guerrilla fighters of the Aberdare mountains was Stanley Mathenge, also from Nyeri district, and whose name figured on the list of people to have been arrested on 20 October.

These guerrilla fighters took as their name "Land Freedom Army", a name which signified clearly the anti-colonial nature of their struggle, their demand for access to the land of their birth. However, until March 1953 the Mau Mau army consisted of several groups, each with a chosen leader, but without any formally centralised leadership. In that month, however, these groups were integrated into several large camps and in May a first Mau Mau general council was

D. Kimathi

held, known as the Ituma Ndemi Trinity Council. This brought together all the fighters from Nyeri district who elected Stanley Mathenge as their president and Kimathi as secretary-general.

Within a few months, however, Kimathi had established himself as the uncontested leader of all the Mau Mau groups. He achieved this through his intimate knowledge of the forest, his organisational talents and his education.

He called a general meeting of all the armed groups operating in the Aberdares, from 16-25 August 1953, on the banks of the River Mwathe, to discuss the structure of the Mau Mau army. About 50 military leaders, accompanied by several hundred armed followers and representing not only Nyeri district but also Fort Hall and the Kikuyu of the "White Highlands", took part. Mathenge, who considered Kimathi as his subordinate, refused to participate.

This meeting decided on the formation of a general council to direct the armed struggle, known as the Kenya Defence Council. In the absence of Mathenge, and as representative of the district which had contributed most men, Kimathi was elected president of the Council, unopposed. The Mau Mau army was divided into eight regiments, and Kimathi was their supreme military commander.

The forest constituted a virtually impenetrable barrier to the British army and with the support of the population of Nairobi and the reserves, the guerrilla forces had little difficulty at first in obtaining supplies. They were, however, not well armed; it was this that made it relatively difficult for them to take the military offensive and forced them to the tactics of surprise attack on European farms or villages loyal to the administration.

The British created a series of "protected" villages, within which the inhabitants were confined and allowed out for only one hour daily under armed escort for the purpose of obtaining food. The counter-offensive aimed against the Mau Mau came in April 1954 when the government launched "Operation Anvil" in Nairobi. 25,000 soldiers and police mounted a round-up operation which lasted several weeks and involved nearly the entire African population of 100,000. The 70,000 Kikuyu were subjected to prolonged checking and interrogation. 28,000 people were subsequently sent to detention camps, and thousands of others sent back to the reserves.

This was a turning point in the anti-Mau Mau campaign; arms, medicines and food gradually ceased to reach the forest. The Mau Mau army was reorganised into small, independently-operating groups of about 50 men.

The military authorities, having realised that conventional military tactics could not be successfully employed against the guerrillas, recruited ex-Mau Mau fighters to infiltrate these groups which added to the internal tensions within the Mau Mau. In May 1955 a group led by Stanley Mathenge and including other more "traditionalist" leaders, entered into open hostilities against Kimathi and his men.

Kimathi was finally captured in October 1956, after a 10-month man-hunt directed at him personally. Having recovered from the wound received at the time of his capture, Kimathi was put on trial in November 1956 and condemned to death by hanging. He was executed by the British colonial authorities in Nairobi prison on 18 February 1957. ∎

Kimba, E. (1926-66)

KIMBA, Evariste (1926-66).

ZAIREAN leading politician, Foreign Minister in the secessionist Katangan government of Moise Tshombe (q.v.) and founder and president of the *Mouvement Populaire d'Union Africaine* (MPA). He was born on 16 July 1926 in Nsaka in the Bukama district, Congo (now Zaire). After primary schooling in Elisabethville (now Lubumbashi) he had his secondary education at the Institut Saint Boniface in the same city. He then continued his post-secondary education through evening lessons while working at the *Compagnie du Chemin de Fer du Bas Congo au Katanga*.

He left the company in 1954 and entered the field of publishing as an editorial staff on the Elisabethville newspaper, *Essor du Congo*, where he soon proved to be a brilliant journalist. Through that organ he was exposed to the political, social and economic realities of his country and the interactions between the various ethnic

E. Kimba

groups on the one hand and between them and the Belgian colonial authorities on the other. In 1958 Kimba joined the *Confédération des Associations Tribales du Katanga*, or the Conakat as it was popularly called, a political party formed in Katanga (now Shaba) on the eve of national independence. He soon became a leading personality in the party, though he held no executive position.

In February 1960 he was appointed chief deputy in the colonial administration, followed in May of the same year with his election as a senator for Katanga to the national Parliament in Leopoldville (later renamed Kinshasa). Like all other Conakat parliamentarians Kimba withdrew from the activities of the national authority after independence was proclaimed in June 1960, as a prelude to the Katangese secession the following month. He and his Katangese political colleagues, Moise Tshombe, Jean-Baptiste Kibwe and Godefroid Munongo, led the province out of the Congo on 11 July 1960 and established a rebel administration in which Kimba became Minister of Foreign Affairs. This was a difficult posting in the circumstances leading to the rebellion, exacerbated by the Congo government's outright rejection of secessionism and the enormous interest shown in the affair by the international community. The consequence of all this was a devastating blow to the newly independent country that suffered the loss of its first Prime Minister, Patrice Lumumba (q.v.), and a bloody civil war that employed the services of European mercenaries and the involvement of the United Nations troops, and culminated in a military dictatorship. Kimba travelled extensively in Europe and the Americas to solicit support for his rebel government while at home, after initially making efforts to resolve the differences between the Katangese and the Congolese governments through internal negotiations, he took a very hard line towards any settlement. Through his diplomatic efforts Katanga won the tacit support of the Western countries, but in 1963 the rebel forces were defeated by the Congo national government; it was Kimba who, after Tshombe had fled from Katanga into exile, formally handed over power to the central authorities. He and Tshombe were later absorbed into the national government, the latter even becoming Prime Minister in July 1964.

In 1964 Kimba formed the *Mouvement Populaire d'Union Africaine* (MPA) and won election on its platform to Parliament. Following the dismissal of the Tshombe government in October 1965, Kimba was appointed by President Kasavubu (q.v.) to form a government. He twice presented his nominations to Parliament and was twice turned down by his numerous adversaries in the pro-Tshombe lobby. The Prime Minister and President Kasavubu were subsequently overthrown by Joseph Mobutu. Kimba was implicated in a plot to topple the Mobutu government in 1966; he was sentenced to death at an open-air trial in Kinshasa and executed by hanging on 2 June 1966. ■

Kimbangu, S. (c. 1887-1951)

KIMBANGU, Simon (c.1887-1951).

ZAIREAN religious leader. He was born about 1887-89 in N'kamba, in the part of the Bakongo people's area then newly occupied by the Congo Free state (later the Belgian Congo, now Zaire). Brought up by an aunt after the early death of his parents, he was converted as a young man by the Baptist Missionary Society which was important in the Lower Congo, and baptised in 1915 with his wife Marie. Then, in 1921, he began a remarkable independent mission, preaching Christianity on his own initiative with great success. After receiving (so he claimed) repeated calls from God, which he vainly tried to resist by escaping to seek work in Leopoldville (now Kinshasa) he began his ministry on 6 April 1921 by healing a sick woman.

He preached the doctrine of one God according to Christian teaching, and his teaching was in general thoroughly Christian; he said Christ was healing sick people through him. He also practised faith healing and thousands flocked to his village at N'kamba to be healed from illnesses as well as to hear his teaching; missions and hospitals for miles around were almost deserted. He preached against the traditional beliefs and their objects of worship ("fetishes"). And unlike many African independent church prophets, he preached against polygamy.

Despite this rigorous Christian teaching, Kimbangu's phenomenal success over a few months was greeted with dismay by the missionaries who saw him as a threat to their religious denominations, and by the Belgian colonial authorities. Of the missionaries, the Baptist ones seem to have been relatively moderate in their hostility, the Catholic ones ferocious, urging his arrest by the Belgian Congo government. On 2 June 1921

S. Kimbangu

an order for his arrest was given. He escaped but then returned to N'kamba and gave himself up in September; and was put on trial for subversion, with some of his apostles. At his trial he admitted he was a "prophet". He was sentenced on 3 October 1921 to one hundred and twenty lashes, to be followed by execution. He was a man whose dignity of bearing at the trial was outstanding and of whom it could not be shown that he had actually caused or intended harm to anyone. The Belgian King commuted the death sentence, but Kimbangu was flogged as sentenced and then sent to life imprisonment in Elisabethville (now Lubumbashi), where he died on 12 October 1951.

In the years following his imprisonment his followers were persecuted intensely, but they remained loyal to his teaching. After Simon Kimbangu's death, his apostles sought to operate legally and, after a final persecution in 1957, were legalised in 1959; they were headed by the prophet's three sons, Charles Kilolokele, Solomon Kiangani Dialungana, and Joseph Kiangienda. The "Church of Jesus Christ on Earth through the Prophet Simon Kimbangu" became the second largest in Zaire, with several million followers.■

King, C.D.B. (1871-1961)

KING, Charles Dunbar Burgess (1871-1961).

LIBERIAN statesman. He was born on 12 March 1871 in Monrovia. His parents came from Sierra Leone and he was educated at Powell Elementary School, Monrovia, and at Freetown Grammar School in Sierra Leone. He then studied law under Chief Justice F.E.R. Johnson.

On completing his legal studies on 13 December 1897 he joined the legal profession, rising to be Counsellor-at-Law in the Supreme Court of Liberia in February 1900. During this period he was also President of the National Bar Association. He later joined the State Department, serving as Chief Clerk for a while, after which he was appointed Attorney for Montserrado County by the President of the Republic. He was promoted to the Cabinet position of Attorney-General, and in 1912 he became Secretary of State, a position he held throughout the First World War.

The President was very impressed with his diplomatic handling of difficult situations during this period, and recommended that King be nominated his successor. Subsequently King was elected President of the Republic of Liberia in May 1919 and was inaugurated into office on 1 January 1920, having meanwhile represented Liberia at the Paris Peace Conference.

When he came into office, the country was in a difficult economic situation and he immediately tried to rectify this. He headed a

Commission to the USA to negotiate a loan but as this was unsuccessful, he adopted various austerity policies to gradually return the nation to economic solvency.

Despite these austerity programmes and the shortage of money for governmental expenditure, he initiated many public works projects, among which were the first road-building programmes in the country, the introduction of electricity in Monrovia and the construction of lighthouses to protect shipping. He also established a hospital in Monrovia and founded the Booker Washington Institute, Liberia's first technical school.

King was also interested in administrative reforms and during his presidency the country was divided into two administrative areas — the hinterland, which was mainly populated by the indigenous ethnic groups, and the County districts. He did this because he believed that the indigenous peoples required special attention to their problems and needs. In 1923 he convened a Grand Council of hinterland chiefs and government officials. This conference was in session for one month, discussing rules and regulations for the administration of the native districts and the appointment of commissioners for each hinterland district to provide a two-way communication link between the traditional chiefs and the government.

Meanwhile an American company, Firestone, had been conducting surveys around the world for areas politically and agriculturally suited for the production of rubber. Liberia was considered to be very suitable and in 1926, a 99-year lease for up to one million acres of Liberian land was negotiated at a rent of 6 cents per acre per year, with a further one per cent duty payable on rubber exports. King managed to overcome opposition fears that this concession would reduce Liberian independence and after the agreement was ratified he also managed to secure a loan of $5 million through the Finance Corporation of America, an organisation created by the Firestone Company, gaining a breathing space for the country's economic difficulties.

In 1927 King was re-elected President amidst some controversy that the ballot boxes had been interfered with. This was followed by the more serious allegations that King and other very senior Government officials were involved in a form of slave trading, forcing people to work on plan-

C.D.B. King

tations in Fernando Po in very primitive and often fatal conditions. This was a particularly serious accusation as the Republic of Liberia had been founded by the descendants of freed slaves in search of liberty and caused a public outcry, both in the country and internationally.

King denied these allegations and requested an official investigation by the League of Nations to prove them false. A three-man Commission was established, composed of a representative from the USA, Britain and Liberia, and began its inquiries on 7 April 1930. After four months of investigation, the Commission reported that there was no slavery as defined by the Anti-Slavery Convention, but that several important Government officials were involved in compulsory recruitment of labour to Fernando Po for their own profit. The Government was also criticised for its treatment of the indigenous population and various recommendations were put forward to overcome this.

In response to this report, King began to prepare a schedule of political reforms, but feelings were running high in the country, and a great deal of pressure was being placed on the Government. The resignation of the Vice-President, a prominent figure in the scandal, was called for, and on 3 December 1930 King also resigned, partly because of opposition and partly because he felt that his administration was involved by implication although he was personally cleared of any involvement in the matter.

After his resignation, King retired to private life on his rubber plantation, and gradually the antagonism over the slave trade scandal disappeared and he gained the respect of an elder statesman whose advice was often sought.

In 1947 he resumed public service with his appointment as first Liberian Envoy Extraordinary and Minister Plenipotentiary to the USA, a particularly important post because of the country's close links with America. His position was upgraded to Ambassador in 1950 and he remained in this post for a further two years before he retired. He was also Liberia's first Permanent Representative to the United Nations during this period.

Throughout his life he retained his interest in civic affairs and was president of Liberia College's Board of Trustees as well as becoming vice-president and acting president of the College for a while. In addition to this, he gave financial assistance to Cuttington College, where he was a member of the Board of Trustees, and to the Booker Washington Institute, where he was chairman of the Board of Managers. He was also a member of the Order of Ancient Free and Accepted Masons, and rose to the position of Most Worshipful Grand Master between 1922-28.

In the course of his career he received three Liberian honours: Knight Great Band of the Humane Order of African Redemption, Grand Band of the Order of the Star of Africa and Grand Cordon of the Most Venerable Order of Knighthood of the Pioneers of the Republic. He also received decorations from France, Haiti, Holland, Italy, Lebanon, Peru, Spain, Sweden and the Vatican.

He was a devout Christian and was a former choir director, vestryman and warden in the Protestant Episcopal Church. He also wrote the music for the hymn *My God, My Father, While I Stray*. He died on 4 September 1961. ■

Kisenge, E.A. (1912-80)

KISENGE, Elias Amos (1912-80).

TANZANIAN politician and an important political organiser in the struggle for Independence. Born in Usangi, Mwanga District, son of a Luteran Church elder, he went to a local primary school where, despite grave shortages of teachers (he himself helped to teach junior pupils), he passed his Standard V examination in 1929 and went on to Tabora Government Senior Secondary School.

Kisenge joined the then Provincial Administration and was posted as a clerk in the Provincial Commissioner's Office, Arusha where he joined the Tanganyika African Civil Servants Association (TACSA) and became the secretary of the local branch. When he was found openly to sympathise with the Mbiru uprising (1944-45) when the Pares (his people) rose against the British authorities in protest against graduated taxation, the colonial government sent him away from Arusha to the out-stations to frustrate him. Everywhere he went, he

E.A. Kisenge

motivated Africans to campaign for their political rights. Eventually, he was posted to Dar-es-Salaam on promotion, and was immediately elected secretary-general of the TACSA.

When the Tanganyika African National Union (TANU) was formed, Kisenge resigned from the colonial service to join the movement, promoting its aims (at first secretly, but later openly) despite intimidation from the colonial authorities. Such was the fury of the District Commissioner on Kisenge that he was prevented from being elected paramount chief (Sekiti) of Pare.

In April 1956 Kisenge was elected provincial secretary of TANU with Mwalimu Kiheri as his provincial chairman. After the famous Tabora TANU Conference, at which TANU, contrary to the expectation of the colonial government, accepted the detested Tripatite Voting System in order to destroy it, Kisenge was given the onerous job of reopening banned TANU branches in Sukumaland; TANU had been banned in Usukuma (the home of the biggest single ethnic group in Tanganyika) for fear that it could be the beginning of a movement similar to the Mau Mau in Kenya. On the very first day that he arrived in Mwanza about 40,000 shillings were collected on the spot for TANU, and membership of the movement increased rapidly in the three months Kisenge was in Usukuma.

He returned to Tanga as provincial secretary thereafter and it was here that he made perhaps his greatest contribution to the liberation of Tanganyika. This was the time when the colonial government was determined to introduce "multi-racialism" (with the European and Asian minorities sharing power more or less equally with the great African majority) in the country in order to destroy TANU. To do so they encouraged and financed the formation and the consolidation of the United Tanganyika Party (UTP). TANU was, however, able to win all the seats in the subsequent crucial general elections. Kisenge was unopposed as member for Same constituency, in 1960, and was appointed junior Minister in the Prime Minister's Office in 1961. He was transferred to the Ministry of Local Government in 1962, at the time when chieftaincy was abolished, but was transferred to the President's Office and made deputy secretary-general of the party as well. When he was later transferred to the office of the Vice-President, he also

became chairman of the Civil Service Staff Council. He lost in the 1965 general elections but was appointed deputy chairman of the Transport Licensing Authority as well as a member of the Civil Service Commission.

He later retired to Tanga where he was made general manager of the Tanga African Motor Transport Company. He died in 1980. ■

Kiwanuka, B.K.M. (1922-72)

KIWANUKA, Benedicto Kagimu Mugumba (1922-72).

UGANDAN lawyer and politician; he was his country's first Prime Minister at self-government in 1962. He was born in May 1922 at Kisawaba village in Masaka, Buganda. He received his early education in Uganda in Catholic Mission schools up to junior secondary level. In 1950 he left Uganda for Lesotho where he studied Latin, matriculating in 1951. He studied law from 1952 at the University of London, and was called to the Bar in 1956, returning to Uganda the same year he set up a law practice.

He joined active politics during the struggle for political independence in the country, becoming president of the Democratic Party (DP), one of the political parties which existed in Uganda up to the military coup of 1971. In September 1959 he left his law practice in order to become a full-time politician. The following year he came into conflict with Mutesa II (q.v.), the Kabaka of Buganda, on what position the Kingdom of Buganda would occupy in a self-governing Uganda. The Kabaka, in an attempt to force the British colonial government to accept a federal system of government for Uganda, ordered Buganda voters not to register for the 1961 general elections. The elections were held in March 1961 and won by the Democratic Party, with the result that Benedicto Kiwanuka became the head of government, assuming the title of Chief Minister.

A constitutional conference to produce a constitution that would pave the way for full self-government and independence was held in London in 1961. One major feature of the 1961 constitution was that it gave Buganda the option of nominating its representatives to the National Assembly.

Uganda attained self-government in March 1962 with Benedicto Kiwanuka as Prime Minister. In a general election held a

The period between 1962 and 1971 saw his political fortunes decline, until the military coup of 1971, when General Idi Amin, who had become President, appointed him Chief Justice of Uganda. During the second half of 1972, after a disagreement with President Idi Amin, he was arrested in his chambers and never seen alive in public again. ■

B.K.M. Kiwanuka

Kiwanuka, J.W. (1915-72)

KIWANUKA, Joseph William (1915-72).

UGANDAN politician, founder member of the Uganda National Congress, the country's first national political party. He was born in October 1915 in Mengo, near Kampala, son of a former official in the government of the Kabaka of Buganda. He was educated at King's College, Budo, and at Makerere College where he trained as a civil engineer.

He began his career as a surveyor with the British colonial administration, later serving with the East African Army Service Corps during the Second World War. Kiwanuka was demobilised at the end of the war and went into journalism, editing the *Matalasi* (Messenger) newspaper. In 1949, he interrupted his editorship for a two-year course in journalism in Britain.

On his return to Uganda in 1951, Kiwanuka embarked on a political career, joining Milton Obote (later President of Uganda), Ignatius Musazi and Abu Mayanja in the formation in March 1952 of the Uganda National Congress (UNC). The party was founded on a nationalist platform with the declared objectives of uniting the people of Uganda and achieving independence for the country. Its fortunes as a mass movement were enhanced with the deportation of Mutesa II (q.v.), the Kabaka of Buganda, in 1953 and his exile in Britain. The UNC led the campaign for the Kabaka's return, while becoming more critical of British rule.

Kiwanuka and other leaders of the UNC were sent to exile, or imprisoned for their part in the struggle. Kiwanuka was deported to the West Nile District where he remained confined until the Kabaka was

month later, the Uganda People's Congress (UPC), led by Dr. Milton Obote, won. The Democratic Party led by Benedicto Kiwanuka became the opposition party, with the notable absence of Benedicto Kiwanuka from Parliament as he did not gain his parliamentary seat. His party had to choose another man. Mr. Bataringaya, to become the parliamentary leader of the party.

returned to Uganda in 1958. He became a member of the Lukiko (the Buganda Parliament), but was soon expelled for anti-monarchy views. He was subsequently charged for an alleged attempt to assassinate King Mutesa for which he was sentenced to fifteen years' imprisonment. The sentence was quashed on appeal.

The political fortunes of Kiwanuka, now leader of the UNC, took another nasty turn in 1959 when the UNC split, with Obote and Mayanja breaking to form the Uganda People's Congress (UPC). The truncated UNC suffered further decline in strength in the 1961 general elections where it won only one seat out of 81. Kiwanuka himself was defeated in the poll.

Following the unsuccessful bid for parliament on the eve of Uganda's independence, Kiwanuka went into business, running an enterprising nightclub, the White Nile Club, in Kampala. After the military coup of 25 January 1971, Kiwanuka re-emerged briefly in the political arena but soon fell out with President Amin. He left Uganda and went into exile in Kenya where he died in 1972. ■

M. Koinange

Koinange, M. (1907-81)

KOINANGE, Mbiyu (1907-81).

KENYAN politician, founding father of modern Kenya, he was among those that joined Jomo Kenyatta (q.v.) in the country's nationalist struggle for independence against the British. Koinange co-founded the Kenya African Union (KAU), Kenya's first national political party in 1946 and for nearly two decades after had a lifelong working relationship with Kenyatta who became the first president of independent Kenya. He served Kenyatta as Minister of State in the President's Office and in that post built a reputation as one of the nation's most powerful politicians.

Koinange was born in 1907 in Njunu in the Kiambu District near Nairobi. His father was a chief, one of the most respected Kikuyu leaders who was interned between

1952 and 1962 for involvement in the Mau Mau movement. Koinange was educated at the Church Missionary Society mission schools in Kiambaa, Nairobi, Kabete and Mombasa, finishing at the Alliance High School in Kikuyu in 1926. The following year he entered Hampton Institute, Virginia, USA, and in 1936 graduated from Ohio Wesleyan University with a BA degree in Sociology and Political Science. He did a post-graduate course in education at St. John's College, Cambridge, Britain, and at the Institute of Education, University of London. While in London he also did the same Social Anthropology course as Kenyatta. In 1947 he returned to the London School of Economics and Political Science for a PhD.

In the intervening years he returned to Kenya, and in 1939, despite his extensive qualifications was offered a job at a lower salary than that paid to Europeans. Koinange refused the offer and threw himself into establishing the Kenya African Teachers' College at Githunguri to train teachers for the Kikuyu independent schools which expressed African discontent with mission institutions. He became its first Principal.

KAU was Kenya's pioneering political party whose anti-colonial campaign resulted in the development of mass political consciousness in the country as well as independence in 1963. Successor to Kikuyu Central Association and forerunner of Kenya African National Union (KANU), KAU was the first national movement formed to campaign for reform of the colonial constitution and against the appropriation of African land by European settlers. Under the leadership of Jomo Kenyatta, who was its first President, Harry Thuku (q.v.), James Gichuru (q.v.), Oginga Odinga and Koinange, the movement grew rapidly into a mass organisation claiming in 1959 a membership of 150,000 across the country. It soon developed into a formidable opposition to British rule and when, in 1952, the Mau Mau movement was launched its leaders were interned. Koinange was not among those arrested, because he was in London petitioning the British Colonial Secretary. He remained there until 1959, serving as KAU's representative in Europe. During this sojourn he took a course in trade unionism at the Department for Extra-Mural Studies of the University of London.

In September 1959 he returned to Africa, going to Accra at the invitation of Kwame Nkrumah (q.v.). He was made one of the directors of the Ghanaian Bureau of African Affairs with responsibility for the Congo, East and Central Africa. He was at this post when he was invited in January 1960 to become adviser to the African delegation to the Kenya Constitutional Conference at Lancaster House, London. The colonial authorities, persuaded by the settler delegates to the Conference, refused to allow Koinange to participate, and a major row erupted. This was solved by a compromise, which enabled him to enter Lancaster House but not into the conference room.

Koinange returned to his post in Ghana and remained there until 1961 when he went back to Kenya. He was soon arrested but with independence approaching was released to contest election to the House of Representatives. He was elected member for the Kiambaa Constituency which he represented until 1979. At independence he became a member of Kenyatta's administration, serving as Minister of State in the Prime Minister's Office with responsibility for Pan-African Affairs.

In 1964 he became Minister of Education until May 1966 when he reverted to Minister of State in the President's Office where he was responsible for Provincial Administration and then Foreign Affairs. He was widely tipped to succeed Kenyatta when the President died in August 1978. But it was Vice-President Daniel arap Moi who, under the terms of the constitution, took over from Kenyatta. Under the new President, Koinange became Minister of Natural Resources. He held that post until he failed to win re-election in November 1979. He then retired from politics and went into private business. He died in Nairobi on 2 September 1981. ■

Koko, King F. (c1853-98)

KOKO, King Frederick William (c1853-98).

NIGERIAN traditional ruler, he led the people of Brass, an Ijaw "city-state", in the attack on Akassa, the Royal Niger Company trading depot and port, on 29 January 1895, one of the major acts of resistance by Nigerians to the imposition of European rule.

Brass was a trading state which sold slaves and later palm produce to Europeans, sometimes selling to them via Bonny and New Calabar (Elem Kalabari) to which it is linked by the creeks and estuaries of the Niger Delta. Nembe was the capital of the state, with Twon and Okpoama subordinate towns. After a late end to the slave trade Nembe traded in salt and fish from the nearby coasts, and yams and cocoyams among other goods. It was ruled for a long time by one king, in the part of Nembe called Ogbolomabiri. Then a revolt led to a separate dynasty of kings being established at Bassambiri. In 1907 (after Koko) it was stated that there had been 16 kings of Ogbolomabiri and nine of Bassambiri. The former clearly enjoyed a higher status. As titular ruler of all Brass, the king of Ogbolomabiri allowed the Church Missionary Society (CMS), under Bishop Crowther (q.v.), to preach at Brass from 1864. King Ockiya, who died in 1879, was a Christian.

After the death of Ockiya chief Igbeta was regent, refusing to be king. He died in 1888, and then his nephew Koko became ruler, again refusing to be King. Then aged about 35, Koko was a Christian, but on acceding to the effective government of Brass he reverted to the traditiional religion. He had not been a head of any of the "Houses", the main traditional units of society in the Ijaw trading states (essentially they were extended families organised as trading concerns, under a powerful head).

In 1884 the Brass government, when asked by the British Consul to sign a treaty like other coastal states' governments between Warri and Cameroons (Douala), reacted warily, like Jaja (q.v.) of Opobo. It signed a treaty to last six months only, and then renewed it in 1885 on the understanding that the British government would protect its interests against the National African Company. However, that company, renamed the Royal Niger Company (RNC), soon started ruining the trade on which Brass depended.

Brass was not under RNC rule, being instead included in the Oil Rivers Protectorate (1891) and Niger Coast Protectorate (1893). But the complete monopoly of trade, as well as domination in every other sphere, which the RNC imposed along the Niger up to Lokoja destroyed the Brassmen's trade. Brass canoes were effectively prevented from carrying goods to and from Oguta, and even more distant trading centres, as they had done before. The Brassmen complained to the British government, saying they would have to "eat sand", and although there was criticism in Britain of the RNC, nothing was done to help Brass. Then anger mounted against the company, which had an important port and depot for shipment of goods coming or leaving by ocean shipping, at Akassa in the Delta, about 35 miles as the crow flies from Nembe.

Driven beyond endurance, Koko and his people decided to take action, after one leading chief opposed to such a course died in 1894. He persuaded or forced Okpoama, a semi-autonomous part of the Brass kingdom, to join him. He also appealed, but without success, for help from Bonny and from the newly divided New Calabar state. On their own the Brassmen went into action in late

King Koko

January 1895. About 1,500 soldiers, on 30-40 canoes, moved on Akassa through the creeks, inlets and swamps they knew intimately.

On 29 January 1895 the Brass force, evading a British patrol sent out in response to a warning of the attack, landed at Akassa, destroyed the stores, and killed 25 people, captured 70 men, all Africans, killing 43 later at Nembe. The attack shocked the British. Although the Brassmen said they were quarrelling only with the RNC, not with the Queen, the British government ordered a punitive raid on Nembe. A naval force broke through the barrier on Nembe creek, captured Sacrifice Island against strong resistance, and, beating further resistance, occupied Nembe town and burned it down. This took place between 24 and 26 February 1895. The chiefs were forced to free surviving prisoners and told to return the money and property taken at Akassa, but this was returned only later and in part. Many British people believed that Brass had had genuine grievances against the RNC and an inquiry was ordered. Its report in 1896 hastened the end of the Company's oppressive Charter.

Koko, however, fled from Nembe, and went into exile at Etiema. He died on 25 February 1898 having apparently committed suicide. ■

Kom II (1889-1942)

KOM II, Mogho Naba (c. 1889-1942).

Burkinabe traditional ruler. He succeeded his father, Mogho Naba Sighiri, who died in 1905. The French, who had just conquered the Mossi people, prevailed on the kingmakers to choose the young Saido Congo, as he was then called, wanting a young man to occupy the most important Mossi throne after Sighiri had used his position to lead a resistance to French rule. The kingmakers were reluctant to choose

Mogho Naba Kom II

someone aged only 16, but were obliged to submit.

The Mogho Naba was one of the most important traditional monarchs in French Africa and remained so in Kom's reign and later, partly because his great traditional prestige – based on an old religion which to this day has remained influential and resistant to Christianity and Islam – encouraged the French to rule through him. They did, however, seek to reduce his power.

In 1907 the French carried out a reorganisation, removing some non-Mossi peoples and remaining provincial ministers. This considerable interference with the established administrative system under the Mogho Naba led to a revolt. This was suppressed and Mogho Naba Kom had to submit to French measures.

In fact he eventually adapted himself cleverly to French rule so as to retain considerable power. While no longer able to preside over traditional ceremonies surrounding his kingship, he retained loyalty, and after all chiefs' courts were abolished in French West Africa in 1912 cases were still taken to the Mogho Naba secretly. The French tolerated this because it was found useful to rule through a still venerated king.

Kom helped the French recruit soldiers for the First World War and forced labourers for Senegal and especially Côte d'Ivoire. The French allowed Kom to celebrate the *Basgha*, a yearly ritual in honour of the ancestors, and in the 1930s supported the chiefs in a conflict with the Catholic mission (over traditional distribution of girls as gifts by chiefs). Mogho Naba Kom, who never became a Catholic, supported the chiefs and gave a chieftaincy to the anti-Mission writer Dim Delobsom, author of a book on the Mogho Naba's throne.

Kom helped in the building of a capital for the new Upper Volta (now Burkina Faso) colony in 1919 at Ouagadougou, his traditional capital. But in 1932 he protested at the abolition of Upper Volta, whose territory was mostly allotted to Côte d'Ivoire. In 1938 he went to Abidjan and pleaded successfully for a special French official to be sent to Ouagadougou.

Early in 1942 Mogho Naba Kom died. There were rumours that he had committed suicide because of restrictions imposed by the Vichy French authorities, or of pressure by the Catholic mission to abandon all his wives but one; these were not proved. He was widely mourned; one funeral speech said "He loved us all, not as a chief, but as a father of a family." He was succeeded by one of his sons (for whom he had allowed Western schooling, but not baptism); this was Mogho Naba Sagha II, who reigned until 1957. ■

Konate, M. (1897-1956)

KONATE, Mamadou (1897-1956).

MALIAN politician. He was born at Kati, Mali, in 1897. After attending local primary schools he went to Senegal to study at the Ecole William Ponty in Dakar, and then became a teacher. By the time he was 37 he had become the principal of the *Ecole*

M. Konate

Rurale in Mali which was, after his death, renamed *Ecole Mamadou Konate*. He had very radical political views and was involved in organising the first union of African teachers.

After unsuccessfully standing for election to the first French Constituent Assembly in 1945, he joined forces with Modibo Keita (q.v.) and established the *Union Soudanaise* (US), a Socialist party that was affiliated to the *Rassemblement Démocratique Africain* (RDA). Konate be-

came secretary-general of the organisation and over the next nine years worked to increase support for the party, first in urban districts and later in the rural areas, so that it gradually became a major political influence in the country. In the November 1946 elections to the French National Assembly he won one seat for the party.

When the French indicted Keita on a charge of contempt in 1947, Konate accompanied him to Paris in an attempt to have the indictment dropped, but Keita was subsequently imprisoned. Under Konate's secretaryship the US began to develop its ideas and spread its influence. Unlike its rival the *Parti Progressiste Soudanais* (PSP) led by Fily Dabo Sissoko (q.v.) that drew its support from pro-French elements, the US made its gain in the towns among the educated elite and in the rural areas where there had been resistance to French occupation. For its radical leadership, the party was constantly under French surveillance and its members spent considerable lengths of time in detention or exile.

In the 1956 elections the *Union Soudanaise* won all but six of the seventy seats in the Territorial Assembly and Konate and his colleague Keita were elected. Konate was chosen as president of the Assembly. However, shortly afterwards he became ill with hepatitis, and died later in the year.■

Kone, M. (1932-79)

KONE, Maurice (1932-79).

IVORIAN poet. He was born on 11 November 1932 at Bouaké, a major town in the centre of Côte d'Ivoire, son of a Lebanese trader, Touffik Moussa, and a woman from the Senufo country, Moussokro Kone.

He went to primary school at Bouaké until 1949, but gave up schooling early to earn his living from numerous jobs including being an apprentice mechanic, a plumber, a sheet iron worker, a driver and from 1958 to 1960 an assistant at Le Vox cinema. In 1961 he got a clerical post at the Bouaké town hall. With a fairly secure job, he set himself to work and prepared for his primary and elementary school certificate (CEPE) examination, which he passed the same year.

Maurice Kone began his literary career in 1961. That year, he published *La guirlande des verbes*, a 32-page collection of poetry, in the Number 22 anthology of "new poetry", brought out by the J. Grassin publishing company in Paris. In the succeeding two years he published another collection of poems, *Au bout du Petit-Matin*, published in 1962 by Jean Germain at Bordeaux, and his first novel, *Le jeune*

M. Kone

homme de Bouaké – an autobiographical novel – published by Grassin in 1963.

A characteristic trait of all these works is a deep sensitivity which Maurice Kone's poetic talent turns into a simple, clear language. It depicts daily life mingled with the stifled cries of the under-privileged. Other poems followed, inspired by the human condition of the downtrodden such as *Au Seuil du crépuscule* (Rodez, Subervie, 1965); *Poèmes Verlainiens* (Milan, Aveyron, 1969), and *Poèmes* published in 1969 by the Commercial Press of Abidjan; *Les voix du silence*, and *Poivrosage* published by P.J. Oswald.

Maurice Kone won many prizes such as the Prize for Côte d'Ivoire's French-language Poets (1963), the Catholic Poetic Horizons Prize (1967), and the *mention très honorable* awarded at the Touraine art and poetry competition in France in 1972. And

although he was called "the great Ivorian poet", it was not until early 1970's that his fame began to increase in Côte d'Ivoire, when his writings were regularly published in the local newspapers.

The human condition is at the centre of all Kone's work, with a stress on human despair and also on fear of death, of which the poet spoke in his last poem, *Le regret de mourir*, published shortly before his death in the weekly *Bingo*. This poet of everyday life and suffering died in his native Bouaké on 4 June 1979. His last collection of poems, *L'argile du rêve*, was published by *Nouvelles Editions Africaines* in Abidjan. ■

Korsah, K.A. (1894-1967)

KORSAH, Sir Kobina Arku (1894-1967).

GHANAIAN lawyer, the first Chief Justice of independent Ghana. Born 3 April 1894, the son of a wealthy merchant in the fishing port of Saltpond in the east of Cape Coast, Korsah had his early education at the Mfantsipim School in Cape Coast. He entered Fourah Bay College, Freetown, Sierra Leone, where he obtained a BA degree in 1915, and proceeded to Durham University in England for his legal studies, graduating in 1917. In 1919 he earned the LLB from the University of London, was called to the Bar at the Middle Temple Inn, and returned home that same year.

Back in the Gold Coast Korsah practised at the Bar, making commercial law his area of specialisation, but soon abandoned legal practice for full-time politics. He had been active in anti-colonial activities, with fellow African students and intellectuals, during his studies in Britain. In 1922 he joined the National Congress of British West Africa of Joseph E. Casely-Hayford (q.v.) and became assistant secretary of its Cape Coast branch.

Later that year he was elected to the executive committee of the Aborigines' Rights Protection Society, a pressure group of chiefs and politicians aimed at campaign-

Sir Arku Korsah

ing against oppressive measures. Korsah was elected to the Legislative Council as the member for Cape Coast in 1922 and served in the legislature until 1940 when he lost the seat and was then appointed to the governor's Executive Council. During this period he served on various parliamentary committees and won a reputation in the legislature for his criticism of colonial measures which encroached on the rights of Africans and for his effort in fostering unity among the African members of the Council in order to present a united front.

Korsah was a member of the 1934 delegation which visited London to protest against two proposed legislations, one of which sought the extension of the definition of sedition and the other seeking to transfer the responsibility for the costs of water supply from the government to the taxpayers. Though the protest was rejected by the Colonial Office, Korsah returned home undeterred in his campaign which, at this time, had included a call for the Africanisation of the civil service. In 1942, a three-man committee in which Korsah was a member

(the other members were J.B. Danquah (q.v.) and Kojo Thompson) recommended a ministerial form of government for the Gold Coast, with African ministers.

Korsah was as interested in the development of education in his country as he was in its politics. In 1943-44 he served on the Elliot Commission which was appointed by the British government to study the question of higher education in the West African colonies and whose report recommended the upgrading of then existing colleges in Nigeria, Sierra Leone and the Gold Coast to university status. He later served on the Gold Coast Board of Education, and on the Central Advisory Committee on Education. He was appointed chairman of the Council of the University College of the Gold Coast in 1951, retaining the office after it became the Council of the University College of Ghana until 1961 when he was dismissed by the government.

Korsah became a puisne judge between 1945 and 1956 when he was appointed the first African Chief Justice of the Gold Coast, and succeeded in becoming the first Ghanaian to hold the post after independence in 1957. He also served as acting Governor-General of Ghana until 1960 when he was appointed Chief Justice of the Republic of Ghana.

In these capacities, Korsah was required to sign legislation and government orders which were often criticised by opponents of the Nkrumah (q.v.) administration. It was under Korsah's tenure as Governor-General that the 1958 Preventive Detention Act came into effect. Later as Chief Justice he had to preside over two treason trials, both in 1963. In one of these, the Chief Justice acquitted three former government officials – former Foreign Affairs Minister Ako Adjei, former Information Minister Tawia Adamafio and former CPP's executive secretary H.H. Coffie-Crabbe – who were charged with plotting to overthrow the government.

Korsah was dismissed from office on 11 December 1963. He was arrested in 1964, and placed under house arrest until 1966 when he was freed by the new military regime that toppled the civilian administration in February.

He however did not play a prominent role under the new government, living in partial retirement until his death on 25 January 1967.■

Kosoko (died 1872)

KOSOKO, King (died 1872).

NIGERIAN traditional ruler of Lagos in the nineteenth century. The son of King Idowu Ojulari who reigned from 1819 to 1832, he was born in Lagos when the slave trade was at its most profitable on the West Coast of Africa. He became involved in the contest for the throne made vacant by his father's death, not as a pretender but as an active partisan supporting one faction's claim. After his side had failed to stop their rival, Oluwole, who became King of Lagos in 1834, Kosoko conspired to overthrow the new monarch but the plot was foiled. Kosoko and his collaborators were deported from Lagos to Porto Novo. He later went to Whydah where he became acquainted with Portuguese slave dealers, with whom he was to establish a lasting relationship.

In 1841, his uncle Akitoye succeeded Oluwole as King of Lagos (Eleko). The new ruler declared a general amnesty to facilitate the return of his nephew, Prince Kosoko, to the island. Kosoko returned from exile in 1845 but that same year led a rebellion against Akitoye for admitting the British into Lagos and agreeing to abolish the slave trade. This culminated in a civil war which lasted twelve days in Lagos and at the end Kosoko emerged to become King. He deported Akitoye to Abeokuta, and kept his usurped throne until 1851 when he was dethroned by the British.

A man of great organisational ability, Kosoko soon consolidated his position. Conscious of the intentions of the British, he built up a formidable military force for the defence of Lagos, using the expertise and assistance of his allies, the Portuguese traders whom he had invited to his domain. His influence quickly spread beyond the island to the neighbouring states which included Akitoye's refuge, Abeokuta. Akitoye was later escorted out of Abeokuta to Badagry. King Kosoko's reign over Lagos was characterised by flourishing trade in slaves.

In 1851 the British representatives in the Bights of Benin and Biafra, John Beecroft, attempted to install the exiled Akitoye. The military attack on Lagos was repulsed with heavy defeat for the British Navy. Later in the same year they tried again and succeeded in forcing King Kosoko and his supporters to flee Lagos for Epe from where they continued their campaign.

In 1862, after Britain declared Lagos a Colony in 1861, Kosoko returned to Lagos from his second exile. He did not, however, reclaim the throne which was then occupied by Dosunmu, Akitoye's son. Kosoko's eminent place in the history of Lagos revolves around his contribution to the development of legitimate commerce in particular and the growth of Lagos in general. The trading port he established in Palma during his exile in Epe led to a boom in Lagos trade as much as it facilitated the annexation of both Palma and Epe to the colony of Lagos by the British. ■

Kotane, M.M. (1905-78)

KOTANE, Moses Mauane (1905-78).

SOUTH AFRICAN politician who served as general secretary of the Communist Party of South Africa for many years and was a member of the national executive committee of the African National Congress (ANC). He was born on 9 August 1905 in Tamposstad in the district of Rustenburg in the Transvaal, South Africa. He was fifteen years old when he commenced formal schooling at a mission institution where he spent only two years; he continued his education in the Communist-run adult education institute in Ferreirastown in Johannesburg, where he did evening studies while working in the mines during the day.

In 1928 he joined the African National Congress (ANC) and the African Bakers' Union, a Communist Party founded union which was affiliated to the Federation of Non-European Trade Unions. The following year Kotane became a member of the Communist Party which soon elected him both vice-chairman of the Federation of Non-European Trade Unions and a member of the political bureau of the party. In 1931 he relinquished all other duties to become a full-time party functionary and as the first generation of African members of the Communist Party he was encouraged to study in the Soviet Union where he spent a year in the early 1930s. He was elected general secretary of the party in 1938, and held the post until his death.

He retained his position of prominence in the ANC throughout that period and he is renowned for having participated in most of its major deliberations. In 1941 he attended the All-African Convention Conference in Bloemfontein; two years later he served on the Atlantic Charter Committee of the ANC which drew up its *African Claims* and the *Bill of Rights*. He was elected to the national executive committee five years later, working closely with Alfred Bitini Xuma (q.v.) who was then president of the movement. Kotane served on subsequent bodies which drafted the ANC's Programme of Action and constitution in 1958.

As a central figure in the ANC and the Communist Party he was constantly being arrested by the authorities, beginning in 1946 when he faced legal proceedings after the African workers' strike. Following the banning of the Communist Party in 1950 and the coming into effect of the Suppression of Communism Act, which he ignored to lead the Defiance Campaign in June 1952, he was arrested and given a suspended sentence. He was among those arrested in 1956 and prosecuted in the infamous Treason Trial which lasted until April 1958. Though the charges against him were dropped in November he was placed under house arrest for four months under the State of Emergency regulations. He left South Africa for Tanzania in 1963, following the proscription of the ANC a year earlier, and became external treasurer of the movement.

Kotane was awarded the ANC highest award, Isitwalandwe Seaparankoe, on 9 August 1975 on the occasion of his 70th birthday. Isitwalandwe Seaparankoe means the wearer of the feather of a rare, legendary bird, and is awarded to the bravest warriors. In its citation during the award the ANC said that it was in recognition of Kotane's outstanding contribution to and role in the South African revolution and for his long, tireless and consistent record as a fighter for the birthright of Africans.

He died on 21 May 1978 in Moscow where he was hospitalised following a stroke. He is buried at Novodevichy Cemetery in Moscow, alongside John B. Marks (q.v.), another veteran South African political

M.M. Kotane

leader who died in the Soviet Union in 1972. ■

Kotoka, E.K. (1926-67)

KOTOKA, Major-General Emmanuel Kwasi (1926-67).

GHANAIAN military officer who led the 1966 putsch against President Kwame Nkrumah (q.v.). He was born in September 1926 in Fiahor in the Volta region and had his education at the Presbyterian School in Anloga. His first profession was teaching, which he left in July 1942 to enlist in the army. Four years later he was made company sergeant-major of the Second Infantry Brigade in the Royal West African Frontier Force. He trained at the Ghana Military Academy, Teshie, before proceeding to Eaton Hall in Chester, England, for an advanced military training; he later did a three-month attachment service with the First Battalion King's Shropshire Light Infantry that was stationed in Germany before returning to his company in Kumasi. He was commissioned as a lieutenant on 20 November 1954, and returned to Britain for a specialist mortar course.

Major-Gen. E.K. Kotoka

In 1958 Kotoka was promoted to captain, and then major in the same year. He was posted, with his battalion, to the Congo in 1960 as part of the United Nations Peace Keeping Force. At the end of his third tour of duty in the Congo which ended in 1963, he returned to Ghana in August of that year and for his gallant role in the war in the Congo was awarded the Ghana Service Order. He was also elevated to the rank of colonel and assigned to command the Second Infantry Brigade Group. In 1965 Kotoka

became general staff officer grade one, after having served as quarter-master general.

Colonel Kotoka was at this posting when he joined a dissident faction in the Ghanaian army to overthrow the administration of Kwame Nkrumah; it was he who announced the coup d'etat over Radio Ghana on 24 February 1966. "Kwame Nkrumah is dismissed from office. All ministers are also dismissed. The Convention People's Party is disbanded with effect from now. It will be illegal for any person to belong to it," he told Ghanaians in the early morning broadcast of that day.

He soon became a figure of central importance in the new military regime, the National Liberation Council (NLC), which recalled retired Lieutenant-General Joseph Arthur Ankrah who had been dismissed by the Nkrumah government to head the new ruling organ. Kotoka was given the portfolios of Defence and Health in the new administration and promoted to the rank of major-general. In addition to the above Ministries he also took on the responsibilities for Labour and Social Welfare.

A year later, on 27 April 1967, a counter-coup led by Lieutenant Sam Arthur took place. Though it did not succeed Kotoka and two other officers were killed in the fighting.■

Kouame, A.E. (1932-70)

KOUAME, Adolphe Edo (1932-70).

IVORIAN broadcaster and journalist, often known by his assumed name of Pol Amewe. He was born on 2 November 1932 at Aby Aty, in the Adieke sub-prefecture of Aboisso department. He went to primary school at Agboville, about 100 kilometres from Abidjan, and later went to France in 1949 for secondary schooling. Six years later, in 1955, he was admitted for law studies at the Faculty of Law in Paris. Two years later he went on to the radio organisation for the French colonies, SORAFOM (at one time also called OCORA; now absorbed into the French broadcasting service, Radio-France Internationale). He received a year's training in journalism there and was then appointed to the staff of Radio Fort-Lamy in Chad. For a year he served there as editor of the current affairs programme.

He returned to the head offices of SORAFOM in Paris where he was secretary to the editorial office and a general reporter.

E.A. Kouame

When independence came for the French African territories, Adolphe Edo Kouame was assigned the task of covering the independence ceremonies for SORA-FOM. A year after the independence of his country, Adolphe Edo Kouame returned there in July 1961. He went to work immediately for Côte d'Ivoire Radio, where he produced and organised many broadcasts. In 1963 his busy professional career was crowned by his appointment as director of Côte d'Ivoire Radio. He held this major position of responsibility until 1965, after which he became director of Programmes of Côte d'Ivoire Radio and Television.

The day after his death, at the age of 37, on 24 January 1970 he was awarded the posthumous honour of Knight of the National Order by the government. Kouame was buried on 28 January 1970 at his home village, Aby Aty. ■

Koulsoum (1896-1975)

KOULSOUM, Oum (1896-1975).

EGYPTIAN singer and actress. She was born in Tamay el-Zahaira in the Nile Delta, Egypt, in 1896 into a poor peasant family. From an early age she showed an enthusiasm for singing and was encouraged by her father who was also a singer. By the time she was ten years old, she had already sung before public audiences on several occasions, dressed as a boy initially as it was against tradition for girls to do this. In the early years of her career she sang mainly at weddings and religious festivals, but gradually her talent was recognised and by the early 1920s she had moved to Cairo and become a career singing star.

As her fame and popularity increased, she became known beyond Egypt's borders throughout the Arab world. In 1935 Radio Cairo sponsored her to peform monthly concerts that were also broadcast, and these became so popular that people were prepared to pay a lot of money to see her live performances. These monthly concerts continued until 1972 when she retired.

Many famous poets and writers composed songs for her to sing and although they

Oum Koulsoum

were mainly love songs, some also covered nationalist and religious themes. The tone and range of her voice had the great ability to stir audiences and her fans included late Presidents Nasser and Sadat. The latter named her the People's Artist.

In recognition of her great voice she was awarded many honours, including the Order of al-Kamal in 1965 and the Order of the Cedar from Lebanon, where she was the Egyptian *Prima Donna* at the Baalbek Festival; she received the keys of the City of Alexandria in August 1967, and won the Gold Medal, July 1968, and the Grand Cordon of the Nile in 1969.

Although she was primarily famed for her singing, she also starred in a number of films, beginning with *Wadad* in 1935; *Mashid and al Amal*, 1936; *Dananir*, 1940; *Aida*, 1943; *Salama*, 1944; *Fatima*, 1947 and *Samirami* in 1967. By the time of her retirement she was a millionairess and her fame was such that she was nicknamed "Star of the Orient". She died on 3 February 1975 after a brain haemorrhage.

Kountche, S. (1931-87)

KOUNTCHE, Major-General Seyni (1931-87).

NIGER's president for thirteen years, who had a reputation for quiet efficiency and integrity, Seyni Kountche came to power in a military coup in 1974 and his regime, for the first seven years especially, had a good image. He was seen as an important stability factor in the Sahel zone.

Seyni Kountche was born in 1931 in Fandou into a family of traditional rulers, members of the Djerma clan which at the time completely dominated the Niger army officer class though they made up less than ten percent of Niger's 6.3 million. He attended the primary school in Filingue and then went to Mali to the Kati school for servicemen's children. In 1947 he attended secondary schools in St Louis, Senegal, and joined the French colonial army in 1949.

Kountche was an energetic officer who spent most of his army career in the field, not in the office. In 1957, by then first sergeant, he went to the Military Training Academy in Frejus, France, and graduated as second lieutenant in 1959. He saw active service with the French Army in Indochina before returning to his homeland in 1961, a year after the country had gained independence from France.

In Niger Kountche continued his military career and served with the newly created Niger army in Zinder and Agadez. He received more training in staff colleges in France, following which he was promoted to the post of deputy chief of staff in 1966. He became a major in 1968 and was made chief of staff in 1973. A year later, on 15 April 1974, he led the military coup that ended the rule of Hamani Diori (q.v.).

Seyni Kountche became president of the Supreme Military Council and head of state of Niger. Support for the coup was immediate nationally. It was staged in the midst of rumours of widespread corruption in high places, mismanagement of world drought aid pouring into Niger, and neglect of domestic problems with over involvement in foreign affairs. Most government structures were abolished after the coup and high officials placed under house arrest. A commission of inquiry later believed that most of Diori's cabinet and associates were involved in massive embezzlement and fiscal irregularities.

The emphasis that Kountche's government immediately placed on dealing with the worst ravages of the drought that at the time affected the country gained it considerable goodwill. Another one of his actions on assuming power was to invite back to Niamey exiled opposition groups, with the proviso that they would not carry on political activity.

Though at first Kountche's direct manner, strict morals and simplicity sustained him, his high demands of work from those under him made him enemies too, and on 15 March 1976, there was an attempted coup against his regime in which eight soldiers were killed.

The foiled coup benefitted Kountche who gained in popularity; the coup instigator, Bonkano, his former right hand man, was unpopular. However, a certain unrest remained in the army corps with the occasional mutiny.

Kountche, after the coup, made several tours of the region, which perfected his image as "the man of the people". He remained an energetic army officer, but as the years went by, more and more civilians were incorporated into the government and there was a progressive distancing of the military from power.

Kountche instituted an economic recovery programme to tackle the problems that were accentuated by the geographical situation of his country in the Sahel region, and 1000 km from the sea posed. On its implementation, the country became known as one where things got done. Foreign aid was efficiently used, and the economy boosted with the mining of uranium.

On the international scene there was the desire to hold the best possible relations with neighbouring states. Kountche was seen as industrious, and was liked by Nigeria, Niger's southern neighbour. There was a "normalisation" of relations with Libya in 1984, after the explusion of Libyan diplomats in Niamey in 1981 for conducting "without prior consultations with the authorities, activities which were incompatible with their status". He gave wise counsel on ECOWAS, the OAU, the Chad Basin Commission, and the Niger River Authority. His own practised austerity gave him credibility. In France he was recognised as a plain speaker without pretensions, who was industrious and efficient.

In 1983 Kountche survived another coup attempt. Referring to previous attempts to overthrow his regime on that occasion – there was one in 1975 and another in 1976 – he said he was pleased that these "unfortunate and stupid interruptions caused by some megalomaniacs in search of power and glory had been unable to prevent the authorities from pursuing their objectives." In April 1984 he released former president Hamani Diori, and the former secretary general of the progressive party, *Sawaba*, Djibo Bakary.

Throughout his thirteen years in power, however, the country had no constitution until 1983 when a National Council of Development presided over by a civilian was set up for the formulation of a National Charter. Kountche was believed to be reluctant to return to civilian, democratic politics. The council was not the result of general elections, though it was representative of the ethnic diversity of the country as well as of the traditional and new forces within the country.

S. Kountche

The National Charter, which was four years in the making, was a pre-constitution document outlining national goals and objectives to be embodied in the new constitution which was to replace the suspended 1974 one. However, in spite of the provisions of the Charter, the military remained in control, and democratic elections did not immediately follow. In June 1987, the Charter was approved in a referendum.

That same month Kountche underwent surgery to have a cyst removed from his head. He subsequently made several visits to France for medical checks during the last of which on 10 November 1987 he died in a Paris hospital. ■

Kouyate, T.G. (1902-1942)

KOUYATE, Tiemoko Garan (1902-1942).

MALIAN politician. He was one of the first Africans to espouse Communism in response to Europe's colonization of Africa. Others included notably I.T.A. Wallace-Johnson and E.F. Small (qq.v.).

A Bambara, born at Ségou on 27 April 1902, he attended the William Ponty Teachers' Training College at Dakar and worked as a teacher in Côte d'Ivoire from 1924 to 1926. Having obtained a scholarship for further training, he then left for Aix-en-Provence in France. There he joined the anti-colonial groups which had emerged after the First World War.

Kouyate attended the Brussels Conference of 1927 where the League Against Imperialism (LAI) was founded. When Lamine Senghor (q.v.), another militant opponent of French colonial rule at that time, fell seriously ill later that year, Kouyate replaced him as secretary-general of his *Comité de Défense de la Race Nègre*. He renamed this the *Ligue Nationale de Défense des Intérêts de la Race Noire or Ligue de Défense de la Race Nègre* (LDRN), formed to agitate against colonial injustices. He headed this, in France, for several years. It was a small group of committed opponents of colonial rule, Africans and West Indians. Although few, they seriously alarmed the French colonial rulers. However, in France itself they were free to operate and publish their revolutionary anti-colonial newspaper, *La Race Nègre*, edited by Kouyate. He was well-known among the Africans in France at the time.

Germany was an important base for the anti-colonial radicals then, especially for their leading figure, the West Indian George Padmore (1902-59). The LAI held a second Congress at Frankfurt in 1929, and Kouyate spoke there. In 1930 there was an important meeting at Hamburg, organised by the International Trade Union Committee of Negro Workers (ITUC-NW), an affiliate of the Red International Labour Unions, set up to encourage revolutionary trade unionism among Africans and other Black workers in white or white-ruled countries. Kouyate was elected to the ITUC-NW Executive Committee.

By then he had come close to the Communist movement. He at first opposed French Communist Party moves in 1929 to control the LDRN, but in that year he travelled to the USSR, went on a tour of that country, and was promised aid by the Communist International (Comintern). He was for several years thereafter a great admirer of the Soviet Union. The LDRN and its newspaper had by 1931 become allies of the Comintern, after members who disagreed with this tendency had left in 1930. The newspaper was in 1931 renamed *Le Cri des Nègres*. The LDRN, which had a branch in Germany, denounced colonial rule, especially French rule, and called for active resistance. Kouyate and others called specifically for strike action. The ITUC-NW tried to organise such activity, and Padmore's newspaper *The Negro Worker* called for it. Kouyate contributed to this newspaper, published at Hamburg in the early 1930s. In France a major activity of Kouyate was among Black seamen and dockers, especially at Marseilles. Many of them agreed to take *Le Cri des Nègres* to Africa to distribute, as it was banned in the colonies.

In 1932 he and Padmore helped organise a dockers' and seamen's conference at Hamburg. Later in that year, he led a delegation to the US Embassy in Paris as part of worldwide protests at the Scottsborough Negroes case (a notorious case of a false charge of gang-rape in the Southern USA).

In 1934 Kouyate was expelled from the Comintern. Both Kouyate and Padmore criticised the world communist movement for playing down anti-colonialism, at Soviet orders, at that time. Kouyate remained in France, still a radical critic of colonial rule. He was prominent in protests at the invasion of Ethiopia in 1935.

After the German occupation of France in 1940 he was killed by the Nazis in obscure circumstances. ■

Krim, B. (1922-70)

KRIM, Belkacem (1922-70).

ALGERIAN politician who played a prominent role in the struggle for independence. He was born at Ait Yahia Moussa in Grand Kabylie. He served in the Algerian Infantry during 1942-45, rising to the rank of corporal, and went on to gain other military skills which proved to be of great value to him during the struggle for Algerian independence.

After the Second World War he became secretary of the Dra-el-Mizan Municipal Council. He joined the nationalist struggle and became a member for the *Parti Populaire Algérien* (PPA) and its successor, the *Mouvement pour le Triomphe des Libertés Démocratiques* (MTLD). In 1947 he left the Municipal Council after being accused by the French colonialists of organising resistance against the French in the Kabylie area.

He insisted on the necessity of military action to achieve Algerian independence, and in May 1948 joined the *Organisa-*

Belkacem Krim

tion Spéciale (OS), a clandestine paramilitary force consisting of a breakaway group of the MTLD. The OS was banned by the French in 1950, and in 1954 its members regrouped into the *Comité Révolutionnaire d'Unité et d'Action* (CRUA), the most militant wing of MTLD. Belkacem was a core member of the CRUA, and along with eight other members of the organisation, became known as the "historic chiefs" who would not compromise on the question of armed struggle to achieve liberation.

During the summer of 1954 the CRUA held secret meetings both in Algeria and abroad to plan the resistance against the French which began on 1 November 1954. By this time, the CRUA had broken irreconcilably with the MTLD and Belkacem Krim became one of the founding members of the *Front de Libération Nationale* (FLN) that emerged in this period to unite the various Algerian political organisations. The FLN divided Algeria into six *Wilayas* (military districts), and when the war broke out, Belkacem Krim was the military commander for the Kabylie *Wilaya*. He had been organising resistance there since 1947 and was sentenced to death *in absentia* five times by the French.

In August 1956 he helped organise a congress at Soummam to establish the political organisation of the FLN. This congress set up the *Conseil National de la Révolution Algérienne* (CNRA) as the organisation's legislative body and the *Comité de Coordination et d'Exécution* (CCE) as its executive organ. Belkacem Krim was a founder member of both, as well as being responsible for liaison and co-ordination between the CCE and the *Wilaya*. Soon after the congress, Krim relinquished his position of military commander in Kabylie and moved to Algiers with the other four members of the CCE.

Early in 1957, the CCE decided to increase its military activity while the General Assembly of the UN was in session. In February it called a general strike which lasted eight days while urban guerrilla warfare around the capital was intensified. This resulted in increased French repression and Krim, along with the other members of the CCE, moved to Tunisia.

In September 1958 the CCE was superceded by the *Gouvernement Provisoire de la République Algérienne* (GPRA) in Tunis. The GPRA went further than the CCE as it was not only the directorate of the revolutionary war but also regarded itself as the legitimate Government of the Algerian nation. Several Afro-Asian and Socialist states recognised this Government in which Belkacem Krim was appointed Vice-President and Minister of the Armed Forces. thus being responsible for all resistance operations in Algeria.

In the GPRA reshuffle of February 1960, Belkacem Krim became Minister of Foreign Affairs and Vice-President, and he was transferred to the GPRA office in Cairo. Within the GPRA a *Comité Interministériel de Guerre* was formed, with Krim as one of its three members, and in May 1960 he visited China, North Korea and Vietnam to seek material assistance.

When the peace talks were resumed with the French Government in May 1961 Krim, as Minister of Foreign Affairs, led the Algerian delegation and although his portfolio was changed in August 1961 to Minister of the Interior, he continued to lead the peace talks until their conclusion with the signing of the Evian Agreement in March 1962.

The concessions granted by Algeria in the Evian Agreement caused Krim to clash violently with Ben Bella (who had been released from prison after the agreement had been signed at a Revolutionary Committee meeting at Tripoli in May 1962). By the time Algeria gained independence in July 1962 there was a struggle for power among the various nationalist leaders from which Ben Bella emerged victorious. Although they had recently been opponents, Ben Bella nominated Krim to stand in the September 1962 elections so that his opposition to government policies could be conducted within the FLN framework, and on 20 September 1962 he was elected a member of the National Constituent Assembly. He was very critical of the Government, and shortly after the 1963 elections, he was one of the five deputies that the National Assembly excluded from its ranks.

In June 1965 the Government was overthrown and President Boumedienne (q.v.), with whom Krim had clashed in pre-independence days, came to power. Krim left Algeria and in October 1967 formed the Democratic Movement for a New Algeria in opposition to Boumedienne's regime.

In April 1969 he was sentenced to death *in absentia* by a court at Oran for allegedly conspiring to assassinate an FLN party leader. He was found strangled on 20 October 1970 in Frankfurt, West Germany. He was survived by a wife and four children. ▪

Kudjoe, H.E.B. (1918-86)

KUDJOE, Hannah Esi Badu (1918-1986).

GHANAIAN politician, pioneer of the emancipation and advancement of Ghanaian women and founder and first national organiser of Day Nurseries in Ghana. Née Dadson, she was born on 1 December 1918 at Busua in the Ahanta District of the Western Region of Ghana, the tenth child of John Peter Joanah Dadson. Being staunch Methodists, her parents enrolled her in the Busua Methodist School where she started her elementary education. She then left for the Methodist School in Sekondi and stayed with her cousin, Mrs Dorothy Vardon, a strict disciplinarian.

After leaving school, she trained as a seamstress specialising in tea cosies and that was how she earned a living until she married J. C. Kudjoe, one of the first African managers of the Abontiakoon Gold Mines at Tarkwa.

However, her marriage was a disaster and she left her husband to live and work with her brother E. K. Dadson who owned and managed a printing press at Tarkwa. She led an ordinary and simple life working at the press and keeping house for her brother until 1948 when she met Kwame Nkrumah (q.v.), Ghana's first president who had just returned to the Gold Coast at the invitation of the founders of the United Gold Coast Convention (UGCC), a movement which at the time was fighting for the liberation of the Gold Coast from British colonial rule. Nkrumah had arrived to assume the office of General Secretary in order to strengthen the executive of the UGCC.

Kudjoe met Nkrumah at her brother's house, and he talked her into joining the independence struggle. That meeting actually changed her life completely.

She took inspiration from Nkrumah's call on women to participate actively in politics. She was also inspired by what she read at the time about women in other parts of the world who were taking the initiatives towards attaining equal rights with men. She thus abandoned her 'safe' life to become the first woman member of the UGCC. Her zeal and dedication earned her prompt recognition and popularity in the movement, and she quickly rose to become its organising and propaganda secretary.

Her work in that capacity took her all over the Gold Coast. Hopping from bus to bus, travelling on trains, on lorries, walking long distances, resisting the brutalities of the colonial police and colonial agents, she spread the idea of independence and advanced the cause of the UGCC. She formed branches of the UGCC throughout the Gold Coast and educated the people about the urgency and advantages of self-government.

In her determination to carry the message of independence across to every town and village in the Gold Coast she travelled to the "impenetrable" Transvolta-Togoland (now Volta Region) regarded in pre-independence days as "hostile territory" because of its rejection of the independence struggle. She bravely ignored the insults and jeers that accompany women who broke away from the status quo then in force in a bid to liberate her country from colonialism.

In 1949 when internal power struggles within the UGCC culminated in the dismissal of Nkrumah from the Movement, with her characteristic enthusiasm and energy she quickly convened a meeting of the UGCC's committee on youth organisation at Saltpond to redress the effects of Nkrumah's dismissal on the independence cause. This meeting gave birth to the Convention People's Party which led the Gold Coast to independence in 1957.

Kudjoe played a significant role in a committee of ten appointed at the meeting to chart a course for the CPP, whose work resulted in a mass rally which announced the formation of the CPP. She retained her post of organising and propaganda secretary in the CPP and continued to organise and address rallies, launch appeals for funds and engage in income generating activities for the CPP.

It was through the effectiveness of the CPP's propaganda machinery which she established almost singlehandedly that the first ever general elections in the Gold Coast held on 8 February 1951 were overwhelmingly won by the party and Nkrumah became

H.E. Kudjoe

leader of Government Business in the new Legislative Assembly.

In 1957 she formed the All Africa Women's League, an organisation devoted to African women's rights. In recognition of her organisational abilities and her singular achievements within the CPP she was appointed chairwoman of the political bureau of the newly formed National Council of Ghana Women (NCGW). She was a believer in unity and encouraged other women's organisations to affiliate themselves to the NCGW to ensure better co-ordination of, and solutions to, women's issues. She also mobilised the council's members for political work and "educated" them on civic issues,

One particular cause she championed and won in the early sixties was maternity leave with full pay for working mothers throughout the country. Hitherto women were receiving only half their salary when on maternity leave. Under the aegis of the NCGW she played a key role in improving the lives of women in the Northern part of Ghana. Between 1953 and 1957 she toured the Northern Territories (now Northern and Upper East and West Regions) extensively. The naming of a cloth after her by people in the North was an expression of their appreciation of her efforts. Even today, the name Hannah Kudjoe is a household word in many parts of the Northern and Upper East and West Regions of Ghana.

Another notable achievement of hers was the establishment of day nurseries and day care centres throughout the country. She is generally acknowledged as the founder of these institutions; and in recognition of her services in the social welfare field she was appointed Chief Social Advancement Officer in the Ministry of Social Welfare during the First Republic. As a social worker she organised seminars and other public functions aimed at eradicating illiteracy, disease, hunger and ignorance.

Kudjoe's social and political work took her to other countries. She visited many African and Eastern and Western European countries, as well as China and Japan. In those countries she portrayed the Ghanaian woman's way of dressing.

Her last attempt at mobilising Ghanaian women for national development was the formation of the Ghana Women's League for Social Advancement. As Director-General of the League, which was a voluntary organisation, she spearheaded a literacy campaign for women to enable them to participate more meaningfully in the political, social and economic reconstruction of the country.

She made her last public appearance on 8 March 1986 at a symposium by the New Democratic Movement, a political organisation, to mark the 20th anniversary of the overthrow of Kwame Nkrumah. There, she gave a passionate account of her political life which earned her a standing ovation. She died suddenly two days later, on 10 March 1986. ■

Kutako, H. (1870-1970)

KUTAKO, Chief Hosea (1870-1970).

NAMIBIAN traditional ruler. Hosea Kutako was born in the Okahanja District of South West Africa (Namibia) at Okahurimehi in 1870. His family belonged to the prosperous, cattle-farming Herero people and his father, having been converted to Christianity, worked at the Omburo Rhenish Mission Church.

In 1884 the Germans took over the administration of South West Africa and began to impose harsh rule over the indigenous population. As the situation worsened and the Herero people rose up in 1904 in an attempt to regain their freedom, Kutako, at this time 34 years old, fought in the rebellion and was taken prisoner. He was released at the end of the uprising in which around 65,000 out of 80,000 Hereros were killed and most of their cattle confiscated or destroyed.

Kutako then went to the Omarur District and worked there as a teacher for two years, after which he moved north to Tsumeb to work in the mines. Meanwhile the Germans suspected that the large number of Hereros who had escaped to Bechuanaland (Botswana) during the rebellion were preparing to return with the help of their sympathisers within the country. As a result, Kutako was once again taken prisoner, but he managed to escape, taking refuge in the mountains.

During the First World War, the Germans were defeated by South African troops, and, as the leader of the Herero people, Kutako was appointed its representative and spokesman. Two years later he became the Paramount Chief of the Herero

Chief H. Kutako

people in South West Africa with the agreement of the Herero Chief in exile. Meanwhile South West Africa had become a Mandated Territory of the League of Nations under the administration of the Union of South Africa, and it was soon clear that the South African Government would not return lands that the indigenous population had lost under the previous German administration.

After the end of the Second World War South Africa continued to administer South West Africa and Kutako was told that the Hereros would be resettled further north so that whites could settle in their present territory. Kutako inspected the area that was to be allotted to his people and rejected the settlement proposals on the grounds that the new area was much too small and isolated. He also turned down proposals that South West Africa should become part of the Union of South Africa and decided to appeal to the UN to establish a Trusteeship admin-

istration over the country as a step towards its eventual independence, but the South African Government refused to issue passports to Kutako or any of the other South West African leaders.

In 1947 he commissioned a sympathetic English clergyman to put his people's case before the UN. In the following years Kutako continued to place petitions before the UN and in this way played a major role in bringing the plight of South West Africa to international prominence. He also continued to oppose South African efforts to move his people to the Omaheke region that South Africa had designated to be the Herero people's homeland and to incorporate South West Africa into South Africa.

He died on 20 July 1970. A man of great courage and strength of character, he strove consistently throughout his life for the independence of his people in the face of great pressure exerted by the South African Government.■

L

Ladipo, D. (1931-78)

LADIPO, Duro (1931-78).

NIGERIAN playwright, producer, actor, and founder of the Duro Ladipo National Theatre which made an innovating contribution to the revival of traditional theatre in Nigeria in the mid-twentieth century. Duro Ladipo employed his native Yoruba language and the use of Yoruba musical instruments, chants and dance to create, according to Yemi Ogunbiyi's essay in the book *Dance and Theatre in Nigeria*, "a different kind of Yoruba theatre, self-consciously traditional (in the best of the word), invigorating, intense and with a charm of its own. Imbued with a genuine sense of cultural revivalism, Ladipo reached beyond the morality plays characteristic of the forerunners of Yoruba travelling theatre, into the new territory of Yoruba historical drama".

Duro Ladipo was born in Oshogbo on 18 December 1931, the son of a local Anglican church official. Despite his parents' intention for a strict Christian upbringing, young Duro Ladipo showed keen interest in traditional Yoruba festivals and rituals, "as exemplified by the fact that I followed closely the activities of different masquerades and cultists", he said later in describing his childhood. He nevertheless attended local mission schools, becoming in the 1950s a pupil-teacher at the Holy Trinity School at Ilesha. From there he went to Kaduna in the north of Nigeria, as a teacher at the United Native Anglican School whose dramatic society he founded and launched with a production of his interpretation of Shakespeare's *As You Like It*.

He returned to Oshogbo in 1956, still as a teacher but now with a profound interest in dramatic productions. In June

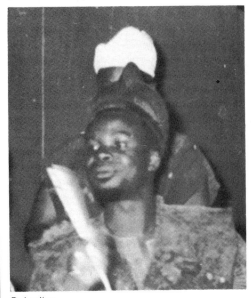

D. Ladipo

1960, he produced his Easter Cantata at the All Saints Church in Oshogbo, amidst considerable controversy over his use of the Yoruba talking drums in the church. The authorities considered the instruments incompatible with the Christian religion because of their use in traditional festivals and rituals. A reviewer in the *Daily Service* said at the time that Ladipo's production was "truly Yoruba in character and a welcome change from the usual dreariness of the English hymns. The Church authorities hardly appreciated the importance and significance of his work. They insisted on having conventional English hymns incorporated into the performance, thus ruining the artistic effect of the work." His attitude could be summed up in his phrase: "If Christianity is to survive in Nigeria, it must undergo the general process of Nigerianisation".

From that point, Ladipo sought new avenues for his productions in schools, on television and elsewhere by performing plays on a purpose-built wagon which his group used as a mobile stage. In December 1961 the Duro Ladipo Company produced a Christmas Cantata at the newly founded Mbari Club in Ibadan.

On 2 March 1962 Ladipo founded in Oshogbo the Mbari-Mbayo Cultural Centre, emulating the example of the Ibadan intellectuals and artists who had opened the Mbari Club. Soon his Mbari-Mbayo, meaning in Yoruba "when we see it, we shall be happy", became the home base for his company as well as the focal point of a new artistic expression – the Oshogbo School – exemplified by Jimo Buraimoh, Twin Seven-Seven and other Yoruba painters.

Having launched the Centre with his first musical play *Oba Moro* in 1962, Ladipo celebrated Mbari-Mbayo's first and second anniversaries with the production of *Oba Koso* and *Oba Waja* respectively. Of the trilogy on the Oyo empire, *Oba Koso* is best known, having been performed more than 2,000 times in at least fifteen countries before Ladipo's death in 1978. *Oba Koso* won the first prize at the 1964 Berlin Theatre Festival and was enthusiastically received in Britain the following year at the Commonwealth Arts Festival. Also that same year, 1965, Ladipo himself was made a member of the Order of the Niger by his country's Government, in recognition of his impressive contribution of some twenty full-length plays and over fifty sketches to the Nigerian theatre. The *Oba Koso, Oba Waja* and *Oba Moro* trilogy has become classics of the Nigerian traditional theatre, expounding Yoruba dramatic ideas and rituals to an increasing international audience through world-wide productions and literary criticism.

True to his dedication to the growth and promotion of the traditional theatre Ladipo, in the later part of his life, took up a research appointment with the Institute of African Studies, University of Ibadan, where he engaged in research work on Yoruba history and mythologies. He was doing this, in conjunction with running the Ladipo Theatre company, when he died on 11 March 1978. The Company continues to exist and perform Ladipo's works under the headship of his wife, Abiodun Ladipo, also a renowned artist in her own right. ■

La Guma, J.A. (1925-1985)

LA GUMA, Justin Alexander (1925-1985).

SOUTH AFRICAN militant, writer, secretary-general of the Association of Afro-Asian writers, who died in October 1985 in Havana, Cuba, where he was the representative of the African National Congress (ANC). He is recognised as one of the most accomplished South African short story writers. His stories deal with apartheid victims, "ordinary people with their human failures in their daily life, vividly described, who become heroes by virtue of their heightened sense of honour and morality and their sensitivity". Angus Calder's comments in the *New Statesman* about his novel *In the Fog of the Season's End* published in 1972 by Heinemann, London, and in 1973 by Third Press, New York, sum up his writing: "This book unequivocally sides with hurt people against the race-based class which hurts them. It is propaganda, and so it should be. But it is humane, careful and very moving; it is propaganda for the truth, and a work of art."

La Guma's writing was banned in the Republic of South Africa, but in 1962 Mbari Press in Ibadan, Nigeria published his first novel *A Walk in the Night* – the story of "a coloured boy fired from his job for talking back to his white foreman. Set in Cape Town's toughest quarter, District Six, the story is evocative of the feelings of despair and violence that are commonplace in the town". It was reissued simultaneously in 1967 by Heinemann and Northwestern University Press together with six other short stories.

Born in Cape Town, South Africa on 20 February 1925, the son of Jimmy La Guma, one of South Africa's leading figures in the Black Liberation Movement who was President of the South African Coloured People's Congress and a member of the Central Committee of the Communist Party, Alex La Guma was raised in a highly politically conscious environment and from the outset planned an active political career for himself. He was educated at Trafalgar School and Cape Technical College, both in Cape Town. He first worked as a clerk, then in a factory and as a book-keeper before becoming a journalist. As a young man La Guma joined the South African Communist Party and was a member of its Cape Town district committee until 1950 when it was banned by the government.

In 1955 he joined the staff of *New Age*, a progressive newspaper where he worked until August 1962, while continuing his political involvement. He helped to draw up the South African Freedom Charter (a declaration of rights). In 1956, along with Nelson Mandela, Oliver Tambo and Walter Sisulu, he was among the 156 accused in the notorious Treason Trial, but the charge was dropped five years later. By 1960 he had become an executive member of the Coloured People's Congress and was one of the 2,000 political prisoners detained for five months in the state of emergency that followed the Sharpeville massacre and the violent incidents at Langa. In prison, Alex read voraciously and wrote. A year later he was again arrested, this time for his part in organising a strike in protest against Verwoerd's (q.v.) introduction of a Republican constitution. In December 1962 he was put under house arrest without trial under South Africa's Sabotage Act. He was confined to his house for 24 hours a day, every day for 5 years.

Before the 5 year period was up, a No-Trial Act was passed and Alex and his wife were arrested and confined to solitary imprisonment. His wife, Blanche Valerie Herman whom he married in 1954, was released after a short time but La Guma was detained further and then released on bail, charged with possessing banned literature, and again subjected to house arrest.

La Guma wrote his first full-length novel *And a Threefold Cord* during his initial house arrest and it was published in 1964 in East Germany. This was a grim presentation of the degradation of human life under apartheid in the slums on the edge of Cape Town. His own experiences in prison resulted in the dedication of *The Stone Country*, published by Seven Seas Books, Berlin, East Germany, in 1967 and by Heinemann, London, in 1976, "to the daily average 70,351 prisoners in South African gaols in 1964." South African prison life is vividly portrayed in the novel. The publication by Heinemann, London, of *Time of the Butcherbird*, in 1979 coincided with the heights of the South African government's enforced resettlement schemes. It is the "story of the

A. La Guma

tragedy and conflict that grip the Black community in a small South African town faced with forced removal and resettlement bring out the complexity of life in South Africa, against a background of racist laws"; the humanity of ordinary people is vividly portrayed.

La Guma and his family arrived in Britain in 1967, and he soon established himself as a short story writer with *A Glass of Wine* and *Slipper Satin* which appeared in the early issues of *Black Orpheus*. Later years saw the publication of *At the Pottagees*, *Blankets* and *Tattoo Marks and Nails*. *A Matter of Honour* appeared in *The New African* and magazines in South America, Germany, the US and Sweden. Other stories of his are featured in numerous collections. His two non-fiction works are *Apartheid* and *A Soviet Journey*. La Guma was awarded the Lotus Prize for Literature by the Afro-Asian Writers' Association in 1973.

La Guma continued to be politically active while writing and worked within the ANC in Britain and in the early 80s, a few years before his death, he became the ANC's representative in Cuba. ∎

Langa, F. (died 1980)

LANGA, Francisco (died 1980).

MOZAMBICAN politician. An early militant in the struggle for the liberation of Mozambique, he was arrested by Portuguese political police (PIDE) in 1961 and held incommunicado for eight months. In 1964 he joined the recently created FRELIMO and escaped in 1965 from Mozambique into Tanzania where he underwent military training with the National Liberation Army of FRELIMO. He fought in Niassa in 1966 and was appointed a member of the Liberation Army High Command. From 1966 onwards Langa played a leading part in the opening of new fronts in the armed struggle against Portuguese colonialism, culminating in 1967 in the extension of the war to the Tete Province and later to the Manica, Sofala and Zambesia regions.

With the declaration of independence, in June 1975, the National Liberation Army became the new national army of Mozambique and Langa was appointed a member of its High Command. In the third congress of FRELIMO held in February 1977, he became a member of the Central Committee and was elected to the People's National Assembly in 1979. He was very much involved in the forging of relations with other liberation movements in Africa and, for that reason, was given a leading post at the Centre for Support to Refugees and Liberation Movements, which he held until May 1979.

Langa's life was characterised by patriotism and sobriety. He committed suicide by shooting himself on 20 May 1980, after criminal proceedings had been started against him for embezzling state funds.■

Lansana, D. (1922-75)

LANSANA, Brigadier David (1922-75).

SIERRA LEONEAN military officer who was his country's first brigadier and Commander of the Army. He was born on 27

March 1922, in Baiima in the district of Kailahun, and was educated at the Central School and at the Union College in Bunumbu, Kailahun. He enlisted in the colonial Royal Sierra Leone Military Force and was sent for military training at Eaton Hall in Cheshire, England, and later at the Officers' Training School in Chester, also in England. In 1952 he became a commissioned officer and on 1 January 1965 was made brigadier and Commander of the Sierra Leonean army.

Brigadier Lansana attempted to seize power from the civilian administration in 1967, following the inconclusive results of the general elections of that year. The 21 March elections were won by the All People's Congress (APC) of Siaka Stevens, but shortly after Stevens was sworn in as Prime Minister, he and the governor-general, Sir Henry Lightfoot-Boston (q.v.), were arrested on the order of Brigadier Lansana who declared that the polls had "reflected not political opinions but tribal differences." The head of the Army proclaimed martial law, explaining that the governor-general had acted unconstitutionally after rejecting his warning as head of state security that it was not in the interest of Sierra Leone to make any appointment when a "dangerous situation would be created". At the time he put the

Brig. D. Lansana

country under martial law Brigadier Lansana said, "I want to make it clear that the Army – and I say this after consultation with my senior officers – does not, I repeat, not, intend to impose a military government on the people of Sierra Leone. This country has a record for Constitutional Government."

Four people were killed in the riots that followed the declaration of martial law, and two days later, Brigadier Lansana and Dr. Albert Margai (q.v.), leader of the Sierra Leone People's Party (SLPP), were arrested by junior army officers, who also suspended the constitution, banned all political parties, and invited Lieutenant-Colonel Andrew Juxon-Smith to head a military government, under the National Reformation Council (NRC). Lansana was later appointed to a diplomatic post in New York by the NRC.

Following the overthrow of the NRC government in 1968 by a dissident section of the army who reinstated Siaka Stevens' APC to power, Lansana fled from his New York posting to Liberia where he sought political asylum. He was extradited at the request of the new government and put on trial on charges of illegal assumption of power, convicted and sentenced to a prison term. Pardoned in the general amnesty for all political prisoners in the wake of the May 1973 elections which returned the APC to power, Lansana was again rearrested in 1974 when the home of a government leader was attacked in what was seen as an attempt to overthrow the government. Lansana and 14 others were tried for treason and he was executed on 19 July 1975. ■

Lat Dior (died 1886)

LAT DIOR, Damel of Kayor (died 1886).

SENEGALESE monarch. His full name was Lat Dior N'Gone Latir Dyop. He was King (Damel) of the old Wolof kingdom of Kayor (Cayor), one of several kingdoms all nominally under the supreme ruler of the Wolofs, the Bourba Jolof.

When he came to the throne in 1862 the French in the nearby Senegal settlements (St. Louis being the major one) had begun expansion inland. Various Islamic rulers had been expanding their states, also, including Ma Bâ (q.v.). In 1864 the French attacked Kayor, near their settlements, and drove out Lat Dior. He sought refuge with Ma Bâ, who offered help on condition that he became a Moslem, which he did.

Ma Bâ was killed in action against Sine in 1867, but four years later Lat Dior was able to return to Kayor, because of a temporary retreat by the French. From 1871 to 1882 he ruled as an ally of France.

In 1877 the French informed Lat Dior of their plan to build a railway from Dakar to St. Louis, crossing his territory. He signed a convention on the building of the line on 30 September 1879, but his people then revolted; peace was temporarily restored with the aid of a French mission, but the Wolofs of Kayor and their ruler were now suspicious of France. In the next two years hostility grew, and Lat Dior stopped the transit of produce across his territory for sale to the French.

Lat Dior

In 1882 Lat Dior refused to agree to any railway, and promised to resist the French in alliance with the Bourba Jolof, Ali Bouri, and the ruler of Futa-Toro, Abdul Boubakar. In December 1882 the French went to war with these Senegalese leaders. Swiftly they occupied Kayor and in January 1883 deposed Lat Dior. A relative, Samba Yaye, was installed in his place.

While the French were busy fighting other African forces and building their railway, they could not immediately pursue and capture Lat Dior who gathered a guerrilla force around him and harassed French forces for over three years. The Moslem preacher Amadou Bamba (q.v.) was with him for a time and Lat Dior was said to have gone to consult him before the final battle. In October 1886 Lat Dior was killed in action against the French. He is now the best remembered Senegalese resistance leader.■

Lattier, C. (1925-78)

LATTIER, Christian (1925-78).

IVORIAN artist and considered one of Africa's and the world's foremost sculptors, born on 25 December 1925. He went, at the age of seven, to the Catholic primary school at Abidjan. Three years later his father, a doctor, sent him to France to continue his schooling. He went to St. Chamond College in the Loire region, run by the Marist fathers, and studied there for ten years. He then passed the entrance examination for the Art School at St. Etienne, where he was taught by the sculptor Henry Barthélemy and the modeller Joachim Durand.

In 1947, Lattier was admitted to the Paris Art School where he studied for six years under the guidance of the modellers Niclause and Saupic. With the latter he learned wood carving. Then he followed Dometh-Smith's courses in Architecture and later joined Yancesse's modelling studio. There he was guided by Janniot, sculptor for the Palais de Chaillot and many other public buildings in France. The experience acquired in working with these great masters

decided his choice of career and he dedicated his whole life to creative art.

From 1953 Lattier decided to work in modern sculpture, using string around a wire frame. This was his distinctive art form which made him very original. He placed a string coat around a wire "skeleton" to make, according to the artist's inspiration and approach, masks which he called *bonhommes* with human or animal features.

A champion experimenter, a tireless creator, Lattier completed every year nearly 3,400 designs. He destroyed many thousands with his own hands, always seeking better quality and anxious to achieve artistic distinction. Thus, in applying the use of string to sculpture, Lattier achieved a "revolutionary" success in his career. A creative genius, he made with his materials an exemplary and unique masterpiece, a leopard three and a half metres long. This made his name; despite the controversy aroused by his artistic revolution, his leopard won the first Chevenard prize in 1954.

A year earlier he had successfully proved his talent and genius by winning, by unanimous verdict, the French Cathedrals Grand Prize, awarded by the Fine Arts Academy every five years and previously awarded to artists working in plaster. When Lattier won the prize it had not been awarded for ten years as no artist had been found worthy of it. The award to Lattier confirmed the recognition of his artistic talent and revolutionary approach, and also showed he had acquired and mastered the secrets of artistic theory. Doors which had been closed to him were now wide open, including that of work on the restoration of French Cathedrals, Romanesque and Gothic. So from 1956 he joined in and worked on the restoration of Chartres Cathedral.

A year later, at the invitation of Professor Leygue, he joined the sculptor Guillaumel and Georges Fabre in work on the external decoration of the Abidjan city hall. Earlier, when in Janniot's studio, Lattier was in 1955-6 *Massier des Beaux Arts de Paris*; then, in 1959-60 he was *Grand Massier des Beaux Arts de France* (these are special offices of treasurers for collective budgets of French artistic groups). This showed the popularity he enjoyed among his colleagues, and the trust they put in him, all through his career in France.

These followed years of exhibitions; the first was in 1959, at the Fine Arts Gallery in Paris. The same year he exhibited a portrayal of Christ at the Abbey of Jouarre in France. Then he took part in the Young Sculptors' Exhibition at the Musée Rodin in Paris, and the first Biennale exhibition, also in Paris. Invited to the "France-Africa" conference at Royaumont in 1960, he exhibited his work there. Later he exhibited a Pietà at the church at Meaux. The same year he won the first prize for sculpture at Asnières, and the gold medal of the town of Taverny, where he had already won the bronze medal a year earlier. Before returning to Côte d'Ivoire permanently in 1962, he took part in 1961 in the Comparative Modern Art Exhibition.

On his return to Abidjan in 1962 he was appointed professor of Sculpture at the *Ecole Nationale Supérieure des Beaux Arts* at Abidjan, now called the *Institut National des Arts* (INA).

He took part in the World Festival of Negro Arts at Dakar, Senegal, in 1966, where he won the first World Prize for Negro Arts (all disciplines) for the whole of his work. His work, called *The Orchid*, was among those he presented to the Festival. So Lattier was recognised by the world as the most representative Black artist. It was the climax of the career of a man who refused to be carried away by this triumph. He was rather inhibited by it and withdrew to reflect and continue studies of the use of a new material based on laterite. He joined in the Pan-African Festival in Algiers in 1969 and was appointed to the panel of judges for sculpture and painting. Working without a break, he succeeded in perfecting his new artistic material, based on laterite and as hard as stone, in 1973.

Many of Lattier's works now adorn Côte d'Ivoire's public buildings: his *Christ* in the Eloka chapel in the suburbs of Abidjan at Bingerville; a big string-design mural called *Les trois âges de la Côte d'Ivoire* in the main hall of Abidjan airport; and *La Côte d'Ivoire en l'an 2000* (metalwork) and *Aviation* (concrete) at the same airport. As his contribution to the decoration of the Price Stabilisation Fund office block at Abidjan, he completed in 1970 a bas-relief 17 metres long depicting scales. He helped decorate the *Conseil de l'Entente* offices at Lomé, especially the Côte d'Ivoire pavilion, and the Assinie holiday village. He also created an iron bas-relief for the Engineers' House at Treichville in Abidjan.

C. Lattier

He died in hospital at Abidjan on 23 April 1978, in relative obscurity in his country where he is often described as a bitter and lonely artist. But even though his work aroused no strong admiration or sympathy among his countrymen, many artists strove to copy his pattern. Lattier, a creative genius, revolutionised sculpture and was accorded worldwide recognition.■

Laye, C. (1928-80)

LAYE, Camara (1928-80).

GUINEAN writer, widely known for his first novel, *The African Child*. The eldest of seven children of a goldsmith, Laye was born on 1 January 1928 in Kouroussa, northern Guinea, where he had his elementary and Koranic education. He later studied engineering at the Collège Poiret (now Lycée Technique) in Conakry and won a scholarship to study motor mechanics in Paris. After graduating he worked for sometime in a car factory in France before embarking on a literary career.

L'Enfant noir, Laye's first novel published in 1953 (translated as *The African Child* in 1955), idolised his childhood in colonial Guinea, without recourse to the politics of the day. The novel received critical acclaim but was castigated by Laye's

African contemporaries for its lack of commitment to the cause of African nationalism. Of it, *Présence Africaine* said: "Has this young Guinean, of my own race, who it seems was a very lively boy, really seen nothing but a beautiful, peaceful and mater-

C. Laye

nal Africa? Is it possible that Laye has not once witnessed a single minor extortion of the colonial authorities?".

A second novel, *Le Regard du Roi*, appeared in 1954 and was translated as *The Radiance of the King* two years later. Though a more complex work than its predecessor, the work suffered the same fate for the repeated lack of commitment to the ideological directives of the militant nationalism of Negritude. Yet in 1955 Laye returned to Guinea, and after the country's independence in 1958 he joined the government of Sekou Toure as director of the Ministry of Information's Study and Research Centre.

He later fell out with the government and left Guinea in 1964 for exile in Senegal where he wrote his third book, *Dramouss*, in 1966 (translated as *A Dream of Africa* in 1968). He died there in February 1980. ∎

Leakey, L.S.B. (1903-72)

LEAKEY, Louis Seymour Bazett (1903-72).

KENYAN archaeologist who, with his wife Mary, found in 1959 the important fossil remains of pre-historic man now known as *Australopithecus boisei* in Tanzania, which reinforced the thesis that Africa was the cradle of mankind.

Of British origin, Louis Seymour Bazett was born on 7 August 1903 at Kabete, near Nairobi, to a missionary family serving among the Kikuyu. After informal early education in East Africa, privately conducted by his father, he went in 1920 to Weymouth College in England.

In October 1922 he entered St.John's College, Cambridge, but interrupted his studies the following year for field work with a British Museum archaeological team that was excavating for dinosaurs in Tanganyika. From this 1923 expedition that was led by the Canadian archaeologist W. Cutler, Leakey acquainted himself with the techniques of collecting and preserving fossils. He returned to Cambridge in 1924 to read Modern Languages, taking a first class there and another first in Archaeology and Anthropology in 1926. He was made a Research Fellow of St. John's three years later and achieved his PhD.

From Cambridge he undertook the first of four major excavations in Kenya and in the Olduvai Gorge in northern Tanzania, one of the world's most important early Palaeolithic sites. During these excavations Leakey established the sequence of prehistoric cultures in the region, using as his guide the climatic changes during the Pleistocene. Among his early finds were the Kanam jaw and the Kanjera skulls.

From 1937 and through the Second World War years he worked in Nairobi, as a trustee of the Corydon Museum of which he later became curator, and as head of the African section of British CID in Kenya. During this same period Leakey organised, in 1947, the first Pan African Congress on Pre-history in the Kenyan capital. The deliberations of the Congress and consequent sponsorships made possible the excavation in western Kenya which led to the

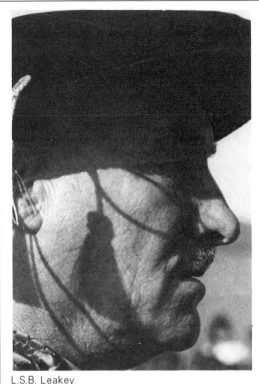

L.S.B. Leakey

Age activities but also that the continent had been the centre from which hand-axe culture evolved and spread to other regions of the world. This notion has been supported by Leakey's subsequent discoveries, like the oldest known remains of man's ancestors, found in the East African region in November 1975.

Leakey received several awards for his archaeological and anthropological work and wrote books on the subjects. These include *The Stone Age Cultures of Kenya Colony*; *The Stone Age Races of Kenya*; *Adam's Ancestors*; *Stone Age Africa*; *Mau Mau and the Kikuyu*; and *Olduvai Gorge*.

He died in London on 1 October 1972, leaving his wife who carried on excavations at the Olduvai. His son, Philip, was elected to Kenya Parliament a few years after independence and made a junior minister in 1979.

The Louis Leakey Memorial Institute for African Prehistory in Nairobi has been established and named after him. The Institute houses one of the world's best collections of fossil man, his early technology, and all the remains of animals that existed then. It is the first international centre for research into the origins and development of man and his environment. Its establishment in Nairobi is largely due to the pioneering work of Dr. Leakey. He had insisted since the 1930s that the eastern Africa region was the birthplace of man, an opinion that at first was not generally shared by scientists. But in the course of his excavations he had drawn the attention of the world to Africa as the most productive source of knowledge concerning our ancestors. ∎

discovery of the earliest ape, *Proconsul Africanus*.

Having also studied the Kikuyu community and their customs between 1937 and 1939, he was highly regarded in British circles and worked in various capacities for the colonial authorities. He was official interpreter at the trial of Jomo Kenyatta (q.v.) in the wake of the so-called Mau Mau uprising. Thereafter he and his family returned to the Olduvai Gorge for large scale excavations, resulting in 1959 in the discovery of the skull of prehistoric man later named *Australopithecus boisei*. In 1960 the Leakeys found the important remains of a more human-like creature which is now called *Homo Habilis*. That same year Leakey made another important find, the fossil of a tool-using creature which was named *Homo Erectus*.

These discoveries challenged an earlier theory that man may have originated in Asia because, apart from findings themselves, the presence of numerous Acheulian sites in Africa suggests not only early Stone

Lefela, J. (1885-1965)

LEFELA, Josiel (1885-1965).

LESOTHO politician and founder of the first political movement in the country, *Lekhotla la Bafo* (the Commoners' Association). The son of Molebo, he was born in 1885 in Maponteng in the Berea district. After a brief spell in the mines in Witwatersrand, South Africa, the young man returned home to campaign for equal opportunities for his compatriots under British colonial rule.

At the same time he set up in private business, farming and running a provisions store in Maponteng.

In 1913 Lefela established *Lekhotla la Bafo* to campaign for African participation in government. The constitution of the movement stated that the lack of parliamentary representation hindered the rights of Africans to make known their opinion and aspirations. It called for a constitutional rearrangement of the Basutoland National Council, which he saw as a body of nominated chiefs, to include elected representatives.

Changes, however, were not implemented by the colonial authorities until the 1940s when, contrary to African expectation, the British imposed severer control over the chiefs and headmen. This was seen by the *Lekhotla la Bafo* as a direct assault on a sacred Basotho institution and the fears were confirmed in 1948 and 1949 when several chiefs were hanged for activities against colonial rule.

Now a member of the National Council, Lefela accused the British authorities of trumping up evidence against the chiefs who were charged in the Liretlo murder cases. For this he was dismissed from the Council and imprisoned. He had been arrested and detained during most of the years of the Second World War when he demanded that the Basotho in the British army should be given adequate facilities and opportunities like their European counterparts.

A patriot and a dynamic force in the nationalism of his days, Lefela sought the co-operation of his counterparts in South Africa in his campaign for independent Lesotho. He allied with the then biggest workers' organisation in South Africa, the Industrial and Commercial Workers' Union of Africa, and became its spokesman in Basutoland, and with the African National Congress (ANC) that was being presided over by Josiah Tshangana Gumede (q.v.). In August 1928 Lefela invited Gumede to speak at the congress of the *Lekhotla la Bafo*. With the development of political parties in Basutoland many of the movements's supporters joined the new parties and Lefela's political influence declined considerably. He died in 1965, a year before Basutoland became independent Lesotho. He is widely remembered in the country as a hero of the struggle against British rule. ■

Leigh, L.W. (1921-80)

LEIGH, Leslie William (1921-80).

SIERRA LEONEAN police officer who became his country's first Commissioner of Police. He was born on 23 February 1921 in Freetown. He attended St. Anthony's Primary School, from where he went to St. Edward's Secondary School in Freetown. On completion in 1941, he joined the Sierra Leone government service as a third grade clerk in the Public Works Department. In 1942, he made his way to Britain where he joined the Royal Air Force (RAF), and later graduated as pilot with Bomber Command. He ended the war with the rank of Flight-Lieutenant.

On demobilisation in February 1947, he joined the Colonial Police Service and was posted to the Gold Coast (now Ghana), under probation. In 1948 Leigh was posted to the Sierra Leone Police Force as an Assistant Superintendent of Police. His service in Sierra Leone was one of distinction, dedication and loyalty. He negotiated the various overseas training courses with ease, covering all the higher disciplines in police professional work. Leigh was much respected by Interpol and other international

L.W. Leigh

security organisations. He was a familiar figure at police and security conferences which gave him the opportunity of wide travel, particularly in North and Latin America. He played a major part during the Queen's visit to Sierra Leone in 1961 and was awarded the honour of membership of the Royal Victoria Order (MVO) by the Sovereign, and also the Queen's Police Medal. He became Commissioner of Police in 1963.

Leigh's career, however, was clouded by political upheavals in Sierra Leone in 1967. He joined the National Reformation Council (NRC) which seized power then, and was appointed deputy chairman and commissioner for External Affairs in the NRC regime. When the NRC lost power in 1968, he was sentenced to death for the David Lansana coup, but the sentence was commuted by Prime Minister Stevens after an appeal. Leigh was a devout Catholic and was able to draw upon his religious beliefs during a most difficult time. He served three years in jail and was then officially retired from the police force.

In 1972, he was invited to assume an appointment within the Ministry of Justice by the then President of Liberia; and he subsequently became Director of Liberia's National Public Safety Institute. He demonstrated his great resources in the matter of security for the Heads of State and their suites during the 1979 OAU Conference in Monrovia, the success of which earned him a special Presidential commendation. He died of a heart attack in Monrovia on 13 April 1980. Bill Leigh is survived by his wife, Saka, whom he married in 1953, his daughter Mrs. Roberts and sons Antonio and Martin. ■

Lembede, A.M. (1914-47)

LEMBEDE, Anton Muziwakhe (1914-47).

SOUTH AFRICAN lawyer and politician, the first President of the ANC Youth League at its formation in 1944 and member of the national executive of the African National Congress. An exceptionally brilliant mind, he went through college in a record time and earned the BA and LL.B degrees of the University of South Africa

through correspondence with distinction. He brought that combined brilliance and industry to bear on both his legal practice and the ANC.

Son of a Natal peasant father and a teacher mother, he was born in 1914 in the Georgedale district of Natal. After primary education in a local mission school he gained a bursary to Adams College for a three-year teachers' course but finished the training in two years. He then taught for a short time in a Roman Catholic Mission school, while undergoing private studies for his matriculation which he again did within a space of two years. His next appointment was as a secondary school teacher in the Orange Free State where again he undertook correspondence courses for his law degrees.

In 1943 he went to Johannesburg to serve articles in the law firm of Pixley Ka Izaka Seme (q.v.) and qualified as an attorney in 1946. He became a junior partner in the office of Seme from whom he picked up the Africanist ideas – except that his were of more radical persuasions than his mentor's. Lembede believed that Africans should move on to a new "era of African Socialism", based on African principles rather than on foreign ideology, "because no foreigner can ever truly and genuinely represent the African spirit".

A. Lembede

These militant ideas were shared by other younger members of ANC who included Asby Peter Mda, Nelson Mandela, Walter Sisulu, Govan Mbeki, Oliver Tambo and Ntsu Mokhehle. Together with A. P. Mda, Lembede attacked the ANC leadership under Dr A.B. Xuma (q.v.), which they said was failing to "give positive leadership". With that came the need to establish the Youth League as the "brain-trust and power-station of the spirit of nationalism". Thus was the League created in 1944, and Lembede was elected its first President and Tambo its Secretary at its innaugural conference in Johannesburg.

In 1946 Lembede was elected to the national executive of the ANC – he was its youngest member and also one of its most articulate spokesmen. By virtue of his offices he automatically became a member of the ANC national working committee, through which he came into close contact with other senior members of the organisation who were also members of the Communist Party. Lembede was opposed to the communists' membership of the ANC and overtly advocated their expulsion. But in 1947 he died suddenly, aged only 33. His radical ideas were, however, drawn up in the Youth League Manifesto in 1948.

The Youth League Manifesto states that every African had an "inalienable right to Africa which is his continent and motherland" which will be transformed to a "people's free society where racial oppression and persecution will be outlawed".

In 1949 the Manifesto was presented to the ANC annual conference and was accepted as the parent organisation's policy. His premature death at 33 robbed both the ANC and Africa of a visionary and an able politician.∎

Lemma, M. (1927-88)

LEMMA, Menghistu (1927-88).

ETHIOPIAN poet, playwright, scholar and wit. An intellectual deeply schooled in traditional Ethiopian church culture, at the same time a modern thinker, a man of letters and a master of humour, Menghistu Lemma was, as he always claimed, if not a socialist, at least a "supporter of socialism".

Menghistu Lemma, described as the "Molière of Ethiopia" but who should be more accurately called its Bernard Shaw, was born in Addis Ababa and brought up in Harar where his father, Aleka Lemma Hailu, was a learned cleric. Young Menghistu received a traditional Ethiopian Orthodox Church education, specialising in *Qené*, or ecclesiastical poetry, and *zema*, or music. He subsequently travelled to Addis Ababa to attend the prestigious Haile Sellassie I Secondary School. There he gained a reputation for his poetry which he recited to his fellow students every Sunday. He later received an Ethiopian Government scholarship to study in England. He joined the Regent Street Polytechnic before gaining admission to the London School of Economics where he was an avid reader of French and Russian novels and plays as well as works on economics and politics.

During his years in England Menghistu emerged as one of Ethiopia's first student activists. Using the pseudonym Etyopis, he wrote a seminal article entitled "The Best System of Ideas" for the *Lion Cub*, the magazine of Ethiopian students in Britain, urging them to concern themselves not only with their formal studies but also with the social and political transformation of their country. While in England he also produced his first dramatic sketch. Written to entertain his fellow Ethiopian students on one of their holiday gatherings, it featured a discussion between a traditional Ethiopian cleric and a European philosopher. The former held the old view that the world was flat and stationary, while the latter argued that it was round and rotated round the sun. Both protagonists drank copiously, and by the last scene were sprawling on the floor. At that point the merry priest conceded that he could see that the world was "really going round."

Menghistu provided Sylvia Pankhurst with a detailed account of traditional Ethiopian church education – a subject then virtually unknown outside the country – for her book *Ethiopia: A Cultural History* (1955) which also included two little known drawings by the youthful Menghistu.

On returning to Ethiopia in the early fifties Menghistu was assigned to his country's Civil Aviation Department, but devot ed his attention primarily to literary affairs. In 1960 he published his first book, a collection of traditional Ethiopian stories, *Tales of the Fathers*, retold in Amharic verse. The work appeared in 1960 without the portrait of the Emperor which it was then customary to place as a frontispiece in all Ethiopian publications. For this act of *lèse-majesté* the author was despatched to the Ethiopian Embassy in India. There he served under the monarch's progressive cousin, Ras Imru, and was able to observe a Third World country in Asia. This was another formative period in his life.

Returning to Ethiopia in the early sixties Menghistu was attached to the Ethiopian Ministry of Foreign Affairs, but continued to be mainly concerned with literature and scholarship. He wrote two comic plays, *Marriage by Abduction* (1963) and *Marriage of Unequals* (1964). Both deal with the clash of values between traditional Ethiopians and members of the modern foreign-educated generation who reject such time-honoured customs as arranged marriages. These plays, like most of Menghistu's writings, conformed to his dictum that Ethiopian literature should be "nationalist in form and progressive in content". They were first written in Amharic, for their author held that Ethiopian, and by extension other African, authors should write for their compatriots in their own native languages; their works should later be translated into foreign languages to reach a wider audience. In keeping with this view he duly produced English versions of both his plays. The first appeared in *Ethiopia Observer* while the second was published by Macmillans.

During this period Menghistu began recording the memories of his aged father from which he eventually published extracts in 1966. They constitute a document of unique interest from historical, religious and linguistic points of view. Collaborating with Dr Richard Pankhurst, director of the Institute of Ethiopian Studies, Addis Ababa, he collected and published several hundred traditional Ethiopian poems in a mimeographed periodical, *Qené Collections*. Menghistu wrote an important study on the Technical Aspects of Amharic Versification, and, making use of both traditional and foreign verse forms, composed a number of poems of his own. His deep interest in the literary achievements of others led him to translate their works. These include those by Chekhov

M. Lemma

and J. B. Priestley. In this period Menghistu was appointed to head an Amharic Language Academy and later received the Haile Sellassie I Prize for Ethiopian literature.

After the Ethiopian Revolution of 1974, Menghistu was recognised as one of his country's pioneer advocates of social change. He was elected to the provisional Shango, or Parliament, which drafted the first post-revolutionary legislation, introducing, for example, full formal equality between Christians and Muslims. He later joined Addis Ababa University where he taught drama, and proved a dedicated and inspiring teacher. During this period he continued to develop his theatrical talent, and completed a play about the Italian fascist occupation of his country. He was, at all times, a perfectionist, repeatedly working over his drafts before permitting performance or publication. He persuaded the Ethiopian Ministry of Culture to begin two major enterprises: the recording of traditional Ethiopian interpretations of the Bible, and the collection, publication and translation into modern Amharic of traditional *Qené*, poetry, with the intention of making it accessible to a wider public. A first volume of this poetry appeared under his editorship in early 1988, and won him a prize from the Ministry of Culture. He died in July 1988.

Menghistu Lemma was throughout his life a keen and often sardonic observer of his country's social scene and will long be remembered as one of Ethiopia's great men of letters and social critic. ■

Lenshina, A.M. (c.1924-78)

LENSHINA, Alice Mulenga (c.1924-78).

ZAMBIAN religious leader, head of the Lumpa Church or the Lenshina Movement, which she founded in 1953 when she claimed to have received a calling from Jesus Christ himself to become a prophetess. Lenshina said this happened near a river where, she claimed, she died on four occasions, each time resurrecting again. She claimed she was instructed by God, who she said had spoken to her in Heaven during one of these deaths, to return to earth to help eradicate witchcraft and sorcery. Thus was the Lumpa (a Bemba word meaning "better than all the rest") Church begun in September 1953 at Kasomo which she renamed Zion.

Alice M. Lenshina

Of Bemba origins, she was for a time a catechumen of the Church of Scotland Mission to the Bemba, the major ethnic group of eastern Zambia. She married Petros (Peter) Chintankwa Mulenga and was called, in full, Alice Lenshina Mulenga Mubusha when she rose to fame. Largely illiterate, she continued to receive instruction from the Presbyterians for a time after her prophetic experiences and was baptised at Lubwa by an African minister, the Rev. Paul Mushindo, in November 1953. But already many people were following her because of her own experience and the preaching for which she said she had been given instruction in the vision.

By 1955 Alice Lenshina had broken with the Presbyterian Mission at Lubwa. She and her husband were excommunicated. Great numbers of Presbyterians followed her, believing in her divine inspiration. She had her own ministers and baptised people. By 1959 an organisation had grown up among those who followed her doctrines, expressed mainly in hymns which were very important in her movement. She preached against polygamy, alcoholic drink, and witchcraft. Her doctrines were basically Christian but there was no Communion, and Baptism was of a special sort and administered commonly, if not exclusively, by Alice Lenshina herself.

In 1956 one of her followers was gaoled for accusing an African Catholic priest of sorcery. Demonstrations at Chinsali followed, and led to the imprisonment of many of the new movement, including Petros Chintankwa, sentenced to two years' gaol. But from her base at Kasomo Alice Lenshina continued to win followers; many people travelled to see her. The church, known by 1956 as the Lumpa Church, spread to the Copperbelt. Deacons in black gowns ran services in mud-built churches and the prophetess herself went on tours. A big church at Kasomo was completed in 1958. By 1959 the Lumpa Church had between 50,000 and 100,000 members.

With its considerable power the Church threatened the authority of the chiefs, encouraging its adherents to form new villages. Its main centre at Chinsali was a place of strong nationalist feelings by the 1950s; the church itself could to some extent satisfy those feelings as a breakaway from a white-run church, and Dr. Kenneth Kaunda's brother Robert joined it, but later the church was a rival to the United National Independence Party (UNIP) for Africans' loyalty fuelled by the church's defiant refusal to recognise any earthly authority.

In 1963 incidents between UNIP and Lumpa supporters multiplied. Both groups used violence and brutality, and efforts to restrain them by the new African government failed. In December 1963 Alice Lenshina then met Dr.Kaunda and agreed to tell her followers to leave the new Lumpa villages and return to their home villages. They did not, and some of the villages were fortified with stockades. In the months leading to Zambian independence the Lumpa followers were worked up into a state of religious exaltation and enthusiasm for the fight against their "enemies". In July 1964 fighting broke out. Police were ordered to tell people to leave the Lumpa villages. There was fierce resistance; eventually hundreds were killed in suicidal resistance to the police and the troops who reinforced them. The Lumpa villages were broken up and inmates taken to camps and after a final battle on 10 October the resistance was ended. On 3 August 1964 the Lumpa Church was banned. Alice Lenshina surrendered on 11 August and was interned with her husband and children.

She was released in 1975 but temporarily restricted to the Lusaka area. In 1977 she and 47 of the followers of her still banned church were charged with attending a meeting of an unlawful society, but acquitted. Early in December 1978 she died. ■

Lewanika (c.1830-1916)

LEWANIKA, King Lubosi (c.1830-1916).

ZAMBIAN monarch. He was a grandson of King Mulambwa, the greatest of the Luyi who were the forerunners of the Lozis of present day western Zambia.

Mulambwa's death in 1830 led to a drawn-out internecine succession dispute which left the kingdom vulnerable to external invasion. In 1838 the Kololo, a clan that was fleeing from Chaka (q.v.) of the Zulus, conquered the Lozis and set up their own dynasty. All the members of the Lozi royal family fled north to Kabompo to live among the Luvales of north-western Zambia.

In 1865 Sipopa, one of the exiled princes of the defeated Lozi monarchy, organised an army from Kabompo that was to successfully dislodge the Kololo. Sipopa, however, proved to be too cruel for his people, and was driven into exile where he died. His nephew, Ngawia, who took over from him, was deposed by his cousin, Lubosi, whose rule was to span from 1870 till his death in 1916. He changed his name to Lewanika on assuming power.

Lewanika sought to re-establish the Lozi hegemony over the Ilas and Tokas to the East and the Luvales to the North, a hegemony which had lapsed with the arrival of the Kololos. His assumption of power coincided with the period of increased search for colonies and mineral prospecting in central and southern Africa by Europeans. He decided to take advantage of this situation, and was determined to use the Europeans in his bid to stay in power.

In the meantime Lewanika's cruelty had worsened so much that Mataa led a successful rebellion in the southern part of the kingdom in what is now known as the Caprivi Strip of Namibia. In retaliation the king marched on the rebels in 1885. So fierce was the counter-attack that some say that the event was the "bloodiest scene" ever witnessed in Barotseland.

With his overlordship once more confirmed Lewanika now turned to the search for permanent security in his kingdom. In spite of the fact that Lobengula (q.v.) had sent a delegation offering friendship and imploring Lewanika to join him in his anti-European crusade, the latter remained suspicious of the Ndebele chief. Lewanika had earlier sent an emissary to Khama of the Bamangwato in Bechuanaland (now Botswana) who had agreed to let his kingdom become a British protectorate, to inquire about the sincerity of the Europeans. Khama replied positively and added that, "they not only offered the Queen's protection but they also showered you with gifts."

Lewanika allowed François Coillard of the Paris Evangelical Missionary Society to set up a mission immediately, and asked him to write a letter on his behalf to Sydney Shippard, the administrative commissioner for the Bechuanaland Protectorate, offering to accept the protection of Queen Victoria. Within the same year, 1889, he granted a prospecting concession to a British explorer, Harry Ware. Ware later sold his rights to a group of speculators in October of the same year, from whom the British South Africa Company (BSAC) in turn bought the concession a few weeks afterwards. The BSAC, led by Cecil Rhodes, had a royal Charter granting it the right to enter into territorial treaties on behalf of the British imperial sovereign. Rhodes was so excited when the news of Lewanika's swing to the British side reached him that in March 1890 he despatched an emissary, one F.E.Lochner, to conclude a formal treaty with the Lozi king. This was done on 27 June 1890. Lewanika presented Rhodes's envoy with two elephant tusks for transmission to Queen Victoria as a sign of his appreciation for the "protection" granted. It was, however, to take seven years before a resident Commissioner, an essential part of the treaty, was to arrive in 1897, in the person of Robert Coryndon.

Perhaps nothing demonstrated Lewanika's shrewdness more than his treaty with the BSAC. Insisting that he controlled a vast territory, he not only secured a £2,000 fixed annual payment but also demanded the insertion of a clause promising royalty payment for any minerals exported from the territory. This clause was to prove a thorny issue nearly seventy years later when Northern Rhodesia attained independence in 1964, and Lewanika's successor refused to cede his payments to the national treasury.

Barotseland was formally made a British protectorate in 1900 by Order-in-Council.

Although he disliked what he termed the "white man's religion", it is clear that Coillard's influence on the Lozi king was considerable. In 1897, Lewanika cancelled a planned military expedition against the Ilas in the East. In the same year he passed a law making witch-hunting illegal and laying down that any witch doctor caught would be sentenced to sweeping the streets of the palace at Lealui. The following year he let his son Litia be baptised. In 1906 he showed his belief in modernisation and development by freeing over 30,000 slaves including some from his royal household.

The amalgamation of Barotseland with North Western Rhodesia and North-Eastern Rhodesia in 1911 extended the "protection" of the British over a larger area. Lewanika died in February 1916. ■

Lewis, S. (1843-1903)

LEWIS, Sir Samuel (1843-1903).

SIERRA LEONEAN lawyer who in 1882 became acting Chief Justice of his country. He was born in Freetown on 13 November 1843, the son of the Creole Recaptive trader William Lewis (d.1901). After attending the Church Missionary Society Grammar School he joined his father's business before going to England in 1866 for law studies. He was called to the Bar at the Middle Temple in 1871. He returned to Sierra Leone and married Christiana Horton in 1874.

He was then among the first practising lawyers in Sierra Leone, practising also in Lagos and The Gambia. He became a temporary police magistrate in 1874, Acting Queen's Advocate in 1877-86 and again in 1895, and Acting Chief Justice of Sierra Leone in 1882 and 1894. After appearing in several important cases, he became a well known lawyer in British West Africa. From 1882 to 1903 he was a member of the Legislative Council. As such he was a loyal critic of the government.

Sir Samuel Lewis

Lewis was among several Creoles who believed in expanding agriculture as a new source of wealth for their people and went in for farming himself. A practising Methodist, he helped start the Wesleyan Educational Institution in Freetown.

In 1893 Freetown was created a Municipality, and in the local elections in 1895 Lewis became Mayor. He was re-elected in 1896 and 1897. Later he became Mayor again after the death of his successor, T.C. Bishop. It is as Mayor of Freetown, and the first West African to receive a British knighthood (in 1896), that he is remembered most. Sir Samuel Lewis died in Britain on 9 July 1903. ■

Lightfoot-Boston, H.J. (1898-1969)

LIGHTFOOT-BOSTON, Sir Henry Josiah (1898-1969).

SIERRA LEONEAN lawyer, politician and the first African Governor-General of his country. He was born on 19 August 1898 in Bullom, Sierra Leone. His family was fairly wealthy and his father was a church minister.

Henry Lightfoot Boston received his early education at the Cathedral Boys' Primary School and the Church Missionary Society Grammar School in Freetown, after which he continued his studies at Fourah Bay College, graduating with a BA degree in 1919 and an MA degree the following year.

On leaving college he joined the Treasury Department of the colonial civil service, and at the same time began to study law in his spare time as an external student of the University of London. Two years later he left Sierra Leone and became a full time student at the University of London where he obtained the LLB and BCL degrees in 1925. He was called to the Bar at Lincoln's Inn, London, in January 1926.

He then returned to Sierra Leone and established a private legal practice. He became justice of the peace in 1935 and took up the position of police magistrate in 1946. He was later promoted to senior police

Sir Henry Lightfoot-Boston

magistrate and was appointed registrar-general of the Supreme Court of Sierra Leone in 1954, later becoming a puisne judge in that court.

Between 1957 and 1962 he was Speaker of the House of Representatives, after which he was appointed the first Sierra Leonean Governor-General of the country. He received a knighthood from the British Government later in the year and remained as Governor-General until 1967. After the 1967 elections he was asked to choose the new Prime Minister because of the closeness of the results. He selected the former leader of the opposition, Siaka Stevens, but shortly afterwards the government was taken over by the military and Lightfoot-Boston was placed under house arrest. He was detained for one year, during which time, his health deteriorated, and in 1968 he travelled to London for treatment. He died there on 11 January 1969, aged 70. ■

Lobengula (c.1836-94)

LOBENGULA, King (c.1836-94).

ZIMBABWEAN traditional ruler, the last independent ruler of the Ndebele kingdom. He was born near the Upper Marico River in Western Transvaal, South Africa. His mother, Fulata, was the daughter of a chief and his father, Mzilikazi (q.v.) a leader of the Ndebele people.

His family moved northwards to Zimbabwe where his father founded the Ndebele kingdom in Matabeleland in 1839, based in the region around present-day Bulawayo. As

King Lobengula

a young man he became a member of an *ibutho*, a group of men formed by the King to raise cattle and perform police and military functions for the state in Mahlokohloko.

On the death of his father in 1868 there was uncertainty as to who should succeed him as King. Lobengula's half-brother, Nkulumane, was the heir to the throne, but he had not been seen or heard of since the late 1830s. Until the matter could be resolved Mncumbathe, the hereditary chief adviser in the kingdom, became regent and delegations were sent to Natal to see if any information could be found regarding Nkulumane's whereabouts. As Nkulumane could not be found, Mncumbathe nominated Lobengula to succeed his father. The majority of the influential chiefs supported this move and in January 1870 Lobengula was proclaimed King during the *inxwala*, an annual religious festival of the Ndebele.

However, the Ndebele in the Zwangendaba *ibutho* did not support Lobengula's accession to the throne and refused to accept his authority, partly because they did not believe rumours that Nkulumane was dead and also they thought he had been passed over because of his mother's Swazi origins. Lobengula immediately began to marshal his forces, and with an army of around 5,500 men he attacked and defeated the rebels at Zwangendaba in June 1870. The rebel leader was killed in the battle along with 400 of his supporters, and many others involved in the rebellion fled to the Transvaal. Although Lobengula did not carry out harsh reprisals against those who remained, many of them continued to work against him in conjunction with those in exile, throughout his reign.

Around the time of his father's death, gold had been discovered at Tati and in the area between the Gwelo and Hunyani Rivers. When Lobengula came to the throne many prospectors were flooding into the area trying to gain permission for mineral exploration and exploitation. At the same time a man named Kanda claiming to be Nkulumane had allied with the eldest of Lobengula's half brothers, Mangwane, and the two sought European support for their claim. Partly to ensure against this, Lobengula awarded the first written mining concession to a British explorer, Thomas Baines, in 1871.

During the *inxwala* in the following January, the royal pretender attempted to invade Matabeleland, hoping that Lobengula would be caught off-guard during the festival. However, at the last minute a number of his supporters let him down and Lobengula was easily able to overcome the invasion and scatter the enemy, with the royal pretender fleeing to western Transvaal.

The kingdom that Lobengula had inherited had been built on a military framework with which he organised many cattle raids on his neighbours, particularly in Mashonaland to the north and east, Botswana and western Zambia. Lobengula himself ruled as an absolute monarch.

He strictly controlled the movements of European traders, hunters and missionaries in the area. He personally regulated the flourishing trade with the Europeans, who were protected in his territory so long as they came in peace. In 1878 a party of Europeans under Patterson died in Matabeleland. Officially their deaths were said to have been caused through drinking water at a poisoned well, but there were rumours that they had been killed after Patterson, who was on a semi-official mission to investigate alleged ill-treatment of Britons in the kingdom, tried to put pressure on Lobengula by suggesting that the British Government might support the cause of the royal pretender who had attempted to invade the country six years previously.

During the 1880s competition among the imperial powers in this region intensified, partly to curtail Afrikaner expansion to the north of the Limpopo River but also to gain access to the mineral wealth. In July 1887 an agreement was supposedly reached between Lobengula and the Transvaal Government, making the countries firm allies and extending considerable rights to Afrikaners in Matabeleland. However, Lobengula later denied signing this agreement and in the following February he signed a treaty of friendship with the British. This was known as the Moffat Treaty after its main negotiator, and provided that land-grants and treaties agreed with non-Ndebele interest would not be finalised without the agreement of the British High Commissioner based in South Africa, thus laying the foundations for the creation of a British sphere of influence in the area.

Shortly afterwards negotiations began for mineral exploration and exploitation rights, and on 30 October 1888 Lobengula signed the Rudd Concession on the advice of J.S. Moffat, a missionary of the London Missionary Society. In return for the payment to Lobengula of £100 per month plus 1,000 rifles and 100,000 rounds of ammunition, Lobengula assigned "unto the said guarantees, their heirs, representatives and assigns, jointly and severally, the complete and exclusive charge over all metals and minerals situated and contained in my

Kingdom, principalities and dominions together with full power that they may do all things they may deem necessary to win and procure the same. . ."

The Rudd Concession was written in English, and owing to an incorrect translation Lobengula did not realise the extent of the concession he had granted, believing it to be limited in both the area covered and the number of prospectors allowed. Once the misconception was uncovered, Lobengula denied the validity of the concession and sent a delegation of senior chiefs to London in early 1889 to the Queen of England and the British Government. They returned with the Colonial Secretary's advice to be cautious in making extensive concessions to a single syndicate. In the meantime Rhodes had established the British South African Company (BSAC) on the strength of the Rudd Concession, and was granted a Royal Charter in 1889, empowering the company, among other things, to take over the administration of the area concerned and set up a police force. He also sent his agent, Jameson, to re-open talks with Lobengula who, fearing British hostility if he refused to discuss the issue, attempted to negotiate a more limited agreement. However, once again he was misled and the points he ceded were magnified beyond recognition by Rhodes who claimed later that he had reaffirmed the original concession.

The BSAC claimed that the concession covered Mashonaland as this territory was under Lobengula's control. Rhodes sent the Pioneer Column, a group consisting of military experts, mercenaries and white South Africans into Mashonaland, a move which started white settlement in Rhodesia and later caused the war of 1896.

As Lobengula began to appreciate the full implications of the Moffat Treaty and the Rudd Concession, he started to look for ways to neutralise the BSAC's authority. He negotiated with the Germans and signed the Lippert Concession on 17 November 1891. Under this agreement Lobengula, believing he was dealing with Rhodes' rivals, granted Lippert sole rights for the allocation of European land titles in the territory under BSAC control. However, shortly afterwards Lippert sold the concession to the BSAC, thus greatly enhancing their position.

By 1892 around 1,500 Europeans from South Africa had settled in Mashonaland. The following year, boundaries between

Mashonaland and Matabeleland were drawn up by Jameson, then the BSAC administrator. A few months later, in July 1893, Lobengula's forces crossed this boundary in a raid against the Shona in Fort Victoria who had refused to pay tribute to Lobengula. The incident was blown into a major crisis and war was declared on Lobengula by the British, who were pleased for the excuse to overthrow him. By early November 1893 the British had defeated Lobengula and taken over Bulawayo, his headquarters. Lobengula fled towards Zambia but died of smallpox about 40 miles south of the Zambezi River, near Kamativi, in February 1894. ■

Luke, E.F. (1895-1980)

LUKE, Sir Emile Fashole (1895-1980).

SIERRA LEONEAN jurist, acting Chief Justice of the country and later the Speaker of the House of Representatives. He was born on 19 October 1895 in Freetown. Educated at Ebenezer School, Methodist Boys' High School, and Fourah Bay College, he proceeded to Lincoln's Inn, London, in 1922 to read law. He was called to the Bar in

1925. From 1926 he was a practising barrister till 1943 when he was appointed assistant magistrate. Two years later Luke was made police magistrate, and in 1949 he became senior police magistrate.

He was appointed a judge in 1953. He rose progressively on the bar and bench to the position of puisne judge. In 1957 Luke became acting Chief Justice of Sierra Leone. In 1960 he was made Justice of the Court of Appeal, holding this position until 1964.

Sir Emile became the Speaker of the House of Representatives in 1968. This office he held until 1973 when he retired.

Sir Emile served as a councillor of the Freetown City Council from 1940 to 1944. He was a member of the Royal Commonwealth Society, and was conferred with a degree of Doctor of Civil Law by the University of Sierra Leone. A keen scouter, he served as Chief Commissioner of the Sierra Leone Boy Scouts Association from 1954 until 1969, when he became Chief Scout. He represented the Scout Movement at several international conferences and jamborees and was awarded the highest world scout award – the Bronze Salver – at the Boy Scouts World Conference in Tokyo, Japan, in 1971.

Emile Luke became a Commander of the British Empire in the Queen's Honours' List in 1959 and Knight Commander of the Most Excellent Order of the British Empire (KBE) in 1969. He also won the Grand Cordon of the Cedar of Lebanon award in 1971. Sir Emile was a Freemason of international repute and held the position of District Grand Master for Sierra Leone. He died in January 1980, aged 84, leaving behind three children. ■

Sir Emile Luke

Lule, K.Y. (1912-85)

LULE, Professor K. Yusufu (1912-85).

UGANDAN statesman, a distinguished academic and leader in many fields of Ugandan life, though he was a short-lived president. He became political leader of the National Resistance Movement which, under its military commander, Mr Yoweri Museveni, a former Minister of Defence and now President of Uganda, became the ruling party.

Yusufu Lule was born on 10 April 1912 in Buganda. He went to King's College, Budo, Uganda, from 1929 to 1934, then to Makerere University College (later Makerere University), Kampala, from 1934 to 1936, Fort Hare College, South Africa, from 1936 to 1939, where he took a degree in Chemistry. He returned to Uganda in 1940 to teach science at King's College. In 1948 he went to Britain to take a diploma in Education at the University of Bristol and a Master in Education degree at the University of Edinburgh. Back in Kampala in 1951 he became a lecturer in Education at Makerere University College, a post he occupied until 1954. In 1955 he entered the Colonial Government as Minister of Education and Community Development, the first African to reach such a rank in Uganda.

When Milton Obote became Prime Minister in 1961, Lule was Chairman of the Uganda Public Service Commission and from 1963 to 1970, principal of Makerere University College, University of East Africa. He left Makerere because of disagreements with Dr Milton Obote and was out of the country when Idi Amin took over in a military coup of 1971. He was then appointed assistant secretary-general of the Commonwealth Secretariat, with special responsibilities for educational and legal affairs, in London.

After two years in that post Lule became secretary-general of the Association of African Universities and was based in Accra until 1978. Lule retired after that to live in London, but went back to Uganda when in 1979 border fighting between Tanzania and Uganda led to full scale invasion by Tanzanian forces which brought Amin's fall. The leaders of the 18 groups opposed to Amin gathered at Moshi, Tanzania in March 1979 and chose Professor Lule as chairman leader of the Ugandan National Liberation Front.

In April 1979 Lule returned to Kampala in triumph. However, his term as president did not last long; he was president for only 68 days. In June the same year he was forced to resign. Difficulties arose over appointments to his government. He refused to have the National Consultative Council (Interim Parliament) sanction his appointments and he was seen as being dictatorial. Amin's tyranny had made politicians very sensitive on this matter. A motion of no

Prof. Y. Lule

confidence was passed by the newly-established National Consultative Council and he was replaced by Godfrey Binaisa, who was in turn later replaced by the Military Commission, an organ of the Uganda National Liberation Front.

After a period when he was under some sort of house arrest in Tanzania, Lule returned to exile in London. Less than a year after general elections were held in December 1980, Dr A. Milton Obote's UPC Party won and he became President. The elections were observed by a team of Commonwealth officials. Professor Yusufu Lule and his supporters contested the results of the elections though Professor Lule did not personally participate in the elections due to difficulties within his party, the Democratic Party. In his last years in exile in London, he was bitterly opposed to the government of former President Obote, canvassing against it in Britain and Europe.

Lule died in a London hospital on 21 January 1985, at the age of 72. He is survived by his wife, Hannah, and five children. ■

Lumumba, P. (1925-61)

LUMUMBA, Patrice (1925-61).

ZAIREAN statesman. He led the struggle for his country's independence from Belgium and what is now accepted as the most oppressive colonial administration in the continent. Lumumba became his country's first prime minister, and although he lasted just over six months before being brutally murdered, his political career has made him a Pan-African hero and a major symbol in the conflict between neo-colonialist forces and African nationalist aspirations of the early 1960s.

Lumumba was born in Wembonya village in the Katoko-Kombe District of Sankuru, Central Kasai province and edu-

P. Lumumba

cated in both Roman Catholic and Protestant schools. Up to the age of 14 he attended a Catholic missionary school after which he decided, against the wishes of his Catholic father, to go to a Protestant one. His wider knowledge came later through private studies assisted by Protestant missionaries who introduced him to liberal and radical European thinkers such as Sartre and Karl Marx. Lumumba emerged as a religious freethinker.

After his studies, Lumumba joined the Belgian administration as a filing clerk in the tax office, later transferring to the post office where he rose to the rank of assistant postmaster. Lumumba was one of the intellectuals, known as *évolués*, who were quick to respond to Professor A. A. J. van Blisen, a Belgian who in 1954 published *A Thirty Year Plan for the Political Emancipation of Belgian Africa*. During the 11 years he spent in the Colonial Service, he wrote for periodicals such as *La Croix du Congo* and *La Voix du Congolais*, campaigning for immediate independence of his country, and in 1956, he wrote the book *Is the Congo, the land of the future, threatened?* He was also active in two *évolués* organisations, the *Cercle Libéral* and the Association of Congolese Government Employees. Lumumba's serious political involvement began in the African Staff Association at Stanleyville (now Kisangani). The Belgians allowed such associations, regarding them as a harmless outlet for African grievances. These inevitably developed into political organisations.

Lumumba moved from Stanleyville to Léopoldville (now Kinshasa) and in 1957 became commercial director of a brewery. The Belgians, at the time still hoping to contain the growing political movements, sent Lumumba on a goodwill tour to Brussels.

In August 1958 General de Gaulle paid a visit to Congo-Brazzaville across the river from Léopoldville, and offered the French Congo the choice in a referendum between membership of the French Community as an autonomous republic and complete independence. This had an immediate impact on the opinion in Belgian Congo. Two days later a group of influential *évolués*, led by Lumumba, addressed a firm memorandum to the governor-general of the Belgian Congo, demanding outright independence and the inclusion meanwhile of representative African leaders in the study group set up in

Belgium to formulate a new policy for the Congo.

Lumumba and the other signatories followed up their demands with the establishment, in October 1958, of a political party, the *Mouvement National Congolais* (MNC) whose programme was "to prepare the masses and the élite to take control of public affairs, to spread the process of democratisation, to implement the Declaration of Human Rights, and by peaceful means to free the Congo from colonialism". This was the first supra-ethnic political party in the country. The other main party was ABAKO (*Alliance des Bakongo*), led by Joseph Kasavubu (q.v.); it consisted of the Bakongo people and was organised on an ethnic basis in the Léopoldville Province.

In December 1958, Lumumba attended the Accra All-African People's Conference (AAPC), where he met Kwame Nkrumah and many other African nationalist leaders. On his return Lumumba addressed a mass rally in Léopoldville in which he declared that "independence was not a gift to be given by Belgium, but a fundamental right of the Congolese people". Two days later, the rising political tension, heightened by a ban on ABAKO, erupted in riots. The mass protest was severely repressed by the Belgians who, however, realised the combined commitment of the MNC and ABAKO to independence, and agreed to the idea of early independence, to be preceded by local elections. A further concession was that, during 1959, 700 Africans would be appointed to senior civil service posts previously reserved for Europeans with the promulgation of a strong law against racial discrimination.

Throughout most of 1959 Lumumba worked hard at absorbing other growing nationalist movements into the MNC. At the MNC congress of 29 October 1959, the party was joined by the *Centre du Regroupement Africain*, the *Parti du Peuple*, the *Union de la Jeunesse* and the *Union Nationale du Ruanda*. All of them agreed to boycott the local elections scheduled for June 1960 and passed a resolution for immediate independence. This congress was followed by another wave of violent protests and on 1 November 1959, Lumumba was arrested and held responsible for various incidents in the course of which the Belgian authorities had killed several Congolese.

Lumumba was released to attend the Round Table Conference in Brussels in January 1960. At the conference the MNC formed a united front with other nationalist movements, and in the face of it, the Belgians agreed for the Congo to become independent on 30 June 1960, preceded in May by elections to provincial and national parliaments. Parties such as Kasavubu's ABAKO and Moïse Tshombe's (q.v.) CONAKAT (*Confédération des Associations du Katanga*) which favoured loose federalism for the independent Congo, were also represented at the conference.

Though the MNC had suffered a setback in mid-1959 when some central committee members led by Joseph Ileo broke away to form a new party – later joined by Albert Kalonji, the MNC leader in Kasai Province – known as the MNC-Kalonji, it nevertheless grew in popularity and the Belgian authorities in an attempt to curtail the movement, imposed emergency regulations for the campaigns for the national elections of May 1960. Armed reinforcement was sent in from Belgium, curfew was in force and assemblies of more than five persons were made illegal, but Lumumba defied them.

In those elections, the MNC which had campaigned for a united Congo had the largest number of seats – 37 out of 137 – in the National Assembly, compared with 12 for Kasavubu's ABAKO, while Tshombe's CONAKAT failed initially to win enough seats to form the provincial government, and only did so after a change in the law by Belgium. Lumumba was appointed Prime Minister and Kasavubu became President.

On 30 June, King Baudouin of Belgium, speaking at the independence celebrations in Léopoldville, said the granting of independence was "a deliberate act of policy rather than the scuttle it had been taken for", and he "advised" the new parliament not to "compromise the future with hasty reforms and replace organisations which Belgium is handing over to you until you are sure of being able to do better." In a powerful speech Lumumba challenged the alleged benefits of Belgian rule, concluding that "no Congolese will ever forget that independence has been gained by a struggle paid in tears, fire and blood. The wounds are too fresh and painful, after 80 years of colonial government, for us to drive them from our memories."

But the circumstances in which Lumumba found himself were not easy. As a consequence of a deliberate policy of denying Africans access to modern education, the Congo had not a single qualified medical doctor or lawyer or architect, and only one engineer at independece. But there was the *Force Publique*, an army specifically built to oppress and control political activities in the 1940s, which at independence consisted of 24,000 African soldiers commanded by 1,000 Belgians.

On 5 July, five days after independence, a mutiny broke out against the European officers in the *Force Publique*. The Belgian government reacted by sending troops, allegedly to protect Belgian nationals in the Congo against the growing anti-white opposition; Lumumba, seeing this as a blatant violation of the sovereignty of the Congo, demanded that the Belgian troops leave and appealed for an immediate despatch of United Nations troops to protect his country against the invasion.

On 11 July Lumumba had to face another crisis. Tshombe proclaimed Katanga's (now Shaba) secession and independence, declared a state of emergency and appointed a Belgain army officer to supervise the army and police.

Tshombe was believed to have received aid from the rich *Union Minière*, the European multi-national company, which controlled most of the mineral resources of the Katanga; and the secession cut off from the Central Government the bulk of the national earnings from the copper-rich province. On 14 July Lumumba broke off diplomatic relations with Belgium and demanded the withdrawal of all Belgian troops within 12 hours. On 16 July UN troops began to arrive in accordance with a unanimous Security Council resolution that all Belgians should leave and that the UN force should assist the Central Government in maintaining law and order. But when the UN forces failed to evict the Belgian forces, Lumumba canvassed for African support, and threatened to invite the help of the Russians. Ghana's response soon came, President Nkrumah announced that "in the event of the UN failing to effect a total and unconditional withdrawal of Belgian troops from the Congo", Ghana would provide any assistance "even if this meant Ghana and the Congo had to fight alone against Belgium."

In the midst of the crisis, on 5 September, Kasavubu announced that he had dismissed Lumumba as Prime Minister,

to which Lumumba reacted by dismissing Kasavubu from the Presidency. The Congolese parliament cancelled both dismissals. Lumumba then called for the withdrawal of UN forces on the grounds that they had failed in their mission, having won a vote of confidence in the Congolese Senate. This call followed the drastic UN action of closing all Congolese airfields and ordering Léopoldville radio station to stay off the air, which was explained as a move to prevent the arrival of Russian military aid solicited by Lumumba.

But Lumumba had no chance to follow this up for on 14 September Colonel Joseph-Désiré Mobutu announced that the army was taking over until 31 December. Mobutu, formerly of the *Force Publique* now reconstituted as the *Armée Nationale Congolaise* (ANC), announced his personal promotion to Commander-in-Chief of the ANC, and ordered the closure of the East European embassies and the withdrawal of the Ghanaian contingent of the UN forces.

On 15 September Lumumba asked for UN protection after he had been seriously assaulted by ANC soldiers. He was guarded by UN troops, for nearly two months during which he was rendered politically powerless while Mobutu strengthened his position in alliance with Kasavubu.

In the division of international opinion that followed, Ghana led an Afro-Asian group of countries, backed by the Soviet Union, demanding at the UN the recognition of Lumumba's as the only legitimate government.

Under house arrest in Léopoldville, Lumumba was said to have escaped from his official residence and from UN guards on 27 November and to be heading for Orientale Province, the centre of his political support where his close friend and Deputy Prime Minister, Antoine Gizenga, had set up a rival regime in Stanleyville. But some believed that the UN handed him over to Mobutu's troops who later claimed to have arrested him. Lumumba was severely beaten up before being jailed in Thysville, pending trial.

A couple of weeks later came the announcement from the Katangese regime that Lumumba, while trying to escape on 13 February, had been "massacred" by persons in an unnamed village of Katanga. Later an Elizabethville (now Lubumbashi) evening newspaper proclaimed the murder with the headline: "Justice is Done".

The news of what many saw as Lumumba's assassination provoked demonstrations outside Belgian embassies in a number of countries. Inside and outside the UN, the Secretary-General was attacked for failing to ensure the safety of Lumumba. In the Congo, the removal of Lumumba strengthened the Kasavubu-Mobutu alliance to eventually defeat the Gizenga's pro-Lumumba movement that continued to have the support of Ghana and many other countries.

Lumumba's death was and still is regarded by many on the African continent and outside, as martyrdom, the sacrifice of African nationalism to colonial intervention and ethnic separatism. He is remembered as a very active pan-Africanist, who advocated the unity of Africa, as reflected in his fight for the unity of the Congo. "This conference", he had said at the AAPC in Accra in 1958, "reveals one thing to us. Despite the boundaries that separate us, despite our ethnic differences, we have the same awareness, the same soul plunged, day and night, in anguish in the same anxious desire to make the African continent a free and happy continent that had rid itself of unrest and of fear and any sort of colonialist domination." The Russians honoured him by naming a Moscow University after him. Dr Nkrumah's book, *I Speak of Freedom*, was dedicated to "Patrice Lumumba, the late Prime Minister of the Republic of the Congo and all those who are engaged in the struggle for the political unification of Africa". ■

Chief A.M. Luthuli

Luthuli, A.M. (1898-1967)

LUTHULI, Chief Albert Myumbi (1898-1967).

SOUTH AFRICAN politician, a leading figure in the struggle for the independence of South Africa, he has the reputation of being the father of Black nationalism in his country. He was born in 1898 in Salisbury (now Harare), Zimbabwe, where his father was a preacher. The family returned to South Africa in 1908 where the young Luthuli entered the Mission school in his home town, Groutville. He later trained as a teacher at Adam's College in Natal, where his academic brilliance was rewarded with a bursary to Fort Hare University; however, he rejected this in order to work and earn money to support his family. He taught at Adam's College until 1936, when he was made Chief by his people, the Abasemaklolweni Zulu.

He entered politics in 1945 as a member of the African National Congress (ANC) and was elected the next year to the Native Representative Council. Rising quickly through the ranks of the ANC, of whose Natal branch he became President in 1951, Chief Luthuli threw his influence as traditional ruler behind the struggle against the apartheid government of South Africa. As a chief, his involvement in nationalist politics was objected to by the government; in 1952 the authorities asked him to choose between his chieftainship and the ANC. He opted for the struggle and was stripped of his chieftaincy by the government. In December of the same year he was elected President-General of the ANC, a role he continued to play, despite frequent imprisonment, until his death.

In November 1952 Chief Luthuli was served with a banning order for two years, renewed in 1954 after he had campaigned against a scheme which deprived Africans of their few remaining land rights. In 1956 he was arrested, along with 145 other leaders of ANC, on allegations of high treason; but he was released one year later with 66 others. In 1959 he was again placed under house arrest in his village and banned from all gatherings for a further period of five years. This order was extended in 1961 under the Suppression of Communism Act, which confined him to a smaller area of his home, banned him from receiving visitors, and forbade him to make statements or attend church services.

Chief Luthuli was not discouraged by these rigid restrictions. Rather, his resolution to fight for full political, economic and social rights for the oppressed Africans was not only strengthened but made him a national hero and brought international respect and support. At the early stage of the struggle before the ANC was proscribed, Chief Luthuli made two trips abroad to present the movement's case. In 1938 he attended the International Missionary Conference in Madras, India. In 1948 he went on a lecture tour of the United States under the auspices of American church organisations. The situation changed and became more difficult after the ANC was banned in South Africa in 1960, and its leaders were barred from travelling abroad.

On 26 March 1960, while his restriction order was suspended to enable him to travel to Johannesburg to testify at the continuing "treason trial", Chief Luthuli publicly burnt his pass as a protest against the massacres of hundreds of Africans on 21 March 1960 during a peaceful demonstration in Sharpeville. He called on South Africans to observe a national day of mourning on 28 March in honour of the Sharpeville victims, to which the government replied on 29 March with his detention, along with 2,000 others, for five months under the State of Emergency declared on 30 March 1960.

Chief Luthuli was awarded the Nobel Peace Prize in 1960, and after mounting pressures from the local and international community the government permitted him to travel to Norway to receive it. He was not allowed to visit any other country whilst outside South Africa. He regarded the award as "a recognition of the sacrifices made by the people of all races in South Africa, particularly the African people who have endured and suffered so much for so long". In 1962 he was elected Rector of the University of Glasgow, but was not allowed to travel to Britain for the installation ceremony. His autobiography, *Let My People Go*, published the same year, further enhanced his reputation, both for what it said and its scholarly approach which gave Luthuli the added credential of a man of letters. Chief Luthuli died on 21 July 1967, while still under a restriction order. The white authorities claimed he was hit by a train while crossing a railway line in the area to which he was confined, but many South Africans believe he was murdered by the South African apartheid regime. ■

Luwum, J.K. (1924-77)

LUWUM, Most Reverend Janani Jakaliya (1924-77).

UGANDAN clergyman, he was one of the most influential leaders of the modern church in Africa. Born in Uganda in 1924, he joined the Anglican Church in Uganda and became a deacon in 1955. The following year he was ordained a priest and between 1956 and 1961 he worked in the Upper Nile Diocese. In 1961 he became priest of the Diocese of Mbale. Four years later he was appointed examining Chaplain under the Bishop of Mbale.

On 25 January 1969, he was consecrated Bishop of Northern Uganda at Gulu. After five years he was appointed the Archbishop of the Metropolitan Province of Uganda, Rwanda, Burundi and Boga-Zaire, the second African to hold this position.

Archbishop Luwum was a leading voice in criticising the excesses of the Idi Amin regime that assumed power in 1971. In December 1976, in a broadcast Christmas sermon, he attacked the regime, making reference to Christian victory achieved through suffering; the broadcast was abruptly taken off the air. As a further protest against the harassment of Christians in Uganda, the Archbishop threatened to lead a march through Kampala to petition President Amin.

On 5 February 1977, security forces raided Luwum's home. In response Luwum and 17 other Anglican bishops in Uganda sent an open letter to the President with copies sent to government ministers, other church leaders and the All-Africa Conference of Churches in Nairobi. This letter protested about the security forces' treatment of the Archbishop, and also accused the government of abusing its power, adding, "we have buried many who have died as a result of being shot and there are many more whose bodies have not been found. . the gun which was meant to protect Uganda as a nation, the Ugandan citizen and his property, is increasingly being used against the Ugandan to take away his life and his property!" This was the first time any members of the church had publicly criticised the military regime so strongly.

Shortly afterwards, on 14 February, Amin publicised his "knowledge" of a "conspiracy" against the state in which Luwum was alleged to have been involved. Luwum and his wife were interviewed by Amin in the presidential palace near Lake Victoria, and after denying any involvement in a plot to overthrow the government, Luwum was advised to concentrate solely on his religious functions.

Two days later the Archbishop and other leading churchmen were invited to a large rally in Kampala. During the ceremonies, confessions were read out by three other alleged conspirators and Luwum was named as one of those involved, as well as accused of being a key figure in smuggling arms into the country in preparation for a coup against Amin. Luwum firmly denied these allegations but later in the day he was arrested along with two government ministers. On the same day, 16 February 1977, he died at the age of 52, leaving a widow and five children.

Archbishop J.K. Luwum

According to the government, he was killed in a car crash while on the way for interrogation. He had apparently tried to overpower the driver with the help of the two ministers arrested with him, and this had caused the fatal collision. However, other sources have said that the damage to the car did not correspond to the official version of the accident and that Luwum was shot dead by the security forces. His body was buried secretly and there was no inquest. ∎

M

Mabathoana, E.G. (1904-66)

MABATHOANA, Most Reverend Emmanuel Gregory (1904-66).

LESOTHO linguist and clergyman who, on being consecrated the first Archbishop of Maseru and Metropolitan of Basutoland in 1961, became the first African head of the Catholic Church in the Southern African region. Archbishop Mabathoana was also the first African to serve on the executive of the Southern African Bishops' Conference.

Archbishop E.G. Mabathoana

A great grandson of King Moshoeshoe I (q.v.), the founder of the Basotho nation which later developed to become modern Lesotho, Mabathoana was born on 29 December 1904 in Mokhokhong in Roma, Lesotho. After primary education in Marist Mission institutions he entered St. Joseph's Training College, also in Roma, before going into the St. Teresa Seminary in 1924. In 1932 he made his oblate novitiate, and in June 1933 he was ordained, becoming the first Mosotho oblate priest and the second Mosotho to enter into priesthood, after the Reverend Raphael Mohasi.

He taught at the Roma Minor, later at the Major, Seminary where he spent a considerable number of years. He later went to teach African languages at the Pius XII Catholic University College in Roma, after having completed further studies in Rome, London and at the Villa Nova University in America. His lectureship at the Pius XII University College lasted for eight years.

On the creation of the diocese of Leribe in December 1952, Mabathoana was elected the first Bishop of the new Catholic diocese. His consecration, which took place on 25 March 1953, was performed at St. Monica's Mission in Maseru before an estimated crowd of 15,000 members of the Church and his countrymen. In January 1961 he was created the first Archbishop of Maseru and Metropolitan of Basutoland and was installed in April of that year. As Archbishop of the new Archdiocese, Mabathoana again became the first African South of the Zambezi to be elevated to such a position in the Catholic Church in the region. In June 1963, on the occasion of the centennial celebrations of the Catholic Church in Lesotho, Archbishop Mabathoana was conferred with the Commander of the Order of the British Empire (CBE) by the British Queen, Elizabeth II.

He was proficient in Latin, Greek, Italian and German but his reputation as a linguist derived from the extensive work he did on all the major southern African languages, which culminated in his translation of the Bible into Sotho. He also composed numerous hymns for the Catholic Sesotho Hymn Book. Earlier in 1956 he had served on the Basutoland Council which prepared the revised Southern Sotho Orthography. He travelled extensively within and outside his diocese, visiting numerous countries in Africa, Europe, Asia and the Americas on Church business. In 1963 he visited Rome as a member of the Board of the Commission on Missions during the Vatican Council of that year. His visit to Bombay in India in December 1964 was on the occasion of the Eucharistic Congress, where he preached on the Lay Apostolate.

Archbishop Mabathoana died on 19 September 1966, while travelling on a plane from Maseru to Pretoria where he was to attend a meeting of the Southern African Bishops' Conference.∎

Mabhida, M. (1924-86)

MABHIDA, Moses (1924-86).

SOUTH AFRICAN political leader, former secretary-general of the South African Communist Party (SACP) of which he was a member for over 40 years. For the last 25 years of his life he lived in exile, rallying international opinion and organizing international mobilization for the African National Congress (ANC). At his death on 8 March 1986 the South African Communist Party said: "The SACP dips its revolutionary banner in solemn tribute to a great freedom fighter whose life and work are an example and inspiration to all his comrades and to all who love peace and social progress."

Born in 1923 in Natal, he was nineteen when he joined the South African Communist Party. A Durban trade union leader, Mabhida was secretary of the Natal South African Congress of Trade Unions (SACTU) in the late 1950s. Meanwhile, the SACP had gone underground following the South African Suppression of Communism Act of 1950. Mabhida's involvement in trade unionism

and the communist movement was intense and he often participated in political activities directed at the apartheid government.

He was very much involved in the preparations for the historic Congress of the People in 1955 where the Freedom Charter

M. Mabhida

was adopted. SACTU was formed in 1955 and Mabhida took part in its first congress (Johannesburg, March 1955); he was elected one of the four vice-presidents. After the Sharpeville shootings of 1960 – by which time Mabhida was acting President of the Natal ANC as well as elected chairman of SACTU – there was a state of emergency and the leadership of SACTU was banned; the organisation went underground and Mabhida went into exile. In those five years, however, he had played a key part in building up the trade union movement in Natal and was prominent in the political campaigns of the time.

In exile, as a member of the national executive committee of the ANC, which he had become by 1960, he was appointed political commissar for ANC's armed wing, *Umkonto we Sizwe*, and from 1963 worked full time for it, helping to co-ordinate the ANC's military strategy. He also presented the case of the Black South African unions to the International Labour Organization (ILO) and for some time he worked as SACTU's representative at the World Federation of Trade Unions. He became SACP's secretary-general in 1981.

Mabhida had the reputation of being highly committed and his work contributed enormously to the establishment of the international campaign against apartheid in South Africa. He died of a heart attack in Maputo, having been ill since he suffered a stroke in 1985, and was buried on 29 March 1986. ■

Macaulay, H.S.H. (1864-1946)

MACAULAY, Herbert Samuel Heelas (1864-1946).

Herbert Macaulay

NIGERIAN surveyor and politician, the leader of Nigeria's first political party who is remembered for his very prominent role in the early days of his country's nationalist movement. He was born in Lagos on 14 November 1864, the grandson of the first African Bishop in West Africa and the child of the first principal of the first Grammar School in Nigeria. He attended the Lagos Grammar School and became the first Nigerian to be sponsored by the colonial government for a professional course abroad when he won a scholarship to study land surveying and civil engineering at Plymouth, England, in 1890.

Returning to Nigeria in 1893, Macaulay joined the colonial civil service as government surveyor in charge of Crown Grants, a function which not only introduced him to the land situation in Lagos but also gave him an insight into the injustices of the colonial administration. Originally an ardent empire loyalist – in 1887, he masterminded the celebration of Queen Victoria's Golden Jubilee in Lagos – he continued to serve the government until he became disenchanted with its racist policies. Macaulay's first personal experience of colonial injustice was when as surveyor he was given a salary of £120 per annum, as compared with £250 being paid to his British colleagues. This, and a succession of events of broader nation-

al importance, led to his resignation from the service in 1899 and to his setting up private practice in Lagos. Thus also commenced his campaign against discrimination and colonial rule, which stirred many Nigerians into nationalist consciousness.

In 1912 Macaulay led a delegation to protest against the government's decision to place lands in the Northern Provinces of Nigeria "under the control of the Governor who shall hold and administer them for the use and common benefit of the natives" and to do likewise in the Southern Provinces. Failing to gain a favourable response from the Lagos government, he decided to visit London to lobby the Colonial Office, but this plan was foiled by his arrest for an alleged misappropriation of public funds. He was subsequently tried and imprisoned.

The next confrontation with the government centred on the celebrated case of Chief Amodu Oluwa, a titular head of a Lagos family whose land had been acquired by the government in return for inadequate compensation. After an unsuccessful fight in the Nigerian courts, the Chief, with Macaulay as Secretary, visited London in 1920 to lodge an appeal before the Privy Council who ruled in their favour; the Lagos colonial authority was ordered to pay Chief Oluwa the sum of £22,500 in contrast to £500, which had given rise to the appeal.

This verdict gladdened Nigerians but infuriated the colonial government whose immediate response was to deport the Oba (Eleko) of Lagos to Oyo for having lent his support to Chief Oluwa's claim. Macaulay's perception of the political implications of the deposition led to the formation of the Ilu Committee of prominent Lagos citizens to oppose the deportation order. In 1922, Macaulay founded the Nigerian National Democratic Party (NNDP), Nigeria's first political party of which he was General Secretary. The Ilu Committee and the NNDP teamed up and fought successfully for the restoration of the Oba in 1931, after a period of eleven years.

This marked a turning point in Nigerian politics, with Macaulay leading subsequent campaigns against discrimination and for self-government. His NNDP won all three seats for Lagos in the elections to the Legislative Council in 1923, 1938, 1943 and 1948. When Dr. Nnamdi Azikiwe formed the National Council for Nigeria and the Cameroons (NCNC) in 1944 to accelerate the process towards the country's independence, Macaulay was made its first national President. It was in the course of leading the party in a nationwide campaign tour in 1946 that he was taken ill and died in Kano on 7 May 1946.■

Macaulay, T.B. (1826-78)

MACAULAY, Reverend Thomas Babington (1826-78).

NIGERIAN churchman, remembered notably as the founder and first principal of the historic Church Missionary Society (CMS) Grammar School in Lagos. He was one of the many distinguished people born in Sierra Leone, of "Recaptive" parents, originally from what is now Nigeria, who later went to live in their parents' country of origin. In some cases the recaptives themselves, i.e. people freed from slave ships and settled in Freetown, such as Bishop Samuel Ajayi Crowther (q.v.) went back to settle in the land from which they had been captured. Macaulay was the eldest of the three sons of Ojo Oriare, a Recaptive originating from Ore

Aganju in Ikirun district, and Kilangbe, from Oyo, a granddaughter of the founder of the Ile-Ogo. They lived at Kissy in the Sierra Leone Colony, where the father was named "Daddy Ojo", after being enslaved, rescued, resettled, and married. Thomas Macaulay was, like very many children of Recaptives, brought up by the CMS.

He attended the Fourah Bay Institution, then run by the CMS, and was then sent to the Church Missionary College run by the Society in Islington, London, where Crowther had been a few years before. This was under a CMS scheme started in 1845 for technical training for West Africans, which included training partly in Britain. T. B. Macaulay returned to Sierra Leone, and worked as a tutor at the CMS Grammar School from 1849 to 1851. Then, while not yet in orders, he was put in charge of the Anglican Mission's pastoral work at Regent, one of the Recaptives' villages just outside Freetown proper.

In 1852 he was transferred to the "Yoruba Mission" which the CMS ran with many Sierra Leonean clergymen and other assistants, including Crowther who was Bishop of Western Equatorial Africa in 1864. The mission was based mainly at Abeokuta, where missionary work had started in 1845. Macaulay was sent there and put in charge of the Christian Institution, a school set up for industrial and other practical training in particular.

In 1854 he was ordained. Then he married Abigail Crowther, the second daughter of Rev. Samuel Crowther. Their children included the famous politician Herbert Macaulay (q.v.), renowned in Nigeria for his strong opposition to British rule.

Rev. Macaulay ran the CMS' Mission stations at Igbein and at Owu, both in Abeokuta. Then, in 1859, he founded the new CMS Grammar School in Lagos. This was in response to a growing need for secondary schooling for the children of Christians; the Sierra Leone-born (Saro) community in Lagos gave its full support to its establishment. In 1867 a fund for a new building was launched, on the initiative of J. P. L. Davies (q.v.).

The school, where Nathaniel Johnson (brother of Samuel Johnson (q.v.)), went to help Macaulay as tutor in 1870, had 28 pupils at that time. In the years following the number varied between 25 and 40. Later it was to increase greatly as the Grammar

School became one of Nigeria's leading secondary schools. Its founder, T. B. Macaulay, was also noted for his contributions to the translation of the Bible into Yoruba. He died an early death on 17 January 1878, in a smallpox epidemic. ■

Machel, J. (1945-71)

MACHEL, Josina (1945-71).

MOZAMBICAN politician and prominent member of the movement that led to her country's independence. She was born on 10 April 1945, in the Inhambane province in the south-east of Mozambique. Most members of her family were active in the struggle for independence. Her father was arrested in 1965 and imprisoned for political

J. Machel

activities while her uncle, Mateus Sausoio, who was a member of the Central Committee of FRELIMO, was killed in 1968.

After primary education she went to Lourenço Marques (now Maputo) in 1956 to pursue a four-year course in secretarial studies but soon abandoned this in favour of the nationalist politics aimed at winning independence from Portuguese colonialism. She was very involved in the clandestine movement that was developing while overt political activities were forbidden and, with the formation of FRELIMO, became a member and organiser of an underground cell.

She attempted to leave the country in early 1964, but was intercepted at Victoria Falls by the Rhodesian security forces who handed her over to the Portuguese political police (PIDE). She was detained in Lourenço Marques and released in August 1964 as a result of an international campaign against Portuguese repression. Josina succeeded in escaping to Tanzania in May 1965 where she had military training.

In August 1965 she was appointed organiser of political education in the liberated province of Niassa. She was a delegate to the second congress of FRELIMO in 1968, after which she became an official of the newly created Women's Department with responsibility for social affairs. In May 1969, Josina married Samora Machel, who was then leader of FRELIMO and who later became the first President of independent Mozambique.

Josina Machel participated in the September 1970 second conference of the Department of Education and Culture where it was decided to expand the scope of the Women's Department. In December 1970 she organised a programme for the orphans of the armed struggle against the Portuguese forces. At that time she herself was beginning to suffer from poor health, but carried on to participate in the second conference of the Defence Department of FRELIMO held in February 1971. She was taken ill soon after the conference and was hospitalised in Dar-es-Salaam, where she died on 7 April 1971.

Josina Machel's life has become a symbol of women's contribution to the political and armed struggle for Mozambique's independence. The date of her death, 7 April, is now commemorated each year as Women's Day in independent Mozambique. ■

Machel, S. M. (1933-86)

MACHEL, Samora Moises (1933-86).

MOZAMBICAN nationalist, statesman, leader of the National Liberation Movement, *Frente de Libertação de Moçambique* (FRELIMO), which won independence for his country and first President of the People's Republic of Mozambique. A charismatic figure, Samora Moises Machel was renowned for his ability to communicate with the people, his military skills and his commitment to the eradication of colonialism from Africa and the socialist transformation of Mozambique. Throughout his remarkable career Machel was a severe critic of all forms of corruption and misuse of power.

Machel was born on 29 September 1933 at Chilembene in Mozambique's south-western province of Gaza. His parents were peasant farmers, and the family had a long tradition of resistance to colonialism. He had his early education at local schools run by the Catholic Church, although he came from a Protestant family background. Having completed his primary education, he refused the offer by Catholic missionaries to continue his studies in a minor seminary, and decided to go to work, finishing his secondary education through private study. He trained as a male nurse and worked for some time at the Central Hospital in Maputo (then Lourenço Marques).

His political career began in earnest when FRELIMO was founded on 25 June 1962, under the leadership of the late Eduardo Mondlane (q.v.). Samora Machel immediately joined it. In 1963, he went into exile to Tanzania from where he proceeded to Algeria to undergo military training. He was among the first group of Mozambican combatants to be trained militarily.

He returned to Tanzania and played an active part, at Kongwa, in the preparation for guerrilla warfare against Portuguese colonialism. The armed struggle was launched on 25 September 1964 when FRELIMO forces attacked several colonial posts in northern Mozambique.

Machel organised the opening of a new front in the eastern part of Niassa Province in 1965. Thereafter, he was put in charge of the establishment of FRELIMO's main rear base, the Centre for Political and Military Training at Nachingwea in Southern Tanzania. He assumed the overall command of FRELIMO's fighting forces in 1966 upon the death of Filipe Magaia who had been the commander. Under his leadership, the Mozambique People's Liberation Force (FPLM), as FRELIMO's armed forces movement came to be known, rapidly grew in size and enlarged its area of operations.

When FRELIMO's first president, Eduardo Mondlane (q.v.), was assassinated in February 1969, Machel was elected one of the three members of the Presidential Council formed then; he was the Secretary for Defence. This triumvirate was dissolved in May 1970 and Samora Machel was elected President *ad interim* by FRELIMO's Central Committee. It was at FRELIMO's Third Congress in February 1977 that he was unanimously endorsed as President of the FRELIMO Party, a position to which he was re-elected at the Fourth Congress in April 1983. Under the Constitution, the elected President of the FRELIMO Party becomes the Head of State and is also Commander-in-Chief of the Mozambican Armed Forces.

After the collapse of the fascist regime in Portugal in 1974, Samora Machel led the FRELIMO delegation in the talks with the

S. Machel

new Portuguese government in Lusaka. These negotiations laid the basis and established the framework for Mozambique's accession to independence on 25 June 1975. Samora Machel was elected President of the People's Republic by the Seventh Session of FRELIMO's Central Committee. In September 1975, Machel married Graça Machel, Mozambique's Minister of Education and Culture with whom he had two children; he had been married before to Josina Machel (q.v.) who died in 1971.

As President of Mozambique, Machel's major task was to revive the country's economy which had been brought nearly to its knees by the mass exodus of Portuguese farmers, manufacturers and technicians during the period of transition to independence. It was in this context that the "dynamising groups" (*grupos dinamizadores* – GDs) were set up in workplaces, urban neighbourhoods, and villages in late 1974 and they took over the functions of the Portuguese administration, serving as local councils, police and courts, as well as the management in business, and acting as an organ of popular democracy on independence.

The GDs were undoubtedly successful in limiting sabotage, in politicising people and in boosting the administration. But they always remained *ad hoc* committees, and during the following five years they were slowly replaced by more conventional bodies.

Its experience in the liberation struggle led FRELIMO to put the stress on services, because under colonialism peasants and urban workers had been badly discriminated against. So in July 1975, just a month after independence, law, medicine, education, and funeral services were all nationalised. There were to be no private lawyers and no separate ethnic or customary law; similarly there would be no private or mission education and health services. Banks, insurance, the strategic refinery in Maputo and land and rented property were also nationalised.

Great stress was put on expanding health and education and providing at least minimal services in rural areas. A major literacy and numeracy programme was launched. The main stress was put on primary education, and the number of primary school pupils jumped from 671,000 in 1975 to 1,495,000 in 1979.

Similarly, FRELIMO stressed primary health care; a basic training for large numbers of health workers was started and by 1982 more than 4,000 had been trained, of whom over a 100 were doctors. At the same time, the number of rural health posts increased from 326 in 1975 to 1,130 in 1984.

Under Machel's radical government, other policies such as "socialisation of the countryside" which believed that "state-owned enterprises are the quickest means of responding to the country's food requirements", were adopted.

In 1977 FRELIMO held its third Congress, where it was agreed to transform the movement to a "Marxist-Leninist Vanguard Party". Those who had been in FRELIMO during the armed struggle automatically became members of the new party. Machel had always encouraged the people to participate in the "governing" of the country, though Mozambique is a one-party state. New candidates were chosen in a unique way; anyone could be put forward for membership, but they had to be approved at mass meetings and at workplaces. Only the most "exemplary" were to be selected, and people at the meetings discussed the candidates' attitudes and conduct towards workmates, as well as their home life. Literacy and knowledge of Marxism-Leninism were no criteria.

Despite these changes, Machel's task was still a very difficult one. The shortage of skilled manpower and of finance and the war of liberation going on at the time in the then Rhodesia, to which he gave his wholehearted support, were real impediments to the country's dream of "victory over underdevelopment".

Nevertheless, when the United Nations called for economic sanctions against the White minority regime of Prime Minister Ian Smith in Rhodesia, Machel did not hesitate to close Mozambique's border with Rhodesia in March 1976 even though his country did lose, as a result, millions of dollars in foreign exchange from the disuse of Beira port and the Beira-Umtali railway on which most of Rhodesia's exports and imports were transported. His commitment to the wars of liberation did not allow him to look back. And when Zimbabwean nationalists sought the protection of Mozambique as a rear-base in their guerrilla war against the Smith regime, Machel proved a staunch ally, thereby exposing his country to many risks and infrastructural destruction. Mozambique itself at the same time was torn by civil war and the rebel Mozambique National Resistance (MNR) was supported by the Smith regime in its attempts to destabilise the Mozambican state.

A ten-year development plan (1981-1990) was launched and Mozambique set about earnestly building up its economy when Rhodesia became independent Zimbabwe in 1980. That same year Mozambique joined with Zimbabwe and the seven other majority-ruled states of the region to form SADCC, the Southern African Development Coordination Council, whose goal was to increase economic development within the region by reducing economic dependence on South Africa and increasing economic cooperation on a planned basis within the nine. But a series of crises began to loom which prevented the execution of the plan. Foreign exchange shortages were exacerbated by the oil price rise and the costs of the Rhodesia war. Then in 1982 and 1983 Mozambique and the rest of southern Africa were hit by the worst drought of the century.

Moreover, the financing and logistical leadership of the MNR passed on to South Africa's White minority regime in retaliation for the granting of facilities to African National Congress (ANC) fighters by Mozambique. However, the pressure of the years of war made Machel's government agree to suspend support for the fighters operating from each other's territory. So, the Nkomati non-aggression treaty was signed with his country's implacable enemy, the South African regime, in March 1984. The treaty was decried by most of Africa as an unfortunate move by the Mozambican leader.

Members of the ANC were expelled from Maputo and the government in Pretoria promised to end its support for the MNR. But after a brief lull, the war in Mozambique continued, Pretoria alleged that ANC freedom fighters were still being given facilities in Mozambique before crossing into South Africa to plant land mines while Samora Machel accused South Africa of infiltrating commandos into the south of Mozambique to help the MNR destabilise the country. The failure of this compromise convinced Machel of the need to take an unswerving stand against Pretoria and its apartheid policies. With increased pressure for international mandatory economic sanctions against South Africa of which he became an outspoken exponent, he closed ranks with the other Frontline States' leaders. The sanctions crusade and a stepped-up freedom campaign by the ANC in South Africa, especially along the border with Mozambique, singled out Machel for more accusations of aiding the freedom fighters by Pretoria.

Machel was killed in an aircraft crash on South African soil on 19 October 1986 on his way back to Mozambique from a Frontline States' leaders summit meeting in Zambia. Two weeks before, the South African Defence Minister, General Magnus Malan, had issued threats against Mozambique and its leadership. It was against this background of tension between the two neighbouring countries that Machel's sudden death took place, robbing Mozambique of a leader who had devoted his whole life to trying to establish security and restore economic order in his motherland. ∎

Macias Nguema, F. (1922-79)

MACIAS NGUEMA, Francisco (1922-79).

EQUATORIAL GUINEAN statesman, his country's first President. He was born in 1922 in Nsegayong village in Rio Muni where he attended local Catholic Mission schools. He commenced a civil service career at the age of 22, in the Spanish colonial administration as an orderly with the Department of Forest Service and Public Works in Bata. After passing the examinations that eventually made him an "emancipated" African, in line with the policy of *emancipado* of the colonial regime, he was promoted to senior administrator, a post which he held from 1964 to 1969. A year after his promotion, he became a member of the militant *Idea Popular de la Guinea Ecuatorial* (IPGE) formed in 1960. Nguema rose through the ranks of the IPGE to become leader of Equatorial Guinea's first political party.

Changes in the colonial constitution in 1963 brought him into the government when, as a member of the eight-man governing council instituted in the wake of self-rule, he was elected Vice-President of the country in 1964. Bonifacio Ondo Edu (q.v.), leader of the pro-Spanish *Movimiento de Unión Nacional de la Guinea Ecuatorial*

(MUNGE), was made President. Their alliance was short-lived, for the parties' ideological differences, fuelled by conflicting personal interests, brought increased hostility by early 1968, resulting in the suspension of the Constitution which had brought internal autonomy.

The subsequent August 1968 referendum favoured total independence from Spain. In the 29 September 1968 elections, Nguema was elected President. On 12 October 1968, when independence was formally proclaimed, President Nguema formed a coalition government, consisting of the three main parties including the *Movimiento Nacional de Liberación de la Guinea Ecuatorial* (MONALIGE) formed in 1964 by Atanasio Ndongo (q.v.) who was appointed Foreign Minister. Macias Nguema kept the additional portfolio of Defence.

But stability eluded the country, for only a few months after independence the rivalry between the groups escalated and culminated in the killing of Foreign Minister Ndongo in March 1969 for allegedly plotting to overthrow Nguema. Meanwhile, President Nguema called on the Spanish government to withdraw its troops from Equatorial Guinea. The Spanish resisted this call and riots followed. Believing that members of the Spanish business community instigated the riots he ordered the expulsion of several of them and by April 1969 most of the 7,000 Spanish residents and all the troops had left the country. The cumulative effect of this was a crippling shortage of trained personnel which, in the immediate years following the expulsion, brought the economy on the verge of collapse. Relations between Equatorial Guinea and its former colonial master became strained.

On 2 February 1970 he merged all the political parties into the *Partido Unico Nacional* (PUN), later named *Partido Unico Nacional de los Trabajadores* (PUNT), making Equatorial Guinea a one-party state. On 14 July 1972 President Nguema was made Life President, following which he promulgated a new Constitution in July 1973. This brought fundamental changes in the country: the country's currency was given a new name, *ekpwele*, in place of the peseta; the island of Fernando Po, apart from having its name changed to Macias Nguema Biyogo after the President, had its autonomous status which it had enjoyed under the 1968 Constitution abolished.

Rio Benito was changed to Mbini and Santa Carlos to Luba. This indigenisation of names and titles was taken further later in 1976 when Nguema decreed that all non-national names of Equatorial Guinean citizens should be changed within six months. Penalty for non-compliance, the presidential decree warned, was a fine of between 100,000 and one million *ekpwele*.

Ensuing years were characterised by rumours of attempted coups and reports of killings of people either suspected of or convicted for engaging in anti-government activities. Prominent on this list were the former Vice-President, Miguel Eyegue (q.v.), who was killed in 1975. By August 1974 Equatorial Guinean opponents of the regime who had fled the country and formed the National Alliance for the Restoration of Democracy (NARD) put the number of leading personalities killed since 1969 on the President's orders at 93.

Forced labour became government policy in 1976 as part of a desperate effort to boost cocoa production which had slumped from its pre-independence rate of 50,000 tons to 7,000, especially after the evacuation of some 20,000 Nigerian workers by their

F. Macias Nguema

government in the wake of the severe ill-treatment and the killing of 11 Nigerians by Equatorial Guinean soldiers in January 1976. A presidential decree of March 1976 compelled all able-bodied citizens over the age of 15 to render part of their labour on the farms. The policy of coercion and forced labour caused many Guineans to flee the country.

Meanwhile internal and external opposition to the regime escalated, culminating in the October 1976 coup attempt. Externally, the exiled political opponents, operating under NARD, led a delegation to Paris in 1976 to "alert French public opinion to the terrible repression now raging throughout Equatorial Guinea". They stated that a quarter of Equatorial Guinea's population was living in exile. In an earlier plea to the EEC, NARD had urged the community to "exclude the bloody police regime" of President Macias Nguema from the benefits of the Lomé Convention signed by members of the EEC and African, Caribbean and Pacific (ACP) countries. Spain, the former colonial authority, which had contributed a substantial quota of aid to the country, responded to the plea by reducing its economic involvement. In March 1977 the Spanish ambassador to Equatorial Guinea was recalled.

But despite these external pressures Nguema remained in office until 3 August 1979 when he was ousted in a military coup by his nephew Teodoro Obiang Nguema Mbasogo. Nguema was arrested by the new regime and charged with bringing the country "under a state of total anarchy, terror, assassinations, maladministration, misery, systematic and persistent violation of the fundamental rights of Guinean and foreign citizens and oppression of all kinds – economic, social, cultural and religious". He was found guilty, sentenced to death by firing squad, and shot on 1 October 1979. ∎

Mahabane, Z.R. (1881-1970)

MAHABANE, Reverend Zaccheus Richard (1881-1970).

SOUTH AFRICAN clergyman and politician; he was twice President of the African National Congress (ANC). Of Sotho

origin, his father being a Sotho from Basutoland, he was born in 1881 in the Barolong "reserve" at Thaba Nchu in the Orange Free State, South Africa. After elementary education at a local Methodist Mission school he went to Morija in Basutoland (now Lesotho)

Rev. Z. R. Mahabane

for post-primary education and, at the age of twenty, qualified as a teacher at the Morija Mission Institute where he was a contemporary of Don Davidson Tengo Jabavu (q.v.), another prominent South African political leader and educationist.

After a stint as a teacher and later interpreter, Mahabane began training for priesthood at the Healdtown Methodist Institution in the Cape, and was ordained in 1914. His first appointment as minister was in 1916 in the Cape Town African township where some African politicians had been active. The political leader and a founder of the Wilberforce African Methodist Episcopal Church, Charlotte M. M. Maxeke (q.v.), and her husband were active here during Mahabane's posting and Maxeke's political dynamism left a deep impression on the young cleric. In 1916 Mahabane joined the Cape branch of the African National Congress and two years later became the branch President.

Though a man of great energy and determination, Mahabane was a gradualist in his earlier approach to politics, encouraged by a deep belief in Christian morality whose rejection by the white supremacy regime forced him, and indeed the entire African population, steadily towards radicalism. By 1920 Reverend Mahabane was telling the annual conference of the ANC that the South African whites had rejected the Christian doctrine of universal brotherhood and in its place adopted a new creed: "God Our Father, Whiteman our Brother and the Blackman an Outcast". Four years later he was to succeed Sefako Mapogo Makgatho (q.v.) to the presidency of the ANC and directed its campaign until 1927 when he lost the post to Josiah Tshangana Gumede (q.v.).

In 1937 Reverend Mahabane was re-elected President of the ANC and held the position for three years. In the period following his defeat in the 1940 elections to the leadership of the ANC he turned to clerical duties for the organisation as chaplain. Between 1937 and 1954 he served as President of the All-African Convention whose several deputations to the government he was part of. He worked at effecting unity between South African non-whites and also devoted a great time to the activities of the Inter-denominational African Ministers Association of which he was president for several years. He died at his Kroonstad home, South Africa, in 1970.■

Maharero (c. 1820-90)

MAHARERO, Chief (c.1820-90).

NAMIBIAN traditional ruler who was responsible for the consolidation of the Herero kingdom, now in central Namibia. A powerful and successful leader, popularly known and called "Kamaharero" by his people, he led the Hereros in the Nama-Herero wars. These disputes arose over control of the grazing land in central/southern Namibia. He freed the Hereros from the political domination of their former Nama overlords, and through doing so, strength-

Chief Maharero

ened his position as an effective paramount chief, moulding the previously disparate Herero communities into a more homogenous and cohesive group.

Severe drought in 1830 brought the Hereros and their herds of cattle south from the central plateau in search of grazing land. The Namas feared that their pastures were being encroached upon, and what ensued was a period of endemic warfare between the Namas and the Hereros and the Damaras who also lived in the central area. The Namas used their monopoly of firearms and horses, acquired through trade with European settlers from the south and the Cape, to establish effective control of the area, extending north as far as Okahandja.

By the 1840s European traders and missionaries were penetrating Namibia, seeking to secure their interests by playing off local leaders against each other. The pressure of the traders turned the intermittent fighting between Namas and Hereros into long years of warfare.

As a young man in the 1840s, Maharero accompanied his father Tjamahua to

Otjomuise (Windhoek) where he was exposed to wider influences and experiences and witnessed the Namas' skilled use of horses and firearms. When his father died in 1859, Maharero became ruler of one of the many Herero communities. He was committed to resisting Nama domination, and in 1863 he launched a protracted armed campaign for Herero independence, which was to last for seven years. The Nama leader, Jonker Afrikaner, was a personal friend whom he had come to know in Otjomuise. Thus, despite their bitter battles, when a truce was declared in 1870, after Nama control had been broken by Maharero, he leased Otjomuise to Jonker Afrikaner. Maharero himself then stood as the single most powerful figure between the Orange and Cunene rivers.

In the latter years of his reign Namibia was increasingly prey to European expansion and settlement. Persistent rumbling disputes between Namas and Hereros brought in the Europeans on one side or the other. Maharero asked the British administration in Cape Town for help in dealing with the European traders and settlers, but the response was merely to send out a resident magistrate.

In his efforts to co-exist with the increasingly large European community, Maharero signed a treaty of protection with the Germans in 1885, who had established their presence in Namibia the preceding year, in 1884. However, he remained unhappy with this situation, changing his mind about the treaty because he saw no real benefit to his people from it, but realising also the overwhelming strength of the Germans and their increasing colonial entrenchment in Namibia.

He died in 1890 and was succeeded by his son, Samuel Maharero (q.v.).■

Maharero, S. (c. 1854-1923)

MAHARERO, Chief Samuel (c.1854-1923).

NAMIBIAN chief of the Hereros, anti-colonial fighter. He succeeded his father, Maharero (q.v.), in 1890. During the early period of his reign he attempted rapprochement with the German colonial authorities in South West Africa (Namibia). However, as German rule became more entrenched and more brutal and unbearable, he changed his position, and eventually led the Herero people in the bitter war of resistance against German rule from 1904 until 1907.

On his father's death there was a dispute over the succession. Among the Chief's Council, made up of prominent Herero local leaders, were people who felt that they were more qualified than Samuel Maharero to take the role of overall leader of the Herero people. However, Samuel's mother played a significant part in ensuring her son's accession.

Samuel Maharero used the German patronage afforded by the treaty of protection, signed between his father and the German colonial authorities, to consolidate his position and to move against those who had opposed him. The Germans, however, then used him, promoting him as paramount chief while trying to gain greater control over central Namibia. This further alienated Samuel Maharero from the local Herero leaders, especially Nicodemus and Kahimemua.

The increasing threat to the survival of Namibian communities posed by German

Chief S. Maharero

rule, its land expropriations, forced labour system and repressive colonial legislations, finally led to the outbreak of organised armed resistance. On 12 January 1904 Samuel Maharero launched an attack against the colonial forces, which marked the beginning of the war of resistance. The day before the launching of the struggle against the Germans, Samuel Maharero sent a message to Hermanus van Wyk, leader of the Rehoboth community, and to Hendrik Witbooi (q.v.), chief of the Namas, calling for united action. He wrote: "It is my wish that we weak nations should rise up against the Germans. Either we destroy them or they will all live in our country. There is nothing else for it." He also requested Witbooi, although the two communities had for long been antagonistic to each other, to "Let us rather die together, and not as a result of ill-treatment, prison, or all the other ways."

Maharero's request for unity did not get to Witbooi, for van Wyk betrayed the letters to the Germans. Yet although Witbooi's forces did not join the Hereros from the beginning, they later entered the war. The Damaras also entered the war alongside the Hereros, and these combined forces together fought determinedly against the Germans, using both orthodox and guerrilla tactics. The Ovambo kings in the north also joined the uprising by attacking the German fort at Namutoni and giving asylum and aid to the Herero forces.

The German Imperial Command was reinforced in the face of these attacks. The new command was under General von Trotha, who issued the following "extermination order" in 1904: "Within the German boundaries, every Herero, whether found armed or unarmed, with or without cattle, will be shot – I shall not accept any more women and children. I shall drive them back to their people, otherwise I shall order shots to be fired at them. These are my words to the Herero people."

Retreating in the face of German military supremacy, Samuel Maharero and his people fled to British held Bechuanaland (now Botswana) and to safety, believing that a people are only defeated if their leader is captured. Thousands died, not only in battle but also from thirst and hunger, as they made their way across the Kalahari Desert to sanctuary. Almost eighty percent (60,000 out of 80,000) of the Herero population were thus massacred. By 1907, out of the entire population of the area under German control, 140,000 in 1904, sixty percent had lost their lives.

Samuel Maharero, and those who successfully crossed the Kalahari, settled in Botswana. Among the Herero commanders who survived and remained in Namibia was Hosea Kutako (q.v.), who played a major role in rallying together the survivors of the war and in liaising with Samuel Maharero in exile. In the absence of Samuel Maharero, Kutako became the leader of the Herero people, though still recognising the authority of the exiled ruler, and after his death in 1923, of his successor, his son Frederick. Maharero is revered in Namibia.∎

EL-Mahdi, Abd-el-Rahman (1885-1959)

EL-MAHDI, Abd-el-Rahman (1885-1959).

SUDANESE political leader. He was born in June 1885, a few days after the death of his father, Muhammad Ahmad el-Mahdi (q.v.), the famous religious leader of the nineteenth century. Abd-el-Rahman came into limelight during the British occupation of the Sudan. The Islamic state set up by the Mahdi had come to an end in November 1899 on the death of his successor el-Khalifa (q.v.) and two of Abd-el-Rahman's brothers at the battle of Umm Diwaykrat at the hands of the British.

After the collapse of the Mahdist state, in the defence of which, as a mere boy of thirteen, he had sustained a serious injury, Abd-el-Rahman embarked on a new strategy. He re-established mahdism on a new basis and persuaded his followers, the Ansar as they were called by his father, that the struggle was best pursued on moral grounds than by military resistance. He secured recognition for his group in return for co-operation with the British to suppress the pro-German revolt during the Second World War and was knighted by the British King, George V. His involvement in business made him quite wealthy and supplied the resources to finance and administer his religious and political organisations. Under his administration the Ansar became a political as well as a religious force.

Abd-el-Rahman travelled to England

Abd-el-Rahman El-Mahdi

ners, Abd-el-Rahman concealed a firmness and an astuteness which were the secret of his success. ■

El-Mahdi, H.A. (1915-70)

El-MAHDI, Hadi Abd-el-Rahman (1915-70).

SUDANESE religious leader. He was born in the Sudan in 1915, the grandson of the great nineteenth century Mahdi Muhammad Ahmad. His father, Abd-el-Rahman el-Mahdi (q.v.), reactivated the Ansar movement in modern Sudan. El-Mahdi was educated in the Islamic tradition that prepared him for his future role as Imam of the Ansar, which he became in 1961 when he succeeded his nephew Siddick el-Mahdi (q.v.).

Early in his headship of the movement the Imam had a passing interest in politics, but as head of the powerful Ansar successive Sudan governments sought his support and patronage. The movement supported the Umma (Community) Party which in the 1950s advocated a separate, independent Sudan, and el-Mahdi was made an ex-officio patron of the party after his succession as the

in 1946 to pursue Sudanese opposition to the draft clause about Sudan in the Anglo-Egyptian treaty and was able to argue Sudan's case during his meetings with the British prime minister and foreign secretary. His politico-religious views were opposed by more orthodox Muslims under the leadership of Ali Ibn Mirghani (q.v.). On the eve of independence, they campaigned against the bid of his supporters to make him king of Sudan, preferring King Farouk of Egypt (q.v.) as a token monarch to him.

Abd-el-Rahman remained politically active throughout this time. Faithful to his father's legacy, he stood firmly for independence from Egypt as well as from Britain. He founded Sudan's first political paper and gave the Umma party, on its foundation in 1945, his patronage and support. The "Umma", which is an Arabic word meaning community or nation, advocated a separate and independent Sudan and under Abd-el-Rahman's leadership, spearheaded the demand for self-determination and self-government for Sudan. Its first secretary-general, Abdallah Khalil, became the second prime minister of the Sudan which regained her independence in 1956.

Abd-el-Rahman died in 1959, leaving behind a political party which was to remain a powerful force in the Sudan. Behind a cultured, gentle bearing and pleasant man-

Hadi El-Mahdi

spiritual leader of the Ansar. In later years however he became active in the leadership of the Umma Party when a clash between him and Siddick el-Mahdi who was head of the party caused a split in the 1960s. The Siddick section of the party was advocating a more active modernisation policy while the Imam and his followers took a traditionalist line. They reconciled early enough for the Umma party to team up again with the National Unionist Party (NUP) in a coalition government.

In May 1969 the government was overthrown in a military coup d'état that brought Colonel (later General) Gaafar Mohammed Nimeri and his Free Officers' Movement to power. After the coup all political organisations were disbanded and several officials of the deposed administration were tried on charges of bribery and corruption. Private property of some individuals, including the Mahdi family, was seized.

The Imam el-Mahdi himself relocated his base in Aba Island in the White Nile from where he and his Ansar supporters organised resistance against the Nimeri government. An open military clash between the Ansar and the government forces took place in 1970 and the Mahdists were defeated. Later, on 31 March of the same year, President Nimeri announced that the Imam el-Mahdi had been killed by government forces who fired at his car in Kurmuk on the Sudan-Ethiopia border. The President said that el-Mahdi's car failed to obey orders to stop at the border post and, in the ensuing chase, fire from the car was returned. Later the guards "identified Hadi Abd-el-Rahman among the dead passengers", President Nimeri's broadcast added.■

El-Mahdi, M.A.A. (1848-85)

EL-MAHDI, Muhammad Ahmad ibn el-Sayyid Abdullah (1848-85).

SUDANESE religious leader and politician. He was born in 1848 at Darar. He grew up in a religious environment and after attending a Koranic school in Omdurman he joined the Ismailiyyah religious order under which he continued his religious studies. Although he quickly built up a reputation for devoutness, he later terminated his studies, feeling that his teacher was too worldly. He then became a member of the Summaniyyah brotherhood.

By the beginning of the 1880s el-Mahdi, a strong nationalist, became very critical of the way Egyptian officials were administering his country according to European ways, with Europeans working among them. He also believed that it was his divine mission to restore Islam in the Sudan, and gathering his supporters at Aba, an island in the Nile, he began a revolt against the Egyptian authorities in May 1881. He claimed to be the Mahdi, whose coming near the end of time, to install a reign of justice, is forecast in Islam; his followers, the Mahdists, called themselves Ansar.

The Mahdist movement rapidly gained support. He quickly organised his forces, defeated several expeditions sent by the Egyptian government against him, and gathered more followers. After victories in December 1881 and May 1882 his troops suffered a minor setback at el-Duwaim, but then they placed el-Ubaiyed (el-Obeid) under siege, overcoming its resistance in January 1883. They occupied Darfur, and defeated major Egyptian forces under the British

M.A.A. El-Mahdi

officer Hicks Pasha in November 1883. Under the leadership of the Mahdi, as he was now known around the world, the Ansar continued to score victories over the Anglo-Egyptian forces, and during 1884 they closed in on Khartoum.

After prolonged resistance led by General Gordon, the capital was captured in January 1885, by which time the Mahdi was in control of most of the country. He made his headquarters at Omdurman and began to organise the country according to the principles of Islam. But he died on 22 June 1885, just after the virtual completion of his conquest of the Sudan. He was succeeded, as he had wished, by the Khalifa Abdullahi (q.v.). His own son and grandson were later leaders of his movement when it was revived peacefully under Anglo-Egyptian rule after 1898. ■

El-Mahdi, S. (1911-61)

EL-MAHDI, Sayed Siddick (1911-61).

SUDANESE politician and religious leader. Siddick el-Mahdi was born in the north of Sudan in 1911. His family was very rich and powerful and his father, the son of the famous Mahdi who led the 1881 revolt, was the Imam of the Ansar, the Mahdi's followers.

After completing his primary and secondary education, Siddick el-Mahdi went to study at the Gordon Memorial College in Khartoum. From an early age he developed an interest in politics and while he was at this college he organised the students to strike against suggested changes in the working conditions of the Civil Service.

He believed in non-violent political change towards the total independence of Sudan, and like his father, he opposed proposals for a union between Sudan and Egypt. To establish a political platform for these views Siddick el-Mahdi and his father were among the founders of the Umma (Community) Party in 1945. This party, with Siddick el-Mahdi as its President, pressed for the eventual independence of Sudan through co-operation with the British administration, rather than by more militant means.

As President of Umma Siddick el-Mahdi wielded political influence in the ensuing years, although he preferred to remain in the background. The Umma Party, working with the British, played an important part in drafting the Self-Government

Siddick el-Mahdi

Statute of 1952. The following year the Umma Party accepted amendments that would ensure the co-operation of the newly established Egyptian government for Sudanese self-determination, and later in the same year elections were held. The Umma Party did not gain a majority in these elections but continued to influence government decisions, particularly by the demonstration held in early 1954 at the opening of the new Parliament, which indicated the large measure of support for its policies of independence for Sudan and rejection of union with Egypt.

Shortly after independence was achieved in 1956 a coalition government was formed, lasting until November 1958 when, after rising political tensions, a military coup took place and all political parties were banned. Siddick el-Mahdi and his followers initially accepted the military government on condition that it kept its promise to restore a system of democratic government as soon as it was feasible, while in the interim period maintaining independence and order in the country.

The following year his father died and he took over as Imam of the Ansar. In this position he had a great deal of influence, becoming not only the spiritual leader of the vast number of Moslems belonging to this sect but also the commercial and financial administrator of the movement. He also inherited vast sums of money as well as the large cotton estates to the south of Khartoum and his father's overseas interests.

His opposition to the military government began in 1960 when he joined other leading political figures in calling for national elections to end military rule. He then became one of the organisers of a national opposition front despite economic pressures applied by the government against his and his family's interests. In July 1961 many political leaders were arrested and as Siddick el-Mahdi was not among these, he began to campaign actively for their release. He died on 2 October 1961, at the age of 50.

A quiet and reserved man whose personality commanded a great deal of respect and loyalty among his large following, he wielded great influence but was content to remain in the background of the political arena, campaigning for independence and political change through non-violent methods.■

Mahgoub, R. al- (1926-90)

MAHGOUB, Rifaat al- (1926-90).

EGYPTIAN politician and academic. Born in the Nile Delta area, he studied Law at Cairo University and later was awarded a PhD in Economics at the Sorbonne in Paris (1953). He worked for many years at Cairo University, as a Lecturer in Economics and later Professor of Economics.

He began his political career as Secretary for Ideology, Religion and Propaganda of the Arab Socialist Union (ASU), the ruling and at the time sole legal party in

Egypt. In 1973 President Sadat (q.v.) appointed him Minister for Political Affairs in the Presidency. Besides holding this important post he was also appointed to the Committee to draft revision of the National Charter, and to the High Council of Culture, in the same year. There followed appointments as a

R. al-Mahgoub

member of the National Council for Production and Economic Affairs (1974) and Deputy Prime Minister for Political Affairs in the Presidency (1975). In 1975-76 he was First Secretary of the ASU.

For some years after this he concentrated on his academic work, being appointed Dean of the Faculty of Economic and Political Sciences at Cairo University in 1981. But his political career was not yet over. In May 1984 he was elected to the People's Assembly (parliament), in general elections in which several parties were allowed to compete. The ruling party, since 1978 renamed the National Democratic Party (NDP), won most of the seats. Dr. Mahgoub became President (Speaker) of the new parliament.

He was also on the political bureau of the NDP, and was accused at one point of favouring that party in his role as President. For six years, during which new elections were easily won by the NDP in 1987, he remained President of the Assembly. As such he was by law second only in the order of precedence to the President of Egypt, Hosni Mubarak, for after Mubarak succeeded the assassinated Sadat in 1981 he appointed no Vice-President.

On 12 October 1990, the day after a referendum approving dissolution of the Assembly and new elections, Dr. Mahgoub was shot dead in a street in Cairo. The killers were assumed to be Muslim fundamentalists or other opponents of President Mubarak's rule, perhaps opposed particularly to his support of the UN and Western action against Iraq's occupation of Kuwait.■

Mahjub, A. (1927-71)

MAHJUB, Abd-el-Khalik (1927-71).

SUDANESE leader of the Communist party, whose predecessor, the Sudan Movement for National Liberation, he co-founded in 1946. He was born in 1927 in Sudan and had his education in Cairo, Egypt. Generally regarded as the most influential spokesman for the Communist movement in the Arab world, his career had its roots in the early radical opposition to British rule. He was associated with the Anti-Imperialist Front of the mid-1940s, the movement which developed to become in 1946 the Sudan Movement for National Liberation of which Mahjub was Secretary-General. The movement had only one elected member in Parliament, but its political strength rested largely on the trade unions and the peasantry from which it drew support.

Outlawed by the colonial authorities, its leaders went underground but reappeared as the Communist Party of Sudan (CPS) when Sudan became independent of Britain on 1 January 1956. At first it was permitted to operate freely but with the military coup d'état of November 1958 came suppression of all political activities in the country. The CPS was suspended and it went underground again; fifty-six of its leading members were imprisoned without trial in May 1959 and Mahjub who was its Secretary-General was detained until December 1960.

After his release he worked actively in the plot that ended the regime of General Ibrahim Abboud in 1964. The CPS and Mahjub enjoyed widespread but brief popularity in the immediate aftermath of the 1964 Revolution and played an important role in the subsequent administration. During this period the Communists contested elections freely and Mahjub himself stood, unsuccessfully, against Ismail el-Azhari (q.v.) in the Omdurman constituency in the 1965 elections. He was, however, elected in the 1968 elections when he stood as an independent candidate. The CPS had been banned again in November 1965 following widespread disturbances for which the Communists were blamed.

In the early days after the May 1969 coup d'état which brought Colonel Gaafar Mohammed Nimeri and his Free Officers' Movement to power, Mahjub had a working relationship with the new regime. Colonel (later General) Nimeri said then that his regime was committed to "Sudanese socialism", and renamed the country the Democratic Republic of the Sudan. The new government, after a month in office, announced that the 15-year-old civil war in the south must be ended, not by military means but by negotiated settlement with the rebels who demanded regional autonomy for the south. It established a Ministry for Southern Affairs and appointed a member of the Communist Party, Joseph Garang, as its head. Such was the influence gained by the CPS in the post-Revolution years, and Mahjub and his supporters rallied round the government of Nimeri during the 1970 Mahdist rebellion in Aba Island on the White Nile.

The Communist leader however disagreed with President Nimeri on the question of setting up a one-party system for the

Sudan, which Mahjub viewed as the start of a dictatorship. He fell out with the government and left the country in April 1970 for Cairo. He returned home, following reconciliation, but was arrested in November of 1970 and detained until 29 June 1971 when he escaped from prison. The following month, on 19 July, an attempt was made to overthrow the Nimeri government, in which Mahjub was implicated. Rebel troops, led by Major Hashim el-Atta, and Colonel Osman Hussain, commander of the Presidential Guard, had seized and held Nimeri captive in his palace in Khartoum; but 72 hours later loyal troops had overpowered the mutineers and restored the President to power.

The leaders of the abortive coup and some leaders of the CPS were rounded up and executed; among the Communists hanged were Joseph Garang and Mahjub. The latter was arrested on 24 July 1971 and tried by a military tribunal which sentenced him to death. He was hanged early on the morning of 28 July 1971. During the trial, according to Radio Omdurman, Mahjub denied any part in the coup but admitted that a central committee of the CPS meeting on 19 July had decided to support any change-over to a left wing government.■

country, Mahlangu became more and more involved in the organisation of the demonstrations that were taking place simultaneously in the schools and streets of Soweto and other African townships.

S.K. Mahlangu

Mahlangu, S.K. (1956-79)

MAHLANGU, Solomon Kalushi (1956-79).

SOUTH AFRICAN freedom fighter who became part of the struggle as a student activist in the resistance against the imposition of the Afrikaans language as a medium of instruction in African schools.

Mahlangu was born on 10 October 1956 in Mamelodi near Pretoria, South Africa. He was attending school in the African township when students revolted against the compulsory introduction of Afrikaans in June 1976; his activities in the subsequent mass protest by Africans marked him out as a hero of the struggle for freedom. As the student rebellion spread in the

The revolt was more than a protest against the Afrikaans language; it was basically a rebellion against the general inadequacies of the African education system that sought to maintain the status quo. During the widespread revolt students boycotted classes and in the Sibasa area alone eleven schools were affected when 115,000 children refused to attend lectures, precipitating the closure of their institutions. In Soweto, where the demonstration began on 16 June 1976 when about 3,000 African High School pupils marched on the Phefeni School in the Orlando West district of Johannesburg, public buildings were burnt and about 23 people were killed in the first two days of clashes between students and police.

It was during this period that Mahlangu joined the ANC, and in October 1976 left South Africa to join its external wing. While outside he received political and military training. In June 1977 he returned to South Africa as a militant in the ANC military wing, *Umkhonto we Sizwe*; he was arrested by government authorities that month following a shooting incident in Goch Street in Johannesburg in which two Europeans were killed. He was in the company of two armed ANC militants and, although armed himself, did not fire a shot. A government statement at the time said that 600 guerrillas had been trained in Angola as part of a renewed campaign of sabotage and subversion. It added that the guerrillas who had infiltrated into South Africa planned a three-phase campaign concentrating on the alienation of the African population, the economic and diplomatic isolation of the Republic, and the infiltration of the trade unions. The statement said that 38 guerrillas had been arrested.

Mahlangu was sentenced to death on 2 March 1978, though the court accepted that he had not fired a shot himself. He became a martyr to the liberation struggle when the apartheid regime hanged him in Pretoria Central Prison on 6 April 1979. On the eve of the execution the United Nations Security Council held an emergency meeting, at the request of its African members, where the world body registered its protest against the death sentence. In Africa and Europe calls were made by governments, institutions and individuals for clemency, all of which the South African authorities ignored. The execution provoked equal immediate international protests, which the South African Foreign Minister, Roelof Botha, denounced.

Though Mahlangu's body was secretly buried at the Mamelodi cemetery by the authorities, over 2,000 people attended his memorial service, organised by the Soweto Students' League, at St. Francis of Assisi Church in Rockville. His mother, Martha Mahlangu, told the congregation, "I firmly believe that my son left one day and decided he should do something to help free his people from suffering. I see contrary reports as mere propaganda designed to instil fear into those youths who may follow in his footsteps." The execution of Mahlangu prompted a new wave of international condemnation of South Africa's apartheid policy and the brutal force with which it sought to implement it. ∎

Makaman Bida, A. (1907-80)

MAKAMAN BIDA, Alhaji Aliyu (1907-80).

NIGERIAN politician who was the first Minister of Education of Northern Nigeria. He was known by the title of a high traditional office, the *Makama*, under the Etsu Nupe, the Emir of Bida. The old and powerful Nupe kingdom had been absorbed into the Hausa-Fulani empire in the 19th century and its institutions had been affected accordingly.

Aliyu, born at Doko, rose within that traditional system, being helped by a nobleman who held the title of *Maaji* (treasurer) under the Etsu, and in whose house Aliyu's father lived. The *Maaji* helped him to become one of the few Moslem Northerners at that time to receive Western education, at Bida Middle School and then at Katsina College, the major school for such education in Northern Nigeria. He qualified as a teacher and then taught at Bida Middle School, eventually becoming the headmaster.

In 1938, Aliyu was given the *Makaman Bida* title, which ensured him prominence

Alhaji Aliyu Makaman Bida

and influence in Nupe affairs despite his relatively humble birth. He was on the Etsu Nupe's Council with responsibility for district administration and education in Bida "Native Authority", from 1942 to 1951. In 1945 he was appointed to the Niger Province Development Committee. As the leading Western-educated member of the "Indirect Rule" local government system in Bida, he attended a Local Government training course in 1945-46.

In 1947, when the Richards Constitution came into force, he was chosen as one of the Northern members of the Legislative Council. This was the start of a rapid rise to political power as a leading member of the Northern People's Congress (NPC) and the right-hand man of Sir Ahmadu Bello (q.v.). When the first Nigerian government of the Northern Region was formed in 1951, with Sir Ahmadu Bello, Sardauna of Sokoto, as Premier, Aliyu Makaman Bida was appointed Minister of Social Services, with responsibility for education and health. Soon afterwards he became head of a separate Ministry of Education, a post he held for four years (1952-56) during which he sponsored and encouraged a rapid spread of western education in Northern Nigeria. As a devout Moslem who went to Mecca frequently, he was one of the main believers in the compatibility of Islam and modern education.

In 1957, after serving briefly as Minister of Trade and Industry, he was promoted to the Ministry of Finance. He continued to hold the portfolio in the post-independence government of the North, often acting as Premier, after the Constitutional Conferences (which he attended from 1953) had led to Nigeria's independence in 1960. He was also the main liaison officer between the NPC secretariat and the government in Kaduna. In January 1966 that government fell in the coup led by Major P.C.K. Nzeogwu (q.v.).

Later Makaman Bida played a prominent role in the revival of civilian party politics at the end of the era of military rule when he was chosen as Patron of the National Party of Nigeria (NPN) formed in 1978. The NPN won the largest number of votes in the 1979 elections and its candidate, Alhaji Shehu Shagari, was elected President of Nigeria. But six months after the return to civilian rule under the new President on 1 October 1979, Alhaji Aliyu died at Kaduna. He had four wives and five children. ■

Makgatho, S.M. (1861-1951)

MAKGATHO, Sefako Mapogo (1861-1951).

SOUTH AFRICAN politician and president-general of the African National Congress (ANC) from 1917 to 1924. Son of a minor chief, Makgatho was born in 1861 in Mphahlele in the northern Transvaal, South Africa. He attended the newly created Methodist Training Institute in Kilnerton, near Pretoria, and proceeded to Britain in 1882 for a course in education which took him three years. On his return to South Africa he took up a teaching post at his former school in Kilnerton, remaining on its staff from 1887 until 1906.

After his resignation from Kilnerton, he worked as a real estate agent in Pretoria but soon became active in the political agitation against the repression of the settler regime. He had founded the Transvaal African Teachers' Association during his stay at Kilnerton, with the aim of securing better conditions of service for the African teachers in the province. In 1906 he formed the Transvaal Native Political Union which he brought into the Transvaal Native Congress to form the South African Native National Congress; that in turn developed to become the ANC, the first national movement representing African opinion in the country. He succeeded Reverend John Lengalibalele Dube (q.v.) to the presidency of the ANC in 1917 and retained the office of president-general until 1924.

Makgatho's energies and great political acumen were devoted to rebuilding the leadership of an ANC that appeared to have lost direction because of his predecessors' indecision over how Africans should oppose the regime's new land policies. His presidency saw an increase in membership as well as the successful campaigns against the extension of the Pass Laws to include women, and a proposed tax increase in the Transvaal.

Makgatho was also active in journalism, having been involved with the production of the *Native Advocate*, a nationalist paper founded by Alfred Mangena (q.v.). He also collaborated with Pixley Ka Isaka Seme (q.v.) in launching the *Abantu-Batho* in 1912.

During the latter's presidency of the ANC between 1930 and 1937, Makgatho served in the executive committee of the movement as treasurer-general. He continued to exercise great influence in the affairs of the ANC until his death in Pretoria in 1951. ■

Makongoro, M. (1893-1958)

MAKONGORO, Chief Mohammed (1893-1958).

Tanzanian traditional ruler who defied colonial regulations to become actively engaged in the struggle of the Tanganyika African National Union (TANU). Chief of Ikizu, one of the chiefdoms of the Zanaki area, he was a prominent figure in the early days of the struggle for independence. Though Chief Makongoro, like all other chiefs and Africans in the colonial civil service of Tanganyika, was forbidden by the administration to participate in the anti-colonial movement of the time, he flouted the regulations by not only encouraging TANU's activities in his chiefdom but also by subscribing to party membership himself.

Political activities in the Zanaki area were intensified when Nyerere, who had been elected president of TANU in 1954, returned home temporarily in 1955 following a forced resignation from his post of history teacher at St. Francis College in Pugu, near Dar-es-Salaam. The resignation of Nyerere and other leading TANU members followed in the wake of the Societies Bill, introduced by governor Edward Twining on 14 April 1954, which made it compulsory for all organisations to register the names of officers, rules and regulations with the authorities. Nyerere's presence in his Zanaki home during this time facilitated TANU's activities in the area, and from then on a lasting working relationship existed between Chief Makongoro and Nyerere, encouraged more by their common desire to achieve independence for Tanganyika rather than by their ethnic affiliation.

Faced with the increased momentum of the TANU campaign and the party's growing popularity in the country, the government set out to introduce elements of non-racial policy for representation at the

Chief M. Makongoro

local council level. For this it needed the support of the chiefs; thus in early 1957 a meeting of all important chiefs in the country was convened at Mzumbe, in the Morogoro region. Chief Makongoro and other heads from the Musoma district attended the meeting with specific instructions from the Musoma district commissioner, F.B. Weekes, to endorse the government policy of creating multi-racial local councils whose African, Asian and European members would be chosen under a tripartite voting system. The chiefs were also directed by the district commissioner to report to their people, on their return from the Mzumbe conference, that the policy was unanimously endorsed by the participants. At the subsequent official reception organised for the Musoma chiefs, Chief Makongoro told the district commissioner that the people of Musoma, like their chiefs, would not lend their support to the government policy. Few days later Chief Makongoro was arrested for alleged criminal offences; he was subsequently sentenced to six months' imprisonment and a fine of 4,201 shillings, following which he was deposed as chief of Ikizu. Replaced temporarily with a British district officer as head of the Waikizu, Makongoro was subsequently deported from his home to which he was only allowed to return after a successful appeal in the Tanganyikan High Court.

His trial, sentence and deposition further aggravated the anti-British sentiment in the country, spearheaded by TANU and Chief Makongoro's people. On 26 May 1958, the No 29 issue of *Sauti ya Tanu* (Voice of TANU), the party newspaper, carried an unsigned article critical of the case and other similar punitive measures being taken against other dissenting chiefs in the Musoma and Geita districts by resident commissioners F.B. Weekes and G.T.L. Scott. Nyerere was later accused of writing the alleged libellous article, which he denied during his trial in July and August 1958. Chief Makongoro was the key witness for Nyerere at the trial, and such was his evidence that he was served with a deportation order again, while the trial was still going on, to the Tanduru district in southern Tanganyika. Nyerere was ordered to go to prison or pay a fine; it was said that, fearing the repercussions of sending him to prison, the authorities persuaded Nyerere to pay the fine of 3,000 shillings which was collected on the spot by his supporters who were present at the trial.

In his exile, as he had done in his chiefdom, Chief Makongoro remained supportive to TANU's cause until his death in 1958. ∎

Makonnen, E. (1926-74)

MAKONNEN, Endalkatchew (1926-74).

ETHIOPIAN politician, born in Addis Ababa in September 1926. His parents belonged to an aristocratic Amhara family and his father, a close friend of Emperor Haile Selassie I (q.v.), served as Prime Minister and President of the Ethiopian Senate for a number of years.

After attending the Haile Selassie I Secondary School in Addis Ababa, Makonnen travelled to England where he studied politics, economics and philosophy at the University of Exeter, and later at Oriel College, University of Oxford. He then returned to Ethiopia where he became an attaché in the Ministry of Foreign Affairs. He was promoted to Chief of Protocol in 1953 and the following year he was appointed

E. Makonnen

vice-minister of Foreign Affairs. While in this position he attended the Bandung Conference in 1955, and a year later he was sent to London as part of an Ethiopian delegation to the Suez Canal Conference.

In 1958 he left the Ministry of Foreign Affairs to become Deputy Minister of Education, but the following year he returned to his old Ministry and took up the position of Ambassador to Britain, where he gained a reputation as an able diplomat. He returned to Ethiopia in 1961 following his appointment as Minister of Commerce, Industry and Planning. While in this position he also served as chairman of the Ethiopian Coffee Board.

He resumed his diplomatic activities in 1966 when he became Permanent Representative to the United Nations and in the three years that he held this post he was President of the Security Council twice between 1967-69. In 1969 he was appointed

Minister of Communications, Telegraphs, Telecommunications and Posts, a post he held until 1974.

When U Thant resigned in 1971 Makonnen stood as Africa's candidate for the post of Secretary-General of the United Nations, but was unsuccessful.

During 1973 there was a severe drought in Ethiopia, leading to a famine in which several thousands of people died. This increased the general feeling of discontent with the Government as it was believed that bureaucratic mismanagement had exacerbated the effects of this disaster. There was also mounting unrest in the Armed Forces over pay and conditions and on 28 February 1974 the Government resigned. On the same day, Makonnen was appointed Prime Minister by the Emperor.

As Prime Minister, he announced sweeping reforms in April 1974. Among these were land reforms whereby excess land that was not being cultivated would be taken by the Government, after appropriate compensation, and allotted to others to be farmed. However, these reforms did not satisfy the opposition who wanted specific policies on overcoming corruption, and clear guidelines as to how future droughts would be handled. By June 1974 the Armed Forces Committee had become a permanent body working with the Cabinet and was gradually gaining control of the country.

On 22 July 1974 Makonnen, up to this time the only member of the previous Government to escape being purged by the military, was dismissed from his post by the Emperor. He was later detained while a Commission of Inquiry into Corruption and Maladministration by Government Officials was held, the findings of which were reported on 13 November 1974. He was executed ten days later on 23 November 1974, for gross abuse of authority, along with 28 other civilians and several members of the military.■

Malan, D.F. (1874-1959)

MALAN, Dr. Daniel François (1874-1959).

SOUTH AFRICAN clergyman and politician who strongly believed in Afrikaner

Dr. D.F. Malan

nationalism and apartheid. Daniel François Malan was born on 22 May 1874 at Riebeeck West, Cape Province, South Africa. He was educated locally, after which he attended the Victoria College in Stellenbosch where he passed his matriculation examinations. In 1901 he travelled to Holland to study at the University of Utrecht, graduating four years later in 1905.

On his return to South Africa he became a preacher in the *Nederduitse Gereformeerde Kerk* (NGK) (Dutch Reformed Church). He remained in this position for several years during which time he travelled extensively, preaching to NGK congregations in Southern Rhodesia (now Zimbabwe) and the Belgian Congo (now Zaire) as well as in South Africa.

His interest in politics developed against a background of Afrikaner identity. He became a member of the National Party in 1915 and was appointed the editor of *Die Burger*, a newspaper published by Afrikaner nationalists in Cape Town who were opposed to the Government fighting on the side of Britain during World War I. He was later elected chairman of the Cape Province branch of the National Party, and although he was defeated in the 1915 parliamentary elections, he was offered a seat when a successful candidate stepped down in his favour.

By the end of the First World War

support for the National Party was growing, partly owing to the Government's unpopular handling of a miners' strike in 1922. In the 1924 elections the nationalists gained a majority of the parliamentary seats and Malan became Minister of the Interior, Education and Public Health in the new government.

He began to introduce proposals to realise his nationalist beliefs and ideals. He amended the 1911 South Africa Act to include a clause which stated that the people of the Union of South Africa "recognise the sovereignty and guidance of God", reflecting his own deep religious beliefs, while also altering the electoral laws and making Afrikaans the official language of South Africa. He introduced a law which demanded that during parliamentary elections, all newspaper articles which sought to influence opinion must bear the name and address of the writer.

In 1926 he married Martha Margaretha Elizabeth van Tonder, née Zandberg, with whom he had two sons before her death four years later. Meanwhile, the National Party had been successful in the 1929 elections and Malan continued to hold his ministerial position. However, the Wall Street crash of 1929 and the ensuing world economic recession, combined with drought, had an adverse effect on the South African economy.

In 1933 the National and South African Parties formed a coalition government. Malan, although remaining in the government, did not approve of this coalition as he disagreed with the South African Party's policies.

The following year the South African Party and the National Party merged into the United South African National Party. Malan, objecting to the merger, kept the National Party alive supported by 19 other members of Parliament who shared his views on Afrikaner nationalism, the necessity of racial segregation and the eventual establishment of an Afrikaner Republic of South Africa. Although the United South African National Party retained white popular support, the National Party's capture of an extra seven seats in the 1938 elections showed that the latter was gaining more white support. During this period Malan married Mana Ann Sophia Louw, and later adopted a daughter.

On the outbreak of the Second World War in September 1939 the internal political differences increased with many dissident nationalists from the United Party joining Malan to form the *Herenigde Nasionale* Party (Re-united National Party). Malan's party in the meantime increased the number of seats it held in Parliament to 43 in the 1943 elections.

In the post-war period tension between the various races in the country increased. Malan and his supporters advocated the introduction of apartheid under which the political, cultural and social development of all the races would be subordinated to white supremacy. By the time of the 1948 elections the two Afrikaner nationalist parties had overcome their differences and agreed to work together. Support for Afrikaner nationalism among the white population had grown to the extent that the two nationalist parties managed to gain an overall majority in Parliament, with Malan becoming Prime Minister.

In this position he began to implement his nationalist and apartheid policies. So as to overcome remaining elements of British imperialism in the country, Union nationals became South African citizens instead of British subjects in 1949 and the following year the British Privy Council was removed as the highest court of appeal. Also in 1949 he moved to link Namibia (South West Africa) permanently with South Africa and members of Parliament representing Namibia, all of whom belonged to the *Herenigde Nasionale* Party, joined the South African Assembly in 1950. The following year the two Afrikaner parties merged into the National Party and won the 1953 elections with an increased majority. The implementation of the Government's policy of apartheid in 1950 saw the endorsement of residential segregation, the prohibition of sexual relations and marriage between people of different races, and the classification of all adults by race in the new popular register. In 1950 Malan appointed Dr. Hendrik Verwoerd (q.v.) as Minister of Native Affairs, in which position he became the architect of apartheid. Malan also feared "communist" influence and sponsored the enactment of the Suppression of Communism Act in 1950. Three years later the Criminal Law Amendment Act was passed under which a state of emergency could be called at any time if the government thought the situation so required.

Malan saw the emergence of African

states as a threat to the white race and proposed that the European colonisers of the continent should ensure that Africa developed as part of western Christian civilization. He justified the apartheid policy on the argument that African people were backward and their development needed to be supervised by the white race.

After a long political career during which he had remained constantly committed to the objectives of Afrikaner nationalism, Malan retired from the office of Prime Minister in 1954 at the age of 80. He died five years later on 7 February 1959, at Stellenbosch. ■

Maliki, A. (1914-69)

MALIKI, Alhaji Abdul (1914-69).

NIGERIAN diplomat; he was his country's first High Commissioner to the United Kingdom. Born in 1914, he was a son of the Attah of Igbirra, traditional ruler of the Igbirra group in what is now Kwara State, and a brother of Abdul Aziz Atta (q.v.). He was educated at Katsina Training College. He taught at Okene Middle School in his home area in 1934-35, and was then appointed supervisor of Native Authority Works, a post he held from 1936 to 1939.

He held other posts in a rapid rise in the service of the colonial administration in the Northern Provinces. In 1939-40 he was Provincial Clerk in Katsina, an important post for a Nigerian in the colonial government service at that time. In 1940 he was appointed to an even more important post, that of Chief Executive Officer of Igbirra N.A. He also became chairman of Okene Town Council, the first elected municipal council in the former Northern Region. He was thus one of the most prominent members of the Igbirra (or Ebira) community, while in the Public Service. He went on a Local Government course in Britain in 1950.

He was a member of the Northern Region House of Assembly and then of the Federal House of Representatives from 1952 to 1955. He was a member of the Northern People's Congress (NPC). In 1955 he was appointed Commissioner to the United King-

Alhaji Abdul Maliki

dom for Northern Nigeria; he held this post until 1958, and during this time was made Commander of the Order of the British Empire (CBE).

He joined the Federal diplomatic service in 1958. On the independence of Nigeria in 1960 he was appointed the first High Commissioner to the United Kingdom. He served for six years in what was then the most vital diplomatic post representing Nigeria overseas. In mid-1966 he was transferred to France as ambassador there, a difficult post because of France's support for the secessionists in the civil war then still raging. He died in the middle of 1969 while on leave at home. ■

Mally, T. (1913-73)

MALLY, Théophile (1913-73).

TOGOLESE politician and his country's first Minister of the Interior. Born of an Akposo family at Gode-Admiabra in 1913, he was a farmer until the rise of nationalism in the 1940s. He then joined the *Comité de l'Unité Togolaise* (CUT) headed by Sylvanus Olympio (q.v.).

After Togo's independence, Mally joined M. Olympio's government as Minister of the Interior, Press and Information in May 1960, in 1962 his portfolio became the Ministry of the Interior only. As such he was seen as responsible for the internal policies as a result of which many opponents of Olympio were arrested or driven into exile, usually Ghana. He was thus a particularly hated member of the Olympio regime. But he escaped when that regime fell in January 1963, and fled to Nigeria, and later Guinea (whose president had been shocked by the murder of President Olympio).

He rivalled Noe Kutuklui for leadership, from exile, of the CUT, until Gen. Eyadema took over power in 1967. Then he returned under an amnesty and held several positions. He joined President Eyadema's party, the *Rassemblement du Peuple Togolais* (RPT), created in 1969. In March 1973 it was announced that he had died in prison after being gaoled on 28 February for passing a cheque that "bounced". ■

Malula, J. A. (1917-89)

MALULA, Cardinal Joseph Albert (1917-89).

ZAIREAN Catholic clergyman, a renowned advocate of the Africanisation of Christianity, who lived through the turbulent years preceding and following his country's independence.

He was born on 12 December 1917 in Kinshasa, then Léopoldville, to a mother from the Equateur Region and a Baluba father. He was educated at the Petit Séminaire in Bolongo and the Grand Séminaire in Kabwe where he studied the classics and humanities for eight years.

Malula started his clerical career as a priest in the parish of Christ-Roi. As the first black parish priest in Kinshasa, he became dissatisfied with the paternalistic attitudes with which both the church and the Belgian colonial authorities treated Africans. In 1959, just a year before the independence of the then Belgian Congo (renamed Zaire in

October 1971), Malula became the auxiliary Bishop of Kinshasa. He remained in that position until July 1964 when he was appointed Archbishop of Kinshasa. He was created a Cardinal in April 1969.

Cardinal Malula became especially renowned as a result of his efforts to indigenise the Catholic church in Zaire and to help achieve its autonomy. He called for the Africanisation of the liturgy and for the use of valid elements in traditional religions by the church. With changes of this kind, he hoped Africans would be able to make the Catholic religion their own. Malula also became an advocate of the dignity of women, denouncing whatever turned them into "slaves or instruments of lust". Moreover, he denounced tribalism as the curse of Africa. However, his pursuit of change and "authenticity" — as he described his call for Africanisation — did not include giving up

J.A. Malula

Christian names and replacing them by African ones. So when President Mobutu launched his "Authenticity" campaign by changing the country's name to Zaire and his own from Joseph-Désiré Mobutu to Mobutu Sese Seko, Malula led the church in criticism of the regime. (He saw this campaign as an extreme interpretation and its implementation as undemocratic.) The Catholic church was — and still remains — a very powerful force in Zaire with over 40 per cent of the population as members.

Malula refused to obey the order to Zairean citizens to give up the use of Catholic Christian names. He also disagreed with proposals that the youth wing of the ruling *Mouvement Populaire de la Révolution (MPR)* should establish cells within all religious institutions throughout the country. The state took over all Catholic and other mission schools and banned religious instruction in schools, and although the schools were returned to church control later, religious instruction was not allowed and all Christian festivals ceased for years to be public holidays. Supporters of the regime reacted fiercely and there were threats to the churchman's life.

Malula's clashes with the Mobutu regime led to his exile to Rome for five months, from January to May 1972. The political bureau of the MPR accused the churchman of subversion, while the state press drummed up a campaign against "counter-revolutionaries". Malula was allowed to return to Zaire after he had virtually capitulated to the government on most of the policy measures in dispute. The papal visit to Zaire in May 1980, during which Cardinal Malula joined President Mobutu to welcome Pope John Paul II, was seen by some as an indication of the reconciliation between the state and the church.

Malula after that had to deal with more problems from the Vatican. He would have liked to see married men ordained priests, and, as this was not allowed, he encouraged the elderly natural leaders of the communities to become catechists. His great project, however, in the last decade of his life, on which he spent a great deal of his time, was to establish a "council of the African Church" which would formally work through the problems of combining Africanness and Christianity. It was his hope that such a council would eventually lead to the synthesis of the valuable elements of African traditional ways of life with Christianity, which has been seen as desirable since the Second Vatican Council. Malula was awarded his country's highest honour, the Order of the Grand Leopard.

He died on 12 July 1989 in a clinic in Brussels.■

Malvern, Viscount (1883-1971)

MALVERN, Viscount (1883-1971).

ZIMBABWEAN settler politician; he was a believer in racial segregation who became the first Prime Minister of the Federation of Rhodesia and Nyasaland (now Malawi) from 1953 to 1956 after previously being Prime Minister of Southern Rhodesia (Zimbabwe) for 20 years. He was born as Godfrey Martin Huggins at Bexley in Kent, England, on 6 July 1883. He was educated at Malvern College and at St. Thomas' Hospital, London, where he qualified as a doctor in 1906.

After working at the Hospital for Sick Children in Great Ormond Street in London he was forced by ill health to emigrate "for a rest and a change"; he settled in Southern Rhodesia in 1911 and set up a private medical practice. Interrupting his medical practice on the outbreak of the First World War, Huggins joined the Royal Army Medical Corps, became a captain, and served in Britain, France and Malta. In 1921, he entered politics and was elected member of the Legislative Council of the Rhodesia Party, which he left in 1931 to join the Reform Party.

In the general elections of 1933, Huggins campaigned strongly for the introduction of segregationist laws and won the election for his Reform Party, with 16 seats more than the Rhodesia Party's nine. He became Prime Minister and also took charge of the portfolio of Native Affairs in order to facilitate the implementation of his racist policies. He believed that Africans and Europeans should develop separately in two pyramids which would meet at the top in a common legislature. Following the example of the accentuation of apartheid policies in

South Africa, Huggins ended the Africans' right to vote in Rhodesia. Although the right was restored (for a few only, later) in 1950, Huggins described it as involving Africans and Europeans going the same way in a "rider and horse" fashion.

Yet, two years later, in 1952 when he visited London to press for the federation of Southern Rhodesia, Northern Rhodesia and Nyasaland, Huggins took with him Joshua Nkomo and Jasper Savanhu to represent

Viscount Malvern

African opinion. The Federation was created in 1953 and Huggins relinquished his Southern Rhodesian premiership to become the first Federal Prime Minister as well as Minister of Defence. Once in power, Huggins continued his opposition to Africans' participation in government, arguing that they were "quite incapable of playing a full part". He believed that the economic and social advancement of the Africans was of greater importance than their political advancement, and that this advancement would eventually herald political development. Huggins was created a peer in 1953, becoming the first Viscount Malvern of Rhodesia and Bexley.

Lord Malvern retired from politics on 1 November 1956, being succeeded by Sir Roy Welensky as Prime Minister of the Federation. In retirement, Lord Malvern was actively involved in Rhodesian politics, making frequent trips to London to present the federation's case. In the wake of the declaration of a state of emergency in March 1959, he went to London to participate in a House of Lords debate on the situation. He is reported to have said that "Africans, until they are very much advanced, are all liars." In latter years, he was to emerge again into the political arena to attack Ian Smith's unilateral declaration of independence and the declaration of a republic. In line with his pro-British tradition, he attacked the illegal regime for abolishing the Union Jack and adopting a new flag which he described as "pagan". He died in Salisbury, now Harare, on 8 May 1971. ■

Mandume (c.1890-1917)

MANDUME, Chief (c.1890-1917).

NAMIBIAN traditional ruler. He was the last king of the Cuanhama group of the Ovambo people. The Ovambos were in 1886 divided between the territories of Portuguese Angola and German South-West Africa. They did not come under effective occupation until some time later, especially in Angola. The Ovambos there, including the Cuanhamas (who were on both sides of the border), remained independent until the 20th century. Brief contact with the Portuguese government of Angola and Catholic missionaries under King Nambade (1882-85) ended after his reign for a time. His successor Weyulu ruled an independent state from his capital, Ngiva.

Missionaries returned to Cuanhama territory in Weyulu's reign. German Protestant missionaries were in South-West Africa and young Mandume went to one of their schools. Traders, including gun-runners, also went to the Cuanhama country. Consequently the Cuanhama warrior caste, accustomed to raiding over long distances, now acquired better guns; when raiding had to be restricted, the guns were kept and eventually used

Chief Mandume

against the Portuguese. But for long these presented no threat; it was only with great difficulty and very slowly that Portugal, itself weak and bankrupt, conquered the vast country of Angola, and this required numerous expeditions. In the Ovambo area they attacked first the Cuamato group, neighbours of the Cuanhama, whose rulers, Weyulu (1885-1904) and then Nande (1904-1911), helped the Portuguese against their fellow Ovambos.

In 1904 the Cuamatos defeated a Portuguese force, but a larger force returned and subjugated them by 1907. Even then the Portuguese, with many other areas resisting them in Angola then, had to leave Cuanhama alone for several years more. During those years Nande was succeeded by Mandume.

Mandume imposed his power ruthlessly, killing and banishing opponents. Although mission-educated, he was very anti-European, and drove out the Holy Ghost Fathers' Catholic mission in 1912. He was fiercely determined to maintain full independence. Despite his harsh leadership this aim had much support and his people bought arms with money earned on the German side. Mandume's people raided extensively when famine hit southern Angola after

1911. Portugal could not at first stop this raiding, nor make its nominal rule over the Cuanhamas effective.

After the outbreak of the First World War there was a German raid into Angola, although Portugal was neutral then. The Cuamatos rose in revolt, and other risings followed in other parts of Angola. In 1915, while the Germans in South-West Africa succumbed to an attack by South African forces, the Portuguese sent an expedition led personally by the Governor-General to the unoccupied Ovambo country. In the great battle of Mongua, in August 1915, Mandume had a vast force, estimated at over 40,000 and many had modern rifles. But mistakes by him led to the defeat of his greatly superior force. He fled into the "neutral zone" between Angola and South-West Africa, now under South African occupation, while the Portuguese occupied his capital Ngiva.

Only about 2,000 Cuanhamas remained with Mandume, and this defender of African independence continued to be feared and respected by all. His force attacked some Portuguese and its activities led to summonses to appear before the South African authorities at Windhoek. When these were ignored a South African expedition defeated and killed him on 6 February 1917. ∎

Mañe, A. (died 1958)

MANE, Acacio (died 1958).

EQUATORIAL GUINEAN resistance leader and leader of the *Cruzada Nacional de Liberación de Guinea Ecuatorial* (CNLGE). A Fang, of Cameroonian origin, Mañe was a pioneering figure in the nationalist struggle against Spanish colonialism in Equatorial Guinea. A most daring politician and dynamic personality in the early days of the struggle, he was among the first to voice claims for independence, defying the repressive measures instituted by Spain against such demands.

In 1947 Mañe co-founded the CNLGE, the first organised anti-colonial movement in the colony and he became its president. The CNLGE operated clandestinely until the early 1950s when a teachers' strike over low wages and bad conditions of service brought its activities into the open. Mañe addressed the demonstrating teachers in 1950 and accused Spain of failing to meet their demands that had been accepted by the colonial authority. From then on he travelled through the mainland Rio Muni, expounding his movement's policy and winning new members. Among his early recruits was Miyone Atanasio Ndongo (q.v.), first Minister of Foreign Affairs of independent Equatorial Guinea, who joined the CNLGE in 1952.

By 1955 when Spain became a member of the United Nations, Mañe and his followers in the anti-colonial movement had become a force to be reckoned with. Internally the increased tempo of their demand for independence had brought equally increased repression by the colonial authorities who refused to recognise any nationalist movement. In 1955 Mañe presented a memorandum to the United Nations calling on Spain to withdraw from the territory. It was partly in reaction to the pressures of the Afro-Asian bloc, generated by Mañe's memorandum, at the United Nations that Spain began making arrangements for the country's independence which, beginning with "provincialisation" and leading through autonomy between 1964 and 1967, was achieved in 1968.

Mañe was arrested by the Spanish Civil Guards on 20 November 1958 and was assassinated in Bata. His body was thrown in the ocean. He was succeeded as president of CNLGE by Sikacha Maho who later passed the leadership to Ndongo under whose direction it became the *Movimento Nacional de Liberación de la Guinea Ecuatorial* (MONALIGE). Acacio Mañe was proclaimed a national hero and martyr of independence shortly after the Spanish withdrew from Equatorial Guinea in October 1968. ■

Mangena, A. (1879-1924)

MANGENA, Alfred (1879-1924).

SOUTH AFRICAN lawyer and politician, the first African in South Africa to qualify as an attorney; he was a founder member of the African National Congress

(ANC) which he served as vice-president. Mangena was born in 1879 in Eastcourt in the Natal Province of South Africa. After primary school in his home province he went to Cape Town in 1900 for further education, sponsoring himself in private tuition. It was during this period that he first involved himself in the struggle against the segregation measures of the South African government – he participated in the resistance to a relocation scheme that was being introduced in Cape Town. He travelled soon after to Britain to read Law at Lincoln's Inn, London.

While he was in London the trial of the Africans who had revolted with Chief Bambata in 1906 opened in South Africa. The Bambata Rebellion, often regarded as the Zulus' last major military attempt to challenge the European occupation, alarmed the British colonial authorities who ruthlessly suppressed it. Chief Bambata of the Zondi people in Zululand, then under the kingship of Dinuzulu (1884-1913), was killed by British forces during the unrest which spread throughout the empire. Dinuzulu was exiled as a result, after standing trial for high treason. During the trial in Natal, Mangena petitioned the British government on behalf of the accused. At the same time he challenged the legality of the authority of the colonial administration in Natal to declare martial law in the territory. Mangena soon gained recognition both in Britain and South Africa for his intellectual and fearless criticism of the colonial authorities. Before returning to South Africa in 1910 Mangena joined a multi-racial delegation that was appointed by the Transvaal Native Congress to protest against the Act of Union.

Back in his native South Africa, Mangena, the first black to qualify as an attorney in the country, had to overcome the racial policies of the regime that banned Africans from professions reserved for the Europeans. He however got admitted to the profession and established a private practice in Pretoria which soon grew to be a successful concern, with a branch office in Johannesburg.

Through his work as a lawyer in the services of Africans he realised the need for Africans to organise themselves in pursuit of their rights, and in 1912, in association with others, founded the South African Native National Congress (SANNC) which was succeeded by the African National Congress (ANC). Mangena was elected one of the first four vice-presidents of the movement. And in that same year,with Sefako Mapogo Makgatho (q.v.) who became president-general of the ANC (1917-24), he established the Pretoria-based newspaper, the *Native Advocate*.

In 1913 he served on the SANNC body which petitioned the government over the 1913 Land Act on which he took an uncompromising stand. Three years later he co-founded with Pixley Seme (q.v.) a law partnership in Johannesburg. He died in 1924 in Umtata. Mangena remained dedicated to the cause of the Africans throughout his life, on whose behalf he acted fearlessly in the face of repressive measures. Of him, the *Africa Yearly Register: An Illustrated National Biographical Dictionary of Black Folks in Africa* (*1930*) said that Alfred Mangena was a fearless man whose "life was in danger more than once because of his success". ■

Mangena, R.A.N. (1945-78)

MANGENA, **Rogers Alfred Nikita** (1945-78).

Z IMBABWEAN politician and a celebrated military commander of the liberation forces. Rogers "Alfred Nikita" Mangena was born Rogers Mangena at Fort Rixon near Filabusi in March 1945. He was the youngest of eight children of Bakayi Mangena. In the early 1950s, his family, together with other people in the region, moved to Namande in Mazetese area to make way for European farmers. His mother died when Rogers was two years old.

Mangena attended Namande Primary School, and with the help of the missionaries went to Musume boarding school, where he was first in every class. By this time his leadership qualities had begun to show. Rogers was school captain for all the years he was at Musume. Because of his limited means Rogers seldom went home during the holidays but remained at the mission to earn some of his fees by working for the missionaries. His political inclinations became appa-

rent during school debates when he showed a mastery of current events over other students.

Mangena later transferred to Chegato Secondary School, where he was again school captain. In 1964 there was a strike by the students over increased fees. The mission authorities accused Mangena, the captain, of leading the strike and expelled him from the school. At the age of 19 he crossed the border into Zambia at the start of the liberation war.

R.A.N. Mangena

By this time, the Zimbabwe African People's Union (ZAPU) had approached several countries for the training of their cadres in preparation for armed conflict in Zimbabwe. Algeria was then the only country on the African continent that had gained its independence through armed struggle and Mangena was sent there for training. He assumed the *nom-de-guerre* Alfred Nikita and soon impressed his instructors with his leadership qualities. On his return he helped prepare other cadres for the struggle as a military instructor.

ZAPU underwent a major crisis during 1970-71, culminating in a group of men taking the law into their own hands and arresting the leadership of ZAPU, including "Nikita". At the end of the crisis, the ZAPU leadership decided to reorganise the Party and Alfred Nikita was appointed the army commander. The whole training syllabus was reorganised as part of the task of restoring discipline in the Zimbabwe People's Revolutionary Army (ZIPRA).

In 1974 the detained ZAPU leadership in Rhodesia (now Zimbabwe) was released as part of the abortive "détente" exercise. They travelled to Zambia where it was decided to merge the two armies of ZANU and ZAPU. Nikita became the Chief Political Commissar of the combined armies called ZIPA – Zimbabwe Peoples' Army. But because of political problems in the new grouping it proved very difficult to merge the two armies. The problem was accentuated by the insistence of some of the commanders on denouncing their political leaders.

Nikita, who refused to go along with these as well as other demands, then led the ZAPU section of ZIPA out of Mozambique and back to Zambia and once again set about rebuilding the army. One of the problems for Mangena was that of size and the need to maintain high training standards with a much larger force.

During the 1976 Geneva conference on Zimbabwe, Nikita formed part of the ZAPU delegation, as well as at the subsequent Malta conference.

As Commander of ZIPRA, Alfred Nikita was editor of the ZAPU armed forces magazine, the *Combat Diary*. In it he wrote a powerful poem "Forward", extolling the struggle to destroy the fascist dictatorship in Salisbury (now Harare). Alfred Nikita adopted Marxism-Leninism as his philosophy and made it compulsory teaching in the ZAPU army.

In March 1978 he survived an assassination attempt which seemed to originate from elements bent on putting a brake on the military efforts which Mangena saw as necessary in the changed Rhodesian circumstances. Just after the signing of the 2 March agreement in Salisbury and before the attempt on his life, Mangena had written in the ZIPRA *Combat Diary* that "Our patience is at an end. Let us strike mercilessly at the enemy, an enemy who is now clearly defined. Now is the time for mass revolutionary action."

After receiving treatment in Lusaka and the Soviet Union, he was soon back in command of the forces, and was killed in June 1978 when a vehicle in which he and three others were travelling hit a land mine believed to have been laid by soldiers of the Smith regime. Mangena was first buried in Leopards Hill Cemetery, Lusaka, before his remains were removed to Heroes' Acre in the Zimbabwean capital, Harare.■

Mangoaela, Z.D. (1883-1963)

MANGOAELA, Zakea Dolphin (1883-1963).

LESOTHO literary figure. Born in February 1883 to a Christian family in Hohobeng in the Cape Province of South Africa, he gained his primary school certificate in 1895 at the early age of twelve. A brilliant student, he had to wait for two years to attain the required age before entering the Basutoland Training College, where he graduated with a teaching diploma in 1902.

His first job was with mission schools in the Moloti Mountains region of his country where he taught briefly while at the same time working with a government commission to produce teaching materials. Among these were three graded readers including *Lipaliso tsa Sesotho*, which was published in 1903. Four years later, he joined the staff of the Koeneng Mission School, and simultaneously launched his writing career with articles on local history and fictional stories in the *Leselinyana* (The Little Light) journal.

Mangoaela left Koeneng in 1910 to teach at Morija, a job he combined with another as book-keeper and translator at the Morija Sesuto Book Depot, the publishers of the *Leselinyana* journal whose fortunes he helped to shape. He became the paper's chief editor in 1954, holding the position for four years. In 1911 he published a study of his country, *Lesotho's Progress (Tsoelopela ea Lesotho)*, which was followed the following year by a collection of tales and folklore entitled *Among the Wild Beasts, Large and Small (Har'a libatana le linyamatsane)*. He achieved a literary feat in 1921 with the publication of *Lithoko tsa marena a Basotho*, the first collection of Sotho praise songs of the Basotho Chiefs to be published.

A prolific writer of immense ability, he extended his literary prowess in the following years to include a pioneering work on Sesuto's grammar which resulted in the publication of the *Grammar of the Sesuto Language* in 1932, and translations of foreign titles into Sesuto. In 1944 he translated E. Roux's *The Cattle of Khumalo* (*Sebopheho sa bokreste*) and in 1960 H. Stephen's *Christian Character.* His scholarship was rewarded in 1932 when he was made a member of the Regional Literature Committee for Sotho. Mangoaela died in 1963. ∎

Manuwa, S.L.A. (1903-75)

MANUWA, Sir Samuel Layinka Ayodeji (1903-75).

NIGERIAN physician and administrator. Born on 4 March 1903 at Porogun, Ijebu-Ode, Ogun State, Nigeria, he was educated at Saint Andrew's Anglican School, Aiyesan (1907-11), St. John's School, Aroloya, Lagos (1912-13), CMS Grammar School, Lagos (1913-17), and King's College, Lagos (1918-21). Like many early West African doctors, he studied medicine at the University of Edinburgh from 1921 to 1926. There he was awarded the Robert Wilson Memorial prize and medal in Medicine, and won the Demon-

Sir Samuel Manuwa

stratorship in Human Anatomy. He published the *History of the Development of our Knowledge of the Endocrine Organs* (1924). He went on to the University of Liverpool, England, receiving its Diploma in Tropical Medicine and Hygiene in 1926 and in 1934 its Diploma in Tropical Hygiene.

He was appointed medical officer and senior surgical specialist in the British Colonial Medical Service in 1927 and remained in that service for 21 years. He published *Lymphostati Verrucosis* (1935). He served as senior surgical specialist, Ade-Oyo hospital, Ibadan, from 1944 to 1948 and published *Proocephalosis* in 1947. From 1948 he rose rapidly to high rank in the government medical service of Nigeria. He was deputy director of Medical Services (1948-51), Inspector-General of Medical Services (1951-54) and then Chief Medical Advisor to the Federal Government of Nigeria from 1954 to 1959. He published *The Estimation of Age in Nigerian Children* (1957).

He also took part in political life. He was a member of the central Legislative and Executive Councils (1951-52), a member of the Government's Privy Council (1952-54), a member of the Federal Privy Council (1954-60) and a member of the Federal Public Service Commission. He was pro-chancellor and chairman of the University Council of University of Ibadan from 1961 to 1975. He was a licentiate of medicine of Dublin (1926), a fellow of the Royal College of Surgeons (Edinburgh 1938), a member of the Royal College of Surgeons (Edinburgh 1957), a fellow of the Royal College of Physicians, the American College of Surgeons, and the Royal Society of Arts (London). He was also a member of the American Public Health Association and of the WHO Advisory Committee on Medical Research; and president of the World Federation of Mental Health, 1965-66. He served as president of the Association of Surgeons of West Africa and of the Association of Physicians. He held the traditional titles of Obadugba of Ondo, Olowa Luwagboye of Ijebu-Ode and Iyasere of Iteba. He was a Companion of the Order of St. Michael and St. George, a Member of the British Empire, a Commander of the Order of St. John of Jerusalem; he was awarded the John Holt Medal of the University of Liverpool for services to Tropical Medicine in 1959, and was awarded honorary doctorates by the Universities of Nigeria (Nsukka), Ibadan and Ife.

The publications of this prolific medical writer included *Hernia in the West African Negro* (1929), *Principles of Planning National Health Programmes in Under-Developed Countries* (1961), *Mental Health Programmes in Public Health Training* (1963), *Mental Health is Common Wealth* (1967), *The Training of Senior Administrators for Higher Responsibilities in the National Health Services of Developing Countries* (1967), and *Mass Campaign as an Instrument of Endemic Disease Control in Developing Countries.* He died on 16 September 1975. He was married twice, to Theodora Obafunmilayo Oluwole (marriage dissolved 1944), and then to Isabella Inyang Eyo Ita, who died in 1976.■

M.T. Mapikela

Mapikela, M.T. (1869-1945)

MAPIKELA, Mtobi Thomas (1869-1945).

SOUTH AFRICAN politician, a founder member of the African National Congress (ANC) in which he was active for a quarter of a century. Born in 1869 in the Cape Colony, he was educated in Grahamstown, also in South Africa; thereafter he was apprenticed as a builder and carpenter. He later set himself up in that business in Bloemfontein.

While working as carpenter/builder contractor in Bloemfontein he became a prime mover in the African politics in the Orange Free State, establishing the Native Vigilance Association of the Orange River Colony. At this time there existed also in the Orange Free State, as it did in the Transvaal and Natal, the Native Congress, and Mapikela was president of the Orange Colony Native Congress. In 1909 he led a delegation of the organisation to the national Native Convention which discussed, among other things, the implications and consequences for Africans of the South Africa Act; the National Convention drafted a petition against the anti-African measures in the Union constitution and Mapikela was in the delegation that presented the unsuccessful petition to the British government in London in 1909. He revisited Britain in 1914 as member of another African delegation which protested to the British authorities about

the 1913 Land Act which deprived Africans of land rights outside the "African homelands."

Following the Bloemfontein National Convention, Mapikela played an important part in the efforts to give African opinion cohesion, expressed under a united political platform. Thus on 8 January 1912 the South African Native National Congress, which later changed its name to the African National Congress (ANC), was created at a conference of African leaders in Bloemfontein. Its first president was Reverend John Lengalibalele Dube (q.v.) while the national secretary was Solomon Tshekisho Plaatje (q.v.), and Mapikela was elected to its national executive committee where he was to serve as official spokesman for the next twenty-five years. He was thus closely associated with formulating the early policies of the ANC whose constitution he co-drafted in 1919. He was also co-author of its 1943 *African Claims.*

Having served on the South African Location Advisory Boards Congress (a government agency) as treasurer, Mapikela was elected chairman of the Bloemfontein advisory board at its inception in 1920. Seventeen years later he was elected to represent urban African interests in the

Orange Free State and Transvaal areas in the Natives' Representative Council and remained a member until his death in 1945.

Mapikela was a popular speaker at party rallies and conferences; he was fluent in the major languages of southern Africa, which include Sesotho, Setswana and his native Xhosa.■

Mapondera, P. K. (died 1904)

•MAPONDERA, Paitando Kadungure (died 1904).

ZIMBABWEAN politician and a celebrated soldier for freedom in the 19th century. Born into the Changamira Rozvi royal family, Mapondera is reputed to have inherited the gifts of prowess and bravery as a birthright. His father, Gorenjena, was a great warrior and ruler of the Negomos, in eastern Zimbabwe, who are renowned for their valiant campaigns against both other African communities who threatened the security of the Mazoe district and early European settlers. Against both, Mapondera was to establish himself a leader whose

P.K. Mapondera

military and political exploits won him as much support as successes. Also, Mapondera (his name means "he who vanquishes the stronghold of his enemy"), was to earn himself the praise name "Hugumu" for his conquest of enemy forts.

Mapondera's early recognition came with the Mazoe campaign against Ndebele invaders of Mazoe district. He led the Mazoe forces against the Ndebeles and in the climatic battle killed their leader, Chiyama Makomo, and put an end to the threat to stability and peace in his father's domain. This achieved, Mapondera turned his attention to the Portuguese and British merchants who had entered the district in the last quarter of the 19th century. He immediately established good relations with them, signing a mineral concession with the Selous Exploitation Syndicate in 1891 and engaging in commercial ventures with the Portuguese and their agents.

But Mapondera did not subject his position to the Europeans, nor did he allow his subjects to be subjected to a subordinate status or to the injustices and excesses of the foreigners. His people, he told a Selous mining official, were entirely independent and "had never paid tribute either directly to the Portuguese government or indirectly to any *capitao mor*. . ."

Yet by 1892 the abuses of colonial rule had become commonplace in Mazoe district as the British, in a bid to establish firm control, instituted their administrative machinery. In 1892 British forces attacked Mapondera's village and in the ensuing confrontation his half-brother, Rawanga, was taken prisoner; he committed suicide in prison. By 1894, police patrols were greatly increased as government officials plundered the villages for taxation. These abuses attracted Mapondera's disfavour and his reaction was that he regarded the "Europeans as an enemy, no longer as a friend". He publicly announced his refusal to recognise the authority of the new Southern Rhodesia Native Commission and urged his followers to resist efforts to compel them to acknowledge British suzerainty and pay taxes.

In 1895, in his most defiant act, Mapondera mobilised a force of some forty men to initiate attacks on European holdings and government patrols and their African allies. The movement grew in strength, enjoying the support of the Africans in the immediate Mazoe district as well as in far away Tete district in Mozambique where Mapondera was quickly seen as a symbol of resistance to colonialism.

The Africans not only provided him with food and information on enemy troop movements, but also joined his force in increasing numbers. With the escalation of the war of resistance, Mapondera extended the campaign eastward into Portuguese-controlled Mozambique, which points to a new dimension in his political consciousness. Mapondera's campaign in Mozambique suggests that he had recognised the Europeans, irrespective of their national origin, as the source of African oppression.

Mapondera enjoyed major successes in Mozambique. From his base in Tete, his forces valiantly disrupted trade, fermented anti-colonial sentiment and openly challenged the Portuguese authorities when they supported King Muenemutapa Chioco and Makombe Hanga (qq.v.), the Barue monarch, in their opposition to collaborating with the Europeans. The experience in Mozambique had tremendous influence in Mapondera's later anti-colonial campaign in Rhodesia (now Zimbabwe). Recognising that the colonisers could only maintain their authority by working through subservient chiefs, he returned to Rhodesia in 1900 to wage war against both the European powers and their African allies. He demonstrated his new strategy when he told Chimanda; "You know me of old, Chimanda. I am a powerful man. I am going to free you from the yoke of the White man". Earlier he had told a Shona chief who rebuffed his call for unity that, "You have no excuse now as we warned you years ago against being friendly with the White men in the country. We will kill you when we have killed your White chief."

With the years, Mapondera's movement gained the support of Africans on both sides of the frontier. His alliances with Chioco and Hanga brought him more following, to the displeasure of the authorities. According to European intelligence reports, "the majority who have joined Mapondera in the past . . . will do so again on the first opportunity. They are tired of paying taxes and sooner than paying any more will join Mapondera". Mapondera had established himself as a major anti-colonial figure both in Rhodesia and Mozambique. In 1902 the Portuguese occupied his headquarters and the Barue were defeated. Crossing from Mozambique into Southern Rhodesia, he

gave himself up in 1903 and was sentenced to seven years imprisonment. He died in 1904, through a hunger strike in prison. ■

Margai, A.M. (1910-80)

MARGAI, Sir Albert Michael (1910-80).

SIERRA LEONEAN politician and second Prime Minister of his country. He was a brother and the successor of Sir Milton Margai (q.v.). He was born at Gbangbatok in Moyamba District, the sixth of seven sons of a Mende businessman. As his brother was the first medical doctor from the Sierra Leone Protectorate (declared by Britain in 1896), so Albert was the first lawyer from there. He was educated first at the Catholic Mission School at Bonthe (he always remained a Catholic), and at St. Edward's School in Freetown, after which he worked for twelve years as a male nurse. He qualified as a druggist in 1940. In November 1944, he left Government service to go to Britain to study for the Bar.

He was called to the Bar at the Middle Temple in London in 1947 and returned to Sierra Leone the following year. He enrolled as solicitor and advocate in the Supreme Court of Sierre Leone and set up in private practice. He became a member of Moyamba District Council and in 1949 of the Protectorate Assembly. After initially failing in the Freetown City Council elections of 1950, he successfully went into politics when elective representation was extended to the Protectorate in 1951. This meant a great change after a century in which Sierra Leone Colony (mainly Freetown) had been transformed by education and Christianity and had therefore had active local politics, while the Protectorate was far behind in such developments. When politics developed in the Protectorate the Margai brothers, pioneers there in professions which the Colony Creoles had followed for decades, were natural leaders.

The brothers became leaders of the Sierra Leone People's Party (SLPP) which won the 1951 elections. Albert was elected to the Legislative Council, and in 1952 he joined the first largely African government

449

as Minister of Local Government and Education. In 1957, in new elections to Legco which was now renamed the House of Representatives, he was again elected for Moyamba South. But he was now increasingly opposed to his brother's cautious leadership of the SLPP. He stood as a candidate for the leadership in an election by the party's executive and was actually elected (22 votes to 21), but agreed to stand down in favour of

Sir Albert Margai

his elder brother. He then refused to accept a ministry in the new government, left the SLPP in 1958, and formed the People's National Party (PNP) with Siaka Stevens (q.v.).

The PNP did badly in the District Council elections in 1959, winning only 33 seats (mainly in Albert Margai's own Moyamba District) out of 324. In 1960 Albert Margai allowed his party to join the United National Front formed by Sierra Leonean political parties for the purpose of talks with the British. He broke on that issue with Siaka Stevens who formed his own party, the All People's Congress (APC). After the conclusion of independence negotiations the PNP rejoined the SLPP and Albert Margai became Minister of Natural Resources. With

his brother Sir Milton Margai as Prime Minister, Sierra Leone became independent on 27 April 1961. In 1962, after elections which returned Albert as one of a new SLPP majority in Parliament, he became Minister of Finance.

On 29 April 1964, the day after the death of Sir Milton Margai, Mr. Albert Margai succeeded him as Prime Minister, becoming the second Sierra Leonean to hold the office. There was a strong protest in the SLPP leadership over the correctness of his appointment, and four ministers were dismissed by the new prime minister, including Mr. M.S.Mustapha and Dr. J. Karefa-Smart, who had been interested in the succession. After this difficult start Albert Margai was accepted as leader of the party and the country. In 1965 he was knighted by the Queen of England (still then the constitutional head of Sierra Leone).

Sir Albert was prominent in African and world politics, an example being the Commonwealth summit conference of 1966 when he criticised British policy over Zimbabwe (then Rhodesia). He was friendly with Presidents Nkrumah of Ghana and Touré of Guinea (qq.v.). In Sierra Leone he and the SLPP came to lose support. By 1966 Sir Albert was expressing opinions in favour of a Republican constitution and a one-party state. This aroused fears of dictatorship and increased support for the opposition All People's Congress of Siaka Stevens who used the APC newspaper, *We Yone*, to strongly condemn the idea of a one-party state.

In March 1967 new elections were held. A few weeks earlier Sir Albert's government announced that a plot had been uncovered, and several army officers were arrested; a state of emergency was declared, and Guinea moved troops to the border. But the elections were held and, as it later turned out, led to an APC victory. When the returns indicated this result the Governor-General, Sir Henry Lightfoot-Boston (q.v.), sent for Mr. Stevens, who went to receive the official call to form a new government. But then the Sierra Leone Military Force commander, Brig. Lansana (q.v.), intervened, declaring martial law and arresting Mr. Stevens and Sir Henry. This move was suspected to have been made in Sir Albert's interest. However, although the democratic process was halted Lansana's move did not last long for other officers soon installed a National Reformation Council (NRC).

In 1968 the NRC was overthrown and Mr. Stevens became Prime Minister. An inquiry ordered by the NRC had confirmed that the elections had been extensively rigged, and there was no doubt that despite that they had been won by the APC. Sir Albert's political career in Sierra Leone was at an end and he went to live in Britain. He died during a visit to the USA, in December 1980. ■

Margai, M.A. (1895-1964)

MARGAI, Sir Milton Augustus (1895-1964).

S IERRA LEONEAN statesman, the first Prime Minister of the country. He was born on 7 December 1895 into a merchant family at Gbangbatok, Banta Chiefdom, Moyamba District, Sierra Leone. A member of the Mende ethnic group, his early education took place in Sierra Leone at Evangelical United Brethren Mission Schools, followed by the Albert Academy and the prestigious Fourah Bay College at Freetown. In 1920 he travelled to England to study medicine at the University of Durham, and he was the first African from the Sierra Leone Protectorate to receive MB and BS degrees in 1926.

After spending a brief period in private medical practice, Milton Margai joined the colonial medical service in 1928. For the next 22 years he worked in various parts of the country, gaining a reputation as a highly skilled doctor and surgeon, as well as for organising a highly effective midwifery service. In connection with this he wrote two booklets, *A Primer on Midwifery* and *A Catechism on Midwifery*, to improve local midwifery techniques.

Meanwhile, Milton Margai's interest in politics deepened. In 1946 he founded the Sierra Leone Organisation Society (SLOS) which campaigned for progress and emancipation to be achieved within the traditional framework of the country. In the same year he was elected a member of the Bonthe District Council and later represented Bonthe in the Protectorate Assembly. He established a newspaper, the *Sierra Leone*

Observer, to publicise the political views of his party in 1949, and in 1950 he resigned from the colonial medical service to concentrate on his activities in the political field.

In 1951 the SLOS merged with the People's Party of Freetown to form the Sierra Leone People's Party (SLPP). Following the success of the SLPP in the November 1951 elections, Milton Margai was elected leader of the party and parliamentary leader. From 1951 to 1954 he was first in charge of the Ministry of Health, Agriculture and Forests, and later was made Leader of Government Business. In 1954 he became Chief Minister. The SLPP gained a substantial majority in the 1957 elections, although dissensions were growing within the Party, with the more radical element feeling that Milton Margai's approach was too cautious. This group finally broke away from the SLPP in 1958 to form the People's National Party. Despite this, Margai's SLPP won 232 out of the 324 seats in the 1959 District Council elections. In 1959 he was knighted.

In March 1960, Sir Milton Margai formed a United National Front representing all political parties in the country for

Sir Milton Margai

constitutional talks held in London. When Sierra Leone gained independence on 27 April 1961, Sir Milton became Prime Minister, a position that he held until his death.

Throughout his political life, Sir Milton was a firm believer in democracy, and he strove to ensure that all ethnic groups were represented in the ruling party and the government. He was also against any proposals that would curtail the rights of the Opposition and limit free speech. He played a leading role in the harmonious transition to independence with a minimum of conflict and was a popular figure in Sierra Leonean politics despite the opinion of some that his policies were too cautious and conservative. Although he was no orator, he was a shrewd and tactful politician.

The bases of his policies were the unification of the nation and the economic and social development of the country, and to this end he encouraged proposals of closer regional co-operation and increasing foreign investment. During his prime ministership he also made a great impact on women's social services and a considerable cultural contribution through the encouragement of artists and craftsmen. He died peacefully on 28 April 1964. ■

S.J. Mariere

Mariere, S.J. (1907-71)

MARIERE, Chief Samuel Jereton (1907-71).

NIGERIAN politician who was the first Governor of the Midwest Region, later renamed Bendel State. Born in 1907 at Evwreni, Urhobo Division, in what is now Bendel State, he was educated at St. Andrew's School, Warri and then taught at the African School at Okpari (1927-28). He worked as a clerk, and later as business manager, for Mukoro Mowoe & Co., the firm started at Warri by his relative Chief Mukoro Mowoe, from 1929 to 1938.

He then joined the major firm of John Holt and was made clerk in charge of their Agbor station. He stayed with Holt until his retirement in 1961. He was active in the Urhobo Progress Union, founded in 1931 (Chief Mowoe being its first President-

General), and became its Secretary-General from 1935 to 1938. Later he went into Nigeria's emerging politics as a National Council of Nigerian Citizens (NCNC) member. He was elected in 1953 to the NCNC's Asaba Divisional Working Committee. Standing for election with Holt's permission, he was elected NCNC member of the House of Representatives for Urhobo East (1954) and later for Urhobo Central (1959). He attended a course on parliamentary practice and procedure in the UK. He became treasurer of the parliamentary NCNC party.

On the creation of the Mid-Western Region, of which he had been a leading advocate, he was appointed Deputy Administrator and Commissioner for Chieftancy Affairs on 7 February 1964. Then he became Governor of the Region. After the fall of the civilian regime he, like the other recently removed governors of Regions, was appointed adviser to the Military Governor (1966-68).

Before retiring as adviser in 1968, he was installed Chancellor of the University of

Lagos in January 1968. He was also appointed chairman, State Schools Board, Mid-Western State in 1968. He was elected president of the Christian Council of Nigeria in 1970. He held the traditional titles of Olorogun of Evwreni (1953), Onisogene of Aboh (1964) and Ogifureze of Agbor (1965), and was awarded the honorary LLD degree by the University of Nigeria, Nsukka, in 1964, and the same degree by the University of Ibadan (also 1964). He died on 9 May 1971 as a result of a road accident. ■

Marks, J.B. (1903-72)

MARKS, John B. (1903-72).

SOUTH AFRICAN trade unionist and politician who was prominent in the African National Congress (ANC) and the Communist Party of South Africa, which he served as Treasurer-General and Chairman respectively.

Born on 21 March 1903 in Ventersdorp in the Western Transvaal, Marks was the seventh child of mixed parentage, his father being an African married to a woman of white origin. After obtaining a teacher's diploma from the Kilnerton Teachers' Training College in Pretoria in 1921, he taught in several schools in the Transvaal and the Orange Free State areas.

It was while teaching African miners' children in the Orange Free State that Marks became involved in politics, this led to his dismissal in 1931 by the authorities. Banned from teaching he went into full-time politics, joining the Communist Party of South Africa (CPSA) which had been formed in 1921. The party later sponsored his further education in the Soviet Union where he studied at the Lenin School in Moscow. Returning to South Africa he sought election to Parliament on the Communist Party platform, but was defeated in the Germiston constituency. He however succeeded in getting elected to the party's Johannesburg district committee and later to its central committee.

Marks had been active in the ANC and in the trade union movement. He rose to become Transvaal president of the ANC and later its treasurer-general. In the trade union movement he held several leading positions, which culminated in his presidency of the powerful African Mine Workers Union of which he was a founding member. As leader of the union Marks, who was also chairman of the Council of Non-European Trade Unions, led the miners' strike of August 1946 which saw some 100,000 workers refusing to work unless their conditions of service were improved. The strike was broken by the police after a week, Marks and other leading trade union officials were arrested and charged under the Riotous Assemblies Act, commencing a prolonged legal battle that lasted for more than two years.

Meanwhile, Marks had been elected to the national executive committee of the ANC, playing a leading role in its activities between 1946 and 1952 when banning orders restricted his political activity. In 1952, however, he challenged the regulations to participate in the Defiance Campaign of that year. Subsequent bans forced him to leave South Africa in 1963 to join the external mission of the ANC in Tanzania. In 1969 he was elected the CPSA chairman in exile, while also remaining in the executive committee of the ANC as treasurer-general.

He was taken ill in 1971 and went to Moscow for treatment; he died there on 1 August 1972 and is buried in the Novodevi-

J.B. Marks

chye Cemetery in Moscow where another
ANC leader, Moses Mauane Kotane (q.v.),
was buried six years later.■

Massemba-Debat, A. (1921-77)

MASSEMBA-DEBAT, Alphonse (1921-77).

CONGOLESE politician, born in 1921 in
Nkolo, near Brazzaville where he had his
elementary education and then trained as a
teacher. He began his teaching career in 1934
in Fort Lamy (now Ndjamena), capital of
Chad, then part of French Equatorial Africa.
It was there also, during the same period,
that Massemba-Debat was induced into the
emerging nationalism against French colonialism in Central and West Africa. He
joined the *Parti Progressiste Tchadien* (PPT)
which later became the Chadian section of
the inter-territorial *Rassemblement Démocratique Africain* (RDA). In 1945 he became
general secretary of the *Association des
Evolués du Tchad* which he served until
1947.

A. Massemba-Debat

Returning to Brazzaville in 1947 to
become headmaster of a primary school,
Massemba-Debat took increasing part in the
politics of his country and the following year
joined the *Parti Progressiste Congolais*
(PPC), the local branch of the RDA. In 1956,
when the *Union Démocratique pour la Défense des Intérêts Africains* (UDDIA) of Abbé
Fulbert Youlou (q.v.) succeeded the PPC as
the Congolese wing of the RDA, Massemba-
Debat became an active member of the new
organisation. He subsequently abandoned
teaching in 1957 in favour of full-time
politics, on the eve of the election for
internal self-government which preceded
independence. Though he himself was not
elected to the Legislative Assembly until
1959, he was given an important political
office as assistant to the Minister of Education in 1957.

Between 1959 and 1961 he served as
President of the Assembly. He was appointed
Minister of State in 1961, a year after
independence, and later Minister of Planning and Equipment. He served subsequently as Speaker of the National Assembly and
as Minister of Economic Development until
his resignation in May 1963, when he
opposed President Youlou's excessive pro-
French policies.

On 19 December 1963, following the
forced resignation of the Youlou government in August 1963, Massemba-Debat was
recalled to head a new government. As President of the Republic, he devoted the early
part of his rule to political reorganisation
which gave rise to the adoption of a one-
party system, centred on the *Mouvement
National Révolutionnaire* (MNR) officially
constituted on 2 July 1964. He was elected
the first secretary-general of the party
which sought to unite all the different
political elements in the country and
through which the Congo would progress
toward "scientific socialism" at home while
pursuing an independent foreign policy.

President Massemba-Debat was
overthrown by the more radical elements in
the Congolese army on 4 September 1968, and
was succeeded as Head of State by Major
Marien Ngouabi (q.v.). His deposition threw
him once again into political obscurity.
Later he was arrested and accused in early
March 1977 of alleged complicity in the
assassination of his successor, President
Ngouabi. Massemba-Debat was subsequently
executed on 25 March 1977.■

Masuku, L. (1940-86)

MASUKU, Lookout (1940-86).

ZIMBABWEAN nationalist, the celebrated hero of the Black nationalist war against white minority rule in Rhodesia (now Zimbabwe) and former Deputy Commander of the Zimbabwe National Army. During the liberation struggle, Masuku was Commander of the Zimbabwe People's revolutionary Army (ZIPRA), the military wing of ZAPU. At independence in 1980, he was appointed one of the top five military officers who made up the Joint Military Command (JMC). The body was charged, in addition to normal security duties, with the task of building the new national army through the integration of the Zimbabwe African National Liberation Army (ZANLA), ZANU's military wing, ZIPRA and the former Rhodesian forces of Ian Smith. By the end of June 1981, Masuku and his colleagues had successfully established 18 fully configurated battalions, each equally made up of units from the liberation forces and the Rhodesian forces. The JMC also succeeded in disarming all the former guerillas.

Masuku's war effort was further rewarded with his appointment as Deputy Commander of the new Zimbabwe National Army. He was, however, soon arrested, in 1982, on charges of plotting a coup against Mugabe's government. Tried the following year and acquitted of treason charges, he was again detained until 11 March when he was freed on health grounds.

Lookout Masuku died in the Parirenyatwa Hospital, Harare, on 5 April 1986. Masuku, aged 46, suffered from cryptococcal meningitis, an inflammation of the membrane covering the brain, which caused his admission into the Harare hospital on 9 February. His death came 28 days after the lifting of detention orders which had held him in prison for his alleged involvement in a plot said to have been organized by the opposition Zimbabwe African People's Union (ZAPU), party of Joshua Nkomo, to overthrow the government of Prime Minister Robert Mugabe.■

L. Masuku

Matante, P.P.G. (1912-79)

MATANTE, Philip Parcel Goanwe (1912-79).

BOTSWANA politician who founded and led the opposition Botswana People's Party (BPP). He was born in 1912 in Serowe, in the north of Gaborone, but spent most of his early years in South Africa where he had his education before joining the army in 1939. By the time he left military service in 1947 he had become a sergeant-major in the Army Corps formed in the three British High Commission Territories.

After his demobilisation he became active in South African politics in the early 1950s as a member of the Youth League of the African National Congress (ANC) and later joined the Pan Africanist Congress (PAC). An enigmatic, shrewd organiser and orator, he soon became a figure of central importance in the nationalist movement and, as such, became a target for the South African regime. He fled South Africa in 1956, joining the influx of the politically experienced nationalists who arrived in Botswana in the late 1950s. From 1957 he worked on various projects including a Commonwealth Development Corporation project in Botswana and later became manager of a Francistown general store.

Matante took to full-time politics in 1960 as a founder member of Botswana's first modern political party, the Bechuanaland (now Botswana) People's Party (BPP). He was elected its vice-president, serving with Kgalemang Motsete who was president and Motsamai Mpho, secretary-general, in the leadership of the new party.

He occupied a pivotal position in the evolution of Botswana nationalism; he was strongly influenced by the philosophy of Dr. Kwame Nkrumah and was often described as a man of strong personality, stubborn in his obsession with Pan-Africanism and fierce in attacking his ideological opponents. For this he was known as the 'Lion of Botswana' by his political supporters,but the same militancy had sometimes led some to accuse him of racialism which Matante vehemently denied.

In 1964 he said: "We, the BPP, say that Africa is the land of the Africans, from the Cape to Cairo, from Morocco to Madagascar. Does this suggest that we are racialists? We believe that we are all one race: the human race. We say to hell with multiracialism, because it seeks to entrench racialism in our country".

The BPP was founded on this Pan-Africanist principle, which not only put Botswana on the Pan-African map but also enabled the party to build up a rapid spread of political consciousness in the country. It was partly in reaction to its militancy and partly because of its phenomenal growth that Seretse Khama (q.v.) formed the Botswana Democratic Party (BDP) in 1962. Matante remained as BPP's vice-president until 1964 when the party was split into two sections, with Mpho leading a breakaway group that regrouped as the Botswana Independence Party (BIP). Though Motsete remained president of the BPP, it was only the following year that he lost the presidency to Matante, and no sooner had the latter taken over than the party's programme was given a vigorous revitalisation.

The party made substantial gains in the pre-independence elections of 1965, which, though these gave Seretse's BDP a majority in the National Assembly, left Matante's BPP in control of major commercial centres like Francistown. He himself was elected as one of the members representing Francistown and he became leader of opposition in the parliament. In the subsequent local and national elections in 1969, the BPP retained its stronghold over Francistown, winning both its parliamentary seats and a majority of the seats in the local council. This was repeated in the North-Western District Council, but in both cases Matante's victory was vitiated by the government which increased the number of nominated, as opposed to elected, members of the local council.

P.P.G. Matante

The BPP's success in the 1969 elections confirmed Matante's reputation as a skilled politician who, despite the combined opposition from the BDP and BIP, made his mark in Botswana politics. In parliament, as at political rallies, he was both eloquent and steadfast in his commitment to Pan-Africanism.

Matante remained president of the BPP and leader of opposition in parliament until the October 1979 national elections when he lost his Francistown seat. He died on 24 October 1979, just a week after the elections, in a Gaborone hospital.■

Matatu, G. H. (1947-89)

MATATU, Godwin Herbert (1947-89).

ZIMBABWEAN journalist who made a most significant contribution to African journalism in the 1970s and 1980s. His death at the relatively young age of 42 deprived African journalism of one of its most respected practitioners. Godwin Herbert Matatu was born on 26 May 1947 into a peasant family in Mrewa, Zimbabwe. After primary school, Matatu attended the Goromozi Government School in 1961-2 and the Hartzell High School in 1963-4. He then moved to Europe and studied in Britain, Norway and France, attending Pembroke College, Oxford from 1969 to 1971.

Matatu began his career as a reporter for *Remarques Africaines* in Brussels in 1968, and worked as a research assistant for the Franz Fanon Institute in Milan in 1970. He went to work in Addis Ababa as a feature writer for the *Ethiopian Herald* in 1971. In 1973 Matatu began work for the London-based AFRICA Magazine as a freelance researcher and writer. He later joined the journal on a full-time basis and quickly rose through the ranks to become the senior editor of the magazine between 1974 and 1980. During that time, Matatu became a significant editorial asset of AFRICA Magazine. He established a wide range of contacts with African leaders from all over the continent, and partly as a result of his work, the magazine became the most authoritative voice in African journalism in the 1970s and early 1980s, as it was able to cover most major issues affecting the continent with inside knowledge. Using AFRICA Magazine, with its pronounced pan-African commitment, as his platform Matatu played a most notable role in the field of information and publicity for the Zimbabwean struggle against Ian Smith's UDI (Unilateral Declaration of Independence) government, the struggle against apartheid in South Africa, and the independence struggle in Namibia. This work won Matatu a special award from the OAU.

Matatu also rendered valuable service to a range of professional and political organisations, some of which he helped to found. These included the All African Journalists and Broadcasters Conference, and the Pan African Association of Writers and Journalists. In 1973-4 he also served as the organising secretary of the London branch of the Zimbabwe African National Union (ZANU), the party which eventually formed the government when Zimbabwe became independent in 1980. Matatu returned to

G.H. Matatu

Zimbabwe briefly in 1980, then returned to AFRICA Magazine as Political Editor. He went back to Zimbabwe in 1983 to live in Harare, from where he worked as Africa correspondent for the London-based *Observer* newspaper.

Apart from the eminence he attained in his profession, Matatu was known as a cheerful, easy-going person, very popular in the community of London-based African journalists. Matatu was on assignment in Windhoek, observing the countdown to Namibian independence, when he suddenly died from a heart attack on 24 July 1989. He left behind a widow, Rita, and two sons. ∎

Matenje, D.T. (1929-83)

MATENJE, Dick Tennyson (1929-83).

MALAWIAN politician and educationist who for over ten years was an influential member of government in post-independence Malawi.

Born on 29 January 1929 outside Blantyre, Dick Tennyson Matenje went to Bemvu Primary School and the Henry Henderson Institute (H.H.I.) in Blantyre before he entered Blantyre Secondary School and the Domasi Teachers' Training College where he qualified as a teacher in 1951. He taught for nine years during which time he became headmaster of Namadzi Primary School, and then went to Bristol University, England, where he obtained a Diploma in Education in 1960. Matenje returned to Malawi in 1961 and taught at the H.H.I. until 1962 when he was promoted district education officer for Blantyre. In 1963 he did a course at the University of Perth, Australia, and obtained a Diploma in Education Administration. Back home he joined the Soche Hill Teachers' Training College, becoming the headmaster of the Soche Hill Secondary

D.T. Matenje

School in 1964 at the end of which year he left for Ottawa University in Canada where he graduated with a BA.

On his return to Malawi in 1969, Matenje was appointed education officer in the Ministry of Education before he became principal of Domasi Teachers' Training College in March 1971. It was then that Matenje's career in politics started; that same year he was nominated member of Parliament for Blantyre.

Though his was a late entry into politics, he was in his forties when he joined the government, he was soon promoted to various ministerial posts. It was believed that Matenje's rapid rise to influence was due to his attention to detail, his personal and strong party loyalties and his dedication to his work. He became Minister of Education in February 1972, and was appointed Minister of Finance five months later. In that later capacity, Matenje was able to successfully promote the development of fisheries in Malawi.

When Aleke Banda was dismissed as a minister, Matenje acquired the extra portfolios of Trade, Industry and Tourism in March 1983. Though he did not have any professional qualifications in finance or banking, and indeed was more of an educationist than an economist, he was thought to have been good in these posts, being a man of no impulsive action who resisted being pushed into quick decisions and inspired confidence by his measured style.

Matenje was very much in the news from 1973 onwards when he was appointed Secretary-General and administrative head of the ruling Malawi Congress Party, a position he held until 1975. He was reappointed Minister of Finance before he became again Secretary-General of the Malawi Congress Party and Minister without Portfolio in 1981.

As Secretary-General of the Malawi Congress Party and its administrative head, Matenje theoretically was the most powerful man after Banda, Malawi's President. In the event of Banda vacating the Presidency of Malawi, he would have taken over as Chairman of a Presidential Commission of three cabinet ministers as provided for in the Malawi Constitution, calling three weeks thereafter a convention of the Party to elect a new President of the Party who automatically would have become the new President of Malawi. Thus when Banda intimated that he intended to take a sabbatical leave to Britain after the general elections of June 1983, and that during that period he intended appointing John Tembo, an uncle of Cecilia Kadzamila (the official hostess of Banda) as his successor ad interim, Matenje as Secretary-General of the Party and its administrative head opposed the move on grounds of its illegality as Tembo was not then a cabinet minister and had been, it was alleged, an inefficient governor of the Malawi Reserve Bank. He was joined in this opposition by the former Minister of the Central Region, Aaron Elliot Gadama (q.v.), former Minister of Health, John Sangala and the former Member of Parliament for Blantyre, John Chiwanga.

The four died on 19 May 1983 in what was officially termed an accident. Some saw it, however, as "part of an elimination process to pave the way for John Tembo to take over the leadership after Banda." Indeed, it was also said that their death was the result of an internecine power struggle among senior Malawi politicians.

Dick Matenje died at the age of 53, leaving a wife and several children.∎

Matshikiza, T.T. (1921-68)

MATSHIKIZA, Todd Thozambile (1921-68).

SOUTH AFRICAN composer who wrote the music for the successful play *King Kong* by Harry Bloom. Matshikiza was born in 1921 in Queenstown, South Africa, in a musically inclined family; his father was a church organist. After attending Lyndhurst Road Public School in Kimberley, he went to St. Peter's Secondary School in Rosettenville in Johannesburg and later studied at Adams College, Natal, and at Lovedale in the Cape Province where he obtained a teacher's diploma. He later taught at Lovedale until 1947 when he resigned from teaching. While at school he took piano lessons, both at school and through private tutorials.

Matshikiza then went to Johannesburg to work first as a hotel waiter, then as a messenger, a bookshop assistant and a journalist. He became a full-time journalist in 1951 when he took employment with the *Drum* monthly publication as a reporter. He soon rose to become its features editor but left the magazine to work for the weekly *Post* as news editor. During this period he began playing with a local musical group, the Harlem Swingsters Jazz Band, in the night clubs in Johannesburg.

T.T. Matshikiza

Between 1949 and 1954 Matshikiza was among a group of African musicians who formed an association, the Committee Syndicate of African Artists, with the view of protecting their interests in the harsh, exploitative world of show-business. Soon he began to identify with the aspirations of his fellow Africans in their political campaign against the measures of the white supremacy regime. When the government deported the British clergyman, Reverend Huddleston, following his opposition to some racist measures, Matshikiza wrote a protest song, *Makhaliphile* (The Clever One), in honour of the cleric for his unrepentant stance. In 1956 he wrote another protest song, *Uxolo*, which has since become popular in the Africanist circles.

In 1958 Matshikiza was commissioned to write the music for *King Kong*, a play by Harry Bloom, which tells the story of the famous African boxer, Ezekiel Dlamini. When the play opened in Johannesburg that year, it was acclaimed by critics both for its music and form, and it had the distinction of becoming the first play in South Africa to be performed before mixed audiences in recent years. *King Kong* transferred to London's Princess Theatre in 1961 where it had a successful ten-month run. Matshikiza, who had accompanied the company to London, opted for exile in Britain and took employment with the British Broadcasting Corporation (BBC).

He returned to Africa in 1964 as an announcer/producer in newly independent Zambia. The following year he was among South Africa's black artists who participated in Zambia's first national arts festival. He worked in Zambia until his death in 1968. He was the author of a book, *Chocolates for My Wife*. ■

Matswa, A. (1889-1942)

MATSWA, André (1889-1942).

CONGOLESE politician. Born near Brazzaville, of the Balali people, he was one of the few people in the French colony of Middle Congo (Moyen-Congo) who received some Western education in the early colonial period, when the major concern of the French was the brutal extraction of wealth through forcible rubber collection for Concessionary Companies. Matswa became a mission catechist and a customs officer. He served in the French army in Morocco in 1924-5. On demobilisation, he worked in France as an accountant at a social welfare office in Paris. There he started an organisation called the *Amicale des Originaires de l'Afrique Equatoriale Française* in 1926 (a "friendly society" for "people of French Equatorial Africa origin"), at first non-political, aiming to help Africans in France and approved by the Governor-General of Equatorial Africa. But then it began to call for extension of rights of citizenship to Africans, and to send protests against the Concessionary Companies, the *Indigénat* (the special system of summary justice for Africans), and other oppression.

Matswa's organisation also established branches in the French Middle Congo colony – in the Bakongo, Basoundi and Balali ethnic areas. And the colonial authorities became alarmed at the *Amicale*. The leaders in the Congo were arrested and 100,000

A. Matswa

francs collected in subscriptions were confiscated. Then, in December 1929, Matswa was arrested in France and deported back to Brazzaville. There he was charged with "fraud", a common charge against Africans who collected money for protest activity in French colonies.

On 3 April 1930 he was sentenced to three years' imprisonment and five years' restricted movement. When the conviction was announced there was a big demonstration by Africans outside the court, leading to firing by troops and many arrests. Matswa was sent to Chad. The *Amicale* survived secretly, and was revived openly again for a short time in 1934-5, only to be suppressed again.

Matswa later escaped into the Belgian Congo. He made his way back to France and joined the army there in 1939. In May 1940 he was arrested on a charge of spying and sent back to the Congo. The Free French regime later had him tried and, on 8 January 1941, sentenced to life imprisonment. On 12 January 1942 he died in prison at Mayena in Chad. Officially he was said to have died of dysentery, but it was rumoured that his death was due to beating. ■

Matthews, Z.K. (1901-68)

MATTHEWS, Professor Zachariah Keodirelang (1901-68).

BOTSWANA politician and his country's first Permanent Representative to the United Nations. He was born in Kimberley, South Africa in 1901 where his father combined work in the diamond mines with a small business as a tearoom owner. His early education was at an Anglican school from which he won a bursary to Lovedale Mission. He later went to Fort Hare College where he became the first African to graduate. He was appointed headmaster of Adams College in Natal but decided to study law, later qualifying as an attorney of the South African Supreme Court in the Transvaal Division. At Adams College he married Freda Bokwe, a descendant of the famous writer and musician, John Bokwe (q.v.). Matthews later travelled to the USA where he enrolled at Yale University in New Haven, Connecticut. He left to study at the London School of Economics and Political Science in 1934. He wrote an MA dissertation entitled "Bantu Law and Western Civilisation". His standing in the academic world gradually increasing, he was appointed a research fellow of the International Institute of African Languages and Culture in London. Before returning to South Africa, he was appointed member of the Commission on Higher Education for Africa in East Africa and Sudan by the Secretary of State for the Colonies.

On arriving in South Africa in 1935, he threw in his support against the Hertzog government's disenfranchisement of African voters in the Cape. He joined the South African National Congress (ANC) in 1942 and became an active political campaigner as well as professor of Social Anthropology, Native Law and Administration at Fort Hare University College. He became Head of the Department of African Studies in 1936. In 1941 he was elected to the Native Representative Council, but resigned from this moderate body in 1950. A year before he had become president of the ANC in the Cape Province.

During the Defiance Campaign in 1952-53 Matthews was in New York lecturing at the Union Theological Seminary. On his return he was appointed acting principal of Fort Hare, the position he held when he was arrested in 1956 on charges of high treason. The charges were withdrawn in 1958, but two years later, he was detained under the State of Emergency. He had already resigned from Fort Hare following the Nationalist Government's takeover of the College in order to bring it in line with its apartheid policies in African education. After being held for six months without trial, he came out and established his own law practice in Alice in the Cape.

He later joined the World Council of Churches in Geneva and headed its African Affairs section. He was in this position when the Botswana government invited him to be its ambassador to the UN and USA. Professor Matthews died in Washington in March 1968. ■

Prof. Z. K. Matthews

Maxeke, C.M.M.
(1874-1939)

MAXEKE, Charlotte Makgomo Manye
(1874-1939).

SOUTH AFRICAN social scientist and politician, founder member of the African National Congress Women's League, and the first African woman in South Africa to earn the Bachelor's degree. Born on 7 April 1874 in Ramokgopa near Fort Beaufort in the Pietersburg district, South Africa, she joined an African choir while attending school in Port Elizabeth. It was while touring Europe and America with the choir in the 1890s that young Maxeke was offered a scholarship to study at Wilberforce University in Cleveland in Ohio, USA, an African Methodist Episcopal (AME) institute run by Afro-Americans. Maxeke was later instrumental in establishing a mission of the AME in her country.

She graduated from Wilberforce University with a BSc degree in 1905. It was while studying at the University that she met and married Reverend Marshall Maxeke, a fellow South African who was also a student there. The Maxekes returned to

C.M.M. Maxeke

South Africa and founded the Wilberforce Institute in the Transvaal, which grew to be the leading institution of higher education for Africans. Maxeke also took active part in the establishment of the AME missions in the country and she was later elected president of the Women's Missionary Society by the AME.

From 1919 onwards Maxeke's exceptional talents as a leader and able organiser won her wide respect both among Africans and the authorities who frequently sought her opinion on matters concerning Africans. She was appointed a probation officer, the first African woman to be so appointed, for young people in custody in Johannesburg and among the many recommendations she made in this capacity were the appointment of women magistrates and the creation of juvenile courts that would be better equipped to deal with cases of children and their parents. On 27 July 1930 she told a conference of the European and Bantu Christian Student Associations meeting in Fort Hare that the problems facing the African woman in the home emanated from the migratory system which she described as "the stream of native life into the towns" and from the labour laws which prevent the wife from living with her husband in his place of work. "Thus", she added, "the woman starts on a career of crime for herself and her children, a career which often takes her and her children right down the depths of misery. The woman, poor unfortunate victim of circumstances, goes to prison, and the children are left more desolate than when their parents left them to earn a living."

Her political campaign for African rights dates back to 1919 when she founded the Bantu Women's League to give organised opposition to the proposed extension of the pass system to African women. The League became the women's wing of the African National Congress of which Maxeke was elected its first President. As such she was a leading figure in the ANC's protracted campaign against the pass laws in particular and for the rights and freedom of the African in general. She was described in 1935 by Alfred Bitini Xuma (q.v.) as "the mother of African freedom in South Africa."

Maxeke died in 1939, at the age of 65 long before the ANC adopted its non-passive strategy in the campaign against the measures of the white minority government in

South Africa. The movement was subsequently banned in 1962 and it established its external headquarters in Tanzania, where in August 1980 the Charlotte Maxeke Child Care Centre was opened in memory of the first president of the ANC Women's League. ■

newspapers (which were of high quality) in the late 19th and early 20th centuries. It was edited by J.C. May's brother, Cornelius, who later also became famous as a Mayor of Freetown in the 1920s.

The Rev. May married Christiana Bull and they had seven children. ■

May, J.C. (1845-1902)

MAY, Rev. Joseph Claudius (1845-1902).

SIERRA LEONEAN clergyman and prominent educationist. Born on 14 August 1845 in Freetown, he was the son of a Yoruba Recaptive Creole clergyman, the Rev. Joseph May, who died in 1891. He worked first as a shop assistant until the age of 20, when it was decided that he should follow his father into the Wesleyan (Methodist) ministry. He did so after education in England, latterly at Wesley College, Taunton, Somerset, and Westminster Normal Training School.

He returned to Sierra Leone in 1871. His ordination was delayed by the chairman and general superintendent of the Sierra Leone Methodist Church, the Rev. B. Tregaskis, who had sponsored his studies (and those of Samuel Lewis, q.v.). Tregaskis had for long planned a secondary school to rival the Grammar School of the Church Missionary Society which ran the other major Protestant mission in Sierra Leone, but he delayed its opening until 1874 and the Rev. J.C. May became its first principal. He was ordained in 1880.

For a quarter of a century the Rev. May headed one of the major educational institutions in that early centre of Western education in West Africa. According to Prof. C. Fyfe (*A Short History of Sierra Leone*), "He was a fine teacher, kind and patient, who won the affection of his staff and pupils, and made his school as good as, if not better than, the (CMS) Grammar School." He remained principal until his death on 14 October 1902.

From 1882 to 1888 he was editor of the *Methodist Herald*. And in September 1884, aided by Dr. E.W. Blyden (q.v.), he founded the *Sierra Leone Weekly News*. It was the most famous of all the Sierra Leonean

---

Mazengo (1852-1967)

MAZENGO, Chief (1852-1967).

TANZANIAN traditional ruler. The only child of Chief Chalula whose pre-colonial Wagogo state extended over the Dodoma and Mpwapwa regions, Mazengo was born in 1852. The Wagogo empire was strategically located in today's central Tanzania and thus controlled the then important slave and

Chief Mazengo

ivory trade route from the Indian Ocean coast to the hinterland of East Africa. As a result Wagogo exerted tremendous political and economic dominance in the region before German occupation.

Mazengo succeeded to the headship of Wagogo on his father's death shortly before the Germans arrived. His position was initially recognised by the colonial authorities who conferred on him the title of *Jumbe*, but the chief resented the impudence of being required to subordinate his rule to an alien power. Soon a clash ensued between him and the Europeans, following which Chief Mazengo voluntarily went into hiding. His son Chalula was appointed as successor and served until Germany surrendered Tanganyika to the British after the First World War – Chief Mazengo was subsequently reinstated as head of Wagogo by the new colonial administration.

Once restored by the British, Chief Mazengo began to implement a progressive programme; his reign from then on was marked by a gradual expansion of education and medical facilities in the region. Chief Mazengo's aims were to improve the living standard of his people. He encouraged missionary activities in his chiefdom, facilitating the building of schools and hospitals which include the present-day hospital at Mvumi. Among the education institutions built during this time is the Alliance Secondary School, now re-named after Chief Mazengo. He also encouraged the development of adult literacy education and he himself is reputed to have participated in an adult education course at a very late stage of his life.

In independent Tanzania Chief Mazengo became a strong supporter of the government policy which abolished chieftainship in the country, following which he himself retired. He was one of the two traditional rulers, the other being Chief Petro Marealle of Kilimanjaro, who officiated at the swearing in ceremony of Julius Nyerere as first President of Tanzania in 1964. He strongly supported the government campaign to mobilise the population to live in Ujamaa villages, for which the Dodoma region which was formerly under his jurisdiction attracted one of the largest responses in the country. Chief Mazengo died in 1967, just at the time of the public discussion on moving the country's headquarters from Dar-es-Salaam to Dodoma. ■

Mazerieux, E.C. (1899-1962)

MAZERIEUX, Major E. de Coulhac (1899-1962).

SEYCHELLOIS politician. He was born in 1899. After completing his primary education he attended St Joseph College in Mauritius and then travelled to France to study at a college of higher commercial studies in Paris. On the outbreak of World War I he joined the French Army and was later awarded the Croix de Guerre. During World War II he served as commander of the Seychelles Section of the Royal Pioneer Corps and reached the rank of major.

After World War II he began to develop his business interests in the Seychelles and also became involved in politics, becoming a member of the Independent Party. In 1954 he was elected to the Legislative Council representing the Central District (which included Victoria, the capital of the Islands). He was re-elected to the Legislative Council in 1957 and at the same time was appointed a member of the Executive Council.

The following year he was awarded an OBE by the British Government. He continued to represent Victoria and the outlying islands on both the Legislative and Executive Councils until his resignation early in 1962. He died soon after on 1 May 1962. ■

Mazorodze, S.C. (1933-81)

MAZORODZE, Dr Simon Charles (1933-81).

ZIMBABWEAN physician and politician whose eminence in both fields brought him into the first government of independent Zimbabwe as Minister of Health in 1981. He had a brilliant medical career which took him to the position of District Medical Officer and later Senior House Surgeon at Harare Hospital at a time when the racist policy of the White settler regime barred African progress. Dr Mazorodze combined this with underground supportive activities for the Zimbabwe African National Union (ZANU) during the long-drawn, bitter war of independence. He was a founder-member of that party in 1963.

Simon Charles Mazorodze was born on 29 November 1933 at Nhamo in the Mhondoro Tribal Trustland in Hartley District. His father was a postman and his mother was a local leader of the Methodist Church; she suffered from poor eye-sight when he was still attending local schools and had him read the Bible to her. After schooling at the Mufuka, Chibero and the Marshall Hartley primary schools he completed his studies at the Waddilove Institute in 1949. He then entered the Goromonzi Secondary School from where he was admitted to read medicine at the University of Natal in South Africa. In 1962 he gained the MB. and Ch.B. qualifications but remained in South Africa at the King Edward Hospital for his housemanship.

The following year Dr Mazorodze returned to Zimbabwe to specialise in Obstetrics and Gynaecology at Harare Hospital in Salisbury (now Harare). Soon he became Senior Registrar there, from 1963 for four years – he was transferred in 1967 to the Victoria area as Medical Officer for the Ndanga, Bikita and Gutu districts. Seven years later he left the public service to set up on his own, opening a surgery in Fort Victoria where his affection for patients and the general public alike, plus his clandestine activities among the locals on behalf of ZANU, soon made him a very popular doctor. He responded to the increasing demands put on him by his profession and his party by making himself as readily available at local meetings as was possible.

By that time the armed struggle against the Rhodesian forces of the illegal regime of Ian Smith had entered a crucial and decisive phase with the opening of the northeastern front by the army of ZANU, the Zimbabwe African National Liberation Army (ZANLA). This 1974 offensive was soon extended to cover other parts of the country; such was the intensity of the warfare that the enemy had to deploy most of its forces. The cumulative result was increased casualties on both sides and Dr Mazorodze, whose official appointment had hitherto prevented him from overt involvement in the struggle, became more actively involved.

Dr. S.C. Mazorodze

Now, in addition to organising for ZANU and assisting refugees fleeing the country, he started giving medical treatment to the wounded guerrillas of ZANLA. He used to travel out at night from his Fort Victoria practice to tend these in bush-camps, administering what he described as "cocktail anaesthetics" during major operations. He recalled later that he lost only one patient, "due to excessive bleeding".

He was in regular contact with the ZANU headquarters in Mozambique where the demise of Portuguese rule in April 1974 had allowed for added logistical support for the party's war efforts. He maintained these links with the nationalists throughout this difficult phase, at the risk of his life under the prevailing political system. He was arrested and detained briefly in late 1979 after he had treated a wounded guerrilla.

By then, however, the war was in its final stage and Zimbabweans were organising for their first democratic elections which Mazorodze contested on the ZANU-Patriotic Front ticket. He won his seat in the Victoria constituency and in March 1980 was appointed to the first administration of Robert Mugabe. He was given the post of Deputy Minister of Health; in late 1981 he was made head of the Ministry but died later that same year.■

Mba, L. (1902-67)

MBA, Léon (1902-67).

GABONESE statesman and first President of the Republic. Mba was born on 9 February 1902 in Libreville, the capital of Gabon. A member of the prominent Fang ethnic group, he was educated in a Roman Catholic Mission school in Libreville and later specialised in African customary law.

He began his career working with the French colonial administration in Gabon, rising from an accountant to an administrator of a *canton* in Lower Gabon during the 1930s. In this period he was also a journalist with the *Echos Gabonais*. From an early age, Léon Mba was proud of his African heritage and his concern that colonial rule and European economic penetration would erode his country's traditional life-style led him into politics.

He was in trouble with the government as early as 1922, and was sent into exile in 1933 for obscure reasons. He went to Oubangui-Chari (which later became the Central African Republic) and stayed there for 13 years.

In 1946 Léon Mba returned to Gabon and joined a British trading company, meanwhile continuing his political activities in his spare time. In the same year he founded the *Mouvement Mixte Gabonais* (MMG), which was linked to the *Rassemblement Démocratique Africain* (RDA), a movement seeking autonomy for French Africa. He was also a member of the Working Committee of the RDA, with responsibility for the press. His political status was enhanced by a congress called to resolve Fang Ethnic problems by the Gabon colonial administration in 1947, where he demonstrated his ability to reconcile apparently opposing factions.

After losing in the 1951 elections, Léon Mba was elected a member of the Gabonese Territorial Assembly in 1952, and in 1953 he re-organised the MMG and renamed it the *Bloc Démocratique Gabonais* (BDG). He was also Mayor of Libreville following the 1956 municipal elections.

The BDG defeated the opposition *Union Démocratique et Sociale Gabonaise* (UDSG) in the 1957 territorial elections and

Mba was appointed Vice-President of the Executive Council under the French Governor. His political strength lay in his ability to bring together diverse interest and ethnic groupings, thus allowing the creation of a broad basis of support, together with his ability to placate the opposition. After the elections he selected several ministers from the UDSG party, all of whom subsequently joined the BDG.

L. Mba

Following the elections of July 1958 Mba became President of the Executive Council. In February 1959 he was elected Prime Minister, and when Gabon gained independence on 17 August 1960, Mba was made Head of State. Initially he encountered opposition from those who saw his policies as rather conservative and pro-French, and a six-month state of emergency had to be declared, beginning in November 1960. However, in the February 1961 elections, he was overwhelmingly confirmed as President of the Republic.

By 1964 political tensions were once more apparent, and on 18 February troops captured key points in the capital. Mba was forced to resign and a new Head of State was named. On 19 February, following an appeal from the Vice-President, French paratroopers retook the city and Mba regained the presidency. He managed once again to come to terms with the opposition members in the National Assembly who declared their support for the government.

Apart from this instance, Léon Mba remained President of Gabon until his death. While Head of State, his underlying policy was one of political stability and economic development. Throughout his political career he remained strongly pro-French and a supporter of African freedom, although he preferred loose links of military and economic co-operation rather than a form of federalism involving loss of sovereignty. To this end he joined the Central African Customs and Economic Union (UDEAC), and later, in 1966, he signed the Charter of the now defunct Common Afro-Malagasy Organisation (OCAM). In August 1966, Mba went into hospital in Paris where he died following a long illness on 28 November 1967. ■

Mbacke, A. A. (c.1905-89)

MBACKE, Abdoul Ahad (c.1905-89).

SENEGALESE religious leader. He was the third successor or *Khalife-Général* to the founder of the Mourides Islamic order, Ahmadou Bamba (q.v.), who bore the family name Mbacke. He thus headed the order after Ahmadou Bamba, his father, and two of his elder brothers.

After Ahmadou Bamba Mbacke's death in 1927, his son Mamadou Mustafa Mbacke succeeded him and took the title of *Khalife-Général.* He was recognised as the founder's heir by the French colonial authorities, in preference to the founder's brother Cheikh Anta Mbacke. He presided over continued expansion of the order, whose followers expanded groundnut culti-

vation ever further over Senegal, earning money both for themselves and for the order. He continued the building of the grand mosque and mausoleum at Touba, but died in 1945 before the building could be completed. This was achieved under the next *Khalife-Général,* the founder's second son Falilou Mbacke.

After several decades of cooperation between the Mourides and the French colonial rulers, Falilou Mbacke adapted to the changing situation in Africa and formed an alliance with Léopold Senghor and his party in Senegalese politics. From the late 1950s that party ruled with the very important support of the Mourides, until today (as the *Parti Socialiste,* PS), although the party was led by Senghor, a Catholic, and then by Abdou Diouf, a Muslim but of the Tijaniyya (Tidianes) order. Falilou died in 1968 and then his brother Abdoul Ahad succeeded.

He was the seventh son of Ahmadou Bamba. Under his rule the Mourides remained a major religious, economic and political force in Senegal. In the economic sphere they were affected by the problems Senegalese groundnut farmers faced in the 1970s and 1980s, while payment to the order in kind by farmers was replaced largely by cash contributions; but the Mourides, the richest Muslim order in the country, remained powerful in commerce, Touba being a free trade zone as well as a place of pilgrimage. In politics, *Khalife-Général* Abdoul Ahad told his followers that anyone who opposed President Diouf in the 1988 elections also opposed the founder Ahmadou Bamba.

He began large-scale extensions to the Touba mosque, and rebuilt the library, which had by 1989 over 170,000 books. There was also a printing press which published the writings of the founder among other works. Abdoul Ahad Mbacke had a private airstrip and expensive cars. But accusations that the Mourides exploit their followers are always denied by their defenders, who speak of material as well as spiritual benefits conferred in return for the contributions of the faithful.

Abdoul Ahad Mbacke died on 19 June 1989 and was succeeded by another brother, Abdoul Khadre Mbacke. The influence of the Mbacke family in the religious and political life of Senegal has been seen by many, inside and outside the country, as contributing a stabilising factor in the growth of the nation especially since independence. ■

Mbadiwe, K. O. (1917-90)

MBADIWE, Kingsley Ozuomba (1917-90).

NIGERIAN politician and businessman, famous as a rumbustious and colourful "character" in the First Republic's politics. His home town, with which he was linked closely all his life, is Arondizuogu in Imo State. He was born there on 15 March 1917. He attended several schools: St. Mary's Catholic School at Port Harcourt, the famous Hope Waddell Training Institute at Calabar, the Aggrey Memorial College at Arochukwu, and the Baptist Academy and Igbobi College in Lagos.

He began work as a trader, working as a produce buyer in Port Harcourt. But he also worked as the representative there of the *West African Pilot*, the newspaper just established by Nnamdi Azikiwe. From then on "Zik" was seen as the younger man's mentor, and in 1939 Mbadiwe followed his

K.O. Mbadiwe

example by going to the USA for further studies. He studied at Lincoln University, Pennsylvania; the Columbia University Business College in New York; and New York University, where he was awarded the MA in Political Science and later the PhD.

As a student in the USA he began his political career in African students' activities. He also founded the African Academy of Arts and Research which set up Africa House, a students' hostel in New York; wrote a book *British and Axis Aims in Africa* (1942); and later produced a film, *Greater Tomorrow,* which was shown and widely acclaimed in Nigeria on his return in 1948.

Using the same name, he set up the Greater Tomorrow bus service between Enugu and Onitsha and within Onitsha city. He founded in 1950 the African Insurance Company which remained his main business activity during the subsequent years of political activity. In 1950, too, he married Cecilia Alisah; they had four sons and a daughter.

Mbadiwe's career in Nigerian politics began with his election to the Eastern House of Assembly in 1951, to represent Orlu, and to the Federal Parliament in 1952. A leading member of the National Council of Nigeria and the Cameroons (NCNC) headed by Azikiwe, he became one of the NCNC's Federal Ministers, being appointed Minister of Lands and Natural Resources in 1952, Minister of Communications and Aviation in 1954, and Minister of Trade and Industry in 1957. His ministries' achievements included, for example, the Surulere Housing Scheme in Lagos, started when he was Minister of Lands.

He was a flamboyant character who, as one commentator said, used his powerful imagination "to put colour in Nigerian politics". He called himself once a man "of timbre and calibre", and through confusion of similar words, he was nicknamed "Timber". He was renowned for memorable phrases and came to be known for supreme self-confidence and formidable strength; he was called in Ibo *agada gbachiti uzo,* "the giant tree that blocks the footpath". He was also called "K.O.", to stand not only for Kingsley Ozuomba, but also for "Knockout". This indicated his personification of the rough-and-ready style of politics in the First Republic of 1951-66.

In 1957 he, then second National Vice-President of the NCNC, joined with Kola

Balogun, then the Party's General Secretary, to challenge Dr. Azikiwe's leadership; "Zik" dismissed them both, and when they raised support for another attempt to replace him, they were expelled from the party. Mbadiwe then formed the Democratic Party of Nigeria and the Cameroons in July 1958. But after losing his Federal House of Representatives seat in the 1959 elections, he rejoined the NCNC in 1960. In 1961 he became Adviser on African Affairs to the Prime Minister, Sir Abubakar Tafawa Balewa (q.v.), then Minister of State in the Prime Minister's office, and then Minister of Aviation again later that year. Typical of the style by which the public knew him was the extravagant ceremony he organised in 1964 as Minister of Aviation to inaugurate Pan Am's Lagos-New York route: "Operation Fantastic", in which a cultural troupe including traditional dancers and trumpeters, and some influential Nigerians, were flown to New York.

He remained in the government until it fell in the coup d'état of January 1966. Mbadiwe was prominent among the ministers who handed over power to the army.

In the crisis and civil war which followed Dr. Mbadiwe played the role of elder statesman, spending some time in Biafra but a good deal overseas. He returned to Nigeria from overseas in 1970. In 1977 he became a member of the Constituent Assembly which drafted a Constitution for return to civilian rule. When civilian rule elections approached he joined the National Party of Nigeria (NPN). He stood for the Senate, but in the Orlu senatorial constituency he lost to the candidate of Dr. Azikiwe's party, the Nigerian Peoples Party (NPP). But the new President, Shehu Shagari, then appointed him Presidential Adviser on National Assembly Affairs. In typical style Mbadiwe said, "I lost the tail and won the head; in fact K.O. is O.K.". In October 1983 he was appointed Ambassador Extraordinary and Plenipotentiary, the first to be so appointed in Nigeria. But the military coup of 31 December 1983 soon ended this appointment.

Two years later Dr Mbadiwe declared, "I am laying down the sword of politics, having served successfully and blamelessly in the two civilian republics. There is no other political office for me to capture but to become a statesman and guide the incoming generation". He was writing rules and guidelines for future politicians, and a book called *The Nigerian Destiny,* when he died on 30 August 1990. K.O. is fondly remembered by his compatriots for his robust humour in an otherwise bitter political arena, and abroad for his belief in the destiny of the African and people of African descent everywhere. ■

Mbanefo, L.N. (1911-77)

MBANEFO, Sir Louis Nwachukwu (1911-77).

NIGERIAN jurist and politician, first indigenous Chief Justice of the former Eastern Region. He was born in Onitsha on 13 May 1911, the son of Chief Mbanefo, the Odu I of Onitsha. He was educated at St. Mary's School, Onitsha, and then the Methodist Grammar School and later King's College, both in Lagos. He graduated from the University of London with a Bachelor of Law degree in 1935, and was called to the Bar at the Middle Temple the same year, but instead of going into legal practice he entered King's College, Cambridge, where he graduated in History with a BA and MA in 1937.

On returning to Nigeria he set up a law practice in Onitsha where his hard work and interest in public and Anglican church affairs soon won him a wide measure of respect. In 1939, he became a member of the Onitsha Town Council which reorganised the well-known Onitsha Market and, in 1946, chancellor of the Anglican Diocese on the Niger, an office he held till his death. He was a member of the Eastern House of Assembly from 1950 to 1952 and represented the Eastern Region in the Nigerian Legislative Council in Lagos from 1950 to 1951. However, it was in the legal profession that Mbanefo, the first among the Ibo ethnic community to qualify as a lawyer, first to be appointed as a Magistrate in 1948 and the first Nigerian Chief Justice of Eastern Nigeria, excelled.

In recognition of his competence at the Bar, Mbanefo was appointed judge of the Supreme Court in 1952 and, following the regionalisation of the judiciary, became judge of the High Court of Eastern Nigeria in

Sir Louis Mbanefo

1956. He was later transferred to Lagos in 1958 as judge of the Federal Supreme Court of Appeal. The following year saw him back in Eastern Nigeria as the area's first indigenous Chief Justice. His stature as an eminent jurist led to his appointment in 1961 to the International Court of Justice at The Hague where he served as an *ad-hoc* Judge.

Outside the court, Mbanefo served on various bodies and boards. He was pro-chancellor of the University of Ibadan from 1965 to 1967, founding member and trustee of the Nigerian Institute of International Affairs, and chairman of the Board of Governors of Iyi Enu Hospital in Ogidi, Anambra State, which he helped to rebuild after its devastation during the civil war. The war broke out when Mbanefo was still Chief Justice of the then Eastern Nigeria, a post he continued to hold during the years of hostilities between the break-away Biafra and Nigeria. He was several times a Biafran representative abroad, and in January 1970 he took part in the formal surrender at Lagos.

Mbanefo was invited in 1963 by the government of Trinidad and Tobago to lead an inquiry into trade union problems. Earlier, in 1959, he had led a commission that was established by the Federal Government to review the salaries and wages of civil servants and resulted in the Mbanefo Salary Awards.

In addition to being chancellor of the Anglican Diocese he was legal adviser to the Church, a president of the Christian Council of Nigeria, and president of the World Council of Churches in 1972. In 1961 Mbanefo received a knighthood from Queen Elizabeth II. In 1963 he was awarded the honorary degree of Doctor of Laws by the University of Nigeria, Nsukka, and made a fellow of the University of London in 1972. He died on 28 March 1977. ■

Mbida, A.M. (1917-80)

MBIDA, André-Marie (1917-80).

CAMEROONIAN politician; he was the first Prime Minister in the internal self-government of 1957. Born at Endinding, a village of the Eton people near Obala, he was given a Catholic education including seminary studies. After working as a legal secretary from 1945 to 1950 and then setting up in business in 1951, he entered politics with the 1952 elections to the Territorial Assembly of French Cameroon, to which he was elected as leader of the *Bloc Démocratique Camerounais* (BDC). From 1953 to 1956 he was an elected member of the Council of the French Union in Paris.

In January 1956 Mbida was elected one of French Cameroon's deputies in the French parliament, defeating Dr. Aujoulat, the Frenchman whom he had earlier followed in politics. His BDC was the leading legal party following the banning of the *Union des Populations du Cameroun* (UPC) in 1955 and the failure in 1956 of M. Soppo Priso's plans for a new nationalist alliance. In the elections of December 1956 to a new Legislative Assembly, held in the face of UPC guerrillas calling for a boycott, the BDC won 20 seats out of 70. With the granting of internal self-government M. Mbida became Prime Minister in May 1957. He ruled in alliance with the *Union Camerounaise* (UC) under Ahmadou Ahidjo (q.v.), which had 30 seats, Ahidjo being Vice-Premier in charge of the Interior.

The coalition government collaborated with France against the guerrillas, with little success at first. Disagreements in the coalition were reported to be aggravated by unpredictable and arbitrary behaviour by M. Mbida. Independence was a cause of dispute, M. Mbida having been pro-French and cautious on the ending of France's Trusteeship rule.

A.M. Mbida

In February 1958 Mbida was ousted by the Assembly and then removed from office by the new French High Commissioner, M. Ramadier, and replaced by Ahidjo. Ramadier was recalled for this action but it stood. Mbida went to Egypt to join the UPC leader Félix Moumié (q.v.) and later went with him to Guinea. In 1959 he joined the UPC in denouncing French and United Nations' plans for conceding independence under Ahidjo with the UPC still outlawed and no new elections.

After independence on 1 January 1960, Mbida returned to Cameroon, and in the elections of April 1960 his *Démocrates Camerounais* party won ten seats out of 100. The party formed a coalition with the UC but he did not join the government. The party's relationship with the coalition steadily deteriorated until 1962, when Mbida, with some other opposition leaders decided to form an opposition "national front". They were arrested after issuing a critical manifesto in June 1962 and sentenced to several years' imprisonment each. But two and a half years later they were freed. After undergoing medical treatment in France he returned to his home area, declaring support for the single ruling party of President Ahmadou Ahidjo.

Mbida died in a Paris hospital on 2 May 1980, and was given a state funeral at his home village. ■

Mbikusita, G. (1907-77)

MBIKUSITA, Godwin (1907-77).

ZAMBIAN political leader who was president of the Northern Rhodesian African Congress during the federation of the Rhodesias and Nyasaland. He was also king of Bulozi (known also as Barotseland), which was founded about the 17th century and is now part of the Republic of Zambia. In the latter role, which he performed in the last eight and a half years of his life, he was known as Litunga (king) Godwin Lewanika. He was born into the royal house of King Lewanika (q.v.) (1845-1916) in 1907 and had his elementary education at the Barotse National School before studying social welfare at both the Universities of South Africa and Wales in the United Kingdom.

On graduation, he joined the court of King Yeta III in 1935, serving as the monarch's private secretary until 1938 when Mbikusita exiled himself from Barotseland after the discovery of a plot to overthrow the king. Mbikusita, who was accompanying King Yeta to the coronation of King George VI in London in 1938 when the alleged coup was uncovered, was implicated. He chose to remain abroad until 1941 when, on his return to Zambia, he became a senior welfare officer in the Rhokana Corporation in Nkana.

This was the time when the majority of Africans in the British colonies of Northern Rhodesia (now Zambia) and Nyasaland (now Malawi) were reacting against a proposed merger of their countries into a federation that would include Southern Rhodesia (now Zimbabwe). Despite the opposition the forerunner of the Central African

G. Mbikusita

Federation, the Central African Council, was formed in 1944 while the federation itself was inaugurated in October 1953 to facilitate British rule. These countries were to be ruled by a central parliament based in Salisbury (now Harare). African reaction was manifested in the formation of political parties opposed to the proposed federation. One of the first movements in Northern Rhodesia was the Kitwe African Society (KAS) that was formed at the time the Central African Council was being formulated. Mbikusita was among its founding members and he was elected its first president while Harry Nkumbula (q.v.), another Zambian political leader, became the secretary.

In 1946 the KAS and other "Welfare Societies" in the country grouped as the Federation of African Welfare Societies, and when in 1948 that organisation was reorganised into a Congress of Northern Rhodesia (renamed African National Congress of Northern Rhodesia in 1951) Mbikusita was elected its first president. The ANC of Northern Rhodesia was the country's first political party and forerunner of the United National Independence Party (UNIP) which brought Northern Rhodesia to independence in 1964. The objectives of the ANC were to promote the educational, economic and political advancement of the Africans while reaffirming its commitment to an independent national government, led by Africans, outside the proposed federation. To this effect the ANC, under Mbikusita's leadership, sent a delegation to the British Secretary for the Colonies in 1949 to protest against the federation plan.

In August 1951 the ANC of Northern Rhodesia split over federation with Southern Rhodesia and in the election of that month Mbikusita lost the presidency to Harry Nkumbula (q.v.). Having earlier lost the leadership of the African Mineworkers Union in 1947 to Lawrence Katilungu, he succeeded in becoming leader of the rival union, the Mines African Staff Association, in 1953. A year later Mbikusita founded the Barotse National Association, which later supported a move to take Barotseland from the rest of Northern Rhodesia. He also became a supporter of the Central African Federation, joining the white-led United Federal Party of Roy Welensky as its only African member in 1958. In November 1958 he was elected to the federal parliament in Salisbury, on the party's platform, where, because of his support for the merger, he was made a parliamentary secretary to Prime Minister Roy Welensky. In that capacity, Mbikusita was prominent in the constitutional conferences, held in London and Africa, that paved the way for the dissolution of the federation in December 1963 and subsequently for Zambia's independence the following year.

In 1967 Mbikusita became a member of the Barotse House of Chiefs. His appointment to the House was followed the same year with another by King Mwanawina Lewanika III who made him *Natamoyo* (the minister of Justice) in the Barotseland government. In December 1968 Mbikusita succeeded the king as ruler of the Lozi. He died in 1977. ∎

Mboya, Tom (1930-69)

MBOYA, Thomas Joseph Odhiambo Nienge (1930-69).

KENYAN trade unionist and politician. He was born on 15 August 1930 at Kilima Mbogo near Nairobi. Both his parents were devout but poor Catholics who sent him to the local Roman Catholic schools for his early education. Like his contemporaries, he had to walk a great distance to school where young African boys and girls were mostly taught to recite the Bible and prayer books.

Mboya's further education began in 1942 when he passed the Common Entrance Examination and was admitted to St. Mary's School, Yala, about 200 miles from his home in Kilima Mbogo. Mboya took on odd jobs to earn money for his school fees and other basic expenses. However, his exposure to the white Christian missionaries changed his mind about his boyhood hopes of becoming a priest.

In 1945 Mboya passed the Kenya African Preliminary Examination and was enrolled at the Holy Ghost College, Mang'u, on an African District Council bursary. Two years later he passed his African Secondary School Examination, making him eligible for the Cambridge School Certificate course. However, his academic ambition was temporarily frustrated when he could not raise the tuition fees for the course and was forced to give up his studies.

Mboya applied for admission to the Kabete Sanitary Inspectors' School near Nairobi, to which he was admitted from 1948 to 1950. Such were his personality and abilities that he was soon elected student leader, a position that often brought him into conflict with the colonial school authorities.

Mboya's first paid job was as a sanitary inspector with the Nairobi City Council in 1951. He was elected Secretary of the African Staff Association, the trade union which represented African workers of the Council. In 1952 he founded the Kenya Local Government Workers' Union, serving as its national Secretary-General between 1953 and 1957. About the same time he took over the running of the Kenya Federation of Labour following the detention of some of its

leaders. He was also director of information and acting treasurer of the Kenya African Union, the precursor of the now ruling Kenya African National Union (KANU) party.

Mboya's meteoric rise to national prominence continued with his election as chairman of the Kenya Sanitary Inspectors Association in 1954. Between 1955 and 1956 he studied industrial management at Ruskin College, Oxford, on a scholarship. This period of the mid-1950s was crucial in the political evolution of Kenya. Once the turbulence generated after the declaration of a state of emergency by the colonial administration subsided, Africans began to overtly organise political parties. As an early campaigner for constitutional reform in Kenya, he was largely responsible for the replacement of the Lyttleton Constitution by the Lennox-Boyd Constitution which gave Africans increased participation in the Legislative Council (Legco). Mboya founded the Nairobi People's Convention Party in 1957

Tom Mboya

and was elected member of the Legco. His political constituency was Nairobi.

Upon becoming a member of the Legco, Mboya's colleagues chose him Secretary/ Treasurer of the Pan-African Freedom Movement for East and Central Africa (PAFMECA). In 1958 he was elected chairman of a committee of the International Confederation of Free Trade Unions (ICFTU). On 6 December 1958 he chaired the first all Africa Peoples Conference (AAPC) in Ghana, in many respects the progenitor of the present-day Organisation of African Unity. At the conference, Mboya was elected a member of the AAPC executive council. In recognition of his abilities, Howard University of Washington DC, USA, conferred on him an honorary degree of Doctor of Laws in 1959.

Mboya's rise abroad was equally matched at home. In 1961 he was one of the founder members of KANU. In 1962 he was appointed Minister of Labour in the coalition government formed with the opposition Kenya African Democratic Union (KADU). In the pre-independence elections of 1963 he was elected member of Parliament for the Nairobi constituency of Kamukunji and was appointed Minister of Justice and Constitutional Affairs.

A close associate and for many years a confidant of the first President of Kenya, Jomo Kenyatta (q.v.), Mboya was elected KANU's Secretary-General at the party's national congress in March 1966. He was serving in these and other capacities when he was assassinated on 5 July 1969, while shopping in Nairobi. ■

McKenzie, B.R. (1919-78)

McKENZIE, Bruce Roy (1919-78).

KENYAN politician, the only White politician who served in the post-colonial Kenyan government. McKenzie, who farmed in Kenya, arrived and settled in the country in 1946. He was born in Richmond, Natal, South Africa, in 1919 and was educated at Hilton College, Natal, before attending the Agricultural College in that country. He joined the South African Air Force during the Second World War and did long service with the British Royal Air Force throughout the duration of the war. He was made colonel in the South African Air Force at the age of 24 and was subsequently awarded the Distinguished Service Order (DSO), and the Distinguished Flying Cross (DFC).

B.R. McKenzie

At the end of the war McKenzie settled in Kenya and acquired a farm in Nakuru which he developed into one of the best farms in the Rift Valley. He became a member of the New Kenya Party in 1957 and served in the Legislative Council. In 1959 he was appointed Minister of Agriculture, a post he held until 1961 when he resigned from the New Kenya Party to join the Kenya African National Union (KANU) led by Jomo Kenyatta (q.v.).

He was re-elected to the Legislative Council that year on the Party's platform and became Minister of Agriculture in the Shadow Cabinet of KANU, and later, in the coalition government of 1962, he was made Minister of Land Settlement and Water Development. Following KANU's victory at the 1963 elections, McKenzie was appointed Minister of Agriculture and Animal Husbandry in the government of Prime Minister Kenyatta. He served in that capacity until

1970 when he retired, taking on a number of directorships.

He died on 24 May 1978 when the aircraft in which he was travelling from Uganda exploded in mid-air about 15 miles outside Nairobi. The circumstances in which he died at the age of 59 provoked some political controversy. It was alleged that a bomb was planted on the aircraft while it was stationed at Uganda's Entebbe Airport, but the Ugandan government of Idi Amin refuted the allegations.

In Kenya, where McKenzie had a big following, his funeral at Nairobi Cathedral was attended by a strong delegation of the government and the business community. In his message of condolence, President Kenyatta said he had learned "with deep sorrow of the untimely death of my good friend. He was among the very first Kenyan Europeans to have identified themselves with the African people's struggle for *Uhuru*. His contribution to the agricultural industry of this country, not only in his capacity as the Minister of Agriculture, but also as a farmer himself, will never be forgotten". ■

1942, first to Mali and later on to France where he studied general and tropical agriculture. He returned to Togo in 1953, and as an expert he soon became deputy chief of Agricultural Services in Lomé, Head of the Kluoto Agricultural Promotion in the southwest and director of the Tové Farm School. Under his administration, agricultural performance improved, aided by a French programme of infrastructure investments.

Meatchi was soon drawn into politics, however. In 1956 when Togo was given autonomy by the French and Grunitzky was elected its first Prime Minister, Meatchi was appointed Minister of Agriculture, and a year later was given the Finance portfolio. When fresh elections were held in April 1958 under UN supervision, because Olympio's *Comité de l'Unité Togolaise* (CUT) had contested the legality of the 1956 ones, Meatchi won a seat representing Pagouda in the north while Grunitzky lost to his political rival, Sylvanus Olympio.

Meatchi, himself a Northerner, was able to pull his weight because of the North-South rivalry, and with Grunitzky's retirement from politics and in 1961 his departure to the Ivory Coast (Côte d'Ivoire), he became

---

Meatchi, A.I. (1925-84)

MEATCHI, Antoine Idrissou (1925-84).

TOGOLESE politician, first Vice-President of independent Togo, he was a leading figure in the turbulent politics of his country which led to the assassination of President Olympio (q.v.) and the exile of President Grunitzky (q.v.) in the 50s and 60s; the constitution was amended and the post created to accommodate him in 1963. Meatchi played an important role in the merging of the *Union des Chefs et des Populations du Nord* (UCPN) to which he belonged with Grunitzky's *Parti Togolais du Progrès* to form the *Union Démocratique des Populations Togolaises* (UDPT), a North-South tactical alliance.

Meatchi's political career started late, in 1955, following a long period of study and service in agriculture. He was born in Sokodé on 13 September 1925, and was related to the local royal family. He had his primary education in Togo before going in

A.I. Meatchi

the leader of the UCPN and the leader of the Opposition. Following independence in 1960, certain administrative regulations came into force to crack down on sources of opposition, and Meatchi lost his parliamentary seat in the 1961 elections. Under Olympio that same year the constitution was amended, providing a strong presidential system with wide powers lodged in an executive president. Meatchi spoke out against it, was arrested and accused of plotting against the government. On his release he made his way to Accra where he remained in exile until the 1963 coup d'état that brought him back into a position of power. For a while in Ghana he headed the Bureau of African Affairs which amongst other things supported the liberation movements of the period, becoming a radical politician.

In 1962 Togo became a one-party régime with all parties except the CUT formally banned. Shortly afterwards, in January 1963, disgruntled soldiers mounted a coup, and Olympio was assassinated in the process. Meatchi returned from exile, and was appointed Minister of Finance, Public Works and Post and Telecommunications in the Grunitzky Provisional Government. He assumed the Vice-Presidency, with responsibility for Finance and Economic Planning in the government formed after the 1963 elections, in a split executive government. This constitutional arrangement lasted for four years and proved disastrous. Meatchi was believed to be abrasive and ambitious, and he constantly clashed with Grunitzky. This led to the November 1966 cabinet crisis when the long history of hostility between Meatchi and Grunitzky's loyal Minister of Interior Fousseni Mama came to a head over an accusation of subversive action by the latter. There was a popular uprising soon after that aimed at bringing down the Grunitzky-Meatchi régime, and as a result Grunitzky in an attempt to provide a more assertive leadership and strengthen his position passed a constitutional amendment, by 41 votes for and three against, abolishing the Vice-Presidency, and Meatchi was appointed to head the Ministry of Works, Mines and Transport.

This new government did not survive long; a few weeks later, in January 1967, Lieutenant-Colonel (as he was then) G. Etienne Eyadema overthrew Grunitzky in a military coup. Meatchi, who had lost his

credibility and support too, retired then from active politics and was reappointed Director of Agricultural Services, a post he held for several years thereafter.

He met his death in relative obscurity in 1984.■

Meli, F. (1942-90)

MELI, Francis (1942-90).

SOUTH AFRICAN writer, one of the most distinguished intellectuals of the African National Congress (ANC). He was born on 6 May 1942 in Mdantsame, near East London, to a migrant couple. He lost his parents early in life. In spite of the constraints of the Bantu Education Act, he was able to win a place at the University of Fort Hare. In 1963 he was sent to join the ANC external mission in Tanzania. However, it was in Germany that he completed his degree in History, through the scholarship the ANC secured for him from the German Democratic Republic.

F. Meli

He went on to postgraduate studies and in 1973 he was awarded a doctorate degree for his thesis on the Comintern (i.e. the Communist International of 1919-43) and sub-Saharan Africa.

After his studies he was sent to the ANC camps in Angola and Tanzania where he gave classes to recruits of *Umkhonto We Sizwe* (MK), the ANC's armed wing. His capacity for hard work and committed service to the ANC in conjunction with his enormous ability to build up warm relationships with embattled compatriots went a long way to lessen the tedium and hardship of life in the camps. He became very popular with the new recruits, particularly those who flocked to the ANC camps after the Soweto uprising of 1976.

From 1977 until early 1990, he moved to London where his service to the ANC was no less committed. He was the editor of the ANC's monthly journal *Sechaba* and in 1985 was elected on to the ANC's National Executive Committee. His relationship with the Anti-Apartheid Movement in Britain was one of mutual cooperation and on several occasions he addressed the Annual General Meeting of the Movement. In April 1990 he returned to South Africa under the special amnesty provided for members of the ANC's National Executive Committee after the unbanning of the ANC. Thus ended the painful and rigorous life of exile which circumstances had forced on Meli and many of his compatriots.

Meli's dedication to the struggle was profound and his devotion inspired many people who met him. The degree of his commitment was revealed in his fine book, a history of the ANC entitled *South Africa Belongs to Us* (1988). Despite the pain of life in exile which cut him off from his cultural roots, Meli never lost his warm nature nor his sense of humour. In his speeches and writing, he exhibited a clarity of mind and an incisive intellect combined with wry humour which was always impressive.

Unlike many of his compatriots in exile, he was fortunate to return to his beloved country. Yet it is regrettable that he died on 8 October 1990, barely six months after that historic return. His death thus deprived him and his people of the undoubted contribution he might have made subsequently to the total liberation and rehabilitation of the Black community of South Africa. ■

Mendes, F. (1939-78)

MENDES, Francisco (1939-78).

GUINEA-BISSAU politician. Popularly known throughout his later life by his *nom de guerre*, Chico Te, he was born on 7 February 1939 in Enxude in the Buba region of Guinea-Bissau. After completing primary school, he became one of the few in his country to proceed to secondary education. Following the independence of neighbouring Guinea in 1958 and the establishment of the headquarters of the *Partido Africano da Independencia da Guiné e Cabo Verde* (PAIGC) in Conakry, Mendes quit his studies in order to actively participate in the struggle for independence.

In 1960 he joined the party, and utilising his knowledge of the rural population, helped in the recruiting and training of cadres for the PAIGC. In 1962 he was

F. Mendes

initially appointed political commissar of the Bafata region and later of the Northern Front. The party re-organised itself after the congress at Cassaca in February 1964 and Mendes was appointed member of the Political Bureau. In 1965 he became member of the Council of War, and in 1967 was appointed delegate of the Council for the Northern Front together with Amilcar Cabral (q.v.).

The People's National Assembly, convened after the declaration of Guinea-Bissau's independence in 1973, voted Mendes the chief commissar (prime minister) to head the Council of State Commissars, the government of Guinea-Bissau. At the Third Congress of PAIGC in November 1977, the government which he headed was voted to a second term of office and Mendes was elected to the party's eight-man permanent commission. He was awarded the Amilcar Cabral Medal for distinguished political career.

Mendes' death in a car crash in Bissau, on 7 July 1978, precipitated the re-organisation of government, as demanded by the constitution: an interim commissar was chosen, followed by the dissolution and election of a new government in October 1978. He was succeeded in the post by Bernardo Vieira, former State Commissar for the Armed Forces and President of the People's National Assembly.■

Menelik II (1844-1913)

MENELIK II, Emperor of Ethiopia (1844-1913).

THE third successive Ethiopian monarch of the nineteenth century who reunified the scattered semi-autonomous provinces of the medieval empire and restored the power of the central government. Emperor Menelik founded the city of Addis Ababa and expanded the empire to its modern limits. He was born Sahle Mariam on 17 August 1844, the grandson of Sahle Selassie who was ruler of the Shoa kingdom. His father, Haile Maualok, succeeded to the Shoa throne to which Prince Menelik was heir apparent.

The young prince was brought up in his grandfather's palace where he had private tuition in Amharic and given the kind of general education normally provided for the children of Ethiopian nobility. He was eleven years old when Kassa Hailu ascended to the imperial throne as Emperor Tewodros II in 1855. The emperor's policy was to restore the authority of the central government over the emerging self-governing provinces whose officials were taking advantage of the emperor's weakened position. Thus was Shoa's own semi-independent status threatened by Emperor Tewodros II whose army overran the kingdom; Menelik's father died during the 1855 offensive and the royal heir was taken captive to Tewodros' capital Magdala, where he remained a hostage for nine and a half years. Throughout this period Shoa was ruled by governors appointed by Emperor Tewodros II.

Menelik escaped from captivity on 30 June 1865 and reached Shoa where he was acclaimed king in August of the same year. He soon established his authority over the kingdom, building up an army to fend off any attack from Magdala and encouraging trade with European merchants while seeking the friendship of Britain, France and Italy whose missionaries he welcomed to Shoa. Meanwhile Emperor Yohannes IV had succeeded Tewodros II and, like his predecessor, had as his central aim the reunification of the empire under the authority of the imperial throne. Menelik's activities caused the Emperor great anxiety, for Yohannes not only wanted to restore his authority but also wished to make the empire independent of European powers. In 1878 Emperor Yohannes invaded Shoa where, due to the military superiority of the imperial army, Menelik was forced to make peace at Litche on 20 May 1878. Under the Treaty of Litche Menelik reaffirmed his loyalty to the Emperor, for which in return he was acknowledged and crowned *negus* (king) of Shoa. But Menelik's ambitions included the imperial throne and, as such, the differences between the two rulers remained.

A second treaty in 1882 dealt with the important issue of a successor to the imperial throne after Yohannes. It has been recorded by some accounts that Emperor Yohannes IV agreed that Menelik should succeed him but before his death in 1889 the Emperor named his nephew Mangasha as successor. The deciding factor, however, was military strength and being the most powerful man then in the empire, Menelik usurped the throne and became *negus neghest* (king of kings) as Emperor Menelik II on 3 November 1889.

A man of profound organisational ability with a desire to bring changes to his people and country, the new Emperor introduced a modernisation programme. He established an administrative structure which included a cabinet of seven appointed ministers and administrative units in the provinces. A standing Ethiopian national army was created while a national tax system came into being. Following this, Emperor Menelik made Addis Ababa (which means "new flower") his new headquarters. He had founded the town in 1886 as king of Shoa but as Emperor he built it up into a modern city complete with paved streets, modern buildings and essential amenities like a hospital and the Menelik School which was the first secondary school founded in Ethiopia. He introduced a postal system in Addis Ababa in 1894 and created an Ethiopian currency, the Birr, the same year.

Menelik was as intent on modernisng Ethiopia as he was on defending its independence in the face of European colonial expansion. On this he had to resist the encroachment of the British, the French and the Italians on its borders. In order to limit the latter's advance into Ethiopia's northern province in 1889 he entered into a treaty with the Italian government on 2 May 1889. The treaty, signed in Wichale, was written in both the Italian and Amharic languages, and it ended the state of war between the two countries. In addition, it ceded a part of the northern province to Italy in return for which the Italians would equip the Ethiopian army. Soon however the Italians extended their occupation to Eritrea and even claimed that the Treaty of Wichale transformed Ethiopia into an Italian protectorate, which was certainly not included among the provisions of the Amharic version of the treaty. On 1 May 1893 Menelik declared the treaty to be no longer valid, protesting to Italy and other European powers that "I have no intention of being an indifferent spectator if far-distant powers make their appearance with the idea of dividing Africa". On 1 March 1896 the Italians invaded Ethiopia in an attempt to establish their rule but were decisively beaten at the famous Battle of Adowa in which 4,000 Italians were killed and another 2,000 taken prisoner. As a result of the Italian defeat, both the Italians

Emperor Menelik II

and other major European nations recognised the independence of Ethiopia and soon established diplomatic missions in Addis Ababa.

Emperor Menelik II spent the following years consolidating the independence of his country, safeguarding its frontiers in successive treaties with the French and the British who occupied the neighbouring countries. Weakened by ill health and uncertain of the intentions of the ambitious Europeans the Emperor appointed a cabinet in 1907 to make for the smooth running of the administration after his death. He suffered an attack of paralysis in 1908, following which he named his grandson Lij Iyasu as heir to the throne. He died in December 1913 in Addis Ababa. ■

Messali, B.A. (1898-1974)

MESSALI, Hadj Ben Ahmed (1898-1974).

ALGERIAN resistance leader and founder of the nationalist party *Etoile Nord-Africaine*, Messali Hadj, as he is popularly known, was born in 1898 at Tlemcen, near the Moroccan border with Algeria. He came from a working class background, his father being a shoemaker, and was educated in local schools up to secondary level. Soon after the First World War he briefly joined the French Army and was based in southern France, later moving to Paris where he worked in a Renault car factory whilst

Hadj Messali

attending classes at the School of Oriental Languages at the Sorbonne. During this period he joined the French Communist Party, later becoming a member of its Central Committee.

In 1925 he co-founded the *Etoile Nord-Africaine* (ENA), an organisation committed to Algerian nationalism and the independence of Algeria from France. The ENA was more radical in both doctrine and tactics than any other Algerian political organisation at the time and is often regarded as the pioneer of Algerian nationalism, with Messali Hadj as its patriarch.

He developed the organisational structure of the ENA along the lines of the French Communist Party, establishing well-knit party cells closely controlled by the Central Committee. He also spread the aims of the organisation through a journal entitled *El Ummah* (The Nation), and by 1929, the ENA had around 4,000 active members. However the organisation's extreme anti-colonial stance and its growing support alarmed the French government. In 1929 both the ENA and *El Ummah* were banned and Messali was imprisoned.

In 1930, he organised marches and demonstrations in Paris for Algerian independence and also appealed to the League of Nations for support. These activities led to further antagonism with the French authorities causing Messali to move to Switzerland, where he remained until an amnesty granted by the Popular Front Government enabled his return to France.

Messali revived the ENA in 1933 and was imprisoned for one year in 1934 for his political activities. He was released in 1935, but shortly afterwards the ENA was again outlawed by the French authorities in 1936. In August 1936, Messali returned to Algiers to begin a campaign against the French policy of assimilation and to organise political activity among the workers around the Algerian capital.

He returned to Paris in late 1936 and founded the *Parti Populaire Algérien* (PPA) to regroup his supporters from the outlawed ENA. By this time he had broken his links with the French Communist Party because of its failure to defend the ENA through its members in the French Government. The PPA was a continuation of the ENA, advocating Arab unity and national independence for Algeria, while emphasising the need for agrarian and economic reform. It gained much support both in Algeria and among Algerians living in France; but shortly after its inception, Messali was once again arrested.

After his release he was elected to the Algiers General Council in October 1938, but did not take up his position there as the election was disallowed. By 1939 the membership of the PPA had increased to 10,000 and immediately after the outbreak of the Second World War, Messali was arrested for alleged seditious activities and the PPA was banned. In 1941 he was sentenced to 16 years hard labour, but he was released in 1946.

Meanwhile, after the end of the Second World War, tensions had been growing in Algeria as expectations of reforms, if not liberation of the country, were dashed. On 8 May 1945, Moslem crowds demonstrated, and called, among other things, for the release of Messali and other political prisoners. A shot was fired and violence erupted leading to the death of about 108 Europeans. This resulted in swift and ruthless retribution by the French, and estimates of the Moslems killed range from 1,000 to 45,000. Around the same period, preparations were made by Messali and the PPA for an armed insurrection in Algeria, but these plans were withdrawn.

In October 1946, Messali and the other leaders of the PPA formed the *Mouvement pour le Triomphe des Libertés Démocratiques* (MTLD), to take the place of the outlawed PPA. The Party won five of the 15 seats in the elections of November 1946. However, dissension was growing within the MTLD and between 1948-54 there were a series of internal crises which greatly weakened it. Three distinct groupings began to emerge within the party, all preferring different methods to achieve their goals.

In 1952, Messali was again arrested and taken to France, where he was restricted until 1962. By 1954 the dissension within the MTLD had become irreconcilable and the movement broke up. One of the organisations to emerge from this was the *Front de Libération Nationale* (FLN), which then appealed for unity among the various Algerian political organisations. In response, Messali formed the *Mouvement National Algérien* (MNA) which was opposed to the FLN. The FLN gradually absorbed all the other political groupings in Algeria, and after bitter clashes with the MNA, became the guiding force in the nationalist movement.

Messali was freed after the Evian Agreement in 1962, but he never returned to Algeria. He died in France on 3 June 1974. ■

M'hammedi, D. (1912-69)

M'HAMMEDI, Driss (1912-69).

MOROCCAN lawyer and anti-colonial politician who served as Foreign Minis-

ter and later as Director-General of King Hassan's royal government from 1965 until his death. Born in 1912 in historic Fez, the cultural and spiritual centre of Morocco and seat of one of the world's oldest universities, M'hammedi had a traditional Moslem education in that centre of Islamic learning and later worked as a Koranic tutor there.

During that time the French had firmly consolidated their rule over Morocco, which effectively began under the March 1912 Fez Convention that made the country a French protectorate. "Pacification" soon followed, coming in 1934 when M'hammedi was twenty-two years old. Two years later, and until 1941, he undertook private law studies and in 1941 became a member of the Meknès Bar.

In the same period he also worked in the colonial public service but continuing opposition to French rule now re-appearing under the leadership of young Moroccan intellectuals necessitated his resignation in 1941 from the civil service. He was among the intellectuals who reconstituted the National Party into the Istiqlal Party (Independence Party) in 1944. First under the leadership of Ahmed Balafrej (who was to become independent Morocco's first Foreign Minister) and later led by Mohammed Allal el-Fassi (q.v.), the party was the first Moroccan national movement to issue an Independence Manifesto that called for not just the usual colonial reforms but a termination of the Protectorate agreement with France and independence with King Mohammed V (q.v.) as constitutional ruler of Morocco. Most of the instigators of the Manifesto and leaders of the Istiqlal Party were immediately arrested by the French authorities, but this only served to increase the popularity and strength of the party which soon became a national movement.

Following the arrest and detention, widespread strikes and demonstrations took place in M'hammedi's hometown of Fez and also in Rabat, to which the French responded with further repression. Further mass anti-French demonstrations occurred in 1952, this time in Casablanca where French troops shot and killed 200 Moroccans. The Istiqlal Party was blamed for the riots, and banned. This was followed by the deposition of King Mohammed on 20 August 1953. During this period, beginning from 1941, M'hammedi had set up a private legal practice and became well-known for his conduct of defence in several political trials. He was arrested in 1952, on charges of subversion against the French, and detained for two years.

The period from 1952 saw the tempo of the independence cause increased and encouraged by the continued deposition of the monarch and persecution of political leaders, it soon broke into armed rebellion. In November 1955, the colonial authorities submitted to Moroccans' demands, restored the monarch and began negotiations for the country's independence. M'hammedi, who had been released also, was the King's chief negotiator with the French. The eventual agreement brought Morocco independence on 2 March 1956, and M'hammedi was appointed the country's first Minister of the Interior. He held this office, almost consistently, until 1960 when he became Minister of Foreign Affairs.

As Foreign Minister at that time he had the difficult task of reconciling diverging Moroccan interests in its neighbour, Mauritania. For while the official policy was to re-integrate the country into "Greater Morocco", there was strong opposition to the move in both countries. M'hammedi resigned from the government in 1961 after falling out with el-Fassi who alleged that the Foreign Minister was not showing sufficient zeal in implementing government policy.

In 1963, following King Hassan's re-organisation of government, he was brought out of political retirement and made Director-General of the royal government. A further constitutional re-arrangement in June 1965 saw King Hassan invoke Article 35 of the Constitution and declare a "state of exception" which suspended the Constitution and Parliament and invested in himself all legislative and executive powers, leading to the further consolidation of M'hammedi's prominence in the country.

He remained at this post until he was taken ill early 1969; he died in Paris on 10 March 1969.∎

Micombero, M. (1940-83)

MICOMBERO, Colonel Michel (1940-83).

BURUNDIAN soldier and politician, first President of the Republic of Burundi,

whose seizure of power in 1966 abolished the monarchy.

Belonging to the Hima clan of the Tutsi people, Michel Micombero was born in Musenga, Bururi Province, in 1940. After attending the local Rutovu Catholic Mission School, he studied at the *Collège du Saint-Esprit*, Bujumbura, where he showed great academic promise. In April 1960 he joined the armed forces and proceeded to the Military Academy in Brussels. His course there was interrupted by the advent of independence in 1962 when, along with other Burundians at the Academy, he was summoned as part of an Africanisation programme in the army. Initially serving as a Second Lieutenant, he was promoted Captain shortly before independence was granted on 1 July 1962.

The following year Micombero joined the *Unité et Progrès National* party (UPRONA), which was closely identified with the Mwami (King) of Burundi. He was Secretary of State for Defence between June 1963 and October 1965 when he was appointed Minister of Defence in the aftermath of an unsuccessful Hutu-backed uprising. With the backing of Mwami Mwambutsa IV, he instituted harsh measures against the Hutu people in Muramvya Province where the coup originated, and thousands were reported killed. Shortly after, the Mwami appointed Micombero Chief of the Secretaries of State.

In July 1966, Mwami Mwambutsa IV (who had ruled from Europe since the attempted rebellion) was deposed by his nineteen year old son, Crown Prince Charles Ndizeye, who was proclaimed Ntare V (q.v.). The constitution was suspended and Micombero was appointed Prime Minister. However, almost immediately tension began to grow between Ntare V and Micombero. As relations deteriorated, Micombero ensured the support of the armed forces by either dismissing or arresting the Mwami's chief army supporters. In early October the army foiled an attempt by the Mwami to announce Micombero's dismissal while he was attending an OAU Conference in Addis Ababa. The following month Micombero took advantage of Ntare V's state visit to Zaire to depose him, abolish the monarchy and proclaim Burundi a republic with himself, now a colonel, as President, on 28 November 1966. He was 26 years old. On assuming power he abolished all political organisations apart from UPRONA and established a 12-man

Conseil National de la Révolution (CNR) to assist him in running the country (the CNR was abolished in 1968). He also immediately set about trying to improve the relationship between the Tutsi (around 14 per cent of the population), the Hutu (85 per cent of the population), and the Twa (one per cent). His speeches stressed the need for unity and he ordered the release of several Hutu political prisoners as well as officially proscribing ethnic distinctions. However, the basic tensions created by the rule of the minority (which was itself deeply divided) remained and grew.

In July 1967, shortly after the independence anniversary celebrations, Micombero was involved in a serious road accident, so that the country was governed temporarily by the CNR. Immediately afterwards all suspected monarchists were arrested and the army was mobilized complete with road blocks throughout the country, reflecting the extent of the fear of anti-government activity.

Micombero favoured a socialist domestic policy, and although he was inherently anti-west in his outlook, the extremely poor economic situation in Burundi and the resulting need for foreign aid demanded that he took a more pragmatic approach to the West in his foreign policy.

Between 1968-72 he continued to promote national unity while the underlying ethnic tensions sporadically rose to the surface among students, soldiers and peasants alike. There were various allegations of Hutu plots, and the Hutu people became fearful that the freedoms they had might be curtailed. Meanwhile, in 1971 the divisions among the Tutsi came to a head when Micombero learned that there was a plot to overthrow him by the Banyaruguru Tutsi. Whether there actually was a plot is a matter of some controversy, but Micombero believed it and the alleged leaders were arrested while other Banyaruguru army officers were dismissed. Feelings ran very high during the Banyaruguru trial and Micombero, not wanting to exacerbate an already tense situation, commuted the death sentences of the leaders to various terms of imprisonment, in February 1972.

The following month Ntare V returned to Burundi from his exile in West Germany. Micombero immediately had him arrested and charged with treason; he was executed on 29 April 1972, on which same date Micombero abruptly dismissed all cabinet members. Rumours of plots were rife, and many were arrested during April 1972. Serious fighting broke out, particularly in the south. It emerged that there had been a general uprising of Hutu, in which many Tutsi were murdered. The rebellion was quickly quashed and was followed by a campaign of massive revenge against the Hutu. Several hundreds were thought to have died during the repression while thou-

M. Micombero

sands fled into exile. As a result of this systematic neutralisation, the Tutsi were able to continue their domination of political power in Burundi, but inter-Tutsi rivalry and struggle for power continued. By 1973 Micombero was spending more and more time at Gitega, protected by loyal armed forces.

In December 1973, Micombero became lieutentant-general. The following July a new constitution came into force establishing a one-party Presidential system with Micombero retaining the powers of president until the elections. He was re-elected to a seven year term in October and re-installed as President on 28 November 1974. Although the Hutu population had generally lost faith in Micombero's continued appeals for national unity since the 1972 uprising, he managed slowly to improve relations with Rwanda, which has a large and dominant population of Hutu. In June 1976 he signed an agreement with Rwandan President Habyarimana to strengthen commercial, economic, cultural and social ties, including the establishment of joint agricultural projects.

Meanwhile the army, upon which Micombero depended to remain in power, had become increasingly dissatisfied with his rule and, on 1 November 1976, Micombero was overthrown by a military coup led by Lieutenant-Colonel Jean Baptiste Bagaza. Choosing to live in exile in Somalia, Micombero studied economics and later worked for an international organisation there. He died on 16 July 1983, aged 43. ■

Mingas, S.V.D. (1943-77)

MINGAS, Dr. Siady Vieira Dias (1943-77).

ANGOLAN freedom fighter and politican who became the first Minister of Finance of the Republic. He was born in 1943 in Luanda, where he attended primary and secondary schools, proceeding later to Lisbon for further studies. In 1961 he joined the Popular Movement for the Liberation of Angola (MPLA) and was soon given a scholarship to Cuba where he took a degree and a doctorate in economics. While in Cuba Mingas underwent military training and he returned to Angola to join the fight for the liberation of his country from Portuguese colonialism. His first important engagement was in 1971 as director of the Centre for Revolutionary Instruction (CIR) which was situated in the liberated zone on the eastern front.

In 1972 Mingas was transferred to the external relations department of the MPLA and was appointed as the movement's representative in Stockholm where he took charge of MPLA's interests in the Scandinavian countries. He was recalled after the April 1974 coup in Portugal which brought the liberation war to a dramatic conclusion, and played an important part in the activities of both the transitional administration

succeeding the colonial government and the subsequent independence administration. It was he, as squadron commander, who on 1 August 1974, signed the instrument of office on behalf of FAPLA, the military wing of the MPLA.

Mingas was elected into the Central Committee of the MPLA in September 1974 and in January 1975 appointed Minister of Planning and Finance in the transitional government. After independence was proclaimed on 11 November 1975, he became

Dr. S.V.D. Mingas

Secretary of State for Finance and later the same year Minister of Finance in the first independence government under President Neto (q.v.), and was promoted to the rank of major in the first formal commissionings of the FAPLA in 1976. He was also made a member of the Revolutionary Council, which was provisionally the supreme governing body in the country.

A politician of outstanding ability and intellect, Mingas was also inclined to the world of literary pursuits. He wrote poems which have been published under the name of Gasmin Rodrigues. He was killed on 27 May 1977 in the abortive coup led by Nito Alves (q.v.) against the MPLA government. ■

Mirambo, M. (c.1840-84)

MIRAMBO, Chief Mtemi (c.1840-84).

TANZANIAN traditional ruler. Mirambo was a chief of the Nyamwezi of Urambo in what is now Tanzania's Tabora Region. Little is known about his early life apart from the fact that he was captured when the Tura, a branch of the Ngoni ethnic group, were conquering their way north from southern Tanzania in the 1850s.

He spent his years of captivity learning military tactics and political leadership and in the 1860s he organised a group of warriors to defeat and bring under his control the chiefdoms surrounding his own, Uyowa. Mirambo's forays into neighbouring chiefdoms were motivated as much by his desire to rule a bigger empire as by his determination to forge unity among the Nyamwezi to resist Arab domination.

Tabora was then the principal Arab settlement in East Africa, and the Nyamwezi were performing a useful function to them in their pursuit of slaves and ivory as caravan porters. The Nyamwezi were divided into many small independent chiefdoms – there were 31 in 1859 – which were often at loggerheads with each other. Added to the recurrent political quarrels over succession to the chieftainships, the lack of political unity enabled the Arabs to maintain some influence among some of the Nyamwezi until the European conquest. It was this state of affairs that Mirambo wanted to change.

By 1870 Mirambo had selected a number of men from the chiefdoms that he conquered and given them military training. He taught them how to use guns and travel fast with little food. He built an army of around 5,000 men known as the "ruga ruga", which he used in a series of military campaigns which eventually gained him control of the trade routes and most of the Nyamwezi country. His continuous conflict with the Arabs of Tabora ended in 1876 when he defeated them in battle. After the defeat of the Arabs peace prevailed, and Mirambo was left in control of trade routes to Uganda, Ujiji and Ufipa. He made the Arabs pay tribute to him when using his trade routes, and by the time he died he had succeeded in bringing virtually all the minor chiefs over

most of the area between the southern shores of Lake Nyanza and Lake Rukwa under his control.

In his attempts to maintain his authority over the Nyamwezi, Mirambo was keen to have the goodwill of the British Consul in Zanzibar. But his rivalry with the other major Nyamwezi chief, Isike of Unyanyembe, continued. Mirambo was a great organiser, but failed to train a successor. Thus after his death in 1884 his chiefdom broke up. His desire to have his people educated led him to welcome European

Chief M. Mirambo

missionaries to open up schools in Tabora. Today a secondary school there is named after him, as are the barracks of the Tanzanian People's Defence Force (TPDF).

On his death in 1884, Chief Mtemi Mirambo was survived by a large family among whom was a daughter and later successor, Mtemi Kibete Mwanamirambo, who was a hundred years old in 1972. On the occasion of her one hundredth birthday, when she was honoured by President Julius Nyere, she said in an interview with *Africa Woman* that her father "was very fond of us, though he had a lot of work to do and was involved in a lot of military operations." Her succession to the Nyamwezi chiefdom ended with her dethronement by the British colonial government.■

Mirerekano, P. (died 1965)

MIREREKANO, Paul (died 1965).

BURUNDIAN politician, he was an ardent supporter of traditional monarchy whose values he eulogised in his writing. Mirerekano was a member of the *Parti de l'Unité et du Progrès National* (UPRONA), the neo-traditionalist party, from its formation, serving as a deputy to Prince Louis Rwagasore (q.v.) who was president of the party. He contested the presidency in 1962 but lost to Joseph Bamina (q.v.), partly because of his strong pro-Hutu policies. He then led a breakaway faction of the party of which he was elected president. This, however, was shortlived because the split was resolved in 1964.

Between 1960 and 1961 he liaised between the UPRONA and the Lumumbists'

P. Mirerekano

forces in then Belgian Congo. Following the declaration of independence in July 1962 he was elected Secretary-General and later Treasurer of the UPRONA. He became an antagonist of André Muhirwa, a colleague in the Central Committee of the party, after Rwagasore's assassination in 1961, attacking the succeeding Muhirwa administration for failing to implement the electoral promises which the party had made during the 1961 elections. He published several anti-Muhirwa publications which accused the government of profiting at the expense of the masses. In 1962 he was arrested for anti-government propaganda but later released. He was re-arrested in February 1963 for alleged collaboration with anti-government elements in neighbouring Rwanda. Released on 1 March of the same year he fled to Zaire, returned but fled again in 1964 after the discovery of a plot against the government of Albin Nyamoya who had succeeded Pierre Negendandumwe as Prime Minister.

Mirerekano returned to Burundi in 1965 after Nyamoya had fallen from power. Coming on the eve of the parliamentary elections, he played an important part in the campaign that saw the re-election of the UPRONA. He was the organiser of the Pierre Ngendandumwe's Nationalist Youth, a semi-military arm of the UPRONA which served as both body-guards and propagandists. Having been elected to the National Assembly in May 1965 he became first vice-president of the body, a post he retained until his death.

Mirerekano was perhaps better recognised for his writing which eulogised Burundi's monarchy and traditions. Among his numerous eulogies was *Mbire Gito Canje* (Listen my Son) published in 1961. In the exhortation he said: "Let the Owner of the Drum, the Mwami (king) of Burundi, reign. Let the mwamiship be strong. Let it strengthen public order and the union of all Burundi in peace and justice." Mirerekano continued: "The mwami makes the law for all the Barundi. The mwami holds his power from God. As such he represents all the Barundi. Do not follow the example of neighbouring countries (i.e. republics) or else you will disintegrate like flour scattered on the ground. Do not trip and tumble lest you lose the drumsticks and find yourself unable to get back on your feet. Say to yourself: We are the virgins who serve the Owner of the Drum. The Drum is like the taste of honey to the lips of the Barundi! You must bend your energies around the Drum so as to make possible the strengthening of the established order and the union of all".

Mirerekano was executed in 1965 for participating in the Hutu rebellion of that year. ■

El-Mirghani, S.A.I. (1879-1968)

EL-MIRGHANI, Sayed Ali Ibn (1879-1968).

SUDANESE religious leader. He was born in 1879 in Dongola, the son of the hereditary head of the powerful orthodox Islamic sect, the Khatmiyya, and grandson of its founder Muhammed Osman el-Mirghani, who was an Islamic scholar from Mecca. At the turn of the nineteenth century the sect had some two million followers in the Sudan.

The young el-Mirghani was taken by his parents to Egypt in 1881 to escape the Mahdist movement that later came to power in Khartoum. Mahdism was a rival religious sect headed by the Mahdi (q.v.) who advocated radical changes in the Sudanese society. In Egypt, where el-Mirghani was being given an Islamic education, the family enjoyed the hospitality of the British authorities who regarded them as allies for the future pacification of Sudan and as a counterweight to the Mahdist nationalism. The family returned to Khartoum in 1898 following the reconquest of the Sudan by the British, and el-Mirghani, now the head of the Khatmiyya, was respected by the British who decorated him with honours: in 1900 he was given the CMG, in 1916 the KCMG, and in 1919, during a meeting with King George V in London, he was awarded the KCVO.

From the 1920s to the 1950s, however, the position of el-Mirghani came under severe pressure with the rise of nationalist politics and the re-emergence of the Mahdist movement headed by Abd-el-Rahman el-Mahdi (q.v.). There had emerged in Khartoum two opposing political movements, the Ashigga, known also as the National Unionist Party (NUP) which favoured continuation of the union with Egypt as provided by the Anglo-Egyptian

Treaty of 1936, and the Umma Party, or Independence Party, which demanded immediate independence for the Sudan and negotiations later on the future relations between the Sudan and Egypt. A division had also occurred in the ranks of the religious movements with the Khatmiyya, led by el-Mirghani, backing the call for union with Egypt while the Ansar, the Mahdist followers, led by el-Mahdi, called for complete independence.

Sayed Ali El-Mirghani

El-Mirghani supported the unionist claim during the first Sudanese elections in 1953, which the party he followed, the NUP, won. Later however when the Prime Minister, Ismail el-Azhari (q.v.), changed his policy to support the demand for independence of the Sudan, el-Mirghani withdrew his backing from the government. The Sudanese government's change of policy was more in response to the changed situation in Egypt where King Farouk (q.v.) had been overthrown in a military coup d'état in July 1952. The new military rulers announced on 2 November 1952 that the Egyptian government recognised the Sudanese right to self-determination.

Meanwhile, el-Mirghani encouraged his followers to form the People's Democratic Party (PDP) which, after the attainment of independence in January 1956, joined the Umma Party to form a coalition government in July 1956, forcing the NUP into opposition. The three parties regrouped in a coalition government after the March 1958 elections.

El-Mirghani did not join in the protest that came after the coalition government was overthrown by a military coup on 17 November 1958, nor did he make public his views on the military rule which lasted until 1964. But when the junta was itself toppled by another coup in late 1964, his influence became less prominent and he retired into private life. In December 1967 he supported the re-unification of the PDP and the NUP under the name of the Democratic Unionist Party (DUP).

El-Mirghani died on 21 February 1968 in Khartoum, where his passing was mourned for three days. More than 100,000 Sudanese attended his burial. His eldest son, Sayed Ali el-Mirghani, was declared successor as a leader of the Khatmiyya. ■

Mkandawire, M.
(died 1972)

MKANDAWIRE, Chief Matupi (died 1972).

MALAWIAN politician, who was prominent in the nationalist struggle for independence. In post-colonial Malawi, he maintained his steadfast opposition to foreign domination, notably by wealthy, White-minority ruled South Africa, that has tended to use economic leverage to gain support for its apartheid policy from the Malawian government.

Son of a prominent chief of the Wahenga in northern Malawi, Mkandawire was born in Bolero in the Rumpi district. After completing his formal education in Malawi, he went to South Africa, like most Malawians of his time, for employment under the "migrant labour contract" that had existed between the Nyasaland (now Malawi) colonial administration and South Africa, Southern Rhodesia (now Zimbabwe) and Northern Rhodesia which became independent Zambia. The very bad conditions under which the so-called migrant workers were required to work in the European mines and farms, their poor wages and the attendant social problems and strains in the families left behind at home had since 1895 been criticised by Church and African circles.

Chief M. Mkandawire

Yet by 1914 there were about 40,000 Malawian workers in South Africa and Southern Rhodesia, rising to more than 90,000 and 2,000 respectively in 1970. In April 1974 when 74 Malawian mine-workers died in an air-crash on their way home from South Africa, President Banda imposed a restriction on further recruitment of Malawians for South African mines. In 1975 the President announced that his government was planning to bring migratory workers back "to help build Malawi". By 1977, however, the Malawian government had responded favourably to fresh requests for Malawian workers who, by the middle of that year, had already numbered over 130,000 in South Africa.

Mkandawire returned to Malawi on his father's death, and succeeded as head of the Wahenga chiefdom. Though the colonial authorities forbade chiefs from participating in politics, he joined the Nyasaland African Congress that was opposing the proposed Federation of Rhodesia and Nyasaland and

Thus on 3 March 1959, Governor Robert Armitage ordered a dawn swoop, codenamed "Operation Sunrise", on NAC members. Chief Mkandawire, Dr Hastings Kamuzu Banda, Henry Masauko Chipembere (q.v.), Dunduza Kaluli Chisiza (q.v.) and his brother were among over 200 people arrested in the swoop and flown to detention in Gwelo prison in Southern Rhodesia. A state of emergency was simultaneously proclaimed in the protectorate and in the ensuing protest against the detention of the NAC leaders about fifty Africans were killed by the authorities while over 1,500 were arrested and detained. Chief Mkandawire and other NAC leaders were subsequently released.

At Nyasaland's first general elections in September 1961, he was elected unopposed to Parliament as member for Rumpi West. President Hastings Banda's appeasement of South Africa and Portugal which was engaged in the anti-liberation war with Mozambican nationalists contributed to a Cabinet crisis in 1964, following which he dismissed three ministers for wanting to minimise political contact with the two states. Chief Mkandawire opposed Dr Banda's demanding an end to British rule. He took part in several anti-Federation conferences, for which he mobilised the support of the Council of Chiefs of which he was a leading member. He played an active part in the organisation of the Soche "bush meeting"; where the Nyasaland African Congress (NAC) adopted a militant programme in the campaign against the Federation – the British authorities later alleged that a plot had been hatched at Soche to massacre the governor and all Europeans in the country.
action, and was himself later barred from taking his seat in Parliament and placed in detention where he died in 1972.∎

tance to German occupation. Born in 1855, he was the grandson of the great Kindole, a powerful ruler of the Hehe. His father, Chief Munyingunda, organised the multi-ethnic kingdom into a united and efficient force that proved unconquerable in the inter-state wars with its neighbours whose territories he absorbed. By the time Chief Munyingunda died in 1879, the Hehe empire was a major influence in the politics and trade of the entire east African region.

Chief Mkwawa

Mkwawa, N. (1855-98)

MKWAWA, Chief Ntasatsi (1855-98).

LAST ruler of an independent Hehe empire which is now part of Tanzania. He led the most protracted East African resistance to German occupation.

As a young man, Mkwawa trained in his father's army and had the credit of being a brilliant soldier and military tactician in his first battle experience in the expeditionary war against the Ngoni; Mkwawa's army fought their neighbours to a negotiated truce. After his father's death, Mkwawa fled north to Ugogo to escape the purge of his brother Mhamile who had usurped power. He soon raised an army and returned to reassert his claim, and in 1883 finally forced

Muhenga, another brother who had succeeded Mhamile, into exile in Ukimbu.

As a ruler, Chief Mkwawa pursued the expansionist policies of his father and for this purpose he perfected new military tactics by reorganising the army into six units: the Kitengelumutwa (the Imperial Guard), the Walambo (the shock troopers), the Walaya (crack troopers), the Wanyambwe and Wanyamwami (the infantry), and the Watandisi (the Intelligence unit). The efficacy of this new force made further conquest more feasible; this was recognised in the following years' two-pronged campaign to expand the Hehe empire and to defend its autonomy against encroaching colonial powers.

Mkwawa succeeded in annexing part of Kilombero, Kilosa, Kilimantinde and Manyoni to the north of Uhehe while to the east he despatched an advance column to forestall the progress of the Germans. Germany, having established a base on the coast, had laid claim to Tanganyika and was spreading its influence inland. Chief Mkwawa resented the incursion into his territory and employed administrative measures which were aimed at checking it: for example, he imposed customs duties on goods bought by the Germans in the kingdom. On 17 August 1891 Mkwawa's army of 3,000 men repulsed an advancing German column under the command of Captain von Zelewsky in Lugalo, annihilated the invaders and captured their weapons.

After the Battle of Lugalo, Mkwawa made constant raids into German fortresses at Kilosa and Kilimantinde. The protracted warfare continued until 28 October 1894 when the Germans attacked Mkwawa's headquarters. The fort fell to the Europeans on 30 October, thus signalling the end of the Hehe kingdom. Chief Mkwawa fled and for four years mounted a protracted, bitter military resistance to the German occupation forces. By 1898 the resistance could not contain the superior military power of the colonialists and with defeat imminent Chief Mkwawa, rather than surrender, committed suicide. His skull was taken to Germany for display at the Bremen Anthropological Museum until 1954 when it was returned to British colonial authorities in Tanganyika. Captured and also taken to Germany was his son, Musilamugunda, whose own son Adam Sapi later became Speaker of independent Tanzania's Parliament. ■

Mofolo, T.M. (1875-1948)

MOFOLO, Thomas Mokopu (1875-1948).

LESOTHO writer whose novel, *Chaka*, was the first to be written in Sesotho. He was born on 2 August 1875, in Khojane in the Mafenteng district of Lesotho. He grew up in Qomogomorg and Morija where he attended the Paris Evangelical Missionary Society School. He later studied woodwork at the

T.M. Mofolo

Leloaleng Technical School before proceeding to the Morija Training Institute for a teacher's training course, and he gained a teacher's diploma in 1899. He started teaching at Leloaleng and Bensonvale schools in the Cape Province, South Africa, and continued at Maseru and Morija in Lesotho, but spent some of his time working at the Morija book depot.

It was during this teaching period at Morija that he began his writing career with his first novel, *Moeti Oa Bochabela* published in 1906; it is believed to be the first novel by an African in South Africa. The novel was translated as *A Traveller of the East* in 1934. His second book, *Pitseng* (In the Pot), was published in 1910. Two years later he was appointed recruitment officer for the Native Recruiting Corporation, a South African government agency that recruited Basotho labourers for the South African mines. It came into being in 1911 under the Native Labour Regulation Act, and by that time private recruiters were hiring some 10,000 Basotho workers a year. Mofolo interrupted this to work on his best known novel, *Chaka*, in Morija.

The historical novel, detailing the childhood years of Chaka and his subsequent rise to the leadership of the powerful Zulu kingdom, was published in 1925 and was translated into English, German, French, and Italian. Mofolo also took interest in the nationalist politics that was developing in southern Africa. He became an active member of the Basutoland Progressive Association which was founded in the 1940s as a forum for political expression. Though he did not live long enough to see its development into a political movement, one of his sons used it as a platform to the Basutoland Council in 1948, the year Mofolo died. ■

sympathies became more pronounced, and from 1947, they were unconcealed, to the alarm of the French government and French settlers, who knew the respect of most Moroccans for their traditional monarch.

In the next few years he increasingly clashed with the French. He refused to give his legally required signature to a decree (which like other decrees would be in his name but drawn up by the French Resident and his staff) on local government, and was not mollified by a red-carpet trip to France in 1950. Later in 1950 he ostentatiously received members of the Council of Government who objected to the French budget proposals. But in February 1951 the French, backed by sympathetic Berbers under el-Glaoui (q.v.), forced the Sultan to disavow the Istiqlal nationalist party.

In 1952 the Sultan, recovering from this setback, asked France for complete independence for Morocco. This was refused and the French began to plot the removal of the Sultan. Pro-French Moroccan elements, notably el-Glaoui and his powerful Berber forces in the Atlas mountains, called for the

Mohammed V (1910-61)

MOHAMMED V, King (1910-61).

MOROCCAN monarch. He was born Sidi Mohammed Ben Youssef in 1910, the descendant of Sultan Moulay Ismail who reigned between 1677 and 1727. He was enthroned in November 1927 following the death of his father Sultan Moulay Youssef. At that time he was styled Sultan.

In the 1930s when French colonial ("Protectorate") rule was most firmly established, the young ruler took advantage of the need of the French for him in their government of Morocco, which gave him some leeway, and hinted at sympathy with the growing nationalist movement. When that movement revived during and after the Second World War, under the leadership of Allal el-Fassi (q.v.) in particular, the Sultan's

King Mohammed V

deposition of the Sultan. Eventually the French declared the Sultan deposed and put in his place a relative, Mohammed ben Arafa. In August 1953 France exiled Sidi Mohammed, first to Corsica and later to Madagascar in January 1954.

The tide of nationalism continued to swell, guerrilla fighting broke out, and it soon became clear that Sidi Mohammed's return would be the only realistic response to the demands of the Istiqlal party. In 1955 the French asked Moulay Ben Arafa to step down as part of the new reforms which also created a regency council. The French had in the meantime asked Sidi Mohammed to move from his exile in Madagascar to France. In 1955 Sidi Mohammed's restoration was strongly advocated by el-Glaoui, who had been in the forefront of the demand for deposition in 1953. Sidi Mohammed was restored as Sultan on 6 November 1955. He introduced political and institutional reforms which led to the termination of French and Spanish protectorates over Morocco. The two European powers were asked to commit themselves to Moroccan independence under agreements respectively signed in Paris on 2 March 1956 and in Madrid on 7 April 1956.

In 1957 Sidi Mohammed then took the title of King and dropped that of Sultan. This was in keeping with his desire to introduce western standards in his country ("Sultan" being primarily a religious title, seen by some as outmoded). His concern for modernisation led to maintenance of loose ties with France, even including permission for many settlers to remain, despite the problems caused by the Algerian war. However, King Mohammed backed the Algerian FLN, being particularly angry with France when a plane carrying leaders including Ben Bella was forced down and the leaders arrested, after having conferred with him in Rabat. In succeeding years King Mohammed cultivated ties with Nasser of Egypt and the USSR.

In 1960 a political crisis led to his assuming even more power by taking over the portfolio of Prime Minister after dismissing the Cabinet. He dictated Morocco's policy which was very pan-African, involving ties with radical African governments, hence the Casablanca meeting of January 1961, leading to the "Casablanca Bloc". He was also involved in secret mediation to end the Algerian war. He died on 26 February 1961 of heart failure after an operation. ∎

Mohieddin, F. (1927-84)

MOHIEDDIN, Dr Fouad (1927-84).

EGYPTIAN politician and an excellent administrator. At the time of his death, Dr Fouad Mohieddin was Prime Minister of Egypt and Secretary-General of the ruling National Democratic Party (NDP). His political career which began with the Egyptian

F. Mohieddin

revolution (1952-56) spanned the governments of Presidents Nasser, Sadat (qq.v.) and Mubarak.

Mohieddin was born in 1927 in a small town in the Nile Delta. He came from a wealthy and prominent family whose impact on Egyptian politics has been considerable.

One cousin, Zakaria Mohieddin, served as Prime Minister and Vice-President under Nasser, and another, Khalid Mohieddin, led the Unionist Progressive Party and became one of Egypt's prominent politicians.

Mohieddin studied medicine at Cairo University in the 1940s and early 1950s, qualifying as a physician with a speciality in radiology. He became involved in politics as a member of the student union during the early days of the 1952 revolution when a group of young army officers seized power in Cairo and King Farouk (q.v.) abdicated. On his election to Egypt's first National Assembly in 1957 under Nasser, he abandoned medicine for a political career.

From 1968 to 1973 Mohieddin served as governor of three different provinces including Alexandria and Giza. In 1973 he became Minister of Local Government in Sadat's Cabinet and later became Minister of Health. Sadat appointed him Deputy Prime Minister in 1980, a post he held till Sadat's assassination in 1981.

President Mubarak chose Mohieddin as his Prime Minister in 1982 and asked him to form his first Cabinet. In the reshuffle which followed, Moheiddin said his priority would be "to eliminate corruption and extravagance". Mubarak gave him greater responsibility as Prime Minister than he had had previously. But the real delegation was not of power but of accountability. Criticism of the government could be deflected onto Mohieddin, a relatively safe target.

Mohieddin was an able, hard-working administrator who served governments, rather than a politician who served political deals. He had little popular support; opposition parties saw him as a conservative who blocked economic and political change.

In 1984 Mohieddin led his party, the NDP, to a massive victory in the first parliamentary elections of the Mubarak government. But opposition parties attributed the scale of the victory to vote rigging and voter intimidation. Mohieddin, who was Deputy Secretary-General of the NDP and controlled the day to day workings of the party, received the brunt of this criticism.

He died of a heart attack on 6 June 1984, nine days after the elections, amid rumours that he might be replaced. Mubarak, who posthumously awarded him the Order of the Nile, described Mohieddin as "a dutiful son . . . who had dedicated his life to the service of his homeland". ■

Mojekwu, C.C. (1919-82)

MOJEKWU, Dr Christopher Chukwuemeka (1919-82).

NIGERIAN jurist; he was the first Attorney-General and Minister of Justice of the former Eastern Region of Nigeria. Before that he was a barrister and solicitor of the Supreme Court of Nigeria and, in later years, he served the secessionist regime of Biafra as Commissioner for Home Affairs among other things.

Christopher Chukwuemeka Mojekwu was born in 1919 in the Nnewi locality of Anambra State. He is said to have been related to Sir Louis Odumegwu Ojukwu (q.v.), the successful businessman whose son, Emeka Ojukwu, led the Eastern Region to secession in 1967. Mojekwu's own prominent influence during the duration of Biafra is attributed largely to that relationship.

After formal schooling in Nigeria and legal studies in Europe, C. C. Mojekwu returned to Nigeria to commence practice, serving as a barrister and solicitor of the Supreme Court of Nigeria. He was subsequently appointed Attorney-General and Minister of Justice of Eastern Nigeria. He was the first to hold this position in the region, and he employed his talent in transforming the region's colonial legal structure into one appropriate for an integral unit of independent Nigeria. Soon, however, political and military disturbances in the country, reaching their peak in August and September 1966, saw several thousand Easterners, mostly Igbos, killed. C. C. Mojekwu and many of his leading Igbo kinsmen, failing to get Federal Government assurance that similar incidences would be averted, initiated a move which took the Eastern Region out of Nigeria in 1967.

The birth of Biafra saw him variously as Commissioner for Home Affairs in the secessionist regime and as ambassador-at-large, soliciting international political and material support for the Igbo cause. At the cessation of hostilities in 1970 Dr Mojekwu, like a host of other Biafran leaders – notably Odumegwu Ojukwu and Professor K. O. Dike (q.v.) – went into exile. Like Dike, he settled in the United States of America where he took up a teaching job as Professor of Politics at the Lake Forest College in Illinois. He held this post until his death in 1982 in a motor accident that occurred between his Lake Forest home and the Chicago O'Hare Airport.

Dr Mojekwu's body was flown to his native town Nnewi for burial which attracted a large section of Nigerian society. An exuberant man of many talents, he had served the nation well in several capacities. For besides his legal duties, he was for many years Chief Commissioner of the Boys' Scout of Nigeria. He was also a member of the Federal Public Service Commission as well as Chairman of the Nigerian Flying School.■

Molapo (1814-80)

MOLAPO, Chief (1814-80).

Lesotho traditional ruler. He was a junior son of the famous king of the Sotho, the founder and defender of their nation, Moshoeshoe (q.v.) or Moshesh; his mother, Mamohato, was Moshoeshoe's main wife.

In 1833 Moshoeshoe sent Molapo and an elder son, Letsie, to greet missionaries of the French Protestant missionary society, the *Société des Missions Evangéliques* (SME). These missionaries had a major effect on the Sotho people who were being united, after the chaotic migrations of peoples called the *Mfecane,* to form a state in the mountains under Moshoeshoe's leadership. They helped Moshoeshoe defend his independence against the Boers who were aggressive neighbours from the 1830s. Many Sotho people were converted by the SME.

Moshoeshoe sent Letsie and Molapo to Morija to go to the SME school. After seven years Molapo was converted to Christianity and baptised. The missionaries were impressed by his sincere Christian conviction. Their journal later wrote that he had shown "an astonishing grasp of Bible history, an expansive and scrupulous piety, complete reform of conduct, a zeal both burning and wise." He renounced polygamy and celebrated a Christian marriage with Lydia Mamoussa, converted before him to become the first Sotho Christian woman.

He was said to have been, at first, good at his traditional government duties, giving judgement and commanding in war. However, as a younger brother his role was limited. Moshoeshoe sent him to a northern area where he gradually ceased to be an active Christian, reverting to polygamy, and allowing the revival of traditional customs. Relations were often difficult between him and the mission whose role was so important.

In 1858 the Boers' Orange Free State went to war with Lesotho (Basutoland). Molapo fought with distinction but the war was indecisive. In 1859 he attacked the Boers again and was defeated. In that same year the SME missionary Coillard set up a station at Leribe near Molapo's headquarters. In 1868, following an appeal by Moshoeshoe, Lesotho was taken under British protection. This "Basutoland Protectorate" began as genuine protection against the Boers, and ensured that these would not conquer the Sotho. In March 1870 Moshoeshoe died and was succeeded by Letsie.

In the north which he governed, Molapo followed the policy of collaboration with the British, to whom he handed over a Zulu chief who fled after defying an order for his people to surrender newly acquired weapons. The British, who in 1877 increased their territory in South Africa by annexing the Boer Republics, sought to enforce their rule over Basutoland by ordering its people to surrender arms in 1879. Their refusal led to a war between Britain and the Protectorate in 1879-81. During that "Gun War" Chief Molapo died on 28 June 1880.

The French Protestant mission took part in a Christian burial service, and the body was taken by about a thousand men to the royal tombs at Thaba-Bossiu. He was succeeded by his eldest son, Jonathan Molapo.■

Molema, M.S. (1892-1965)

MOLEMA, Dr Modiri Silas (1892-1965).

Botswana physician, writer and politician who was prominent in South Africa's African National Congress (ANC) in the 1940s. Molema was born in 1892 in Mafeking, the eldest son of Chief Telesho Molema who founded the *Koranta ya Bachuana*, a Setswana newspaper that was edited for sometime by Solomon Plaatje (q.v.). Modiri Molema received his early education in the Cape Province, South Africa, after which he taught at the Lyndhurst Road Public School, Kimberley, South Africa. In 1913 he matriculated at Lovedale College in Alice in the Cape Province. In 1914 he proceeded to the United Kingdom to study medicine at Glasgow University, he qualified in 1919.

It is not clearly ascertained whether Molema's political thinking was directly influenced by the Pan-Africanists who were active in Europe at the time of his studies, but it was during the latter part of his sojourn at Glasgow University that he wrote an important historical document on southern Africa which was published in 1920 as *The Bantu – Past and Present*. He was later to publish other biographical books, *Chief Moroka: His Life and Times, His Country and His People* which came out in 1951, and *Montshiwa, Barolong Chief and Patriot 1815-1893* that appeared in 1966, a year after Molema's death.

Returning to Africa after his studies in Glasgow, he settled in Mafeking where he soon established a successful medical practice; the fact that a substantial proportion of his patients were Europeans may have influenced the cautious, moderate stance he maintained in the early years of his political activity in South Africa. He soon however abandoned that stance when he joined the ANC in 1936 as co-opted member of the committee charged with presenting African views on government new measures against African rights (the "Hertzog Bills").

Following the ANC leadership crisis of 1940 when D.A.B. Xuma (q.v.) succeeded Reverend Zaccheus Richard Mahabane (q.v.) as president, Molema played an important part in the re-organisation after openly criticising the administrative defects of the deposed leadership. At the 1949 annual congress of the ANC he became a member of the Executive Committee following his election as Treasurer-General. He was re-elected to serve a second term of office in December 1952.

He was instrumental in adopting the new strategies which were aimed at frustrating the government racist measures of the

time. These culminated in the Defiance Campaign of 1952 when Africans, Indians, Coloureds and their European sympathisers voluntarily defied the segregation laws. He was among the several African leaders arrested during the Campaign, although he was not tried as a principal defendant. Some records have construed this as the result of his earlier moderate and conciliatory stance in relation to co-operating with sympathetic non-African organisations. He retired from politics in 1953 following a banning order which prevented him from actively carrying on with his work in the ANC. Molema died in relative political obscurity in Mafeking in 1965. ∎

Mondlane, E.C. (1920-69)

MONDLANE, Dr Eduardo Chivambo (1920-69).

MOZAMBICAN freedom fighter, the first leader of FRELIMO. Eduardo Mondlane was born in 1920 in the Gaza district of Southern Mozambique. Like most children of his age he spent the first ten years of his life herding cattle. He entered a mission primary school but as an African he was prevented from going to secondary school. However, he taught himself English and obtained a scholarship to a high school in the Northern Transvaal, South Africa. From there he went to study social science at the University of the Witwatersrand.

While in South Africa Mondlane became interested in the affairs of the Mozambican students studying in South Africa. They organised themselves into a students union body called NESAM. Because of his activities he was arrested by the South African police and handed over to PIDE, the Portuguese secret police, in Mozambique. He later continued his studies in Lisbon on a Phelps-Stokes Fund scholarship.

PIDE continued to harass him and made his medical studies impossible. But his stay in Portugal was far more important than that in South Africa. In Portugal he came into contact with people who had the same colonial experience. He met and talked with men who became future leaders of the nationalist movements in other Portuguese colonies.

After Eduardo Mondlane had transferred his scholarship from Portugal to the United States he studied sociology and anthropology at Oberlin University, where he graduated with a BA degree in 1953. He

Dr. E.C. Mondlane

went on to take MA and PhD degrees in sociology at Northwestern University, Evanston, Illinois. Work in "role conflict research" at Harvard University was followed by an appointment at the United Nations as a research officer in its Trusteeship section.

While at the United Nations he continued to study the situation in his own country and kept himself informed of developments there.

He went back to Mozambique in 1961

and travelled widely throughout the country. On his return to the United States he left the United Nations and took up a professorship at Syracuse University in New York.

He had concluded from talking with Portuguese diplomats at the United Nations that independence for Mozambique could be won only through war. He made open contact with existing Mozambican exile movements but refused to become a member of any of them; he wanted unity of all the movements.

Eduardo Mondlane spent the years 1961-62 campaigning for the unity of all Mozambican political movements and preparing the ground for the formation of a new unified movement. In September 1962 the major organisations in Mozambique, UDENAMO, MANU and UNAMI met in Dar-es-Salaam and formed one organisation, the Front for the Liberation of Mozambique (FRELIMO). Mondlane was rewarded for his hard work in bringing all these organisations together with the first presidency of FRELIMO.

The aims of the new organisation included consolidation and mobilisation, preparation for war, education, and diplomacy.

To mobilise the people, various networks that had been established by the old parties were developed. The networks of the co-operative movements were used for internal mobilisation and the recruitment of youths for the budding FRELIMO army, the People's Forces for the Liberation of Mozambique (FPLM).

In their preparation for war FRELIMO approached Algeria and sent about 50 people for training. In the education field FRELIMO set up the Mozambique Institute in Tanzania for secondary school students.

To facilitate the diplomatic work of FRELIMO, permanent offices were set up outside Tanzania in Cairo, Algiers and Lusaka. They sent delegations to international conferences and printed information pamphlets.

Within two years of its formation FRELIMO made its first military attack in northern Mozambique in September 1964. By 1968 FRELIMO had liberated one third of Mozambique, thus enabling it to hold its second congress inside the country.

Mondlane was re-elected President of FRELIMO. Delegates came from all parts of Mozambique making this congress more representative and democratic than the first one. There were also two delegates from the Afro-Asian Solidarity Committee, the MPLA, the ANC (South Africa), and Zimbabwe.

Mondlane strongly supported joint action by all the liberation movements in the region as well as greater co-operation between all liberation movements in the Portuguese colonies.

On the morning of 3 February 1969, Mondlane was killed in Dar-es-Salaam by a parcel bomb. He was survived by his wife Janet and three children.■

Moodley, M. (1913-79)

MOODLEY, Mary (1913-79).

SOUTH AFRICAN politician who was a founding member and leader of the South African Coloured People's Congress. She gave expression to the aspirations of the country's so-called Coloured community in their struggle against excesses of the white minority regime and, in the process, Moodley became a symbol of the protracted resistance and of unity among the oppressed Africans, Indians and the Coloureds.

Born in 1913 in the Coloured township of Wattville in Benoni near Johannesburg, Moodley's life spanned several years of campaign. Aunty Mary, as she was commonly known, began her political work as an early member of the South African Coloured People's Congress which she helped to form. By the 1950s she had become one of its leading figures, featuring in its campaign in and around Johannesburg. She played an important role in the 1950s campaign against the attempt to impose the pass system, hitherto confined to men, on women. Later when the South African Coloured People's Congress teamed up with other Congresses – the African National Congress, the South African Indian Congress, the South African Congress of Trade Unions, and the Congress of Democrats – to constitute the Congress of the People (COP) in 1955, she was a prominent delegate at the COP's first meeting held in June of that year in Kliptown near Johannesburg.

It was at the Kliptown meeting that the Freedom Charter, which demanded a non-racial and a democratic South Africa, was drawn up. The Charter was aimed "to benefit all classes and groups, and likewise

M. Moodley

the democratic struggle to achieve it", said Nelson Mandela, one of the ANC leaders at the conference. He added that it was "conducted by an alliance of various classes and political groupings amongst the non-European people supported by white democrats. African, Coloured and Indian workers and peasants, traders and merchants, students and teachers, doctors and lawyers, and various other classes and groupings: all participate in the struggle against racial inequality and for full democratic rights". The day the Freedom Charter was adopted, the 25 June 1955, was the third anniversary of the launching of the Defiance Campaign in 1952, and has since been declared and observed as Freedom Day by the ANC.

Earlier in 1954 Moodley had been a prime mover in the mobilisation of all South African women and their various organisations to give organised expression to their campaign. The effort resulted in the formation in 1954 of the Federation of South African Women, a multi-racial front of women's organisations in the country of which Lilian Masebida Ngoyi (q.v.) was elected to the presidency.

Her political activity led to continuous police harassment and banning orders whose culminative effect placed Moodley under restriction for a considerable number of years. She was first confined in 1963 under the Suppresion of Communism Act which forbade her to attend or speak at any public meeting for five years. In 1968 the banning order was renewed for another five-year period, which was again extended in 1973 and 1978 to last until 1983. Moodley, weakened by ill-health, died of diabetes and hypertension on 23 October 1979 in Benoni hospital while serving the fourth instalment of her confinement. ■

He was also honorary treasurer, Boy Scout's Council, 1948-60; he was a member of the Fourah Bay College Council from 1950 to 1954, and of the West African Examinations Council in 1953. In 1956 he was appointed a Temporary Nominated Member of the Legislative Council, and he served there (until 1961).

He was president of the Chemists and Druggists Association; president of the African Chamber of Commerce, 1944-1960; and president of the Chamber of Commerce of Sierra Leone, 1961-1963. He was awarded the MBE in 1944, made a Justice of the Peace in 1952, awarded the OBE in 1959, and awarded the Sierra Leone Independence Medal in 1961. He received his knighthood from the Queen at Buckingham Palace in March 1971. He was made an honorary Doctor of Civil Laws, University of Sierra Leone.

He died in early December 1979. ■

Morgan, E.D. (1894-1979)

MORGAN, Sir Ernest Dunstan (1894-1979).

SIERRA LEONEAN druggist and businessman. Born on 17 November 1894, he qualified as the first Sierra Leonean druggist and from 1921 served as dispenser in various parts of the then Sierra Leone Colony and Protectorate, including Kissy and Nothe. He also served with the "A" Company of the Sierra Leone Military Force at Kailahun until he resigned from government service. Sir Ernest then worked as an independent druggist at Blama, in the then Central Province, until 1936 when he returned to Freetown to open the West End Pharmacy, later named Morgan Pharmacus.

He also ran a public transport service known as Novel Transport, from 1938-1941. Elected a member of the Freetown City Council from 1938 to 1944, he served on numerous government and public committees. He was the first chairman of the Rent Assessment Committee, Central Ward, Freetown, 1941-51. Sir Ernest was one of the first two Sierra Leoneans to serve as members of the Public Service Commission, from 1948 to 1952.

Moroka, J.S. (1891-1985)

MOROKA, Dr James Sebe (1891-1985).

SOUTH AFRICAN politician, ex-President of the African National Congress (ANC) of South Africa, medical practitioner and farmer. Dr Moroka's political career can be said to have begun in 1930 when he agitated against racial discrimination, the pass laws and liquor restrictions. He campaigned against the disenfranchisement of Africans in the Cape Province, the only province where Africans had the vote. In the mid-thirties he joined The All African Convention and immediately became its leader. A delegation led by him confronted Prime Minister Hertzog (q.v.) regarding the Land Act which restricted Africans to 13 per cent of all land, and other discriminatory laws.

Dr Moroka was the great grandson of the Tswana Chief Moroka. Born in 1891 in Thaba Nchu, he was educated at Lovedale Training College in the Cape Province. In 1911 he went to study medicine at the University of Edinburgh, Scotland, where he graduated in 1918. Afterwards he continued his training in Vienna, Austria. He returned to South Africa as one of the first non-White doctors in the country, established his prac tice at his home town of Thaba Nchu, and soon gained the respect of the Whites in his region to the extent that the normally prejudiced Afrikaners became his patients. It is said that at one time he had segregated entrances to his surgery. He often reminded

Dr. J. Moroka

people that he owed a great deal of gratitude to an Afrikaner, Piet Steytler, who had spent over two thousand pounds on his medical education. He in turn assisted four White students and did in fact also help African students. He could well afford this being a very prosperous farmer as well as having a large practice.

In 1942 he was elected to the Native Representative Council (NRC), which was created in 1936 as a sop for the lost Cape franchise. This advisory body was later referred to as "a toy telephone" to the government. He believed that the best way to wreck it was from the inside. In 1946 the South Afrian population embarked on a civil disobedience campaign, the African miners

went on strike, eight were shot and over a thousand were injured. The NRC members decided to adjourn indefinitely. In 1948 they resigned, but Dr Moroka delayed his own resignation until 1950; this gave him problems because by that time he had already served a year as President of the ANC.

In 1949 the Youth League of the ANC, led by the lawyer Lembede (q.v.), Nelson Mandela, Oliver Tambo, Walter Sisulu, and others were disenchanted with the then President, Dr A. B. Xuma (q.v.), who was resisting their call for more militancy through a programme of action that would entail non-co-operation with the government, national strikes and stay-at-homes. An alternative candidate for Presidency needed to be found and Dr Moroka was chosen despite the fact that he was not a member of the ANC. He was a popular leader and enhanced his presidency by addressing meetings throughout the country, having the advantage of being able to afford the expenses.

He readily endorsed the Defiance Campaign that was led by Nelson Mandela in 1952, insisting that it should at all costs be a non-violent campaign, marked by passive resistance. This was after he and Walter Sisulu had written to the Prime Minister Dr Malan (q.v.) pointing out the long history of the ANC's representations to successive governments and its desire for understanding being met with even more repressive laws. The Prime Minister's perfunctory reply was that the ANC did not represent the majority of the people. On 6 April 1952 Dr Moroka addressed a vast gathering in Johannesburg and called on the Africans to "muster all their forces of mind, body and soul to see that this state of affairs, these crushing conditions under which they live shall not continue any longer". He called for 10,000 volunteers to defy apartheid laws.

At the end of November Dr Moroka, Nelson Mandela, Walter Sisulu and other leaders were arrested and charged under the Suppression of Communism Act as a result of organising the Defiance Campaign. Dr Moroka dissociated himself from the other accused, engaging a separate counsel. They were all found guilty of "statutory communism". In mitigation Dr Moroka stressed his friendship with Afrikaners and mentioned how he had assisted them; he was sentenced to nine months' imprisonment, suspended for two years. This trial, however, was to destroy his political leadership. At the annual conference of the ANC in December 1952 Moroka was not re-elected having received only votes from his province of the Orange Free State. He was succeeded by Chief Albert Luthuli (q.v.).

After that though Dr Moroka went on taking an interest in public affairs he did so from the distance of his farm in Thaba Nchu, and continued practising as a doctor. To the end of his life he believed that Blacks and Whites in South Africa needed each other, and he supported the creation of Bantustans saying the "homelands at least gave Blacks a stable home which Whites could not take away".

Confident and dignified, Dr Moroka had the status required for national leadership, but lacked the political sharpness needed to see him through certain situations.

He died in November 1985 at the age of 94. ■

Bishop S.R. Moshi

Moshi, S.R. (1906-76)

MOSHI, Most Reverend Bishop Stefano Reuben (1906-76).

TANZANIAN clergyman, elected first president of the Evangelical Lutheran Church of Tanganyika, now Tanzania, (ELCT) at its formation in 1963. Born into a Christian family in Kotela, Mamba division of Moshi district, on 6 May 1906, he went to school at Gonja where his father was teaching. His family moved back to Kotela where he continued his education until 1922.

That same year he began teaching in a local school, remaining there for four years. In 1927 he did a two-year course at the Marangu Teachers' Training College. He later taught at the college while studying for the London University entrance examinations in which he was successful but he chose instead to enter the theological college in Lwandai in Tanga, Tanzania. He was ordained pastor on 26 December 1949. Between 1952 and 1953 he studied at the Lutheran Bible Institute, Minneapolis, Minnesota, in the United States. He returned to Tanzania and continued to work as a

teacher; he later became principal of the Marangu Teachers' Training College.

In 1955 he left the teaching profession to concentrate on the work of the Church. He was elected assistant, and later vice-president of the Lutheran Church of Northern Tanganyika (which later became the Northern Diocese), of which he became head in 1958; he was also elected, for two years from 1961, president of the former Federation of Lutheran Churches of Tanganyika. When the various Lutheran Church groups in the country united to form the Evangelical Lutheran Church of Tanganyika (ELCT) in 1963, Bishop Moshi was elected the first head of the body.

The membership of the ELCT is estimated at nearly 800,000 and the Church, until 1970, managed several schools and hospitals before they were taken over by the State. As head of the ELCT, and also Bishop of the Northern Diocese (having been consecrated in 1964), Bishop Moshi was a powerful force in and outside the country. He did not pretend to support the notion of "not mixing religion with politics" and often spoke against injustices of governments, as in a

1974 speech to Church leaders in Dar-es-Salaam when he reiterated "the Church's condemnation of atrocities perpetrated by big powers as can be seen in Rhodesia (now Zimbabwe), Mozambique, South Africa, Angola, Guinea-Bissau and elsewhere in the world".

A man of tremendous energy, Bishop Moshi joined and served in many organisations. He became a member of the Christian Council of Tanganyika (CCT) in 1960 and was elected its first African chairman in 1965. He also served as vice-president of the Commission of World Mission of the Lutheran World Federation and as a president of the All-African Conference of Churches for many years. Between 1959 and 1961 he was a member of the Chagga Council and the Moshi Town Council. Bishop Moshi was instrumental in the historic meeting in Moshi of representatives of Churches in East Africa where the East African Venture Company, which published the Church organs *Target* and *Lengo*, was established.

In recognition of his services he was awarded in 1970 two doctorate degrees of Divinity by the Gustavus Adolphus College and the Concordia Seminary, both in America.

Bishop Moshi was on church business in Germany in 1976 when he was taken ill; he was flown to Nairobi, Kenya, for treatment and died in a hospital there on 15 August 1976. He is buried in Kotela, his birthplace, in Tanzania. ■

Moshoeshoe I (1786-1870)

MOSHOESHOE I, King (1786-1870).

LESOTHO statesman and traditional ruler, was born in 1786 in the Caledon River valley in Lesotho. His father, a sub-chief of a people who were mainly cattle raiders, first called him Lepoqo but he later changed his name to Moshoeshoe (the shaver) following his first cattle raid as a warrior against a neighbouring community, during which he is said to have shaved off a rival chief's beard.

Shortly thereafter Moshoeshoe, following tradition, moved away from his father and set up his own village at Butha-Buthe with his followers. In the early 1820s the Sotho-Tswana wars, known as the *Lifaqane*, broke out and for a number of years this conflict was the source of considerable instability on the South African plateau. After Moshoeshoe's settlement at Butha-Buthe had come under constant attack from the Batloka, Moshoeshoe decided that he and his followers should rejoin his father's community. Together they moved into the mountains where they were able to fend off hostile attacks, until the mountain hide-out was attacked and placed under siege by Sekonyela. The siege was ended when Sekonyela was attacked by a neighbouring clan. Moshoeshoe and his father moved their people south to Thaba-Bosiu, which means "mountain at night", a flat-topped, steep-sided mountain in the central Drakensberg range, which provided almost impregnable natural defences.

Moshoeshoe's followers had been swelled by the vast number of refugees that had been scattered and made homeless by Zulu and Matabele raids. Other clans also joined Moshoeshoe and their chiefs became his vassals. This intercourse also led to the introduction of horses, which some clans depended on for mobility in the mountains, and which Moshoeshoe used militarily to control the surrounding valleys. The people of Lesotho are known in Southern Africa for their horse-riding skills. Although for a long period Sekonyela remained Moshoeshoe's enemy, attacking the latter's mountain stronghold, he could not defeat Moshoeshoe. By the middle of the 1830s the *Lifaqane* began to die out.

Moshoeshoe allowed the French Evangelical Church Mission to operate in his territory and established personal ties with two missionaries who became his trusted advisors, particularly in his dealings with the Afrikaners and the British. In 1834, the Afrikaners began what came to be known as the "Great Trek", northwards from the Cape Colony which was under British rule. Many of them settled on Sotho territory. Moshoeshoe initially allowed them to do so, unaware that they intended to remain permanently in the area. Hostility soon developed between the two people with the Sotho raiding Afrikaner cattle as the Afrikaners encroached on more and more of Lesotho territory.

On the advice of the French missionaries, Moshoeshoe appealed to the British for

King Moshoeshoe I

help. Although they demarcated the boundaries between Sotho and Afrikaner territory, the British failed to remove Afrikaners who had already settled on Sotho land. A struggle ensured between the Sotho and the Afrikaners, with the Afrikaners unable to defeat Moshoeshoe's mountain stronghold.

In 1868 Moshoeshoe asked the British to set up a protectorate over his territory. In the negotiations which brought about the end of the Afrikaner-Basotho war, Moshoeshoe lost some of his most fertile territory along the Caledon River. This land, seized by the Afrikaners, remains an issue of conflict between the governments of Lesotho and South Africa today. After handing some power to his eldest son in January 1870, Moshoeshoe died on 11 March 1870.■

Mothopeng, Z. L. (1913-90)

MOTHOPENG, Zephaniah Lekoane (1913-90).

SOUTH AFRICAN political activist. He was of Zulu and Sotho parentage, and was born in September 1913 in eastern Transvaal. He went to St. Peter's Catholic school in Johannesburg, and then qualified as a teacher at Adams College in Natal. For 13 years he taught mathematics and science at Orlando High School in an area later included in Soweto, the vast African "township" of Johannesburg. He conducted the school's choir, which was chosen to sing before King George VI of England on his visit to South Africa in 1947. While working he studied by correspondence for a BA of the University of South Africa.

He became President of the Transvaal African Teachers' Association, and was re-elected several times. In that office he led opposition to "Bantu education", the apartheid system of education for Africans which was explicitly aimed at training them for a permanently subordinate role. He was sacked by the government in 1952, and then concentrated on nationalist politics and on trying to earn a living; he did several jobs before becoming qualified as a law clerk. He was a member of the African National Congress (ANC) for some years. But in 1959 he joined others in breaking away from the ANC, saying it was not militant enough and too influenced by white and Asian Communists. They formed the Pan-Africanist Congress (PAC) and Mothopeng joined its National Executive Committee.

With the PAC leader, Robert Sobukwe (q.v.), he joined in the protests against the "pass" laws which were answered with the killing by the police of 69 people at Sharpeville in March 1960. He was then gaoled for two years for "incitement", while the PAC was banned. After his release Mothopeng (fondly called "Uncle Zeph" by other activists) continued legal studies, but was rearrested a year later, held in detention without trial under the newly passed "90 day" detention law, and brutally treated. Then he was gaoled for three years for working for the PAC and sent to the notorious Robben Island prison.

After his release in 1967 he was first restricted to a rural area, then allowed to live in Soweto but still under "banning" orders, heavily restricting his activity, until 1971. Then he became director of the Urban Resource Centre, a voluntary organisation for adult education and other services for Africans in Kagiso, outside Krugersdorp. He also studied for an external degree in Commerce.

When the Soweto uprising, which spread to many parts of South Africa, was begun by schoolchildren in 1976, Mothopeng was arrested. He was charged with inciting unrest in Kagiso, and with underground activity aimed at overthrowing the apartheid regime; he was said to have worked to help reorganise the PAC. In fact the PAC, in exile, fell into factional infighting and decline about then, while Sobukwe died in 1978. Whatever "Zeph" may perhaps have done to help revive the PAC in South Africa itself, the white-supremacy regime saw him as a fearless opponent. In 1979 he was sentenced to 15 years' imprisonment, but he defiantly wrote, "As the doors of prison lock us in, this time our spirits are very high because we realise that victory is in sight and freedom is on our threshold".

In 1985, when he was over 70 and his health was declining, the government offered to free him, but he refused as he would be required to sign a statement renouncing all violent opposition to apartheid. He was

finally released in 1988 and, despite his age, at once resumed political activity and even became President of the still banned PAC. He received medical treatment in Britain in 1989. In the following year the PAC was legalised again along with the ANC. When Mothopeng died on 23 October 1990 in Johannesburg, change for the better for the Africans of South Africa had begun to appear on the horizon: freedom, it seemed, was on the threshold. But his death left the PAC in continued disarray, with internal and exiled leaders in dispute. In appropriate tribute to him, one of the main leaders of the ANC, Walter Sisulu, said Mothopeng's death left "the people of South Africa, especially the oppressed much poorer". ■

Z.L. Mothopeng

Moumié, F. (1926-60)

MOUMIE, Dr Félix-Roland (1926-60).

CAMEROONIAN politician and physician. He was born at Foumban, Cameroon in 1926. After attending primary and secondary schools in Cameroon, he went to Senegal, where he qualified as a doctor in 1950. He returned to Cameroon and became involved in the *Union des Populations du Cameroun* (UPC), in whose formation he had been instrumental in 1948; the party later became the Cameroon branch of the *Rassemblement Démocratique Africain*, the inter-territorial political movement of French-speaking West Africa, founded in Bamako, Mali, in October 1946, which was lobbying for political change in France's West African territories.

Dr Moumié became Co-President of the UPC in 1952 and was active in promoting the party's aims. These were, principally, the unification of the British and German Cameroons, and independence from France. Despite widespread support, especially in urban centres, the tightly-knit UPC found it impossible to win seats in the Cameroon assemblies. This was partly due to hostility from the French administration and partly to the emergence of anti-UPC groups between 1949 and 1955. The UPC decided, therefore, to adopt a more militant attitude and, on 22

April 1955, it and other affiliated political organisations issued a Joint Proclamation declaring the end of French trusteeship and calling for general elections. In the two months that followed, the UPC launched a series of demonstrations in Douala and Yaounde, which led to its proscription in July 1955.

Dr. F. Moumié

Along with other UPC leaders, Dr Moumié went into exile, first to Cairo, where he set up temporary headquarters, and later to Conakry on the occasion of Guinea's independence in October 1958. During his exile, Dr Moumié was the president of the UPC, and, together with other exiled leaders, directed the party's political activities from abroad. The guerrilla campaign conducted by the UPC's militant wing between 1955 and 1962 came to be known as the "Bamileke Rebellion' after 1958, when most guerrillas except for the Bamilekes surrendered. The UPC conducted a campaign to discourage people from voting in the elections of December 1956. The government which emerged from those elections called on French troops to assist in putting down the UPC-led campaign. This attempt at crushing the UPC was not at first successful, for the guerrillas had thousands of sympathisers, both in the main towns and in the countryside. From exile, Dr Moumié also led a propaganda campaign, petitioning the United Nations constantly for the lifting of the ban on the UPC and for amnesty for its leaders.

East (French) Cameroon achieved internal self-government in 1957, and in February 1958 Ahmadou Ahidjo (q.v.) became Prime Minister. In June 1959 Dr Moumié issued a statement, saying that in spite of Cameroon's independence, which he regarded as "unreal", his movement would continue the revolution. On 27 June violence broke out in the west and the government declared a state of emergency in Douala, the Bamileke country and Yaounde. On 18 August 1959 Dr Moumié issued a joint statement from Conakry to the effect that revolutionary action would be continued until the French agreed to certain stated policies, including abolition of the existing institutions, the ending of a state of emergency and the lifting of the ban on the UPC. They demanded a round-table conference and general elections as a prelude to real independence, but failed to obtain these; the independent Republic of Cameroon was established on 1 January 1960. Once again, violence broke out in Douala and other areas, following the UPC's opposition to independence and the rejection of Dr Moumié's constitutional proposals and political demands.

Dr Moumié was admitted to hospital in Geneva on 16 October 1960, complaining of stomach poisoning. Tests conducted at the Medico-Legal Institute in Zurich produced evidence that he had been poisoned by thalium, a metallic constituent of rat poison, believed to have been administered by "The Red Hand", a French terrorist group which was opposed to Algerian Independence. He died in hospital on 3 November 1960. ■

Moyo, J.Z. (1927-77)

MOYO, Jason Ziyapapa (1927-77).

ZIMBABWEAN politician; he played a prominent role in the formative years of the struggle for independence. He was born in 1927 in Kezi District, Zimbabwe. After attending a mission primary school outside Bulawayo, Moyo went to Mzingwane Government School, Essexvale, where he qualified as a builder and carpenter. He worked in Bulawayo and soon joined the Rhodesia Artisans Union, later becoming its general secretary. He also joined the Bulawayo-based African National Congress and became its secretary and later chairman. When the new African National Congress was formed on 12 September 1957, Moyo became a member and was detained for three months after the party was banned during the state of emergency declared on 26 February 1959. He was later detained in Marandellas Prison from which he was released in 1960. When the National Democratic Party (NDP) was formed, following the banning of the ANC, he was elected to the national executive in November 1960. After the NDP was banned also, Moyo became national treasurer of the newly-formed Zimbabwe African People's Union (ZAPU).

After the split with ZAPU which resulted in the formation of the PCC (People's Caretaker Council) and ZANU (Zimbabwe African National Union), Moyo sided with the PCC and became its financial secretary. Later he was appointed to the Lusaka-based PCC external executive, formed to ensure that possible detention of leaders by the Rhodesian government would not destroy the party. When the Front for the Liberation of Zimbabwe (FROLIZI) was formed to bring together ZANU and ZAPU, "JZ" as he was popularly known, declined to join and took over the leadership of the ZAPU faction. He declined to serve as vice-chairman in the Zimbabwe Liberation Council formed after the African National Council (ANC) had been made umbrella organisation to the Zimbabwe liberation movements in December 1974.

On 12 September 1975 Moyo and three others were expelled from the ANC because it was believed that he had formed a secret ethnic organisation, *"Dengezi"*, aimed at wresting power for itself. On 14 April 1976, Moyo was appointed vice-president of the ANC-Nkomo, charged with external and military affairs. He attended the Geneva Conference as a delegate. He was killed by a parcel bomb in the ZAPU offices in Lusaka on 22 January 1977, becoming a hero of independent Zimbabwe when his body was flown for reburial at the Heroes Acre just

J.Z. Moyo

outside Salisbury (now Harare) on 12 August 1980; the ceremony was attended by some 60,000 Zimbabweans. ■

Mpakati, A. (1932/3-83)

MPAKATI, Dr Attati (1932/3-83).

MALAWIAN politician who was born in Mlanje district in the Southern Region of Malawi, and became involved in the anti-colonial struggle in his teens. He was elected provincial secretary of the Nyasaland African Congress, the dominant political organisation of Africans in Nyasaland (now Malawi) for the then Southern Province in November 1957 and held that position until the organisation was proscribed and he himself, among over 1,500 of its members, was arrested in what was code-named Operation Sunrise on 3 March 1959. With a number of others, he was flown to Zimbabwe (then

Southern Rhodesia) where he was detained at Khan prison near Bulawayo and later Marondella before he was sent to Kanjedza detention camp in Malawi. After his release in July 1960, he was put under restriction at Kuntaja near Blantyre but immediately after the removal of his restriction in 1961, he left the country and found his way to Russia and later Sweden and West Germany where he furthered his education, and eventually obtained an advanced degree in Economics.

Dr. A. Mpakati

Because of his disagreement with Dr Banda, whom he accused of having 'highjacked the Malawi revolution and pawned it to the British', Mpakati did not return to Malawi after his studies and his country's independence in 1964, but worked in various places, as a research fellow in the Department of Economic History at the University of Uppsala, Sweden, at UNESCO's regional office in Lusaka and with the Reserve Bank of Mozambique in Maputo.

When Lesoma, the Socialist League of Malawi, was formed in 1974, Mpakati who was at the time in Maputo, was elected its National Chairman.

As leader of Lesoma, an opposition party in exile to President Banda's Malawi Congress Party, Mpakati had become a target. In February 1979, a parcel bomb sent to him in Maputo, exploded in his hands, blowing off all the fingers on his left hand and three on his right. Later, it was alleged that the Malawi National Assembly members were informed that "the most cunning and troublesome leader of the dissidents is in hospital recovering from wounds." As a result of this act, Lesoma, at its congress in 1980 said to have been held in Dar es Salaam, announced the formation of its military wing and claimed that several young Malawians would be trained in Cuba, though Mpakati is quoted to have said "they do not believe in invading the country." At the inaugural meeting in the British House of Commons of the Labour Party Malawi Support Committee, Mpakati prompted the Labour Party to launch a campaign, which was supported by the Labour Party's international chairman, Joan Lestor, "to fight for the restoration of democracy and human rights in Malawi."

Mpakati believed in forging closer links between Malawi and, what he termed, neighbouring anti-imperialist states and in nullifying "contracts signed between Banda and South Africa". He was, however, deported from Zambia in February 1982.

Mpakati was killed, at the age of 50 on 28 March 1983 in a second attempt on his life in Harare where his body, with a gunshot in the head, was found. Though nobody was charged with his murder, it is commonly believed that he was eliminated by the agents of South Africa.

Mpakati was survived by his Russian wife and their two children.■

Mpande, King S. (1798-1872)

MPANDE, King Ka Senzagakhona (1798-1872).

Zulu king, brother of Chaka (q.v.) and Dingane, whose reign of 32 years (1840-72) was the longest in the history of the Zulu kingdom. During that period he strove to keep the Zulu nation united while repulsing external pressures from the British and the Boers.

Mpande, whose name means the Root, spent his youth in the Zulu army under

Chaka and commanded troops in several campaigns to consolidate the Zulu nation. Following the assassination of Chaka in 1828, Dingane eliminated many men of royal birth whose loyalty he suspected. Fortunately for Mpande he was away on a campaign at that time. He readily swore allegiance to Dingane, his childhood friend, and survived the purge. For the next few years he stayed out of the limelight, living near Eshowe.

Mpande returned to public attention in 1838 during the war with the Boers who had recently settled in Natal. In April he commanded the Injanduna regiment which, along with other Zulu forces, virtually wiped out Robert Biggar's expeditionary force. Shortly afterwards Mpande incurred Dingane's wrath when his troops failed to show up in response to Dingane's call to arms for a campaign against the Swazi people in the North. In September 1839, having been warned of Dingane's intention to kill him, Mpande with his many followers and cattle fled to Natal for safety. Later that same year Dingane was badly defeated at the Battle of Blood River, and a peace treaty between the Boers and the Zulus was signed.

After receiving permission to make camp on the banks of the Thongathi River, Mpande met with the Boer leaders to negotiate for a permanent place to settle with his people. The Boers regarded Mpande's flight as an opportunity to rid themselves of the threat of Dingane once for all. As a result, in October 1839, Mpande, as leader of the Zulus in Natal, formally allied himself with the Boers for the overthrow of Dingane. For the next few months Mpande and his chiefs made military preparation and in January 1940 the Boers, accompanied by Mpande and using as an excuse the non-arrival of cattle agreed in the 1839 peace treaty as compensation, began the invasion of Zululand. After a bitter and bloody battle in which Zulu fought Zulu, Dingane's forces fled into Swaziland and on 10 February 1840 Mpande was installed King of the Zulus. The death of Dingane a few months later strengthened Mpande's position, especially as many of Dingane's followers returned to Zululand and swore allegiance to him.

During the early years of his reign Mpande embarked on re-uniting the Zulu nation. He relied on the support of his chiefs to maintain his position and to some extent political power was decentralised. In 1842 the British annexed Natal and the Boers

King Ka S. Mpande

moved over the Drakensberg Mountains to the Central Plateau, north-west of Zululand. Both white groups coveted areas of Zululand though for differing reasons, but were deterred from declaring war against Mpande because of the strong military and economic infrastructure of his kingdom. Mpande was able to manipulate alliances with both the Boers and the British, and at the same time keep the kingdom intact.

Meanwhile his father's sister, Mawa, and his brother, Gqugqu, were organising support for Mpande's overthrow. He dealt with this challenge in 1843 by killing Gqugqu and his followers, and confiscating their property. Mawa and her supporters escaped and sought asylum in Natal. There they were able to remain, although Mpande demanded that the cattle they had taken should be returned. At the same time, Mpande and the British in Natal agreed that the Thukela and Mzinyathi rivers would form the new boundary between their two territories. As the Boers had moved away, their former agreements with Mpande concerning land were abrogated.

Mpande's rule for the next 12 years was stable. The peace was then shattered by the bitter rivalry between his two eldest sons, Cetshwayo (q.v.) and Mbuyazi, as to who should inherit the throne on his death. Both sons enjoyed a great deal of support in the country. The matter was finally resolved at the end of 1856 when both sides, having amassed their forces, met in battle at Ndondakusuka. After a bloody struggle in which thousands were killed including Mbuyazi, Cetshwayo emerged the victor. An uneasy truce existed between Mpande (who had supported Mbuyazi) and Cetshwayo. However, Cetshwayo continued to respect Mpande as King while becoming more involved in the affairs of state. During the 1860s the tension created by the increasing border disputes with the Boers in the Transvaal, coupled with general economic depression in Zululand, helped to ensure that Mpande and Cetshwayo worked closer together. In 1872 Mpande died of natural causes. He was buried at Nondwengu and Cetshwayo succeeded him as King of the Zulu nation.■

Mqhayi, S.E.K. (1875-1945)

MQHAYI, Samuel Edward Krune (1875-1945).

SOUTH AFRICAN poet, who wrote some of the stanzas to *Nkosi Sikelel I Afrika* (God Bless Africa) which has been chosen by the African National Congress (ANC) as their national anthem.

S.E.K. Mqhayi

Mqhayi was born on 1 December 1875 in Gqumahashe in the Tyumie Valley, Cape Province. His father was a preacher and teacher and his great-grandfather was the chief of the Amacira people. His family moved from the Tyumie Valley when Mqhayi was nine years old, interrupting his schooling which he continued in Kentani in the Transkei, their new home. Between 1891 and 1895 Mqhayi attended Lovedale Mission, Alice, where he studied for a teacher's diploma. On completion, he taught for some time at the West Bank Location in East London before entering journalism, as a literary correspondent of the *Izwi Labantu* (The Voice of the People). His praise songs, later collected, were first published in that journal, where he worked as a sub-editor between 1897 and 1900.

Later in 1900 Mqhayi returned to teaching at Kentani and later at Mopongo, before finally giving up the profession because he disapproved of the distorted perspective being given to African history. In 1920 he became editor of *Imvo Zabantsundu*, serving there until 1922 when, turning down an invitation to work at Lovedale Press, he embarked on writing. A novel published during this period, as *Ityala Lamawele*, in Xhosa and later translated as *The Case of the Twins*, became a success and soon established Mqhayi in the literary world. He followed this up in 1929 with *U-Don Jade*, a novel published in three parts that won the May Esther Bedford Prize in 1935.

In 1927 he wrote seven stanzas to *Nkosi Sikelel I Afrika* (God Bless Africa), which was composed that year by Enoch Sontonga (q.v.) who also wrote the first stanza. "Of late the Black races of the Union and the Protectorates have somehow by tacit assent adopted it as their recognised national anthem, sung before Royalty and on big public occasions", wrote Davidson Don Tengo Jabavu (q.v.), the South African educationist whose father John Tengo Jabavu (q.v.) was the proprietor of *Imvo Zabantsundu*, in 1935. The song has been chosen by the ANC as the anthem of South Africa.

Mqhayi's works of biography include *U-BomiBom-Fundisi u J.K. Bokwe* (*The Life of the Rev. John Knox Bokwe*) published in 1925; *U-Sogqumahashe* (*The Life of Chief Cyril Mhalla*) and *Isikhumbuzo sika Ntsikana* (*The story of Prophet Ntsikana*). He also translated, among other books, *Aggrey of*

Africa into Xhosa as *U-Aggre um-Afrika* in 1935. His autobiography, *U-Mqhayi wase-Ntab' ozuko* (Mqhayi from the Mountain of Glory), was published in 1939.

Mqhayi died on 29 July 1945 in Ntab'ozuku, near King Williams Town, South Africa. ■

Mswati II (c.1820-68)

MSWATI II (c.1820-68).

KING of the Swazis who unified the nation into modern Swaziland. He was born in about 1820, the son and heir to King Sobhuza I who founded the Lobamba city (known now as Old Lobamba). Like his father whom he succeeded to the throne in 1836, Mswati continued his predecessor's military exploits and annexed formerly independent neighbours whom he defeated to his kingdom. For this he had the distinction of not only being regarded as the greatest soldier, after King Chaka of the Zulu, in the entire southern Africa region, but also as the founder of today's Swaziland. The country's name is derived from a European corruption of his name, Mswati, which the foreigners called Swazi, hence "Swaziland."

his defences and country but also encouraged the successful military raids he made into Zulu territories. He reorganised the army, modelling it on the efficient Zulu force, he also recruited non-Swazis, like the Sothos and the Ngunis, into his forces.

With these armies King Mswati, while generally avoiding confrontation with border states, exerted indirect influence on his neighbours by despatching his soldiers to settle internal disputes among the chiefs. In the 1850s however his armies clashed with invading forces of the Zulus in the Battle of Lubuya. King Mswati succeeded in getting a peaceful withdrawal of the invaders with the aid of the British representative in Natal.

His relations with the Europeans were functional. In 1840 he signed a non-belligerance treaty with the Afrikaner Voortrekkers who were occupying the Transvaal. Despite this, however, the king was to provide refuge for Mawewe who had been deposed by the Portuguese in Gazaland,

Mswati came to power at the time of the decline of the Zulu empire, which facilitated his rise to eminence in the region. The absence of continuous harassment from the Zulus not only enabled the king to build while zealously protecting his own kingdom from the Europeans. Though he was the first Swazi ruler to welcome European missionaries, he succeeded in protecting Swaziland's independence until his death in 1868 in Hhohho. He was succeeded as king by his son Mbandzeni. ■

Muenemutapa Chioco (died 1902)

MUENEMUTAPA CHIOCO (died 1902).

MOZAMBICAN King of the ancient kingdom of Muenemutapa who was leader of rebellions against Portuguese and British colonial administrations.

In the mid-nineteenth century the Muenemutapa kingdom in Tete was disseminated by the Portuguese forcing the Muenemutapa Dudza and his successor Chioco to flee into exile. They regrouped their forces and persuaded several Tawara chiefs to join them in rebellion on the Mozambique and Southern Rhodesia border. In 1870 Chioco also established contact with Chief Mapondera (q.v.) who had sought refuge along with his regiments with the Barue after his defeat by the British. That year, with the support of Hanga (q.v.) of the Barue, Chioco and Mapondera formed an alliance. Chioco started liberating the Tete Tawara. He destroyed Portuguese estates and military bases. The following year the area between the town of Tete and Chicao was liberated.

In 1900 he joined up with the Massangano and the Barue and forced the European renters on the Mozambique/Rhodesian border to flee, and precipitated a number of uprisings against the Portuguese administration. In 1901 the Portuguese army was forced to withdraw and Chioco's forces surrounded the last Portuguese stronghold in the middle-Zambezi and established territorial links with the Massangano and Barue.

Throughout this period Chioco envisaged recreating the Great Muenemutapa kingdom which would include the Tawara living in Southern Rhodesia. In 1898 and 1899 the British sent delegations to warn him against interfering in Southern Rhodesia where the Tawara were already refusing to pay taxes. He ignored these warnings and appointed Mapondera commander of the Tawara forces. The powerful spirit mediums were said to support the cause and helped persuade several chiefs to join the alliance. Hanga provided war materials. They liberated the border regions and threatened the Portuguese from Sena to Zumbo and in Eastern Mashonaland, Rhodesia.

In 1902 Hanga and his vast army had to defend themselves against the Portuguese whilst Mapondera and Chioco were routed by the British. Chioco died in the battle but Mapondera survived with a small following.■

Muhammad Bey (1881-1962)

MUHAMMAD El-AMIN BEY (1881-1962).

TUNISIAN monarch. Son of Muhammad el-Habib bin Mamun Bey, who occupied the traditional throne of the Beys of Tunis (dating back to 1705) from 1922 to 1929. He was born on 4 September 1881 at Kasr-el-Said. As a young man he fell desperately in love with Djeneina, a palace laundress who was the daughter of a Sudanese palace slave, and against strong opposition he married her at Monastir in 1920. She was his only wife; they had twelve children.

The French colonial regime in Tunisia left the Bey with considerable influence though little real power, and as the throne represented continuity with the pre-colonial past, nationalist feelings were for a time centred around it. In 1942 Sidi Muhammad el-Moncef Bey, on accession, voiced the demands of Tunisian nationalists. He petitioned the Vichy French authorities then in control, for sweeping reforms. He then formed an "independent" government with widespread support. While he did not seriously attempt to re-establish an independent state definitively, his activities angered the Free French. Their government, headed by de Gaulle and Giraud, occupied Tunisia after its re-occupation by the Allies, and forced Moncef Bey to abdicate in May 1943.

Although Moncef had changed the law of succession to introduce primogeniture, the French ignored this and appointed Muhammad el-Amin (often called Lamine). For five years the new Bey was handicapped because many did not see him as the rightful ruler. Although banished by the French to Algeria and then to France, Moncef did not recognise Lamine as his heir until shortly before he died in 1948. Even after that

Muhammad Bey

Lamine was unable to revive nationalist feelings around the throne as Mohammed V of Morocco (q.v.) successfully did. The rise of the Neo-Destour as a mass nationalist party, and its clashes with the French, put the monarchy to the back of the stage. However, France allowed the formation of a half-French, half-Tunisian government, headed by Muhammad Chenik. The efforts of the French to introduce self-government in controlled stages involved an increasing role for the Bey.

But those efforts were opposed by the Neo-Destour. In 1952 the Bey refused to sign some French reform decrees until threatened with deposition, but the decrees were rejected by the Neo-Destour as inadequate. Even so, when France eventually conceded independence and the Neo-Destour under Bourguiba took power, it seemed as if the monarchy was still acceptable to most nationalists.

Not long after independence in 1956, however, the Bourguiba government was clearly moving towards abolition of the monarchy. Sidi el-Amin therefore abdicated on 24 July in favour of his heir Sidi Husayn en-Nasr (a son of Muhammad en-Nasr Bey who reigned from 1906-22; Sidi el-Amin's own sons being excluded from the succession). Sidi Husayn immediately abdicated in turn in favour of his son Rechad el-Mahdi, aged 10. The Bourguiba government,unaware of these abdications, proclaimed the deposition of Sidi el-Amin and the abolition of the monarchy on 25 July 1957. Rechad, who was styled "King" by his supporters, fled to the stronghold of those supporters at Kairouan, the religious centre, where he was crowned; but then he had to flee again. Muhammad el-Amin, the last effective Bey, died in Tunis on 30 September 1962. ■

Muhammed was appointed Aide-de-camp (ADC) in 1962 to the Administrator of the Western Region of Nigeria, where the Regional Government had been suspended by the Federal Government following a political crisis and public disorder which threatened the stability and unity of Nigeria.

In 1963 he was made Officer-in-Charge of the First Brigade Signal Troop in Kaduna, returning to Catterick later in the year for a course on more advanced telecommunications techniques. In 1964 he was promoted to Major and made the Officer Commanding, One Signal Squadron in Apapa, Lagos. Muhammed became Acting Chief Signals Officer of the Army in November 1965, on the eve of the military coup of January 1966 which saw his elevation by the new leader, General Aguiyi-Ironsi, to the rank of Lieutenant-Colonel. His new appointment was Inspector of Signals, based in Lagos where

---

Muhammed, M.R. (1938-76)

MUHAMMED, General Murtala Ramat (1938-76).

NIGERIAN military ruler whose short reign had a major impact on the country's subsequent development. Muhammed was born on 8 November 1938, one of eleven children of Risqua Muhammed and Uwani Rahamat, in the Kurama Quarter of the ancient trade centre of Kano. He was educated at Cikin Gida and Gidan Makama primary schools in Kano. After gaining his school certificate at the Government (now Barewa) College in Zaria in 1957, Muhammed enlisted in the Nigerian Army and was sent to Britain for training at Sandhurst Royal Academy as an officer cadet. His training completed in 1961, he returned to Nigeria as a commissioned 2nd Lieutenant and was posted to the Army Signals.

After spending one year at the Catterick School of Signals in England, he went to the Congo (now Zaire) where he served with the United Nations' Peace-Keeping Force. On his return from Zaire,

Gen. Murtala Muhammed

the second military coup of July 1966 found him among the young officers who formed the next military administration under General (then Colonel) Gowon.

When war broke out between the Federal forces and the army of the breakaway Biafra, Muhammed led Nigeria's newly-created Second Infantry Division, for which he was appointed the first General Officer Commanding, in August 1967, against the Biafrans. On 20 September 1967 his troops pushed the Biafrans out of the Mid-West (now Bendel) State but were less successful in their efforts to storm Onitsha, across the River Niger, in the then East Central State. After three unsuccessful attempts, Muhammed led his troops northwards, crossed the Niger at Lokoja and marched down to take Onitsha. He returned to Lagos in March 1968 to be again appointed Inspector of Signals and became a full Colonel in April. He was promoted Brigadier in October 1971, after a year at the Joint Services Staff College in England, and took his first political appointment as Federal Commissioner for Communications on 7 August 1974, which he combined with his military duties at the Army Signals Headquarters in Apapa. He was holding both offices when he was named Nigeria's new Head of State and Commander-in-Chief of the Armed Forces on 29 July 1975, following the coup against Gowon who was attending the 12th Summit meeting of the Organisation of African Unity (OAU) in Kampala.

The new Head of State said that "the nation had been groping in the dark and the situation would inevitably result in chaos and bloodshed unless arrested. . . After the civil war the affairs of state, hitherto a collective responsibility, became characterised by lack of consultations, indecision, indiscipline and even neglect. Indeed, the public at large became disillusioned and disappointed by these developments. The trend was clearly incompatible with the philosophy and image of our collective regime". He instituted mass retirement and dismissals of about 10,000 officials from the armed forces and civil service for incompetence and corruption, immediately introduced measures to decongest the ports, to remedy the petrol shortage and reduce inflation. He outlined a political programme that included the creation of seven more states, the drafting of a new constitution and the organisation of state and national elec-

tions as prelude for a return to civilian rule on 1 October 1979. He acted quickly on the issue of Lagos as the Federal capital in view of its congestion and dual role as headquarters of the Lagos State administration and of the national census. He disposed of the emotive issue of properties abandoned during the civil war. He announced that the Federal capital would be moved from Lagos to Abuja in a more central part of the country. On the national census, General Muhammed stated that the 1973 census, whose results had never been made public, would be cancelled and that the 1963 figures would be used for planning purposes. These measures were enthusiastically welcomed by Nigerians who not only felt motivated but also became committed to a new order with a clear-cut policy and a goal to achieve. Even the large-scale purge of public employees, whose scope was broad enough to allow for victimisation and a subjective rather than objective approach, was taken in good stride, enhancing General Muhammed's "no-nonsense", business-like attitude.

While giving Nigerians the confidence and lead in tackling their problems, Mohammed also impressed on Africa and the world that it was time Africans took decisions and worked together for their own interests. Taking the initiative in November 1975, the government of General Muhammed recognised the MPLA Government of President Neto as the legitimate authority in Angola. In a diplomatic offensive matched only by its dynamism in local affairs, the Lagos Government mobilised African opinion on behalf of the MPLA and against the FNLA-UNITA coalition supported by South Africa and western powers. "Africa has come of age", General Muhammed said. "It is no longer under the orbit of any extra-continental power. It should no longer take orders from any country, however powerful. The fortunes of Africa are in our hands to make or mar". General Muhammed thus brought Africa's most populous and one of its richest nations out of its erstwhile vacillating approach to African and foreign issues to play a more active role. Guided by pragmatism, this energetic feature of Nigeria's diplomacy has continued even after the death of Muhammed.

A simple, unostentatious and devout Moslem who discarded the pomp and trappings of office, General Muhammed regarded himself as working for the overall interest of

Africa, much in the same context as he saw himself in Nigeria. He shunned the protective cavalcade of escort troops while going about his business. This very simplicity which won him the trust of Nigerians was ironically to make him an easy prey for the dissidents in the army who ambushed and shot him on his way to work in Lagos on 13 February 1976. He left a widow, Ajoke, who is a close relative of General Olusegun Obasanjo, General Muhammed's right-hand man and successor. ■

El-Mukhtar, S.U. (c.1862-1931)

EL-MUKHTAR, Sidi 'Umar (c.1862-1931).

LIBYAN resistance leader. A Bedouin, like many other Bedouins of his time, he attended an Islamic school run by the Sanusiyya Order (*see* el-Sanusi). Then he studied at the Order's university at Jaghbub,

'Umar el-Mukhtar

and was later appointed Sheikh of the el-Qasur monastery (*zawiya*) of the Order.

He went to Kufra in southern Libya to help organise resistance to the French occupying Chad further south, early in the 20th century. About 1906 he returned to el-Qasur. Then, when the Italians invaded Turkish Libya in 1911, the Sanusiyya became the leaders of guerrilla resistance by the Arabs, and el-Mukhtar became one of the most prominent.

By 1917, when the Sanusiyya had forced the invaders to accept a truce leaving them for the moment masters of much of Libya, el-Mukhtar was in charge of some of the Sanusiyya war-camps. Later, when the head of the Order, Idris el-Sanusi, was away in Egypt, el-Mukhtar led the fierce and prolonged resistance against Italian military suppression.

He was styled *el-Naib el-Amm*, "Representative-General", of the Sanusiyya whose head remained in contact with him during the eight years' war. He was the leader of the Sanusiyya guerrillas. Using the Bedouin's intimate knowledge of the desert and age-old skill at defeating sedentary governments, and inspired by fierce hatred of Italian rule and Sanusiyya preaching, the guerrillas fought one of the strongest campaigns of resistance in any part of Africa. Each Bedouin tribe had a guerrilla band of between 100 and 300, while most of the population supported the resistance, including those living in Italian-controlled areas and even the chiefs appointed by the colonial rulers.

However, the guerrillas were slowly worn down and in 1929 Sidi 'Umar approached the Italians for a truce. For several months in 1929 there was a truce accompanied by talks. El-Mukhtar and the Italians could not agree on terms and fighting resumed in January 1930. Sidi 'Umar himself was wounded then. Finally, General Graziani began a new and extremely brutal campaign to crush the Sanusiyya guerrillas. His forces put all the Bedouins into concentration camps and built long barbed-wire barriers to impede the guerrillas. Gradually ally these measures succeeded. Sidi 'Umar el-Mukhtar was wounded and captured on 11 September 1931, and on 16 September 1931 he was hanged at Suluq before a crowd of 20,000. The resistance ended a few months later. ■

Mulder, C. P. (1925-88)

MULDER, Dr Cornelius Petrus (1925-88).

SOUTH AFRICAN politician, who achieved international notoriety by being at the centre of the Muldergate scandal in the late 1970s.

C. Mulder

"Connie" Mulder, as he was known, was an Afrikaner, born on 5 June 1925 at Warmbaths in the Transvaal, the youngest of ten children. He was educated at Krugersdorp and then at Potchefstroom University, where he was awarded a BA in 1944. After teacher training he taught at Randgate from 1946, and then from 1925 to 1958 at Riebeeck Secondary School at Randfontein. In his spare time he studied for a doctorate at the University of Witwatersrand, which he obtained in 1957 for a thesis on the influence of the Bible on the character of the Afrikaners, whose ideology rests on their peculiar interpretation of the Bible.

He entered politics by being elected to the Randfontein City Council in 1951, and was its mayor from 1953 to 1957. In 1958 he was elected National Party MP for the same town. He became assistant information officer in 1966, and chief information officer in 1967, of the National Party, the Afrikaner party in power in South Africa since 1948. On 12 August 1968 he entered the cabinet of the apartheid regime as minister of Information and soon showed his communicating skills by establishing better relations with the press. He was also minister of the Interior and held for some years the portfolio of Immigration. In September 1972 he became leader of the National Party in its main stronghold, Transvaal. In this powerful position he was for long considered to be well placed to move on to succeed B. J. Vorster (q.v.), eventually, as prime minister.

In 1972 Dr Mulder appointed Dr Eschel Rhoodie as secretary for Information. Rhoodie had ambitious ideas for publicising the apartheid regime's case and countering worldwide condemnation; Mulder and Vorster approved these ideas and large-scale secret use of government funds for putting them in operation. For six years millions of Rands were secretly used by the Department of Information for projects including efforts to win over some politicians in independent Africa and to buy control of newspapers and magazines overseas. One major project was the launching, in 1976, of the *Citizen* as a new English-language newspaper in South Africa, to support the Afrikaner Nationalist government, with massive supplies of money from the Department of Information later estimated at 32m Rands.

After rumours about the *Citizen* reached a leading anti-government newspaper, the *Rand Daily Mail*, in 1977, gradually more and more details of the Information Department's secret activities came out. The press and the Auditor General revealed the extent of the secret expenditure, the loss of considerable amounts of money, and use of some on high living in many parts of the world; in addition, large-scale fraud and deceit were uncovered. This was the scandal which, on the analogy of "Watergate" in the USA was called "Muldergate" after Dr Mulder.

Dr Mulder dismissed the affair, twice, as a "storm in a teacup" but as revelations followed one another in 1978 he came under greater pressure and was removed from his posts, though at first he remained in the cabinet as minister for Plural Relations. Vorster, whose role had not yet been fully exposed, announced his resignation as prime minister on 20 September 1978. In the election of a new prime minister by National Party parliamentarians and senators, Mulder won 72 votes out of 172 on the first ballot, 74, on the second, despite the scandal which, however, prevented him from winning.

P. W. Botha became prime minister. More facts emerged about "Muldergate", which caused convulsions among the Afrikaners because the corruption and deceit went against their impression of their own rectitude. On 7 November 1978 Mulder was forced to leave the cabinet and the Transvaal National Party leadership.

An interim report of the Erasmus Commission inquiring into the scandal said Dr Mulder had wrongly interpreted his function as minister and had, "to say the least, fulfilled it incompetently"; he had been lax and negligent in giving Rhoodie "almost unlimited discretion in dealing with public funds." He was expelled from the National Party, and on 24 January 1979 he announced his resignation from the Cape Town parliament.

Later in 1979 "Muldergate" reached a climax when Vorster resigned as State President. But that same year Mulder began his moves to return to the political arena; he said he had been made a scapegoat and hinted that others, including P. W. Botha, had been implicated. Later he joined the hard-line Afrikaners who believed that Botha, in his constitutional changes and noticeably in giving political representation to Coloureds and South African Asians, was "betraying White South Africa"; they formed the new Conservative Party in 1982. On 6 May 1987 Dr Mulder was returned to parliament by the White voters of Randfontein again, this time for the Conservative Party. He said he would make further revelations about the scandal called after him. But on 13 January 1988 he died after a long illness without fulfilling that promise. He left a wife and four children, two sons being active in the Conservative Party.■

Mulele, P. (1929-68)

MULELE, Pierre (1929-68).

ZAIREAN politician and first Minister of Education in the government of Patrice Lumumba (q.v.). He attended the Kinzambi Catholic seminary but was expelled in 1947, and then attended a "middle school" for junior office staff in the Belgian Congo (now Zaire). After two years' compulsory military service he worked for the Public Works Department at Leopoldville (now Kinshasa). He was active in the civil servants' trade union, APIC, and pursued private studies helped by the Czech Consul.

He also joined in Leopoldville a mutual

P. Mulele

aid society for people from his home area of Kwango-Kwilu, who later supported him when he went into politics. He was a leading member of the *Parti de la Solidarité Africaine* (PSA) with Sylvain Kama and Antoine Gizenga; the party, founded in February 1959, won early support in the Kwango-Kwilu area.

In 1959-60 Gizenga and Mulele travelled abroad, seeking support for the struggle against Belgian rule. Mulele visited Guinea, Belgium and the USSR before he returned to help organise the PSA in preparation for independence which the Belgians, very unexpectedly, had agreed to grant on 30 June 1960. In the pre-independence elections the PSA came second after Lumumba's MNC. When Patrice Lumumba formed a coalition government, Mulele was appointed Minister of Education.

After the dismissal of Lumumba, Gizenga went to Stanleyville (now Kisangani) to form a rival government to the new one in Leopoldville. In mid-1963 after a visit to Egypt and China, Pierre Mulele came back and started the first of the revolutionary uprisings that were to shake the Congo for a number of years. His "Kwilu rising" was the longest (1963 to 1970). It was directed against the Leopoldville government and what he termed its repressive actions and its Western backers. Fighting began in December 1963, apparently in response to police actions by the government. While there were few battles the rising spread rapidly as the government troops' conduct drove the people on to the side of the guerrillas. Mulele organised his guerrillas well, creating a rival administration. But starvation eventually forced many people to desert the guerrillas, whose own conduct also lost them some support.

Later, with his guerrilla resistance gradually declining, Mulele left for the Congo (Brazzaville). There the Congo (Leopoldville) government urged him to return under a general amnesty. He did so in October 1968. But soon afterwards President Mobutu returned from an overseas trip, and it was announced that Mulele had been tried and executed. The full facts about Pierre Mulele's return under this general amnesty, followed by his almost immediate execution, have never been fully revealed. It was suspected that he was killed before the report on 9 October 1968 of his execution by firing squad.■

Muntassir, M. (1903-70)

MUNTASSIR, Mahmoud (1903-70).

LIBYAN politician and diplomat and the first Prime Minister appointed by King Idris (q.v.) after independence. He was born in 1903 and had his university education in Rome. In 1936, he became chairman of the Muslim High School Council whose aim was to provide facilities for the education of Libyan children who were deprived of formal schooling by the policies of the Italian colonialists. By 1951, when Libya achieved its independence from Italy, he had distinguished himself in local and national politics.

In 1950, he was elected vice-president of the Administrative Council of Tripolitania, one of the three provinces of the federation of Libya, and was also elected to the National Assembly in Tripoli. In March 1951, he became a minister in the government of Tripolitania holding the portfolios of the Interior, Education and Justice. On 24 December 1951, Libya became independent with King Idris installed as ruler of a federated kingdom consisting of Tripolitania, Cyrenaica and Fezzan. Muntassir was made Prime Minister, thus becoming the first to head the government of the independent state. He was also Minister of Foreign Affairs, holding the two offices until 1954.

M. Muntassir

The immediate post-independence years were fraught with political crisis emanating largely from the rivalries between the three components in the federation. Only one year after independence the disagreement between the anti-federal and anti-monarchist forces on the one hand and the pro-unitary elements on the other in the Federal Chamber of Deputies came to a head when the government outlawed the anti-federal National Congress Party and dissolved the Tripolitania provincial government where the party had a strong base. By the end of 1952, the trouble had spilled into Cyrenaica and King Idris declared a state of emergency there.

The other sensitive issue of the day concerned the various military agreements which Muntassir's government made with the countries of Western Europe and the USA. In 1953 the government signed a twenty-year treaty with Britain, which provided for a military base for Britain, in return for which Libya was promised £1 million annually for development. A similar agreement was entered into with the USA in 1954, all to the vocal disapproval of radical politicians and students. Muntassir resigned from the government in 1954.

He was appointed ambassador to the UK later the same year and recalled in 1957 to serve as personal adviser to King Idris. In 1958, he was re-appointed ambassador to Italy, Greece and later Yugoslavia. On 22 January 1964, Muntassir was appointed to his second term as Prime Minister. The former premier had resigned in the wake of student demonstrations against the continuance of Libya's military agreements with the West. In February 1964, Muntassir announced that Libya would terminate forthwith all existing military treaties with Britain and the USA. He also stated that his government would evolve a more Arab-centred foreign policy which resulted in a meeting of Arab states, Morocco, Algeria, Tunisia and Libya in September of the same year. The countries agreed to set up a special relationship amongst themselves.

In October 1964, elections for the Libyan Parliament took place (a unitary state having been created by a decree), with most of the 103 seats going to moderate candidates. But King Idris dissolved the Parliament on 13 February 1965, following allegations of irregularities in the election procedures, and Prime Minister Muntassir was again forced to resign from office. Later in the same year he was appointed chief of the Royal Household. He was serving in this capacity when he was arrested in 1969 in the wake of the 1 September coup d'état which brought Colonel Muammar Gaddafi to power. Mahmoud Muntassir died in prison in Tripoli on 3 October 1970. ■

Musungu, C.K. (1890-1965)

MUSUNGU, Chitimukulu Kafula (1890-1965).

ZAMBIAN traditional ruler, was born in 1890 into the Bemba royal house. He succeeded to the royal title of Chikwanda, a

Chief C.K. Musungu

most revered junior chieftainship among the Bemba, at an early age in 1910. He rose to the next highest rank of rulers in 1934 when he became Chief Nkula. In June 1946 he attained the coveted title of Chitimukulu.

As Paramount Chief, Chitimukulu's office was soon to become a decisive factor in the emerging nationalists' campaign to wrest independence from the colonial government which, on the other hand, sought the loyalty of the chiefs in order to perpetuate its rule. Some chiefs reaffirmed their allegiance to the colonial authorities, but the Chitimukulu rejected official directives and declared his support for the African National Congress (ANC) which had come into being two years after his accession. He not only refused to ban the new party in his area but indeed encouraged its activities.

His intransigence towards the colonial administration assumed a new dimension in 1952 when he publicly rejected the idea of amalgamating Northern and Southern Rhodesia and Nyasaland (now Zambia, Zimbabwe and Malawi respectively) into a Central Africa Federation. To this end he was among the delegation of chiefs and politicians from the three territories that visited London in 1952 to petition the British government.

Even after the Federation was imposed in 1953, the Chitimukulu continued to make his opposition felt. In March 1953, he joined 129 other chiefs in the country in petitioning the Queen not to merge the territory with Southern Rhodesia. So strong was his opposition to the Federation that even five years after it came into being, the Chitimukulu refused to meet its Prime Minister, Roy Welensky, during the latter's visit to the Bemba area in 1958.

Though these actions endeared him more to the Africans, the government took extreme exception to the Chitimukulu's "misconduct", culminating in the allegation of incompetence. He was subsequently stripped of his powers and downgraded, which led to unrest among his people. Chitimukulu Musungu remained undeterred in his support for the nationalist cause which brought Zambia to independence in October 1964, when his powers were restored. He died in 1965. Chitimukulu Kafula Musungu is still very much respected in independent Zambia, where he is fondly remembered as a progressive traditional ruler and a patriot. ∎

Mutara III (1913-59)

MUTARA III, Mwami Rudahigwa (1913-59).

RWANDAN monarch. He was born in Rwanda in 1913, the son of Mwami (King) Yuhi IV Musinga. His family belonged to the Tutsi ethnic group which had, despite their numerical minority, established a feudal system over the centuries which enabled them to control all positions of power in the country.

His father was deposed in 1931 and Mutara succeeded him as Mwami of Rwanda. By this time, although Belgian colonial (Mandate) rule was firmly established in the country, the Mwami was still powerful, owning all the land and having firm control over the population through his dominance of the feudal chiefs.

Within this framework of colonialism Mutara was able to maintain his authority over the Hutu ethnic group which constituted a large percentage of the population.

Mwami Mutara III

After the Second World War the Belgians were granted a Trusteeship over the country by the United Nations, with the Mwami being answerable to the Belgian Commissioner. In the ensuing period, although the Mwami and his Tutsi chiefs exercised a great deal of administrative and judicial control, the Belgian administration introduced reforms to try and improve the position of the Hutu people, such as providing them with education in the Roman Catholic Mission Schools and generally paving the way for a more democratic system.

Mutara remained very much opposed to these changes. By 1956 the Hutu people were beginning to organise themselves into movements aimed at achieving social and political equality. However, he managed to contain these movements and there were no major changes until after his death on 25 July 1959. He died in Bujumbura, of a heart attack according to the Belgian administration, although some people believe he was poisoned.■

Mutesa I (1838-84)

MUTESA I, Kabaka (1838-84).

KING of Buganda, Mutesa was born around 1838, son of Kabaka Suna, who reigned over Buganda from 1824-1856. When Kabaka Suna died of smallpox, contracted while engaged on a military expedition in a distant part of the kingdom, Mukabya (Prince) Mutesa was eighteen. The Kabakaship did not automatically pass to the Kabaka's eldest son and Mukabya Mutesa was one of 60 to 100 eligible candidates. He owed his election partly to the fact that Kayira, the Katikiro (one of the Kabaka's chief officials whose functions were that of prime minister and minister of justice), believed that the election of a young prince would be less likely to entail the loss of his authority. Mutesa's chief rivals were exiled to an island on Lake Victoria where they organised a rebellion that was quickly crushed by Mutesa.

Kabaka Mutesa became ruler of a kingdom with a highly centralised administration. Apart from the principal officers of state (who included the Katikiro) and five provincial governors, there was the *saza* chiefs, with whom the Kabaka remained in close contact. The *bataka*, or clan chiefs, were named by the Kabaka and therefore owed him close allegiance. Finally, there were the *batongole*, favourites to whom the king granted land, and who were therefore not only more intimately linked to him than other chiefs, but also more powerful. All had to pay tribute to the king – this could take various forms, livestock, slaves, ivory or agricultural produce. The kingdom was administered from the king's palace, where hundreds of people lived, including the Kabaka's many wives.

Mutesa was not a soldier, and once he had succeeded in putting down the various revolts which followed his succession, he devoted himself to the kingdom's internal affairs. The first Europeans to reach Buganda were astonished at the king's administrative control which was based on, among other things, a highly developed road system and a network of informers. Mutesa's father, the Kabaka Suna, disillusioned in his first contacts with Arab and other Islamic visitors to Buganda, had issued an edict in the 1840s, forbidding foreigners to enter the country, an edict which was maintained until 1861, despite the negative effect this had on trade.

It was in 1861 that Mutesa received word, through the very effective spy network he maintained beyond the frontiers of the kingdom, that two white men had been seen at the southern extremity of Lake Victoria. These were the British explorers, Speke and Grant, in search of the source of the River Nile. Although such foreigners might represent a threat to the king's sovereignty, Mutesa was nevertheless extremely curious to meet the two white men. Speke, leaving Grant, who was injured, in the kingdom of Karagwe to the south of Buganda, arrived in Mutesa's capital on 19 February 1862 and was amazed at the sophistication of its construction. Speke's intention had been, firstly, to make contact with a group of white explorers whom he had heard were in the adjacent kingdom of Bunyoro, to the north-east of Buganda, to get help to the injured Grant in Karagwe, and most importantly to him, to continue this journey northwards, up the Nile. Mutesa, however, had become worried by the coincidental arrival of several white explorers in the area and kept Speke in a state of uncertainty for several months, withholding permission to continue his journey. It is believed that Speke and Grant (who had joined him on 7 May) were finally permitted to leave because of the intervention of the queen mother, who persuaded the Kabaka that the opening of a route towards the north would mean a flow of gifts from England. The two explorers left on 7 July 1862, having impressed Mutesa with their diplomatic behaviour, though this respect was mutual.

Shortly after Speke's departure, Mutesa was afflicted by an illness which was to considerably restrict his movement for the rest of his life. Mutesa had been frustrated by the lack of a common language in dealing with the English explorers and had tried to learn a little Swahili. Now that he was more or less confined to his palace he used the opportunity to get traders from Zanzibar to teach him the Arabic script, and showed much interest in the Koran. The Zanzibari traders became favourites and some were even nominated chiefs. With the arrival of another English explorer, Samuel Baker, in Bunyoro, as well as powerful groups of traders from Khartoum in the north, these Swahili speakers assumed greater importance because of the arms they supplied.

Buganda's intervention in the Bunyoro war of succession ended in a humiliating defeat; the victorious Kabarega had been supported by arms and troops supplied by the Khartoum traders, a situation which served to accentuate Mutesa's isolation. Towards the end of 1873, having received courteous messages from Sultan Seyyid Barghash of Zanzibar, he dispatched emissaries laden with ivory to make contact with the Sultan and form an alliance.

At this point news was received that Samuel Baker was in Bunyoro again. By 1872 he was in the service of the Khedive of Egypt; his official mission was to halt the slave traffic on the Nile, but in reality he was charged with securing the annexation of all countries to the south of Egypt as far as the Equator. Mutesa was informed that Baker had raised the Khedive's flag not far from Masindi, capital of Bunyoro, and he then received a personal letter from Baker, couched in the most flattering terms, and requesting him to investigate what had become of the missionary explorer, David Livingstone, who had disappeared in East Africa. Mutesa sent an encouraging reply, urging Baker to come and visit him; Baker did not receive this reply until after he had been driven out of Bunyoro into Acholi, to the north, having first set fire to Masindi. On his return to England, Baker denigrated the Kabarega, King of Bunyoro, but painted a flattering portrait of Mutesa of Buganda, whom he had never met, as a great and generous king.

The mission which the Khedive had entrusted to Baker was taken up by General Gordon. In 1874 Gordon sent one of his lieutenants, Chaille-Long, an American, on a mission to Mutesa, to cede to Egypt the course of the Upper Nile, and, consequently, the Kingdom of Buganda. Mutesa had been badly served by his Zanzibari advisors, who certainly had not understood the implications of the treaty signed by Mutesa. Gordon requested permission from the British government to follow up this triumph and extend the Khedive's influence as far as Mombasa, thereby demonstrating his ignorance of the true extent of the Sultan of Zanzibar's power.

In 1875 Gordon dispatched another emissary to Mutesa, Linant de Bellefonds, a Belgian Calvinist, accompanied by two Moslem scholars who were to introduce him to the Koran, as well as artisans to build a European-style palace. Mutesa learnt that yet another Englishman (this was Henry Morton Stanley) was at Kagera, and prudently requested Bellefonds to defer his arrival for a few days, so that he could first ascertain the reasons for Stanley's visit.

Mutesa showed interest both in Stanley's Christianity and in the Islamic beliefs outlined by Linant de Bellefonds' Moslem scholars; his court became the theatre of lengthy religious discussions, in which he himself was to take pleasure right up to the end of his life, though he never became a convert to either of the two religions.

When Linant de Bellefonds left Buganda, Stanley sent with him a letter, addressed, in Mutesa's name, to the *Daily Telegraph* in London, requesting that Christian missionaries be sent to the kingdom. This letter was to have serious consequences for the future of Egyptian imperialism. Stanley himself spent several months in Buganda, during which time he created a most favourable impression with the Baganda, before leaving for the west coast of Africa, via the River Congo.

Mutesa wrote a conciliatory letter to Gordon, appealing to him not to intervene in Bunyoro, a request which Gordon treated with contempt, having no regard for Mutesa. Nuer Aga, Gordon's Egyptian commander, was sent with a detachment of Acholi soldiers to raise the Khedive's flag over Buganda. However, he could only enter Buganda under the Kabaka's escort and, although he raised the Egyptian flag, Mutesa, who at this stage called himself "His Most Christian Majesty", raised his own flag in retaliation, following this up with the dismissal of Nuer Aga's Acholi porters, taking the soldiers prisoner and finally authorising Nuer Aga to leave the country.

Gordon who had himself set out for Buganda, began to understand just what manner of man he was dealing with in Mutesa. To obtain the release of Nuer Aga's soldiers, he sent Emin Pasha, a German doctor who had been converted to Islam. Emin was courteously received by Mutesa, requested to explain the relative merits of Christianity and Islam, and then sent back to Gordon with the Egyptian soldiers. Gordon, embarrassed at receiving a letter from the Khedive congratulating him on his glorious conquest of Buganda, wrote to Mutesa, recognising Buganda's independent status and offering to accompany two Baganda to Egypt as ambassadors. Mutesa chose to ignore this proposal and instead asked Gordon to pray for him and to provide him with arms! During leave in England in 1876, Gordon was strongly advised against attacking Buganda by the British government.

July 1877 saw the beginning of a new era in Buganda's history with the arrival of two Anglican missionaries of the Church Missionary Society, Shergold Smith and C.T. Watson. Mutesa was disappointed to find that they were not going to supply him with arms. Their assurance, however, that the powerful Queen Victoria wished only for the prosperity of Buganda, prompted Mutesa to authorise the entry of other missionaries. Shergold Smith wrote to the British consul in Zanzibar, urging him to dissuade the Khedive of Egypt from annexing Buganda. Kirk, the consul, had already joined with the Sultan of Zanzibar in protesting against the sending of troops by the Khedive to the mouth of the river Juba, in Zanzibari territory, at the prompting of Gordon. The British government now made it clear in no

uncertain terms, that any attempt by the Khedive to annexe Buganda would be viewed with the gravest displeasure.

The first two Catholic missionaries, French White Fathers, arrived in 1879, with the backing of the Vatican, who had decided that the region of the Lakes should be attributed to Cardinal Lavigerie's order. The Verona Fathers, who had already established their influence further up the Nile, had obtained promises of assistance from General Gordon. Mutesa had hitherto been unaware of the existence of France and wondered whether it might not be to his advantage to reach an understanding with the French missionaries, since the English missionaries were clearly unwilling to furnish him with arms. Having been reassured that the White Fathers had no connection with Gordon, Mutesa decided to encourage them.

There was thus serious conflict between the Catholic and Anglican confessions at the Kabaka's court. Both were detested by the Moslems, since the Christian churches were at least agreed on putting an end to the slave trade, vital for Moslem interests. They were detested equally by the traditional chiefs who continued to adhere to the kingdom's traditional religious beliefs; the missionaries' physical safety, indeed their very presence in the kingdom can be attributed to Mutesa's astute political sense, whereby he played one group off against another. The English missionaries' suggestion that a mission of Baganda be sent to England was countered by Mutesa with a proposal that a mission be sent to France. The French missionaries, however, received no reply from the French government when they wrote suggesting such a mission, and thus a delegation of Baganda left for an official visit to England, which gave a corresponding boost to the political weight of the British in Buganda.

Kabaka Mutesa died in the autumn of 1884; there are suggestions that his wives may have deliberately hastened his death in order to save him unnecessaryy suffering. Mutesa had managed to maintain the territorial and political integrity of his kingdom and the administrative structures still retained their traditional form. That this was so, despite increasing pressure from the colonising powers, is doubtless in large measure attributable to Mutesa's receptiveness to new ideas and to an innate political flair, a mixture of caution, diplomacy and shrewdness, which enabled him to maintain peace by giving equal encouragement to all who would otherwise have been Buganda's conquerors. It can be argued that it was on the basis of these early "peaceful" relations with the European powers that Uganda was later given protectorate status. His death, however, was followed by years of civil war, in which the British intervened. The victorious faction in which Apolo Kagwa (q.v.) was prominent collaborated with the British and secured considerable privileges, under colonial rule, for Mutesa's successors, down to Mutesa II (q.v.). ■

Mutesa II (1924-69)

MUTESA II, King Edward Frederick (1924-69).

THE 36th and last Kabaka of Buganda and the first President of post-colonial Uganda. Born Edward William Frederick David Wagulembe Luwangula Mutebi on 19 November 1924, he was the son of Sir Daudi Chwa II, the 24th hereditary ruler of Buganda, and Lady Irene Drusila Namaganda. He succeeded his father in November 1939, at the early age of 15, but deferred his coronation until 1942. Instead he continued his education at King's College, Budo, and at Makerere College, both in Uganda, before entering Magdalene College, Cambridge, in England in 1945 to read history and economics. He served a short course of military training in Britain with the Brigade of Guards and in 1947 became an Honorary Captain in the Grenadier Guards.

His kingdom was the largest of the four kingdoms of Uganda, comprising 2,000,000 people, and enjoyed a semi-autonomous status within the British protectorate. A British government proposal in 1953 to effect constitutional changes that would make Uganda a unitary state was opposed by the whole of Buganda, with Mutesa II at the front of the opposition. The Kabaka demanded that his kingdom be placed under Foreign Office control and granted independence within a stated period. He rejected British demands to appoint Buganda ministers to the Legislative Council, a step which was considered to be essential for the unification of Uganda. He maintained his opposition to the policy, which he considered a threat to Bugandan independence, throughout the negotiations. On 30 October 1953 the British Governor, Sir Andrew Cohen, had him summarily dismissed as Kabaka, and deport-

King Edward Mutesa II

ed to London for refusing to co-operate with the Protectorate Government. In London, the exiled ruler was given a pension of £8,000 a year tax-free by the British government.

The Kabaka's deposition elicited widespread protest among the Baganda who rallied to his support. His sister, the Nalinya, was reported to have fallen dead at the moment she heard the news of his banishment. The Governor established a Regency and twice imposed a State of Emergency in the kingdom, but the pro-Mutesa protest continued. The Kabaka was allowed to return to Uganda on 7 October 1955, after accepting an agreement which promised Buganda limited autonomy within Uganda.

He returned to his kingdom with greatly increased influence and popularity as a national hero. With Uganda moving closer to independence, the Kabaka took a

leading part in the constitutional arrangements that preceded it. He encouraged the
alliance of a royalist party, with the nationalist party of Dr Milton Obote, the Uganda
People's Congress (UPC). Through this alliance, Mutesa was not only able to consolidate Buganda's partial autonomy in post
colonial Uganda but indeed become the
country's first non-executive president in
1963 when the last British Governor-
General left Uganda.

His dual position as Kabaka and Head
of State was a difficult one in the immediate
aftermath of a nationalist struggle whose
protagonists wanted to break down the
colonial barriers that had isolated them from
their contemporaries in neighbouring countries. His role as a constitutional monarch
was seen by the pan-African politicians in
the government as an impediment on the
path of bringing Uganda to join a wider East
African federation. To this effect the government of Milton Obote sought to amend the
1962 independence constitution, which the
Kabaka contested, claiming that it contained certain "entrenched provisions" that
safeguarded "Buganda and the Kabakaship"
and that any attempt to amend them would
be illegal. Nevertheless in 1966 the government introduced a new constitution which
provided for an executive Head of State and
Obote became the president. The Kabaka
denounced the constitution and requested
Obote to withdraw his administration from
the soil of Buganda as it was no longer
enjoying the confidence of his people. The
government ordered the arrest of the Kabaka. In the attack on his palace on Mengo
Hill, on 27 May 1966, Colonel Idi Amin who
later became President of Uganda led the
army, but Mutesa II escaped to London to
commence a second term of exile. In 1967 he
published *Desecration of my Kingdom*. He died
in London on 21 November 1969, aged 45.∎

Mwezi Gisabo (1830-1908)

MWEZI GISABO, King (1830-1908).

BURUNDIAN monarch. He ruled Burundi
between 1852 and 1908 in continuation
of the dynasty of the Baganwa into which

he was born and which was founded at
the end of the 17th century by King Ntare
Rushatsi. The kingdom inherited by Gisabo
Mwezi was roughly the same size as the
present day Burundi, with a population of
about one million. However, territorial considerations were less important than the
spiritual power vested in the King, who was
regarded as a deity – the King was consi-

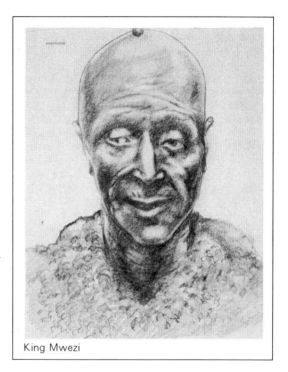

King Mwezi

dered as the guarantor of his people's prosperity and fertility; his spiritual role was
symbolised not only in the sacred rituals at
his enthronement and death, but also during
his lifetime whenever the annual planting
feast was held.

Gisabo Mwezi is reputed to have led a
simple life for a King: he lost one eye early in
life and was paralysed in one leg following a
fighting contest. He spent a lot of time in the
central region of Muramvya where most of
his agricultural lands were situated. He
maintained his power and influence through
various clans, each of whom specialised in
performing a particular duty or service for
the King. The King's personal domains were
administered by Hutu or Tutsi chiefs, known
as *Bishikira*, while the rest of the country
was administered by the Baganwa, members

of the royal family each of whom exercised virtual sovereignty in his own chiefdom.

When Gisabo Mwezi ascended the throne, he was faced with opposition because, although he had been King Ntare's favourite son, he was not first in line of succession to the throne and therefore not the heir apparent. When the news of Mwezi's enthronement was known, opposition erupted but it was quickly brought under control. But as Mwezi's reign advanced, various contenders for the throne appeared, the opposition becoming more effective in the 1880s, at the time of European penetration.

The kingdom also had to defend itself against attack from outside. Between 1855 and 1858 Burundi had been the victim of repeated aggression from the Batuta. The Austrian explorer, Oscar Baumann, was the first European to visit the kingdom of Burundi. But missionary White Fathers were the first Europeans to actually settle in Burundi. Gisabo Mwezi made known his extreme displeasure at these developments, because it appeared to the King that the missionaries were part of a European penetration of his kingdom. The King himself was growing old and a series of calamaties had hit the country after 1880. There had been a famine, invasion by locusts, an eclipse of the sun (considered a bad sign) in 1889, the country's cattle were stricken with bovine plague in 1890 and there was a smallpox epidemic in 1892. The Germans then set up their first military command post at Kajaga in 1896, from which a series of military incursions into Burundi were later made.

In 1889 Gisabo Mwezi and the Germans reached a provisional agreement. The King was determined to resist the Europeans. In 1902 the Germans again attacked him after forming alliances with two rebel chiefs. In April 1903 four columns attacked Mwezi's headquarters, forcing him to retreat to Burunga, where he surrendered. The Germans extracted a number of concessions from him: he had to recognise the Usumbura military station and the Mugera mission; he had to hand over 424 head of cattle; Kirma and Maconco, who had collaborated with the Germans in defeating the King, were respectively installed as chiefs at Bukeye and Muramvya.

This treaty, signed on 6 June 1903, marked the end of the independent Kingdom of Burundi. Until his death, however, Gisabo Mwezi remained King of Burundi. From 1904 onwards, the Germans adopted a new policy, which favoured monarchical and traditional rule. They let Mwezi recover Muramvya and Bukeye from his rivals in 1905. Between 1905 and 1907 the policy of encouraging the insubordination of the north-eastern Batare chiefs was finally brought to an end. On 8 October 1905 Mwezi was recognised officially as King of a reunited Burundi.

He died on 21 August 1908. ∎

Mxenge, G.M. (1938-81)

MXENGE, Griffiths Mlungisi (1938-81).

SOUTH AFRICAN political activist who was a prominent Durban attorney. Mxenge was a member of the ANC from the early 1960s when he was a student at Fort Hare. Held under the 180-day law in 1966, he went on a hunger strike in protest. Sentenced to two years' imprisonment under the Suppression of Communism Act for membership of the ANC, he was released in 1969 but immediately banned under the same act. In 1973 his ban was renewed for five years.

Born into the Xhosa ethnic group in 1938, he was married to Victoria Nonyamezelo Mxenge (q.v.) who was murdered four years later at the age of 43 outside her home. She was a civil rights lawyer. They had four children.

A large portion of Mxenge's work was acting for political prisoners. In 1976 he acted as the family attorney for Joseph Mdluli who died in detention in March 1976. A few days after Mdluli's death, Mxenge was detained and held without trial for 103 days. This did not, however, deter him, after his release he went on as instructing attorney in many political trials, in Durban, Pietermaritzburg, East London and Johannesburg. He acted for the family of Mapetla Mohabi, secretary-general of the banned South African Students' Organisation (SASO) who died in detention in Port Elizabeth in August 1976. In 1978/79, he was the defence attorney in the Pan African Congress Bethal trial, during which he received written death threats. Undeterred, early in 1980 he represented Chief Sabata Dalindyebo, paramount Chief of the Tembus in the Transkei.

Mxenge, was arrested on 24 November 1981, following a police raid on his office. He was detained under Section 22 of the General Law Amendment Act which allows detention without trial for 14 days. The police seized pamphlets advertising a memorial service for Mxenge which was to be held on 26 November. Mxenge's funeral itself took place on 6 December near King Williams Town and was attended by thousands of mourners. ▓

G. Mxenge

Outside his legal activities, he was very much involved in other political activities, though the two were entwined. He was treasurer of the Release Mandela Committee, a leading activist in the campaign for the demands of the Freedom Charter, and campaigns to boycott the Republic Day Celebrations and the South African Indian Council Elections (which was a success with less than 15 per cent of the people voting). He was also responsible for attempting to get the bodies of those killed in the South African raid on the homes of the ANC members in Matola Mozambique) for burial in South Africa. When this failed, he made arrangements for the families of the dead to travel to Maputo for the funeral.

Mxenge's murder on 20 November 1981, in Durban was a shock, though it came in a series of killings and violent actions against opponents of the South African regime. His mutilated body was found at a cycling stadium at Umlazi, Durban. On the day before his two dogs had been found poisoned at the family's home. His murderer was never found. A big demonstration was held in Durban to protest and show the African's anger at such brutal actions against opponents of the apartheid regime.

People were detained in connection with the organisation of memorial services, which took place in Durban and other towns. Patrick Maqubela, a lawyer articled to

---

Mxenge, V.M.T. (1941-85)

MXENGE, Victoria Nonyamezelo Tsaba (1941-85).

SOUTH AFRICAN leading Black civil rights lawyer. She was killed by four men in the driveway of her home in Umlazi, a township on the outskirts of Durban, on 1 August 1985 only days before the resumption of the trial of United Democratic Front (UDF) members. She was an instructing attorney and therefore a vital member of the team defending the 16 UDF members in the Pietermaritzburg treason trial accused of plotting to overthrow the state.

Victoria Mxenge was fully aware that the work she did in apartheid South Africa put her life daily at risk, nevertheless she was determined to do it as she and her husband, G. M. Mxenge (q.v.), had done together before he was brutally murdered in 1981. She had said at the time "If by killing my husband they (the oppressive minority regime of South Africa) thought the work he was doing would come to an end they have made a mistake. I'll continue even if it means I must also die."

Born in 1941/42 at Tamara, near Zwelitsha, she was the second child of Wilmot Gosa and Nobantu Ntebe, both teachers. She had her primary education locally and then went to Forbes Grant Secondary School, Ginsberg, and Healdtown Institution near Fort Beaufort. She trained as a nurse at Lovedale Hospital and did a midwifery course at King Edward VIII Hospital, Pietermaritzburg. After working as a nurse for ten years, she went on to study law and was called to the bar in 1981; she joined her husband's legal practice.

After his murder, she went on working as a political lawyer, defending those who had been banned, placed under house-arrest, detained or imprisoned. She was no stranger to the hardships and sacrifices of commitment to the South African struggle for freedom and for justice, and "though she never held a gun, she confronted the country's apartheid regime daily by what she represented." Throughout her life great demands were made on her and she faced them bravely; she was the wage-earner when her husband was studying to be a lawyer and went through hard times when he was detained in 1964 and later sentenced to two years' imprisonment on Robben Island.

Victoria Mxenge's murder came in a long series of killings, which reached new heights after the South African government imposed a state of emergency in Black townships around Johannesburg and in the Eastern Cape on 21 July 1985. Her eldest son rushed her to hospital when she was shot as she returned home from a meeting, but she apparently died on the way. Her murder heightened suspicions that alleged death squads of the Botha regime were steadily eliminating political activists with the tacit approval of the authorities. The African National Congress, in a statement, said Mxenge's murder "was deliberately planned both to get rid of this immensely humane, peace-loving but militant anti-racist mother of four children and to terrorise the rest of the democratic leadership of our country into a state of panic-striken paralysis." It went on to urge the international community to increase the isolation of South Africa in response to the murder.

Victoria Mxenge was a senior member of the Natal Organisation of Women and a senior executive member and treasurer of the Natal Branch of the UDF. She often spoke at the funerals of apartheid victims, and was secretary-treasurer for the Release Mandela Committee. ■

V. Mxenge

Mzilikazi, K. (c1795-1868)

MZILIKAZI, Khumalo (c1795–1868).

ZIMBABWEAN Zulu chief who established the Matabele Nation.

Mzilikazi, meaning the Great Way, was the son of Mashobane, chief of the Khumalo Clan of the Zulus. In 1818 Mashobane was captured and decapitated by Zwide, chief of the Ndwandwe Clan. Mzilikazi was made chief of the Khumalos by Zwide, but he feared for his life and fled, seeking sanctuary with Chaka (q.v.), King of the Zulus. Before long Chaka was impressed with his bravery and his qualities of leadership. He installed him as commander of one of the regiments and became his closest friend. In 1822 Chaka allowed him to return to his home and become the chief of the Khumalos once more under his protection. He also ordered him to proceed to the Western border with his regiment and destroy the Sotho chief Ranisi and to deliver the captured cattle to him. Mzilikazi defeated Ranisi but absconded north with the cattle. This made him a sworn enemy of Chaka.

With only three hundred warriors Mzilikazi attacked Sotho clans, incorporating the able-bodied men into his army, and capturing the livestock. He continued his conquests further north in what is now the Transvaal. He conquered some of the Pedis and Kgatlas who were fragmented and absorbed them, teaching the men Zulu military tactics and the use of the short spear and large shield. In 1825 he established his capital Mhlahlandlela in the western Transvaal. His army had swelled to 1,400. He was now able to extend his raids as far as the Shonas north of the Limpopo. He also repulsed an invasion by the Giquas led by Bloem and Berends.

In 1832 Dingane who had become King of the Zulus, having murdered Chaka in 1828, attacked Mzilikazi and his Ndebele people. In the confusion of the battle the Pedis fled and returned to their home territory, free from Mzilikazi. Mzilikazi decided to distance himself from the powerful Zulus and fled west.

In 1829 two Scottish traders befriended him and supplied him with firearms and also introduced him to the missionary, Robert Moffat. His interest in Moffat was to get advice on how to deal with Europeans and ways of acquiring guns. He resisted Christianity. Meanwhile Boer trekkers were entering his country without permission. As the numbers grew he became annoyed. In August 1831 one of his patrols wiped out several Boer families and their servants. In 1836 he committed his entire army of 4,000 against the Boers in the Northern Free State. He failed to penetrate the Boer laager and lost 430 men, but he captured 100 horses, 4,600 cattle and 5,000 sheep and goats. This action discouraged the Boer infiltration until 1837 when a Boer commando invaded and killed 400 of his men and hundreds of women and children and captured 6,000 cattle. This defeat made him decide to retreat further north, across the Limpopo. Whilst preparing for the long migration north the Boers attacked again and this time they killed 3,000 Ndebeles (Matabele). In twelve months he had lost half his army.

Mzilikazi was a brave leader who could be ruthless, but his main intention was to create a Ndebele nation from the original three hundred and the many differing people he conquered and absorbed, these ranging from the Sotho in the south to the Shona in the north.

King Mzilikazi

For the journey north he split the Ndebeles into two groups, each taking a different route in order to find sufficient water. He led the one and Chief Gundwane led the other. Mzilikazi also entrusted his heir Nkulumane to Gundwane. Two years later, in 1840 the two groups made contact. Gundwane and some of the chiefs with him had installed Nkulumane King of the Ndebeles in place of Mzilikazi. Mzilikazi executed the conspirators and possibly his son too.

The migration had depleted what remained of his cattle after the defeat by the Boers. He rebuilt his stock by attacking the Shonas. He also carried out his policy of conquering and absorbing. Again his kingdom expanded as more Shonas joined the Ndebeles.

He was the father of the nation. He had control of many aspects of his people's lives. He organised an administration that was centralised. Each region being administered by a senior chief who was also head of the regional regiments. There were two councils, one composed of members of the royal family and chosen wise elders, and the other was made up of chiefs. He presided over both. He tried to introduce the Tswana God, Modimo, his doctors were Shonas and he followed Zulu customs.

In 1859 he allowed missionaries to settle in his country but they failed to proselytise the people. They blamed Mzili-kazi who in fact never interfered nor discouraged the people. The people were not interested in a religion that amongst other things condemned polygamy.

Mzilikazi died in 1868, aged around 70 years. By then he had built the powerful Ndebele nation by welding various ethnic groups into one. ■

N

Nagogo, U. (1905-81)

NAGOGO, Alhaji Sir Usman, Emir of Katsina (1905-81).

NIGERIAN traditional ruler, he succeeded his father Muhammadu Dikko (q.v.) as the tenth Fulani ruler of the Katsina emirate in 1944. Katsina came under Fulani influence at the beginning of the reign of the Habe kings; the last Habe king was Magajin Halidu. The throne of Katsina was then granted to a disciple of the Jihad, Umaru

U. Nagogo, Emir of Katsina

Dallagi, who in 1806 became the first Fulani ruler of Katsina.

Nagogo's family, the Sulibawa, did not however become a ruling house until a hundred years later. For though Usman Nagogo's grandfather Gidado and great grandfather Dahiru had been prominent in the court where they served respectively as Durbi (Gidado was also a noted soldier) and collector of tolls, it was not until 1906 that the British appointed Muhammadu Dikko as Emir, in succession to the deposed Emir Yero. Dikko thus became the first Emir from the Sulibawa house and the ninth Fulani Emir of Katsina.

Usman Nagogo was born in Katsina, a year before his father succeeded to the throne. After attending the Old Katsina Provincial School his education followed the Moslem traditional pattern of Koranic studies, and he became learned in Arabic as well as in Hausa. In 1921, with his father, he visited Mecca to perform the Hadj. At 24 he was made the first head of the Katsina Native Authority Police, a newly created independent local force whose formation was precipitated by the creation of Katsina Province from Zaria Province in 1921. This position brought him into public attention and he was to serve in that capacity until 1938.

From 1938, for six years, Nagogo served as Magajin Garin Katsina – councillor for Katsina township, which ensured him influence in the affairs of a province that was fast becoming one of the leading emirates in northern Nigeria. In earlier times Katsina had been an important trade route for the regions north and south of the Sahara. It was also, and still is, renowned for its leather work and for its tradition of scholarly pursuits. The latter, among other considerations, led to the establishment in 1921 of the famous Katsina Training College which for many years was the premier institution of superior education in the North. The College has since transferred to Zaria where it is now known as Barewa College. With these came political influence which in the succeeding years saw Katsina as the seventh emirate, coming after Sokoto, Bornu, Gwandu, Kano, Bauchi and Adamawa, in order of precedence in the northern hierarchy. Thus by 1944 when Usman Nagogo became the tenth Emir of Katsina he was a force to reckon with in the politics of both the North and the entire country.

One of his first assignments in 1944 was a British-sponsored morale-boosting tour of Burma where he visited West African soldiers. In 1948, he was one of the Nigerian delegation to the African Conference held in London. Following constitutional changes in Nigeria Usman Nagogo became one of the first batch of northern representatives in the Nigerian Executive Council. That same year, 1954, he was appointed a Central Minister without Portfolio.

He reverted to regional politics in 1956, and again was made Minister without Portfolio in the government of Sir Ahmadu Bello (q.v.). There, in the shadow of the Sardauna of Sokoto, the role of Emir Nagogo, like that of other northern leaders of the time, was overtly secondary. But as one of the Premier's trusted lieutenants Nagogo played a prominent role in the political development of the North whose interests he represented effectively throughout his reign.

Emir Usman Nagogo was not too enthusiastic about rapid changes, but he encouraged many developments in his emirate. A much loved Emir, respected by many in Nigeria and knighted by the British, he died in 1981, aged 76. He is survived by many children, among them General Hassan Katsina who became Chief of Staff of the Nigerian Army. ■

Nahas Pasha, M. (1876-1965)

NAHAS PASHA, Mustafa (1876-1965).

EGYPTIAN politician. Born in 1876 at Samanoud, he was educated at government schools and then at Cairo law school, where he graduated in 1900. He became a judge in 1904, while also supporting the nationalist movement against the British occupation. He joined the Wafd, the main nationalist party of the post-First World War era, led by Zaghlul Pasha (q.v.), and was deported with him to the Seychelles on the

M. Nahas Pasha

eve of legal independence, which was proclaimed in March 1922 but with serious restrictions which made it seem to the Wafd to be not true independence. The two returned in 1923. While not satisfied with the constitution, they worked with it for a while.

In 1924, when Zaghlul Pasha was Prime Minister after a Wafd victory in elections, Nahas was Minister of Communications. After the fall of the Wafd government, he worked as secretary of the party and also in private legal practice. He was re-elected to Parliament in 1926 and became Second Vice-President of the Chamber. In 1927, on the death of Saad Zaghlul Pasha, Nahas became leader of the Wafd, a position he was to hold for 25 years.

He also became Speaker of Parliament then, and on 18 March 1928 he formed his first government, following the resignation of Prime Minister Sarwat. Now, and later, he clashed with both the British, still dominating Egypt with powers reserved to them since 1922, and the King. The British forced his government (a coalition including Liberal Party leaders) to drop bills they disliked, while the King took advantage of the publication in newspapers of certain documents incriminating Nahas (said by Nahas to be forged) to dismiss him in July 1928.

He became Prime Minister for the second time on 1 January 1930 and soon announced the intention of holding talks with Britain on the "reserved powers" of 1922. The talks broke down over the question of Egypt's claim to the Sudan. Then, once more, Nahas clashed with the monarch, King Fuad, who objected to two government bills and dismissed the government, calling on Sidqi Pasha (q.v.) to form a new one.

In 1936 Nahas led a delegation for talks with Britain which led to a new Treaty, signed on 26 August 1936. This recognised Egypt's independence more fully, while allowing Britain to retain troops in the country. At elections held during the talks the Wafd won and Nahas Pasha became Prime Minister for the third time. In 1937 he secured a further success in reducing the foreign domination of Egypt, his party's constant aim, with an international agreement to end the system of special courts for foreign residents, the "Capitulations".

The new King, Farouk, began to clash with the Wafd as his father had done, in alliance with many Moslem zealots, especially at the ancient el-Azhar University. Tension arose between these elements and the Wafdist government in late 1937, when the party leadership split, with Nokrashi Pasha (q.v.) and others leaving, according to one account, because of Nahas's demand for total obedience to himself by the party. Nahas encouraged student demonstrations and a "Blue Shirts" organisation of party militants, but these methods were then used against him. A "Young Egypt" organisation opposed him with those methods and one of its members attempted to kill him in November 1937. In December 1937 he was dismissed by Farouk (q.v.).

The Wafd lost heavily in the 1938 elections, but Nahas remained an influential figure, continuing his strong criticisms of British domination from 1938 to 1941. But when the Second World War broke out

Britain enforced its control over Egypt more than ever, determined to keep the strategically placed country for the purposes of the war. For all the Wafd's criticisms of Britain, the British needed to see a strong government in Egypt, ·which it could effectively control, and saw that the government in power was ineffective. Thus the British ambassador, with a show of armed strength, forced King Farouk on 4 February 1942 to appoint Nahas Prime Minister, in a famous incident showing who really ruled Egypt.

Nahas ruled for over two years. But there were splits in the Wafd, and the general-secretary, Makram Obayd, after being expelled in 1942 published in 1943-44 two editions of a *Black Book* denouncing Nahas' government. It accused the government of massive corruption, which did go on though Nahas was said not to have been corrupt himself, and of subservience to Britain. At the same time King Farouk intrigued to make it possible to dismiss the Prime Minister whom he had appointed only by Britain's order. After quarrels between Nahas and the King, and increasing opposition to the Prime Minister, Britain eventually ceased to care about him and in October 1944 he was dismissed.

In opposition he became an ultra-nationalist again. He ordered his followers to boycott the 1945 elections, and later said only the Wafd represented Egypt. In 1946 he refused to join the delegation for talks with Britain on another Treaty revision unless he led it. Though he later agreed to join the government, and the talks, he remained critical of the policies of the other parties. He therefore remained a leader of the increasingly strong opposition to British interference. Riots and strikes were directed against the presence of British troops until these were withdrawn from all areas except the Suez Canal by 1947. Increasing tension and violence in succeeding years included eight attempts on Nahas Pasha's life. But he remained a popular figure with exceptional powers of oratory, and well liked personally.

In January 1950, after a Wafd victory in elections, he became Prime Minister for the fifth time. His government started some social reform measures, including a plan for major land reform. It also voiced the Egyptian protests against Israel, which had defeated Egypt in 1948-49, and Britain. In 1951 the Wafd government encouraged guerrilla attacks on British forces in the Canal area, to back up a call for total withdrawal, after the failure of talks in 1950-51.

On 8 October 1951 Egypt abrogated the 1936 Treaty and the Sudan Condominium Agreement. King Farouk joined in the nationalist policy. But the ordinary Egyptians' feelings began by early 1952 to turn against the King and the government. On 20 January 1952, after the British had occcupied the Ismailia area in retaliation against guerrilla attacks, mobs burned down a large area of Cairo. King Farouk immediately sacked Nahas Pasha.

This did not save the monarchy, which was overthrown on 23 July 1952 to congratulations from Nahas. He played no part in politics after the revolution and lived a relatively obscure life until his death in Alexandria on 23 August 1965.■

Naicker, G.M. (1910-78)

NAICKER, Dr Gangathura Mohambry (1910-78).

SOUTH AFRICAN political leader of the South Africa Indian Council. He strongly advocated the unity of Africans, Indians and Coloureds in the struggle against apartheid and the white-minority regime. "Monty", as he was generally known, was born in 1910 in Durban, a second-generation of an Indian family who had settled in South Africa. After elementary education in Durban he went to Scotland in Britain in 1927 for his secondary education. There he later studied medicine, returning to South Africa in 1934 as a qualified medical practitioner. He opened a surgery in Durban, where he inevitably became involved with the social and political problems of his numerous Indian patients.

Together with other political activists in the Indian community he co-founded the Anti-Segregation League to give organised opposition to the government measures which sought to restrict Indian landownership rights under the Pegging Act. And critical of the cautious leadership in the Natal Indian Congress (NIC), Naicker joined the younger progressive elements in the League to seize control of the movement. He

was elected its President in October 1945 and in December of that year he united the Indian masses in the Transvaal Indian Congress (TIC). Following the protracted campaign by Africans, Indians and Coloureds against the late 1940s segregationist

Dr. G.M. Naicker

measures, Naicker and Yusuf Dadoo (q.v.), another Indian leader, visited the newly independent India to solicit support for their cause. India subsequently broke diplomatic and economic links with South Africa. On 9 March 1947 he and Dadoo led the Indian Congress into a pact with Alfred Bitini Xuma (q.v.) who was President of the African National Congress (ANC). The two leaders issued the Joint Declaration of Co-operation which sought to present a united African/Indian front. The pact subsequently led to the formation of the Congress Alliance in 1955, and thus began a working relationship that survived all political vicissitudes.

In the wake of the Defiance Campaign of 1952, where he led the Natal demonstrators, he was among the more than 8,000 Africans, Indians and Coloureds arrested, following which he was sentenced to prison for a month. He had earlier served various terms of imprisonment for his political activities and in 1956 he was again arrested and charged with high treason, but the charges against him were dropped in 1958. The following years were a period of continual banishment under the South African banning orders which cut him off from any political activity. He succeeded Dadoo as president of the South African Indian Council after the former had been restricted. He also remained the head of the NIC until his death on 12 January 1978 in Durban. ■

Naicker, M.P. (1920-77)

NAICKER, Mariemuthoo Pragalathan (1920-77).

M.P. Naicker

SOUTH AFRICAN trade unionist and journalist who was Director of Publicity and Information for the African National Congress (ANC) and editor of its organ, *Sechaba*. Of Indian descent Naicker, known to many of his colleagues as "MP", was born in 1920 into a working class family in Durban. He was forced to abandon primary schooling because of lack of funds and started working in a Durban factory at an early age.

At eighteen, while working as a Durban van driver, he began trade union activities among sugar workers and was elected secretary of the Natal Sugar Workers Union. A young, energetic, and brilliant organiser, he was appointed in 1946 secretary of the Passive Resistance Council which sought to oppose the 1946 "Ghetto Act" which forbade property deals by Asians, and was imprisoned for four months for defying the law. Following this he was elected secretary of the Natal Indian Congress (NIC) and played a key role in transforming it into a mass movement committed to militant campaigning and the unity of South African non-whites.

Following the passage in 1952 of the Suppression of Communism Act, Naicker was forced to end political and trade union activities. He went into journalism as editor/ manager of the *Guardian* newspaper which,

because of its radical editorials, was constantly banned by the authorities. The newspaper, however, survived several bannings by changing its name after each prohibition until it was finally crushed by the government in 1963. Naicker had himself defied banning orders to lead the 1954-55 Defiance Campaign in Natal, for which he became one of the 156 accused in the Treason Trial of 1956-61. Though the charges proffered against him were later dropped, he was detained for several months without trial during the 1960 State of Emergency which preceded the Sharpeville Massacre. Subsequent banning orders forced him into exile in 1965 when he joined the external wing of the ANC.

In exile Naicker was appointed Director of Publicity and Information in the London office of the ANC. He also became editor of *Sechaba*, the organisation's organ which was being printed in Berlin, Germany. He died in the plane on his way there to submit editorial materials for printing on 29 April 1977, aged 56. He was buried in London on 8 May before a large gathering of colleagues. Among those who paid tribute at the funeral was Oliver Tambo, acting President of the ANC, who said: "He died whilst on a mission on behalf of our movement. Like those forces that advanced onto Berlin thirty-four years ago to liberate Germany, he was advancing onto Berlin in the service of our struggle to liberate South Africa and fell in battle just like any member of Umkhonto we Sizwe" (the military wing of the ANC).

Another tribute, by Yusuf Mohammed Dadoo (q.v.) of the South African Communist Party, read: "The loss of MP will be surely felt throughout the movement. There is no campaign in the South African struggle since the 1940s which does not bear the imprint of his valuable contribution."

Naidoo, S. (1937-89)

NAIDOO, Most Rev. Stephen (1937-89).

SOUTH AFRICAN clergyman and educationist who became the Roman Catholic Archbishop of Cape Town and was known for his opposition to apartheid. Naidoo was born on 23 October 1937 in Durban, Natal, to parents who came from India. He had his primary and secondary schooling in South Africa and was taught by Christian missionaries, before going to Britain for the Redemptorists' noviceship at St. Mary's, Kinnoull Hill, Perth. He then studied theology at Hawkstone Park in Shropshire.

Naidoo decided that he needed to learn Tamil also if he were to be able to do his work more effectively, so he spent some time in Bangalore, India, learning the language. After that he took a doctorate in Canon Law at the Dominican Angelicum University in Rome.

In 1968 Naidoo returned to South Africa after a period of teaching liturgy at Hawkstone. He immersed himself in church work, learning a lot about his country in the process, visiting households in African townships and observing at first hand the problems of the Cape Town Coloureds and other minorities. The inequities of the apartheid regime became even more apparent to him and his stand against it, though it did not make headlines, was nonetheless firm.

In 1973 Naidoo succeeded Cardinal Owen McCann as the first "non-White" Archbishop of Capetown. He may not have been as outspoken in his opposition to apartheid as his Anglican counterpart, Archbishop Desmond Tutu, but he also became known for his vigorous denunciation of it. In April 1987 he teamed up with Tutu and others in St. Mary's Anglican Cathedral in a prayer service for detainees. At the time, there was a ban on "joint action" for detainees; Naidoo described the ban as a "manifest nonsense". He spoke on South African problems at the October 1987 Synod on the Laity in Rome, and achieved a high-profile exposure to the universal church. At the end of the Synod he was elected one of the three African representatives to the Synod board where he was said to have made a good impression with his courtesy and quick wit.

He died on 1 July 1989 at Merton Park in Surrey, England, after an attack of angina.

Nana (1852-1916)

NANA of the Itsekiri (1852-1916).

NIGERIAN traditional ruler. Nana was born in 1852 at Jakpa, mid-western Nigeria. His father was a wealthy trader belonging to the powerful House of Ologbotsere of the coastal Itsekiri people, while his mother was a member of the neighbouring Urhobo ethnic group.

From his early years, Nana learned trading from his father's business. At the time there was a great deal of rivalry among the various trading families in this area, and he soon realised that to be successful, a trader must also be a fighter. In order to protect his expanding business, his father founded a settlement that could easily be defended at Ebrohimi, and when Nana was a young man the family moved to this town.

Soon he began to work with his father, and although he was not the eldest son he became his deputy, having distinguished himself through great bravery and intelligence. On his father's death in 1883 Nana succeeded him as head of the family, becoming one of the richest and most powerful men in the area. At the same time he also became Governor of the Benin River, a highly respected post that had also been held by his father. At that time Europeans traded in the Delta area but did not yet rule. In the position of Governor of the Benin River, Nana was responsible for collecting customs duties as well as ensuring peaceful trade between the British and Itsekiri.

Shortly after he became head of the family he declared war on the Eku people when they shielded one of his half brothers who had fled after committing adultery with one of his father's wives. Despite the support of the Abraka people, the Eku were defeated and many of their menfolk were taken prisoner by Nana.

During the period British strength in West Africa greatly increased and in 1884 Nana, as head of the Itsekiri owing to his great wealth and position as Governor, along with other Itsekiri elders, agreed to a "protection treaty" with the British. This treaty established Britain's exclusive trading rights in the area. Nana and the other chiefs were allowed to continue as before, provided they did not do anything to incur the disapproval of the British, who would in return guarantee protection for them. Two clauses were removed from the treaty before Nana and the other Itsekiris would agree. One concerning missionary activity in the area which they did not want because of its opposition to polygamy. The other related to British trading activities in the interior, the Itsekiris insisted that they must remain the middlemen in the trade between the people of the interior and the British.

After the treaty was signed the British made no immediate attempt to establish a government in the area and in the ensuing period Nana's power and influence greatly increased, as did the respect in which he was held. In late 1886 and early 1887 Nana organised a boycott of trade with the Europeans after they offered very low prices for the palm produce. Trade was only resumed after Nana had threatened to go to war. However, the British traders began increasingly to complain about Nana's power, and by 1890 the British decided to establish a colonial government in the area.

The British then set about decreasing Nana's influence so as to increase their own authority, they, for example, took over the collection of customs duties from Nana. They

Nana of the Itsekiri

also began to extend their influence and establish a trading station in the interior at Sapele. However, Nana was anxious to avoid conflict with the new government and modified his trading activities to suit this new situation and even sent his agents to trade at the Sapele trading station.

In November 1893 Nana's agents refused to trade with the British Vice-Consul who was visiting the Urhobo area, as they had had no instructions in this matter from Nana. The British Vice-Consul was incensed at this defiance of British authority and began to criticise Nana. The underlying problem was that Nana's power and influence in the interior exceeded that of the British colonial government there. Nana's wealth and authority as head of the Itsekiri had earned him powerful enemies among his people and these now decided to ally with the British to bring about his downfall.

In April 1894 Nana was informed that he was no longer Governor of the Benin River and should cease to act as such. The following month trade in the Abraka area was upset and Nana was accused of taking many slaves from this area. He denied this accusation, stating that he had only taken pawns (men who were given over to a creditor until debts were paid) in the customary fashion as the people of Eku owed him a great deal of oil.

The British tried to arrange a meeting with Nana, but he could not leave his town at the time because of a number of deaths there and as they would not deal with his messengers, they sent him a series of stipulations and threatened to stop him and his people using the rivers if he failed to carry them out.

Although Nana began to comply with these demands Ebrohimi, his home town, was placed under blockade so that no canoes could use the river. He protested and stated that he did not want to fight with the British, but to no avail. His enemies among the Itsekiris were spreading false rumours as to his intentions and the British prepared for battle. A meeting of British and Itsekiri elders was called in August 1894 but Nana, fearing that he would be seized and deported, did not attend. As a result he was forbidden to use the rivers and was informed that canoes belonging to his people would be attacked.

Realising that conflict was inevitable, Nana barricaded the creek entrance to his town. This was destroyed by the British on 4 August 1894 and the war began. Ebrohimi was in a very advantageous position but on 25 September the town fell after the British received reinforcements and two gunboats. Nana escaped to Lagos, where he surrendered to the British authorities. He was taken to Calabar to stand trial and was found guilty of breaking his treaty with the British, disturbing the peace and causing war, after which he was sentenced to exile for life. For two years he stayed in Calabar and then he was sent to Accra.

During exile he was converted to the Christian faith. He sent several petitions to the British Government to be pardoned so that he could return home. In 1906 his fourth petition was granted and on 8 August he arrived at Koko. Despite his twelve-year exile he received a great welcome on his return home and many people travelled to Koko to greet him and bring him gifts. He had retained the people's admiration and respect for standing up for his rights even though he had lost all his wealth and power by doing so.

He began to build up a settlement near Koko called Nana Town and, like Ebrohimi, it was developed as a model of good planning and great cleanliness. He once again began to build up a trading concern and attracted a great deal of business to Koko, increasing the town's importance, while also working as a government contractor. Nana remained there for the rest of his life, dying on 3 July 1916 at the age of 64.■

Nasser, G.A. (1918-70)

NASSER, Gamal Abdul (1918-70).

EGYPTIAN soldier and statesman, the first President of Egypt, one of the founders of the Non-Aligned Movement and the Organisation of African Unity. A staunch proponent of Arab nationalism, he was born on 15 January 1918 in Bani Murr, in the province of Asyut in northern Egypt. Nasser's father was a post office official. His early childhood was spent in Alexandria, before the family moved to Cairo. From Ras-el-Tin Secondary School, Alexandria, he joined the army and entered the Military College. After graduating in 1938 he was promoted captain and became instructor at the College in 1942. He graduated from the Staff College in 1947 and fought in the 1948 war against Israel.

The aftermath of the war, which among other things saw martial law as well as government suppression of anti-British guerrilla activity, led Nasser and a number of others to form the Free Officers Committee. Its principles included the elimination of British imperialism, the abolition of feudalism and capitalism and the creation of a more democratic government. Following the coup d'état of 23 July 1952, Nasser was appointed Minister of the Interior in 1953, and Prime Minister on 18 April 1954.

In 1952 a series of controversial land reforms were introduced, aimed at redistributing large land-holdings to small landowners. The same year also saw the formation of a party which became the National Socialist Union in 1961 and the Arab Socialist Union in 1965. Nasser believed that for Egypt to become a modern industrialised state, it had to distance itself from the kind of fundamentalism preached by the Moslem Brotherhood, a secret organisation founded in the 1920s.

On assuming the premiership, Nasser began negotiations with the British for a phased withdrawal from the Suez Canal zone. The draft agreement, signed in July 1954, which provided for an evacuation phased over 20 months, was criticised on the grounds that it did not challenge British interests. The outlawed Moslem Brotherhood violently attacked the agreement and was alleged to be behind the plot to assassinate Nasser in October 1954.

As part of Nasser's drive to modernise and industrialise Egypt, plans were drawn up for the construction of a high dam at Aswan, which would supply electricity for the country's industrial efforts. In early 1956, agreement was reached in principle with the International Bank for Reconstruction and Development (IBRD) for the financing of the dam and later with Britain and America. In July 1956 the US withdrew its offer, followed by the IBRD and Britain. Nasser was angered by what he regarded as reprisal for the arms agreement he had negotiated with Czechoslovakia earlier in the year and Egypt's anti-Israeli stance. This loss of Western support prompted Nasser to nationalise the Suez Canal on 26 July 1956. The military intervention of Britain, France and Israel between 29 October and 6 November 1956 was condemned by the UN General Assembly, which demanded their withdrawal in favour of an international emergency force.

The withdrawal of the aggressors left Egypt's and Nasser's prestige greatly enhanced in Arab eyes. Nasser was inspired both by the vision of a socially just and economically strong Egypt which could also play the role of leader of the Arab world. In his book *Egypt's Liberation: The Philosophy of the Revolution* (Washington, Public Affairs Press, 1956), he says: "I review our circumstances and discover a number of circles within which our activities inescapably must be confined and in which we must move . . . Can we fail to see that there is an Arab circle . . . Can we possibly ignore the fact that there is an African continent which fate decreed us to be part of and that it is also decreed that a terrible struggle exists for its future – a struggle whose results will be either for us or against us, with or without our will? Can we further ignore the existence of an Islamic world with which we are united by bonds created not only by religious belief but also re-inforced by historic reali-

ties? It is not without significance too that our country lies in north-east Africa, overlooking the Dark Continent, wherein rages a most tumultuous struggle between White colonizers and Black inhabitants for control of its unlimited resources."

Nasser realised that the viability and stability of Egypt depended in part on a strong and united Arab front to resist Western imperialist and Zionist interests.

G.A. Nasser

Thus, during 1954-57, he lent strong support to the Algerian Revolution. The years 1955-56 were characterised by his opposition to the Baghdad Pact concluded between Iran and Turkey on 24 February 1955 with Britain, Pakistan and Iran as associate members. It became known as the Central Treaty Organisation (CENTO) in 1958, with headquarters in Ankara. Following the withdrawal of Iraq, Nasser's opposition to CENTO culminated in February 1958 in the establishment of the United Arab Republic consisting of Egypt and Syria.

When Yemen joined the Union a month later the name was changed to the United Arab States. The establishment of the Union had a number of important consequences. The Syrian · Communist Party, which was opposed to the Union, encouraged communist opposition in Egypt, leading

Nasser to launch anti-communist measures in 1959. The Union was not to last very long. Syria seceded from it on 28 September 1961 after a military coup. Three months later, the Union was formally dissolved but Egypt continued to use the name United Arab Republic.

From 1962 to 1967, Egypt's support of the Yemeni Revolution led to strained relations with Saudi Arabia from whom the Yemeni royalists were receiving support, as well as with Britain.

Together with India and Yugoslavia, Egypt under Nasser became one of the moving forces behind the formation of the Non-Aligned Movement.

During the early 1960s Nasser initiated a series of measures to strengthen the Egyptian Revolution and set the country on the path of socialism. He initiated a new phase in the Egyptian Revolution, moving away from centralised state control to a broader grass-roots involvement. By 1963 a total of 405 companies including all banks, heavy industry and key enterprises had come under state control. Medium-sized enterprises had to accept a 50 per cent state participation and 38 parastatal bodies were created.

In May 1963 a National Charter was adopted following a six-month national debate that involved all levels of Egyptian society. The construction of socialism became the country's political objective. Half of the Arab Socialist Union's party officials and future members of the National Assembly were to be workers or peasants. In 1966 Nasser introduced measures against the continuing resistance of large landowners and the Moslem Brotherhood to his socialist orientation. He created the Political Organisation within the Arab Socialist Union and consisting of communists, intellectuals and trade unionists.

In November 1966 Egypt and Syria signed a five-year defence agreement. Mounting tension between Israel and Syria and a build-up of Israeli armed forces along the Syrian-Egyptian border led Egypt to order a general mobilisation in May 1967. Egypt requested the withdrawal of the UN Emergency Force from its territory, reoccupied Sharm-el-Shaikh and threatened to close the Gulf of Aqaba to Israeli shipping. These measures were deemed aggressive and provocative by Israel and led to the Six-Day War of June 1967. By the time of the cease-fire agreement of 8 June 1967, Israeli troops were in occupation of the Sinai peninsula, as far as the east bank of the Suez Canal, and the Gaza Strip. Following this Egyptian setback president Nasser offered his resignation, but popular demonstrations persuaded him to remain in office. At the Arab Summit in Khartoum during August-September 1967, Saudi Arabia, Kuwait and Libya agreed to give financial assistance to Egypt for its war losses.

On 28 September 1970 Nasser died following a heart attack, just as he had finished helping make peace between the Palestinians and King Hussain of Jordan. His funeral was attended by four million Egyptians. ■

Ndawa (c.1855-88)

NDAWA of Wonde (c.1855-88).

SIERRA LEONEAN soldier. He was of the Mende people, today the dominant people of the southern part of Sierra Leone. When he was born, about 1855, they were not included in Britain's possession of Sierra Leone but had a number of chiefdoms and a very powerful Poro Society, which was their effective government. They had close contact with Sierra Leone Colony, and by the time Ndawa grew up the British were intervening with increasing frequency in Mende affairs, mainly to try to stop wars which harmed British trading efforts in the area.

Born at Majoru, in the modern Kenema district, he had a very active childhood, like other Mende boys. A traditional account quoted by Professor K. Little in *The Mende of Sierra Leone* says, "Ndawa was of middle height, brown skinned, thickly built, had powerful arms, and a scar on his forehead. He was handsome and very lively in spirit."

For being too friendly with the wife of Chief Ganglia, he was sold into slavery by that chief to Sellu Tifa. As a slave he refused to do farm work and insisted on becoming a soldier, despite flogging. He was re-sold to Chief Macavoreh of Tikonko, who employed him as a soldier. From then on he was a professional warrior. He is remembered by

Ndawa of Wonde

the Mendes as a great fighter in local wars.

With another war leader, Kai Lundo of Luawa, he fought against Benya, chief of Blama, in the Kpove War of the 1870s; Benya was driven out of Macavoreh's lands and the grateful chief gave Ndawa his freedom. Then Ndawa fought as a freebooting war leader as far as the Liberian border (fixed on the map in 1885) and Pendembu. In 1885 he and Makaya of Largo raided Sulima and Mono-Salijah. These had made treaties with the British, who intervened regularly in interior wars against such war leaders as Ndawa who attacked their allies. But it seems that no important British expedition was directed against Ndawa.

Ndawa became an independent chief for practical purposes; he told Governor Rowe in 1887, "Macavoreh is my father, but I am not in his hand." He built a capital for himself at Wonde or Wende, said to consist of thirteen towns. In 1887 he and Makaya were allies again in a war in the Gallinas and the Kityam. Chief Makaya (Makaiah) of Largo seems to have been considered more dangerous to the British who, concerned that his war disrupted trade though he had not attacked them, sent an expedition in 1888. The commander, exceeding his instructions, attacked and defeated Makaya.

It seems to have been just about then, in 1888, that the renowned warrior Ndawa

was killed. There seems to be some uncertainty about the date, but there is a detailed traditional account of how he died. His enemy Jami Lenge laid an ambush in which Ndawa was wounded. Then a young man sought to kill him but he called out, "Come Jami Lenge, come and finish me off, lest posterity should say that a small unknown boy killed the Great Ndawa." ■

Ndongo, A.M. (died 1969)

NDONGO, Atanasio Miyone (died 1969).

EQUATORIAL GUINEAN politician and leader of the *Movimiento Nacional de Liberación de la Guinea Ecuatorial* (MONALIGE). Atanasio Miyone Ndongo was born in Rio Benito on the west coast of Rio Muni, Equatorial Guinea mainland area. He was educated at the Catholic Mission School in Banapa, southwest of Malabo. He left school after a student strike and went to Gabon where he became a member of the police force in Libreville.

It was during this time that he met and married one of Leon Mba's (q.v.) daughters. (Mba became President of Gabon in 1961). It was also during this period that he became influenced by the nationalism that was reacting against European colonialism in West Africa. He subsequently spent several years as an activist in Cameroon where he renewed contact with the socialist leader Félix Moumié (q.v.) whom he had met in Gabon.

In 1952 he joined the *Cruzada Nacional de Liberación de Guinea Ecuatorial* (CNLGE), an anti-colonial movement founded in 1947 and presided over by Acacio Mañe (q.v.), a Fang of Cameroonian origin. Ndongo co-signed with Mañe a CNLGE memorandum to the United Nations urging Spain to withdraw from Equatorial Guinea. Mañe's arrest on 20 November 1958 and his subsequent assassination in Bata by the Spanish Civil Guard who threw his body into the ocean signalled Ndongo's rise in the party hierarchy.

Mañe was succeeded as President of CNLGE by Maho Sikacha in 1960 but he was forced to flee Spanish persecution the same year when he took refuge in Cameroon, and the leadership fell to Ndongo under whom the CNLGE became the MONALIGE in 1962.

Under constant threats himself from the Spanish authorities, Ndongo fled to Gabon where in September 1962 he presented a memorandum at the Heads of State Conference of the African and Malagasy Union, announcing the formation of the Liberation Committee of Spanish Guinea and requesting assistance for Guinea's independence. In February 1963 he became Secretary-General of the Co-ordination Bureau of Spanish Guinean Movements, based in Cameroon. Although this body split up in June, the activities of the group triggered off the beginning of the constitutional process that led to autonomy and later independence in 1968. Ndongo and his MONALIGE opposed the autonomous government which Spain set up between 1964 and 1967, demanding total and immediate independence for the country.

He went to Ghana shortly after the collapse of the Co-ordination Bureau and in Accra in October 1964 founded the *Frente Nacional Popular de Liberación de Guinea Ecuatorial* (FRENAPO), a cell of MONALIGE. In March 1965 Ndongo published the FRENAPO programme which requested expropriation without compensation of all Spanish possessions in Equatorial Guinea and their transformation into co-operatives. He later left Accra for Algeria, returning to Cameroon where he married Marthe Moumié, widow of Félix Moumié, his political ally who had been assassinated by French agents in Geneva.

Ndongo returned to Equatorial Guinea in 1966 to participate in the Constitutional Conference convened by Spain. His party having come third in the first ballot of the pre-independence presidential elections of September 1968, he withdrew in favour of Macias Nguema (q.v.) who became Equatorial Guinea's first president. He joined the Nguema administration and was appointed the country's first Minister of Foreign Affairs. In this capacity he played an important role in the international relief flights that were transiting through his country bound for the victims of the Nigerian civil war that was raging then. After a meeting in New York with the Secretary-General of the United Nations, U Thant, Ndongo ordered the interruption of the Red Cross flights to the then Biafra in order to maintain his country's neutrality.

The Foreign Minister soon fell out with President Nguema who on 5 March 1969 had Ndongo arrested for an alleged plot against the administration. He was taken to a Bata prison where he died, reportedly killed on President Nguema's order. In 1976 the President moved the Independence Day celebrations, due on 12 October, to 5 March to commemorate the failure of the alleged Ndongo coup d'état. ■

Neal, D.F. (1928-80)

NEAL, D. Franklin (1928-80).

LIBERIAN economist and politician; he was Chairman of the Council of Ministers of the Mano River Union and alternate Governor of the World Bank. Born on 24 November 1928 in Harper, he attended the University of Liberia in 1951, from where he went to the University of Manitoba, Canada, in 1956. In 1957 Neal was at the University of

Dr D.F. Neal

Michigan, Ann Arbor, Michigan, USA. Later he went to the London School of Economics and Political Science, England. Returning home, he worked in the Ministry of Finance as an economist in 1960, and a research officer, Office of National Planning and Statistics in 1961.

He was director, Project Preparation and Evaluation, Office of National Planning and Statistics in 1962, and became assistant to the administrative Head, Office of National Planning and Statistics in 1964. After two years, he was made deputy to Administrative Head, National Planning Agency until 1970, when he became deputy to Administrative Head, Department of Planning and Economic Affairs. He was appointed Managing Director of the National Port Authority in 1971. In November 1972 he became Minister of Planning and Economic Affairs. He was also Chairman of the Council of Ministers of the Mano River Union, later an alternate Governor of the World Bank, and a Governor of the African Development Bank.

He was a board member of the Liberian-American-Swedish Minerals Company (LAMCO), one of the largest of the five foreign mining companies in the country then, and of the Bong Mining Company. He was also area chairman of the boards of many corporations, including the Liberia Water and Sewer Corporation, the Liberia Social Security and Welfare Corporation and the Liberia Development Corporation. He served on the boards of the Liberia Electricity Corporation, the Forestry Development Authority, the Liberia Produce Marketing Corporation, the National Port Authority, the National Housing and Savings Bank and the Monrovia Tobacco Company.

Neal was executed on 22 April 1980 after the overthrow of President William Tolbert (q.v.) and was survived by his wife and four sons. ∎

Nenekhaly-Camara, C. (1930-72)

NENEKHALY-CAMARA, Condetto (1930-72).

G UINEAN writer and politician. He was born in Beyla, Guinea, on 10 September 1930. He was educated at local primary schools after which he went to Senegal and attended the Ecole William Ponty in Dakar. He then travelled to France to study at the University of Paris, and later graduated in both English and modern literature, as well as gaining a Diploma from the Paris Institute of Ethnology. During that period he was an active member of the General Union of West African Students, the Union of Black Students in France and the Student Union of Revolutionary Africa, being appointed the Guinean representative of the last body at the Havana Cultural Congress.

In 1955 Nenekhaly-Camara joined *Présence Africaine* publication in Paris, writing political and critical articles for this journal until 1958. He also wrote a number of articles for other journals and in 1956 La Courneuve in France published a collection of his poems called *Lagunes*. This was later republished by P.J. Oswald under the title *Poèmes pour la Révolution*.

He returned to Guinea after independence was achieved in 1958 and held several positions in the Office of the President before being appointed Minister of Scientific Research. In the meantime he pursued his interest in African history and culture, and apart from his political writings, he wrote two plays, *Amazoulou*, about Chaka, the great nineteenth century Zulu king, and *Continent-Afrique*. These two works were published in one volume by P.J. Oswald in 1970. He died two years later in August 1972, at the age of 41. ∎

Neto, A.A. (1922-79)

NETO, Dr. Antonio Agostinho (1922-79).

A NGOLAN statesman, the founder of modern Angola. A poet and freedom fighter, he steered the armed struggle that led to the liberation of his country and the emergence of the People's Republic of Angola. The first President of Angola was born on 17 September 1922, in Kaxikane in the Icolo e Benyo region. He had his secondary education at the Liceu Salvador Correia in Luanda where his father was a Methodist pastor. From 1944 to 1947, he worked in the Portu-

Dr A.A. Neto

guese colonial health services. At the same time, he was deeply involved in the movement of cultural nationalism that was developing as overt political organisations were forbidden by the Portuguese rulers. The cultural upsurge was the precursor of the political awakening that culminated in the formation of the *Movimento Popular de Libertação de Angola* (MPLA) in 1956.

Through the force of his personality, and with the help of a modest grant from the people of his village, Neto went to Portugal in 1947 to study medicine at the University of Coimbra where he qualified as a doctor in October 1958.

His undergraduate years were interrupted by spells of imprisonment for political activities in the anti-colonial cause and for his politically perceptive poetry. He was first arrested in 1951 and detained for three months at Caxias Prison in Lisbon; again arrested briefly in 1952; and re-arrested in February 1955 and imprisoned until June 1957 when, under enormous international pressure from intellectuals, artists and liberal politicians, the Portuguese authorities were persuaded to release him.

In Lisbon Neto associated with other future freedom fighters from the other Portuguese colonies, including Amilcar Cabral (then also a student) with whom he cofounded the *Movimento Anti-Colonialista* (MAC). The unity spawned in MAC has effectively continued until today with the common programmes of MPLA in Angola, FRELIMO in Mozambique, and the PAIGC in Guinea-Bissau.

Dr. Neto returned to Angola in 1959. He rejected the privileged position available to him in the public health service where there were only 203 medical practitioners, almost all of whom were Europeans treating only European and "assimilado" African patients. He started a private medical practice in Luanda where he treated both Africans and Europeans; the practice also provided cover for his underground political work for the MPLA.

On 8 June 1960 the Portuguese authorities moved to suppress MPLA militants; Neto was arrested in his consulting room by the Portuguese political police (PIDE). He was first deported, in chains, to the Cape Verde islands in 1961 and, later, following the outbreak of the armed struggle on 4 February 1961, was transferred to Aljube Prison in Lisbon. In March 1962 he was released from prison and placed under house arrest from where he escaped to Leopoldville (now Kinshasa), where the MPLA then had its headquarters. Neto soon became President of the movement.

This was a time of considerable difficulties for the MPLA. Factionalism had led to defection in May 1962 when its Secretary-General since 1956, Viriato da Cruz, led some dissident members out of the movement to join the *Frente Nacional de Libertação de Angola* (FNLA), the other Congo-based organisation of Holden Roberto. At the time the FNLA, with a "government-in-exile" in Leopoldville, enjoyed the goodwill and encouragement of the Congo government and the recognition of the Organisation of African Unity(OAU), which were all denied the MPLA.

Inside Angola, however, the MPLA had a more popular appeal for Angolans who responded to its ideological orientation towards an egalitarian society without distinctions of race and social status. This did not only facilitate its war efforts but indeed transformed it into a mass movement with a multi-ethnic base, thus rejecting the notions of anti-White racism and elitism. The guiding principle was that independent Angola should not duplicate the class patterns of the colonial period, and the MPLA opted for socialism as the mechanism through which the new society might be created.

As head of the movement, Neto took charge of the political and military components of the struggle, holding the cadres together by example and political leadership. He travelled widely in Africa, Eastern and Western Europe, and the Americas, marshalling support for the Angolan cause. By 1965 the MPLA had proved, both on the diplomatic and military fronts, to be the most effective movement in the country. The OAU recognised these achievements that year by granting the movement official status as a genuine liberation movement; and it reconfirmed that judgement in 1968 by withdrawing recognition for the FNLA's "government-in-exile".

On 13 December 1972, under the auspices of the OAU, Neto led the MPLA into a unity pact with FNLA. The agreement, calling for the establishment of a Supreme Council for the Liberation of Angola, and for a Unified Military Command, had not been implemented before the April 1974 coup in Portugal which dramatically changed the entire situation. On 4 February 1975, Neto returned to Luanda to a mass welcome from almost the entire city. On 11 November 1975, when independence was proclaimed, he became President of the People's Republic of Angola, a post he held until his death on 10 September 1979.

Neto was essentially a private personality for whom the public role of a Head of State seemed burdensome. His inclination was to the world of ideas and intellectual pursuits, and in his lifetime he deservedly won international acclaim for his poetry. His poems, many of which were written in and smuggled out of prisons, are the best known of Angolan poetry and form the basis of popular songs and political mobilisation both nationally and internationally. His work has appeared in many editions and languages, including English, Chinese, French, Italian, Romanian, Russian, Serbo-Croat, Spanish and Vietnamese.

But overriding these individual pursuits and desires was the compelling sense of duty to his country and people. It was this that propelled him from his student days in Portugal through his medical work in Luanda, the difficult days of the armed liberation struggle and finally to the victory that was consummated with the proclamation of the People's Republic of Angola. His intellectual strength guided the guerrillas in the armed struggle against Portuguese colonialism and the soldiers of the post-independence Angolan armed forces who successfully fought against South African expeditionary forces that had entered Angola to assist UNITA and FNLA, which had been defeated in their attempts to challenge, militarily, the ascendancy of the MPLA.■

Neway, G. (1924-60)

NEWAY, Girmame (1924-60).

ETHIOPIAN politician, Governor-General of Harar Province, a man of great scholarship, he identified Ethiopia's development problems at the time with the feudal system of government. He was a leading theorist of the movement for social and political change. In 1960 he and his brother, Brigadier-General Mengistu Neway (q.v.) of the Imperial Guard, led an abortive coup against Emperor Haile Selassie I (q.v.); though they failed, their ideals inspired the generation that finally ended Ethiopia's feudal rule in 1974.

Girmame Neway was born in 1924 at Laketch where his father was Dean of St. George's Cathedral in the Ethiopian capital. His mother, a great-grandchild of Dejazmatch Girmame, named him after her illustrious ancestor who was adviser to the ruler of Shoa, Sahle Mariam, who later became Emperor Menelik II (q.v.) of the Ethiopian Empire. Unlike his brother Mengistu, whose early military career took him to exile with the Ethiopian army during the Italian invasion, Girmame spent his childhood in occupied Addis Ababa. He attended the Tafari Makonnen School and the Haile Selassie I Secondary School from where he was sponsored, with four others, by Crown Prince Asfa Wossen to study in America. Girmame read Politics at the universities of Wisconsin and Columbia. At the latter he presented a thesis, entitled *The Impact of the White Setlement Policy in Kenya*, for his Master's degree.

During that time Girmame was active

in student affairs, being President of the Ethiopian Students' Association of America, a regular contributor to the *Ethiopian Student News*, and an ardent exponent of pan-Africanism which he espoused in writings as well as in speeches. He shared the ideas of pan-African unity with similarly minded African students in America and that country's Black intellectuals and politicians.

His further studies there were interrupted in 1954 when he was recalled by the Addis Ababa government to join its service. Eager to serve his country and clearly aware of the challenge in the building of a new society, he returned to take a post at the Ministry of the Interior. He worked hard there, dedicating himself to the problems of poverty and of how best and quickly reforms could be effected. But soon he became disillusioned with the bureaucracy and with the self-seeking officials and the small group of aristocratic landowners who dominated the government and held office only because of their loyalty to Emperor Haile Selassie. He admired and respected the Emperor's personal political skill and reformative zeal, just as much as he disapproved of the corruption and indifference of the officials who advised him. Girmame Neway began to explore ways of exerting pressure on the Emperor to institute social and economic reforms.

Towards the end of 1955, he and fellow former students of the Haile Selassie Secondary School formed the institution's *alumni* association as a forum for persuading the Emperor to initiate reform. Girmame Neway was elected its first President. The Former Students' Association soon grew to include many Ethiopians who had studied abroad and others drawn from the University College of Addis Ababa and the Church, and it became known as the Union of the National Church. Their meetings and the speeches of members like Girmame, especially in the spheres of land tenure and education, caused disquiet in Court circles, and the organisation soon suffered degeneration partly because of internal divisions encouraged by the authorities and partly because of fear of intimidation.

Girmame himself fell foul of the regime and was posted to Walamo in the Sidamo Province as Governor. There, as before, he concerned himself with the plight of the underdog whose conditions he set out to improve. He built several schools, dug water-

holes and encouraged the use of modern storage methods for grain, all financed by contributions extorted from the rich landowners and nobility. To the poor peasants he allotted unutilised land for cultivation, which earned him the dislike of the aristocracy who protested to the Emperor. He was recalled to Addis Ababa to answer before the Emperor; Girmame Neway replied that he allocated the land because "the people had nothing to eat because they had no land".

He was withdrawn from Walamo and sent to Jijigga, capital of the Harar Province. As the Governor-General of the Harar Province he devoted his energies to providing clinics and waterholes. He made frequent visits to Addis Ababa to request funds and equipment, but met with marginal success. During one of these trips in December 1960, while Emperor Haile Selassie was on a state visit to Brazil, he and his brother Mengistu made a bid to overthrow the imperial government. With the support of progressive officers in the army and members of the government, they rounded up several leading ministers, forming a 25-man Council of the Revolution which proclaimed Crown Prince Asfa Wossen the King and Head of State in place of Emperor Haile Selassie. The coup failed, crushed by loyal forces, and its ringleaders were executed for treason. As they fled into the mountains Girmame shot Mengistu and later committed suicide. However Mengistu survived, was captured, tried and hanged on the Emperor's order, outside St. George's Cathedral in the capital, Addis Ababa.

Many years later, in 1974, the ideals and aspirations of the Neway brothers were effected by the regime of the Provisional Military Administration Council, later named the Derg and now led by Lt-Colonel Mengistu Haile Mariam, which overthrew the imperial government of Emperor Haile Selassie. ■

Neway, M. (1919-61)

NEWAY, Brigadier-General Mengistu (1919-61).

ETHIOPIAN military officer; the Commander of the Imperial Guard who in

December 1960 turned the guns of the royal army on Emperor Haile Selassie 1 (q.v.) and his regime in a revolt against the excesses of the feudal order.

Mengistu Neway and his brother, Girmame (q.v.), a forceful exponent of the movement for social and political change, led the 1960 abortive coup that was the first serious internal challenge to the Emperor's authority, and the beginning of fierce criticism and rebellion that culminated in the coup of 1974. Though they themselves died as a result they are revered in post-feudal Ethiopia as heroes of the Revolution which ended the Solomonic dynasty with the deposition of Haile Selassie in 1974.

The Neway brothers hailed from a family of considerable influence in Moja in the Shoa Province. Aleka Neway, their father, was Dean of St. George's Cathedral at Laketch. Their mother's family had a long association with Ethiopian monarchs, being the great-grandchild of Dejazmatch Girmame who served as adviser to Emperor Menelik II (q.v.) when he ruled Shoa as Sahle Mariam. Thus Dejazmatch Girmame, whom Mengistu's brother was named after, had been instrumental in Ethiopia's past efforts to maintain its independence, culminating in the famous decisive 1896 Battle of Adowa in which an Italian military expedition was defeated. Mengistu himself was old enough to participate in the second war (1935-41) against the Italians, again successfully repelled by the Ethiopians.

He was born in 1919 and entered the army, after formal education, and training at the Holeta Academy for cadets. Soon the Italians invaded and occupied Ethiopia, and Mengistu went into exile with Emperor Haile Selassie and the imperial army. He spent his exile in Sudan where he underwent further military training at the Soba Academy in Khartoum. With the war against the Italians gaining momentum he joined the Ethiopian Patriot forces in the campaign to dislodge the invaders. Remarkably handsome, young and able, he was soon recognised by his superiors.

Thus when his country's independence was restored in 1941 Mengistu was among the Patriot officers who became Emperor Haile Selassie's confidants. He was made Colonel and training-officer of the Imperial Guard, a feudal force which he built into a modern fighting unit. He used the Guard to suppress a revolt against the

Emperor in 1951, after which he was made its Commander (1955) and promoted Brigadier-General in 1956. By that time he had earned a reputation as an able officer, having commanded the Ethiopian contingent, under UN auspices, in the Korean War (1950-53).

Meanwhile his brother Girmame had started to agitate for political and social reforms, to redress the growing inequality between the ruling aristocracy and the Ethiopian peasant society. There were regular weekly luncheon meetings at Mengistu's house where Mengistu espoused his radical ideals of the new society. Mengistu and his other guests seemed to have been influenced by these and, together, they planned to overthrow the regime of Haile Selassie.

The coup, executed on 13 December 1960 while the Emperor was on a state visit to Brazil, was crushed on 16 December by loyal troops, aided by the USA. The plotters took control of Addis Ababa and proclaimed a Council of the Revolution with Crown Prince Asfa Wossen as Head of State and King of Ethiopia, in place of the absent Emperor. But by the next day a counter-revolution had been organised; it engaged the plotters in a decisive battle which lasted through the 15 and 16 December and left several leading members of the government dead. Some of the coup leaders were killed in the battle of Addis Ababa; but Mengistu and his brother fled the capital into the hills. They were about to be captured on 24 December when Girmame shot and seriously wounded his brother before committing suicide.

Mengistu survived his wounds to be tried for, among other charges, "armed uprising" and "killing dignitaries". His trial drew widespread interest inside and outside Ethiopia, which gave the General a ready ear for his grievances. He conducted himself with utmost dignity at the proceedings, taking responsibility for almost everything. He spoke of the backwardness of Ethiopia, the inefficiency of the feudal administration, maldistribution of land and the resulting misery of the peasants, and the indifference of the ruling aristocracy including the Emperor whom, Mengistu said, had not acted on the countless complaints made to him repeatedly by aggrieved Ethiopians. At the end he told the Court: "I shall not appeal, and am quite satisfied ... I did all this for the sake of the Ethiopian people and pray that God soon gives true judgement to the

Ethiopian People." He was sentenced to death and, stripped of his rank and decorations, hanged in public in Addis Ababa on 30 March 1961.

Soon after his execution a succession of rebellions and crises, by senior military officers as well as students and intellectuals, became the political feature in Ethiopia. And Ethiopians, the Emperor and his citizens alike, knew then that a cause had not only been defined for their country but had also acquired an irrevocable dimension. They knew, too, that the new political awakening had found its heroes in the Neway brothers; and thus it was they who inspired the 1974 Revolution which deposed Emperor Haile Selassie and ended Ethiopian monarchical tradition.■

R.G. Ngala

Ngala, R.G.(1922-72)

NGALA, Ronald Gideon (1922-72).

KENYAN politician. He was born in 1922 in Mombasa, Kenya, and was educated at Kaloleni School, Kilifi, and Alliance High School, Kikuyu (near Nairobi), and then at Makerere College, Kampala, where he qualified as a teacher. He went to teach at his old school at Kaloleni in 1946, after which he was appointed headmaster of Buxton School, Mombasa in 1952. On his return from Britain, where he attended a short course at Redland College, Bristol, he became Inspector of Schools in the Mombasa area. Ngala's debut in politics came in 1953 when he was made a member of the Mombasa African Advisory Council.

The following year he became a member of the Mombasa Municipal Board. In March 1957 he was elected to represent the Coast Rural constituency under the Lyttleton Constitution which was the first colonial constitution to allow Africans direct elections to the Legislative Council (Legco). One of the original eight African elected members, he won wide public esteem for his personal qualities and thorough commitment to African self-government.

In 1957 Ngala was among those Kenyans who journeyed to London to demand a more liberal constitution for their country.

Unable to wring further constitutional reforms from Britain, Ngala returned to Kenya a disenchanted politician. He was increasingly at loggerheads with the leadership of the African members of Legco.

He was instrumental in the formation of the multi-racial Kenya National Party, an organisation he stuck to even when other popular nationalists broke away to found the Kenya Independence Movement. It was, nevertheless, a mark of his stature in independence politics that when the two parties created a common front for another constitutional conference in London, Ngala was elected its chairman. The move was also designed to remove the wedge that was threatening to tear the African body politic apart. At the conclusion of the constitutional conference, however, Ngala seemed more than ever before the "dissident" he had become. Shortly after his return from London he caused a political shock by forming the Kenya African Democratic Union (KADU).

It was Ngala's reply to the Kenya African National Union (KANU) which had been recently set up by his political rivals, who saw the way to Kenya's independence in terms different from those envisaged by

Ngala. Unknown to Ngala KANU, which included such political heroes of the day as Oginga Odinga, Tom Mboya (q.v.) and James Gichuru (q.v.), was to emerge victorious in the power struggle that was about to ensue.

Not unexpectedly, however, given the immense popularity he commanded in his home, Ngala was overwhelmingly elected for Kilifi in the first general elections to provide for an African majority rule in Legco in February 1961. His party KADU fared poorly, winning only 11 seats against KANU's 18.

Paradoxically Ngala, who had briefly served as Minister of Labour in the outgoing government, resigned his post after the elections in protest at the British refusal to release Jomo Kenyatta (q.v.) from detention. This despite the fact that, even in jail, Kenyatta was known to favour KANU's programmes for the country's independence. Other biographies have explained Ngala's political paradoxes as in essence a manifestation of his total commitment to African self-government, differing from others only on the means to be used.

He, however, rescinded his decision in March 1961 and joined the new Government as the Leader of Government Business and Minister of Education. In a bid to popularise his party, Ngala claimed responsibility for Kenyatta's release from restriction not long before, the credit for which KANU also claimed.

With Kenyatta's release and his assumption of the presidency of KANU, the stage had been set for the tumultuous political events leading to independence. KADU, despite prolonged peace talks with KANU, remained intransigent. The party demanded a federal constitution for Kenya based on ethnic regionalism. KANU, on the other hand, insisted on a strongly centralised unitary government.

Ngala waged a relentless campaign against KANU, arguing that "Kenyatta's party" was dominated by Kenya's two largest ethnic groups, the Kikuyu and the Luo, and would therefore militate against the interests of the country's other ethnic groups. Further, Ngala claimed that his party was the more moderate of the two and could be trusted with safely midwifing Kenya's independence. KANU sought to counter these arguments by presenting itself as a multi-ethnic movement, and dismissed KADU's fears of domination as unfounded.

Ngala's political philosophy of *Majimbo* (literally "regions" in Kiswahili) suffered its first serious setback when in February 1962, in London, KADU agreed to a compromise plan calling for the formation of a coalition government. In the Government formed in April 1962, although the Cabinet was equally divided between KADU and KANU, and Ngala held the influential post of Minister of Constitutional Affairs and Administration jointly with Kenyatta, differences persisted.

In December 1963 Kenya became independent, but not before KADU was defeated by KANU in the general elections of March of the same year. KADU's defeat was largely due to KANU's popularity, but also to its having espoused what may be described as a narrow nationalism, and it failed to convince the electorate of its longer term interest. The party was dissolved in November 1964 "in the interests of national unity" and most of its members in Parliament, including Ngala, crossed the floor to join the Government and KANU.

Ngala, a keen sports promoter in the country, held the post of Minister of Co-operatives and Social Services. He was later made Minister of Power and Communications and was holding this portfolio when he died tragically in a car accident near the Kenyan capital on Christmas Eve, 1972. His name will always be associated with his country's politics, for both his independent views and pragmatism.∎

Ngcebetsha, C.C. (1909-77)

NGCEBETSHA, Charlton Cezani (1909-77).

ZIMBABWEAN politician, the first Secretary-General of the African National Council (ANC). He was born on 18 February 1909 in Butterworth in the Transkei, South Africa, into a leading Fingo family. His parents were teachers, a profession which Ngcebetsha was later to follow. He attended Lovedale mission in Alice in the Cape Province and trained for a teacher's diploma. After joining the Presbyterian Church he was chosen as part of a group to go to Rhodesia (now Zimbabwe) to teach. He was assigned to the Ntabasinduna Presbyterian Church Mission School (later changed to the David Livingstone Memorial Mission) where he taught for some years before joining the Department of Native Affairs. One of Ngcebetsha's pupils at school was William Henry Kona who later became his colleague in the nationalist struggle for Zimbabwe's independence and the deputy national chairman of the ANC.

Before entering into politics in the 1940s Ngcebetsha established himself in private business in Mzilikaze township in Bulawayo where he ran a grocery store. Between 1953 and 1965 he was editor of the *African Home News*, as well as being an active official in the football organisation based in Bulawayo. He was also active in civic and voluntary organisations, becoming chairman of the Township Advisory Board and of the African Welfare Society for a number of years.

Though he had been active in politics as a member of the old African National Congress then led by the Reverend Thompson Douglas Samkange (1887-1956), his influence was not felt until the formation of the Zimbabwe African People's Union (ZAPU) which he served as a national councillor from 1962. Following the split within ZAPU in 1963, he sided with the group which later formed the People's Caretaker Council (PCC). He however later became involved in the deliberations to bring about a united front, and when ZAPU and ZANU merged on 16 December 1971 as the African National Council, Ngcebetsha was elected its first Secretary-General. He was arrested by the Smith regime in early 1972 and interned until November 1975. Ngcebetsha died two years later, on 11 March 1977 in Bulawayo. ∎

P. Ngendandumwe

Ngendandumwe, P. (1930-65)

NGENDANDUMWE, Pierre (1930-65).

BURUNDIAN politician, deputy Prime Minister and Minister of Finance. He was born in 1930 of a well-known Hutu family in Ngozi province. He was educated in Catholic schools and the University of Lovanium in Leopoldville (Kinshasa), where he obtained a degree in administration and political science. On returning to Burundi he took up a post as assistant territorial administrator in the colonial administration.

Ngendandumwe's political career began with the founding by Prince Louis Rwagasore (q.v.) of the *Parti de l'Unité et du Progrès National* (UPRONA) in 1959, for he soon became one of Rwagasore's close associates. In the 1961 Government of national union led by Rwagasore, Ngendandumwe served as Minister of Finance. Following the assassination of Rwagasore in October 1961, André Muhirwa became Prime Minister and in 1962 Ngendandumwe was appointed both deputy Prime Minister and Minister of Finance. Muhirwa resigned in June 1963, at the request of Mwami (King) Mwambutsa IV, the Head of State, who was disturbed by the growing hostility towards Muhirwa on the part of Hutu members of the Government and Parliament.

Mwami Mwambutsa's invitation to Ngendandumwe to form a government, in

June 1963, was an attempt to prevent overt conflict between Burundi's opposing ethnic and political forces. Ngendandumwe's Government, formed in June 1963, and whose slogan was "bread and peace", had a balanced ethnic composition. It was Burundi's recognition of the People's Republic of China, allegedly engineered by the Tutsi members of the government, that led Mwami Mwambutsa to request Ngendandumwe's resignation in April 1964, after less than 10 months in office. This followed diplomatic pressure on the part of the Belgians and the Americans against allowing the Chinese to establish an embassy in Bujumbura.

The King recalled Ngendandumwe, however, and invited him to form another government on 11 January 1965, but on 15 January four days later, he was assassinated as he was leaving the hospital, where his wife was in maternity confinement after the birth of a son. ■

Ngouabi, M. (1938-77)

NGOUABI, Major Marien (1938-77).

CONGOLESE soldier and statesman. He was born in 1938 in Ombele near Fort Rousset in northern Congo. After finishing his primary and secondary education he joined the Congolese army in 1960 and trained at the Coetquidan Inter-Services School before attending courses in Strasbourg and at the St. Cyr Military Academy, France, where he graduated in 1962.

He returned to the Congo the same year and was commissioned as a second lieutenant and placed in charge of the Pointe Noire garrison in the south of the country. In 1963 Ngouabi was promoted to the rank of captain and relocated to the capital, Brazzaville, to take charge of the newly-established paratroop battalion which he commanded for five years.

Between 1963 and 1966 Ngouabi developed his political ideas which encompassed Marxist-Leninist principles. During the time he also built up comradeship with fellow officers of similar political leaning – an alliance which led to the army mutiny of June 1966. Captain Ngouabi was later demo-

ted following his refusal to accept a new military posting and his opposition to a Government proposal to incorporate the army in the militia, though the army-militia proposal was subsequently dropped. Again, in July 1968, Ngouabi's arrest by President Massemba-Debat (q.v.) was preceded by an

Major M. Ngouabi

army rebellion and after a few days of unrest in the capital, President Massemba-Debat emerged with Ngouabi who had been promoted Chief of Staff.

On 4 September 1968 the Massemba-Debat regime fell, succeeded by the Revolutionary Council headed by Ngouabi, now elevated to the rank of major, and later President of the People's Republic of the Congo. From his personal analysis of his predecessor's downfall, the new head of state said that only a more progressive party adhering to the principles of Marxism-Leninism could provide motivation for building a truly socialist and strong Congo. On 31

December 1969 President Ngouabi dissolved the *Mouvement National de la Révolution* (MNR) formed by Massemba-Debat in 1964, and replaced it with the *Parti Congolais du Travail* (PCT) to "ensure with fierce jealousy the fruits of the revolution". In 1970 a new constitution was drawn up and its massive acceptance in a referendum in 1973 formally established the country's new socialist status and the PCT as the sole legal political party, whose leader also had to be the President of the Republic.

To win wider support from the population after three unsuccessful coup attempts (1969, 1970 and 1972), President Ngouabi began to implement some of the radical measures he had preached, and convened extraordinary sessions of the PCT congress to consult party and public opinion about the policies of the Government. In 1972 he introduced controls on the repatriation of profits of foreign businesses and took over France-Cable and the relay station of Free French Radio in Brazzaville.

Two years later he nationalised all foreign oil distributing companies, with the exception of Agip, the Italian company in which the Congolese Government had a 50 per cent share. But, after a quarrel with the company in 1975, President Ngouabi took over Agip's interests in the country without compensation. A presidential decree to the effect, issued on 12 April stated that Agip's shares, goods and property had been taken over by the state-owned oil company, Hydro-Congo. Earlier, US oil interests in the country had been acquired, followed by a bitter controversy which culminated in the withdrawal of tariff preference granted by America to the Congo.

In 1972 the Government had also abolished the bride-price, becoming the first Congolese authority to look at a hitherto undiscussed family taboo in relation to political ideology.

Under President Ngouabi, the Congolese armed forces became one of the most politicised armies on the African continent. The revived youth wing of the PCT, *Union de la Jeunesse Socialiste du Congo* (UJSC), was absorbed into the regular army, the civil defence corps, the gendarmerie and the police force. Apart from providing national security, the new force's duties included carrying out the "political tasks of the revolution" as well as contributing to Congo's construction and production.

Following the adoption of the Constitution after the 1973 referendum, a People's National Assembly was established and an office of Head of Government, centred on the Prime Minister, created. President Ngouabi made Henri Lopes the first incumbent and re-appointed him in January 1975, but he was replaced in December by Major Louis-Sylvain Goma. On 9 January 1975 Ngouabi was re-elected for a second term of office as President and Chairman of the PCT. In his swearing-in speech, he promised "to be guided by Marxist-Leninist principles, to defend the stature of the party and constitution and to devote all my strength to the triumph of the Congolese people's proletarian ideals in work, democracy and peace".

A brilliant and articulate theoretician, his skill at assimilating the revolutionary style of Brazzaville into a static body politic won him admiration at home and abroad. He was a strategist whose ideology, though most often submerged by his revolutionary harangues, never clouded his pragmatism, as shown in his relations with Congo's neighbours and to France.

On 18 March 1977 President Ngouabi was assassinated in Brazzaville. Former President Massemba-Debat and four others were later executed for his death. His successor, Colonel Yhombi-Opango, declared a full month of national mourning in the wake of the assassination.■

Ngoyi, L.M. (1911-80)

NGOYI, Lilian Masediba (1911-80).

SOUTH AFRICAN politician; she was a staunch anti-apartheid activist and founder member of the Federation of South African Women (FSAW). Born in 1911 in the village of Gamatlala near Pretoria, her primary education at Kilnerton was terminated in Standard Six because her parents could not afford to support her. She then went to work as a trainee nurse, having worked as a domestic servant previously in 1935. She married Ngoyi, a van driver, who died early.

In 1945 Lilian had to take a job in a clothing factory as a machinist until 1956

L.M. Ngoyi

Experiencing the conditions under which Black people work and the exploitative wages, she joined the Garment Workers Union and later became one of its important branch leaders who vigorously organised the workers to struggle against destitution and humiliation.

In September 1952 Lilian became a member of the African National Congress (ANC), taking part in the 1952 Defiance Campaign against the race laws; her contribution to the campaign was to defy the apartheid laws by using "Whites Only" post office facilities, for which she was arrested and given a prison sentence. Her organisational ability and oratory soon won her rapid recognition and she was duly elected the President of the ANC Women's League, later becoming the first woman to be elected to the ANC National Executive Committee in December 1956. Earlier, in 1954, when the Federation of South African Women was formed, Lilian was appointed one of its National Vice-Presidents. In August 1956 she became the President of the organisation, a post she held until her death in 1980. She represented the FSAW at the conference of the Women's International Democratic Federation in Europe in 1955. After the conference she visited Russia, China and other Eastern bloc countries as a guest of the authorities.

Back home she led the mass demonstration against the legislation that compels African women to carry passes. This is commonly known as the "women's anti-pass demonstration", which in 1956 culminated in one of the largest demonstrations in South African history; Lilian led her followers to a mass rally at the Union Buildings in Pretoria. In December of that year she was arrested and charged with high treason, but with the other main accused she was acquitted in March 1961, after having served five months in prison during the 1960 State of Emergency. She spent 71 days of that prison term in solitary confinement.

Influential and outspoken critic of the apartheid regime, she was served with banning orders in October 1962 and restricted to her Orlando home near Johannesburg. She was forbidden to be active in public. Her banning orders were lifted in 1972, but renewed again for a further five-year period in 1975. During her temporary release in 1972 she said in an interview with the South African *Drum* magazine that "My spirits have not been dampened. This girl is still her old self if not more mature after the experiences. I am looking forward to the day when my children will share in the wealth of our lovely South Africa".

Lilian's 1975 banning orders confined her to her home, where she died on 12 March 1980. ■

Nhlapo, J.M. (1904-57)

NHLAPO, Jacob Mfaniselwa (1904-57).

SOUTH AFRICAN educationist and journalist, editor of the *Bantu World* (later known as the *World*) which he served from 1953 until his death three years later. He was born in 1904 in Reitz in the Orange Free State, South Africa, the son of a Methodist family whose early association with the missionaries influenced Nhlapo's interest in education. After some time at the Bensonvale Institution he went to Lovedale,

J.M. Nhlapo

district in the Western Transvaal. He relinquished the position in 1940 following his appointment as principal of Wilberforce Institute in Evaton, a comprehensive Mission institute consisting of a primary school, a secondary school and a department where church ministers were trained.

It was during his tenure at Evaton that Nhlapo evinced interests in the politics of the African National Congress (ANC). He joined the movement and was later elected to its National Executive Committee as Director of Information. An untiring activist who combined his teaching with his work with the ANC, which included the drafting of some of its important petitions in the 1940s and early 1950s, Nhlapo was also active in the Transvaal African Teachers Association (TATA) until 1950 when he and other senior members of the association were edged out of its leadership as a result of internal disagreements.

Between 1951 and 1952 he was a visiting lecturer at Selly Oak College in Birmingham in England. Still unsettled in his academic pursuits, he entered journalism in 1953 as editor of the *Abantu Batho* which later became the *Bantu World*. The newspaper which in its time became the most influential African organ in South Africa, had its name changed to the *World*. Nhlapo retained its editorship until his death in 1957 at the age of 53. ■

a reputable mission institute in Alice in the Cape Province, where he obtained a teacher's diploma. He gained the BA degree in 1936 through private studies, a diploma in Bantu studies from the University of South Africa, and a doctorate degree in psychology. Nhlapo also obtained the LLB and a doctorate in jurisprudence through correspondence courses in America.

Meanwhile he had been teaching at schools in the Orange Free State where he also took an active part in Church affairs as a member of the provincial Orange Free State Synod. He became headmaster of Moroka Primary School in the Orange Free State, and later went to become the first headmaster of the newly established Methodist Boistshoko Institution in the Ventersdorp

Nico, "Docteur" (1939-85)

NICO, "Docteur" (1939-85).

ZAIREAN musician, a prominent guitarist of the 1960s and 1970s whose Orchestre African Fiesta became one of the most famous in the area of African popular music. His work still has great influence on many of the young musicians of today's Africa as well as those outside the continent.

He was born Nicolas Kasanda on 7 July 1939, in the Kasai Province of Zaire into a family of musicians. He demonstrated exceptional musical talent in his early years. But "Docteur Nico", as he later became known after establishing himself, remem bered too the external influence on him; he was to recall the impact of the great musicians that developed the modern dance music of Zaire that swept through Africa as 'Congo music': Wendo, the popular singer and guitarist of the 1940s and 1950s; Jhimmy, a guitarist; and the great Kabasele (Kallé), a vocalist and later collaborator of Nico in the seminal group African Jazz, were these pioneers and Nico's mentors. He paid tribute to them in an album 'Hommage au Grand Kallé'.

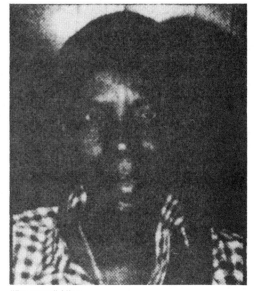

"Docteur" Nico

It was when Nico played with Kabasele and the African Jazz group in Brussels in 1960 that he got the nickname "docteur". The band whose current hit was Independence Cha Cha, was invited to entertain the delegates to the round table conference on independence for Zaire (then the Belgian Congo). The Belgian radio announcer dubbed Nico "docteur" because of his virtuosity with the guitar.

Nico's Orchestre African Fiesta evolved from the African Jazz group to become one of the most popular bands to emerge from Kinshasa onto the African music stage in the 1960s and dominated the scene for another decade. With its Belgian recording company collapsing and Nico's own problem (he suffered from a blood disorder which had troubled him for a long

time), the band's influence diminished. By the early 1980s however Nico was making a comeback, producing five albums between 1983 and the time of his death.

His later releases were waxed on the Africa New Sound Label, a Togolese recording company with major distribution outlets in Africa. Still aiming for wider exposure for his music, Nico made his first American release in 1985 through the African Music Gallery. That was his last personally supervised produced work, but by the time of his death in November 1985 in Brussels where he was being treated, he had recorded enough material for up to a dozen albums. Nico thus left a musical legacy for his numerous fans inside and outside Africa who had held and still hold him in great reverence as one of Africa's most brilliant artists this century. ∎

N'Jie, A.B. (1904-82)

N'JIE, Alhaji Alieu Badara (1904-82).

GAMBIAN politician and civil servant who in 1959 was appointed his country's first Registrar of the Supreme Court. He was hardworking, committed and able, all of which contributed to making him one of the best administrators in the Government of his time.

Of a prominent Wolof family, N'jie was born in 1904 in Banjul, formerly Bathurst, and attended the Stanley Street Methodist Primary School from 1917 to 1922. Although he had been influenced early in life by Islam he continued his education at mission schools, entering the renowned Wesleyan Boys High School in the Gambian capital in 1922 and completing his postprimary education there in 1925.

Like many of his contemporaries among the small educated elite in Banjul, N'jie entered the Colonial Civil Service in the then British colony of The Gambia in 1925. Soon he began to show the exemplary qualities that were to become the traits of his 33 years in the Service. He held various senior posts including that of Municipal Counsellor of Banjul. He helped form Gambia's first political party, the Democratic

Party, in February 1951, which merged with the Moslem Congress Party (MCP) in 1960 to become the Democratic Congress Alliance, but it lost the elections of that year to Dawda Jawara's People's Progressive Party. Though a devout Moslem, N'jie had opposed the MCP when it was formed in 1951; he saw it*as divisive.

A.B. N'jie

He retired in 1958 from the Public Service where he had achieved the distinction of being the first Wolof to head a Government department. He was also the first Moslem to have risen to prominence in the Public Service. He did not, however, remain long outside the Government, in 1959 Alhaji Alieu N'jie was recalled from retirement and made Registrar of the Supreme Court.

Despite his party's electoral defeat Alhaji Alieu N'jie was brought into the Government. He served successively as Minister of Works and Services, Minister of External Affairs as well as Resident Minister in Dakar, Senegal, before being appointed Minister of State in the President's Office in 1970. Between 1977 and 1978 he was Vice-President of the country.

Alhaji Alieu N'jie died in April 1982 when the helicopter in which he was travelling with President Jawara crashed near Brikama, The Gambia. He was the only casualty out of the 16 people in the plane. ■

N'jie, M. M. (c.1913-90)

N'JIE, Momodou Musa (c.1913-90).

GAMBIAN businessman. He became a legendary business operator after starting out humbly and with no modern-style education. He was of a Fula cattle-rearing family at Basse, and was born probably as early as 1908, the exact date being unknown. He never learned to write but signed cheques besides placing his thumbprint when he developed his business activities. He began, after working for a while with his father, as an assistant in a Lebanese trader's shop.

He then worked with the leading Lebanese traders in The Gambia, the Madi family, but after 1940 he left them and did business on his own. He moved to the capital, Bathurst (now Banjul), in 1948, and began buying property and trading in commodities. Successfully challenging the Lebanese, he became the leading market dealer in sugar, rice, flour, cement (this coming from neighbouring Senegal), and other goods. He was said to buy rice on credit and resell it at 100 per cent profit to repay the purchase price. His credit was excellent and the Bank of West Africa regarded him as a very good

M.M. N'jie

customer. He himself gave credit to others, and acted as a business agent for other Gambians.

He travelled widely in West Africa and traded across borders easily. He did plenty of currency dealing, involving CFA francs. At one time, the British colonial authorities suspected him of forgery of currency notes, but a raid on his home in 1952 confounded the suspicion. He did not enter groundnut buying, but was involved in the long-distance cattle trade. He was said to be involved in diamond dealing, but denied it in an interview in the 1960s. He once denied the suggestion that he was the richest man in The Gambia, but it was commonly believed that he was. He had expensive properties in the capital and elsewhere—half of all the city centres in the country, it was estimated.

Momodou Musa N'Jie went on the Pilgrimage in 1951, and later paid for many relatives and friends to go to Mecca; he built mosques and schools. He had four wives, 18 sons and 20 daughters; although himself an ardent traditionalist, he had his children educated on Western lines as he had not been, and many obtained high academic qualifications.

In politics he took no active part himself, but was allied at first with P.S. N'Jie, who defended him as a lawyer, and then with the Peoples Progressive Party (PPP). That party, which took The Gambia into independence in 1965, thus benefited from his widespread business network, and through his influence an MP in the Basse area, Momodou Modi Cham (who had been raised as a son by Musa N'Jie) crossed over from P.S. N'Jie's United Party to the PPP. At independence in 1965 Musa N'Jie donated £1,000 (at that time a considerable sum) to his country. His daughter Chilel married President Dawda Jawara. N'Jie died in London on 4 July 1990, leaving a large fortune. ■

Njoku, E. (1917-74)

NJOKU, Professor Eni (1917-74).

NIGERIAN educationist and politician. He was born on 6 November 1917 in

Ebem, Ohafia in Imo State, Nigeria, and was educated at Ebem Primary School which he entered in 1922 and at the Hope Waddell Training Institute in Calabar from 1933 to 1936. The next year saw him at the Yaba

Prof. E. Njoku

Higher College in Lagos, then Nigeria's highest educational institution. He went to read Botany at the University of Manchester in England, where he graduated with first class honours in 1947, and remained there for an MA degree in 1948. He obtained a doctorate in 1954 from the University of London.

Njoku returned to Nigeria to take up teaching at the University of Ibadan, first as a lecturer, then senior lecturer and later professor, head of department and Dean of the Faculty of Science, holding the latter post from 1959 to 1962. In 1956 he was appointed chairman of the Electricity Corporation of Nigeria. He relinquished both offices in 1962 to assume a new appointment as the first Vice-Chancellor of the University of Lagos. He resigned in 1965, after a major crisis over his proposed re-appointment, to become visiting professor at the Michigan State University, USA. In 1966 he was made Vice-Chancellor of the University of Nigeria, Nsukka, where he was when the Civil War broke out in 1967. Njoku was deeply affected by the dilemma posed by the events which led to the war between the secessionist Ibo community of which he was a member and the Federal authority which he had served as a Nigerian.

As a former parliamentarian and central government Minister of Mines and Power between 1952 and 1953, he was first elected to the Eastern House of Assembly, then to the Federal House of Representatives where he served in the Balewa administration. He was also a member of the Senate, Nigeria's upper chamber in the federal legislature from 1960 to 1961.

The outbreak of the hostilities convinced him that the basis for Nigerian unity had been wrecked and he joined the Biafran cause, becoming a prominent member of the breakaway regime. Yet his involvement did not cloud his dedication to a peaceful solution in pursuit of which he led many delegations to several African and overseas countries. At the end of the war he declined offers of posts abroad and remained in Nigeria where he played an important part in reconstruction and reconciliation. He returned to his professorship of Botany at the University of Nigeria.

Under his leadership both the Universities of Lagos and Nigeria became outstanding not only in Africa but internationally. His capacity for work led to various academic engagements in and outside Nigeria. He was a member of the Federal Scholarship Board, and of the University of Ibadan Council while, at the same time, serving on the Boards of the Commonwealth Scientific Committee, the United Nations Advisory Committee on the Application of Science and Technology, and the UNESCO Advisory Committee on Natural Sciences. Njoku was also on the Councils of the Universities of Zambia and Zaire. He was a fellow of the Science Association of Nigeria and wrote several books and articles in international professional journals.

In 1964 he received the honorary Doctor of Science Degree from the University of Nigeria; in 1966 Michigan State University conferred on him an honorary Doctor of Law Degree, and in 1973 he was awarded an honorary Doctor of Science Degree by the University of Lagos. He died in London, where he had been receiving medical treatment, on 22 December 1974.■

Njoku, R.A.(1915-77)

NJOKU, Raymond Amanze (1915-77).

NIGERIAN lawyer and politician. He was born in August 1915 in Emekuku in Owerri, to the family of Chief Njoku Ndudu of Emekuku. He had his primary education at Our Lady's School in Emekuku from 1922 to 1929 and attended the Ahiara Catholic Secondary School from 1929 to 1936, before proceeding to St. Charles College, Onitsha, where he won the Buckley Prize while

R.A. Njoku

training as a teacher. In 1939 he was appointed tutor at St. Charles College, resigning in 1943 to join the staff of St. Gregory's College, Lagos. He left Nigeria the same year to read Law at the University of London and was called to the Bar at the Middle Temple in 1947.

Returning to Nigeria in 1947 Njoku went into private legal practice in Aba where he also took an active part in the politics of the district. From 1952 to 1954 he was chairman of the Aba Community League; he joined the National Council of Nigerian Citizens (NCNC) in 1952 and became chairman of the Eastern Region Working Committee of the party. Njoku was unsuccessful in his first attempt to get elected to the then Eastern House of Assembly in 1951 but his fortunes improved three years later when he became member for Owerri Division in the regional chamber. In 1951 he was elected to the Nigeria Legislative Council in Lagos where he was made Minister of Commerce and Industry in the Federal Council of Ministers.

In 1955 he became the Federal Minister of Trade and Industry, followed in September of the next year with the portfolio of Transport. In October 1955 Njoku was elected Second National Vice-President of the NCNC. Following his re-election at the eve-of-independence federal polls of 1959, Njoku was re-appointed Minister of Transport in the Northern People's Congress (NPC) and NCNC coalition government under Prime Minister Abubakar Tafawa Balewa (q.v.). In 1964 he was appointed Minister of Communications and Aviation, a post he held until the government was overthrown in a military coup on 15 January 1966. A much respected and likeable parliamentarian, he was Vice-Chairman of the Commonwealth Parliamentary Association. He returned to legal practice in 1966 when the new military administration suspended political activities in the country. He died on 21 September 1977.

Njoku was a devout Catholic whose services to the church included his chairmanship of the National Catholic Laity Council of Nigeria. He was honoured by Pope John XXIII with the Knight Grand Cross of the Order of St. Gregory the Great. He was also decorated by the Nigerian government with the national honour of Commander of the Federal Republic of Nigeria, for his outstanding services to the country. ∎

Njoya (c.1875-1933)

NJOYA, Ibrahim, Sultan of Bamoun (c.1875-1933).

CAMEROONIAN traditional ruler, remembered for launching his own religion and an alphabet for the Bamoun language. He was the 16th Sultan of the state of Bamoun, powerful for several centuries but in the 19th century engaged in conflicts with Fulani states to the north. Sultan Nsangou died in 1888 and his son, Njoya, took over the government, after two years' regency by his mother, in 1890.

In the 1890s the German colonisers of Cameroon encountered the Bamoun kingdom and its ruler Njoya, who co-operated with them as long as he was allowed to retain some of his power. He was a man of remarkable talents. Having inherited the traditional religion of his people, he came under the influence of German Protestant Mission which reached his capital, Foumban, early in the 20th century; but he then decided to create his own religion, incorporating elements of Christianity, Islam – which was already influential in the area – and the traditional beliefs.

Sultan Ibrahim Njoya

Njoya also invented his own script for his people's language, with 83 letters and 10 numbers. He had a *History of the Customs and Laws of Bamoun* written down in that script; it has been preserved and translated as a major source of historical knowledge of the area. His alphabet was almost the only locally developed one in pre-colonial Africa (the Vai people of Liberia having produced another).

Njoya also built a large palace at Foumban; drew up a list of standard dosages of medicines for use in Bamoun; built a mechanical grain mill; and drew the first maps of Bamoun. Besides the *History* he wrote a compilation of Bamoun legends and stories. He founded a private museum of art and crafts, his people being then and now famous for wood carving, bronze casting and other crafts. The museum still exists and receives many visitors.

When the Germans with whom he had developed close relations were expelled in the 1914-18 war, Njoya attempted to forge an alliance with the British. But his kingdom was added to French Cameroon in 1916. In that year Njoya gave up his own religion and became a Moslem with the name Ibrahim; his people are largely Moslem now.

Such an intelligent and traditionally-minded ruler did not suit the French, who suppressed chieftancy over most of their colonial territories. In 1923 they deposed him and split his state into 17 chieftancies. In 1931 they deported him to Yaounde, where he died on 30 May 1933. But the cultural strength of his state ensured its survival under French rule and it is still an important traditional kingdom under one of Njoya's family.■

Nkrumah, Kwame (1909-72)

NKRUMAH, Dr Kwame Francis Nwia Kofie (1909-72).

GHANAIAN statesman, the first President of Ghana, the foremost exponent of African unity and Pan-Africanism, one of the founding fathers of the Organisation of African Unity (OAU) and a leading member of the Non-Aligned Movement. Born on 21 September 1909 at Nkroful, south-western Ghana, he spent eight years of primary school at the Roman Catholic Church School in Half-Assini where his father was a goldsmith. In 1930 he qualified as a teacher at the Government Training College in Accra;

Dr Kwame Nkrumah

he taught there until 1935. He then left for the USA where he graduated in 1939 from Lincoln University, Oxford, Pennsylvania with a major in economics and sociology. He also studied theology and obtained post graduate degrees in education and philo sophy from the University of Pennsylvania in Philadelphia.

He was later appointed lecturer in Political Science at Lincoln University where he was also elected President of the African Students Organisation of America and Canada. In June 1945 he went to study at the London School of Economics and Politi cal Science and to read law at Gray's Inn. H was elected Vice-President of the West African Students Union and in October c the same year was elected co-Secretary of the Fifth Pan-African Conference held at Manchester, England.

The Pan-African movement inspired many future leaders of Africa, including Nkrumah, to champion the cause of freedom and independence on the continent. At the Manchester Conference he largely wrote the agreed "Declaration to the peoples of the colonies", calling on them to organise to end colonial rule. Nkrumah was elected Secretary-General of the Working Committee established by the Fifth Pan-African Conference and also Secretary of the West African National Secretariat. At the same time, he became editor of the *New African*, a radical Pan-African publication for African students in Britain.

Writing later about the years he spent abroad, Nkrumah said, "Those years in America and England were years of sorrow and loneliness, poverty and hard work. But I have never regretted them, because the background that they provided had helped me to formulate my philosophy of life and politics."

On 14 November 1947 he returned to the then Gold Coast, and became General Secretary of the United Gold Coast Convention (UGCC). He began to implement some of the political principles which had been part of his political education while abroad. One of the crucial elements included the creation of a mass political party which could be mobilised for "positive action" in the struggle for independence. Following demonstrations by ex-servicemen and workers against high prices, and the boycott of European and Syrian traders, Nkrumah was detained on 12 March 1948 in the Northern Territories.

His arrest, with those of five other UGCC leaders, followed allegations that the UGCC was to blame for the agitation and riots in which the colonial administration had shot dead 29 Africans and injured 237. In his autobiography, Nkrumah stated that in the UGCC itself some elements placed the blame on him. "There appeared to be a general belief among them that the whole tragedy of our arrest and suffering was my fault, and they began to make it plain that they regretted the day they had ever invited me to take up the Secretaryship of the UGCC."

Differences between Nkrumah and the UGCC leadership became aggravated in the face of evidence submitted before the Watson Commission, set up to inquire into the causes of the recent disturbances. The UGCC leadership resented Nkrumah's plan for a Union of African Socialist Republics and the contacts he maintained with Pan-African organisations abroad. But Nkrumah was a most hard-working Secretary-General, having helped to establish 209 UGCC branches throughout the country.

The rest of the UGCC leadership was torn between the inclination to expel Nkrumah, thereby losing the benefit of his dynamism, on the one hand, and maintaining him in his position and risking being identified with his militant views, on the other. More important, the UGCC leadership was unsure of the forces which Nkrumah might unleash in a possible confrontation in the party. Nkrumah's belief in mobilising as many people as possible had resulted in the raising of consciousness among Ghanaians, many of whom soon began to articulate political demands which were ahead of the UGCC. Whereas the latter's policy was centred on "self-government within the shortest possible time", demands were already being made for "self-government now".

The party decided to demote him to the post of Honorary Treasurer. On his release from detention Nkrumah, now virtually excluded from the UGCC, organised the Committee of Youth Organisation (CYO) and founded the Accra *Evening News*. These two events led to calls for his complete expulsion from the UGCC. The calls increased following Nkrumah's open criticism of the UGCC's policies. In the same month – September – that the *Evening News* and the CYO were formed, the colonial administration announced that a committee would be formed to examine the constitutional proposals of the Watson Commission. In the eyes of the more militant members of the CYO, the UGCC's acceptance of membership in the resulting Coussey Committee, to which Nkrumah was not invited, identified the Convention with moderate demands in an atmosphere which was increasingly anti-colonial.

Attempts to heal the rift between the UGCC and Nkrumah led to the reconstitution of the CYO in February 1949 as part of a sub-committee of the UGCC. This, however, did not prevent further disagreements. The final break came on 12 June 1949 when the formation of the Convention People's Party (CPP) was announced before an audience of

about sixty thousand people – "on behalf of
the CYO, in the name of the chiefs and the
people, the rank and file of the Convention,
the Labour Movement, our valiant ex-servicemen, the youth movement throughout the
country, the man in the street, our children
and those yet unborn, the new Ghana that is
to be, Sergeant Adjetey and his comrades
who died at the cross-roads of Christianborg
during the riots of 12 June 1948, and in the
name of God Almighty and humanity."

The CPP issued a six-point programme:
1. To fight relentlessly by all constitutional
means for the achievement of full "Self-
Government Now" for the chiefs and the
people of the Gold Coast;
2. To serve as the vigorous conscious political vanguard for removing all forms of
oppression and for the establishment of a
democratic government;
3. To secure and maintain the complete unity
of the chiefs and the people of the Colony,
Ashanti, Northern Territories and Trans-
Volta;

4. To work in the interests of the trade union
movement in the country for better conditions of employment;
5. To work for a proper reconstruction of a
better Gold Coast in which the people shall
have the right to live and govern themselves
as free people;
6. To assist and facilitate in any way possible
the realisation of a united and self-governing
West Africa.

Following the release of the Coussey
Report, Nkrumah convened on 20 November
1949 a Ghana Peoples Representative Assembly to which were invited members of the
CPP, CYO, trade unions, farmers, ex-servicemen and youth organisations. The purpose of
the meeting was to formulate a collective
response to the colonial government and to
demand "self-government now", the point
on which the Assembly differed fundamentally from the Coussey Report.

In agreeing to the Report's recommendations, the chiefs and others, Nkrumah
argued, had sabotaged the wishes of the

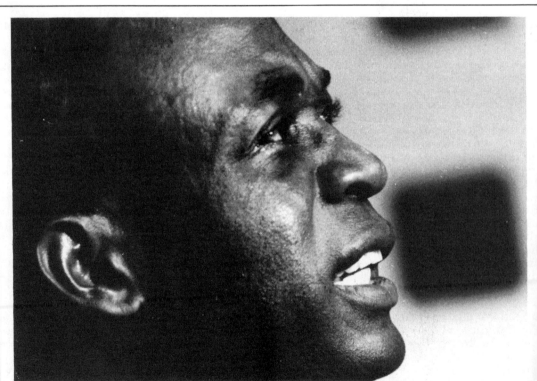

Nkrumah . . . "Our political independence will be meaningless unless we use it so as to obtain economic and financial independence".

people for self-government. The *Evening News* also criticised the Report. Nkrumah, as he had done before, then toured the country urging "positive action". When the chiefs in Ashanti joined the members of the dwindling UGCC in supporting the Coussey Report, the division with Nkrumah was further accentuated. The other leaders accused Nkrumah of undermining law and order in calling for positive action, a policy of non-violent civil disobedience and non-cooperation. In response, Nkrumah and his supporters accused them of sympathising with the fears of the colonial administration.

On 25 December 1949 Nkrumah made a speech in which he urged that people remained organised and resolute. This was to prepare the people for the advent of positive action which Nkrumah was concerned should proceed with the maximum success in order to convey to the colonial administration a clear and unequivocal wish for self-government from the people. "We prefer self-government with danger," Nkrumah said, reiterating the motto of the *Evening News*, "to servitude in tranquillity." Regarding the question of organisation, the Accra *Evening News* had stated on 18 May 1949 that "The history of colonial liberation movements shows that the first essential thing is ORGANISATION. Some may say unity, but unity presupposes organisation. At least, there must be organisation to unify the country; one person cannot do it, a few leaders cannot do it, but when the masses and the leaders share common ideals and purposes they can come together in an organisation, regardless of tribal and other differences, to fight for a cause."

On 6 January 1950 the Trade Union Congress (TUC) called a general strike in support of the meteorological workers who had begun their own strike in December 1949. On 8 January 1950 railway workers went on strike. On the same day, after a meeting of the CPP executive, Kwame Nkrumah announced the inception of the campaign of "positive action" against the colonial administration. Positive action led to a wave of strikes throughout Gold Coast. The administration ordered the army to take over Accra and the police forces were increased. This followed the declaration of a state of emergency on 11 January 1950. All meetings were banned, CPP organs were suspended or closed and leaders were arrested. Nkrumah was arrested on 21 January

1950, convicted and sentenced to three years' imprisonment. On appeal, the High Court reaffirmed the judgement of the magistrate's court.

While Nkrumah and other leaders were in prison, the CPP continued to function, benefitting from the momentum which the demand for "self-government now" had generated among the people. The party emerged victorious in both the municipal and general elections of February 1951. Campaigning from prison, Nkrumah won the Accra central constituency by polling 22,780 votes out of 23,122 cast. The colonial administration, which had claimed that its clampdown on the CPP had been done on behalf of "a very large body of moderate and responsible people who are utterly opposed to the methods of the Convention People's Party," now recognised that without Kwame Nkrumah "the contitution would be stillborn and if nothing came of all the hopes, aspirations and concrete proposals for a greater measure of self-government, there would no longer be any faith in the good intentions of the British Government."

On 12 February 1951 Nkrumah was released from prison to become Leader of Government Business, a title which was changed to Prime Minister in March 1952. Speaking on 10 July 1953 in the Assembly during the Motion of Destiny under which independence was claimed from the colonial power, Nkrumah said that "The right of a

Nkrumah at the inaugural Summit of the OAU in 1963..."Africa must unite".

President Nkrumah, the statesman, with Non-Aligned leaders: (l to r) Prime Minister J. Nehru of India, Kwame Nkrumah, President Nasser of Egypt, President Sukarno of Indonesia and President Tito of Yugoslavia.

Nkrumah leading Ghana to independence in 1957..."We would be judged by our achievements".

people to govern themselves is a fundamental principle, and to compromise on this principle is to betray it." He continued: "If there is to be a criterion of a people's preparedness for self-government, then I say it is their readiness to assume the responsibility of ruling themselves. For who but a people themselves can say when they are prepared? Self-government is not an end in itself. It is a means to an end, to the building of the good life for the benefit of all, regardless of tribe, creed, colour or station in life. Our aim is to make this country a worthy place for all its citizens, a country that will be a shining light throughout the whole continent of Africa, giving inspiration far beyond its frontiers. And this we can do by dedicating ourselves to unselfish service to humanity. We must learn from the mistakes of others so that we may, in so far as we can, avoid a repetition of those tragedies which have overtaken other human societies."

During the elections of June 1954, the CPP won 72 out of 104 seats, the others going to the opposition which was increasingly consolidating itself with the help of chiefs and the cocoa growers in the centre. After Nkrumah had announced the introduction of cocoa stabilisation measures in August 1954, opposition flared up in Ashanti, associated with the main opposition party; this caused the colonial administration to call fresh elections in July 1956. The CPP again won 72 out of 104 seats.

On 6 March 1957, Gold Coast became independent Ghana. Nkrumah set about introducing measures aimed at improving the social and economic aspects of Ghanaian life. Laws were passed which opponents pointed to support arguments that Nkrumah was bent on suppressing political opponents. Writing in his autobiography *Ghana*, Nkrumah stated: "Capitalism is too complicated a system for a newly independent nation. Hence the need for a socialist society. But even a system based on social justice and a democratic constitution may need backing up, during the period following independence, by emergency measures of a totalitarian kind. Without discipline freedom cannot survive. In any event, the basis must be a loyal, honest, hard-working and responsible civil service on which the party in power can rely. Armed forces must also be consolidated for defence."

At the opening of the Bank of Ghana in July 1957, Nkrumah said: "Our political independence will be meaningless unless we use it so as to obtain economic and financial self-government and independence." He went on to spell out his objectives in his December 1957 broadcast. "My first objective," he said, "is to abolish from Ghana poverty, ignorance and disease. We shall measure our progress by the improvement in the health of our people; by the number of children in school; and by the quality of the education; by the availability of water and electricity in our towns and villages, and by the happiness which our people take in being able to manage their own affairs. The welfare of our people is our chief pride and it is by this that my government will ask to be judged."

In December 1957 Nkrumah married an Egyptian, Fathia Helen, in a private ceremony attended by close relatives and friends. They had three children.

On 1 July 1959 Nkrumah announced the beginning of the Second Five-Year Development Plan. To ensure its success, he called among other things, for the establishment of a "Grand Alliance" consisting of the CPP, the TUC and the Ghana Farmers' Council. The Plan aimed to see the completion of the Volta River Project, which Nkrumah believed, "would provide the quickest and most certain method of leading us towards economic independence", and the construction of 600 new factories capable of producing over 100 different products.

Throughout his life, Nkrumah was concerned that the party and its functionaries should be capable of instilling confidence in people so as to be able to mobilise them towards desired policies and goals. Speaking on 12 June 1959 at the tenth anniversary of the founding of the CPP, Nkrumah said: "Members of the Party must be the first to set an example of all the highest qualities in the nation. We must excel in our field of work by working really hard. We must produce unimpeachable evidence of integrity, honesty, selflessness and faithfulness in the positions in which we are placed by the party in service of the nation. We must abandon ridiculous ostentation and vanity when the Party has charged us with eminent offices of state, and remember constantly that we hold offices not in our right, but in the right of the total membership of the Convention People's Party, the masses of the people who really matter." He therefore had some functionaries expelled from the party and others forced to scale down their quest for individual benefit and wealth, such as a high ranking official whose wife is said to have purchased a gold-plated bed.

In the meantime, the Opposition continued to consolidate itself through championing the cause of dissatisfied chiefs and intellectuals and the Ewe of Togoland, some of whom resented being included in the union with Ghana. Three non-Ghanaians were deported, two of them for preaching separatism. This led to criticism at home and abroad and Nkrumah became apprehensive that foreigners might use the opposition to prejudice Ghana's image and security.

He felt increasingly justified in this apprehension when subsequent intelligence reports confirmed the connection which some Opposition members had with secret ethnic separatist movements. Another member of the Opposition was found to have purchased, quite within the law, military insignia in London, but for purposes unspecified. However, just before Nkrumah's trip to India in 1958, a report stated that an assassination had been planned to take place as Nkrumah boarded the plane.

In December 1958 the Secretary-General of the United Party and a member of Parliament were held under the recently passed Preventive Detention Act. A tribunal consisting of three lawyers found that the men "were engaged in a conspiracy to carry out at some future date in Ghana, an act for unlawful purpose, revolutionary in character." Nkrumah made available copies of the tribunal's proceedings to members of the International Commission of Jurists and the Western press.

His concern for unity and progress at home was also matched by his desire to achieve Pan-African unity. On the eve of Ghana's independence, Nkrumah had said that "Our independence is meaningless unless it is linked up with the total liberation of the African continent." In April 1958 Nkrumah convened a conference of independent African states in Accra consisting of Egypt, Ethiopia, Liberia, Libya, Morocco, Sudan and Tunisia. Speaking on 15 April 1958 Nkrumah said "We have for too long been the victims of foreign domination. For too long we have had no say in the management of our own affairs or in deciding our own destinies. Now times have changed, and today we are the masters of our own fate."

In December 1958 Nkrumah called the first All-African Peoples Conference, the precursor of the OAU. In his address, he said: "What is the purpose of this historic Conference? We are here to know ourselves and to exchange views on matters of common interest; to explore ways and means of consolidating and safe-guarding our hard-won independence; to strengthen the economic and cultural ties between our countries; to find workable arrangements for helping our brothers still languishing under colonial rule."

In May 1959 Nkrumah helped establish the Ghana-Guinea Union, after he had offered to assist Guinea with £10 million following the latter country's break with France in September 1958. Writing in *I Speak of Freedom*, Nkrumah stated that "we were determined to unite in order to form a nucleus for a union of African states." In pursuit of this goal, he met the leaders of Guinea and Liberia at Sanniquellie, Liberia, in July 1959 and a Declaration of Principles was issued setting out the framework for a Community of Independent African States. However, at the second conference of independent African states held in Addis Ababa on 15 June 1960, opposition to Nkrumah's idea of a union of African states was spearheaded by Nigeria whose delegate argued that it was premature. In November 1960

Nkrumah announced that he would help Mali following that country's break with Senegal and in December a federation of Ghana, Guinea and Mali was formed.

When the Congo crisis erupted in 1960, Nkrumah supported the duly elected Prime Minister of the country, Patrice Lumumba (q.v.). He was angered at the inability of the United Nations Congo Command to prevent the arrest and death of Lumumba and suggested the establishment of an African High Command which could be called upon to repulse any threat to the independence of an African state. First mooted in November 1960 to the leaders of Ethiopia, Guinea, Liberia, Libya, Mali, Morocco, Sudan, Tunisia and the United Arab Republic (UAR), this idea of the High Command failed to take root.

However, it received support in January 1961 at the Casablanca Conference where a Charter was adopted. Among other things, the Charter called for support for the National Front for the Liberation of Algeria and the Lumumbist forces in Congo. The Charter, which also called for the establishment of an African Consultative Assembly, condemned neo-colonialism and urged the promotion of economic, cultural and political cooperation in Africa. The Casablanca Conference was attended by Ghana, Guinea, Mali, Morocco, Libya, UAR and Algeria.

Ghana then became a leading member of one of the two "blocs" in Africa between 1960 and 1963. Nkrumah's approach to African unity was not supported even by his allies in that bloc; his idea of "continental government" was rejected in the discussions leading to the creation of the OAU at Addis Ababa in May 1963. Kwame Nkrumah considered the OAU to be inadequate. He encouraged opposition, legal and illegal, to several independent African regimes through the Bureau of African Affairs (BAA) based on an office originally started by an old friend from his London days, George Padmore (1902-59). Radical policies directed against pro-Western independent governments, as well as colonisation and White settler rule, were expressed by the BAA's newspaper *The Spark*. They were certainly Dr Nkrumah's own policies. However, he agreed to host the 1965 OAU summit in Accra, and did so, though a crisis occurred beforehand because of the guerrillas being trained in Ghana for action in some OAU member states.

On the guerrillas fighting colonia

rule, Nkrumah was followed by general African opinion. He was for years a leader of African criticism of White domination. In December 1965 Nkrumah, who had for long maintained working relations with Britain (and the USA), broke off relations with Britain in accordance with an OAU resolution, ignored by many other OAU members, because of the failure to end the White settler rebellion in Rhodesia (Zimbabwe).

In 1960 Ghana adopted a Republican Constitution and Nkrumah became its first President, defeating Dr J.B. Danquah (q.v.) in an election. He was re-elected unopposed in 1965. In 1961 President Nkrumah ordered a number of changes in the direction of socialism and, in foreign affairs, "non-alignment" with closer ties forged with the Communist countries. Some development in this socialist phase included the creation of many state industries and the Kwame Nkrumah Ideological Institute. Nkrumah and his Socialist followers had, however, to face criticisms, internal and external. The anti-CPP opposition remained, though it was wholly underground after the creation of a one-party state in 1964. In 1961 there were bomb outrages and in 1962 there was an attempt on Dr Nkrumah's life; another attempt followed early in 1964. The CPP itself did not generally follow Nkrumah's ideals, many of its leaders being out to enrich themselves despite the action Nkrumah took in 1961 – with a "Dawn Broadcast" and some sackings – against such activity.

The CPP's rule became authoritarian and corrupt in a way which was certainly beyond its leader's control, though he probably contributed to the worsening situation through weaknesses – such as suspicion, and being easily impressed and flattered – which were exploited by unscrupulous colleagues and supporters.

In February 1966, soon after inaugurating the Volta Dam, Kwame Nkrumah left on a peace mission to end the Vietnam War, accompanied by senior members of his Government. On 24 February 1966, in his absence, he was overthrown by a military coup. A junta of army and police officers, the National Liberation Council (NLC), took over power and the CPP, cut off by now from the ordinary people who suffered from an increasingly bad economic situation, collapsed utterly. Kwame Nkrumah went to Guinea, where he was welcomed and, for a time, entitled co-president to Sekou Toure (q.v.).

For a few months Dr Nkrumah broadcast to Ghanaians calling on them to overthrow the NLC. There was no immediate response, but after a few years Ghanaians began to think better of the founder-President whose fall they had initially celebrated. A few always remained in touch with him. His involvement in the April 1967 attempted coup was not proved, but the NLC, and the civilian government which took over in 1969 under the leadership of Nkrumah's old political opponent Kofi Busia (q.v.), feared his influence greatly. In 1970 Kwame Nkrumah believed his recall to Ghana was imminent; in 1971 stiff penalties were enacted in Ghana for advocacy or any favouring of his return.

Kwame Nkrumah published many books. After *Towards Colonial Freedom* in 1946, and *What I Mean by Positive Action* in 1950, he wrote his autobiography, *Ghana*, published at the time of independence in 1957. While ruling Ghana later he was able to publish *I Speak of Freedom* (1961), *Africa Must Unite* (1963), *Consciencism* (1964) and *Neo-Colonialism: The Last Stage of Imperialism* (1965).

He then wrote *Axioms of Kwame Nkrumah* (1967), with a special edition for the liberation fighters in whom he continued to take a special interest. He also published in 1967 *Challenge of the Congo*, to denounce Western intrigues in the Congo crisis, and in 1968 *Handbook of Revolutionary Warfare*. In 1968 he published *Dark Days in Ghana*, condemning NLC rule as he had done in broadcasts collected in a book, *Voice From Conakry*. Many of his works were brought out by the publishing company he had started in London, Panaf Books. In 1970 he published *Class Struggle in Africa*. His thinking in exile moved towards more orthodox Marxism and rejection of the idea of "non-alignment"; but he remained constant on the twin objectives of the liberation and unity of Africa.

He was deservedly noted as a thinker and writer as well as a politician. In Africa outside Ghana he was very popular, except among the rulers of some countries. His reputation remained, in Nigeria for example, after his fall.

In 1971 his health, poor for years, became worse. He was seriously ill when the second military regime in Ghana, the National Reformation Council (NRC), took over on 13 January 1972. Repudiating Busia and his colleagues, Kwame Nkrumah's opponents for 20 years, the NRC seemed to move slowly towards policies closer to Nkrumah and his ideas. In Ghana public opinion was by now coming to accept widely that he should return, if not to rule again. But on 27 April 1972 Kwame Nkrumah died in a hospital in Bucharest in Rumania. There was prolonged mourning in Ghana. After an argument between the NRC and the government of Guinea, where the former President of Ghana had been first buried, his remains were eventually sent back to Ghana for reburial with full traditional honours amid national mourning.

His mother, Elizabeth Nyaniba, was still alive then and lived for several years afterwards. He left a widow, Fathia, and three children. The NRC set up an inquiry into ways to honour the memory of Kwame Nkrumah; following one of its recommendations, his widow and children returned from Egypt to Ghana. ∎

H.M. Nkumbula

Nkumbula, H.M. (1916-83)

NKUMBULA, Harry Mwaanga (1916-83).

ZAMBIAN politician, one of the fathers of African nationalism in former Northern Rhodesia (now Zambia) and leader of the Opposition in independent Zambia between 1964 and 1972.

Harry Nkumbula was born in January 1916 at Maala, near Nanwala, the son of an Ila Chief. He was educated at local Methodist mission schools and later at Kafue Teachers' Training College, qualifiying as a teacher at the age of 18. He initially taught at schools near his home before moving to Kitwe in 1942. Already interested in politics, he was one of the founders and secretary of the Kitwe African Society, established to promote the interests of Africans.

In 1946 he was awarded a scholarship to study at Makerere College, Uganda, from where another scholarship enabled him to travel to England for a course in Education. Having obtained a Diploma in Education, Nkumbula got a further grant for a degree course at the London School of Economics, but this was withdrawn in 1950 and he returned home without finishing his studies.

Nkumbula was fiercely opposed to any proposals of a federation between Northern Rhodesia, Southern Rhodesia (now Zimbabwe) and Nyasaland (now Malawi) which he was sure would only increase the power of the white settlers in the area. On the strength of this opposition, he was elected President of the Northern Rhodesian African National Congress in 1951. He renamed the organisation African National Congress (ANC) and its militant nationalism won great popular support. In the same year he helped Dr Hastings Kamuzu Banda (who later became President of Malawi) to publish a pamphlet against the federation.

In 1952 he organised a boycott of shops that discriminated between non-African customers who were served over the counter and Africans who were served through a hole in the wall generally at the back. The following year, as part of the continued campaign against federation, he made the symbolic gesture of publicly burning the White Paper on Federation issued by the British Government. Despite the ANC's efforts the Central African Federation was established in October 1953. Nkumbula continued to be active in both promoting African nationalism and opposing discriminatory practices and in 1955 he was arrested along with Kenneth Kaunda, then secretary-general of the ANC, for possessing anti-federation literature and also writings about India's Mahatma Gandhi's campaign of passive resistance. They were imprisoned for two months.

When another White Paper containing proposed changes to the Constitution was published in February 1958, Nkumbula again publicly burned it, and demanded provision in the new constitution for universal adult suffrage and equitable African representation. Though these demands were not met, Nkumbula decided to stand for election to the Legislative Council under the new constitution. Meanwhile Kaunda and the younger more radical members of the ANC had become increasingly disenchanted with Nkumbula's leadership, and this course of action caused them to break away from the ANC and form the Zambia African National Congress (ZANC) in October 1958.

Nkumbula was elected member of the Legislative Council for the South West district in the elections held the following March. ZANC boycotted the elections and the new constitution and gained a great deal of support in the Luapula and Northern Provinces, at the expense of the ANC. This support was such that ZANC was banned in March 1959 and Kaunda, its president, was arrested. Throughout 1959 Nkumbula's popularity within the ANC waned, culminating in another split in the party in September 1959. From this the United National Independence party (UNIP) was established, and this new party also drew in former members of ZANC to become a major political force.

During the following year, the ANC continued to lose support to UNIP. In September 1960, Nkumbula was involved in a road accident in which a man was killed. Found guilty of dangerous driving he was sentenced to one year's imprisonment which he served from April 1961 to January 1962 after losing his appeal, and in the process lost his seat on the Legislative Council.

Elections for the first fully African administration were held in October 1962, with UNIP winning 14 seats, the United Federal Party (UFP) 15 seats, and the ANC 7 seats. In December 1962 UNIP and ANC formed a coalition government and Nkumbula became Minister of African Education.

The Central African Federation was disbanded in 1963 and elections were held early in 1964. UNIP won a resounding majority of 55 seats, compared to the ANC's ten, and thus after independence was granted in October 1964, Nkumbula became leader

of the Opposition. Although his party did slightly better in the 1968 elections gaining 23 seats compared to UNIP's 81, his support came mainly from the south of the country.

A one-party state was established in December 1972, and six months later, Nkumbula joined UNIP. Although no longer a major political force in the country he was held in respect and when he died on 8 October 1983 in Lusaka, there were three days of national mourning. ■

Nokrashi Pasha, M.F. (1888-1948)

NOKRASHI PASHA, Mahmoud Fahmi (1888-1948).

EGYPTIAN politician. Born in Alexandria in 1888, he went to the Higher Training College, Cairo and then to Nottingham University College in England, before working as a teacher in Egypt. He rose to be headmaster of Gammaliya School in Cairo (1914-19). In 1919 he became Director of Education under the Asyut Provincial Council. Then he was transferred to the Ministry of Agriculture and in 1924 he obtained the post of Assistant Secretary-General in the Ministry of Education.

Between 1919 and 1924, he was also active in the nationalist movement. He was a leader of the main nationalist party, the Wafd of Zaghlul Pasha (q.v.), and organised its sub-committees in Cairo and Alexandria. Two years after the nominal independence of Egypt in 1922 the Wafd, which while opposed to the continued predominant role of Britain had decided to take part in politics under the Constitution, won elections and took power. During its brief period in power Nokrashi was Deputy Governor of Cairo and then Under-Secretary for the Interior. He was considered an "agitator" by the British, and when the Wafd government was virtually forced to resign by them after the murder in Cairo of the Governor-General of the Sudan in late 1924, he was arrested for some weeks. He was arrested again in 1925 and charged with complicity in several political crimes. He was acquitted, but much later the British suspected that he had been implicated in the assassination of the Governor-General, Sir Lee Stack.

In 1930 he was Minister of Communications in the Wafd government headed by Nahas Pasha (q.v.) who took over as leader of the Wafd in 1927 on Zaghlul Pasha's death. In 1936 he was a member, with Nahas, of the delegation which negotiated the new Treaty with Britain, recognising something closer to real independence for Egypt. A close associate of Nahas, he was Minister of Communications again in the Nahas government of 1936-37, until a major split occurred in mid-1937 in the Wafdist leadership.

Nokrashi protested at the award of a major contract for the electrification of the old (1902) Aswan Dam to the English Electric Company without invitations to tender. Nahas upheld the award and a quarrel followed which led to Nokrashi's exclusion from the government in a reshuffle in August 1937. He also disagreed with other Wafd leaders over the "Blue Shirts", a paramilitary party organisation.

He and Ahmed Maher Pasha, with others, formed the Socialist Party. For a time, Nokrashi, who refused to be bought over with a sinecure job (he had a high reputation for integrity), was a hero to opponents of Nahas. But Nahas fell later in 1937, and in 1938 a coalition government including the Socialists was formed. Nokrashi was variously Minister of the Interior, Education, and of the Interior again, and in September 1940 Minister of Finance.

After the Wafdist government of 1942-44, ruling with British backing through the most difficult years of the Second World War, Maher Pasha became Prime Minister, but in February 1945, when about to declare war on Germany, he was assassinated. Then Nokrashi took over as Prime Minister. Egypt now entered a turbulent period, with a great deal of political violence, in the course of feuding involving the Wafd, the Communists, the resurgent Moslem Brotherhood (believers in achieving government based on Islamic principles by any means possible) and others. Continual labour unrest also characterised these years, but much of the discontent was channelled against Britain, which still had many troops in Egypt.

Presiding over this troubled situation in 1945-46, Nokrashi tried to discredit and weaken the Wafd, and suppressed mass movements, while seeking to take the lead in the anti-British protest movement so as to control it. These efforts were not wholly successful, and after a major political riot at Abbas Bridge in Cairo in 1946 he resigned and was replaced by Sidqi Pasha (q.v.). Later in 1946 he was recalled by King Farouk (q.v.), and served as Prime Minister for two critical years. He combined the post with various other ministries.

The efforts to reach a definite new agreement with Britain failed. British forces withdrew from all of Egypt except the Suez Canal Zone in 1947, but their presence in the Canal Zone, and the British refusal to recognise Egyptian claims to the Sudan, remained as nationalist grievances. Feelings were then roused further, in 1947, by the Arab-Jewish-British conflict over Palestine. During efforts to solve this in 1947 at the United Nations Nokrashi represented Egypt. He won popularity by his advocacy of the Palestine Arabs, and in 1948 Egypt went to war, with Arab allies, against the newly proclaimed state of Israel. The war went badly and exposed monumental corruption in Egypt, involving people close to the King. Discontent remained and Nokrashi Pasha felt obliged to ban the Moslem Brotherhood early in December 1948. Soon afterwards, a member of the Brotherhood shot him dead, on 28 December 1948. ■

Nokwe, P.P.D. (1927-78)

NOKWE, Philemon Pearce Dumalisile (1927-78).

SOUTH AFRICAN politician and the first African advocate in the country. He was born on 13 May 1927 in Evaton, Transvaal, and had his primary education locally before attending St. Peter's Secondary School in Johannesburg where he was tutored by Oliver Tambo, a later President of the African National Congress (ANC), with whom he was to share a working relationship in the leadership of the movement. After St. Peter's, Nokwe attended Fort Hare University College, graduating with a science degree in 1949 and gaining a teacher's diploma the following year.

He joined the Youth League of the ANC while studying at Fort Hare, where he helped organise the 1949 Programme of Action of the League. In 1950, he took up teaching at Krugersdorp, which he com-

P.P.D. Nokwe

bined with active participation in the campaign of the ANC. But in 1952 Nokwe, who was popularly known as "Duma", short for Dumalisile, was dismissed from teaching because of his involvement in the Defiance Campaign in which 8,500 ANC activists were arrested by the South African authorities for voluntarily violating the apartheid laws.

Nokwe was elected Secretary of the ANC Youth League in 1953, and having been deprived of employment by the government he enrolled at the University of Witwatersrand as a part-time student of law. He gained the LLB degree in 1955, which made him the first African recipient of a Witwatersrand law degree, and also the first African advocate in the country. With this achievement, however, came more rigorous persecution by the apartheid regime which, on the eve of his graduation, served him with banning orders under the Suppression of Communism Act. This ban, extended in 1959 for a second five-year period, made it impossible for Nokwe to travel out of Johannesburg where, at the same time, he was deprived of office premises in the building housing the practices of his white professional colleagues.

In December 1956 Nokwe, alongside other 155 ANC leaders including Chief Albert Luthuli (q.v.), Oliver Tambo, Nelson Mandela and Walter Sisulu, was arrested and charged in the Treason Trial, where he was a member of the defence which ably contested virtually every legal point until they won acquittal in March 1961.

The year 1958 saw his election as Secretary-General of the ANC, a position he held until 1969. Following the 1960 State of Emergency, Nokwe was sentenced to five months imprisonment. On his release he became involved in the organisation of the December 1960 Consultative Conference of African Leaders whose aim was to formulate a common military strategy in the face of South Africa becoming a republic following its expulsion from the Commonwealth. Though Nokwe did not attend the subsequent Maritzburg Conference of March 1961, being still under a restriction order, he was arrested with eleven others and charged with its organisation under the Unlawful Organisations Act. He got a twelve-month sentence which he successfully appealed against.

He was rearrested in 1962 in connection with a manuscript advocating armed struggle, but left South Africa the following year, before the trial had begun, to join the external wing of the ANC in Lusaka. A man of formidable intellectual vigour and commitment, he was soon to prove his capability at the external mission. In 1974 he led the ANC delegation to the United Nations to lobby for the expulsion of South Africa from the world body; the Afro-Asian countries voted overwhelmingly for this during the Security Council debate but South Africa was spared through the triple veto cast by Britain, France and the USA.

Nokwe was appointed the ANC's Director of International Affairs the following year. He combined this office with that of Deputy Secretary-General of the ANC, and performed both functions with unwavering determination. During this time he travelled extensively, addressing meetings in Eastern and Western Europe, the Americas and Africa.

On 8 January 1978 he performed what became his last duty in Lusaka where he was chairman of the meeting commemorating the ANC's 66th anniversary. Four days later, on 12 January, Nokwe died at the University Teaching Hospital in Lusaka, after a brief illness. ■

Ntare V (1947-72)

NTARE V, Mwami Charles Ndizeye
(1947-72).

BURUNDIAN traditional ruler. He was
born on 2 December 1947, the son of
Mwami Mwambutsa IV, King of Burundi
and Head of State until 1966. The Prince
Regent was educated in Lausanne, Switzerland, from where he returned to Bujumbura
in 1966 to depose his father and become
Mwami (King) Ntare V at the age of 19.

Mwami Ntare V

Ntare ascended to the throne on 8
July 1966, at a time when there was considerable political instability in Burundi. In the
four years between independence in 1962 and
the accession of Ntare V, there had been
seven changes of administration in the
country, with three Prime Ministers assassinated. Ntare's father himself narrowly escaped an assassination attempt in September
1965 during an unsuccessful army revolt.
Mwami Mwambutsa left the country immediately for Europe for a prolonged stay. It

was during this period that his son succeeded
him.

On taking power, Ntare V revoked his
father's government, dismissing Premier
Léopold Biha and suspending the Constitution. He appointed Captain (later Colonel)
Michel Micombero (q.v.), a former Minister
of Defence and Chief Secretary of State, to
head a new administration. In a newspaper
interview after the take-over, Ntare V
promised social and economic reforms and
pledged that his administration would ensure justice and eliminate corruption.

But friction soon arose between the
young King and some members of the
Government who accused him of not meeting his obligations and of betraying the
progressive tendencies of the new regime. He
tried on several occasions to purge his critics
in the Government, but failed. On 29 November 1966, when he was on an official visit to
Kinshasa, Captain Micombero seized power
and established a military revolutionary
council. The monarchy was abolished and
Mwami Ntare V was forced to remain in
exile in Zaire. He returned to Burundi in
March 1972, on the eve of the Hutu revolt
against Tutsi domination. Ntare was suspected by the Government to have encouraged the revolt and was executed on 29 April
1972. ■

Ntitendereza, J.B. (died 1963)

NTITENDEREZA, Jean Baptiste
(died 1963).

BURUNDIAN politician. The eldest son of
Chief Pierre Baranyanka of the Abatare
lineage, Ntitendereza was a central figure in
the intra-mural rivalry among the descendants of Burundi's royal houses which
formed a critical factor in the background of
the Hutu-Tutsi ethnic problem. A Hutu, his
political career was shaped and directed by
the struggle for power between his party, the
Parti Démocrate Chrétien (PDC) and the
Parti de l'Unité et du Progrès National
(UPRONA) of the rival Tutsi community.
The parties represented the Batare and Bezi
ruling families respectively. His father was
an influential chief who was highly favoured
by the Belgians who were administering the
country under a Trusteeship.

Ntitendereza was educated at the Groupe Scolaire d'Astrida and entered politics in the 1940s. Like his father he cooperated with the Belgians who in return encouraged his rise in the political leadership of Burundi. He was appointed to the Supreme Land Council which was succeeded by the Interim Commission of which he also retained his membership. In 1944 he was given a chiefdom. With his brother Biroli, who was Burundi's first university graduate, he founded the PDC in December 1959. Ntitendereza succeeded Biroli to its presidency shortly after its formation and the party won the 1960 elections which brought him into the provisional government as Minister of the Interior in 1961.

The PDC's close association with the Belgian administration caused it a great deal of discredit among many Burundians, including some of the party's intellectual functionaries who viewed it as detrimental to winning the support of the masses. Such was the damage to its image that even after the party leadership had lost the support of the Belgians for trying to pursue independent policies, the PDC was unable to retain its dominant position in Parliament in the 1961 legislature elections. It lost the elections to the UPRONA who gained 58 seats out of a total of 64. The elections highlighted the political differences between the two parties, for while the PDC was maintaining that independence was a "long-run objective, not to be attained before the implementation of a double plan of progressive economic and political emancipation", the UPRONA demanded immediate independence for Burundi.

Following the PDC's electoral defeat, there seemed to be a conspiracy to decapitate the UPRONA by assassinating Prime Minister Rwagasore (q.v.), who was shot dead on 13 October 1961. Ntitendereza and his brother Biroli were implicated in the assassination. They were tried by the Belgian authorities and given prison sentences in May 1962, but after Burundi became independent the case was brought up again for a re-trial under the country's new Constitution. Rwagasore's supporters who called for the re-trial, insisted that the Belgians, who were alleged to be connected with the murder, would not have been impartial in the first trial.

Some Burundian constitutional experts however argued that the absence of a jury during the earlier trial, although this was *res judicata*, was in effect a violation of the provisions of the new Constitution. The case was re-opened and on 7 November 1962 the Court of First Instance sentenced Ntitendereza and his accomplices to death for their role in the murder. The Court of Appeal confirmed the judgement of the lower court on 5 January 1963, following which Ntitendereza was hanged publicly in Kitega on 14 January 1963.

According to the International Commission of Jurists "this was the first time that a country passing from the status of a trust territory to that of a sovereign state had considered itself authorised to re-open judicial proceedings closed prior to its independence ... It is a principle of law in all civilised countries that a change in internal or international political status has no effect on the validity of certain decisions which have become *res judicata*." ■

Nyagumbo, M. T. (1924-89)

NYAGUMBO, Maurice Tapfumaneyi (1924-89).

ZIMBABWEAN nationalist and political leader whose life history reflects the country's fight for justice, and whose sudden death in April 1989 robbed the nation of one of its most famous figures in the liberation struggle.

Born on 24 December 1924 in Rusape, in the eastern part of Zimbabwe, the young Nyagumbo had his primary education in the nearby St. Faith's Mission School and then St. Augustine's School in Penhalonga. In 1940 he travelled to South Africa in search of employment and to broaden his horizons. He worked as a waiter and a butler in Port Elizabeth before moving to Cape Town where he embarked on what was to be a lifelong political career. His participation in the activities of the South African Communist Party proved crucial to his growing political awareness. In 1953 Nyagumbo became the secretary of the Central African Social Club, a quasi-political organisation of Zimbabweans working in South Africa that he had helped to found. From then on he devoted his life to the political education and mobilisation of his people.

M.T. Nyagumbo

The South African authorities deported Nyagumbo in 1955 on the allegation of his involvement with Mau Mau elements from Kenya. Back home in Zimbabwe, then Southern Rhodesia, he became one of the founders of the Youth League which is regarded as the country's first modern nationalist movement, and later the Secretary of the Rusape branch of the African National Congress (of Southern Rhodesia) when it was reformed, revitalised and relaunched in 1957 with Joshua Nkomo as president. In a crackdown on heightened nationalist activities by the Rhodesian authorities, who declared a state of emergency following public demonstrations in February 1959, Nyagumbo was arrested and detained in Khami prison between 1959 and 1962 and the ANC was banned. His movements were restricted to Gokwe for many months after his release.

However, this ordeal did not discourage Nyagumbo who played an active role in the formation of the Zimbabwe African National Union (ZANU) in August 1963 under the leadership of Rev. Ndabaningi Sithole and Robert Mugabe. Nyagumbo was elected organising secretary of ZANU. But he was again detained in 1964 along with other African nationalist leaders when ZANU was banned, and he was to become one of the longest serving detainees of the white minority regime of the then Rhodesia.

Nyagumbo was released in late 1974, but rearrested within four months on charges of recruiting people for guerrilla training. He was convicted and given a 15-year gaol sentence. Released in December 1979, he immediately proceeded to London to witness the signing of the Lancaster House Agreement under which Zimbabwe attained black majority rule in April 1980.

In February 1980 Nyagumbo was elected ZANU-PF member of parliament for Manicaland. He was appointed minister of Mines and Energy Resources in the first cabinet of independent Zimbabwe. He later became the senior minister for Political Affairs in the Office of the Prime Minister (later President) Robert Mugabe, charged with the responsibility of overseeing the evolution of a new political order in the country. In this latter capacity, Nyagumbo was closely involved in the negotiations to merge the ruling ZANU-PF with Joshua Nkomo's Zimbabwe African People's Union; towards that end a unity accord was signed in December 1987.

Nyagumbo's life-long commitment to the liberation of Zimbabwe and his contribution to nation building after independence won him much respect and admiration. It therefore came as a shock to many when he appeared to have been implicated in a damaging car racket in early 1989; he resigned from his portfolio as Minister for Political Affairs and his position as a member of the National Executive Committee of ZANU. Unable to bear what looked like his burden of guilt, he committed suicide in April 1989.

Nyagumbo was declared a national hero, honoured with a period of national mourning and buried at Heroes' Acre in Harare. He was survived by his wife, Victoria, and five children. An account of Nyagumbo's life and prison experiences was published by Allison and Busby, London, in an autobiography entitled *With the People* in 1980. ∎

Nzeogwu, P.C.K. (1937-67)

NZEOGWU, Major Patrick Chukwuma Kaduna (1937-67).

NIGERIAN army officer, leader of the coup which ended the first civilian regime in Nigeria in January 1966. Son of parents of the Ibo ethnic group of Bendel State, from Okpanam, he was born in Kaduna in 1937 and grew up in the Northern Region where his parents lived for 34 years. A Catholic, he attended St. John's College, Kaduna, from 1950 to 1955. As an adult he was a practising Catholic, in fact a daily communicant, teetotaller and non-smoker.

He joined the army as a cadet and in 1959 received his commission at the Sandhurst Military Academy. Steadily promoted, by January 1966 he was a Major and senior instructor at the Military Academy at Kaduna. One account says he did well in the Intelligence Division but was thought by some superiors to be too good at such work; he was moved to training assignments, and therefore to Kaduna.

In 1965 Chukwuma Nzeogwu joined other officers, including Major Emmanuel Ifeajuna and Major D.O. Okafor, in a plot to end the regime of the politicians, whom they condemned for dictatorship and corruption. The plot went into effect on 14/15 January 1966. Major Nzeogwu, leader of the plotters, assigned to himself the task of eliminating the leading figure in the Northern People's Congress (NPC) dominated regime ruling the Northern Region and the Federation, Sir Ahmadu Bello (q.v.), Sardauna of Sokoto and Premier of the North. He led forces which stormed the Premier's house at Kaduna and killed him.

Nzeogwu spoke of a "Supreme Council of the Revolution" when he announced his coup on 15 January: "My dear countrymen, no citizen should have anything to fear as long as that citizen is law-abiding. Our enemies are political profiteers, swindlers, the men in the high and low places that seek bribes and demand ten percent, those that seek to keep the country divided permanently so that they can remain in office as ministers and VIP of waste, the tribalists, the nepotists, those that make the country big for nothing before international circles, those that have corrupted our society and put the Nigerian political calendar back by their words and deeds."

Dispelling rumour about the tribal characteristic of the putsch and its victims, he emphasised in the 15 January broadcast that the main aim of the coup was to "establish a strong united and progressive nation free from corruption and internal strife."

Major P.C.K. Nzeogwu

Although he briefly controlled the Northern Region in the absence of immediate opposition, no beginnings of a new government were set up by him there. And in the rest of Nigeria his fellow coup-makers, while they succeeded in killing the Federal Prime Minister, Sir Abubakar Tafawa Balewa (q.v.), and some senior army officers, did not succeed in taking over control. However, they ended a regime which many Nigerians had come to dislike; Nzeogwu himself became a hero to many. As Nzeogwu and the other insurrectionists failed to take over full control of the government of all Nigeria, they had to submit to the military leadership in Lagos that was headed by General Johnson T.U. Aguiyi-Ironsi (q.v.) who, as is now virtually beyond doubt, had been an intended victim of the plot, not a conspirator. General Aguiyi-Ironsi had been head of the Nigerian army during the rule of the ousted civilian administration.

On 19 January 1966 Nzeogwu left Kaduna for Lagos and submitted to Ironsi's authority. He was detained in the Federal capital and later Eastern Nigeria, where he was released in March 1967 by the Military Governor, Colonel Odumegwu Ojukwu. These two, however, did not agree; before the secession of the Eastern Region that was renamed Biafra, Major Nzeogwu publicly opposed such a move, and after the Civil War broke out he was regarded with suspicion, even though he eventually commanded secessionist troops against Federal forces in July 1967, on the Nsukka front. He was killed in action on that front early in August 1967. His body was found by the Federal forces and buried in Kaduna with full military honours, in recognition of his true national spirit.

In an article published by the Federal Ministry of Information at the time of the 1966 coup, Nzeogwu was described as "one of the few astute soldiers Nigeria has ever produced. He is known as a nationalist who is completely detribalised. Adored in the ranks for his bravery and informality and respected (even feared) by his officer colleagues for his skill and persuasive ability, he is one soldier in Nigeria whose name at once invokes love and awe. He is honest and dependable."■

A.T. Nzula

Nzula, A.T. (1905-34)

NZULA, Albert T. (1905-34).

SOUTH AFRICAN politician who was the first African secretary of the South African Communist Party (SACP). Though he died at the early age of twenty-eight, his brief period of political activities was meteoric and spanned such important events as the SACP's transformation from a white-dominated party to a mass organisation with Africans on its executive committee, the adoption by the SACP of the 'Native Republic' slogan, and the first of the mass demonstrations against the pass system.

Albert Nzula was born on 16 November 1905 in Rouxville in the Orange Free State. He was brought up in a humble family; his father was among the early generations of Africans converted to Christianity. Nzula rejected Christianity and European domination at an early age. He attended school at Bensonvale, Herschel and at Lovedale College where he qualified as a teacher. His first teaching post was in Aliwal in the Cape Province where he supplemented his meagre income by acting as a court interpreter. Soon he was attracted to the Industrial and

Commercial Union (ICU) of Clements Kadalie (q.v.), which was then an active political organisation; Nzula was elected secretary of the local branch. This was his introduction to African politics.

At a meeting of the Communist Party of South Africa in 1928 at Evaton where he was then teaching at the Wilberforce African Methodist Episcopate (AME) Mission, Nzula enrolled as a member of the SACP. A month later he wrote to the *Umesebenzi* (Worker) newspaper that no halfway measures would solve the problem of reconciling Marxist ideology with Christian teaching. He soon left teaching and immersed himself in the activities of the SACP, addressing rallies while also pressing persistently for a greater involvement of Africans in positions of responsibility within the movement. His dedication to the Party culminated in his election as General Secretary of the SACP.

Nzula was a delegate to the 1930 annual conference of the African National Congress (ANC) where, with J. T. Gumede (q.v.) who was then President of the ANC, he was weeded out of the organisation by the conservative elements, for their pro-Soviet views. Earlier, in 1929, he and Gumede and other Communist members of the ANC had launched the League for African Rights to campaign for the retention of the franchise for Africans in the Cape and its extension to other provinces, free education, the abolition of the pass laws, and for freedom of speech and association. These aims, in spite of the split at the 1930 ANC conference, continued to attract members of the ANC and ICU to the League. Nzula led the League's mass demonstration against the pass laws in Johannesburg, in which the ANC did not participate. Nevertheless, he persisted with the anti-pass demonstrations, including the one in Durban where 3,000 passes were burnt.

In 1930 Nzula took over the post of General Secretary of the Non-European Federation of Trade Unions. Before long he led a radical faction out of the Union, firmly under his control and named the African Federation of Trade Unions. But this did not have the desired support from Africans, and in August 1931 Nzula left for Moscow under the auspices of the Soviet Communist Party.

He was attached to the Research Association for National and Colonial Problems of the Eastern Workers Communist University in Moscow. Other Africans including Jomo Kenyatta (q.v.), J. B. Marks and Moses Kotane (qq.v.) were to follow Nzula's footsteps at this institution where he was a pioneer. It was there that he met Ivan Potekhin and A. Z. Zusmanovich, both greatly interested in African politics. These three, all in their twenties then, collaborated in the writing of *The Working Class Movement and Forced Labour in Colonial Africa*, which is believed to have been the first book on Africa to be published in Moscow under the Soviet regime.

Nzula died in the Soviet capital on 14 January 1934, of pneumonia according to Moscow sources. But African sources in Moscow at the time believed otherwise; they said that Nzula was eliminated by security agents on the instructions of the Communist Party who feared that his return to South Africa could exacerbate factionalism within the SACP. ■

Ocansey, A.J. (1889-1943)

OCANSEY, Alfred John (1889-1943).

GHANAIAN businessman. Born at Ada, he studied at Basle Mission schools and then worked for some years with the British firm of F. and A. Swanzy (later absorbed into the United Africa Company). From 1910 he was an independent businessman, working at Somanya, then at other towns in the Accra Plains and lower Volta area. He later moved to Accra and made his head offices there in 1918.

Besides ordinary merchant business, he was a pioneer of the sale of cars and car parts. At a time when car sales were small he secured the agency for many of them in the Gold Coast. He was also a pioneer in cinemas. By the 1930s he was the owner of many cinemas and of the Ocansey Stores. He was also an early dealer in record players and radio sets in the Gold Coast.

Ocansey was conscious that despite his own success, African businessmen were finding it hard to compete with European firms. He joined with another African businessman, Winifried Tete-Ansa (1889-1941), to start African ventures to remedy this situation. On entering the cocoa market he joined with Tete-Ansa to form the Gold Coast and Asante Cocoa Federation in 1930, to try to reassert Ghanaian control over the valuable export from their soil. The Federation organised a "Cocoa Hold-Up" in 1930-1, in which sales to firms were withheld. This was the precedent for a more successful "Hold-Up", organised by others, in 1937.

Ocansey became a newspaper proprietor also, and for nationalistic as well as commercial reasons. He had a Palladium Press in Accra, and published first the *Gold Coast Spectator*. In 1934, he invited Nnamdi Azikiwe, returning to West Africa from the USA, to start a newspaper. This was the *African Morning Post*. Ocansey allowed Azikiwe to prominently involve the newspaper in Accra politics. As a result, so Azikiwe recalls in *My Odyssey*, "Accra was now more politically awake. The *African Morning Post* did roaring business. From a circulation of 2,000 in 1934 it had rocketed to 10,000 daily in 1936. This was a record for West Africa then." In 1936, the *Post* carried an article by the Sierra Leonean revolutionary Wallace-Johnson (q.v.) which led to famous sedition trials of himself and Azikiwe.

Ocansey was a member of the Committee of 12 for protests against the Sedition Bill and Waterworks Bill in 1934; the protests failed, and the sedition law was the one under which his newspaper's editor was

A.J. Ocansey

tried in 1936. For a time Ocansey was a member of the Mambii Party in Accra, and of Wallace-Johnson's West African Youth League. He was involved in Ghanaian protests against the Italian occupation of Ethiopia in 1935-6. A.J. Ocansey died in September 1943. ■

Ofori-Atta, W.E.K. (1910- 88)

OFORI-ATTA, William Eugene Kwasi (1910-88).

GHANAIAN teacher, lawyer and a leader of the independence struggle. He was born in Kibi in Eastern Ghana on 10 October 1910, the son of Nana Sir Ofori-Atta I, at the time one of the most powerful of Ghana's chiefs. The Akyem Abuakwa stool is in an area of the country rich in diamonds and gold.

William Ofori-Atta was educated at Mfantsipim and Achimota Schools in Ghana. He then went to Queen's College, Cambridge, UK, and read economics.

His return to Ghana in 1938 marked the beginning of his participation in nationalist activities which eventually led to independence. As a teacher in Achimota School, he was very popular with his students, constantly pointing out the inequities of colonialism, which did not go unnoticed by the authorities. His natural gifts of oratory and his wit brought him to national attention in a series of public lectures he gave on the subjects of colonialism, the cocoa industry and the economy of the Gold Coast (Ghana) under the general theme of "Whither Are We Drifting?" So it was not surprising when he left Achimota to become secretary of state of the Akyem Abuakwa State, and teamed up with his cousin, J. B. Danquah (q.v.), then one of Ghana's leading lawyers, and others to found the United Gold Coast Convention (UGCC) which pioneered the fight for independence. It was the arrest in 1948 of the six leaders of the UGCC by the British Colonial authorities following popular demonstrations against high prices, which sparked the momentum that led to independence.

The six, dubbed the "Big Six" were J.

B. Danquah, Kwame Nkrumah (q.v.), who later became the first Ghanaian prime minister, Obetsebi-Lamptey, Edward Akuffo-Addo (q.v.), E. Ako-Adjei and William Ofori-Atta. One of the allegations was that the UGCC was to blame for the agitation in which 29

W. Ofori-Atta

people were shot dead by the colonial administration, and 237 injured. Disagreement among the leading members of the UGCC upon their release from detention, led Kwame Nkrumah to leave the UGCC and form the breakaway Convention People's Party (CPP).

The UGCC, with which Ofori-Atta sided, saw its support dwindle not only because it was seen by many to represent traditional authority but also because its demands were perceived as moderate. The CPP by contrast championed the cause of the common people and called for immediate self-government, as it put it "now" not "as soon as possible". Nevertheless the UGCC still represented a challenge to the CPP and William Ofori-Atta became a member of the Legislative Assembly for Akyem Abuakwa from 1951 to 1954 under the UGCC banner. He lost his seat in the 1954 elections and left for London to read law at Gray's Inn, interrupting his studies to return to Ghana for the independence celebrations on 6 March 1957.

Finally returning to Ghana in 1958 as a lawyer, he joined the law Chambers of his cousin J. B. Danquah, then leading the opposition parties to Kwame Nkrumah's CPP in independent Ghana. William Ofori-Atta also continued to be opposed to the CPP's policies, arguing that they eroded democracy, the principle of the rule of law and individual freedom, and as a result was in and out of detention.

When Kwame Nkrumah was overthrown in February 1966, Ofori-Atta was appointed to the economic and political committees of the National Liberation Council (NLC), the military junta which governed the country from February 1966 to September 1969. He was also the chairman of the State Cocoa Marketing Board from 1966 to 1968, where he tried to introduce better deals for the cocoa farmers who he believed were not properly compensated though providing sixty per cent of government revenues.

He served as a member of the constitutional commission that drafted the constitution of the Second Republic and also of the Constituent Assembly which reviewed the draft and adopted the constitution.

Ofori-Atta became a founding member of the Progress Party led by Dr K. A. Busia (q.v.) which won the 1969 elections and, in the Second Republic, served in the cabinet as minister of Education and Foreign Affairs. As minister of Foreign Affairs his avowed policy of dialogue with South Africa was not popular, but rather than precipitate a confrontation with Busia, Ofori-Atta attempted to reassure the rest of Africa that Ghana had not abandoned its traditional anti-apartheid stance.

When the government was overthrown on 13 January 1972, Ofori-Atta found himself once again in political detention. Out of jail, he led a quiet life for some time, but in 1977 heeded the call of the many movements that had sprung up to oppose the military government of General I. K. Acheampong (q.v.) and was again detained in 1978 until the coup of June 1979.

When the ban on party political activity was lifted in 1979, William Ofori-Atta broke away from his traditional allies to found the United National Convention (UNC) a party that he hoped would be a fusion of what he regarded as the best of the two strands of politics in Ghana – the CPP and the UP (United Party). This party exemplified the search for middle ground that had ruled William Ofori-Atta's life, but he lost the 1979 presidential elections.

However he led the UNC into alliance with the ruling People's National Party. Appointed chairman of the Council of State, he really came into his own then, serving as the elder statesman.

When that civilian government was also overthrown on 31 December 1981, Ofori-Atta went into retirement, emerging only in 1985 to deliver a series of lectures under the auspices of the J. B. Danquah Memorial Lectures organised by the Academy of Arts and Sciences. Like the series that launched his public life, these lectures were also entitled "Whither Ghana?". In them, he spoke out against arbitrariness and injustice.

William Ofori-Atta was converted to active Christianity during one of his detention periods in 1965 and remained an active Christian for the rest of his life. He was affectionately called "Paa Willie" by everybody and with his wife, the former Mary Amoah, kept an open house where there was a ready welcome for everybody. After the death of his wife in 1987, William Ofori-Atta never recovered his cheerful spirit and died on 14 July 1988. He had one son, Bernard, who is a magistrate. ∎

Ogunde, H. (1916-90)

OGUNDE, Hubert (1916-90).

NIGERIAN dramatist, musician, dancer, actor-manager, film maker and versatile artist. Hubert Ogunde was the doyen of modern Nigerian theatre. He was born in 1916 at Ososa near Ijebu-Ode, Ogun State. His father was a Baptist Minister, Jeremiah Dehinbo Ogunde; his mother was Eunice Owatusan Ogunde. He had a *babalawo* (traditional healer and diviner) grandfather whose influence blended with his Christian upbringing and created in him strong interest in both Christian and Yoruba traditional beliefs. These disparate influences shaped his dramatic output, as can be clearly seen in his early Christian plays and the strong flavour of traditional beliefs in his later plays and films.

H. Ogunde

He had his primary education at St John's School, Ososa (1925-28), at St Peter's Faji School, Lagos (1928-30) and at Wasimi African School, Ijebu-Ode (1931-32). Between 1933 and 1940 he was the choirmaster and organist of Wasimi African School, where he also taught.

He joined the Nigeria Police Force in 1941 and while serving there started (as an amateur) a theatre company called the African Music Research Party, and came out in 1944 with his first "Native Air Opera" called *The Garden of Eden and the Throne of God.* In 1946 he left the police and went professional and stormed the stage with the production of *Tiger's Empire,* an opera which earned him a caution by the police. Later that year, in Jos, his theatre was banned for staging the play *Strike and Hunger.*

Ogunde's theatre progressed through different phases, from the opera concert party to the contemporary theatre it was at the time of his death. These phases are reflected in the different names he gave to his company. In 1945 it was called African Music Research Party, but in 1947 the name was changed to Ogunde Theatre Party. In the 1950s it became the Ogunde Concert Party and it was again renamed The Ogunde Theatre in the 1960s and retained this name thereafter.

The thematic preoccupation of his plays varied; from folklore, he went on to tackle other themes, such as satire, history and politics. The themes that interested him are a reflection of the influences acting on his art. He was influenced by European theatre, an influence which he made use of creatively to come up with a unique theatre all his own. He was, perhaps, more profoundly influenced· by the classical travelling theatre of the Yoruba called the Alarinjo theatre which had its beginnings in the 16th century.

Ogunde's theatre became very popular, especially among his Yoruba audience, because of its preoccupation with cultural nationalism. He catered for the interests of not only the nationalists but also the ordinary people. His theatre came to be closely identified as a vehicle not only for entertainment but also for social comment, political action and instruction. Thus through his theatre he became a leading figure in the nationalist struggle. The colonial government viewed his theatre with disapproval and saw it as an effective voice in the agitation for independence and consequently did what it could to silence it.

Ironically, Ogunde's theatre also suffered persecution in the 1960s after independence was achieved and this time at the hands of the Western Region Government under Chief S. L. Akintola (q.v.) after the staging of *Yoruba Ronu* ("Yoruba Think") in 1964. The theatre was banned for two years until the ban was lifted by the military government of Col. Fajuyi after the 1966 coup d'état.

His theatrical performances were remarkable and memorable; he was a charismatic personality. His usual lively and dynamic presentations held his audience spellbound. His was a fascinating family theatre group constituted by himself and his many wives and children. Ogunde had over eight wives and numerous children, and most of them were members of his theatre. The commitment of Ogunde and his entire family to the theatre company, which was the family business, was profound. Thus his theatre had a cohesion, durability and resilience lacking in many other Yoruba travelling theatres. Ogunde's success in the theatre took him to many parts of Africa, Europe and the Americas where he performed to very enthusiastic audiences.

He was constantly writing and producing new operas and plays all his life. Among the most famous of his operas are *The*

Garden of Eden and the Throne of God (1944), followed by *Worse Than Crime* (1945), *Strike and Hunger* (1946), *King Solomon* (1948), *Bread and Bullet* (1950) and *My Darling Fatima* (1951). Some of his most remarkable plays include *Yoruba Ronu* (1964), *Ayanmo* (1970), *Onimoto* (1971) and *Aiye* (1972). A large number of his political works provoked a ban or caution from the authorities, but many of the political plays were well received by the government of the day. These works include *Song of Unity* (1960), a play commissioned by the Nigerian government to mark independence, *Keep Nigeria One* (1968), *Muritala Mohammed* (1976) and *Nigeria* (1977).

One of Ogunde's major contributions to the history of professional theatre in Nigeria is that he made the theatre accessible to the ordinary people, thus wresting it from the tutelage of court and church. He founded the Union of Nigerian Dramatists and Playwrights in 1971 and by 1990 the union had a membership of over one hundred professional travelling theatres. He founded a film village in his home town of Ososa. In 1979 he set up a film company to record his most successful and popular plays for posterity. At the time of his death he had four screen titles, including *Aiye* and *Jaiyesinmi,* to his name, in addition to 51 stage productions and eleven record titles, produced by his record company.

In 1982 Ogunde was honoured by his country with the award of Member of the Order of the Federal Republic. Ogunde, one of the finest and most productive dramatists Nigeria ever produced, was active as ever in the last years of his life. He wore his age gracefully, and when he died on 4 April 1990 at the age of nearly 74, he was still a very dynamic and tireless actor and producer. ■

Ogundipe, B.O. (1924-71)

OGUNDIPE, Brigadier Babafemi Olatunde (1924-71).

NIGERIAN soldier. He was born in Lagos on 6 September 1924. He attended the Wesley and Banham Memorial School in Port Harcourt, after which he enlisted in the army in 1943 and was posted to India and Burma, where he served with the British during the Second World War.

After the war, he attended the Chester Officer Cadet School in England, the School of Infantry, the Camberley Staff College, and the Imperial Defence College in London. In 1953 he received his commission and returned to active service with the British forces in Germany the same year, making him one of the most experienced officers in the army when Nigeria became independent in 1960.

Brig. B.O. Ogundipe

Brigadier Ogundipe was one of his country's officers who served in the United Nations Peace-Keeping Force in the Congo (now Zaire) between 1960 and 1963. After commanding the Nigerian brigade in Katanga early in 1963, he was from May to December 1963 Chief of Staff of the international force in the Congo operation. On his return to Nigeria he was made commander of the 2nd Brigade of the Nigerian Army; later he became military adviser to the Nigerian High Commissioner in London.

Following the January 1966 military coup, Brigadier Ogundipe became the number two man at the Supreme Military

Headquarters where he was Chief of Staff. After the second military coup of July 1966 he was the most senior surviving officer in the Nigerian Army. He was posted to London as Nigeria's High Commissioner in the same year, serving there throughout the civil war, and was replaced a few months after its conclusion. He died in London on 20 November 1971, and is buried in Nigeria. ■

Ojike, M.M. (1912-56)

OJIKE, Mazi Mbonu (1912-56).

NIGERIAN politician remembered for his cultural nationalism in the struggle for Nigeria's independence. He was born in 1912 in Akeme in Arochukwu, south-eastern Nigeria. He attended the Arochukwu Primary School, finishing in 1926 and taking up a teaching appointment with a mission school. He returned to college in 1929 to train as a teacher at the Church Missionary Society (CMS) Training College in Awka. A brilliant student, he won the 1931 college annual prize which was a book – *Aggrey of Africa*, the biography of the renowned Ghanaian educationist whose ideas of pan-Africanism left a lasting influence on the young Ojike.

M.M. Ojike

On leaving college in 1931, Ojike resumed teaching at the Central School in Abagana. In 1933 he resigned to join the staff of Dennis Memorial Grammar School in Onitsha, becoming one of the few African teachers on the staff.

His involvement in politics commenced in 1936 when he organised a successful teachers' salary strike after senior teachers were granted an increase which excluded junior members of the profession. He resigned from teaching in mission schools in 1938 in preference to private schools. That same year he met Nnamdi Azikiwe with whom he established a long personal and political relationship.

Ojike left for the United States in 1938 to continue his education at Lincoln University. His stay there sharpened his political ideology for it was then that he came in contact with other African students like Kwame Nkrumah (q.v.). Together they formed in 1941 the African Students' Association of America and Canada to campaign against colonialism in Africa and injustices against the Black race in general. Ojike was elected its first President.

His return to Nigeria marked an active involvement in the nationalistic politics spearheaded by Dr Azikiwe who had founded the National Council of Nigerian Citizens (NCNC) and whose newspaper, the *West African Pilot*, had become the vocal organ of the campaign for independence. Ojike joined the NCNC and contributed articles to the *Pilot*. In 1949 he was fined £40 on a charge of sedition because of an article in which he criticised the colonial government for the shooting of 21 miners during a labour dispute at the Udi Coal Mines, near Enugu. In 1953 he was a member of the NCNC delegation to the London Constitutional Conference which paved way for Nigeria's independence in October 1960. The following year he won an election on the platform of the NCNC to the Eastern Region

House of Assembly, becoming the Region's Minister of Finance; he held that office until early 1956.

In 1955 he wrote that British continued occupation of Nigeria was designed solely "to derive huge profits from Nigerian labour, soil, industry and commerce". He added that "Political freedom is a natural right ... It is idiotic for people to speak of attaining readiness for independence. They are born to it". Ojike also wrote that "Nigeria will rise as a nation under the democratic leadership of her citizens. A turtle knows where to bite a turtle".

His nationalist aspirations spread beyond the confines of politics to culture and the arts. An eloquent defender of African traditions, Ojike wrote in his book, *My Africa*, that "Names of persons and places hitherto spelled or called in English should be returned to their Nigerian identities". He did, in practice, generate greater enthusiasm for Nigerian traditional clothes by his "boycott" methods which involved a preference for traditional clothes as opposed to English-styled ones.

Mbonu Ojike died in late 1956. There is now an Ojike Memorial Medical Centre at Arondizuogu, Imo State. ■

Sir Louis Ojukwu

Ojukwu, L.O. (1909-66)

OJUKWU, Sir Louis Odumegwu (1909-66).

NIGERIAN businessman and politician, he combined remarkable success as a businessman with distinguished public service in several fields. He was associated with several philanthropic and cultural organisations to which he made substantial contributions.

He was born in 1909 in Nnewi, southeast of Onitsha in modern Anambra State. After formal schooling he joined the Produce Inspection Service as produce examiner in 1928 and later worked as a clerk with the large West African trading company of John Holt. It was here that the self-made man who later rose to become one of Nigeria's foremost business tycoons and a multi-millionaire developed his business interest. He resigned from John Holt in 1934 to start a transport business with one second-hand truck that later grew into a vast transport enterprise.

He entered politics in 1951 as a member of Dr. Nnamdi Azikiwe's National Council of Nigerian Citizens (NCNC) which included him in the delegation to the London Constitutional Conference in 1951. Four years later Odumegwu Ojukwu was elected to the Federal House of Representatives in Lagos, but resigned in 1956 to become chairman of the Eastern Region Development Corporation. His success, drive and ability led him to a host of other business appointments as chairman of the Eastern Nigeria Marketing Board, chairman of the Nigerian Shipping Line, chairman of the Nigerian Cement Company and director of a number of business concerns including Shell-BP. His last public engagement was as chairman of the Eastern Nigeria Marketing Board. He resigned from this position, and also from the office as chairman of the African Continental Bank, in May 1966 as a result of ill-health.

His own company, founded as the Ojukwu Transport Company in 1934, had at the time of his death in 1966 spread its activities into construction and other areas, growing into a multi-million naira group and employing thousands of workers.

In 1953, he was awarded the Queen Elizabeth II Coronation Medal; he was knighted in 1960. Sir Odumegwu was the father of Lieutenant-Colonel Chukwuemeka Odumegwu-Ojukwu who led Biafra's secession from Nigeria in 1967. In 1963 the University of Nigeria, Nsukka, conferred upon him the honorary degree of Doctor of Law, becoming one of the very first to be so honoured by that University. He died on 13 September 1966 at Nkalagu in his home state, at the age of 57.

Ojukwu's death came a few months after the first Nigerian civilian government was ended by a military coup d'état which saw his son, Lieutenant-Colonel Chukwu-emeka Odumegwu Ojukwu, ascend to office as Military Governor of Eastern Nigeria. Lieutenant-Colonel Ojukwu later declared the region, which he renamed Biafra, independent of the Federation of Nigeria, an action that led to a three-year bitter civil war which ended in 1970.■

R.C. Okala

Okala, R.G.C. (1910-73)

OKALA, René-Guy Charles (1910-73)

CAMEROONIAN politician, founder of the *Union Sociale Camerounaise* party. Born at Bilome (Mbam) he went to the Catholic seminary at Yaounde but left in 1931 to become a teacher. Later he worked for a British firm and, from 1938, as an interpreter for the French colonial administration.

When African politics developed rapidly after the Second World War, Okala was elected to the Territorial Assembly of French Cameroon. He was re-elected in 1949, 1952 and 1956. From 1945 to 1955 he was one of the indirectly elected overseas members of the Council of the Republic (Senate) of France. He founded in 1947 the French Cameroon branch of the SFIO, the French Socialist Party. Then, in 1953, he founded the *Union Sociale Camerounaise*. It tried to establish itself in the Bulu ethnic district and in Douala, but had limited success.

In 1958 he was appointed Minister of Public Works, Transport and Mines in the coalition government of Ahmadou Ahidjo. In 1959-60 he was Minister of Justice, a key post at the time of independence (1 January 1960) amid civil war between the government and the *Union des Populations du Cameroun* (UPC) revolutionaries.

In 1959 he formed a new socialist party, the *Parti Socialiste Camerounais* (PSC). He was elected to the National Assembly in the elections following independence. When President Ahidjo then formed another coalition the PSC leader became Minister of Foreign Affairs, responsible for the new state's policy of close ties with France and most other ex-French states, combined with efforts to seek "reunification" with former British Cameroons which consisted of two provinces, Northern Cameroons and Southern Cameroons. In 1961 referenda there led to Northern Cameroons voting for union with Nigeria, which caused a serious disagreement between Cameroon and Nigeria; while Southern Cameroons voted for union with ex-French Cameroon. Thus the Cameroon Federation came into being on 1 October 1961.

In a reshuffle after that, however, Okala was dropped from the government. He had not joined Ahidjo's *Union Camerounaise* (UC) and in 1962 he made closer contact with other political leaders outside the UC. On 15 June 1962 he, André Mbida (q.v.), Théodore Mayi Matip and Marcel Bebey-Eyidi signed an open letter accusing the government of aiming at a one-party state and dictatorship. With the other signatories he was arrested and imprisoned. On his release in 1965 he helped dissolve the PSC to make way for the one-party regime he had opposed. Then he joined the single party, the *Union Nationale Camerounaise* (UNC).

In 1968 he was appointed Ambassador-at-large by President Ahidjo, but on the creation of a unitary state to replace the Federal system in May 1972 he was dropped from the post. He died over a year later.■

Okigbo, C.I. (1932-67)

OKIGBO, Christopher Ifekandu (1932-67).

NIGERIAN poet, probably the most famous among his contemporaries. Okigbo was born on 16 August 1932 in Ojoto, near Onitsha, in Anambra State, Nigeria. After primary education at a local school, he attended the Government College in Umuahia before reading classics from 1951 to 1956 at the University of Ibadan.

In late 1956 he joined the Federal Nigeria Public Service as personal assistant to the Minister of Research and Information, serving in Lagos until 1958 when he resigned to become vice-principal of Fiditi Grammar School near Ibadan. From there Okigbo joined the staff of the University of Nigeria, Nsukka, as assistant librarian at its Enugu campus from 1958 to 1960. He later became the representative of the Cambridge University Press in Nigeria as well as serving as co-editor of *Transition*, the Pan-African literary quarterly magazine which later changed its name to *Ch'Indaba*. He was also editor of the Ibadan-based Mbari Press.

The first volume of his poetry was published in 1962 as *Heavensgate*, followed two years later by *Limits* and *Silences* in 1965. That same year he participated in the Commonwealth Arts Festival that was held in London where he read some of his poems. In 1967, with another Nigerian author Chinua Achebe, he founded a publishing house in Enugu. The previous year the First Festival of Negro Arts held in Dakar, Senegal, had awarded Okigbo the First Prize for Poetry, but he rejected the award, saying "There is no such thing as Negro art".

C.I. Okigbo

Okigbo's poetry had been likened to European and especially English classics which the poet studied for his BA degree in 1956 and some critics have tended to highlight the so-called exceptional influence of Ezra Pound and T.S. Eliot on his style. But, while not refuting the analogy, Okigbo uses African images of sacred shrines, streams and forests to create a distinctive, if complex, poetic style that sets him in a class of his own in African literature. His poetry is firmly rooted in the reality of his experience. "I believe that writing poetry is a necessary part of my being alive, which is why I have written nothing else," Okigbo said.

Following the outbreak of the Nigerian civil war in 1967 when Lieutenant Colonel Ojukwu, who was Governor of the then Eastern Nigeria, led the region into secession, Okigbo joined the secessionist forces as a major. He was killed in action against the Federal forces in October 1967 on the Nsukka front. A new volume of his poetry was published posthumously in 1971 as *Labyrinths with Paths of Thunder*. His personality and works are the theme of Ali Mazrui's philosophical novel entitled *The Trial of Christopher Okigbo*. Okigbo, generally regarded as one of the finest and most complex of all African poets who employed English as their medium, is widely anthologised.■

Okotie-Eboh, F.S. (1912-66)

OKOTIE-EBOH, Chief Festus Sam (1912-66).

NIGERIAN politician, one of the political leaders in the era of the first Nigerian Republic. He was born on 18 July 1912 in the old Warri province, the son of a chief of the Itsekiri people of latter-day Bendel State. He was educated at the Sapele Baptist School, and after a year as a municipal clerk taught

Chief F.S. Okotie-Eboh

for several years. He joined the Bata Shoe Company in 1935 as a clerk. Through private study and determination he qualified in 1942 as an accountant and was later appointed chief clerk in Lagos. He went on to become a deputy manager of the Sapele branch of the Bata Shoe Company which then sent him to Czechoslovakia, where he studied for and obtained diplomas in business administration and chiropody. He was in that country at the time of the communist coup d'état of 1948.

On his return to Nigeria he resolved to go into business on his own. He became a timber and rubber merchant and opened a chain of schools and enterprises with which he laid the foundations for his own personal fortune. He entered politics in 1951 when he was elected to the Western Region House of Assembly. He had already been chosen the first secretary of the Warri National Union and was secretary-general of the Itsekiri National Society. He moved to the Federal House of Representatives in 1954 as the member for the Warri division and in the same year became the national treasurer of the National Council of Nigeria and the Cameroons (NCNC; the party later changed its name to the National Council of Nigerian Citizens).

Okotie-Eboh was appointed Federal Minister of Labour in 1955. He became Finance Minister in 1957 combining with his duty as leader of the NCNC parliamentary party in the Federal House.

He was a man of influence and power, with considerable financial strength and know-how. He retained the important Finance portfolio until the fall of Nigeria's first civilian administration, during which he was kidnapped and killed by soldiers on 15 January 1966 in the military coup d'état.■

Okot p'Bitek (1931-82)

OKOT P'BITEK (1931-82).

UGANDAN poet, one of Africa's best known literary figures and a trenchant commentator on contemporary culture in the Continent. He was, to many in Africa and beyond, one of the finest poets of the 20th century. Okot p'Bitek was also a novelist, dramatist, philosopher and teacher. His death on 19 July 1982, at the relatively young age of 51, was a great blow for Uganda as well as for Africa. He had been a pivotal figure in the continent's literature with the fusion of the past with the present and the future that he achieved in his own writings.

Okot p'Bitek

He was born in 1931 in Uganda's northern district of Gulu where he received his early education. Following his father, the young Okot chose to become a teacher. After attending King's College, Budo, near the capital Kampala, he undertook, in 1952, a teacher's training course of two years at the Government Training College at Mbarara in western Uganda.

It was Okot p'Bitek who in the 1950s gave impetus to African literature by a series of books which set out very remarkable and distinct markers for the future. His first book, Lack Tar, published in 1953 in the Acholi language, was a pungent rebuff at Africans who severed their links with their ancestral roots and traditions. This was Okot's first assertion of the direction African literature should take, and it was given a definitive mark in his epic-long poem, Song of Lawino, which came out in English in 1966; it blended contemporary satirical ironies into a verse form approximating to Acholi poetry.

Okot p'Bitek repeatedly clashed with "tribalists, shallow-minded traditionalists as much as he did with the half-baked custodians of Western civilization" he so aptly illustrated in his next book Song of Ocol.

For him, the world was Africa, firmly rooted, as he often said, in the "homestead pumpkin" that refuses to be uprooted but one that changes with the times to suit its needs and aspirations. Okot p'Bitek established himself as one of Africa's much loved poets with such classics as Song of the Prisoner and Song of Malaya which jointly won the 1972 Kenyatta Prize for Literature; Horn of My Love (1974); and Hare and Hornbill, published in 1978. He championed the cause of African oral literature, while remaining very vocal about what Nigeria's Chinua Achebe, another great African literary personality, once described as the "burning issues of the day".

Talking of the "African tragedy", Okot once said: "It consists of the endless and often meaningless blood letting, the destruction of the basic freedoms of movement, association, communication: the economic chaos, the fears, frustration, humiliation and uncertainty about tomorrow, all of which have turned the entire Continent into one vast scattered clan, teaming with refugees. In the ensuing confusion, the neo-colonial forces both from the West and the East have entrenched themselves by offering their sophisticated merchandise of death".

In 1964 he presented his thesis on Acholi oral literature at Oxford in Britain. In 1968, he became Director of the Uganda Cultural Centre. But he soon left home for Kenya to work at the University of Nairobi. There, together with Ngugi wa Thiong'o, Kenya's renowned novelist, he was instrumental in the abolition of the English Department and its replacement with the Department of Literature. Together they altered its direction emphasizing the primacy of African studies in relation to all else.

Okot did not stay there long, he refused to become the desk-bound scholar. He chose to return to the village to develop drama from the roots. In the meantime, he had read law, anthropology, sociology and theology after giving up the pursuit of another of his talents – football; he once played for the Uganda national team.

Not long before his death he returned to Kampala to become Professor of Creative Writing at Makerere University where he

587

had taught briefly in 1964. By that time Okot p'Bitek had ten published works to his name including the polemical *East Africa's Cultural Revolution*, published in 1973.■

Okpara, M.I. (1920-84)

OKPARA, Dr Michael Iheonukara (1920-84).

NIGERIAN politician, Premier of the Eastern Region in the First Republic when the country was divided into three and then four Regions. He was born on 25 December 1920 at Umuegwu Okpuala, Ohuhu, in the area of Umuahia (now in Imo State). After schooling at the local Methodist school and the Methodist College at Uzuakoli, he went to Yaba Higher College at Lagos in

M.I. Okpara

1941, and completed medical studies at the Nigerian School of Medicine in 1947.

After working for the government as an Assistant Medical Officer at Maiduguri and Lagos, he set up in private medical practice at Umuahia from 1949 to 1952, and was also honorary surgeon at the Methodist Hospital at Amachara near Umuahia. During that time he also began his political activity. He joined in the widespread protests by Nigerians at the shooting of coal miners in Enugu in 1949, and was arrested and put under surveillance for a time by the colonial authorities.

In 1952 he was elected to the Eastern Region House of Assembly as a National Council of Nigeria and the Cameroons (NCNC; later National Council of Nigerian Citizens) member for Bende, and was appointed Minister without Portfolio in the Regional government at Enugu with responsibility for conducting the 1953 elections. Having supported the NCNC leader, Dr Nnamdi Azikiwe, against a revolt by senior colleagues in the NCNC, Okpara became Minister of Health in the Regional government headed by Azikiwe in 1954. He served as Minister of Production in 1957-58, and Minister of Agriculture in 1958-59.

When Dr Azikiwe resigned in 1959 as Premier of the Eastern Region, Dr Okpara succeeded him. Thus he presided over the Eastern Region from independence in 1960 until the fall of the first civilian regime in 1966. He also became the national leader of the NCNC when Dr Azikiwe became Governor-General in 1960. (Nigeria became a republic on 9 October 1963 and Dr Azikiwe its first President.)

Dr Okpara, who was called "M. I. Power", was a dynamic character, and his government of the Eastern Region was dynamic. Himself owner of a large cocoa farm in his home area, he sought to promote agricultural development; he also promoted many new industries in the region. The large-scale plantations of the Eastern Nigeria Development Corporation were a limited success, but there was considerable development of what had been the poorest region in Nigeria, while the new oilfields began to bring in more wealth in the time of Okpara's government. While the Eastern Region was largely peaceful at that time, it was naturally affected by the growing political tensions of the First Republic. While the NCNC was allied to the dominant Northern People's

Congress (NPC), Dr Okpara led the protests against the accuracy of the 1962-63 censuses which contributed to worsening tension. In the 1964 general elections, the NCNC was allied with the Action Group in the United Progressive Grand Alliance (UPGA), of which Okpara was leader. After UPGA's defeat there was brief talk of secession by the East, now in opposition to the NPC-dominated Federal government.

Within the Eastern Region one political problem was opposition by non-Ibo peoples to alleged Ibo control. Because of this, British Southern Cameroons, which had been joined to the Region for many purposes, voted in the 1961 referendum against union with Nigeria, preferring union with ex-French Cameroon. The Calabar-Ogoja-Rivers (COR) movement called for a separate state for remaining minority peoples in the Region, in areas which were eventually to become the Rivers and South Eastern (later Cross River) States. Dr Okpara favoured the COR state in principle and spoke in 1964 in favour of splitting the Eastern, Western and Northern Regions; the previous year he had supported the creation of the Mid-West out of the Western Region. But the Eastern Premier said he wanted the three regions to be split simultaneously, and in fact they were not split up until 1966.

Okpara was not affected by the general bad reputation which the "old politicians" had acquired, especially because of corruption, by the time of the 1966 coup. But his government, with the other civilian Regional and Federal governments, was sacked by the new military regime of Gen Ironsi (q.v.). In the course of that coup, troops loyal to the plotters were moved to Enugu, but there was no attack on the Premier. This was possibly because President Makarios of Cyprus, who had attended the Commonwealth prime ministers' conference at Lagos just before, was Okpara's guest at Enugu. But some Nigerians suspected that it was because Okpara and the leading plotters were of the same ethnic group. Tension caused by this suspicion and other factors led to the second 1966 coup, the massacres of Easterners in the North, and the civil war. During that period Dr Okpara was arrested for some time in 1966 by order of the Eastern Military Governor, Colonel Ojukwu.

Later, however, Okpara worked with Ojukwu after the declaration of the East's secession in May 1967 as the Republic of Biafra. He was an adviser to Ojukwu and went on missions for Biafra overseas. He left when the Biafrans were re-integrated early in 1970, and went to the Irish Republic, where he did further medical studies and became a Licentiate of Apothecaries Hall, Dublin.

In 1978 Dr Okpara returned from exile. He played only a minor role in politics under the Second Republic (1979-83). But he headed the movement for a new state, Abia State, to be carved out of Imo, and joined the ruling party at Federal level, the National Party of Nigeria (NPN), in 1983, believing that party was best able to satisfy the demands for new states. In his home area he was grand patron of the Ohuhu Welfare Union and founder of the Umuegwu Medical Clinic.

Dr Michael Okpara died on 17 December 1984 while attending his father's funeral at Umuegwu in their home area. He left a widow – Adamma *née* Kanu, whom he married in 1949 – and six children. His funeral a month later was attended by countless mourners; the many eulogies included one from 80-year-old Nnamdi Azikiwe who said, "Irrespective of political persuasion, Nigerians should be honest in frankly admitting without reservation whatsoever that Mike was a political hero." ■

Okwaraji, S. (1964-89)

OKWARAJI, Samuel (1964-89).

NIGERIAN football star. He was born on 20 March 1964 at Umudioka in Imo State. He lost his father at the age of three and was brought up by his mother. After his primary education, he went to Eziachi Secondary School in Orlu and began playing football while there. His performance even at that early stage earned him the nickname "Wasky Pele". Later he played for a neighbouring school—Boys' Secondary School, Nkwerre—in the World Secondary Schools Soccer Competition in Europe.

Okwaraji had already made a name for himself in football in Nigeria before embarking on his brilliant soccer career in Europe. But what is more remarkable was the way he

S. Okwaraji

admirably combined his success in football with a distinguished academic performance in his Law studies. He was already doing postgraduate studies in Law at the time of his premature death.

His soccer career spanned Italy, Austria and West Germany before he ended up in Belgium in 1989. In 1984 he successfully combined his Law studies in Rome with playing occasionally on semi-professional Italian sides like S.S. Macareze. After graduating in Law in 1985, he joined Falcao and Cerezo, the Brazilian internationals, in A.S. Roma, the Italian first division side. From this he moved to Yugoslavia's champion side, Dynamo Zagreb, a year later.

His remarkable talent and expertise in the field of soccer was acknowledged in Austria while he was playing for Klagenfurt, a first division side, and he was popularly acclaimed the local "Pele". Okwaraji's name became a household word among soccer fans and he shared the limelight in popular European journals like *Wierner* with film celebrities such as Klaus Kinski and Marcello Mastroianni.

Okwaraji was a young man who loved his country deeply. He joined the Green Eagles—the national team—in December 1987 in order to use his talent to serve his

motherland. His soccer career in Europe reached its most brilliant stage in 1989 when he left his former club Eintracht Frankfurt for Antwerp, who paid $450,000 to effect his release. Okwaraji was earning a good deal of money too; but in spite of this, his strong sense of patriotism impelled him to answer the call of his motherland when he returned to Nigeria in August 1989 to play in the national team during the match against Angola in the qualifying World Cup series. It was his resolve that Nigeria must feature in the 1990 World Cup in Italy. It was while playing in this match that he suddenly collapsed and died seven minutes to the end of the game, on 12 August 1989.

He was a devoted son and a loving brother and had taken steps to see to the welfare of his family. He was indeed the family breadwinner, and was making arrangements to get married to his girlfriend Beatrice Ohiri from Imo State when death struck. His affection was not limited to the members of his family. His deep love for the people of his community is remarkable for a man of his age—he was only 25 when he died. He gave 10,000 naira to his local community in Umudioka to aid its piped water project. He also gave two post-primary scholarships for his community.

Okwaraji's contribution to soccer in Nigeria was rewarded by the national honours given him after his death. He was given a hero's burial by the government and the Nigerian Football Association (NFA). For a man of his age, Okwaraji could be said to have achieved a lot. His life was cut short at the point when he was poised for even greater achievement and his death was a grievous loss not only to his family but to Nigeria and to Antwerp, his club in Belgium. He will be remembered always as a patriot, a soccer star and a hero.■

Okwei, O. (1872-1943)

OKWEI, Madam Omu (1872-1943).

NIGERIAN businesswoman who crowned a highly successful business career at the great market town of Onitsha by becoming Omu or Queen of her home of Ossomari.

This was a trading town on the Niger, downstream from Onitsha. The Ibos there, as at Onitsha and Aboh, were influenced in the past by Benin and had monarchies, unlike most other Ibos. King (Obi) Nzedegwu of Ossomari, who made various treaties with the Europeans following the major British expedition up the Niger in 1854, had a son Osuna Afubeho, a warrior, who was the father of Okwei. Despite her good family connections she had, in true Ibo fashion, to work her own way to business success; but she was helped by being apprenticed as a child to an aunt in the Igala country to the north.

In 1884 her father died as she returned to her home town. In that same year the National African Company, later renamed the Royal Niger Company (RNC), concluded ambiguous or fraudulent "treaties" with rulers along the Niger, to arrest a claim to sovereignty and a complete trade monopoly. These were enforced with ruthless efficiency and many Africans were deprived of their livelihood from trade in palm produce and European goods. However, from then on Okwei seized with great success all the opportunities that remained to an African trader. She started trading at Atani where she lived with her mother. Later she made contracts with European traders and African agents of firms at Atani for the supply of food in exchange for imported goods.

Against the wishes of her family, she married Joseph Allagoa, a Brass trader, in 1888, but they soon separated. In 1895 she made a second marriage, also opposed by her family, but unlike the first, this was more successful and helped advance her business career. Her husband, Opene of Aboh, was a son of a very wealthy woman, Okwuenu Ezeiwere. He lived at Onitsha and she joined him in that flourishing market town. European firms and Christian missions had been at Onitsha from the 1850s. The firms were incorporated or squeezed out by the RNC from 1884 to 1900, but in 1900, deprived of its charter and monopoly, the RNC became one firm out of many, and other firms and expatriate banks made Onitsha one of their main centres of operations. At the same time the British occupation of Iboland and of Northern Nigeria expanded trade, of which a large part came to pass through Onitsha, handled to a great extent by African traders.

Madam Okwei became an agent for the RNC, selling palm oil and palm kernels to it in exchange for imported goods which she resold widely. According to the historian Felicia Ekejiuba who has studied Okwei's career, her credit value with the company in 1910 amounted to 20,000 gallons of oil or about £400. She expanded operations, sending her own agents to Oguta, an important trading centre near the Niger, and most of the Niger Delta region. Whatever economic changes occurred, she hardly ever lost. When the sterling was introduced in 1902 she used both that and the old cowrie currency in operations until sterling became generalized after 1918.

To some extent expatriates dominated the scene at Onitsha. By 1915 John Holt, Miller Bros., and the RNC were there, and a remarkable independent businessman, John Murray Stuart-Young, known in Ibo as "Odoziaku." Competition was stiff. But African traders aided by expatriate banks did very well. Madam Okwei in particular came to dominate the network of Nigerian links to the firms for supplies and resale.

She established close ties with male business partners who included Chief Quaker Bob Manuel of Degema; Chief Kio Young Jack; Mr. Gascoyne and later Mr. Cooper, RNC managers at Atani; Mr. J. Newton, RNC manager at Onitsha; and an Onitsha bank manager, Mr. J. Windfall.

In the early years of the 20th century the market was held at Onitsha every four days, near the river bank. Aguleri, Asaba and Atani were important alternative trade centres then. But Onitsha soon eclipsed the others. In 1916 the market was moved to a new site on land partly leased by Madam Okwei. Eventually, at her death, she owned a third of all the land near the river bank at Onitsha, leasing it to firms and individuals.

She also did well, after 1920, by loaning money to young traders, and to litigants needing money to bring lawsuits; these were repaid with 60/90 per cent interest. She bought coral beads and ivory to hire out to women for traditional festivals.

Ivory was one article she sold to firms in the 1920s. Among the imported goods she handled, gin was important. 400 gallons of it, with bottle labels translated into Ibo, were sent inland from Onitsha every day except Sunday in peak years. Madam Okwei bought lorries and canoes for trade with Port Harcourt, Calabar and other places.

Immensely rich from her successful trading, Madam Okwei came through the

1930s' economic depression almost unscathed. She was one of the first car owners in Onitsha. At her death she owned over 20 houses in Onitsha.

In 1912 her husband became a member of a "Native Court" established by the British as the main local government institution (at that time) in Iboland. He also became *Eze Otu*, Chief of the "Onitsha Waterside" settlement which in 1931 had about 15,000 inhabitants from various parts of Nigeria, attracted by the city's trade and living away from the old Ibo town. Their son, Peter Opene, worked for the Royal Niger Company and had taken over the management of his mother's business operations by 1935. A son by her first marriage, Francis Allagoa, entered government service and in 1935 became Amanyanabo of Nembe (Brass) in succession to his father.

In 1935 Okwei became Omu or "queen" of Ossomari. Not exactly the wife of the Obi, she reigned with him and was chairwoman and spokeswoman of the traditional "Council of Mothers". There were representatives of the Aboh, Igala, Nupe and Hausa communities at her coronation in Onitsha. She concentrated on her traditional functions and left her son in charge of her business from then on.

Omu Okwei died a very wealthy woman in May 1943. A statue of her was unveiled in Onitsha in 1963. ■

Oloitipitip, S.S. (1927-85)

OLOITIPITIP, Stanley Shapashina (1927-85).

KENYAN politician. Having grasped the reality of British colonialism at an early age, Oloitipitip played a crucial role in organizing his people and awakening them to the possibilities of political independence. Although in essence an ethnic leader in his early political career, Oloitipitip grew into one of the strongest defenders of Kenyan nationalism.

Born at Loitoktok in the Masailand of Kenya, Stanley Shapashina Oloitipitip was one of the most important post-independence Kenyan politicians. He was educated at local colonial government schools, later joining the medical corps of the King's African Rifles in 1943 and qualifying as a nursing orderly. He served with the rank of sergeant in the British colonial army in India, Sri Lanka and Burma where he won the Burma Star for bravery.

S.S. Oloitipitip

After demobilisation Oloitipitip returned to East Africa and soon became leader of the Maasai Moran (initiated warriors) in his home region. During the time (1948-50) he also served as a medical assistant at Munduli Hospital and Loliondo Medical Centre in neighbouring Tanzania. He returned to Kenya and worked at Kajiado District Hospital near his home. In the years leading up to Kenyan independence from British colonial rule Oloitipitip became one of the political leaders of the Maasai. He was elected deputy chairman of the Maasai United Front, essentially an ethnic grouping. Oloitipitip was also a member and later organizing secretary in his district of the Kenya African Democratic Union (KADU), which with the Kenya African National

Union (KANU) was the other major pre-independence Black national political party. KADU was notable for its coincidence of views with the outgoing colonial administration, especially its opposition to a strong central government.

At independence in 1963 Oloitipitip was elected Member of Parliament for Kajiado South, his home constituency, on a KADU ticket, a seat he retained until his expulsion in 1984 from KANU, Kenya's sole and only legal political party. KADU had merged with KANU at independence in 1963 in a show of political unity. Before Oloitipitip's political demise, however, he had a long political career spanning two decades. After his election to parliament he was appointed Assistant Minister of Commerce and Industry and subsequently served as Assistant Minister of Health, Minister of Natural Resources, Minister for Home Affairs and Minister of Local Government. He was also KANU chairman of his home district Kajaido.

A heavily-built man, Oloitipitip was a controversial personality. In 1976, as Minister of Natural Resources under President Jomo Kenyatta, Oloitipitip was instrumental in securing the succession of the then Vice-President Daniel arap Moi to the Presidency. The so-called "Oloitipitip Group" which was composed of many MPs and cabinet ministers, threw its support behind Moi's legal right to the Presidency on the death of Kenyatta, thus helping to stave off pressures within Kenya for amendments to the Constitution, which would have entailed a Presidential election. Oloitipitip had had a long-standing rivalry with a previous Vice-President Oginga Odinga who later became a political opponent of the Kenyatta and Moi regimes.

Oloitipitip, "the uncrowned King of Masailand", like a lot of political figures was, however, eventually to face his political Armageddon. During the Commission of Enquiry in 1984 into the anti-Government activities of the former Attorney-General, Charles Njonjo, he was named with 13 others as co-conspirators in an attempt to overthrow President Moi with whom he had by then become disenchanted. Oloitipitip was allegedly to have become Vice-president under Njonjo. He was expelled from KANU, stripped of his posts and returned, prey to profound depression, to Masailand, where he died on 22 January 1985. ■

Olorun-Nimbe, A.I. (1908-75)

OLORUN-NIMBE, Dr Abubakar Ibiyinka (1908-75).

NIGERIAN doctor and politician, first and only Mayor of Lagos. He attended the Tinubu Methodist School, the Aroloya Government Moslem School, going to CMS Grammar School and King's College where he finished schooling in 1928.

Dr. A.I. Olorun-Nimbe

He graduated in medicine at the University of Glasgow in 1937, and returned to Nigeria in 1938. He joined the government medical service at first, and like other Nigerian doctors soon objected to the conditions of service, which openly discriminated against African doctors. He led a group of doctors in a protest over pay and conditions before leaving government service in 1941 to start his own private clinic at Kakawa Street on Lagos Island.

He was elected to the Lagos Town Council and was already a prominent citizen of Lagos as a doctor and councillor before taking part in nationalist mass politics after 1945. A practising Moslem, he made the pilgrimage to Mecca twice. He was a member of the Ahmadiyya Movement and of the Ansar-ud-Deen Society, both influential among Lagos' many Moslems.

He joined the Nigerian National Democratic Party (NNDP), led by Herbert Macaulay (q.v.), which from 1944 was an affiliate and supporter of the National Council of Nigeria and the Cameroons (NCNC). In December 1945 Olorun-Nimbe, Vice-President of the NNDP, was elected to the Legislative Council for one of the Lagos seats, as the NNDP-NCNC candidate, defeating Mr O. Alakija of the Nigeria Youth Movement. He was re-elected in 1947, the year he also joined an NCNC delegation to Britain.

In 1950 elections were held for the first wholly elected Lagos Town Council. In the polling on 16 October 1950 the "Demo-Labour-Market" alliance, as it was called, a group dominated by the NCNC and the remnants of Macaulay's NNDP, won 18 out of the 24 seats. Dr Olorun-Nimbe became Mayor of Lagos. But his position was before long weakened as a result of his involvement in national politics, and of his municipal government's handling of the affairs of an expanding and complex commercial and administrative capital.

In 1951, while Mayor, Olorun-Nimbe successfully contested one of the five Lagos seats for the Western House of Assembly, for the NCNC. He then insisted on standing for election as a Lagos representative in the Central House of Representatives, although pressed by the NCNC to stand down and accept a large salary (£2,500 p.a.) as Mayor so as to make way for Dr Azikiwe, the NCNC leader, to go to the House of Representatives. For his attitude he was expelled from the NCNC.

From then on he was at odds with the councillors who had been his colleagues, as well as the opposition (affiliated to Awolowo's Action Group) in the Town Council. As the opposition mounted increasing attacks on alleged malpractice, he admitted that "there is organised corruption in the Lagos Town Council." The British government ordered an inquiry which was conducted by Mr Bernard Storey, Town Clerk of Norwich. Its report early in 1953 found that there had been corruption and other irregular and indefensible activities. As Lagos came under the Western Region for such purposes as this, the Premier of the West, Chief Awolowo, took action on the report and dissolved the Town Council.

Fresh elections were held later in 1953, but the system was altered; now there were eight chiefs and the Oba (then Adele II) was President of the Council. There was no longer a Mayor, nor has there been since then. Dr Olorun-Nimbe, the only mayor, retired from active politics. He died in Lagos on 5 February 1975. ■

Olympio, S.E. (1902-63)

OLYMPIO, Sylvanus Epiphanio (1902-63).

TOGOLESE statesman, first President of his country. Offspring of a wealthy family, Olympio was born in Lomé on 6 September 1902, the son of the businessman Epiphanio Olympio (1873-1968). He attended local German primary and secondary schools, as Togo was then a German colony (Germany colonised Togo in 1884, but surrendered it in 1914 to Britain and France who subsequently divided it between themselves).

Olympio went to Austria after his secondary education and studied at the University of Vienna before going to the London School of Economics and Political Science in 1922.

Returning to West Africa in 1926, he joined the United Africa Company (UAC), serving with it in Nigeria from 1926 to 1928, in the then Gold Coast in 1928, and later in Togo between 1928 and 1938 as the district manager for Togo, the highest post held by an African at the time in the foreign multinational firm.

Olympio was active in the pan-Ewe unification movement and had links with the All-Ewe Conference in the British-administered part of Togo and the Gold Coast. This, as well as his criticism of French colonial administration, brought him into conflict with the two colonial authorities. In 1942 he was banished to Djougou, Dahomey (now Benin). His release and subsequent

S.E. Olympio

return to Togo were facilitated by de Gaulle's victory in France at the end of the Second World War.

A founding member of the *Comité de l'Unité Togolaise* (CUT), originated in 1941, Olympio led the party to victory in the French Togo territorial elections of 1946, and became the President of the Territorial Assembly until 1952. Following Olympio's critical speech at the UN in 1947 when he denounced the division of the Ewe community, more ruthless measures were introduced by the French authorities who engineered his transfer to the Paris branch of the UAC. Olympio declined the "promotion", following which he was arrested and convicted of "contravening currency regulations", fined $25,000 and banned from running for elective office. At the same time the French encouraged the growth of more pliable parties, leading to the rise of the conservative *Parti Togolais du Progrès* (PTP), led by the pro-French Nicolas Grunitzky (q.v.). In 1956 the PTP was elected the ruling party with Grunitzky as Prime Minister.

The Grunitzky administration was unpopular because of its conservatism at a time of rising nationalism in the country. The UN refused to end the "Trust Territory" status of the country until properly supervised elections were held. In the subsequent UN-supervised elections of 27 April 1958,

Olympio and the CUT swept into power, winning 33 seats against the PTP's three. The ban on Olympio was lifted and he became Prime Minister. In 1959 he was also elected Mayor of Lomé.

As Prime Minister of autonomous Togo within the French Union, Olympio used his position to campaign for full independence which was achieved on 27 April 1960. A year later, in the elections of 1961, his party won all the seats in the National Assembly, and following constitutional revisions the same year he was unanimously elected the first President of the Republic of Togo.

President Olympio was popular and respected in Togo as the architect of independence. He encouraged foreign investment to exploit Togo's mineral resources, giving rise to the expansion of the phosphate industry which commenced in 1962. However, opposition to the one-party regime was severely repressed. Togo's successive budgets showed austerity and balancing which prevented the integration of the demobilised French colonial soldiers into the new Togo armed forces. The former colonial soldiers had sought to be incorporated in the national army but Olympio argued that his country neither needed a bigger force nor could afford the luxury of veterans of the colonial era. This offended the demobilised soldiers who teamed up with the dissatisfied elements in the NCO and officer corps in the army, who had wanted faster promotion and enhanced status within an enlarged army, to overthrow Olympio. On 13 January 1963 was shot dead in a military coup as he ran for refuge to the American Embassy in Lomé. The President's assassination caused great shock and much mourning especially in Nigeria and Ghana where he had many admirers. ∎

Omo-Osagie, H. (1896-1977)

OMO-OSAGIE, Chief Humphrey (1896-1977).

NIGERIAN politician. An early member of the National Council of Nigeria and the Cameroons (NCNC), through an affiliation with the Benin-based Otu-Edo move-

Chief H. Omo-Osagie

Meanwhile he had been serving on the Benin Divisional Council of which he became Chairman in 1947. He held that office until 1951 and, three years later, was elected to the Federal House of Representatives. He was soon recognized for hard work and organisational skill, and brought into Nigeria's first national administration under Sir Abubakar Tafawa Balewa (q.v.). He was appointed Parliamentary Secretary to the Federal Minister of Finance who then was Chief Festus Okotie-Eboh, a party colleague and fellow Midwesterner – the two men became leaders of the movement for the creation of that state. Omo-Osagie was soon elevated to the post of Minister of State in the same Ministry where he remained until 1963.

It was during this period that the NCNC/Otu-Edo alliance launched the campaign for Benin Province to be created into an autonomous Midwest Region. This was bitterly opposed by the Action Group government in the West, of which Benin Province formed an important part. In the campaign leading to the referendum on the issue Omo-Osagie led his Otu-Edo on a province-wide tour, seeking support for a positive vote. He got it and the Midwest was created in 1964. Soon after he left the Central Government to return to Benin as Deputy Administrator in the new region's interim administration and subsequently a leading member of the NCNC government of Chief Dennis Osadebay.

Shortly afterwards, however, a major rift developed between members of the Otu-Edo and their NCNC allies in the government. There were allegations of a plot to overthrow the administration and assassinate Osadebay, and of replacing the ruling NCNC with a party which would draw support from the Otu-Edo and the prohibited Owegbe society. Under the proposed arrangement, according to the allegations, Omo-Osagie would ascend to a position of authority as Premier of the Midwest Region. These allegations led to a Government-appointed Commission (1964) under Mr. Justice Alexander, which inquired into the activities of the Owegbe, a ritualistic cult which had been banned in 1959, and of its members which included Omo-Osagie and other prominent politicians in the Region.

Omo-Osagie was cleared by the Alexander Commission of any implication in the threat to assassinate Osadebay, but its report

ment of which he was president-general, he was a prime mover in the campaign for the creation of the Midwestern Region from the former West. When that was achieved in 1964 he became deputy leader of the new region. Omo-Osagie was also influential in the Benin traditional government, centred around the Oba who in 1960 made him the Iyasere (the traditional equivalent of Prime Minister) of Benin.

Born in 1896 in that famous seat of the ancient Edo empire but now capital of Bendel State, he was educated locally at Benin Government School. He entered King's College, Lagos, on scholarship and graduated in 1919. Following in the footsteps of the educated elite of the time he joined the colonial public service, working in the Medical Department (later to become the Ministry of Health). He left the Civil Service in 1945 to devote himself to a career in politics; two years later he was elected to the Western House of Assembly as a member of the NCNC/Otu-Edo alliance and was re-elected in 1951.

stressed that the Otu-Edo leaders "demonstrated utter, if not reckless, disregard for established law in that they have continued to foster the activities of the Owegbe society in the full knowledge that the worship and invocation of the Owegbe juju had been prohibited and with the objective of taking over control of the Government by these means."

He was detained briefly, but soon the process of parliamentary democracy was halted by the army intervention of 1966. Omo-Osagie and all other Nigerian politicians were thus relieved of their role and functions. He remained prominent in Benin affairs until his death on 15 September 1977. ■

Onabanjo, V. O. (1927-90)

ONABANJO, Chief Victor Olabisi (1927-90).

NIGERIAN journalist and politician. Born in Lagos on 12 February 1927, of an Ijebu Ode family, he went to the Baptist Academy in Lagos where he was adjudged a particularly bright student. In 1950-51 he studied at Regent Street Polytechnic in London and obtained a Diploma in Journalism. Then he worked for many years as a journalist, but was also involved in politics, first supporting the Nigerian Youth Movement (NYM).

From 1951 to 1953 he was editor of the *Nigerian Citizen* of Zaria, which formed the foundation of New Nigerian Newspapers. In 1953 he became editor of the NYM's newspaper, the *Daily Service.* Later he worked as editor of the *Radio Times,* deputy editor-in-chief of the Nigerian Broadcasting Corporation, a director of Western Nigeria Television and Broadcasting, and Editorial Director of the Express Group of Newspapers (1960-63). In his journalism he became noted for his readiness to defy the politicians and was called *Aiyekoto,* meaning in Yoruba "teller of bitter truths".

He became more active in politics himself, however, after working as media consultant and publicity man for Chief Awolowo (q.v.), leader of the Action Group

V.O. Onabanjo.

party, in the 1959 Federal elections. He became a leading figure in the AG in the 1960s, and was arrested with other AG personalities in 1962; placed first under house arrest in Forcados, he was charged with Chief Awolowo and others, but he was acquitted. In December 1964 he was elected to the Federal parliament to represent his home area of Ijebu Ode.

After the military takeover he served in the Western Region and (after 1967) Western State Governments as Commissioner for Home Affairs and Information, for Health, and for Lands and Economic Planning, from 1966 to 1969. Some years later, as the preparations for return to civilian rule progressed, he became chairman of Ijebu Ode Local Government and was elected in 1977 to the Constituent Assembly. He joined Chief Awolowo in the new Unity Party of Nigeria (UPN) and in 1979 was elected Governor of Ogun State by a huge majority.

As Governor he did what he could to carry out the UPN's programmes of free health and free education, though he was personally lukewarm about socialism as an ideology. But as Nigeria fell into economic crisis from 1982 he ordered salary cuts and privatisation measures. He joined actively in the opposition mounted by non-UPN governors to the policies of the National Party of Nigeria (NPN) which controlled the central government of the Federation. Always concerned with political and ethnic balance in the Federation, he argued for a confederal arrangement for running the affairs of the country. In 1983 he was easily re-elected Governor.

On 31 December 1983, however, the Federal and state civilian governments were overthrown by the military. The regime of Gen. Buhari had many former governors charged before special tribunals and Chief Onabanjo was the first to be convicted, on 31 May 1984. He was convicted of receiving an improper payment of 2.8m naira for the political funds of his party, the UPN. He received a very severe sentence (22 years' imprisonment) but did not serve it for in 1986 he was released and was allowed to go to Britain for medical treatment. He died in a London hospital on 14 April 1990. Onabanjo is remembered for the consistency with which he opposed whatever he perceived as an invasion of the rights of the individual citizen or sections of the citizenry.■

Ondo Edu, B. (died 1969)

ONDO EDU, Bonifacio (died 1969).

EQUATORIAL GUINEAN politician and leader of the *Movimiento de Union Nacional de Guinea Ecuatorial* (MUNGE). He came from the central town of Evinayong on the mainland Rio Muni and had his education at the San Jose mission centre in Evinayong. Like most of his compatriots, he took an interest at an early stage in politics which in the 1950s were centred on winning independence from Spain. The elimination by assassination and imprisonment of the protagonists in the anti-colonial struggle in the country forced Ondo to take refuge in neighbouring Gabon where he founded the *Union Popular de Liberación de Guinea Ecuatorial.*

He returned to Evinayong and from 1960 to 1961 became mayor of the chief town of the country's largest district. In 1963 he founded a new movement MUNGE, which was more moderate in its policies than his earlier organisation. Its formation was encouraged and supported by the Spanish and the *Casas Fuertes*, an organisation of expatriate owners of cocoa plantations and large commercial companies, who felt threatened by the radical nationalism of Atanasio Miyone Ndongo (q.v.) and his *Movimiento Nacional de Liberación de la Guinea Ecuatorial* (MONALIGE). Though MUNGE wanted independence for Equatorial Guinea, it favoured a gradual process towards its attainment and advocated close economic and political ties between Spain and independent Guinea. Thus Ondo Edu was able to enjoy the support of the Spanish authorities who had refused to recognise any nationalist movements in the colony until 1963.

Between 1964 and 1967 when Spain granted Autonomous Government (*Consejo de Gobierno*), Ondo Edu was named head of the administration which was not supported by Ndongo and many other nationalists. In 1966 he reiterated his party's policy of delaying independence until a future date before the United Nations Trusteeship Council. He led his party's delegation to the Constitutional Conference convened by Spain in 1967, though he was in fact leading the official delegation as President of the Autonomous Government. During the conference some dissident members of MUNGE joined the *Secretariado Conjunto* led by Macias Nguema (q.v.), which weakened Ondo Edu's position.

At the subsequent pre-independence general elections which took place in September 1968, his party won only seven of the 35 seats in the *Assemblea de la República*. He himself, though sponsored by the rich and influential members of the *Casas Fuertes* and supported by Spain, lost the presidential elections of the same year to Macias Nguema who beat him in the first and second ballot. Two of his former supporters, Ndongo Engonga and Naba Ada, joined the Nguema administration, becoming Vice-President of the *Assemblea de la República* and President of the Senate respectively.

Ondo Edu left Equatorial Guinea for Gabon shortly after independence on 12 October 1968. After reassurances by President Nguema about his safety he returned home in November 1968 but was soon charged with conspiracy to overthrow the administration. He was placed under house arrest and killed in January 1969, with other leading members of the MUNGE which, like other political parties in the country, was abolished a year later. His former colleague, Ndongo Engonga, and his wife Edelvina Oyana Ondo were among those executed by the regime in a purge in 1969. ■

court's Ibos acted in concert and upon an awareness of their common linguistic and cultural heritage was the occasion of the "welcome home" reception held for Dr Onwu by prominent Ibos there. The success of the Port Harcourt reception was instrumental in the decision to transform the Reception Committee into a permanent Ibo Union, a cultural organisation embracing all Ibo elements in Port Harcourt.

Onwu, S.E. (1908-69)

ONWU, Dr Simon Ezievuo (1908-69).

NIGERIAN physician, the first doctor from the Ibo community whose eminence is reputed to have catalysed the formation of the Ibo Union. He was born on 28 December 1908 in Affa in Anambra State, the son of Chief Onwubunta. His early schooling was at the Government School in Udi and at the Onitsha St. Mary's School where he was brought up as a Catholic. He then entered the Wesley Boys' High School in Lagos, but later transferred to King's College there. He did not, however, complete his secondary education in Lagos for in 1924 he accompanied Chief Onyeama of Eke on an extended trip to the United Kingdom, fulfilling the role of personal confidant to the late traditional ruler.

He returned to Britain the following year to study and in 1927 obtained his London Matriculation Certificate. Later that year he entered Edinburgh University Medical School and obtained the degrees of MB and ChB in July 1932, thus becoming the first medical doctor from the Ibo ethnic group in Eastern Nigeria. Also in 1932 he gained the diploma in Tropical Medicine and Hygiene from Liverpool University. Thereafter he went to Coombe Hospital in the Republic of Ireland and got his Licentiate in Midwifery.

Dr Onwu returned to his country in 1933 and joined the colonial civil service as a junior medical officer in Port Harcourt where he spent the next two years. His return to Eastern Nigeria in 1933 coincided with the emergence of political activities among the Ibos in the new urban setting of colonial Nigeria. It has been documented that the first instance in which Port Har-

Dr. S.E. Onwu

While Dr Onwu's reception provided the immediate incentive for the formation of the Ibo Union, the organisational initiative reflected fundamentally a new political assertiveness on the part of all politically conscious Nigerians. In this connection his return to Nigeria also inspired the formation of similar organisations in Lagos and elsewhere in the country.

As a medical officer he worked, for the next 27 years, in different parts of Nigeria. In 1948 he returned to Britain for a post graduate course and in 1950 became Senior Medical Officer in Aba. He was promoted two years later to the grade of Deputy Director of Medical Services in the Eastern Region. In 1957 he became the first African Director of Medical Services in that region, holding the post along with that of Permanent Secretary in the Ministry of Health until he retired from the Public Service in 1963.

In June 1964 he was appointed chairman of the Eastern Nigeria Housing Corporation, a post he held until his death. In 1965 he was elected the first African vice-president of the International Union of Building Societies.

He travelled extensively, visiting the United States of America, USSR, Germany and India under the auspices of the World Health Organisation and representing his country in many world conferences.

He did not confine his activities to the practice of medicine alone. He was actively involved with a number of charitable and religious organisations in Nigeria: he was chairman of the Red Cross Society, Eastern Nigeria; chairman of Cosmas and Damian; and vice-patron of the Society for the Prevention of Cruelty to Children.

In 1953 Dr Onwu was awarded the Coronation Medal and in 1954 and 1956 Queen Elizabeth II of England conferred upon him the Order of the British Empire (OBE) and Member of the Royal Victorian Order (MVO) respectively in recognition of his contributions and achievements.

He was a highly devoted family man and throughout his life showed a stringent application of Christian principles and an unequivocal pursuit of Christian ideas. In recognition of his devout life he was, in 1965, awarded by Pope Paul VI the Papal order of the Knight of Saint Sylvester. In 1968 he was again honoured by the Vatican by having his name enrolled in the Papal Scroll of Honour.

During the Nigerian civil war Dr Onwu, suffering from a prolonged illness, travelled to London for medical treatment. He died there on 4 June 1969. ∎

Onyekwelu, C.T. (1898-1971)

ONYEKWELU, Christopher Tagbo (1898-1971).

NIGERIAN businessman. Based at the great commercial centre of Onitsha, he was a pioneer of the record business in Nigeria. The son of a farmer, he was born in the Ibo village of Nawafia; he did not finish his primary schooling until he was about 20 years old. He then worked as a catechist for the Church Missionary Society (CMS), a railwayman, a police cadet, and a farmer before starting his business career at Onitsha in 1924.

By that time expatriate firms dominated import and export trade, but African traders could do well by supplying agricultural produce to the firms and distributing their imported goods. Madam Omu Okwei (q.v.) was the most outstanding of many successful traders. However, when they tried to compete with the firms in other sorts of trading they were not so successful, as C T. Onyekwelu found out. After selling palm kernels to exporters, he tried to run his own business of importing rice from Burma; later he began importing spare parts for British bicycles and sewing machines, increasingly used in Nigeria by then. However, this direct challenge to the firms' control of imports was met with their full force, and after one successful year he was forced out of business.

In 1929, C. T. Onyekwelu began importing gramophones and records. There he proved able to outdo the expatriate firms, for he was able to predict the popularity of records. He contacted many overseas suppliers willing to extend credit. From then on, except for a short-lived involvement in a sock-knitting factory project in 1934, he concentrated on importing and distributing records, gramophones and radio sets. He became one of the biggest importers and distributors of these increasingly popular goods in Eastern Nigeria.

In 1939 he branched out further by organising singers and musicians for local functions, and recording their music on tapes, which were sent by the CFAO firm to Europe for the making of records; the records were then shipped to Nigeria and distributed with C. T. Onyekwelu's own label.

In 1952 he bought his own recording machine, but unfortunately neither he nor the British technician he had hired could operate it. Later he made two journeys to Europe, and tried to persuade Decca to be his technical partner for a record-pressing enterprise; Decca refused. Then he decided to build his own studio and record-pressing factory at Onitsha, but he encountered further setbacks.

In 1955 the Eastern Nigeria Development Corporation refused him a £50,000 loan although he could offer as collateral real estate estimated at £100,000. Four years later, he received a £35,000 loan from the Federal Loans Board. Then there were many delays in starting the project. Eventually, Phillips, the leading Dutch firm, provided capital and took over production management. Onyekwelu kept about half of the equity and handled recording and marketing.

Nigeria's record industry thus started at last, essentially through Onyekwelu's pioneering efforts, but his career had shown the difficulties Nigerian businessmen faced in directing importing at the height of the colonial era, and in industrial ventures later. C. T. Onyekwelu, who was decorated by the Nigerian Government with the Order of the Niger, died on 29 June 1971. ■

Opangault, J. (1907-78)

OPANGAULT, Jacques (1907-78).

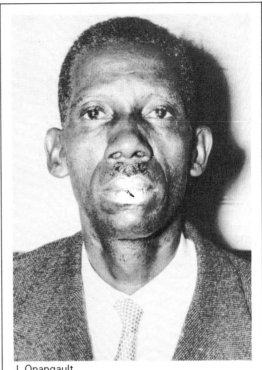

J. Opangault

CONGOLESE politician; president of the *Mouvement Socialiste Africain* (MSA) which was founded in 1946, he agitated for reforms. He was Vice-President of the self-rule government between 1957 and 1958 and later became Second Vice-President of independent Congo. Opangault was born on 13 December 1907 in Ikagna in northern Congo and after early schooling at a local Catholic Mission school in Boundji he went to Brazzaville to continue his education.

He started working as a clerk in the capital in 1938 and interested himself in the socialist ideas of the French Socialist Party (SFIO) with whose assistance he founded in 1946 the Brazzaville branch of the MSA. Initially the movement was largely dominated by European socialists like Cazaban-Mazerolles, a Frenchman who was its early leader, but with gradual Africanisation resulting from increased participation of Africans in politics, Opangault emerged as one of the first leading indigenous politicians and President of the MSA. The party made early gains in the inter-party rivalries between it and another front-runner, the *Parti Progressiste Congolais* (PPC), also formed in 1946 by Félix Tchicaya (q.v.).

Its support was, however, largely drawn from the northern Likouala-Mossaka district where Opangault and his lieutenants in the MSA came from. This ethnic identification was not unique to the MSA for the PPC too relied strongly for its support among Tchicaya's people in the Pointe-Noire region, and it was largely because of its opposition to these ethno-centred parties that the *Union Démocratique pour la Défense des Intérêts Africains* (UDDIA) of Abbé Fulbert Youlou (q.v.) though appearing late in 1956, emerged the most dominant of the three parties, absorbing both the PPC and the MSA.

Opangault's prominence in the late 1940s aided his election in 1946 to the Territorial Assembly; he was returned to the Assembly in the March 1957 elections when his party, gaining the support of independent members of the Assembly, had a narrow lead over the UDDIA. Constitutional rearrangements led to his appointment in May 1957 as Vice-President of the first Congolese government. He later became the Prime Minister in the government but in November 1958, when the country was proclaimed a republic, his majority in the Assembly was offset by the UDDIA whose leader, Fulbert Youlou, became Premier.

This period was followed by increased rivalries between the government and its opponents, resulting in February 1959 in riots in Brazzaville in which some 200 Laris (Youlou's people) and Mbochis (Opangault's people) were reported killed. Opangault and other opposition leaders were blamed for the riots, arrested and detained. Released six months later, Opangualt took his seat in parliament, having been elected in the June 1959 elections *in absentia* while serving his prison term. On the eve of independence in August 1960, he agreed to work with Youlou and brought his MSA into the ruling UDDIA. He was made Minister of State in the administration and later, in January 1961, became Second Vice-President of the Congo Republic with responsibility for Justice. Though he was demoted the following year to Minister of Public Works he remained politically prominent in the country until 1963. His presence in the administration calmed the inter-ethnic rivalries of the post-independence era and he used his influence wisely in appealing for unity of the Congo.

When the Youlou administration was forced out of office in August 1963 Opangault too lost his position. He was again arrested by the succeeding authorities; this was the end of his political career. Following his release he led a quiet and private life. He died in 1978. ■

Oritshejolomi-Thomas, H. (1917-79)

ORITSHEJOLOMI-THOMAS, Professor Horatio (1917-79).

NIGERIAN eminent surgeon, also prominent as a university teacher and administrator, he combined a brilliant medical career with headship of Nigeria's two major universities. He was among the generation of Nigerians who built up University College Hospital, Ibadan, and Lagos University Teaching Hospital and College of Medicine.

Oritshejolomi-Thomas was an Itsekiri, born in 1917 in Sapele in Bendel State where his family owned rubber plantations. After his primary and secondary education in Nigeria, he went to Birmingham University in Britain in 1937, where he read medicine. He subsequently worked for se-

veral medical degrees in Britain, including the fellowship of the Royal College of Surgeons of which, for several years, he was the only Nigerian recipient. For a while, from the time he completed his studies until 1948, he worked as a lecturer in Anatomy at Birmingham University as well as a surgeon in various British hospitals.

He returned to Nigeria in 1949, to become a member of the pioneering staff of University College, Ibadan, that was then just beginning to function under a special relationship with the University of London. At that time there was a growing need in Nigeria to create institutions of higher learning, both to meet individual aspirations and national manpower needs and to enable university degrees to be granted in the country. The new University of Ibadan, though short of adequate facilities, provided the basis for that development. The Medical Faculty of that institution began work in 1949 at temporary premises at the old Yaba Higher College and at Ibadan's Adeoyo Hospital. Oritshejolomi-Thomas who taught surgery was one of the first intakes of its fifteen staff members.

In 1953 he returned to Britain for a specialist course in plastic surgery at East Grinstead, Sussex. He returned home in the

Prof H. Oritshejolomi-Thomas

mid-1950s before the new teaching hospital of the University moved to its permanent site at Agodi in Ibadan. He worked there until the University became an autonomous institution in 1962, rising to become one of its leading heads of department and respected academic staff. In 1962, when the Lagos University Teaching Hospital and the College of Medicine was established by the Federal Government, Professor Oritshejolomi-Thomas was made head of its Department of Surgery. Soon he became head of the College of Medicine, first as Dean of the Medical School and Chairman of Lagos University Teaching Hospital (LUTH) Board of Management and later Provost of the College Medicine. During his seven years' headship of the College, he served for a while as acting Vice-Chancellor of the University of Lagos. He remained head of the College of Medicine for seven years, reverting to his earlier position of head of department in 1969.

In 1972 he was appointed Vice-Chancellor of the country's premier university, Ibadan, whose development owes much to the contributions of the generation of distinguished Nigerian scholars like himself. Professor Oritshejolomi-Thomas held that office until he retired in the 1975 nation-wide purge of public officers by the military regime. He died four years later, in July 1979, survived by his wife and their children. ■

E.W. Oryema

Oryema, E.W. (1917-77)

ORYEMA, Ewinayo Wilson (1917-77).

UGANDAN policeman, first African chief of the Uganda Police Force. He was born on 1 January 1917 in Anaka Payira, in the Acholi District of Uganda. He was educated at Gulu Elementary School in East Acholi from 1925 to 1926, Gulu High School from 1927 to 1931, and Buwualasi Teacher's Training College from 1931 to 1933 where he obtained a Teacher's Diploma. He began his career as a teacher at Gulu Primary School, then Gulu High School, and later Kitgum Primary School in West Acholi, where he taught from 1933 to 1938.

Perhaps the beginning of his promising and most eventful career was when he joined the colonial police force as probation constable in 1939. He was seconded to the then King's African Rifles from 1940-45 and became a sergeant in the Uganda Police Force in 1945, rising through the ranks to become Inspector of Police in 1951, Assistant Superintendent of Police in 1963, and finally Inspector-General of Police in 1964.

A dramatic change in Oryema's career came in 1971 when a military coup toppled the government of Milton Obote, bringing Major-General Idi Amin to power. Oryema was made Minister of Mineral and Water Resources in the military government. His stay in the government as Minister was precarious right from the beginning; it is believed that Amin forced Oryema to join his government in order to secure the support and loyalty of the Police Force. Oryema was killed along with Archbishop Luwum (q.v.) and Mr Oboth-Opumbi on 16 February 1977 by the agents of the government.

In recognition of his services during his lifetime, he was awarded numerous medals and was honoured by Pope Paul VI in 1969 with the order of the Knight of Saint Sylvester. ■

Otu, S.J.A. (1915-79)

OTU, Major-General Stephen J.A. (1915-79).

GHANAIAN military officer. He was born on 23 October 1915 and attended the Abetifi Presbyterian School and Achimota Teachers Training College. He taught briefly before joining the army in 1941, serving with the Army Education Corps of the Royal West African Frontier Force (RWAFF) that was stationed in The Gambia. In 1943 he changed from the Education Corps to Infantry and served as a Platoon and Company commander on the staff of the RWAFF. At the independence of Ghana in 1957 he was promoted commanding officer of the Third Battalion of the Ghana Army.

He served with the United Nations Peace-Keeping Force in the Congo (Zaire) where he was both senior military liaison officer at UN Headquarters in Leopoldville (Kinshasa) and commander of the Ghana Brigade. Promoted Brigadier in September 1961, he was elevated to the rank of Major-

Major-Gen. S.J.A. Otu

General a few weeks later and appointed Chief of Defence Staff of the Ghana Armed Forces, a post he held until he retired from the services in 1965. Otu later served as a diplomatic representative of Ghana in Israel in 1966 and was also Ghana's High Commissioner in India. Until his death in 1979, Major-General Otu was his country's High Commissioner in Kenya. ■

El-Ouali, M.S. (1950-76)

EL-OUALI, Mustafa Sayed (1950-76).

SAHRAWI politician, founder and first leader of POLISARIO. He was born in 1950, of Sahrawi parents, in neighbouring Mauritania. After primary and secondary education in his country of birth he proceeded to read law at the University of Rabat in Morocco which, at the time, attracted many of his countrymen.

Like many of his compatriots who were studying in the neighbouring country he underwent political radicalisation which resulted in opposition to Spanish colonisation of Western Sahara which was proclaimed the Sahrawi Arab Democratic Republic in 1976. The ultimate realisation of this nationalist fervour was the *Mouvement pour la Libération du Sahara* (MLS) which came into being with the aim of forcing Spain to implement the UN resolution recognising the Sahrawi right to self-determination. On 10 May 1973, the MLS regrouped as the *Front Populaire pour la Libération de Saguia El Hamra et Rio de Oro* (POLISARIO) under the leadership of el-Ouali, who was elected its first Secretary-General.

With an area of 266,000 square kilometres, and a population of about 80,000, Western Sahara is the single largest source in the world of phosphates. It was to free the country from Spanish colonialism that POLISARIO launched its armed struggle on 20 May 1973, with an attack on the Spanish military post at Khanga. Their initial military and diplomatic skill would not have enabled them to hold out for so long against the colonial forces had it not been for the daring determination and shrewd leadership of el-Ouali. Within months of POLISARIO's

M.S. El-Ouali

inception he had forged contacts with Sahrawi groups of similar persuasion, effecting a united front under POLISARIO.

El-Ouali worked tirelessly to sustain the momentum of the struggle, travelling across and outside the country to ensure liaison between various cells of POLISARIO and between the movement and its sympathisers in neighbouring and other countries, where he mobilised a diplomatic offensive against Spain. These efforts resulted in the visit of a UN mission in 1975 which later declared POLISARIO as the "dominant political force" in the territory. In October of the same year, the International Court of Justice ruled against Morocco's claim to Western Sahara, and in favour of the Sahrawi right to self-determination. This was followed in January 1976 by the OAU's recognition of POLISARIO as the genuine representative of the aspirations of the Sahrawi population.

Earlier, on 24 November 1975, Spain had instituted a tri-partite agreement with Morocco and Mauritania which placed Western Sahara under their joint rule. POLISARIO rejected the accord and intensified its military operations. On 27 February 1976 el-Ouali proclaimed the Sahrawi Arab Democratic Republic at a ceremony in the libera-

ted zone near the oasis of Mahbes. A provisional government of POLISARIO was formed on 4 March 1976.

The partition was followed by the escalation of the struggle, with Morocco launching a major military offensive against POLISARIO guerrillas. The effect on Mauritania on the other hand had been devastating to its political stability and economic growth. This destabilisation culminated in the overthrow of President Mokhtar Ould Daddah in a military coup in July 1978.

In a major offensive on 8 June 1976 POLISARIO guerrillas, under the personal command of el-Ouali, made a daring attack on the Mauritanian capital, Nouakchott. This attack was expensive for POLISARIO; not only was the whole 150-strong column either killed or captured by the Mauritanians, but el-Ouali himself was killed during the raid. His death deprived POLISARIO of one of its ablest leaders, and the anger and grief over it gave a new impulse and determination to the struggle. The 3rd POLISARIO Congress was convened from 26 to 30 August 1976 to reaffirm el-Ouali's policy of "No peace before the restoration of total independence". ■

Oufkir, M. (1920-72)

OUFKIR, General Mohammed (1920-72).

MOROCCAN military officer. He was born in 1920 and started his military career in the French army and then held powerful positions, related to security, after King Mohammed V (q.v.) was returned to the throne from exile in Madagascar in 1955. At independence in 1956 he was appointed Director-General of National Security, and he became Minister of the Interior in 1965.

In 1965 he was tried *in absentia* by a French court and sentenced to life imprisonment on charges of complicity in the disappearance in Paris of the exiled Moroccan opposition leader, Ben Barka (q.v.). The exiled politician's disappearance after being kidnapped in October 1965 (he was presumably murdered in the French capital) caused a great public scandal in France. Among those accused of the kidnapping in a subsequent

Gen. M. Oufkir

trial that began in Paris in September 1966 were high government officials from Morocco and figures from the French underworld.

In 1971 Oufkir was appointed Minister of Defence and promoted major-general of the Royal Armed Forces, following the July 1971 armed rebellion against King Hassan II which the minister suppressed. On 10 July 1971 several senior military officers had led some 1,400 junior officers in an attempt on the King's life as he was celebrating his 42nd birthday in his palace at Skhirat. In the subsequent clash between the mutineers and loyal forces several people, estimated at about 100, were killed. Four generals, five colonels and a major who were alleged to have led the abortive coup were executed on 13 July 1971.

In a newspaper interview on 15 July 1971 Oufkir named the coup leader as Colonel Mohammed Ababou who was commandant of the Ahermoumou military training institute. Colonel Ababou was alleged to have led the cadets being trained at Ahermoumou in the attack on the Skhirat palace in which the Minister of Tourism, Muhammad Lazraq, General Driss Numaishi, Commander of the Royal Air Force, General Muhammad

Madbouh, Minister of the Royal Military Household who was named as a coup leader, and several other senior military officers and a foreign ambassador were killed. On 14 July 1971 General Oufkir was appointed, with another senior minister, to a three-man tribunal to investigate the cause and wider implications of the plot.

In August 1972 a second unsuccessful attempt was made to assassinate the King during a flight from France, when the royal plane was fired at by its escort fighter planes. General Oufkir, with 220 other officers, was implicated in the coup attempt. On 17 August 1972 a government report announced that General Oufkir had committed suicide "out of shame". The following day, the Minister of the Interior, Dr Mohammed Benhiwa, said, "I am able to certify that the suicide of Oufkir is a suicide of treason and not of loyalty".■

Ouko, R. J. (1932-90)

OUKO, Dr Robert John (1932-90).

KENYAN diplomat and politician. Born on 31 March 1932 at Kisumu, he attended Ogada School in that town and then Nyangori School at Kakamega and Siriba College in Nyanza. He worked as a teacher from 1952 to 1955, and then as a district revenue assistant from 1955 to 1958.

In 1958 he went to Ethiopia to pursue further studies at Haile Selassie I University (as it was called then), taking a BA in public administration, political science and economics in 1962. He was among the first Kenyans chosen for Foreign Service training, as part of the preparations for independence, in 1962; he went to Makerere University College in Uganda for a course in International Relations and Diplomacy. In 1963, the year of independence, he did further Foreign Service training in Rome and London.

He worked as Assistant Secretary in the Department of Foreign Affairs in the office of the Prime Minister in 1962-63, and then, after serving briefly as Senior Assistant Secretary, he became at a young age Permanent Secretary in the new state's

R.J. Ouko

Moi's chairmanship of the OAU (1981-82). He served afterwards as Minister of Labour, and Minister of Planning. At various times he served also on the board of the Tana River Development Co, the East African External Telecommunications Co, and Kenya Polytechnic.

In 1988 Dr Ouko was appointed Foreign Affairs Minister again. But on 13 February 1990 he vanished from his home at Koru in the west of Kenya, and three days later he was found murdered in a sugar cane plantation nearby. The mysterious murder led to protests after his funeral, and some sections of the public voiced their suspicion of official involvement, but the government denied this.

Dr. Ouko, who had a wife and four children, is remembered for his very considerable diplomatic skill and an abiding commitment to African unity.∎

Ministry of Foreign Affairs (1963-64). Later, however, he transferred to other ministries and was Permanent Secretary of the Ministry of Communications and Power (1964-66) and the Ministry of Works (1966-69).

Ouko then began working with the East African Community (EAC) grouping Kenya, Uganda and Tanzania, serving as the EAC's Minister for Finance of Administration (1969-70) and Minister for Common Market and Economic Affairs (1970-71). He also served in the Community's Legislative Council. Like others who helped develop the EAC, Ouko saw all the efforts fail when the Community collapsed because of political disagreement in 1977.

Ouko was then nominated to the Kenyan parliament and appointed Kenya's Minister for Community Affairs, in charge of integrating former EAC services into the Kenya civil service. He was elected to parliament as member for Kisumu Rural in 1979. Then he became Foreign Minister from 1979 to 1983, an eventful period in Kenyan foreign policy which included President

Oumaar, F. (1864-1948)

OUMAAR, Haji Farah (1864-1948).

SOMALI politician and nationalist leader who founded and led the political movement of the Somali Islamic Association. Oumaar followed the tradition of the great nationalist hero of Somalia, Sayyid Mohammed Abdullah Hassan (q.v.), in opposing the progress of British occupation of his country. But whereas the former took up arms against the British the latter applied a non-violent approach, using his persuasive writing power to rouse his compatriots into agitation against British colonialism.

Born in 1864, he joined the colonial administration as an Assistant District Officer around 1910 but soon became disenchanted with its policies. He started urging people to revolt against the injustices and repressive measures of the administration by refusing to pay their taxes. The British responded by transferring him to the Somali military forces with the rank of captain. He resigned after only two years in his new posting and embarked on a full-time political career. Fearful of the impact his nationalism would have in the country, the British exiled him to Aden in the 1920s. There he founded the Somali's claim to independence.

Oumaar visited India around 1930, where he met Mahatma Gandhi; he later adopted Gandhi's non-violent philosophy in his campaign in Somaliland. In 1932 he wrote his first petition to the British government, protesting against the oppression of his people by the British representatives and the anomalies in the colonial administration. He quoted instances where unqualified civil servants, who had never studied law, were appointed to judicial offices in the country. In the petition he referred to the chief secretary to the government who also presided as chief justice.

Like his friend Mahatma Gandhi, Oumaar was to spend most of his life behind bars. He was arrested and exiled again in the 1940s, this time to the Kamaran islands near Aden where he was held until his health started to deteriorate. Oumaar who was now in his eighties defied the threat of British harassment and continued to petition the British government and wrote a letter to the British monarch about Somalia's grievances. After his release he returned to the protectorate, an old man broken by many years of captivity. He died shortly afterwards in 1948 in Hargeisa. He is today regarded as a hero of the country's struggle for independence which was attained in July 1960. ■

Ovonramwen, King (died 1914)

OVONRAMWEN, Oba of Benin (died 1914).

THE last independent ruler of the Edo Kingdom of Benin, now in modern Nigeria. Ovonramwen is renowned for his brave stand against the colonisation of his state by the British, for which he is generally regarded as the last great king of Southern Nigeria in the nineteenth century who attempted to stem the tide of British occupation and conquest. During the nine years (1888-97) he reigned, he sought to preserve the sovereignty of the Edo state as well as its economic interests which, in the end, led to the British armed invasion of Benin in 1897. The Oba (king) lost the battle and was dethroned and banished into exile for life,

Oba Ovonramwen

while his kingdom was merged into a wider political unit under British administration. By 1912 that unit, the Protectorate of Southern Nigeria, had been fused with the Protectorate of Northern Nigeria to become the entity of Nigeria.

"Ovonramwen fell for the same reasons as other great African rulers of the late nineteenth century who represented an age that was fast fading away under the determined thrust of the white man resolved to take over the political and economic control of the African coast and the interior – Pepple of Bonny (q.v.) in 1854, Jaja of Opopo (q.v.) in 1887, Nana the Itsekiri (q.v.) in 1894, King Prempeh of Ashanti (q.v.) in January 1896", writes the Nigerian historian Professor Philip A. Igbafe in his book *Benin under British Administration*. Indeed by the late 1880s during Ovonramwen's father Adolo's reign, Britain had already mapped out Benin state as its area of influence. That was reflected in the visit of Captain H. L. Gallway, the British Commissioner and Vice-Consul of the Benin District of the Oil Rivers Protectorate, to Benin in 1892, four years after Ovonramwen succeeded his father as Oba.

During that visit the British officer signed a treaty with Ovonramwen, for commercial relations between Benin and Britain. Among other clauses the 1892 treaty requested the Oba to co-operate with Britain in the interest of "order, good government and the general progress of civilisation". The implications of these, as later events were to show, were not fully explained to the Oba of Benin. Because for several years after the treaty Oba Ovonramwen continued to rule his state in the tradition of his ancestors, refusing to "compromise his independence in order to pander to the needs of British officials and traders", says Igbafe, adding that "relationship between Benin and the traders on the coast as well as with the British officials during those last two decades of the nineteenth century was particularly productive of friction from the British standpoint. . . . The stage was thus being set for the overthrow of Benin".

It was against that background that Vice-Consul James R. Phillips, going against warnings about the provocation such a visit would cause in Benin, embarked on a mission to assess the strength of the Benin army, and visited Oba Ovonramwen on 18 January 1897. Phillips and a large number of his men were ambushed outside the city, to which the British responded with the punitive expedition of February 1897. Benin fell in that battle and its Oba was dethroned and deported to Calabar where he died seventeen years later, in 1914.

Oba Ovonramwen reigned at a precarious time in the history of Benin. He succeeded to an empire that was on its decline, "probably because of attacks by other indigenous powers on the peripheral peoples of his Empire, which led invariably to a shrinkage of his dominions and possibly too of his throne" (Igbafe again). As Idugbowa, Ovonramwen had to fight off opposition to his accession to the throne of his father in 1888; even after that he could only consolidate his rule through purges and executions.

Yet Ovonramwen was determined from the beginning to make his reign as purposeful as possible by maintaining court in the tradition of his ancestors which he hoped to preserve. The human sacrifices at which the British protested were a part of tradition which the Oba could not abandon. He lost his throne and power in the bid to defend that tradition against foreign aggression. One result of the aggression was the looting of vast quantities of Benin's excellent works of art, now scattered over the world.

In 1914 the monarchy was restored under Ovonramwen's eldest son, Eweka II, who was succeeded in turn, in 1933, by Akenzua II (q.v.).∎

Parirenyatwa, T.S. (1922-62)

PARIRENYATWA, Dr Tichafa Samuel (1922-62).

ZIMBABWEAN politician and physician; he qualified in 1957 to become Rhodesia's (now Zimbabwe) first African doctor. He was born in 1922 in Mrewa, Zimbabwe, and was first educated at Mrewa mission and Howard Institute in the country. He later moved to Adams College, Natal, where he matriculated. After teaching for a year in Zimbabwe, he won a Methodist Scholarship which enabled him to resume studies at the University of Fort Hare, South Africa, where he studied for a science degree. He then transferred to the University of the Witwatersrand to study medicine and qualified in 1957 as a doctor. At Fort Hare and Witwatersrand, Parirenyatwa was an active campaigner against South Africa's pass laws and apartheid.

Parirenyatwa did his housemanship at Harare hospital, Salisbury (renamed Harare in 1981). He later moved to Antelope Mine Hospital near Bulawayo in July 1959, where he served as a medical officer and was in charge of patients of all races.

Dr Parirenyatwa resigned from his post in December 1961 to join active politics. He became the Vice-President of the Zimbabwe African People's Union (ZAPU) when it was formed in 1962. Dr Parirenyatwa wanted the party to have stronger grassroots support and travelled widely throughout the country creating branches. He also made a determined effort to recruit members, winning over many who previously preferred either to remain outside nationalist politics or were members of moderate multi-racial organisations, into the party ranks.

Despite his involvement in politics

Dr. T.S. Parirenyatwa

Dr Parirenyatwa did not neglect his medical practice and ran two surgeries in Salisbury.

Parirenyatwa's career was abruptly cut short when he was killed in a car accident on the Gwelo-Bulawayo road in July 1962. To many his death was suspicious and mysterious. Dr Parirenyatwa was survived by his wife and five children.■

Parkes, J.C.E. (1861-99)

PARKES, James Christopher Ernest (1861-99).

SIERRA LEONEAN administrator; he was one of the early Africans to be employed in the colonial administration. A Creole, son of Thomas Parkes, he went to Britain to study law but was unable to complete his studies because of illness. He returned in 1881 and became a clerk in the Commandant's office at Bonthe, which came under the Sierra Leone Colony. He took an interest in the affairs of the Sherbro country around Bonthe, and wrote articles for the newspapers. In 1884 he was promoted to the Aborigines Branch of the Secretariat in Freetown. This had been created six years earlier out of an informal department responsible for relations with the interior rulers, and headed by T.G. Lawson (1814-91).

Parkes worked at first under Lawson, and helped him compile an official memorandum entitled *Information Regarding the Different Districts and Tribes of Sierra Leone and its Vicinity.* This was printed as a confidential Colonial Office document in 1887. By then the British government was more interested in the interior than ever, because of wars affecting trade there, missionaries' and Creoles' penetration, Creoles' calls for extension of British rule, and the advance of the French further north.

In 1888 Lawson retired and Parkes, who had already visited the interior with Governor May in 1885 and with Governor Rowe in 1887, succeeded him. His department was separated from the Secretariat and renamed in 1891 the Department of Native Affairs, directly under the Governor. As its head Parkes occupied a key position in British expansion into the area allotted to Britain in the 1889 partition agreement with France. He took part in a small expedition in 1889 and visited the interior with May again in 1890. But most of all, from his office and on tours, he was the intermediary between the chiefs and the British. Professor C. Fyfe wrote of him as "the indispensable source of knowledge on the interior." He was able to write good reports (his literary talents were

also shown in poetry, and in a school geography book based on the report by him and Lawson in 1887, and published in 1894).

Most Creoles favoured expansion by Britain as far as the agreed limit, or further. Parkes shared the general view, and helped persuade chiefs to submit to British rule. But he had disagreements with the British. He favoured the continuation of friendly ties with Samory (q.v.), who, besides buying arms in Freetown, had tried to strengthen relations with the British there from the 1880s, hoping to get their help against the French. Parkes shared the common Creole admiration for "Samadu" (as they usually called him), and hoped he could be persuaded by negotiation to withdraw his *sofa* soldiers from areas in the British sphere of influence.

In 1892 a proposal by Parkes for a British protectorate to be run by five "Political Agents", with the new Sierra Leone Frontier Police gradually disbanded, was rejected; the government wanted to keep the Frontier Police, raised in 1890 and often used, and when it was seen that Parkes thought of replacing them with Creole Political Agents, the idea was considered unacceptable. Creoles were losing their prominent role in the government of Sierra Leone; Parkes was by 1896 the most powerful one remaining. In 1893 he argued strongly against an expedition to stop *sofas* attacking people under British "protection", and secured their withdrawal from one area by peaceful means. But the policy of friendship with Samory was being abandoned. For continuing to advocate it Parkes was accused by two British officers of being in league with the *sofas* or in their pay, and employing their spies in his office. The allegations were investigated in August 1894 and disproved. But Parkes had played down reports of *sofa* crimes to defend his policy of friendly relations.

In 1896 Parkes was promoted Secretary for Native Affairs. But the formal creation of the Protectorate in the same year led to a reduction of his role. British District Commissioners in the Protectorate sometimes bypassed him in official matters. The imposition of the Hut Tax, which led to the great uprising of 1898, was opposed by him in favour of a poll tax.

By 1899 Acting Governor Nathan had to give special orders to ensure that Parkes could see District Commissioners' reports: a sign of the Creoles' declining position. Ill with nephritis, Parkes could not accompany Nathan on an interior tour. On 10 August 1899 he died, at the age of 38. "His department", Fyfe recalls, "was wound up, and the last vestige of equal partnership between European and educated African in the development of the Protectorate ceased." ■

Paton, A. S. (1903-88)

PATON, Alan Stewart (1903-88).

SOUTH AFRICAN writer and for a time political leader of White South Africans opposed to the apartheid regime, but better known as one of the country's leading novelists, whose writings exposed the realities of apartheid.

Alan Stewart Paton was born on 11 January 1903 at Pietermaritzburg in Natal. He went to the University of Natal, where he obtained a degree in mathematics and physics and a diploma in education, and then worked as a teacher for twenty years. He taught at the small town of Ixopo and then, from 1928 to 1935, at Pietermaritzburg College. In 1935, when the government transferred the administration of African reformatories from the Department of Prisons to the Department of Education, Paton was appointed principal of the Diep Kloof Reformatory near Johannesburg by the minister of Education, Jan Hofmeyr. A leading colleague of Jan Smuts (q.v.), but more liberal than he, Hofmeyr was a close friend of Paton.

The Diep Kloof institution for African boys, the largest of its sort in South Africa then, was reformed under Paton's administration, which came to be much respected. His work there had an effect on Paton's outlook; he had been an admirer of the Afrikaner cultural revival, even learning Afrikaans, but at the Voortrekker Monument ceremonies in 1938 he recognised the bigotry and intolerance of the Afrikaner nationalist movement; and he came to understand the impact of the oppressive segregation regime on the Black population. In

1946, when on a tour of Scandinavia, Britain and the USA to study penal practices, he wrote his first novel, depicting the lives of Africans and Whites under that regime. Entitled *Cry the Beloved Country*, it was published in 1948, the year of the Afrikaner

A. S. Paton

National Party's election to power and also of the death of Hofmeyr, to whom the novel was dedicated. Later, in 1965, Paton published a biography of Hofmeyr. *Cry the Beloved Country* was a bestseller and remained Paton's best known book.

As the National Party enforced the apartheid system with increasing brutality Paton, who had resigned from the civil service in 1948, joined with other White people opposed to the system to form the Liberal Party, which advocated universal franchise, in 1953. In late 1955 he became president of that party which had Black African members also. He published a second novel, *Too Late the Phalarope*, about love between people of different races, which was banned under apartheid in 1953. He also published *South Africa: The Land – Its*

People in 1955; and, with Don Weiner, *South Africa in Transition* in 1956. An eloquent speaker and pamphleteer, he led the Liberal Party in the 1950s towards close cooperation in anti-apartheid protests with the Congress Alliance including the African National Congress, which was not then banned. He received the Freedom Award in the USA in 1960, and, on his return to South Africa had his passport withdrawn; it was returned ten years later. Besides that award Paton received many honorary degrees starting in 1954, when Yale University in the USA awarded him an honorary LLD. He published a collection of short stories, *Debbie Go Home*, in 1961, and *Instrument of Thy Peace* in 1968.

Paton's first wife, Doris, died in 1967; they had two sons. He married a second wife, Anne Hopkins. His writing career went on into the late 1970s, and honours continued to come to him from several universities, including the University of Natal in 1968 and the University of Durban-Westville in 1986. However, his party political role ended in 1968 when the Liberal Party, faced with a likely ban under a new restrictive act named the Prohibition of Improper Interference Act and aimed at racially mixed political parties, dissolved itself. Paton published *The Long View* in 1969, *Kontakion for You Departed* in 1969, *Apartheid and the Archbishop* in 1973, *Knocking on the Door* in 1975, and in 1981 *Ah, But Your Land is Beautiful*. In 1980 he published his autobiography, *Towards the Mountain*.

Paton's liberal outlook caused him to be detested by the Afrikaner nationalists and their supporters. At the same time, like other such white liberals, he was not fully accepted by African leaders either. In his later years he called for a non-racial federal system for South Africa, and although he saw that the new constitution of 1984 which gave representation to Coloureds and South Africans of Asian origin was far from that idea, he thought there was progress away from "the tiger of white racism" among the Afrikaner nationalists under P. W. Botha. In this attitude, and in his praise for the Zulu political leader Chief Buthelezi and his opposition to international economic sanctions which African leaders were advocating, he parted company with many other opponents of apartheid. But through his writing he had done much to tell the outside world about apartheid. He died on 12 April 1988 at his home in Natal. ∎

Payne, J.S. (1819-82)

PAYNE, Reverend James Spriggs (1819-82).

L IBERIAN clergyman and statesman. James Spriggs Payne was born to freed slaves of African descent on 19 December 1819 at Richmond, Virginia, USA. His father was an ordained minister in the Methodist Church and in this deeply religious environment he grew up to be a devout Christian. When he was nine years old his family decided to return to Africa under the auspices of the American Colonisation Society to start a new life, and they arrived in Monrovia on 21 March 1829, having travelled on the same boat as Joseph Jenkins Roberts (q.v.) and his family.

He was educated in Liberian schools and returned to America in 1840 to be ordained a Methodist minister. For the next nine years he was deeply involved in his church and missionary work, and in 1848 was appointed a presiding Elder by his Church, a position he held until 1858 when his failing voice caused him to give up this duty.

Rev. J.S. Payne

Apart from his religious activities he was also very interested in politics and economics, and became a successful writer on both. This interest resulted in the government selecting him as one of the commissioners charged with organising the details of the separation of the Liberian Commonwealth from the American Colonisation Society.

In the May 1867 elections, he stood as one of the presidential candidates. He received the majority of votes and although his party only gained a minority of seats in the Legislature, the House of Representatives voted to allow him to become the next President of Liberia.

He was concerned about the continuation of slave trading activities along the Liberian coast and shortly after his inauguration in January 1868 his Government bought a gun boat and converted it into a schooner for coastal patrols to help prevent this practice. He also increased and improved foreign trade by creating a system whereby Liberian products were sent direct to foreign markets, rather than through the old barter system used by merchants on the coast.

Payne was anxious to improve and strengthen relations between the central government and the ethnic groups of the interior. He felt that these indigenous peoples had an important role to play in the development of the country and as such ought to be allowed to identify with and become involved in the Government. With this in mind he set up a Department of the Interior to be responsible for the hinterland, and to ensure that adequate educational and other facilities were available to all Liberians, whatever their origins. The Government however was suffering at the time from a shortage of manpower and finance, and this greatly hindered the implementation of Payne's policies.

His first two-year term as President was also marred by the continuation of problems caused by European, and particularly British, traders operating in the northwest of the country near the Sierra Leonean border in virtually complete disregard of the Liberian Government, and often in violation of its laws. In September 1869 a British schooner found illegally trading, was confiscated by the Liberian Government. In response, the British Governor of Sierra Leone travelled to Monrovia accompanied by two British gunboats and demanded the return of the schooner along with compensation of £3,370 9s 11d for the ship's cargo. The Government demurred but had to accept the demands following an ultimatum that if the matter was not resolved, the gunboats would take the necessary action, a situation that Liberia had no means to deal with.

Payne's first term came to an end in December 1870 when he lost the presidential elections; but he was re-elected President of the Republic in May 1875. Immediately after his inauguration in January 1876 he turned his attention to the war that had broken out in Cape Palmas, Maryland County, the previous September. The situation in this area was particularly serious as Britain was supplying ammunition to the contesting parties. Payne appealed to the USA for assistance, and was taken to Cape Palmas to negotiate in an American man-of-war. These negotiations were successsful and a peace treaty was signed on 1 March 1876. Payne returned to Monrovia but his financial scope for policies was greatly reduced during his second term due to the cost of the war, estimated at around £60,000.

On leaving office in 1878, Payne continued his life-long interest and involvement in church work. In 1880 he travelled to Cincinnati, Ohio, USA, as the Liberian delegate at the General Conference of the Methodist Episcopal Church, and on 19 January 1881 he was elected president of the Methodist Annual Conference of Liberia. He was highly respected in Liberia. In January 1882 he was awarded an honorary Doctor of Divinity degree by Liberia College for his service and achievements. He died on 31 January 1882 at the age of 62.■

Payne, J.A.O. (1839-1906)

PAYNE, John Augustus Otunba (1839-1906).

NIGERIAN educationist and leading member of the Sierra Leone (Saro) community in Lagos. He and another Sierra Leonean émigré, Charles Forsythe, founded the Society for the Promotion of Religion and Education, in 1873, which aimed to raise the level of local schools and churches through voluntary efforts. The association was the first national semi-political organisation to be formed in the Lagos colony and it operated independently of the Church Missionary Society (CMS) whose policy then restricted the level of education in Lagos to just above elementary stage.

Otunba Payne was born on 9 August 1839 at Kissy in Sierra Leone. His father, a freed slave resettled in Sierra Leone, was of the Gbelegbuwa royal family, being the brother of the Awujale of Ijebu Ode in Nigeria. This relationship with the royal family explains the name given to the young Payne, Otunba, meaning in Yoruba the adviser of the Oba. His other name, Payne, is a European corruption of the Yoruba name Adepeyin. He attended the CMS Grammar School, Freetown, from 1857 to 1861 and came to Lagos in about 1862. There he spent all his working life, with renowned contemporaries like Sapara-Williams and Henry Carr (qq.v.).

In 1862 he entered the Lagos administration as a police clerk and from then onwards held several jobs connected with the courts. He became Commissioner in the Petty Debt Court in 1836, then Registrar of Births and Deaths (1866-1869), and rose in 1869 to the position of Chief Registrar and Taxing Master of the Supreme Court of

J.A.O. Payne

Lagos, a role in which he was commissioned to conduct the census of Lagos in 1881.

An intellectual with a keen interest in the history of Lagos, his report was to become the vital source of recorded materials of the history of the Nigerian capital. From 1874 he himself began producing *Payne's Lagos and West African Diary and Almanack*, which he published annually until a year before his death. A collection of their contents was published in 1893 as *The Chronological Table of the Principal Events in Yoruba History*.

Payne belonged to several associations in Lagos, to which he gave material and moral support. He also played an active role in Lagos politics; he was a principal signatory to the People's Petition of 1882 which protested against the colonial administration's education policy. He served on the Committee of Leading Citizens of Lagos which in 1890 organised the visit to Lagos of Dr Edward Wilmot Blyden (q.v.). During the visit the Liberian pioneer of West African nationalism stayed with Otunba Payne at his Orange House residence in Lagos.

He retired from active service on 31 August 1899, an occasion which prompted the *Lagos Weekly Record* of September 1899 to write: "Never before in the annals of the British West African Colonies has such an incident been witnessed as that which took place on Monday morning 3 September 1899 at the Supreme Court, a scene in which the whole court assembled to take leave of one who had rendered many years of faithful and valued services to the department.

"His Honour the Chief Justice in thus according a public and marked recognition to Mr Payne for his services, has at once given honour to the ex-registrar and paid a tribute to native capacity, and every native present at the function must have felt that the recognition accorded Mr Payne reflected in a sense upon himself while the effect upon the young would be to kindle them with ardour to merit similar recognition."

During his retirement Otunba Payne was appointed to serve on several government bodies; he was made solicitor of the Supreme Court, member of the Legislative Council (Provisional), of the Board of Trustees, and of the Lagos Race Course Board of Management.

He was murdered on the night of 20 December 1906, by an unknown assassin, in his Lagos residence.∎

Pepple (1817-64)

PEPPLE, King William Dappa (1817-64).

NIGERIAN monarch. He was born on 23 August 1817 in Bonny, a trading post and port in the Niger Delta, the son of King Opubu the Great who died in 1830 when the Prince was 13. After a reign of two regents, he succeeded to his father's throne in 1835. As new king he had to contend with ex-regent Alali who had refused to relinquish his claim to the monarchy. In 1837 Pepple declared war on Alali and, with the assistance of the British government seeking trade concessions in the area, defeated him.

In 1839 the new King signed a treaty with Britain, abolishing slavery and giving Britain more trading concessions in Bonny. But this treaty was never ratified, nor was the 1841 treaty which said "if at any future time Great Britain shall permit the slave trade to be carried on, King Pepple and the chiefs of Bonny shall be at liberty to do the same". Instead, while British commercial interest grew, there was a naval blockade on the mouth of the River Bonny preventing King Pepple from trading openly, though he and his people were able to re-route their exports through Brass. The King's enterprising ability and business acumen, as well as a shrewd sense of political diplomacy, enabled him to launch subtle subversions which threatened British interests in West Africa. Commerce was Bonny's economic mainstay and as a result its position was jealously guarded and contested by indigenes and foreigners alike. King William Pepple's personal yearly income of about £15,000 to £20,000 from the palm oil trade by the middle of the century was as much an indication of the King's success as it was of Bonny's prosperous trading relationship with the outside world.

It was this need for continued prosperity that led to a confrontation with the British. A shrewd politician, King Pepple resented the encroachments of the British into his kingdom. He revoked the treaties with Britain and between 1847 and 1850 employed guerrilla tactics to undermine British interests. He forged an alliance with the supporters of the ex-regent Alali against the British in Bonny. In 1848 he organised

King Pepple

an ambush on the River Calabar in which some British traders were killed. The British retaliated by engineering his dethronement and exile in 1854 after he had been convicted in the Court of Equity presided over by the British Consul in Lagos. King William Dappa Pepple was banished to Fernando Po, where he spent seven years. In 1861 he was allowed to return to Bonny, where he died in 1864.■

Peregrino, F.Z.S. (1851-1919)

PEREGRINO, Francis Zaccheus Santiago (1851-1919).

GHANAIAN journalist and politician, an active pro-Africanist who championed Africans' rights in other parts of the continent besides his native Gold Coast (Ghana).

Born in Accra, he went in his teens to Britain to study, and in 1876 married an Englishwoman, Ellen Sophia, in Birmingham; they had several children. In the 1880s he went to the USA, where he lived for many years. In Buffalo (New York State) he decided to launch a newspaper for Black Americans, called *The Spectator*; it was edited by Peregrino from Albany (New York). In 1898 he was one of a hundred signatories to a petition to the President of the National Afro-American League calling for a meeting of Black American leaders.

In 1900 he attended the first Pan-African Conference in London, organised by Henry Sylvester Williams, a lawyer from Trinidad. The South African War between the British and the Boers (Afrikaners) had started the previous year, and Peregrino later said this event was what gave him the idea of going to South Africa. His son, Francis Joseph Peregrino, was already in South Africa, where he was the principal of an educational and cultural institution for Africans, the Progressive Institute; his lectures there in 1899 were published in 1900 as *A Short History of the Native Tribes of South Africa: Their Manners and Customs.*

The elder Peregrino travelled to South Africa in 1900 and started in Cape Town the newspaper for which he was best known, the *South African Spectator*. A fortnightly, it first appeared on 1 December 1900 and continued until October 1903. It was produced particularly for the non-Whites.

In the Cape Colony under British rule, the non-Whites (Africans and "Coloureds" of mixed descent) had more freedom and rights than in the Boer Republics. Some had the vote, and it was possible to start a newspaper like Peregrino's with few or no restrictions.

The newspaper, much of which the editor wrote himself, highlighted news of the Black Africans' sufferings, and carried articles to "instil if possible a little race pride in the Coloured or Black man", describing famous Africans and people of African descent in history. It covered South African events and from 1901 had a Xhosa section with extra news of African interest. Peregrino had close contacts with the Black South African journalist, A. K. Soga, editor of *Izui*. The *Spectator* highlighted racial discrimination; this was already serious, and Peregrino suffered from it – he was assaulted by a White man and said the police had refused to investigate, and later forced out of his lodgings in 1901. He had to change the *Spectator*'s printers five times. It probably made little or no money; it refused all advertisements of alcoholic drinks and fortune-telling, and the non-White businessmen whose advancement Peregrino backed placed few advertisements.

Besides editing the *Spectator*, and

carrying on some other commercial activity, Peregrino founded in his first year in Cape Town a Coloured People's Vigilance Society. He usually called all non-Whites "Coloured" (not using the term in the modern South African sense), as in the Coloured Refugees Commission of which he was Secretary in 1902, which helped non-Whites who had fled from Transvaal and Orange Free State in the war. The Vigilance Society, of which he was General Secretary, was set up to "foster friendly relations between all people in South Africa who are not white".

Much as he opposed racialism, his concern for the "moral improvement of the poor black man" was believed to have had a tone of superiority; and he had a strong faith in the British government, thinking it would follow up its defeat of the more racist Boers in the war of 1899-1902, by measures to benefit the Africans. In the event, British and Boers were reconciled at the Africans' expense. Before then Peregrino had found he was out of touch with non-Whites' political leaders even in those days, when they, like he, thought petitions could achieve something. However, he joined in a deputation to protest at the virtual exclusion of non-Whites from juries in the Cape; gave evidence to the Native Affairs Commission in 1903; and in November 1907 was invited to the Congress of Native and Coloured People at Queenstown. And in 1906 he took up the cause of the Kingdom of Barotseland, in Northern Rhodesia (Zambia), with the British authorities.

King Lewanika (q.v.) of Barotseland found that, in spite of his treaties in 1890 and 1900 with the British South African Company (BSAC), his traditional powers were being steadily eroded by the BSAC. While initially he had obtained recognition of his rule over a large area in 1905 this was reduced by a change in the frontier with Angola, reached between the colonial powers. Moreover, the BSAC had failed to "establish and maintain" schools as it had promised. Lewanika, who believed in education and modernization, turned to modern African forms of protest against the treatment of his kingdom by the BSAC.

Peregrino offered his services to the Lozis as "the agent of natives in making complaints to the Government"; he added, "The path of the native is difficult. I am a Black man and have acted for years between the Black man and the government in the

Cape Colony with much success". Litia, Lewanika's son and eventual successor, invited Peregrino to Lealui, the Lozi capital, and he travelled there in 1906. He soon prepared for Lewanika a petition to be submitted to Selborne, the British High Commissioner for South Africa. It listed Lozi grievances, and resulted in Lewanika and his chief minister having talks with Selborne at Bulawayo in October 1906, but the High Commissioner rejected all points in the petition but one; he believed that most of the issues were without foundation. And the BSAC encroached further still on Barotseland's traditional government and customs.

While he did not forget his homeland (the *Spectator*'s telegraphic address was "Accra"), Peregrino stayed in South Africa and joined in protests at worsening White misrule. He published important pamphlets: *Life Among the Natives and Coloured Miners of the Transvaal* in 1910; *The Political Parties and the Coloured Vote* in 1915; and *His Majesty's Black Labourers. A Treatise on the Camp Life of the South African Native Labour Contingent* in 1918. The last described the service of Black South Africans as labourers (they were not recruited as soldiers) for the war effort in 1914-18.

Peregrino died of a heart attack in Cape Town on 19 November 1919.■

Pereira, J. (1823-91)

PEREIRA, José de Fontes (1823-91).

ANGOLAN journalist. He was a *mestiço*, half-European, apparently the son of a Portuguese father named João de Fontes and an African mother. He was brought up in the small community of African *assimilados* (people who had adopted Portuguese culture), *mestiços* and Europeans in Luanda, who at that time shared many experiences in common. This multi-racial elite had newspapers from the 1860s and it was with these that José Pereira made his fame.

After being brought up by the Catholic mission, which predominated in Luanda and to which he was always faithful, he obtained a licence for legal practice in Angola, and also joined the civil service as a clerk. But from 1870 he was writing for the Luanda newspapers and also some in Portugal itself. From an early date Pereira was noted as a particularly strong critic of the government. In 1871-72 he protested in the newspaper *O Mercantil* against the regular shipments of labourers from Angola to the cocoa plantations of São Tomé. He continued to protest at this notorious disguised slave trade in *O Cruzeiro do sul*, a "muck-raking" Republican newspaper run by Europeans in Luanda. He also attacked the lack of education, even for local Europeans, in Angola. Pereira's associates were whites, *mestiços* and Africans, and he expressed the still prevalent feelings of common interests among these people in Luanda; but he was also conscious of special grievances of Africans, and wrote about them.

In 1875, after a criticism of the government in *O Cruzeiro*, he was dismissed from the civil service. This was a year of personal tragedies for Pereira: he lost two of his children by his wife Isabel Josephina. He also lost his lawyer's licence in 1875, but regained both that and his job in 1877. Undeterred by what had happened, he continued to criticise the government. He believed Africans could benefit from European influence and from Christian missions, whose work he praised, criticising Portugal's numerous anti-clericals. He favoured colonial expansion to the interior for the development of trade.

When African newspapers developed, written mainly in Portuguese but also in Kimbundu, Pereira placed articles in them, starting in 1882, when he had an article published in *O Futuro d'Angola*. At that time, as Portugal was very gradually extending its rule in Angola, Pereira became more and more the champion of the Africans. He wrote historical articles on Africans' earlier resistance to the Portuguese. He became more and more critical of Portugal, until in 1890, when it was thought Britain wanted to have some of the parts of Africa occupied or claimed by Portugal, Pereira wrote openly in *O Arauto Africano*, saying Africans would welcome such displacement of the Portuguese. He ended by saying of the Portuguese: "Out with them!"

The furious colonial government sacked Pereira from the civil service again. Censorship became somewhat stricter, although the Luanda press continued to flourish and to speak out until the 1920s. José Pereira himself died of pneumonia on 2 May

1891. He had not, in his lifetime, been fully supported or admired by a divided Luanda elite, but his death was mourned by all as the passing of a great crusading journalist.■

north of England and it was while on his way to spend Christmas with them that he had a car accident, resulting in serious injuries from which he died in Carlisle hospital on 29 December 1940.■

Pezzani, E.R. (1885-1940)

PEZZANI, Emile Roger (1885-1940).

MAURITIAN lawyer and politician. He was born in 1885 in Moka, Mauritius. After completing his secondary education in 1904 he went on to study law and was called to the Bar, at the Middle Temple, London, in 1908. He practised law for two years and then went to the Seychelles, also administered by the British at that time, where he worked as a legal counsellor. On returning to Mauritius in December 1911 he continued to practise as a lawyer and soon acquired a reputation as an able legal draftsman.

In 1919 he was elected to the Curepipe Municipal Council, a position which he held until 1921. In January 1926 he was elected to the Legislative Assembly following a successful campaign in Plaines Wilhems, based on a condemnation of the ruling bureaucracy, an appeal to the elite to fulfil their responsibilities and a demand for greater participation by Mauritians in the running of the island's affairs. Although he had a French background, he had an excellent command of English and was thus able to communicate his political views persuasively. Amongst other things, he advocated the admission of qualified Mauritians to senior administrative posts, for the reform of police administration and the development of air communications. In March 1927 a motion in which he called for a representative government was rejected by 10 votes to 5.

In 1930 he went to Europe with his family and retained his seat in the general elections of January 1931 through a proxy. He decided, however, not to return to Mauritius and resigned in 1934. In England he continued to practise law and continued to campaign for the Mauritian cause. His hope of election to the British House of Commons was thwarted by the outbreak of the Second World War. His wife and two children were evacuated from London to the

Phillips, J.T. (1927-80)

PHILLIPS, James T. (Jr) (1927-80).

LIBERIAN agronomist and politician. He was born on 3 December 1927 in Monrovia, and had his early education at the College of West Africa, Monrovia, from where he went to the Tuskegee Institute, Alabama, USA. Then he proceeded to Rutgers University, New Jersey, also in America. On his return to Liberia he was made Head of the Department of Agronomy, Agricultural Experiment Station, Suakoko. He later became Co-ordinator of Technical Services, Department of Agriculture, and served also as assistant Secretary of Agriculture and as Adviser, Department of Agriculture.

Apart from his official duties, Phillips was also a proprietor of estates and farms. He was Secretary of Agriculture for a time and then in 1976 was appointed Minister of Finance. He was a member of the Board of

J.T. Phillips

Trustees, International Institute of Tropical Agriculture (IITA), Ibadan, until 1976. Phillips was the first chairman of the West African Rice Development Association and the chairman of the Board of Directors of the Liberian-American-Swedish Minerals Company (LAMCO); he was also vice chairman of the Board of Directors, Bong Mining Company.

He was executed on 22 April 1980 along with other ministers following the coup that overthrew the government of President Tolbert (q.v.). He was survived by his wife and three sons. ■

Pierre, J. (1908-80)

PIERRE, James (1908-80).

LIBERIAN jurist. He was born on 18 July 1908 in Hartford, Grand Bassa Country, Liberia, and had his early education at Cuttington Collegiate and Divinity School from 1922 to 1928. In 1931 he studied law under Louis Arthur Grimes and Edward I Summerville until 1945. Pierre was a defence

J. Pierre

counsel in 1952, but was appointed Judge of the First Judicial Circuit Court later the same year. After four years as Judge, he was made associate Justice, Supreme Court, in 1956.

In 1964 Pierre became the Attorney-General of Liberia. This post he held until 1971 when he was promoted to Chief Justice of Liberia. He belonged to the World Association of Judges and the International Association of Jewish Lawyers and Jurists. He was a member of the True Whig Party and was accorded national honours – Knight Grand Band of the Humane Order of African Redemption; Knight Grand Band of the Order of the Star of Africa – and foreign honours – Commander of the National Order of Merit, Haiti; Commander of the National Order of Merit, Mauritania; Commander of the National Order of Côte d'Ivoire. Apart from such honours, Pierre was also conferred with an honorary LLD degree, University of Liberia.

Chief Justice Pierre was among the people executed on 22 April 1980 following the military coup that overthrew President Tolbert's government. He was survived by his wife, Rebecca neé Watts, and five daughters and five sons. ■

Pinto, A.R.J.P. (1927-65)

PINTO, Antonio Rudolfo Jose Pio (1927-65).

KENYAN politician and leading member of the Kenya African National Union (KANU). He spent more than five years in detention for his part in the liberation struggle in Kenya and, at independence, was elected KANU member of Parliament. Of Asian origin, Pio Pinto was born in 1927 in the Kenyan capital where his Goan settler father was working; the Pintos were among the thousands of Asian workers who were imported by the British to work in the East African colonies, namely Kenya, Tanganyika (now Tanzania) and Uganda. By the 1960s when Kenya achieved independence there were about 170,000 Asians in that country.

Pinto had his education in India,

attending the Dharwar College, Bombay. He returned to Nairobi in 1949 and worked briefly in the administration of a commercial firm. While in India he contributed immeasurably to the campaign of the Goan National Congress, a nationalist organisation which

A.R.J.P. Pinto

he co-founded to agitate against Portuguese rule of his ancestral country, Goa. During this same period he was serving in the Indian Air Force.

A year after his return to Kenya Pinto was appointed assistant secretary of the Kenya Indian Congress (KIC) which had appeared in 1907 as a reaction by the early generation of Asian settlers against increasing European political domination and racism. The KIC soon affiliated with other Asian organisations in the surrounding colonies, which in 1941 resulted in the formation of the inter-territorial East African National Congress. The KIC succeeded in obtaining electoral representation for the Asian community in Kenya shortly after the First World War and, following the emergence of the Kenya African Union (KAU), began collaborating with Africans in the campaign for political reforms.

With the growth of KAU into a mass movement and the subsequent ferocious campaign leading to the Mau Mau rebellion in 1952, several political leaders were arrest-ed. Two Asians, of whom Pinto was one, were also detained during the State of Emergency. Though charges were never brought against him, he was alleged to have aided the Mau Mau campaign for which he served more than five years in detention. He was arrested in June 1954 and imprisoned on Manda Island and later in northern Kenya.

Released in August 1959, Pinto collaborated with Chanan Singh, another Indian leader, in the formation of the Kenya Freedom Party. Shortly after, he joined KANU whose leaders then included Tom Mboya (q.v.). A past staff member of the *Daily Chronicle*, an Asian newspaper which he edited from 1953 until his arrest, Pinto became manager of KANU's organ, *Sauti ya KANU* (The Voice of KANU). After British withdrawal in 1963, he was elected KANU member of the independent Kenya Parliament and also became Editor-in-Chief of the reconstituted party newspaper which became known as Panafrica.

He was shot dead outside his Nairobi residence on 4 February 1965; his assassination was believed to be politically motivated. He was survived by his wife Emma and three daughters. Soon after the murder, President Kenyatta (q.v.), whom Pinto had worked closely with, said that by his death "our country has lost of one of the most conscientious workers of freedom, who suffered many years in detention for his uncompromising stand in politics." ■

Plaatje, S.T. (1876-1932)

PLAATJE, Solomon Tshekiso (1876-1932).

SOUTH AFRICAN author and founder member of the African National Congress (ANC) of which he was the first Secretary-General. Plaatje was born in 1876, into a Rolong family in Boshof in the Orange Free State, and had his elementary education at the Lutheran Church Missionary School in Barkly West. Between 1890 and 1893 he was an assistant teacher, and early in 1894 he joined the Post Office in Kimberley as a letter-carrier. He was posted in 1898 to Mafeking where he served as interpreter to Lord Edward Cecil at the Court of Summary

Jurisdiction, and later in the Native Affairs Department.

The outbreak of the Anglo-Boer War in 1899 found Plaatje in Mafeking where he wrote a diary of the Boers' siege (1899–1900), his first stint as a writer. In 1901 he left the government service and went into full-time journalism as editor of *Koranta ea Becoana* (The Tswana Gazette), the first Setswana newspaper, which he founded in Mafeking, printed in both Tswana and English. He had established the paper with the financial assistance of Silas Modiri Molema (q.v.). In 1908 Plaatje returned to Kimberley, where he founded another paper, *Tsala ea Becoana* (The Friend of the Bechuana).

He entered politics four years later as a founding member of the South African Native National Congress (SANNC), which later became the ANC. He was elected its first Secretary-General and, as such, was a central figure in its first major campaign which was against the Land Act of 1913 that curbed the rights of Africans to own or occupy land in areas reserved for the Europeans. Plaatje was a member of the ANC delegation which visited London in 1914 to protest, albeit unsuccessfully, against the Act. He remained in Britain, while the rest of the delegation returned to South Africa. He lectured for three years on the plight of his compatriots in South Africa and worked at the University of London as a language assistant. During this period Plaatje wrote three books: *Native Life in South Africa*

before and since the European War and the Boer Rebellion (1916), *The Sechuana Phonetic Reader* (1916), and his famous *Sechuana Proverbs, with Literal Translations and their European Equivalents* (1916) which is a collection of over 700 proverbs.

In 1919 Plaatje joined another unsuccessful SANNC delegation to the Versailles Peace Conference where it was not acknowledged. But while in Paris he took part in the Pan-African Congress organised by William Edward B. Du Bois in February 1919. He returned to London where he met the British Prime Minister Lloyd George and told him of the increasingly oppressive treatment of Black Africans in South Africa. In 1921–22 Plaatje visited America to arrange for the publication of the American edition of his *Native Life in South Africa*.

He returned home in 1923 and continued to write, earning his living as a journalist. He was much involved in social and educational work and became committed to the preservation of his native language, Setswana. To this end he translated Shakespeare's *Comedy of Errors* into Setswana as *Diphoshophosho*, and later *Julius Caesar* as *Dintshontsho tsa Bo-Julius Kesara*. His most famous novel, *Mhudi, An Epic of South African Native Life a Hundred Years Ago*, was published in 1930. An earlier publication, *The Mote and The Beam: An Epic on Sex-Relationship 'Twixt White and Black in British South Africa*, had appeared in 1921. He was still involved in political activities during that time and in 1930 took part in the ANC's protest against the Pass Laws. Plaatje died of pneumonia in June 1932 during a journey from Kimberley to Johannesburg.■

S.T. Plaatje

Pokela, J.N. (1923-85)

POKELA, John Nyathi (1923-85).

SOUTH AFRICAN freedom fighter, one of the founders of the Pan-Africanist Congress (PAC) of South Africa, the movement which broke away from the African National Congress in 1958. Pokela became leader of the PAC in 1981 – but not before he had served 13 years in South Africa's Robben Island jail.

His fight against apartheid White minority rule in South Africa spans more than three decades.

Born in Herschel District, Cape Province, South Africa, in 1923, Pokela grew up in Mokhohlong, a village in Lesotho. He met

J. Pokela

Robert Sobukwe (q.v.) who was to be the founding President of the PAC at Healdtown High School in 1946. After matriculation he continued his education at the University of Fort Hare in South Africa – again with Sobukwe. Their fellow students at that time included Robert Mugabe later to become first Prime Minister of Zimbabwe, Ntsu Mokhehle and the late Herbert Chitepo (q.v.). Pokela played a prominent role in the burgeoning political activities centred on Fort Hare, joining the African National Congress Youth League, led by A. P. Mda, whose nationalist ideas were a strong influence on him. The Youth League Branch of Fort Hare led by Sobukwe pressed the ANC to adopt a programme of positive action at their annual Conference in Bloemfontein in 1949. Pokela was one of the Fort Hare delegates.

Again with Sobukwe, Pokela became a

school teacher in the small town of Standerton in the Transvaal. Now a graduate with a diploma in education Pokela lost no time in helping his colleague to form local ANC Youth League branches. But first Sobukwe, then Pokela in 1957, was expelled from teaching for their political activities.

Two years later he helped Sobukwe form the Pan-Africanist Congress, a breakaway movement from the ANC, whose members, originally known as the "Africanists", had been unhappy at the multi-nationalism of the ANC and rejected non-Black African participation in the South African struggle; the PAC members professed socialism, and believed Africans had to achieve their liberation by their own efforts, their ultimate goal being a "government of the Africans, by the Africans, for the Africans".

Sobukwe became the President of the PAC and Pokela's job was to work behind the scenes, to organize PAC activities in the event of the leadership being suppressed. The PAC's defiance campaign was planned to get people to leave their passes at home, and allow the police to arrest them; it was hoped the South African economy would be disrupted. But the South African police opened fire at Sharpeville and at Langa on 21 March 1960 when the campaign opened; Sobukwe was arrested, and on 8 April the PAC was banned. In 1962 Pokela set up the PAC exile headquarters in Maseru, Lesotho, later fleeing there himself to become acting secretary-general and a member of the Presidential Council, under the leadership of Potlako Leballo. But after the underground military wing of the PAC – called Poqo – carried out a number of military actions inside South Africa, the PAC offices in Lesotho were raided, resulting in thousands of arrests.

In 1966, Pokela was picked up by the South African police – who said he had been lawfully arrested on South African soil. He claimed he had been lured across the border from Lesotho by a police agent. He was charged with recruiting people for training to overthrow the South African Government, attempting to kill white South Africans on 8 April 1963, and to damage and destroy property, and to kill members of the King William's Town police on that day. The charges made it clear that he was not accused of participation in the attacks but of planning them from the PAC Headquarters in Lesotho. He was convicted and sentenced in June 1967 to 13 years' imprisonment under the Sabotage Act and 7 years under the Suppression of Communism Act, the two terms to run concurrently.

He was sent to Robben Island – where he once more joined his friend and colleague Sobukwe.

In 1980 he was released from prison and in January the following year left South Africa for Tanzania. By this time the PAC had become split by factional squabbles, had suffered a severe setback in Swaziland, where its members had been rounded-up and deported in 1978, and in 1979 Leballo was ousted as leader.

On his return to the Headquarters-in-exile of the movement in Dar-es-Salaam Pokela was appointed chairman of the central committee and leader of the movement, from which positions he worked to improve the standing of his organisation.

But Pokela did not live to see the PAC's fortunes revived to a marked degree. In 1985 while on a journey from Gaborone to Dar-es-Salaam, Pokela was taken ill and admitted to hospital in Harare where he died on 30 June 1985.■

Prempeh II

Prempeh II (1892-1970)

PREMPEH II, Otumfuo Osei Agyeman, Asantehene (1892-1970).

GHANAIAN traditional ruler of the fourth largest of Ghana's ten regions. A descendant of Osei Tutu, the founder of the Ashanti empire and first occupier of the Golden Stool, Prempeh II was born in 1892 in Kumasi. He was the nephew of Nana Kwaku Dua III, Prempeh I. He had his elementary education at the Wesleyan mission school in Kumasi and worked as a storekeeper until 1931 when he succeeded to the Golden Stool which the Asantes regard as the guardian of their ancestral spirits. Between his ascension and 1935 the British colonial authorities did not recognise him as the Asantehene (King of the Asantes) and chose to call him the Kumasihene, but in 1935 when the Asante Confederacy was restored his office was accepted.

Prempeh II became head of the Confederacy Council, in addition to becoming the Omanhene of Kumasi. His management of the Council, which he personally supervised, won the admiration of the British authorities. He was given a knighthood in 1937 and in 1947 was invited by the British governor to become an unofficial member of the Executive Council. The Asantehene declined, on the ground that his chieftainship did not allow him to make decisions as an individual.

As the custodian of the Golden Stool, the Asantehene's influence is immense and immeasurable. He is the spiritual head of the Asante religion and the Golden Stool is the most sacred shrine. As the Asantehene, he is the 'most mighty' to whom Asante's 300 paramount chiefs and over 3,000 sub-chiefs swear their oath of loyalty. His office had remained largely undisturbed until 1896 when the British Governor, Sir Frederick Hodgson, totally ignorant of the importance and sanctity of the Golden Stool, made an attempt to take possession of it. The ensuing resistance culminated in a bitter nine-month battle between the Asantes and the British who regained control of the region only in 1897. The then occupier, Prempeh I, was subsequently deported and allowed to return to his kingdom in 1924 and recognised only as the Kumasihene in 1926.

In the latter days however the authority of the Asantehene had been encroached upon by modern institutions. The advent of party politics and democratic representation diminished the Asantehene's control of affairs, further aggravated by wholescale transformation of an hitherto feudal society to an egalitarian one whose values are in the main opposed to chiefs and chieftainship.

Prempeh II was himself very much opposed to radical changes in the administrative structure of Asante. From 1948 onwards his role, and that of his subordinates, was subject to continuous attack by the Asante Youth Organisation, the Committee for Youth Organisation and its successor the Convention People's Party (CPP) of Kwame Nkrumah (q.v.). In 1954 the National Liberation Movement (NLM) was formed, with the backing of the Asantehene, to oppose the CPP. Though the NLM was able to make considerable gains in Asante in the 1956 general elections its fortune changed disproportionately with the CPP's gains in the region in subsequent elections. The NLM had successfully pressed for the establishment of Regional Assemblies and Houses of Chiefs, which temporarily enhanced the Asantehene's position. But constitutional re-arrangements after Ghana's independence ended regional assemblies and inevitably eroded the powers of the chiefs. In 1957 the Asantehene renounced his association with the NLM, thereby consolidating his neutral role as a traditional ruler. His authoritiy remained as such until he died on 27 May 1970 in Kumasi. He was succeeded by his second cousin Opoku Ware II.■

Prest, A.E. (1906-76)

PREST, Chief Arthur Edward (1906-76).

NIGERIAN politician, he became the country's first Minister of Communications in the first Central Cabinet of 1951. A year later he was one of the parliamentarians in the Nigerian House of Representatives who called for an end to colonial rule by demanding self-government from Britain. A former police officer, he was the first Nigerian officer in the Intelligence Division of the Nigeria Police Force.

Arthur Prest was born on 10 March

1906, in the now oil-producing seaport city of Warri in Bendel State. He was a grandson of Chief Ogbe of Warri and the son of a shipping executive. He had his education at Warri Government School and at King's College in Lagos. On leaving the latter in 1926 he

Chief A.E. Prest

enlisted in the colonial police force and rose to the rank of chief inspector. He resigned from the Nigeria Police Force in 1943 to read law at the University of London and was called to the Bar at the Middle Temple Inn in 1946. On his return to Nigeria he set up in private legal practice.

He later went into politics as a founding member of the Action Group (AG) party led by Chief Obafemi Awolowo, the party ruled the then Western Region which also included Chief Prest's Warri constituency before the creation of the Midwest Region (now Bendel State) in 1963; he later became AG's First Vice-President. In the federal elections of 1951 Chief Prest was elected to both the Western House of Assembly at Ibadan and the Federal House of Representatives as member for Warri, and became one of four AG office holders in the Federal Council of Ministers – he was appointed Minister of Communications. Prest was one of the AG and National Council of Nigerian Citizens (NCNC) members of the Federal Parliament who proposed the historic motion calling for self-government in 1953 and served on subsequent delegations to the constitutional talks in London. When new elections were held to start a regime of Federation and more self-government, Chief Prest was defeated by Chief Festus Okotie-Eboh (q.v.). He became a member of the Public Service Commission and was based in London, attached to the Nigerian Mission in the UK.

He was later appointed Agent-General of Western Nigeria in London, and was for a time Acting High Commissioner for the Federation there. Following the creation of the Midwest Region, Prest was appointed to the judiciary of the new region as a High Court Judge. With the suspension of parliamentary democracy in 1966 he returned to private legal practice in Warri. He turned down an invitation to serve in the Law Revision Commission, and remained independent and critical of the government and the state of society which he saw as corrupt. He also started a bakery business at Warri.

He died on 11 September 1976 in Warri. He had 15 children, including Michael Prest who in 1979 became head of the personal staff of President Shagari, and Robert Prest, a senior officer of the Royal Air Force in Britain. ■

Al-Qaddafi, M.A.H.A. (1885-1985)

AL-QADDAFI, Mohamed Abdulsalam Hamid Abumeniar (1885-1985).

LIBYAN nationalist who joined the resistance movement against the Italian occupiers of his country when he was in his late twenties. Abumeniar al-Qaddafi was the father of Libya's Head of State, Colonel Muammar Qaddafi. Abumeniar was 57 years of age when Muammar was born.

Abumeniar, like his wife Aisha, was of the "Khathathfa" ethnic group. A Bedouin who reared a modest herd of goats and camels and followed the rain, he was bound to collide with the Italians, and soon became battle-scarred. He fought against the Italians in many battles, chief among which was the Sirte battle of al-Qurdabiya in June 1915. An accomplished horseman, Abumeniar filled his son's early years with stories of his military encounters with the colonialists. Thus Muammar Qaddafi received his first lessons of Libyan history from his father.

Abumeniar was a true Bedouin who refused to go into exile after the al-Aqqaqir defeat of the Cyrenaica leaders and the capture of the legendary Umar al-Mukhtar (q.v.); he reverted to his pasture farming and rearing of livestock, yet he never abandoned the spirit of resistance against the foreign occupiers.

Because he was forced to move from province to province in search of pasture lands, his son, Muammar, was educated in Sirte, Sebha and Misurata.

Abumeniar, a devout Muslim who was also a Muezzin, instilled in the young Muammar steadfast principles, frugality, asceticism, and a love for the native soil. Despite the country's oil wealth and his son's accession to power after the Al-Fateh Revo-

M.A.H.A. Al-Qaddafi

lution of 1969, he continued to lead a simple life.

Abumeniar may not have been a military strategist, but his intimate knowledge of Eastern Tripolitania and the Fezzan proved of great value in the anti-colonial guerrilla warfare. He was instrumental in the severe defeat of the Italians at Sirte.

He died at the age of 100 on 8 May 1985, and was buried at Sihuga Sidhani cemetery in Tripoli. ■

Qoboza, T. P. P. (1938-88).

QOBOZA, Tselito Percy Peter (1938-88).

SOUTH AFRICAN journalist, the leading Black journalist in his country for many years, best known internationally for his criticism of the South African government in the aftermath of the 1976 Soweto uprising. This led to the banning of his newspaper, the *World*, and his detention without trial for a time.

He was born, son of Sankoela Qoboza, on 17 January 1938 at Sophiatown, a famous African district of Johannesburg. He was educated at Sophiatown and Pietersburg, and at the then Catholic University Institution in Lesotho (now the Lesotho National University) at Roma. He studied for the

P. Qoboza

Catholic priesthood but did not take the holy orders. In 1963 he married Sielatsatsi Anne Moliena; they had a son and four daughters.

In 1963, that same year, he became a junior reporter on the *World*, a newspaper for Black South Africans, published by the Argus company. He rose to be news editor in 1967 and, in 1974, editor. The *World* under his editorship spoke out on controversial issues and the inequities of apartheid and became the largest-circulation Black daily newspaper in South Africa, its circulation eventually reaching about 180,000. He was

able to resist the enormous pressures of the apartheid regime on the press, and became famous for his defiance of the regime. Qoboza was a Nieman Fellow at Harvard University in the USA for a time and travelled to other countries.

In the Soweto uprising in 1976, the *World* was the only newspaper giving first-hand coverage. Qoboza condemned the brutal repression by the police in Soweto. A few months later, in December 1976, he was arrested and put in prison. Later in 1977 he spoke out about the murder of Steve Biko (q.v.), the Black Consciousness leader. The following month, on 19 October 1977, the apartheid regime made a massive crackdown on non-violent Black opposition activities; 18 organisations were outlawed, and the *World* and the *Sunday World* were banned. Qoboza was arrested again. After six months, following worldwide protests, he was freed, without being charged. Qoboza won international recognition in 1978 with the award of the "Golden Pen of Freedom" by the International Federation of Newspaper Publishers.

Although the *World* had been banned, soon the *Post* and *Sunday Post* inherited much of its role and took over much of its readership. Qoboza became editor of the Transvaal editions of both the daily and the Sunday newspaper. In 1980, however, their production was halted by a Black media workers' strike, and after failing as a result to appear at least once a month, the newspapers lost their registration. Before this happened Qoboza went to the USA to assume the newly created post of editor-in-residence of the *Washington Star*. In 1981 he announced his resignation from the *Post* and *Sunday Post*, but continued to be a 'loud' critic of the South African racist regime.

In 1985, back in South Africa, he became editor of the weekly *City Press*. This was owned by the pro-government Afrikaans press group, Nasionale Pers, but it was allowed editorial independence.

So Qoboza continued his outspoken journalism, especially in his own column "Percy's Pitch", condemning violence and corruption by South Africans but in particular condemning the apartheid government and challenging it. However, his career as a crusading journalist was cut short. He became ill in December 1987 and died in Johannesburg on his 50th birthday, 17 January 1988, after raising circulation to a record of over 200,000. ■

Quiwonkpa, T. (1955-85)

QUIWONKPA, Brigadier-General Thomas (1955-85).

LIBERIAN soldier and army commander. During his short but eventful military career, Quiwonkpa was one of the leaders of the 1980 coup which deposed President Tolbert (q.v.), and became a key member of the new regime headed by General Doe. Quiwonkpa later died in an unsuccessful attempt to overthrow General Doe.

He was born on 25 July 1955 in Zurlay, Nimba county. He interrupted his education midway through Barracks Union High School in 1978 to join the army, as did many of his young compatriots in those days, and soon became staff sergeant in the Armed Forces of Liberia. Quiwonkpa is said to have wanted to spend only a few years in the army before returning to his education.

However this was not to be so. Quiwonkpa believed that what he considered the excesses of the Tolbert government imposed serious hardships on Liberian society. The non-commissioned soldiers, who lived and worked under very difficult conditions, seemed to have felt these hardships more than most other groups. Quiwonkpa took advantage of these dissatisfactions to plan the overthrow of President Tolbert in a bloody non-commissioned officers' coup d'état in April 1980. He personally led the troops that captured the Executive Mansion, in which assault Tolbert was killed.

The triumphant soldiers set up a People's Redemption Council (PRC) to replace the deposed government. Quiwonkpa, who was hopeful that the new regime would bring about reforms, was an influential senior member of that Council. In the spate of promotions that followed the coup, he was made Brigadier-General. Despite his new elevated status, it is believed he preferred to stay close to his men and was duly appointed Commanding-General of the Armed Forces of Liberia. That appointment marked the peak of the spectacular rise of the twenty-five year old soldier who only two years before had joined the army as a fresh recruit from high school.

Some believe that, of the coup makers, Quiwonkpa was one of the few who retained

Gen. Quiwonkpa

his idealism and did not abuse his position of power for personal gain, continuing to regard the military government as temporary without losing sight of the aims of the 1980 coup. Once the revolution had set the country on the 'right' path, he wanted a quick return to representative government. And on a personal level, he was concerned with his education. During the period he was Commanding-General, he employed tutors to teach him at home, and he often talked of the day when he would return to formal education.

All these views, often expressed publicly, put him at odds with some of the members of the PRC. Quiwonkpa's disagreements with them, they said, became most pointed over the question of return of the country to civilian rule by 1985, which brought about an increasingly embarrassing situation. They were said to have tried in vain to get Quiwonkpa to rally to their point of view, to involve him more in politics. He was believed to have been offered the job of Secretary-General of the PRC, but when he refused to take it, the split became inevitable. All this affected the government's policies and disturbed running of the country.

In November 1983 Quiwonkpa was accused of plotting to overthrow the government of General Doe (q.v.). He denied knowledge of the plot but for his own safety fled the country to the United States where he lived in Baltimore for the next two years. He is quoted as having said that those were the most difficult two years of his life, being distressed by reports of the deteriorating situation in Liberia. He spoke of his role in the future of Liberia in almost messianic terms. In June 1985 he declared "I staged the 1980 coup to free the people of Liberia from 133 years of oppression, but now Doe has declared war on our people again. I have no other choice but to join my people in their struggle for another freedom."

Accusing the Government of election malpractices, gross mismanagement of the economy and of instituting a reign of "terror, brutality and bloody tyranny", Quiwonkpa returned to Liberia with the aim of overthrowing it. The attempted coup of 12 November 1985 was to be Quiwonkpa's last act in the continuing saga of post-Tolbert Liberia. The attempt failed, with many more casualties than in the coup of 1980. Quiwonkpa himself was caught on 15 November trying to flee the country. He was killed and his bullet ridden corpse was put on public display.■

R

Rabearivelo, J.J. (1901-37)

RABEARIVELO, Jean-Joseph (1901-37).

MALAGASY essayist and poet whose work has been widely acclaimed as a major force in both Malagasy and French literature. He is revered as one of the most important black poets of the French language.

He was born Joseph-Casimir Rabearivelo (he later changed his first names to Jean-Joseph) in Antananarivo (Tananarive) on 4 March 1901, five years after the French had established colonial rule over Madagascar. Though his mother was from a noble Hova family, they were poor and this was to

J.J. Rabearivelo

affect Rabearivelo's short life. His education at the *Ecole des Frères des Ecoles Chrétiennes* in Andohalo and then at the *Collège Saint-Michel* in Ampario was cut short at the age of thirteen, largely because of lack of funds. He spent 1914 and 1915 at the Faravohit government school, and then took a job as interpreter for the head of the administrative centre of Ambatolampy, south east of Tananarive (as the Malagasy capital was then called).

Returning to Tananarive in 1919 he took on various jobs, first as a messenger and then as a clerk. In 1923 he joined the *Imprimerie de l'Imperina* as a proof reader, and three years later he got married to Mary Razafitrimo. It was during this period that he started writing poetry, which was published mainly in a local literary review. Between 1930 and 1931 he was joint editor of a new review *Capricorne*, which he had co-established with another Malagasy poet, R.J. Allain. Although he was in contact with some established poets in France (whose works he admired) during this period, his first major international recognition came in 1933 with the publication of his essay on Malagasy poetry in the Vienna-based literary journal *Anthropos*.

Thus commenced a creative but short-lived career which, by the time of his death saw the publication of several volumes of poetry in both Malagasy and French, and the emergence of a new distinct voice. His collections of poetry include *La Coupe de Cendres, Presqu'en-songes* (which a critic said represents the most beautiful and the most original expression of the cosmic pessimism which is one of the basic elements of Rabearivelo's inspiration), *Sylves chants pour Abeone, Vieilles Chansons des pays d'Imperina, Lova, Des stances oubliées,* and *Enfants d'Orphée.* Most of the poems have appeared in English translation, and in an introduction to some of his poems, included in the *Introduction to African Literature*, Ulli

Beier wrote that "Rabearivelo's world is a world of extreme strangeness and also of extreme loneliness. We seem to be let in for an experience we cannot share with others and the cosmos we see are full of paths deserted by goats, and roads frequented by silence. A recurring image is that of 'birds that have become strangers and cannot recognise their nest'. Rabearivelo's poems are clear and precise visions of a strange and personal world. In his life he has destroyed and dismembered reality. And out of the fragments he has built a new mythical world; it is a world of death and frustration, but also transcended by a sad beauty of its own."

Rabearivelo's life was marked with tragedy and frustration: the death of one of his four daughters, Voahangy, in 1933, from which he never recovered even though he had another daughter in 1936 whom he named Velomvoahangy (Voahangy is re-born); and his unsuccessful bid to get employment in the French colonial civil service in Tananarive, in order to be able to do his writing and to earn enough money to keep his family. In the attempt to escape from this situation he planned to visit France but his efforts were frustrated by the colonial authorities. He committed suicide by poisoning himself on 22 June 1937, two days after receiving a final rejection of his application for employment in the public service.

Three days before his death he had written in his diary that "The truth is I suffer and I suffer all the more because there is no one in whom I can confide completely. I would feel much less alone and my burden of solitude would not be as heavy as it is if at least, O God, I had the will to work". ∎

Rabih bin Fadlallah (c. 1840-1900)

RABIH bin FADLALLAH (c.1840-1900).

SUDANESE soldier and would be empire builder. Born at Halfaya, north of Khartoum, he was said to have joined the Egyptian army at an early age and to have spent some time in Egypt itself. Returning to Sudan, under Egyptian rule, about 1862, he joined a rich merchant, Zubeir Rahmat el-Mansur Pasha el-Abbasi, who had carved out a personal fief in Bahr-el-Ghazal in the south. While acknowledging the authority of the Egyptian government at Khartoum, the trader-ruler Zubeir had about 12,000 personal warriors, *bazinqir*, and employed Rabih as an officer for them. Rabih rose fast to become a senior lieutenant of Zubeir.

Recognised as ruler of Bahr-el-Ghazalin 1872, Zubeir conquered the large Sudanese province of Darfur in 1874. He then clashed with the Governor-General of the Sudan over Darfur, and went to Egypt to present his case, but was detained there. Rabih continued to serve Zubeir's son Sulayman, who was later recognised by Egypt as ruler of Darfur but was in 1879 deposed, defeated in battle and killed by the Egyptian authorities. Rabih and about 1,000 other people went south, back to the Bahr-el-Ghazal, where in the Kreish area Rabih began to emulate Zubeir in creating a personal empire. He proceeded to do this over the next 20 years.

He started by raiding into the upper Ubangi area and the Azande territory to the south, and defeating an Egyptian expedition sent against him in 1880. Then the rising of the Mahdi (q.v.) in 1881 prevented Egyptian operations against him. He was free to expand his territory with the aid of his army, which was stronger than any other force for a long way west of the Nile, and had able officers such as Arbab Babikir, Rabih's highest lieutenant almost until the last. He was able to obtain arms, being always in touch with long-distance traders. Throughout the western march of conquest which he began in 1883, he captured slaves to swell his army and to sell. He thus came to be remembered especially as a slaver, and his efforts were indeed aimed at pure military conquest and domination.

These efforts took him and his army on a remarkable migration westwards from the then Egyptian Sudan. He moved first into the large area (covering much of what is now the Chad Republic) ruled by the ancient state of Wadai. He moved south of the heartland of Wadai and overran Dar Kuti and other areas to the south, recently annexed to Wadai. He installed his own nominee, Sanusi, as ruler of Dar Kuti, but his hold on that and other areas was challenged often in the course of frequent fighting in the 1880s. He did not defeat the Sultan of Wadai fully and the two remained formidable antagonists. Rabih and his force reached the Shari-Logone valley and from 1888 to 1890 were mainly in the Sara people's country.

By 1890 he ruled Dar Kuti, Dar Banda (in the area of the modern Central African Republic), and other regions. There seems to have been little permanent or effective rule by him over areas dominated mainly by fear of his large migrant armed force. This force lived off the land, but some supplies had to be bought, and Rabih apparently traded with Borno for some years.

In 1891 a French expedition from the south, under Crampel, reached Dar Kuti where it was wiped out by order of Sanusi. While not authorised by Sanusi's overlord Rabih, this act delayed the European advance in the area. Then, however, Wadai launched an offensive. Rabih decided to move north and attack Baguirmi, a state lying between the more powerful ones of Borno and Wadai. He captured the Baguirmi stronghold of Manjaffa, on the lower Shari, after a long siege, and after defeating a relieving expedition from Wadai.

By now Rabih had contacted Hayatu bin Said bin Muhammad Bello, a member of the Sokoto Caliphate ruling house who in the 1880s led a revolt in the large territory of the Adamawa Emirate, against the reigning Sultan-Caliph (overlord of the Lamido of Adamawa) and in the name of Mahdism. The influence of the Mahdi had spread far to the west and Hayatu was not his only follower there. He was, however, the most formidable, a challenge to the Sultan of Sokoto and also to the Shehu of Borno, both hostile to Mahdism. Rabih himself had a cautious attitude to Mahdism, at least initially; also envoys sent to him from the Caliphate about 1887 were detained for six years. But later Rabih seemed to have been completely converted to the Mahdist Islamic cause, with his troops. He formed an alliance with Hayatu, who married Rabih's daughter. Then he threatened Borno and thus attracted the worried attention of the Sokoto Caliphate and of the British, whose Royal Niger Company (RNC), as the vanguard of Imperial annexation, was established on the River Benue by 1890.

France, whose representative Monteil went to Borno in 1892, was also concerned about Rabih. But Britain, France and also Germany, whose colony of Cameroon was expanding towards Borno, were too far removed to have any effect on Rabih's final imperial conquest, that of Borno. He clashed with Borno from 1892 and in 1893-94 defeated Shehu Hashimi and then Shehu Kiyari after the great battle of Ngamagui and other battles. By 1894 Borno was occupied, the royal family in flight, and the capital Kukawa destroyed. Rabih set up a new capital at Dikwa.

Rabih's army subjected Borno to a reign of plunder, extortion and crime still remembered with horror today. It harmed Rabih's own interests, as the killing of traders at Kukawa, and general misrule, wrecked the Trans-Sahara trade which had for long gone from Tripoli to Borno. He tried to make peace with Wadai for resumption of trade but without success, and the Sultan of Wadai and the Sanusiyya leader, el-Mahdi el-Sanusi (q.v.), who controlled much of the trade from Kufra, were allied against him. The Sokoto Caliphate was hostile and banned trade with occupied Borno. Rabih invaded the eastern part of the caliphate in 1894-95. His concern was especially to re-open trade with Kano, but this was not achieved. Rabih sent trading caravans to the Niger Company territory on the Benue, and although the company apparently did not sell arms to him direct, gunpowder sold by it probably reached the Sudanese conqueror indirectly via Bauchi and Misau.

Rabih suppressed a rising in Borno and led an expedition to Mandara to the south in 1896. In the following year he attacked the Caliphate again driving the Emir of Bedde out of his capital. By then Emirates along the Benue subject to the Caliphate were drawing closer to the RNC for fear of Rabih. But early in 1897 the RNC attacked Bida and Ilorin. As a result the Sultan and Rabih, though still hostile to each other, both saw the British as the enemy.

In 1891 Rabih had made contact with his former master Zubeir, now living in Egypt under British occupation. Later the British decided to contact Rabih through Zubeir, fearing an alliance between Rabih and the French. Messengers were sent via the RNC territory with a letter from Zubeir advising Rabih to enter into friendly relations with the British. One reached Rabih with the letter in 1894/5, but the ruler furiously rejected the advice. In 1897/8 the RNC planned to attack Rabih, but the plan was dropped. However, Rabih's position was getting steadily worse despite the end of the open hostilities with Sokoto, which still saw him as a threat although he clashed with Hayatu and defeated and killed him. Trade was reopened along the Trans-Sahara route, but not for long. Short of arms, Rabih now had to face the French.

A French expedition under Gentil made a Treaty with Baguirmi in 1897. Rabih attacked Baguirmi and other areas which had received the French well after they left, but later the French planned other expeditions. One under Cazemajou took, as the British had done, a letter from Zubeir, recommending cooperation with the French this time; neither was this letter delivered, as Cazemajou was murdered at Zinder in May 1898. A peaceful French expedition under de Behagle was received by Rabih at Dikwa in April or May 1899. But then three conquering expeditions converged on the Lake Chad area. One under Bretonnet, from the Congo, was defeated on the middle Shari by Rabih in 1899, and Bretonnet was killed. Then Gentil came up from the south and won a costly victory over nearly 13,000 forces under Rabih, at the Battle of Kuno on 29 October 1899. Rabih retreated, and had de Behagle put to death. This could not save Rabih, now cut off from Trans-Sahara supplies, from the forces under Gentil and two other French expeditions, one from the Niger and one from Algeria.

The three expeditions joined and fought about 5,000 troops under Rabih at the Battle of Kousseri on 22 April 1900. The French won and although their commander Lamy was killed, so was Rabih, beheaded by a Senegalese soldier. His son Fadlallah fought on until he was defeated and killed in 1901. ∎

Raditladi, L.D. (1910-71)

RADITLADI, Leetile Disang (1910-71).

BOTSWANA administrator and politician, he was born at Serowe, in the then Bechuanaland, into the royal family of the Bamangwato people in July 1910. He received his early education locally after which he went to South Africa to study at Tiger Kloof High School, Lovedale College and the Fort Hare University College.

On completing his education he re-

turned home, where he remained until 1937 when, following a dispute with the ruling branch of the royal family, he was expelled from Bamangwato territory. He moved to Francistown and joined the Bechuanaland administration as a clerk, later to be appointed secretary to the Queen of Ngamiland. He lived in exile for 20 years and during that period wrote three plays: *Dintshontsho tsa Lorato, Motswasele II*, which won the May Either Bedford Competition, and *Sekgoma*, the winner of the Drama Section of the 1954 Afrikaanse Library Competition. In this competition he also won first prize in the Poetry Section for his anthology *Sefalana sa Menate*.

He returned to Serowe in 1957 and went into private business. He was also appointed secretary to the Bamangwato Council in the Mahalapye District, and prior to the establishment of the Legislative Council he set up the Bechuanaland Protectorate Federal Party (BPFP) in 1959, becoming its president. This party aimed to achieve economic, social and political reforms to unify the country and eventually lead to a democratic African government. In 1961 he was elected member of the Legislative Council and remained on this body for a number of years, although his party did not gain major political prominence. He died in 1971. ∎

Rainilaiarivony (1828-1900)

RAINILAIARIVONY (1828-1900).

MALAGASY politician, Prime Minister for the last thirty years of Madagascar's development and modernisation as an independent state before the French occupation, husband of the three queens who ruled the island kingdom in those years. He was the younger son of Rainiharo, husband and Prime Minister of Queen Ranavalona I (q.v.) (not the mother of Rainilaiarivony and his brother). That queen expelled the British Protestant missionaries who had begun preaching and teaching under her earlier husband, cousin and predecessor, King Radama I (died 1828). But before then the young Rainilaiarivony had some schooling under them. Later he was presented at court, and he and his elder brother Raharo rose in favour and influence.

On the death of Rainiharo in 1852 Raharo became commander-in-chief. His brother accompanied him on an expedition to suppress an uprising: one of many such

Rainilaiarivony

expeditions, for the Merina kingdom based at Antananarivo (Tananarive) never enforced fully its claim to rule over the whole island, and failed completely to control some areas, while others were governed with difficulty.

When Queen Ranavalona I died on 15 August 1861, her son Radama II reversed her policy and welcomed back the missionaries, traders and representatives of the two European powers in the Indian Ocean, Britain and France. However, the rapid changes started by Radama II were too rapid for many. He made Raharo Prime Minister and Rainilaiarivony commander-in-chief, but in 1863 Raharo eventually led a revolt in the capital, during which the King was killed.

When Radama II's cousin and wife, Rasoherina, became Queen she kept Raharo on as Prime Minister and married him. But in 1864 she dismissed him and replaced him, as husband and Prime Minister, by his brother. Rainilaiarivony kept his first wife, by whom he had 16 children, at least for the time being.

From then on Rainilaiarivony was the real ruler of Madagascar. In 1868, when Rasoherina died, the second widow and cousin of Radama II succeeded, by Rainilaiarivony's wish, as Queen, and as his wife also. During her 15 year reign she and her Prime Minister carried out many reforms. Christianity had spread so far that at the Queen's coronation the Bible was used; and on 21 February 1869 she and Rainilaiarivony were baptised, Protestantism having become the state religion. With the spread of the missions, of which the most important was the London Missionary Society which had converted the rulers, came the spread of western education. A literate civil service was developed, and Madagascar began to acquire the appearances of a modern state.

Rainilaiarivony ruled supreme, as the Council which included eight ministers (heads of ministries created in 1881) and clan chiefs, and which advised the Queen officially, did not go against her all-powerful Prime Minister. Thus he led Madagascar into the era of confrontation with the Europeans. Early in the 1880s his government quarrelled with France over Nossi-Bé and over the property of an important Frenchman who had recently died in Madagascar. As France became more of a threat he sent a delegation to Europe in 1882-83, but it received inadequate support even from Britain, where there was much unofficial sympathy for the Malagasys. Then, in 1883, France attacked Madagascar.

Queen Ranavalona II and Rainilaiarivony led the Malagasys in defiance of the aggressors, and they fought well. The Queen died soon after the outbreak of fighting; Ranavalona III (q.v.) succeeded her and kept Rainilaiarivony on as Prime Minister and royal husband. After two years of fighting the French held only points on the coast, but were able to prevent Madagascar from continuing the struggle. As a result of a peace agreement concluded on 17 December 1885, France obtained the right to supervise Madagascar's foreign relations and represent Madagascar overseas, and was promised a huge war indemnity.

Rainilaiarivony later disagreed with the French over interpretation of the treaty. He tried to maintain the country's independence, but the war indemnity made it difficult to pay for effective administration. Government authority began to decline in many places. In 1890 Britain allowed France a free hand in Madagascar. In 1894 a French mission went to Tananarive for talks, which were unsuccessful. Then the French parliament voted funds for an expedition; a French force took the port of Tamatave (now Taomasina) in December 1894, and war broke out. During 1895 the French advanced inland, slowed down mainly by the problems of road-building and by disease. Madagascar's forces could not resist them and on October 1895 the French captured the capital.

Rainilaiarivony was deported in February 1896 and sent to Algiers. While he was there his wife Ranavalona III was deposed and deported in 1897. The Prime Minister lived in banishment in Algiers until he died there on 17 July 1900. His remains were taken back to Madagascar and buried before a large crowd on 4 October 1900. His former palace is now the residence of the President of Madagascar.■

Ralaimongo, J. (1884-1943)

RALAIMONGO, Jean (1884-1943).

MALAGASY journalist and politician. In his childhood, his home area, that of the Betsileo people, was in a state of some disorder as the power of the Queen of Madagascar declined in the area, and there were many brigands. Some of these captured Ralaimongo at the age of nine and sold him into slavery. He was adopted as a son by his owner, but in 1898, following the French occupation of Madagascar, he was able to return to his family.

Western education had spread among the Malagasys for decades, but at first Ralaimongo's family did not want him to go to school. After marrying, and learning to read and write with his wife, he eventually went to the teacher training college at Fianarantsoa, run by the French Protestant Missionaries and headed by Pastor Henri Randzavola in 1899. After obtaining his primary school teachers' certificate in 1902 he worked at Ikalamavony, near his home town, as a teacher for the French Protestant Mission, which had largely taken over from the British missions working before 1896.

Then he went to a new French government school, the François de Mahy School, at Fianarantsoa.

He helped, as an interpreter, the French forces "pacifying" areas which revolted in 1904, but worked mainly as a government school teacher, for some time at the François de Mahy School. He started a lifelong friendship at that time with Jules Ranaivo, then a police inspector. In 1910 he went to France, where he obtained a *brevet*. But on his return he found that his qualification was ignored when he obtained a new teaching post near Majunga (now Mahajanga). Out of frustration he left teaching and did clerical jobs. But in October 1916 Ralaimongo volunteered for service in the French forces in the First World War.

After the war he succeeded, with great difficulty, in obtaining discharge in France, where he remained. With the help of one of his French friends he obtained a job with cooperative wholesale stores. He later had a great interest in cooperative ideas. He also felt the influence of socialist ideas spreading by the end of the war. He joined the movement of various Frenchmen and some people from the French colonies, in France after 1918, to protest against the abuses of colonial rule. For Madagascar a group called the "French league for granting of French citizens' rights to the Madagascar natives" was started in 1919.

Ralaimongo contributed to a French newspaper *l'Action Coloniale*, which criticised misrule in the colonies and called for better conditions, and more spread of formal education, within the French empire. These ideas, which seem subservient today, were regarded as very dangerous by the colonial authorities at the time. Thus he was received with suspicion by the government, and abused by the virulent white settler press, when he returned home in 1921 on an investigative mission for his "league." He was offered money, a job and even French citizenship in return for giving up his critical ideas, but he refused. He sought information above all on the imprisonment of members of a secret organisation, the *Vy Vato Sakelika* (VVS), in 1915-16. His report on the case, after his return to France, helped start a protest campaign which led to the release of the VVS convicts including Joseph Ravoahangy (q.v.).

He returned to Madagascar again in 1922, with his wife, to organise the work of a cooperative he had started while in France for the marketing of Malagasy produce and giving aid to farmers. The Governor-General ordered his banishment to Mayotte in the Comoro Islands. He went back to France, where he had the banishment order lifted, allowing him to return permanently to his country in 1923.

His cooperative venture failed, but another venture started in France, a new French-language newspaper for Madagascar called *Le Libéré* did better. He edited it and had it circulated in Madagascar before his own return. Once there, he decided to start a new newspaper. This plan encountered many obstacles, as the government and settlers called him a "Communist." Their hostility to him increased when he moved from Tananarive to Diégo-Suarez (now Antseranana), in the north, and studied the problem of expropriation of land in that area, to write protests afterwards. In 1925 he was sentenced on a "fraud" charge (this charge was used in French colonies against Africans collecting or receiving money for political or similar activity). But he was acquitted on a similar charge, and won an appeal against the conviction on the first, in 1926.

He tried again to start a marketing cooperative, but deliberate opposition by the settlers, because of their own interests, prevented its success. However, despite similar opposition, his newspaper, *L'Opinion*, was launched on 27 May 1927. It attacked forced labour and expropriations and soon incurred the anger of the French. Both Ralaimongo and Ravoahangy, who worked with him on the paper, spent periods in prison. But the paper survived and sold well. And Ralaimongo and Ravoahangy, with a French lawyer, Paul Dussac, went on to organise a "Petition of the Natives of Madagascar," calling for French citizenship and equal treatment for the Malagasys, to be followed later by Republican institutions and French social legislation.

In May 1927, when a meeting organised by Dussac was banned in Tananarive, a demonstration followed, leading to repression. This fell on Ralaimongo and Ravoahangy in 1930 after they republished the Petition. Ralaimongo was sent to Port-Bergé for five years' forced residence. While there he remained active, writing many newspaper articles and helping local people with complaints. In his absence Ranaivo refounded *L'Opinion*. Ralaimongo turned

more towards general denunciaton of colonialism, losing some of his faith in the possibility of colonial reform to give equality to "natives". But in 1935, in an article saying that a French official had killed his French wife because she protested at ill-treatment of Africans, he urged his readers to see her as a sign that the French were not all oppressors. That article led to a libel action which Ralaimongo lost. While waiting for his appeal he began another newspaper *La Nation Malgache* with Ravoahangy and Dussac, but after losing his appeal he went to prison for six months.

He was freed after the Popular Front (of left-wing parties) won the 1936 elections in France. There were high hopes placed in the Popular Front government in Madagascar and other French colonies. Dussac, who renamed the newspaper *Le Prolétariat Malgache*, was pro-Communist in accordance with widespread feelings at the time, and Ralaimongo seems to have shared some of his ideas at least temporarily. But the suspension of colonial repression caused by the left-wing victory in France was short-lived. Ralaimongo returned to prison as he had not paid the fine imposed with the gaol sentence in the libel case. Some Europeans assaulted him in late 1937, and were acquitted at a trial.

Ralaimongo had ceased to be active in politics when World War II led to the severities of the Vichy and Free French colonial regimes. He died on 10 August 1943. ■

Ramanantsoa, G. (1906-79)

RAMANANTSOA, General Gabriel (1906-79).

MALAGASY soldier and statesman. He was born on 13 April 1906 in Tananarive (now Antananarivo), the son of a wealthy gold prospector, and was educated locally before being sent to Marseilles, France, where he completed his secondary education. He enrolled at the *Ecole Spéciale Militaire* in Saint-Cyr where he was the first Malagasy to study at the prestigious French military academy, graduating in 1931 as a second lieutenant in the French colonial army.

In 1932 he was assigned to the Colonial Infantry Regiment of Morocco stationed at Aix-en-Provence, France. Later that year, until 1935, Ramanantsoa was made assistant

Gen. G. Ramanantsoa

head of the *Ecole Militaire Préparatoire des Enfants de Troupe*. He rejoined his regiment in 1936 and served in Tunisia until 1940 when he returned to an embattled France where he took part in the war against Germany. A gallant soldier who had taken command of his battalion following the death of his commander at the battle-front, he was rewarded with promotion to captain in 1940. He was reposted to Madagascar the same year and there he supervised the establishment of the *Ecole Supérieure d'Education Physique* at Fianarantsoa, whose commandant he became in 1943.

Ramanantsoa returned to Paris in

1946 to serve at the headquarters of the Colonial Troops in the Ministry of Defence. In 1948, he went to Tananarive as officer-in-charge of war veterans attached to the French High Commission. After three more years at the Ministry of Defence in Paris, Ramanantsoa, now a major, went in 1953 to Indochina with the French army in north Vietnam, where he commanded African and French troops. He later served in the French headquarters in Hanoi and Haiphong before returning in 1955 to the Defence Ministry in Paris as lieutenant-colonel.

He became colonel in 1959 and after a senior officers' course at the Institute for Higher Studies in National Defence returned to Madagascar in June 1960 when the country became independent of France. He was involved in the negotiations for Madagascar's independence, serving as military adviser to his country's delegation to the constitutional conferences in Paris. At independence, he became the first Malagasy commander-in-chief of the new armed force. He was promoted in July 1961 to brigadier-general, and six years later became lieutenant-general.

His involvement in the island's politics began on 18 May 1972, when power was handed over to him after a general strike and workers' riot had precipitated the collapse of the government of President Philibert Tsiranana (q.v.) whose policies had alienated a large section of the Malagasy community. Opposition to Tsiranana Government centred on its excessive dependence on France and increasingly more economic and diplomatic ties with South Africa. Matters came to a head in May 1972 when the Government split after a series of protest demonstrations by students and workers culminated in the shooting of about 400 demonstrators, and the detention of political opponents – which included the vice-president André Resampa. President Tsiranana was then forced to hand over power to Ramanantsoa.

General Ramanantsoa's first act on taking office was the restoration of law and order, followed in June by the release of all political detainees. He instituted reforms by raising minimum wages by five percent; abolishing the head and cattle taxes that had caused widespread dissension; increasing annual holidays to thirty days; depoliticising the civil service; imposing penalties for misappropriation of public funds and introducing austerity measures which pegged prices and brought him nation-wide support.

In July 1972 the government announced the Malagasisation of education and the civil service where serving Frenchmen of all grades were replaced by Malagasy citizens. The government also set up the National Commission of Language and Civilisation whose terms of reference included the formulation of an inventory of local dialects that would serve as the basis of a common national Malagasy language.

In foreign affairs Ramanantsoa reversed his predecessor's policy, which not only involved re-negotiating existing agreements with France but also the breaking of ties with South Africa which the government described as proving "an apple of discord". In June 1972 the government severed relations with Pretoria and embarked on creating closer ties with Black Africa which culminated in Madagascar's payment of nine years' arrears of subscriptions to the OAU liberation funds.

On 8 October 1972 Ramanantsoa led the country to a referendum which gave him a mandate to govern for a five-year period, following which Tsiranana formally bowed out from the presidency on 11 October. Post-referendum politics saw Ramanantsoa embark on more directional alterations to Madagascar's policies. After protracted discussions to re-negotiate co-operation agreements with France, the erstwhile officer in the French army ordered the closure of French military bases and the withdrawal of troops from the island. Also, France was made to surrender all public property which it had held on the island since independence. In August 1973 Madagascar withdrew its membership of the African and Mauritian Common Organisation (OCAM) and left the franc zone in order to be able to control its own currency and foreign exchange reserves.

The early months of 1974 saw the introduction of the "Green Plan" programme aimed at boosting agricultural production by putting large but hitherto uncultivated arable land into use for the first time. This was also designed to provide employment for a large number of people in the rural areas.

By April 1974 however, the government was meeting opposition from the new party formed by former President Tsiranana and his ex-Vice-President Resampa, the Mal-

agasy Socialist Union (USM). There was an unsuccessful military attempt to topple the government in December 1974, to which General Ramanantsoa responded on 25 January 1975 by dissolving his government. He warned that the country was on the verge of civil war. On 5 February it was announced that the former Interior Minister, Colonel Richard Ratsimandrava (q.v.), had assumed the full powers of state and government, displacing Ramanantsoa. Ramanantsoa died on 9 May 1979 in a military hospital in Paris.■

Ramgoolam, S. (1900-85)

RAMGOOLAM, Sir Seewoosagur (1900-85).

MAURITIAN politician, statesman, leader of the Mauritian Labour Party (MLP), Prime Minister and Governor-General of Mauritius and the dominant figure in Mauritian politics since the early forties. Sir Seewoosagur led Mauritius to independence in 1968 and was the Prime Minister from 1967 to 1982 and chairman of the OAU for 1976-77.

Born in Belle Rive on 18 September 1900, of humble parents who saved to send him to school, Seewoosagur Ramgoolam came from a rural background. After attending the Royal College in Curepipe he travelled to England to study medicine at the University of London. He not only qualified as a doctor but he used his spare time to read widely in English literature and socialist work and to become active in student politics – he was the organising secretary of the Indian Students' Union. Through his position in the Union he was able to meet Indian political leaders like Gandhi, Nehru and Krishna Menon who influenced his political thoughts.

When he returned to Mauritius, Ramgoolam practised as a doctor but soon came to be active in local politics, becoming involved in helping the workers in the sugar plantations, Mauritius's main agricultural activity, achieve larger participation in the country's economic and political life. In 1940 he was elected to the Port Louis municipal council, and nominated as a member of the Legislative Council by the British administration to represent their interests. In 1948, under a new constitution (the old one had lasted for more than 60 years) he was elected as member for a northern constituency. In 1953 he joined the Labour Party (*Parti Travailliste*) set up by Maurice Curé (q.v.) in 1936 to press for worker participation in government.

In the 1955 elections, the Labour Party won 13 out of 19 seats, and following its success demanded constitutional changes

Sir Seewoosagur Ramgoolam

that would guarantee universal adult suffrage, the introduction of the ministerial system and a clear limitation of the government's powers. In 1958, on Guy Rozemont's (q.v.) death, Ramgoolam became leader of the party, and led the MLP to victory in 1959 in the first elections held under universal suffrage. In 1961 he became Chief Minister of Mauritius and in 1965, Premier.

Ramgoolam proved to be a skilful politician, steering a middle course between the radical proposals of the militant wing of his party, encouraging many opponents to join his coalitions, and ensuring Mauritius a

smooth path to independence in 1968, and a steady economic course after that. His feat was to have managed to reassure the economically powerful White minorities and integrate them into the new social and economic order. He became a bonding force in the nation, rallying round all the different ethnic groups that make up Mauritius's population and building a Mauritian nation with emphasis on the common heritage and culture. Ramgoolam came increasingly to be regarded as a fatherly figure and was known as "Chacha" (Uncle) by all Mauritians.

His foreign politics were equally pragmatic and moderate; it was he who set Mauritius on a non-aligned path. He became Chairman of the Organisation of African Unity in 1976 and Vice-President of the Afro-Arab summit in 1977, and was awarded the 1973 United Nations Prize for his defence of human rights. He was a Commonwealth leader of influence in Africa as well as in Asia.

By the late 70s, however, the older generation of politicians was seen as outmoded and corrupt. A new generation of vocal, educated and politically aware electorate challenged Ramgoolam's government. The *Movement Militant Mauricien* (MMM), which was founded in 1968, became the voice of that opposition. The coalition government broke in 1973, and after the 1976 elections when Ramgoolam was able to retain his position through another coalition, the disenchantment with his government grew. Faced with increasingly articulate opposition, industrial unrest, the Diego Garcia problem and a worsening unemployment situation, his party was swept away completely in the 1982 elections, and the MMM party came to power with new radical policies. Although the MMM's period in power lasted barely two years, Sir Seewoosagur's time as an active politician was over. Many hoped to see him as Mauritius's first President but the new coalition government of Aneerood Jugnauth failed to bring in a Republican constitution in 1983 and Sir Seewoosagur moved into "Le Réduit", the old French Colonial mansion, as Governor-General.

During his lifetime he had received many honours, the Médaille de l'Assemblée Nationale Française, 1971, the Grande Croix, Ordre National du Lion de la République du Sénégal, 1973, the Grande Croix, Ordre National du Bénin, 1973, the Grande

Croix de l'Ordre du Mérite de la République Centrafricaine, 1973 and was decorated Grand Officer, Légion d'Honneur de la République Française in 1973. He received a honorary doctorate from the University of Delhi, India, and was also a Licentiate of the Royal College of Physicians, England, and a member of the Royal College of Surgeons.

Ramgoolam died, aged 85, on 15 December 1985, mourned by his country and by many friends throughout the world. He was cremated at Pamplemousses Botanical Gardens on 17 December 1985. ■

Ranavalona I (c.1788-1861)

RANAVALONA I, Queen (c.1788-1861).

QUEEN of Madagascar. She was the wife of King Radama I, who consolidated the achievements of his father, the conquering Andrianampoinimerina. The Merina kingdom, expanded by the latter king to cover much of the island, entered in Radama's reign into relations with Britain and France, especially the former, and European influence, especially Protestant religion and education, began to spread. In 1828 Radama died and his widow became Queen. She called herself Rabodonandrianampoinimerina, "The beloved daughter of Adrianampoinimerina."

She was the first Queen of Madagascar and the last absolute ruler; the Malagasy historian Raymond Rabemananjara said of her, "Never would there be another Malagasy sovereign so absolute in authority, so firm in decisions, so rigorous in principles" (*Madagascar: Histoire de la Nation Malgache*). She sought not only to maintain the authority of the monarchy, but also to respect tradition. Hence while wanting more modernisation, she wanted it to be in accordance with ancestral traditions, and thus without Christianisation.

She maintained her rule for 33 years with a firm hand, executing a number of her opponents. She favoured some education to spread useful European knowledge, but soon showed increasing hostility to the London Missionary Society, the main Protestant missionary body allowed to preach and teach

Queen Ranavalona I

by Radama, and to Christianity in general. Aspects of the traditional religion were maintained, and after first restricting missionary work, from 1835 Ranavalona decreed death for followers of the "new religion".

Ranavalona was also hostile to any undue encroachments by the British and French, who from their nearby island colonies (Mauritius and Réunion) traded with Madagascar and sought to have influence there. France showed aggressive intentions as early as 1829-31, with a brief occupation of a port. In 1841 France established a "Protectorate" at Nossi-Bé by agreement with the Sakalavas, but Ranavalona claimed that the agreement was invalid as the Sakalavas were her subjects. However, one Frenchman, Laborde, lived in Madagascar from 1837 and helped carry out the Queen's policy of independent development. He manufactured arms and gunpowder, while a Scotsman, Cameron, organised mining under royal supervision. The Queen helped Laborde found an industrial centre at Mantasoa.

Ranavalona aimed at self-reliance, and had some success with the help of such entrepreneurs, but could not refuse trade with other countries and did not seek complete isolation. However, she quarrelled with Britain as well as France, and those two countries, often rivals in Africa, joined in bombarding Tamatave (now Toamasina) in 1845. In response she closed the ports to trade. Smuggling went on, and in 1853 overt trade resumed. Then the British attempted to improve relations.

However, in 1857 there was an attempted coup d'état by supporters of Ranavalona's son Rakoto. In an angry reaction the Queen ordered the expulsion of all foreigners; even the useful Laborde had to leave. The ageing queen became increasingly tyrannical. She had always been a dynamic, restless and vigorous character, fond of travelling and hunting. In her old age she was more oppressive than ever. But on 15 August 1861 she died, the last defender of the old order which after then changed rapidly.■

Ranavalona III (1861-1917)

RANAVALONA III, Queen (1861-1917)

QUEEN of Madagascar. Born on 11 November 1861, she was of the royal family of the powerful kingdom of Madagascar, but of a branch excluded for some time from the succession. However, after being educated by the Protestant mission, which had great influence then, she became Queen on the death of Ranavalona II on 13 July 1883, in the middle of the first French war against the island kingdom. Previously named Razafindrahety, she now took the same name as her predecessor.

That war ended in a treaty on 17 December 1885, in which Madagascar made many concessions but remained independent. The Prime Minister who handled the negotiations, Rainilaiarivony (q.v.), married the young Queen. He had been the dominant figure in Malagasy politics since 1864, as the husband and Prime Minister of Queens Rasoherina and Ranavalona II, and remained so as the consort and Prime Minister of Ranavalona III. The Queen was determined to maintain the power of her throne and the independence of her kingdom. Recalling her predecessor Radama I (died 1828), she declared at her coronation, so

the historian Raymond Rabemananjara tells us in his book *Madagascar: Histoire de la Nation Malgache*, "Radama I devoted himself body and soul to create one single kingdom from all the territories surrounded by the sea. . . Therefore, if anyone wants to

Queen Ranavalona III

take from me one bit of it, however small, I shall defend our common country . . . as if I were a man".

Unfortunately, this stand was hard to maintain against France, which won in 1885 the right to control Madagascar's foreign policy. The Queen and her Prime Minister wanted to maintain as much independence as possible, but had to face increasing French interference after 1885, and after 1890 their ally, Britain, left Madagascar to the French. Finally a major French expedition occupied Madagascar in 1895. The Queen surrendered after the fall of Tananarive on 30 September 1895. She kept her throne at first, but Rainilaiarivony was deported; in 1900 he died in Algiers.

After the "Menalamba" uprising in 1896, the French in February 1897 ended the monarchy, deposed Queen Ranavalona, and deported her. She was sent to Réunion and then in 1899 to Algiers, where she died on 23 May 1917. Her body was reburied in Madagascar in 1938. ■

Ransome-Kuti, I.O. (1891-1955)

RANSOME-KUTI, Reverend Israel Oludotun (1891-1955).

Rev. I.O. Ransome-Kuti

NIGERIAN eminent churchman, educationist and administrator, he was founding president of the Nigeria Union of Teachers (NUT). This Union is Africa's largest movement of any professional group; it was formed on 8 July 1931 and Ransome-Kuti was elected its first president. He remained at the head of the movement until 1954 when he retired at the age of 63.

He was born on 30 April 1891, to a prominent Egba family in Abeokuta. His father was Reverend Canon J. J. Ransome-Kuti (q.v.), well-known for his outstanding administrative competence as well as a singer which earned him the nickname "the Singing Minister". Israel Oludotun was born at the Anglican Parish of Gbagura, Abeokuta, where his father was serving as a teacher/catechist. After attending the Suren Village School there he went to the Lagos Grammar School, but returned to his home town to complete his secondary education at the newly opened Abeokuta Grammar School. He was the first pupil to be enrolled at the school in 1908.

In 1913 Ransome-Kuti matriculated at the Fourah Bay College, Freetown, and returned to his country in 1916 with a B.A. degree. He began work in Lagos, as a teacher at his former Grammar School from 1916 until 1918 when he left for Ijebu-Ode. For thirteen years he was Principal of Ijebu-Ode Grammar School, which had been established in 1912 to provide the only secondary education for the whole Ijebu Province. Among Ransome-Kuti's innovations at this pioneering institution was the first Boy Scout troupe he formed there. This became known in the Province as the first Ijebu-Ode Troupe.

Ransome-Kuti's great intellect and sensitivity towards people soon won him the admiration and respect of the Ijebus. He became their spokesman, pleading their cause with the British colonial resident in the Province. His greatest achievement in Ijebu was to break down the myth that his own Yoruba group, the Egbas, could not work among the Ijebus. Through his example, and the utmost concern for all, he was able to draw the two groups together. His departure from Ijebu was marked with a wide-spread expression of feeling of loss. Of his successor at the Ijebu-Ode Grammar School, the people used to say: "This new Kuti is not as the old one".

On leaving Ijebu-Ode in 1932, Reverend Ransome-Kuti returned to Abeokuta where for the next 22 years he served as principal of the Abeokuta Grammar School. During that period he visited Britain in 1939 and again between 1943 and 1945; he spent the latter years as a member of the Elliott Commission reviewing higher education in West Africa.

It was during his posting at Ijebu-ode that Ransome-Kuti founded an association of local teachers known as the Association of Headmasters of Ijebu Schools. This was in May 1926, a year after a similar association had been formed in Lagos by another renowned Anglican clergyman, Reverend J. O.

Lucas, who inaugurated the Lagos Union of Teachers in May 1925. These two bodies became the base from which the idea of a national organisation that could embrace teachers from all parts of Nigeria grew and culminated in the formation of the NUT on 8 July 1931. At its founding that year, in Lagos, Ransome-Kuti was elected its first national President. He was returned at successive elections to that post which he held until his retirement in 1954. A man of strong and forceful personality, also charismatic, he guided the Union in its early campaign for improved conditions of service for teachers in particular and against colonial education policy in general.

Ransome-Kuti and his colleagues in the NUT Executive, notably A. A. Ikoku, E. E. Esua (qq.v.) and the Reverend (later Bishop) S. I. Kale, succeeded in winning recognition from the British colonial authorities, and also benefits for their members, which by October 1948 were said to number 20,000. With the improved conditions the Union grew rapidly to become by the 1960s the largest professional organisation in Africa, with a membership that exceeded a quarter of all the teachers in the continent. Today education is still the largest single employer in Nigeria, touching more Nigerians directly than any other service, and the thousands of teachers who joined the NUT annually soon found not only respectability but also strength in their Union. It was the foresight and dedication of Reverend Ransome-Kuti that led to both that dignity and unity.

His wife was the famous women's rights' leader, Mrs. Funmilayo Ransome-Kuti (q.v.), who bore him four children, all prominent in Nigeria.■

Ransome-Kuti, J.J. (1855-1930)

RANSOME-KUTI, Reverend Canon Josiah Jesse (1855-1930).

NIGERIAN clergyman and administrator. He was born on 1 June 1855 at Igbein, Western Nigeria. His parents belonged to the Egba Yoruba ethnic group, his father being a weaver, soldier and Egba

diplomat. His mother was an early convert to Christianity and from an early age he was influenced by her deep religious beliefs despite opposition from both her family and her husband.

At the age of nine he began to attend the Church Missionary Society (CMS) Training Institution at Abeokuta. He did very well in his studies, excelling particularly in music. In 1871 he continued his education at the CMS Training Institute in Lagos. He successfully completed his studies there in December 1876 and then became a teacher at St Peter's School in Ake, Abeokuta. After three years he went to teach music at the CMS Girls' School in Lagos. He remained in this position for seven years and during that period he married Bertha Anny Erinade Olubi on 2 May 1882. They had two daughters and three sons.

Throughout this time his religious beliefs had deepened and in 1891 he was appointed catechist at the Gbagura Church Parsonage at Abeokuta. One of his first tasks was to found the Gbagura Church. Initially the services were held in the open air, but later, with the help of the village people, he was able to construct a building

Rev. J.J. Ransome-Kuti

for the church. By this time he was an accomplished musician and singer. He improved the quality of church music and was able to attract many people, some of whom became converted to the Christian religion. He also carried out much charitable work and although he was often short of money he refused an offer of a job in one of the big Lagos commercial concerns.

In 1895 he became a deacon and the following year he was transferred by the Church authorities to the Sunren-Ifo district, an area of 60 square miles where law and order had virtually broken down after a recent war. Initially the people were suspicious of him and his ideas, particularly after he had refused their welcoming gifts, suggesting that they should be sold and the proceeds put into a common fund for the needy. Meanwhile the Egba District government, impressed by his intelligence and capabilities, increased his administrative responsibilities in the district.

He was ordained a priest in 1897 and between 1902 and 1906 he was also appointed a district judge. His sense of fairness and justice greatly increased the people's respect for him. In 1903 he became superintendent of the Abeokuta Church Mission and was also granted a mandate from the Egba District government to act as its representative in cases of emergency in the area. Gradually success in his administrative position enhanced respect for his religious activities and led to increased church attendance. He spent much time trying to overcome resistance to changing traditional forms of worship. He took many boys and girls into his house to provide them with elementary training.

By 1906 he had established 25 new churches in the Sunren-Ifo district, initially superintending them all and later helped by an assistant. He secured permission from the Olu of Ilaro for Christians to use umbrellas, a right that had previously been reserved for the Olu. This caused widespread discontent among the people and some Christians left the church as they felt it was abrogating royal tradition. Ill feeling towards Reverend Ransome-Kuti grew and on his next visit to Ilaro he was attacked and severely wounded. The attackers on being arrested said that they had mistaken him for a burglar. At the same time 100 armed men from Ifo decided to avenge this attack and marched on Ilaro. On their arrival, Reverend Ransome-Kuti per-

suaded them to return home in peace. Shortly afterwards another force of 200 armed men under British command arrived at Ilaro with the same intent and once again, after lengthy negotiations, he was able to convince the soldiers to desist from violence. His diplomacy in dealing with these incidents so as to avoid bloodshed greatly enhanced his reputation, both in Ilaro where a church was constructed on the spot where he was attacked, and in Nigeria generally.

In 1911 he was appointed pastor of St Peter's Church, the leading church in Ake, while remaining a government official. At this time the Church authorities began to apply their rules more strictly and Reverend Ransome-Kuti was later suspended from his duties for three months after baptising children whose parents had not been married either in church or court, without first gaining special permission from the Bishop. His parishioners were very angry about this and wanted to break their connection with the diocese, but Reverend Ransome-Kuti managed to avert this confrontation and calm the situation.

The Egba state lost its independence in 1914 when British rule was imposed. In the resulting upheavals Ransome-Kuti played a major role in mediating between various opposing elements; although the situation stabilised, in 1918 there was an indigenous uprising against the British and also against literate Africans and Christians. Once again Ransome-Kuti played a mediating role, he was the only minister to visit the troubled area, at great risk to himself, to perform services for the Christians there.

In 1922 he visited the Holy Land and on his return he was made a Canon of the Lagos Cathedral Church of Christ, and also resumed his position as pastor of St Peter's Church, remaining there until his death on 4 September 1930 at the age of 75.

From an early age he had been deeply committed to Christianity and through his life's work became a prominent African missionary of his time. He was deeply interested in African history and customs and used this understanding, combined with his musical talents, in his religious work. He composed and sang many indigenous songs to increase awareness of Christian beliefs, several of which were recorded on gramophone and compiled into hymn books. His son Josiah was also a famous churchman.■

Ransome-Kuti, O. (1900-78)

RANSOME-KUTI, Chief Olufunmilayo (1900-78).

NIGERIAN teacher and politician, one of the most outstanding women in the recent history of Nigeria. A champion of women's rights, she was born on 25 October 1900, in Abeokuta, daughter of Chief and Mrs Thomas. She attended the Anglican Church Primary School and later the Abeokuta Girls' Grammar School before proceeding to Manchester, Britain, in 1920 to study domestic science and music at Wincham Hall College.

On her return to Nigeria, having qualified, she taught at the Abeokuta Girls' Grammar School in 1923-24. Then she married the Reverend Israel Ransome-Kuti (q.v.), son of the clergyman Josiah Ransome-Kuti (q.v.), who was from 1918 to 1932 principal of Ijebu-Ode Grammar School. Reverend Israel Ransome-Kuti later became principal of Abeokuta Grammar School until his retirement in 1954; he was the first president (1931-54) of the Nigerian Union of Teachers, and died on 6 April 1955.

In the 1940s she became known as a politician in her own right. She founded a Ladies' Club for educated women and, with the Club, started a club for market women. Adult education for them was started under the name "Social Welfare for Market Women". This merged with the Ladies' Club to form the Egba Women's Union.

During the Second World War market women at Abeokuta suffered from the effects of enforcement, by the Alake (King), of British food trade regulations. The Alake, Oba Ademola II (q.v.), had sweeping powers as "Sole Native Authority" under the British and the women accused him of abusing those powers, while also criticising the poll-tax imposed on women regardless of their circumstances. Women also complained at discriminatory pay in employment and called for the right of women to vote.

The effect of her Egba market women's campaign resulted in the temporary exile of the Alake of Abeokuta on 29 July 1948, by the British Resident who deported him to Oshogbo in the interests of peace. The Alake's deposition was followed by major reforms in the taxation policy of the Egba Native Authority which brought relief to the market women.

During that period Mrs Ransome-Kuti joined the National Council of Nigerian Citizens (NCNC), led by Dr Nnamdi

Chief O. Ransome-Kuti

Azikiwe; she had the distinction of being the only woman delegate to the Constitutional Conference in London in 1947. As a party activist she was entrusted with responsible offices both at the local and national level. She was elected the treasurer of the NCNC in Egba Division and also served as a National Executive member of the party. Speaking later about her NCNC membership, she said that many believed that the party "was more liberal and thought more of the common man. I joined the NCNC because I wanted to see what I could do for the common man rather than to think of myself alone". She added that being a woman made her "unwanted in the political circle then largely dominated by men and this made me unhappy and decided that I would fight to force a change of attitude towards women".

This dedication led to further involvement in Nigerian politics which was shaken by her campaign for the extension of the vote to women. Though she succeeded in bringing about the enfranchisement of women, Mrs Ransome-Kuti was still dissatisfied with the chauvinism of the Nigerian male in particular, and of the African man in general. She travelled widely in Africa, West and East Europe and the United States, representing women's interests at international seminars and conferences.

She was honoured with several awards which included the Order of the Niger in 1963, an honorary Doctorate of Laws by Nigeria's premier educational institution, the University of Ibadan, and the Lenin Peace Prize, both in 1968. She also had the distinction of being one of the first Nigerian women to hold a chieftancy title. Mrs Ransome-Kuti died on 13 April 1978, survived by four children: Dolupo Ransome-Kuti (the eldest), a nursing sister, the renowned musician, Fela Anikulapo-Kuti, Professor Olikoye Ransome-Kuti, a paediatrician, and Dr Beko Ransome-Kuti.■

people. He wrote a Mpongwe dictionary published in two volumes in 1934 and 1963.

After retiring from active priestly duties at the age of 70, he devoted his time to writing. He worked with the French ethnonaturalist Roger Sillans from 1950, and their joint efforts produced the books *Plantes utiles du Gabon* in 1961 and *Rites et croyances des peuples du Gabon* in 1962. He contributed to the magazine *Réalités Gabonaises* started in 1959. In 1960 he published a major historical work, *Notes d'Histoire du Gabon* (with an emphasis on the Omyenes).

After Gabon's independence Mgr. Raponda-Walker protested at the worsening dictatorship of President Mba (q.v.) following his reinstatement by French forces in 1964. Supporters of the President attacked him at one point, although he was in his 90s, and burned many of his books. However, he was able to bring out a large collection of folk stories from all parts of Gabon, *Contes Gabonais*, published in 1967 by Présence Africaine. He died in 1969.■

Raponda-Walker, A. (1871-1969)

RAPONDA-WALKER, Mgr. André (1871-1969).

GABONESE churchman and writer. Born on 19 June 1871 in Libreville, he was the son of Robert-Bruce Walker and a Mpongwe mother related to traditional rulers in the French colony, then confined to the Libreville area. After a year in England with his father, he had primary and secondary education back in Gabon with the Holy Ghost Fathers Catholic Mission. On 23 July 1899 he became the first Gabonese to be ordained to the Catholic priesthood.

Besides working as a priest he studied the customs and languages of the peoples of Gabon, which had been occupied by France largely in the 1880s and 90s, and the animal and plant life of the country. He travelled all over the country as a priest; later he recalled that many took him for a trader. In 1937 he wrote a grammar of the language of the Mitsoghos for whom he was the first Catholic preacher. But his writings on history and customs dealt especially with his own Mpongwe people and the other Omyene

Ratsimandrava, R. (1931-75)

RATSIMANDRAVA, Lieutenant-Colonel Richard (1931-75).

MALAGASY soldier and statesman. He was born on 21 March 1931, the son of a Tananarive (now Antananarivo) school teacher. He was educated locally at the *Lycée de Tananarive*, then went to France to study at the Military College in Saint-Cyr. After graduation he continued military studies at the *Ecole Supérieure de Gendarmerie* at Melun, south of Paris, and was commissioned into the French Gendarmerie in 1954.

He served in France before being posted to the Gendarmerie in Morocco and Algeria from where he returned to Madagascar in June 1960, when the Indian Ocean island got its independence from France. He was promoted in 1962 to the rank of captain in the country's new Gendarmerie, and six years later was promoted lieutenant-colonel. In 1968 he became the first Malagasy to command the Gendarmerie, when the French commander left the island.

Lieutenant-Colonel Ratsimandrava

was at his post until 1972 when President Tsiranana handed control of government to the army following a nation-wide strike and workers' uprising which brought down the regime. On 18 May 1972 General Gabriel Ramanantsoa (q.v.), the Commander-in-Chief

Lt-Col. R. Ratsimandrava

of the Armed Forces, assumed powers of government and the first appointment he made was that of Colonel Ratsimandrava who became minister of the Interior. He was chosen a week ahead of all other ministers, which was an indication of the esteem in which he was held in military circles.

One of his first acts in office was to release the jailed Vice-President André Resampa and 200 others held in detention since the 1971 unrest. The freeing of all the political prisoners in the country made him very popular. Yet he did not exhibit any ambition for office or show any sign of disloyalty to General Ramanantsoa's administration. By 1975, however, with the government facing serious opposition from former President Tsiranana and his ex-Vice-President, Resampa, who had formed the Malagasy Socialist Union (USM), Ramanantsoa announced that he was dissolving his

administration because the country was on the brink of civil war. On 25 January 1975 the government resigned, after a reported coup attempt by some military officers.

On 5 February 1975 Ratsimandrava assumed full powers of state and government. But the 43-year old Colonel was assassinated only six days later in an ambush as he drove to his home in the Malagasy capital. His Cabinet co-ordinator, General Gilles Andriamahazo, succeeded the dead leader and imposed martial law. The new ruler announced that 297 people, including Tsiranana and Resampa, had been arrested and charged with complicity in the assassination. Their trial ended on 12 June 1975, with the acquittal of all the accused – except three officers in the Mobile Police Commando Unit that was alleged to have carried out the assassination of Colonel Richard Ratsimandrava on 11 February 1975. ■

Ravoahangy, J. (1893-1970)

RAVOAHANGY, Dr Joseph (1893-1970).

MALAGASY doctor and politician. He came from a prominent family of the Merina aristocracy, powerful until the French conquest in 1895. He went to a school run by the French Protestant Mission and then the François de Mahy regional school. Throughout his life he was a convinced Protestant, a man of simple ideas and an opponent of violence in the independence movement, of which he became a leader.

He was studying medicine at Tananarive (now Antananarivo) when a nationalist organisation, *Vy Vato Sakelika* (VVS), was founded by him and others. They were arrested in late 1915 and Ravoahangy, although he had not gone in for undercover activity as some others had, was sentenced to hard labour for life. He was imprisoned at Dzaoudzi in the Comoro Islands. He was eventually freed through the efforts of Jean Ralaimongo (q.v.), another early nationalist, then in France. He finished his medical studies in 1923.

Before then he had given Ralaimongo material from the VVS which was published in Ralaimongo's newspaper *Le Libéré*. Dr

Ravoahangy was closely associated with Ralaimongo after the latter's return from France, and went to Diégo Suarez (now Antseranana) to join him. He was forbidden to practise as a doctor there, but at Ralaimongo's request he took over the newspaper *L'Opinion* in 1927. For three years he published attacks on France's colonial oppression and contacted farmers to help organise opposition to seizures of land.

After the nationalist demonstrations at Tananarive on 13 May 1929, Ravoahangy, who had gone to the capital, was sent to

Dr. J. Ravoahangy

Maintirano and restricted there for several years. He was forbidden to engage in political activity, but he was allowed to practise as a doctor and thus made contact with the local Sakalava people, while doing some secret political writing.

In 1936 he was allowed to return to Tananarive. He published the newspaper *La Nation Malgache* and helped organise trade union activity under the relaxed colonial system of the French Popular Front period. In 1938, after some delay, he was allowed to set up in private practice. Between 1940 and 1942, when Madagascar was under repressive Vichy French rule, he was under

surveillance but not arrested. After the replacement of the Vichy authorities by the Free French and the British (1942), Dr Ravoahangy, then secretary of the farmers' trade union, emerged in 1943 as a leading critic of the equally repressive Free French regime. He married Flora, daughter of Pastor Joel Rabesandratana in 1938 and they had five children.

In 1945/46 he was elected by large majorities to the two French Constituent Assemblies and then the first National Assembly of the Fourth French Republic. He was usually treated with hostility by the government. On 29 March 1947 a major uprising was started by members of the *Mouvement Démocratique de la Rénovation Malgache* (MDRM). Two weeks later Dr Ravoahangy, although he condemned the many killings committed by the rebels, was arrested.

He was detained and tortured and his protests were ignored, while the rebellion spread rapidly but eventually succumbed to brutal repression. From July to October 1948 Ravoahangy, with Joseph Raseta (another deputy in the French parliament) and other prominent Malagasys, was tried for conspiracy to launch the uprising which had led to tens of thousands of deaths. He was sentenced to death but he was reprieved in 1949 and served several years in prison, mostly in Corsica (France).

In 1956 he was given a conditional release; he was allowed to practise freely as a doctor, but forbidden to leave France. In 1958 all the remainder of his sentence was dropped but he still had to stay in France. By then Madagascar had full self-government. In the 1958 referendum Ravoahangy had let it be known he favoured a "No" vote in Madagascar, which could have meant independence against French wishes (as happened in Guinea). In fact a majority voted for membership of the French Community. But independence came on 26 June 1960. The following month he and other exiles flew home with President Tsiranana.

Dr Ravoahangy, highly respected as a veteran nationalist, was elected member of Madagascar's National Assembly for Tananarive. He then became Minister of Health and later, in 1965, Minister without Portflio "delegated to the Presidency"; he was reappointed to that post in 1969. He died on 21 August 1970 and received a state funeral. ■

Reindorf, C.C. (1834-1917)

REINDORF, Carl Christian (1834-1917).

GHANAIAN churchman. He was the son of a Dane resident at Accra and his wife Anowah Cudjoe, a Ga woman. Born on 31 May 1834, at Prampram, he was at first put under the care of a shrine of the traditional religion of his mother's people, but then fled

C.C. Reindorf

and went to school in Accra at Christiansborg where Christiansborg Castle belonged to Denmark from the 17th century to 1850. Baptised in 1844, he received schooling from the Basle (Presbyterian) Mission, and traded for a time in an interval in his schooling. The Mission made him a catechist; he taught literacy in Ga and helped interpret the Bible.

He worked in the Krobo district for the missionary Steinhauser, and became a full catechist in 1857. In 1860 he became an assistant teacher at the Akropong Seminary.

He retired briefly to his farm, called Hebron, near Aburi in 1862, but later resumed missionary work; two efforts to convert the people of Teshie were fruitless at that time. He taught at the new Basle Mission School at Christiansborg, then under British rule.

With British rule still only informal except in forts like Christiansborg, wars broke out in the coastal or nearby areas of Gold Coast before 1874. In two such wars near Accra, the Ada-Awuna War of 1866 and the Ga-Akwamu War of 1869-70, Reindorf (not yet a full minister) served in the forces of the side he supported, apparently as a non-combatant assistant surgeon. In 1869-70, the British at Accra backed the Gas and commended Reindorf's work.

On 13 October 1872 he was ordained a full minister. He worked at Mayera near Accra, first starting a school there and about 1882 moved to Christiansborg where the Castle was the seat of government. In 1893 he started a new mission in Accra proper, then separated from Christiansborg. He retired to his farm in 1893 but headed a nearby mission at Adenkrebi.

He published a work for which he is most famous, *A History of the Gold Coast and Asante*. This painstaking work, based on oral information among other sources, is still useful today. He finished it in 1889.

He was recalled to Christiansborg in 1907, and helped complete the new Ga Bible, published in 1912. He died on 1 July 1917. He had married Ayikai Mansah Djebi in 1856, and had eleven children including a famous medical doctor, Dr Charles Reindorf, who died in 1968. ■

Rennat, M.M.A. (1905-77)

RENNAT, Muhammad Mustafa Abu (1905-77).

SUDANESE jurist; he was Chief Justice of Sudan from 1955 until 1964. He was born in 1905 in Nahud in western Sudan, to a family of the Shaiqi ethnic group who had settled in the West from the Nile Valley. He was educated at the Gordon Memorial College, and at the School of Law, both in Khartoum. Beginning his career as a translator between 1925-1933, he worked his way up to clerkship in 1933, and became a district judge from 1938 to 1944, then department assistant, Legal Section. As a judge he had a reputation of incorruptibility.

Following a five-year assignment as

M.M.A. Rennat

inspector of Native Courts, he studied in England during 1949-50 and on his return was appointed Chief Justice of Sudan in 1955, a post that he held for nine consecutive years. On the eve of General Abboud's takeover in 1958 he agreed to stay on as Chief Justice, thus neutralising legal opposition to the military government. For six years thereafter, he was one of a handful of men, all Shaiqi, who ran the country. He presided over changes in the structure of national and local government permitting the introduction of controlled representation. The structure failed to mature before the Abboud regime was swept from power in October 1964. In that year he was elected member of the United Nations Sub-Committee on the

Prevention of Discrimination and Protection of Minorities, with headquarters in Geneva, Switzerland, and in May-July 1965, he sat on the Constitutional Committee for British South Arabia.

Judge Abu Rennat's reputation did not collapse with the government with which he was associated. He was a respected lawyer and businessman in Khartoum and his advice was internationally sought on legal and constitutional matters and on issues of human rights. On 2 October 1977 Rennat died in London.■

Ribadu, M. (1910-65)

RIBADU, Alhaji Muhammadu (1910-65).

NIGERIAN politician, who was first Minister of Defence after independence. Born in 1910 at Balala in what is now Gongola State, he was educated at Yola Middle School and taught there from 1926. Later he left teaching and joined the colonial local government administration in 1931, as chief accountant to the Yola Native Administration. He was made district head of Balala in 1936, and also became treasurer of the Adamawa Native Authority Treasury. In 1946 he became the first Nigerian to be sent on a local government course in Britain, sponsored by the British Council.

Returning to Nigeria the following year, he was active in politics in the Northern Region and entered the Northern House of Assembly in Kaduna in 1947. Thus began a political career in which he rose rapidly. He soon became a leader of the Northern People's Congress (NPC), founded in 1949 as a cultural organisation but soon turned into a political party in order to meet the requirements of the Macpherson Constitution. Under the leadership of the Sardauna of Sokoto, Sir Alhaji Ahmadu Bello (q.v.), the NPC won all the Northern seats in Nigeria's first general elections of 1951-52, and Alhaji Muhammadu Ribadu was one of the Northern candidates who won the election to the Federal House of Representatives in Lagos where he was appointed Minister of Natural Resources. He was previously a director of the Nigerian Produce Marketing Company, but resigned this post on becoming a minister.

In 1954 he was appointed Federal Minister of Land, Mines and Power; he served in that ministry until 1957 when he was transferred to the Portfolio of Lagos

Alhaji M. Ribadu

Affairs. He was second Vice-President of the NPC, and one of the most influential leaders of the NPC-dominated regime in the Federation. He received a British decoration, being awarded the MBE in 1952.

In September 1960, on the eve of Nigeria's independence in October, he was appointed Federal Minister of Defence. In that vital ministry he presided over the complete Nigerianisation of the armed forces, culminating in his own choice of Major-General Aguiyi-Ironsi (q.v.) to be commander of the Nigerian forces in February 1965.

Alhaji Muhammadu Ribadu was very powerful in the federal government and was referred to as a "deputy prime minister" to Alhaji Abubakar Tafawa Balewa (q.v.). He died on 1 May 1965, shortly before the Balewa administration was ended by a military coup d'état. ∎

Robert, S. (1909-62)

ROBERT, Shaaban (1909-62).

TANZANIAN poet, novelist and essayist, whose works are a major contribution to the modern development of Kiswahili language. He was born on 1 January 1909 in Vibambani in the Ganga region of Tanganyika (now Tanzania). He attended schools in Msimbazi and later in Dar-es-Salaam where he was a pupil at the Central School from 1922 to 1926. On leaving school he joined the colonial government service as a revenue clerk in the Customs Department, serving in Pangani from 1926 until 1944. He was deployed to the Games Department as secretary in the veterinary station in Kikombo, Mpwapwa, in 1944, and in 1952 was reposted to the Provincial Commissioner's Office in Tanga. Though Robert was frequently transferred from one government department to another until his retirement from the service in 1960, he did not make any significant rise in the colonial service structure because, as he stated in his autobiography *Maisha Yangu na Baada ya Miaka Hamsini*, he was regarded essentially as a poet.

Indeed, Robert is regarded as one of the most distinguished and prolific literary figure in East Africa. He wrote many volumes of poetry, stories, essays and novels in Swahili, all published as complete works issued in thirteen volumes under the title *Diwani ya Shaaban*. Twelve of his books are standard textbooks used in schools and colleges in East Africa. A fervent Pan-Africanist, Robert's writings protest at Africans' subjugation to European colonialism, depicting their courageous reactions to the forms of adversity which assail them in their oppression. But he also dwelt on a broad spectrum of contemporary themes which give his works a wider appeal.

His first poems were published in a volume entitled *Pambo la Lugha* (The Embellishment of Language) in 1948 and had been reprinted in three subsequent editions. *Utenzi wa Vita Uya Uhuru* (The War for Freedom), published after his death, is an epic about the Second World War and is generally considered as Robert's greatest poetic work. In 1952 he published two works, *Adili na Nduguze* (Adili and His Brothers) and a translation into Swahili of the *Rubaiyat* of Omar Khayyam, the famous Persian poet, as *Khayyam kwa Kiswahili*, which was a novelty in Swahili literature. Other works include *Kielezo cha Fasili* in 1954, *Masomo Yenye Adili* in 1959 and *Insha na Mashairi* in 1960.

In addition to his creative activities Robert was a member of the Inter-Territorial Language Committee for East Africa, the East African Literature Bureau, the Tanganyika Languages Board, and the East

S. Robert

African Swahili Committee which he joined in 1952 and whose chairman he became in 1961. In recognition of his achievements he was honoured with a British knighthood, the Knight of the British Empire (KBE) and won, among other literary awards, the Margaret Wrong Medal and Prize in 1962 shortly before his death on 20 June 1962 in Tanga. In a tribute to Shaaban Robert, the *East African Committee Journal* wrote: "Sheikh Shaaban was the undisputed Poet Laureate of the Swahili language and a pioneer in the development of this language.

He opened up new ways of expression, new modes of thought. He will for ever be known as a turning point in the evolution of the Swahili language. His work will remain a link between the classical literature of the past and the modern Swahili of the future". ■

Roberts, J.J. (1809-76)

ROBERTS, Joseph Jenkins (1809-76).

LIBERIAN statesman, the country's first President. Joseph Jenkins Roberts was born in Norfolk, Virginia, USA, on 15 March 1809. He grew up in a devout Methodist household, and on the death of his father, he helped his mother to support the family by working on a flat-boat which travelled up and down the James and Appomattox Rivers. He showed an eagerness to learn and used any spare money he had on books to gain more knowledge.

On hearing of the American Colonisation Society, the family applied to be assisted in settling in the new settlements in Africa. After their application was accepted they set sail for Liberia on 9 February 1829. The voyage lasted 40 days and they landed at Monrovia on 1 March 1829.

Roberts became a trader and did business both locally along the coast and with American and British companies. His activities as a merchant brought him into contact with the indigenous peoples of Liberia. In 1836 the Liberian government asked him to assist in collecting overdue debts from the chiefs of Bassa. He was given promises which were not kept. In 1838 the government again asked for his assistance, authorising him to propose that land would be an acceptable alternative for the money owing. The chiefs refused and Roberts returned with a force of 70 men. They then agreed to pay their debts with land. On 12 April 1838 the land was taken over by the government in the name of the American Colonisation Society.

As a soldier in the Liberian Militia he distinguished himself in combat along the St Paul River in 1839 during the armed conflict against the indigenous groups. In the same year he became Vice-Governor of the Liberian Commonwealth, a position in which he worked closely with the Governor especially in matters related to the indigenous population.

He became Governor of the Liberian Commonwealth in 1841 on the death of the previous incumbent. In 1843 he convened a council of ethnic leaders from North and West Liberia to discuss ways of settling disputes and inter-ethnic problems. One of the achievements of this meeting was that the ethnic leaders pledged to present their grievances to the government in Monrovia before resorting to any other action. For its part, the Liberian government undertook to promote the material and spiritual development of the indigenous people as part of the general growth of the country. Roberts introduced laws for the protection of ethnic apprentices and workers and, by 1845, around 300 indigenous men were enfranchised.

Throughout the period when Roberts was Governor his authority was repeatedly challenged, particularly by the British. Constant appeals to the British government to restrain its nationals from engaging in criminal activity, especially smuggling, were ignored. At that time Britain did not recognise Liberia as a sovereign state but regarded the country as a private philanthropic organisation carrying out private commercial enterprise. In 1843 British and French traders were even advised that they were not legally bound to pay customs duties owed to Liberia.

Much of the confusion over the legal status of Liberia stemmed from the involvement of the American Colonisation Society which had organised the original settlements. In 1846 its Board of Directors held a meeting at which it was agreed that the Society should sever its control of the colony to enable Liberia to proclaim its independence. These proposals were passed on to Roberts who called a referendum of the settlers on 27 October 1846. The results showed that the people firmly supported independence, in spite of fears in some quarters that without an effective army the new state would be vulnerable.

In January 1847 a convention was established to draft a new constitution with the help of a Harvard University academic, Professor Simon Greenleaf. Modelled on the Constitution of the USA, it was signed on 26 July 1847, the day the Republic of Liberia's independence was declared. Elections were held in October and Roberts standing as the candidate for the True Republican Party was elected first President of Liberia. The Republic was then bigger than the original colony, because throughout his governorship Roberts had bought land for the country.

Before his inauguration on 3 January 1848, Roberts travelled to England to meet Queen Victoria. During the meeting Britain officially recognised the Republic of Liberia and Roberts was presented with a ship to help patrol coastal waters against slave traders and smugglers. He was re-elected President in the 1849, 1851 and 1853 elections.

During his presidency he strengthened the international status of the Republic. Domestically small settlement holdings were encouraged as a first step to large farms and increased productivity leading to a growth in trade, particularly between Britain and Liberia.

His administration was particularly successful in suppressing slave trading activities and in dealing with the resultant hostilities of the coastal populations who had acted as middlemen in this business since the 16th century. By 1853, over 80,000 slaves had been freed, slave trading along the Liberian coast had been stopped and the coastal traders had signed treaties undertaking to have no further involvement in the business.

The size of the country was also further expanded in the West to the border of Sierra Leone with land acquired from agreements that had been previously negotiated with the indigenous chiefs as well as new ones. In April 1855 Roberts went to Robertsport, Cape Mount, in the West of the country to help establish a new settlement there. Shortly after his return to Monrovia an inter-ethnic war broke out, placing the existence of the new settlement in jeopardy. Following his failure to be re-elected in the May 1855 elections, he returned to Robertsport to settle the dispute successfully by arbitration.

After handing over the presidency in January 1956, Roberts was briefly appointed Chargé d'Affaires to France. Later in the year he travelled to America and during his stay there he acted on behalf of the Board of Trustees of Donations for Education in Liberia. He returned to Liberia in December 1856 with building materials for the project.

Meanwhile ethnic problems had caused Maryland to join the Republic of Liberia and on 11 February 1857 Roberts, now a major-general in the Liberian Militia, went to Maryland with a force of 115 men to try to settle the dispute. In the following year he remained closely involved in government affairs, while also supervising the construction of the Liberia College which was opened in 1863. In 1869 he went to the USA to raise funds for the College, of which he remained president until his death, and from there went to England, returning to Liberia in 1871.

The political situation in the country had meanwhile become unstable, leading to the deposition of President Roye (q.v.). Roberts was declared President of the Republic by the Legislature on 4 December 1871. He was re-elected in the 1873 elections. During his last term he increased his efforts to integrate the indigenous people into Liberian society. He also organised prospecting parties in the interior of the country, through which large mineral deposits were later discovered.

He declined renomination as presidential candidate in the 1875 elections, and after an illness he died in Monrovia on 24 February 1876, having served his country well for many years. An orator with a tall dignified appearance, together with an unpretentious manner, keen shrewdness and clearly expressed views, he was popular with the people. He was dedicated to the development of his country and before his death made a will providing $10,000 and a coffee farm to be used to assist the growth of education there. ■

D. Rodrigues

Rodrigues, D. (died 1966)

RODRIGUES, Deodolinda (died 1966).

ANGOLAN resistance leader who was active in the organisation of women during the struggle against Portuguese colonialism. A member of the Popular Movement for the Liberation of Angola (MPLA), she was proclaimed a national heroine of the independence struggle after the withdrawal of Portugal. The country's Women's Day 2 March commemorates her disappearance in 1966 when she was abducted and later murdered by the rival National Front for the Liberation of Angola (FNLA) forces on the northern border with Zaire. She is also remembered in her country as a dedicated freedom fighter who gave her life to the cause of the Angolan Revolution.

Rodrigues was born in Luanda but the family moved from the Angolan capital to the countryside where she spent her first seven years. They returned to Luanda where she was educated to secondary school level. At school she came under the influence of two teachers who, like most of their educated countrymen then, were working clandestinely for the emerging nationalist movement. Thus Rodrigues was given early encouragement to develop her militancy in the face of the excesses of Portuguese rule. During this period she went on an excursion tour of rural Angola which she recorded later as "an awareness of the calamitous state of Angola and of the sufferings of its people".

After graduation she joined the MPLA, taking active part in its clandestine deliberations in the capital. She escaped arrest by the colonial authorities and fled north to the Zairean border where the MPLA forces were in active combat against the colonial forces. There Rodrigues soon became a central figure in the activities of the Angolan Women's Organisation (OMA), a wing of the MPLA. The organisation had been set up to coordinate the activities of women in the liberation struggle, while at the same time promoting both their emancipation and their integration in the Revolution. Through these activities Angolan women played an important part in the struggle where they were active in the forefront of the armed resistance as well as in other inter-related areas. In the post-colonial years the OMA reconstructed itself into seven departments: political, organisation, foreign relations, productive and social work, information, finance, and education, with the aim of mobilising Angolan women, with emphasis on the peasant women in rural Angola, into a mass movement.

Rodrigues did not live to see the aims of the organisation develop after independence; for on 2 March 1966 she and several other colleagues in the MPLA were kidnapped by the forces of Holden Roberto's FNLA and taken to the Kinzuku military base where she was reported killed. After Angola ascended to independence under the MPLA in November 1975, Rodrigues was declared a heroine of the resistance. ■

Roye, E.J. (1815-72)

ROYE, Edward James (1815-72).

LIBERIAN statesman. Edward James Roye was born on 3 February 1815 in Newark, Ohio, USA. His family was fairly wealthy and his father owned land in Illinois. After attending Newark High School, he went to study at the University of Athens in Ohio for three years, graduating in 1835. He then became a teacher in Chilicothe while saving money to start a business. He later left teaching to become a sheep trader.

In 1837 he moved to Terre Haute and opened the city's first bath-house, a venture that proved very successful. He then arranged for his widowed mother to join him, and cared for her until her death in 1840. Five years later he joined the Masons fraternity of America, but despite his flourishing business he was unhappy over the

E.J. Roye

prejudice and denial of opportunities to Afro-Americans in the USA and decided to move to Haiti, then changed his mind and emigrated to Liberia.

He arrived in Monrovia on 7 June 1846 and rapidly built up a prosperous mercantile business, his ships being the first to sail to America and Europe under the Liberian flag. He was later elected to the Liberian House of Representatives, becoming Speaker of that body in 1849. After a while he was elected a member of the Senate and in 1864 he was appointed Chief Justice of the Supreme Court of Liberia.

A member, and later leader, of the True Whig Party, Roye unsuccessfully campaigned for the presidential candidacy in both the 1855 and 1867 elections. In May

1869, however, he was elected President of the Republic with great popular support, having inspired the people with his campaign for Liberian development.

At the time of his presidency the Liberian economy was facing financial difficulties, mainly caused by falling export prices, obsolete shipping facilities, inadequate infrastructure and a limited commercial base for operating in the country. To help rectify this situation Roye drew up an ambitious plan covering agricultural and agro-industrial development, the creation of a more effective transportation system, and the restructuring of the financial economy, including the establishment of a national banking system, and the growth of an efficient education system. In addition he also called for the advancement of the indigenous population, seeing Liberia's future as a prosperous, educated and civilised Black community, with all its people, whatever their origin, playing a full role in the affairs of the country.

After his inauguration in January 1870 he enlarged his Cabinet by two members, a Secretary of the Interior and a Secretary of Education, to help the development of education and facilitate the integration of the nation. He began a common school system that would be compulsory for all children in the country, establishing a Commissioner for Education in each district to ensure that adequate educational facilities were available.

To carry out the rest of his plan he proposed that foreign capital should be sought to help develop Liberian resources and establish a foundation from which the economy as a whole could grow. There was some opposition to this as it was feared that it could, among other things, lead to a loss of sovereignty. On 28 January 1870 the president received the Legislature's approval for negotiating a foreign loan provided it did not exceed $500,000.

In June 1870 Roye visited England to try and settle the long-standing dispute over Liberia's border with Sierra Leone in the North West. He was unable to reach an agreement that was acceptable to the Legislature and began negotiations for a foreign loan, leaving delegates to continue while he went briefly to America to encourage foreign investment in his country.

Meanwhile his progressive policies were arousing strong opposition from some leading Liberian figures. This opposition flared up over the issue of the presidential term of office being extended from two to four years. In the 1869 elections a special poll was held on this issue, with a majority of those who voted being in favour of the extension. There was a disagreement over whether the constitution should be amended and it was decided to hold another special referendum on the matter in May 1870. The Legislature did not count the votes as required by the constitution but, in November 1870 Roye prematurely stated publicly that the term had been extended.

The matter was put to the Legislature, but as the opposition failed to get the necessary two-third majority against the constitutional amendment, Roye felt that the amendment had become law. His opponents refused to accept this, saying that he did not have general support for this move, and began to stir up opposition against him, portraying him as a dictator who was determined to keep power. The opposition was strong enough to demand elections in May 1871, but Roye refused to participate, saying that he intended to remain in office for his full 4 years.

In August 1871 a private loan of £100,000 was finalised with a group of London Bankers. As Liberian credit at that time was poor, the conditions of the loan were very harsh with £30,000 being retained by the bankers as advance interest. The loan was repayable in 15 years at the rate of 7 per cent interest per annum. Roye's opponents were extremely critical of the terms of the loan, arguing that they were unfavourable and not in the best interests of the country.

Opposition to Roye was strengthening over both the loan and whether the presidential term had been extended, and during the constitutional crisis that emerged, impeachment proceedings against him began. In October 1871 violence broke out in Monrovia between the opposing factions and Roye's house was attacked. On 26 October 1871 Roye, along with some of his supporters, was arrested and imprisoned. A Provisional Government was established under his Vice-President who had joined Roye's critics.

On 11 February 1872 the High Court of Impeachment found Roye guilty. That evening, before sentence had been passed, he escaped from prison and attempted to leave the country. He was unsuccessful and died the following day. Accounts vary as to the cause of death. Some say that he was shot while waiting for a boat to carry him to a British steamer, others say that he was drowned after his canoe capsized, possibly because it had been fired on, while another version holds that he nearly drowned but was rescued, dying a few hours later. Yet others say that he was drowned while trying to swim to a boat. ■

Rozemont, M.J.G. (1915-56)

ROZEMONT, Marie Joseph Guy (1915-56).

MAURITIAN trade unionist and politician, Guy Rozemont was born on 15 November 1915 in Port Louis. He attended Saint-Enfant-Jesus primary school in Rose-Hill, the Collège Royal and Collège St. Joseph. He had to give up his secondary studies in 1931 when his father died, in order to take whatever employment he could find. In 1939 he applied to join the police force but was turned down.

In 1940 he joined the labour movement after securing a job on the militant *Peuple Mauricien* newspaper, edited by Emmanuel Anquetil, the trade union leader. Anquetil became President of the Labour party on 1 May 1941 and made Rozemont the party's Secretary-General. Together they launched a vigorous union recruitment campaign aimed at workers in the towns and rural areas.

During the Second World War years he served as an ambulance driver at Curepipe barracks.

In December 1946 he unsuccessfully stood as a candidate in the municipal elections. When Anquetil died in 1947, Rozemont became President of the Labour Party and intensified political action. He successfully stood as a candidate for Port Louis in the general elections of August 1948 and became the capital's first deputy. In the August 1953 elections he was returned with an increased majority. An eloquent speaker, he consistently promoted the interests of the island's workers in the Legislative Assembly and in the Municipal Council to which he was elected in December 1950.

In 1955 he travelled to London as a member of the Labour Party delegation to the constitutional conference. On his return to Mauritius he became seriously ill and was admitted to Victoria Hospital where he died on 23 March 1956. ■

Rubusana, W.B. (1858-1936)

RUBUSANA, Walter Benson (1858-1936).

SOUTH AFRICAN politician, who was the first African member of the Cape Provincial Council. The son of a Denge Councillor, he was born in 1858 in the village of Mnandi, Somerset East District, in the Cape Province of South Africa. In 1874, at

W.B. Rubusana

the age of sixteen, he commenced formal schooling at the Peelton Congregational Mission Primary School and in 1876 won a scholarship to Lovedale in Alice, Cape Province, where he trained later as a teacher; he qualified in 1882. During the next two years he underwent training in preparation for ordination in the Congregational Church; he was ordained in late 1884 and served as a junior minister under Reverend Richard Birt in the Somerset East District. He was later posted to the East Bank African Location in East London where he was instrumental in the establishment of an African newspaper, *Izwi Labantu*, in 1898.

Following his visit to Britain in 1904 when he joined the entourage of Chief David Dalindyedo of the Tembu to the coronation of Edward VII, Rubusana went into politics; he was a member of the Cape delegation to the inaugural meeting of the South African Native Convention which was held in Bloemfontein in March 1909. At the first elections held on that occasion he was elected President of the Convention and was, as such, a leading figure in the succeeding years' skilful deliberations that resulted in the formation of the African National Congress (ANC) in 1912. A year earlier he had participated in the Universal Races Congress, held in London, which was attended by several pan-Africanists. As President of the Convention he had also headed its delegation to London to protest against the anti-African clauses contained in the Act of Union, but though the delegation was received, the British government did not accede to its demands for modification.

In 1910 he was supported by the white-led Progressive Party in the election to the Cape Provincial Council, which he won as a representative for Tembuland contituency. His election thus gave him the distinction of being the first African to be elected to the Council and, following his defeat in the 1914 elections when another African candidate, John Tengo Jabavu (q.v.), contested and split the African vote, became the only member of his race to serve in the body. At the formation of the ANC in 1912 he was elected a Vice-President and was co-author of its constitution.

An expert on Xhosa literature and language, he edited the revised Xhosa Bible and supervised its publication in 1905. He himself wrote several hymns in Xhosa which were collected as *Zemka Inkoma Magwalandini* in 1906, and published a *History of South Africa from the Native Standpoint* for which he received an honorary doctorate degree from McKinley University in America. Rubusana died in 1936 in East London, South Africa. ■

Rupia, J. (1904-79)

RUPIA, John (1904-79).

TANZANIAN politician, the first First Vice-President of the Tanganyika African National Union (TANU) which led the country to independence. Born on 19 May 1904 at Kiserawe in the Lutheran Mission area, his father was a trader before and during the German occupation of Tanganyika and his mother was from Zaire. John went to a German school and finished in Standard Six, then the highest class obtainable in the country, and spoke brilliant German. Thereafter he went to the famous UMCA Mkunazi High School in Zanzibar. At that school John changed from the Lutheran to the Anglican denomination. When the First World War broke out, however, anxious parents demanded the return of their children from the island, and thus John returned to the mainland without having completed his education. But with sufficient knowledge of English he became one of the first Africans to be employed in the British colonial civil service (Tanganyika, at this time, had become a British mandated territory).

J. Rupia

Rupia was employed in the Revenue Office, in what was then a very small secretariat in Dar-es-Salaam. He later moved to the Magogoni district of the capital where he lived with his mother, his father having died when he was only three years old. This was the time however when the British were dividing the African area of Dar-es-Salaam into separate quarters for Moslems and Christians. These areas were further subdivided into areas for particular denominations.

He soon left the civil service to open up a business selling building materials in Dar-es-Salaam, in conjunction with running a bus service from Dar-es-Salaam to Mondromango. He also had a cotton farm in the Morogoro area. No doubt adversely influencd by the harsh regime of the Germans and the equal humiliation under the British, Rupia also began to take an active part in politics. He was a founder member of the Tanganyika African Association (TAA), a quasi-political body of which he eventually became its Treasurer and Vice-President. He held these posts until the TAA became TANU on 7 July 1954. One of the 17 founder members of TANU, Rupia was elected its first Vice-President (with Nyerere as President) and, as such, did not only become a close associate of Julius Nyerere who at independence became the country's first leader, but was also an important figure in the party's organisation and activities that brought Tanganyika to independence in 1961.

He also took immense interest in education; thus when TANU opened schools to cater for the needs of Africans he was one of the pillars behind the Tanganyika African Parents' Association (TAPA) established by the party to run the schools. He toured the country to give inspiration to communities to build their own schools, even though the British authorities viewed these as possible breeding places for insurgents like the Mau Mau then making headway in the neighbouring territory of Kenya. It was in recognition of this service that Rupia was one of the first five leading personalities (the others being President Julius Nyerere, Sheikh Aboud Jumbe, Rashid Mfaume Kawawa and President Samora Machel of Mozambique) who were given honorary membership of TAPA. John Rupia was also involved in many other activities; he was president of the Tanzania Red Cross Association, chairman of the Mwananchi Development Corporation (TANU's economic wing), and a member of the TANU Board of Trustees. He was founder member of the Pan-African Freedom Movement of East, Central and Southern Africa, and of the Chama Cha Mapinduzi which TANU became in 1977. He died in 1979 and was buried with full party honours before a large crowd of government officials and members of Tanzania's business community. ■

Rwagasore, L. (1932-61)

RWAGASORE, Prince Louis (1932-61).

BURUNDIAN politician and Prime Minister. He was born on 10 January 1932 at Gitega, the son of Mwami Mwambutsa IV and Therese Kanyonga. His early education was at Catholic mission schools in Bukeye, Kanyinya and Gitega and from 1945 he

Prince Louis Rwagasore

studied at the GSA for six years. He attended university for a short time in Belgium, but returned to Burundi in the same year to commence a career in politics. His attempt to create African cooperatives was opposed by the Belgian colonial administration which suppressed the initiative in 1958.

Prince Louis had been given the command of Butanyerera chiefdom by his father, but after entering politics and creating the *Parti de l'Unité et du Progrès National* (UPRONA) in 1959 he gave up this traditional post. Rwagasore strove to make UPRONA a party of national unity. Unlike the *Parti Démocrate Chrétien* (PDC) which favoured a republican constitution, UPRONA favoured the continuation of the monarchy.

It was, however, the PDC which won the elections of 1960 and formed the pre-independence government. This victory, it was alleged, was in large part due to manipulation by the Belgian authorities. Rwagasore was able to ally himself with Dr Julius Nyerere and the Tanganyika African National Union (TANU). The latter was instrumental in organising support for UPRONA at the United Nations and in sponsoring the General Assembly's resolution declaring the 1960 elections void. In the UN-supervised elections of 1961 Rwagasore's UPRONA registered a resounding victory and Rwagasore was appointed Prime Minister on 19 September 1961.

In appointing his Cabinet, Rwagasore was at pains to achieve an ethnic balance between the country's two main ethnic groupings, the Tutsi and the Hutu, and promised that members of opposition parties would gradually be integrated into the administration. He favoured a federation of Tanganyika, Burundi and Rwanda. The new Burundi government had no control over matters of defence, foreign affairs or technical assistance, all of which remained in Belgian hands, a situation which Rwagasore was very anxious to change.

He was assassinated in a Burundian restaurant on 13 October 1961, less than a month after taking office. There has been an official cult of his memory since then in Burundi.■

Sadat, M.A. (1918-81)

SADAT, Colonel Mohammed Anwar (1918-81).

EGYPTIAN soldier and statesman; he succeeded Abdul Nasser (q.v.) to the presidency in 1970, becoming the second President of Egypt.

Anwar Sadat was born on 27 December 1918 in Mit Aboulkom in the Nile Delta. His mother was of Sudanese extraction and his father, an army hospital clerk, gave him an early Islamic education at the Tala Koranic School. From there he went to Cairo for primary and secondary education, gaining admission, in 1936 to the Abbatieh Military Academy in the Egyptian capital where he was a contemporary of Nasser.

Together, they founded a secret revolutionary organisation at Manqabad, which became the nucleus of the Free Officers' Movement launched in the 1950's to liberate Egypt from British colonialism. His anti-British activities led to his being court-martialled, dismissed from the service, and imprisoned in October 1942. Two years later Sadat escaped from prison and went underground until the end of 1945. But he was again soon imprisoned in 1946 for complicity in attacks on pro-British officials. He served this term until 1949 when he was freed. He then worked briefly as a journalist. In 1950 his friends used their influence to have his commission restored. He was posted to Rafah in Sinai, where he resumed active membership of the Free Officer's Movement. On 23 July 1952 the Free Officers' Movement seized power and King Farouk (q.v.) had to abdicate.

Although one of the members of the new ruling Revolutionary Command Council, with whom real power lay after the 1952

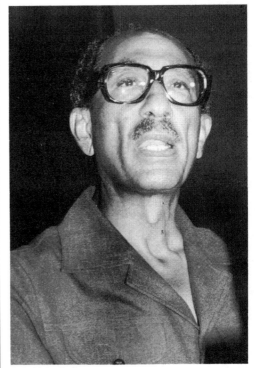

Col. M.A. Sadat

coup, Sadat was not at first given a key post in Government. From 1952, for two years, he was Editor-in-Chief of the official *Al-Goumhouriya* newspaper and Director of the Armed Forces Public Relations; from 1954 to 1956, Minister of State; from 1956 to 1961 Secretary-General of the Islamic Congress and Egyptian National Union (later to be known successively as the Arab Socialist Union and the National Democratic Party); and in 1960 Head of the Afro-Arab People's Solidarity Council. Between 1961 and 1968 his duties included the Presidency of the National Assembly and, from 1964 until 1967, the Vice-Presidency of Egypt when he served as one of the four deputies to Nasser. He became sole Vice-President in December 1969, nine months before Nasser's death.

After the death of the President on 28 September 1970, he was chosen interim President. On 7 October 1970 he was nominated by the Egyptian Parliament to succeed Nasser, and on 15 October had his nomination approved by a popular referendum.

On 14 May 1971 Vice-President Ali Sabri and other Nasserites were arrested and sentenced to death on treason charges; the sentences were later commuted to life imprisonment. But opposition continued in the various strata of Egyptian society, as Sadat moved to replace the socialism of Nasser with an "Open Door" economic policy and a rapprochement with the West. In 1972, 20,000 Soviet military advisers were expelled from Egypt as a consequence of this shift in policy.

Despite the internal problems he took very bold steps towards solving the Arab-Israeli crisis. When his 1971 proposals for an interim solution failed, he led his country in a daring attack across the Suez Canal in October 1973. Egypt's gallantry in the Yom Kippur War destroyed the myth of Israeli invincibility. President Sadat became a national hero and gained credit for restoring Arab morale and pride, shattered by previous defeats at the hands of the Israelis.

In June 1975 he re-opened the Suez Canal, closed to international shipping in the wake of the 1967 Six-day War. On that occasion Sadat declared that the canal was being re-opened to "what it was always intended to be, a passageway to peace and an avenue for prosperity and co-operation among mankind." He crowned his diplomacy in November 1977 with an historic visit to Jerusalem where he addressed the Israeli Parliament, the Knesset, on his desire for peaceful co-existence. This move was widely condemned in the Arab world. Undeterred he continued direct negotiations and, on 17 September 1978, signed two peace agreements with Prime Minister Menachem Begin of Israel at Camp David under the auspices of America. However, the Camp David accords were rejected by the Arabs as a betrayal. Sadat's Egypt was thrown out of the Arab League and isolated diplomatically. But for his peace initiatives of 1978 Sadat received the Methodist Peace Prize and shared the 1978 Nobel Peace Prize with Begin. Thus admired by his allies as a harbinger of peace and chastised by his Arab

critics as a traitor, he continued his chosen way, undoubtedly endowed with great courage, and in April 1979 he ratified the peace treaty. Then in 1981, the President arrested about 1,600 religious and political opponents for alleged political offences; the Coptic Pope was banished to a desert monastry and replaced by a government-appointed committee. On 6 October 1981 Anwar Sadat was assassinated by a member of the Egyptian army at a military parade. He was succeeded by Hosni Mubarak. ∎

Salem, M. (1918-88)

SALEM, Mamdouh (1918-88).

EGYPTIAN former police officer who was responsible for modernising his country's security network and introducing some democratic reforms when he became Minister of the Interior and Prime Minister under Anwar Sadat (q.v.) in the 1970s. Mamdouh Salem remained throughout his career a man of action, efficient and loyal to his principles.

He had a great talent for identifying problems, discerning trouble and dealing

M. Salem

with them swiftly. Mamdouh Salem was considered by all to be a "liberal policeman"; in adversity as in success he remained level-headed, never to be tempted by luxuries or corruption, despite available opportunities.

A bachelor, he lived in a small flat in the centre of Cairo and did not hesitate to walk in the streets unaccompanied and mix with the crowd.

Born in 1918 in Alexandria into a modest family, he graduated from the Police Academy in 1940 and began his career at the Customs Office in Alexandria. There he gained wide experience in investigating clandestine operations and security matters, which proved extremely useful afterwards.

He acquired a reputation for diligence and moved into the higher ranks and was soon promoted to chief of Investigations in Alexandria. In 1954 he took an active part in the enquiry relating to the Lavon Affair, a spying ring believed to be organised by the Israeli Secret Services, under the guise of trading in horses, whose principal aim was to discredit the new republican regime of Gamal Abdel Nasser.

In recognition of his effective role in that affair he was promoted chief of the special squadron of body-guards to the President. In that capacity he reorganised the Egyptian security forces.

More concerned with the welfare of his fellow countrymen and their criticism of the political leadership, he concentrated his efforts on fighting crimes, particularly the parallel (black) market and smuggling.

In 1967 he was made Governor of Asiut (Upper Egypt) by President Gamal Abdel Nasser, and was able to put into execution his campaign against drug smugglers. In the space of two years he established one of Egypt's most efficient anti-drug networks. This covered the desert region between the Red Sea and the Libyan borders. During his governorship much of the narcotics smuggled into the country was tracked down – an effective operation which brought him many enemies while smashing the long established drug rings in the area.

Later in 1970, as Governor of Alexandria, his home-town, he organised a similar operation called "Cleaning up", which chased all petty criminals, exploiters and drug pushers, away from the streets.

In 1971 he was appointed Minister of the Interior by President Anwar Sadat following the arrest of the pro-soviet nasserite group of Vice-President Ali Sabri, Shaarawi Gomaa and Sami Sharaf, who were later accused of preparing a mini palace coup.

As Minister of the Interior, Mamdouh Salem gradually restricted the activities of the police force in Egypt, especially those of the notorious *Moukhabarat* (Secret Police). In this task he had the full approval of President Sadat who was eager to show to the international community his new liberal policies. The particular surveillance operations of the organisation were reduced and only individuals likely to belong to the opposition or to subversive groups, or people suspected of working against the national security remained its sole targets.

In spite of the hard-line position taken by him during the 1974 students' riots against a background of popular unrest, Mamdouh Salem succeeded in regaining the confidence of the Egyptian people who began to acknowledge his dedication to their cause. They stopped fearing the formidable machinery of the state as he liberalised the security forces of the country. By abolishing secret arrests and torture, closing down concentration camps and releasing political prisoners, Mamdouh Salem set the pace for a return to democratic life. This was to be the start of the "*infitah*" (open door) policy of President Sadat.

However, the democratic and liberal attitude which prevailed in the country since 1971 was to get its first blow in 1973. The disciplinary committee of the Arab Socialist Union (ASU) which was sitting in permanent session announced the elimination from the ASU of a large number of left-wing elements, among them were journalists, writers, university professors, lawyers. Taking over the premiership temporarily and declaring himself Military Governor-General, President Sadat appointed Mamdouh Salem as his deputy to be in charge of internal affairs and external security, thus making him second in command after himself.

It was in this capacity that Mamdouh Salem, in 1974, ordered the closure of the magazine *Al Kateb* under the provisions of a law passed in 1972 which provided for penalties up to life imprisonment for offences endangering national unity.

Later, however, he continued working towards more liberalisation and steered the Assembly to giving more democratic rights to the Egyptian people. An amnesty was extended to political prisoners and more than 2,000 persons accused of political offences were released from prisons in April of the same year. Freedom of the press was restored and some 8.5 million Egyptians endorsed the economic and social reform programme of the government.

In 1976 President Sadat called for elections for the People's Assembly, the first ever since 1952, which returned Salem as Prime Minister. Under pressure for his liberal attitudes Mamdouh Salem was forced again to tighten the internal security which led him to ban another magazine, *Al Talee'a*, and was not unconnected to the food riots of of 1977, involving his home town where some 80 people were killed by the security forces.

Salem enjoyed the full confidence of President Sadat who relied more than once on his organisational abilities and coolness in dealing with emergencies, and could count on his loyalty.

In 1978, at the height of his career, Mamdouh Salem was to face his first set-back when Anwar Sadat who had introduced a multi-party system, announced his plans to form the National Democratic Party. The outcome was political disaster for Mamdouh; for his party (the Arab Socialist Party) lost its parliamentary majority. No longer Prime Minister, Mamdouh Salem, from 1978 until his death in London in February 1988, held the honorary post of assistant at the presidency. ■

Samba, M.P. (c.1870-1914)

SAMBA, Martin-Paul (c.1870-1914).

CAMEROONIAN soldier and traditional chief. He was of the Bulu people in the southern forest area, occupied in the 1890s by the Germans moving inland from Kribi. He was born in the area of Ebolowa, now the chief Bulu town, but was taken with his family, when a child, to Akok in the Kribi area. There he was taken into the service of the German Curt von Morgen, passing through Kribi in the course of enforcing German rule over Kamerun (Cameroon).

Morgen took Samba, then apparently between 15 and 20, to Buea and then to Germany, where a few other Cameroonians had already gone for studies (e.g. Rudolf Douala Manga Bell, q.v.). He spent three years at a German school, and then three more at an officers' training academy. He was one of the few Africans of any European colony at that time to be trained as an army officer; he reached the rank of *Hauptmann* or major.

In 1895 he returned to Cameroon. He was said, in one later legend, to have brought back a handkerchief from Germany as a good luck charm. However, the many legends about him are mostly unbelievable, e.g. the story that the Kaiser gave him letters appointing him governor of Cameroon but he lost them on the voyage home.

On his return he was a chief among the Bulus for many years. He helped enforce German rule over his people, who resisted it strongly, launching a major uprising from 1898 to 1901. But at some date, for some reason, this much-favoured protégé of the Germans turned against them. The Germans accused him of plotting in 1914. One account says that Rudolf Manga Bell contacted him about a plot, but the story of that Douala chief's alleged plot is doubtful. The full facts

M.P. Samba

about Samba appear to be still very unclear. According to the version taught to Cameroonian school children today, he contacted the French forces attacking German Kamerun on the outbreak of the First World War, but the message was intercepted.

At any rate, on 8 August 1914 Martin Samba was executed by firing squad. According to legend, he waved his German handkerchief and so caused the bullets to miss, but then said he was not afraid to die, put the "magic" handkerchief away, and faced death. Legends about him among the Bulus showed for decades afterwards the impression he had made on his people. ■

Samory Touré (c. 1830-1900)

SAMORY TOURE (c.1830-1900).

GUINEAN soldier and leader. He was born near Sankoro in Guinea around 1830. From an early age he displayed great organisational and leadership abilities and by the age of 20, having been a trader for only three years, he had established a wide commercial network extending to Freetown in Sierra Leone. At this time the region in which he lived was unsettled by religious wars and when he was 23 years old he was taken prisoner by the Sise people and sent to Madina. He remained there for five years during which time he joined his captor's army and learnt a great deal about warfare. His military ability was such that when he left Madina he became a warchief among the Berete people until a strong disagreement caused him to return to his own Konyan people (of Malinke origin), where he rejoined members of his family and quickly gathered a large military following.

Over the years his military prestige and strength grew and in 1874 he established his own state with its capital at Bissandugu. He had retained his involvement and interest in trade and his primary objective was to protect the commercial activities in his new state. He continued to build up the strength of his army and overpowered local non-Moslem rulers who had closed trading routes, then going on to conquer more territory including the gold fields at Bure.

By 1879 the boundaries of the area under his control extended from the Liberian forests through Upper Guinea to Bamako in present-day Mali. As head of this state he took the military title of Faama and under his rule trade flourished in a wide variety of commodities.

As he gained more territory, prisoners were given the option of joining his army which was well-equipped, well-ordered and well-disciplined, forming the basis of his power. He had earlier reverted to his ancestors' Islamic faith and in 1884 he decided to establish a Moslem state, changing his title to Almami. Two years later all the people under his control were ordered to convert to this faith and he began to etablish schools and mosques in most parts of his empire. This decision helped to unify the peoples from different ethnic groups and add to the existing cohesion of the army which was already run along non-tribal lines.

The empire was divided into ten administrative provinces with Samory personally controlling two of these, which formed the nucleus and where the central army was based, while the other eight were

Samory Touré

sub-controlled by military administrators, each with a force of around 5,000 men. When not at war, the soldiers spent half the year training and the remainder working for the state, usually in the agricultural sector. There was a system to provide for the maintenance of trained reserves and this overall administration made Samory's territory exceedingly strong and unified into an empire what had once been minor warring states. Modern firearms were bought from Sierra Leone, where local opinion admired "Samadu" as they called him.

In 1881 Samory began to clash with French troops and this continued sporadically over the next few years. However at that time it suited both sides not to become engaged in outright conflict as their armies were tied up elsewhere, and after lengthy negotiations the Treaty of Bissandugu was signed on 23 March 1887. Under this agreement the boundaries between Samory and the French were agreed to run from the source of the Tinkisso to the River Niger and on to Nyamina, with Samory relinquishing his claims to the left bank of the Niger, placing his territory under French "protection" and allowing the French to trade, unmolested in his territory, while the French agreed that while the terms of the treaty were adhered to, their forces would not cross over to the right bank of the Niger into his territory.

However the French continued to try and undermine Samory, feeling that he was too powerful. Samory's appeals for help in his war with Sikasso were unheeded and instead the French supplied his enemy with arms and protection. In August 1888, after a long, hard struggle in which heavy losses were incurred, Samory's troops returned unvictorious to Bissandugu and relations with the French deteriorated. The following year Samory signed the Convention of Niako with the French, once again delimiting the territory of both parties, with their armies being restricted to their respective sides of the River Niger. However, shortly afterwards both parties claimed that the other had broken, and therefore nullified, the treaty and in 1891 war broke out.

Samory's great organisational abilities enabled him to resist the French effectively for a number of years. His army was very strong and effective, and he was able to ensure adequate supplies through his extensive trade network. He had established bases that could manufacture and repair arms for his troops and the administration of his empire was such that he was able to easily change the location of his headquarters after defeat. He also employed guerrilla tactics and as he retreated he strategically ordered crops to be burned so that the advancing French forces could not use them as food supplies.

In the face of French victories he began to establish a new empire to the east of his old territory. In order to maintain and recruit troops he demanded food, arms and men from local rulers, but his tactics led to strong opposition. Although he was able to repel a French attack in 1895, he had difficulties in consolidating his position in his new empire and this, along with the heavy losses sustained by his armies, led him to once again begin negotiations with the French. These negotiations were finally broken off when a French party was massacred by a section of Samory's troops. During the rainy season of 1898, Samory's army was weakened by half as they crossed the mountainous region of Man on their way to Guinea and shortly afterwards, on 29 September 1898, he was captured by the French in a surprise attack at Gueole. He was sent into exile at Ndjolé in Gabon, and he died there on 2 June 1900. ■

Sankara, T. (1949-87)

SANKARA, Thomas (1949-87).

BURKINABE soldier and revolutionary leader, Captain Thomas Sankara was the forceful President of Upper Volta, which he renamed Burkina Faso (meaning land of incorruptible men), and was renowned for his forthright approach to politics and commitment to participatory democracy.

Born on 21 December, 1949, into a Catholic peasant family, he attended primary school at Gaoa in Poni province. From there he went to the military secondary school at Kadiogo where he passed the baccalaureate. In 1972 he passed out of the military academy at Antsirabé in Madagascar, with the rank of sub-lieutenant. Two years later he returned home, having attended two parachute courses, one at the parachute school at Pou in France and another at the parachute centre in Rabat.

Ouagadougou, at the time of his return, was replete with various trade union and leftist organizations whose meetings he made a habit of attending. One such group was LIPAD (*La Ligue Patriotique pour le Développement* or Patriotic League for Development). In the military, Sankara met a number of like-minded young men and together they formed a loose nationalist grouping. Its leading members were Blaise Compaoré, Jean Baptiste Lingani, Henri Zongo and Abdul Salan Kabone.

In 1974 Mali and Upper Volta fought a brief war in which Sankara distinguished himself and came to the notice of his superiors. Two years later he was posted to the parachute institute at Po, 150 km south of Ouagadougou, as a parachute instructor and leader of the parachute commandos there. When in 1981 a military coup brought Colonel Saye Zerbo to power, Sankara was appointed to the ministerial position of secretary of state in the president's office, in charge of information. He encouraged the press to adopt an investigative and critical approach to national issues and also marked himself out by adopting the practice of going to work on a bicycle.

He resigned from the government in April 1981, denouncing it as corrupt and incompetent at a news conference. For this he was stripped of all responsibility and sent to Dedougou, a small town 200 km out of Ouagadougou. During that year Sankara spent some months in prison.

By now Upper Volta had become decidedly unstable with a number of coup plans being discussed by various groupings. In November 1982, a motley group of soldiers seized power and after some deliberation, settled on a compromise candidate, Jean Baptiste Ouedraogo, as the new head of state to replace Colonel Saye Zerbo. Although Sankara and his associates were members of the 120-man ruling council, they initially refused government posts. In January 1983, however, they accepted positions in the government and Sankara became prime minister.

A rift soon developed between the conservative head of state, Ouedraogo, and his radical prime minister. On 17 May 1983, the prime minister's house was surrounded. After a few hours Sankara ordered his men

Capt. T. Sankara

to surrender. Along with Lingani, whose house had also been surrounded by tanks, he was arrested and interned in a military camp in Ouahigouya, while Captain Compaoré remained free and in command at Po.

There followed a period of virtual dual power, with sections of the military loyal to Sankara, Lingani and Compaoré and others to Ouedraogo. Following popular demonstrations by students and workers' organizations Sankara was released and put under house arrest. This confusing state of affairs was ended on 4 August 1983, when he was set free by Blaise Compaoré and other members of the group. A National Revolutionary Council (CNR) was set up with Sankara as chairman.

The political line of the CNR was set out in his "political orientation speech" delivered on 2 October 1983. In it he characterised the "August Revolution" as "democratic" and "anti-imperialist". Its primary purpose, he said "is to take power out of the hands of our national bourgeoisie and their imperialist allies and put it in the hands of the people." To this end what were termed Committees for the Defence of the Revolution (CDRs) were formed in villages and towns, communities and work places. Sankara promoted the development of the CDRs and encouraged community discussion of collective actions, which helped to mobilise large portions of the population until then politically marginalised. This approach was of particular use in July 1985 when the country was hit by a drought which threatened the lives of half a million people.

A "popular development programme" was put into account for the period October 1984 to December 1985. The programme resulted in over 250 water storage tanks being built by local communities. Between June and December 1984, a mass vaccination campaign immunised three million children and made the country's health statistics compare favourably with those of industrial nations. A major literacy drive was launched in 1986 to combat the 90 per cent illiteracy rate prevailing in the rural areas. An internationally acclaimed tree-planting exercise was launched to stem the advance of the Sahara desert.

The CNR nationalised all land and natural resources in the country, and adopted a development strategy of integrated agricultural and industrial development based primarily on collective production for the domestic market, its main source of financial support coming from non-governmental international organizations.

The budget was made the subject of popular discussion, with the result that a structural deficit was transformed into a surplus by 1985. All wage earners were asked to give varying proportions of their month's income to support the national effort. This caused disquiet in certain sectors and resulted in the teachers calling a strike of their members. They were sacked and made to reapply for their jobs.

Relations with the civilian wing of the CNR, particularly with LIPAD, became strained during the first year of Sankara's regime. LIPAD's leading members objected to the pre-eminent position occupied by the military in the CNR and challenged them in some urban CDRs. A number of trade unionists, for their part, felt the CDRs were being given greater prominence than the unions, and the rural population priority over urban workers. As a result of these tensions, in the second government formed a year after coming to power, leading members of LIPAD were removed from government

positions. Throughout that time there were a number of attempts to overthrow the CNR, the most notable being in May 1984. Seven people were executed as a result.

In the international arena Sankara developed warm relations with Algeria, Ghana, Uganda and Libya inside Africa and with Cuba, Nicaragua and North Korea outside. Burkina adopted a hitherto unaccustomed high profile in international organizations both regionally and globally.

In the eyes of many, Sankara's pan-African credentials were tarnished when on Christmas day 1985, war once again broke out between Burkina and Mali over the longstanding border dispute which had caused the two countries to fight in 1974. Fighting, however, was brief and the two leaders undertook to seek a political solution. In February 1985 an unexplained explosion in the hotel where Sankara was staying during an official visit to Yamoussoukro, Côte d'Ivoire, narrowly missed killing him. The incident stretched already strained relations with Côte d'Ivoire. These strained relations overshadowed summits of various regional, political and economic groupings. By the end of 1985 Burkina Faso had become somewhat isolated regionally. Sankara failed for example, to assume the chairmanship of ECOWAS even though it was Burkina Faso's turn. Further afield, relations with the Western powers, particularly France, were uneasy.

By May 1987 internal tensions culminated in the arrest of a number of trade unionists who were accused of subversion. Some CDRs called for their execution, and reportedly had Sankara's support. Compaoré, however, in the powerful position of minister of Justice, disagreed and ordered the release of some of those detained, providing public evidence of the rift within the CNR.

Matters came to a head in mid-October. Sankara, it was alleged, was about to order the arrest of Compaoré and others who disagreed with him when he was killed in a shoot out between troops loyal to him and those loyal to Compaoré.

The CNR was replaced by the Popular Front (*Front Populaire*) in which Sankara's former colleagues, Lingani and Zongo were prominent members with Compaoré as leader. In a statement issued on 15 October 1987, the Popular Front accused Sankara of dictatorship, suppression of left wing organizations and ambition to lead a single party state.

Sankara's death was seen by many, however, as an unnecessary and unpleasant outcome of a power struggle. He was mourned in many countries and posthumously honoured by Ghanaian head of state Jerry Rawlings. He is remembered as a symbol of a new breed of young African leaders, uncompromising in their determination to mobilise the peasants to improve their lot and for African people to free themselves from foreign political and economic exploitation.■

Under el-Mahdi's administration, travellers and traders were protected and customs dues levied as a source of revenue. Though the order did not control the trade in the new settlement, this was its primary source of revenue as it depended on the levies. El-Mahdi forged links with neighbouring villages in order to defend the vital trade routes.

A few years later, however, he was again forced to abandon Kufrah by the French who viewed the renewal of anti-colonial activities as the result of Sanusi teaching. El-Mahdi moved the sect's centre to Chiru, north of Borku, where he died shortly afterwards, in 1902.■

El-Sanusi, M. el-Mahdi (1844-1902)

EL-SANUSI, Mohammed el-Mahdi (1844-1902).

LIBYAN religious leader. He was born in 1844 in the Cyrenaica province in north-east Libya. The second son of Sayyid Muhammad (q.v.), the Grand Sanusi and founder of the Sanusi sect which preached devotion to orthodox Islam, and who was a temporal as well as a spiritual ruler, el-Mahdi devoted his early years to religious studies.

He succeeded his father in 1859, but at first there was a regency. By the time he became effective head of the order there were 38 Sanusi *Zawiyas* or colleges and monasteries teaching Sanusi doctrine in Cyrenaica, though its influence was already widespread in the neighbouring Tripolitania province, Egypt, Tunisia and Algeria. It was el-Mahdi however who brought the order to the height of its pre-colonial power in the eastern Sahara. He was thus the architect of the order's political and commercial influence whose growth and expansion brought confrontation with advancing colonial powers.

In 1894, faced with Italian and French penetration from the north, the Soudan, Senegal, Algeria and Tunisia, el-Mahdi moved the headquarters of the Sanusi sect from Jaghbub to Kufrah, a remote oasis in southern Libya. Kufrah had been a stronghold of bandits, being located on a strategic point on the Wadai-Benghazi trade route.

El-Sanusi, S.M.A. (c.1787-1859)

EL-SANUSI, El-Sayyid Muhammad bin Ali (c.1787-1859).

LIBYAN religious leader, famous as the founder of the Sanusiyya order of Moslems. Born near Mostaganem in Algeria, he studied at that town and at Mazum, and then at Fez in Morocco, a leading centre of Islamic learning; he was said to have shown an interest in mysticism while there. Then he went on the pilgrimage, and on the way began gathering disciples by his preaching. He spent six years in Arabia, then returned to Mostaganem about 1829.

He went back to Arabia, between 1833 to 1841, and there made a reputation as a preacher of reform and began to gather a permanent body of disciples around him. He was himself a leading disciple of the Moroccan reformer Ahmed bin Idris, who was then at Mecca. When Ahmed bin Idris was forced into exile for two years in Yemen, el-Sanusi accompanied him; and then, on the reformer's death, two of his disciples formed religious orders, one being the Sanusiya of Muhammad el-Sanusi. The Sanusiya was thus started near Mecca in 1837.

About 1841 the founder of the order left to return to Algeria. On the way, hearing of the advance of the French in his homeland, he decided to stop in Cyrenaica, a part of Libya (then a Turkish province). In 1843 he founded in Cyrenaica, near Cyrene, the first lodge or monastery (Zawiya) of the order in Libya, called the "white lodge" (*el-zawiya el-baida*). It was the beginning of a rapid expansion of the order in that area. The Sanusiya were Moslems dedicated to

M. bin Ali el-Sanusi

following their religion in a particular way, living as "brothers" (*ikhwan*) in the *zawiyas*. Their leader did not preach any departure from orthodox Islam. Their version of Islam was strict but did not involve any aggressiveness against others, until these attacked the area.

The order established good working relations with the Turks. Its brothers were respected for piety by the independent-minded nomadic Bedouin Arabs, who took their disputes to them. The Sanusiyya lodges became important centres in the Bedouin country; they were major centres of trade, being themselves dependent on it for supplies. They helped the Turks maintain some rule over the recalcitrant Bedouin. Eventually the Sanusiyya became the real power in a large part of Libya.

The Grand Sanusi, as the founder was called, returned to Mecca again from 1846 to 1853. On returning to Cyrenaica he moved his central *zawiya* to Jaghbub in 1856. At his headquarters he had a library of 8,000 books and he started a Moslem university which came to be regarded as second only to al-Azhar in Cairo. He died at Jaghbub on 7 September 1859. His son, named el-Mahdi (q.v.), succeeded him as head of his order.■

Sapara, O.O. (1861-1935)

SAPARA, Dr Oguntola Odunbaku (1861-1935).

NIGERIAN medical practitioner. He was born on 9 June 1861 in Freetown, to Nigerian "Recaptive" Creole parents in Sierra Leone. After primary and part secondary schooling in Freetown, he migrated to Nigeria at the age of 15 where he completed his education at the Lagos CMS Grammar School.

His first job was in 1878 as a technician in a government department, but he left this employment in 1881 to train as a dispenser at the Lagos Colonial Hospital where he was subsequently appointed a dispenser and storekeeper. He resigned from the public service in 1885 and set up a private practice in the Gold Coast (Ghana).

In 1887 Sapara took a course at the St Thomas Hospital School of Pharmacy in London, where he also specialised in midwifery, and proceeded to Edinburgh and Glasgow for specialist medical studies which, six years later, made him a Licentiate of the Royal College of Surgeons (LRCS) and of the Royal College of Physicians (LRCP).

Returning to Nigeria in 1896 he was appointed Medical Officer for the Lagos Colony, serving in various medical institutions in Badagry, Abeokuta, Ijebu-Ode, and at the Massey Dispensary in Lagos. In 1901 Dr Sapara had sat on a government commission which examined the causes of high infant mortality rate in Lagos. The commission reported that, among other reasons, the lack of "proper management of the infants at birth and of mothers in the puerperal state" was an important factor in infantile mortality which must be remedied.

The recommendations were not however favourably received by the government and, after a prolonged period of inaction, Dr Sapara embarked on a one-man campaign for their acceptance and implementation. In addition, he requested the government to provide training facilities for midwives and nurses who were equally invaluable in containing the problem. In order to facilitate this scheme he, at his own financial expense, organised the training of two Nigerian midwives in Britain.

The gesture, an eloquent testimony of Dr Sapara's innovations, was to signal the establishment of the first maternity hospital in Nigeria and the commencement of the training of midwives and nurses in the country.

It was at this time that he began his pioneering research into the causes and prevention of smallpox, tuberculosis and syphilis, which led to major medical reforms in the country. Dr Sapara's first experiments were on smallpox, which he found was being spread by sufferers as they came into contact with the public. In 1909 his recommendations to the government on how the disease could be contained were embodied in the Southern Nigeria Order-in-Council which was the first government attempt to eradicate smallpox.

Next, Sapara turned his attention to the perennial scourge of tuberculosis and syphilis whose wide spread, he found, was not unconnected with the method of "arm-to-arm" vaccination that was being used in Lagos. He recommended its abolition, in favour of a more hygienic method that was subsequently adopted in 1912; in that same year he returned to Britain and did post graduate studies and subsequently became a fellow of the Royal Institute of Public Health.

In 1913 the government requested him to convert the Massey Dispensary into a maternity hospital, with facilities for an in-service training scheme for nurses and midwives. As in other things, Dr Sapara effected the project with vigour and made such a success of it that it became the main achievement for which he was remembered in later years. He was honoured by the government who renamed the main approach to the hospital after him.

He retired from public service in 1928 but continued to play an active role in society. First, he established the so-called

Dr. O.O. Sapara

"Baby Week", a forum for the propagation of the ideas of infant welfare – he was, until his death in 1935, its chairman. Dr Sapara also became a member of the Society of Native Medicine Men and Herbalists whose president he was. Under the society's auspices, he conducted research into the curative qualities of local herbs and established that some of the traditional mixtures extracted from these have remedial qualities. Among his discoveries is the still very popular children's mixture which is produced under the trade name of YARO ("boy" in the Hausa language). Thus does the name of Dr Sapara still live on in Nigeria.

For his life and work he had gained respect and esteem and had received several honours. In 1923 he was made Companion of the Imperial Service Order (ISO) by the colonial government, followed with the royal honour from the Alake of Abeokuta who made him the Adahunse Alake ati Ijoba Re (Honorary Consulting Physician to the Alake of Egbaland). In 1924 Dr Sapara was given the chieftaincy title of Isida of Ilesha by the Oba (Owa) of Ilesha. He spent his retirement years in Lagos where he died on 4 June 1935. His brother Christopher Sapara-Williams (q.v.) was also a very prominent Lagos citizen. ■

Sapara-Williams, C.A. (1855-1915)

SAPARA-WILLIAMS, Christopher Alexander (1855-1915).

NIGERIAN lawyer. He was one of the Sierra Leone Creoles, children of Yoruba "Recaptives", who went back to their parents' Yoruba homeland after education in Sierra Leone and did well there. His father was an Ijesha Yoruba Recaptive, Orisha Saparoda, who took the name Alexander Charles Sapara-Williams after being rescued from a slave ship in 1815 and resettled in Freetown. His children by his wife Nancy Tejumade included the famous Nigerian doctor Oguntola Sapara (q.v.) as well as Christopher, who was born on 19 July 1855.

He went to the Church Missionary Society (CMS) Grammar School in Freetown and after moving to Lagos in 1871, to the CMS Grammar School there. Then he entered government service as a clerk, with the Customs and subsequently at Government House. In 1875 he went to Britain where, after studying briefly at Wesley College in Sheffield, he became the first Nigerian to complete full British legal studies from 1876 to 1879. After being called to the Bar at the Inner Temple on 27 August 1880, he was enrolled as the first indigenous barrister and solicitor of Gold Coast Colony, to which Lagos Colony was then attached.

He practised at Accra, Cape Coast and Elmina in Gold Coast proper, and married the daughter, Sophia, of a prominent Gold Coaster (Ghanaian), Robert Hutchinson. But in 1888 he moved permanently to Lagos, now a separate British Crown Colony. For the next fifteen years he was one of the outstanding African lawyers there; he and the only two other such lawyers at that time, Kitoyi Ajasa (q.v.) and Joseph Egerton Shyngle, were an eminent "legal triumvirate."

There was plenty of work for these private lawyers, as the flourishing trade of Lagos, involving many Africans and expatriate businessmen and firms, gave rise to many commercial lawsuits, which in fact occupied most of the lawyers' time; while modern development also led to land tenure problems and considerable property litigation. Criminal cases were fewer but the government made Sapara-Williams defence counsel for some indigent defendants. Sapara-Williams won a high reputation for his knowledge of case law. He is considered one of the founders of modern Nigerian law. He acted as legal adviser to the Owa of Ijeshaland, the Oba of his home area, and was sometimes solicitor to the semi-independent Abeokuta government of 1893-1914. He handled cases in the south-eastern part of Nigeria after it came under British rule. His reputation for competence and knowledge of the law was undoubted. He was well versed in customary matters as well as British law.

He helped form the Ekitiparapo Society, an association of Ekiti Yorubas, in 1881, and became its president. This, and his position as adviser to the Owa (which the British disliked), involved him in events in the interior of Yorubaland. In Lagos politics he joined in some of the elite's collective actions, including a meeting in 1897 to declare loyalty to Britain and deny rumours of a plan to attack Europeans, a protest in 1899, which he led, against a Criminal Code Bill (which was withdrawn), and the 1900 protest at the Forest Bill.

C.A. Sapara-Williams

In 1901 he was appointed a member of the Legislative Council (Legco), where he remained until his death. He was also a member of the Lagos Municipal Board. In Legco he was often critical of the government, as in his opposition to plans for a separate church for Europeans. But he did not seek or get mass support, and refused to join in the agitation against the proposed Water Rate.

Sapara-Williams was appointed in 1914 to the Nigerian Council set up (with little effect) by Governor-General Lugard, while remaining in Legco. He died on 14 March 1915. ■

Sarbah, J.M. (1864-1910)

SARBAH, John Mensah (1864-1910).

G HANAIAN lawyer and writer. Son of John Sarbah, a merchant of Anomabu and Cape Coast, who was a member of the Legislative Council of Gold Coast Colony and who died in 1892, he was born on 3 June 1864 and went to the Wesleyan High School in Cape Coast and then a secondary school at Taunton, England. He studied for the Bar at Lincoln's Inn, London, and in 1887 became the first fully qualified Gold Coast (Ghanaian) barrister.

After setting up in legal practice back home, he also took part in Gold Coast Colony politics. He was one of the main organisers of the Mfantsi Amanbuhu Fekuw, the Fanti National Political Society, founded in 1889. He became noted for his studies of customary Fanti law and his nationalist views, which he expressed partly in those studies. His books, *Fanti Customary Laws* (1897) and *Fanti National Constitutions* (1906), were widely admired in West Africa at the time, especially by followers of the movement to retain or revive traditions, inspired by Dr E.W.Blyden (q.v.) in particular.

In 1897 Mensah Sarbah became a leader of the agitation of elite and traditional leaders against the proposed Lands Bill of the British Government. He and others formed the Gold Coast Aborigines Rights Protection Society (ARPS), which was influential for long after its successful campaign against the Lands Bill. Sarbah considered the ARPS to be a continuation of the earlier Fekuw. In 1900 he was appointed an Extraordinary Member of the Colony's Legislative Council (Legco), for the debate on a Concessions Bill dealing with some of the matters which the abortive Lands Bill would have covered. It was less potentially dangerous to African interests and was passed. In 1901 Mensah Sarbah was appointed as a permanent member of Legco.

In the Council he criticised the Native Jurisdiction Bill of 1906, which sought to base administration on traditional rulers. Sarbah, with J.E. Casely-Hayford (q.v.) and others, opposed these ideas as contrary to genuine tradition and as arising from a British preference for chiefs to educated Africans; there were other reasons also for the protests which were to continue against "Indirect Rule" ideas. Sarbah was noted for his expert knowledge of true traditions which added force to his protests. He wrote of traditional government as essentially democratic. However, he also believed in modernisation and saw both the educated

J.M. Sarbah

elite and the British as agents for this. After a visit to Europe in 1903 he and William Edward Sam promoted the "Fanti Public Schools Ltd.", which founded the famous Mfantsipim Secondary School in Cape Coast.

When the Native Jurisdiction Amendment Bill was passed in August 1910 Sarbah was criticised by some Africans who were opposed to the bill and did not know of the changes he had helped to secure in it. Amid this misunderstanding he died on 6 November 1910. He had married in 1904 Marian Wood, daughter of Benjamin Wood of Accra, and left three children. ◼

Savage, R.A. (1874-1935)

SAVAGE, Dr. Richard Akinwande (1874-1935).

NIGERIAN doctor and journalist. He was born in 1874 in Lagos, the son of Josiah Alfred Savage, a merchant of Sierra Leone Creole and Egba origins. He attended the CMS Grammar Schol and then went in 1895 to the University of Edinburgh in Scotland where he studied medicine.

Besides successfully completing his studies, he was active in student affairs, including student journalism, which launched him on his journalistic career. He was sub-editor of *The Student*, the Edinburgh Students' Union magazine, from 1898 to 1900, and joint editor in 1899/1900 of the *Edinburgh University Handbook*. He was a member of the students' representative Council of the same Scottish University from 1897 to 1900. And in 1900 he was one of two delegates of the Afro-West Indian Literary Society of Edinburgh to the first ever Pan-African Conference held in London.

He was awarded the M.B. Ch. B of Edinburgh apparently in 1900 though one biography gives the date as 1905. He entered the British government service in West Africa in 1901 as Assistant Colonial Surgeon; he was the last African to hold such a high post in the government medical service. After that they were subjected to systematic discrimination. He served for ten years in the Gold Coast (now Ghana), where he was for a time Medical Officer of Health at Cape Coast Castle. He also set up in private practice in the Gold Coast, and he was commended by the Colonial Secretary in London for his work during a plague epidemic.

Savage's entry into politics began in the Gold Coast when he became a member of the Sekondi Town Council. In the Gold Coast he had written regularly for newspapers and made friends with Mr. J. E. Casely-Hayford (q.v.) (1866-1930), the famous lawyer and nationalist, with whom he worked on regular contributions to the *Gold Coast Leader* in 1912-13. In 1914 the two men launched the idea of a conference of Africans from the four British West African colonies (Nigeria, Gold Coast, Sierra Leone, Gambia). They wrote letters to several distinguished West Africans and contacted the Gold Coast Aborigines Rights Protection Society (ARPS) about the idea in 1915. They wanted a meeting of leading, educated men i.e. the elite of lawyers, doctors and businessmen, already numerous by then – to discuss their position under British rule.

Soon after returning to Lagos in December 1915 Dr. Savage called a meeting which set up a committee to help prepare such a conference; he and Thomas Horatio Jackson, son and successor of the editor J. P. Jackson (q.v.), became its secretaries. Despite the first World War, in which Savage and others of the elite expressed their fervent loyalty to Britain, he and Casely-Hayford continued to promote the idea of a West African conference. Soon after the end of the war the committee set up earlier in Lagos was on 24 January 1919 turned into the Provisional Committee of the West African Conference, Lagos Branch; Dr. J. K. Randle, another doctor who was deeply involved in politics, was chairman, and Dr Savage secretary. On 28 March 1919 the Committee became the Lagos Committee of the West African Conference. Randle and Savage had disagreements which led to Randle resigning while Savage remained secretary.

As a result of the efforts of Casely-Hayford, Savage and others, the National Congress of British West Africa (NCBWA) was formed at an inaugural meeting in Accra from 11 to 29 March 1920. It made many demands for reforms to benefit Africans, all moderate and combined with expressions of loyalty to the British monarch. The British considered that the participants of the conference were not representative of the country at large as they claimed to be. The NCBWA had only limited success, because of the British attitude but also because of the internal feuds among the coastal elite. These were especially intense in Lagos. Many opposed Savage and the NCBWA, and ultimately the Congress became peripheral to Lagos politics, in which there were more important parties and issues in the 1920s.

Dr. Savage, however, soon reached the height of his influence on the Lagos scene by starting, on 19 May 1923, his own newspaper, the *Nigerian Spectator*. It was a successful newspaper for some years, though it ended its life early, the last issue being on 27 December 1930. Those seven years were long enough for Savage to be noted as one of the founders of modern Nigerian journalism. Nnamdi Azikiwe considered him as such and, in *My Odyssey*, quoted a large part of Savage's first editorial, in which he stated his broad political view: "It is hardly necessary to remind ourselves that the goal of British West Africa is to develop gradually her political system until she attains in due course full representative institutions, giving her the dominion status within the British Empire. It will not be tomorrow, or the next day. But that it is sure to come, no one can deny." In that editorial Savage said Nigeria's own disunity was to blame for the failure to obtain from the British any more representation than had recently been accorded.

While Dr. Savage's talents were recognised all around, he had many enemies, and according to the study of the history of Nigeria's press by Omu, Savage "was in fact an intemperate, self-assertive and self-satisfied man with a penchant for mud-slinging and abuse." In spite of this, and of the early death of his journal, he is recalled as a pioneer editor along with James Bright Davies (q.v.) and the Jacksons, father and son.

A daughter of Dr. Savage, Agnes Yewande Savage, was born to a Scots mother in 1906 and educated in Scotland, finishing at Edinburgh where she followed in his footsteps, qualifying as a doctor in 1929. She can be considered the first lady Nigerian doctor, but as almost none of her life (1906-54) was spent in her father's country, that distinction is often accorded not to her but to Dr. E. A. Awoliyi (q.v.). Dr. R. A. Savage died in October 1935. ∎

Savi de Tove, J. (1895-1971)

SAVI DE TOVE, Jonathan (1895-1971).

TOGOLESE politician. He was co-founder and Secretary-General of the *Comité de l'Unité Togolaise* (CUT) which led the country to independence in 1960. Born on 15 August 1895 at Tove, he worked as a lawyer's clerk in Cameroon then, like Togo, under German rule. He later became personal secretary to the last German governor of

J. Savi de Tove

Kamerun and accompanied him on his retreat before the Allied forces in 1914-16, following him to Spanish Guinea where the remaining German forces withdrew in February 1916. Later the former Governor, Ebermaier, was moved to Spain, accompanied by his secretary. The latter visited Germany before returning to the part of Togo allotted to France as a Mandated Territory in the 1919 peace settlement.

He worked as a teacher and was for a time a director of Protestant schools in the 1920s. He helped the famous German linguist Westermann to compile a grammar of the Ewe language. He supported French rule which some of the elite, German-trained and under some Gold Coast and British influence, disliked. In 1928 he became secretary of the Council of Elders, started as a powerless consultative body by the French in Lomé. He went into business and became a leading merchant. In 1933 his house was burned in anti-French riots in Lomé.

From 1936 to 1941 he was head of the Press and Information services of the colonial government. In 1941 he was co-founder and Secretary-General of the CUT, encouraged by the French at that time. He played a major role in the rapid rise of the CUT in the next few years, when its candidate Martin Akou (q.v.) was elected to the French parliament. In 1946 Savi de Tove was elected to Togo's own assembly, and in 1947 he was indirectly elected as a member of the Council of the Republic (Senate) of France.

For a few years after 1946 the CUT collaborated with the All-Ewe Conference which sought the union of the Ewes – separated by two borders and living in the Gold Coast Colony, British Togoland and French Togo – under British tutelage. Savi de Tove supported this idea strongly. The French became cool towards the CUT because of its Ewe unity policy, but the All-Ewe Conference lost importance later. Savi de Tove remained in the Assembly and in 1958, when full internal self-government was accorded to French Togo, became President of the Assembly. He also served as editor of *Unité Togolaise* and *le Guide du Togo*, while continuing to work as a language teacher.

Under the CUT government of President Olympio (q.v.) Savi de Tove returned to Germany, as Ambassador in Bonn (1961-64). He was appointed chairman of an organisation for "Cultural Exchanges" with other countries in 1971, but died later that year.■

Sawyerr, H. A. E. (1909-86)

SAWYERR, Rev. Canon Prof. Harry A. E. (1909-86).

SIERRA LEONEAN clergyman and educationist, who worked for most of his life on the academic staff of Fourah Bay College, now part of the University of Sierra Leone, and was vice-Chancellor of that University from 1970 to 1972. As a lecturer in theology, he brought a certain sense of excitement to his teaching of christianity, and the "philosophical reasoning" that he translated into his understanding of the religion has left its marks on the many that went through that educational institution.

Rev Sawyerr was born on 16 October 1909, in Freetown, to a leading Creole family of Aberdeen, Sierra Leone. His father, the Rev. O. A. D. Sawyerr, was an Anglican clergyman who worked in the Protectorate from 1898, and the young Harry Sawyerr thus grew up in the Protectorate and began his schooling there. In 1920 he went to the Government Model School in Freetown, and then, in 1927, to the Prince of Wales School. From 1927 to 1929 he worked as a laboratory assistant while studying for a London examination, but eventually, in 1929, went to Fourah Bay College, on a scholarship provided by the Creole businessman P. J. C. Thomas. He studied first for the General Arts degree and then for the Diploma in Education which he was awarded in 1934. He had wanted to take Holy Orders of the Church of England like his father, but could not study theology at the time, so he postponed this aim and became a teacher.

From 1933 to 1941 Sawyerr worked as a tutor at Fourah Bay College, the famous educational institution started by the Anglican Church Missionary Society (CMS) in 1827, which was affiliated to the University of Durham, England, from 1876. It was moved to its present site on Mount Aureol in Freetown after the Second World War.

Following the report of the Fulton Commission in 1954, the Sierra Leone Government took over responsibility for the College from the CMS; it became the University College of Sierra Leone in 1959 and in 1966 a constituent college of the new University of Sierra Leone, awarding its own degrees, Sierra Leone having by then been independent since 1961.

Sawyerr then left for two years to take charge of the professional teacher training courses at Union College, Bunumbu. During those years he did his postponed training for the ministry and was ordained. He returned to Fourah Bay as chaplain in 1943 and worked there until 1945, when he went to Britain to study theology for three years at the University of Durham. Back in Freetown in 1948 he resumed his functions of chaplain while also working as a lecturer in theology. He was appointed senior lecturer in theology in 1952 and held that post for ten years, seven of which, from 1955 to 1962, as dean of the Faculty of Theology, and, from 1954 to 1958, as vice-principal of the College.

Parallel to his career at Fourah Bay, Sawyerr worked as a clergyman of the Church of England, serving as examining chaplain to the bishop as early as 1948; in 1961 he became a Canon of St George's Cathedral, Freetown. He edited the *Sierra Leone Bulletin of Religion* from 1962 to 1964. Sawyerr was a member of the World Council of Churches Commission on Faith and Order and a member of its working committee. He wrote *Creative Evangelism* in 1968, *The Spring of Mende Belief and Conduct* in 1968 and *God: Ancestor or Creator?* in 1970.

Canon Sawyerr was one of the most distinguished public figures in Sierra Leone for a quarter of a century; he became known for his independent mind, his wit and socio-cultural patriotism. At University College he was appointed professor of Theology in 1962 and served as dean of the Faculty of Arts from 1962 to 1964. The University was created in 1966, while Sawyerr was serving a second term as vice-principal from 1964 to 1968. He was then appointed pro-vice-chancellor of the University from 1968 to 1970, and finally, from 1970 to 1972, headed the University of Sierra Leone as vice-chancellor.

He retired from the University in 1973 and worked for some time at the famous Codrington College in Barbados. He returned to Freetown to become head of Theological Hall. He remained active to the last, serving in the last months of his life on the planning committee on a proposed rural secondary school for the mountain villages near Freetown. This work concluded a lifetime's service to education in Sierra Leone, during which he had trained very many distinguished Africans and acquired a wide reputation. One of his pupils, Prof Eldred Jones who also had a distinguished career at the University of Sierra Leone, wrote after Sawyerr's death in August 1986, "earlier generations of Fourah Bay College students whom he taught during the 1930s and 1940s would remember him as a polymath who taught at one time or the other almost the whole range of liberal arts subjects with competence and devotion. ... His vigour, his enthusiasm and his total devotion to the cause of education and religion, made him a household name and almost a legend in his lifetime." ■

Schimming, H.R.H. (1935-75)

SCHIMMING, Dr Harold Rudulf Haki (1935-75).

NAMIBIAN physician, the first indigenous Namibian to qualify as a medical doctor. He was born on 17 July 1935 in Windhoek, the second of eight children, and received his early education in Windhoek at M.H. Greef Primary School, a 'coloured' (mixed blood) school. He then went to Cape Town and studied at the Zonnebloem Secondary School and Trafalgar High School. After matriculating he enrolled at the University of Cape Town for medical studies. He successfully completed his studies in 1960 and did his housemanship in Port Elizabeth before returning to Namibia in 1962.

Schimming's return to Namibia aroused great enthusiasm amongst black people in the country, especially in his hometown, Windhoek. To many Namibians, Schimming's success was not only a personal achievement, but also a national one in that it inspired many of his countrymen and helped to reinforce their sense of national pride and confidence.

The South African occupation of Namibia has been notorious for its denial of educational, social, and medical facilities to the Namibian people. In line with the apartheid ideology of the ruling Afrikaner Nationalist Party, the South African regime in Namibia treated Namibians as manual labourers to work the mines, farms and factories owned by white settlers. Freedom of movement, the right to choose a job, where to live, and so on were denied to Namibians. Similarly, South African educational policy was to provide an education "fitting" for a manual labourer, to ensure that Namibians did not aspire to a world in which they were not allowed to participate.

Dr. H.R.H. Schimming

Schimming's achievement in wrenching from South Africa both a personal education and a skill which he could use to help his countrymen was a major breakthrough. There was no opportunity for Shimming to work in a local hospital in Namibia as medical facilities for black and white were segregated, and the white medical staff at the black hospital in Windhoek would not work with him. He was therefore forced to go into private practice, and he opened a surgery in the Old Location – the black township of Windhoek.

As the only black doctor in the whole country at that time, he took on an immense work load and was kept busy at his consulting room for thirteen uninterrupted years. He responded to the increasing demands put on him by the public by making himself as readily accessible to patients as was possible. Although he wanted to return to South Africa to specialise in surgery, the lack of

alternative medical treatment for Namibians kept him in Windhoek. Eventually he was able to work in the local black hospital, but he continued to maintain his private practice.

Schimming was also politically active. He was a member of the South West African People's Organisation (SWAPO), the Namibian national liberation movement dedicated to the complete overthrow of the South African administration. Through his work and his commitment to Namibian freedom and independence, he won the admiration and respect of many people, who used to refer to him affectionately by his middle name, Haki.

After 13 years of uninterrupted work, he took his first holiday in July 1975, to visit his sisters who were studying in Germany and Sweden, and friends in Britain. He returned to Namibia in August 1975 and died the morning after his arrival, of a lung disease. He was survived by his wife, whom he married in 1961, and three children.■

Seeneevassen, R. (1910-58)

SEENEEVASSEN, Renganaden (1910-58).

MAURITIAN lawyer and politician. He was born on 11 April 1910 in Port Louis. He received his primary education at the Church of England Aided School, the Central Boys Government School and Sunnee Surtee Aided School, after which he went to the Royal College for his secondary schooling. Having decided to study law, he had to wait until 1935 to begin his studies because his family could not afford to send him to England and he had to raise the money himself. At the London School of Economics and Political Science, he was taught by Professor Laski who may have generated his interest in socialism. While president of the Indian Students Union in Britain he met Mahatma Gandhi, Nehru and Patel. After graduating in 1939 he was called to the Bar at the Middle Temple, London, on 17 April the following year.

He returned to Mauritius later in 1940 and became an advocate of the Supreme

Court on 2 December. Six years later he was elected to the Municipal Council, to which he continued to be re-elected until his death. Following his election to the Municipal Council, he was offered a nominated seat on the Legislataive Council, thus inaugurating his career in national politics.

R. Seeneevassen

The new Constitution of 1948 provided for general elections. Seeneevassen successfully stood as a candidate for Port Louis. He was re-elected in 1953 and was chosen as one of Mauritius's representatives at the coronation of Her Majesty Queen Elizabeth II of England. The year 1955 saw him in London again, this time as a member of the delegation to the constitutional talks. He, as one of the leaders of the Mauritius Labour Party, believed that the British constitutional proposals did not go far enough in meeting his party's demands. A second delegation was sent to London in 1957, after which a commission visited Mauritius to inquire into the constitutional crisis. Seeneevassen was chosen by the Labour Party to put their case to the commissioners.

When the first Mauritian cabinet was formed in July 1957, Seeneevassen became Minister of Education. Towards the end of 1957 he went to Burma on a trade mission involving rice imports for Mauritius.

He died suddenly in Port Louis on 5 June 1958 and was survived by a wife and three children. He had been a much loved and respected figure; the crowd of mourners at his funeral was estimated at 50,000. ■

Sekyi, K. (1892-1956)

SEKYI, Kobina (1892-1956).

GHANAIAN writer and early nationalist politician. His original name was William Essuman Gwira Sekyi. He was born on 1 November 1892, son of William Gladstone Sackey (Sekyi). He went to the Wesleyan Primary School and then the famous Mfantsipim Secondary School, both in Cape Coast. He left Mfantsipim as a student in 1908 but remained as a teacher until 1910.

Then he studied philosophy at University College, London, and was awarded a degree in 1914. He had to interrupt further studies to return home on the death of the uncle who had been sponsoring him, in 1915. Then he began a career as an active and, for those early days, very radical nationalist.

He formed, with J.C. de Graft-Johnson, a Cape Coast branch of Casely-Hayford's (q.v.) Gold Coast Research Association. That branch used the Fanti language at meetings, and called for revival of tradition and rejection of European customs. Sekyi believed in this, and adopted the new forename of Kobina and wore traditional dress. In 1918 he published a series of articles in *West Africa* magazine entitled "The Anglo-Fanti", denouncing the imitation of British ways by the main ethnic group of Gold Coast Colony.

In the same year he returned to Britain for more philosophy studies, sponsored by another uncle. He also read for the Bar at the Inner Temple in London, to which he was called in 1919. He practised as a lawyer back in Gold Coast but was more noted as a militant nationalist. He joined the National Congress of British West Africa

(NCBWA) headed by Casely-Hayford, but later he criticised the acceptance by Casely-Hayford and others of the constitutional changes under Governor Guggisberg. He was a leader of the Aborigines Rights Protection Society (ARPS) for years and in

K. Sekyi

1928 led the ARPS campaign against the Native Authority Ordinance. He published an anti-colonial article, "Our White Friends", in *West Africa* in 1925, and a very polemic book, *The Parting of the Ways*, about the same time. He also wrote a play criticising Europeanised Fantis, *The Blinkards*, published after his death.

He joined in the ARPS protest at the Sedition Bill in 1934, and was a patron of the West African Youth League's Ethiopia Defence Committee, protesting at the Italian invasion of Ethiopia, in Accra in 1935. In the 1940s he was President of the ARPS for a time. An ardent nationalist, he agreed to serve on the Gorman Commission of Inquiry into a mine strike in 1947. Two years later he served on the Coussey Committee of Inquiry into constitutional changes. He was on the Council of the University College of the Gold Coast from 1948 to 1951. He died on 5 October 1956. ■

Selem, K. (1924-81)

SELEM, Alhaji Kam (1924-81).

NIGERIAN police officer, of noted professionalism and quiet industry, who worked his way up from a constable to succeed Louis Edet (q.v.) in 1966 as Inspector-General of the Nigerian Police Force (NPF). He was the second Nigerian to head his country's police force, and earlier in 1962 Kam Selem had distinguished himself as the first Nigerian to take command, as regional commissioner of Police, of the Northern Region – he was the third Nigerian to attain the rank of Commissioner.

He was born in 1924 in Dikwa in the Bornu Province in northeastern Nigeria. Kam Selem's father, Mallam Bashir, was a Moslem teacher of distinction and he himself was a devout practising Moslem throughout his life, performing the pilgrimage to Mecca. After attending the Dikwa Elementary School he went to the Bornu Middle School in Maiduguri where his brilliance earned him the distinction of the "best all-round pupil" in 1941. On 24 April of the following year Kam Selem enlisted in the Police Force and did the basic training at the NPF Northern Training School (now Police College), Kaduna. He then worked as a constable and later as a detective in Kano, following which he became a law instructor and prosecutor at the Kaduna magistrate's court.

In April 1950, for three years, he was a sub-inspector; he became an assistant superintendent in 1953. He was promoted deputy superintendent in 1955. During that period he served in various postings in the Northern Region where, after an officers' course at Rython-on-Dunsmore in Britain in 1956, he continued to serve. He returned to the United Kingdom for further training in 196 when he attended the Senior Police Course at the Scottish Police College, and again in 1961 and 1963 for two specialist courses. Meanwhile in 1958 he earned a nation-wide reputation when he investigated and broke up a counterfeiting gang, in the course of

Alhaji K. Selem

which he travelled to the Middle East for investigation. He was rewarded with a promotion to the rank of superintendent.

Further promotions came to Kam Selem in quick succession: in 1960, the year of Nigeria's independence, he was made chief superintendent and in December 1961 he attained the rank of assistant commissioner. In March 1962 he rose to the post of deputy commissioner and, six months later, became commissioner in command of the Northern Region. He was promoted deputy inspector-general in 1965. Then following the military coup of January 1966 and the second coup of July 1966 after which Louis Edet retired in August, Kam Selem was made Inspector-General of Police. As head of the police force he became a member of the Supreme Military Council and the Federal Executive Council. He was appointed Commissioner for Internal Affairs in June 1967 in the regime of General Yakubu Gowon; he fell with that government when it was overthrown in 1975.

Like most members of the ousted regime Kam Selem retired to his home base, but he soon started again in public service as a member of the Constituent Assembly which drafted Nigeria's new constitution and paved the way for the return to civilian rule. He served there from September 1977 until 1978. That same year he became a founding member of the National Party of Nigeria (NPN) that won the subsequent elections and formed the first government when the army stepped down in October 1979. He himself did not however succeed in his bid for the governorship of Borno State, but he remained a leading party member until his death in early 1981.

Kam Selem is well remembered for his services in the force, for which he received several awards and decorations including the Nigeria Police Medals for Meritorious Service. He worked hard at maintaining the integrity of the Police as a non-partisan force at a time when the country faced serious political crises. Indeed his main achievements as head of the force was the integration of the local government police authority in the North into the national police force. Kam Selem was president of the Nigerian branch of the International Police Association and a member of the International Association of Chiefs of Police.■

Seme, P.K.I. (1880-1951)

SEME, Pixley Ka Izaka (1880-1951).

SOUTH AFRICAN lawyer, politician and editor of the *Abantu-Batho*, the first African newspaper in South Africa, which he founded. Seme was born in Zululand in 1880. He obtained his primary education at a local mission school and went to the USA where he studied at Columbia University, New York. He then went to Oxford, England, where he read law, and was called to the Bar at the Middle Temple, London. At the American University, Seme won the first prize of the Curtis Medal Orations for his oration *'The Regeneration of Africa'* which called for acknowledgement and recognition of Africa's past great civilisation, as a basis for understanding the modern African and his aspirations.

On his return to South Africa in 1910 he set up in private practice in Johannesburg. This was at the time of the creation of the Union of South Africa, following the Anglo-Boer War (1899-1902) and the Treaty of Vereeniging of 1902. This was fought between the British imperial forces which at the time controlled the Cape Province and Natal, and the Afrikaners (Boers) who were resisting British sovereignty and had declared independent republics in the Transvaal and Orange Free State.

P.K.I. Seme

The Afrikaners were opposed to the attitude of the British administrators towards Africans. They considered South Africa their promised land which they were not willing to share with anybody. They therefore advocated the separation of the races. This was in fact incorporated in the Vereeniging Treaty, which was very generous to the defeated Afrikaners and sealed the political fate of the Africans. Non-integration of races at all levels was enshrined in the Treaty.

Thus, although Seme's first political involvement was with Zulu nationalism, the political demands of the period called for a more comprehensive and integrated approach against white monopoly, of the social, economic and political rights in South Africa. Seme was one of the founders of the South African Native National Congress which was formed in Bloemfontein on 8 January 1912. It was renamed the African National Congress (ANC) in 1923. At its inaugura meeting attended by 100 delegates J.L. Dube (q.v.) was elected its first President and Seme became the Treasurer-General.

Seme was also by then the editor of Abantu-Batho, which had a nationwide circulation and was printed in Zulu, Xhosa Sotho and English. Seme also helped to establish the African Native Farmers' Association which served both as a pressure group and a forum for discussion on development issues.

He received an honorary doctor's degree from Columbia University in 1928. In 1930 he was elected President of the ANC Earlier, Sobhuza II, King of Swaziland, had appointed Seme as his legal adviser. In 1926 Seme had represented the King before the Privy Council in the case of Sobhuza II v Miller and the Swaziland Corporation Limited, which was concerned with land rights.

Seme's leadership style was considered conservative by some and as a result he lost the presidency of the ANC in 1936. At the same time his paper Abantu-Batho declined in popularity and went out of circulation. After that though no longer in the forefront of South African politics, he continued to be involved in ANC activities until his death in 1951. ■

Sendwe, J. (1917-64)

SENDWE, Jason (1917-64).

ZAIREAN politician who served as Deputy Prime Minister under Cyrille Adoula (q.v.). A member of the Ba-Luba ethnic group in Northern Katanga, he was born in 1917 in Kabongo. His primary and secondary education was begun and ended in local Protestant mission institutions; he then studied medicine and became a medical assistant and later a teacher. From 1942 he worked in the church administration, becoming a member of the Protestant Council for the Congo.

Soon Sendwe became a member of the Amitiés Belgo-Congolaises, a cultural association formed at the time when Africans were forbidden to organise themselves politically. By August 1959, when the Belgian colonial authorities were compelled to revoke th restriction on African participation in politics, many Congolese had indeed already clandestinely, but on a regional basis, begun organising their people. Thus were the chances of a national consciousness for the Congo frustrated at the early stages of its political life; and the subsequent tragic ethnic rivalry, encouraged by European opportunism, that led to a bitter civil war at independence was only a chapter in that history in which Jason Sendwe and his contemporaries featured prominently.

Among these early ethnic political groupings was the *Association des Ba-Luba du Katanga* (Balubakat), formed in 1957 by Sendwe to facilitate unity of his Katanga Ba-Luba people. With increasing relaxation of Belgian control other political groupings emerged in the Katanga Province, notably the *Fédération des Associations de Ressortissants du Kasai et du Katanga* (Fedeka) founded by Isaac Kalonji, and the *Association des Tshokwe du Congo, de l'Angola et de la Rhodésie* (Atcar) of the Ba-Tshokwe ethnic group. Also appearing at the time was the *Confédération des Associations Tribales du Katanga* (Conakat), formed in 1958, with Moise Tshombe (q.v.) as its leader from December 1959, with the assistance of Belgian settlers and business organisations who encouraged it in a secessionist programme.

Sendwe initially agreed to work with the Conakat whose early aim, like that of the Balubakat, was to encourage unity of the Katanga Province. But he soon fell out with Tshombe when the latter began to advocate provincial autonomy and close co-operation with Belgians.

Shortly before the May 1960 general elections, Sendwe's Balubakat merged with Fedeka and Atcar in the Balubakat Cartel against the Conakat whose policy of "Katanga for the Katangans" they believed could only serve the interests of the colonialists. Sendwe, who was elected president-general of Balubakat Cartel, told *L'Echo du Katanga* then that he was strongly opposed to secession which he considered suicidal for the country, and he also declared himself in favour of a united Congo with a strong central government. In January 1960 he headed the Balubakat Cartel delegation to the Round Table Conference held in Brussels to discuss Congo independence.

He was elected for Elisabethville in the May elections to the National Assembly. There, where his party won six seats to

J. Sendwe

Conakat's eight out of a total of 137 for the country, he formed a parliamentary alliance with the *Mouvement National Congolais* (MNC) of Patrice Lumumba (q.v.) which won thirty-three seats. He was appointed State Commissioner for Katanga in the coalition government formed by Lumumba after the elections.

In the Katanga Provincial Assembly, the Balubakat Cartel succeeded in gaining twenty-two seats while its rival Conakat won thirty-eight of the sixty seats. The Balubakat Cartel deputies rejected Conakat's majority and refused to participate in government as they continued their opposition to the secession of Katanga. They subsequently formed an alternative administration in north-east Katanga. On 11 July 1960 Tshombe announced the secession of the Province and throughout the ensuing crisis Sendwe and the Balubakat Cartel remained loyal to Lumumba.

Following Lumumba's murder in January 1961 and the formation of the Cyrille Adoula coalition government in August, Sendwe was appointed Deputy Prime Minister. He was later made minister extraordinary for Kalemie (former Albertville in Katanga, now Shaba). Sendwe was killed in June 1964 while trying to calm dissident groups in the army in the Katanga Province. ■

Senghor, L. (1889-1927)

SENGHOR, Lamine (1889-1927).

SENEGALESE politician and prominent critic of French colonialism. He was born in 1889 in Senegal, where he was brought up and given his early education. In 1909 he was conscripted into the Senegalese Rifles, an elite colonial army corps. At the outbreak of World War I, Senghor was sent to the front, where he discovered that, horrific though conditions may have been for all the soldiers, those from the colonies were worse off than their European companions in arms.

He was demobilised in 1919 with the rank of Sergeant and officially designated as disabled. He found employment as a post office official, working in the 9th District of Paris. In April 1923 he enrolled at the Sorbonne (University of Paris) and also joined the French Communist Party (PCF). His free time was spent campaigning to raise the awareness of Africans in French provincial towns concerning the continuing evils and injustices of colonialism and imperialism. Such activity inevitably drew the attention of the authorities who came to regard him as subversive and placed him under police surveillance.

In 1926 he broke with the PCF and founded the *Comité de Défense de la Race Noire* (CDRN – Committee for the Defence of the Black Race), which aimed to direct its activity specifically towards the struggle of black people as an oppressed group, both in the metropolis and in the colonies. The CDRN was the successor to the *Union Intercoloniale*, a PCF-controlled umbrella organisation of militants from France's African and Asian colonies. Senghor's break with the PCF followed his unsuccessful call for autonomy within the organisation for Africans, arguing that their struggle had a unique character. However, he continued to retain his membership of the *Union Intercoloniale*.

In February 1927 Senghor attended the first meeting of the League Against Imperialism held in Brussels. The same year he published an anti-colonialist pamphlet entitled *La Violation d'Un Pays* (The Rape of the Country) in which he strongly criticised Blaise Diagne (q.v.), Senegal's African deputy to the French Parliament, for his collabor-

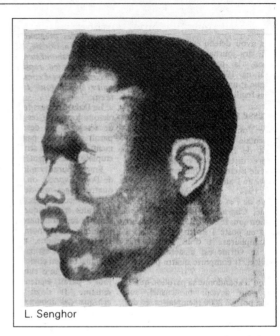

L. Senghor

ation with the French colonial authorities. A militant critic of oppressive French rule, he said at Brussels, "The Negroes have been asleep for too long. But beware, he who has slept too well and then awakes will not fall asleep again."

Lamine Senghor died in November 1927, at Fréjus in the south of France, aged 38, as a result of an illness that was not unconnected with gas poisoning he experienced on behalf of France during the War. ■

Shabou, A.K. (1925-71)

SHABOU, Colonel Abd-el-Kader (1925-71).

ALGERIAN soldier and politician who was prominent in the resistance against French rule. After independence he emerged as one of the most influential members of the government where he served as secretary-general at the Ministry of Defence. Born Abd-el-Kader Mouley in 1925 in the mountainous Aurès province in northern Algeria, he changed his surname to Shabou after deserting the French Army in 1957 to become a member of the Algerian resistance movement; it was a strategy to evade arrest by the French colonial authorities. After formal education in Algeria he joined the French colonial force and was sent to France for military training and, on completion, was commissioned lieutenant.

In 1958 he left France, declaring support for his compatriots in the *Front de Libération Nationale* (FLN) which had established a government-in-exile in neighbouring Tunis on 18 September 1958. With his military experience, gained in the French Army, he was an asset to FLN's armed forces, the *Armée de Libération Nationale* (ALN). He was posted to Tripoli, Libya, using Shabou as his *nom de guerre*. At the time the ALN forces were operating across the borders with Libya and Tunisia, and in 1959 Shabou was made instructor in the "Frontier Army" in that region. The ALN troops on the border had the task of containing the forces of the colonial authorities who in 1957 had barricaded the Algeria/Tunisia boundary with electrified barbed wire and mines. In 1960 he was promoted to the rank of major and made assistant to the head of Intelligence in the ALN.

When independence was formally gained on 3 July 1962, Shabou became the *Chef de Cabinet* at the Ministry of Defence in Algiers. A confidant of Colonel Houari Boumedienne (q.v.) whose administration came to power in June 1965, Shabou was later promoted to the post of Secretary-General of the same ministry and, in this capacity, headed important missions to the Soviet Union and Morocco. He was promoted colonel in June 1969, and in August 1970 he was made a member of the Revolutionary Council.

Colonel Shabou died on 1 April 1971 in a plane crash, 20 miles west of Algiers, in which two other senior military officers were also killed. ▪

Shafik, D. (1919-75)

SHAFIK, Dr Doria (1919-75).

EGYPTIAN journalist, writer and politician. Doria Shafik was born in Egypt in 1919. After finishing her early education in Egypt she travelled to France to study at the

Dr. D. Shafik

Sorbonne University in Paris from which she graduated with a Doctor of Philosophy degree.

On her return to Egypt she became editor of a twice-yearly French periodical *La Femme Nouvelle* in 1944, a position she held until her death. She was also editor of the Arabic publications *Bint el-Nil* (from 1946), *Katkout* and *Doria Shafik Magazine*.

She was a determined campaigner of women's rights, both socially and politically, and was active in the demand for the right of women to vote in Egypt. In 1948 she founded the *Bint el-Nil* (Daughter of the Nile) Union, a movement which not only strove for better conditions for women but also trained its members in guerrilla warfare to help the nationalist cause.

In 1951 *Bint el-Nil* organised 1,500 women to march into the Egyptian Parliament, disrupting the proceedings there as part of the campaign to gain women's suffrage. The movement followed this with demonstrations and other activities including a hunger strike by Doria Shafik and her supporters which lasted for one week. Eventually women were enfranchised in Egypt in 1956.

After this success, Doria Shafik continued to campaign for what she believed in, but criticism of President Nasser's Government and repeated demands for democracy in Egypt turned official, and to some extent public, opinion against her.

She wrote several books including *La Bonne Aventure, L'Esclave Sultane, L'Amour Perdu, L'Art dans l'Egypte Antique, La Femme et l'Islam, La Femme Egyptienne* and *Voyage autour du Monde*. She was married to Dr Noureddine Ragai and had two daughters. She died after falling from her sixth-floor apartment in Cairo in September 1975.■

Shangali, A.(1903-76)

SHANGALI, Chief Abdiel (1903-76).

TANZANIAN paramount head of the Chaggas. Born in 1903 in Machame, a rich coffee-growing area on the western slopes of the Kilimanjaro, Abdiel Shangali received his early education locally before attending the Government Secondary School in Tanga. His education was interrupted in 1924 when he was recalled home to become chief of Machame, at the age of twenty-one.

Under his chieftainship, Machame became the first Chagga chiefdom to allow activities of the Lutheran Church which facilitated rapid introduction of Western education and modern medical services. Under his rule Machame's school attendance exceeded that of any other chiefdom. Also, a coffee farmer himself, Chief Shangali encouraged the expansion of the coffee industry, the mainstay of the Chaggas and one of Tanzania's main crops and revenue earners. He encouraged the application of modern farming methods while advocating collective agricultural projects. Thus, the young Chief was soon to gain recognition for his progressive ideas from the British colonial authorities. He received honours, the King's Medal in 1934 and the Coronation Medal in 1937, and was taken under British supervision in 1943 on a morale-boosting visit to the East African soldiers who were serving in the Middle East with the colonial army. He was also appointed to the Makerere College Council; the college was the highest educa-

tional institution for East Africa, namely Kenya, Tanzania and Uganda.

In 1944 he became chairman of the Chagga Local Executive Committee on African education. The following year he became one of the first Africans, the other being Chief Kidaha Makwaia of the Wasukuma, to

Chief A. Shangali

be nominated to the Legislative Council of Tanganyika. Their nominations followed African demands for participation in the process of government, provoked by the upsurge of nationalism in the East African region at the end of the Second World War. Further constitutional re-arrangements in 1948 saw Chief Shangali's appointment to the Central Legislative Assembly which dealt with matters concerning the three East African colonies of Kenya, Uganda and Tanganyika. The Chief was the first African to serve in this Assembly.

At about this time, the chiefdoms in Chagga were being reconstituted into one administrative division, to be headed by one paramount chief. Shangali was appointed the divisional chief of Chagga in 1946, thus ending his headship of the Machame, but retained the chieftainship of Chagga until 1961 when the Independence Constitution abolished chieftainships. He was later appointed to various public bodies like the Tanganyika (now Tanzania) National Tourist Board where he served as executive chairman. He died in 1976.■

Al-Sharif al-Sanusi, A. (1873-1933)

Al-SHARIF   AL-SANUSI,   Ahmad (1873-1933).

LIBYAN nationalist who as head of the Sanusi Order was the leader of the resistance to Italian occupation in Cyrenaica.

On 29 September 1911 Italy declared war on the Ottoman Empire which nominally ruled Libya, and landed troops along the Libyan coast. The Ottoman rulers, in turn issued a decree on 15 October 1911 granting full autonomy to Tripolitania and Cyrenaica. Al-Sharif and the other Tripolitania leaders regarded this action as a declaration of their country's independence, and now opposed the Italian invaders.

When in 1913-1914 the Italians moved systematically to occupy Cyrenaica, al-Sharif's forces resorted to guerilla warfare and harassed the Italians. In July 1915, he was nominated Governor of Cyrenaica and of the dependent regions and undertook to continue the war as the Sultan's (Libya was nominally ruled by Turkey at the time) representative.

During 1915 Turkish and German officers landed from submarines on the Marmarican coast, bringing arms and other supplies to al-Sharif's camp. Al-Sharif himself took to the field and offered his followers great moral encouragement. The Italians suffered heavy losses in their confrontation with Libyan leaders such as him, Sulayman al-Baruni (q.v.) and Ramadan al-Suwayhili (q.v.).

To free Libya, al-Sharif accepted help from Turkey and external Arab groups. However, during World War I when the Ottoman Porte tried to urge the Sanusi followers to attack the British in Egypt, al-Sharif at first tried to establish peaceful relations with the latter. But when Cyrenaica was included in the area under British blockade, he became more dependent on Ottoman supplies and, together with Umar el-Mukhtar (q.v.), agreed to war to thwart the British.

The Sanusi force, commanded now by Turkey, crossed the Egyptian frontier on November 1915 and advanced as far as Sallum, but after the British forces counter-attacked in January 1916, the Sanusi army was forced to withdraw. Defeated by the British at al-Aqqaqir on 26 February 1916, al-Sharif retreated with a small bodyguard to Siwa Oasis and finally to al-Dakhla.

Following the retreat, al-Sharif transferred the political and military leadership of the Sanusi to Mohamed Idris, later King Idris I (q.v.), and left for Jaghbub and later for Sirte from where in September 1918 he went to Istanbul.

Al-Sharif never returned to his country. He spent the war years in Turkey and the greater part of the inter-war years in Damascus and the Hijaz, until his death in Medina on 10 March 1933.■

Al-Shawish, A.A. (1876-1929)

AL-SHAWISH, Abdul Aziz (1876-1929).

EGYPTIAN journalist and politician. Son of a Tunisian immigrant to Alexandria, he was educated at the famous al-Azhar Islamic University at Cairo and then in Britain, where he went to Borough Road Teacher Training College, London. Later he taught Arabic at both Oxford and Cambridge Universities.

Back in Egypt, where British rule was now firmly established, el-Shawish became Inspector of Religious Instruction at the Ministry of Education. He also became a strong nationalist and Pan-Islamist, a supporter of the Sultan of Turkey as Caliph of Islam in opposition to European imperialism. In 1905, at a Congress of Orientalists, he met Muhammad Farid, son of a distinguished family, who had been a public prosecutor before resigning and joining the Nationalist Party under Mustafa Kamil (q.v.). After this meeting he was offered the editorship of the Nationalist newspaper *al-Liwa'* but he did not accept it because of disagreement over the terms of the contract. But he remained an active nationalist and, after the death of Kamil in 1908, became editor of *al-Liwa'*.

Under his editorship a*l-Liwa'* continued to oppose British rule vigorously. In response the British Agent and Consul-General, Gorst, and the government headed in 1909-10 by Boutros Ghali Pasha (q.v.) revived a law of 1881 on the press, providing for action against critical journalists. When charged with publishing a false report of the summary execution of 70 Sudanese by the British, he was acquitted as he was held to have written in good faith. But later he was tried and gaoled in 1909 for an article attacking Boutros Ghali and Ahmed Fathi Zaghlul for their role in the hanging of villagers in 1906 for a small attack on British troops (the "Dinshawai Incident"). The newspaper had appointed an Egyptian who claimed American nationality as political director, in the hope that he would come under the jurisdiction of one of the consular courts, so that the press law could not be invoked. This hope was not realised.

However, despite problems which included the withdrawal of support by Khedive Abbas (q.v.) and a strike of the newspaper's staff in 1908, the Nationalists did well for a time under el-Shawish, *al-Liwa'* and Farid. *Al-Liwa'* remained outspoken and more nationalist newspapers were started in 1909. However, the British government became more hostile to the nationalists after the murder of Ghali Pasha by one of their supporters in 1910. Then, too, *al-Liwa'* was seized by a court order following a lawsuit by heirs to Kamil, and, although it went on appearing for some time, during 1910 it split with the Nationalist leader Farid. Relations between him and al-Shawish worsened in the succeeding years, although in 1910 both were jailed (al-Shawish for three months) for writing prefaces to a book of poems by another anti-British Egyptian.

After the Italian invasion of Libya in 1911 al-Shawish, one of many Egyptians who supported the Libyan and Turkish resistance to Italy, left Egypt, first to help arms shipments to Libya. Then he settled in Turkey. The Committee of Union and Progress (CUP), formed by the "Young Turks", had for some time after 1908 repudiated Pan-Islamism and the Egyptian Nationalists; but by 1911-12 they and their German allies were interested again in such anti-British leaders as el-Shawish. He was appointed editor of the CUP's Arabic-language newspapers.

During the 1914-18 war el-Shawish went to Germany where he edited a Turkish CUP periodical in German, *Die islamische Welt*. By 1918 he, Farid and Abbas were all agreed again on a common nationalist programme for which they sought German and Turkish aid. But earlier disagreements had damaged the prospects, which a number of North African nationalists had seen in 1914, of seeking liberation from colonial rule by supporting Turkey – which many such people respected as the champion of Islam, as el-Shawish did – and the other enemies of the colonial rulers. And in 1918 those enemies of Britain, France and Italy were defeated.

Al-Shawish stayed on in Germany for some years. In 1924, two years after Egypt's independence, and soon after the election of the Wafd government which under Zaghlul Pasha (q.v.) called for complete independence, it was reported that el-Shawish was returning home. Prime Minister Zaghlul gave orders to stop him landing, but he slipped through to Cairo. There, in surprising contrast to his earlier activity, he accepted the post of Controller of Elementary Education, a post he held until his death on 25 January 1929. ■

Shermarke, A.R.A. (1919-69)

SHERMARKE, Dr Abdul Rashid Ali (1919-69).

S OMALI statesman, the first Prime Minister of his country. He was born at Harardera in northern Somalia in 1919. His family was fairly wealthy and belonged to the large Darod ethnic group. After attending the Harardera Koranic Primary School he went to the Mogadishu Government School and on completing his education became a clerk in the civil service. He remained in this position for a year, after which he left government administration and established his own private business.

In 1944 he became a member of the Somali Youth League. In the same year he rejoined the civil service where he remained for six years, working in various positions.

He went to study at the Mogadishu School of Political Administration in 1950 and was awarded a Diploma of Political Administration two years later. In 1953 he continued his studies in Italy and the following year he enrolled at the Somali Institute of Law and Economics, later receiving a Diploma with distinction from there. He then returned to Italy to study political science at the University of Rome, and after graduating with first-class honours he continued to study at the university and was awarded a PhD for his thesis on "The Cessation of Trusteeship" in 1958.

During this period abroad he had retained his interest and involvement in Somali nationalist politics and had become a leading member of the Somali Youth League. After receiving his doctorate he returned to Somalia and in 1959 was elected to the Legislative Assembly, representing the Gardo constituency.

Meanwhile preparations were under way for the independence of Somalia, but British and Italian efforts to increase social services and educational facilities, while gradually transferring political and administrative authority, were unable to make the country economically viable by the time of independence. Added to this was the problem that both the Italians and the British had established different administrative institutions in southern and northern Somalia respectively, leading to regional differences when the two areas merged into the Republic of Somalia on 1 July 1960.

Shermarke was chosen to become the first Prime Minister of the new Republic, remaining in this position until 1964. His primary concerns were to overcome inherited administrative differences and thus create a cohesive government in the country, while at the same time reducing political divisions and promoting unity and development.

During his term as Prime Minister he appealed to Britain, Russia, China, the USA, Italy, West Germany and the EEC for financial and development assistance. He was able to overcome Western fears of a growing communist influence in the country, and with this international help many development schemes were initiated, particularly in the agricultural and communications sectors.

By the end of 1963 the political divisions within the Republic had been considerably reduced. To an extent this was the result of a strong nationalist commit-

Dr. A.A. Shermarke

ment to regain ethnic Somali-inhabited territory under the administration of bordering countries and France. Some argued that internal unity was being developed at the expense of external antagonism with the Republic's neighbours. Feelings ran very high on this issue and in 1963 Somalia broke off relations with Britain for allowing the Somali-populated areas of Kenya to be included in the newly independent state of Kenya despite Somalia's claims to them.

The growing unity in the country was reflected in the Somali Youth League gaining a majority of seats in the March 1964 elections, but following a leadership struggle within the party, Shermarke was not selected to continue as Prime Minister. However, he remained a member of the National Assembly and was elected President of the Republic by this body in 1967. By that time it was apparent that campaigns to extend Somalia's boundaries to incorporate territory under the administration of neighbouring states had been unsuccessful. In the wake of this there was a re-emergence of ethnic divisions in the Republic. Public discontent grew against the government, and in the resulting factional quarrels Shermarke was assassinated on 15 October 1969, during a tour of the drought-stricken northern region.■

Sibai, Y.M. (1917-78)

SIBAI, Youssef Mohammed (1917-78).

EGYPTIAN politician, author, and publisher and editor-in-chief of *al-Ahram*. He was born in December 1917 and educated at the Military Academy and University of Cairo, both in the Egyptian capital. On leaving the university he chose the teaching profession, lecturing in military history from 1943 to 1952 when he was appointed director of the Military Museum in Cairo.

He abandoned teaching in 1953 for journalism, having already proved his talent for writing while at the university, and was appointed editor-in-chief of *Arrissala al-Gadida*. He served in that position until 1956 when he became secretary-general of the Higher Council of Arts, Letters and Social Science. The following year he was appointed President and Secretary-General of the now established Afro-Asian People's Solidarity Organisation (AAPSO), a permanent liaison body aimed at forging close economic, social and cultural links between the peoples of Africa and Asia. The body had 75 national committees and affiliated organisations and had its headquarters in Cairo where it published a monthly bulletin *Solidarity*. A man of great intellectual depth whose political commitment to the aims of the AAPSO was reflected in his lasting connection with the organisation, Sibai remained the head until his death.

In the early 1970s his intellectual capacity and his extensive academic experience were deemed the right mixture for him to be a moderating influence in the clash between students and the establishment. He was appointed to the Cabinet on 27 March 1973 by President Sadat (q.v.), who made him Minister of Culture. Sibai's appointment was generally welcomed in literary and academic circles, but as a writer with an independent mind his posting was somewhat challenging.

It was an uphill task to which he dedicated himself. He remained in the Cabinet until March 1976 when, following re-organisation of the Egyptian press, he succeeded Ihsan Abdul-Quddous as chairman of the board of *al-Ahram*, becoming also its editor-in-chief. He was appointed chairman of the board of the Unified Arab Press Organisation at the same time.

Throughout these engagements Sibai found time for his literary pursuits, producing novels, short stories, plays and film scripts which brought him the reputation of one of the most outstanding authors of his generation. His novels include *Death of a Water Carrier, Among the Ruins* and *Land of Hypocrisy*. A collection of his short stories has been published as *A Nation that Laughed* while two of his plays, *Behind the Curtain* and *Stronger than Time*, have been performed to critical acclaim. His film script for *Rodda Qalbi* won the Ministry of Culture's prize for the best film story and an award for the best dialogue. Sibai was also honoured with Italian awards.

On 18 February 1978 he was shot dead by two Arab gunmen in Nicosia, Cyprus, where he was attending a meeting of the AAPSO. The two gunmen, Samir Kadar, a Jordanian, and Hussein el-Adi, a Kuwaiti, murdered Sibai in a hotel and later seized 11 other delegates and demanded to be flown out on a Cypriot airliner which the Cyprus government had provided for them. In the bid to try to rescue the hostages the Egyptian government sent troops to storm the airliner at Larnaca Airport on 19 February but instead they clashed with Cypriot national guardsmen who killed 15 Egyptian soldiers.

Y.M. Sibai

The assassination of Sibai and the death of the 15 officers caused considerable anger and demonstration in Egypt. Amid calls for "revenge" President Sadat recalled the Egyptian diplomatic mission in Nicosia and ordered all Cypriot diplomats out of Egypt. ■

Sibeko, D.M. (1938-79)

SIBEKO, David Maphunzana (1938-79).

SOUTH AFRICAN political leader; he was the first leader of a liberation movement from Africa to address the Security Council of the United Nations. Born on 26 August 1938 in Sophiatown near Johannesburg, South Africa, he was educated first at St Cyprian's Anglican School and later at Madibane High School. David Sibeko was exposed at an early age to the disparity between the living standards of Africans and whites. He was only eleven years old when the Programme of Action of the ANC Youth League was adopted, and fourteen when in 1952 the country-wide Defiance Campaign was launched. He joined *Drum* magazine in 1955 as a switchboard operator but later moved to the ranks of reporters and advertising agents.

In 1958 Sibeko joined the United Wide Aid Services and Insurance company. After becoming a member of the Pan-Africanist Congress of Azania (PAC) in 1960 he rejoined *Drum* and also became part of the reporting staff for *Post* the same year.

Journalism provided an excellent cover for his political activities. He later moved to Evaton from Orlando, and became chairman of the PAC in the Vaal Region. In 1963 he was arrested under the notorious Sabotage Act which had been promulgated in 1962, and kept in prison for seven months. Because of insufficient evidence, he was discharged on 1 December 1963.

In 1964 Sibeko left the country through Botswana for military training in Tanzania. On his arrival in Dar-es-Salaam, the external headquarters of the PAC, the party sent him on a six month course in journalism to the People's Republic of China, during which time he travelled to various parts of Asia including Vietnam.

On his return he was appointed Chief Representative of the PAC in East Africa, based in Dar-es-Salaam, a position he held till 1968, concurrently with that of liaison officer of the PAC to the Liberation Committee of the Organisation of African Unity (OAU).

He left Tanzania to take up the post of head of PAC Mission to Europe and the Americas. His efforts led to the expansion of the PAC European Mission to include a London office and one for the Nordic countries. In Europe he worked hard to bring back disaffected members of his organisation, and for a united front among all organisations fighting against the racist regime in South Africa. On the question of "disinvestment" Sibeko believed that far from being detrimental to the struggle, it would be of some service to the oppressed people in that country.

In 1975 he was appointed Permanent Observer to the United Nations and also a member of the Central Committee of the PAC and Director of Foreign Affairs. He participated in UN and many other international conferences including non-aligned countries' conferences, and became the first leader of a liberation movement from Africa to

D.M. Sibeko

address the Security Council of the United Nations.

Apart from international conferences he also addressed audiences at institutes of learning such as Oxford, Harvard, Yale, Columbia and Dar-es-Salaam universities.

On 1 May 1979, after P.K. Leballo was removed from the leadership of the PAC, David Sibeko was elected member of the three person Presidential Council assigned to carry out the function of the "Chairman of PAC". Sibeko was assassinated in Dar-es-Salaam, on 12 June 1979, and was buried in Botswana. He was survived by his wife, Elizabeth, and four children.■

Sidqi Pasha, I. (1875-1950)

SIDQI PASHA, Ismail (1875-1950).

EGYPTIAN politician. Of Turkish descent, he was born in Alexandria, son of Ahmed Shukry Pasha, at one-time Under Secretary of State in the government of Egypt. He obtained a diploma at the Collège des Frères in 1889 and won honours at the Khedivial Law School in 1894. After working in the public Prosecutor's office, he became administrative secretary to the Alexandria Municipal Commission in 1899.

He was Minister of Agriculture and then of *Waqfs* (religious institutions) in 1914-15, when Egypt was declared a British Protectorate, but resigned in 1915. In 1916-17 he headed a Committee on Commerce and Industry, examining ways to encourage Egyptian indigenous enterprise. This led to the creation of a Bureau of Commerce and Industry in 1920.

In 1918-19 Sidqi emerged as a leading figure in the new Wafd nationalist party, headed by Zaghlul Pasha (q.v.). In 1919 he was deported to Malta for a time, with Zaghlul, by the British. Not long afterwards, however, he broke with the Wafd, whose determined enemy he remained for years.He was said to be an autocrat and of an independent mind by inclination, and to have found the Wafd's demagogy uncongenial. He was Finance Minister in 1921, and was on the Egyptian government delegation whose talks in London, boycotted by the

Wafd, led to legal independence under severe conditions in 1922.

Following the fall of Zaghlul Pasha's government in late 1924, Sidqi became the Interior Minister in the Zihar government, and the real power in the country. He purged the provincial administrations of Wafdists, and sought to influence the 1925 elections by warning the new appointees that the Wafd would remove them if elected. But he lost power after the second elections in 1925. Later he was leader of the Liberal Party, but a rival of its other leaders, and not really content to wear a party label at any time.

In July 1930 he formed a government and promptly began to install an undemocratic regime in collaboration with King Fuad. The King prorogued Parliament; the Wafd

I. Sidqi Pasha

protested and riots followed in Cairo and
Alexandria, leading the British to send
warships to threaten Egypt. In October 1930
the 1923 Constitution was abrogated and
Parliament dissolved. A new Constitution,
giving more powers to the executive, and a
new Electoral Law, designed to stop the
Wafd winning elections, were enacted by
royal decree. For elections in early 1931 Sidqi
formed his own People's Party, *Hizb al-
Shaab*; with other parties loyal to his
government it controlled the new Parliament, as both the Wafd and the Liberals
boycotted the elections. Sidqi ruled as Prime
Minister with considerable power, but there
was persistent unrest in 1931/2, including
attempts on Sidqi's life and other violence.
No complete dictatorship was established,
and press restrictions did not prevent a
scandal over a Ministry of Justice "cover-
up" of a torture case, which led to Sidqi's
resignation in 1933. He went overseas for
medical treatment early in 1933 and resigned
in the following September.

After leaving office he went into
business and became very rich. He was a
director of the Suez Canal Company. He was
Finance Minister for a short time in 1937,
and thereafter remained politically active,
criticising the British still dominating Egypt
during the Second World War. In the
turbulent political situation after the war he
became Prime Minister again in February
1946. He also held the Interior and Finance
ministries in government composed otherwise of Liberals and Independents. Reputed
as Egypt's "strong man", he brought the
rioting, which had been directed mainly
against the British, and had gone out of
hand, under control, still allowing some to
help him put pressure on the British for
evacuation of their own forces from Egypt;
in July 1946 he ordered mass arrests of
Communists. He arranged for talks which
went far towards agreement on the
withdrawal of British troops and the future
of the Anglo-Egyptian Sudan. But although
a draft treaty was drawn up, progress was
halted by differing interpretations of an
agreement reached on the Sudan. Following
a statement by the British Governor-General of the Sudan, Sidqi Pasha made a reply
contradicting it and then, on 8 December
1946, resigned. No agreement was signed at
that time, though British forces did withdraw to the Canal Zone in 1947. Sidqi Pasha
died in Paris on 9 July 1950. ■

Silundika, T.M.G. (1929-81)

SILUNDIKA, Tarcisius Malan George
(1929-81).

ZIMBABWEAN politician whose activities during the war for independence
made him a prominent figure. When independence was achieved in 1980 Silundika
was a member of the first government of the
Republic of Zimbabwe, serving as Minister of
Roads and Road Traffic and Posts and
Telecommunications.

Silundika was born in Plumtree on 1
March 1929. He received his early education
at Empandeni Mission, and in 1945 proceeded to St. Francis's College, Marianhill, in
Natal, South Africa, for secondary educa-

T.M.G. Silundika

tion. He was admitted to the University of Fort Hare in 1951 for a preparatory course for a medical degree. However, he spent just one year at the University before being expelled for political activities. He was subsequently deported in 1953 by the South African authorities who sent him back to Zimbabwe. In 1954 he enrolled at Pius XII University College (now University of Botswana), Roma, in Lesotho, but left after a year due to lack of financial support.

George Silundika returned to Zimbabwe and taught for two years at Empandeni Secondary School. He joined the Federal Broadcasting Corporation in 1958 but soon left it for the University College of Rhodesia and Nyasaland (now University of Zimbabwe) where he became a Research Assistant in the Department of African Studies.

Two years later he began an active political career when he co-founded the National Democratic Party (NDP); this party succeeded the African National Council (ANC) that had been banned by the white settler regime of Edgar Whitehead (q.v.). The NDP's first congress was held in October 1960, where Silundika was electd its first Secretary-General, alongside Joshua Nkomo who was made its President. The party was a highly disciplined and motivated organisation and, unlike its predecessor, adopted a more militant approach to its demand for radical constitutional and political change for the realisation of a just and democratic Zimbabwe. But it too, like the ANC, was suppressed; it was banned on 9 December 1961 and all its assets were confiscated.

By that time however, Silundika had demonstrated the remarkable organisational and leadership qualities that won him widespread admiration as well as a place in Zimbabwe's later politics. In July 1960 he had led the famous Salisbury (now Harare) march of 7,000, in protest against the arrest of three NDP leaders. The march soon took the form of an effective strike action, involving over 40,000 NDP supporters, and spreading from Salisbury to other centres in the country. The authorities responded with characteristic repression and violence, killing eleven people and injuring several others as police charged on demonstrators. By 9 December the NDP was proscribed; but its leadership regrouped in a new movement, the Zimbabwe African People's Union (ZAPU).

Shortly afterwards Silundika was an adviser to the nationalist delegations at the Federal Review Constitutional Conference in London, as well as a delegate to the 1961 Southern Rhodesia Constitutional Conference in Salisbury.

Meanwhile, he had also been serving as external representative of ZAPU in London. When that party split in 1963 he joined forces with the pro-Nkomo elements and was elected Publicity Secretary of the People's Caretaker Council (PCC). With the imminent proscription of the PCC, Silundika went to work at the party's external headquarters in Lusaka.

An ideologist and a persuasive writer who articulated the case of majority rule, most of the time he spent in the Zambian capital was as ZAPU's Information and Publicity Secretary. He supervised the production of the party's publications, including its official organ, *The Zimbabwe Review*. He also represented ZAPU at several international conferences and was a delegate to the 1976 Geneva Conference and the Lancaster House Conference of 1979 which provided the basis of the independence constitution.

Silundika left Lusaka for home in 1980 to be elected to the first Parliament of the Republic of Zimbabwe. He won his seat on the ZAPU – Patriotic Front (PF) ticket and was one of the few members of that party who was appointed a minister in the ZANU (Zimbabwe African National Union) – PF-led government of Prime Minister Robert Mugabe. Unfortunately he died not long after in 1981, leaving a wife and children. ∎

Silwizya, G.B. (1932-79)

SILWIZYA, Greenwood Bwembya (alias Chikalamo) (1932-79).

ZAMBIAN politician and administrator; he later served as a minister in the independent government. He was born on 12 April 1932 in Kasama, Northern Zambia. His education was at primary schools at Kasama (1938-39), Mpika (1940-41), and Mbala (1942-46), and then at Lunzuwa Upper Primary School (1947-49), Chalimbana (JTC) Junior Secondary School (1950-51) and Munali Secondary School (1952).

He was a member of the African National Congress from 1952 to 1957. However, in 1955 he joined the colonial Customs service of Northern Rhodesia (Zambia). Two years later he transferred to the service of Mufulira Copper Mines Limited for which he worked as Assistant Welfare Officer and then Welfare Officer (1960-62). He was a

G.B. Silwizya

member of the Zambian African National Congress from 1958 to 1960, and in 1960 joined the United National Independence Party (UNIP). He studied at Oppenheimer College of Social Service, Lusaka, from 1962 to 1964, before becoming sectional senior personnel officer for Mufulira Copper Mines (MCM) (1964-66).

In 1966 he returned to the service of the government, now the independent Zambian government. He was a Foreign Service Officer in the UK and West Germany for two years. But in 1968 he returned yet again to the service of MCM, now as assistant personnel manager, while also starting part-time studies at the University of Zambia, which he continued for two years. He became MCM's personnel superintendent from 1969 to 1972. Then he was managing director of Belmont Limited and Marwood Limited at Mufulira in 1972-73.

In 1973 he joined the government as Minister of State for Social Affairs. Then he was appointed Minister of State for Foreign Affairs in 1974, and he held that post until he

died, of brain haemorrhage, in a Nairobi hospital, while attending a meeting of the OAU Council of Ministers in 1979.

He was a member of the Greenlands Association of the UK, of the Institute of Personnel Management of Zambia, and of the executive committee of the Zambia branch of the Commonwealth Parliamentary Association. He had four sons and two daughters by his wife Margaret, née Chibale. ■

Singhateh, F.M. (1912-77)

SINGHATEH, Alhaji Sir Farimang Mamadi (1912-77).

GAMBIAN pharmacist and first Gambian Governor-General; he held the office until its abolition in 1970. Alhaji Farimang was born in 1912 in Georgetown, near the Gambian capital, Banjul, then Bathurst. He attended Catholic and Methodist Mission schools and later took a job in the Gambia Medical Department. It was while working there that he developed an interest in pharmacy which he later studied. After qualifying as a druggist, he went into private practice, opening a drug store in Banjul, known locally as "Farimang's Hospital".

He became a member of the ruling People's Progressive Party of Dawda Jawara, but remained much in the background. He was a devout Moslem who performed the holy pilgrimage to Mecca, becoming Alhaji. He was best known in the country for his drug store before his appointment as the first Gambian to succeed the last British Governor-General in 1966. His appointment came after the government of Prime Minister Jawara failed in 1966 to muster enough votes to introduce a republican constitution.

But in 1969 Parliament adopted a republican constitution, and it was approved in a national referendum in April 1970. The country was formally declared a republic on 24 April 1970 when Jawara became its first President and Sir Farimang retired as Governor-General, having been the only Gambian to hold the office. He devoted his latter years to his business, and died in Banjul in 1977, at the age of 65. ■

Sissoko, F.D. (died 1962)

SISSOKO, Fily Dabo (died 1962).

MALIAN politician. He was born at Bafoulabe in the Kayes region of western Mali. He was educated at local schools after which he went to Senegal to study at the Ecole William Ponty in Dakar. He then returned to Mali and became a teacher at the Bafoulabe Regional School. After teaching for some years he was appointed a regional administrator at Niambia in 1933 and towards the end of the 1930s he became involved in Popular Front activities in the country.

He was elected member of the first Constituent Assembly in 1945 and the following year he was one of the founders and the leader of the *Parti Soudanais Progressiste* (PSP), a conservative political party which gained the support of the French administration and many of the traditional rulers in the country. His party continued to hold a

majority in the Territorial Assembly for the next ten years, but during that period its influence was gradually declining and in the 1956 elections the PSP won only six seats out of 70 in the Assembly. Its rival, the *Union Soudanaise* (US) of Modibo Keita (q.v.), won all other seats. Unlike the PSP, the US was popular among the educated African elite and in the rural areas where there had been opposition to French occupation.

The PSP was further weakened by reforms under the 1956 *loi-cadre*, and in 1958 Sissoko changed the party's name to the *Parti du Regroupement Soudanais* (PRS). Later on, in December 1958, the PRS was merged into the dominant *Union Soudanaise* party.

In 1962 the government withdrew Mali from the *Communauté Financière Africaine* (CFA) grouping and began to isssue its own currency. A series of riots followed this move and Sissoko was arrested and charged with treason for his alleged involvement in inciting these riots. He was sent to the Kidal area in the north east of the country where at that time there was an armed revolt against the government, and was assassinated shortly afterwards in what the government said two years later was a rebel ambush. But doubts remained about his death, which was said to have been due in reality to quiet deliberate murder by the authorities. ■

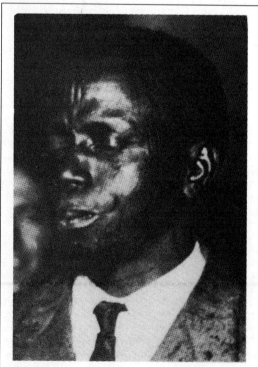

F.D. Sissoko

Sithole, E.F.C. (1935-75)

SITHOLE, Edson Furatidzayi Chisingaitwi (1935-75).

ZIMBABWEAN politician and barrister. He was born on 5 June 1935 in Zimbabwe. He commenced primary education in Bikita in 1943 and continued at Chikore Mission School in Chipinga until 1949. Forced to work on a farm for three months in 1950, he escaped to Salisbury (now Harare) in 1951 and enrolled at St Peter's School, where he combined night schooling with odd jobs as kitchen boy, waiter and factory hand. On the eve of the creation of the Federation of Rhodesia and Nyasaland, Sithole entered politics as a member of the Nyasaland

African National Congress, there being no active political party in Southern Rhodesia then. This led him later to participate in the formation of the City Youth League (CYL) of which he was interim Secretary-General until 13 May 1956. After briefly working as a clerk with the American Board Missions in Chipinga, he returned to Salisbury in 1957 as Secretary of the CYL Harare branch, a post he continued to hold under the new (Southern Rhodesia) African National Congress (ANC), formed on 12 September 1957.

On 26 February 1959, Sithole, along with about 500 other ANC leaders, was detained when the party was banned. He was held first in Khami prison, Bulawayo, then in Selukwe, Que Que, Salisbury and Marandellas prisons. Between June 1961 and July 1962 Sithole was detained with 14 others at Gokwe prison. While in prison, he was appointed Deputy Secretary of the Zimbabwe National Party (ZNP), formed in June 1961 in opposition to the National Democratic Party's first acceptance of the 1961 constitutional proposals, attacked by many as a derogation from the principle of "one man, one vote". When the ZNP merged with the Southern Rhodesia African Trade Union Congress to form the Pan-African Socialist Union in September 1962, Sithole was appointed its Secretary-General and served in that position till the party's demise in December 1962. In June 1962 Sithole obtained the LLB degree from the University of London, and on 4 July he was called to the Rhodesian Bar, becoming the second African in Zimbabwe, after Herbert Chitepo (q.v.), to achieve the status.

In May 1964 Sithole was appointed Publicity Secretary of the Zimbabwe African National Union, formed on 8 August 1963. On 26 September 1964 he was arrested and restricted to Wha Wha and Sikombela for one year, during which time he studied for and obtained the LLM degree from the University of London.

On 5 December 1964 he was moved to Sikombela and on 4 June 1966 to Salisbury prison. On his release on 15 March 1971 Sithole was restricted to a three-mile radius of the Harare police station to which he had to report daily as well as observing a 7 pm curfew. When the African National Council was formed on 16 December 1971, Sithole was appointed its Publicity Secretary.

On 20 June 1974 he was detained at Gatooma prison for allegedly torpedoing an

E.F.C. Sithole

agreement said to have been reached between the African National Council and the Rhodesian government. A month before that Sithole had been awarded the degree of Doctor of Laws by the University of South Africa on the basis of a thesis entitled "A Comparative Study of the Republican Constitutions of Zambia and Malawi". On 3 December 1974 Sithole was taken from prison to attend the discussions which led to the signing of the Lusaka Declaration of Unity on 7 December 1974, under which the African National Council was made an umbrella organisation to the Zimbabwe liberation movements led by James Chikerema, Joshua Nkomo and Ndabaningi Sithole.

On 15 October 1975, Sithole disappeared in his country (having returned home after the Lusaka conference), amid fears that the Rhodesian government had kidnapped him in order to eliminate him. He has not been seen or heard of since. ■

Slim, M. (1908-69)

SLIM, Mongi (1908-69).

TUNISIAN politician, one of the most influential leaders in the campaign for independence, who subsequently held important ministerial and diplomatic posts. Mongi Slim was born in Tunis in September 1908. He attended local primary and secondary schools, after which he travelled to France in 1933 to study mathematics and law at the University of Paris. Three years later he graduated with a law degree and then

M. Slim

returned to Tunisia, where shortly afterwards he was called to the Bar at Tunis.

He joined the Neo-Destour Party, an organisation which campaigned for Tunisia's national independence. After becoming a qualified legal practitioner he took up the position of permanent secretary of the Neo-Destour's National Council with responsibility for the organisation of the party.

In 1938 the Neo-Destour Party began a campaign of demonstrations against French rule. Tension rose and in April 1938 police

fired on marchers in Tunis, sparking off serious riots. The trouble was quickly suppressed and the leading members of the Neo-Destour Party, among them Slim, were arrested. The party was banned but it continued to operate as a clandestine movement because of its wide popular support. Slim was court martialled and detained in the south of the country until 1939 when, on the outbreak of World War II, he was moved to France, to Fort St. Nicholas prison in Marseilles. He remained there until 1943 when he was sent back to Tunisia, and then released by the Germans.

He continued to work for the nationalist movement and was appointed to the party's Political Committee in 1945. In 1951 tension once again grew in the country owing to a lack of political agreement concerning eventual self-government. As a result Slim was once again detained along with other leaders of the party. Despite these arrests the struggle continued and he was released in 1954 after the French government recognised the right of Tunisian self-government. He played a leading role in the ensuing autonomy negotiations which were concluded in June 1955. In the new Tunisian government, Slim was appointed Minister of the Interior, and in this position continued to be very involved in the negotiations which led to Tunisia's complete independence from France in March 1956.

In July 1956 he was appointed Tunisian Ambassador to the USA, concurrently accredited to Canada while also serving as Permanent Representative to the UN. He remained in these positions until 1962 during which time he had become a leading spokesman in the UN General Assembly on African affairs, and particularly on independence for the colonies. As well as belonging to the UN Africa Committee, he was also a member of the UN Commission on the 1956 Hungarian Revolt, and was elected President of the UN General Assembly between 1961 and 1962.

He returned to Tunisia in 1962 to become Secretary of State for Foreign Affairs, a position which he held until 1964. He then became the personal and roving representative of the President of Tunisia for two years, after which he was appointed Secretary of State for Justice in 1966. He continued in this position despite a heart attack in 1968, until his death, caused by hepatitis, on 23 October 1969. ■

Small, E.F. (1890-1957)

SMALL, Edward F. (1890-1957).

GAMBIAN journalist and trade unionist. He was born on 29 January 1890 in the Gambia and educated locally in Banjul schools. He was a clerk and later a teacher before founding the *Gambia Outlook* newspaper in 1922. A supporter of pan-Africanism, in 1920 he joined the National Congress of British West Africa (NCBWA), an organisation established in Accra to promote the political, social and economic aspirations of Africans in British-ruled West Africa. He went on the NCBWA delegation to London in 1920-21.

He organised the first Gambian labour union, the Bathurst Trade Union, in 1929. Shortly after the union's formation in November 1929, the first strike in the country's history was organised by river craft workers and artisans. This strike led to the workers achieving their demands for higher pay. Small continued to be active in the union, which was the only expression of organised labour in the country at that time and for the next twenty years. Despite its success, the strike did not enable the union to grow into a strong organisation, partly because of the prevailing world depression but also owing to the opposition of the British administration.

In mid-1930 Small attended the Hamburg conference of the International Trade Union Committee of Negro Workers (ITUC-NW), a subsidiary of the Communist "Red International of Labour Unions"; other delegates included Jomo Kenyatta (q.v.). Small joined a new executive committee of the ITUC-NW. He edited the *Gambia Outlook* which published revolutionary material submitted by the Communist *Negro Worker* newspaper, for which Small acted as a correspondent.

About the same time, the Rate Payers' Association (RPA) was established, and became a very influential pressure group in the Gambia until the mid-1930s. Small was appointed chairman of the RPA and although the association later declined he continued to be politically active and was later nominated a member of the Legislative Council. Between 1945 and 1957 he was a member of

E.F. Small

the executive council of the International Confederation of Free Trade Unions (ICFTU), and in 1947 he was re-elected a member of the Legislative Council, serving on this body until 1951. He died in 1957.■

Smuts, J.C. (1870-1950)

SMUTS, General Jan Christiaan (1870-1950).

SOUTH AFRICAN lawyer, soldier and Afrikaner nationalist politician. He played an important part in the creation of the Union of South Africa, becoming one of its early Prime Ministers. On the international plane he was instrumental in the formation of both the League of Nations and the United Nations. Jan Christiaan Smuts was born on 24 May 1870 at Bovenplaats, Cape Province, South Africa. His ancestors had moved to South Africa from Holland in the 17th century and his father, a farmer by occupation, was also a representative for Malmesbury in the Cape House of Assembly. He spent his childhood on the farm, receiving elementary education from his mother until the age of 12 when he was sent to boarding school and later to the Victoria

College in Stellenbosch where he passed his matriculation examination with distinction in 1887.

After matriculation he studied literature and science at the University of the Cape of Good Hope, graduating in 1891 with a double first class combined degree in these subjects and also winning an Ebden Scholar-

Gen. J.C. Smuts

ship. He then travelled to England where he enrolled at Christ's College, University of Cambridge, to study law in October 1891. After passing his examinations with first class honours and also achieving the highest marks in his class, he enrolled at the Middle Temple Inn of Court in October 1894, and was called to the Bar three months later. During his law studies he wrote an unpublished manuscript, *Walt Whitman: a study in the evolution of personality*.

On completing his studies he returned to South Africa and went into legal practice in Cape Town. He maintained his early interest in politics, becoming an Afrikaner nationalist and republican in 1896 in reaction to the Jameson Raid, and contributing political articles to the newspapers *Ons Land* and the *South African Telegraph*. He married Sybella Margaretha Krige in 1897 and moved to Johannesburg where he continued to practise law. The following year he was appointed State Attorney of the Transvaal Republic and legal adviser to the Republic's Executive Council. While in this position he was involved in the abortive negotiations between the British government and the Transvaal. After the outbreak of the Anglo-Boer war in October 1899 he began to advise on military and political strategy.

As the war continued, Smuts organised the transfer of the Transvaal's substantial reserves from Pretoria to Middleburg before the capital was taken by the British. He then became assistant to the General in charge of the Western Transvaal area, helping to organise commando units. His skill and knowledge of military operations earned him the position of General, in which capacity he commanded the military activities around Gatsrand.

In August 1901 he set out with a force to attack the British in the Cape Colony. He established a base in the North Western Cape for coastal attacks, mounted with the aid of increased reinforcements and volunteers. The following April he attended a conference at Vereeniging as legal adviser to the Transvaal Government. He reluctantly agreed to the ending of the war and the abrogation of the Transvaal Republic's independence.

He resumed legal practice in Pretoria and his involvement in politics waned until 1905 when, in opposition to various British policies in the Transvaal, he became one of the leaders of *Het Volk*, an Afrikaner political party similar to the Cape *Afrikaner Bond*. He travelled to England later in the year to campaign for the self-government of both the Transvaal and the Orange Free State. As a result elections were held in which *Het Volk* was successful and he was appointed Minister of Education and Colonial Secretary in the Transvaal in 1907. He then began to work towards a union of four British South African colonies (Cape Province, Natal, Orange Free State and the Transvaal) and drafted a unitary constitution that was flexible enough to be acceptable to all parties, resulting in the establishment of the Union of South Africa in 1910. *Het Volk* merged with the *Afrikaner Bond*, the South African Party and the Orangia-Unie to form the South African National Party which quickly became known as the South African Party (SAP), representing Afrikaners and some British interests.

After the elections Smuts was appointed Minister of Defence as well as Minister of the Interior and Minister of Mines. In 1912 he lost the latter two portfolios but received that of Finance. During the same year the Defence Act that he had drawn was passed by Parliament, providing for the reorganisation of the country's defence and military service. Two years later some of these forces were employed to maintain order and to break a general strike of miners and railwaymen in Witwatersrand. Although his methods of dealing with the strike were endorsed by the South African Parliament, they were considered harsh in some quarters and lost the government some popularity.

On the outbreak of the First World War, the newly established Afrikaner National Party demanded that the Union should remain neutral despite the Government's decision to ally with Britain against Germany. Violence erupted over this issue in October 1914, but by January of the following year government troops had restored order and Smuts became the Commander of the southern army in an offensive against German South-West Africa. With the help of the northern army this campaign was successfully completed and Smuts left South Africa in February 1916 to take up the command of East African operations, having been promoted to the rank of Lieutenant-General in the British Army. He remained in Tanganyika (Tanzania) until January 1917 when he was sent to represent South Africa at the Imperial War Conference in London. During this conference he succeeded in opposing proposals for closer links between Britain and the dominions and instead advocated a "British Commonwealth" consisting of independent nation states.

For the following 18 months he remained in Britain, and after rejecting an offer of the military command in Palestine and the Middle East in June 1917 he became a member of the British War Cabinet. He then became involved in a variety of projects and committees, including those responsible for providing war priorities and policies, as well as leading the committee that organised the establishment of the Royal Air Force in Britain. He was also active in the peace negotiations on the European continent.

In 1918 he published *The League of Nations, a Practical Suggestion*, which helped form the basis of the League of Nations that was later established.

In August 1919 he returned to South Africa and shortly afterwards became Prime Minister on the death of the former incumbent, Mr Louis Botha. By the time the elections were held in 1920, the Nationalists, taking advantage of economic discontent, had gained such support that the SAP had to rely on the Unionist Party to retain its parliamentary majority. The following year the two parties merged in order to contain the rising militant Afrikaner nationalism. In the 1921 elections Smuts' parliamentary majority was enlarged by the merger.

During the period when he was Prime Minister, the economy was suffering from a general economic crisis, with falling prices, rising unemployment and the closure of some mines. These economic problems caused a general discontent against the government. In May 1921, 163 Africans belonging to a religious sect were killed and many more were wounded after police moved in to evict them from a Bulhoek farm which they had taken over. Smuts was severely criticised for the way the police had behaved.

In March 1922 there was a general strike by white workers in the Witwatersrand. Believing the strike to be a communist-inspired attempt to overthrow the government, Smuts declared martial law in the area and personally commanded the troops sent in to suppress the strike. Both sides suffered heavy casualties. Two months later he ruthlessly crushed Hottentot resistance and arrested some members of the African group for allegedly breaking the law.

Smuts tried to reduce his increasing unpopularity with an attempt to get Southern Rhodesia to join the Union, but his proposals were rejected by the white Rhodesians in a referendum held in 1922. The Nationalist and Labour Parties' alliance won the 1924 elections; the SAP suffered heavy losses and Smuts failed to win his Pretoria West seat and had to be given the

Standerton seat by a successful candidate so that he could become leader of the Opposition, representing the interests of the English-speaking section of the population. Although he basically agreed with the concept of segregation between black and white, he was opposed to the proposed Native Bills which he helped defeat when they were introduced in Parliament.

The world economic crisis which followed the Wall Street crash in 1929 also affected the South African economy whose agriculture sector was also hit by drought. To overcome these problems, a coalition government was formed in February 1933 by the SAP and the National Party. Smuts, who was Deputy Prime Minister and Minister of Justice in this Government, supported this move and the fusion of the two parties the following year into the United South African National Party (known as the United Party), because he believed in the unity of white South Africa. However, some white nationalists who did not join in the United Party kept the National Party going as a separate entity.

The United Party alliance lasted until the outbreak of the Second World War in September 1939, when the question rose of whether South Africa should join the Allies or remain neutral. A strong nationalist element opposed South Africa's involvement but after a long debate, Parliament voted to enter the war on the side of the Allies. Smuts once again became Prime Minister, also holding the posts of Minister of Defence and Commander-in-Chief of the South African Armed Forces.

Smuts sent South African forces to help in the re-conquest of Ethiopia from Italian occupation, and played an important role as counsellor on Allied strategy, particularly in the Middle East. On 28 May 1941 the British government made him a Field-Marshal in the British Army.

South Africa's industry was stimulated by war production, and although the internal political division in the country intensified, the opposition was weak. This opposition weakness, coupled with the victories in North Africa, helped Smuts to win the 1943 elections, becoming Prime Minister for another five-year term.

Smuts participated in the establishment of the United Nations at the end of the Second World War, drafting the UN Charter's Declaration of Human Rights. Later he was to have doubts as to the effectiveness of such an organisation, given the complexities of the post-war world, the rising influence of the Soviet Union and increasing international tension. He opposed any role for the UN in relation to South-West Africa.

Shortly after the Second World War he received two honours in recognition of his contribution in international affairs. In 1947 he was awarded the Order of Merit by King George VI, and the following year he received an honorary LLD degree from the University of Leyden.

In the post-war period the South African economy which had been stimulated by the war saw a period of economic and industrial development but most of the problems encountered by Smuts during this period were of a political nature. In 1946 the Asiatic Land Tenure and Indian Representation Act were passed, concerning Indian representation and property rights. This law was rejected by the Natal Indian Congress with the support of the government of India which not only broke off relations with the Union, but also took up the case of the South African Indians at the United Nations in 1946.

Opposing the revised Native Acts of 1936 on the basis that they were outmoded in the context of rapid industrialisation, Smuts urged a more liberal approach to race relations. However, his proposals met with opposition, not only from the nationalists but also from Africans who pointed out that his ideas did not go far enough to meet their demands of full political equality and trade union rights. Smuts' party was defeated in the 1948 elections and he lost his seat.

This election defeat was a great blow to a man who regarded himself as a fighter for the unity of white South Africans. It was obvious that he had under-estimated the appeal of the Afrikaner nationalists to a part of the white electorate. Despite his disappointment and disillusionment he accepted another seat in Parliament and once again became leader of the Opposition, hoping to be able to take a stand against the policies of extreme nationalism.

In June 1948 he was elected chancellor of the University of Cambridge. He was taken ill in January 1950. Shortly after his 80th birthday he suffered from coronary thrombosis and died of a heart attack on 11 September 1950 at Doornkloof. He was survived by his wife and six children. ∎

Sobhuza I (c.1795-1836)

Sobhuza II (1899-1982)

SOBHUZA I, King (c.1795-1836).

KING of the Swazis and founder of the kingdom. Born in about 1795, he descended from a Dlamini (Ngwane) chiefdom. Sobhuza's mother was Somnjalose Simelane and his father Ndvungunye ruled the Swazis from about 1780 to 1815 when he was killed by lightning. Ndvungunye created the first Swazi army. Sobhuza succeeded his father as king in 1815, taking the titles Ngwane IV and Somhlolo. His other official title was Ngwenyama (king) of the Swazis.

From the early years of his reign he continued his father's policies of strengthening the armed forces, which he successfully used to annex neighbouring countries. The army, well-trained and armed with weapons forged from the country's rich deposits of iron, strongly resisted Zulu attacks from the south, but were slowly pushed northwards. In about 1820 Sobhuza built a new settlement in the north of the country in Lobamba which is today known as Old Lobamba. From there he expanded his kingdom northwards to include areas which now form modern Swaziland. Clans were absorbed and Sobhuza's following grew dramatically. He built other major villages at Zulwini and Langeni.

Friction with his southern neighbours, however, continued, especially with Chief Zwide of Ndwandwe. Through shrewd diplomacy, Sobhuza made a truce with the Ndwandwes by marrying Chief Zwide's daughter, Thandile, who became mother of his son and successor, the great Swazi king, Mswati II (q.v.). He forestalled further Zulu attacks on his territory by making friends with King Chaka and his successor Dingane; Sobhuza is said to have visited Zululand as the guest of Chaka.

But the two countries went to war after Chaka's death when Dingane ordered the destruction of the Swazis in 1836 for raiding his cattle. Sobhuza himself died in 1836 and was buried in Mbilaneni. He was succeeded by Mswati II. The new King came under increased pressure from the Zulus, and later from the Boer settlers in the Transvaal, although, at the same time, he conquered and annexed Sotho peoples to the north. ∎

SOBHUZA II, King (1899-1982).

KING of Swaziland. He ruled the small southern African kingdom of Swaziland from 1921 until his death on 21 August 1982, as Africa's oldest statesman and one of the modern world's longest reigning monarchs. Sobhuza also had the distinction of being one of the few traditional rulers to have retained real political power in post-colonial Africa.

The concrete achievements of his reign however rest on leading Swaziland to

King Sobhuza II

independence in 1968 and on regaining Swazi land ceded to Europeans during the colonial period. The King also had the satisfaction of seeing the economy of his landlocked country flourish, despite the difficulties of lying close to South Africa whose apartheid policy is a cause of political friction in the region.

King Sobhuza was born Nkhotfotjeni on 22 July 1899 at Zombodze, the son of King Bhunu, who died five months later, and

Queen Lomawa Nxumalo. He was chosen to succeed his father but because he was still a minor, his grandmother, Queen Labotsibeni, acted as Regent. The king-designate was educated at Zombodze National School that was built by Labotsibeni to assure his education. In 1916 Nkhotfotjeni left Zombodze for the Lovedale Institute in Cape Province, South Africa, for secondary education but was recalled in 1918 to prepare for kingship. He was crowned on 6 December 1921 and took the name Sobhuza II; he was also known, among other names, as Ngwenyama (the Lion).

The kingdom Sobhuza inherited at the age of 22 had been a British Protectorate since 1903. At the time of his accession nearly two-thirds of what is now Swaziland were lost to the Swazis, ceded, according to British sources, to European settlers by his father who was reported to have said: "If I do not give whites rights here, they will take them. Therefore I give them when they pay". The new King, however, thought differently. With a single-minded dedication of purpose he concentrated his efforts on regaining the land.

In December 1922 he sailed to London at the head of a delegation to King George V that Swaziland had been illegally acquired by the British. His protests both to the monarch and his Secretary of State for the Colonies were unsuccessful; even the Special Court of Swazi land was to dismiss the claim the following year. But Sobhuza pursued his quest by appealing to the Privy Council in March 1926. This court, too, found against him.

Undeterred by these rejections he persisted with the case for the next fifteen years, culminating in a petition to the new British monarch, King George VI, in 1941. It was not until the Second World War, however, that Sobhuza had an opportunity to make a deal with Britain; the British sought and got Swaziland's assistance in the war against Germany in return for a scheme whereby land was rebought from the Europeans and reassigned to Swazis. By the time he died in 1982 nearly two-thirds of Swazi land had been repossessed, but the King did not see the fulfilment of his ultimate plan to regain the 2,000 square miles of land still claimed by South Africa. But he died with the satisfaction of witnessing his land campaign result in bold agricultural schemes like the Usutu commercial pine and eucalyptus

forests which had been expanded to become the largest man-made forests in Africa.

Sobhuza was a modernist, in spite of his fondness for dressing in the Swazi traditional attire of loincloth and feathers. He actively promoted new farming methods and encouraged the development of the Ngwenya iron ore mines which made mining the leading export earner in the 1970's.

Politically, he bequeathed to his 600,000 citizens a machinery blending Swazi customs with selected aspects of modern politics. He had ruled the country autocratically since independence was achieved from Britain in 1968, employing his remarkable skill and the shrewdness of an arch traditionalist to make himself the chief of a somewhat unique system in modern Africa. In the first post-independence elections of 1972 he used this position to secure complete control of Parliament for his *Imbokodvo* (Royal) Party which he formed in 1964. In April 1973 he suspended the independence constitution and decreed that the country would be ruled by the King through a National Council made up of his nominees. From then on, he had exercised almost absolute power over his subjects who, in return, regarded him with tremendous affection.

King Sobhuza travelled out of Swaziland only twice during his reign, in 1922 during the land campaign and the second time in 1953 when he attended the coronation of Queen Elizabeth II of England. Yet he was widely respected outside his kingdom, as was evident when he celebrated the Diamond Jubilee of his reign in 1981 which attracted some 22 foreign Heads of State to Swaziland. The king died a year later on 21 August 1982, aged 83.∎

Sobukwe, R.M. (1924-78)

SOBUKWE, Robert Mangaliso (1924-78).

SOUTH AFRICAN politician who became the first President of the Pan-Africanist Congress (PAC). He was born on 5 December 1924 at Graaf-Reinet, Eastern Cape, South Africa. His Xhosa parents were very poor but his intellectual aptitude at various mission schools enabled him to win a scholarship to Lovedale College where he studied until 1945. He then went to Fort Hare University College at Cape Province to study history, literature and education, and graduated with an honours degree and a diploma in Education in 1949. During that time his interest in nationalist politics developed. He joined the Youth League of the African National Congress (ANC), and in 1949 he became the chairman of its Victoria East (Fort Hare) branch.

In 1950 he became a teacher in Standerton, a position he held until he was dismissed two years later because of his activities in the 1952 Defiance Campaign in the region. The following year he joined the Department of Bantu Studies at the University of the Witwatersrand in Johannesburg as a language assistant, and remained in this post until 1960. His involvement in the African nationalist movement during these years greatly increased, and in 1957 he became editor of the *Africanist*, the official organ of the ANC. Also during this period Sobukwe and many other younger members of the ANC began to be disenchanted with the development of the movement. It was felt that the increasing aid to the organisation by the Communist Party, with the corollary of increasing political influence, was obscuring its policies, while the growing multiracial character of the organisation was adversely affecting the development of black consciousness and aspirations. As a result, Sobukwe and many others left the ANC in 1958 and founded the PAC. This organisation, which was inaugurated on 6 April 1959 with Sobukwe elected its President, was aimed at overcoming the inequities of the apartheid system and establishing a new society in South Africa based on African nationalism.

Sobukwe believed that in order to overcome racial inequality in South Africa, the Africans had to regain their dignity and self-respect so as to receive respect from other races. He was convinced that liberation could only be achieved by the black people themselves. This was the essence of the difference between the ANC and the PAC, and led to his being accused of racism by his opponents, despite his commitment to the establishment of a non-racist, democratic and socialist society after the destruction of the apartheid system. His belief in the necessity of developing black awareness was

R.M. Sobukwe

also one of the sources of inspiration to the later evolution of the Black Consciousness Movement under Stephen Biko (q.v.).

The PAC built up a large following among the black masses and began to organise a campaign against the Pass Laws, the removal of which it considered would be a major step towards achieving its aims. Mass demonstrations were arranged in various places for 21 March 1960 and Sobukwe was arrested at Orlando during a Soweto demonstration. He was charged with incitement and was sentenced to three years' hard labour, being held in Stofberg Prison in Orange Free State until April 1961 when he was transferred to Pretoria Prison. At the end of the sentence Sobukwe was further detained at the maximum security prison on Robben Island, where he remained in solitary confinement for six years. During this time he read for a degree in economics from the University of London by correspondence.

On his release in May 1969 he was served with a five year banning order which placed him under house arrest in Kimberley, Northern Cape. This order was renewed in 1974 for another five years. Meanwhile he continued with his correspondence studies, this time reading for a law degree which he obtained in 1975. At this time too he had begun to suffer from a lung illness for which he underwent chest surgery at Groote Schuur Hospital in Cape Town in September 1977, but his health did not significantly improve. He died in a Kimberley hospital on 27 February 1978.

A committed African nationalist, he was also a great believer in the principles of Pan-Africanism and the eventual liberation and unity of African peoples all over the continent. His dynamic personality combined with his great organising abilities and oratorical skills made him a great leader and a powerful influence in South African nationalist politics despite his imprisonment and later restrictions which made it very difficult for him to communicate effectively with many people. ■

Socé Diop, O. (1911-73)

SOCE DIOP, Ousmane (1911-73).

SENEGALESE writer, politician and veterinary surgeon. Born on 31 October 1911 at Rufisque, he was educated at a Koranic school and then at the French Lycée in Dakar and the famous William Ponty Teachers' College in Senegal. From there he went to France for further studies. He could not obtain a scholarship to study medicine as he had hoped to do, so he studied veterinary medicine, on a scholarship, at France's National Veterinary College at Alfort and then (1930) at the Institut de Médecine Vétérinaire Tropicale in Paris, where he was awarded a diploma.

In France he also studied for a Teachers' Certificate, which he was awarded in 1935; and began literary efforts, while meeting some of the other young Africans and West Indian literary figures in Paris at the time, a small but influential group (Léopold Senghor, Aimé Césaire and others) who developed the philosophy of *Négritude*. In 1935 Ousmane Soce Diop, who, as a literary figure, was to be known simply as Ousmane Soce, published his first novel, *Karim*. The second, *Mirages de Paris*, followed in 1937.

Soce obtained a job as a veterinary surgeon at the French Army's Cavalry Academy at Saumur in 1937. Later he was head of the cattle inspection service in Senegal for some time. In 1946, after the introduction of representation of the colonies in the French parliament with the vote accorded to Africans, Ousmane Soce was elected a representative of Senegal in the French Senate; he was a member of the French Socialist Party (SFIO).

In 1948 *Karim* was awarded a French literary prize for overseas writers. He continued his literary activity in the next few years, publishing a collection of poems, *Rhythmes du Khalam*, in 1956. But for some years he was preoccupied with politics and journalism. From 1952 to 1957 he edited the newspaper *le Phare du Sénégal*, and in 1953 he founded *Bingo*, a popular magazine for Francophone Africa. In 1956 he joined the *Parti Sénégalais de l'Action Socialiste* of Lamine Gueye (q.v.), but then he joined Senghor's *Bloc Démocratique Sénégalais* (BDS) on its foundation, and became editor of the BDS newspaper *le Regroupement*.

He was elected a BDS member of the Senegal Assembly in 1958 and then entered the government headed by Senghor, following the attainment of full self-government within the French Community. In 1959 he became Senegal's representative in the Senate of the French Community. But the Community was formally dissolved after the independence of most French African colonies (including the Mali Federation, from which Senegal broke off to become independent on its own) in 1960 deprived it of any meaning it had had.

In 1959-60 Soce Diop (he used both names in politics) was Assistant Secretary of Senghor's party, then renamed the *Union Progressiste Sénégalaise* (UPS). In 1960 he was appointed Ambassador of the newly independent state to the USA and the UN. In 1968, however, approaching blindness forced him to return to his home town of Rufisque.

He published a famous work, *Contes et Légendes de l'Afrique Noire*, in 1962, and a new edition of *Rhythmes du Khalam* in the same year. *Mirages de Paris* was republished in 1965. Ousmane Soce was one of the leading literary figures in Senegal and in French-speaking Africa until his death in Dakar on 26 October 1973. He is also held in high esteem for his contribution to the evolution of Senegal's politics. ■

Soga, T. (1829-71)

SOGA, Tiyo (1829-71).

SOUTH AFRICAN writer, also well known for his work with the Scottish mission. Tiyo Soga was, most likely, the first African missionary, and could have been the inspiration for Reverend John Laputa in the novel *Prester John*. He was a man of two worlds, an African who believed that his people, the Xhosas, had to be "civilised to enable them to be converted to Christianity". He was a missionary of the old school that was prepared to sacrifice their lives to convert the "natives". Late in life Tiyo Soga also preached Black Consciousness.

He was born in the eastern frontier of the Cape Colony in South Africa. This was a period of frontier wars when the Xhosas were resisting the encroachment of white settlers and suspicious of the motives of the missionaries who were widely regarded as agents of the colonial government.

Tiyo Soga was born into an enlightened family. His father sent him to Tyhume Mission school, later known as Lovedale College, which was run by the Glasgow Missionary Society. This was a multi-racial school and all the pupils were children of missionaries. In 1846 his education was interrupted by a frontier war. The principal of the school resigned and returned to Scotland with young Tiyo. Four years later he was baptised and returned to South Africa. He joined the staff of the Tyhume School for a brief period, then transferred to Uniondale where his Christian zeal and loyalty to the colonial government made him extremely unpopular with the people. His life was threatened and he had to flee to Grahamstown. He was persuaded, against his father's wishes, to return to Scotland.

He studied theology at Glasgow University. He was in great demand as a speaker. It was during this period that he experienced racial prejudice in Scotland. This was most likely the seed that was to blossom in his ideas in later life. In 1856 he was ordained a minister of the Presbyterian Church. By this time he was suffering from tuberculosis, which was to be the ultimate cause of his death.

T. Soga

A year later he married a Scots girl, Janet Burnside, and returned to South Africa with her. This shocked and disgusted the Whites, and confused his fellow Africans. But there was still no reconciliation between him and his people, who were now even more convinced that he was a missionary like all the other White missionaries and was part of their machinations.

In 1860 Prince Alfred and the Governor of the Cape Colony visited his mission and were so impressed with him that they invited him to join the royal party to Cape Town. Tiyo Soga was always loyal to the Crown and Colony.

Later in life Tiyo devoted a great deal of his time to writing. In 1866 he translated *The Pilgrim's Progress* into his native Xhosa. He was on the board that was revising the Xhosa Bible. He also felt it was his duty to record Xhosa fables, proverbs and customs, and the genealogy of Xhosa chiefs. But his most gratifying task was writing hymns, which are still used in South Africa.

His most important political contribution was an article he wrote for a newspaper on pride of colour, race and history. To his children he said: "For your own sakes, never appear ashamed that your father was a Kaffir (Black man), and that you inherited African blood. It is every bit as good and as pure as that which flows in the veins of my fairer brethren."

His children all grew up to be dedicated missionaries like their father after their Scottish education. Soga died in 1871. ■

Soglo, C. (1909-83)

SOGLO, General Christophe (1909-83).

BENINESE soldier and politician, leader of three successful coups, and President between 1965-67. Soglo, who was born on 28 June 1909 at Abomey, capital of the Zou Departement (administrative region), had started his military career in 1931 when he joined the French Army. During the Second World War, he was a sub-lieutenant in Morocco, and also in Corsica and France. After the war he was promoted lieutenant and appointed military adviser to the Minister for French Overseas Territories. He later became captain and, in 1956, received the Croix de Guerre for bravery during the Franco-Indochina War. Promoted major and posted to Senegal, Christophe Soglo returned home in 1960 when his country became independent. His first appointment in the new Republic of Dahomey, as Benin was known until November 1975, was as military adviser to President Hubert Maga, and in 1961 he was promoted lieutenant-colonel and appointed chief of staff of the newly formed Dahomeyan Armed Forces. President Maga's régime gradually lost popularity, not least because of high-cost prestige projects alongside austerity measures for the ordinary man; unrest grew and there were a number of trade union and student demonstrations and a general strike in the southern part of the country in October 1963. Soglo, as chief of staff, staged a successful and bloodless coup on 23 October 1963.

Initially he tried to hand over power to a triumvirate of the three leading politicians – Maga, Apithy and Ahomadegbé – but this failed because of the unpopularity of Maga, who was then placed under house arrest. Soglo acted as temporary head of state while he arranged elections that brought Apithy (q.v.) to power in January 1964, with Ahomadegbé as vice-president and prime minister.

Returning to his regular army duties, Soglo was promoted general in February 1964. However the uneasy alliance of the two political leaders he had handed over to lasted less than two years. By the middle of 1965 unrest was once again growing, and demonstrations and disturbances were finally sparked off by a disagreement between Apithy and Ahomadegbé over who had the constitutional right to appoint Supreme Court personnel. As violence grew between supporters of the two leaders, Ahomadegbé, ignoring Soglo, appealed directly to his supporters in the army to deal with Apithy's followers. Soglo intervened and removed both Apithy and Ahomadegbé from office on 29 November 1965.

He initially asked the President of the National Assembly, Tahiru Congacou, to form a new government, but finally staged a third coup on 25 December 1965, when Congacou was unable to form a viable government reflecting the ethnic and political situation in the country. This time Soglo retained power and became head of state.

Gen. C. Soglo

Soglo aimed to change the nature of post-independence politics, which he felt were centred around personalities rather than political programmes. His was a government of technical experts and soldiers. He published a five-year development programme early in 1966 and instituted austerity measures. As part of the development plan, operation "Return to the Fields" was launched to boost agricultural production during 1966, with Soglo and some of his ministers joining the farmers in the fields. Likewise when the "Operation Roads and Bridges" campaign was instituted, Soglo joined in the efforts to show an example of hard work creating results.

Despite these efforts, Soglo failed to alleviate the financial and economic problems of the country, and the austerity measures became increasingly unpopular with the people. Although political activity was formally banned, the trade union movement was active. By the end of 1967 growing unrest in the towns, and a strike threat forced Soglo to revoke a decree limiting that his administration was becoming "unmilitary" and corrupt, and on 17 December 1967, Soglo's régime was overthrown by young fellow army officers led by Major Kouandété, and Soglo had to leave and go into exile to France. After the December 1969 coup, however, he was able to return home, which he did in 1970.

He lived quietly in retirement until his death on 7 October 1983, at the age of 74. ■

Soilih, A. (1938-78)

SOILIH, Ali (1938-78).

COMORO statesman and its President. He was born in 1938 in Madagascar, then governed jointly with the Comoro Islands by France; the Comoros were separated from Madagascar in 1946. He studied at the Institute of Agriculture in Madagascar and later at the Institute of Tropical Agronomy at Nogent in France, where he qualified as an agronomist. Soilih entered politics in 1968 as a deputy in the Comoros Assembly and a member of the

Umma party which was part of the National United Front (FNU). Between 1970 and 1972 he served in the government of President Prince Said Ibrahim as Minister of Public Works.

Early in 1972 the Comoros Democratic Union (UDC), the Comoros People's Democratic Rally (RDPC) and the Comoros Demo-

A. Soilih

cratic Rally (RDC) made a joint demand for independence. The Umma party to which Soilih belonged called for a compromise with France and was defeated in the referendum that was conducted on the issue of independence. The history of the Comoro Islands was to centre on the problem of Mayotte in years to come as well as on the ethnic composition of the islands whose people are derived from a complex of Polynesian, African, Arab, Dutch, French, Chinese and Indian origins.

When it became apparent that France was about to organise separate referenda for different islands and to call a constitutional conference, Ahmed Abdallah (q.v.), the islands' leader, unilaterally declared inde-

pendence from France on 6 July 1975. In
August Ali Soilih staged a coup against
Abdalla and announced his intention to seek
a compromise with Mayotte. Prince Said
Mohammed Jaffar was made President and
because of his central role in the uprising,
Ali Soilih became Minister of Defence and of
the Interior.

On 21 November Soilih led an unarmed landing on Mayotte but had to call it
off owing to the opposition on the island. All
French property in the other three Comoro
Islands was nationalised and French officials
expelled. In January 1976 Soilih was elected
President of Comoro Islands.

While France conducted a referendum on Mayotte in February, Soilih applied
revolutionary reforms in the independent
Comoros. The civil service was dismantled,
all French records publicly burned, and old
ministries abolished, to be replaced by only
three departments attached to the
presidency.

The country was declared a "democratic secular socialist republic". The central
feature of Soilih's policies was the new local
administration called the *"Mudiria"* – small
units economically self-sufficient with three
or four villages of 6,000 people. These were
intended to be the nuclei of all essential
services such as grocery stores, government
offices, electricity generators, law courts,
telephone exchanges, and so on. Each citizen
was given a parcel of land on which to farm.
The creation of the new ruling groups owed
little to foreign influence. The most notable
of these groups were the *"mudirs"*, consisting of local chiefs, students and youths who
were given the main administrative tasks
and were also responsible for internal
security.

Soilih's hope of changing the thinking
of the people from what he called colonial
and feudal attitudes in two years proved to
be a gigantic task. Although proclaiming his
adherence to Islam, Soilih attempted to
eliminate some of its aspects, such as the veil
and "Grand Marriages".

A bad harvest in 1977 caused many
shortages, and created a crisis which the
opposition tried to exploit. Soilih had survived four coup attempts in his four year
rule. In May the opposition secured the
support of Belgian, French and German
mercenaries led by the notorious ex-
Congo, ex-Biafra mercenary Colonel Bob
Denard.

Soilih was overthrown on 13 May 1978
and placed under house arrest. He was shot
dead on 29 May 1978 for allegedly trying to
escape. ■

Sokambi, R. (died 1957)

SOKAMBI, Chief Raymond (died 1957).

CENTRAL AFRICAN REPUBLIC paramount chief. He ruled over the Banziri
people from 1912, when he was appointed by
the French who had recently included the
territory of the Banziris and their neighbours
the Langbassis and Yakpas in their colony
of Ubangi-Shari (now Central African
Republic). According to traditional accounts, he was born south of the Ubangi
River, in what became the Belgian Congo
(Zaire), but later went north to his mother's
home country around Kouango, north of the
Ubangi. "Because he was a courageous man,
the first Portuguese merchants noticed him
and hired him as an assistant. There Sokambi sold cloth and beads which his boss
entrusted to him, in exchange for rubber.
After the departure of these Portuguese,
who went from place to place to buy rubber,
Sokambi remained and went to build his
village not far from that of his uncle's on the
Gbabiti near the Ouaka river" (B. Weinstein, *Eboué*).

Wild rubber was the main product
attracting the Europeans in that area then.
After the Portuguese and other small
traders, large concessionary companies appeared with official help, in Ubangi-Shari as
in Middle Congo and also across the Ubangi
in the pre-1908 "Congo Free State." These
companies were given full rights over wild
rubber and allowed to force the Africans, by
all possible means, to find it. The *Compagnie
du Kouango Français* (CKF) was one such
company in the Banziri people's area. Sokambi helped it obtain rubber and ivory, and
also assisted in the recruitment of canoe
paddlers for the French administration.
These services were rewarded by his appointment as chief.

Two years later Félix Eboué became
the French administrator at Kouango, and
collaborated with Sokambi to enforce

French rule. Sokambi became a personal friend of Eboué, who was from French Guiana and was to become famous as Governor-General of French Equatorial Africa (including Ubangi-Shari) from 1941 to 1944. Eboué, praised by some French people as an exemplary "Black Frenchman", preferred to work with chiefs like Sokambi, in a kind of French "indirect rule" during his services to the French Colonial Administration.

Eboué and Sokambi worked to enforce one of the most oppressive colonial regimes in all Africa. They suppressed a rising by the Langbassis in 1915. Sokambi, who once saved Eboué's life, was made ruler over the Langbassis and Yakpas as well as his own people. He was allowed to have a modern rifle and helped to build a solid house. Sokambi, to whom Eboué had handed over captured rebels in 1915, was later suspected by another French official of slave-trading, and the Governor of Ubangi-Shari was concerned over the power given him. Sokambi helped Eboué collect taxes. Taxation and forcible rubber collection caused extreme suffering. In 1917 an epidemic among the Langbassis was attributed to starvation due to the rubber collection, which was suspended for a time.

About 1920 Sokambi's power extended even further, during a temporary shortage of French staff he actually ran Kouango subdivision. By trading and hunting he angered the CKF, but Eboué though at Bambari, defended him. He later helped Sokambi's oldest sons receive a French education in the colony.

As a loyal servant of the French, Sokambi, though allowed more power than most chiefs in French Africa, retained his chieftaincy and power until his death in 1957. His family remain important in the CAR.■

Sokoine, E.M. (1938-84)

SOKOINE, Edward Moringe (1938-84).

TANZANIAN politician who was his country's Prime Minister for seven years. He was noted for his hard work and his intolerance of laxity and laziness and his period of office was marked by major administrative structural changes in an effort to achieve greater efficiency and improve performance.

Born in 1938 in Monduli, a district town in Tanzania's northern Arusha Region. He attended Monduli Primary School and Umbwe Secondary School before joining the Mzumbe Local Government Training School in Morogoro, about 120 miles from Dar es Salaam, along the country's Central Line railway.

His first job was as administrative officer in Masasi, southern Tanzania. A respected member of his ethnic group, the famous Masai, Sokoine was conferred the title "Haingwanani" or elder of the Kisongo area. Part of his early government service included a brief period as executive officer with the Masai District Council, in which post his background as a Masai proved invaluable.

Sokoine joined the Tanganyika National Union (TANU) in its early days and along with Julius Nyerere, Tanganyika's first prime minister, played a prominent role in the struggle for independence which was attained in 1961.

In 1965 he was elected Member of Parliament for Monduli. Two years later he was appointed Parliamentary Secretary in the Ministry of Commerce, Transport and Labour as well as Chairman of the Transport Licensing Authority. One of his briefs as Parliamentary Secretary was to negotiate with the Chinese for the construction of the Tanzania-Zambia railway (now completed and functioning), a job he carried out with patience and dedication.

Sokoine's great capacity for sustained hard work became known, and he quickly rose to cabinet rank after serving from 1970 to 1972 as Minister of State in the Vice-President's Office. In 1972 he was appointed Minister of Defence and National Service, a portfolio he held until 1977. During that period there was a concerted programme to both politicize and expand the Armed Forces. Sokoine's plain speaking and his direct approach to problems made him very popular with the men in the forces. When in 1977 TANU became *Chama cha Mapinduzi* (CCM) Sokoine continued to hold high office in it.

It was partly his outstanding performance as Minister of Defence and National Service and partly his honesty and sense of

E. Sokoine

death, the then President Julius Nyerere decided to implement most of Sokoine's recommendations. Nyerere's successor, President Ali Hassan Mwinyi, served notice to inefficient government managers that they either shape up or go. Sokoine had, before him, threatened to sack half of the civil servants unless they improved their efficiency.

Unfortunately, Sokoine's career was cut short when he was killed in a car accident in April 1984 while travelling from Dodoma, Tanzania's proposed new capital, to Dar es Salaam. He was also at the time of his death Secretary of the powerful Defence Committee of the National Executive Committee of the ruling and only political party of Tanzania, *Chama cha Mapinduzi* (Revolutionary Party). It was widely believed that he would have succeeded Julius Nyerere as President of the United Republic of Tanzania, a post for which many Tanzanians believed Nyerere was grooming him. ∎

purpose that singled him out as next in line for the job of Prime Minister in 1977. His premiership was a period marked by radical change in the attitude towards work by members of the Civil Service and state organizations. Sokoine soon became known variously as "the Action Man" or "No-nonsense" Prime Minister. He insisted on hard work and accountability. It was not unusual during that time for ministers to work until the early hours of the morning.

It was when he was Prime Minister that the government embarked on an ambitious campaign against corruption and black marketeering. In the police round-up of suspects that followed, a number of prominent politicians were detained. Sokoine resisted strong official pressure to treat these politicians on a preferential basis, and his contempt at attempts by senior government officials to pervert the cause of justice in these cases endeared him greatly to the people.

Again as Prime Minister, he fought very hard to slim down and streamline the Civil Service and to do away with loss-making parastatal organizations, a fight which he won posthumously when, after his

---

Solanke, L. (c. 1880-1958)

SOLANKE, Ladipo (c. 1880-1958).

NIGERIAN lawyer and nationalist, famous as the founder and leading figure of the West African Students' Union (WASU) in Britain. He was born at Abeokuta at a date variously given as 1880 or 1884. He went to Ake Primary School in Abeokuta and then to the celebrated Fourah Bay College in Sierra Leone, where he was awarded the BA of Durham University (England). In 1917 he began teaching at the Leopold Educational Institution in Freetown. Then, in 1922, he went to Britain, where he was to spend most of the rest of his life.

He studied law at London and qualified, and also gave Yoruba lessons at the School of Oriental Studies (now School of Oriental and African Studies). Although a qualified lawyer he devoted the rest of his life to a new student organisation founded through his initiative on 7 August 1925, and named the West African Students' Union (WASU). It was the biggest and most lasting and influential of the groups formed by the West African students who had been going to Britain in considerable numbers since the 1870s. One other, the Nigerian Progress Union, was founded by Solanke only a year earlier, in 1924, but was then replaced by WASU, as were the Union for Students of African Descent, founded in 1917, and the Gold Coast Students' Association. WASU was later opened to other African students besides West Africans, but it was mainly a body for English-speaking students from the West Coast.

The importance of WASU in the political development of British-ruled West Africa was immense. Through it the students from there in Britain, much fewer then than now, could meet and discuss all sorts of issues, and have some early political experience. While Solanke remained honorary secretary and later General Secretary, other posts in the union executive changed hands frequently, so that many leading figures in West Africa held office in WASU in their student days. WASU published a magazine reflecting the ideas of these students and future leaders. From the start its tone was critical of colonial rule, though the criticism was at first combined with expressions of loyalty as was normal then. It aimed at ultimate freedom and unity, and also sought to change the Europeans' attitude to educated Africans, something closely affecting the elite whose sons ran WASU.

J.E. Casely-Hayford (q.v.), whose ideas WASU followed to some extent, was one of the first patrons. Other prominent Africans supported the union. In 1929 Solanke set out on a tour which eventually lasted three years, to publicise WASU and raise funds for a students' hostel. He travelled all over British-ruled West Africa and was favourably received. In 1932 he returned to London with about £600 net of travel expenses. On 1 January WASU opened its hostel at 62 Camden Road. The matron was Olu Obiasanya, who became Solanke's wife.

The hostel's rent was high and WASU proceeded to raise funds to buy property for a new one. Companies such as United Africa Company (UAC) and Elder Dempster contributed; as did the Oni of Ife, the Alake of Abeokuta, and the Asantehene. In 1937 the Colonial Office, after initial reluctance, agreed to make a contribution for the hostel. The British administration in Nigeria sent money later. On 1 June 1938 the WASU hostel moved to its new freehold site at 1

L. Solanke

South Villas, Camden Square, it was called Africa House.

While Solanke won official approval for his efforts for the West African students, WASU was wholly independent in its policy and contacts. Its house was a centre of activity for Africans in London, and others such as Marcus Garvey and Paul Robeson prominent personalities of Africans in the diaspora in the West Indies and United States. For a time Solanke had links with left-wing anti-colonial activity. Solanke and WASU were well-known for nearly two and a half decades to all Africans and people concerned with Africa in Britain; for years many Labour politicians like Reginald Sorensen were closely linked with WASU, and outside London there were many active WASU branches.

In the 1940s WASU had an important role in the rise of nationalism, sending many resolutions to the British government. In 1944-45 Solanke, who was Warden of Africa House, made another publicity tour of West Africa, leaving his countryman H.O. Davies as Acting Warden.

Ladipo Solanke lived to see the progress of British West Africa in the direction of independence, which Ghana achieved in 1957; and the great increase in the numbers of West African students in Britain in the 1950s. Eventually WASU lost its relative importance with that swelling of numbers; its heyday had been when the students were fewer and knew each other. But Solanke remained a well-known and popular figure until his death on 2 September 1958, and his funeral at the Great Northern London Cemetery was attended by many prominent members of the black community.■

Somé, Y.G. (died 1983)

SOME, Colonel Yorian Gabriel (died 1983).

BURKINABE politician, former Chief of Staff and Minister of Defence. After the independence of Burkina Faso (known as Upper Volta until 1984), Somé became a very influential member of the government and the armed forces. He held important ministerial and other government posts, and during the régime of Major Jean-Baptiste Ouedraogo, he was the second most powerful man in the country. With his reputation for integrity, strength and patriotism, Somé weathered the storms of a succession of governments.

During the Mali Federation of Senegal, Mali and Upper Volta, Somé, a veteran of the French army, represented the Diébougou area in the Territorial Assembly from 1957 to 1959. Upper Volta seceded from the Federation in 1959 and in 1960 became independent. Soon after, the then President Maurice Yaméogo came under considerable opposition, and the army assumed power on 3 January 1966. Colonel Somé, one of the leaders of this coup, was instrumental in the establishment of General Sangoulé Lamizana, who was Head of the Armed Forces, as Head of State. He himself became a member of the Supreme Council of the Armed Forces in a government which was two thirds military and one third civilian. However, in 1974, Lamizana dismissed all the civilians after the army had declared them incapable, and formed a Government of Reconstruction which was military. Somé had been Minister of the Interior and Security from 1971 to 1973, a post which he again occupied from 1976 until 1978.

In 1977, after a new constitution was drawn up, Lamizana resigned from the army and stood for President. He was elected in June 1978, but on 24 November of that same year, he was overthrown by the army. The former military Foreign Minister Colonel Sayé Zerbo led the coup and with thirty-one other officers, Somé amongst them, formed the Military Committee for National Recovery and Progress. Six months later Somé was appointed Chief of the Armed Forces.

Colonel Zerbo himself was overthrown in a near bloodless coup led by Captain Thomas Sankara in November 1982, but that was not the end of Somé's political career. Major Jean-Baptiste Ouedraogo became the new Head of State, and Somé, Chief of Staff and Secretary-General for National Defence, was the President's closest adviser. Many believed him to be the real source of power in the Ouedraogo government. Captain Sankara, who had had to stand down from his post of Secretary of State for Information in Colonel Zerbo's régime, became Prime Minister. But after only three months as Prime Minister, Sankara was dismissed by the President, a move which, it had been suggested, was the work of Colonel Somé.

In August 1983, Captain Sankara organised and led a coup against Ouedraogo. Sankara, who called his coup a "revolution to restore dignity to the people", is said to

Col. Y.G. Somé

have believed both Ouedraogo and the pro-Western Somé to be reactionaries. Somé was placed under house arrest outside the capital Ouagadougou. Members of the armed forces still loyal to him rescued him a few days later, and he led them on a march to the capital. In an exchange of fire with forces supporting the Sankara coup, Somé was accidentally shot and killed. Despite their conflict, Captain Sankara is said to have been dismayed when he heard of his death. ■

Sontonga, E. (died 1897)

SONTONGA, Enoch (died 1897).

SOUTH AFRICAN teacher and music composer who wrote Nkosi Sikelel I Afrika (God Bless Africa), which has become accepted as the national anthem of the nationalist organisations in South Africa. Nkosi Sikelel I Afrika is also, with local variations, the national anthem of Tanzania and Zambia.

Sontonga was a member of the Mpinga ethnic community among the Tembu group in the Witwatersrand. Like other Africans of his time who went to school, he was educated at Mission institutions. He later took to teaching, working in a Methodist Mission school in one of the so-called Bantu townships around Johannesburg. Nancefield, where he was teaching, is among the many of the Bantu townships that were established during the last quarter of the 19th century in the wake of the combined British and Boer conquest of South Africa after many years of protracted African resistance. Subdued by the superior military power of the Europeans, the Africans came under settler paramountcy, with over 87 per cent of the arable and mineral-rich lands passing to European ownership. The Africans, at best, were relocated to new, hostile settlements and, at worse, forced to become landless helots.

Sontonga grew up and was educated during this period and, as such, could not have escaped the devastating effects of the racist measures of the settlers. As indicated by the words, Nkosi Sikelel I Afrika, composed in 1897, was an expression of the despair felt by the Africans. "The composition was inspired by a depressed heart, and the refrain testifies to a somewhat melancholy strain. The black folk around Johannesburg were, at the time, far from happy, by reasons of straightened circumstances and because they felt they were not getting a square deal from the powers that be", wrote Davidson Don Tengo Jabavu (q.v.), the South African educationist, in 1934.

Sontonga wrote the music and the first stanza, the last seven being written in 1927 by the Xhosa poet, Samuel Edward Krune Mqhayi (q.v.). The piece was at first sung in African schools but was later introduced to a wider audience by the Ohlange Zulu Choir. In 1899, two years after Sontonga had died, Nkosi Sikelel I Afrika was

E. Sontonga

given its first public professional performance during the ordination of an African,
Reverend M. Boweni, as a Methodist minister in Johannesburg. According to D.D.T.
Jabavu, "When the African National Congress (ANC) flourished its leaders adopted
this piece as a closing anthem for their
meetings and this soon became a custom. Of
late the black races have somehow by tacit
assent adopted it as their recognised anthem,
sung before Royalty and on big public
occasions".■

Stevens, S. P. (1905-88)

STEVENS, Siaka Probyn (1905-88).

SIERRA LEONEAN politician who for 17
years was one of the dominant personalities in his country's politics, first as Prime
Minister from 1968 to 1971 and then as
President from 1971 to 1985. A staunch
advocate of African unity and non-alignment, he made significant contributions to
the OAU and the Non-Aligned Movement.

Siaka Stevens, known as "Shaki", was
born on 24 August 1905, according to official
reckoning, in Moyamba District, son of a Vai
mother and a Limba father, a sergeant in the
Royal West African Frontier Force. He
attended the Albert Academy in Freetown
and joined the police in 1923 rising to the
rank of sergeant-major while serving with
the Court Messenger Force, the main police
force in the then Sierra Leone Protectorate
under British rule. In 1930 he obtained a job
on the construction of the new railway from
the Marampa iron ore mines of the Sierra
Leone Development Co. (Delco) to the terminal at Pepel, and was later promoted station
master.

His job with Delco led him into trade
unionism, in which he was prominent for
years and which paved his way into nationalism and politics. He became fully involved,
and later full-time secretary of the Marampa
Mineworkers Union. When this was merged
with other mine unions to form the United
Mineworkers Union, Stevens became its
secretary-general and was identified as a
leader of the workers. He also served as a
district and city councillor, and in 1945 he

was appointed to the new Protectorate
Assembly, set up by the British, as a workers'
representative. He spent nine months in
Britain at Ruskin College, Oxford, studying
industrial relations, in 1947.

Stevens went into politics as a
founder member of the Sierra Leone Organi-

S. Stevens

sation Society, which merged with the
People's Party in 1951 to form the Sierra
Leone People's Party (SLPP) with Sir Milton
Margai (q.v.) as the leader. He was elected to
the Legislative Council in the 1951 elections,
which were won by the SLPP. In 1953 he
became minister of Lands, Mines and Labour. He was re-elected to the Council in
1957 but was unseated by an election petition. Then he left the SLPP to join the
People's National Party (PNP) and became
its deputy leader.

When all the parties, including the
PNP, formed a United Front to negotiate on
independence from Britain, Stevens was
chosen as a member of the Front's delegation
in 1960 to the Constitutional Conference in
London. He objected to decisions taken there
and said the SLPP government of Sir Milton
Margai was unrepresentative, and demanded fresh elections before independence. He
refused to sign the Conference report, was

expelled from the PNP and went to form the Elections Before Independence Movement (EBIM), which, in May 1960, became the All People's Congress (APC). Stevens spent independence day, 27 April 1961, in prison, but a sentence passed for libel and conspiracy was quashed on appeal. In 1962, when Sir Milton called elections, the APC and its ally the Progressive Independence Movement won 14 seats, the independents 14 and the SLPP 28. Stevens led the opposition as leader of the APC, and vigorously denounced the government headed by Sir Milton and, after his death in 1964, by his brother Sir Albert Margai (q.v.). Siaka Stevens was Mayor of Freetown in 1964-65.

In new elections on 17 March 1967 the APC won a majority; the Governor-General appointed Stevens as prime minister, but the commander of the Sierra Leone Military Force, Brigadier David Lansana, intervened to stop him taking over the government. The military officers then took power and formed a National Reformation Council (NRC). Stevens went to Britain and then to Guinea, where he prepared to return home, while in Sierra Leone an inquiry found that the APC had indeed won the elections. In April 1968 junior officers and common soldiers overthrew the NRC, and Siaka Stevens returned in triumph to take over as prime minister and form a government on the basis of the 1967 election results.

After a brief coalition between the SLPP and APC, the APC ruled alone. Tension between SLPP and APC supporters, led to a state of emergency in 1970, while a new opposition party, the United Democratic Party, formed in 1970 was soon banned. After an unsuccessful coup attempt on 23 March 1971, Stevens' government introduced a Republican constitution; on 21 April 1971 he was sworn in as the country's first Executive President.

In the succeeding years there continued to be uneasiness in the country, which led the SLPP to boycott the elections in 1973; and after a bomb explosion in 1974 at the home of C. Kamara-Taylor (q.v.), one of Stevens' closest colleagues, a number of people were detained and those found guilty of treason were hanged in 1975. The 1977 elections were fiercely contested. In 1978 Sierra Leone was turned into a one-party state under the banner of the APC. Stevens remained President of State.

There developed a large personality cult of "Pa Shaki", and as the years went by, he became gradually alienated from his trade union beginnings. Opposition, however, continued and showed itself in sporadic student demonstrations and other protests, while Stevens became preoccupied with consolidating his personal position and power. To this end he used his mixed ethnic background, and came to rely on a small group of people close to him. In the meantime Sierra Leone underwent difficult economic conditions which resulted in a general strike in 1981.

In 1980 the OAU summit was held in Freetown and as OAU chairman for the year, Siaka Stevens played a prominent role in African affairs.

After elections with one party but several candidates, in 1982, the question of succession to the ageing Stevens was a subject of speculation for years. Eventually his term of office, expiring in June 1985, was extended by six months, but then, in October 1985, he finally retired. He handed over power to the armed forces commander, Brigadier Joseph Momoh. Siaka Stevens still retained some influence, but gradually his successor distanced himself from him. He died on 28 May 1988. He had a wife, Rebecca, and several children, including some sons active in politics.∎

Sukati, M. (1910-77)

SUKATI, Msindazwe (1910-77).

SWAZI educationist and diplomat. He was born on 11 June 1910 at Zabeni Royal Village, Manzini district, Swaziland, and was educated at Zambode National School, Swaziland and the Lovedale Institute, Alice, Cape Province, South Africa. Then he went to University College of Fort Hare in South Africa, becoming the first person from Swaziland to obtain a matriculation certificate in 1932.

Three years later, he became a revenue clerk at Mankaiana and continued his studies, obtaining a BA degree from the University of South Africa in 1940. In 1950 he was appointed administrative officer and later establishment officer. Before becoming clerk to the Legislative Council, 1965-67, he had worked as an aide de camp to King Sobhuza II and had participated in the 1963 London Constitutional discussions preceding Swaziland's independence. Later he was appointed Speaker of the first session of Parliament under the self-government Constitution on 8 May 1967.

M. Sukati

In 1968 Sukati was honoured by the University of Botswana, Lesotho and Swaziland, which conferred on him an honorary LLD. That same year, following Swaziland's independence, he was appointed Ambassador to the USA and later Swaziland's Ambassador's to Mozambique. The highly respected diplomat returned to his country in October 1973 and was made chairman of the National Industrial Development Corporation of Swaziland.

Sukati died in Mbabane in March 1977 and was survived by his wife and eight children. ■

Suluku, A. (c. 1820-1906)

SULUKU, Almamy (c.1820-1906).

SIERRA LEONEAN traditional ruler, the last independent ruler of Biriwa Limba, a chiefdom situated strategically on a trade-route in the centre of modern Sierra Leone. Born in about 1820, the second son of Sankailay who himself succeeded his father Hoseya as chief of the Biriwa Limba country, he was of the Limba Konte ancestry. As a young man Suluku trained in his father's army that was stationed in the headquarters of Biriwa, Bumban. He later rose to prominence as both a military commander (*kurugba*) and chief (*gbaku*) of the Biriwa dynasty, where his exploits and shrewd diplomacy in the relations with his neighbours and the Europeans marked him as a remarkable leader of his era.

Unlike his brothers, who were given important chiefdoms in the Biriwa country, Suluku (or Amadu as he was known before acquiring the nickname of "Suluku", meaning wolf) was assigned the task of organising the defence of the country. Thus he was a figure of central importance in the execution of his father's policies, which sought to extend and sustain Biriwa's political dominance over neighbouring countries. It was under Suluku that the Biriwa forces brought the Saffroko Limba and Loko kingdoms under the rule of Bumban, and such was the success of his military campaigns that by the end of the 1860s Suluku had almost eclipsed his father as a ruler.

He succeeded to the headship at his father's death in 1873, despite Sankailay's wish to be succeeded by his elder brother Bubu. As ruler he pursued his predecessor's expansionist policies, but, unlike his father, instituted a centralised administrative structure which allowed him a position of prominence in the affairs of the country. His innovatory measures included the setting up of a council of headmen and chiefs at his Bumban headquarters, which met as the governing body of Biriwa Limba, and of provincial capitals to which he appointed governors who were directly responsible to the *gbaku*. With this came the development of Biriwa's agriculture and trade that were the mainstay of the economy, bolstered by the taxes derived from transiting traders using this vital route between Falaba to the north and Freetown to the south of the country. Biriwa's prosperity was sustained until 1884 when the country was attacked and occupied by the powerful forces of Samory (q.v.).

The occupation lasted from October 1884 to March 1888 when, with the assistance of the British, Chief Suluku regained control of his country. His position, however, had not only been weakened by the occupation of the *sofas*, Samory's forces, but the entire kingdom had become subservient to Samory's empire and the British who were seeking to establish control over the region. To the former, Biriwa surrendered its sovereignty and suffered conversion to Islam; Chief Suluku himself became a Moslem, taking the religious title of Almamy in 1884, and sent his son Dekor for Koranic education at Futa Jallon. From the British, despite the earlier suspicion of Britain's intentions and the subsequent passive resistance to its establishment of colonial rule over Biriwa, Chief Suluku sought and got aid which was followed in 1888 with an Anglo-Biriwa treaty of friendship. He remained essentially co-operative with Britain though he was known to have given support to Bai Bureh (q.v.) in the 1898 struggle against the British. His own efforts to keep the British out of Biriwa through tactful diplomacy, which when viewed against the background of the raging armed resistance to European occupation in other West African empires gave the notion of appeasement, failed in 1896 when all the inland areas of modern Sierra Leone were declared a British Protectorate. His influence waned considerably from then, though he was allowed to remain head of the Biriwa chiefdom. He died in 1906. ■

R. Al-Suwayhili

coastal region of Misurata. When World War I broke out in July 1914 the Italian colonizers began to face difficulties in Libya. Their dependence on friendly native chiefs did not help because of nationalists like Ramadan al-Suwayhili. In June 1915 he lured the Italians into an attack against Sirte and inflicted a devastating defeat on them, capturing substantial munitions. This battle became known as the battle of al-Qurdabiya.

After this victory Suwayhili sought to extend his leadership over the whole of Tripolitania and challenged the authority of other Sanusi leaders. One of them, Safi al-Din, was defeated in a battle in 1916, and had to withdraw to Cyrenaica.

Suwayhili refused to accept the Grand Sanusi leadership and to cooperate in the formation of an army under the aegis of Sayyid Idris (q.v.). Instead, Suwayhili, with another leader Sayyid Murayyid, formed the Tripolitania Committee and asked permission from the British authorities to form a separate Tripolitanian Army. Suwayhili believed Sayyid Idris had misled his countrymen into fighting with Britain by not obtaining a definite pledge of independence beforehand, and for his alleged failure to consult the Joint Advisory Committee prior to his decision to collaborate with the British, and applying the term 'Sanusi' to all

Al-Suwayhili, R. (1881-1920)

AL-SUWAYHILI, Ramadan (1881-1920).

LIBYAN nationalist who was also known as al-Shutaywi, he was among the most prominent Tripolitanian leaders at the time of the Italian invasion. He also challenged Ottoman rule over his country from the those who desired to collaborate without prior agreement by them.

Although Italy was rapidly occupying the country by force, it was, however, difficult to control or subdue some of the people with strong leadership. Ramadan al-Suwayhili, whose force joined with that of the Sanusi leader, Sayyid Safi al-Din, launched an attack from Cyrenaica. During this period of unity between the Tripolitanian and Cyrenaican leaders the Italian forces made no headway.

Though the Treaty of Ouchy of 19 October 1912 ended the hostilities between Italy and Turkey, the resistance led by Sanusi guerillas went on for another decade. Ramadan al-Suwayhili refused to go into exile as the Italians gradually gained ground and continued to oppose the Italian occupiers and fought until together with many of his colleagues he died at the battle of Misurata at the age of 39. He was later interred in the cemetery of martyrs in Tripoli. ■

Swart, C.R. (1894-1981)

SWART, Charles Robberts (1894-1981).

SOUTH AFRICAN lawyer and politician; he was one of the architects of apartheid which he introduced as Minister of Justice in 1948. In 1961 he became South Africa's first State President, when in the face of opposition to the country's racial policies from the Commonwealth it withdrew from the organisation and became a republic.

He was born on 5 December 1894 at Morgenzen in the Orange Free State. After matriculating at the age of 13 he entered the University of the Orange Free State, Bloemfontein, from which he graduated with the BA and LL.B degrees. He then taught law for one year from 1917 at the University and in 1919 became an advocate of the Supreme Court. He had been called to the Orange Free State Bar in 1918, and in 1919 was appointed private secretary to General James B. M. Hertzog (q.v.).

Charles Swart was a South African steeped in the die-hard white South African nationalism which he had fiercely advocated

since the 1920s. He upheld white supremacy over the majority African population. He was a founding member of the Nationalist Party whose coming to power in 1948 gave him, as Minister of Justice, the responsibility for drafting and applying the tyrannical

C.R. Swart

laws of apartheid, built around the Group Areas Act of 1950. Also, as ministerial head of the Police Department, Swart introduced reforms which extended corporal punishment to a long list of offences, and piloted through Parliament the notorious Suppression of Communism Act and a revised Immorality Act that gave the government vast powers over the freedom of the citizen. In addition to the long series of security laws he, moreover, abolished South Africans' appeals to the Privy Council.

In ministerial office as well as in other State functions he continued to uphold policies that eventually led to the ostracisation of South Africa by the international community. When South Africa withdrew from the Commonwealth in 1961, Swart became the first President of the Republic on 10 May 1961, a post he occupied until 1967. Before that he had been the last Governor-

General of the Union of South Africa for the short time running up to the declaration of the republic.

Before then Swart had occupied other prominent positions; he was Minister of Justice from 1948 to 1949, Minister of Education, Arts and Science from 1949 to 1950, Deputy Prime Minister and Leader of the House of Assembly from 1954 to 1959, and acting Prime Minister when Dr Malan (q.v.) was absent for a few months in 1958. He later contested for the position of Prime Minister and leadership of the Nationalist Party and lost, but was made Governor-General in 1960 and Chancellor of the University of the Orange Free State from 1950 to 1976. Swart received several honorary degrees from South African universities. He was decorated with the Medal for Meritorious Service for South Africa in 1972, years after he had retired from active politics.

He died on 16 July 1981, aged 87.■

T

Taha, M.M. (died 1985)

TAHA, Mahmud Muhammad (died 1985).

SUDANESE politician who all his adult life was a consistent patriot and a passionate advocate of a liberal and humane Islam. He was opposed both to colonialism and to violence. His execution in January 1985 for "Heresy, rebellion against the Sharia [Islamic], incitement to hatred and advocating the violent overthrow of the [Nimeiri] Government" will be seen historically as one of the least justifiable actions of that military regime.

Taha first came to political prominence in the nineteen-forties when Sudanese nationalism was seeking to bring an end to British Administration of the Sudan. There were at the time many different parties advocating independence, and many different prescriptions for the methods by which it should be pursued, and for the sort of regime which should replace the British when they had been induced to depart. Taha advocated a non-violent approach and in 1945 he founded the Republican Party to pursue national liberation by non-violent means. It remained independent of other political parties or alliances and had no electoral success. It did achieve some acceptance among the more thoughtful members of the intelligentsia, however, and was represented in some all-party consultations such as the National Constitutional Committee of 1956.

Taha himself had been trained as an engineer, but he left his employment in 1948 to work full-time for the independence of his country. In the closing years of the British administration he suffered some harassment as a result. When Independence was achieved in 1956 Taha founded the *Ikhwan al Jamhuriyin*, the Republican Brothers' Party, devolving out of the Republican Party.

Taha saw the Sudan, having achieved its immediate goal of independence, as now needing to improve and develop its social structures in the context of a more modern and open Islam. Ever since the Turko-Egyptian period of rule in the Sudan during the nineteenth century, the rival Islamic parties of the *Khattmiya* and the *Ansari* (the followers of Muhammad Ahmad the Sudanese Mahdi (q.v.)), had had a great importance in the political as well as religious affairs of the Sudan. More recently the Muslim Brothers have pursued a stricter and more fundamentalist form of Islam. By contrast Taha advocated a more liberal Islam, with, for example, greater equality between men and women and a society more open in general to influence from the outside and the Western

M.M. Taha

world. While such an approach did gain some support from the more enlightened and educated segments of the Sudanese élite, especially in the capital Khartoum, it was not always so acceptable to the more traditionalist and powerful political and religious parties.

The period of the First Sudanese Republic following independence in 1956 was, however, brief. The considerable differences between the many civilian parties, religious orders and factions were brought to a summary end by the imposition of military rule by the Army in 1958. During the following six years, while the religious orders continued in existence, political parties as such were without any direct power. Taha himself concentrated his energies on Islamic reform and his movement emerged without a party-political organisation as such after Abboud and the military were overthrown in the Revolution of October 1964.

With the restoration of civilian government the multiple divisions of Sudanese political opinion became apparent once again, especially in the then long-enduring Civil War in the Southern part of the country. Even when tentative agreement was reached on the Southern problem, this was again put in jeopardy by moves towards an Islamic Constitution. Against this background Taha's publication in 1965 of a book inviting people to read the Koran in a new light, and his opposition to the imposition of Sharia Law, seemed a sensitive and intelligent attempt to present an Islam with a "human" face, a "faith" which would not antagonise the non-Muslim South or inhibit the "modernisation" of the North.

The Third Republic was also short-lived and the Fourth, "Democratic" Republic, came into being with a bloodless military coup in May 1969. Headed by a group of young radical officers calling themselves the Free Officers Movement (inspired by a similar movement in Egypt some years previously), the Army took power with considerable popular support and Nimeiri at the head, and once again civilian political parties were out of favour, even though again the religious orders survived. One source of politico-religious traditionalist opposition was overcome with the defeat of the leader of the Ansari, Al Hadi al Mahdi (q.v.), at Aba Island in 1970, and his subsequent death. Taha's movement continued to attract a number of followers, but for several years, though quietly active, was not so prominent.

In September 1983, however, when President Nimeiri introduced Sharia Law, Taha expressed his strong opposition to this course. He denounced Sharia as a "shameful law for Islam and humiliating for the Sudanese people". He thought that "limb cutting and flogging did not illustrate the true message of Islam". The introduction of Sharia was, in fact, contrary to everything he had been advocating for many years. He saw it as a retrograde step which would (as it did) antagonise the South and do nothing to modernise the North or improve relations between the Sudan and the outside world. He also strongly denounced corruption in the Army and among civil servants.

Taha was arrested in October 1983 and sent to Kober Central Prison, where he was allowed no visitors and no daily exercise. Freed on 19 December 1984, he continued to advocate the policies in which he believed, and addressed a meeting of several hundred students at the University of Khartoum the following day. He was re-arrested on 23 December and sent back to Kober. On 7 January 1985 he was tried with three other Republican Brothers and all were condemned to death by hanging. All Mahmud Muhammad Taha's books and writings were condemned to be burnt. Execution was postponed by the court for 30 days to allow the accused the time to repent and so perhaps avoid the death penalty, but on 17 January 1985 Nimeiri ordered Taha's immediate execution which was carried out the following day. ■

Taitu Betul (1853-1918)

TAITU BETUL, Empress (1853-1918).

WIFE of Emperor Menelik II (q.v.); in her own right she was an influential figure in Ethiopian politics and one of the most powerful women in Africa in her time. She had vast holdings to manage, an autonomous squad of palace staff to command and even a private army which she personally led in 1902 to put down a Tigre rising against her husband. Empress Taitu gave the name Addis Ababa (meaning 'new flower' in Amharic) to Ethiopia's capital which she influenced Menelik to establish in 1887.

She was born in 1853 at Gondar to a Semen noble family; her father was Dejazmatch Betul Haile Mariam and mother Woizero Yubdar. Taitu, whose baptismal name was Walatta Mikael, had a sister, Desta, and two brothers, Alula and Wele. All, by virtue of their noble birth, were given private education as was the practice of the nobility in feudal Ethiopia, and Taitu was as literate in Amharic as she was adept at Ge'ez literature.

In 1844 her brothers and Menelik, who was then a prince and heir apparent to the throne of Shoa, were imprisoned at Magdala by Emperor Tewodros II after overrunning Shoa province. The Prince escaped to Shoa in 1865 to later become Emperor and on 29 April 1883 married Taitu who was crowned Queen of Shoa. Both had been married several times before; Taitu was Menelik's third wife while he was the last of many husbands. Her former husbands included a general in Emperor Tewodros's army whom she married in 1866; a nobleman from the court of Emperor Yohannes IV (they were married in 1870); and a provincial governor whom she married twelve years later.

Through these associations Taitu gained great influence and valuable experience which she put to use during her husband's campaign for the emperorship of Ethiopia. That achieved, in 1889, she was sworn in as Empress of Ethiopia just two days after Menelik had been crowned on 3 November. Soon her influence grew even more. According to a study of her, Taitu had a strong influence on her husband, and was always at his side. She was "conversant with Ethiopian law, religious doctrine, and internal and foreign affairs. She did not share her husband's liberal attitude towards innovation, nor his interest in foreigners. Visitors and diplomats often found her hostile, though she frequently said she approved of the marriage customs of Europe. Her hostility to Italians was well founded, as the misunderstandings over the Treaty of Wichale concluded in 1889 between Ethiopia and Italy, resulted in the war of 1895-96, in which she put her own life in danger at the battles of Meqelle and Adwa".

Empress Taitu had no children by Menelik but she supervised the welfare of the children of the nobility who were brought up at the palace. In 1907 she was instrumental in the establishment of a mixed school for boys and girls in Addis Ababa. She also built the first hotel in the capital; she had had much to do with its establishment when Menelik decided on moving his headquarters from Entotto in 1887.

From 1906, following her husband's ill-health, the Empress became the most influential political figure in Ethiopia. By 1910, however, her authority had been undermined by the Council of Ministers created that year. She then left Addis Ababa for Entotto where she died on 11 February 1918. ■

Takawira, L. (1916-70)

TAKAWIRA, Leopold (1916-70).

ZIMBABWEAN politician and the first Vice-President of the Zimbabwe African National Union (ZANU) which he co-founded in 1963. He was born in 1916 at Chirumanzu, Zimbabwe. He was educated at primary schools in Salisbury and at Marianhill College in Natal, South Africa. After qualifying he worked for many years as a teacher and later as headmaster at Chipembere Government School in Highfield, Salisbury (Harare).

Takawira resigned from teaching to become the executive secretary of the Capricorn Africa Society, a multi-racial society consisting of educated members of all races. Later he resigned from this society and helped to found the National Democratic Party (NDP), which was formed to replace the banned African National Congress. Leopold Takawira became the NDP's Harare branch chairman and was arrested together with other nationalist leaders on 19 July 1960, under the Public Order and Unlawful Organisations Act. This arrest led to a demonstration of more than 7,000 people protesting against the arrests.

On 21 September 1960 Takawira was elected Acting President of NDP until the party congress in November 1960. He became the chief representative of NDP in London and Western Europe. Following the acceptance by the NDP delegation of the 1961 constitutional proposals, giving Africans 15 out of 65 seats, Takawira cabled a strongly worded condemnation of the acceptance. It read: "We totally reject the Southern Rhodesia Constitution arrangements as treacherous to the future of the three million Africans. Agreement is diabolical and disastrous. The outside world was shocked by NDP docile document." This telegram led to his suspension from the party. However, the

L. Takawira

NDP's position over the constitutional proposals was later reversed.

Takawira joined the Zimbabwe African People's Union (ZAPU) on its formation and became Secretary for External Affairs. During 1961 Takawira and others became disenchanted with the party's leadership. In April of 1962 the ZAPU executive moved to Tanganyika (now Tanzania) to form a government in exile. This was done to facilitate contact among the executive members and away from the harassment of the Rhodesian government. The move however was criticised by some executive members who saw

the party as deserting the people inside the country.

Later, Takawira and others who disagreed with the strategy of a government in exile, were accused of being rebels; this caused a serious split within ZAPU which led to the formation of a new party, ZANU, on 8 August 1963. Leopold Takawira became Vice-President and other executive members included Robert Mugabe as Secretary General, later first Prime Minister of Zimbabwe, and Herbert Chitepo (q.v.) as National Chairman.

Late in 1964 Takawira was detained. He was initially confined to Sikombela, but was later transferred, together with other ZANU leaders, to Salisbury Central Prison. Takawira's diabetic condition deteriorated in prison and many people believe that he was purposely left unattended because even in prison, he remained opposed to policies which did not guarantee majority rule. He died in 1970. ■

Tall, S.U. (c.1794-1864)

TALL, Al-Hajj Saidou Umar (c.1794-1864).

SENEGALESE religious reformer and military leader who founded a new state through a *jihad* (a war in the cause of Islam) in the Upper Senegal and Niger valleys. This state, one of several created by *jihads* in West Africa in the 19th century, lasted until the French colonial occupation in the 1880s and 1890s. In this history of Islam in West Africa Umar was also important for spreading the Tijaniyya school of Moslem belief and worship.

He was of the Tukulor (Toucouleur) people of Fouta Toro, on the bank of the Senegal river. Closely related to the Fulanis they were similarly prominent in Islam in all the savanna regions of West Africa. Early in the spread of Islam a clerical caste, the Torodbe (sing: Torodo), became prominent among the Tukulor, and spread Islam. Umar belonged to that caste.

Born at Halwar, Umar received an Islamic education and was already noted for his religious learning before setting out, about 1825, to make the Mecca Pilgrimage. After several years in Mecca and Medina, Umar returned, with the title al-Hajj, to West Africa, having joined the Tijaniyya brotherhood and been appointed its representative or Khalifa for the Western Soudan (as Europeans called the area around the

Saidou Umar Tall

Upper Senegal and Niger Valleys). The Tijani "way" of Islam, founded by the Algerian al-Tijani (1737-1815), brought a special approach to the religion and its observance and Umar may have joined it before his pilgrimage. On his return journey he stopped for six or seven years in Sokoto, capital of the new Islamic Caliphate then ruled by Muhammed Bello (q.v.), one of whose daughters he married.

He was also said to have married a Hausa woman who bore him his son Ahmadu. He left Sokoto a rich man with a large following, in 1838. He spent some months in Masina, another state created by a Fulani Moslem *jihad*; with its capital at Hamdallahi, it had defeated the neighbouring Bambaras of Ségou (in modern Mali). These were still Masina's enemies and they detained Umar when he passed through their country.

He returned to his home region, Fouta Toro, in 1840, but soon afterwards went south to Fouta Djallon. In that upland area, now in Guinea, another Islamic *jihad* led by

a Torodo Tukulor had created a Moslem state in the late 18th century. Umar was allowed to settle in that strongly Moslem country, and he established a *Zawiya* (a religious community of his disciples) at Dyegounko, near the capital, Timbo.

As a revered preacher, said to have a special blessing or *baraka*, Umar attracted many students. Besides teaching and writing several books on Islam, he was also a prosperous trader. He traded in gold dust and in arms and ammunition bought from European settlements and trading posts on the coast. His religious writings showed a concern to reform Islam and he believed that the whole of society must be based on that amended form of Islam. He believed that previous *jihads* and other efforts had not done enough, and that Tijaniyya belief and worship were superior to the Qadiriyya form prevalent in West Africa at the time.

When the Almamy of Fouta Djallon became suspicious of Umar's doctrines and his wealth and power, Umar left Dyegounko and went to Dinguiray where he established a military base and bought more arms. He prepared to fight a *jihad* against neighbouring states, with a considerable body of recruits of whom many were his countrymen from Fouta Toro. His military preparations alarmed rulers of states in the area. Tension led to clashes in 1851 and then open war in 1852, when Umar claimed to have had a vision in which he was told to begin his war against the "unbelievers". The occupation of Tamla and Merieng by the *jihad* forces in 1852-53 began the creation of Umar's new Moslem state.

Umar moved his base to Tamba, capital of Tamla, in 1854, but in succeeding years he accompanied his armies on campaigns which were initially directed northwards into the Upper Senegal Valley. The states in the area were affected by internal fighting and tensions which helped Umar to extend his control over their subjects and beyond to Fouta Toro. However, the French had reached that area through penetration up the river, on whose banks they had established forts, and they saw Umar as a rival for power in the area. Each sought to win over chiefs and to exploit local rivalries. Umar and his forces advanced in 1854 against Khasso, Bundu, later occupying Ka'arta, a state centred on Nioro.

In 1855 Sambala, a chief defeated by Umar, reached an agreement with the

French, under which the latter built a fort
on the river bank at Médine. In 1857 Sambala
and his people, and the French were besieged
by Umar's forces. The siege of Médine, a
celebrated episode in Al-Hajj Umar's campaign lasted from April to July 1857, when
the French governor of Senegal, Faidherbe,
led a relief force. The French did not want an
all-out war with Umar, but they continued
to help his African enemies. These were
many, for Umar was a conqueror whose
forces killed large numbers and regularly
destroyed villages.

In his native Fouta Toro which he had
reached by 1858, the Almamy opposed Umar.
Others also opposed him, and the Moors in
Ka'arta to the north (in modern Mauritania)
and the states of Ségou and Masina to the
east sent help to the forces resisting Umar.
However, he defeated them all in 1858.
Umar's forces were constantly replenished,
mainly by recruits from Fouta Toro and
Fouta Djallon, and by 1858, 40,000 people
from areas (now in Senegal) were believed to
have responded to a call to leave home and
join him. The troops had firearms of which
many were manufactured or repaired by
local blacksmiths.

These forces fought the French again
in late 1859 at Guémou, but then there were
proposals for peaceful relations in 1860, and
although a French delegation to Umar did
not leave Senegal until 1863, the two sides
largely left each other's spheres of influence
alone, while Umar turned his attention to
the east. He advanced to the Niger River
fighting the state of Ségou which, in response, reached an agreement with its enemy
Masina. Their forces were defeated by Umar
near Sansanding, early in 1861, and in March
of that year Umar occupied the Ségou
capital.

Everywhere he went, Umar promoted
Islam, and in Ségou he ordered the destruction of shrines of the traditional religion. In
1862 he went on to the conquest of Masina
itself. He entered the territory with his army
in late April and by mid-May had defeated
the ruler, Ahmadu, who was killed not long
afterwards, and occupied Hamdallahi. Thus
ended the Masina *jihad* state after about
forty years. Al-Hajj Umar's empire now
stretched over much of what is now the
western part of Mali.

However, wherever his forces conquered, resistance began again quickly, and
in May 1863 an uprising broke out in

occupied Masina led by two uncles of the late
ruler Ahmadu and by the scholar al-Bakkai
of Timbuctoo. The Tukulor forces found it
difficult to contain the rising. Finally, in
early February 1864, Umar escaped from
Hamdallahi to the Bandiagara cliffs, where
he and some others entered the cave of
N'Goro. Soldiers pursuing him lit a fire at
the entrance, and al-Hajj Umar, two of his
sons, and some military commanders died in
the blaze on 12 February 1864.

Umar left about fifty other children,
half of them sons, and this led to disputes
which made it difficult for his successor
Ahmadu to control the empire won by his
father. The Ségou Tukulor Empire was
precariously maintained, but it lasted until
the French occupation in 1890-93. However,
al-Hajj Umar's work in spreading Tijaniyya
Islam proved more lasting. It continued to be
spread by his descendants in Nigeria as well
as Senegal, and an outstanding leader was
Umar's grandson Seydou Nourou Tall
(q.v.)■

Tall, T.S.N. (1863-1980)

**TALL, Al-Hajj Thierno Seydou Nourou
(1863-1980).**

SENEGALESE religious leader. He was
born at Nioro to the family of al-Hajj
Umar Tall (q.v.) (died 1864), the famous
Tukulor scholar and warrior of the Tijaniyya Islamic Order. Umar occupied a large
empire in the Upper Niger and Senegal
valleys, ruled after his death by Ahmadu, one
of his sons by a daughter of Sultan Bello
of Sokoto (q.v.). Another son by the same
wife was the father of Nourou Tall, who became a spiritual successor of al-Hajj Umar
for the Tukulor Tijaniyya Moslems in Senegal itself.

Thierno Seydou Nourou Tall studied
at Kayes, Tivaouane, Boghe, St Louis and
other places. The combined effect of his
Islamic learning and his descent gave him
great influence over Senegal's Moslems.
Many of these were of the Tijaniyya group
based at Tivaouane. The Tijaniyya of Senegal were headed by al-Hajj Malick Sy (died
1923) and then Seydi Babacar Sy, his son

Al-Hajj T.S.N. Tall

(died 1957), and later the Khalifa-General, al-Hajj Abdoul Aziz Sy, while Nourou Tall was Grand Marabout of Dakar and "Spiritual Father of the holy family of the Tijaniyya." Seydou Nourou Tall's influence all over Senegal was due also to his leadership of a major ethnic group, the Tukulor, and their association, the *Union Générale des Originaires de la Vallée du Fleuve*, and to his generally co-operative attitude towards the French. In the 1920s and 30s, when Senegal was administered by France, he was often called upon to serve as mediator between the colonial government and marabouts or between different marabouts. He also travelled outside Senegal, throughout French-speaking Africa, at the government's request and expense, settling disputes and promoting larger plantations of groundnut for Western markets. In 1949 the French allowed him to visit troops in Cameroon and to preach to the Moslem soldiers among them. By 1957 he had been decorated 24 times for outstanding services, including the award of the *Légion d'Honneur* by the French.

In the fifties, when Senegal was about to attain independence, Seydou Nourou Tall was among those responsible for the organisation of a *Conseil Supérieur des Chefs Religieux* aimed at securing religious interests in the constitution and new government. This has remained an influential body.

During that time Seydou Nourou Tall also lent his support and that of the Tukulor to Léopold Senghor and his party, and thus helped decisively to ensure their victory. He was a close ally of the Senghor government from then on, until he died on 25 January 1980 at the age of 117. His wife, named Gogo, came from Mali and was a businesswoman in Dakar. ■

Tanzi, M. (1933-74)

TANZI, Mandrandele (1933-74).

ZAIREAN politician, who was also a very able administrator. He was born on 20 March 1933 in Watsa, the only son of a Logo-Ogambi family. After primary education in his birthplace, he proceeded to the College Notre Dame at Dungu for advanced education which took him to the Lovanium University in Kinshasa in 1955. He graduated, in 1960, with a degree in political science, becoming one of the first group of his countrymen to receive university education.

Like most of the small educated elites of the time, he was absorbed into the government administration and made director of the Ministry of Internal Affairs. In 1961 he was appointed director general of the National Water and Power Distribution Authority. Successively, he served as administrator of Lovanium University from 1964 until 1970, administrator of the National Bank between 1964 and 1965, and administrator of the National Institute for Agronomic Research from 1964 for three years. Alongside these functions he had other numerous official engagements; he was president of the Zaire Trust Company, and a member of the Government commission for Air Zaire.

The formation of the *Mouvement Populaire de la Révolution* (MPR) in 1967 saw Tanzi in a new role. As a member of the party and a loyal supporter of its leader, President Mobutu Sese Seko, he was appointed to its politicl bureau where he articulated the MPR's policies. Soon he was made its First National Secretary, then its political Director and later People's Commissioner. Not long after taking on the last responsibility Tanzi died, on 12 February 1974. ■

733

Tarka, J.S. (1932-80)

TARKA, Joseph Sarwuan (1932-80).

NIGERIAN politician. The son of Chief Tarka Nachi, a former district head of Mbakor and past chairman of the Inyamat-sen District Council, Tarka was born on 10 July 1932 in Igbor, Tiv Division, in what is now Benue State of Nigeria. After elementary education at Gboko Primary School,

J.S. Tarka

which he attended between 1937 and 1942 and at the Katsina-Ala Middle Secondary School, he trained at the Bauchi Teachers' Training College. He joined the teaching staff of the Benue Provincial Secondary School where he taught until 1956.

Interested in politics at an early stage, he formed the United Middle Belt Congress (UMBC), of which he became the President-General, with the main objective of campaigning for the creation of a Middle Belt

State. In the 1954 elections he won a seat in the Federal House of Representatives for the UMBC. Once there, and in an attempt to further the campaign for the extraction of a Middle Belt State from the Northern Region, he allied his UMBC with the Action Group (AG) of Chief Obafemi Awolowo, presenting a co-ordinated opposition to the Government of Alhaji Abubakar Tafawa Balewa (q.v.). He was made a Federal Vice-President of the AGUMBC alliance and also became the shadow Minister of Commerce and Industry.

Tarka led the UMBC delegation to the Constitutional Conferences on Nigeria's independence, held in Lagos and London in 1957 and 1958. An able parliamentarian, respected for his skills as much as for his resourcefulness, he served on his country's various parliamentary delegations abroad and attended the Pan-African Conference in Accra in 1959.

In 1962 Tarka, with Chief Awolowo and other prominent members of the AG, was arrested and charged with plotting to overthrow the Federal Government. He was discharged and acquitted for want of sufficient evidence about his role in the abortive attempt to dislodge the Tafawa Balewa administration.

Following the subsequent overthrow of the government in 1966 when the army took control of Nigeria, Tarka was appointed a member of the four-man delegation of the Northern Region to the All-Nigeria Constitutional Conference where he had the opportunity to argue the case for the establishment of states in the federation. He was also appointed to the new Federal Executive Council where he served first as Commissioner for Transport and later for Communications in the regime of General Yakubu Gowon, until he was forced to resign, following serious allegations of corruption, in 1974.

Before his resignation, however, Tarka's primary political objective had been effected by the military regime with the restructuring of Nigeria's four regions into 12 states on 27 May 1967. Thus were his endeavours rewarded with the creation of Benue Plateau State.

He went into private business in 1974, setting up a lucrative enterprise in manufacturing and contracting. For one who said that he was "a teacher by profession, a politician by choice and a businessman by necessity", the rapid achievement Tarka made in the short time he established his commercial enterprise demonstrated his enormous skills and capability.

This business success notwithstanding, Tarka returned to his first love in 1979 with the re-emergence of parliamentary democracy in the country. He co-founded the National Movement which gave birth to the National Party of Nigeria (NPN), the party that won over its rivals in the 1979 general elections to become Nigeria's first civilian government after 13 years of military rule. He was elected a National Vice-Chairman of the NPN, but lost a campaign for the presidential candidacy in the party's convention to Alhaji Shehu Shagari who was eventually elected President of Nigeria. Tarka, however, opted for a senatorial role, successfully winning a seat in the Senate on the NPN's ticket. He died in a London hospital on 30 March 1980. ■

Tavares, E. (1867-1930)

TAVARES, Eugenio (1867-1930).

CAPE VERDEAN poet. He was born on the island of Brava in the Cape Verde group. After educating himself locally in the Portuguese colony he left for the USA, intending to settle in New England. However, once there, he found as much racism as he had encountered in his birthplace. Demoralised and angry, he returned to Cape Verde to work in the colonial civil service.

It was at this time that Tavares began to write his poetry in the island patois, Creole. His area of concentration encompassed the strength of love, the painful experience of separation and the sad memory of a lost heritage. But the verses, accompanied by guitars for the local dance, the *morna*, were popular among Africans and Portuguese settlers alike. His first major works, *The Love That Saves* (*Amor que salva*), and *The Crown of Thorns* (*Mal de amor: coroa de espinhos*) were published in 1916, followed by another important work, *Listless Airs: Creole Songs* (*Mornas: cantigas Crioulas*), which came out in a book of the same name two years after his death.

A man of immense literary talent,

Tavares was also an essayist of classical Portuguese. This won him the admiration of Portuguese intellectuals and government officials, including Governor Guedes Vaz of Cape Verde, himself a poet, who encouraged the civil servant in his writings. In 1916 Tavares's poems were published in Lisbon and in the Cape Verdean pioneering literary journal, *Almanach Luso – Africano*, which was founded in 1894. He died in his birthplace island of Brava in 1930. ■

Tchikaya, F. (1903-61)

TCHIKAYA, Félix (1903-61).

CONGOLESE politician; his career was rooted in the southern ex-French Congo where he founded the *Parti Progressiste Congolais* (PPC). Born on 9 November 1903 in Libreville, Gabon, Tchikaya rose to prominence in the early politics of Congo where he went after completing his education at the famous William Ponty Teacher Training College in Dakar, Senegal.

F. Tchikaya

He later worked on various jobs, first as an accountant and then as a journalist. He joined the French army during the Second World War and fought with the Free French army to liberate France. From the French radical movements of the time Tchikaya had learnt techniques of party management and returned to the Congo to launch the PPC in 1946. The previous year he had been a member of the French Constituent Assembly, which also brought him into contact with other African leaders in inter-territorial politics.

On the platform of his newly created PPC he sought and won election as deputy for the Congo to the French National Assembly in 1946. These elections also saw the rise of another early prominent Congolese politician, Jacques Opangault (q.v.) and his *Mouvement Socialiste Africain* (MSA) which was also founded in 1946. The two parties were to dominate the political scene for the next ten years, with Tchikaya and Opangault leading the stage. The parties, like their leaders, drew their support mainly from their home bases: the MSA enjoying the overwhelming support of Opangault's home district in northern Congo while Tchikaya's PPC depended heavily on the strength of its massive backing from the people of Pointe-Noire in the south.

Tchikaya participated in the 1948 congress of the inter-territorial *Rassemblement Démocratique Africain* (RDA) that was held in Bamako in what was then French Soudan (now modern Mali). It was at this congress that he affiliated the PPC to the RDA whose president was Félix Houphouet-Boigny, later first President of the Republic of Côte d'Ivoire. Also founded in 1946, the RDA was the first all-African political movement which demanded constitutional safeguards for the rights of Africans in the French colonies. It sought to "free Africa from the colonial yoke by the affirmation of her personality and by the association – freely agreed to – of a union of nations".

The PPC's influence in the Congo began to wane in the mid-1950s with the emergence in 1956 of another Congolese party, the *Union Démocratique de Défense des Intérêts Africains* (UDDIA) of Abbé Fulbert Youlou (q.v.), which replaced it as the RDA local section. Before then, however, Tchikaya retained his prominence throughout the late 1940s and early 1950s. He was elected member of the Grand Council for

French Equatorial Africa in 1952, re-elected that same year and again in 1956 to the National Assembly.

His declining influence was facilitated by the absorption of such notable leaders of the PPC like the Mayor of Pointe-Noire, Stéphane Tchichelle, into the UDDIA. By the time of the 1957 elections his leadership had come under serious challenge from emerging younger politicians from the Pointe-Noire region. He failed to get the PPC's nomination in that election and later retired into political oblivion in Pointe-Noire where he died on 15 January 1961, six months after the Congo became independent of France. ■

Teelock, L. (1909-82)

TEELOCK, Sir Leckraz (1909-82).

MAURITIAN diplomat who, while serving as his country's first High Commissioner to the Court of St. James, London, became doyen of the Diplomatic Corps as well as Dean of the Organisation of African Unity (OAU) group of ambassadors in the United Kingdom.

Teelock was born in 1909 in Mauritius where he was educated at the Royal College in Curepipe. In 1931 he went to Britain to further his education, receiving the MB and ChB medical degrees from Edinburgh University in 1937. Two years later he gained a Diploma in Tropical Medicine from Liverpool University, followed by a Licentiate in Midwifery from Dublin in Ireland.

Returning to Mauritius in 1939 he started his career as a General Practitioner and his devotion to the people soon won him widespread respect and affection. Later he became a member of the Mauritius Labour Party (*Parti Travailliste*). The party, formed in 1936, was for a long time the sole political organisation in the country. It had strong roots in the poorest sections of the community which, with the harsh conditions for workers in the sugar plantations, constituted an ideal breeding ground for the fermenting of agitation for improved conditions and political rights. The party won considerable concessions from the British

Colonial administration, including universal adult suffrage which was introduced in 1947.

Twelve years later, in 1959, Teelock was elected a member of the Legislative Assembly where he remained until 1963.

Sir Leckraz Teelock

During that period the Labour Party had become the vanguard of the movement for independence from Britain, and Teelock was a leading voice in the demand. In addition to his parliamentary duties, he took close interest in the works of the Mauritius Family Planning Association of which he was a founder member and Chairman from 1959 to 1962. From 1940 up to 1962 he also served as Director of the Free Press Service Limited. In addition he was a co-founder of the Triveni Cultural Association.

In 1964 Teelock was posted as Commissioner for Mauritius to London, where he was closely involved in the independence constitutional talks with the British Government. When independence was achieved in March 1968, he remained in Britain becoming Mauritius's first High Commissioner. He was honoured by the British Queen that year with the Commander of the British Empire and in 1972 received a knighthood.

Teelock was also accredited as Ambassador Extraordinary and Plenipotentiary to

the Holy See, Holland, Luxembourg, Denmark, Sweden, Norway and Finland. From 1971 to 1975, he was also Ambassador Extraordinary and Plenipotentiary to Belgium and the EEC. In this later accreditation, he played a prominent role in the negotiations which led to Mauritius's membership of the Yaoundé Convention and subsequently the Lomé Convention.

Sir Leckraz was highly respected in the diplomatic community, not only by those he was closely associated with in Europe but also by others in America and Africa. For years he remained the Dean of African Ambassadors and High Commissioners in the UK, while being the Doyen of the Diplomatic Corps in the country. On several occasions he accompanied his Head of State, Seewoosagur Ramgoolam (q.v.), for bilateral talks to many countries including the Soviet Union, China, America, India and Canada.

Sir Leckraz Teelock died in active service at his London base in 1982. He was survived by his lawyer wife, Vinaya Kumari, and their son and daughter.■

Telli, B.D. (1925-77)

TELLI, El-Hadj Boubacar Diallo (1925-77).

GUINEAN diplomat, was the first Secretary-General of the Organisation of African Unity (OAU). He was born in 1925 in Poredaka, a member of the nomadic Fulani ethnic group in Guinea. His academic record was marked with a series of "firsts". The young Telli came first in the Poredaka primary school which he attended, first at the Ecole William Ponty in Dakar, and had a first from Paris University where he took his law degree. And in 1951 he became the first African to enter the prestigious French training institution for senior administrators, the *Ecole Nationale de la France d'Outre-Mer*.

He worked as a magistrate at Thiès in Senegal and Cotonou in Dahomey (now Benin Republic), and then became *chef de cabinet* to the French High Commissioner for West Africa and, in 1957, Secretary-General to the Grand Council of French West Africa. When Guinea became independent in October 1958, Telli became a Roving Ambassador for the new state, then Permament Representative to the UN from 1958 to 1964. He was for a time Chairman of the UN's Committees on Decolonisation and on South African Apartheid.

El-Hadj Diallo Telli

In 1962 he travelled around Africa as a representative of President Touré (q.v.), who did much then to prepare the ground for the Addis Ababa Summit of May 1963 where the OAU was founded. Then, at the Cairo Summit of the OAU in 1964, Diallo Telli was elected Secretary-General of the Organisation on 21 July.

He was re-elected in 1968. For eight years he was constantly in the news as a spokesman for the OAU and for Africa. He was criticised at times for being also a spokesman for Guinea, and for being particularly forceful in expressing some policies (though these were agreed OAU policies). But he had the respect of many African governments. In 1972, however, he failed to be re-elected at the Rabat OAU Summit.

He then returned to Guinea and was appointed Minister of Justice. He served as minister for four years but was said to have been on bad terms with President Sékou Touré. He was awarded a gold medal at the

celebrations of the OAU's tenth anniversary in 1973.

In July 1976 Diallo Telli was arrested with some other leading politicians after the announcement of a "Fulani plot" to overthrow the government. For some time afterwards there was a fearsome purge of Fulanis, who were sacked and gaoled in large numbers, but little was said officially about the leaders of the alleged plot. The Touré regime kept silent on the fate of the former OAU Secretary-General, although Presidents Nyerere and Boumédienne (q.v.) made inquiries and questions were asked at the Libreville OAU Summit in 1977. But "confessions" by the alleged plotters were broadcast over Conakry radio. Nothing was ever announced about their fate, but it is assumed widely that Diallo Telli is dead, and in late 1978 a Paris newspaper noted for its anti-Touré policy gave a circumstantial account confirming his death.

According to this account, after his arrest on 24 July 1976 Telli was brutally tortured after questioning by senior members of the government, until he was forced to sign a confession. Then the order was given for him and his fellow "plotters" to be deliberately starved to death in prison, and Diallo Telli was found dead in his cell on 25 February 1977. President Touré never admitted this explicitly but said, "Those who are condemned to death are dead". ■

Tenreiro, F.J. (1921-63)

TENREIRO, Francisco José de Vasques (1921-63).

SAO TOME writer, geographer and leading critic of Portuguese colonialism. Born in São Tomé in 1921, he was a geography graduate of the Higher School of Colonial Administration in the Portuguese Colony. He entered the Centre of Geographic Studies in Lisbon and later proceeded to the London School of Economics and Political Science for postgraduate studies and research.

Returning to Portugal, he was made assistant professor of Human Geography in the Arts Faculty of the University of

Lisbon. This was where Tenreiro produced his authoritative study of the geography of his native São Tomé, which was published in 1962. In addition to being a brilliant scholar he was also a poet whose remarkable eloquence and powerful enunciation of the African aspirations made him a leading critic of Portuguese colonialism. Drawing on the concept of *Négritude* he attacked European degradation of African culture, arguing, for example, in *The Island of the Holy Name* (*Ilha de nome santo*) published in 1942, that every culture is conscious. He wrote that being Black was a positive attribute, in an effort to combat the negative portrayal of African culture by the Portuguese.

The Island of the Holy Name, a long poem which gives its name to one of his books, was preceded by a collection of short stories, *The Ballad of one Silva Costa* (*Romance de seu Silva Costa*). A sketch of the Portuguese trader in São Tomé, the book depicts vividly the contrast between the trader's affluent life and the miseries of the African wallowing in both sorrow and anger.

Tenreiro's writing is regarded as the first major work of *Négritude*, which won him a large following in Europe and in the Portuguese colonies where he was held in high esteem in both intellectual and political circles.

Tenreiro also wrote critical essays and produced a pioneering anthology, *Negro Poetry in Portuguese* (*Caderno de poessia negra de expressão portuguesa*), published in 1953 and re-issued as the *Anthology of Negro Poetry in Portuguese* in 1958. His literary work took him to the Americas, resulting in the publication in 1945 of *Panorama of North American Literature. Courage in Africa* (*Coração em Africa*), a collection of his poetry, was published four years after his death in Lisbon in 1963 at the age of 42. ■

El-Hadj A.A. Tha'Alibi

Tha'alibi, A.A. (1876-1944)

THA'ALIBI, Abdul-Aziz ben El-Hadj (1876-1944).

TUNISIAN politician who also achieved fame as Islamic reformer. He was said to have been of Algerian descent, more precise-

ly, according to one account, the grandson of an Algerian *qadi* (Moslem judge). Born in Tunis on 15 April 1876, son of a notary, he studied at the historic Mosque-University at Tunis, and went into journalism at a young age. In 1896 he founded an Arabic-language newspaper, *Sabil Erreched*. In this journal he showed a particular interest in Islamic doctrinal matters.

He continued to show this special interest when he travelled to Egypt and was deported for his expressions of ideas on Islam. But he had been able to meet Sheikh Muhammad' Abduh (q.v.), the outstanding religious leader in Egypt then. Later his ideas showed some of the influence of Abduh, who subsequently visited Tunisia. He (Abduh) preached the revival of Islam through a return to correct teaching and understanding which would help resist European domination while accepting useful change coming from Europe, The young Tha'alibi, who also visited Turkey, declared support after returning home (about 1902) for the ideas of the Egyptian nationalist leader Kamil (q.v.). He preached Islamic doctrines which angered the revered marabouts who, as in Algeria, were local leaders of Islam but were condemned by reformers such as Tha'alibi for preaching a superstitious version of the religion. This won him two months in prison. He was accused of heresy but wrote a book in his defence. In French North Africa generally, 20th century nationalism was linked to religious criticism of the marabouts who aided submission to French rule.

Tha'alibi joined the Young Tunisian movement and was a very active member. In 1912 this movement, already regarded with hostility by many Frenchmen despite its loyalty to France, was suppressed fiercely after it supported a strike in Tunis. Tha'alibi was deported with another leader of the movement, Ali Bach Hamba, but was allowed to return in 1913. He was not among the Tunisians, led by Ali and Mohammed Bach Hamba, who worked closely with the Turkish and German enemies of France in the 1914-18 war in the hope of liberating their country. But he is said to have sympathised with them and particularly with Turkey, whose historic links with Tunisia, still close, encouraged there the ideas of an Islamic peoples' solidarity with Turkey, a kind of "Pan-Islamism". During the war Tha'alibi, it is said, spread Pan-Islamic ideas in Tunisia. As there were in fact uprisings in southern Tunisia in 1915-17, encouraged and aided by Turkey and Germany, this activity of Tha'alibi must have remained unknown to the French authorities as he apparently escaped arrest then.

With the end of the war in 1918, and the collapse of hopes placed in the defeated side, many Tunisians saw possibilities of reform in the victors, particularly in the post-victory inclination of some Frenchmen to reward the people of their colonies for help in the war and in the ideas of President Wilson of the USA, who came to Paris for the Peace Conference. Tha'alibi was the leader of those Tunisians who came forward in 1919 in the hope that a re-ordering of the world would benefit their country.

He went to Paris in August 1919 and worked with Ahmed Sakka, who had gone there earlier, on a book completed later in 1919 and called *La Tunisie Martyre: Ses Revendications*. Tha'alibi wrote a good deal of this work, though a considerable amount was contributed by Sakka who wrote the final French version, and by others. In 14 chapters the book denounced French misrule, especially the seizure of Tunisians' land, the denial of education, and discrimination in the civil service; it declared, "....

the Tunisian, in his own country, lives like an undesirable alien among citizens!" There was a final declaration of demands, including freedom of speech and the press, equality before the law, recruitment for the civil service on the basis of merit only, and a Supreme Council, largely elected by universal legislation, for legislative purposes. These demands bypassed the question of French rule but were sufficiently radical to arouse the opposition of the French authorities.

In Tunisia the remnants of the Young Tunisians became the *Parti Libéral Constitutionnel*, later renamed the *Parti du Destour*. It seems to have come into being early in 1920, with Tha'alibi among its outstanding leaders. The ideas in his book were those advocated by the party, which used the Arabic word for Constitution, *Destour*, and centred its demands on a self-governing constitutional régime for Tunisia. The leaders in Tunisia, where the French had ruled by martial law for years, avoided open calls for independence, Tha'alibi, in Paris, agreed with their approach, though the militant exiled leader Mohammed Bach Hamba, in Switzerland, urged him to call for full independence. In France Tha'alibi made many contacts with the press, with Socialist politicians, and with groups and individuals sympathetic to colonial subjects' demands. In Tunisia the Destour Party in its early days aroused wide support, especially from traders, artisans and farmers, particularly in the capital and Sahil region (which led in educational progress).

In mid-1920 the party presented a petition to Muhammad en-Nasr Bey, who had some sympathy with its claims. Another was presented in Paris, by Tha'alibi and others who had joined him from Tunisia, to the President of the Chamber of Deputies and to the Chamber's Commission on the French colonies. It recalled Tunisians' service in the War, with 45,000 casualties, and called on France to recompense Tunisia, by granting rights and freedoms. A second delegation under Hassouna Ayachi (q.v.) and others made a similar call. The Destour Party leaders, who were from well-off families like Tha'alibi's, were cautious, however, they came to encourage the continual popular demonstrations staged in Tunis from early 1920, and the strong nationalist feelings at their followers' meetings. This strengthened French hostility to them.

Police searched Tha'alibi's Paris residence in June 1920, and on 31 July 1920 he was arrested on charges of contact with the enemy and anti-French activity. The charges arose partly from letters from Bach Hamba. He was taken to Marseilles, where he was said to have been roughly treated, and then back to Tunis, where he appeared before a military court. When martial law was lifted early in 1921 the case against Tha'alibi, and some others with him was continued. But in the end all charges were dropped.

The Destour Party continued to agitate for reforms despite French refusal to consider the demands made in 1920. In April 1922 Bey presented a list of 18 demands drawn up in collaboration with the Destour Party, including general legislative elections, more power and responsibility for ministers, full citizenship rights for all Tunisians, compulsory education, and freedom of the press and of association as in France. The French Resident-General, M. Saint, forced the nominal ruler to withdraw the demands. Soon afterwards Tha'alibi and his fellow Destour leaders disagreed over the visit of the French President; he wanted a boycott of the visit but the others published a contrary decision. Later in 1922 en-Nasr Bey died; France created a Grand Council which by giving some representation, however small (18 Tunisians as against 44 Frenchmen) to the Moslems, satisfied some protests; and the party leadership quarrelled.

A congress on October 1922 re-elected Tha'alibi and others to the leadership, with Tha'alibi becoming Assistant Secretary-General, but soon afterwards there was a major breakaway. During 1923 the split led to a decline in the nationalist movement. Tha'alibi led one of the two rival groups whose bickering became more and more intense. He sent representatives to the interior to raise support and cash, without success. As his supporters left him, to the delight of M. Saint who may have helped foment the split, the French governor suggested Tha'alibi might do well to leave Tunisia. On 26 July 1923 he did leave, to travel to the Middle East. Tha'alibi visited Turkey and India among other countries.

He was away for 14 years, during which the Destour revived but was then harried by repression before being challenged, in the 1930s, by the Neo-Destour, formed by younger nationalists including Habib Bourguiba at the Ksar-Hellal Congress of 1934.

In 1937 the Neo-Destour, rapidly expanding with the initial tolerance of France's Popular Front government and under the leadership of Bourguiba, grew in strength to about 100,000 members in 400 branches. To challenge its spread the "Old Destour" arranged, with French cooperation, for Tha'alibi to return. He landed on 8 July 1937. He was welcomed by the Neo-Destour leaders and they at first agreed to cooperate with him. But Tha'alibi sought a reunified Destour Party led by him and with a pronounced Pan-Arab and Pan-Islamic character, and condemned the Neo-Destour's secularism. Soon the Neo-Destour turned against him and the "Old Destour" leaders who now followed him again.

When Tha'alibi went on an interior tour to rouse support, the Neo-Destour systematically disrupted meetings he addressed. His tour was quickly ruined, and he eventually had to leave Mateur under police protection. In 1938 a complaint he made to the police against the Neo-Destour was published by the more militant party; and he gave evidence about M. Bourguiba when the latter was arrested by the French after riots and the killing of demonstrators in April 1938. After these Tha'alibi's popularity declined rapidly. He died in relative obscurity on 1 October 1944. ■

Thema, R.V.S.(1886-1955)

THEMA, Richard Victor Selope (1886-1955).

SOUTH AFRICAN politician. He was one of the founder members of the African National Congress (ANC) of South Africa, and despite his conservative and Africanist stance regarded the ANC as the sole political mouthpiece of South Africans.

He was born on a farm in Pietersburg in the northern Transvaal. His education at a mission school was interrupted when he was compelled to work as a labourer in the dispensary of the Imperial Military Railways during the Boer War. After the war he used his meagre savings to continue his education at the Lovedale Missionary College, where at the age of twenty-one he obtained his Junior

Certificate. He then worked as a clerk at the Pietersburg mine recruiting corporation.

About 1915 he was employed by one of the first African lawyers in South Africa, Richard W. Msimang. This was to be Selope Thema's introduction to the new phase of

R.V.S. Thema

the African political struggle. At the time Msimang was heading the drafting committee for the ANC constitution. His dedication to the struggle soon catapulted him to the position of secretary of the ANC Transvaal branch, and for periods he acted as Secretary General of the movement.

In 1919 he was a member of an ANC deputation to Britain and the League of Nations to explain the plight of the Africans and extract support, especially from Britain because of its imperial relations with South Africa. Needless to say, the deputation returned to South Africa without the support it had hoped for. Selope Thema took advantage of the trip and enrolled for a course at the London School of Journalism. He thus became the logical choice to edit the ANC newspaper *Abantu-Batho*. It was moderate in its politics, reflecting the stance of its editor who believed in dialogue with the government.

He soon became recognised by the government as a leader and was invited to participate in several conferences to discuss

pending legislation for the Africans based on the policy of segregation. When *Abantu-Batho* finally closed, he involved himself with the Johannesburg Joint Council, which was an organisation of selected prominent Africans and Whites. The purpose of the Council was to discuss conditions of Africans in Johannesburg and make representations to the authorities. The Council was not supported by the ANC because it was a talking shop and merely scratched the surface of the degradation and oppression of the people.

He then became editor of *Bantu World*, a white-owned newspaper for Africans. This gave him the opportunity to propagate his Africanist and conservative position.

In 1935 he was a founder member of the All African Convention (AAC), an umbrella organisation to co-ordinate strategy. Organisations in it included the ANC, the Communist Party, and the Industrial and Commercial Workers Union. The AAC was conceived because of an urgent need to mobilise against several drastic bills about to be enacted. These were the Native Trust and Land Bill which was to allocate only 13.5 percent of the land to Africans, the Riotous Assemblies Bill which was designed to ruthlessly suppress any demonstrations and strikes, and the Native Service Contract Act and Pass Laws which controlled and restricted the movement of Africans within the country, in particular the freedom to work where they want and their rights of tenure. Selope Thema devoted his energies to the AAC, perhaps believing that it could become the all-embracing political organisation for the Africans, even though he was ill at ease with the participation of the Communist Party.

In 1937 he was elected to the Native Representative Council (NRC), an indirectly elected body which included nominated chiefs, a body that was spawned by the 1936 bills and which removed all possibilities of direct representation. The NRC was an advisory body to the Minister of Native Affairs. It was at first approved by the All African Convention. The ANC became increasingly hostile to this instrument of indirect rule, and eventually demanded that the members boycott the Council, which they did; in 1951 the Afrikaner nationalist government dissolved it.

In 1940 Selope Thema became Speaker of the Cabinet of the ANC; he remained in the National Executive until 1949. During this period he was violently opposed to the alliance of the ANC with the Communist Party and the Indian National Congress. Through *Bantu World* he propagated his Africanist beliefs despite the radical changes in the ANC. J.B. Marks (q.v.), a member of the Communist Party, was elected Secretary of the Transvaal province and a younger, more militant leadership emerged – Mandela, Sisulu, Tambo and others. He formed a "national minded block", but this received no support in the organisation. He also opposed direct action by the ANC, still believing in dialogue with the government. This was confirmed by his opposition to the Defiance Campaign in 1952. In that same year he retired as editor of *Bantu World*, becoming in his last days a spokesman for Moral Re-armament. He will always have his place in the history of the ANC, as a leader during a particular phase of the struggle. ■

Thomas, B. (1921-53)

THOMAS, Chief Bode (1921-53).

NIGERIAN politician; he was a leading figure in the movement for Nigeria's independence, although he was to die seven years before Britain granted independence in 1960. He was a founder member of the defunct Action Group (AG) party, of which he was elected the first national deputy to Chief Obafemi Awolowo. His brilliance and dynamism were quickly rewarded, and he became at the early age of 30 one of the first Central Ministers of Nigeria. As a lawyer too, Bode Thomas was very successful, and this success enabled him to co-found in 1950 the firm of Thomas, Williams and Kayode which was one of the leading indigenous legal firms in Nigeria at the time.

Bode Thomas was born in 1921 in Lagos, of an Oyo family, and was educated in the Nigerian capital until 1937 when he left the Lagos CMS Grammar School. He joined the Nigerian Railway, as a clerk earning two shillings a day. In 1939 he left for the United Kingdom to read Law, and he was called to the Bar at Middle Temple three years later. It was while he was studying in London that

he became involved in the nationalism of other Nigerian and African students who were campaigning against British colonial rule.

Returning to Nigeria in 1942, he set himself up in private legal practice in Lagos, where he soon built a reputable career as a barrister. His success enabled him to form, with other Lagos lawyers, a partnership of barristers in January 1950. Their company, the Thomas, Williams and Kayode group soon became one of the leading firms in Nigeria, and after acquiring a reputation as

Chief B. Thomas

a lawyer, Bode Thomas took to full-time politics.

He had joined the Nigerian Youth Movement (NYM) on his return from Britain in 1942. The NYM was a major platform for the young nationalist intellectuals and lawyers who, alongside the National Council of Nigeria and the Cameroons (NCNC) of Dr. Nnamdi Azikiwe, sought independence from Britain.

Bode Thomas had hoped then that these two movements, the NYM and the NCNC, would come together to hasten the cause of independence and unity of the country. To this end, he took interest in the activities of Azikiwe and his party. Of this,

Bode Thomas said later: "A united Nigeria was essential. I did try to understand what the NCNC stood for and to see if there would be any likelihood of merging together the two parties, but I found that their ideals were poles apart".

He left the NYM in 1950 and, with Awolowo, launched the Action Group in March of the following year; he was elected the first deputy leader of the party and remained so until his death. Following subsequent constitutional rearrangements that paved the way for the first general elections of 1951/52, Bode Thomas was among the AG members elected to the Western Region House of Assembly. From there he was one of the four members nominated to the national legislature in Lagos where he was made Minister of Transport in the 1951 Central Council of Ministers. But in 1953 he resigned from the Council over the rejection of the AG/NCNC sponsored Bill which called for self-government in 1956. Bode Thomas was among the ministers who proposed the historic motion, moved by his party colleague Anthony Enahoro. But their demand was opposed by the four Northern ministers supported by the six British officials in the Council – the Northerners had favoured a gradual approach until self-government was practicable. As a result Thomas, his three AG ministerial colleagues and the NCNC ministers resigned temporarily from the Council. He was later made Minister of Works and held this office until his death on 20 November 1953, aged 32.

The career of Bode Thomas exemplifies both the growth of political consciousness in his country and the collective determination of the nationalists to lead their country to freedom. For this he gave up a lucrative legal practice in order to devote his time to full-time politics. A charismatic politician, able and dynamic, his death in 1953, seven years before Nigeria's independence, was received with unrestrained national mourning. In private life he did not give the impression of possessing intense ardour and an aggressive drive. Rather Chief Bode Thomas carried himself with the dignity of the high traditional office holder he was – he was made the Balogun of Oyo in 1949. This appointment gave him a seat in the Oyo local administration and there, too, Chief Bode Thomas made a tremendous contribution to the affairs of the Yoruba city. ∎

Thuku, H. (1895-1970)

THUKU, Harry (1895-1970).

KENYAN politician, one of the pioneers of African nationalism in Kenya. He came from Mbari ya-Gathirimu, in Kikuyu province in northern Kenya. Born in 1895, into a poor farming family in a village about two miles from Kambui Hill, he left home while young to attend a Gospel Missionary Society (GMS) mission. Throughout his four years' stay at the GMS with the missionaries Mr and Mrs Knapp, he served them with extreme diligence. There he learned how to read and write.

In 1911 he left the mission to seek employment in Nairobi. Thuku's first job was at the Standard Bank, Nairobi, where he worked briefly as a messenger. But he was convicted and imprisoned for fraud. On his

H. Thuku

release in 1913, he took up another appointment as a clerk to do hut-counting, and in 1914, he joined the *Leader of British East Africa* newspaper, where he learned printing, he also became a compositor and learnt to print maps and sketches of war positions. He left the *Leader* in December 1917 and the following year got a job with the Government Treasury as a telephone operator, which he later resigned to enter politics.

While Thuku was with the *Leader* he developed a special interest in some of the troubles of Africans, especially the question of forced labour, a system whereby law-abiding Africans were used by foreigners in manual labour, with no sexual discrimination as both men and women were involved. With this developing political sentiment, Harry Thuku began to know a number of people, mostly Indians. Perhaps the most intimate was M.A. Desai from whom he acquired some political experience.

Another problem was the introduction in 1919, of what was called *kipande*; this was Swahili for a container in which a registration paper was carried. This *kipande* was only for Africans and actually restricted them to a precise foreign employer who was the arbiter of his employees' fate. His remark on the registration paper determined whether the African could be employed by another employer. After increasing the tax burden on Africans, the colonial government decided to reduce African wages by one third.

These grievances were discussed at a meeting held in a Nairobi suburb in 1921, leading to the formation of Kenya's first political organisation, the Young Kikuyu Association. It soon became the East African Association (EAA) and formed branches in many parts of the country. With Thuku as its first President, the EAA started the first organised campaign against colonial measures: it sent a petition to the Colonial Secretary in London while in Kenya it held protest meetings against the allocation of much of the fertile land to Europeans. Following this Thuku was arrested in March 1922, and during demonstrations against the arrest, troops fired and killed 20 people in Nairobi. He was deported to Mombasa from where he was taken to Kismayu Island. This was to cut off Harry Thuku from all political contacts, as the British saw he was an impediment to colonial exploitation. He spent almost nine years in detention.

From Kismayu, he was deported to Marsabit, where he gained a lot of experience especially in agriculture. In Kismayu, he had organised lessons for children to sustain his living. At the end of his detention he immediately took to farming, while he was still active in politics.

Harry Thuku, among other things, stopped women's forced labour before his arrest in 1922. When he returned in 1930, he continued to work towards his people's political freedom. He was dynamic, persistent, prudent and hospitable. He sent his wife Tabitha to England in 1957 for a farm management course aimed at ensuring adequate administration of his farm.

He rose to become one of the wealthiest farmers of his time, so much that the government came to seek his advice. His love for his country was evident when he destroyed about sixty thousand seedlings of his coffee plantation in order to help Kenya keep within its coffee export quota in the world market. He was the first African director of the Kenya Planters Coffee Union (KPCU).

Harry Thuku's opposition to the colonisation of Kenya had in no small measure contributed to the early realisation of the need for political emancipation. He died on 14 June 1970. ■

Tiger, D. (1929-71)

TIGER, Dick (1929-71).

NIGERIAN professional boxer, he became a world champion. He was born Richard Ihetu on 14 August 1929 in Aba, Imo State, Nigeria. After attending local primary school he began petty trading in the town, dealing in empty bottles which he collected and re-sold to distillers and brewers. It was at that time that the stoutly-built trader took an interest in boxing.

He began his boxing career in 1950 but it was not until 1952, at the age of 23, that he abandoned trading to turn to professional boxing. He made his way through a maze of local boxers to become the Nigerian, and subsequently the Commonwealth, middleweight boxing champion. His next attempt was at the world middleweight title which he wrested from Gene Fullmer in San Francisco on 23 October 1962. In 1963 the new middleweight champion of the world successfully defended his crown against Fullmer in the first world title fight in Africa, staged in Lagos before his jubilant

Dick Tiger

compatriots. On 7 December 1963, however, he was defeated by Joey Giardello in Atlantic City, New Jersey, USA, but he regained the title from the American in a re-match on 22 October 1965. Dick Tiger thus became the first man to win the middleweight boxing crown twice.

On 25 April 1966 Tiger was defeated by Emile Griffith who was the first opponent to floor the Nigerian. The dethroned champion was not too long in the cold, the next year saw him in a different category as world light-heavyweight boxing champion, having defeated José Torres.

Tiger returned with his new title to a Nigeria engulfed in the civil war. He joined the forces of Biafra and was commissioned lieutenant and placed in charge of giving physical training to the soldiers. In 1968 he left for America to defend his title which he lost to Bob Foster in a punishing duel in which he suffered his first knock out in the fourth round. He remained in the USA but did not fight until July 1970 when he had his last contest which he lost to Emile Griffith in New York's Madison Square Garden.

In 1971 he returned to Nigeria and announced his retirement after 21 years in the ring during which he had 64 victories, 26 of them by knockout, and 17 losses. Dick Tiger died in Aba at the end of 1971 following a brief liver ailment. ■

Tinubu (died 1887)

TINUBU, Madame (died 1887).

NIGERIAN businesswoman and patriot, after whom a prominent Lagos landmark, "Tinubu Square", is named. She lived in the 19th century and was born in Abeokuta, western Nigeria, to a trading family. After a period of business apprenticeship under her mother, Tinubu went to Badagry, an important trading post on the outskirts of Lagos, where, despite her lack of formal education, she soon established a flourishing trade in tobacco and salt. The enterprising Tinubu was later to expand her trade, which brought her into contact with the European slave dealers, with whom she dealt as a middleperson.

In 1846 Tinubu, now a successful businesswoman, played hostess to the exiled King Akitoye of Lagos who sought refuge in Badagry; she used her influential position to inaugurate a pro-Akitoye movement dedicated to the eventual return of the King to the throne in Lagos. Thus commenced her involvement in the politics of Lagos, which was dominated by men of wealth and education. In 1851 Akitoye regained his throne and Tinubu was invited to Lagos where she soon transferred her business activity. She strengthened her position as an intermediary in the trade between the expatriate community and the indigenous population of Lagos on the one hand and the interior, which included her birthplace, Abeokuta, on the other.

Her influence in the court of Akitoye grew to such an extent that she was often accused of being the power behind the throne, a belief which in 1853 led to the rebellion of two prominent chiefs. By 1853, when Akitoye was succeeded by Prince Dosunmu, Tinubu's influence grew even more. In 1855 she led a campaign against the

Brazilian and Sierra Leonean immigrants in Lagos for using their wealth and power against the King and for subverting the ancient customs of the island, thus displaying a degree of nationalism which worried the British. The latter retaliated with mass arrests of the organisers, followed by expulsion from Lagos. Tinubu and her followers were deported to Abeokuta in May 1856.

In Abeokuta Tinubu expanded her business activities to include a wide range of wares such as gunpowder and bullets. In time her influence began to be felt also in Egba politics in which she played two important roles; her contribution to the successful defence of Egbaland during the Dahomean invasion of 1863 following which she was awarded the title of *Iyalode* (First Lady) in 1864. In the Alake succession crisis of 1877 her chosen candidate was installed. The conferment of the title of *Iyalode* placed her in a position of power, which she was denied in Lagos, for, by virtue of it, she not only acquired a constitutional right to participate in Egba affairs but was also accorded honour and esteem in the community.

She died in 1887 when she was at the height of her popularity. Today in Abeokuta a monument stands in the town square named after her, Ita Iyalode (Iyalode Square). ■

Tippu Tib

Tippu Tib (c. 1830-1905)

TIPPU TIB (c.1830-1905).

TANZANIAN merchant and ruler. His original name was Hamed bin Mohammed. He was born in Zanzibar, son of an Afro-Arab planter and caravan trader, Mohammed Bin Juma, and of a Mrima mother. He learned trading and accompanied caravans with his father and then with Said bin Omar, another organiser of the inland caravans from the East African coast. Then he traded on his own. By 1865 he was selling ivory in the Ruemba region, near the eastern shore of Lake Tanganyika. There he began to establish his own trading state, after capturing a town, and so began the series of conquests which were to lead to his ruling a large new state west of the lake, in the upper Congo basin (in modern Zaire).

He first intervened in the affairs of the Rua people, and then went to Maryema, where he had heard much of the ivory came from. He became ruler over 30-40,000 people by telling the old Chief, Kasongo-Ruchie, that he (Hamed) was the grandson of his long-lost sister, so that the chief abdicated in his favour. He advanced to Nyangwe in 1874 and then was elected Governor by the Arab traders at Kasongo. Those two towns became the capital of his unusually large trading empire. While respecting the authority of the Sultan of Zanzibar, Hamed bin Mohammed was the effective ruler over a large area, though he was content with a loose rule through vassals, enough to ensure profitable trade.

Ivory, ultimately for European use, was the main object of trade, but the need for slaves to carry ivory tusks led to massive slave trading. The military activity and destruction which resulted caused havoc. While the Arab rulers in the eastern Congo basin established plantations of many crops and brought some other benefits, their slave trading was very oppressive and from the 1870s was exposed and denounced by Livingstone, Stanley and other European travellers. "Tippu Tib", as Europeans called him, helped such travellers and they spoke well of his ability while making his name notorious as a slave-trader.

Tippu Tib ruled as far as Stanley Falls by 1883; he had fifteen relatives and allies as commercial representatives at various centres. For his trade route to the East coast he made alliances with Rumaliza (Mohammed bin Ghelfon) of Ujiji and the Nyamwezi ruler Mirambo (q.v.). In 1883 he was visited by H.M. Stanley, now representative of the association formed by King Leopold II of the Belgians for the purpose (then concealed) of occupying the Congo basin.

Another representative of Leopold II made a treaty with one of Tippu Tib's lieutenants, but he repudiated it. In 1885 Leopold II was recognised in Europe as personal ruler of a vast Congo Free State. Being within the borders of this proposed state, Tippu Tib was ready to reach an agreement with the Europeans, whose activities he well knew and understood. At first, however, he clashed with them in 1886, when the Free State representative was driven out of Stanley Falls.

In 1887 Stanley passed Zanzibar, en route to the Congo mouth to start an expedition to bring Emin Pasha (a European who had been a governor under the Egyptians) out of the Southern Sudan, and met Tippu Tib, on a visit to his homeland. On behalf of King Leopold II, Stanley made Tippu Tib Governor of the Stanley Falls. This recognised and possibly extended Tippu's rule over the upper Congo basin, putting some other Arab trader-rulers (Kibonge, Mohara, Said bin Abibu) under him. In Europe opponents of the slave trade denounced Leopold II for this move, which was an early sign of the deceitful nature of Leopold's "humanitarian" pose, later to be fully exposed. Tippu Tib, however, promised to restrict slave trading and did try to restrict the Arabs' caravan traffic, on his return to the Falls area. This helped to provoke resistance to him, and Said bin Abibu defied him, claiming to be the representative of the Sultan of Zanzibar; when he died in 1889 Mohara continued this defiance. Meanwhile Stanley's expedition passed through Arab ruled Congo territory but, so Stanley said, did not receive the promised help from Tippu. In 1890, after Stanley had accused him after the completion of the expedition, Tippu left for Zanzibar to answer the accusations. He left his nephew Rashid in charge at Stanley Falls.

In his absence the Congo Free State's representatives turned against the Arabs, while Leopold II called for European support for action against the slave traders. His agents started to enforce a Free State government monopoly of trade, which was to subject the Congolese to oppression worse than Arab slavery. One step in this direction was reported in 1891 to Tippu, who informed the British Consul in Zanzibar, then a British Protectorate. He did not return, and in 1892 the Arabs went to war with the Free State in the Upper Congo. When Ngongo Letete, an ally of the Arabs and (according to one account) a personal slave of Tippu, made peace with the Europeans and Mohara, Rashid, and Tippu's son, Sefu, demanded his return. After two years of war the Arabs were defeated by Free State forces under Dhanis. Fearsome misrule then descended on Tippu's former domain.

Tippu Tib remained in Zanzibar, where he died in 1905. ■

Tlili, A. (1916-67)

TLILI, Ahmed (1916-67).

TUNISIAN trade unionist and prominent activist in the anti-colonial campaign. Ahmed Tlili was born at Gafsa in central Tunisia in 1916. He attended local primary schools after which he went to study at Sadiqiya College. On leaving school he joined nationalist politics and at the age of 21 became a member of the Neo-Destour Party, a nationalist organisation committed to the achievement of Tunisian independence. He also became increasingly involved in trade unionist activities, being a member of the *Union Générale des Travailleurs Tunisiens* (UGTT), later becoming the Gafsa branch secretary of this organisation.

In 1947 he was elected to the Steering Committee of the UGTT, and the following year he became secretary of the Gafsa branch of the Neo-Destour Party. In 1951, in the face of a slowing-down of French reforms towards Tunisian autonomy, the Neo-Destour Party resumed its active struggle for independence. As a result strikes and demonstrations broke out and many leading members of the party, including Tlili, were arrested.

He was detained until 1954, by which time the continuing struggle had caused the

A. Tlili

French to recognise the country's right to self-government. On his release he became a member of the party's Political Bureau and the following year he was elected Secretary of Finance at the Neo-Destour Party Conference held at Sfax.

When Tunisia became independent in 1956 Tlili was appointed secretary-general of the UGTT. He was chosen for this position by the President who preferred his moderate views to those of the former trade unionist leader who was forced to resign. Later he also became Vice-President of the International Confederation of Free Trade Unions and for a period he was President of the African Trade Union Congress. Both of these organisations were affiliated to the trade union movements of the Western countries.

Tlili was opposed to the establishment of an independent all-African federation of trade unions.

In 1959 he was appointed First Vice-President of the National Assembly. He held this position until 1965 when he was removed because of his opposition to the government's economic policies. He was also expelled from the Neo-Destour Party and shortly afterwards he moved to Switzerland.

He returned to Tunisia in May 1967 and was readmitted as a member of the party. By this time he was very ill, suffering from cancer of the liver, and in early June he travelled to Paris for treatment at Saint Antoine Hospital. He underwent an operation but died shortly afterwards, on 25 June 1967. ■

Tolbert, S.A. (1922-75)

TOLBERT, Stephen Allen (1922-75).

LIBERIAN businessman and politician. The younger brother of President William Tolbert (q.v.), Stephen Tolbert was born in Bensonville (now Bentol City) on 16 February 1922. He was educated in White Plains and went to Liberia College in 1936. In 1941 he obtained a BA degree from the University of Liberia, Monrovia, and in 1944 took a BSc and MA in forestry at Howard and Michigan Universities in America.

On his return in 1949 Stephen Tolbert became the first Director of the National Forest Service. He founded the Faculty of Forestry Studies in the University of Liberia and became its first dean. Having earned a reputation for his innovatory work in the School of Forestry, he was invited into the Government in 1950. He was given the portfolio of Deputy Minister of Agriculture and Commerce which he held until 1956 when he resigned to devote his time to a business career begun in 1955.

His company, the Mesurado Fishing Company, grew to become one of Liberia's most successful commercial ventures, spreading into a whole range of activities, including cold stores, soap making, feed mill and shrimp exports. It had subsidiaries in Sierra Leone, Nigeria and Britain. By 1978, the Mesurado Group was employing some 3,500 workers and selling over $3 million worth of shrimp and fish exports alone. A multi-millionnaire businessman, Tolbert was also involved in other public responsibilities. From 1958 to 1960, he was President of the Liberian Chamber of Commerce. Between 1956 and 1972 he was Director of the Bank of Liberia. He was appointed to the governing

S.A. Tolbert

body of the United Nations Food and Agriculture Organisation (FAO), becoming Chairman of the Second Commission of the FAO General Conference in 1965.

His business success and ability led to another invitation to serve in government in 1960 when he was appointed Minister of Agriculture and Commerce. On 10 January 1972 he became Minister of Finance.

Tolbert's influence was soon to be felt in Liberia's foreign policy. Against most African opinion, he advocated dialogue with apartheid South Africa and was instrumental in bringing about South African premier John Vorster's (q.v.) visit to Liberia in 1975. Amidst ensuing domestic and foreign criticism, Stephen Tolbert retained the confidence of the Government until his death in a plane crash in May 1975. ∎

Tolbert, W.R. (1913-80)

TOLBERT, William Richard (1913-80).

LIBERIAN statesman, President of Liberia 1971-80; he was also Chairman of the Organisation of African Unity (OAU) at the time of his death. He was born on 13 May 1913 in Bensonville (now Bentol City), Montserrado County, son of William Richard Tolbert Snr., who served as member of the House of Representatives and National Chairman of the True Whig Party, and Mrs Charlotte Hoff-Tolbert. He had his early education at Government Elementary School in Bensonville and at the Protestant Episcopal High School in Clay-Ashland. On completion he proceeded to Liberia College (now University of Liberia) where he obtained a BA degree in 1934.

In 1935 he was appointed a disbursing officer in the Treasury Department of the Bureau of Supplies, a post he held until 1943 when he was elected member of the House of Representatives. He was elected Vice-President of Liberia in 1951 serving under William Tubman (q.v.) and the same year he was made president of the Liberia Baptist Missionary and Education Convention. He was vice-president of the Baptist World Alliance in 1960-65 and president from 1965-1970. He was the chairman of the Bank of Liberia and a director of the Mesurado Corporation until July 1971 when he became the President of the Republic of Liberia on the death of President Tubman.

As Vice-President of the Republic, he travelled widely, personally representing President Tubman at major African and international conferences and on important goodwill missions. He represented his country at the independence celebrations of Ghana, Togo, Senegal, Nigeria, Tanzania and several other African nations, thus cultivating a personal relationship with several African leaders. This, and his stated belief in good relations with all countries and the settling of differences by negotiation, led to profound diplomatic activities during his years as President. He reactivated diplomatic relations with the Soviet Union, leading to the opening of a Soviet Embassy in Monrovia, and opened relations with several communist bloc countries including East

Germany, Cuba, North Korea and Rumania. In October 1973 President Tolbert signed the Mano River Union Declaration, establishing the Mano River Union (MRU) between Liberia and Sierra Leone. By 1979 the sub-regional economic grouping had, through his personal initiative, expanded to include the Republic of Guinea though the latter formally joined the MRU a few months after Tolbert's death in 1980.

In February 1975 President Tolbert met John Vorster (q.v.), the South African Prime Minister, in Monrovia for talks on the situation in Southern Africa. Vorster's visit, arranged by the Liberian Minister of Finance and the President's brother Stephen Tolbert (q.v.), took place against a background of fierce opposition in several African countries and in liberation movements' circles. But defending the meeting, President Tolbert reiterated his preparedness to go anywhere and talk with anyone if his declared criteria were met to contribute to peace, progress and security. In a statement issued later in Monrovia he said that Mr Vorster had agreed that the whole of Namibia (South-West Africa) must be given independence. Tolbert said that the South African leader also told him that the Bantustan policy was designed to provide independence for Africans in areas occupied by them in South Africa. Vorster, he added, had admitted certain injustices of the policy but gave assurances that his government would do all it could to remove them in stages.

President Tolbert said that he agreed to the talks after approaches were made to him by representatives of South Africa during a visit to Lesotho in July 1974. He had earlier met with the African leader, Chief Gatsha Buthelezi, and the president of the South-West African People's Organisation (SWAPO), Sam Nujoma.

Also in 1975 President Tolbert signed the Treaty of the Economic Community of West African States (ECOWAS), making Liberia a founding member of the 16-state regional grouping. That same year he initiated fresh diplomatic activities in the region, aimed at reconciling Guinea's President Sékou Touré (q.v.) and his counterparts in Senegal and Côte d'Ivoire. This resulted, in May 1978, in what was described then as the Monrovia Miracle which saw the Liberian President bringing together Touré, Léopold Senghor and Félix Houphouet-Boigny, thus

W.R. Tolbert

signalling an end to a long-standing verbal hostility.

He was re-elected President of Liberia twice, in 1975 and 1978. He began his presidency in 1971 with a determination to bridge the gap between the descendants of the liberated American slaves who founded Liberia and led it to independence in 1847, and the indigenous Liberians who, until the 1940s, suffered serious discrimination. He launched a number of campaigns to achieve these goals, often with catchy titles like "From Mat to Mattress", "War on Ignorance, Disease and Poverty", "Total Involvement" and the like. Despite these many reforms of the situation inherited from his predecessor and the success of his astute diplomacy, his regime was shaken by the "rice riots" of April 1979, and conditions grew worse. He was elected Chairman of the OAU in July 1979.

As OAU Chairman Tolbert was a leading figure in the continental politics of the time, centred on economic co-operation and the liberation of Africa. He played an important role in the OAU efforts to resolve the dispute between Morocco and the Sahrawi Arab Democratic Republic (SADR). On 12 April 1980 President Tolbert was killed in a coup d'état that removed his entire administration from power, making him the first incumbent Chairman to fail to complete his term. President Tolbert's assassination was met with widespread condemnation by many governments in Africa.

He was survived by his wife Victoria, six daughters and two sons. He was conferred with honorary DCL and DD degrees by the University of Liberia. Tolbert was also accorded national honours – Grand Band of the Star of Africa, Grand Band of the Humane Order of African Redemption, Grand Cordon of the Most Venerable Order of the Knighthood of the Pioneers – and foreign honours: Knight Commander of the Order of St Michael and St George (KCMG, British), Grand Cross of the Order of Merit of the Federal Republic of Germany, Grand Cross (first class) of the Equestrian Cavalier Order of Pope Pius X (Vatican), Knight Commander of the Legion of Honour (France), Grand Orient of Italy, Grand Cross of the Order of Orange of Nassau (Netherlands), Grand Cordon of the Yugoslav Flag (Yugoslavia), Collar of the Republic (Egypt), and Grand Officer of the Republic (Guinea). ■

Tombalbaye, N. (1918-75)

TOMBALBAYE, Ngartha (1918-75).

CHADIAN statesman, first President of the country who is noted for having sought to achieve national unity in a country divided by the effects of French colonialism. He was born on 15 June 1918 in Bessada in southern Chad, into a protestant family. After his primary and secondary education in Brazzaville, he taught at various schools in Ndjamena, Fort Archambault (now Sarh), Koumra and Kyabe between 1946 and 1949 before going into politics.

In pre-independence days, he was engaged in trade union organisation, becoming in 1946 the president of the *Syndicat Autonome du Tchad*, an independent union, in Sarh where he also organised the formation of the local branch of the *Parti Progressiste Tchadien* (PPT) which he helped to found. The PPT was the Chadian branch of the *Rassemblement Démocratique Africain*

(RDA) launched to fight for independence in French Africa.

In 1946 Tombalbaye headed the Sarh branch of the PPT, and succeeded in increasing the party's popularity in Chad and earning himself the dislike of the French colonial administration. The latter deprived him of employment in the public service, so that he had to do other work, including manufacturing bricks in 1951.

Tombalbaye was elected councillor for Middle Chari to the Territorial Assembly in the elections of 30 March 1952 when the PPT began making the first strides towards breaking the political stronghold of the French and Moslem parties in the country, culminating in the first autonomous government after the territorial elections for self-rule in 1958. Tombalbaye was re-elected in 1957, and again in 1959 and 1962. Following the 1957 elections, he was appointed Higher Councillor for Chad in the General Council for French Equatorial Africa, of which he later became the Vice-President. This Council brought together all of France's four Equatorial Africa colonies.

A brilliant organiser and hardworking politician, he rose rapidly through the ranks of the PPT, serving between 1957 and 1959, alongside his parliamentary duties, as the Ideological Secretary of the party. He succeeded Gabriel Lisette as Prime Minister

N. Tombalbaye

in 1959, and in August 1960 rose to the post of President of the Republic, Chairman of the Council of Ministers, and Minister of National Defence.

Growing opposition from the *Parti National Africain* (PNA) made Tombalbaye intensify moves towards national unity in 1960. On 18 March 1961 the two parties merged to form the *Union pour le Progrès du Tchad*. This union left the remaining small opposition parties unable to offer what the Government called "constructive opposition". In early 1962 Tombalbaye announced the dissolution of Parliament and called for new elections.

On 4 April 1962 the National Assembly approved a change in the constitution which involved a new presidential system of government. On 22 April Tombalbaye was elected President, and re-elected for a second seven-year term in 1968. In that year he called on French forces to help fight the guerrillas of FROLINAT, a group opposed to his rule and active since 1966. The war and the tension between the north and the south persisted later. Then, in August 1973, there were sweeping changes in which the PPT was replaced by the *Mouvement National pour la Révolution Culturelle et Sociale* (MNRCS).

At that time (1973) Tombalbaye also introduced a policy of "authenticity", charting Chad's course of cultural revolution. The President took the lead by dropping his first name, François, for Ngartha, to be prefaced with "Citizen" instead of "Monsieur", and ordered his countrymen to do likewise. Streets, cities and districts bearing French names throughout the country were changed to Chadian names. Fort Lamy, the capital, became Ndjamena. Along with the programme of Chadianisation were started *Yondo* initiation rites, requiring all male government employees and all Sara adult men to undergo the traditional ceremonies.

President Tombalbaye also launched "Operation Agriculture" which was aimed at boosting production of the country's main commodity, cotton, to about 750,000 tonnes a year. Even after his overthrow, the influence of his Chadianisation policy could be seen in the programme of his successors who shortly on assuming office introduced the "Commercial revolution" which was aimed at putting Chad's trade into the hands of its nationals. But the more extreme policies of Tombalbaye, including the cotton programme, were dropped then.

Tombalbaye's problem of maintaining national unity persisted, re-inforced by the guerrilla activity of FROLINAT. In December 1972 President Gaddafi of Libya halted his backing for the movement, granting Chad some 23,000m CFA francs in aid. This pact apparently led to Libyan occupation of a part of northern Chad, but not to the end of the guerrilla war. President Tombalbaye was assassinated in a coup on 13 April 1975. ■

Tongogara, J.M. (1938-79)

TONGOGARA, General Josiah Magama (1938-79).

ZIMBABWEAN soldier and hero of the armed struggle for independence. He was born and educated in Zimbabwe, and moved to Lusaka, Zambia, in January 1960 to take up employment as an accounts clerk in a brewery firm. He joined the Zimbabwe African National Union (ZANU) at its inception in August 1963, becoming chairman of the

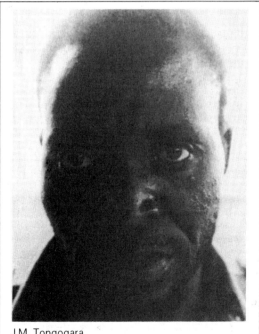

J.M. Tongogara

Lusaka district branch in 1964. The following year he resigned his brewery job to work for the party. He was sent to Tanzania for military training for a year, and then to China for nine months of specialist training. He was the first of four cadres from the Zimbabwe African National Liberation Army (ZANLA), the military wing of ZANU, to train in China.

In 1966 Tongogara became a member of the Military Committee of ZANU's Revolutionary Council after ZANLA had fired the first shots in the Zimbabwe war for independence on 29 April of that year. In June 1967 he was made deputy chairman and chief of operations of the newly constituted Military Planning Committee, and by 1968 he had risen to become Chief of Defence Staff and Secretary for Defence in the Central Committee, posts he held until his death.

While he was propelled to eminence through the ranks of the liberation movement's fighting force, Tongogara was not just a military man in the conventional sense. He was first and foremost a politician, a quality he combined with his military ability to become one of the most influential personalities in ZANU's Central Committee. His influence also spread beyond the confines of his party, and transcended the partisan nature of Zimbabwe's politics. Thus, in 1975 Tongogara was instrumental with Jason Moyo (q.v.) of the Zimbabwe African Peoples' Union (ZAPU) in forging the joint military command that later became known as the Zimbabwe People's Army (ZIPA). Though ZIPA did not survive long, it released the tensions between the two parties, laying the foundations for the establishment of the Patriotic Front in 1976. Tongogara was as pragmatic as he was uncompromising towards his foes – an attribute which some of those who worked with him saw as ambition and hunger for power.

In 1974 ZANU went through a turbulent period with an internecine struggle that culminated in the assassination of Herbert Chitepo (q.v.) in Lusaka in 1975. Tongogara, along with other party cadres, was detained and indicted for complicity in the affair. He was acquitted by the Zambian Supreme Court in 1976. His blend of pragmatism and military skill enabled him to play a crucial role in the negotiations for a settlement in Zimbabwe, from the abortive Geneva to the successful Lancaster House conferences. He died on 26 December 1979 in a motor accident

in Mozambique, shortly after returning from the Lancaster House meeting. Tongogara was made a national hero of the revolution after Zimbabwe became independent in 1980. His body was flown home from Mozambique for re-burial at Heroes Acre outside Salisbury (now Harare) on 11 August 1980, before a crowd of 60,000 Zimbabweans. ■

Touré, A. S. (1922-84)

TOURE, Ahmed Sékou (1922-84).

GUINEAN nationalist, pan-Africanist, one of the most radical of the leaders in French-speaking Africa during the struggle for independence in the 1950s, who was the President of the Republic of Guinea for 26 years. The "symbol of a certain African dignity" though later also a certain form of dictatorship, Sékou Touré was a charismatic, respected, admired politician as well as a most controversial figure. A hero, when he led Guinea to independence in 1958, he enjoyed the passionate and almost unanimous admiration of his people. He was a brilliant organizer and shrewd politician who knew when to be tough and when to compromise. He was the only national leader in the French African territories with the single-mindedness and self-confidence to opt for complete independence and severance of ties with France in the referendum of 1958. But, unfortunately, in later years he became known as one of Africa's most oppressive rulers, although "a moderate" in international affairs.

Guinea at the time of Sékou Touré's birth on 9 January 1922 in Faranah, near the source of the River Niger, in a modest family, was (and still is) a predominantly Moslem country, but superimposed on the traditional society were all the structures and pressures of the French colonial system. Educated at Koranic and then the local primary school, followed by the regional school at Kissidougou, Sékou Touré soon gained a reputation for hard work; he was one of the brightest students, interested in everything, and a voracious reader. In 1936 he went to the Ecole Georges Poiret in Conakry, but was expelled a year later for leading a food strike.

Between 1938 and 1940 he did various jobs while continuing to educate himself through correspondence courses.

At eighteen, in 1940, he was employed by the Compagnie du Niger Français and in 1941 he joined the Post and Telecommunications (PTT) Department. He was by that time already showing his organisational abilities and an active interest in the labour movement. Four years later, in 1945, he formed the PTT Workers' Union, the first trade union in Guinea, of which he became the secretary-general in 1946. He helped to form the Federation of Workers' Union of Guinea, closely associated with the *Confédération Générale des Travailleurs* (CGT), the French Communist trade union movement, and the World Federation of Trade Unions. In 1946 he joined the Treasury Department and was elected secretary-general of the Treasury Employees' Union; that same year he also became a founder member of the inter-territorial *Rassemblement Démocratique Africain* (RDA) formed in Bamako under the leadership of Côte d'Ivoire's Houphouët-Boigny.

When Sékou Touré lost his job in the Treasury for his political activities, he devoted his time to the national trade union movement, and rose to a position of power within Guinea as well as French West Africa (AOF – Afrique Occidentale Française), becoming in 1948 secretary-general of the Coordinating Committee of the CGT in the AOF, and in 1952 secretary-general of the Guinea branch of the RDA, the *Parti Démocratique de Guinée* (PDG), which had by then become a powerful mass movement under his leadership. In 1953 he was in the forefront of a wave of strikes from which he emerged as the idol of the Guinean workers, his reputation greatly enhanced.

That same year he was elected to the Territorial Assembly, and became the Guinea deputy to the French Assembly in the January 1956 elections, having been elected Mayor of Conakry in the 1955 municipal elections. The PDG-RDA in 1957 won 56 of the 60 seats in the then newly established territorial assembly, following the "loi-cadre", which Sékou Touré saw as an opportunity for African nationalists to establish a power-base on their own ground. He was then the undisputed leader of Guinea, drawing his strength from popular support and party organisations. His prestige devolved outside Guinea, and in January 1957 he

formed the *Union Générale des Travailleurs d'Afrique Noire* (UGTAN) which aimed "to unite and organise the workers of Black Africa, to coordinate their trade union activities in the struggle against colonialism and all other forms of exploitation . . . and to affirm the personality of African trade unionism". UGTAN soon attracted the vast majority of workers in the AOF, and in May 1957, Sékou Touré became a member of the Grand Council of French West Africa.

At that time there was a lot of controversy within the RDA as to whether the French African colonies should stay together in a federation within the French Community or move towards balkanisation, with each country linked directly to France. Sékou Touré was a strong advocate of the first option, in opposition to Houphouët-Boigny, but at the 1957 Bamako conference a compromise was reached, and Sékou Touré was elected vice-president of the RDA. The split, however, became again evident when in early 1958 Guinea led by him decided alone of all French Black Africa colonies to vote "no" in French President de Gaulle's referendum between limited autonomy and complete independence, and was expelled from the RDA; Sékou Touré declared that "Guinea prefers poverty in freedom to wealth in slavery".

And so on 2 October 1958, Guinea became an independent republic with Sékou Touré as its President, and the French pulled out of Guinea within days, taking with them their administrative machinery; for more than a decade after that there were no official relations between the two countries.

Sékou Touré, at the beginning, enjoyed the respect of other countries and was particularly close to Nkrumah (q.v.) with whom he had much in common and who at the time of Guinea's independence struggle had also been battling for full independence of Britain's Gold Coast as Ghana was then. Ghana came to Guinea's help with a loan, and considerable aid was also given by the East European countries. Both Sékou Touré and Nkrumah were enthusiastic supporters of pan-African aspirations and conferences, and in November 1958, they formed the Ghana-Guinea Union as a beginning for a Union of West African States, as they saw it. In 1960 the Ghana-Guinea-Mali Union went a further step towards common pan-African and socialist objectives. In January 1961, Sékou Touré attended a summit conference

Sékou Touré

at Casablanca of Heads of State from Ghana, Mali, Guinea, Morocco, the United Arab Republic and the Provisional Government of the Algerian Republic, together with the Foreign Minister of Libya and Ceylon's Ambassador to Cairo. The Casablanca States – as they came to be called – attacked "neo-colonialism", supported the Lumumba (q.v.) forces in Congo, and established a Joint African High Command, and launched committees for economic, political and cultural cooperation. Nkrumah went into exile to

Guinea and was welcomed by Sékou Touré, when he was overthrown in 1966.

However, with time Touré's image in Africa began to suffer. His régime became increasingly marked by plots, repression, lack of capital and expertise needed to back a state-controlled economy and above all the initiative to develop and market the country's economic resources; corruption, profiteering and smuggling became a constant challenge. Touré became disillusioned with Soviet aid, but it was not until the 1980s that he "resigned" himself to encourage US investment and allow the French to come back, having made his peace with them.

He also became increasingly obsessed with the fear of plots against him, and was preoccupied with his own domestic problems, but still managed to remain in office. From 1964 to the end of his days in 1984 large-scale arrests and executions and prison deaths marked the régime and Guinea earned the reputation of being a repressive state and became more and more isolated. Some one million Guineans were believed to be living in exile at the time of his death.

Sékou Touré attributed the economic problems of his country to "enemies and saboteurs". Loyal to his dreams, he "fought" on for several years; he had believed at the time of independence that the "Guineans were going to show how self-confidence and reliance were going to triumph". He had friends, Kwame Nkrumah of Ghana, Modibo Keita (q.v.) of Mali and the Algerians who were fighting for their independence. Guinea was to have a wholly new administrative framework, traditional chieftancy was abolished, village councils had been elected and established, the civil service had been africanized. The Guineans were with him and he had hopes. But somehow it did not work, what followed was a period of disenchantment, first in Guinea itself.

So in the early 80s, Sékou Touré having had to reconcile himself to the harsh realities of low achievements in all fields, opened out the country to improve its economic situation and set out to attract Western and Arab investment to exploit Guinea's reserves of bauxite, diamonds, iron and, potentially, oil. He visited the United States in 1982 to promote business support for development projects. On the international stage in his last years, he was regarded as a "moderate" Islamic figure, though as far back as 1971, he had embarked on a new friendly foreign policy, welcoming many old "rivals" to Guinea, including Congo's President Ngouabi (q.v.), Liberia's former President Tolbert (q.v.), Cameroon's former President Ahidjo (q.v.) in 1972, and Zaire's President Mobutu that same year as well as Côte d'Ivoire's Houphouët-Boigny. He sought better relations with Ghana. He was closely associated with King Hassan of Morocco, whose cause he championed over Western Sahara (the Sahrawi Arab Democratic Republic – SADR). In 1982 he led the delegation sent by the Islamic Conference Organisation to attempt mediation in the Iraq-Iran war, and, in 1984, he played an important role in securing Egypt's re-admission to the Islamic Conference. He was expected to host the OAU 20th anniversary summit in Conakry in 1984, thereby becoming its next chairman, while trying to mediate in the SADR dispute which threatened the OAU's existence and credibility, when he died.

Sékou Touré's belief in pan-Africanism, the picture of Africa he evoked, alone has earned him a place in history. Senegalese President Abdou Diouf, on the announcement of his death spoke of "the historic stature and the exceptional qualities of a man who will later be seen as a courageous and indomitable fighter and intransigent defender of the dignity, the independence and the freedom of Africa, its people and its causes".

The Moroccan daily's *Le Matin du Sahara* editorial said that "with President Sékou Touré's death, Africa has lost one of its historic liberation leaders, the Guinean people have lost an intransigent nationalist, Islam a revolutionary believer ... In voting for independence and against neo-colonialism a little more than 25 years ago, he not only rendered a great service to his country but also to all Africa. In effect, he speeded up the decolonisation process; he was one of the most eminent forgers of African independence as well as one of the most active".

Sékou Touré died of heart failure in an American hospital on 26 March 1984 after an emergency overnight flight from Conakry, where his body was later returned for burial. His close associate and friend, Prime Minister L. Beavogui (q.v.) became interim leader under the constitution, but a few days later Radio Conakry reported that the armed forces had seized power in a bloodless coup and established a "Military Committee for National Redress". ∎

Tovalou Houenou, M.K. (1877-1936)

TOVALOU HOUENOU, Marc Kodjo (1877-1936).

BENINESE politician and author of anti-colonial publications. Born in April 1877, he was the son of a leading merchant, Joseph Tovalou-Padanou-Quenum (died 1925). He was sent to Bordeaux in France for secondary schooling. He stayed in France to study law and was accepted as a member of the Paris Bar Association in 1911. He lived for some time as a rich and smart society man in France, apparently well adapted to French life. In the 1914-18 war he served in the French army.

In 1921 he published a book entitled, *L'Involution des Métamorphoses et des Métempsychoses de l'Univers*, a book of philosophy, theology and comparative linguistics with implicit expressions of opposition to European domination. In the same year he revisited his home country, where there was considerable unrest that culminated in riots in Porto Novo in 1923. Tovalou Houenou, back in France, became increasingly critical of colonial rule. He became a radical critic after an incident in a restaurant in Montmartre, Paris, when he was refused service because of his colour; he sued the management and won. Then he worked closely with other left-wingers from the French colonies living in Paris. With them he formed in 1924 the *Ligue Universelle pour la Défense de la Race Noire*.

This was the first of several small radical anti-colonial groups in France in the inter-war period. It was strongly against French colonial rule, especially such aspects of it as forced labour. Tovalou Houenou said he was basically loyal to France and believed in French ideals, while condemning acts contradicting those ideals. He called for extension of citzenship to Africans generally. His ideas were radical for the period, and feared as such by the French colonial rulers, who were aware of support for such ideas in Dahomey (now Benin), which had the main concentration of Western educated Africans in French Africa outside Senegal.

Tovalou Houenou also started a newspaper, *Les Continents*. It expresed, among other attitudes, the common resentment of many Africans against Blaise Diagne (q.v.), the Senegalese deputy in the French parliament, whose attitude was perceived as being too co-operative with the colonial rulers. An attack on him by *Les Continents* led to a successful libel action. Diagne joined the French colonial rulers in hostility to Tovalou Houenou and his colleagues, who were suspected of Communist links.

In 1925 Tovalou Houenou set out for Africa in an attempt to do something in Dahomey. What his plans were is unclear, but he was arrested in neighbouring French Togo. He later went to Senegal, where he was active in politics, supporting Diouf (q.v.) against Diagne in the French parliamentary elections of 1928 and 1932. In 1936 he died in Dakar; his death was allegedly caused by injuries in a fight at an election campaign meeting. ■

Townsend, E.R. (1923-80)

TOWNSEND, Edison Reginald (1923-80).

LIBERIAN politician. Born on 23 July 1923 in Schiefflin, Marshall Territory, Liberia, he attended the Lott Carey Mission School between 1937 and 1939 and then taught at the J.B. McCritty Elementary School, from where he entered Liberia College, Monrovia, in 1940. After his secondary education in 1943 he joined the Liberia Civil Service as a clerk of the House of Representatives until 1947. He was also the business manager at the President's Executive Mansion.

Townsend was the Press Secretary of the President of Liberia until 1950 when he left for higher studies at the American University, Washington DC. On completion in 1952, he proceeded to Michigan State University, Lansing, where he obtained his Masters' degree in 1953.

On his return that same year Townsend was appointed the adviser of the Bureau of Information, Department of State, retaining this post until 1957. In 1958 he was made the First Secretary of the Department of Information and Cultural Affairs. He was later appointed Minister of State for Presidential Affairs. This post he held until 1972

when he became President of Liberia Enterprises Limited. Townsend was a member of the Fraternal Order of the United Brothers of Friendship (UBF), and general grand patron of the Order of the Eastern Star, 1959-64.

His major appointment was as First National Vice-Chairman of the True Whig Party (TWP) of Liberia. As a leader of the TWP he was one of the important politicians in the country.

He edited some publications: *President Tubman Speaks* (London), *The Official Papers of William V.S. Tubman, President of the Republic of Liberia* (Longmans Green). During his lifetime he won many national honours – Commander and Grand Commander of the Order of the Star of Africa, Liberia; Knight Commander of the Order of the Pioneers of Liberia; Knight Commander of the Humane Order of Redemption, Liberia; and foreign honours – Knight of the British Empire; Grand Commander of the Star of Africa (France); Knight of the Order of the Vatican, Order of Orange of Nassau (Netherlands); Bundesverdienstkreuz (Order of Merit, Federal Republic of Germany); and Order of Merit (Italy).

E.R. Townsend

Like most of his colleagues who had served in the administration of President William Tolbert (q.v.), Townsend was arrested in early 1980 when the government fell in a military coup. He was executed on 22 April 1980, for alleged corrupt practices by the ousted regime in which he had been very influential. Edison Townsend was survived by his wife Evelyn and two daughters and six sons. ∎

Tshombe, M.K. (1919-69)

TSHOMBE, Moïse Kapenda (1919-69).

ZAIREAN politician, who unsuccessfully attempted to lead Katanga (now Shaba) into secession from Belgian Congo. He was born in November 1919 at Musamba in Katanga into a rich commercial family related to the royal house of the Lunda ethnic group.

Educated at the American Methodist mission, he took an accountancy course by correspondence and later went into commerce. He was not very successful and declared bankrupt on three occasions.

In 1951 and 1953 he was a member of the Katanga Province Council and in July 1959 helped to found the *Confédération des Associations Tribales du Katanga* (Conakat) whose main support came from the Lunda. Also supported by the Belgian government and Union Minière, the company controlling the rich copper mines of the province, he succeeded in becoming President of Conakat. In December 1959 he went to Brussels to press for elections and a constitutional conference.

In January 1960 at the Brussels Round Table Conference Tshombe demanded a federation for the Congo (now Zaire) but was denounced as being "big-business controlled" and ignored even by the Belgian government. In May 1960 he was a member of the Round Table Economic Conference and travelled to America on a US government invitation.

In the May 1960 elections Conakat won eight of the 137 seats in the National Assembly and gained 25 of the 60 seats in the Katanga Provincial Assembly; Tshombe was elected Provincial President and formed a Conakat administration. On 11 July 1960, less than two weeks after the establishment of the Democratic Republic of the Congo (now Zaire), Tshombe declared the secession of Katanga. On 8 August he was elected Head of State by the Katanga Provincial Assembly. On 6 September he supported Kasavubu (q.v.) in demanding a confederal solution to the Congo crisis.

At the end of February 1961 Tshombe signed a defence agreement with Albert Kalonji and Joseph Ileo, Kasavubu's nominee as premier of the Central Government. On 5 March he attended the conference of Congo politicians in Tananarive (Antananarivo). On 4 April at a second Round Table Conference in Coquilhatville, Tshombe walked out because Kasavubu had agreed to the presence of UN troops in the Congo. The next day he was arrested at the airport while trying to leave for Elisabethville (now Lubumbashi).

M.K. Tshombe

On 30 April the central government announced that he would be put on trial for various acts of treason, including "Katanga secession and counterfeiting". He was released after he had signed an 11-point agreement with representatives of the Congo's central government in Leopoldville (now Kinshasa). This agreement was rejected on 4 July 1961 by the Lower House of the Katanga "parliament", after the President of the Chamber told deputies that Tshombe had signed it "to gain his liberty".

In August 1961 the Congolese Central Parliament met without the representatives of the Tshombe regime in Katanga. Tshombe maintained the secession of Katanga with the aid of mercenaries and foreign advisers in spite of efforts by the UN to remove them. On the morning of 28 August UN troops occupied key points in Elisabethville and began arresting mercenaries and foreign officers. Fighting continued and Tshombe announced that he would wage total war on the UN. Dag Hammarskjöld, the Secretary General of the UN, arrived in Leopoldville on 13 September and on 16 September he stated that he would go to Rhodesia to meet Tshombe to arrange a cease-fire. His plane left Leopoldville the next day but crashed soon afterwards, killing him.

Mahmound Khiari of the UN resumed the peace talks with Tshombe later. An agreement was signed between the two for a cease-fire to come into force on 21 September. By early November both the UN and Katanga were accusing each other of breaking the cease-fire.

On 24 November the Security Council approved a resolution demanding an end to the Katanga secession and authorising the Secretary-General to use force to remove the mercenaries. Tshombe's reaction was to call on the people of Katanga to take up arms. Fighting broke out in Elisabethville. On 15 December, he sent a telegram to President Kennedy agreeing to meet Adoula (q.v.), the central government premier, provided that the US could guarantee Tshombe's safety and the fighting would stop in Elisabethville.

On 20 December a delegation met in Kitona and on 21 December Tshombe issued an eight-point declaration which reflected the balance of forces which had been established by the 24 November resolution and by the UN operation of 5 December. On 16 February 1962 Adoula proposed a meeting

with Tshombe to examine the means of implementing the Kitona declaration. On 15 March Tshombe agreed to visit Leopoldville. The discussions began on 18 March and dealt with the future Congolese constitution and with a transitional period. The attempts at conciliation failed and on 26 June the discussions ended. After the failure of the Adoula-Tshombe talks, the UN was convinced that the only way of ending Katanga's secession was by bringing economic pressure to bear on Tshombe. But this tactic failed as the *Union Minière*, the largest holding company in Belgium, financed Tshombe's government.

On 11 July celebrations were held in Elisabethville to commemorate the second anniversary of Katanga's secession. On 25 July Tshombe announced that Katanga would adopt guerrilla warfare if the UN attempted to use force to integrate Katanga with the rest of the Congo. He rejected the UN's plan to tax Katanga's mineral resources in order to finance the central government. U Thant, the new UN Secretary-General, continued to try to get British, American and Belgian support for economic pressure against Tshombe. But only the American government was in favour of the plan.

This division encouraged Tshombe to claim that he had enough money and arms to carry on a guerrilla war for years. On 29 July Adoula proposed a federal constitution for the Congo consisting of 21 provinces. This was a significant concession to Tshombe, who received the news with much enthusiasm. However, on 16 October, when the proposed federal constitution was handed to the President, Tshombe was not there.

Fighting broke out again in north Katanga and Tshombe's planes bombed villages in the area. On 19 December Tshombe declared at Kolwezi that he would resort to a "scorched earth" policy rather than accept reintegration by force. After anti-American demonstrations had erupted in Elisabethville a US military mission arrived in the Congo on 21 December. Fighting broke out in Elisabethville on 28 December, when UN troops were ordered to attack in self defence against Katangese soldiers.

On 14 January 1963, the day on which an agreement was reported to have been reached between the central government and the Union Minière on a division of revenue and tax payment, Tshombe was said to be in Kolwezi, having flown there from Ndola. On 16 January he officially informed the central government, in a written statement, that the secession was at an end. Two days later, UN forces entered Kolwezi without fighting. Shortly afterwards Tshombe announced that he was leaving Katanga for health reasons.

By the middle of March Tshombe returned to Elisabethville, having paid a visit to Salisbury (now Harare). Throughout May, June, and July there was increasing unrest in the Congo. At the beginning of June Tshombe went into exile; on 16 June he arrived in France and was detained. On 26 June he was removed as head of the Katanga government.

With UN troops gone and rebel activity reported in the north-east the situation deteriorated even further in 1964. Tshombe was asked to come back as it was thought that he was the only politician able to control the situation. He arrived in Leopoldville on 26 June. On 10 July he was sworn in as Prime Minister of the Congo. Most of Africa's leaders attending a meeting of the OAU were horrified at this appointment and refused to allow him to join the conference in Cairo.

Tshombe was unable to restore order. He appealed to America for military aid and recruited white mercenaries to strengthen his army. In November 1964 he authorised the Belgians to send in paratroops to save white Belgians. In spite of attempts by the OAU to mediate, bitter fighting on both sides continued. The revolutionaries were, however, driven back in 1965. On 13 October Kasavubu invoked his constitutional powers to force Tshombe to resign. On 24 November General Mobutu and his army seized power, alleging that the Kasavubu-Tshombe rivalry might have led to 1960-style bloodshed. Tshombe went into self-imposed exile in Madrid.

Tshombe had lost his seat in the Congolese Parliament, and in March 1966 charges of high treason were filed against him. After he was kidnapped on board an aeroplane which he had hired in Spain, on 30 June 1967, he was held prisoner in Algiers. Congo applied for his extradition on 2 July 1967 but this was refused by Algeria, where Tshombe died in captivity in July 1969; he was buried in Belgium. He was survived by his wife, a daughter of Chief Bako Ditende, and 10 children. ■

Tsiranana, P. (1912-78)

TSIRANANA, Philibert (1912-78).

MALAGASY statesman, first President of Madagascar. Born in 1912 in Ambarikorano, a small village in the north-eastern province of Majunga to a peasant family, he spent his early years tending his father's flocks until he was sent to school at the age of twelve. In 1930 he went to Tananarive (now Antananarivo) where he qualified as a teacher at the Ecole le Myre-de-Vilers, and then taught for twelve years. He interrupted his teaching career and went to Montpellier in France where he obtained a diploma in technical education teaching.

P. Tsiranana

From this humble background Tsiranana rose, through a rather convulsive political career spanning 20 years, to be the first President of Madagascar from 1959 to 1972. He made his debut in politics in 1952 when he was elected unopposed to the Provincial Council of Majunga (now Mahajanga). Four years later he was elected deputy to the French National Assembly and founded the

Madagascar Social Democratic Party (SDP), the ruling party at independence in 1960.

As President, Tsiranana chose to remain in the French fold after independence and maintained close links with the former colonial power. Yet President Tsiranana was a major force in the union of the majority of French-speaking states. In March 1961 he presided over a conference of 12 African states in Yaoundé, paving the way for a later conference in Tananarive in 1965 which led to the formation of the *Organisation Commune Africaine et Malgache* (OCAM).

President Tsiranana is said to have once remarked that he was "100 per cent socialist", yet he had strong anti-communist sentiments which in 1966 prompted him to denounce Chinese activities in Africa. "We will not accept the admission of Communist China to the United Nations, even if we should be the only country left to oppose them", he said. Tsiranana also defied most African opinion and traded with apartheid South Africa thereby tainting the Pan-African esteem which he shared with other founding fathers of the Organisation of African Unity (OAU).

In 1965 he was re-elected President for another seven-year term, and re-elected again for a third term on 30 January 1972. According to official results, President Tsiranana's SDP won 99.9 per cent of all the votes cast by 86 per cent of the electorate that went to the polls. He said in a victory speech that the vote was a popular endorsement of his policies which were opposed by many in the country. Hardly had the post-election euphoria subsided than an alliance of students and workers sparked off unrest in Tananarive; he was accused of excessive dependence on the French and of unacceptable closeness of relations with South Africa. The unrest continued for three days, during which 34 demonstrators were killed and many were wounded. On 18 May President Tsiranana was forced to hand over power to the army.

The ex-president's exit from power and relegation to political obscurity did not constitute a final departure for the ageing Tsiranana. On 21 March 1975 he was charged, in the company of 296 others, with complicity in the assassination of Colonel Ratsimandrava (q.v.), Ramanantsoa's (q.v.) successor. Tsiranana was acquitted and returned once more to relative obscurity until his death from a multiple heart attack in May 1978. ∎

Tubman, W.V.S. (1895-1971)

TUBMAN, William Vacanarat Shadrach (1895-1971).

LIBERIAN statesman. He was born on 29 November 1895 in the south-east of Liberia at Harper, Cape Palmas, in Maryland County. His parents were both Americo-Liberians and his father, a former Speaker in the Liberian House of Representatives, was a minister in the Methodist Church, while his mother was an evangelist worker. From this religious environment Tubman grew up to be a devout Christian.

W.V.S. Tubman

He was educated at Cape Palmas Methodist Seminary and Cuttington College Divinity School until 1913 when he became a teacher. He supplemented his income by working as a tailor while also studying law under the famous Munroe Cummings. He was called to the Bar in 1917.

For some time he practised law in his home town, and gained a reputation not only as an able lawyer but as the "poor man's friend", owing to the large number of cases he pleaded for people with little or no money. He was also appointed a recorder in the Monthly and Probate Court and later became a collector of Internal Revenues.

In 1923 Tubman, already a member of the ruling True Whig Party, was elected to the 10-man Senate representing Maryland County, becoming at the age of 28 the youngest senator at that time. As a senator he was one of the staunch supporters of the proposed Firestone Concession to produce rubber on one million acres of Liberian land which, despite opposition, was ratified in 1926.

Tubman became a lay preacher in the Methodist church. In the same year he represented Liberia at a Methodist conference in Kansas City, USA. He was re-elected to the Senate in 1929 but resigned the following year in the face of scandal concerning the export of slave labour from Liberia, when both the President and the Vice-President of Liberia resigned. Tubman had acted as legal adviser to the Vice-President. Maryland County re-elected him to the Senate in 1934, where he remained until 1937 when, at the request of President Barclay (q.v.), he left to become an associate justice in the Supreme Court of Liberia, a position he held until 1943.

On 6 May 1943 he was elected President of the Republic of Liberia, having stood for election with the support of the outgoing President. He was inaugurated on 3 January 1944. Immediately afterwards Liberia joined the Allies in the Second World War and declared war on Germany and Japan. From that time Tubman took keen interest in international as well as domestic affairs where he left an indelible personal imprint. In the same year his wife Martha died, leaving four children. Four years later he married Antoinette Padmore and had one daughter by her.

During the first term of office the country's Constitution was amended to enable him to stand for re-election after serving in office for eight years, previously the maximum term for a president. Tubman was re-elected President in 1951 and was the successful candidate in all the ensuing presidential elections during his lifetime, making his administration the longest in the history of Liberia.

One of Tubman's main concerns on becoming President was to facilitate the development of Liberian resources. With this in mind he put forward a series of Five-Year Plans during his presidency aimed at improving communications infrastructure, the educational system, the Civil Service, agricultural and industrial development, foreign relations and the exploitation of the country's mineral resources. The economic development of the country was greatly aided by the opening of the deep Free Port of Monrovia and the discovery of large high-grade iron ore deposits.

His "open door" policy, which included offering attractive tax concessions to new enterprises, exemption of import duty on capital goods and no restrictions on the repatriation of profits, encouraged foreign investment. During his term of office both levels of employment and income increased as did Liberia's revenues except during the early sixties when a sharp decline in the price of rubber on the world market and delays in iron ore production caused budget and payments difficulties.

Under Tubman's administration the Constitution was amended to allow the indigenous population to be represented in government. The vote was extended, not only to the indigenous peoples but also to women. Although these initiatives did not by themselves suffice to bridge the gulf between the Americo-Liberians and the indigenous population, Tubman achieved immense respect for his efforts to narrow the divisions and lessen the bitterness between them. In foreign affairs, Tubman travelled extensively, strengthening diplomatic ties and international economic links. He supported the drive for independence on the African continent and in 1960 he joined Ethiopia in contesting the legality of South Africa's administration of Namibia (South West Africa) at the International Court of Justice at the Hague.

Together with Kwame Nkrumah (q.v.) of Ghana and Sékou Touré (q.v.) of Guinea, he organised the 1958 Accra Conference of Independent African States and the 1959 Sanniquellie Conference in Liberia where unity and economic cooperation were discussed for the first time.

In 1961, along with Cameroon, Nigeria and Togo, he helped organise the first conference of independent African Heads of State in Monrovia, to promote African unity and cooperation. Of the 28 Heads of State at that time, 21 attended or sent representatives to the meeting, forming what came to be known as the "Monrovia Group" as distinguished from the group of more militant states known as the "Casablanca Group". The conference supported the concept of African unity, which was envisaged in terms of common aspirations and actions rather than political integration on a continental basis.

Tubman was delighted with the resolutions of the conference as they endorsed his views on African unity; that economic ties and cooperation should be strengthened in all practical fields among independent African states, leading to a uniformity and co-operation of interests, while each nation retained its political sovereignty.

In 1963 Tubman was one of the 32 Heads of State at the Addis Ababa Summit Conference that gave birth to the Organization of African Unity.

A very popular President at home, Tubman was however not without opponents. A new political organisation, the Independent True Whig Party, was formed to contest the 1955 elections. It began its campaign rather late and gained very few votes. At a gathering following the announcement of Tubman's re-election, an attempt was made on his life. The would-be assassin was captured and it was alleged that leading members of the Independent True Whig Party had organised the attempt. The plotters were all arrested, except two who were killed while trying to escape, and were later sentenced to death. However, Tubman did not sign the death warrants of the accused, most of whom were released in 1958.

In September 1961 a strike flared up in Monrovia, bringing commerce and industry in the capital to a virtual standstill. On 11 September about 15,000 striking workers were held throughout the country, as they marched to the Presidential Palace. The following day Tubman called on the Legislature to pass legislation conferring special emergency powers to deal effectively with threats to public safety and the security of the state.

Another assassination plot was uncovered just before the 1963 presidential campaign, and five people were arrested, including the commander of the Liberian National Guard. When Tubman expressed his willingness for the party to select another candidate for the elections, huge demonstrations were held throughout the country calling him to stand for re-election. He reiterated his willingness to step down from office on his 71st birthday in 1966, but again pressure was put on him to remain President.

He was concerned to bring about greater equality between Americo-Liberians and the majority of "countrymen", but the measures he took still left a wide gap. There was hidden opposition to Tubman's government-by-patronage system, the virtual one-party state, control of the press and secret police activity. In 1968 Henry Fahnbulleh, a diplomat, was condemned for another plot.

President Tubman was a Past Grand Master of the Ancient Free and Accepted Masons of Liberia and was awarded honorary LLD degrees by Liberia College and Wilberforce University in Ohio, USA. He also received honorary PhD and DCL degrees from the University of Liberia. His stature as leader and statesman were such that by the time of his death, he was internationally recognised as one of the elder statesmen of the African continent. He died on 23 July 1971 in a London hospital. ◼

Tunsele, M. (c.1830-98)

TUNSELE, Chief Mukengea (c.1830-98).

ZAIREAN traditional ruler of the Lulua, who was noted for his resistance to Belgian occupation. Born in about 1830 in the Kasai province, Tunsele came from the Bena Kashyye ethnic group whose settlement prospered from the 18th and 19th centuries' commerce on the Kasai River. As such the Lulua polity became very powerful, exerting both political and military influence over the whole region. By 1875 Chief Tunsele, also known as Kalamba (without peers), had successfully subdued mutinous chiefs in his country and annexed formerly independent states into his realm. Also he had established contacts with the agents of the emerging Congo Free State, which was formally proclaimed in 1885 by the Berlin Conference placing the entire area of modern Zaire under King Leopold II of Belgium.

The Europeans' initial interest in Lulua was trade, as seen in their early dealings with Chief Tunsele. The Chief welcomed the opportunity and granted facilities which included escorts for the agents through and out of Lulua. In 1884 Tunsele provided land in Katanga for the *Association Internationale du Congo*, a concern belonging to the King of the Belgians, to build a trading post. From 1890, however, the encroachment of the Belgian colonial authorities on Lulua brought friction between Chief Tunsele and the Europeans who sought to establish effective control through the imposition of taxes, to be paid directly to the colonial government, the appropriation of all the tribute destined for Tunsele, and the implementation of measures which forced the Chief's men to work in government industries.

In 1891 Chief Tunsele revoked the concessions he had granted the Europeans and ordered the government agents and their African allies to leave Lulua. In retaliation the colonial troops attacked Lulua, forcing Chief Tunsele and his army out of the land in 1891. For the following three years the Lulua army mounted a campaign against the occupation forces and made the decisive attack in June 1895 in the Battle of Mukabua. The attack on the government post in Mukabua resulted in heavy losses, and a retreat, for the Belgian troops who were commanded by Michaux. Tunsele made another daring attack on the government forces in July 1896 but his troops were forced

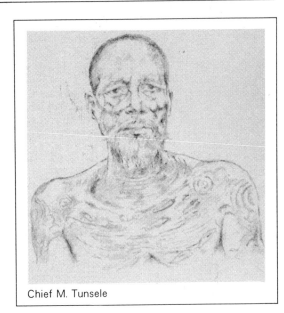

Chief M. Tunsele

to surrender to the superior power of the Belgians' newly introduced Nordernfeld cannon.

Following the last unsuccessful bid to regain his land, Tunsele went into exile where he died in 1898. He was succeeded by his son Tshisungu as Chief of the Lulua people who, until the early 1900s, resisted the Belgian occupation of their land. Tshisungu was given official recognition by the Belgians in 1909 and ruled until his death in 1916. ■

U

Um Nyobe, R. (1913-58)

UM NYOBE, Reuben (1913-58).

CAMEROONIAN politician, leader of armed resistance to French colonial rule. He was born in 1913 at Boumnyebel in the then French Cameroon. His family belonged to the Bassa ethnic group. He received his early education in local schools and then went to a teacher training school for one year before joining the colonial government civil service. He became a member of the Cameroon trade union body linked to the *Confédération Générale du Travail* in 1947 and together with a number of fellow trade unionists he formed the *Union des Populations du Cameroun* (UPC) on 10 April 1948, becoming its president. The UPC advocated that the British and French Cameroons should be united and be granted independence as a unit.

Shortly after its inception the UPC affiliated with the *Rassemblement Démocratique Africain* (RDA) and began to publish the monthly *Voix du Peuple du Cameroun*, its party paper. In 1951 the UPC broke its relationship with the RDA, preferring to maintain its connection with the French Communist Party. Um Nyobe continued to head the organisation and the following year unsuccessfully appealed to the United Nations for political support.

Meanwhile the UPC was gradually gaining in urban support, although the French colonial administration was opposed to its activities. In conjunction with other trade union movements the UPC called on the government to organise general elections as a precursor to independence by the end of 1955. As a result the UPC and other organisations were banned in July 1955 and Um Nyobe, along with other UPC leaders, fled to British-ruled Cameroon.

He returned later in the year and began to organise military operations against the French colonial authorities. A state of emergency was declared in the territory and elections were announced for December 1956. Um Nyobe and the UPC organised a partially effective boycott of

R. Um Nyobe

these elections which they opposed as long as the state of emergency was not lifted. For the next two years he continued to organise military campaigns, supported by many, particularly in the Bassa Region, where he was killed in action near his birthplace on 13 September 1958. The two territories were united three years later. ■

Urabi Pasha, A.
(c.1842-1911)

URABI PASHA, Ahmed (c.1842-1911).

EGYPTIAN soldier and nationalist politician. The son of a farmer of the village of Heyha, he was conscripted into the army after an ordinary Koranic education, and later was able to rise to officer rank. He was one of the first Egyptians of indigenous descent to do so, after a change of government policy allowed it. The officer class was of alien origin, with Turks and Circassians (a people originating in the Caucasus mountains and prominent in the Ottoman Empire) predominant in it, under the ruler (called Khedive from 1867) who was of alien Ottoman origin himself.

By the 1870s, however, Urabi and some other Egyptians had risen to high ranks in the army and had become the most determined leaders of indigenous opposition to the ruling class. Meanwhile increasing British and French control over the country, due mainly to debts incurred on projects started by Khedive Ismail (q.v.) and the European powers' rival active interests in Egypt's fate, culminated in the dismissal of Ismail in 1879 and the imposition of Anglo-French "Dual Control." Foreign control of the country's finances was complete and this virtual occupation aroused Egyptian opposition. Urabi and other officers led this opposition, which was also directed at the Khedive (the Europeans' nominee Tewfik) and his autocratic government.

The nationalist movement led by Colonel Urabi, Colonel Ali Bey Fehmi, and others advanced steadily from the start of 1881. Urabi and Fehmi signed a petition and then, when summoned to a meeting where they were to be arrested, told their troops to follow them. The troops did so, freed their two popular colonels, and forced the dismissal of the Minister of War. Urabi Pasha insisted on the appointment of Mahmud el-Barudi, officer and poet, as the new Minister. The soldiers presented demands regarding pay and promotions, generally agreed by April 1881.

Later in the year, the insurgent officers protested at the punishment of some mutineers; as a consequence Barudi was sacked. The officers were an independent power now, beyond the control of the Khedive, his government and his European controllers. Attempts to curb them led to a virtual coup d'état on 9 September 1881, when, however, they did not seize power for themselves. Their support soon fell and Sherif Pasha took over as Prime Minister without accepting all their earlier demands. The government, including Barudi as War Minister again, sent Urabi away from Cairo, to Zagazig, for a time. But his journey there was a triumphal procession as the officers' protests had massive popular support; Egyptian feelings were aroused not only by local grievances but also by the French conquest of their fellow Arabs in Tunisia in 1881.

Early in 1882 Urabi returned to Cairo and was appointed Under-Secretary for War. Then Britain and France, anxious about developments, sent a Joint Note assuring Khedive Tewfik of their support. The tone of this note aroused Egyptian feelings still further. For some months Urabi and his nationalists were the real power. Barudi became Prime Minister and Urabi, Minister of War. After a report of a plot, 48 Turkish

A. Urabi Pasha

and Circassian officers were arrested and sentenced. But Tewfik, hostile to the nationalists, refused to approve the sentences. Some "notables" who had favoured the new government later turned against it. In May 1882 the British and French, who had sent war fleets to Alexandria, demanded the resignation of the government and the banishment of Urabi. But Urabi responded by denouncing Anglo-French plans to occupy Egypt and also denouncing Tewfik. The government did resign, but the army forced the reappointment of Urabi as Minister of War.

Rising tension broke out in a murderous riot directed against Christians in Alexandria. Following this the British ships (the French ones deciding to back out) bombarded Alexandria on 11 July 1882. Urabi declared war on Britain. Tewfik, at Alexandria, dismissed him, but Urabi secured a judgement of three *Sheikhs* (learned teachers of Islam) at the distinguished el-Azhar Islamic University in Cairo, declaring Tewfik deposed. But the popular backing for his cause did not help Urabi Pasha against a British force of 20,000 which landed in August 1882 under the command of Sir Garnet Wolseley. They defeated his troops at Tel-el-Kebir on 13 September 1882, and marched on to Cairo where Urabi surrendered.

At a trial later in the year Urabi was sentenced to death, but the sentence was immediately commuted to life banishment. He was sent to Ceylon (now Sri Lanka). He was pardoned in 1901 by Abbas II (q.v.), and allowed to return to Egypt. There he died on 21 September 1911.■

Usman Dan Fodio (1754-1817)

USMAN DAN FODIO (1754-1817).

NIGERIAN Islamic scholar politician, and crusader whose *Jihads* – holy wars – were responsible for the spread of Islam in Nigeria in particular and neighbouring West African countries. He was born in December 1754 in the small Fulani village of Maratta in Gobir, northern Nigeria. The family moved to Degel where Usman grew up and received a traditional Moslem education in Islamic sciences, law, theology, grammar and mysticism. Important early influences came from his father and uncles and later a renowned Agades (Niger) teacher, Mallam Jibril, who led an abortive *Jihad* against the Tuaregs.

By the time Usman returned to Degel to begin his teaching career in 1774, he was determined to revive Islam and to set up an Islamic system of government and social order along the orthodox lines which he regarded as sacred. Soon afterwards he toured Hausa kingdoms, preaching against the infidelity of the kings and the harsh and illegal taxes they imposed on their subjects. His fame and reputation won him a large following of Fulani and some Hausa who were dissatisfied with Hausa rule. This too brought him to the notice of King Nafata of Gobir who appointed him tutor to his sons. The King conceded some of Usman's demands for reform by giving Moslems the freedom to worship and to wear turbans and veils. More significantly, the King agreed to reduce taxation. These measures were however soon suspended in 1802 when Yunfa succeeded his father to the throne of Gobir. Also in the same year the new King deported his former tutor to Degel for fear that his teachings might incite open rebellion.

In Degel, Usman dan Fodio continued his criticism of the rulers for permitting an

Usman Dan Fodio's tomb in Sokoto

impure form of Islam. This was met with threats to his life and attacks on his followers which forced them to flee from Degel to Gudu on 21 February 1804. This flight, *Hijra*, still honoured in the Moslem calendar in Nigeria, has significance for the Fulani because of its similarity with the flight of Prophet Mohammed from Mecca to Medina in the 7th century. Usman's followers saw the *Hijra* as the final justification for launching a *Jihad*. Usman dan Fodio was elected caliph and given the title of *Sarkin Musulmi* (Commander of the Faithful) and had the political title of Shehu bestowed upon him, in preparation for the wars against the Hausa rulers.

In February 1804 the first attack was made against the King of Gobir but the state did not fall to the Fulani until 1808. However, by 1804 they had captured Zaria and Katsina, paving the way for the taking of all Hausaland in 1809 and the emergence of the Fulani empire which later spread southward as far as the Oyo Kingdom in Yorubaland. In later stages, the *Jihad* lost most of its original religious character; what had begun essentially as a clash between Usman dan Fodio and the rulers of Gobir turned out to encompass a revolutionary movement, led by intellectuals, with far-reaching political consequences. The *Jihad* thus resulted in a system of government, based on Islam, in place of the traditional dynasties south of the Sahara.

Although Usman's personal involvement in the wars decreased with age, he was the mastermind behind the movement whose spirit and intentions he articulated eloquently in his writings. It was he who guided his son, Muhammadu Bello (q.v.) and his brother, Abdullahi, during the invasions of Hausaland. With the war won and the new Fulani Empire established, Usman divided it into two dynasties, Sokoto under Bello and the other, Bornu, under Abdullahi. He retired from politics in 1809 and went to Sokoto where he died at the age of 63, in April 1817.■

Vales, S. (1951-77)

VALES, Sita (1951-77).

ANGOLAN politician and Head of the Department of Mass Organisation (DOM) of the *Movimento Popular de Libertaçao de Angola* (MPLA). A militant from her teens, she played a key role in the 1977 coup attempt to overthrow President Agostinho Neto.

She was born on 23 August 1951 in Cabinda of a middle class family, the daughter of Goan Indians. After her primary education, she left Cabinda to continue her studies in Luanda, later entering Luanda University as a medical student. Active early in her life in nationalist politics, she was forced to leave Angola before obtaining her medical degree. She went to Portugal, enrolling at Lisbon University, where in November 1971, she joined the Portuguese Communist Party, working within the Communist Student's Union (UEC), and became one of the leaders of the Faculty of Medicine Students Association for the following three years. Having displayed her exceptional organizational ability Sita was soon appointed to the secretariat of the Communist cell at her university.

In 1973 she was elected to the Central Committee of the UEC which was still legal at the time. A year later, in April 1974, she was elected a member of the executive of the Central Committee. It was after this election that she devoted herself to full-time politics.

In the beginning of 1975, Nito Alves (q.v.), a member of the MPLA Central Committee, a Minister and leader of the nitista faction, encouraged her to return to Angola which she did, becoming affiliated to the party. Nito Alves appointed Sita head of MPLA's Department of Mass Organisation (DOM). With Sita at the top and some other fifteen militants trained by Nito's controlled Centre for Revolutionary Instruction (CIR) forming the core of the department, the Nitista faction exercised an overall control of this body.

In a few months Sita had built an extra-legal secretariat running parallel to the existing structures and functioning as an agency for establishing nitista cells in all mass organisations, notably the youth movement (JMPLA), the women's movement (OMA) and the trade unions. This clandestine structure was headed by Nito Alves himself, and there were Nitistas in control of many subordinate departments. Sita herself, through the "group study practice", recruited young, newly politicized militants to join the faction. In 1975 Sita married José Van Dunem (q.v.), member of the MPLA's Central Committee, and second to Nito Alves in the Nitista faction.

At the Central Committee meeting of October 1976 to discuss factionalism within the Party, Sita was deposed from the DOM. She was believed to have carried working on clandestine activities while working as a doctor in a Luanda hospital. A few months later, in May 1977, Nito Alves and Van Dunem were also expelled from the party, having been found guilty of factionalism. The three of them then conspired against the government and planned to overthrow it.

Sita was said to have written the text for the first broadcast Nito would have made announcing his take over and his immediate decisions. The document was later found by the MPLA and used as evidence against Sita and the Nitistas.

The attempt to overthrow the government failed and Sita and Van Dunem were arrested a few days after it, during which time she tried to send a letter to the Russian embassy in Luanda asking for political asylum which was intercepted.

No formal statement was ever made by the Angolan government on Sita's fate after imprisonment, but she is believed to be dead. Sita and José Van Dunem had a son who was born on 8 February 1977. ■

Van Dunem, J. (1949-77)

VAN DUNEM, José Jacinto da Silva Vieira Dias (1949-77).

ANGOLAN politician, former member of the *Movimento Popular de Libertaçao de Angola* (MPLA) Central Committee, of the Political Commissariat of the party's Armed Forces (FAPLA) and one of the leaders of the factionalist group (the nitista) which attempted to overthrow Agostinho Neto's (q.v.) government in Angola in May 1977.

He was born in Angola on 29 August 1949. Involved in politics from a young age, in 1966, he was arrested, together with a number of other MPLA militants and sent to the prison camp of São Nicolau, in the south of the country.

In São Nicolau Van Dunem managed to build up a strong clandestine structure, having won, it is said, the confidence of many of the six thousand Angolans imprisoned with him. This network was related to the CRL (Revolutionary Committee of Luanda) which was an organization linked to the MPLA but which had a fairly independent nature. Many CRL members were later to join the Nitista faction of the MPLA.

Van Dunem was released shortly after 25 April 1974 and headed straight for Luanda. In the capital he met Nito Alves (q.v.) the then Commander of the MPLA's First Politico-Military Region, Dembos Forest, in Northern Angola, and organized with some friends Nito's trip to Lusaka to participate in the MPLA Congress.

The MPLA leadership, unhappy with the failure of the Lusaka Congress to reunite the Party, organized another meeting, this time inside Angola, which Van Dunem attended. He was appointed member of the Central Committee and of the Political Commissariat of the FAPLA.

Within a few months of working in the FAPLA, Van Dunem, who enjoyed the trust of the Chief Political Commissar, Jika, was able to install his own "Nitista" network within the Commissariat. He also succeeded in appointing nitistas to control the People's Defence Organisation (ODP, a kind of militia) and the recently created Military Police.

In 1975 he married Sita Vales (q.v.), head of MPLA's Department of Mass Organisation (DOM) and a very important leader of the Nitista faction.

That same year Jika died, but Van Dunem's lack of military experience disqualified him from becoming Chief Political Commissar and the post went to Bakalov. Van Dunem had nevertheless strong power in the FAPLA. Together with Bakalov he was in charge of a number of Centres for Revolutionary Instruction (CIR), where MPLA militants were trained in military matters. At the head of the Sangue do Povo CIR where the first Commanders of post-independence Angola were trained, was Amadeus Neves, one of Van Dunem's men. In the Kimpuanza CIR, a centre for training soldiers on strategic weaponry, there were seven members of Van Dunem's own family.

The Central Committee Plenary meeting in October 1976, which discussed the nitista faction, launched an attack on the behaviour of the FAPLA National Political Commissariat. It was decided that the General Staff of the forces should exercise a greater control over the Commissariat. After this meeting the Nitistas started building a stronger clandestine network, and from time to time would openly challenge the government. Van Dunem and Bakalov used their power to its full extent, instigating acts of insubordination and near mutiny in the army.

The Central Committee meeting of May 1977 to discuss the report of the Commission of Inquiry into the Nitista faction, found Nito and Van Dunem guilty of factionalism, and expelled them from the party. A plan to overthrow Neto's government was then drafted by Nito, Van Dunem, Sita Vales and a number of top Nitista people. It was believed Van Dunem was to become Prime Minister of this new government.

At first the coup was to take place on 25 May 1977, the FAPLA being of key importance to the success of the exercise.

Van Dunem was responsible for assuring the Army's support. However, at the last moment, the military Nitistas, realising that Nito's plan seriously over-estimated their strength, refused to go into action. The coup was then postponed to the 27 May; Van Dunem tried to patch up the weakness of the previous plan. He formed three "Death Commandos" that were assigned to kill specified members of the Central Committee, DISA (Department of Information) and the FAPLA General Staff.

The entire operation hinged on a mass demonstration which turned out to be far smaller than expected by the Nitistas. They had failed to gather enough mass support. Only one barracks fell to them, the Ninth Armoured Brigade, and a fort on the outskirts of Luanda was captured, but soon the Nitistas had to surrender to the much stronger loyal forces of the government. Moreover, most political commissars outside Luanda were neutralised before that date.

Van Dunem and his wife, Sita Vales, went into hiding immediately after the failed attempt, and managed to avoid arrest for two weeks. Even though no formal statement was ever made by the Angolan authorities on Van Dunem's fate, he is believed to be dead. ■

Dr H.F. Verwoerd

Verwoerd, H.F. (1901-66)

VERWOERD, Dr Hendrik Frensch (1901-66).

SOUTH AFRICAN settler politician, principal architect of apartheid. Hendrik Verwoerd was born in Amsterdam, Holland, on 8 September 1901. Two years later his family moved to South Africa where his father, a missionary of the Dutch Reformed Church, opened a grocery shop in Cape Town. His early education took place at Wynberg High School in Cape Town, Milton High School at Bulawayo in Southern Rhodesia (now Zimbabwe), and Brandfort High School. He then went to study at the University of Stellenbosch in Cape Province, and in the tradition of Afrikaner intellectuals he finished his studies at the Universities of Hamburg, Leipzig and Berlin, after turning down an Abe Bailey Scholarship to study at the University of Oxford in England. In 1927 he married Elizabeth Schoombee, with whom he had seven children.

On his return to South Africa he joined the University of Stellenbosch as professor of Applied Psychology between 1927-32, and professor of Sociology and Social Work from 1933-37. He was one of a deputation of professors from the University who protested to the Prime Minister against a government decision to give asylum to German Jewish refugees, and as his interest in politics increased, he became a member of the National Party and the *Broederbond*, a secret society of influential Afrikaners.

In 1936 he was one of the main organisers of the National Conference on the Poor White Problem at Kimberley and became chairman of its Continuation Commission. In 1937 he left the University of Stellenbosch and became editor-in-chief of the Afrikaans daily *Die Transvaaler* in Johannesburg. He stayed in this position until 1948, during which time he became known for the anti-British, anti-Semitic and pro-Nazi views which his paper promulgated. In 1943 he sued the Johannesburg *Star*, a rival newspaper, for damages after being attacked for his Nazi sympathies. He lost the case, the judgement being that he did support Nazi beliefs.

Dr Verwoerd stood as a candidate for the Alberton constituency in the 1948 elections and after his defeat, he was nominated to join the Senate, where he led the National Party between 1950 and 1958. He was also appointed Minister of Native Affairs in October 1950, a post which he held until 1958, during which time he became the chief architect of apartheid, determining the pattern of the Government's Bantu policies.

He expressed apartheid as territorial separation, with each race developing through its own institutions and by its own powers. This concept was justified through his belief that although God had created all men to be equal, they must develop separately. In this way the Africans could be excluded from a voice in South African politics and denied the right to hold property outside their allotted territories. Thus in reality it stripped South Africa's non-white population of their political rights and economic security.

In the April 1958 elections he was elected to Parliament, for the Heidelberg constituency, and in September of the same year he was elected leader of the National Party and Prime Minister on the death of his predecessor, Strijdom. It was clear that he intended to continue promoting the policy of white supremacy in South Africa and shortly afterwards legislation was introduced causing the choice of three white parliamentarians and the four members of the Senate representing African interests to be discontinued.

Meanwhile feeling was growing against the government's racial policies, and on 21 March 1960 the Pan Africanist Congress (PAC) organised a protest meeting against the laws at Sharpeville. Around 5,000 Africans attended this meeting, and although the crowd was peaceful, the police reacted by firing into it, killing 67 men, women and children and wounding over 300 others. In response to this, the African National Congress (ANC) called a stay-at-home day of mourning on 28 March, and the Government received protests against their action from all over the world. On 30 March the Government declared a state of emergency, outlawing both the ANC and the PAC. Hundreds of opposition politicians from all races were detained without charge or trial for several months.

On 9 April 1960 there was an assassination attempt against Dr Verwoerd while he was attending a Transvaal Agricultural Show in Johannesburg. He was shot in the head by David Pratt, a white English-speaking farmer, but was not seriously hurt and recovered within two months. Pratt, who was found to be mentally unbalanced, later committed suicide.

During 1960 Dr Verwoerd raised the issue of whether South Africa should become a republic, and a referendum in which only the whites voted was held in November 1960. Of those who voted 52 per cent were in favour of the creation of the Republic of South Africa. With the preparations for the establishment of the republic underway, Verwoerd attended the Commonwealth Prime Ministers' Conference in London in March 1961 to apply for continued membership of the Commonwealth. While at the conference he described apartheid as a domestic policy of good neighbourliness, but in the face of the considerable and fierce debates that this issue caused, he formally withdrew his application.

The opposition United Party were bitterly critical of his decision to withdraw from membership of the Commonwealth. The Republic of South Africa was formally established two months later on 31 May 1961. The October 1961 elections confirmed his white support in the country with the National Party increasing its majority in most of its constituencies and gaining three more seats in the Assembly.

During his tenure as Prime Minister he continued the formulation of his policy of separate development through the establishment of Bantustans, areas within South Africa that would be assigned to Africans on the basis of ethnicity. The first step in the creation of these homelands was announced in January 1962, and in 1963, the Transkei was established as a territorial authority with a legislative assembly. However, the South African government retained control over defence, foreign affairs, internal security, posts, telegraphs, public transport, immigration and some financial matters, as well as requiring all laws passed by the Transkei parliament to be submitted to the President of South Africa for his approval.

The intensified policies of apartheid during this period led South Africa to become even more diplomatically isolated in the world, while internally the country was increasingly becoming a ruthless police state. There was a great increase in the number of Africans killed or imprisoned for opposition to his policies, and he firmly rejected taking a more liberal stance on the racial issue, believing that any concession could lead to more demands and to the final erosion of white supremacy in the Republic.

On 6 September 1966 he was stabbed to death while seated in Parliament by a white man who had recently secured employment as a parliamentary messenger.■

Vieira, O. (1938-73)

VIEIRA, Osvaldo (1938-73).

GUINEA-BISSAU soldier and hero of the armed struggle for independence in which he distinguished himself as military commander of the Northern Front and later as Chief of General Staff in charge of the entire military operation. Popularly known in political circles as Ambrosio Djassi, he was among the first cadres of Guinean youth to embrace the ideology of the *Partido Africano da Independencia da Guiné e Cabo Verde* (PAIGC) and respond to its call for national liberation. The PAIGC was founded on 19 September 1956 by Amilcar Cabral (q.v.) to mobilise the people of Guinea-Bissau and Cape Verde for the campaign for independence. Because the Portuguese forbade African political organisation at the time the party operated clandestinely, first among urban workers and then the people in rural Guinea. The party's strategy was a long term programme which involved preparing the peasants for revolution before rather than after launching the struggle for independence, so that the diverse material interests and aspirations of the different groups could be united against Portuguese colonialism. This programme soon won popular support for the PAIGC which in 1959 created a special school for the training of cadres drawn from wage-earners, members of the petty bourgeoisie, merchants and peasants. The party rapidly became a major force in the country, demonstrated by the fact that just after three years of launching the armed

struggle, in 1963 it had over two-thirds of Guinea-Bissau under its control.

Vieira joined the PAIGC in 1959, at the age of 21. After studying at the PAIGC ideology school where he was also taught military tactics, he received advanced military training in China and in the Soviet Union. He returned to Guinea-Bissau to take the important post of Military Commander of the northern region where the PAIGC combatants had opened a second front in the protracted campaign against Portuguese occupation.

Soon he was moved to the external base of the PAIGC, as head of the military programme which was being directed in Algeria. From that position he was appointed into the War Council and made Inspector-General (Chief of General Staff) in charge of all PAIGC military operations.

Osvaldo Vieira died of cancer in 1973 and was widely mourned as a national hero.■

Vorster, B.J. (1915-83)

VORSTER, Balthazar Johannes (1915-83).

SOUTH AFRICAN politician, for twelve years prime minister of South Africa and the embodiment of the apartheid régime and ideology of the Afrikaner Nationalists. He was born at Jamestown in the Eastern Cape on 13 December 1915 and went to Stellenbosch University, a cultural centre of the Afrikaners who were then advancing steadily towards domination over the other Whites and over the majority non-White people.

Vorster first practised as an attorney in Port Elizabeth, but soon became involved in politics when Smuts (q.v.) took South Africa into the Second World War on the side of Britain in 1939. When the cabinet voted by a narrow majority for war against Germany, Hertzog, who defended Germany and wanted South Africa to remain neutral, was replaced by Smuts. Afrikaner nationalism, with its belief in the superiority of one race and its destiny to dominate, and its anti-semitism and advocacy of total subjugation of the Black African, had much in common with Naziism, and in 1938 some of the more extreme and militant Afrikaners formed the *Ossewabrandwag* (ox-wagon guard), a Nazi-type quasi-military formation.

B. J. Vorster joined this organisation and was an outspoken supporter of Hitler in the war years. Pro-Nazi Afrikaners launched

B.J. Vorster

a campaign of sabotage to impede Smuts' war effort; telegraph and telephone wires were cut, post offices blown up. Vorster, a "General" of the *Ossewabrandwag*, was in the thick of this activity, and on 26 September 1942 he was sentenced to 17 months' imprisonment; he was held at Koffiefontein in Orange Free State. A few years after the war Vorster joined the National Party and in 1953 he was elected to parliament and soon acquired a reputation as a skilful orator. He entered the National Party government in 1958, and in 1961 was appointed Minister of Justice and Police in Dr Verwoerd's (q.v.) government. In that important post he became notorious all over the world as the man mainly responsible, with Verwoerd, for the intensified repression following the Sharpeville shooting of 1960 and the subsequent unrest

which badly shook the white-supremacy regime. He strengthened the security police and had their powers much increased by the notorious "Sabotage Act" of 1962. Detention without trial and other methods were used to suppress the African National Congress (ANC) and the Pan-Africanist Congress (PAC) and other Black opposition groups. Having said in his first speech, "the rights of free speech, assembly and protest are getting out of hand", Vorster proceeded to curb them by several means, notably the use of "banning" orders. In 1963-64 Nelson Mandela and other ANC leaders were arrested and gaoled.

After the assassination of Verwoerd (which Vorster's security services had failed to prevent) in 1966, Vorster became prime minister. For the next twelve years he headed the apartheid regime, proving himself more pragmatic than his predecessor in his endeavours to maintain it. He adopted the viewpoint of those called in Afrikaans *Verligte* (the enlightened), believing in a more subtle and apparently conciliatory enforcement of apartheid than the intransigent methods favoured by the others called *Verkrampte* (the narrow-minded). While the dispute was intensely felt by Afrikaners, some of whom left the National Party to form a new *Herstigte Nationale Partie* (HNP) in 1969, in reality the quarrel was only about slightly differing means to the same end.

Vorster, for all his strong attack on the HNP, believed firmly in the extremism and enforcement of apartheid, with only the most trifling changes aimed at deception of some outside South Africa. The white voters returned his party to power to pursue those policies in 1970, 1974 and 1977. At the core of those policies was the creation of "Homelands" or "Bantustans", to which Black Africans would be considered to "belong" while most of the country was treated as the white man's, with Africans allowed to live and work only under rigid controls enforced by the infamous "Pass Laws". Vorster pursued this policy until Transkei became "independent" in 1976 and Bophutatswana in 1977. The enforcement of police controls over Africans' movements was unabated, and as prime minister Vorster continued, as before 1966, to give the police more power to detain, torture and harass. Back in 1969 Vorster had created a new Bureau of State Security (BOSS) headed by Hendrik Van den Bergh, who had shared imprisonment with him. In 1976 hundreds of Black Africans were killed in the suppression of mass protests in Soweto.

In 1975 Vorster went to Israel; some Israelis protested at his visit, but the Israeli government made an alliance with South Africa to the benefit of both. Other countries continued to deal with South Africa, even with some arms sales, and trade between South Africa and the rest of the world, particularly western Europe and North America, boomed, with the Rand gold industry as its base. Vorster and his Defence Minister, P. W. Botha, presided over a massive rearmament programme including domestic arms production which by 1978 met virtually all the régime's needs. Despite its economic and military strength, Vorster's régime could not ignore the independent African states and their united condemnation of apartheid. It helped the rebel white Rhodesian régime and the Portuguese colonial authorities to fight against African nationalists. The independence of Angola and Mozambique in 1974-75, however, was immediately followed by a period of what was called détente when he met President Kaunda of Zambia in 1975 in the course of efforts to secure a Rhodesian settlement. These efforts came to nothing, and Vorster continued to defy African and world opinion in continued occupation of Namibia, and sent an expedition into Angola in 1976. In Namibia he sought to set up a client régime including Africans as an alternative to the South West African People's Organisation (SWAPO). He met the Presidents of Côte d'Ivoire, Senegal and Liberia in 1974-75 as part of a policy of trying to establish contact in independent Africa which however did not succeed.

Vorster's policy of trying to evade criticism of apartheid culminated in secret government payments for favourable press coverage in a new local newspaper, *The Citizen*, and foreign newspapers. In 1978 illegal and secret overspending in the Department of Information, which came under the ministry headed by Dr. Connie Mulder, was exposed. The ensuing scandal, "Muldergate", shook the apartheid régime and on 20 September 1978 Vorster resigned as prime minister, officially for health reasons. He was then chosen as President to replace Dr. Diederichs who had just died. But a few months later the Erasmus Commission investigating "Muldergate" found that Vorster had known about the secret operations. Its final report criticised him and on 4 June 1979 he resigned as President. Vorster, who had a wife and two sons, then retired from politics. But he came out to denounce the plans of his successor, Botha, for a constitutional change introducing elective representation of Coloureds and Asians. He died on 10 September 1983. ∎

W

Wallace-Johnson, I.T.A. (1894-1965)

WALLACE-JOHNSON, Isaac Theophilus Akunna (1894-1965).

SIERRA LEONEAN pan-Africanist, trade unionist, politician and eminent journalist who used his pen to oppose colonial domination of Africa. He was born into a poor Creole family on 6 February 1894 at Wilberforce Village, Freetown. He went to a local primary school and the Centenary Tabernacle School in Freetown after which, lacking the formal qualifications to become a church minister, he worked for a variety of commercial concerns. He joined the Customs Department of the colonial service in 1913 and while he was in this position he began to utilise his organisational and oratorial abilities to help establish a workers' movement. The following year he helped to lead a strike for better conditions and increased wages and as a result he was dismissed from his job.

He was reinstated but shortly afterwards in 1915 he was transferred to the Carrier Corps of the British Army, working as a records clerk in various parts of Africa for the remainder of the First World War and until his demobilisation in 1920. He then returned to Sierra Leone where he joined the Freetown City Council until 1926 when, once again becoming unpopular with the authorities through his continuing campaigns for better pay and working conditions, he left to become a merchant seaman. While in the Merchant Navy he became a member of the British National Seamen's Union and contributed to *The Seafarer*, a news magazine for sailors.

Wallace-Johnson later returned to West Africa and worked on the Lagos *Daily Times* in Nigeria. He returned to Sierra Leone and attended the First International Conference of Negro Workers held in Hamburg in 1930, as the unofficial representative of the Sierra Leone Railroad Workers' Union. The following year, after organising and acting as Secretary-General of the African Workers' Union, Nigeria's first labour organisation, he went to Moscow to attend the International Labour Defence Congress and then studied at the People's University there under the name W. Daniels.

By 1933 he had become editor of the *Nigerian Daily Telegraph* and also contributed under pseudonyms to the *Negro Worker*. An able and militant writer, he soon became unpopular with the authorities and eventually moved to Accra. He became a regular

I.T.A. Wallace-Johnson

contributor to the *African Morning Post*. The British authorities in the then Gold Coast soon regarded him as a "potential troublemaker". In 1936, he was arrested for alleged sedition following the publication of an article in the *African Morning Post* entitled "Has the African a God?". He was fined £50 and then travelled to England to appeal to the Judicial Committee of the Privy Council. However he lost his appeal after the Judicial Committee decided that although the article was not seditious, it was an unwarranted attack on religion, and held that the sentence should stand. He remained in England until 1938 and worked as General Secretary for the International African Service Bureau. While in England he renewed his acquaintance with George Padmore and Jomo Kenyatta (q.v.), both of whom he had met at the 1930 Hamburg Conference, and worked with them to help establish a Pan-African Federation to promote the interests of African workers. He also set up two newspapers, *The African Sentinel* and *Africa and the World*, to help publicise his political beliefs.

In April 1938 he returned to Freetown, taking with him 2,000 copies of *The African Sentinel*. These were confiscated by the Customs Department on his arrival, but this only added to his popularity. He immediately established the West African Civil Liberties and National Defence League and shortly afterwards founded the West African Youth League (Sierra Leone), becoming its Secretary-General. The West African Youth League aimed to appeal to people of all levels in Sierra Leone. Through the *African Standard*, a newspaper which was established the following January to publicise the views of the League, criticism was made of the country's economic and social problems. The paper called for the establishment of trade unions and the extension of civil liberties.

The West African Youth League gained much mass support, enabling all four of its candidates to win in the November 1938 elections for the Freetown City Council. After Wallace-Johnson had helped in organising eight separate trade unions in the country, the British authorities in Sierra Leone became increasingly worried about his activities and growing influence. Their suspicion that he was receiving help from Communist sources was later proved to be unfounded. During 1939 there were a series of strikes by unions affiliated to the West African Youth League. These strikes, and Wallace-Johnson's articles in the *African Standard*, caused the colonial administration to pass three bills concerned with sedition, undesirable literature and deportation.

In September 1939 Wallace-Johnson was arrested on charges of criminal libel following publication of an article in the *African Standard* headed "Who killed Fonnie?", which implied that Fonnie, an African who had died while being flogged, had been killed by the colonial District Commissioner who had ordered the beating.

Following the outbreak of the Second World War, Wallace-Johnson was detained under the emergency Colonial Defence Regulations. Until 1940 he was held at a temporary internment camp after which he was transferred to Pademba Road Prison where appalling conditions led him to write a series of poems about the prison. He called these works *Prison in the Muse* and after their publication an official investigation was held which resulted in some improvement of prison conditions.

During this period he suffered from bad health and in March 1942 he was transferred to Bonthe on Sherbro Island, where he remained until his release in 1944. In the following February he went to London to represent Sierra Leone at the World Trade Union Congress and later on in the year he was elected to the Executive Committee of the World Federation of Trade Unions Congress. He was also involved in the organisation of the 1945 Pan-African Congress in Manchester.

In 1951 he became a leading member of the National Council of the Colony of Sierra Leone (NCCSL), a political organisation which was the result of the merging of a number of political movements, including the West African Youth League. In the same year he was elected member of the Legislative Council for the Wilberforce and York constituency and became an active member of the Opposition. In 1956 he broke away from the NCCSL and was one of the founders of the United Progressive Party (UPP). The UPP quickly gained much popular support and the following year he was re-elected to the House of Representatives. But by 1959 he had left the UPP which had disintegrated through internal rivalries, and founded the Radical Democratic Party. In 1960 he was one of the delegates to the London Constitutional Talks for Sierra Leonean independence. He died in a car accident in Accra, where he was attending a labour conference, on 16 May 1965, aged 71. ■

Whitehead, E.C.F. (1905-71)

WHITEHEAD, Sir Edgar Cuthbert Fremantle (1905-71).

ZIMBABWEAN settler politician. The son of a Chancellor of the British Embassy in Berlin, he was born on 8 February 1905. He was educated at Shrewsbury School, England and later went to read history at University College, Oxford. In 1928, as a result of ill health, he left for Southern Rhodesia (now Zimbabwe) where he joined the Civil Service. From 1930 to 1939 he engaged himself in farming in Vamba, and was a prominent member of the Umtali District Farmers Association and the Eastern Farmers Federation.

In 1939 he was elected Member for Umtali North to the White-dominated Parliament. With the declaration of the Second World War in 1939, he joined the armed forces in England. He left the army after the war with the rank of Lieutenant-Colonel and was made High Commissioner for Southern Rhodesia in London. He later returned to Southern Rhodesia to become Minister of Finance from 1946 to 1953. He was a figure of considerable controversy during his tenure of office as Finance Minister, for the hitherto unrestrained white businessmen in the territory were brought to obedience. He insisted on a closer link between Southern Rhodesia, Northern Rhodesia (Zambia) and Nyasaland (Malawi); like others he favoured this idea (eventually achieved in the Federation from 1953 to 1963) in order to ensure a larger internal market. He had to resign because of poor health and sight in 1953 and returned to his farm.

Despite his poor health, from 1954 he served as the first representative of the Federation of Rhodesia and Nyasaland in Washington. Whitehead was Southern Rhodesia's Prime Minister from 1957 to 1962. His tenure of office could be regarded as marking a change from the more radical policies of Garfield Todd, whose period as premier had led to the revolt of some white politicians who formed the United Federal Party. Under Whitehead the political position of the African in Southern Rhodesia deteriorated, though his policies later seemed quite moderate compared with what followed.

On 26 February 1959 he declared a State of Emergency in Southern Rhodesia, using the Nyasaland disorders as an excuse, irrespective of the fact that there had been no political unrest in Southern Rhodesia. He proscribed the African National Congress and detained 495 people. He proposed six draconian laws to fortify the security legislation, but was forced to modify them in response to the protests of academics and renowned members of the legal profession. The 1960 riots in Salisbury (Harare), which spread to Bulawayo and led to the killing of twelve Africans and the arrest of three senior leaders of the National Democratic Party (NDP), emanated from the unjustified policies of Whitehead. The NDP was banned.

In 1961 the "Whitehead Constitution" was introduced giving Africans slight-

Sir Edgar Whitehead

ly increased representation, which would be slightly and gradually increased later. The African nationalist leaders denounced this constitution. But white settlers also turned against Sir Edgar (knighted in 1957), many believing him to be too ready to accept British policies favouring concessions to the Africans. In 1962 his party was defeated in the settler elections. Sir Edgar was Leader of the Opposition from 1962 to 1965. He died in England on 23 September 1971.■

Witbooi, H. (1840-1905)

WITBOOI, Chief Hendrik (1840-1905).

NAMIBIAN traditional ruler. He was born in the southern part of Namibia (South-West Africa). Witbooi was an outstanding leader who played an important role in both shaping and leading the anti-colonial war against the Germans. The German colonialists are said to have selected him and his army as their first target in their invasion of Namibia.

Leutwein, the German representative at the time Germany was planning to colonise Namibia, sent an ultimatum to the Namibian leader in August 1894 in which he stated, "You have so utilised two months of consideration given to you that you still refuse to recognise German supremacy. The times of independent chiefs of Namaqualand (or the Southern Namibia) are gone for ever. . . In comparison with the German Emperor you are but a small Chief. To submit yourself to him would not be a disgrace but an honour".

Witbooi's reply to this was: "You say that it grieves you to see that I will not accept the Protection of the German Emperor, and you say that this is a crime for which you intend to punish me by force of arms. To this I reply as follows: I have never in my whole life seen the German Emperor; therefore I have never angered him by words or by deeds. God the Lord has established various kings on the earth, and therefore I know and believe that it is no sin and no misdeed for me to wish to remain the independent Chief of my land and my people. If you desire to kill me on account of my land,

and without guilt on my part, that is to me no disgrace and does no damage, for then I die honourably for my land. But you say that 'Might is Right' and in terms of these words you deal with me because you are indeed strong in weapons and all conveniences. But, my dear friend, you have come to me with armed power, and declared that you intend to shoot me. . . I will shoot back, not in my name, not in my strength, but in the name of the Lord, and under His power. . . So the responsibility for the innocent blood of my people and of your people which will be shed does not rest upon me as I have not started this war."

Chief H. Witbooi

Witbooi was later killed in the battle-field and Leutwein wrote about him: "A born leader and ruler, that's what Witbooi was; a man who probably might have become world famous had it not been his fate to be born to a small African throne".■

Wobogo (died 1904)

WOBOGO, Mogho Naba (died 1904).

RULER of the Mossi kingdom of Ouagadougou. The 30th Mogho Naba (King) of the state of Ouagadougou (now part of Burkina Faso) who is renowned for his fierce resistance to French efforts to colonise his kingdom.

He was the second son of Koutou who was the 28th king of Ouagadougou and was given an Islamic education at the Koranic School in Sarabatenga where he was taught to read and write Arabic. Boukari Koutou, as he was known before he ascended to the throne as Wobogo, competed unsuccessfully for the crown against his older brother Sanem at their father's death in 1871. It took several months for the council of electors to resolve the succession dispute between the two brothers. Boukari led a civil war, equally unsuccessful, against his brother who had become the 29th Mogho Naba. However, following Naba Sanem's death in 1889, Boukari returned to Ouagadougou, accompanied by his troops, to reassert his right to the throne which was now being contested by his remaining brothers. He forced the electoral college to name him the new Mogho Naba, assuming the name Wobogo, meaning elephant.

Mogho Naba Wobogo's reign was occupied with suppressing the Lalle rebellion which had broken out in the northern part of the kingdom under his predecessor and with resisting European encroachment on his state. For the former he solicited, and got the help of the Zerma warriors who came from the area of modern Niger. His opposition to European colonialism was however the biggest test of his rule. He resisted successive attempts by the French and the British to establish contact with his kingdom, although he welcomed individual European visitors to the state. In September 1890 he received in the Mossi capital of Ouagadougou François Crozat, a French medical doctor who brought a message from the French government. The following year Mogho Naba Wobogo barred another French emissary, Monteil, from entering his capital, maintaining his suspicion of the intentions of the Europeans.

He however entered into a friendly treaty with the British government in July 1894. The alliance with Britain was the result of negotiations by a Gold Coast (Ghanaian) Fanti surveyor and cartographer, George Ekem Ferguson, who acted as British agent in West Africa in the nineteenth century. His suspicion of European intentions was confirmed when the French army invaded Ouagadougou in 1896. Led by Paul Gustave Lucien Voulet, the invaders captured the capital, which they burned when Mogho Naba Wobogo tried to resist the invasion. The King remained in the city to do battle with the French but was forced to retreat when his vassal kings surrendered to the French army. He fled to Nobere where he was welcomed by Naba Kaglere. From there he led several attacks on French military positions. He was formally deposed in 1897 and replaced by his youngest brother Sighiri as the 31st Mogho Naba.

The provinces of Manga and Busansi remained loyal to Mogho Naba Wobogo during the period of his deposition, which encouraged him to raise an army against the French. He appealed to the British government for assistance, in respect of the 1894

Mogho Naba Wobogo

treaty, but was turned down. Mogho Naba Wobogo continued his campaign against the French until his army was defeated. He took refuge in the Gold Coast from where he made a desperate and final attack to retake his capital in 1897. Halted by the French just 40 kilometres (24 miles) south of Mossi, he retreated to Zangoiri in the Gold Coast where he died in 1904.

Mogho Naba Wobogo is seen in retrospect as an unfortunate ruler who reigned at a most difficult time in African history. His consistent refusal to deal with the Europeans is now considered as shrewd political calculations to keep the colonial powers at bay, but his resources could not match the military might of the French when the latter resorted to armed incursion.■

Xuma, A.B. (1893-1962)

XUMA, Dr Alfred Bitini (1893-1962).

SOUTH AFRICAN politician and physician; he was President General of the African National Congress (ANC) from 1940 to 1949. He was born in 1893 in the Transkei into an aristocratic Xhosa family. He was educated locally and, after working as a teacher, went to the USA where he studied agricultural science at the Tuskegee Institute in Alabama. Later he enrolled for a medical course at the University of Minnesota. After receiving the Doctor of Medicine degree from Northwestern University, Evanston, Illinois, Dr Xuma went to Europe where he specialised in gynaecology. He also took some courses at the universities of Glasgow and Edinburgh.

On his return to South Africa in 1927 he opened a surgery in Sophiatown in Johannesburg. He concentrated on his medical practice at first, while joining the Johannesburg Joint Council. As the Africans' political position steadily worsened under the government of J.B. Hertzog (q.v.), he became more involved in African protest. He was elected Vice-President of the All African Convention when D.D.T. Jabavu (q.v.) became its President.

In 1940 he was elected President General of the ANC. He worked hard to transform the ANC into a mass movement. Xuma recognised the special role of young people in a revolutionary struggle for national freedom. During his leadership many young people were brought into the fold of the ANC. According to Albert Luthuli (q.v.), the presence of young people dynamised the activities of Congress. A Youth League sub-committee was constituted in 1944 and led by Nelson Mandela, Walter Sisulu and Oliver Tambo. These young men advocated more militant programmes that did not receive full endorsement from Xuma.

Dr Xuma encouraged links between the ANC and other political groups. Relations were developed with the Indian National Congress which was also campaigning against the exclusive social, political and economic rights of white South Africans. At the United Nations, Dr Xuma strongly opposed the incorporation of the Mandated Territory of South West Africa (Namibia) into South Africa.

Dr A.B. Xuma

Because of his relatively moderate approach, Dr Xuma's standing within the ANC began to ebb. In 1949 he was replaced by J.S. Moroka (q.v.) as President of the ANC; Moroka's nomination was sponsored by the Youth League. He helped to lead a protest against the application of apartheid in Johannesburg, where Sophiatown was declared a white area, in the 1950s. Dr Xuma died on 28 January 1962. ∎

Y

Yall, A. (1940-85)

YALL, Abdoulaye (1940-85).

MAURITANIAN army officer and Minister who was one of the leading figures from southern Mauritania in the military and political set-up dominated largely by the Moors of the north. Born on 2 March 1940 at Bogné on the border with Senegal, he was brought up mainly in the north, living among the Moors and learning their language. That up-bringing became an invaluable asset in later years as it enabled him to penetrate the tight leadership circles of Mauritania.

After completing secondary school, the young Yall entered the army, training in various military academies in Senegal and France. He returned to Mauritania in 1965 and was immediately appointed assistant to the Commanding Officer of the First Reconnaissance Squadron, a post he held until 1966 when he was appointed Commanding Officer of the Specialised Unit at Gom.

Yall returned to the Reconnaissance Squadron in 1967 as Commanding Officer, before moving on to the General Headquarters in Nouakchott in 1970 to take charge of the Personnel Division. But he was soon appointed to head the Chancellery of the Ministry of Defence, and then in 1973 became Commanding Officer of the Military Company at the General Headquarters.

His brilliant performance at this command post earned him commission of the second military sector in the mineral-rich zone around Zoueraté. It was while he was there that the war over the Western Sahara broke out and Yall's troops were in the front-line of the fighting. As Commanding Officer, he emerged from the war with his reputation greatly enhanced. He was promoted to Co-lonel and, in 1977, appointed Deputy Chief of Staff in the General Headquarters in Nouakchott. The following year Yall was sent to Morocco as Military Attaché, with the extra responsibility of commanding all Moroccan troops stationed in Mauritania as a result of the war.

The coup d'état that took place in Mauritania in early 1979 brought Yall back home to join the ruling Military Committee of National Salvation as Inspector of the National Guard. Membership of the Military Committee gave a new political dimension to Yall's career. In January 1984 he was appointed Army Chief of Staff, and two months later he joined the Government itself as Minister of the Interior.

Though a very able administrator, Yall was more of a leader; in the barracks he was able to bring together the different ethnic groups in the army and maintain stability. So he asked to be returned to military command, and was duly appointed Commander-in-Chief of the National Gendarmerie in December 1984.

In May 1985 he was returned to an even more central role as Chief of Staff, Supreme Headquarters, a post he held until his death on 29 October 1985. An official three-day mourning was decreed throughout the country in his honour, as one of the most prominent army officers from southern Mauritania.■

Yaya, A. (died 1912)

YAYA, Alfa (died 1912).

GUINEAN traditional ruler. He emerged in the confusion which arose in the Moslem Fulani state of Fouta Djalon in the

1880s and 1890s, and which helped the French to occupy a once powerful kingdom slowly but with little difficulty. The state was ruled by an Almamy, supposed to be chosen alternatively from two families for a limited term of office. A war over the succession in 1896 was followed by French occupation of the capital, Timbo, and a treaty establishing French control on 6 February 1897.

Alfa Yaya

In the years before this Alfa Yaya, who bore the title Alfa Mo Labe and ruled a large area around Labe, collaborated with the French against the Almamys, whose authority his family had long resented. He obtained power after killing his brother Aguibou and then a rival claimant to the chieftancy, Alfa Gassimou (1892). After co-operating with the French Alfa Yaya was recognised in the 1897 treaty as "permanent chief of the Labe, the Kade and the N'Gabou". He was still nominally subject to the Almamy then, but in 1898 this subjection was ended and Alfa Yaya became "King of Labe" directly under the French governor.

After a few years the French began to disagree with him. The French made Labe a *région* with six *cercles* (1902-3). Locally Alfa

Yaya was the effective power, but the French began to make difficulties over his appointments of chiefs, and there were also problems over taxes which he collected for the government. In 1905 some of Alfa Yaya's territory was transferred to Portuguese Guinea. And so Alfa Yaya turned against the French. In response, the French invited him to meet the governor at Conakry for a talk, it was a trick to get him to leave his stronghold, and he was arrested as he left the governor's palace. He was deported to Dahomey (now Benin) for five years, accompanied by his son Aguibou.

The French then split up his kingdom and distributed its territory among four chiefs, rivals of Alfa Yaya. But Alfa Yaya's influence was still so powerful in his home area that the French were unwilling to let him return. He promised to submit to the French and live back home as a private citizen when he finally returned to French Guinea. But he was accused of plotting to return to power in Labe; the plot stories are doubtful. He was arrested in Conakry on 9 February 1911, without returning to Labe, and condemned for the alleged plot and deported again, this time to Mauritania. He died there of scurvy, a year later. In the same year, 1912, the French completed their suppression of Fulani authority in Guinea.

Alfa Yaya is remembered as a national hero in independent Guinea; his remains were brought back from Mauritania for reburial, as Samory's (q.v.) were from Gabon.■

Youlou, F. (1917-72)

YOULOU, Abbé Fulbert (1917-72).

CONGOLESE statesman, first president of the independent Republic of Congo. Fulbert Youlou was born at Madingou in the south of the Congo Republic on 9 June 1917. His family belonged to the Lari ethnic group and his father was a merchant. From early childhood he wanted to become a priest, and he entered a seminary school at the age of 12 in Brazzaville. He later continued his studies at Akono and Yaoundé in the then French Cameroons, and after teaching in the Congo he completed his studies in Libreville and Brazzaville.

He was ordained a priest of the Roman Catholic Church in June 1946 and became the priest in charge of the St. Francis parish in Brazzaville. He was involved in the work of many Catholic organisations and also became known locally for his activities as chaplain in a local hospital and for his involvement in various youth movements. In the 1955 elections he stood as an independent candidate for the French National Assembly and although he was unsuccessful he received many votes and was widely regarded as the leader of the Lari people in the south of the country.

In 1956 he founded the *Union Démocratique pour la Défense des Intérêts Africains* (UDDIA), and he also began publishing a magazine called *Cette Semaine* to publicise his political views to the people. Meanwhile senior church officials, displeased with what they considered his lack of zeal and discipline, suspended him from priestly functions. He carried on his campaign for public office in spite of Church disapproval of these activities. However, he continued to use his religious title and his popularity increased, resulting in his election as Mayor of Brazzaville in November 1956.

In March 1957 elections were held for deputies to the Territorial Assembly. By this time Youlou's party had increased in popularity and it gained 21 of the 45 seats. The opposition party also gained 21 seats and received support from two of the three independent deputies, thus gaining an overall majority. The support that Youlou had resulted in his being made Minister of Agriculture in the new government.

The UDDIA became affiliated in August 1957 to the *Rassemblement Démocratique Africain*, an inter-territorial political organisation encompassing trade unions, political parties, religious and cultural groups in French-speaking Africa. In the September 1958 referendum concerning the future status of the Congo, Youlou and his party campaigned vigorously to remain in the French Community with partial autonomy rather than for complete independence, a view which received the majority of votes.

Two months later the Republic of the Congo was created and Youlou, having gained a majority in the Territorial Assembly by receiving support from a deputy of the other party, became Prime Minister on 28 November. Tensions began to build up between the opposing political factions in

Abbé F. Youlou

the country, leading to riots in both Brazzaville and Pointe Noire in January 1959 during which 200 people were killed. As a result several members of the opposition party, including its leader, were briefly imprisoned. The situation soon stabilised and by June 1959 an agreement was reached whereby the two parties merged into one.

Meanwhile, Youlou's popularity was growing and in the June 1959 elections, the UDDIA gained all but ten of the 61 seats. After agreements were signed for the transfer of sovereignty with continued co-operation with the French on matters of defence and foreign affairs, the Republic of Congo became independent on 15 August 1959, with Youlou as its first President, duly elected on 21 November 1959. He was re-elected President for a five-year term in March 1961, after receiving 97 per cent of the votes. During this period he also held the portfolios of Defence and Internal Affairs.

Realising the importance of co-operation with neighbouring states, he put forward proposals for a union of Central African Republics. However, this association floundered because of internal difficulties and the disparate economic strengths of the countries involved. He also attempted to solve the troubles of the neighbouring Belgian Congo (now Zaire) and organised two conferences in Brazzaville in 1960. From one of these conferences the "Brazzaville Bloc" of 12 countries emerged, all of them moderate and pro-West. Youlou's support of Tshombe (q.v.), the leader of the secessionist Katanga Province, eventually led to the closure of the border between the two Republics.

During his term of office many ambitious economic projects were initiated. Early in 1962 mineral explorations revealed large iron-ore deposits. He secured French and German finance towards the proposed Kouilou dam and hydro-electric plant for an aluminium smelter. However, the country's economic difficulties continued, such as a continuous trade deficit and high levels of unemployment.

In an attempt to overcome unemployment Parliament decided that unskilled and unemployed youths should be trained for work in the Civic Service where they would be able to contribute to the economic life of the Congo. The International Labour Organisation charged, and the government denied, that these plans resulted in the institution of forced labour.

Meanwhile, opposition to Youlou was growing in the country. His pro-French policy was resented as neo-colonialist and he was accused of political oppression, nepotism and corruption. The increasing economic problems cost him the support of the trade unions and on 13 August 1963 a general strike was called. Rioting broke out in Brazzaville and Youlou appealed to France for help. French troops were sent in to protect their nationals' property and to restore order, but did not give him the support he needed to retain power and on 15 August 1963, after long talks with the union leaders in the face of violent demonstrations, he resigned the presidency and was detained in a military camp.

He remained in detention until March 1965 when he escaped and fled to neighbouring Zaire where he was given refuge by his old ally, Tshombe. He left the country following Tshombe's resignation as Prime Minister and after being refused asylum in France, he went to Spain where he stayed for the rest of his life. During this period he wrote a book *J'Accuse La Chine* (Paris, 1966), accusing Communist China of causing many of the troubles in post-independent Central Africa. He died on 6 May 1972 at the age of 54.■

Z

Zaghlul Pasha, S. (c.1857-1927)

ZAGHLUL PASHA, Sa'ad (c.1857-1927).

EGYPTIAN politician. Born at Ibiana village in Gharbiyya province in the Nile delta, he was the son of a big landowner and village headman. He was educated at a village school and then, from 1871, at the famous Islamic University of al-Azhar, Cairo. He joined the group of followers of two leading Moslem reformers, al-Afghani (in Egypt in the 1870s) and Muhammad Abduh (q.v.), and was closely associated with Abduh. The latter had a profound influence on Egypt, for his calls for the reform and purifying of Islam were coupled with acceptance of modernisation on Western lines, which Egypt had been pursuing in the 19th century. In 1880 Zaghlul became assistant to Abduh in editing the *Official Gazette*.

Zaghlul entered government service and worked in the early years of the British occupation. He worked in the judicial branch and became interested in legal reform, following the ideas of Abduh and others on that subject. He became a judge in the Court of Appeals in 1892. Having learned French, he studied in the French Law School in Cairo. In 1906 he married the daughter of the pro-British Prime Minister, Mustapha Fahmi Pasha. This made him known to the court of the Khedive and to the British. At the suggestion of Consul-General Cromer, he was appointed Minister of Education in 1906.

He had shown his interest in education earlier, as in the Moslem Benevolent Society founded in 1892 by Abduh, himself and others. As Minister of Education until 1910, he organised an increase in the number of schools, and the introduction of night schools for adults; he pushed for greater use of Arabic instead of English, and employed more Egyptians as school inspectors. In 1908 a Supreme Council of al-Azhar and councils for some other Moslem institutions were started; this move, and the school for training of Sharia judges under government supervision, were given a mixed reception by the al-Azhar scholars, centre of a powerful pressure group. Zaghlul was on poor terms with the Khedive too, and this led him, as Minister of Justice after 1910, to oppose British moves to give the ruler greater power.

He resigned from the government in 1913 and stood successfully for election to the new Assembly (called "Legislative" but with no real power) campaigning on a platform of greater Egyptianisation of the administration. He was a Vice-President of the Assem-

Zaghlul Pasha

bly during its short life in 1914, and made his mark as a leader of opposition to the government, the upper classes, and (by implication) the British. He had already projected his image for years with a view to a later political career.

That began in 1918 when, at the end of the First World War, he led a delegation to the British Resident (Egypt having been declared a Protectorate in 1914), and then formed a permanent "Egyptian Delegation", al-Wafd al-Misri, to present Egyptian demands in the post-war peace settlement. The Wafd became the main nationalist party, and Sa'ad Zaghlul Pasha the main nationalist leader.

When Zaghlul and others were prevented from travelling to Europe early in 1919, a massive show of support, leading to unrest and violence, forced the British government to let them go, after briefly deporting them to Malta. They failed initially to end the protectorate but in 1920 Britain agreed in principle to this, while being ready to negotiate it with the politicians in power and not the Wafd, which was on increasingly bad terms with those politicians. Prime Minister Adli Yeken left on 1 July 1921 for talks with Britain which Zaghlul refused to join. He continued to arouse strong support in Egypt and was deported to Aden and then to the Seychelles, in late 1921. After this Britain promised independence on condition that important British interests were safeguarded. Independence was declared on 15 March 1922.

With Britain still controlling Egypt's foreign policy and maintaining a large number of troops, Egypt did not have the independence Zaghlul had called for. But he returned in 1923 and worked within the situation of incomplete independence. The Wafd won an overwhelming victory in elections in January 1924 and on 28 January 1924 Sa'ad Zaghlul Pasha became Prime Minister. In power he found it difficult to satisfy the expectations of a great mass of followers, especially in the rural areas who revered him as the *za'im el-umma*, the national hero. He made several compromises, finding the aim of complete independence difficult in practice then. The Wafd resorted to authoritarian measures against opponents. Then, on 19 November 1924, the British High Commissioner in the Sudan (whose status was one Egyptian nationalist grievance) was murdered in Egypt. In a furious reaction the British made demands on the Egyptian government which Zaghlul could not accept entirely. So he resigned on 23 November 1924.

New elections were later held under a changed electoral process intended to prevent a Wafd majority. A narrow Wafd majority was in fact elected but a coalition of other parties took over the government in March 1925. Then Zaghlul was elected Speaker, and Parliament was immediately dissolved again. Despite further measures to prevent a Wafd majority in new elections, yet again it won a majority in May 1926. Zaghlul, however, agreed to a coalition of the Wafd and the Liberals under the Liberal leader Adli Yeken. He became Speaker again. On 23 August 1927 he died.■

Zakara, M. (1916-77)

ZAKARA, Mouddour (1916-77).

NIGER politician. Born in 1916, at Digina in Filingue District, Niger, he was one of the nomadic Tuareg people who are numerous in the Sahel and Sahara of Niger. After his primary education in Niamey, between 1925 and 1932, he became a clerical officer at the Treasury in Niamey (1932-38)

M. Zakara

and was posted as clerical officer to the French District Administration at Tahoua (1938-40). He worked as interpreter at the Sub-Division for Nomad Affairs in the French colonial government from 1940 to 1947. In 1947 he was appointed special agent in Tahoua, and in 1952 head of Imanan district, Filingue division. In 1952 he became a chief of the Imanan Tuareg; he was also Amenokal (paramount ruler) of one of the largest Tuareg confederations, the Ouilliminden Kel Dinnik.

He was elected a *Parti Socialiste Africain* (PSA) member and Vice-President of the Territorial Assembly of Niger, 1957-58, and member for Tahoua in the National Assembly in 1958. When Niger obtained self-government he became Secretary of State for Internal Affairs, 1958-62. He was also Minister of Saharan and Nomad Affairs from 1959 to 1974, combining this post with successive other ones, he was Minister of Posts and Telecommunications from 1965 to 1970. He was then appointed Minister of Finance from 1970 to 1974.

Mouddour Zakara received the National Order of Niger and honours from African and other countries, including Egypt, Côte d'Ivoire, Morocco, Belgium, France and West Germany. He was a striking figure dressed in Tuareg traditional robes, and a major power behind the scenes in the regime of President Diori (q.v.). He was the Treasurer and main leader of the Association of Traditional Chiefs of Niger. However, his fellow Tuareg suffered terribly in the drought and famine which led to the fall of the Diori regime. Zakara was arrested following the coup d'état of April 1974. He died in Niamey hospital in May 1977, survived by his two wives and three children. ∎

Zaouche, A. (1873-1947)

ZAOUCHE, Abdeldjelil (1873-1947).

TUNISIAN politician. He belonged to one of the aristocratic families of Tunisia which had, even before the establishment of the French "Protectorate" following the occupation in 1881, accepted Western education and forms of modernisation as good for their people. He went to the Lycée St. Charles in Tunisia and then to the Faculty of Law at the Paris University, where he obtained a degree in 1900, being one of the first Tunisians to qualify as a lawyer (the very first being Ahmed Chattas, 1875-1926).

He practised as a lawyer back in Tunis, but only very briefly, before joining M. Ramella to start a modern flour mill. He ran it profitably for 20 years, being interested not only in his own business success but in the general encouragement of business enterprise by Tunisians to improve their situation under French rule.

Zaouche was one of an important group of followers of the reforming Prime Minister of pre-occupation days, Khair el-Din (q.v.), all initially willing to tolerate French rule as an aid to necessary modernisation. Their attitude was made easier by France's policy of leaving the Bey of Tunis and much of his traditional administration alone, while effectively ruling Tunisia herself. From 1891 the Bey had a Consultative Conference, and in 1907 this was reorganised to include 16 Tunisian Arab representatives, of whom Zaouche was one.

A. Zaouche

In 1907 Zaouche joined about ten others of the group just mentioned to found a weekly newspaper in French, *Le Tunisien*. It proclaimed co-operation with France but sought to improve the position of the Arabs under a continued French Protectorate. This general policy was put forward by the same people, with others, in a small political group called the Young Tunisians. Zaouche and several Young Tunisians' leaders attended a conference on North Africa in Paris in 1908. Their speeches there made a good impression on many Frenchmen.

However, like very many Africans in the colonial era, they found that proclamation of co-operation did not always raise them above the suspicion of many of the European settlers. In Tunisia the settlers, who already owned considerable amounts of good land, were hostile to all Arabs with education who could make articulate grievances over land and other issues. Although the Young Tunisians were the target of attacks from these arch-colonialists, Zaouche remained a respected member of the Tunis Municipal Council. He also continued to encourage and help practical efforts to improve the Arabs' situation, particularly through cooperatives.

In 1911 there was a crisis in Tunis over a decision to expand a stone quarry on to the land of a cemetery. Zaouche persuaded his fellow members of the Municipal Council to drop the idea, but this decision was not conveyed to the angry Moslem crowds who, infuriated by the plan to encroach on sacred ground, fought with police. Zaouche rushed to make peace but could not prevent more clashes. Nine Europeans were killed and probably many more Moslems.

From 1917 Zaouche held many posts in the traditional government headed by the Bey. He became Caid, traditional governor, of Sousse in that year; Caids still had a role, though local French officials really ruled. In 1934 he was appointed to the high traditional office of Sheikh el-Medina, and in 1935 he became "Minister of the Pen". The following year he was made Minister of Justice. He retired on 1 January 1943, during the German and Vichy French occupation which a few months later led to the dismissal by the Free French of Muhammad el-Munsif Bey. Zaouche lived to see the subsequent birth of nationalism as a mass movement; he died early in 1947. ■

Zarruq, M. (1916-65)

ZARRUQ, Mubarak (1916-65).

SUDANESE politician, famous for anti-colonial agitation. He later served as his country's Minister of Communications. He was born in 1916 in the Sudan, graduated from Gordon College in the Sudanese capital Khartoum and went to work, between 1934 and 1939, for the Sudan Railways. He then studied law and went into practice as an advocate in 1943.

Zarruq became active in the early nationalist and intellectual organisations contesting the British occupation of the Sudan. He served on the Executive Committee of the Graduates Congress formed in 1938 to demand independence for the country. In 1944 Zarruq was among the radical elements led by Ismail el-Azhari (q.v.) who formed the Ashigga Party, or Blood Brothers, to oppose any official collaboration with the British while supporting the union of the Sudan with Egypt. He became a member of the Omdurman Municipal Council in 1950.

M. Zarruq

An able politician with radical leanings, he co-founded the United Front for Sudanese Liberation, an organisation of the radical pro-independence parties which included Communists, students and workers' associations. The objectives of the Front included immediate termination of the British-sponsored condominium which placed the Sudan and Egypt, under one central British control, with King Farouk (q.v.) as King of Egypt and the Sudan. The Front also rejected any form of dealing with the British. Zarruq acted as its secretary before joining the National Unionist Party (NUP) in 1952, taking most of his Front colleagues into the new party.

The NUP won a majority of seats in the parliamentary elections of 1953, and Zarruq was elected to Parliament. He was appointed Minister of Communications in the government headed by el-Azhari – this government led the Sudan to independence in January 1956. The el-Azhari government fell later that year, following a split within the ranks of the NUP, and after which Zarruq went into opposition with the former Prime Minister. He participated in the 1964 Revolution that forced the Ibrahim Abboud government out of office and, for his part, he was placed in charge of the important Finance portfolio in the transitional administration that served in 1964-65. Mubarak Zarruq died in 1965 before the general elections of that year.■

Zeleke, B. (1895/96-1948)

ZELEKE, Dejazmatch Belay (1895/96-1948).

ETHIOPIAN resistance leader who fought in the war (1936-41) to defend his country's independence against Italian colonialism. The exploits of his small band of guerrillas who routed the Italian occupation troops, and his administration from the Gojam Province in north-east Ethiopia marked him out as an outstanding patriot leader. For this he is fondly remembered in Ethiopia as *Atse Bagulbatu* (self-made emperor); he was in fact given the honorific title of *Dejazmatch* and made Governor of

Gojam by Emperor Haile Selassie I (q.v.) after the re-establishment of independence in 1941.

Belay Zeleke was born in 1895 or 1896, to a proletarian family and grew up in the humble surrounding of rural Welo, a province north-east of Addis Ababa. In his youth, according to Ethiopian sources, he ran away from home after accidentally killing his uncle. He was said to have settled on the bank of the River Abbay in southern Gojam. where his wife joined him. Soon his household grew in numbers, to include both members of his family and others who all paid allegiance to him. Belay Zeleke reigned over this community until the Italians invaded Ethiopia in 1935.

During their military occupation the following year Zeleke and his band were said to have attempted to submit themselves to the authority of the Italian provincial appointee in Debre Marqos. But they were attacked by Italian troops at Bichana in July 1936, and Zeleke's irregulars responded with a counter-attack. They defeated the Italians and hanged their leader. After that Zeleke decided, on his own initiative, to continue to fight the Italians. He and his small band of followers, though less equipped than their European adversaries, made slow but steady progress in a guerrilla campaign in southern Gojam. As the campaign intensified they started making daring attacks on Italian columns in the region. Their successes rekindled the flame of nationalism among Gojam patriots who joined Zeleke's army in large numbers. Soon he was at the head of a considerably large army of patriots and, as such, was respected, and was referred to by many as an emperor. He restructured his army and appointed officers on whom he confirmed the titles of *Balambara* and *Ras*, an act which was the prerogative of Ethiopian emperors.

Meanwhile his activities intensified, gaining momentum and widespread support in Gojam until the whole province revolted against the Italians. Their success, apart from ending the Italians' occupation of Gojam, gave further impetus to the national struggle, and by 1939 when the Italians made overtures for a negotiated settlement, Zeleke was one of the patriot leaders who opposed negotiations. By 1941 the Italians were defeated and Ethiopia's independence restored. Following that Zeleke was given the title of *Dejazmatch* and appointed Governor of the province he had liberated from the Italians. Soon however, he refused to accord recognition to those he said did not contribute to the struggle for Ethiopia's independence, for which he was charged with treason. Arrested and imprisoned, he tried to escape and was shot in 1948. ■

Zogbo, S.B. (1929-80)

ZOGBO, Sylvain Bailly (1929-80).

IVORIAN journalist. Better known by his pen-name Kack Edim, he was born in 1929 at Kibouo, a village about 10 kilometres from Daloa, a town in the south of Côte d'Ivoire. After successfully completing primary and secondary education, the young Zogbo went to the studio-school of the Maison Laffitte in Paris, where he was trained as a journalist. He was then appointed in 1957 Director of Programmes of Radio Dahomey (now Radio Benin).

On his return to Côte d'Ivoire in 1958 he occupied the post of Director of Programmes at Radio Abidjan, until 1963. Some of the broadcasts he started and produced

S.B. Zogbo

still remain famous – *La terre au soleil* and *La famille Yao*. His human and professional qualities helped him attain several responsible positions in the course of his journalistic career, which was very full. Then, in 1963, the Minister of Information, M. Amadou Thiam, brought him into his Cabinet as *chargé de mission*. Two years later he returned to Côte d'Ivoire Radio-Television, but this time as Assistant Director of Programmes.

From that new appointment Kack Edim's career was one of well-deserved progress. After five years as Assistant Director he was appointed Director of Ivorian Radio-Television in 1970. He began to reap the rewards of his ability, and was Head of Broadcasting for four years, until 1974. In 1978 Sylvain Bailly Zogbo was promoted to the important post of Director of the CPAAP (Permanent Centre for Audio-Visual Current Events Reporting and Further Training), for training of radio, television, and newspaper staff.

In 1980, after an illness of several months, the director of the CPAAP went to Paris for treatment. On 10 May 1980, while Côte d'Ivoire was preparing to welcome Pope John Paul II, the bad news came: Sylvain Bailly Zogbo died that morning in Paris, as a result of his illness.

The news caused consternation among Ivorian journalists. Some hesitated to believe it, just as they did after Pol Amewe (Adolphe Edo Kouame, q.v.), another equally famous broadcaster, had died. Zogbo was buried on 24 May 1980 at the small cemetery of his home village, Kibouo. ■

Zungur, S. (1915-58)

ZUNGUR, Sa'adu (1915-58).

NIGERIAN politician. A native of Bauchi, son of the Limanin Bauchi, he became a Koranic scholar and also acquired Western education at a time when few Moslems in Northern Nigeria had it. He was at Yaba Technical College in Lagos in the 1930s. Later he was a teacher at the Kano School of Hygiene from 1930 until 1940 and then at the Zaria School of Pharmacy, becoming head of this in 1941. He formed a Zaria Friendly Society there and, while in Zaria, formed a close friendship and alliance with Aminu Kano (q.v.). This continued at Bauchi, where he had to return after falling seriously ill with lung trouble.

While at Bauchi he formed, in association with Abubakar Tafawa Balewa (q.v.), Aminu Kano and some other politically inclined Northerners, the Bauchi General Improvement Association, one of the first political organisations in Northern Nigeria. In 1949 Aminu Kano and Tafawa Balewa were among the founders of the Northern People's Congress (NPC) which was to dominate the governments of the Northern Region and of the Federation. The Bauchi General Improvement Association was a vehicle for expressing Zungur's radical views, opposed to the autocracy of the Emirs and the British Indirect Rule system. He called for modernisation through adoption of Western education.

Zungur never recovered his health fully, but he entered nationalist party politics at an early stage; he was a member of the National Council of Nigeria and the Cameroons (NCNC). In 1948 the NCNC elected him as General Secretary, under the presidency of Dr Nnamdi Azikiwe. For a short time Zungur worked in Lagos in this post, showing his and the party's commitment to the unity of Nigerians. Later he joined the Jami'yyar Mutanen Arewa in 1949, the organisation which became the NPC, believing the NCNC was neglecting the North's special problems. But after working with the NPC from 1951 to 1954 he left it and worked

S. Zungur

for Aminu Kano's Northern Elements Progressive Union (NEPU), closer to his radical ideas and run by his disciple, being too ill to play an important role.

Zungur remained influential behind the scenes in Northern Nigeria for a while longer, and was also noted as a poet. He died in 1958, two years before Nigeria achieved independence. ∎

Acknowledgements

SOURCES CONSULTED INCLUDE:

Africa Yearbook and Who's Who 1977. Africa Today (1st Edition 1981). *Africa Who's Who* (1st Edition 1981). Armah, K., *Nkrumah's Legacy.* Asante, S.K.B., *Pan-African Protest.* Ayandele, E.A., *Holy Johnson.* Banks Henries, A.D., *Presidents of the First African Republic.* Bechtold, P.K., *Politics in the Sudan.* Berque, J., *Egypt.* Bridger, P., *et al, Encyclopaedia Rhodesia.* Burke's Peerage Ltd., *Burke's Royal Families of the World.* Castagno, M., *Historical Dictionary of Somalia.* Clark, E., *Hubert Ogunde: The Making of Modern Theatre in Nigeria.* Clifford, M., *Land and People of Liberia.* Coleman, J., *Background to Nationalism in Nigeria.* Colvin, L.G., *Historical Dictionary of Senegal.* Courrière, Y., *Les Fils du Toussaint.* Courrière, Y., *Le Temps des Léopards.* Crowder, M. *The Story of Nigeria.* Crowder, M., and Ikime, O. (eds.), *West African Chiefs.* Cruise O'Brien, D., *The Mourides of Senegal.* Daily Times of Nigeria Ltd., *Nigeria Yearbook* (1974; 1975; 1976; 1977-8; 1979; 1980). R. Danziger, *Abd al-Qadir and the Algerians.* Davies, H. O., *Memoirs.* Decalo, S., *Historical Dictionary of Dahomey (Benin).* Decalo, S., *Historical Dictionary of Niger.* Decalo, S., *Historical Dictionary of Togo.* Delano, I., *The Singing Minister of Nigeria.* Dickie, J., and Rake, A. *Who's Who in Africa.* Ducoudray, E., *El Hadj-Omar.* Dudley, B.J., *Parties and Politics in Northern Nigeria.* Duse Mohammed Ali, *In the Land of the Pharaohs* (and introduction to 1968 Cass edition, by Khalil Mahmud). Encyclopaedia Africana (Ghana), *Dictionary of African Biography* (Volume on Ghana & Ethiopia; Volume on Sierra Leone & Zaire). Evans-Pritchard, E.E., *The Sanusi of Cyrenaica.* Feinstein, A., *African Revolutionary.* Foray, C.P., *Historical Dictionary of Sierra Leone.* Furneaux, R., *Abdel Krim: Emir of the Rif.* Fyfe, C., *Africanus Horton.* Fyfe, C., *A History of Sierra Leone.* Gailey, H.A., *Historical Dictionary of the Gambia.* Geiss, I., *The Pan-African Movement.* Grotpeter, J.J., *Historical Dictionary of Zambia.* Gwam, L.C., *Great Nigerians.* Hahn, L., *North Africa: Nationalism to Nationhood.* Hahn, L. and Muirragui, M., *Historical Dictionary of Libya.* Haliburton, G.M., *The Prophet Harris.* Hargreaves, J., *A Life of Sir Samuel Lewis.* Herdeck, D.E., *African Authors.* Hogben, S.J., and Kirk-Greene, A.H.M., *The Emirates of Northern Nigeria.* Holden, E., *Blyden of Liberia.* Holt, P.M. (ed.), *Political and Social Change in Modern Egypt.* Hooker, J., *Black Revolutionary.* Hoskyns, C., *The Congo since Independence.* Igbafe, P., *Benin under British Administration.* Ikime, O., *Merchant Prince of the Niger Delta.* Jackson, H., *The FLN in Algeria.* Jahn, J., *et al* (eds.), *Who's Who in African Literature.* Johnson, W., *The Emergence of Black Politics in Senegal.* Julien, C.A., *et al* (eds.), *Les Africains* (12 vols.). Kadalie, C., *My Life and the ICU.* Karis, T., and Carter, G.M. (eds.), *From Protest to Challenge,* Vol. 4 ("*Political Profiles*"). Kay, E. (ed.), *Dictionary of African Biography 1971-72.* Keppel-Jones, A., *South Africa.* Kimble, D.A., *Political History of Ghana 1850-1928.* Kopytoff, J.H., *Preface to Modern Nigeria.* Kraiem, M., *Nationalisme et Syndicalisme en Tunisie 1918-29.* van Kricken, C.S., *Khayr al-Din et la Tunisie 1830-1881.* Langley, J.A., *Pan-Africanism and Nationalism in West Africa.* Lejri, M.S., *Evolution du Mouvement National Tunisien.* Lemarchand, R., *Rwanda and Burundi.* Lewis, I.M., *The Modern History of Somaliland.* Liniger-Goumaz, M., *Historical Dictionary of Equatorial Guinea.* Little, K., *The Mende of Sierra Leone.* Lynch, H., *Edward Wilmot Blyden, Pan-Negro Patriot.* Macdonald's Encyclopedia of Africa. Magbaily Fyle, C., *Alimamy Suluku of Sierra Leone c.1820-1906.* Marcum, J., *The Angolan Revolution.* Martin, M.L., *Kimbangu.* McFarland, D.M., *Historical Dictionary of Upper Volta.* Merand, P., and Dable, S., *Guide de Littérature Africaine.* Miners, N.J., *The Nigerian Army.* Mortimer, E., *France and the Africans.* Mveng, E., *Histoire du Cameroun.* Oberle, P., *Afars et Somalis.* Omu, F., *Press and Politics in Nigeria 1880-1937.* Pélissier, R., *Les Guerres Grises.* Perham, M. (ed.), *Ten Africans.* Post, K.W., and Jenkins, G.D., *The Price of Liberty.* Quandt, W.B., *Revolution and Political Leadership: Algeria 1954-68.* Rabemananjara, R., *Madagascar.* Rasmussen, R.K., *Historical Dictionary of Rhodesia/Zimbabwe.* Rézette, R., *The Western Sahara and the Frontiers of Morocco.* Rivière, L., *Historical Dictionary of Mauritius.* Rosenthal, E., *Encyclopedia of Southern Africa.* Rotberg, R., *Black Heart.* Rotberg, R., and Mazrui, A.A. (eds.), *Protest and Power in Black Africa.* Rudin, H., *Germans in the Cameroons.* Sampson, M., *Gold Coast Men of Affairs.* Segal, R., *Political Africa.* Selvon, S., *Ramgoolam.* Seychelles Government, *Annual Reports.* Sharwood Smith, B., *But Always as Friends.* Simoes, *Politics and Decolonization.* Simpson, C.L., *Memoirs.* Skinner, E.R., *The Mossi of Upper Volta.* Smerli, Z., *Les Successeurs.* Smyke, R.J., and Storer, D.C., *Nigeria Union of Teachers.* South Africa 1975 (Official Annual). Spitzer, L., *The Creoles of Sierra Leone.* Suret-Canale, J., *French Colonialism in Tropical Africa.* Tamuno, T.N., *Nigeria and Elective Representation 1923-47.* Taylor, S. (ed.), *The New Africans.* Theobald, A.B., *Ali Dinar.* Theobald, A.B., *The Mahdiyya.* Thompson, V., and Adloff, R., *Djibouti and the Horn of Africa.* Thompson, V., and Adloff, R., *Historical Dictionary of the People's Republic of the Congo.* Thuku, H., *An Autobiography.* Times Newspapers Ltd., *Obituaries from The Times* (Vol. 1, 1961-70; Vol. II, 1971-5). Vatikiotis, P.J., *The Modern History of Egypt.* Voll, J.O., *Historical Dictionary of the Sudan.* Weinstein, B., *Eboué.* Weinstein, B., *Nation-Building on the Ogooué.* Weinstein, W., *Historical Dictionary of Burundi.* Whitaker, C.S., *The Politics of Tradition.* Willan, B., *Sol Plaatje.* Wilson, E., *Russia and Black Africa before World War II.* Zartmann, I.W., *Morocco: Problems of a New Power.* Zell, H., and Silver, H. (eds.), *A Reader's Guide to African Literature.* Zell, H., Bundy, C., and Coulon, V. (eds.), *A New Reader's Guide to African Literature.*

Articles in Learned Journals: Adeleye, R.A., "Rabih ibn Fadlallah . . .", *Journal of the Historical Society of Nigeria* (vol. V no. 2 and no. 3, 1970). Domenichini, J.P., "Jean Ralaimongo (1884-1943)", *Revue Française d'Histoire d'Outremer* (vol. LVI, no. 204, 1969). Duffield, I., "The Business Activities of Duse Mohammed Ali", *Journal of the Historical Society of Nigeria* (vol. IV no. 4, 1969). Ekejiuba, F., "Omu Okwei, the Merchant Queen of Ossomari: A Biographical Sketch", *Journal of the Historical Society of Nigeria* (Vol. III, no. 4., 1967). Hess, R.L., "The 'Mad Mullah' and Northern Somalia," *Journal of African History* (vol. V. no. 3, 1964). Hopkins, A.G., "R.B. Blaize", *Tarikh* (Nigeria, Vol. 1 no. 2).

PERIODICALS AND NEWSPAPERS CONSULTED

Africa (1971 ff). *Africa Diary* (1961 ff). *Africa Research Bulletin* (Africa Research Ltd. 1964 ff). *Afrique* (1977 ff). *Afrique Asie* (1985-86). *Ambassador International* (Vol. 2/1, 1985). *Arab Report and Record* (1966 ff). *Commonwealth Currents* (1979). *Fraternité-Matin* (Abidjan). *Guardian* (London). *Independent* (London). *Jeune Afrique* (1960 ff). *Sechaba* (1983 ff). *Le Soleil* (Dakar). *The Times* (London). *West Africa* (1917 ff).

SOURCES OF PHOTOS INCLUDE

Abba, ABC, Africpress, Agence France Presse, ANC (South Africa), Argus Africa News Service, Associated Press, BBC Hulton Picture Library, Camerapix, Camera Press, Central Press, Daily Times of Nigeria, Drum Publications, Frank-Robert Faes, Ghana Ministry of Information, Alan Hutchinson, Illustrated London News, International Defence and Aid Fund for Southern Africa, Keystone Press Agency, Mansell Collection, Mary Evans Picture Library, Namibia Support Committee, Nationphoto, Panaf Books, Popperfoto, Press Association, Sipa Press, R. Shanu-Taylor, Frank Spooner/Gamma, Sudanow, Tanzania Ministry of Information, QT Vincent, Roger Viollet, West Africa Publishing Co.